CONTEMPORARY
FASHION

CONTEMPORARY ARTS SERIES

CONTEMPORARY
FASHION

FIRST EDITION

Editor:

Richard Martin

ST. JAMES PRESS

An International Thomson Publishing Company

Changing the Way the World Learns

NEW YORK • LONDON • BONN • BOSTON • DETROIT • MADRID
MELBOURNE • MEXICO CITY • PARIS • SINGAPORE • TOKYO
TORONTO • WASHINGTON • ALBANY NY • BELMONT CA • CINCINNATI OH

STAFF

Richard Martin, *Editor*

Colin Naylor, Lee Ripley Greenfield, Jackie Wrought, Janice Jorgensen, *Project Editors*

David Collins, Margaret Mazurkiewicz, Michael J. Tyrkus, *Associate Editors*
Nicolet V. Elert, James F. Kamp, *Contributing Editors*
Whitney Blausen, *Editorial Assistant*

Peter M. Gareffa, *Managing Editor, St. James Press*

Mary Beth Trimper, *Production Director*
Shanna Heilveil, *Production Assistant*
Cynthia Baldwin, *Art Director*
Sherrell Hobbs, *Macintosh Artist*
Pamela A. Hayes, *Photography Coordinator*

Laura Standley Berger, *Desktop Publisher*

Victoria B. Cariappa, *Research Manager*
Barbara McNeil, *Research Specialist*
Marlene Lasky, *Permissions Manager*

∞™ This book is printed on acid-free paper that meets the minimum requirements of American National Standard for Information Sciences—Permanence Paper for Printed Library Materials, ANSI Z39.48-1984.

Cover photo reproduced with permission. Dress by Donna Karan, Fall 1994 collection; neutral longsleeve scoopneck tie-front umbrella dress. Model: Shalom Harlow.

Library of Congress Catalog Number 95-23329
ISBN 1-55862-173-3
Printed in the United States of America

I⟨T⟩P™ Gale Research Inc., an International Thomson Publishing Company.
ITP logo is a trademark under license.

10 9 8 7 6 5 4 3 2 1

CONTENTS

INTRODUCTION

While it may seem flattering to a speaker to say that he or she needs no introduction and reference books customarily require no introduction, *Contemporary Fashion* may be the atypical example of a reference book that demands brief preamble and proposition. Its subject has sometimes been dismissed as indescribable; its application of designer "identity" is spurned by some who regard fashion as a vitiated commercial enterprise.

Fashion has seldom been viewed with the seriousness of purpose—and substantial documentation—of other arts. Its association with ephemerality has led to its mistrust as a negligible flickering; traditionally, fashion's identification as women's expression has caused it to be less powerful than the visual arts identified with men; among the arts, fashion has always seemed one of the most commercial; and fashion's indivisible link to the body has carried the stigmas of vanity, sexuality, and dependence. Yet, none of the prior justifications to ignore or disparage fashion can seem compelling to us today. On the contrary, the issues of fashion are singularly important to late twentieth-century culture.

Fashion has probably always occasioned a great deal of talk, but some of the talk is inevitably trivial. That some of what we say and hear about fashion is inconsequential should not, however, lead us to believe that nothing of consequence can be said or written about fashion. Fashion's generally complimentary press is not, in fact, so markedly dissimilar from art criticism's often obsequious generosity or theater reviewing's propensity to favor and flatter. *Contemporary Fashion* has no agenda to praise and even less to delude. Rather, it attempts to provide and index information and ideas in a field where these are rare presences.

Should we abandon fashion and say that its too laudatory press, its extravagant lifestyle, and its patently commercial motives render it forbidden and unspeakable? On the contrary, knowing about fashion enables us to speak not only of garments, but of the ancillary elements of fashion that mark contemporary culture. Advertising image, self-expression, body cognizance, gender, implicit elements of class and money, and the transferals between high art and quotidian culture are all in the purview of contemporary fashion. We could not avoid fashion today if we tried: fashion constitutes the pervasive and persuasive culture of our time. *Contemporary Fashion* attempts to be an intelligent, clarifying, trustworthy guide to this inescapable contemporary art.

—Richard Martin

EDITOR'S NOTE

This volume is dedicated to Colin Naylor (1944-1992), who initiated the publication and was its editor until his early death. Colin's distinguished contributions to the arts—as editor of *Art and Artists* and as editor of indispensable reference volumes published by St. James Press/Gale Research Inc.—resonate with his lively sense of the role of contemporary arts. He rejected hierarchies and predetermined categories in modern art, relishing arts of performance, integrated decorative arts, collage and other hybrid forms, as much as the sacrosanct fine arts. I had the privilege of writing for him at *Art and Artists* more than 20 years ago and began on this volume in order to be involved again with an old friend and an inspiring editor. While he is not present for its outcome, *Contemporary Fashion* will always bear Colin's sense of adventure, scope of interest, and unceasing imagination about both the intellectual referencing and interpretative and bibliographic realization of works of art. *Contemporary Fashion* is, I hope, no less Colin's book and Colin's dream for his aching absence upon its fulfillment.

Contemporary Fashion seeks to provide information on and assessment of fashion designers active during the period from 1945 to the present. International in scope in accordance with fashion's wide resourcing and dissemination, this volume attempts to provide dependable information and substantive critical appraisal in a field often prone to excessive praise and hyperbolic language. Each entry consists of a personal and professional biography; bibliographic citations by and about the designer; when possible, a statement by the designer on his or her work and/or design philosophy; and a critical essay by a scholar or critic in the field of fashion and costume history. The book's emphasis is on the design creativity and distinction; in instances of a corporation, family business, design house, or other collective enterprise, we have attempted to hone in on the distinguishing attributes of the design tradition, as we would have if thinking about the della Robbia heritage or the Skidmore, Owings, and Merrill aesthetic or the traits of the Carracci. Much literature from specialized periodicals is assimilated in the critical essays and listed in the bibliographies, offering this volume's reader access to a wide variety and deep concentration of specialized literature.

Special appreciation is owed to the designers and design houses who generously supplied statements, information, and visual documentation. Virtually everyone in the civilized world talks about fashion. It is an area in which most of us consider ourselves knowledgeable, if only as a function of making our own clothing decisions on a daily basis. *Contemporary Fashion* gives value to the data and ideas of fashion discussion; it is intended to aid the discourse about apparel and edify the lively fashion conversation. *Contemporary Fashion* is to stand as a solid reference where no other comparable volumes exist and to make a contribution to fashion study and fashion's myriad allied expressions.

—Richard Martin

CONTRIBUTORS

Kevin Almond
Rebecca Arnold
Andrea Arsenault
Therese Duzinkiewicz Baker
Whitney Blausen
Sarah Bodine
Carol Mary Brown
Jane Burns
Marianne T. Carlano
Barbara Cavaliere
Hazel Clark
Debra Regan Cleveland
Linda Coleing
Elizabeth A. Coleman
Arlene C. Cooper
Caroline Cox
Fred Dennis
Jean L. Druesedow
Doreen Ehrlich
Mary C. Elliott
Alan J. Flux
Mary Ellen Gordon
Roberta Hochberger Gruber
Yoko Hamada
Chris Hill

Nancy House
Betty Kirke
Janet Markarian
Lisa Marsh
Richard Martin
Elian McCready
Sally Ann Melia
Janet Ozzard
Kathleen Paton
Angela Pattison
Alan E. Rosenberg
Susan Salter
Margo Seaman
Molly Severson
Dennita Sewell
Madelyn Shaw
Gillion Skellenger
Montse Stanley
Valerie Steele
Teal Triggs
Vicki Vasilopoulos
Gregory Votolato
Myra J. Walker
Melinda L. Watt
Catherine Woram

CONTEMPORARY FASHION

LIST OF ENTRANTS

Joseph Abboud
Adolfo
Adri
Gilbert Adrian
Agnès B.
Akira
Azzedine Alaia
Walter Albini
Victor Alfaro
Linda Allard
Ally Capellino
Hardy Amies
John Anthony
Aquascutum, Ltd.
Junichi Arai
Giorgio Armani
Laura Ashley
Christian Aujard
Sylvia Ayton
Jacques Azagury

Badgley Mischka
Cristobal Balenciaga
Pierre Balmain
Banana Republic
Jeff Banks
Jeffrey Banks
Jhane Barnes
Sheridan Barnett
Rocco Barocco
Scott Barrie
John Bartlett
Franck Joseph Bastille
L.L. Bean
Geoffrey Beene
Bellville Sassoon-Lorcan Mullany
Benetton
Laura Bigiotti
Bianchini-Férier
Dirk Bikkembergs
Dorothée Bis
Sandy Black
Manolo Blahnik
Alistair Blair
Bill Blass
Blumarine

Bodymap
Willy Bogner
Marc Bohan
Hugo Boss AG
Tom Brigance
Brioni
Brooks Brothers
Donald Brooks
Liza Bruce
Burberrys
Stephen Burrows
Byblos

Jean Cacharel
Calugi e Giannelli
Roberto Capucci
Pierre Cardin
Hattie Carnegie
Carven
Joe Casely-Hayford
Bonnie Cashin
Oleg Cassini
Jean-Charles de Castelbajac
Catalina Sportswear
Jean Baptiste Caumont
Nino Cerruti
Sal Cesarani
Champion
''Coco'' Gabriel Bonheur Chanel
Caroline Charles
Chloé
Liz Claiborne
Ossie Clark
Cole of California
Nick Coleman
Jasper Conran
Corneliani SpA
Giorgio Correggiari
Victor Costa
Paul Costelloe
André Courrèges
Enrico Coveri
Patrick Cox
C.P. Company
Jules François Crahay

Lilly Daché
Wendy Dagworthy
Sarah Dallas
Danskin
Oscar de la Renta
Ann Demeulemeester
Myrène de Prémonville
Jacqueline de Ribes
Elisabeth de Senneville
Jean Dessès
Christian Dior
Giorgio di Sant'Angelo
Dolce & Gabbana
Adolfo Dominguez

Perry Ellis
David and Elizabeth Emanuel
English Eccentrics
Erreuno SCM SpA
Escada
Esprit
Jacques Esterel
Luis Estevez

Fabrice
Nicole Farhi
Kaffe Fassett
Jacques Fath
Fendi
Han Feng
Fenn Wright and Manson
Louis Féraud
Salvatore Ferragamo
Gianfranco Ferré
Andrew Fezza
David Fielden
Elio Fiorucci
John Flett
Alan Flusser
Anne Fogarty
Brigid Foley
Fontana
Mariano Fortuny
Diane Freis
French Connection
Bella Freud
Giuliano Fujiwara

James Galanos
Irene Galitzine
John Galliano
The Gap
Sandra Garratt

Jean-Paul Gaultier
Genny SpA
Rudi Gernreich
Ghost
Bill Gibb
Romeo Gigli
Marithé & François Girbaud
Hubert de Givenchy
Georgina Godley
Madame Grès
Jacques Griffe
Gruppo GFT
Gucci
Guess, Inc.
Olivier Guillemin

Halston
Katharine Hamnett
Cathy Hardwick
Holly Harp
Norman Hartnell
Elizabeth Hawes
Edith Head
Daniel Hechter
Jacques Heim
Sylvia Heisel
Gordon Henderson
Hermès
Carolina Herrera
Tommy Hilfiger
Hobbs Ltd.
Pam Hogg
Peter Hoggard
Emma Hope
Margaret Howell
Barbara Hulanicki

Sueo Irié
Isani

Betty Jackson
Marc Jacobs
Jaeger
Charles James
Jan Jansen
Jantzen, Inc.
Eric Javits
Joan & David
John P. John
Betsey Johnson
Stephen Jones
Wolfgang Joop
Joseph
Charles Jourdan
Alexander Julian

Gemma Kahng
Bill Kaiserman
Norma Kamali
Jacques Kaplan
Donna Karan
Herbert Kasper
Rei Kawakubo
Patrick Kelly
Kenzo
Emmanuelle Khanh
Barry Kieselstein-Cord
Anne Klein
Calvin Klein
John Kloss
Gabriele Knecht
Yukio Kobayashi
Yoshiyuki Konishi
Michael Kors
Hiroko Koshino
Junko Koshino
Michiko Koshino
Lamine Kouyaté

Lachasse
Lacoste Sportswear
Christian Lacroix
Karl Lagerfeld
Ragence Lam
Kenneth Jay Lane
Helmut Lang
Lanvin
Guy Laroche
Byron Lars
André Laug
Ralph Lauren
Mickey Lee
Hervé Léger
Jürgen Lehl
Judith Leiber
Lucien Lelong
Lolita Lempicka
Tina Leser
Levi-Strauss & Co.
René Lezard
Liberty of London
Stephen Linard

Walter Ma
Bob Mackie
Mad Carpentier
I. Magnin
Mainbocher
Mariuccia Mandelli
Judy Mann

Mary Jane Marcasiano
Martin Margiela
Marimekko
Marcel Marongiu
Mitsuhiro Matsuda
Maxfield Parrish
Max Mara SpA
Vera Maxwell
Claire McCardell
Jessica McClintock
Mary McFadden
Nicole Miller
Missoni
Issey Miyake
Isaac Mizrahi
Edward H. Molyneux
Mondi Textile GmbH
Claude Montana
Popy Moreni
Hanae Mori
Robert Lee Morris
Digby Morton
Franco Moschino
Thierry Mugler
Jean Muir
Muji
Mulberry

Josie Cruz Natori
Sara Navarro
New Republic
Next PLC
Nikos
Norman Norell

Bruce Oldfield
Todd Oldham
Benny Ong
Rifat Ozbek

Jenny Packham
Mollie Parnis
Jean Patou
Guy Paulin
Sylvia Pedlar
Pepe
Elsa Peretti
Bernard Perris
Andrea Pfister
Paloma Picasso
Robert Piguet
Gerard Pipart
Arabella Pollen
Carmelo Pomodoro
Thea Porter

Prada
Anthony Price
Pringle of Scotland
Emilio Pucci
Lilly Pulitzer

Mary Quant

Paco Rabanne
Sir Edward Rayne
Georges Rech
Red or Dead
Maurice Rentner
Mary Ann Restivo
Zandra Rhodes
Nina Ricci
John Richmond
Marina Rinaldi SrL
Patricia Roberts
Bill Robinson
Marcel Rochas
Rodier
Carolyne Roehm
Christian Francis Roth
Maggy Rouf
Cynthia Rowley
Cinzia Ruggeri
Sonia Rykiel

Gloria Sachs
Yves Saint Laurent
Fernando Sanchez
Jil Sander
Arnold Scaasi
Jean-Louis Scherrer
Elsa Schiaparelli
Carolyn Schnurer
Mila Schön
Ronaldus Shamask
David Shilling
Simonetta
Adele Simpson
Martine Sitbon
Sophie Sitbon
Graham Smith
Paul Smith
Willi Smith
Per Spook
Stephen Sprouse
George Peter Stavropoulos
Stefanel SpA
Robert Stock
Helen Storey
Strenesse Group
Anna Sui

Alfred Sung
Sybilla
William Tang
Gustave Tassell
Chantal Thomass
Vicky Tiel
Jacques Tiffeau
Tiktiner
Timney Fowler Ltd.
Ted Tinling
Zang Toi
Isabel Toledo
Yuki Torii
Torrente
Transport
Philip Treacy
Pauline Trigère
Trussardi, SpA
Sally Tuffin
Richard Tyler

Patricia Underwood
Emanuel Ungaro
Kay Unger

Valentina
Valentino
Koos Van Den Akker
Joan Vass
Philippe Venet
Gian Marco Venturi
Joaquim Verdù
Roberto Verino
Gianni Versace
Sally Victor
Victorio y Lucchino
Madeleine Vionnet
Adrienne Vittadini
Roger Vivier
Michaele Vollbracht
Diane Von Furstenberg
Louis Vuitton

Catherine Walker
John Weitz
Vivienne Westwood
Whistles
Workers for Freedom

Kansai Yamamoto
Yohji Yamamoto

Ermenegildo Zegna
Zoran

ABBOUD, Joseph.

American designer

Born: Boston, Massachusetts, 5 May 1950. **Education:** Studied comparative literature, University of Massachusetts, Boston, 1968-72; also studied at the Sorbonne. **Family:** Married Lynn Weinstein, 6 June 1976; children: Lila Faith, Ari Rachel. **Career:** Buyer, then director of merchandise, Louis of Boston, 1968-80; designer, Southwick, 1980; associate director of menswear design, Polo/Ralph Lauren, New York, 1980-84; launched signature menswear collection, 1986; designer, Barry Bricken, New York, 1987-88. J.A. (Joseph Abboud) Apparel Corporation, a joint venture with GFT USA, formed, 1988; Joseph Abboud Womenswear and menswear collection of tailored clothing and furnishings introduced, 1990; opened first retail store, Boston, 1990; collections first shown in Europe, 1990; JA II line introduced, 1991; fragrance line introduced in Japan, 1992, in America, 1993; introduced J.O.E. (Just One Earth) sportswear line, 1992; designed wardrobes for male television announcers for 1992 Winter Olympics, Albertville, France, 1992; Joseph Abboud Environments bed and bath collection launched, 1993; *Joseph Abboud Fragrance* launched, 1994. **Awards:** Cutty Sark Award, 1988; Woolmark Award, 1988; Menswear Designer of the Year Award from Council of Fashion Designers of America Award, 1989, 1990; honored by Japanese Government in conjunction with the Association of Total Fashion in Osaka, 1993; Special Achievement Award from Neckwear Association of America Inc., 1994. **Address:** 650 Fifth Avenue, New York, New York 10019, USA.

Publications:

On ABBOUD:

Articles

Dolce, Joe, "Last of the Updated Traditional," in *Connoisseur* (New York), March 1987.
Saunders, Peggy, "Joseph Abboud," in *Boston Business,* July/August 1987.
"A Man's Style Book, Joseph Abboud," in *Esquire* (New York), September 1987.
de Caro, Frank, "Men in Style: A Designer to Watch," in *The Baltimore Sun,* 24 September 1987.
"Designers Are Made as Well as Born," in *Forbes* (New York), 11 July 1988.
Carloni, Maria Vittoria, "Da commesso a mito," in *Panorama,* 27 November 1988.
LaFerla, Ruth, "Past as Prologue," in *New York Times Magazine,* 19 February 1989.

Wayne, Hollis, "Fashion Forward—the 90s," in *Playboy* (Chicago), March 1989.
Stern, Ellen, "Joseph Abboud, Down to Earth," in *GQ* (New York), October 1989.
"The Word to Men: Hang Looser," in *People Weekly* (Chicago), Spring 1990.
Burns, Robert, "Abboud Takes on Classics in a Big Way," in *Los Angeles Times,* 8 June 1990.
Hatfield, Julie, "Abboud Brings Worldly Styles Home," in *Boston Globe,* 5 September 1990.
Conover, Kirsten A., "Abboud Sets Tone for '90s Menswear," in *Christian Science Monitor* (Boston), 5 November 1990.
Roosa, Nancy, "Much Abboud about Clothing," in *Boston,* January 1991.
Fenichell, Stephen, "The Look of the Nineties: Four Designers Lead the Way," in *Connoisseur* (New York), March 1991.
Hancox, Clara, "And Now, the First Joe Abboud," in the *Daily News Record,* 15 July 1991.
"Joseph Abboud's Next Step," in *Esquire* (New York), August 1992.

*   *   *

Joseph Abboud has said that his clothing is as much about lifestyle as design. Since 1986, after breaking away from Ralph Lauren, he has filled a niche in the fashion world with his creations for both men and, more recently, for women. For the contemporary individual seeking a façade that is as casual, elegant, and as international as the accompanying life, the Abboud wardrobe offers comfort, beauty, and a modernity that is equally suitable in New York, Milan, or Australia. Abboud was the first menswear designer in the United States to revolutionize the concept of American style.

Born in Boston, Abboud is hardly provincial. Something of an outsider, he did not come to fashion through the usual design school training and had no pre-established world in which to fit. Instead he made his own. His approach to fashion was via studies in comparative literature, followed by study at the Sorbonne in Paris. His fall 1990 menswear collection Grand Tour pays homage to that experience with its romantic 1930s and 1940s designs, reminiscent of Hemingway, while his own rich ethnic background provided the depth of appreciation for global culture inherent in his work. Coming of age in the 1960s, Abboud began collecting early Turkish *kilims* (flat woven rugs) with their salient handcrafted quality and stylized geometric patterns. These motifs form a recurring theme in his work, from the handknit sweaters to the machine knit shirts. The rugs themselves, in muted earthtones, complement the calm, natural environment of the Abboud stores. For Abboud, the presentation of the clothing mimics the aesthetics of the garments: soft, casual, and elegant in its simplicity.

Color, texture, and the cut of Abboud fashions express a style that lies between, and sometimes overlaps, that of Ralph Lauren

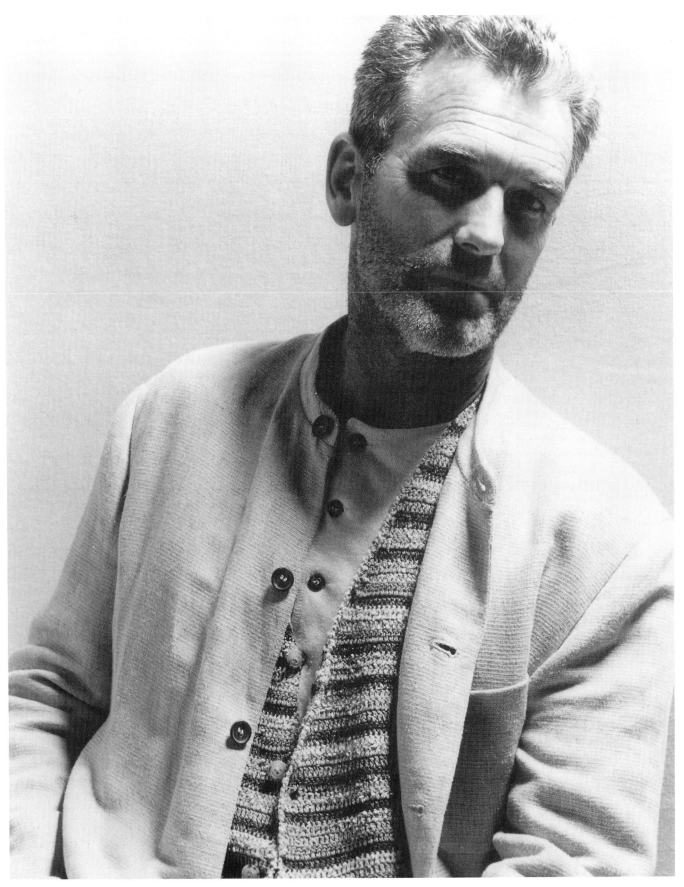

Joseph Abboud: Spring 1995; band collar jacket, linen bib-front shirt, and crochet vest.

and Giorgio Armani. The palette of the Joseph Abboud and the 1992 J.O.E. (Just One Earth) lines for both sexes is more subtle than the traditional Anglo-American colors of the preppie or Sloane Ranger genre, yet more varied in tone and hue than the sublimely unstated Armani colors. Neutrals from burnt sienna to cream, stucco, straw, and the colors of winter birch, together with naturals such as indigo and faded burgundy, are examples of some of the most alluring of Abboud dyestuffs.

The Pacific Northwest Collection, fall 1987, manifested rich hues, from black to maroon, but even these were harmonious, never ostentatious. The black of his leather jackets, fall 1992, appears like soft patches of the night sky due to the suppleness and unique surface treatment of the skins. The fabrics for Abboud designs represent the artist's diligent search for the world's finest materials and craftsmanship. His respect for textile traditions does not mean that his work is retrospective but that his inventiveness is grounded in the integrity of the classics. His interpretation of tweed, for example, although based on fine Scottish wool weavings, which he compares to the most beautiful artistic landscapes, differs from the conventional Harris-type tweed. Silk, alpaca, or llama are occasionally combined with the traditional wool to yield a lighter fabric.

Unique and demanding in his working methods, Abboud is at the forefront of contemporary fashion-fabric design. His fabrics drape with a grace and elegance that is enhanced by the oversize cut and fluid lines of his suits. His characteristically full, double-pleated trousers, for example, are luxurious. The romantic malt mohair gossamer-like fabrics for women in the fall 1993 collection are cut simply with no extraneous details. Even the intricate embroideries that ornament the surfaces of many of his most memorable designs, from North African suede vests with a Kashmiri *boteh* design to the jewel-like beadwork for evening, have a wearability uncommon in the contemporary artistic fashion.

Nature is Abboud's muse. Beyond the obvious J.O.E. line appellation, the theme of the bucolic environment provides inspiration for the garments. Country stone walls, pebbles on a beach, the light and earthtones of the Southwest are interpreted in exquisitely cut fabrics that embrace the body with a style that becomes an individual's second skin.

—Marianne Carlano

ADOLFO.

American designer

Born: Adolfo F. Sardiña in Cardenas, Cuba, 15 February 1933. **Education:** B.A., St. Ignacious de Loyola Jesuit School, Havana, 1950. Immigrated to New York, 1948, naturalized, 1958. **Military Service:** Served in the United States Navy. **Career:** Apprentice millinery designer, Bergdorf Goodman, 1948-51; apprentice milliner at Cristobal Balenciaga Salon, Paris, 1950-52, and at Bergdorf Goodman, New York; designed millinery as Adolfo of Emme, 1951-58; also worked as unpaid apprentice for Chanel fashion house, Paris, 1956-57; apprenticed in Paris with Balenciaga; established own millinery salon in New York, 1962, later expanding into women's custom clothing; designer, Adolfo Menswear and Adolfo Scarves, from 1978. Perfume *Adolfo* launched, 1978. Closed custom workroom to concentrate on his Adolfo Enterprises licensing business, 1993. **Exhibitions:** *Fashion: An Anthology,* Victoria &

Albert Museum, London, 1971. **Collections:** Metropolitan Museum of Art, New York; Smithsonian Institution, Washington, D.C.; Dallas Museum of Fine Arts; Los Angeles County Museum of Art. **Awards:** Coty Fashion Award, New York, 1955, 1969; Neiman Marcus Award, 1956. Member of the Council of Fashion Designers of America. **Address:** 36 East 57th Street, New York, New York 10022 USA.

Publications:

On ADOLFO:

Books

Morris, Bernadine, and Barbara Walz, *The Fashion Makers,* New York 1978.
Diamonstein, Barbaralee, *Fashion: The Inside Story,* New York 1985.
Milbank, Caroline Rennolds, *New York Fashion: The Evolution of American Style,* New York 1989.

Articles

"Adolfo," in *Current Biography* (New York), November 1972.
Friedman, Arthur, "Always Adolfo," in *Women's Wear Daily* (New York), 21 July 1992.
Friedman, Arthur, "Adolfo Closing His RTW Salon After 25 Years: Golden Era Ends," in *Women's Wear Daily* (New York), 18 March 1993.
Schiro Anne-Marie, "Adolfo Decides It's Time to Stop Designing," in *New York Times,* 19 March 1993.

*

To make clothes that are long-lasting and with subtle changes from season to season—this is my philosophy.

—Adolfo

* * *

In April of 1993, Adolfo closed his salon on New York's East 57 Street, after more than 25 years producing his classically elegant knit suits, dresses, and eveningwear. The outcry from his clientèle was emotional and indicative of the devotion that his clothes inspired in his "ladies":

"It's just a tragedy for me. He has such great taste, style, and manners. I don't know what I'm going to do. I've been wearing his clothes for years; they suit my lifestyle. He designs for a certain way of life that all these new designers don't seem to comprehend."—C.Z. Guest

"I'm devastated.... It's terrible. I adore him. He's the sweetest most talented man. You know when ladies say, 'Oh I just don't know what I'm going to wear!' With Adolfo, you always have the right thing to wear."—Jean Tailer.

These loyal clients were among the many who returned to Adolfo season after season for clothes that they could wear year after year, clothes that looked stylish and felt comfortable, style and comfort being the essence of his customers' elegant and effortless lifestyle.

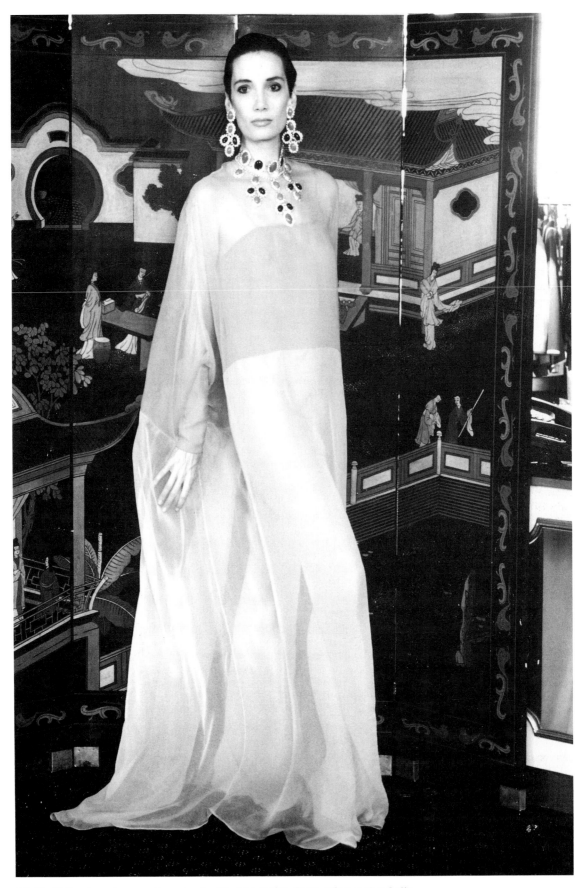

Adolfo: Yellow to red mousseline, round-neck, long-cuffed sleeve caftan and red slip.

Adolfo began his career as a milliner in the early 1950s, a time when hat designers were accorded as much respect and attention as dress designers. By 1955, he had received the Coty Fashion Award for his innovative, often dramatic hat designs for Emmé Millinery. In 1962, Adolfo opened his own salon and began to design clothes to show with his hat collection. During this period as women gradually began to wear hats less often, Adolfo's hat designs became progressively bolder. His design point of view was that hats should be worn as an accessory rather than a necessity, and this attitude was carried over into his clothing designs as well. His clothes of the late 1960s had the idiosyncratic quality characteristic of the period and, most importantly, each piece stood out on its own as a special item. This concept of design was incongruous with the American sportswear idea of coordinated separates but was consistent with the sensibility of his wealthy customers who regarded clothes, like precious jewelry, as adornments and indicators of their social status. Among the garments that captured the attention of clients and press during this period were felt capes, red, yellow, or purple velvet bolero jackets embroidered with jet beads and black braid, studded lace-up peasant vests, low-cut floral overalls worn over organdy blouses, and extravagant patchwork evening looks.

Adolfo remarked, in 1968, that "today, one has to dress in bits and pieces—the more the merrier." By 1969, he described his clothes as being "for a woman's fun and fantasy moods—I don't think the classic is appealing to people any more." Just one year later, however, he changed his point of view and at the same time increased the focus of his knits that had been introduced in 1969. In a review of Adolfo's fall 1970 collection Eugenia Sheppard, writing in the *New York Post,* declared that "he has completely abandoned the costume look of previous years." Adolfo was always responsive to his customers' needs and this sudden change of direction probably reflected their reaction to the social upheavals and excesses of the last years of the 1960s.

By the early 1970s, the 1930s look, inspired by films such as *Bonnie and Clyde* and *The Damned,* swept over fashion, drowning out the kooky individualism of seasons past. His explorations of this look led Adolfo, in 1973, to hit on what would become his signature item. Taking his cue from Coco Chanel's cardigan style suits of the 1930s, Adolfo translated the textured tweed into a pebbly knit, added a matching silk blouse, and came up with a formula that his clients came to him for over and over again until his recent retirement. These revivals of a classic became classics in their own right and the look became associated, in America, with Adolfo as much as with Chanel. Adolfo's collections were not limited to suits. When other American designers abandoned dresses for day in favor of sportswear separates, Adolfo continued to provide his customers with printed silk dresses appropriate for luncheons and other dressy daytime occasions. Adolfo's clients also relied on him for splendid eveningwear that often combined luxury with practicality. Typical evening looks included sweater knit tops with full satin or taffeta skirts, fur trimmed knit cardigans, silk pyjamas, and angora caftans.

The designer has remarked that "an Adolfo lady should look simple, classic, and comfortable." Adolfo brought those modest and characteristically American design ideals to a higher level of luxury and charm, combining quality and style with comfort and ease.

—Alan E. Rosenberg

ADRI.

American designer

Born: Mary Adrienne Steckling in St. Joseph, Missouri, 7 November 1934. **Education:** Attended St. Joseph Junior College, 1953; studied retailing and design, Washington University (School of Fine Arts), St. Louis, 1954-55, and fashion design at Parsons School of Design, New York, 1955-56; studied at the New School for Social Research, New York, 1956-57. **Family:** Married Fabio Coen in 1982. **Career:** Guest editor, *Mademoiselle* magazine's college issue 1955; design assistant for Oleg Cassini, Inc., New York, 1957-58. Design assistant, later designer, B.H. Wragge, New York, 1960-67; opened Adri Designs Inc., 1966-67; formed Design Establishment, Inc. with Leonard Sunshine and the Anne Fogarty Co., New York, for the Clothes Circuit by Adri and Collector's Items by Adri division of Anne Fogarty, 1968-72; partner with William Parnes in Adri label for Paul Parnes's Adri Sporthoughts Ltd 1972-74; designed for Ben Shaw company, 1975-76; Adri for Royal Robes, leisurewear, under license, 1976-77; Jerry Silverman Sport by Adri label, 1977-78; ADRI label collection for Jones New York, 1978-79; ADRI collection marketed by Habitat Industries, 1980-83, and by Adri Clotheslab, 1983-87; designs several designer sportswear collections a year, selling to smaller specialty stores and private customers. From 1994 corporate name changed to Adri Studio Ltd. Designer Adri patterns for Vogue, 1982—. Japanese licensee N. Nomura & Co. Ltd, 1982-87. Critic, Parsons School of Design, 1982—; On its faculty, 1991—. **Exhibitions:** *Innovative Contemporary Fashion: Adri and McCardell,* Smithsonian Institution, Washington, D.C., 1971. Various shows, Fashion Institute of Technology, New York City. **Awards:** Coty American Fashion Critics "Winnie" Award, 1982; "International Best Five," Asahi Shimbun, Tokyo, 1986. Member, Council of Fashion Designers of America. **Address:** 143 West 20th St., New York, NY 10011, USA.

Publications:

On ADRI:

Books

Lambert, Eleanor, *World of Fashion: People, Places, Resources,* New York 1976.
Morris, Bernadine, and Barbara Walz, *The Fashion Makers,* New York 1978.

Articles

"The Find: Adri," in *Women's Wear Daily* (New York), 7 November 1966.
"Adri Opens the Door," in *Women's Wear Daily* (New York), 30 October 1968.
Banik, Sheila, "The Adventures of Adri: A Designer Goes From Wragge to Riches," in *Savvy* (New York), October 1980.
Burggraf, Helen, "Adri: Soft and Easy Designs for the Fast-Paced 80's," in *New York Apparel News,* Spring 1982.
Morris, Bernadine, "Banks and Adri Win Coty Awards and Cheers," in the *New York Times,* 25 September 1982.
Morris, Bernadine, "From Ellis, a Casual Whimsicality," in the *New York Times,* 27 October 1982.

Adri: "Body Rapping," 1982.

Morris, Bernadine, "A Sportswear Preview: Fall on Seventh Avenue," in the *New York Times,* 5 April 1983.

*

I believe in a "design continuum" of clothing that is essentially modern, that reflects the changing patterns of living, evolving gradually but continually.

Good design can be directional *and* timeless, functional and innovative in the tradition of American sportswear, and responsive to the needs of a woman equally committed to professional responsibilities and an enduring personal style.

—Adri

*   *   *

From the moment she fell in love with her first Claire McCardell dress while still a teenager—a dress she copied for herself many times because it fit her so well—Adri (Adrienne Steckling-Coen) idolized McCardell who, coincidentally, was one of her lecturers at Parsons School of Design, New York. Adri's early years with B.H. Wragge taught her the principles of tailoring and mix-and-match separates, long a staple of American sportswear. Designing for Anne Fogarty reinforced the feminine focus of Adri's design philosophy. Always, she returned to McCardell's tenet of form following function. Shapes were simple, skimming the body without extraneous detail or fussiness, often based on the practicality of athletic wear. While McCardell favored dresses, Adri emphasized trousers, later designing skirt-length trousers, or culottes, for variety.

From the beginning Adri utilized soft, pliable fabrics such as knits, jerseys, *crêpe de Chine,* challis, and leather. Her clothes were identified by their floaty qualities and she maintained that this softness made them easy to wear and provided relief from the frequent harshness of modern life. They were also ideal for tall, long-limbed, slender figures like her own. During the late 1960s Adri presented V-necked short dresses with high waists or wrapped fronts, in solid colored synthetic jerseys. Natural fibers, such as unbleached linen, came of use in the 1970s and knits continued to be staples for Adri skirts, trousers, and tunics in various lengths. By 1980 a typical Adri evening look consisted of silk trousers topped by a strapless chenille top and fluid lace jacket.

Interchangeable neutral solids such as beige, black, and white were combined with bold primary colors so that Adri's customers could collect the separates throughout the years and create their own ensembles, without having to purchase a new wardrobe each year. The simple timelessness of the designs, their easy cut and fit, also made this possible. Prices were in the moderate to better sportswear range.

Adri wore her own apparel to accept her Coty Award in 1982: a belted silver-grey (she called it "platinum") mohair sweater over midcalf culottes made of grey suede. Soon afterwards she branched out into menswear, creating unisex sweaters, cardigans, and vests. Evening looks continued to be based on day shapes, but fabricated of highly colored striped shiny rayon or mohair. Pullovers, jackets, and vests were frequently long, and Adri kept experimenting with new materials, such as eelskin, for her contrasting boldly colored belts, or handloomed Japanese fabrics with interesting textures. A touch of the opulent 1980s was evident in her use of tapestry jackets to be worn with velvet trousers, as well as damask and silk Jacquard.

Clothes like these can be easily adapted for homesewers, and Adri contracted with Vogue Patterns during the mid-1980s for a relationship that continues into the 1990s. The same McCardell-inspired sporty yet fluid lines are evident. Shirtwaist dresses with topstitching detail, softly gathered jackets, shaped hemlines with gracefully flounced skirts, cummerbund accents to shorten the appearance of tall, slim figures, gently gathered waists, and easy wrap dresses are some of the offerings available to seamstresses wishing to recreate Adri's classic multifunctional designs.

—Therese Duzinkiewicz Baker

ADRIAN, Gilbert.

American designer

Born: Gilbert Adrian Greenburgh in Naugatuck, Connecticut, 3 March 1903. **Education:** Studied at Parsons School of Design, New York and Paris, c.1921-22. **Family:** Married Janet Gaynor in 1939; son: Robin. **Career:** Film and theater designer, New York, 1921-28; designer, MGM studios, Hollywood, 1928-39; ready-to-wear and custom clothing salon established, Beverly Hills, 1942-52; fragrances *Saint* and *Sinner* introduced, 1946; New York boutique opened, 1948; retired to Brasilia, Brazil, 1952-58; film designer, Los Angeles, 1958-59. **Exhibitions:** Retrospective, Los Angeles County Museum, c.1967; retrospective, Fashion Institute of Technology, New York, 1971. **Awards:** Coty American Fashion Critics Award, 1944. *Died* (in Los Angeles, California) *14 September 1959.*

Publications:

By ADRIAN:

Articles

"Do American Women Want Clothes?," in *Harper's Bazaar* (New York), February 1934.
"Garbo as Camille," in *Vogue* (New York), 15 November 1936.
"Clothes," in Stephen Watts, ed., *Behind the Screen: How Films Are Made,* London 1938.

On ADRIAN:

Books

Powdermaker, Hortense, *The Dream Factory,* Boston 1950.
Riley, Robert, *The Fashion Makers,* New York 1968.
Lee, Sarah Tomerlin, editor, *American Fashion,* New York 1975.
Lambert, Eleanor, *World of Fashion: People, Places, Resources,* New York and London 1976.
Pritchard, Susan, *Film Costume: An Annotated Bibliography,* Metuchen, New Jersey and London 1981.
Milbank, Caroline Rennolds, *Couture: The Great Designers,* New York 1985.
Maeder, Edward, et al., *Hollywood and History: Costume Design in Film,* New York 1987.
Milbank, Caroline Rennolds, *New York Fashion: The Evolution of American Style,* New York 1989.
Leese, Elizabeth, *Costume Design in the Movies,* New York 1991.

Articles

Gordon, James, "One Man Who Suits Women," in *American Magazine* (Philadelphia), March 1946.
Obituary in the *New York Times,* 14 September 1959.
Sims, Joseph, "Adrian—American Artist and Designer," in *Costume,* 1974.
Kinsey, Sally Buchanan, "Gilbert Adrian: Creating the Hollywood Dream Style," in *Fiberarts* (Asheville, North Carolina), May/June 1987.
Lambert, Gavin, "Janet Gaynor and Adrian," in *Architectural Digest* (Los Angeles), April 1992.

*   *   *

By the time MGM costumer Gilbert Adrian went into business for himself in the middle of World War II, his potential customers were already familiar with his work. For over a decade American women had been wearing copies of the clothes he had designed for some of the most famous movie stars of all time. Adrian's ability to develop a screen character through the progression of costumes, be they period or modern, was translated into costuming the modern woman for her new role as career woman while men were away at war.

Adrian was primarily an artist, having trained in France, and was able to perceive Greta Garbo's true personality—aloof, mysterious, earthy—and change the way the studios dressed her; insisting upon genuine silks, laces, and jewels to lend authenticity to her performances. For all the stars he dressed, Adrian believed that the quality of materials that a woman wore affected how she behaved in the clothes, even if the details were not immediately obvious. He brought the same philosophy to his custom and ready-to-wear creations. Of course the copies MGM permitted to be made of Adrian's costumes, timed to coincide with the releases of the films, were not always of the same fine quality as the originals, but the overall looks were what women were after. While films provided a great escape from the dreariness of the American Depression, a dress such as the famous white organdy with wide ruffled sleeves that Adrian designed for Joan Crawford in the movie *Letty Lynton* offered cheer and flattery. Macy's New York department store alone sold nearly half a million copies in 1932. The artist's eye perceived the need to balance Crawford's wide hips, thus the broad shouldered typical "Adrian silhouette" started a fashion revolution in America and abroad.

For Jean Harlow in *Dinner at Eight,* Adrian created another widely copied sheer white bias-cut satin ballgown. Though Madeleine Vionnet invented the bias cut and Elsa Schiaparelli was credited with padded shoulders, at least in Europe, Adrian had the awareness to bring high fashion and glamor to the screen. Joan Crawford praised Adrian's emphasis on simplicity to make a dramatic point, as in the suits she wore in her later films. Even in lavishly costumed period dramas, Adrian was able to stop short of excess. Often, as in Garbo's *Mata Hari,* the character's evolution into purity of spirit would be expressed through increased simplicity of costume. Adrian's understanding of light and shadow made possible dress that, due to clarity of line, looked as well in monochrome film, as later black and white photographs of his commercial designs would show. His eye for perfect cut was impeccable. A day suit consisting of a beige wool jacket trimmed with loops of black braid, paired with a slim black skirt, black gloves, and beige cartwheel hat, looks as crisp and smart today as it did when featured in *Vogue* in 1946. Fluid floor-length crêpe gowns would dramatically yet whimsically be decorated with asymmetrical motifs of horses, cherubs, or piano keys, or else his taste for modern art would be indulged in gowns made up of abstract jigsaw puzzle shapes in several colors.

Just as in films Adrian worked within themes, so did his collections for Adrian, Ltd. develop according to such themes as Grecian, Persian, Gothic, Spanish, or Americana. For the latter he appliquéd Pennsylvania Dutch designs on gowns and made tailored suits and bustled evening gowns out of checked gingham, echoing the gingham checks worn by Judy Garland in *The Wizard of Oz.* Adrian costumed Garbo as the essence of romance in *Camille,* not only in 19th-century crinolines, but in a death scene white nightgown which could have been any female viewer's late day dinner dress. For his average American customer, Adrian recommended clothes like the "costumes worn by the heroines of light comedies laid in moderate-sized towns." Katharine Hepburn in *The Philadelphia Story* was dressed by Adrian as the ideal girl next door, while conservative Norma Shearer in *The Women* mirrored the sophisticated simplicity of Adrian's future well-heeled Beverly Hills clients.

The spare, padded-shouldered, narrow waisted and skirted silhouette of the 1940s was the ideal medium for Adrian's artistry with fabric, while conforming to the wartime L-85 restrictions on materials—the U.S. government limitation on the amount of fabric used in a civilian garment for public consumption. The color inserts, appliqués, mitering of striped fabrics and combinations of materials in one ensemble allowed for savings in rationed fabrics, while creating the trademark Adrian look that was desired then and is still sought after by vintage clothing collectors. Old time movie glamor would resurface in some of Adrian's elegant columns of crêpe, diagonally embellished by headed bands of ancient motifs, or thick gilt embroidery on dark backgrounds. Diagonal lines and asymmetry also lent interest, as in a short sleeved wartime suit that was sewn half of plaid fabric—one sleeve and half the bodice culminating in a bow at the opposite hip, the other half of plain wool—completed by a hat trimmed with the plaid used as edging. Having grown up observing his father's millinery trade, Adrian had included hats in his movie stars' costumes, such widely copied designs as Garbo's slouch, cloche, and Eugenie in the 1930s.

Adrian unsuccessfully resisted Dior's round-shouldered New Look. Women returned to the home. Thirty years later, with the resurgence of women into the workforce, Adrian's broad shouldered looks enabled women to compete confidently with men, as designers resurrected the masterpieces of this truly American fashion virtuoso.

—Therese Duzinkiewicz Baker

AGHION, Gaby. See **CHLOÉ.**

AGNÈS B.
French designer

Born: Born Agnès Troublé in Versailles, France, 26 November 1941. **Family:** Married Christian Bourgois, 1958 (divorced); married Jean René Claret de Fleurieu, 1980; has five children from her marriages. **Career:** Junior fashion editor, *Elle* magazine, Paris, 1964; designer, press attaché and buyer for Dorothée Bis, Paris, 1965-66; free-lance designer for Limitex, Pierre d'Alby, V de V and Eversbin, Paris, 1966-75; set up CMC (Comptoir Mondial de Création) holding company for Agnès B., 1975; established first Agnès B. boutique in Les Halles, Paris, April 1975; opened second-hand shop in same street as boutique, 1977; created American subsidiary of CMC, and first American boutique in SoHo, New York, 1980; opened men and childrens' boutique Agnès B. Enfant, Paris, 1981; licence with Les Trois Suisses for mail order of selected items, 1982; opened Agnès B. "Lolita" boutique for teenagers, also opened la Galerie du Jour art gallery/bookshop, Paris, with ex-husband, 1984; launched perfume, *Le B,* skincare and cosmetics range and also a maternity collection, 1987; launched ranges of sunglasses and watches, 1989; launched perfume for children, *Le petit b.b.,* 1990; launch of perfume *Courant d'air,* 1992; has also established many shops in France and worldwide, including 26 in Japan, two in London, and four in USA. **Collections:** Musée des Arts de la Mode, Paris; Musée du Louvre, Paris. **Awards:** Order of Merit for Export, Paris. **Address:** 17 rue Dieu, 75010 Paris, France.

Publications:

On AGNÈS B.:

Articles

Voight, R., "Succès par excellence," in *Passion* (Paris), March 1983.
Jonah, Kathleen, "How to Live Straight from the Heart," in *Self,* October 1983.
Petkanas, Christopher, "Agnès B. from A to Z," in *Women's Wear Daily* (New York), 22 April 1985.
Bleichroeder, Ingrid, "A Certain Style: Agnès B," in *Vogue* (London), January 1986.
"Agnès B," in *Cosmopolitan* (London), September 1987.
Tretlack, Philippe, "Agnès B: Chez les Soviets," in *Elle* (Paris), 26 October 1987.
"Agnès B. Good," in the *Daily News Record* (New York), 2 May 1988.
Bucket, Debbie, "French Dressers," in *Clothes Show* (London), March 1989.

Tredre, Roger, "A Design Plan for No Seasons," in *The Independent* (London), 16 November 1989.

* * *

Agnès B. is a French sportswear designer who has catapulted herself to fame by challenging the need for fashion in clothing design. She denies that clothes must be stylized, highly detailed, and ephemeral in order to catch the public imagination. Her ascent began in the mid-1970s when, after only a few years in the fashion business, first as junior editor at *Elle* magazine and then briefly as an assistant to Dorothée Bis, she opened her own boutique in a converted butcher shop in Les Halles, Paris, to sell recut and redyed French workers' uniforms, black leather blazers, and T-shirts in striped rugby fabric. Her reputation grew as one of the first young French clothing designers to sell fashion to those who do not want to look too fashionable. In fact, her clothes, while identifiably French in their no-nonsense cut, simple, subdued colors (often black), and casual mood, have a timeless quality that keeps them current. The wrinkling common to natural materials and the already worn look that characterized the hippie ethos were translated by Agnès B. into a timeless chic, combining common sense with flair.

In the age of name identification and personal marketing, Agnès B. is as respected for her business sense as for her relaxed fashion designs. The spontaneous, childlike hand with which she quickly fashioned the logo for her stores belies a sophisticated business sense. Retaining her own independent boutique rather than being swallowed up in larger department stores, she astutely perceived that the non-design of her clothes was too inconspicuous, that they would blend in with other, trendier lines and be lost. She has opened over a dozen shops in France, of which seven are in Paris, with branches in Amsterdam, London, Tokyo, and the United States: two in New York, one in Boston, and one in Los Angeles.

Her understated approach to design for real people (men and children, as well as women) extends to her shows, which she calls working sessions, where professional models are rarely used, and her stores, in which casual and friendly salespeople mix their own antique or mod clothes with her separates. All the stores exude the same comfortable look, with pale wooden floors, white walls, and the occasional decorative tile. The flimsy curtain that separates the display area from the communal dressing rooms is an implication of the marginal distinction between Agnès B. clothes and what everyone else is wearing.

Agnès B. strikes a commercial and creative balance—a radical chic. "I have no desire to dress an elite," she states. "It's all a game. I work as if I were still in my grandmother's attic, dressing up. Clothes aren't everything. When they become too important, when they hide the person wearing them, then I don't like them. Clothes should make you feel happy, relaxed, and ready to tackle other problems."

—Sarah Bodine

AKIRA.

Japanese designer

Born: Maki Akira, Oita, Japan, c. 1949. **Education:** Graduated from Oita University; worked for, and studied fashion with, Reiko Minami, Tokyo. **Career:** Moved to New York, 1974; tailor, Halston, 1976-81; showed first own collection, 1982. **Address:** 200 West 57th Street, New York, New York 10019, USA.

Publications:

On AKIRA:

Articles

Hyde, Ann, "Akira on Bias," in *Threads* (Newtown, Connecticut), October/November 1991.

* * *

In the romantic imagination, the artist thrives on alienation, a critical distancing of an "other." Akira is of two worlds. In Japan, he is addressed by his surname Maki; in America he uses his first name Akira. These are social conventions of two cultures, but they are also theses and antitheses that propagate Akira's fashion. An American designer when he designs ready-to-wear clothing in Japan, Akira is conversely viewed in America as a Japanese designer working for the American custom market. In fact, he is both and neither. His state is only relaxed elegance. After studying and first designing in Japan, he was inspired by the work of Halston that he found in American fashion magazines to come to New York to work with Halston. Today, after working with him until 1981, when he established his own business, Akira is a designer of two identities, with businesses in two countries, and a single design philosophy, a synthesis of East and West.

In Akira's custom business in New York, he creates out of the most distilled, almost astringent, principles of design that he has maintained since working for Halston, with stress on bias cut, quality materials, color, and timeless elegance. His American custom client comes to Akira for a sense of personal comfort and self-assured dignity. While some of his American dresses, often bridal gowns, are adorned with beadwork and other decoration, their principle is in the cut. His is the abiding modernist conviction of truth to material and essential geometries of cut that animated Halston. An external simplicity, like that of a composed Japanese interior or a modern Western painting, is achieved through decisive reductivism and the primacy of the fabric. In his Japanese production, Akira is creating clothing for young women of Japan no less elegant than their American counterparts, but perhaps more fashion-forward. His suits for daywear and early evening emphasize a comfortable, soft shaping inspired in part by Claude Montana. American sportswear inspirations obtain for the collection in Japan, especially Claire McCardell, for what Akira acknowledges is a "very American look" reflective of the emergence of Japanese women in the 1980s and 1990s into active, comfortable American lifestyles.

Ann Hyde has pointed to the seeming contradiction between Akira's intellect in design and his sensuous achievement. "He is a rationalist at heart," argues Hyde, referring to his intense interest in the underlying mathematics and geometry of the garment, but he is also supremely the designer of elegance and grace (*Threads*, October/November 1991). The unifying factor, like that of Renaissance architecture, is proportion, indivisibly a coolly mathematical calculation and a supremely romantic sensibility.

Citing that he learned from Halston the value of the designer looking in the mirror, seeing front, back, and side in Cubist simultaneity, and seeing thereby the garment as paramount, not the wearer,

Akira points out the mirror's impression is more canny than the human eye in discerning proportion and balance. Work in the custom design studio of Halston and in his own design business in New York reinforces Akira's principle of design specific to the client, but generic to the design ideal in proportion. The same idea is carried through in the ready-to-wear collections in Japan. In the understanding of the mirror's perception and metaphor of the clothing, Akira also places the designer as an observer. Mirrors and worlds reflect off one another in Akira's soft, stately synthesis.

Bias is an essential feature of Akira's design, allowing both the design primacy that he upholds and the comfort in wearing. Recalling Halston's layered chiffons as "outrageously beautiful" in color and draping, Akira uses bias to wrap the form, conceiving of fashion not as a series of planes, but as a continuous volume realized three-dimensionally in the twist and torque of bias.

Recent collections have been inspired by Byzantine art and Turkish culture and by early Netherlandish painting, especially the work of Jan van Eyck.

If East and West, reason and style are the antipodes of Akira's work, there is synthesis in Akira's garments. It is an impressive joining of Japanese formality, American plainness, the restraint of design, and the universal common sense of comfortable, wearable clothing.

—Richard Martin

ALAIA, Azzedine.

French designer

Born: Tunis, Tunisia, c.1940. **Education:** Studied sculpture, École des Beaux-Arts, Tunis. **Career:** Dressmaker's assistant, Tunis, then dressed private clients before moving to Paris in 1957; part-time design assistant, Guy Laroche, Thierry Mugler, 1957-59; also housekeeper and dressmaker for the Marquise de Mazan, 1957-60, and for Comtesse Nicole de Blégiers, 1960-65; designer, custom clothing, from 1960; introduced ready-to-wear line, Paris, 1980, and New York, 1982; opened boutiques, Beverly Hills, 1983, Paris, 1985, and New York, 1988-92. **Exhibitions:** Retrospective, Bordeaux Museum of Modern Art, 1984-85. **Awards:** French Ministry of Culture Designer of the Year Award, 1985. **Address:** 7 rue de Moussy, 75002 Paris, France.

Publications:

On ALAIA:

Books

Howell, Georgina, *Sultans of Style: 30 Years of Fashion and Passion 1960-1990,* London 1990.

Articles

"Fashion Meets the Body: Azzedine Alaia on Splendid Form," in *Vogue* (London), July 1985.
White, Lesley, "At Long Last Alaia, the Chic of Araby," in *Elle* (London), November 1985.
Buck, Joan Juliet, "Body Genius," in *Vogue* (New York), November 1985.

"The Azzedine Mystique," in *Vogue* (New York), February 1986.
Arroyuelo, Javier, "L'art de vivre d'Azzedine Alaia," in *Vogue* (Paris), March 1986.
Dryansky, G. Y., "An Eye for Allure," in *Connoisseur,* August 1986.
Worthington, Christa, "The Rise and Fall of Azzedine Alaia," in *Women's Wear Daily* (New York), 17 October 1986.
"3 créateurs: Leur classiques. Azzedine Alaia, la perfection des lignes," in *Elle* (Paris), 10 November 1986.
"Alaia: La passion du vert," in *Elle* (Paris), March 1987.
Dries, Deborah, "The Defiant Ones," in *Art in America* (New York), September 1987.
"Alaia: The Total Look," in *Elle* (Paris), 26 October 1987.
"Finally Alaia Shows—to Mixed Reaction," in *Women's Wear Daily* (New York), 13 November 1987.
"The New Spirit of Azzedine Alaia," in *Vogue* (New York), February 1988.
"La femme un peu provocante d'Alaia," in *Elle* (Paris), 4 April 1988.
"Atmosphère Alaia," in *Vogue* (Paris), August 1988.
"Alaia e Gaultier: Due stilisti a confronto," in *Vogue* (Milan), October 1988.
"24 heures de la vie d'un tailleur," in *Elle* (Paris), 24 October 1988.
Nonkin, Leslie, "Azzedine Addicts: Affection Turns to Affliction for Alaia's Curvaceous Clothes," in *Vogue* (New York), November 1988.
Lalanne, Dorothea, "Mon coeur ... est à Papa," in *Vogue* (Paris), February 1989.
"Le printemps d'Azzedine Alaia," in *Elle* (Paris), 20 February 1989.
Maiberger, Elise, "Azzedine Alaia's Late Late Show," in *Vogue* (London), March 1989.
Scott, Jan, "Call This Man Alaia," in *Paris Passion* (Paris), March/April 1989.
"All About Alaia," in *Elle* (New York), April 1989.
Roberts, Michael, "Alaia, Alaia, Style on Fire," in *The Sunday Times Magazine* (London), 25 March 1990.
Lennard, Jonathan, "Alaia," in *Paris Passion* (Paris), July 1990.
Howell, Georgina, "Acting up for Azzedine," in *The Sunday Times Magazine* (London), 7 October 1990.
Schnabel, Julian, "Azzedine Alaia," in *Interview* (New York), October 1990.
"Azzedine Alaia," in *Current Biography,* October 1992.
Sischy, Ingrid, "The Outsider," in *The New Yorker* (New York), 7 November 1994.

*   *   *

Dubbed the King of Cling by the fashion press in the 1980s, Azzedine Alaia inspired a host of looks that energized high street fashion, including the stretch mini, Lycra cycling shorts, and the body suit.

His designs were renowned for the display of the female body they afforded and, accordingly, bedecked the bodies of off-duty top models and stars such as Tina Turner, Raquel Welch, and Brigitte Nielsen. Alaia's clothes caught the mood of the times when many women had turned to exercise and a new, muscled body shape had begun to appear in the pages of fashion magazines. Many women wanted to flaunt their newly toned bodies, helped by recent developments in fabric construction that enabled designers to create clothing that would accentuate the female form in a way unprecedented in European fashion.

Following in the footsteps of the *ancien régime* of Parisian haute couture, Alaia is a perfectionist about cut, drape, and construction, preferring to work directly onto the body to achieve a perfect fit. Tailoring is his great strength—he does all his own cutting—and, although his clothes appear very simple, they are complex in structure. Some garments contain up to 40 individual pieces linked together to form a complex mesh that moves and undulates with the body. The beauty of his design comes from the shape and fit of the garments, enhanced by his innovative use of criss-cross seaming.

His method of clothing construction includes repeated fitting and cutting on the body. His technique of sculpting and draping owes much to Madeleine Vionnet, the great *tailleur* of the 1920s, famed for the intricacies of her bias-cut crêpe dresses that moulded closely to the body. Vionnet applied the delicate techniques of lingerie sewing to outerwear, as has Alaia, who combines the stitching and seaming normally used in corsetry to achieve the perfect fit of his clothes. Combined with elasticated fabrics for maximum body exposure, his garments hold and control the body yet retain their shape.

Although at first sight his clothes seem to cling closely to the natural silhouette of the wearer, they actually create a second skin, holding in and shaping the body by techniques of construction such as faggoting. This body consciousness is further enhanced by using materials, such as stretch lace over flesh-coloured fabric, to give an illusion, rather than the reality, of nudity.

Alaia introduced his first ready-to-wear collection of minimalist clothes in 1980, and continued to work privately for individual customers until the mid-1980s. Although his clothes are indebted to the perfection of the female body, and indeed at times expose great expanses of skin, he manages to avoid vulgarity with muted colours and expert tailoring.

Based in Paris, Alaia shows regularly but nevertheless seems above the whims and vagaries of the fashion world, producing timeless garments rather than designing new looks from season to season, and inspiring the adulation from enthusiastic collectors that was once reserved for Mariano Fortuny.

—Caroline Cox

ALBINI, Walter.

Italian designer

Born: Born Gualtiero Albini in Busto Arsizio, near Milan, 9 March 1941. **Education:** Studied fashion and costume design, Istituto Statale di Belle Arti e Moda, Turin, 1959-61. **Career:** Illustrator for *Novità* and *Corriere Lombardo* periodicals, Milan, and free-lance sketch artist, Paris, 1961-64; free-lance designer for Krizia, Billy Ballo, Basile, Callaghan, Escargots, Mister Fox, Diamantis, Trell, Mario Ferari, Lanerossi, Kriziamaglia, Montedoro, and Princess Luciana, Milan, 1964-83; established Walter Albini fashion house, Milan, 1965; signature ready-to-wear collection introduced, 1978; Walter Albini Fashions branches established, London, Rome, Venice. *Died* (in Milan) *31 May 1983.*

Publications:

On ALBINI:

Books

Vercelloni, Isa, and Flavio Lucchini, *Milano Fashion,* Milan 1975.
Mulassano, Adriana, *The Who's Who of Italian Fashion,* Florence 1979.
Soli, Pia, *Il genio antipatico,* Venice 1984.
Buiazzi, Graziella, ed., *La moda italiana: Dall'antimoda allo stilismo,* Milan 1987.
Sozzani, Carla, and Anna Masucci, *Walter Albini,* Milan 1990.

Articles

"Walter Albini," in *The Sunday Times* (London), 15 October 1972.
"In Focus: Walter Albini," in *International Textiles* (London), No. 523, 1975.
Etherington-Smith, Meredith, "Albini's New Image," in *GQ* (New York), October 1976.
"Walter Albini, the Designer's Designer," in *Manufacturing Clothier,* 1976.
"Lo stile multimaglia in sfumature rare," in *Vogue* (Milan), October 1978.
"Walter Albini: Italian RTW Designer Is Dead," in *Women's Wear Daily* (New York), 3 June 1983.
"Walter Albini, Men's Wear Innovator, Dies at 42," in the *Daily News Record,* 3 June 1983.
Skellenger, Gillion, "Walter Albini," in *Contemporary Designers,* London 1990.

* * *

In William Shakespeare's *Richard II,* "report of fashions in proud Italy" are the vanguard for what comes to England only in "base imitation." Walter Albini epitomizes the brilliant epoch of Italian fashion in the 1970s, when it seized the international imagination. At least as much as any other designer, if not more, Albini had the Italian spirit *con brio.* Journalists compared him to Yves Saint Laurent and Karl Lagerfeld, designers whose careers outlasted Albini's flash of brilliance. Albini brought his obsession with the 1920s and 1930s to the elongated line and youthful energy of the 1970s; his collections of 1969 and 1970 tell the story of his encapsulation of the time: Gymnasium and Gypsy and China in 1969; Antique Market, The Pre-Raphaelites, Safari, Military, and Polaroid in 1970.

Sadly, Albini so brilliantly embodies the 1970s for Italy (as one would perhaps say of Halston in the United States) because of the détente of his work by 1980 and his death in 1983, just after his forty-second birthday. His Gatsby-like style and passion for life were fulfilled in prodigious achievement—once even, in five simultaneous collections, in romantic brevity, and in the youthful exuberance immortalized by his early death.

Isa Vercelloni and Flavio Lucchini described Albini's mercurial and gifted personality and habits: "From adolescence he still retains the capacity of dreaming, but with the ability of giving body or a semblance of reality to his world of dreams. He has the rare quality of even doing this without spoiling it. This is why women like his dresses so much. They recognize immediately that imagination is given power" (*Milano Fashion,* Milan 1975). It was a wide-ranging imagination, indicative of the 1970s in its travelogue-inspired wanderlust, that captured the vivacity of Diana Vreeland's *Vogue* of the 1960s. Like Vreeland, Albini loved the 1920s and extolled the freedom of women and reminded them of their liberation during that period. Also like Vreeland, Albini was smitten with North Africa and the potential for exoticism. He played with paisley and was fascinated by the pattern and design asymmetry as well as the mysterious women of China. His pragmatic exoticism is evident in a spring 1980 T-blouse and party skirt combination, described in advertising copy in *Harper's Bazaar* (March 1980) as "the mystique of madras. A bit sophisticated for midnight at the oasis ... but divine for sunset on the patio."

So many collections were produced in his own name and others between the late 1960s and 1980 that he touched upon many themes, but he returned consistently to the 1920s and 1930s. He had moved to Paris because of a lifetime preoccupation with Chanel, whom he had glimpsed during her late years, but he more substantively used her as a touchstone for his collections. His fall 1978 knits, as photographed by David Bailey, intensified the luxury of Chanel tailoring, although slightly oversized, in a palette of bronze and browns. For his Mister Fox line in beautiful geometrics, he approximated Sonia Delaunay, but echoed the feeling of Chanel. His movie and fashion magazine passions would encompass Katharine Hepburn and Marlene Dietrich, but for Albini these merely confirmed the role of Chanel in freeing women to be comfortable in sportswear- and menswear-derived styles that were luxuriously tailored for women.

Besides Chanel, Albini's other passion was for ancient Egypt, for which he felt mystical affinity and which served as an inspiration for his men's and women's fashions—especially his fashion drawings. By the mid-1970s, Albini's style was predominately an amalgam of ancient Egyptian motifs (although often attributed elsewhere in the East) and Chanel, using the Chanel suits and proportions with the accommodations of wrapping *à la Egyptienne* and the excuses of Venice, North Africa, and India for billowing harem pants and other pantaloons of which Chanel would scarcely have approved. In 1978 a riding skirt, with its fluid drape, was teamed with a short cropped jacket, combining tradition with contemporary 1970s style.

In some ways, Albini was the precursor of Gianni Versace. His intensely personal style respected many historical exemplars and was passionately defended and highly expressive. Like Versace, Albini combined a studious infatuation with the past with a passion for his own synthesis of styles and a comprehensive style attainment and conviction that was his own; he created this with a fervor approaching fanaticism that reinforced the sense of abiding adolescence and keenest ebullience for the work.

Vercelloni and Lucchini asked Albini what his motto was. He said, "Enjoy today and leave unpleasant things for tomorrow." For Albini and the extravagant fashion that he created, fate held no tomorrow and no unpleasantness.

—Richard Martin

ALFARO, Victor.

American designer

Born: Mexico, c.1965. **Education:** Attended Univeristy of Texas, 1982; graduated from Fashion Institute of Technology, 1987. Immigrated to the United States, 1981. **Career:** Assistant to Mary Ann Restivo, late 1980s, and Joseph Abboud, 1990; established own business, early 1990s. **Awards:** Best new talent award, 1995, Council of Fashion Designers of America. **Address:** 130 Barrow Street, New York, NY 10014, USA.

Publications:

On ALFARO:

Articles

Hochswender, Woody, "Patterns: An American Alaïa," in the *New York Times,* 7 April 1992.
Hochswender, Woody, "Tufts and Tacks, Bells and Beads," in the *New York Times,* 9 April 1992.
Lee, Ricky, "New York to Mexico," in the *New York Times,* 2 August 1992.
Fischer, Laura, "The Thrill of Victor," in *Avenue* (New York), March 1993.
Spindler, Amy M., "For Next Wave, Attitude Counts," in the *New York Times,* 2 April 1993.
Spindler, Amy M., "Fresh Talents Dig Up Tasty Design," in the *New York Times,* 5 November 1993.
Foley, Bridget, "Alfaro Sprouts," in *W* (New York), March 1994.
"Alfaro: Beyond the Pale," in *Women's Wear Daily* (New York), 9 August 1994.
Torkells, Erik, "The Night Is Young," in *Town & Country* (New York), September 1994.
"New York: Victor Alfaro," in *Women's Wear Daily* (New York), 4 November 1994.
Spindler, Amy M., "Learning from Las Vegas and Show World," in the *New York Times,* 5 November 1994.
Min, Janice, and Allison Lynn, "Fitting Pretty," in *People* (New York), 20 March 1995.

*   *   *

Bare simplicity and an equally frank sexuality inform Victor Alfaro's dresses for cocktail and evening. Bridget Foley predicted in *W* (March 1994): "The heir apparent to Oscar and Bill? Perhaps. Victor Alfaro may be New York's next great eveningwear designer." If Alfaro is the torchbearer of style for New York nights, his role betokens a shifting sensibility, one that pointedly exalts the body and seeks out youth and one that takes risks. Skilled in the vocabulary of separates (he worked for Mary Ann Restivo and Joseph Abboud), Alfaro eagerly draws upon the street for inspiration and demands a body consciousness that has made some call him the American Alaïa. In a first recognition as designer for celebrities, photographed by Francesco Scavullo for covers of *Cosmopolitan* in New York, Alfaro flirted with attention-getting vulgarity, though his collections have come to represent a more natural, but nonetheless wilfully seductive, sensuality.

Amy Spindler reported in the *New York Times* (2 April 1993), "Victor Alfaro's clothes come with plenty of attitude." The attitude is, of course, of post-feminist women's individuality and options, including a very 1990s reexamination of the possibilities of seductive, relatively bare clothing in the most luxurious fabrics. One needs a self-confidence approaching attitude to wear dresses and outfits of such body-revealing form, but one also needs a distinct segregation of Alfaro's partywear from day-to-day clothing. His clothes are not for the timid, but neither are they for showgirls.

Amy Spindler refers to his "sex-kitten clothes," but their relative austerity, depending entirely upon textile and shape, keeps them from being vitiated by Las Vegas.

In fact, Alfaro raises provocative issues of women's overt and self-assured physicality and sexuality more than of sexual license. To be sure, short skirts, bared shoulders, lace in direct contact with skin, leather notes, and sheer, skimming fabrics suggest fetishes, but there is always something strangely wholesome about Alfaro's sensibility. The singer Mariah Carey is quoted as saying very aptly that Alfaro's "clothes are fierce." Their ferocity resides in the fact that they define strong women.

According to Ricky Lee (*New York Times,* 2 August 1992), Alfaro was counseled by one buyer from Chicago that in order to succeed he should add more suits to his line. But Alfaro rightly declined, knowing that he is not creating professional clothes or daywear basics. He eschews sobriety and, with it, tailoring. Rather, he is responding to sexuality's siren and creating the sexiest siren dresses for young New Yorkers of the 1990s. He is dressmaker to the legendary "Generation X." At least at this moment, Alfaro is defining a strong personal style and a clientèle that is generationally, visually, and libidinously nurtured on MTV and informed by multicultural street smarts. Woody Hochswender reported in the *New York Times* (9 April 1992) that Alfaro's collection "suggested sex—in a voice loud enough to clear a disco. There were lace chaps and fake snake chaps, worn over bodysuits. Skintight snakeskin jeans were zipped all the way from front to back, reason unknown. Rib-knit sweater dresses were worn with harnesses of metal mesh, Mr Alfaro's version of the bondage look that is sweeping fashion."

Explaining his relative restraint and deliberate avoidance of vulgarity in his fall/winter 1993-94 collection to Bridget Foley, Alfaro explained: "I didn't want it to look cheap. Buyers see every trick in the book, and they want clothes that are wearable." Alfaro has consistently made unencumbered clothing, emphasizing minimalist sensibility and cut and employing luxurious materials. In these characteristics, he is a designer in the great American tradition. His distinctive deviation from that tradition might seem to be his hot sexuality, the body-tracing and body-revealing simplicity of his clothes. But again and again 20th-century American designers have been dressing advanced new women of ever-increasing power and self-assurance.

Alfaro is creating the post-feminist fashion sensibility, consummately beautiful in execution, infinitely skilled in construction, and assertively avant-garde. Even as some critics dismiss his work as offensive, Alfaro is a true fashion risk-taker and visionary. He is defining and dressing today, and will dress hereafter, the bravest woman of the future.

—Richard Martin

ALLARD, Linda.

American designer

Born: Akron, Ohio, 27 May 1940; grew up in Doylestown. **Education:** Studied Fine Arts, Kent State University, Kent, Ohio, 1958-62. **Career:** Design assistant, Ellen Tracy, New York, 1962-64, then director of design, from 1964; Linda Allard label introduced, 1984; design critic, Fashion Institute of Technology, New York; visiting professor, International Academy of Merchandising and Design, Chicago; board of directors, Kent State University; member of The Fashion Group International, Inc., Council of Fashion Designers of America. **Awards:** Dallas Fashion Award, 1986, 1987. **Address:** 575 Seventh Avenue, New York, NY 10018, USA.

Publications:

On ALLARD:

Articles

Daria, Irene, "Linda Allard: Growing up with Ellen Tracy," in *Women's Wear Daily* (New York), 2 June 1986.
Caminiti, Susan, "A.K.A. Ellen Tracy," in *Savvy* (New York), October 1988.
Kantrowitz, Barbara, "The Real Designer Behind that Ellen Tracy Label: Linda Allard Focuses on Clothes that Work," in *Newsweek* (New York), 24 October 1988.
"Linda Allard," in *Accessories,* December 1988.
Schiro, Anne-Marie, "Designed for Retailers and Real Women," in the *New York Times,* 5 April 1995.

*   *   *

Linda Allard is the woman behind Ellen Tracy. In fact, there is no Ellen Tracy—there never was. The company was founded in 1949 by Herbert Gallen, a juniors blouse manufacturer, who invented the name Ellen Tracy for his fledgling firm. Gallen hired Allard in 1962, fresh out of college, as a design assistant. Quickly, she expanded the line to include trousers and jackets. Two years later, she was made director of design and a new Ellen Tracy was born. Since then, under Allard's artistic leadership, Ellen Tracy has become synonymous with top quality fabrics, clean lines, and the concept of a complete wardrobe for the working woman.

Linda Allard grew up in Doyleston, Ohio in a hundred-year-old farmhouse with five brothers and sisters. Like many women Allard was taught to sew at the age of ten by her mother and quickly began designing garments for her dolls. "Even before I could sew, I was always designing clothes for my paper dolls," she said. After receiving a Fine Arts degree from Kent State University in 1962, she moved to New York, where she received her first job offer from Gallen.

Shortly after Allard joined the firm, Ellen Tracy moved away from junior clothing to apparel designed for the newly established female workforce of the 1960s. Allard was one of the first designers to address the new shifting demographics, creating a professional look, stylish yet appropriate for the workplace. Eventually, by the mid-1970s, the company moved into the bridge market. The bridge collections—which fill the gap between upper-end designer lines and mass-market brands—have since become the fastest-growing area of the women's fashion market, key to Ellen Tracy's success, with the company's volume nearly tripling over the following decade.

As the creative force behind Ellen Tracy, Allard has transformed the company into one of the key anchor designers in the bridge market. To give the collection more of a designer feel, Allard's name was placed on the Ellen Tracy label in 1984. Nonetheless, Allard believes high fashion has little relevance to most women's lives. "The extreme end of fashion is over-rated," she said. "It gets a lot of coverage by the press, but it doesn't mean anything to a lot of women. We mean more to real women."

Linda Allard: For Ellen Tracy, Fall 1994; double breasted pant suit with a v-neck cardigan.

Today, working with a 12-person design team, Allard is responsible for the entire Ellen Tracy line. For Allard, designing begins with an emphasis on high-quality fabrics and specific color grouping. "We start with color and a sense of the flavor of the collection. Will it be fluid or rigid, soft and slouchy or tailored? The focus is on easy dressing and effortless shapes. We develop the fabrics first, finding the texture that expresses the attitude we feel, and then comes the styling. Fabrics make the collection unique." There are three Ellen Tracy collections each year. To ensure the clothes work well with each other, each garment is sold separately. "The modern woman buys a wardrobe of jackets that work well in a variety of pairings," says Allard.

One of the keys to Allard's success has been her ability to diversify. In 1981, Ellen Tracy launched a petits division and in 1985 a successful dress division. To cater to the more leisure-oriented customer, Ellen Tracy launched its latest extension, a sportswear line, Company, in the fall of 1991. Allard says her intent is to provide "the same level of quality for the woman who doesn't need strictly career clothes, or whose career offers more fashion choices than the tailored suits we're known for." In 1993, the company introduced a large-sizes division and sophisticated evening dress collection. A perfume line was launched in 1992. Ellen Tracy also has licensing agreements to produce scarves, shoes, eyewear, hosiery, and handbags.

Allard lives and works in Manhattan and spends weekends in her new country home in Washington, Connecticut set on 60 acres of rolling countryside. She designed the house with her brother David Allard, an architect. The house is a 5,500 square feet Palladian-inspired villa, complete with studio and guest quarters. "When we were designing my new house, I challenged my architect brother to take strong classical designs of the past and make them livable for today," she explains.

When asked in an interview with *Women's Wear Daily* if there were a missing ingredient in her life, she replied, "I've always thought about the idea of having children, but I think children need to be nurtured, and I don't think you can do that from five to six at night." In another interview she said, "from the age of ten I always wanted to design. I never excluded having a family, but my work is so demanding. I'm happy that I have a lot of nieces and nephews, so I can enjoy family life and kids, and that's a lot of fun."

—Janet Markarian

ALLY CAPELLINO.

British design firm

Founded by Middlesex Polytechnic graduates Alison Lloyd and Johnathan (Jono) Platt, 1979. After graduation, worked for Courtaulds, then Platt worked for Betty Jackson and Lloyd made hats and jewellery at home. Designed accessories, selling to Miss Selfridges chain, 1979; developed clothing range, 1980; collection for Olympic Games, Moscow, 1980, which received critical attention; introduced childrenswear line, Mini Capellino, 1981; menswear line launched, 1986; signed licensing agreement with CGO Co., Japan, 1987; opened flagship store, Soho, London, 1988; launched diffusion sportswear line, Hearts of Oak, 1990; signed agreement with textile firm Coats Viyella for promotion and marketing, 1992; design consultants to the firm, from 1992; introduced

Ally-T range of T-shirts, 1993; collaboration with Jones Bootmaker to develop dual label shoes, 1994. **Address:** N1R, Metropolitan Wharf, Wapping Wall, London E1 9SS, England.

Publications:

On ALLY CAPELLINO:

Articles

"Influences: Ally Capellino," in *Women's Journal* (London), April 1985.
Tyrrel, Rebecca, "Rival Look on the City Streets," in *The Sunday Times Magazine* (London), 4 September 1988.
"No Business Like Show Business," in *Fashion Weekly* (London), 9 March 1989.
Dutt, Robin, "Ally Capellino," in *Clothes Show* (London), October/November 1989.

*   *   *

In the early 1990s a truce seemed to have been called between British fashion designers and clothing manufacturers. Large manufacturers such as Coats Viyella and Courtaulds had previously viewed the fashion designer as a suspicious entity. However, a change in consumer needs and public taste has forced many companies to rethink their strategies. High Street retailers, such as Miss Selfridge or Top Shop, are demanding short runs of stock in response to swiftly changing trends. This very much reflects the designer's needs for small quantities of product that are often difficult and expensive to produce. Ally Capellino is one of the designer names to bridge the gap between these problems. In 1992 the company signed an agreement with Coats Viyella, Britain's largest textile company, to promote and market their brand name and give them access to Coats Viyella's design and production facilities, which are amongst the most advanced in technological development in the world. In return Ally Capellino would bring a more fashion-orientated handwriting to the business through acting as design consultants. This would, in turn, hopefully avert the criticism aimed at British clothing manufacturers, for producing unadventurous products.

Ally Capellino was founded in 1979 by Alison Lloyd and Jono Platt, both graduates from the BA fashion course at Middlesex Polytechnic. Initially selling accessories to British fashion chains Miss Selfridge and Elle, the company developed a distinctive clothing line that includes children's, men's and womenswear, with simple, well-cut lines and cotton separates. This was developed and sold to an international market, predominantly in Italy, the United States and Japan.

In 1987 the company signed a licensing contract with the GCO Company in Japan, which aimed to achieve optimum positioning of the label in terms of retail, public relations, and advertising exposure. This was followed, in 1988, by the opening of the Ally Capellino store in Soho, London which has since developed into an emporium for clothing, childrenswear, and lifestyle items. Hearts of Oak, a diffusion sportswear collection, was introduced in 1990, followed by the launch of Ally-T, a unisex range of T-shirts, in 1993.

Alison Lloyd sees herself as one of a new breed of fashion designers, far more commercially and market-orientated, as she said when interviewed in *The Independent,* London: "We are sensible

Ally Capellino: Winter, 1994.

rather than outrageous. We have made many mistakes in the past, but we have learned from them, and we made them with our own money rather than relying on handouts." This is a very positive attitude in light of the agreement made between the company and Coats Viyella. Many previous associations between industrial giants and designer names have become stifled rather than creative. Ally Capellino want to retain independence but capitalize on the commerciality of their association.

Ally Capellino seems to have found the perfect solution to a classic problem. With the potential to become one of the top designer names in Europe, the company has established a business association which recognizes the fact that designer fashion represents the tip of a six billion pound industry, in terms of prestige and kudos. The company is set to develop its brand name towards the extensive licensing opportunities available to a designer name.

—Kevin Almond

AMIES, Hardy.

British designer

Born: Edwin Hardy Amies in London, 17 July 1909. **Education:** Studied at Brentwood School to 1927. **Career:** School teacher, Antibes, 1927; office assistant, Bendorf, Germany, 1928-30; trainee, W. & T. Avery Ltd., Birmingham, England, 1930-34; managing designer, Lachasse, 1934, managing director, 1935-39. Served in the British Army Intelligence Corps, 1939-45; lieutenant colonel; head of Special Forces Commission to Belgium, 1944. Designed for Worth and for the British government Utility Scheme during the war; established own couture business, Hardy Amies Ltd., 1946; introduced ready-made line, 1950; dressmaker by appointment for HM Queen Elizabeth II, England, from 1955; added menswear, 1959; firm owned by Debenhams, 1973-81, re-purchased by Amies, 1981. Also menswear designer for Hepworths, from 1961. Vice-chairman, 1954-56, and chairman, 1959-60, Incorporated Society of London Fashion Designers. **Awards:** Named Officier de l'Ordre de la Couronne, Belgium, 1946; Royal Warrant awarded, 1955; *Harper's Bazaar* Award, 1962; Caswell-Massey International Award, 1962, 1964, 1968; *Ambassador* Magazine Award, 1964; *The Sunday Times* Special Award, London, 1965; Commander of the Royal Victorian Order, 1977; Personnalité de l'Année (Haute Couture), Paris, 1986; British Fashion Council Hall of Fame Award, 1989; Knight Commander of the Victorian Order, 1989. **Address:** Hardy Amies Ltd., 14 Savile Row, London W1X 2JN, England.

Publications:

By AMIES:

Books

Here Lived..., Cambridge 1948.
Just So Far, London 1954.
The ABC of Men's Fashion, London 1964.
Still Here, London 1984.

Articles

"A Century of Fashion," in the *RSA Journal* (London), March 1989.

On AMIES:

Books

Lambert, Eleanor, *World of Fashion: People, Places, Resources,* New York and London 1976.
McDowell, Colin, *A Hundred Years of Royal Style,* London 1985.
Milbank, Caroline Rennolds, *Couture: The Great Designers,* New York 1985.

Articles

"Hardy Country," in *Vogue* (London), March 1975.
Boyd, Ann, "Hardy Amies, Haute Couturier," in *The Observer* (London), 3 February 1980.
"Happy Birthday Mr. Amies," in *Vogue* (London), July 1989.
Ginsburg, Madeleine, "Tailor-made," in *Country Life* (London), 13 July 1989.
Lambert, Elizabeth, and Derry Moore, "The Reign of Hardy Amies: The Queen's Couturier in London and Gloucestershire," in *Architectual Digest* (Los Angeles), September 1989.
"Hardy Perennial," in *Fashion Weekly* (London), 19 October 1989.

*   *   *

Hardy Amies began his career as a couturier when he was brought in as managing designer at Lachasse, in London, after the departure in 1933 of Digby Morton. He acknowledges that by examining the models left by Morton he learnt the construction of tailored suits. The 1930s was an auspicious time for the new generation of London couture houses that had begun to emerge, for the British tailored suit reigned supreme in America. Amies's contribution to the construction of the tailored suit for women was to lower the waistline of the jacket, which he believed Morton had always set too high, thus giving the "total effect of a more important-looking suit." His fashion philosophy, that elegant clothes must have a low waistline, has characterized his work ever since and his clothes are always cut just above the hipline rather than on the natural waistline. Working on his theory that fashion design should be a process of "evolution rather than revolution," Amies concedes that his duty as a designer is to vary the cut and design of the tailored suit to make it as feminine as possible, without departing from the canons of good tailoring.

Like his counterparts in the London couture, Amies's work was always tempered by the requirements of the private couture customer who formed the main part of the business. Unlike the Paris couture houses who enjoyed the support of large textile firms, who saw the link with couture as a beneficial form of publicity, as well as backing from the French Government for its *industrie de luxe,* the London couture houses did not benefit from such aid. Thus the main role of the London couture was not to create what Amies has described as avant-garde clothes for publicity purposes but to design for the individual customer.

Amies is perhaps best known for his work for Queen Elizabeth II for whom he began a long association as a royal dressmaker in 1950 when he made several outfits for the then Princess Elizabeth's royal tour to Canada. Although the couture side of the Hardy Amies business is the less financially successful area today, it has nonetheless given his house a degree of respectability as a royal warrant holder. One of Hardy Amies's best known creations is the gown he designed in 1977 for Queen Elizabeth's Silver Jubilee portrait which, he says, has been "immortalized on a thousand biscuit tins." However, while Amies's royal patronage has clearly enforced his international image, the couture side of his business is less financially successful than his menswear and related fashion spin-offs such as licences. These include small leather goods, ties, knitwear, and shirts which are produced under licence in various countries including America, Canada, Australia, and Japan where the Hardy Amies label has become a household name with his association with Diatobo.

Another side of Hardy Amies's work is seen in his designs for corporate uniforms for the service industries, such as hotels and airlines, where his reputation both as a designer of tailored clothes and his royal association have undoubtedly made him an appealing choice.

Hardy Amies is one of Britain's best known establishment designers. He has weathered the transformation of London's fashion image as the home of the thoroughbred tailored suit to a veritable melting pot of creativity, during the course of a career which has spanned more than half a century.

—Catherine Woram

ANSELM, Marilyn and Yoram. See **HOBBS LTD.**

ANTHONY, John.

American designer

Born: Gianantonio Iorio in New York, 28 April 1938. **Education:** Studied at the Accademia delle Belle Arti, Rome, 1956-57; graduated from Fashion Institute of Technology, New York, 1959. **Family:** Married Molly Anthony; son: Mark. **Career:** Designer, in New York, for Devonbrook, 1959-68, and Adolph Zelinka, 1968-70; John Anthony, Inc., established in New York, 1971-79, and from 1986. **Awards:** Maison Blanche Award, New Orleans, 1964; Silver Cup Award, Kaufmann's Department Stores, Pittsburgh, 1964; Mortimer C. Ritter Award, Fashion Institute of Technology, New York, 1964; "Winnie" Coty Award, 1972; Coty Return Award, 1976.

Publications:

On ANTHONY:

Books

Morris, Bernadine, and Barbara Walz, *The Fashion Makers,* New York 1978.

Milbank, Caroline Rennolds, *New York Fashion: The Evolution of American Style,* New York 1989.

Articles

Larmoth, Jeanine, "Haute Couture American Style: The Free Spirit," in *Town and Country* (New York), May 1991.

*   *   *

John Anthony believes that designing clothes is a fusion of function and purpose. The function appears to be his logical, wearable approach. The purpose lies in his pared-down minimalist ideas. He edits collections down to their bare essentials.and, whilst other designers often show over 100 styles per collection, he makes his statement in under 50. His subtle, understated clothes are designed for a young, sophisticated woman. He uses natural fabrics like wool crêpe, chiffon, jersey, satin, and menswear fabrics. He is particularly noted for his cardigan sweaters or pullovers teamed with skirts and his pared-down gala evening gowns, in contradictory daywear fabrics.

Educated at the Accademia delle Belle Arti in Rome, and the Fashion Institute of Technology in New York, Anthony worked for several wholesale companies before opening his own house with the manufacturer Robert Levine in 1971. He immediately marketed his look towards the top end of ready-to-wear, establishing a glossy, up-to-the-minute fashion image and selling to leading retail stores.

John Anthony's first collection was an edited Marlene Dietrich look, featuring masculine tailoring in pinstripe and herringbone wools, softened with blouses underneath, or pleated and smocked crêpe dresses. By 1976 he was showing the soft, liquid separates that became his trademark; ice cream colours seemed to melt into clothes that were so light they almost floated.

His modern understatements have brought him commissions from high profile clients like US presidents' wives Betty Ford, Rosalynn Carter, and Jacqueline Kennedy Onassis, who needed to attract attention through impeccable taste rather than outrageous overstatement. Performers Lena Horne and Audrey Meadows have also been customers, comfortable with the John Anthony style philosophy.

Muted colour is another strong feature of his work. He believes the colour palette in a collection should intermingle, so that one item can easily go with everything else. His first collection was predominantly black with white, navy, and red. He claims to hate shock colours like turquoise or fuchsia and has usually been faithful to a range of beiges, christened with names such as peanut and cinnamon.

Anthony considers the designer's job to be to make things easy for the customer. However, behind this ease lies a renowned skill for cutting, tailoring, and overall dedication to developing a specialist style, which has won the designer Coty Awards.

Born Gianantonio Iorio in Queens, New York, to a metalworker, John Anthony has evolved into a dress designer who uses the most luxurious fabrics in the simplest shapes with unequalled taste. He was one of the first designers to promote the idea of easy-to-travel clothes that can be rolled up in a ball and thrown into a suitcase, with no danger of wrinkling. He recommends that his customer buys a few things that work for her each season, then interchanges and adapts these garments to create several different looks.

—Kevin Almond

Aquascutum, Ltd.: "Paisley/Charlbury" trenchcoats.

APOSTOLOPOULOS, Nikos. See **NIKOS.**

AQUASCUTUM, LTD.

British ready-to-wear firm

Founded by John Emary in London, 1851; early firsts include rain-repellent woollen cloth, the raglan sleeve and the trench coat. Manufacturer of outerwear, from 1851; introduced womenswear, 1909; New York showroom opened, 1948; manufacturing outlet in Canada opened, 1949; Manchester and Bristol shops opened, 1950s; added suits for men, 1951; introduced full line of women's fashions, 1986. Granted royal warrants, 1897, 1902, 1903, 1911, 1929, 1949, 1952. **Awards:** Clothing Oscar, 1958; Queen's Award for Export Achievement, 1966, 1967, 1971, 1976, 1979, 1990; British Knitting and Clothing Export Council Export Award, 1986. **Address:** 100 Regent St., London W1A 2AQ, England.

Publications:

By AQUASCUTUM:

Books

The Story of Aquascutum, London 1959.
The Aquascutum Story, London 1976, 1991.

On AQUASCUTUM:

Books

Adburgham, Alison, *Shops and Shopping,* London 1964.
Hobhouse, Hermione, *A History of Regent Street,* London 1975.

Articles

"Aquascutum—100 Years Proof," in *Vogue* (London), March 1976.
York, Peter, and Page Hill Starzinger, "Americans Have Often Taken Fashion Inspiration from the British," in *Vogue* (New York), February 1990.
Fallon, James, "Aquascutum Accepts $121m Buyout Offer," in the *Daily News Record* (New York), 25 April 1990.
Taylor, John, "The Aquascutum Heritage," in *British Style,* No. 3, 1990.

*　　*　　*

Aquascutum's distinctive name is two Latin words meaning "watershield"—a name which has become synonymous with the best of traditional British clothing. Aquascutum originated as a name for the finely tailored coats made of showerproof natural fabrics developed by a small tailoring firm based in London's Regent Street. They were ideal protection from England's inclement weather, and, like many ostensibly functional items of clothing and footwear, the Aquascutum raincoat or cape also achieved high fash-

ion status, worn even in fine weather. Today's equivalent may be seen in the likes of the Burberry jacket, originally created for "huntin', shootin' and fishin'" but as likely to be seen worn over a city suit as on the moors. Timberland and Dr Martens boots were also developed originally as work footwear but have achieved cult fashion status.

A royal customer has always been an important asset to any business, and Aquascutum was fortunate in attracting the custom of Edward VII, Prince of Wales, who wore both greatcoats and capes made of the miraculously rain-repellent cloth. In 1897, the company was awarded its first royal warrant as "Waterproofers" to HRH The Prince of Wales.

For the first 50 years of business, Aquascutum was involved solely in the production of clothing for gentlemen. In 1909 the company launched its first collection of womenswear, prompted by the increasing popularity of sportswear for women. The often-romanticized imaged of the landed gentlemen and his tweed-clad lady have become potent symbols of English culture, and a persistent element in Britain's international fashion image. It is interesting to note that when fashion designer Katherine Hamnett first showed her collection in Paris in 1989, *Le Figaro* remarked upon the fact that England now produced clothes other than cashmere sweaters and raincoats. In this light it is understandable that, when foreigners refer to English style, they are usually implying the quintessentially English look of companies such as Aquascutum or Burberry, rather than the avant-garde style of contemporary designers. Aquascutum represents the traditional image of thoroughly good British taste which lent itself perfectly to the sporting events that dominated the English Season.

While Aquascutum is perhaps best recognized for its clothing, it is in fact the company's technical achievements in the textiles field that are most remarkable. The 1950s were an important period for the company in terms of textile developments. In 1955 Aquascutum introduced an iridescent-toned cotton gabardine for men's and women's raincoats. Three years later they launched a black evening coat made of showerproof wool and mohair fabric which won the company a clothing Oscar. In 1959 the Aqua 5 rainproof cloth was introduced which eliminated the need for re-proofing after dry cleaning and which resulted in worldwide acclaim for Aquascutum. The company's continuing commitment in today's textile field sees development in the latest microfibre fabrics which are now incorporated into both the menswear and womenswear collections.

Today Aquascutum produces an extensive collection of clothing and accessories for men and women—a full range of womenswear was introduced in 1986. Accessories include handbags and travel bags, umbrellas, hats, scarves and small leather goods, many of which bear the company's coat of arms. As a company that originated producing clothing that protected its wearer from an unruly native climate, Aquascutum has since become a recognized brand label at international level.

—Catherine Woram

ARAI, Junichi.

Japanese textile designer

Born: Kiryu City, Gunma Prefecture, 13 March 1932. **Education:** Trained in weaving at his father's textile factory, 1950-55; also studied at the Theater Arts Institute, Tokyo, 1953. **Family:** Married Riko Tanagawa in 1958; children: Motomi and Mari. **Career:** Independent textile designer in Tokyo, from 1955; developed new metallic yarn techniques, 1955-66; worked with fashion designers Rei Kawakubo, Issey Miyake, Shin Hosokawa, and others, from 1970; produced computer-designed woven fabrics, from 1979; founder, Anthology studio, 1979, and Arai Creation System company, 1987; opened Nuno fabrics shop, Tokyo, 1984; advisor, Yuki Tsumugi Producers Assn., Japanese Ministry of Trade, and International Wool Secretariat from 1987. Also formed Tomodachi Za puppet theater group, 1950. **Exhibitions:** Gen Gallery, Tokyo, 1983; Nichifutsu Gallery, Kyoto, 1984; Sagacho Exhibition Space, Tokyo, 1984; Shimin Gallery, Sapporo, 1985; Axis Gallery, Tokyo, 1986; Rhode Island School of Design, Providence, 1988; *Hand and Technology: Textiles by Junichi Arai 1992,* Yurakucho Asashi Gallery, Asashi, Japan; Pacific Art Center, Los Angeles, 1993. **Awards:** Mainichi Fashion Award, Tokyo, 1983; Honorary Royal Designer for Industry, London, 1987. **Address:** K.K. Arai Creation System, 301 Esyc Heights, 5-16-8 Roppongi, Minato-ku, Tokyo, Japan.

Publications:

By ARAI:

Articles

"Nuno Choryu," in *Ginka Bunka Shuppan,* No. 63, 1985.

On ARAI:

Books

Tulokas, Maria, ed., *Fabrics for the 80's* (exhibition catalogue), Providence, Rhode Island 1985.
Sutton, Ann, and Diane Saheenan, *Ideas in Weaving,* Loveland, Colorado and London 1989.
Arai, Junichi, Jack Lenor Larson, Akira Mishima, and Reiko Sudo, *Hand and Technology: Textiles by Junichi Arai 1992* (exhibition catalogue), Asashi, Japan 1992.

Articles

Tulokas, Maria, "Textiles for the Eighties," in *Textilforum* (Hanover, Germany), September 1985.
Cannarella, D., "Fabric about Fabric," in *Threads* (Newtown, Connecticut), November 1985.
Popham, P., "Man of Cloth," in *Blueprint* (London), December/January 1987/88.
Tulokas, Maria, "Textiles by Junichi Arai, 1979-1988," in *Textilforum* (Hanover, Germany), June 1989.
"Junichi Arai," in the *New York Times,* 16 April 1990.
Smith MacIsaac, Heather, "Arai Arrives," in *HG* (New York), August 1990.
"Junichi Arai and Reiko Sudo," in *Design Journal,* No. 42, 1991.
Livingston, David, "Junichi Arai's Creations Provoke, Mystify," in *The Globe and Mail* (Toronto), 16 January 1992.
Pollock, Naomi R., "Dream Weavers," in *Metropolis,* September 1992.
Louie, Elaine, "A Fabric that Is Light, in Both Senses," in the *New York Times,* 25 March 1993.

*   *   *

Junichi Arai creates the stuff of dreams, fabrics never seen before. His work is a true collaboration: innovators in yarn and slit film production, in computers, and in loom technology are essential partners. But the finished product, the textiles "like stone" or "like clouds" created for Issey Miyake at his suggestion, or the fabrics Arai calls "Spider Web," "Titanium Poison," and "Driving Rain," are pure Arai in inspiration, imagination, and execution. They could only have been created in Japan.

The great-grandson and grandson of spinners, and the son and nephew of weavers, Arai was born and raised in Kiryu, an historic textile center north of Tokyo. Steeped in Japanese textile tradition, he nevertheless dreamed of becoming an actor. Instead, at the age of 18, he began working in his father's factory, weaving *obi* and *kimono* cloth, including one that involved the twisting of gold or silver fibers around a core of silk yarn. The family firm also made synthetic and metallic fabrics for the United States cocktail dress market. In developing these fabrics, he acquired 32 patents. The eight years he spent helping run the business provided him with technical expertise but little satisfaction. They paved the way, however, for his years of experimentation, teaching him the rules he would later break.

Long-time colleague Reiko Sudo wrote in *Hand and Technology: Textiles by Junichi Arai 1992,* an exhibition catalogue, "He is truly the *enfant terrible* of Japanese textiles, delighting in snubbing convention, a naughty boy playing with ultra-high-tech toys." His genius consists of what Milton Sonday of the Cooper-Hewitt Museum, New York, terms "pushing the limits" of both new and traditional technology, having the vision to take it one step further, or to combine fibers and technologies in new ways. The digital computer is his drawing board, freeing him to explore design possibilities and select the best ones. With it and the Jacquard loom, Arai hopes someday to create a fabric whose pattern changes as subtly as the days in a lifetime, never exactly repeating. For a recent exhibition Arai concentrated on the combination of high technology and hand craft, using two different kinds of warp and weft, woven by the same machine, and limiting himself to two weave structures.

Fashion designers like Miyake, Rei Kawakubo, and Yoshiki Hishinuma, a former Miyake apprentice, are among the collaborators whose imaginations he has challenged. Some of his fabrics are suitable for home furnishings; these are sold in Nuno showrooms in Tokyo, New York, Los Angeles, and Chicago. End use, however, is not really an Arai concern. In fact, some of his fabrics may only be suitable for museum installations, but that is quite beside the point of Arai's work.

Tiny print at the bottom of a hang tag, from a scarf purchased in an Issey Miyake boutique, whispers, "This work is the product of a weaving technology invented by Junichi Arai." As an innovator in weaving technology and the creation of new fabrics, he has no equal; in his work, the future is now.

—Arlene C. Cooper

ARMANI, Giorgio.
Italian designer

Born: Piacenza, Italy, 11 July 1934. **Education:** Studied medicine, University of Bologna, 1952-53; also studied photography. **Military Service:** Served in the Italian Army, 1953-54. **Career:** Win-

Giorgio Armani: Men's collection, Spring/Summer 1995.

dow display designer, La Rinascente department stores, 1954; stylist, menswear buyer, La Rinascente stores, 1954-60; menswear designer, Nino Cerruti, 1960-70; free-lance designer, 1970-75; introduced Armani menswear collection, 1974; introduced womenswear collection, 1975; introduced Emporio Armani and Armani Jeans, 1981; introduced less expensive womenswear range, Mani, c.1987; introduced Giorgio Armani Occhiali and Giorgio Armani Calze, 1987; introduced sportswear range, and Emporio Armani shops selling younger collection launched in London, 1989; Giorgio Armani USA company formed, 1980; AX, Armani Exchange, boutiques introducing lower-priced basic quality clothes launched in the United States, 1991. Fragrances include *Armani le Parfum,* 1982, *Armani Eau pour Homme,* 1984, and *Gio,* 1992. **Exhibitions:** *Intimate Architecture: Contemporary Clothing Design,* Massachusetts Institute of Technology, Cambridge, 1982; *Giorgio Armani: Images of Man,* Fashion Institute of Technology, New York, 1990-91, travelled to Tokyo, Paris, London; retrospective *Armani: 1972-92,* Palazzo Pitti, Florence, 1992. **Awards:** Neiman Marcus Award, 1979; Cutty Sark Award, 1980, 1981, 1984; *Gentlemen's Quarterly* Manstyle Award, 1982, Grand'Ufficiale dell'Ordine al Merito Award, Italy, 1982; Gold Medal from Municipality of Piacenza, 1983; Council of Fashion Designers of America International Designer Award, 1983, 1987; L'Occhio d'Oro Award, 1984, 1986, 1987, 1988, 1994; Cutty Sark Men's Fashion Award, 1985; Bath Museum of Costume Dress of the Year Award, 1986; named Gran Cavaliere della Repubblica, Italy, 1987; Lifetime Achievement Award, 1987; Christobal Balenciaga Award, 1988; Media Key Award, 1988; Woolmark Award, 1989, 1992; Senken Award, 1989; Honorary Doctorate from the Royal College of Art, 1991; Fiorino d'Oro award, Florence, 1992; Golden Effie Award, United States, 1993; Aguja de Oro Award, Spain, 1993; Academia del Profumo Award, Italy, 1993. **Address:** Via Borgonuovo 21, 20122 Milan, Italy.

Publications:

On ARMANI:

Books

Combray, Richard de, and Arturo Carlo Quintavalle, *Giorgio Armani,* Milan 1982.
Hayden Gallery, Massachusetts Institute of Technology, *Intimate Architecture: Contemporary Clothing Design* (exhibition catalogue), Cambridge, Mass. 1982.
Barbieri, Gian Paolo, *Artificial,* Paris 1982.
Alfonsi, Maria-Vittoria, *Leaders in Fashion: I grandi personaggi della moda,* Bologna 1983.
Milbank, Caroline Rennolds, *Couture: The Great Designers,* New York 1985.
Perschetz, Lois, ed., *W, The Designing Life,* New York 1987.
Coleridge, Nicholas, *The Fashion Conspiracy,* London 1988.
Howell, Georgina, *Sultans of Style: 30 Years of Fashion and Passion 1960-1990,* London 1990.
Martin, Richard, and Harold Koda, *Giorgio Armani: Images of Man,* New York 1990.

Articles

Hamilton, Rita, "Giorgio Armani's Fine Italian Hand," in *Esquire* (New York), 22 May 1979.

Cover story, in *Time,* May 1982.
Barbieri, Giampaolo, "La moda diventa arte," in *Amica* (Milan), December 1982.
Teston, E., "Architectural Digest Visits Giorgio Armani," in *Architectural Digest* (Los Angeles), May 1983.
"Armani: Success, Tailor Made," in *Vogue* (New York), August 1984.
"Il nuovo studio di progettazione di Armani," in *Vogue* (Milan), September 1984.
Mower, Sarah, "Giorgio Armani: A Man for All Seasons," in *Woman's Journal* (London), April 1986.
Thurman, Judith, "A Cut Above," in *Connoisseur* (New York), August 1986.
Romanelli, Marco, "Giorgio Armani: Il progetto dell'abito 1988," in *Domus* (Milan), January 1988.
Brantley, Ben, "The Armani Mystique," in *Vanity Fair* (New York), June 1988.
Brantley, Bill, "The Emperor of New Clothes," in *The Daily Telegraph Weekend Magazine* (London), 17 December 1988.
Mower, Sarah, "Emperor Armani," in *Vogue* (London), January 1989.
Keers, Paul, "The Emporio of Style," in *GQ* (London), February/March 1989.
Kostner, Kevin, "The Emporio Strikes Back," in *Sky* (London), March 1989.
West, Carinthia, "Giorgio Armani," in *Marie Claire* (London), April 1989.
Cohen, Eddie Lee, "Giorgio Armani," in *Interior Design* (New York), April 1989.
Jones, Nick, "Eagle's Spread," in *Building Design* (London), 28 April 1989.
Furness, Janine, "Alluring Armani," in *Interior Design* (London), May 1989.
"Giorgio Armani," in *Axis* (Tokyo), Summer 1989.
Cohen, Eddie Lee, "Emporio Armani," in *Interior Design* (New York), September 1989.
Brampton, Sally, "Armani's Island," in *Elle Decoration* (London), Autumn 1989.
Polan, Brenda, "The Genius of Giorgio Armani," in *Options* (London), December 1989.
Martin, Richard, "'What Is Man!'—The Image of Male Style of J. C. Leyendecker and Giorgia Armani," *Textile & Text,* 13 January 1990.
Howell, Georgina, "Armani: The Man Who Fell to Earth," in *The Sunday Times Magazine* (London), 18 February 1990.
Mardore, Lucienne, "La storia di Giorgio Armani," in *Marie Claire* (Paris), May 1990.
Borioli, Gisella, "Giorgio Armani: This Is the Real Me," in *Donna* (Milan), October 1990.
LaFerla, Ruth, "Sizing Up Giorgio Armani," in the *New York Times Magazine,* 21 October 1990.
"The King of Classic: Armani," in *Elle* (New York), March 1991.
Gerrie, Anthea, "Giorgio Armani," in *Clothes Show* (London), June 1991.
Michaels, James, "To Give and to Take Away," in *Forbes* (New York), 28 October 1991.
Friend, Ted, "The Armani Edge," in *Vogue* (New York), March 1992.
"Armani on Armani," in the *Daily News Record* (New York), 25 June 1992.
Doyle, Kevin, "Armani's True Confessions," in *Women's Wear Daily* (New York), 25 June 1992.

Hutton, Lauren, "Giorgio Armani," in *Interview* (New York), April 1993.

"Giorgio Armani," in *Playboy,* May 1993.

Forden, Sara Gay, "Numero Uno: Giorgio Armani, the World's Most Successful Designer, Still Isn't Satisfied," in *Women's Wear Daily* (New York), 26 October 1994.

Schiff, Stephen, "Lunch with Mr. Armani, Tea with Mr. Versace, Dinner with Mr. Valentino," in *The New Yorker* (New York), 7 November 1994.

Menkes, Suzy, "Armani's Off-the-Rack Mozart," in *International Herald Tribune* (Paris), 17 January 1995.

Forden, Sara Gay, "According to Armani," in *Daily News Record* (New York), 19 January 1995.

Menkes, Suzy, "World Class Armani Show Wraps Up Italian Season," in *International Herald Tribune,* 11-12 March 1995.

Spindler, Amy M. "Armani and Ferré: A Study in Contrast," in the *New York Times,* 11 March 1995.

*   *   *

Giorgio Armani is a design colonialist responsible for the creation of an aesthetic in both menswear and womenswear that had a firm grip on international style in the 1980s. Renowned for his use

Giorgio Armani: Women's collection, Autumn/Winter 1994/95.

of fabric and expertise in tailoring, he is a world leader in menswear design who was responsible for the wide shouldered look for executive women. His pared-down unstructured silhouette moved away from the standard tailored look that had epitomized menswear since the 19th century. By eliminating interfaces, linings, and shoulder pads, Armani restructured the jacket, creating a softly tailored look.

Although Armani produces entire ranges of these functional, adaptable, flexible items of clothing that seem almost throwaway in their simplicity, they are, in fact, luxurious designs made of high quality cloth. His clothes, however, although expensive, have their own understated glamour and could never be described as ostentatious. Neither trend nor tradition, the Armani style draws a fine line between the two. His designs seem to have little to do with fashion. Notwithstanding, each season he introduces understated alterations, albeit irrespective of the more compulsory fashion changes that affect other designers. Eschewing change for its own sake, he believes in quality rather than invention. Correspondingly, his collections are redefinitions of a soft, unstructured style, playing with layers of texture and colour but constantly renegotiating proportions. Elegant, understated rather than "important" clothes, they have a timeless quality, a classicism emphasized in the nostalgic advertising campaigns that use images by the Italian photographer Aldo Fallai.

Born in Piacenza, Italy, in 1934, Armani's first taste of the fashion industry was with La Rinascente, a large Italian department-store chain where in 1954 he worked on the window displays. He then transferred to the Office of Fashion and Style where he had an invaluable training in the use of fabrics and the importance of customer profiling and targeting. After seven years he left to design menswear for Nino Cerruti, a textile and garment firm, and for a month worked in one of their textile factories where he learned to appreciate fabric, the skills that went into its production, and the techniques of industrial tailoring.

In 1974 Armani launched his own label, which was to become incredibly successful—the biggest-selling line of European design in America. His first designs revolved around the refining of the male jacket, which he believed to be the most important invention in the history of dress being both versatile and functional and suited to all social occasions. His idea was to instil the relaxation of sports clothing into its tailored lines. He later applied similar notions to womenswear, evolving a new way of dressing for women that was not just a simple appropriation of items from the male wardrobe but the use of them as a source upon which to build. He developed a style for the working woman that had an understated, almost androgynous chic that was so discreet in its detailing that it was almost perverse.

At this time his designs were very expensive, being made out of the most luxurious materials such as alpaca, cashmere, and suede. To expand his customer base and to meet the increasing demands of a fashion conscious public for clothes with a designer label, he produced a cheaper womenswear range entitled Mani, made out of synthetics so advanced they could not be copied, together with the popular Emporio Armani range of sportswear. His styles for women include Peter Pan collars on simple blouses, classics such as navy blazers and matching skirts, or tailored trousers whose cut may change slightly each season while the range of garments remains essentially the same. For men he produces items such as the same definitive navy blazers, crumpled linen jackets, leather blousons, which he introduced in 1980, and oversized overcoats and raincoats. Impeccably tailored, with faltering cut, easy lines, and subtle textures, patterns, and colours, he introduces twists such as lowslung button placement on double breasted suits for men and experimental blends of fabrics such as viscose with wool or linen with silk.

Armani's clothes seem anonymous, suited to life in the city—the epitome of post-modern style.

—Caroline Cox

ASHLEY, Laura.
British (Welsh) designer

Born: Laura Mountney in Dowlais, Glamorgan, Wales, 7 September 1925. **Education:** Attended Marshall's School, Merthyr Tydfil, Wales, until 1932; mainly self-taught in design. Served in the Women's Royal Naval Service. **Family:** Married Bernard Albert Ashley in 1949; children: Jane, David, Nick, and Emma. **Career:** Worked as secretary, National Federation of Women's Institutes, London, 1945-52; founder and partner, with Bernard Ashley, Ashley-Mountney Ltd. printed textiles, 1954-68, in Kent, 1956-61, and in Carno, Wales, from 1961; established Laura Ashley Ltd. in 1968; opened first retail outlet, London, 1967, then Edinburgh, Bath, Cheltenham, Cambridge, Norwich, Oxford, Aix-en-Provence, Munich, Vienna, etc.; opened first United States shop, San Francisco, 1974; New York shop opened, 1977; established 185 retail outlets worldwide by 1985. **Awards:** Queen's Award for Export Achievement, 1977. *Died* (in Coventry, Warwickshire) *17 September 1985.* **Address:** 27 Bagley's Lane, London SW6 2AR, England.

Publications:

On ASHLEY:

Books

Carter, Ernestine, *Magic Names of Fashion,* Englewood Cliffs, New Jersey 1980.
Dickson, Elizabeth, and Margaret Colvin, *The Laura Ashley Book of Home Decorating,* London 1982, New York 1984.
Sebba, Anne, *Laura Ashley, A Life by Design,* London 1990.

Articles

"Queen Victoriana," in *Sophisticat* (London), November 1974.
"The Laura Ashley Look," in *Brides* (London), Spring 1975.
Dumoulin, Marie-Claude, "Chez Laura Ashley," in *Elle* (Paris), 11 October 1976.
Gould, Rachael, "From Patchwork to a Small Print to World Wide: How the Laura Ashley Family Business Grew Up," in *Vogue* (London), 15 April 1980.
Cleave, Maureen, "Makers of Modern Fashion: Laura Ashley," in *The Observer* colour supplement (London), 12 October 1980.
Sheffield, Robert, "The Twist in the Tail," in *Creative Review* (London), January 1984.
"Young Nick," in *She* (London), April 1984.
Slesin, Suzanne, "Laura Ashley, British Designer, Is Dead at 60," in the *New York Times,* 18 September 1985.
Dickson, Elizabeth, "Laura Ashley: Her Life and Gifts, by Those Who Knew Her," in *The Observer* (London), 22 September 1985.
Sulitzer, Paul-Loup, "Laura Ashley: Une impression d'éternité," in *Elle* (Paris), 4 August 1986.
"The Ashley Empire," in the *Sunday Express Magazine* (London), 25 September 1988.
Ducas, June, "Inside Story," in *Woman's Journal* (London), October 1988.
"Laura Ashley, A Licensing Legend," in *HFD—The Weekly Home Furnishings Newspaper,* 26 December 1988.
Finnerty, Anne, "Profile of Laura Ashley," in *Textile Outlook International* (London), January 1990.
Fernaud, Dierdre, and Margaret Park, "After Laura," in *The Sunday Times* (London), 4 February 1990.
Grieve, Amanda, "Clotheslines," in *Harpers & Queen* (London), April 1993.
Bain, Sally, "Life Begins at 40 for Laura Ashley," in *Marketing,* 13 May 1993.

*   *   *

Welsh designer Laura Ashley developed and distilled the British romantic style of neo-Victorianism, reflecting past eras in clothing, textiles, accessories, and furnishings and demonstrating classic country styling.

Her approach to design was inspired by her environment, the surrounding Welsh countryside, and her yearning to return to all things natural. Integrating ideas adopted from the designs and qualities of past eras, she combined elements to create a look of nostalgic simplicity and naive innocence. Floral sprigged cotton fabrics, often directly adapted and developed from 18th- and 19th-century patterns, paisleys, and tiny prints worked with romantic detailing to create a style that was original and easily recognized.

Her style possesses old world charm with individual rustic freshness, reflected in traditional beliefs of bygone days. Victorian nightshirts, Edwardian-style dresses, the introduction of the long smock in 1968, delicately trimmed with lace, pin tucked bodices, tiered skirts, and full puffed sleeves are her trademark, aimed at the middle market and retailing at affordable prices.

Laura Ashley rose from the modest beginnings of a small cottage industry, producing a simple range of printed headscarves and table mats in her kitchen, to the development of a company that became a huge enterprise of international renown. It was a fairy story in itself.

Her self-taught skill produced ranges of womenswear, childrenswear, bridalwear, accessories, and furnishings. She established home interiors consisting of coordinated ranges of bed linens, wall tiles, curtains, cushions, and upholstery. Her brilliant concept of fabrics, her discerning research of past eras for new inspiration, and her study and re-interpretation of antique textiles led to the success of the Laura Ashley label.

Traditional floral prints combined together, printed in two colours and various colour combinations, distinguished her work. However, through the technical expertise and experimentation of Bernard Ashley, Laura's husband and business partner, new developments and improved machinery extended versatility: new and subtle colour combinations were produced, often to Laura's own design. Natural fibres, crisp cottons, and lawn fabrics expanded to include ranges in twill, silk, wool, crêpe, velvet, corduroy, and eventually jersey fabrics.

Along with the 1960s youth revolution came a move towards romanticism, conservation, and world peace, an alternative to modern living, pop culture, mass-produced clothing, and vivid Parisian

Laura Ashley: Spring/Summer, 1994; mint silk georgette dress.

fashions. Due to her convincing beliefs in past values, quality, and the revival of romantic simplicity, Ashley's success has been overwhelming. Bernard Ashley's perceptive business brain and Laura Ashley's determination and enterprising mind led to the development of excellent marketing techniques. Retail settings, complementary to the old world style of neo-Victorianism, promoted a look of individuality and quality.

Throughout the 1980s and into the 1990s, the style retains its unique and easily recognizable image. The style, however, has evolved, extending to all ranges to incorporate contemporary fashion ideas, including the introduction of jersey for practical and easy-to-wear clothing. The Laura Ashley style remains unchanged, incorporating the same ingredients, but with a newer, fresher approach.

The phenomenal success of this closely knit family firm, from a chain of boutiques to a multi-faceted company expanding from Europe to Canada, the United States, and Australia, has continued to grow after Laura Ashley's tragic accidental death in 1985, with the style maintaining its international appeal. Her legacy is a multi-million-dollar empire in clothing and coordinated furnishings, constantly updated but withstanding the passage of time.

—Carol Mary Brown

AUJARD, Christian.

French designer

Born: Brittany in 1945. **Family:** Married Michele Domercq in 1972; children: Richard, Giles. **Career:** Worked as a delivery boy, stock clerk, then financial manager for Charles Maudret wholesale ready-to-wear firm, 1964-67; formed own ready-to-wear company with Michele Aujard, 1968; first free-standing boutique opened, Paris, 1978; company purchased by Société Bic, 1983; fashions manufactured and distributed by Guy Laroche. Firm carried on by widow. *Died* (in Paris) *8 March 1977.* **Address:** 15 rue de Tournon, 75006 Paris, France.

Publications:

On AUJARD:

Articles

"Christian Aujard," in *Sir,* February 1982.
Hyde, Nina, "Continuing the Aujard Collection," in the *Washington Post,* 23 September 1978.

*   *   *

From the moment Christian Aujard premiered his first women's ready-to wear collection in Paris, his designs were acclaimed for their youthful appeal, vibrant colors, and lively prints. The Aujard label quickly became recognized for its fresh attitude toward contemporary, updated sportswear. Aujard's first collection, directed towards the young, fashion-conscious consumer, successfully blended both classic and innovative elements into chic, wearable clothes, and thus instantly established his talent among the fashion world.

Michele Domercq, a former art student, began as Christian Aujard's designer of silks before becoming his wife and business partner. Combining her styling skills with his vision, the couple's ready-to-wear line for women took off as it was eagerly embraced by upmarket retailers, first in Europe and then in America. Aujard won acclaim for his upbeat attitude toward the tried-and-true, with youthful trench coats, blazers, trousers, pleated skirts, and shirtdresses. The clothes were tailored but relaxed, with features like elasticized waistbands and dolman sleeves that allowed ease of movement. Detailing was a focus, with interesting yokes and seams, and fagoting was a favored trim. Another Aujard hallmark was his use of natural fibers. Cotton, cashmere, linen, silk, wool tweed, crepe, and mohair—all found expression, as in his soft beige Honan silk blouson sweater and trousers of 1972.

In the 1960s and 1970s when women began to ask for access to the power traditionally enjoyed by men, designers answered with menswear styles for women, and Christian Aujard's lines were no exception. But his menswear-inspired designs remained resolutely feminine, as seen, for example, in the best-selling Officer's Pantsuit. This ensemble, a double-breasted blazer over wide-legged trousers in a navy/white nautical palette, transformed the notion of an authoritative military uniform into a charming, yet provocative daytime look. Aujard also won much attention for his man-tailored oxford cloth shirts, as well as for crisp shirtdresses in dotted silk and wrinkled linen, and praise was garnered for his double-faced beige wool wrap coat which reversed to tweed.

Women's eveningwear included elegant, refined short cocktail dresses of silk inset with bands of lace. The special domain of Michele, the silk clothes for evening were so successful that she spun off a separate label under her own name. It was understood between the couple that Christian designed daywear and Michele designed eveningwear, and often they did not see each other's collections until they premiered.

Aujard ventured into men's ready-to-wear a few years after his womenswear. The collections for men featured both dress suits and casual separates, and continued the philosophy of elegant simplicity updated with youthful vigor. Vibrant, rich color, lively patterns, and prints became a signature, allowing men a wide range of fashion expression. Checks mixed with plaids and houndstooths, bright dotted patterns, and unexpected combinations created a cheerful, yet sophisticated look. In menswear, Aujard's typical attention to detail, use of fine materials, and witty attitude was translated, for example, into a glamorous double-breasted suit of unexpected and dazzling white wool.

At the time of her husband's accidental death, Michele took over the business and continued designing under the Christian Aujard name. At first she did not change the spirit of the Aujard collections, but by the late 1970s the lines were totally of her design. For both mens and womenswear she favored a mixture of textures and a palette of soft, saturated hues. Muted colors were chosen so that separates—jackets, sweaters, shirts, trousers, or skirts—would all coordinate. Crisp lines gave way to less constructed pieces in yielding fabrics like wool challis and satin. And while styling and managing the Aujard lines, Michele Aujard continued to oversee her own label.

The Christian Aujard name continued to thrive as Michele invested ordinary styles with new life. For menswear she created wildly patterned waistcoats and drapy pleated pants, and she let color loose, using daring palettes considered taboo for men. She might mix violet, red, and emerald with gray, or playfully contrast textures, as in a rust tweed blazer against a persimmon satin shirt.

Casual separates, such as a royal blue sport jacket over pale lemon trousers, glowed with intensity and radiated novelty, so that perceived boundaries between appropriate colors for men and women were blurred. The sweater woven with painterly motifs in brilliant color combinations also became a hallmark of Aujard.

The company's formula for success was the ability to push fashion limits while essentially remaining within the boundaries of convention. The Christian Aujard label, as promoted by the couple together and then by Michele Domercq on her own, stood for sophisticated, affordable, and stylishly upbeat ready-to-wear clothing for men and women.

—Kathleen Paton

AYTON, Sylvia.

British designer

Born: Ilford, Essex, England, 27 November 1937. **Education:** Attended Walthamstow School of Art (N.D.D.), 1953-57, and the Royal College of Art, London (Des RCA), 1957-60. **Career:** Freelance design work from 1959-63 includes B.E.A. Air Hostess Uniforms, 1959, clothing for B. Altman and Co. (New York), Count Down and Pallisades stores (London); worked Costume Museum, Bath, England, 1960; designed hats for film *Freud,* 1960; formed partnership with Zandra Rhodes to open Fulham Road Clothes Shop, London, 1964; outerwear designer for the Wallis Fashion Group, Ltd., London, from 1969; free-lance designer and pattern cutter for Keith Taylor, Ltd., London, 1975-80. Part-time lecturer at Kingston Polytechnic (London), 1961-65, Ravensbourne College of Art and Design (London), 1961-67, Middlesex Polytechnic 1967-71; also external assessor for BA (Hons) fashion and textile courses from 1976. **Awards:** Fellow, Royal Society of Arts, 1986; awarded MBE (Member of the British Empire), 1990. **Address:** c/o The Wallis Fashion Group Ltd., 22 Garrick Industrial Centre, Garrick Road, Hendon, London NW9 6AQ, England.

Publications:

On AYTON:

Books

Mulvagh, Jane, *Vogue History of Twentieth-Century Fashion,* London 1988.
Lebenthal, Joel, *Radical Rags: Fashions of the 60's,* New York 1990.
Debrett's *People of Today,* London 1991.

Articles

Palen, Brenda, "Fashion on Fire," in *The Guardian* (London), September 1984.

*

I design for a chain of High Street shops, so I sell to a very wide range of customers who expect well designed, well made and well priced garments.

The coats and raincoats I design must be extremely "wantable." My aim is to make thousands of women feel wonderful by providing garments that are not too boring, too safe, or too extreme but sharp, minimal, very functional, uncontrived, all very easy but with an element of surprise.

I am a perfectionist. I care desperately about the shapes and proportions of my designs. I care about every detail, every stitch, button, and buckle. If the design is easy on my eye it will also please my customer.

I don't design to a theme or for myself. Most of my ideas evolve from season to season, or a new idea just flashes into my head. I am very aware of my customers' lifestyle, and, as fashion is constantly evolving, I must be aware of the changing needs of women, and yet remain creative, experimental, and forward thinking. I design for a type of woman, not for an age group, and I become that woman as I design.

I believe there are basically three types of women—the feminine woman; the classic woman; the fashion woman—and I feel that she stays that type all of her life, whether she is 16 or 60.

I adore designing. I am always enthusiastic about my work, and get great joy from seeing so many women wearing my clothes. It is my job and my joy to make her feel good and very special, and to encourage her to return to the shops to buy again and again.

—Sylvia Ayton

*   *   *

The name Sylvia Ayton probably means little to most British women, yet for the last 25 years she has had a significant influence on what they wear. As outerwear designer for the Wallis Fashion Group Limited, Ayton produces fashion ranges in good quality fabrics at reasonable prices. Over the years her coats and suits have gained a rightful place in the forefront of high street fashion.

Ayton's original ambition was to make women feel wonderful and special, as if each one were a "fairy princess." She dressed her first "fairy princesses" in the 1960s when she worked with Zandra Rhodes, Marion Foale, and Sally Tuffin. Some were private customers but, to her surprise, Ayton found that working for one person did not always provide satisfaction. During her career she has found the greatest fulfilment in designing a coat that will give pleasure to nearly five thousand women. At Wallis, she produces two annual outerwear collections, mainly coats and suits. The cloth provides the starting point. Each season there are new fabrics and colours that must be the right quality and price. These are used to create garments that are fashionable, but realistic. The typical Wallis customer is Ms. Average, but each woman has her own personality and lifestyle. Ayton finds it most accurate to divide women by type, rather than age group. She categorizes them as "feminine," "classic," or "fashionable" types. This guides her attitude to her collections and dictates shapes and details. Each season there are the classics: wool velour winter coats, gabardine trench styles, blousons. There are always new ideas, unexpected twists, trims, or fabrics, or completely experimental designs manufactured in small numbers for a few outlets. Alpaca wool coats are, for example, a luxury item featured only in a small number of shops. Ayton is constantly checking what the customer buys and weekly sales figures are an important guide. Sales influence her ideas as much as the latest design intelligence.

Ayton is a realist who knows that business awareness is essential for the designer. This lesson was first learned in the 1960s when

Sylvia Ayton.

she opened the Fulham Road Clothes Shop with Zandra Rhodes, creating garments from fabric designed and printed by Rhodes. The press loved them, but their lack of backers, finance, and business sense proved fatal. Today when she is designing she thinks like a buyer. She is pragmatic in seeking the best quality at a sensible price, and the customer is always the most important consideration.

Sylvia Ayton works unstintingly with British fashion design courses to instil high standards and to provide students with a realistic view of the industry. Annually, she organizes placements in the Wallis design studio and pattern cutting rooms. Upholding standards is, in her view, essential. Having found her "fairy princess," she teaches young designers how to do the same.

Working exclusively for a company label means that Sylvia Ayton's name is not used to sell her designs. However, her work has not gone unnoticed. She has received many awards, including the MBE for her services to fashion. The accolades are well deserved: as a designer Sylvia Ayton has the right combination of qualities. She is a perfectionist and an idealist, but one with a very firm grasp of reality.

—Hazel Clark

AZAGURY, Jacques.

French fashion designer working in London

Born: Casablanca, Morocco, 1956. **Education:** Studied at London College of Fashion, 1972-73. Finished education at St Martin's School of Art, London. **Career:** Worked for dress company in London's East End, 1972. Began own business, 1975; closed after one year. Opened again, 1977; joined London Design Collections, 1978. **Address:** 50 Knightsbridge, London SW1, England.

Publications:

On AZAGURY:

Articles

Dutt, Robin, "Jacques Azagury," in *Clothes Show* (London), April/May 1990.
"How the Glamour Boys Are You," in *Cosmopolitan* (London), December 1987.
"Relative Values," in *The Sunday Times Magazine* (London), 29 August 1993.
Rodgers, Toni, "Double Vision," in *Elle* (London), March 1991.

*   *   *

Jacques Azagury is a designer of spectacular eveningwear for high profile clients including the Duchess of Kent, Joan Collins, and Selina Scott. His glamorous style was perhaps best epitomized by the Princess of Wales in the summer of 1994 when she walked out of the Ritz Hotel in London, to be met by the glare of the awaiting paparazzi, in a stunning Azagury black, graphite, and bugle bead sheath, with sensuous side split.

Glamour and exoticism have always been part of the Azagury mystique. Born in 1950s Casablanca, he describes this environment as being exactly like a Hollywood film set. The precedent set by Ingrid Bergman in the film *Casablanca* or Lauren Bacall in *To Have and Have Not,* established a culture that demanded a fabulously chic approach to dress. This was the ideal breeding ground for a fledgling fashion designer and Jacques Azagury often attributes his sources of inspiration to a collection of photographs of his mother and her friends, lunching and partying in chic Casablancan style.

The Azagury family moved to London in the early 1960s, so that the children could benefit from an English education. Jacques Azagury's enthusiasm for fashion and style eventually led him to study the subject at London's St Martin's College of Art; after graduating, he quickly established his own label. Browns in London was one of the first high fashion retail outlets to place an order. Joan Burstein, the owner of the boutique, recognized that the Azagury signature had an individual sophistication and luxury that easily complemented the slick appeal of her other labels, such as Claude Montana or Thierry Mugler.

Azagury began his own retail operation in London's Knightsbridge. As well as specializing in exclusive cocktail and special occasion wear for private clients, he also sells pieces to other fashion stores and top couture retailers throughout the United Kingdom. The operation is as chic as any Parisian couture salon and is now complimented by Azagury's sister Elizabeth's exclusive floristry business, Azagury Fleurs, run from the basement of the shop. His brother's shoe design label, Joseph Azagury, is run from premises nearby.

Azagury does not design for one particular type of woman, preferring to appeal to a huge cross-section from the ages of 13 to 60. He is adamant that what a woman does not want when purchasing eveningwear is fancy dress. Some eveningwear designers layer sequins, frills, ruching, and draping to create an overstated, unflattering fantasy but Azagury uses sequins and frills with taste and discretion. The clothes never make major fashion statements but veer instead towards the classic and flattering. Their innovation and style come from Azagury's respect for cut and fit, and he devotes a great deal of time to getting this right.

The Azagury family are a closely linked unit. As well as Elizabeth, two further sisters, Solange and Sylvia, and their father are involved in the companies. Creatively, what links the family together and motivates it is a united quest for design perfection.

Grown-up, sexy sophistication sums up Azagury's style. Never extreme but exquisitely made and fitted, whether it be a short, silver sequin cocktail dress, a cross-over blouse in peacock silk, or a fabulously expensive full-length evening gown. Azagury never wants to compromise his look. "I don't like to see my clothes worn with other things," he declared in a *Clothes Show* magazine interview. He is protective of his designer's vision and does not want his customer to make sartorial mistakes, which epitomizes Jacques Azagury's continuing pursuit of chic and glamour in special occasion dressing.

—Kevin Almond

B

B., AGNÈS. See **AGNÈS B.**

BACHELLERIE, Marithé. See **GIRBAUD, Marithé & François.**

BADGLEY MISCHKA.

American design team

Mark Badgley born in East Saint Louis, Illinois, 12 January 1961; raised in Oregon; studied business, University of Southern California, to 1982; graduated from Parsons School of Design, New York, 1985. James Mischka born in Burlington, Wisconsin, 23 December 1960. Studied management and art history, Rice University, Houston, Texas, to 1982; graduated from Parsons School of Design, 1985. Before forming own company, Badgley designed for Jackie Rogers and Donna Karan, New York, 1985-88; Mischka designed for Willi Smith, New York, 1985-88; Badgley Mischka Company established, New York, 1988; financed by Escada USA, from 1992. **Awards:** Mouton Cadet Young Designer Award, 1989; Dallas International Apparel Mart Rising Star Award, 1992. **Address:** 525 Seventh Avenue, New York, NY 10018, USA.

Publications:

On BADGLEY MISCHKA:

Books

Stegemeyer, Anne, *Who's Who in Fashion* supplement, New York 1992.

Articles

Starzinger, Page Hill, "New Faces," in *Vogue* (New York), March 1990.
"Badgley Mischka: A Single Focus," in *Women's Wear Daily* (New York), 4 June 1990.
"Great Expectations," in *Women's Wear Daily* (New York), 11 June 1991.
Kazanjian, Dodie, in *Vogue* (New York), July 1991.
Lear, Frances, in *Lear's* (New York), September 1991.

Campbell, Roy H., "First Lady Liked Them but Turned Them Down—She Thought They Were European Designs," in the *Philadelphia Inquirer,* 26 February 1993.
Barbee, Pat, "Glamour Boys: Badgley Mischka," in *Beverly Hills 213* (Los Angeles), 21 July 1993.
Torkells, Erik, "The Night Is Young," in *Town & Country* (New York), September 1994.

*   *   *

Lilly Daché (couture hat and style maker of the 1950s) writes in her 1956 *Glamour Book* (Daché, Lilly and Dorothy Roe Lewis, New York 1956) that glamor "means making the most of what you have" and "the consciousness of looking her best often touches off a woman's inner mainspring of joyous self-confidence and—presto!—all of a sudden she is glamorous." Designers Mark Badgley and James Mischka say of their clothing, "one zip and you're glamorous." Dee-luxe and de luxe, their clothing radiates youthful confidence. Fanciful but realistic, their designs recall the elegance of an age when one dressed for evening. The two young designers, who introduced their first collection in 1988 in New York, make glamor attainable by demystifying and simplifying it.

Uptown diners and downtown executives alike would find something appropriate and pleasing in Badgley Mischka designs. Evening suits and dresses are refined and uncontrived: form fitting wool jersey, cotton brocade, faille, re-embroidered lace, silk, and baby bouclé are used to create suits with long fitted jackets (worn underneath: sexy, long silk scarves instead of the predictable blouse), and pencil-thin or swingy full short skirts. One versatile wool jersey dress, perfect for career dressing, looks like two pieces, with a rib knit turtleneck and either a permanently pleated or straight wrap skirt, in gray or pale yellow. The combination of fine crisp and softly draping fabrics (bouclé and silk, velvet trimmed wool, organza and silk chiffon) adds dimension and drama. Fitted, empire, or lowered, waistlines are superbly shaped. Expertly mixed cocktail dresses—with evocative cocktail names such as the Tom Collins, the Delmonico, the Bacardi—are off-the-shoulder, *décolleté,* bowed, lacy, or beaded and above the knee. All are subtly provocative, feminine, and flirtatious. The bridal gowns almost make you want to be wed, soon, just so you may show off your never-seen-so shapely shoulders and waist in a V-backed ivory lace and silk-crêpe dress, or choose the off-white silk brocade coatdress, with front wrap and jeweled buttons. The bridal dresses are for the grown-up sweet tooth, confections which allow the beauty of the wearer to shine through the frills.

American *Vogue*'s Dodie Kazanjian (July 1991) looked to six designers (including Bill Blass, Donna Karan, and Michael Kors) for the perfect "little black dress," and found hers at Badgley Mischka, which "felt new without straining for newness." Frances Lear agrees, choosing a Badgley Mischka wool jersey as *Lear's* "Relevant Dress," stating that it is "... reminiscent of other seminal

Badgley Mischka: Fall 1994; bronze beaded Byzantium cocktail dress (left); Hermatite beaded Chaucer vest tunic, black tuxedo crepe skirt (right).

dresses, yet is perfectly contemporary ..." and "as comfortable as your own skin" (New York, September 1991). There is a sense of ease and balance in Badgley Mischka designs. They create something expertly vital without superfluidity or trendiness; the design team is restrained in their creation, offering designs appealing in their modernity and lack of excess.

Lilly Daché further states, "real fashion begins with simplicity." Mark Badgley and James Mischka employ this mandate, creating clothing that is beautifully made and beautiful and glamorous to wear. Badgley Mischka make glamor easy.

—Jane Burns

BALENCIAGA, Cristobal.

Spanish designer

Born: Guetaria, San Sebastian, 21 January 1895. **Education:** Studied needlework and dressmaking with his mother until 1910. **Career:** Established tailoring business, with sponsorship of the Marquesa de Casa Torres, San Sebastian, 1915-21; founder, designer, Elsa fashion house, Barcelona, 1922-31, and Madrid, 1932-37; director, Maison Balenciaga, Paris, 1937-40, 1945-68; spent war years in Madrid; fragrances include *le Dix,* 1948, *Quadreille,* 1955, and *Pour Homme,* introduced by House of Balenciaga, 1990; couture house closed, 1968. Retired to Madrid, 1968-72. House of Balenciaga managed by German group Hoechst, 1972-86; Jacques Bogart S.A. purchased Balenciaga Couture et Parfums, 1986; Balenciaga ready-to-wear collection launched, 1987; reopening of Balenciaga stores launched, 1989. **Exhibitions:** *Balenciaga,* Bellerive Museum, Zurich, 1970; *Fashion: An Anthology,* Victoria & Albert Museum, London, 1971; *The World of Balenciaga,* Metropolitan Museum of Art, New York, 1973; *El Mundo de Balenciaga,* Palacio de Bellas Artes, Madrid, 1974; *Hommage a Balenciaga,* Musée Historique des Tissus, Lyon, 1985; *Balenciaga,* Fashion Institute of Technology, New York, 1986; *Cristobal Balenciaga,* Fondation de la Mode, Tokyo, 1987; *Homage to Balenciaga,* Palacio de la Virreina, Barcelona, and Palacio Miramar, San Sebastian, Spain, 1987. **Awards:** Chevalier de la Légion d'Honneur; named Commander, L'Ordre d'Isabelle-la-Catholique. *Died* (in Javea, Spain) *23 March 1972.*

Publications:

On BALENCIAGA:

Books

Lyman, Ruth, *Paris Fashion: The Great Designers and Their Creations,* London 1972.

Vreeland, Diana, *The World of Balenciaga* (exhibition catalogue), Metropolitan Museum of Art, New York 1973.

Milbank, Caroline Rennolds, *Couture: The Great Designers,* New York 1985.

Musée Historique des Tissus, *Hommage à Balenciaga* (exhibition catalogue), Lyon 1985.

Fondation de la Mode, Tokyo, and Musée de la Mode et du Costume, Palais Galliera, *Cristobal Balenciaga* (exhibition catalogue), Paris, Tokyo 1987.

Jouve, Marie-Andrée and Jacqueline Demornex, *Balenciaga,* New York 1989.

Howell, Georgina, *Sultans of Style: 30 Years of Fashion and Passion 1960-1990,* London 1990.

Healy, Robin, *Balenciaga: Masterpieces of Fashion Design,* Melbourne 1992.

Articles

"Cristobal Balenciaga" (obituary), in the *New York Times,* 25 March 1972.

"Cristobal Balenciaga: A Most Distinguished Couturier of His Time," in *The Times* (London), 25 March 1972.

Berenson, Ruth, "Balenciaga at the Met," in *National Review* (New York), 31 August 1973.

Mulvagh, Jane, "The Balenciaga Show," in *Vogue* (London), March 1985.

"Homage to Balenciaga," in *Art and Design,* October 1985.

Savage, Percy, "Balenciaga the Great," in *The Observer* (London), 13 October 1985.

Braux, Diane de, "L'Exposition en hommage à Balenciaga," in *Vogue* (Paris), December/January 1985/86.

"Nostra Lione: Grande esposizione consacrata a Balenciaga," in *Vogue* (Milan), February 1986.

Martin, Richard, "Balenciaga," in *American Fabrics and Fashions* (New York), September/October 1986.

Koda, Harold, "Balenciaga and the Art of Couture," in *Threads* (Newtown, Connecticut), June/July 1987.

Paquin, Paquita, "Le Ceremonial de Cristobal Balenciaga," in *Vogue* (Paris), November 1988.

Baudet, Francois, "Leur maître à tous," in *Elle* (Paris), 19 December 1988.

McDowell, Colin, "Balenciaga: The Quiet Revolutionary," in *Vogue* (London), June 1989.

Howell, Georgina, "Balenciagas Are Forever," in *The Sunday Times Magazine* (London), 23 July 1989.

Auchincloss, Eve, "Balenciaga: Homage to the Greatest," in *Connoisseur* (New York), September 1989.

Morera, Daniela, "Balenciaga lo charme del silenzio: Il grande couturier spagnolo," in *Vogue* (Milan), September 1990.

*   *   *

Cristobal Balenciaga's primary fashion achievement was in tailoring, an art that was for the Spanish-born couturier a virtuoso claim to knowing, comforting, and flattering the body. He could demonstrate tailoring proficiency in a *tour-de-force* one-seam coat, its shaping created from the innumerable darts and tucks that shaped the single piece of fabric. His consummate tailoring was accompanied by a pictorial imagination that encouraged him to appropriate ideas of kimono and sari, return to the Spanish vernacular dress of billowing and adaptable volume, and create dresses with arcs that could swell with air as the figure moved. There was a traditional Picasso-Matisse question of post-war French fashion: who was greater, Dior or Balenciaga? Personal sensibility might support one or the other, but it is hard to imagine any equal to Balenciaga's elegance, then or since.

Balenciaga was a master of illusion. The waist could be strategically low, it could be brought up to the ribs, or it could be concealed

Cristobal Balenciaga: Summer 1994.

in a tunic or the subtle opposition of a boxy top over a straight skirt. Balenciaga envisioned the garment as a three-dimensional form encircling the body, occasionally touching it and even grasping it, but also spiraling away so that the contrast in construction was always between the apparent freedom of the garment and its body-defining moments. Moreover, he regularly contrasted razor-sharp cut, including instances of the garment's radical geometry, with soft fragile features. A perfectionist who closed down his business in 1968 rather than see it be compromised in a fashion era he did not respect, Balenciaga projected ideal garments, but allowed for human imperfection. He was, in fact, an inexorable flatterer, a sycophant to the imperfect body. To throw back a rolled collar gives a flattering softness to the line of the neck into the body; his popular seven-eighths sleeve flattered women of a certain age, while the tent-like drape of coats and jackets were elegant on clients without perfect bodies. His fabrics had to stand up to his almost Cubist vocabulary of shapes, and he loved robust wools with texture, silk gazar for evening, corduroy (surprising in its inclusion in the couture), and textured silks.

Balenciaga's garments lack pretension; they are characterized by self-assured couture of simple appearance, austerity of details, and reserve in style. For the most part, the garments seem simple. American manufacturers, for example, adored Balenciaga for his adaptability into simpler forms for the American mass market in suits and coats. The slight rise in the waistline at center front or the proportions of chemise tunic to skirt make Balenciaga clothing as harmonious as a musical composition, but the effect is always one of utmost insouciance and ease of style. Balenciaga delved deeply into traditional clothing, seeming to care more deeply for regional dress than for any prior couture house. As Marie-Andrée Jouve has demonstrated, Balenciaga's garments allude to Spanish vernacular costume and to Spanish art: his embroidery and jet-beaded evening coats, capelettes, and boleros are redolent of the *torero,* while his love of capes emanates from the romance of rustic apparel (*Balenciaga,* New York 1989). Chemise, cape, and baby doll shapes might seem antithetical to the propensities of a master of tailoring, but Balenciaga's 1957 baby doll dress exemplifies the correlation he made between the two. The lace cage of the baby doll floats free from the body, suspended from the shoulders, but it is matched by the tailored dress beneath, providing a layered and analytical examination of the body within and the Cubist cone on the exterior, a tantalizing artistry of body form and perceived shape.

The principal forms for Balenciaga were the chemise, tunic, suit—with more or less boxy top—narrow skirt, and coats, often with astonishing sleeve treatments, suggesting an arm transfigured by the sculptor Brancusi into a puff or into almost total disappearance. Balenciaga perceived a silhouette that could be with or without arms, but never with the arms interfering. A famous Henry Clark photograph of a 1951 Balenciaga black silk suit focuses on silhouette: narrow and high waist with a pronounced flare of the peplum below and sleeves that billow from elbow to seven-eighths length; an Irving Penn photograph concentrates on the aptly named melon sleeve of a coat. Like a 20th-century artist, Balenciaga directed himself to a part of the body, giving us a selective, concentrated vision. His was not an all-over, all-equal vision, but a discriminating, problem-solving exploration of tailoring and picture-making details of dress. In fact, Balenciaga was so very like a 20th-century artist because in temperament, vocabulary, and attainment, he was one.

—Richard Martin

BALMAIN, Pierre.
French designer

Born: Saint-Jean-de-Maurienne, Savoie, 18 May 1914. **Education:** Studied architecture, École Nationale Supérieure des Beaux-Arts, Paris, 1933-34. **Military Service:** French Air Force, 1936-38, and in the French Army Pioneer Corps, 1939-40. **Career:** Free-lance sketch artist for Robert Piguet, Paris, 1934; assistant designer, Molyneux, Paris, 1934-38; designer, Lucien Lelong, Paris, 1939, 1941-45; founder, director, Maison Balmain, Paris, 1945-1982, Balmain Fashions, New York, 1951-55, Balmain Fashions, Caracas, 1954; Director General, Balmain S.A., Paris, 1977-82; ready-to-wear line launched, 1982. Fragrances include *Vent Vert,* 1945, *Jolie Madame,* 1953, *Miss Balmain,* 1967, *Ivoire,* 1980; fragrance business purchased by Revlon, 1960. Also stage and film designer, from 1950. **Exhibitions:** *Pierre Balmain: 40 années de création,* Musée de la Mode et du Costume, Palais Galliera, Paris, 1985-86. **Awards:** Neiman Marcus Award, Dallas, 1955; Knight of the Order of Dannebrog, Copenhagen, 1963; Cavaliere Ufficiale del Merito Italiano, Rome, 1966; Officier de la Légion d'Honneur, 1978; Vermillion Medal, City of Paris. *Died* (in Paris) *29 June 1982.* Firm continued after his death. **Address:** 44 rue Francois-1er, 75008 Paris, France.

Publications:

By BALMAIN:

Books

My Years and Seasons, London 1964.

On BALMAIN:

Books

Latour, Anny, *Kings of Fashion,* London 1958.
Lynam, Ruth, ed., *Paris Fashion: The Great Designers and Their Creations,* London 1972.
Milbank, Caroline Rennolds, *Couture: The Great Designers,* New York 1985.
Musée de la Mode et du Costume, *Pierre Balmain: 40 années de création,* Paris 1985.
Maeder, Edward, et al, *Hollywood and History: Costume Design in Film,* New York 1987.

Articles

Verdier, Rosy, "Balmain: le décor total," in *L'Officiel* (Paris), April 1985.
"Le point sur les collections: Pierre Balmain," in *L'Officiel* (Paris), March 1986.

*   *   *

"Dressmaking is the architecture of movement." This was the philosophy of French couturier Pierre Balmain. His mission, as he saw it, was to beautify the world just as an architect does. The relationship between architecture and couture was emphasized throughout Balmain's career. He initially studied to be an architect. The beauty of couture, Balmain often argued, was when it was brought to life on the human form. He also stated, "nothing is more important in a dress than its construction."

The House of Balmain opened, with great acclaim from the fashion press, in 1945. Alice B. Toklas wrote, "A dress is to once more become a thing of beauty, to express elegance and grace." Prior to opening his own house, Balmain apprenticed with couturier Captain Edward Molyneux, in Paris, for five years. It was these years with Molyneux that taught him about the business of couture. Molyneux was at the height of his success during that time and Balmain defined him as a true creator. He learned there about the elegance of simplicity which is so evident in his later designs under his own name. After leaving Molyneux, Balmain joined the firm of Lucien Lelong, where he worked from 1939 to 1944 off and on during the war and the German Occupation. In 1941, the House of Lelong reopened and Balmain returned to work with a newly hired designer, Christian Dior.

Balmain credited himself with the now famous "New Look" and cited his first collection (1945), pictured in American *Vogue,* as evidence. These designs did illustrate the feminine silhouette of longer, bell-shaped, higher bustlines, narrow shoulders, and smaller waists. The collections of Jacques Fath and Balenciaga were also reflective of the New Look silhouette with which Christian Dior was ultimately credited.

Pierre Balmain believed that the ideal of elegance in clothing was achieved only through simplicity. He detested ornamentation for the sake of making a garment spectacular and offended the American fashion press by stating that Seventh Avenue fashion was vulgar. As a couturier he was not interested in fashion *per se;* rather he sought to dress women who appreciated an elegant appearance and possessed sophisticated style. Balmain once stated, "Keep to the basic principles of fashion and you will always be in harmony with the latest trends without falling prey to them."

The basic Balmain silhouette for day was slim, with that for evening being full-skirted. He was credited with the popularization of the stole as an accessory for both day and evening. Balmain also used fur as trim throughout his collections. He was also remembered for his exquisite use of embroidered fabrics for evening.

After the war, Balmain toured the world giving lectures on the virtues of French fashions. He promoted the notion that French couture defined the ideal of elegance and refinement. The French couture was virtually shut down during the war and these visits did much to revive the industry. As a result of these lectures, Balmain recognized the potential of the American market and opened a boutique in New York, offering his distinctly French fashions.

Balmain was one of the few French couturiers of his generation to also design for the theatre, ballet, and cinema, and also for royalty. Balmain was commissioned by Queen Sirikit of Thailand in 1960 to design her wardrobe for her official visit to the United States.

Pierre Balmain died in 1982. His high standards of elegance were well regarded in the world of couture and he did much to revitalize the French couture industry abroad.

—Margo Seaman

BANANA REPUBLIC.
American clothing store chain and mail order company

Founded by Mel and Patricia Ziegler in Mill Valley, California, in 1978. First Banana Republic Travel Bookstore opened, San Francisco, California, 1978; Travel Bookstore Catalogue first published, 1986; quarterly travel magazine, *Trips,* introduced, 1987. Business acquired by The Gap, Inc., 1983; founding partners Mel and Patricia Ziegler resigned from firm, 1988. **Awards:** Direct Mail Marketing Association Gold Echo Award, 1985, 1986; American Catalogue Gold Award, 1987. **Address:** 1 Harrison Street, San Francisco, California 94105, USA.

Publications:

On BANANA REPUBLIC:

Books

Ziegler, Patricia, and Mel Ziegler, *Banana Republic Guide to Travel and Safari Clothing,* New York 1986.

Articles

Gammon, Clive, "Banana Republic's Survival Chic Is Winning Bunches of Trendy Buyers," in *Sports Illustrated* (New York), 19 August 1985.
Weil, Henry, "Keeping Up with the (Indiana) Joneses," in *Savvy* (New York), February 1986.
Grossberger, Lewis, "Yes, Do We Have Bananas!," in *Esquire* (New York), September 1986.
"From Jungle to Drawing Room," in *Economist* (London), 14 March 1987.
"Banana Republic Founders Quit Firm," in *Women's Wear Daily* (New York), 22 April 1988.
"Ripe Banana," in *Women's Wear Daily* (New York), 17 March 1992.
Articles also in *Newsweek* (New York), 28 September 1987, *Daily News Record* (New York), 21 April 1988, and *Women's Wear Daily* (New York), 9 March 1989.

*   *   *

Banana Republic was a creative fashion adventure in the United States that began when writer Mel Ziegler needed a new jacket. He wanted one without extraneous zippers or buttons, and not made in bright-colored polyester. While on assignment in Sydney, Australia he bought three British Burma jackets. His wife Patricia, an artist, restyled the three jackets into one, using the various parts to make necessary repairs. She added elbow patches, horn buttons, and a wood buckle. Friends and acquaintances liked Mel's "new" jacket and inquired about purchasing one. It seems other people wanted clothing that was usable and stylish, without designer labels. Seeing a potential market, the Zieglers set off in search of other army surplus, and items that could be converted into usable clothing. They traveled to South America, Africa, London, and Madrid, searching out usable goods. According to their book *Banana Republic Guide to Travel and Safari Clothing,* their motto became, "in surplus we trust."

At first they marketed their finds at flea markets, selling the surplus as it was or restyled. Basque sleeping bags became Basque sheepskin vests. Shirts with tattered collars were given new ones.

Eventually the market grew so much that the Zieglers moved into a store front in Mill Valley, California.

This became the second part of the Ziegler adventure in fashion and merchandising. Lacking funds for extensive decorating, they painted the walls in a zebra stripe, and added other decor to create the image of a jungle trading post. The background music was provided by their personal tapes of 1940s and 1950s jazz. They created a theatrical setting for their surplus and redesigned surplus clothing.

The third part of this fashion adventure was the non-traditional catalog the Zieglers developed to sell their product to both men and women. Due to limited funding, Patricia drew pictures of the clothes. Mel wrote the text that went beyond bland descriptions of the clothes, to include their place of origin, or how to use the items.

Calling their enterprise Banana Republic to denote change, the Zieglers began a unique merchandising adventure. People liked the stylish, rugged surplus goods sold at relatively low cost. The Zieglers sold the business to The Gap, Inc. in 1983. The Gap provided the business know-how, which the Zieglers admittedly lacked, allowing the Zieglers to concentrate on the creative end of the business, at which they excelled.

When demand outpaced the supply of surplus goods, Patricia designed clothing which was then manufactured for Banana Republic. The clothes and accessories were always stylish, comfortable, and of a high quality. The designs suggested travel, safari, and camping. They were made of khaki and other neutrals, in natural materials.

Walking into a Banana Republic store was like walking on to a movie set for a jungle outpost, an African hunting lodge, or British officers' club. Mock elephant tusks were hung and jeeps became part of the decor, as did old furniture and luggage. The original 1940s and 1950s jazz was augmented by animal sounds from the jungle.

The catalog now had fashion descriptions written by a number of professional writers and journalists. The text included background stories, and endorsements written by famous people. Drawings were still used for the clothing but were now in color. Photographs of people in various places, wearing the same or similar clothes, were included. The catalog was an adventure to read.

Banana Republic emerged at a time when there was a general shift away from all-purpose department stores, towards smaller stores which concentrated on doing one thing well. They were one of the first stores to concentrate on clothing made of natural fabrics, in stylishly rugged designs. Catalog selling was an important part of their merchandising operation. Their customers were not concerned with the dictates of the fashion world.

Through Banana Republic, Mel and Patricia Ziegler filled a niche for comfortable, rugged, yet stylish clothes. They marketed their product through a catalog that was interesting to read, and at stores that were an adventure to enter. After the Zieglers left Banana Republic, the store no longer used surplus goods, and became less theatrical in the way merchandise was presented.

—Nancy House

BANKS, Jeff.

British designer, retailer, entrepreneur

Born: Ebbw Vale, Wales, 1943. **Education:** Studied textile and interior design, Camberwell School of Art, 1959-62, and St. Martin's School of Art, 1962-64. **Family:** Married Sandy Shaw (divorced). **Career:** Opened first shop, Clobber, 1964; free-lance designer, Liberty, London, and Rembrandt manufacturers, 1975-78; launched Warehouse chain of stores, 1978, and Warehouse Utility Clothing Company catalogue, early 1980s; designed bed linen collection, 1978. Also host and co-producer, *The Clothes Show* for BBC television. **Awards:** *Woman* magazine British Fashion Award, 1979, 1982. **Address:** 21 D'Arbley St., London W1V, England.

Publications:

On BANKS:

Articles

"Jeff Banks Designs," in *The Sunday Times* (London), 11 January 1976.
McCartney, Margaret, "Mr. Banks Bounces Back," in *The Sunday Times* (London), 11 January 1976.
McCormack, Mary, "Trend Setter," in *Annabel* (London), June 1983.
"Behind the Scenes—Fashion Line-up: The Entrepreneur," in *Living* (London), October 1983.
Hennessy, Val, "Banks, the Scruff Fashion Designer," in *You,* magazine of the *Mail on Sunday* (London), 11 December 1983.
Brooks, Barry, "Banking on Fashion," in *Creative Review* (London), October 1984.
"Influences: Jeff Banks," in *Women's Journal* (London), April 1985.
Mower, Sarah, "Dennis and the Menace," in *The Guardian* (London), 9 January 1986.
Rumbold, Judy, "Listening Banks," in *Company* (London), December 1986.
Robson, Julia, "Will Men Buy It?," in *The Sunday Telegraph Magazine* (London), 9 August 1987.
"Banks's Shock Exit," in *DR: The Fashion Business* (*Drapers Record*) (London), 15 July 1989.
Brennon, Steve, "Banking on the Future," in *Fashion Weekly* (London), 26 October 1989.
McCooey, Meriel, "Be Prepared," in *The Sunday Times Magazine* (London), 15 April 1990.
Tredre, Roger, "Out of the Warehouse and into the News," in *The Independent* (London), 5 May 1990.
Barber, Richard, "Jeff Banks: Back Where He Belongs," in *Clothes Show* (London), March 1992.

*   *   *

For many Britons Jeff Banks is the face of fashion. *The Clothes Show,* the television magazine that he devised and co-presents, has helped to democratize and demystify fashion. It has spawned a monthly magazine, generated its own annual exhibition, and has sponsored student fashion shows. The programme epitomizes Jeff Banks's non-elitist attitude to fashion. His career has been devoted to making fashion available to a wide range of people.

Jeff Banks's greatest successes have been in the High Street. Clobber, his first London shop, carried the work of young designers such as Foale and Tuffin, and Janice Wainwright. Over ten years later, in the late 1970s, his Warehouse Utility Clothing company introduced designer looks at non-designer prices. An initial setback—when the first London Warehouse shop and its contents were destroyed by fire—did not quell Banks's irrepressible energy.

From their beginnings in London, the Warehouse shops have gained a national and international reputation. Started as a means of combatting wastage, the company utilized stocks of fabrics piling up in warehouses all over Europe. The resulting collections were retailed at almost wholesale prices. The shops, which have a distinct design and style, sell only Warehouse merchandise, created by a team of designers. The interiors are minimal and logically planned, and the merchandise reflects the current fashion look, without being too extreme for the High Street. Ranges are regularly updated. Warehouse equals lively, fresh ideas, translated into womenswear: the formula has proved attractive. Warehouse shops can be found in most major UK shopping venues, and in the mid-1980s outlets were opened in the United States.

The Warehouse concept helped to revolutionize shopping by post. Freemans, a traditional mail order company, launched Bymail, which brought the Warehouse style to a wider range of customers. The venture was a great success and was quickly followed by Classics Bymail and Men Bymail. With an emphasis on fabrics and cut, the classics included the perennial trenchcoat, suits, dresses, and separates in versatile and interchangeable dark and soft colours. The catalogues set new standards for mail order. Created by top models, stylists, and photographers, the visually attractive spreads helped to sell the clothes. Like the shops, they had their imitators, both good and bad.

Sound team work has provided the essential back-up for Jeff Banks's ideas, and he has inspired many people over the last 30 years. Variety has been a mark of his career. As a designer, illustrator, retailer, manager, design director, consultant, and educator he has helped improve fashion attitudes and awareness. Business training is for him an important part of design education, and he has made his views known by acting as consultant and examiner for several British fashion degree courses. Fashion graduates are employed straight from college by Warehouse.

Jeff Banks's greatest achievement is in promoting genuine fashion awareness, and he has the ability to fire up others with his own enthusiasm. Fashion has come down off its pedestal and become available to everyone. Jeff Banks has helped to make it happen.

—Hazel Clark

BANKS, Jeffrey.

American designer

Born: Washington, D.C., 3 November 1955. **Education:** Studied at Pratt Institute, Brooklyn, New York, 1972-74; graduated from Parsons School of Design, New York, 1977. **Career:** Part-time assistant to Ralph Lauren, New York, 1972-74, and to Calvin Klein, New York, 1974-76; designer, Nik Nik, 1976-77; designer in New York for Concorde International, Alixandre, Merona Sport, 1977-c.1980; launched own menswear company, 1980; introduced boyswear collection, 1980; formed joint venture for designer line with Takihyo, Inc., Hong Kong, 1988; design consultant, Herman Geist, New York, 1990; designer, Jeffrey Banks label for Hartz & Company, New York, beginning in 1984; Jeffrey Banks menswear, neckwear, and eyewear licensed for production in Japan, beginning in 1982; menswear consultant, Bloomingdale's, New York, beginning in 1993. **Awards:** Coty American Fashion Critics Award, 1977,

1982; "Earnie" Award for boyswear, 1980; Cutty Sark Award, 1987. **Address:** 12 East 26th Street, New York, New York 10010, USA.

Publications:

On BANKS:

Books

Trachtenberg, Jeffrey A., *Ralph Lauren: The Man Behind the Mystique,* New York 1988.

Articles

Bloom, Ellye, "Jeffrey Banks: To Boyswear with Love," in *Teens and Boys* (New York), October 1979.
Kleinfeld, N. R., "Jeffrey Banks Suits the Mood," in the *New York Times Magazine,* 2 March 1980.
Gruen, John, "The Designer's Eye for Timeless Fashion Photography," in *Architectural Digest* (Los Angeles), September 1989.

*   *   *

At the age of 15, Jeffrey Banks was working as a salesman at the menswear store Britches of Georgetown, where he already had been a regular customer since he was 12. "He was surely the only high school student in Washington, D.C., with his own subscriptions to *Daily News Record* and *Women's Wear Daily,*" recounts Jeffrey Trachtenberg in *Ralph Lauren: The Man Behind the Mystique.* Banks is the consummate clothing *aficionado* and stylist, one who is positively obsessed with fashion. For some, apparel is simply the family business or narcissist's self-realization. For Banks, clothing is an ecstatic vocation.

A devoted movie fan since childhood, Banks has made his cinematic dream come true in clothing that evokes the Golden Age of Hollywood, in nuanced references to such stars as Audrey Hepburn (later a friend), and in a styling of menswear in the tradition of the debonair man about town. When Ralph Lauren visited Washington, Banks was chosen to pick him up at the airport. Fully dressed in Lauren clothing, Banks appeared as a precocious high school student and was asked by Lauren to come see him for a job when he came to New York for design school. While still in art school, Banks became Lauren's assistant and protégé in fulfillment of his sensibility for the interpretation of the traditional in menswear and in continuing development of his talents as a designer and stylist.

Banks has subsequently designed furs for Alixandre, apprenticed with Calvin Klein, and designed for Merona sportswear. Even at Merona, his style was considered spectator sportswear, meaning the extended vision of sportswear, but also the sportswear edited by Banks's keen eye to what is being worn and how it can be subtly improved. His deepest affection is, though, as it always was: to the romantic tradition of tailored clothing, a debonair style burnished by a sense of artisto nonchalance. In sportswear, Banks's strong sense of color is notable, but even for color his tailored clothing is his more natural medium. He calls himself a romanticist but the term is weak for one so smitten by the passion for traditional clothing that he makes clothes that work for the most conservative gentleman but can be assembled with panache for the urbane sophisticate. Even more outside of his own country, Banks's clothing in Japan epitomizes the grand sensibility of menswear brought into a fresh American focus.

Walt Whitman argued that American democracy promotes uniformity, even a sense of unimportance in individual citizens. American menswear in the second half of the 20th century has been internationally effective in seeking differentiation and distinction within the homogeneity of modern appearance. Designers such as Lauren, Banks, and others address the social need and solve the aesthetic problem in presenting clothing of traditional demeanor and gentry aspiration that will not disturb the standard of uniformity, albeit with a kind of smartness of detailing that is distinguished without being dandified. Both have, of course, learned a great deal from images in film and photography as well as keenly observing men of classic style. They have then reinterpreted and refined that style.

Some would argue that the designer's transformative skill is honed in part by being an outsider—by observing that which cannot be possessed in its present form and by inherently needing and seeking change. Banks, an African-American, has given significant personal inflection to inbred, rarefied traditions of menswear, often connoting class. His customer—probably younger, because of his palette, than Lauren's—buys not to social-climb, but to be subsumed in a fantasy of best-dressed nattiness, perfect in effortless grooming, and informal high style.

Banks's work is infused with his passion for tradition. Even as it incorporates standards of an elite, Banks gives his designs something more pleasant and less vacant. He has a rich sense of clothing's thrill and imagination. His is not aspiring clothing in the sense of seeking class elevation; Jeffrey Banks creates clothing of dreaming, of the fantasy that surpasses class to identify a good life. Stewart Ewen in *All Consuming Images* points to Roland Barthes's model of a "dream of wholeness" and style's struggle to realize that dream. Jeffrey Banks creates men's style of that ideal aggregate.

—Richard Martin

BARNES, Jhane.

American designer

Born: Jane Barnes in Phoenix, Maryland, 4 March 1954. **Education:** Graduated from Fashion Institute of Technology, New York, 1975. **Family:** Married Howard Ralph Feinberg, 1981 (divorced); married Katsuhiko Kawasaki, 1988. **Career:** Menswear company established as Jhane Barnes Ltd, 1977; President, Jane Barnes for ME, New York 1976-78, and Jhane Barnes Inc., from 1978; introduced women's collection, 1979; neckwear line by Zanzara introduced, 1989; footwear collection launched, 1991; clothing licensed by American Fashion Company, San Diego, California, from 1990; leatherwear licensed by Group Five Leather, Minneapolis, Minnesota, from 1994. Also designs furnishing fabrics marketed by Knoll International, from 1989. **Awards:** Coty American Fashion Critics Award for Menswear 1980; Cutty Sark Most Prominent Designer Award, 1980; Cutty Sark Outstanding Designer Award 1982; Coty Return Menswear Award, 1984; Council of Fashion Designers of America Award, 1981, 1984; Contract Textile Award, American Society of Interior Designers 1983, 1984; Product Design Award, Institute of Business Designers, 1983, 1984, 1985, 1986, 1989. **Address:** 575 Seventh Avenue, New York, NY 10018, USA.

Publications:

On BARNES:

Articles

Burggraf, Helen, "Jhane Barnes," in *Men's Apparel News,* 14 October 1980.

Ettorre, Barbara, "Success Looms," in *Working Woman* (New York), June 1981.

"Jhane Barnes: A Material Force," in *GQ* (New York), November 1981.

Fendel, Alyson, "Jhane Barnes: 'For Inspiration I Look to the Future, Not the Past'," in *Apparel World,* 22 March 1982.

Groos, Michael, "Loosening Up: A New Look in Menswear for Fall," in the *New York Times,* 5 January 1988.

"The Americans: Jhane Barnes," in the *Daily News Record* (New York), 15 August 1989.

"Tiny Pieces of Fabric," in *The New Yorker,* 29 October 1990.

Furman, Phyllis, "Resuiting American Men," in *Crain's New York Business,* 15 July 1991.

Maycumber, Gray, "Fabrics a Weapon at Jhane Barnes: Designer Sees Textiles Winning Half the Men's Fashion Battle," in the *Daily News Record* (New York), 15 October 1992.

"New York Reviews: Jhane Barnes," in *DNR* (New York), 11 August 1994.

*   *   *

DNR (11 August 1994) reported of Jhane Barnes's 1995 collection, "Jhane Barnes's spring sportswear collection is designed for a city sophisticate, one who appreciates unstructured silhouettes, rich textures, and cerebral prints for shirts." In fact, Barnes's work has been consistently about a cosmopolitan view of texture, bestowing on menswear a stony, flecked range of earth, grain, and granite hues.

Describing her work for interiors with Knoll, *The New Yorker* (29 October 1990) chronicled: "And the main thing about the Jhane Barnes approach is that it is a modernist approach to nature. For instance, she decided on the design for one fabric, called Aerial View, while she was noticing how the earth looked from an airplane. She has also been influenced by time spent in her country house, in South Salem [New York]." One imagines the inspirations coming so effortlessly from Barnes's observations of informal beauty, whether the aerial landscape or ripe plums or passages of deteriorated façade. Barnes's design exudes its humanism, its earthy and natural bent, and its sense of the easygoing and comfortable. Her knit sweaters are never the artistic geometries of Missoni; instead, they suggest leafy surrounds and irregular patterns in nature. Her propensity to loose, even amorphous, shapes, along with the organics of color, would settle any of her garments into a comfortable camouflage at Walden Pond. In a menswear world of aggressive self-assertion and power, Barnes speaks quietly and with nature's sweet sounds. Her scumbled knits seem like the residue from an artist's palette and her wondrous colors could forecast overcast skies more than any Pantone swatch. Her name could hardly be more apt, her colors and interest suggesting the nostalgic, weathered old barns of rustic life now bygone and prized by urban recollection.

Barnes attempted to re-do menswear from the foundation, accepting none of the conventions or principles of power when she began in the late 1970s. As she admitted to Michael Gross (*New*

York Times, 5 January 1988), "I was way too early," though Barnes can be said to anticipate many of the softened, cozy changes to menswear tailoring and palette in the late 1980s. "Now," she told Gross, "I try to be innovative and interesting, but not trendy or classic. I like a man to be noticed across the room, but not across the street." In fact, Barnes is a chastened designer even in the era of dress clothing for men being more and more reconciled with casual wear. Her clothing always has great dignity and reserve; her beckoning nature seems always to be flinty, cautious New England, not the epic Great Plains of Ralph Lauren or the steamy tropics of Gianni Versace.

Touch and the tactile are leitmotifs of Barnes's work: among menswear designers, she is uncommonly sensitive to hand and feel. Barnes's work—often esteemed almost as much as works of art as garments—has attracted an ardent and loyal clientèle, even if her efforts to reach a mass market have always been strangely out of synch with market trends. Perhaps too urban and unconventional for some and too modest for others, Barnes is making a menswear that may never be wholly mainstream. Nonetheless, her rich earthy design is as fresh, colorful, and splendid as a sunrise garden.

—Richard Martin

BARNETT, Sheridan.

British designer

Born: Bradford, England, 1951. **Education:** Studied at Hornsey and Chelsea Colleges of Art, 1969-73. **Career:** Designer for Quorum, 1975-76; first collection under own label, 1976; designer, Barnett and Brown (with Sheilagh Brown), 1976-80; taught fashion at St. Martin's School of Art, and textiles at Chelsea College of Art; free-lance designer, Jaeger, Norman Hartnell, Salvador and Annalena, beginning in 1980; also designed own label range for Reldan. **Awards:** Bath Museum of Costume Dress of the Year Award, 1983.

Publications:

On BARNETT:

Articles

Brampton, Sally, "Showing the Rest of the World," in *The Observer* (London), 20 March 1983.
Jones, Mark, "Followers of Fashion," in *Creative Review* (London), December 1984.
Mower, Sarah, "The Trick Up His Sleeve," in *The Guardian* (London), 21 August 1986.
"Sheridan Barnett with a Twist," in *Vogue* (London), April 1987.

*   *   *

"We are dressmakers," insisted Sheridan Barnett in an interview with journalist Sarah Mower. "I think it's ludicrous that designers should be made into superstars when they're just out of college. Nobody's a true dress designer until they've worked in the industry at least three years" (*The Guardian,* London, 21 August 1986). Barnett believes passionately in the value of training, practice, and apprenticeship to the designer. To him design is a practical, problem solving exercise that should be approached with organized dis-

cipline. He is not a prima donna, distracted by the whims and extravagances of an often superficial business. His first consideration is his customer and the practical needs they have, rather than the advancement or hype of his own name and talent. This could be one of the reasons why, outside of the fashion business, Barnett is one of fashion's best-kept secrets.

Barnett first produced a collection under his own label when he left the design group Quorum in 1976. He quickly established a reputation for very wearable, simple, and affordable clothes and was always one step ahead of other designers, not only in ideas but also in his work. He introduced oversized jackets and ankle-length skirts that were a year ahead of the catwalk and two years before the High Street had caught on to the look. He also introduced silk pajamas before Parisian designers had even considered them. In many ways he seemed to be developing a new modern formula to shape 1980s fashion and style. "It had to be interesting, well cut, original, comfortable—and a good fit," he declared.

Sheridan Barnett aims for a spareness of design, achieved through a process of elimination. Removing the frills, trims, and fuss that he claims to hate, he believes that customers should add their own style to the clothes to complete a look or change it from day to day. He strongly adheres to perfection in cut, sometimes spending a week over one sleeve, resetting it over a hundred times according to his perception of how it should fit. "Of course nothing's ever perfect," he once declared, emphasizing the fact that a designer should never be satisfied as it breeds complacency.

Barnett regards himself as a professional free-lance designer, a position that he feels strongly suits his temperament. Apart from his own label collections, however, he has collaborated in several successful design liaisons during his career. During the 1970s he was in partnership with designer Sheilagh Brown, trading as Barnett and Brown and designing their own collections. During the 1980s he produced collections for Jaeger and Norman Hartnell, as well as his own label range for Reldan; he also worked variously as a lecturer in fashion schools. The early 1990s saw him take a position as designer for the Marks and Spencer suppliers Claremont.

Barnett claims not to mind that he has not become a household name in Britain, as have designers such as Bruce Oldfield and Jean Muir. He is regarded within the industry as one of the best designers around. Although he admits that things may have been different had he worked in America, his love of London and British culture is a major influence in his work and something he would have had to sacrifice had he gone abroad.

Sheridan Barnett's ultimate contribution to fashion is the longevity his clothes have and his simplistic taste and style. He has remained a rare and constant favorite with customers, and, amazingly, fashion editors, the people most likely to blow with the fashion wind. This reinforces his original aim for clothes that always look interesting and last for many years. "You can only achieve that quality if you eliminate what is superfluous," he declared.

—Kevin Almond

BAROCCO, Rocco.

Italian designer

Born: Naples, Italy, 26 March 1944; christened Rocco Muscariello. **Education:** Attended Accademia delle Belle Arti, Rome, 1962 (Fine Arts). **Career:** Sketch artist, De Barentzen, 1963-65; joined group

Rocco Barocco: Fall/Winter 1993/1994.

to form *atelier* producing high-fashion collections under Barocco label; disbanded 1974. Independent designer using Barocco label, from 1977; Rocco Barocco ready-to-wear line added, 1978; knitwear and children's lines introduced 1982. Produces ready-to-wear, jeans, knitwear, scarves, leathergoods, accessories, perfume, porcelain tiles and linens. Produces fragrance *RoccoBarocco III*. **Exhibitions:** *Italian Fashion in Japan,* Daimaru Museum, Osaka, 1983; *Italian Fashion Design,* Italian-American Museum, San Francisco, and Pacific Design Center, Los Angeles, 1987; *La Sala Bianca,* Palazzo Pitti, Florence, 1992, and the Louvre Museum, Paris, 1993. **Awards:** Senior Singer Company Award, New York, 1969. **Address:** Barocco Roma Srl., Piazza di Spagna 72a, 00187 Rome, Italy.

Publications:

On BAROCCO:

Books

Bianchino, G., and A. Quintaralle, *Fashion—from Fable to Design,* Parma 1989.
Bottero, A., *Nostra Signora la Moda,* Milan 1979.
Giacomoni, S., *The Italian Look Reflected,* Milan 1984.
Giordani Aragno, B., *40 Years of Italian Fashion,* Florence 1983.
Italian Fashion in Japan, Osaka 1983.
McDowell, Colin, *Directory of Twentieth Century Fashion,* London 1984.
La Sala Bianca, Milan, 1992.
Zito, Adele, *Italian Fashion: The Protagonists,* Italy 1993.

Articles

"La botte secrete de la mode romaine," in *Paris Capitale,* May 1994.
Gargia, Massimo, "Barocco ou l'amour des passions inutiles," in *L'Officiel* (Paris), September 1979.
"Italy's Passion for Fashion," in *Sunday Morning Post* (South China), 1 December 1991.
Lanza, S., "The A.W. Collections from Italy," in *The Sunday Times* (London), 2 September 1990.
Melendez, R., "Best of Italy," in *Women's Wear Daily* (New York), 26 August 1989.

*

I started my career very young and so it is natural that I should have a certain leaning towards the avant-garde.

My first creations were challenges to the styles of the period and very courageous. Technique and experience combined with my taste for the daring in fashion have led to the birth of a clearly defined style that can be recognized in my often repetitive choice of colours: black, black/white and optical effects.

In my latest collection a floral *leitmotif* (a rose in particular) appears, inserted into spotted or striped designs (leopards, zebras, tigers). The rigorousness of my cut can be recognized in the jackets and cloaks which in their different inspirations (oriental, African, military) always reveal a search for perfect construction.

I have a predilection for soft and sumptuous materials, for embroidery and for gold in particular.

If we want to define the Roccabarocco style we must use words like rigour, humour, audacity, and poetic imagination.

—Rocco Barocco

* * *

Rocco Barocco, or Rocco Muscariello as he was christened, is an Italian ready-to-wear designer who creates men's, women's, and childrenswear in a variety of ranges from jeans and knitwear to eveningwear. Born in Naples in 1944, he moved to Rome in order to follow his chosen career path. After apprenticeship and training at the city's leading *ateliers,* he eventually opened his own *atelier* in the Piazza di Spagna in 1968. Success was immediate and his popularity with the Roman jet set increased his fame throughout Europe. He was soon exporting clothes to France, the United States, and Japan.

Rocco Barocco defines his style as being rigorous, humorous, impudent, and poetically imaginative. He has a taste for the daring and avant-garde in design and detailing, such as his bright red chiffon evening gowns with bold, asymmetrically draped necklines. He also enjoys working with embroidery and gold, in particular. A distinctive sequin and embroidered jacket from his spring-summer 1993 collection paid joint homage to the stars and stripes of the American flag and the daring circus performers from Elsa Schiaparelli's Circus collection of the late 1930s. Barocco prefers to work in soft and sumptuous materials like *paillettes* and satins or cashmeres and crêpes. His favourite colour combinations are black, black and white, or optical effects, combinations that have been repeated themselves through numerous collections and help to define the Rocco Barocco style.

When he began designing, Rocco Barocco's intention was to challenge established silhouettes and shapes with a search for perfection in cut, construction, and symmetry. Examples of his cutting skills are displayed in his jackets and coats. His autumn-winter collection for 1989 showed long, swinging, dove grey cashmere coats, perfect in balance and proportion and trimmed in fur. His fitted, shawl collared jackets and suits hinted at masculine classics, but exuded femininity in their curvaceous cut, proportion, and detailing. Barocco represents a unique Mediterranean flavour in contemporary fashion. He enjoys taking strong colour and style combinations and mixing them in a diverse Mediterranean way. For instance, floral motifs such as roses or sunflowers are inserted into spotted and striped tiger, zebra, and leopard print designs.

Barocco is also inspired by Hollywood, which he views as a fascinating land of unsettled heroes and heroines and a cornucopia of visual reference for high fashion. Hollywood movie stars and fashion in the movies have always been over the top. This undoubtedly contributes to Rocco Barocco's taste for the daring in fashion, exemplified in his new notorious swimwear-to-lingerie collection.

The Rocco Barocco label is also found on ranges of leather goods, handbags, hosiery, jewellery, umbrellas and shoes. His perfume and toiletry line, *RoccoBarocco III,* has had lasting success and the designer has recently branched out into designs for the home, including household furniture, porcelain tiles, and refined ceramics. Barocco views his success as transitory, accompanied by inevitable changes. However, from an outsider point of view these changes only result in further expansion of the business, ultimately promoting the name of Rocco Barocco on a wider scale.

—Kevin Almond

BARRIE, Scott.

American designer

Born: Nelson Clyde Barr in Philadelphia, 16 January 1946. **Education:** Studied applied arts at Philadelphia Museum College of Art, and fashion design at Mayer School of Fashion, New York, mid-1960s. **Career:** Designer, Allen Cole boutique, New York, 1966-69; co-founder, Barrie Sport, Ltd., New York, 1969-82; menswear collection and Barrie Plus collections introduced, 1974. Also designed dresses for S.E.L., mid-1980s, loungewear for Barad, and furs for Barlan. Moved to Milan, 1982; formed Scott Barrie Italy SrL, in partnership with Kinshido Company, Ltd., of Japan, 1983; designer, Milan D'Or division for Kinshido, 1983-91; designer, signature line for Kinshido, 1983-91; free-lance designer, Krizia, Milan, 1986-88. *Died* (in Alessandria, Italy) *8 June 1993.*

Publications:

On BARRIE:

Books

Morris, Bernadine, and Barbara Walz, *The Fashion Makers,* New York 1978.
Milbank, Caroline Rennolds, *New York Fashion: The Evolution of American Style,* New York 1989.

Articles

White, Constance C. R., "Scott Barrie: Back and Renewed," in *Women's Wear Daily* (New York), 20 November 1989.
White, Constance C. R., "Scott Barrie Dies at 52; Made Mark on S.A. in 70's," in *Women's Wear Daily* (New York), 10 June 1993.
Schiro, Ann-Marie, "Scott Barrie is Dead; Designer, 52, Made Jersey Matte Dresses," in the *New York Times,* 11 June 1993.
"Fashion Designer Scott Barrie Dies," in *Jet* (Chicago), 28 June 1993.

* * *

Scott Barrie was one of a group of brassy and vibrant black designers and models to establish themselves on New York's Seventh Avenue in the late 1960s. Influenced by his godmother, who had designed and made clothes for the sonorous and volatile jazz singers, Dinah Washington and Sarah Vaughan, Barrie began designing in 1966. Although he graduated from the Philadelphia College of Art and the Mayer School in New York, his mother was not initially encouraging about his future in fashion designing for Seventh Avenue. "Blacks don't make it there," she warned her son—Barrie quickly proved her wrong.

Describing himself in the 1970s as being midway between the crazy extremes of Zandra Rhodes and Herbert Kasper, Barrie quickly established himself as a designer of sexy, often outrageous clothes. His eveningwear was particularly noteworthy: skinny gowns sprinkled with *paillettes* and dangerously high splits, or jersey slips that slid tantalizingly over the figure.

He began making clothes in his New York apartment, with a makeshift cutting table and domestic sewing machine. His first orders were from small independent boutiques but success came when prestigious stores Henri Bendel and Bloomingdale's in New York placed orders for his sparse and revealing jersey dresses. By 1969 he had christened his company Barrie Sport and moved into spacious workrooms at 530 Seventh Avenue.

Barrie's forte was the sensuous use of jersey, cut in inventive and unexpected ways, from which he created elegant and often risqué eveningwear. Popular devotees of the Barrie look have been Naomi Sims, an extravagantly beautiful black model, who always ordered her clothes in white, and Lee Traub, wife of the president of Bloomingdale's.

Barrie also designed ranges of loungewear, furs, and accessories and was involved in costume design, creating clothes for films and the costumes for the Jeffrey Ballet's production of *Deuce Coupe.*

The intermingling of culture and race on New York's Seventh Avenue in the 1960s brought a new sort of creative energy that challenged accepted standards. Barrie's models did not parade the catwalk with elegance; instead they boogied wildly and arrogantly, with a streetwise brashness. It was a testimony to the changing times that the clothes were accepted at the higher end of the ready-to-wear market.

Scott Barrie enjoyed being a fashion designer, but acknowledged the hard work and competitive nature of the business. In the 1980s he ceased designing under his own name, taking a position with the dress firm S.E.L. as a designer.

—Kevin Almond

BARTLETT, John.

American designer

Born: Cincinnati, Ohio, c. 1964. **Education:** Graduated from Fashion Institute of Technology and Harvard College. **Career:** Worked for Ronaldus Shamask and WilliWear; established own menswear line, 1992; clothing sold at Barneys New York, Bergdorf Goodman Men, and Saks Fifth Avenue. **Awards:** Perry Ellis Award for New Fashion Talent, 1994, Council of Fashion Designers of America. **Address:** 48 W. 21st St., New York, NY 10011, USA.

Publications:

On BARTLETT:

Articles

Spindler, Amy M., "Menswear Expands the Notion of Basics," in the *New York Times,* 3 August 1993.
Shaw, Daniel, "Rookie of the Year," in the *New York Times,* 5 December 1993.
Horyn, Cathy, "Crusoe for the Modern Man," in the *Washington Post,* 6 February 1994.
"Sharkskin Bites Bartlett," in the *Daily News Record* (New York), 29 July 1994.
Martin, Richard, "Style Is as Style Does: The 'Forest Gump' Look," in *Mondo Uomo* (Milan), November-December 1994.
Ezersky, Lauren, "Bringing Up Bartlett," in *Paper* (New York), December 1994.

* * *

John Bartlett's fashion is driven by ideas—astute ideas—about men and about clothes. For example, his spring-summer 1994 collection was for a man, as Bartlett said to Amy Spindler, "daydreaming about cashing in his Gucci loafers for a lean-to on Easter Island" (*New York Times,* 3 August 1993). Bartlett's volitional Robinson Crusoe would have assembled an elegant mix of tribal tattoos, gauze tunics, and rough silk-twine jackets. As Spindler noted, "It is an ambitious designer who will take on Jean-Jacques Rousseau, but Mr Bartlett did it with fervor." Bartlett never lacks fervor: he is determined—with a missionary's zeal—to make clothing meaningful.

Bartlett is a designer of convictions and of compellingly suggestive and allusive menswear. His spring-summer 1995 collection demonstrated the designer's learned and connected awareness of culture. A runway show that began with clothing inspired by the summer 1994 movie *Forrest Gump* in its nerdish normalcy, in distinctive mint greens, continued into navy-and-white evocations out of Jean Genet (Edmund White's biography had just been published), sharp sharkskin two-button suits, and *tour de force* cross-dressing. Bartlett is a reader, observer, assimilator of contemporary culture in the best sense, bringing his acute sensitivity to contemporary culture into his design. His earlier shapeless structures were being updated into piquant reinterpretations of earlier silhouettes with trousers either cigarette thin or perfectly tubular and shown on models as high-water pants. *Daily News Record* (29 July 1994) enthused about the 1995 collection, "In just four short seasons, this glamour-boy designer has established himself as the *enfant terrible*—the Gaultier, if you will—of American men's wear." If there is a fault to Bartlett's work, it is that he is the best and consummate stylist of his own clothing. Few menswear customers will actually carry off the clothing with the full styling and intellectual jolt Bartlett imparts. But, of course, one might say the same of the ever-influential and beguiling Gaultier. One could easily imagine Bartlett fully assuming the Gaultier role of polite *provocateur,* a function woefully absent from American fashion. Bartlett's 1995 ventures into womenswear will expand the designer's capacity.

Dan Shaw (*New York Times,* 5 December 1993) calls Bartlett's design "a sort of no-fashion fashion for men who don't dress to impress." To call Bartlett no-fashion is like calling conceptual art no-art. His design is cerebral and yet he delights in the cut, materials, and masculinities of menswear. Clearly, though, Bartlett is not out to impress in any ostentatious way. However, to create monks' robes, paradise fantasies, uncompromised sarongs for men, and fictional heroes is, in its own way, most impressive. Rather than flamboyant, Bartlett's clothing is pensive and passionate. His historicism is enlightened: his 1995 argyles are light and pastel and his sheer nylon knee socks make both hairy legs and the 1950s into an irresistible irony. Bartlett's lively, optimistic intelligence does not, however, ever become the impediment that Vivienne Westwood's punk pessimism or John Galliano's melancholic historicism is. Rather, Bartlett relishes the menswear visual and structural options that make clothing wearable and comfortable as much as he adds concept to menswear: as a designer, he thinks through wearing the clothing even as he offers trenchant ideas and provocative allusions. If Bartlett's Harvard education honed his lampooning and imaginative wit, the Fashion Institute of Technology, Williwear, and Ronaldus Shamask added a Seventh-Avenue savvy. Bartlett's logo is the pear that plays on his surname: he practices the Surrealist and dandy inventions that obsessed Magritte, but still keeps the clothing foremost and wearably wonderful.

On winning the Council of Fashion Designers of America's 1994 Perry Ellis Award for New Fashion Talent (presented by actors Joe Mantello and Stephen Spinella of *Angels in America*), Bartlett showed at the awards ceremony a video paean to men's bodies in motion, including nudity and his own nudity, culminating in the dress of a man. His clothing addresses such a fundamental and ritualistic assessment of clothing in which Bartlett, more than any other major American designer in menswear, is examining the basic tenets of men's bodies and their identity in dress. Bartlett's "become yourself" philosophy is inexhaustibly optimistic. His clothing is so idiosyncratically shrewd and seductive that one could wish that many more would choose either to become themselves or, perhaps even better, to realize the ideal, thinking men that Bartlett creates.

—Richard Martin

BASTILLE, Franck Joseph.

French designer

Born: c.1964. **Career:** Known for whimsical designs and embroidered motifs; clothing sold at Galeries Lafayette, New York, among other places. **Exhibitions:** *Fashion and Surrealism,* New York, 1987. **Address:** 13 rue de la Roquette, 75011 Paris.

Publications:

On BASTILLE:

Articles

"Bastille's Day," in *Elle* (New York), July 1989.
Petkanas, Christopher, "Nouvelle Chic," in *Harper's Bazaar* December 1991.

*   *   *

Irreverent is the word for the designs of Franck Joseph Bastille. In the best tradition of Elsa Schiaparelli, whose whimsical and dreamlike designs shocked and delighted earlier fashion audiences, Bastille's witty collections launched him into the limelight as one of Paris' rising young stars. The presentation of his new ideas each season, often shown in an offbeat, trendy venue, invariably spurred fashion headlines, due in no small part to the ironic flourishes which have become his trademark.

Embroidered quotes from the animal kingdom have figured largely in Bastille's *oeuvre*. Lizards and lobsters, ants and rats, fish and cats—all have found their way onto his clothes. A thigh-high skirt might sport a creature snaking along the hem, or a plain vinyl shift may be stitched all over with a bright menagerie. Never one to be limited by convention, Bastille has been known to embroider frogs on a black vinyl coat and then upholster a chair with the same material.

Like his young Parisian peers he finds inspiration in a multitude of sources, sifting through a postmodern melange of ideas and adapting some directly, borrowing from others quite loosely. One fashion show had as its theme the permutations of water, from the beauty of the shimmering sea to the murky mystery of the subterranean underworld. Bastille showed a range of clever, bold clothes, including seaweed-hued frocks decorated with plastic fish, and his own kitschy interpretation of the sort of studded denim resort clothes worn on the Riviera. Other visual puns have included, for example, a black suit appliqued with silver guns, and a simple shift dress with a cut-out heart over the chest. And he is not above the sly tongue-in-cheek gesture, as in his wedding gown embroidered all over with the word *oui*.

Like many young designers, Bastille has rummaged about in the past for ideas, and references to different style periods can be discerned in his clothes. He became identified with 1950s-60s trapeze shapes and princess cuts for a time, but has also toyed with the body-revealing, sexy clothing of the 1980s and the decade's preoccupation with physical fitness. A collection that included clingy little body suits, short shorts, wispy slips, and satin bustiers showed that his clothes were not for the conservative customer, nor for one of advancing age. Pieces such as these demonstrate that Bastille is designing for a young, daring, and fashion-forward buyer who considers clothing a form of provocative personal expression.

Bastille has been called "fearless, with a touch of elegance." He has been known to turn a simple suit into an arch statement with the use of riotous color, as in his peacock-feather printed suit. In addition to appliques and cut-outs he has experimented with "out of context" fabrics, using slippery synthetics, shiny satins and crushed velvets for daytime wear, home-furnishing fabrics for clothing designs, and vice versa. Bastille might cover a blazer with sequins or fashion a strappy shift out of black vinyl, making a bold statement about the allure of "bad taste" while erasing demarcations between clothes for different events or times of day. He has crafted separates out of multi-hued patchwork fabric comprised of satin, floral print, and sequined squares, giving literal form to the bricolage cultural trend so prevalent in the late-twentieth century. In short, the imaginative, playful designs of Franck Joseph Bastille aim to startle and amuse, asserting that fashion does not have to be such serious business.

—Kathleen Paton

L.L. BEAN.

American clothing manufacturer and mail order company

Founded in 1912 by Leon Leonwood Bean (1872-1967), in Freeport, Maine, for mail order sales of Maine Hunting Shoe, patented 1911. Camping and fishing equipment offered, from 1920s; bicycles, cookware, watches, luggage offered, from 1930s; casual apparel offered, from 1980s. Retail salesroom added to manufacturing plant, 1945; offered 24 hours a day, 365 days a year service from 1951. First branch store opened, in Japan, 1991. **Awards:** Coty American Fashion Critics Award, 1975; American Catalogue Awards Gold Award, 1987, 1989, for hunting specialties catalogue; American Catalogue Awards Silver Award, 1989; American Catalogue Awards Gold Award for women's outdoor specialties catalogue, 1989. **Address:** L.L. Bean, Inc., Freeport, Maine 04033, USA.

Publications:

On L.L. BEAN:

Books

Montgomery, M. R., *In Search of L.L. Bean,* Boston, Massachusetts 1984.

Griffin, Carlene, *Spillin' the Beans,* Freeport, Maine 1993.

Articles

Dickson, Paul, "L.L. Bean," in *Town and Country* (New York), February 1977.
Crews, Harry, "L.L. Bean Has Your Number, America!," in *Esquire* (New York), March 1978.
Longsdorf, Robert, "L.L. Bean: Yankee Ingenuity and Persistence Transformed This Little Maine Boot Shop into a Veritable Sportsman's Candy Store," in *Trailer Life* (Agoura, California), May 1986.
Kerasole, Ted, "L.L. Bean: 75 Years," in *Sports Afield* (New York), October 1987.
"Bean Sticks to Its Backyard," in *Economist* (New York), 4 August 1990.
Kaplan, Michael, "Gumshoe," in *Gentlemen's Quarterly* (New York), October 1992.
Hirano, Koji, "L.L. Bean's First Japan Store," in *Daily News Record* (New York), 13 November 1992.
Zempke, Ron, and Dick Schaaf, "L.L. Bean," in *The Service Edge* (Minneapolis, Minnesota), 1989.

* * *

The assimilation of the work of L.L. Bean into the world of fashion design is a direct result of the eclecticism in late 20th century culture. Sportsman, businessman, and inventor, Leon Leonwood Bean stood outside the world of fashion during his lifetime. His mail order company, based in Freeport, Maine, began before World War I selling sporting garments and accessories which were innovative, durable and, once perfected, consistant in appearance over many decades. They were, initially, the epitome of anti-fashion.

Founded on the innovative design of the Maine Hunting Shoe, patented in 1911, L.L. Bean's range of clothing came to include traditional articles such as leather moccasins, based on American Indian footwear, long red woollen underwear, and collections of well-made weekend clothes for sportsmen and sportswomen. The appeal was their comfort, durability, and timelessness of appearance.

Bean's early business success was aided by the United States Post Office's introduction in 1912 of a cheap parcel post service. Similarly, the construction of the national highway network and the expansion of private car ownership in the 1910s and 1920s promoted recreational travel for sportsmen and helped to create a need for the specific kinds of garments sold by Bean. Their shop in Freeport was open for business around the clock, 365 days a year, demonstrating a genuine devotion to customer service and an understanding of the particular needs of their specialist clientèle. Through its marketing policies, L.L. Bean has come to represent solid, ethical values of conduct in commerce. The personification of integrity, L.L. Bean tested his own equipment prior to marketing, as the company president does today.

A notion of the L.L. Bean style had developed by the 1920s, when the company's catalog was known worldwide. The catalog had, from the start, a unique look and quality. Written in L.L. Bean's personal descriptive style, it was presented in a casual, scrapbook format, with its familiar Cheltenham typeface, plain wholesome models, and cover illustrations by America's foremost painters of outdoor life. By the 1980s, the catalog had become an institution and a symbol for a particular lifestyle. It attracted references in publications such as Lisa Birnbach's *The Preppy Hand-book,* which dubbed Bean "Preppy Mecca," and it was parodied in a National Lampoon "Catalog" which featured a range of items including an "Edible Moccasin" and a "Chloroform Dog Bed." The genuine catalog layout contains such surrealist juxtapositions as jackets, trousers, and duck decoys.

Following the death of L.L. Bean in 1967, the business passed into the hands of his grandson, Leon Gorman, who expanded and modernized both the operation and its products while maintaining its essential character, rooted in Down East hunting and fishing culture. But modernization had its dangers. Enthusiasm for their newly developed synthetic fibres, useful in extreme weather conditions, had carried over to the range of casual clothing of the 1960s and 1970s. However, during the 1980s, in keeping with the rising tide of environmentalism and a new public appreciation of the natural, as opposed to the synthetic, L.L. Bean returned to 100 per cent natural materials in their traditional clothes.

Expansion from shoes and outdoor clothing to accessories and equipment such as snow-shoes, fishing gear, and canoes showed a keen awareness of links between apparel and the utilitarian accoutrements of modern life. Later catalogs acknowledge the rise of the fitness movement, with new lines of garments for exercising, water sports, and accessories for activities such as roller skating and cross-country skiing.

In 1975, L.L. Bean was recognized as a bona fide member of the fashion world when it received the prestigious Coty Award. This accolade signified an expansion of the meaning of fashion and confirmed its role as a mirror on contemporary culture. The genius of L.L. Bean had been to recognize the recreational potential in his local surroundings and to invent ways to cater, through clothing, first for the growth of outdoor sporting activities and, later, to the booming leisure market. Throughout the 20th century, L.L. Bean clothes have reflected the social attitudes, leisure pursuits, and health awareness of America while also embodying a dream about the unspoiled American landscape and the values it represented.

—Gregory Votolato

BEENE, Geoffrey.

American designer

Born: Haynesville, Louisiana, 30 August 1927. **Education:** Studied medicine, Tulane University, New Orleans, 1943-46, University of Southern California, Los Angeles, 1946; studied fashion, Traphagen School, New York, 1947-48, Chambre Syndicale d'Haute Couture and Académie Julien, Paris, 1948. **Career:** Display assistant, I. Magnin, Los Angeles, 1946; apprentice tailor, Molyneux, 1948-50; assistant to Mildred O'Quinn, Samuel Winston, Harmay, and other New York fashion houses, 1950-51; assistant designer, Harmony ready-to-wear, New York, 1951-58; designer, Teal Traina, New York, 1958-63; founder-director, Geoffrey Beene Inc. fashion house, beginning in 1963; showed first menswear collection, 1970; Beenebag sportswear collection introduced, 1971; established Cofil SpA, 1976, to manufacture for Europe and the Far East; first freestanding boutique opened, New York, 1989; home furnishings collection introduced, 1993. Fragrances: *Gray Flannel,* 1975; *Bowling Green,* 1987. **Exhibitions:** *Geoffrey Beene: 25 Years of Discovery,* Los Angeles, 1988, Western Reserve Historical Society, Cleveland,

Ohio, 1988, National Academy of Design, New York, 1988, and Musashino Museum, Tokyo, 1988; *Geoffrey Beene Unbound,* Fashion Institute of Technology, New York, 1994. **Awards:** Coty American Fashion Critics Award, 1964, 1966, 1968, 1974, 1975, 1977, 1981, 1982; National Cotton Council Award, 1964, 1969; Neiman Marcus Award, 1965; Ethel Traphagen Award, New York, 1966; Council of Fashion Designers of America Award, 1986, 1987, 1989, Special Award, 1988. **Address:** 550 Seventh Avenue, New York, New York 10018, USA.

Publications:

On BEENE:

Books

Morris, Bernadine, and Barbara Walz, *The Fashion Makers,* New York 1978.
Milbank, Caroline Rennolds, *Couture: The Great Designers,* New York 1985.
Diamonstein, Barbaralee, *Fashion: The Inside Story,* New York 1985.
Coleridge, Nicholas, *The Fashion Conspiracy,* London 1988.
National Academy of Design, New York, *Geoffrey Beene: The First 25 Years* (exhibition catalogue), Tokyo 1988.
Milbank, Caroline Rennolds, *New York Fashion: The Evolution of American Style,* New York 1989.
Martin, Richard, *Beene: 30 Years,* New York 1993.
Fashion Institute of Technology, *Geoffrey Beene Unbound* (exhibition catalogue), New York 1994.
Cullerton, Brenda, *Geoffrey Beene,* New York 1995.

Articles

Bowles, J., "It's a Beene," in *Vogue* (New York), January 1977.
"Geoffrey Beene: Maître incontesté de la couture," in *L'Officiel* (Paris), September 1985.
"Modern Attitude: The Essence of Geoffrey Beene," in *Vogue* (New York), February 1986.
Hyde, Nina, "Geoffrey Beene, Simply Elegant. The Designer and His Lifetime Devotion to Fabric," in the *Washington Post,* 19 April 1987.
Bryant, Gay, "Living for Fashion," in *Connoisseur* (New York), May 1987.
Monget, K., "Designer Profiles: 1988 Marks 25th Year in American Fashion for Geoffrey Beene," in *New York Apparel News,* May 1987.
"The World of Geoffrey Beene," in *Vogue* (New York), September 1987.
"Vogue's Spy: Geoffrey Beene," in *Vogue* (London), October 1987.
"View: High Jumps," in *Vogue* (London), February 1988.
Morrisroe, Patricia, "American Beauty: The World of Geoffrey Beene," in *New York Magazine,* 30 May 1988.
Buck, Joan Juliet, "The Eye of Geoffrey Beene," in *Vogue* (New York), September 1988.
Blane, Mark, "Mr. Beene: The First 25 Years," in *Harper's Bazaar* (New York), October 1988.
Armstrong, Lisa, "The Thoroughly Modern Mr. Beene," in *Vogue* (London), April 1990.
Betts, Katherine, "Showstopper," in *Vogue* (New York), September 1991.
Donovan, Carrie, in the *New York Times,* 9 May 1993.

Geoffrey Beene: Winter 1995. *Photograph by Andrew Eccles.*

Beard, Patricia, "Beene There, Done That," in *Town and Country* (New York), July 1993.

Hirst, Arlene, "Mr. Beene: America's New Homebody," in *Metropolitan Home* (New York), July/August 1993.

Morris, Bernadine, "Beene: If Ever a Wiz There Was," in the *New York Times,* 5 November 1993.

Livingstone, David, "Beene Unbound, Grace Regained," in *The Globe and Mail* (Toronto), 5 May 1994.

Trittoléno, Martine, "L'Elégance Radicale," *Vogue* (Paris), June/July 1994.

Beckett, Kathleen, "Runway Report: In-Kleined to Wow Fans: Geoffrey Beene," in the *New York Post,* 1 November 1994.

Spindler, Amy M., "Beene: Innovative and, Yes, Intellectual," in the *New York Times,* 8 April 1995.

Menkes, Suzy, "A Crisis in Confidnece: Reiventing the American Dream," in *International Herald Tribune* (Paris), 11 April 1995.

*   *   *

"Among the fashion *cognoscenti,* [Geoffrey] Beene has long been acknowledged as an artist who chooses to work in cloth," reports Carrie Donovan in the *New York Times* (9 May 1993). "Every season his work astounds as he ingeniously shapes the most modern and wearable of clothes." For some, the designation of fashion as art is simply an encomium, a way of saying "the best." Geoffrey Beene is one of the best designers today—arguably the greatest American designer living—but also one of the most artistic. His art resides in certain principles and preoccupations: reversibility and alternative reading in Yin-Yang twins; surgically clean cutting, but a fluidity of cloth to body in the manner of Vionnet; an origami-like three-dimensionality that approaches sculpture; a propensity for Cubism, piecing the garment from regular forms in a new tangency and relationship one to another as if in the simultaneity of Cubism; and a modernist indulgence in the medium, relishing the textiles both of tradition and of advanced technology that he selects.

Such abiding elements of art in his work do not mitigate other elements. History may be seized, as in a remarkable Confederate dress inspired by the gray uniform of the Southern Army in the American Civil War. Sensuous appreciation of the body is ever present in Beene's work (he initially went to medical school and always demonstrates his interest in the body and ergonomics). His lace dresses expose the body in underwear—defying gyres of inset lace, a *tour de force* of the exposure of the body and of the security of the wearer in the dress's perfect and stable proportions. In 1988 his virtuoso single-seam dress was minimalist in design, but one never forgot that it was sensuous and clinging on the body. He shifts, conceals, and maneuvers the waist as no other designer has since Balenciaga.

Born in the South, Beene's personal style is of utmost charm, and his clothes betray his sense of good taste, though often with gentility's piquant notes. His 1967 long sequined football jersey was sportswear with a new goal in the evening and played with the anomaly of the simple style with its liquid elegance. Sweatshirt fabric and denim would be carried into eveningwear by Beene, upsetting convention. A brash gentility combines leather and lace; a charming wit provides for circus motifs. In particular, Beene loves the genteel impropriety of stealing from menswear textiles (shirting fabrics and gray flannel) for women's clothing.

Beene has a profound affinity with his contemporary Southerner Jasper Johns, who practices consummate good taste in art but with the startling possibilities of popular-culture appropriations, new dispositions to familiar elements, and a strong sense of contemporary cultural pastiche. Like Johns, Beene is always fascinated by *trompe l'oeil* and continually plays with illusions. Specific illusions of a tie and collar on a dress are the most obvious, but other wondrous tricks of illusion in clothing are found in three-dimensional patterns replicated in textile and vice versa. His bolero jackets so effectively complement the simplicity of his dresses that jacket and dress become an indistinguishable ensemble. Even his preoccupation with double-faced fabrics and reversible abstract designs are sophisticated illusionism.

Optically, Beene demands both near- and far-sight. Even before the most fluid forms emerged for Beene in the 1970s and 1980s, he had been influenced by Op Art to create apparel that was graphically striking. His frequent use of black and white is a treatment that can be read across a room and acts as sign. But one can approach a Beene composition in black and white close up with the same scrutiny of a Frank Stella black painting: there is a fascination up close even more gratifying than the sign from afar. In Beene's case, texture is an important element, and the distant reading of graphic clarity becomes far more complex when disparate textures are mingled. Like reversibility, the near-far dialectic in Beene is provocative: utter simplicity from a distance becomes infinite technicality up close. In the 1990s Beene has often eschewed the catwalk showing of new collections, preferring to display the garments on static dress forms, thus allowing the viewer to examine the garment attentively and immediately, as one might appreciate painting or sculpture.

Art, to describe Beene's clothing, is not vacuous or striving to compliment. Rather, art recognizes a process and suite of objectives inherent in the work. In a discipline of commercial fulfillment, Beene displays the artist's absolute primacy and self-confidence of design exploration.

—Richard Martin

BELLVILLE SASSOON-LORCAN MULLANY.

British couture and ready-to-wear firm, Bellville Sassoon & Bellville Sassoon-Lorcan Mullany, respectively

Belinda Bellville founded own company, 1953, joined by designer David Sassoon to form Bellville Sassoon, 1958; Bellville retired from company, 1983; Bellville Sassoon-Lorcan Mullany founded, 1987. **David Sassoon** born in London, 5 October 1932. Attended Chelsea College of Art, 1954-56, and Royal College of Art, London, 1956-58. Served in the Royal Air Force, 1950-53. **Lorcan Mullany** born 3 August 1953. Trained at Grafton Academy, Dublin. Worked for Bill Gibb, Hardy Amies, and Ronald Joyce in London before producing collection under his own name in 1983. Joined Bellville Sassoon in 1987. Ready-to-wear collection sold in, among others, Sak's Fifth Avenue, Bloomingdale's, and Henri Bendel, New York, and Harrods, Harvey Nichols, London. Also flagship store in Chelsea, London. **Exhibitions:** *Fashion: An Anthology,*

Bellville Sassoon-Lorcan Mullany: 1991.

Victoria and Albert Museum, London, 1971. **Address:** 18 Culford Gardens, London SW3 2ST, England.

Publications:

On BELLVILLE SASSOON:

Books

O'Hara, Georgina, *The Enyclopaedia of Fashion,* New York 1986.

Articles

Thomas, Jacqueline H., "Profile," in *Vogue Pattern Book* (New York and London), 1984.
Holder, Margaret, "That Sassoon Touch," in *Royalty* (London), 1989.
Griffiths, Sally, "Well-Dressed Surroundings," in *House and Garden* (London), 1991.
Polan, Brenda, "Vital Sassoon," in the *Tatler* (London), September 1992.

*

I like clothes that flatter a woman and are sexy. If a woman feels good in the clothes I design, she looks good.

I enjoy designing cocktail and eveningwear with my co-designers Lorcan Mullany and George Sharp. We work together as a team to produce ready-to-wear dresses, sometimes in a romantic mood, sometimes whimsical or sexy. I do not like unkind clothes that are ugly and do not flatter a woman.

I love colour and beautiful fabrics. Each season we try to do something different, but always with a distinct Bellville Sassoon-Lorcan Mullany handwriting, which our buyers always look for. Our collection is sold internationally and each country looks for a different fashion concept, so our collections are always varied, never sticking to one theme. I do not like to philosophize about clothes; they are, after all, only garments to be worn and discarded as the mood of fashion changes.

—David Sassoon

*   *   *

The company of Bellville Sassoon-Lorcan Mullany is currently jointly run by David Sassoon who owns the company, designing the couture, and Lorcan Mullany who joined in 1987 and is responsible for the ready-to-wear. Together they provide a very English version of glamorous occasion dressing and eveningwear, uncomplicated, clear, and immensely flattering clothes worn by society ladies and the international jet set: the Princess of Wales, Ivana Trump, Shakira Caine, Dame Kiri Te Kanawa, and The Countess von Bismarck, to name but a few. The company is also renowned for its glamorous and romantic wedding dresses, designed to order, and the selection of designs available in the *Vogue Pattern Book*'s designer section, which are on sale internationally.

"You have to find your own niche," declared David Sassoon when questioned about his approach to design. "You cannot be all things to all markets. My philosophy of fashion is that I like to make the kind of clothes that flatter. I am not interested in fashion

for its own sake. If you make a woman feel good, she looks good automatically" (*Tatler* [London], September 1992). On leaving the Royal College of Art fashion school in the late 1950s David Sassoon was recruited as Belinda Bellville's design assistant. She recognized in him a designer who had a strong, distinctive signature and a simple approach that was romantic in style but dramatic and very feminine. Together they became business partners, naming the company Bellville et Cie, to capitalize on the prevalent conception that all smart clothes were French. From the start it attracted vast attention from press and buyers. "We gave our first show in my grandmother's house in Manchester Square and the next day there was a queue outside the shop, with Bentleys blocking the street," declared Belinda Bellville.

Sassoon identifies the peak of his career as being the period between the late 1960s and 1970s when he believed that the taste for high romanticism and fantasy clothes endorsed his style. The company was constantly featured in the pages of glossy magazines, sharing the stage with contemporaries such as Zandra Rhodes, Gina Fratini, and Bill Gibb. Sassoon regrets the fact that the British fashion press often flippantly discards designers as no longer newsworthy, comparing this with the American press who always acknowledge good design. Bill Blass and Oscar de la Renta, he declares, may no longer be in the forefront of fashion but the press still regards them as newsworthy.

In the 1970s emphasis on couture was dwindling and the company realized that in order to survive, the ready-to-wear line had to be built up. This was verified by Sassoon's belief that couture runs the risk of turning into a little dressmaker. The decision proved correct as business for the company is very large in America and is promoted with fashion shows across the United States and at trade fairs in London, Paris, New York, Munich, and Dusseldorf. Their agents have had little problem building a strong and impressive clientele.

Lorcan Mullany, who joined the company on Belinda Bellville's retirement in 1987, has a strong background in occasion and eveningwear. He trained at the Grafton Academy in Dublin and, before joining David Sassoon, worked for Bill Gibb, Ronald Joyce, and Hardy Amies. The label now bears the joint name Bellville Sassoon-Lorcan Mullany, justifiably crediting all designers for the product.

Today, Bellville Sassoon's clothes represent the top end of British occasion dressing, from sumptuous ballgowns to flirty cocktail dresses. Frills, sinuous draping, ruching, streamlined side splits, and plunging backs evoke memories of Hollywood in its glamorous heyday. Tulle, encrusted embroideries, taffetas, duchesse satin, mink, and double silk crepes are representative of the luxurious fabrics used. Unlike some eveningwear, the clothes are never gaudy and overstated; their success is reliant on a streamlined sense of style.

—Kevin Almond

BENETTON.

Italian sportswear firm

Founded by Giuliana (1938—), Luciano (1935—), Gilberto (1941—), and Carlo (1943—) Benetton, in Treviso, in 1965 as Maglificio di Ponzano Veneto dei Fratelli Benetton. First Benetton outlet opened in Belluno, Italy, 1968; launched major European expansion campaign, from 1978; first US outlet opened in New York, 1979; first Eastern European outlet opened in Prague, 1985. **Address:** Via Chiesa Ponzano 24, 31050 Ponzano Veneto, Treviso, Italy.

Publications:

On BENETTON:

Books

Baker, Caroline, *Benetton Colour Style File,* London 1987.

Belussi, Fiorenza, *Benetton: Information Technology in Production and Distribution,* Brighton 1987.

Aragno, Bonizza Giordani, *Moda Italia: Creativity and Technology in the Italian Fashion System,* Milan, 1988.

Articles

Withers, Jane, and Anthony Fawcett, "Family that Fashioned Universal Flair," in *The Times* (London), 24 August 1984.

Bentley, Logan, "The Tight-knit Benetton Clan Has Stitched Together a Multimillion-dollar Fashion Empire," in *People* (Chicago), 15 October 1984.

Lee, Andrea, "Being Everywhere: Luciano Benetton" (profile), in *The New Yorker,* 10 November 1986.

Coleman, Alix, "A Colourful Career," in the *Sunday Express Magazine* (London), 20 September 1987.

Fierman, Jaclyn, "Dominating an Economy, Family-style: The Italians," in *Fortune* (New York), 12 October 1987.

Finnerty, Anne, "The Internationalisation of Benetton," in *Textile Outlook International* (London), November 1987.

Tredre, Roger, "Bold Is Beautiful," in *Fashion Weekly* (London), 21 January 1988.

"Alessandro Benetton," in *Interview* (New York), April 1988.

Gastellier, Fabian, "Luciano Benetton: un homme aux couleurs de son temps," in *Elle* (Paris), 19 September 1988.

Fuhrman, Peter, "Benetton Learns to Darn," in *Forbes* (New York), 3 October 1988.

Griggs, Barbara, "The Benetton Fratelli," in *Vogue* (London), October 1988.

Tornier, François, "Les 25 ans de Benetton," in *Elle* (Paris), 1 October 1990.

Baker, Lindsay, "Taking Advertising to Its Limits," in *The Guardian* (London), 22 July 1991.

Kanner, Bernice, "Shock Value," in *New York,* 24 September 1992.

Waxman, Sharon, "The True Colors of Luciano Benetton: Industrialist with a Soul? Naked Self-promoter? Or Both?," in *The Washington Post,* 17 February 1993.

"Benetton Buys Consumer Magazine," in *Advertising Age* (New York), 21 June 1993.

*   *   *

In recent years the Benetton Group of Italy has progressively become better known for controversial advertising campaigns than for the brightly coloured knitted sweaters with which the company was founded in 1965. As part of a well defined global strategy to make the Benetton name as well known as McDonald's or Coca-Cola, the sibling members of the Benetton family—Giuliana, Luciano, Gilberto, and Carlo Benetton—have created a multi-billion *lire* business with over four thousand shops in one hundred countries. The company today is a leader in creating and producing casual apparel and licensed accessories such as cosmetics, toys, swimwear, eyeglasses, watches, stationery, underwear, shoes, and household items. All are sold through the United Colors of Benetton, Sisley, and 012 brand names.

Giuliana Benetton is chief designer and directs the Group's creative research, coordinating over two hundred young assistants. The collections are aimed at young people and children, but over the years have been adopted by consumers of all ages. United Colors of Benetton attempts to transcend gender, social class, and nationality by manufacturing knitwear that exemplifies a philosophy of life. This is reflected explicitly in Oliviero Toscani's advertising campaign "Benetton—All the Colors of the World" (1983). The campaign depicts groups of children representing all walks of life wearing colourful Benetton garments. Subsequent campaigns have increasingly commented on current political and social issues including terrorism, race, and AIDS, without depicting actual Benetton garments. A number of controversial campaigns have been banned by advertising authorities, fuelling unprecedented media coverage.

Benetton's collection is similar in attitude to the California-based Esprit company, and epitomizes values of a new generation of young, socially aware consumers. Garments are designed to be fun—casual with an easy-to-wear cut. Inspiration is often drawn from past sentiments but produced with a contemporary twist. For example, 1950s ski fashions in high-tech synthetic ice-pastel fabrics; 1960s couture of tailored suits in herringbone; miniskirts and leggings, and 1970s disco garments with sequins and leather combined. Other collections are based on themes such as the Nordic for little girls, designed in new fabrics like blanket cloth and fleecewear; Blue Family, which includes jeans; and Riding Star, drawn from the world of horseback riding. In keeping with the company's cosmopolitan attitude, stimuli for collections are often drawn from Benetton family travels. One of the most frequented is Peru where colours and designs of traditional South American garments provide inspiration.

In the beginning, Benetton sweaters were hand-knit by Giuliana in bright colours which distinguished them from existing English-made wool sweaters. The first collection consisted of 18 pieces, the most popular item being a violet pullover made from cashmere, wool, and angora. Benetton's sweaters are created from natural wool and cotton yarns which are dyed in small batches, in response to shop reports which monitor prevailing local tastes and trends. High-tech manufacturing and innovative sales and marketing strategies have made Benetton one of the most progressive clothing manufacturers in the world.

—Teal Triggs

BENTZ, John C. See **CATALINA SPORTSWEAR.**

BET, Xüly. See **KOUYATÉ, Lamine.**

BIAGIOTTI, Laura.

Italian designer

Born: Rome, 4 August 1943. **Education:** Studied literature and archeology in Rome, 1960-62. **Family:** Married Gianni Cigna in 1992; daughter: Lavinia. **Career:** Worked in Biagiotti family ready-to-wear firm, Rome, 1962-65; free-lance designer for Schuberth, Barocco, Cappucci, Heinz Riva, Licitro, and others, 1965-72; founder-designer, Laura Biagiotti Fashions, Rome, from 1972; took over MacPherson Knitwear, Pisa, 1974; established headquarters in Guidonia, 1980; Rispeste collection introduced, 1981; Laurapiu collection introduced, 1984; diffusion knitwear collection for Biagiotti Uomo introduced, 1985; Biagiotti jeans collection introduced, 1986; Biagiotti Uomo collecton introduced, 1987; launched perfumes *Laura,* 1982, *Night,* 1986, *Roma,* 1988, and *Venezia,* 1992; signed licensing agreement for Biagiotti shops in China, 1993; opened LB shop in Beijing, China, Bangkok, Thailand, 1994, and in Moscow, Russia, 1994. **Awards:** Golden Lion Award for achievement in linen, Venice, 1987; named Commendatore of the Italian Republic, 1987; Marco Polo Award for high achievement in diffusing Italian style worldwide, 1993; Frenio Fragene for fashion achievements, 1994. **Address:** Biagiotti Export S.p.A., via Palombarese Km, 17.300, 00012 Guidonia, Rome, Italy.

Publications:

On BIAGIOTTI:

Books

Mulassano, Adriana, *The Who's Who of Italian Fashion,* Florence 1979.
Alfonsi, Maria-Vittoria, *Leaders in Fashion: I grandi personaggi della moda,* Bologna 1983.
Steele, Valerie, *Women of Fashion,* New York 1991.

Articles

Gargia, Massimo, "Laura Biagiotti, Stylish et Italienne," in *Vogue* (Paris), August 1978.
Petroff, Daniela, "Women Designers," in the *International Herald Tribune,* 3/4 October 1981.
"Laura Biagiotti: Bianco per tutte le mode," in *Vogue* (Milan), October 1984.
"The House of Biagiotti," in *House and Garden,* December 1986.
"I cashmere ricamati di Laura Biagiotti," in *Donna* (Milan), October 1987.
"Laura Biagiotti: I piaceri naturali," in *Donna* (Milan), February 1988.
"Laura Biagiotti," in Bonizza Giordani Aragno, ed., *Moda Italia* (Milan), 1988.
Menkes, Suzy, "Couture's Grand Ladies," in *Illustrated London News* (London), Spring 1990.
Skellenger, Gillion, "Laura Biagiotti," in *Contemporary Designers,* London 1990.
Lender, Heidi, "Biagiotti's U.S. Invasion," in *Women's Wear Daily* (New York), 12 February 1992.
Costin, Glynis, "Laura Biagiotti's China Syndrome," in *Women's Wear Daily* (New York), 21 May 1993.

Cover story on Laura Biagiotti, in *Fashion Magazine,* September 1994.

*   *   *

Indisputably Italian, trained by her tailor-mother to admire the couture of France but also witness to the quality of her mother's work and employed early on in Schuberth's elegant Italian ready-to-wear, Laura Biagiotti might seem the quintessential European. Her devotion to fine materials, almost eponymously as she is sometimes called the Queen of Cashmere, may also seem devotedly Italian. Close family ties reinforce the image and Biagiotti's selection of Isabella D'Este as her ideal would seem to substantiate the nationalism of this designer's spirit. One Biagiotti fragrance is named *Venezia.*

When one looks at Biagiotti's clothes, however, one cannot help but think of America. Like Giorgio Armani, Biagiotti bespeaks Italian fashion, but is redefining Italian fashion in the last quarter of the 20th century in a sense of sportswear, separates, menswear influences, and quality materials for the standardizing templates of clothing. Biagiotti tells the story that at the time of her first show in 1972, she had so few pieces that she showed one white jacket three times, once with a skirt for morning, once with a day dress, and finally with a shiny skirt for evening. "Unintentionally I had invented the use of only one item for morning to evening," she said. If Biagiotti was, as she professes, initially inadvertent, her concept has become canny and global; her invention is necessarily as smart as it is coy. Her collections in the 1980s and 1990s have sustained a sense of the marketably traditional, always freshened with insights and style inflections to become one of the most effective designers of the era.

Biagiotti's spring-summer 1990 collection, built around navy, red, and white (admittedly with other pieces as well, but carefully constructed around the red-white-and-blue core), not only anticipated 1993 merchandising of Carolyne Roehm, but offered its clothes as wardrobe builders as well as dramatic outfits. In exposition of her work, Biagiotti told Valerie Steele, "Elegance, taste, and creativity have belonged to the Italian tradition and character for centuries and I share this privilege with all other Italian designers" (*Women of Fashion: Twentieth-Century Designers,* New York 1991). Biagiotti has studied archaeology and now is much engaged with the arts and architecture through generous support of archeology and conservation. Yet again, her work is as much divorced from the historical past as one could imagine. It is as if she has chosen to restore the edifice (and she does live and work in what Gillian Skellenger, in *Contemporary Designers,* rightly calls the factory-castle of Marco Simone near Rome, a Romanesque-era edifice), but her decision is a gutted rehabilitation, putting everything new inside. There are no marks of historicism in her clothing, even in the fall-winter 1985-86 collection when her monastics seem as much about Claire McCardell as about medievalism; her abiding preference for white is symbolic of her *tabula rasa* in her clothing, so clean, notably modern in style; her sensible knits address manifold uses for contemporary working women; and, as Skellenger has noted, "Biagiotti reveals a mania for research," committed to new fabric study.

Biagiotti has spoken of her work as a personal projection, thus inevitably being fit for a modern, self-confident, and business-aware woman. If she is the ideal client for her own clothing, her personal sensibility is toward simple, almost reductive, shape carried in luxury materials, an ethos sounding like three generations of American sportswear-to-evening designers. The women's clothing can be slightly flirtatious in the American mode while her evening looks express her Roman sophistication, always with a reserve and sense of good taste. Biagiotti has come to represent decorum and fashion nuance unerring in its mainstream elegance, again a characterization she would share with Armani. What she does not share with Armani is his intense interest in menswear *per se;* while Biagiotti has designed menswear for many years, it seems even safer than her women's clothing and the epitome of conservative good taste.

Biagiotti has said, "There are some beautiful dresses designed by others that are so important that you cannot always wear them. If you are in a bad mood or tired, if you have some problems, everyone understands that what you are wearing is simply dressing you up. But this does not happen with my designs. In fact, I would define my creations with the slogan, 'A dress for when you want to be yourself.'" Biagiotti has rendered the specific garment unimportant, but she attaches utmost importance to clothing as a value-laden social frame to the portrait of the modern woman. In fact, Biagiotti creates a spare, quiet, comfortable clothing, the essence of late 20th-century dressing, even as she inhabits and works from a medieval castle. The combination is mesmerizingly romantic.

—Richard Martin

BIANCHINI-FÉRIER.

French textile manufacturer

Founded c.1880 by Charles Bianchini and partners; changed name to Bianchini-Férier with partnership of M. Férier, c.1900. **Address:** 4 rue Vaucanson, 69283 Lyon Cedex 01, France.

Publications:

On BIANCHINI-FÉRIER:

Books

Crawford, M. D. C., *The Ways of Fashion,* New York 1948.
Musée de L'Impression sur Étoffes, *Raoul Dufy* (exhibition catalogue), Mulhouse 1973.
Musée Historique des Tissus, *Les folles années de la soie* (exhibition catalogue), Lyon 1975.
Arts Council of Great Britain, *Raoul Dufy* (exhibition catalogue), London 1983.
Galeria Marcel Bernheim, *Raoul Dufy et la mode: ancienne collection, Bianchini-Férier* (exhibition catalogue), Paris 1985.
Deslandres, Yvonne, and Dorothee Laianne, *Paul Poiret: 1874-1944,* London 1987.
Mackrell, Alice, *Paul Poiret,* New York 1990.
Schoesser, Mary, and Kathleen Dejardin, *French Textiles from 1760 to the Present,* London 1991.

Articles

Dufy, Raoul, "Les tissues imprimés," in *Amour de L'Art,* No. 1, 1920.
Vallotaire, Michel, "New Textiles from France," in *Studio,* December 1928.
"Bianchini-Férier ou la créative continue," in *Vogue* (Paris), November 1988.

* * *

From its beginnings in the 1880s the House of Bianchini-Férier has been associated with the world's most luxurious silks. The Lyonnais firm first achieved widespread recognition for a collection of silk velvets and brocades shown at the Paris Exposition of 1889. A few years later Charles Bianchini and his partners opened a sales office in Paris. Offices in London, Geneva, Brussels, Montreal, Toronto, New York, Los Angeles, Chicago, and Buenos Aires quickly followed.

Working in close association with the leading couturiers of the day, Bianchini-Férier created fabrics which are today considered standards but for which the company held the original copyright. Among them are *charmeuse georgette,* and the semi-sheer crêpe Romaine.

Undoubtedly one of the best known collaborations between an artist and a manufacturer was that between Raoul Dufy and Bianchini-Férier. Dufy first designed textiles for Paul Poiret in 1911. Failing to imitate his bold hand wood-blocked patterns, Bianchini went to the source and in 1912 signed Dufy to an exclusive contract. This was renewed annually to c.1928. For Bianchini, Dufy created brilliant florals in the palette of the Fauve painters. He designed geometrics using blocks of opposing colors in which the design is created equally by the object and by the negative space enclosing it, and he continued to execute the large scale block-prints worked originally for Poiret.

Poiret continued to use Dufy's designs for Bianchini in his collections; his summer 1920 collection employed Dufy's fabrics exclusively and Dufy himself sketched part of the collection for the May issue of the *Gazette du Bon Ton.* Theirs was surely one of the most significant collaborations between artist, couturier, and manufacturer of the period.

Whereas many establishments geared to the luxury market were forced to close or reorganize during the Depression, Bianchini not only survived, but continued to experiment with new fibers and weave structures. Consequently when silk became unobtainable during World War II, Bianchini had the technology in place to increase its production of rayon. And because the firm had opened a mill in Port Jervis, New York, in 1921 to replicate patterns and textiles originating from Lyons, they did not wholly lose their overseas market during the war.

Within the industry, Bianchini was known especially for silk velvets and silk and metal brocades for haute couture. After the war the firm increased its efforts to reach the discerning home sewer who could provide an expanded market for their collections of silk and rayon prints. A 1949 collaboration with Vogue Patterns paired a collection of garments designed especially for Bianchini with a group of specific hand-screened prints. The March American *Vogue* claimed that these private edition prints were available in no more than 20 dress lengths each, to be distributed to select stores around the country. The advertising copy read "For the Woman Who Wants to Be Exclusive—A Couture Plan for Your Personal Dressmaking." The implication is that the ability to dress in high style was no longer the sole province of those women who had the good fortune to view the spring or fall collections at first hand.

Dirk Bikkembergs: Spring/Summer 1994. *Photograph by Guy Marineau.*

For more than 100 years Bianchini-Férier has set the standard for fine fabrics which combine invention and artistry in equal measure.

—Whitney Blausen

BIKKEMBERGS, Dirk.

Belgian designer

Born: Flamersheim, Germany, 3 January 1962. **Education:** Studied fashion at the Royal Academy of Arts, Antwerp. **Military Service:** Served with Royal Belgian Army, in Germany. **Career:** Free-lance designer for Nero, Bassetti, Gruno and Chardin, Tiktiner, Gaffa, K, Jaco Petti, 1982-87; launch of Dirk Bikkembergs-Homme Co., with DB shoe line for men, 1985; knitwear introduced, 1986; first complete menswear collection introduced, 1988; first womenswear line Dirk Bikkembergs-Homme Pour La Femme presented in Paris, 1993. **Awards:** For menswear collection, winter 1985-86, several Belgian fashion industry awards, including Golden Spindle. **Address:** Dirk Bikkembergs Hommes BVBA, Kidorp 21, Belgium.

Publications:

On BIKKEMBERGS:

Articles

"Foreign Affairs—Antwerp," in *Blitz* (London), February 1987.
Mower, Sarah, "Six Romp," in *The Guardian* (London), 12 February 1987.
"Fashion," in *Interview* (New York), July 1987.
Ankone, Frans, "De trots van vlaanderen," in *Avenue* (Antwerp), September 1987.
Tredre, Roger, "Belgians Go Branche," in *Fashion Weekly* (London), 10 September 1987.
Grauman, Brigid, "The Belgian Connection," in *Elle* (London), October 1987.
Lobrano, Alexander, "The Young Belgian," in *DNR* (New York), October 1987.
Fierce, Brad, "Il menestrello della moda," in *Vanity* (Milan), February 1988.
"Nouvel homme: Dirk Bikkembergs," in *Profession Textile* (Paris), 24 June 1988.
Grauman, Brigid, "Seam Stress," in *The Face* (London), August 1988.
Cocks, Jay, "A Look on the Wild Side: Two Young Designers Liven Up a Group Fashion Scene," in *Time* (New York), 16 January 1989.
LaChapelle, David, "Dirk Bikkembergs," in *Interview* (New York), October 1989.
Rumbold, Judy, "Dirk Bikkembergs: Clean Cuts," in *Arena* (London), November 1990.
Valli, Jacopo, "The Antwerp Five," in *Donna* (Milan), January 1991.
Summers, Beth, "Obsession," in *i-D* (London), February 1991.
Tredre, Roger, "From Belgium but Far from Boring," in *The Independent* (London), 2 July 1992.
"Dirk Bikkembergs," in *L'Uomo Vogue* (Milan), September 1992.

*

I design clothes for men and women that have a special, strong attitude. For a younger, future-minded generation for whom fashion has become a way to express themselves; to give shelter and strength and the feeling of looking good. A generation that has risen above the question of fashion, sure about its quality and style and their own; celebrating life.

I design collections that give one whole strong look, a vision of life, men and women with items that are nonchalant and easy to mix, give freedom and don't restrict the wearer; but there are always special pieces that are stronger and more defined, marking a certain period of time and setting a sign.

My clothes are never retro. I hate the idea of looking back. I don't have any idols from the past. I do strongly believe in tomorrow and the future of the human race. To achieve this I devote a lot of attention to the cut and fabric that I use. Yes, I tend to think about my clothes as fashion and I'm not afraid of that, nor are my clients.

I design strong clothes for strong individuals rather than wrapping up pretentious nerds in sophisticated cashmere. Nothing is so boring as a "nice and neat" look. Life is just too good and too short for that.

—Dirk Bikkembergs

*   *   *

Heavyweight fabrics and macho imagery quite literally dominate Dirk Bikkembergs's work. His best designs convey a solidity through their layering of leather and thick knitwear, while still retaining the feeling of minimalist restraint which has come to be associated with Belgian fashion. Bikkembergs, although not the most prominent of the designers who formed the Belgian avant-garde of the later 1980s, is nonetheless a significant purveyor of their ideals. His clothing consists of dark and muted toned separates which provide strong images of modern living: although his own work does not so frequently contain the deconstructed edge of his counterparts.

The most influential area of his work has been footwear. A specialist in the field, he has brought together the traditions of well made hardwearing shoes made up for him by Flanders craftsmen, with the late 1980s/early 1990s obsession with workwear. His designs are inspired by classic functional styles. He constantly reworks the clearly defined shapes of 1930s football boots, making them into neat, round-toed lace-up urban footwear in 1987. In 1993 he tampered with the weighty infantryman's boot, stripping it of its utilitarian status, when, with a deconstructivist flourish, he removed the eyelets which normally punctuate the boot and accommodate the distinctive high lacing. Instead a hole was drilled into the sole through which the laces had to be threaded and then wrapped around the boot's leather upper to secure it to the foot. The style soon became *de rigueur* for both men and women in fashion circles, with copies being sold in High Street chains.

Like all his work, they were based on familiar designs which convey traditional notions of masculinity, conjuring up images of sporting and military heroics. Such ideals pervade his menswear.

His carefully styled shows send musclebound models down the catwalk, clad in the obligatory biker boots and black leather which have now become a staple of the late 20th-century male wardrobe. This machismo continues in his signature knitwear range. Heavy rib V-necks are worn with lightweight jogging bottoms or matching woollen leggings. His work may not show the more slimline feminine notes which have been gradually breaking through the previously limited spectrum of menswear designs, but have still had influence. He helped to widen the scope of knitwear with witty takes on classic Aran jumpers and cardigans, and by using decorative detailing to add interest to simple designs: in 1992 with bright blue zips on either side of burnt orange sweaters, and in 1987 by adding them to high necked jumpers which were popular at the time.

Although he works best with these winter weight fabrics, he still adds twists to his summer collections. In 1988 he produced collared linen waistcoats which could be layered over long sleeved shirts, or worn alone to give interest to plain suits. It was in the late 1980s that his designs were most attuned to the *Zeitgeist.* He provided the overblown masculine imagery which was popular then. This was encapsulated in his distinctive marketing, which demonstrated the same eye for detail. The catalogues produced for each range show in grainy black and white his tough masculine ideals with his commandeering of popular stereotypes like the biker.

Despite this concentration on menswear, his work has extended to a womanswear range. In 1993 his first collection was warmly received, bringing together both his love of strong silhouettes and a deconstructed minimalism to provide a twist to basic shapes. The natural counterpart to his masculine lines, it carried through his use of sturdy footwear and accessories which had always been popular with women as well.

As part of the rise in status of Belgian fashion since the late 1980s, Bikkembergs's work appeals to the fashion *cognoscenti.* The overt masculinity of his designs is combined with a knowledge and exploitation of traditional styles to provide stark modern imagery. If not as well known as contemporaries like Dries Van Noten, he has still carved a niche for his work and heralded a fresh slant to his output with his recent divergence into womenswear.

—Rebecca Arnold

DOROTHÉE BIS.

French fashion house

Founded in 1962 by Jacqueline (designer) and Elie (manufacturer) Jacobson; became known for casual knitwear; boutiques have been found in Henri Bendel and Bloomingdale's, New York. **Address:** 17 rue de Sevres, 75006 Paris, France.

Publications:

On DOROTHÉE BIS:

Articles

Snead, Elizabeth, "In Paris, Short Cuts to the '60s," in *USA Today,* 18 October 1990.
"Paris Now," in *Women's Wear Daily,* 19 October 1990.

Parola, Robert, "Sportscast," in *Daily News Record,* 25 August 1993.

*   *   *

Dorothée Bis, the Paris ready-to-wear house, was founded in 1962 by Jacqueline and Elie Jacobson, and quickly and firmly established its now longstanding reputation for unusually stylish and wearable contemporary sportswear, particularly for knits of every variety and description. The jargon of a 1978 Macy's New York, advertisement for the firms' clothes sums up the Dorothée Bis look: "Easy fashion with all-over chic appeal. The kind of clothes that you know look right. Anytime, anyplace."

Since the 1960s, the firm has been presenting clothes that manifest contemporary trends in a sophisticated and wearable way. Dorothée Bis was among the first houses to present styles such as the long and skinny maxi look in knit coats and vests in the late 1960s, the peasant look in the early 1970s, the layered look in the mid-1970s and the graphic color block look of the late 1970s and early 1980s. Generally these looks have been presented in a particularly Parisian way, as total ensembles (as opposed to the American idea of mix and match), with coordinating accessories. For example, a knit dress and coat shown with a hand knit shawl and beret in the same yarn and matching belt, bag, and fashion jewelry.

Bernadine Morris, writing for the *New York Times,* described Dorothée Bis as one of "the quintessential Paris ready-to-wear houses aiming at the young swinging crowd who prefer to chance their style every season if not oftener." Indeed, in 1969 and 1970, while the hemline debate was fought by other designers, Jacobson satisfied her customer's shifting desires by giving her the mini, the midi, and the maxi all in the same collection. By 1972, those debating skirt lengths had reached a momentary consensus at midknee, leaving the design agenda open for a new focus on silhouette. Freed from the hemline discourse, with its implied bourgeois conflict between "appropriateness" and fashion, Jacobson continued enthusiastically to develop her concept of dressing in layers, a look that reflected women's growing liberation consciousness. The feminist theory of the day proposed that as women entered the work force in rapidly expanding numbers, and in a wide variety of career options, they would no longer need to seduce men in order to obtain financial support and would therefore no longer be compelled to wear seductive, figure revealing clothes. Dorothée Bis's layered look evolved from the skinny knits of 1972-73, to the ethnic layers of the mid 1970s, and culminated in the extreme and voluminous layers of 1976-77, in which a typical outfit might consist of a boldly patterned cardigan coat, over a belted, striped tunic dress, over a full gathered skirt, over wide legged or sweat style trousers, with a knit scarf and hat to match. Although that may sound cumbersome the look's appeal lay in its ease and comfort and in Jacobson's ability to give it all a Parisian stylishness.

In the 1980s, with the rise of conservatism in culture and politics, there was a return to conventionally body revealing fashions. Many women began to feel that in their adherence to orthodox feminism, they had abdicated the power inherent in their sexuality, and sought to regain that sense of power through their dress. Dorothée Bis was right in step with this trend with a new focus on dresses, especially in the firm's signature knits. A typical Dorothée Bis outfit of the period, a navy and white striped wool knit two piece dress with deep V neckline and padded shoulders, is described in a Macy's advertisement of 1986 as evidence of "a new body emphasis ... curve conscious and deserving of its stripes."

With the firm's emphasis on its highly adaptable and appealing signature knits, Dorothée Bis has been able to remain at the forefront of stylish and realistic fashion for more than 30 years.

—Alan E. Rosenberg

BLACK, Sandy.

British knitwear designer

Born: Leeds, Yorkshire, 17 October 1951. **Education:** Educated in Leeds; studied mathematics, BSc(Hons), University College, London, 1973, MA in Design Studies, Central St. Martins, London, 1994. **Career:** Free-lance knitwear designer, 1973-79; designer and director, Sandy Black Original Knits Ltd., selling fashion knitwear collections worldwide, 1979-85; designed and published Sandy Black Knitting Patterns and Sandy Black Knitting Kits and Yarns, sold in prestigious stores in London, Japan, USA, Sweden, Germany, Australia, and Canada; introduced knitting kits for *Woman* magazine (London), 1983; Sandy Black Studio—Knitting Kits mail order business. Free-lance knitwear designer for, among others, Rowan, Jaeger, and BBC television, beginning in 1985. Principal lecturer and course leader, University of Brighton, Sussex, beginning in 1990. **Exhibitions:** *Much Ado about Knitting,* ICA, London, 1981; *One-off Wearables,* British Crafts Centre, London, 1982; *The Knitwear Review,* British Crafts Centre, London, 1983; *Knitting— A Common Art,* Crafts Council Touring Exhibition, 1986; *Fashion in the '80's,* British Council touring exhibition, 1989; knitwear exhibition, Hove Museum, Sussex, 1990; *Contemporary Knitwear,* Pier Arts Centre, Orkney, 1994. **Address:** Flat 3, 15 Davigdor Road, Hove, East Sussex BN3 1QB, England.

Publications:

By BLACK:

Books

The Numeracy Pack, with D. Coben, London 1984.
Black, Sandy, *Sandy Black Original Knitting,* London 1988.

On BLACK:

Books

Sutton, Ann, *British Craft Textiles,* London 1985.

Articles

Phillips, Pearson, "The Hills Are Alive with the Sound of Knitting," in *The Telegraph Sunday Magazine,* 7 September 1980.
Lynam, Ruth, "Cast on a New Look," in *The Telegraph Sunday Magazine,* 7 September 1980.
"An Individual Approach to Fashion," in *Fashion and Craft,* November 1980.
Knitwear profile, in *Ons Volk* (Belguim), 29 December 1981.
Jeffs, Angela, "Exclusively Sandy Black," in *Fashioncraft,* February, 1984.
Polan, Brenda, "Looping the Loop," in *The Guardian Women,* 19 July 1984.

Rumbold, Judy, "The Wonder of Creation," in *The Guardian Style,* 20 June 1988.
Samuel, Kathryn, "Those Who Can—Teach," in *The Daily Telegraph,* 20 June 1994.

*

Although I learnt to knit and crochet as a child, it was whilst at university studying math that my interest in knitting really developed, and I started to design and make unusual and interesting clothes. At first these were hand knitted or crocheted, but I soon bought my first knitting machine and by the time I finished my degree, I had decided to make knitting a full-time career, though I wasn't sure how! Being self-taught, I was not restricted by any boundaries and felt I could translate any idea into knitting by working out a logical way of doing it. This approach clearly owed something to my mathematical background and for me there was a natural relationship between the two. I often put many ideas and techniques together to create complex designs. I only became aware of their complexity when I had to train other people to knit them for me!

My work covers a wide range of designs, from casual sweaters to glamorous angora evening coats. *Original Knitting* shows some of this variety and gives an insight into the thinking behind the designs. One of the most important factors is the blending of colour, shape, texture, and pattern to create each individual design, whether it's a bold geometric, a pretty floral, or an intricate stitch pattern. Fashion buyers talk of designers' "handwriting" by which they identify their work. I have often thought that I must have several different signatures! I have always enjoyed working in a great variety of themes, colours, and yarns, inspired by anything which catches my eye or simply the pleasure of combining wonderful materials and textures. I like my designs to be non-repetitive, and view the body as a canvas to be adorned with beautiful stitches and patterns, sometimes subtle, sometimes bold, but always with an underlying logic which combines colour, texture, and form so completely that the result should appear totally natural.

Knitting continues to be for me the perfect blend of creative and technical skills, which my education seemed to want to separate. It used to be the poor relation of the textile crafts but has now grown to be properly recognized, and has a vital part to play in fashion. I know I shall continue to design as long as I can still be excited by a ball of yarn or inspired to develop a new stitch pattern from some unlikely detail I have seen—a mosaic shopfront, a stonecarving, or a wallpaper pattern, for example. I am equally happy designing for hand knitting, machine knitting, or industrial production. One of the greatest attractions of knitting is the fact that the fabric is created from nothing but a length of yarn; everything is within the designer's control.

In my workshops and lecturing I try to convey my own enthusiasm and enjoyment in creating fabrics, garment designs, and structures, and their realization in three dimensions around the body. I am particularly interested in the sculptural potential of knitting; a unique medium with endless possibilities.

—Sandy Black

*   *   *

Sandy Black helped lead the knitwear revolution of the 1970s. Out went the cozy image of old ladies making socks around the fire,

Sandy Black: 1989; "Traveling Vine Tunic"; handknit, 100% wool twist. *Photograph by Paul Dennison.*

in came fashion knitwear, and a craft was turned into an art. For Black it was a logical development of a childhood love of old needlework shops where she bought 1940s knitting patterns, buttons, and yarns to knit and crochet. Using skills learned from her mother and grandmother, she produced traditional hand knits. Having studied mathematics, knitting proved an ideal way of combining her creative and logical instincts. She was able to chart out pictorial knits and to originate the landscape sweaters that became so popular in the mid-1970s. A natural wit emerged. Leopard skin-look sweaters and a knitted armadillo wrap illustrated an appealing sense of humour. Patterned angora jackets, stunning to the eye and to the touch, showed the luxuriance that hand knitting could achieve. Designer knitwear had arrived.

Major international fashion retailers, including Browns and Harrods in London, Isetan in Tokyo, Saks Fifth Avenue, and Bloomingdale's in New York, bought Sandy Black Original Knits. Their quality and details put them way beyond the purse of most shoppers, including the designer herself. To make her designs more widely available Black employed her math training to create her own knitting patterns. By using larger needles and straigtforward instructions, she tried to make her patterns as accessible as possible. They were complex, but not too difficult for the determined knitter. The results justified the effort involved. Black's hand knits were distinctive and unique. Another breakthrough came in 1983, when she designed a knitting kit as an editorial offer for *Woman* magazine. Its success stimulated the Sandy Black Knit Kits, which were retailed in Liberty, Harrods, and John Lewis in London, and in Sweden, Germany, and Canada. She controlled the whole process, creating the patterns, supervising the dyeing of the yarns and designing the packaging. She also produced her own range of yarns. Each step meant that she was able to have greater responsibility over the whole process, from the idea to the finished garment. Her first book of patterns, *Sandy Black Original Knitting,* published in 1988, is an excellent testament to her originality and creativity and provides insight into her inspiration. Whatever the design, a bold geometric, a pretty floral, or something understated, the consistent factor is the blending of colour, texture, and pattern to create an individual design. Variety is a mark of her creativity. By seeing "the body as a canvas to be decorated and adorned with beautiful patterns, sometimes subtle, sometimes bold," she has extended the existing boundaries of knitwear.

Black has been able to convey her obvious enthusiasm to others. Television shows, international lecture tours, workshops, and consultancies have all helped to promote her ideas. She has become increasingly involved in teaching. This is an ideal, if exhausting, means of continuing what she started 20 years ago. In her workshops and as a lecturer to textile and fashion students, she teaches about the dual importance of design and technique. Experimentation is an important way of building ideas and encouraging originality. She gives others the confidence to follow her example, to break down boundaries, and to cast aside preconceptions. Sandy Black has helped to take knitting from the fireside into the artist's studio.

—Hazel Clark

BLAHNIK, Manolo.

Spanish footwear designer

Born: Santa Cruz, Canary Islands, 27 November 1942. **Education:** Educated at home, then at the University of Geneva, 1960-65; studied art in Paris, 1965-70. **Career:** Jeans buyer for Feathers Boutique, London, early 1970s; encouraged to design shoes by Diana Vreeland; first collections for Zapata Boutique, London and for Ossie Clark, early 1970s; opened London firm, 1973 with subsequent shops in New York and Hong Kong. Also furniture designer. **Awards:** Fashion Council of America Award, 1988, 1991; British Fashion Council Award, 1991; Balenciaga Award, 1991; American Leather Award, New York, 1991; Hispanic Institute Antonio Lopez Award, Washington, DC, 1991. **Address:** 49-51 Old Church St., London SW3, England.

Publications:

On BLAHNIK:

Books

Trasko, Mary, *Heavenly Soles,* New York 1989.
McDowell, Colin, *Shoes, Fashion and Fantasy,* London 1989.

Articles

Lester, P., "Manolo Blahnik," in *Interview* (New York), July 1974.
Brampton, Sally, "Well-Heeled," in *The Observer* (London), 2 September 1984.
Burnie, Joan, "Upon My Sole: Best Feet Forward," in *You* (London), 5 January 1986.
Infantino, Vivian, "The Gift of Avant-Garde," in *Footwear News* (New York), July 1987.
Simpson, Helen, "Manolo Blahnik's London Lobby," in *Vogue* (London), August 1987.
Campbell, Liza, "World at His Feet," in *Vogue* (London), September 1987.
Picasso-Lopez, Paloma, "Manolo Blahnik," in *Vogue* (Paris), April 1988.
Fallon, James, "Blahnik Keeps Moving," in *Footwear News* (New York), February 1991.
Roberts, Michael, "Manolo," in *Interview* (New York), September 1991.
"Feets of Brilliance," in *Vogue* (New York), March 1992.

*   *   *

Established in the 1970s, Manolo Blahnik is world famous. His beautiful shoes exude a level of craftsmanship which has become a rare commodity in today's age of mass production, and he has a wonderful sense of line and silhouette. These talents, combined with the other footwear sense that he displays and exploits, have ensured his rightful position as a true genius in his field, worthy of sharing the mantle worn by the other brilliant shoe designers of the 20th century, Yanturni, Vionnet, Perugia, Ferragamo, and the genius he most admires, Roger Vivier.

Manolo Blahnik was born in 1942 in Santa Cruz, in the Canary Islands, of a Czech father and Spanish mother. This slightly exotic and romantic start to his life possibly determined the pattern his future was to assume. His awareness of shoes was an early memory. His mother, who had a fondness for satin and brocade fabrics, had her footwear made by Don Christino, the island's leading shoemaker. Blahnik inherited her love of the unconventional and remembers seeing a trunk containing shoes by Yanturni, the Russian designer and one-time curator of the Cluny Museum in Paris. The shoes, in brocades, silks, and antique lace, trimmed with buckles, were elegant and light; attributes which Blahnik later sought to achieve in his own creations.

Blahnik studied law, literature, and Renaissance art in Europe before settling in London in 1970. His portfolio of theatrical designs was seen by the photographer Cecil Beaton, and Diana Vreeland of American *Vogue* who particularly admired his shoe designs and encouraged him to concentrate on this aspect of his work. His subsequent footwear collections were to prove how astute had been their instincts for this extraordinary talent.

The mood of the 1970s was lively, adventurous, and colourful. The advent of the mini skirt had focused attention on the legs and consequently on original interpretations of footwear. Creative thought had produced new materials for shoes and a climate in which fresh ideas could flourish, and Blahnik dramatically interpreted these trends. Flowers appeared at the ankles, there were cutout shapes and appliqués. Purple was the "in" colour; ankle boots, lace-ups with small, chunky heels in stacked leather or shiny veneer, crêpe soles and a new craze for "wet-look" leather, all appeared in his collections. Footwear was zany, feet were in fashion and it required endless imagination to stay in front.

Blahnik chose "Zapata" as the name of his first shop, opened in London in 1973. He now uses his own name but, from the beginning, his tiny, personalized salon has continued to be a mecca for devotees from all over the world. His shoes are worn by friends and socialites and always attract media attention.

A shoe designer's handwriting is as distinctive as that of a couturier. It will evolve and embrace the newest developments of fashion but, once established, it will not radically change and will continue to be instantly recognizable. Manolo Blahnik has a deep understanding of contemporary trends and a genuine feeling for his clientèle and what they seek in a shoe. Constantly featured in the world's most prestigious fashion magazines, it is easy to see why his imagination and ability to translate fantasy into delectable and desirable foot coverings have won him such acclaim. His designs are always immensely complimentary to the feet. His philosophy is that fashion should be fun and his ebullient and energetic designs have always reflected this. He considers shape, material, and decoration with great care and combines hand-craftsmanship with modern techniques. A master of materials, he handles leather, suede, velvets, silks, and the unconventional and unexpected with equal flair and panache, paying exact attention to detail and creating fine, elegant footwear with glamour and refinement. His shoes have a weightless

Manolo Blahnik.

quality and a seemingly ethereal atmosphere often pervades his collections.

Many styles are deliberately kept exclusive, with only small quantities produced, and his instantly recognized style remains constant, regardless of the fashion climate. Over the years he has designed collections to enhance the work of, amongst others, Yves Saint Laurent, Emmanuel Ungaro, Calvin Klein, Perry Ellis, Bill Blass, Fiorucci, Isaac Mizrahi, Ossie Clark, Zandra Rhodes, Jean Muir, Jasper Conran, and Rifat Ozbeck. One of his most famous individual clients is the fashion eccentric, Anna Piaggi. She invariably selects a pair of Blahnik's shoes to complement the other wonderful items in her wardrobe. The following is a typical description of her appearance: "Black velvet coat by Lanvin, c.1925; T-shirt in cotton jersey by Missoni, c.1975; Harem trousers made out of a silk kimono; Grey suede shoes trimmed with mink by Blahnik; the jewel, a crystal iceberg with an orange bead by Fouquet."

Wherever they are featured, Blahnik's shoes are a copywriter's dream. Frequently executed in vivid colours, magenta, deep purple, bright scarlet, orange, emerald green, or saffron yellow, they retain a certain theatrical fantasy—"Red mules with high, knotted vamps;" "jewelled satin shoes for the summer collection;" "Ribbon wrapped ankles for watered silk dancing shoes;" "Sketch for the glove shoe;" "The Siamese twin shoe." Completely original combinations of wit, sex, and allure. With their reference to history they nevertheless remain entirely contemporary whilst catching the spirit of both.

Manolo Blahnik is a distinctive personality, much travelled, intelligent and well educated, in demand for his opinions, wit, energy, and style. Like many true originators, he could probably have been a successful designer in another field. His distinctive sketches, for example, transmit a real feeling for his shoes and are used for his company publicity. They serve to underline how very individual his work is. He clothes some of the world's best dressed feet. He makes shoes for all occasions. He has an international reputation and a clientèle worldwide. His shoes are worn, and adored, by film stars, celebrities, socialites, and those who just love what he offers. He has an intrinsic feeling for the moment, and a foresight into what will come next. His shoes are provocative and dashingly extrovert; almost, but not quite, too beautiful and desirable to be worn.

—Angela Pattison

BLAIR, Alistair.

British designer

Born: Scotland, 5 February 1956. **Education:** Graduated from St. Martin's School of Art, London, 1978. **Career:** Assistant to Marc Bohan, Dior, Paris, 1977; design assistant, Givenchy, Paris, 1978-80; assistant to Karl Lagerfeld, Chloé, Paris, 1980-83; designer, Karl Lagerfeld, New York, 1983-84; designer, Alistair Blair, 1985-89. Free-lance designer and design consultant to Jaeger, Balmain, Complice, Turnbull and Asser, beginning in 1989; knitwear designer, McGeorge, beginning in 1988; designer, Ivoire ready-to-wear collection, Balmain, Paris, 1990-91; designer, Ballantine, beginning in 1989; creative director, Balmain, Paris, 1991; design consultant, Cerruti, Paris, beginning in 1991; design consultant to Valentino, Rome, beginning in 1993. **Address:** 4 Belmont Court, Pembroke Mews, London W8 6ES, England.

Publications:

On BLAIR:

Articles

Kellett, Caroline, "Cue: The Return of Alistair Blair," in *Vogue* (London), June 1986.

Irvine, Susan, "British Style, the Designer Star: Alistair Blair," in *Vogue* (London), February 1987.

"Solid Talent (British Too) Pendrix," in *Connoisseur*, February 1987.

Hume, Marlon, "Backstage with Blair," in *Fashion Weekly* (London), 16 October 1987.

"Alistair Blair to Design for McGeorge," in *Fashion Weekly* (London), 29 October 1987.

Hillpot, Maureen, "Alistair Blair: Going for It!," in *Taxi* (New York), May 1988.

"Blair Quits Beleaguered Bertelsen as Hamnett Sues," in *The Independent* (London), 8 July 1988.

"Blair, with Backer, Plans Spring Relaunch," in *Women's Wear Daily* (New York), 29 September 1988.

"Backing for Blair," in *Options* (London), December 1988.

Du Cann, Charlotte, "Return of the Pragmatic Professional," in *The Independent* (London), 18 March 1989.

*　　*　　*

When Alistair Blair showed his first collection in London in 1986, he was testing very tepid water. At that time, British designer fashion was recognized for its youth and eccentricity, fun and witty clothes, often unwearable and badly produced. Blair, complete with impeccable fashion credentials (a first class degree from St. Martin's School of Art in London, followed by training at Dior and Givenchy in Paris, then as design assistant to Karl Lagerfeld), seemed to pose little threat to this established reputation in terms of making a valid fashion statement. However, Alistair Blair realized that there was a gap in the British fashion market for a look of continental couture at ready-to-wear prices, a gap that became the philosophy for the company.

This singular marketing notion met with immediate fashion applause at the first season's launch. "Blair has arrived as quite simply the most stylish designer in London," raved *Fashion Weekly* (16 October 1987). Things very quickly went from strength to strength. Support came from top international stores: Saks Fifth Avenue and Henri Bendel in New York, Fortnum and Mason and Harrods in London, and Seibu in Tokyo were quick to place orders. Possibly the greatest publicity came when the Duchess of York ordered her engagement outfit from him.

Alistair Blair's backer was Peder Bertelsen, the Danish oil millionaire. Blair, who was considering an offer to work for Royal couturier Norman Hartnell, was advised by a friend to discuss the move with Bertelsen. "Before I knew where I was he was suggesting that he would back me and I was agreeing," he was quoted as saying. Bertelsen was perhaps British fashion's most important asset in the mid-1980s. He injected a great deal of money into his creation of a fashion empire, buying several prestigious stores including Ungaro, Valentino, and Krizia, and backing John Galliano. In his analysis of British designer fashion he concluded that it fell into two categories: old and new money; old money was the Establishment, including the landowners; new money was in the City or in oil and each identified with its own dress designers. Blair was categorized as Bertelsen's designer for the Establishment.

There was certainly something chic yet traditional about Blair's clothes, even in his luxurious choice of fabrics: alpaca, cashmere and lambswool mixes, duchesse satin and satin backed crêpe, expensive soft suedes and kid leather, even sumptuous embroidery from the Royal embroiderer's Lock Ltd. Dog-tooth check wool coats, flannel jackets, and wool crêpe evening dresses in sharp, florid colours always incorporated a section in Blair's signature colours of orange and black. Each collection evoked a grown-up sensuality, with obvious visual references to the soigné looks of French film stars like Michele Morgan or Catherine Deneuve, prompting Andrée Walmsley from Fortnum and Mason to enthuse, "He has a very French handwriting, which I adore." The catwalk shows enlivened British Fashion Weeks with their no-expense-spared glamour. A coterie of international models, from Linda Evangelista to Cindy Crawford, was flown in to promote the clothes as the *paparazzi* enthused that Paris had firmly established itself in London.

Even though Blair edited the collections with business-like alacrity, the Bertelsen empire was losing money. Bertelsen admitted to *Business Magazine* in December 1987 that he had lost one million on his first set of accounts. This non-accumulation of profit eventually led to Bertelsen pulling out as Blair's backer. Even though Blair subsequently found alternative backing, it was not enough to keep the company afloat and it eventually folded. Despite the hype and publicity behind the name, this perhaps exemplifies a problem experienced by many British fashion companies: without the backing of huge textile conglomerates as happens in France, and the vast income earned from licensed goods such as perfume or cosmetics, sole clothing companies often struggle to survive. As Blair has said: "It's a business. At the end of the day you have to make money for a lot of other people as well."

Fortunately for Alistair Blair, his design handwriting was a much respected commodity, and this has led him to design consultancies with Jaeger, Pierre Balmain, and Complice.

—Kevin Almond

BLASS, Bill.

American designer

Born: William Ralph Blass in Fort Wayne, Indiana, 22 June 1922. **Education:** Attended Fort Wayne High School, 1936-39; studied fashion design, Parsons School of Design, New York, 1939. **Military Service:** Served in the United States Army, 1941-44: Sergeant. **Career:** Sketch artist, David Crystal Sportswear, New York, 1940-41; designer, Anna Miller and Company Ltd., New York, 1945; designer, 1959-70, and vice-president, 1961-70, Maurice Rentner Ltd., New York; Rentner company purchased and re-named Bill Blass Ltd., 1970; Blassport sportswear division introduced, 1972; signature perfume introduced, 1978. Licensed products include menswear, women's sportswear, candies, furs, swimwear, jeans, bedlinens, shoes, perfumes, and an automobile. **Awards:** Coty American Fashion Critics "Winnie" Award, 1961, 1963, 1970, Menswear Award, 1968, Hall of Fame Award, 1970, and Special Citations, 1971, 1982, 1983; Gold Coast Fashion Award, Chicago, 1965; National Cotton Council Award, New York, 1966; Neiman

Marcus Award, Dallas, 1969; Print Council Award, 1971; Martha Award, New York, 1974; Ayres Look Award, 1978; *Gentlemen's Quarterly* Manstyle Award, New York, 1979; Cutty Sark Hall of Fame Award, 1979; Honorary Doctorate, Rhode Island School of Design, 1977; Council of Fashion Designers of America Award, 1986. **Address:** 550 Seventh Avenue, New York, New York 10018, USA.

Publications:

On BLASS:

Books

Bender, Marilyn, *The Beautiful People,* New York 1967.
Morris, Bernadine, and Barbara Walz, *The Fashion Makers,* New York 1978.
Diamonstein, Barbaralee, *Fashion: The Inside Story,* New York 1985.
Milbank, Caroline Rennolds, *Couture: The Great Designers,* New York 1985.
Perschetz, Lois, ed., *W, The Designing Life,* New York 1987.
Coleridge, Nicholas, *The Fashion Conspiracy,* London 1988.
Milbank, Caroline Rennolds, *New York Fashion: The Evolution of American Style,* New York 1989.

Articles

"Dialogue with Bill Blass," in *Interior Design,* June 1973.
"Bill Blass: Real American Class," in *American Fabrics and Fashions* (New York), Fall 1974.
"A Different Glamour at Bill Blass," in *Vogue* (New York), September 1985.
Collins, Amy Fine, "Sequinned Simulacra," in *Art in America* (New York), July 1988.
Prisant, Carol, "Top Blass," in *World of Interiors* (London), October 1990.
Morris, Bernadine, "With Blass, Spontaneity Has Returned to Style," in the *New York Times,* 30 March 1993.
Orlean, Susan, "King of the Road," in *The New Yorker,* 20 December 1993.
Schiro, Anne-Marie, "'Tasteful' Comes in Many Colors," in the *New York Times,* 4 November 1994.
DeCaro, Frank, "Hairy Situations and Hula Baloos: Bill Blass," in *New York Newsday,* 4 November 1994.
Beckett, Kathleen, "Runway Report: My One and Only Hue: Bill Blass," in *New York Post,* 4 Nobember 1994.
"New York: Bill Blass," in *Women's Wear Daily* (New York), 4 November 1994.
Schiro, Anne-Marie, "Chic and Quality from Bill Blass," in the *New York Times,* 7 April 1995.
"New York: Bill Blass," in *Women's Wear Daily* (New York), 7 April 1995.

*   *   *

"Like most people who seem to be most typically New York, Bill Blass comes from Indiana," wrote native Midwesterner Eleanor Lambert in an early press release for Blass when he worked at Maurice Rentner. Blass reigns as an American classic, the man who abidingly exemplifies high style because his work plays on the sharp edge of glamour, but never falls into the abyss of indecency.

Likewise, it defines sophisticated style because it has elements of the naive and the crude in impeccable balance. Blass is the perfect example of fashion's deconstructivist internal oppositions of real, hyper-glamour, and style synthesis.

Although Blass believes in eliminating the superfluous and stressing the essentials of clothing, he is no Yankee skinflint or reductive modernist and aims to beguile and flatter, adding perhaps a flyaway panel, not necessary for structure, that would never appeal to a Halston or a Zoran. He aims to create a fanciful chic, a sense of glamour and luxury. It may be that these desires are fashion's game, but it is undeniable that Blass is the expert player. Everything he does is suffused with glamour, and he creates evening gowns that would stagger Scarlett O'Hara. His shimmering Matisse collection, embroidered in India, transformed the client into the conveyer of masterpiece paintings.

Blass is an indisputable enchanter, a man who loves being with the ladies he dresses. Correspondingly, they love being with him, but the relationship is not merely indicative of the elevation of fashion designer from dressmaker to social presence. Blass learns from his clients and, in learning, addresses their needs and wishes. In designing separates, he describes what he likes with a certain top, admits that one of his clients prefers to wear it otherwise and acknowledges that it looks better as she wears it. The client is supreme not in a manner of subservience, but in adaptability, as if the composer of modern music sought fulfillment in the musical interpretation through performance and some degree of improvisation.

There are essential leitmotifs in Blass's work. Recalling Mainbocher, he invents from the sweater and brings insights of daywear into the most elegant night-time presentations. Blass imports menswear practicality and fabrics to womenswear. His evening gowns are dream-like in their self-conscious extravagance and flattery to the wearer. He can evoke Schiaparelli in the concise elegance of a simulated wood embroidered jacket. A succulent slice of watermelon for a rever may emulate Schiaparelli, but there is also something definably Blass about the gesture. In a very old-fashioned way, he celebrates life with none of the cynicism of other designers. He is audacious in mixing pattern and texture, though generally with the subtlety of his preferred palette of dove, gray-green, and muted color. Texture is equally important, a red wool cardigan resonant to a red silk dress or the complement of gray flannel trousers to fractured, shimmering surfaces for day and evening. Layering is essential to Blass: whether it is a cardigan teamed with a blouse or sweater or gauzy one-sleeve wraps for evening, Blass flourishes in layers.

It is conventional wisdom to say that Blass has become the superb licensing genius and dean of American fashion designers, implying an inconsequential creative impulse. Blass's attainment, however, is to imagine. His is an intensely pictorial imagination, one that conjures up the most romantic possibilities of fashion. He maintains an ideal of glamour and personal aura, redolent of socialites and stars of screen and stage. He plays with the reconciliation of nonchalant comfort for the wearer and the impression his clothing conveys to the spectator.

There is little in Blass's work that is truly unique to him and not practiced by any other designer, yet one would never mistake a Blass for a Mainbocher or a Schiaparelli, nor for any of his contemporaries. The characteristic glamour and star-quality grandeur that he gives to clothing, while maintaining a level of refinement, is distinctively Blass. He is, as Eleanor Lambert said of him when he was still at Rentner, quintessentially New York. A crossroads city, a striving place, and a dreaming desire inform Blass's work. Beguil-

ing charm and glamorous seduction are perhaps easy to envy and easier still to criticize, yet the extraordinary consistency and quality of Bill Blass is not easily achieved.

—Richard Martin

BLUMARINE.
Italian fashion design company

Founded in Carpi, Italy, 1977, by Anna Molinari, chief designer and artistic director, with husband Gianpaolo Tarabini. First catwalk show in Milan, 1981; The Anna Molinari line presented twice a year in Milano Collezioni shows, from 1986; two lines, Blumarine Folies and MissBlumarine, added, 1987; Blumarine licensing deals, for perfume, handbags, belts, ceramic tiles, glasses, stationery, leathergoods, home furnishings, furs, shoes, swimming costumes, costume jewelery, and scarves, 1987; flagship store opened, in via Spiga, Milan, 1990. **Awards:** Best Designer of the Year, Modit Milan, 1980; "Griffo d'oro" award, Imola, Italy, 1981; Rotary Club gold award, Carpi, 1991; Lions Club "Carpione d'oro" award, 1992. **Address:** Press Office, via Borgospesso 21, Milan, Italy.

Publications:

On BLUMARINE:

Books

Gastel, M., *Designers,* Milan 1994.
The Best in Catalogue Design, London 1994.

Articles

Pardo, D., "Modelle d'Italia," in *L'Espresso* (Rome), January 1993.
Mari, L., "Helmut Newton 1993," in *Vogue* (Milan), March 1993.
Staples, K., "Italy's Newest Line," in *Mademoiselle* (New York), March 1993.
Cavaglione, P., "Il mio profeta," in *Amica,* August 1993.
Szlezynger, T., "Stilisti e designer," in *Vogue Sposa* (Milan), March 1994.
Gagliardo, P., "Vogue Erfolg," in *Vogue* (Munich), August 1994.

*

The stylistic concept of Anna Molinari is very simple: fantasy, passion, curiosity, fascination, and romanticism. Evolution coherent with the research for "femininity" assimilating aesthetic influence from the past re-invention of ideas in favour of the dream, of seduction, and joy of living.

It's easy to describe the typical Blumarine woman: one has only to look to Anna Molinari, her intelligence, vivacity, creativity, femininity and passion: a vibration between angel and femme fatale. Helmut Newton, one of the world's greatest fashion photographers, has perceived this essence and, guided by the modernity of Anna Molinari, has created a new concept of feminine power.

—Blumarine/Anna Molinari

*   *   *

The Blumarine collection is designed by the company's founder and owner, Anna Molinari. Based in Capri in Italy, the collection is shown seasonally twice a year in Milan. Since its 1977 inception, the company has built up a steady international following that includes recent openings in the United Kingdom and the United States.

Blumarine collections are young, fun, and throwaway. Kitsch and naughty, sexy yet prudish, the clothes always represent an appealing ambiguity. For example, a Blumarine promotional piece gives a peek-a-boo glimpse at a little girl plundering her elder sister's wardrobe and emerging half innocent, half saucy into the sophisticated world. There is also a hard-edged defiance about the clothes, designed by a woman who combines her intelligence with the feminine powers of seduction.

The fashion photographer Helmut Newton has created a strong image for Blumarine since he began styling and photographing the company's promotional material. Whether it's set in the seedy world of the back street hotel, complete with tacky 1970s decor, or on the shores of a trashy Mediterranean seaside resort, there are always strong sexual connotations in the imagery. Clothes are styled with revealing accessories: suspender belts, the spiked patent stilettos of the dominatrix, or dog collars as chokers. The poses of the models, particularly Nadja Auerman, who resembles an early 1980s Debbie Harry, tantalize. Whether they are lying with schoolgirl innocence on a bed or in an embrace—one model in a short, flirty black lace dress, the other in drag in a man's tuxedo—the images are always provocative.

Anna Molinari likes to emphasize the female figure. This is often achieved by exaggerated feminine styles. Very popular is her tutu mini skirt, which features a tiny cinched waist that suddenly explodes into a full bell skirt, and layer upon layer of net and lace petticoats. The line also features delicate black lace baby doll dresses cut dangerously short, laced bustiers, short, striped milkmaid dresses, tiny cardigans, and figure-hugging sweaters, always worn in a way that reveals a lacy bra top or satin-trimmed slip.

Popular fabrics are lace, brocade, chiffon, and fake fur either as a trim or made into a figure-hugging jacket. Accessories are important: bo-peep caps worn with schoolgirl pigtails, large feather boas, or top hats. Ruffles often reoccur in collections, on shirts or as flounced cuffs and necklines. Colour mixes are always refreshing and unexpected: ice blues mixed with burgundy, peach, and cream, or chocolate brown mixed with sky blue and tangerine; dominating, though, is black, always sexy and suggestive.

Blumarine also explores many directional fashion themes in collections. For Spring/Summer 1995 Anna Molinari exploited the most accurate depiction of that season's "Disco Diva" look, with short, pleated-on-the-knee pencil skirts in sherbet satin, combined with fitted jackets, good-time hot pants, and kitsch-print lurex T-shirts.

Blumarine collections exploit in their design what Anna Molinari believes to be the dual personality in every woman: coyness combined with passion, or the little girl combined with the temptress. The company has steadily increased its influence and is now recognized as one of the more directional, risk-taking fashion names in the world, with showrooms in Milan, New York, and Paris and a steadily increasing coterie of boutiques in Hong Kong, Milan, and London.

—Kevin Almond

BOCHER, Main Rousseau. See **MAINBOCHER.**

BODYMAP.
British design team

Owned by Stevie Stewart and David Holah. Stewart born in London, 1958; studied at Barnet College. Holah born in London, 1958; studied at North Oxfordshire College of Art. Both studied fashion at Middlesex Polytechnic, 1979-82; graduation collection purchased by Browns, London. Firm founded in 1982, expanded from 1985 to include Bodymap men's and women's collection, B-Basic junior line, Bodymap Red Label, and Bodymap swimwear. **Awards:** Martini Young Fashion Award, 1983; Bath Museum of Costume Dress of the Year Award, 1984. **Address:** 93 Fortress Road, London NW5 2HR, England.

Publications:

By BODYMAP:

Articles

Stewart, Stevie, "Mapping the Future: Talking 'bout My Generation," in *Fashion '86,* London 1985.

On BODYMAP:

Books

McDermott, Catherine, *Street Style: British Design in the 80's,* London 1987.
Coleridge, Nicholas, *The Fashion Conspiracy,* London 1988.
Evans, Caroline, and Minna Thornton, *Women and Fashion: A New Look,* London 1989.

Articles

Warner, Marina, "Counter-couture," in *Connoisseur* (London), May 1984.
"Bodymap: British B.C.B.G. Version B.D.," in *Elle* (London), September 1984.
Jones, Mark, "Followers of Fashion," in *Creative Review* (London), December 1984.
Cleave, Maureen, "Leading Them a Dance," in *The Observer* (London), 18 May 1986.
Mower, Sarah, "Off the Map," in *The Guardian* (London), 5 June 1986.
Jeal, Nicola, "Bodymap," in *The Observer* (London), 12 June 1986.
Tredre, Roger, "Body Style," in *Fashion Weekly* (London), 28 September 1989.
Elliot, Tom, and Robin Duff, "Rise and Fall," in *Blitz* (London), November 1989.

*   *   *

"Barbie Takes a Trip," "Querelle Meets Olive Oil," "The Cat in the Hat Takes a Rumble with the Techno Fish," are just some of the bizarre titles of previous Bodymap collections. The company, a male-female partnership between Middlesex Polytechnic graduates, David Holah and Stevie Stewart, was one of the brightest design teams to emerge during the 1980s. By the middle of the decade London was being promoted by the media as a trendy hothouse of bright young things. Bodymap was regarded as being amongst the brightest of all, turning the Establishment upside-down with wild, young, and unconventional clothes. Fashion editors were clamouring for more, declaring Bodymap to be the hottest fashion label of the decade.

Founded in 1982, the name of the company was inspired by the Italian artist Enrico Job, who took over a thousand photographs of every part of his anatomy, then collaged them together, creating a two-dimensional version of a three-dimensional object; in other words, a body map. A similar philosophy was adapted in Stewart and Holah's approach to pattern making and garment construction. Prints, knits, silhouettes, and shapes were restructured and reinvented to map the body. Stretch clothes had holes in unexpected places, so that the emphasis was transferred from one place to another. Pieces of flesh were amalgamated with pieces of fabric in an effort to explore new areas of the body, previously considered unflattering.

Awarded the Individual Clothes Show prize as the "Most Exciting and Innovative Young Designers of 1983," Bodymap clothes have always been for the young, avant-garde, and the daring. Working predominantly in black, white, and cream, a familiar theme involves the layering of prints and textures on top of one another, to create an unstructured look, redefining traditional body shapes, overemphasizing shapeliness or shapelessness so that both the overweight and underweight, plain or beautiful can wear and be comfortable in an outfit.

Bodymap described themselves in the 1980s as being a young company that employed other young people to mix creativity with commerce. They worked very closely with textile designer Hilde Smith, who has created many Bodymap prints and has helped bridge gaps between fashion and textile design. The film and videomaker John Maybury was responsible for Bodymap's outrageous fashion show videos, featuring dancer Michael Clark, singers Boy George and Helen Terry, and performance artist Leigh Bowery. Photographer David La Chappelle was responsible for many of the visual stills used in magazines.

While still at Middlesex Polytechnic, Bodymap recognized the importance of moving in a circle of talented, creative people. Holah and Stewart were part of the young 1980s generation that attracted worldwide attention for London as a vibrant centre for creative energy and ideas, not only in fashion but music, painting, video, and dance.

—Kevin Almond

BOGNER, Willy.

German sportswear designer

Born: Munich, 23 January 1942. **Family:** Married Sonia Ribeiro in 1973. **Career:** US subsidiary, Bogner of America, formed, 1976, Newport, Vermont. Also Olympic skier and film maker. **Address:** Willy Bogner GmbH & Co. KG, Postfach 80-02-80 Sankt-Veit Strasse 4, 8000 Munich 80, Germany.

Publications:

On BOGNER:

Books

Lambert, Eleanor, *World of Fashion: People, Places, Resources,* New York and London 1976.

*   *   *

The Bogner ski and sportswear company has been run by the Bogner family since its founding by Willy Bogner Sr. in 1936. "The Dior of ski fashion" and the "Coco Chanel of sports fashion" are phrases that have been used to describe Willy Bogner and his wife, Maria. Bogner's status as producer of the most stylish skiwear available is practically unrivaled. But in addition to a high fashion look, Bogner products have become famous for their unparalleled fit and quality workmanship. The successful combination of design, cut, and technically advanced skiwear fabrics has earned the Bogner company loyal customers throughout Europe and North America.

The Bogner name has stood for innovation in the skiwear field since the introduction of Maria Bogner's stretch trousers design in 1948. The trousers were immediately popular owing to their feminine look, as compared to previously available women's skiwear which was decidedly masculine and unflattering. Devotees of the new "Bogners," as they were known at the time, included internationally recognized women such as Marilyn Monroe and Ingrid Bergman. The Bogner company also pioneered the development of the one-piece ski suit and the use of stretch fabrics. Their first one-piece racing suits were worn by the 1960 West German Olympic ski team; the team has been outfitted and sponsored by the Bogner company since 1936.

Willy Bogner Jr. joined the company in the early 1970s and continues the tradition of design innovation. During this time the variety of Bogner products has grown to include cross-country skiwear, tennis, golf, and swimwear, and general sportswear and accessories. In 1973 Bogner of America was founded as a subsidiary of Willy Bogner GmbH of Munich. While the company has expanded to include a complete line of sportswear, the skiwear line remains the foremost vehicle for creative expression by its design team, headed by Willy Bogner Jr. He is a high energy personality with multiple interests, from his own skiing career as a member of the West German Olympic ski team in 1960 and 1964, to film making (the opening ski chase scenes from four James Bond films were filmed under his direction), to his energetic surface designs on skiwear. His varied interests are reflected in the range of motifs that appear as decoration for the skiwear. Some collections have included the following: Egyptian designs on jumpsuits complete with detachable feathers; the Topkapi collection of pieces with exotic embossed designs and turban-like headgear; a one-piece Jukebox suit that actually plays music; and his Fire and Ice collection of 1992 with combinations of contrasting motifs such as the "angel-ogre" parka. For the 1994-95 season, Bogner plans to incorporate snowboarder's garb (until recently, the equivalent of street fashion on the slopes) into the vocabulary of mainstream ski fashion. Willy Bogner Jr.'s wife Sonia has joined the design team to help inspire and create a more classic and feminine part of the collection that bears her name. Her styles are for the more subdued and sophisticated female customer and include details such as cashmere linings and real fur trimmings.

Despite the often outrageous decorative themes, the purpose of the skiwear is never forgotten. A fabric may be printed to look like a silk brocade or embroidered with an intricate design, but it will still be wind and water resistant. It is this attention to practical needs and the desire for style that has continued to make Bogner fashions stand out in the world of sportswear and continue to live up to their reputation as the haute couture of skiwear.

—Melinda L. Watt

BOHAN, Marc.

French designer

Born: Marc Roger Maurice Louis Bohan in Paris, 22 August 1926. **Education:** Studied at the Lycée Lakanal, Sceaux, 1940-44. **Family:** Married Dominique Gaborit in 1950 (died, 1962); married Huguette Rinjonneau (died); daughter: Marie-Anne. **Career:** Assistant designer in Paris to Robert Piguet, 1945-49, and to Molyneux, 1949-51; designer, Madeleine de Rauch, Paris, 1952; briefly opened own Paris salon, produced one collection, 1953; head designer for couture, Maison Patou, Paris, 1954-58; designer, Dior, London, 1958-60, and head designer and art director, Dior, Paris, 1960-89; fashion director for Norman Hartnell, London, 1990-92. **Awards:** *Sports Illustrated* Designer of the Year Award, 1963; Schiffli Lace and Embroidery Institute Award, 1963; named Chevalier de la Legion d'Honneur, 1979; Ordre de Saint Charles, Monaco.

Publications:

On BOHAN:

Articles

Devlin, Polly, "The Perfectionists," in *Vogue* (London), September 1974.

Kellett, Caroline, "A Celebrated Stylist: Marc Bohan Commemorates 25 Years at Christian Dior," in *Vogue* (London), June 1983.

Verdier, Rosy, "Marc Bohan: j'aime vivre dans l'ambre," in *L'Officiel* (Paris), August 1986.

"A Dior Original," in *The Observer Magazine* (London), 29 March 1987.

McColl, Pat, "Bohan: The Power Behind Dior," in *Harper's Bazaar* (New York), September 1987.

Michals, Debra, "Bohan Speaks Out: 27 Years of Fashion," in *Women's Wear Daily* (New York), 12 November 1987.

"Bye-bye Bohan," in *Time* (New York), 22 May 1989.

Mulvagh, Jane, "Hartnell's New Marc," in *Illustrated London News,* No. 1098, 1990.

Wheeler, Karen, "Marc Bohan: New Heart to Hartnell," in *DR: The Fashion Business* (London), 7 July 1990.

Friedman, Arthur, "Hartnell's Silverman: Building on Bohan," in *Women's Wear Daily* (New York), 18 September 1990.

Reed, Paula, "New Look for the Royals," in the *Sunday Times Magazine* (London), 27 January 1991.

Armstrong, Lisa, "Making His Marc," in *Vogue* (London), February 1991.

Grice, Elizabeth, "Designing for the Young at Hartnell," in the *Sunday Express Magazine* (London), 17 February 1991.

Smith, Liz, "Hartnell Goes High Street," in *The Times* (London), 21 January 1992.

Miller, Jeffrey, "House of Hartnell," in *Interview* (New York), January 1991.

Fallon, James, "Bohan Talks with Hartnell on Early End to His Career," in *Women's Wear Daily* (New York), 16 September 1992.

*   *   *

"N'oubliez pas la femme," Marc Bohan's much quoted comment in *Vogue* magazine in 1963, is the tenet which underscores all his work. It has brought his success throughout his lengthy couture career, his design always based on the grown-up female form and a recognition of his customers' needs rather than an overriding desire to shock and provoke headlines in his name. From his early days at Molyneux he learned a sense of practicality, as well as an appreciation of the flattering potential of luxurious fabrics and good fit. His perfectionist zeal and attention to detail, and especially in the 1960s and 1970s at Christian Dior, a good fashion sense, have been at the foundations of his reputation.

It was at Dior that Bohan's talents were established, winning him international acclaim. He enabled the house to remain at the forefront of fashion while still producing wearable, elegant clothes. To achieve this end, Bohan combined innovation with repeated classic shapes and styles, reworked to express the current mood. In 1961, Dior included some of the briefest skirts of the couture collections, but the neat black and white tweed fabric of these little suits enabled Bohan to please the established clientèle, as well as attracting new customers with use of wit and modernity. His suiting always showed the most directional styles and cut, which others would follow.

This ability to ease normally cautious clients towards new, more radical styles by carefully balancing all the elements of a design was seen again in his 1966 collection, when he showed the by then *de rigueur* mini with longer coats, promoting a shift in hemlines gradually rather than dictating a change.

It is this desire to coax and flatter which distinguishes his couture work. His sensitivity to the needs of women has prevented him from trying to mould them into ever-altering silhouettes, or forget their desire to look grown up and elegant even when fashion promoted girlish styles in the 1960s. His use of decoration is equally discreet. He prefers the demure wit of pussycat bows on simple silk blouses and shirtwaist dresses or naturalistic floral prints to add interest to his creations, rather than any overblown gestures that might render the garments less easy to wear, making the client self-conscious.

He has always been unafraid to tell his customers what is most flattering for them and they appreciate his honesty; his rich and famous client list remained faithful even when he switched from one house to the next. His eveningwear is, with his clever suiting styles, his greatest strength, with an understated sense of style allowing the luxurious fabrics and subtle detailing to shine through the simple forms he prefers.

This was seen both in his work of Dior and his later creations for Norman Hartnell. At the former he presented stark modernist

shapes, like the angular ivory silk evening tunic and matching cigarette trousers (1965), with rich red floral design creeping over its
surface. At Hartnell he again excelled at reviving the spirits of an
established couture name. He developed his pared-down style to
fulfill the house's design brief, attracting a younger audience with
his first collection, combining flirtatious shaping with classic styles.
In 1991, he showed the sophisticated chic of black sheath dresses
with diamanté buttons next to witty fuchsia silk scoop-necked
dresses with short, very full skirts that harked back to the bubble
dresses that had reinvigorated his work for Dior in the late 1970s.
Again he provided choice for his customers and commercial designs
which were well received by the press.

Bohan's time at Hartnell was brief, curtailed by the recession of
the early 1990s which caused the decline in interest in couture,
precipitating the demise of several of the smaller houses and leading
to cutbacks in all areas of fashion. His sense of elegance remained
undiminished. If his suits were the most innovative area of his
work, he balanced their fashion-led cut with well-constructed, feminine separates and striking eveningwear which had the lasting appeal characteristic of all good design.

—Rebecca Arnold

HUGO BOSS AG.

German menswear fashion house

Founded in Metzingen, Germany, by Hugo Boss, 1923, to manufacture work clothes and uniforms. Subsequently taken over by
Siegfried Boss and son-in-law Eugen Holly (1948-72) and in 1972
by grandsons Jochen Holly and Uwe Holly. Introduced men's and
children's lines, 1948. Began export to Belgium and Netherlands,
1973, Scandinavia and England, 1975, USA, 1977, Canada, 1982,
Italy and Japan, 1985, Spain, 1986, Portugal, 1987, Taiwan and
Korea, 1988. Added men's shirts, 1981, sportsclothes, 1984, and
women's wear, 1989; Hugo and Baldessarini lines for men introduced, 1994. Licenses include Boss cosmetics, 1984, leather goods,
from 1986, and Boss sunglasses, from 1989. Subsidiaries: Hugo
Boss SARL, Paris, formed 1977; Hugo Boss Inc., United States,
formed in New York, 1986; Hugo Boss Italia in Milan and Hugo
Boss Japan in Tokyo formed, 1991. Firm acquired by Japanese
investment group Leyton House, Ltd, 1989, and by Italian manufacturer Marzotto & Figli, SpA, 1991. **Address:** Dieselstrasse 12,
72555 Metzingen, Germany.

Publications:

On BOSS:

Articles

Syedain, Hashi, "What Suits Boss," in *Management Today* (London), June 1989.
"Modest Boss," in the *Daily News Record* (New York), 25 January
1991.
Deeny, Godfrey, "The World According to Boss," in the *Daily
News Record* (New York), 1 April 1991.
Protzman, Ferdinand, "Hugo Boss: A Fading Status Symbol," in
the *New York Times,* 23 June 1991.
Deeny, Godfrey, "Redirecting the Empire: Hugo Boss Adjusts to
the 'Values' of the 90's," in the *Daily News Record* (New York),
5 August 1993.
Levine, Joshua, "I Am the Boss," in *Forbes* (New York), 25 October 1993.

*   *   *

A company originally producing workwear in the 1920s, Hugo
Boss now designs uniforms for the aspiring executive. In the 1960s
Uwe and Jochem Holy, grandchildren of the company's founder,
saw a place in the market for a mid-range version of the kind of
fashionable clothes they enjoyed wearing from Pierre Cardin. Since
then the continuing success of the company and the incursion of
similar German middle market concerns into the European clothing
industry, producing relatively small batches of garments in upmarket styles at affordable prices, has resulted in top German designers and fashion groups like Jill Sander, Mondi and Hugo Boss
becoming international brand names.

Using new technology and the strategy of subcontracting, together with high quality materials, stringent quality control and the
business acumen of the company directors, Boss has become almost a household name; acknowledging the powers of advertising,
particularly the use of product placement, in the creation of an
image. In the early to mid-1980s Boss became associated in the
public eye with the hard metropolitan chic of the ubiquitous yuppie,
through male characters sporting a variety of Boss garments on
television's *Miami Vice* and *L.A. Law.* The popular conception of
the Filofax-toting, mobile-phone wielding entrepreneur living in a
warehouse apartment, surrounded by matte black accoutrements,
was conflated by the young(ish) European man with Hugo Boss
suits, although in reality if the yuppie existed in great numbers he
was far more likely to frequent Paul Smith or Armani. Nevertheless
the sharp Boss suit, styled by businessmen rather than tailors,
became a metonymic signifier for the world of work and its connotations of materialism and power for large numbers of European
men, as increasing sales figures throughout the 1980s proved.

The Boss look, based on a traditionally masculine 20th- century
silhouette, revolved around variations on the wide-shouldered suit,
usually double-breasted with front pleated trousers; the Euroman
adding his own styling by rolling up the sleeves of the jacket à la
Don Johnson. More recently the Boss logo has appeared at prestigious sporting events, not so much because the company is interested in producing a line of sportswear to rival those of the German
firms Puma and Adidas, but because of the glamour image and
athletic machismo associated with Formula One racing and Davis
Cup tennis. This was subsequently reflected in the marketing of
Boss Sport; "fragrance and bodycare for the confident man leading
an active lifestyle."

The company has responded well to the so-called New Age
1990s. Export success has remained constant, although for a time
the name Boss was seen in Germany as somewhat downmarket.
Rather than just concentrating on export and weathering the storm,
Boss responded by quickly withdrawing deliveries from a number
of German retailers who did not fit in with their current image,
prepared to accept a loss of revenue rather than downgrading—a
strategy which has appeared to work as the company has recently
very successfully gone public and taken over United States clothing
manufacturers Joseph and Feiss. As for the image which seemed to
be so squarely rooted in the 1980s? The suits have rather more
rounded shoulders but the advertising and brandnaming give more

Hugo Boss.

of a clue. Now Europeans are being introduced to the Boss man who has "a new attitude and vision" encapsulated in the latest fragrance and marketing angle, "Boss Spirit."

—Caroline Cox

BRIGANCE, Tom.

American designer

Born: Thomas Franklin Brigance in Waco, Texas. **Education:** Attended Waco Junior College; studied in New York at the Parsons School of Design, 1931-34, and the National Academy of Art; studied in Paris at the Sorbonne and at the Academie de la Grande Chaumière, Paris. **Military Service:** Served in the United States Air Corps Intelligence Service, South Pacific, 1941-44, decorated for bravery. **Career:** Worked in Europe as free-lance fashion designer, designed in London for Jaeger and for Simpson's of Piccadilly, late 1930s; designer, Lord & Taylor, New York, 1939-41 and 1944-49; opened own firm, 1949; also designed in New York for Frank Gallant, and free-lanced for Fonde, Sportsmarket, and designed swimwear for Sinclair and Gabar, Water Clothes, 1950s. **Awards:** Coty American Fashion Critics Award, 1953; International Silk Citation, 1954; National Cotton Award, 1955; Internazionale delle Arti Award, Italy, 1956. *Died* (in New York City) *14 October 1990.*

Publications:

On BRIGANCE:

Books

New York and Hollywood Fashion: Costume Designs from the Brooklyn Museum Collection, New York 1986.
Milbank, Caroline Rennolds, *New York Fashion: The Evolution of American Style,* New York 1989.
Stegemeyer, Anne, *Who's Who in Fashion,* supplement, New York 1992.

Articles

Sheppard, Eugenia, "What's Coming Next? ...," in the *Herald Tribune,* 28 October 1947.
"Designer Brigance Speaks to a Mill," in *American Fabrics and Fashions* (New York), No. 25, 1953.
Schiro, Anne-Marie, "Thomas F. Brigance Dies at 70: Designed Sophisticated Swimwear," in the *New York Times,* 18 October 1990.

*   *   *

Eleanor Lambert's 1951 press release for Tom Brigance quotes the young designer: "Good American clothes should be able to go anywhere. They should not be designed with a single town or section in mind. They should be appropriate for the American woman's mode of living, expressive of her individual personality, and suitable for the climate she lives in." Brigance spoke and designed with the plain common sense of Will Rogers and the utmost simplicity of the American ethos. No one could more readily have

epitomized the main-street ideal of an American fashion designer than Brigance. From Waco, Texas, slim, dark, and charming, Brigance became a recognized designer in 1939, while still in his twenties, as part of Dorothy Shaver's campaign to create American designer identities at Lord & Taylor.

His first success was in active sportswear and beachwear. In an advertisement in *Vogue* (15 May 1939), Lord & Taylor boasted of its new American hero, "When you come to the World's Fair be sure to visit our Beach Shop on the fifth floor, home of creations by Brigance, one of our own designers, whose ideas enchant even the blasé Riviera." Anne-Marie Schiro reports in Brigance's obituary in the *New York Times* (18 October 1990) that the Duchess of Windsor bought half a dozen outfits from his first beachwear collection in 1939, a formidable endorsement for any young designer. Brigance remained a designer at Lord & Taylor until 1949. Although he later designed a full spectrum of clothing, including eveningwear, his forte through his retirement in the late 1970s was sportswear, especially playsuits, beach- and swimwear. At Brigance's death in 1990 Schiro reported: "He retired in the late 1970s after a two-year stint with Gabar whose owner, Gabriel Colasante, said this week that a Brigance-designed skirted swimsuit is still one of his company's best-selling styles. 'It sells no matter what print I do it in,' he said."

Brigance was at his best when at his most simple. His employer Lord & Taylor boasted of Brigance in advertising in the *Herald Tribune* (14 September 1947): "His suits and coats have the distinctively American lines that inspire individuality with accessories." Like Claire McCardell, Brigance used fabric ties and sashes to shape waists and create form; his coats and suits were uniformly unadorned, but inflected with relatively large buttons in interesting placement. By the late 1940s, he was acknowledging the New Look, not in its extreme forms, but in a modified version in which the skirt or peplum flared with pockets, adding practicality to the gesture of the wider skirt. His play clothes were his most imaginative, suggesting the spectrum of leisure from beach pajamas through halter tops and playsuits with shorts and skirts. For summer, his preference was generally for colorful cottons, often with dots. His swimwear presaged the American idiom of dressing in warm climates in clothes as suitable for the street as for the beach and swimming.

Distinctively, Brigance enjoyed pattern mixes more than most of his contemporaries. Today his surprising combinations of florals, geometrics, and exotics are strikingly bold and seem more advanced as textile fusions than others of his generation. While his ideological interest was reductive, his style was always to supply plenty of material and ample coverage. He kept a loyal, even aging, clientele because he flattered the body with informal exposure that was never scanty, even in swimwear and playsuits. One could be unfailingly modest and self-assured in Brigance. His design sensibility for minimalism was aided in another way by his interest in fabric technology: his nylon swimsuit of 1960 exploited the fast-drying material. In 1955 he was the only man among seven American designers, including Anne Fogarty, Pauline Trigère, and Claire McCardell, to style interiors for Chrysler Corporation cars.

Eugenia Sheppard, writing in the *Herald Tribune* (28 October 1947), claimed that Brigance had Aristotle's phrase "nothing is permanent but change" set over the mirror in his design workroom at Lord & Taylor. Change for Brigance was ever modest; sportswear was also a credo, believing in the practical aspects of clothing. Less adventurous than McCardell or Cashin, Brigance (along with John Weitz) anticipated the emergence of great male designers in the 1970s and 1980s era of American sportswear. Like them, he was his own best salesperson and a kind of native hero, the man who not only dressed the American ideal woman of suburban chic, but also the man for whom she dressed. His 1949 dinner separates in pleated jersey exemplify Brigance's contribution to design: a quintessentially American look that is informal, sporty, innovative, open, and yet demure.

—Richard Martin

BRIONI.

Italian fashion house

Founded by tailor Nazareno Fonticoli and entrepreneur Gaetano Savini in via Barberini, Rome, 1945. First men's tailored clothing show, Palazzo Pitti, Florence, 1952; launch of accessory line, 1952; first men's runway show in New York, 1954; first show in Britain, 1959; manufacturing company, Brioni Roman Style, launched in Penne, Italy, with 45 workers, 1960; neckwear collection launched, 1979; Penne factory established tailoring school, 1980; first American free-standing Brioni store opened, Park Avenue, New York, 1982; company acquired Burini of Bergamo, 1991, and controlling interest in Sforza of Bologna, leather creator, 1994. Also: ready-to-wear line, Brioni Roman Style, produced in Penne, Italy. **Awards:** *Esquire* (New York) Award for valued contribution to menswear, 1959; International Fashion Council Award, 1962. **Address:** via Barberini 79-81, Rome, Italy.

Publications:

On BRIONI:

Books

Schoeffler, O. E., and William Gale, *Esquire's Encyclopedia of 20th Century Men's Fashion,* New York 1973.

*   *   *

Brioni was the definitive Roman tailoring establishment of the "Continental look" of the 1950s. The silhouette was immediately identifiable, with its pitched shoulders, tapered waist, and narrow hips and trousers, suggesting the architectural purity and astringency of the post-war Italian aesthetic. Brioni's sensitive tailoring was also one of the first post-war softenings of men's tailored clothing, bringing immediate pliability in slim silhouette and delicate drapery. The fabrics advocated by Fonticoli and Savini borrowed from womenswear for a beautiful hand and lush suppleness also brought color to the sober traditions of men's tailoring. American film stars—Clark Gable, Henry Fonda, John Wayne, and Kirk Douglas, among others—had suits custom-made by Brioni: these avatars of masculinity were important in introducing American men in particular to the comfort of Brioni's labor-intensive and meticulous tailoring. America was very important to Brioni's image and business: the American tendency to men of big frame and naïve awkwardness was superbly civilized by the sophistication of Brioni tailoring. Moreover, American masculinity's embrace of the lean Italian style created an alliance powerful enough to serve as an alternative to Savile Row, softening the structure of the suit and

allowing the heretical interventions of style and fashion to come into men's tailored clothing. Brioni is said to be the first men's tailor to employ raw silks and rich brocades in men's tailoring: these innovations in men's tailoring may seem less than radical today, but in the 1950s Brioni was a thorough innovator in the stolid world of tailoring.

The slim modesty of the Brioni "continental" silhouette encouraged the experimental play of textiles, and the suit's clean modernism allowed for color as eye-opening as color-field paintings. Even today, Brioni tailoring is among the most tactile and luxurious in the world. One line of suits, known as Vaticano, employs the dense but silky fabrics traditionally used for priests' robes. Brioni and Sorelle Fontana often showed together in fashion shows, so pronounced was the affinity between the most extravagant style of Roman fashion for women and Brioni's ideal tailoring for men. Today, Brioni tailoring is not limited to the signature silhouette and offers options in construction and silhouette, but the ethos and glory in craft still reside in men's suitings pleasurable to touch, the discernible difference of labor and quality in handmade buttonholes, and the composition of a suit as a perfect harmonics of proportion. Brioni attests to 10 hours of handsewing, 18 hours of fine craftsmanship, 42 pressing stages, and 186 manufacturing phases for a suit today.

Now diversified into casual slacks, distinguished shirts, and excellent suedes and leathers, Brioni has surpassed the suit alone, but the perfect suit has always remained the corporate grail. Edward Tivnan in his essay "A Touch of Vanity" in the *New York Times About Men* book (1987) describes his quest, "Like every good man, I strive for perfection, and, like every ordinary man, I have found that perfection is out of reach—but not the perfect suit." Brioni makes the suit for such aspiration. Today, the corporate statement describes: "The Brioni man, who can be 45 and up, is not a fashion enthusiast nor does he care about fashion trends. His only concern is personal style, the best possible service and impeccable tailoring." In this, Brioni still conceives of the absolute anonymity of style and the prodigious importance of the exceptional man who knows what a work of art and what a cultural statement a great suit can be.

—Richard Martin

BROOKS BROTHERS.

American clothier

Firm established in New York as Brooks Clothing Company by Henry Sands Brooks, 1818; renamed Brooks Brothers, 1854. First American firm to market such staples as the button-down collar shirt and the polo coat; has also sold womenswear from 1940s; opened womenswear department in own New York store, 1976. Firm sold to Marks and Spencer, PLC, by the Campeau Corporation, 1988. **Address:** 346 Madison Avenue, New York, New York 10017, USA.

Publications:

On BROOKS BROTHERS:

Books

Brooks Brothers Centenary, New York 1918.
Roscho, Bernard, *The Rag Race,* New York 1963.
Fucini, Joseph, and Suzy Fucini, *Entrepreneurs,* Boston 1965.
Boyer, G. Bruce, *Elegance,* New York 1985.
Milbank, Caroline Rennolds, *New York Fashion: The Evolution of American Style,* New York 1989.

Articles

Millstein, Gilbert, "The Suits on the Brooks Brothers Men," in *New York Times Magazine,* 15 August 1976.
Attanasio, Paul, "Summer of Size 42," in *Esquire* (New York), June 1986.
"Taking Over an American Tradition," in *Management Today,* May 1988.
Graham, Judith, "Brooks Bros. Spiffs Up Its Image," in *Advertising Age,* 30 October 1989.
Barron, James, "Pleats? Cardigan Cuddling? Brooks Brothers Unbuttons," in *New York Times,* 11 November 1989.
Schecter, Laurie, "View," in *Vogue* (New York), February 1990.
Barmash, Isadore, "Brooks Brothers Stay the Course," in *New York Times,* 23 November 1990.
Better, Nancy Marx, "Unbuttoning Brroks Brothers," in *M Inc.,* March 1991.
Palmieri, Jean E., "When Brooks Put Fashion on the Front," in the *Daily News Record* (New York), 11 March 1991.
Guzman, "He Ain't Stuffy, He's Brooks Brothers," in *Esquire* (New York), September 1991.
Palmieri, Jean E., "An American Icon Celebrated a Milestone; Brooks Brothers Still Spry at 175," in *DNR,* 31 May 1993.
Bhargave, Sunita Wadekar, "What's Next, Grunge Bathrobes?," in *Business Week,* 21 June 1993.
Plimpton, George, "Under the Golden Fleece," in *American Heritage,* November 1993.

Articles also in—

Life (New York), 5 April 1954.
New York Times, 8 May 1976.
Daily News Record (New York), 9 January 1989.
Daily News Record (New York), 7 April 1989.
Daily News Record (New York), 3 May 1989.
Newsweek (New York), 4 December 1989.
New York Times Magazine, 28 March 1990.
Forbes (New York), 9 July 1990.
Daily News Record (New York), 1 November 1990.
Daily News Record (New York), 9 May 1991.
Daily News Record (New York), 18 September 1991.
Daily News Record (New York), 13 November 1991.

*   *   *

Brooks Brothers is one of the oldest clothiers in America. The company has developed a distinctive image of quiet good taste. Henry Sands Brooks first opened the store under his own name in 1818. In 1854 his sons, Henry, Daniel, John, Elisha, and Edward, officially changed the name to Brooks Brothers.

Since the beginning, Brooks Brothers has been innovative. When he first opened his doors in New York, Henry Sands offered ready-to-wear clothing for sailors who were in port for short periods of time and who did not have time to have their clothing custom tailored. Henry Sands also offered bespoke or custom tailored clothing for the gentry, professionals, and the well-to-do.

For more than one hundred years Brooks Brothers made military uniforms, including those for Civil War Generals Lee, Sheridan, Grant, and Custer. George Bush is one of the many presidents of the United States who have worn Brooks Brothers' clothes, while President Abraham Lincoln was wearing a Brooks Brothers' frock coat the night he was shot.

Brooks Brothers introduced many new styles to men's fashion. They adapted the button-down collar from shirts the English wore playing polo. They introduced the so-called sack suit, which had as little padding as possible and became a staple of businessmen's wardrobes with its understated design. In 1890 they introduced madras clothing, in 1904 Shetland wool sweaters, in 1910 the camel hair polo coat, in 1930 the lightweight summer suit, and in 1953 they introduced the wash and wear shirt. Mainstays in the Brooks Brothers line include the foulard tie, khakis, and the navy blazer. These are all part of the so-called Ivy League styles associated with the Ivy League schools of America. People who wear Brooks Brothers clothes are not concerned with fashion, but want to look good. Lawrence Wortzel sums up the look by saying in *Forbes* magazine that "if Brooks dressed you, no one would laugh."

The Brooks image is so distinctive that American authors use it in their work. Mary McCarthy wrote a short story called, "Man in the Brooks Brothers Suit." F. Scott Fitzgerald dressed his characters in Brooks clothes, and they were worn by John O'Hara's good guys.

Brooks Brothers has always been a clothier for men and boys. Surreptitiously women also bought their clothes for themselves, often resorting to purchasing their goods in the boys' department for sizing. They, too, wanted good quality and good design. Brooks Brothers did provide clothing for women as early as the mid-1940s, introducing Shetland wool sweaters. In 1949 *Vogue* magazine showed a model wearing a pink Brooks Brothers button-down collar shirt. It was not until 1976, however, that Brooks Brothers officially opened a small women's department at the back of their store in New York. One of their first offerings was a more femininely cut, pink, button-down collared shirt.

Known throughout the world, Brooks Brothers is now owned by the English concern of Marks and Spencer, with stores in Tokyo as well as throughout the United States. No matter where they are found, the style is Brooks Brothers, and no adjustments are made for regional or national differences.

In a *New York Times* article, Lawrence Van Gelder called Brooks Brothers a "bastion of sartorial conservatism." It would be easy to classify Brooks Brothers as stodgy, old-fashioned, and showing little concern for fashion, but this would be erroneous. They are not revolutionary when it comes to design, but evolutionary. They are not in the forefront of fashion, but quietly maintain a classic style that evolves to meet the needs of the times. In the 1918 *Brooks Brothers Centenary,* Brooks Brothers advised that one "be not the first by whom the new is tried, nor yet the last to lay the old aside."

—Nancy House

BROOKS, Donald.

American designer

Born: New York City, 10 January 1928. **Education:** Studied art, Syracuse University, Syracuse, New York, 1947-49, and fashion design and illustration, Parsons School of Design, New York, 1949-50. **Career:** Designed for a series of New York ready-to-wear firms, c.1950-56; other work in New York includes designer for Darbury, 1956; partner and designer, Hedges of New York, 1957-59; designer, own label for Townley Frocks, 1958-64; designer, custom apparel, Henri Bendel department store, 1961; owner and designer, Donald Brooks, Inc., 1964-73; launched Boutique Donald Brooks line, 1969. Designed sweaters for Jane Irwill, 1965; shoes for Newton Elkin, 1966; furs for Coopchik-Forrest, Inc., 1967; furs for Bonwit Teller department store, 1969; robes and sleepwear for Maidenform, shoes for Palizzio; drapery fabrics and bedlinens for Burlington, 1971; DB II line introduced, c.1980; Donald Brooks ready-to-wear, 1986; consultant for fabric and colour design, Ann Taylor stores, from 1990. Also: theatre, film, TV, and custom clothing designer from 1961. **Awards:** Coty American Fashion Critics Award, 1958, 1962, 1967, 1974; National Cotton Award, 1962; New York Drama Critics Award, 1963; Parsons Medal for Distinguished Achievement, 1974; Emmy Award, 1982. **Address:** c/o Parson's School of Design, 66 Fifth Avenue, New York 10011, USA.

Publications:

On BROOKS:

Books

Maeder, Edward, et al., *Hollywood and History: Costume Design in Film,* New York 1987.
Owen, Bobbie, *Costume Designers on Broadway: Designers and Their Credits 1915-1985,* Westport, Connecticut 1987.
Milbank, Caroline Rennolds, *New York Fashion: The Evolution of American Style,* New York 1989.
Leese, Elizabeth, *Costume Design in the Movies,* New York 1991.

Articles

"Designers Who Are Making News," in *American Fashions and Fabrics* (New York), No. 37, 1956.
"Donald Brooks," in *Current Biography* (New York), March 1972.
Morris, Bernadine, "A Return to Fashion Staged with Flair by Donald Brooks," in the *New York Times,* 14 May 1986.

*   *   *

Staying power characterized Donald Brooks every bit as much as the simply cut, easy fitting dresses in distinctive fabrics for which he is best known. A summer job in the advertising and display department at Lord & Taylor let him into ready-to-wear, first as a sketch artist and subsequently as designer for a series of undistinguished manufacturers. After a stint as designer at Darbury and Hedges of New York, where his work was admired by the fashion press, Brooks moved to Townley Frocks as successor to Claire McCardell. There, Brooks was given his own label as well as the chance to develop his own prize-winning printed fabrics.

By the mid-1960s, Brooks was one of the few American designers to have financial control of his own business. From that base he diversified along the usual lines, designing sweaters, shoes, swimsuits, furnishing fabrics, and other items under a multitude of licensing agreements. At the same time he built a secure base for his custom-made clothes that would stand him in good stead throughout the recession years of the 1970s and 1980s. Brooks also developed a parallel career, interpreting the contemporary scene for television, film, and the theater, beginning in 1961. His many stage credits include the musical *No Strings,* which earned him a New York Drama Critics Award, 1963, and a nomination for the Antoinette Perry, or "Tony," Award. For his film design Brooks received four Oscar nominations. The parallel careers often supported one another, as when Brooks's clothes for the film *Star,* set in the 1920s and 1930s, provided the direction for his 1968 ready-to-wear collection.

Donald Brooks's clothes are known for their clean lines, often surprising colors, and for their distinctive fabrics, most of which he designs. There is a boldness about a Brooks design that makes an impact and makes his contemporary dresses for the stage particularly successful.

The Parsons Medal for Distinguished Achievement has been awarded less than half a dozen times in almost as many decades. Brooks received it in 1974, to join a roster that singles out Adrian, Norman Norell, and Claire McCardell as especially noteworthy American designers.

—Whitney Blausen

BRUCE, Liza.

American designer working in London

Born: New York, 1955. **Family:** Married Nicholas Barker. **Career:** Designed high-end bathing suits, c.1982; began designing ready-to-wear, 1988; works in London. **Address:** 37 Warple Way, London W3, England.

Publications:

On BRUCE:

Articles

Polan, Brenda, "So Long as the Octopus Giggles," in *The Guardian* (London), 6 June 1985.
"Creative Collaborators," in *Harper's Bazaar* (New York), June 1989.
Starzinger, Page Hill, "Out of the Water, onto the Street: Liza Bruce, Known for Swimwear, Takes the Plunge into Ready-to-Wear," in *Vogue* (New York), June 1990.
Jeal, Nicola, "Truly, Madly, Modern," in *Elle* (London), May 1993.
Baker, Lindsay, "A Room of My Own," in *The Observer Magazine* (London), 10 June 1993.
Spindler, Amy M., "Color It with Silver and Spice," in the *New York Times,* 4 November 1993.

*   *   *

Lean, pared-down shapes, devoid of decoration or unnecessary seams dominate Liza Bruce's work. Shaped with Lycra, her clothes cling to the body. She has removed tight clothing from its conventional daring context and defined the mid-1980s notion of simple stretch garments as the basis for the modern wardrobe. Her designs are founded on the flattering silhouette they produce, emphasizing shape while narrowing the frame.

Her background in swimwear design, which continues in her collections, has given her a confidence in working with the female form. Although at first her stretch lustre crêpe leggings made some women feel too self-conscious and underdressed, they became the ultimate example of this 1980s innovation and were soon a staple in the fashion world, taken up by the 1984 revival interest in synthetics.

Minimalist shape was one of the early examples of her highly recognizable style. She has built on the garments that supplement her streamlined swimwear range, originally modelled on bodybuilder Lisa Lyons, who embodied the toned strength of Bruce's design. Her swimming costumes and closely related bodies produce the characteristic smooth line that pervades her work, some in stark black and white with scooped out necklines, in 1989, others more delicate and decorative. In 1992, soft peach bodies were sprinkled with self coloured beads across the bust area.

Bruce's detailing maintains the aerodynamic line of her clothes, while adding definition and interest to their usual matt simplicity. In 1992 she also produced column-like sheath dresses and skirts that clung to the ankle like a second skin, punctuated by beads at regular intervals down their sides, which were quickly copied in the High Street. The subtle sophistication of such tubular styles avoided the pervasive retro fashion of that year. Indeed, Bruce's work, based as it is on easy-to-wear, timeless separates, pays only lip service to current trends. In 1990 this took the form of black crêpe and Lycra mix catsuits with fake fur collars, while her 1993 collection nodded towards deconstructionist styles, with shrunken mohair jumpers, crumpled silk shifts, and narrow coats with external seams. It was perhaps inevitable that her work would incorporate such touches as her outerwear range, begun in 1989, expanded.

Bruce's signature is most strongly stamped on the lean, sculptured stretchwear she consistently produces. It presents an ideal of modernity in its streamlined design, confident shape, and essential minimalism. She has been able to build on these basic garments as her confidence as a designer of outerwear grew, enabling her to incorporate contemporary fashion preoccupations into more tailored pieces that complement and expand upon the post-modernist tenets of her style. Her popularity in the fashion world is established and her appeal to confident, independent women who appreciate simple yet sexy clothes bereft of unnecessary detail continues to grow.

—Rebecca Arnold

BURBERRYS.

British clothier

Originally a draper's shop in Basingstoke, Hampshire, founded by Thomas Burberry (1835-1926), in 1856, specializing in waterproof overcoats. Opened London store in the Haymarket, 1891; Burberry established as a trademark, 1909; women's clothing lines added, and Paris branch opened, 1910; New York branch opened, 1978; toiletries line introduced, 1981. **Exhibitions:** Victoria and Albert Museum, London, 1989. **Address:** 18-22 Haymarket, London SW1Y 4DQ, England.
Publications:

On BURBERRYS:

Books

Burberry & Co. Ltd., *Burberrys: An Elementary History of a Great Tradition,* London.
Garrulus, Coracias, ed., *Open Spaces,* London.

Articles

Brady, James, "Going Back to the Trenches," in the *New York Post,* 10 October 1978.
Morris, Bernadine, "Coat Maker Marks 125 Years in the Rain," in the *New York Times,* 21 January 1981.
Gleizes, Serge, "Burberry's Story," in *L'Officiel* (Paris), October 1986.

*   *   *

Burberrys was founded by Thomas Burberry (1835-1926), the inventor of the Burberry waterproof coat. The origin of the term Burberry to describe the famous waterproof garments is thought to have derived from the fact that Edward VII was in the habit of commanding, "Give me my Burberry," although Burberry himself had christened his invention "Gabardinee."

The original shooting and fishing garments were produced in response to the perceived need for the ideal waterproof: one that would withstand wind and rain to a reasonable degree and yet allow air to reach the body. From Thomas Burberry's original draper's shop in Basingstoke, Hampshire in 1856 to the opening of Burberrys' present prestigious premises in London's Haymarket in 1891, Burberry have employed what the trade journal *Men's Wear* of June 1904 termed "splendid advertising media" to promote their clothing. Some of the earliest advertising read, "T. Burberry's Gabardinee—for India and the Colonies is the most suitable of materials. It resists hot and cold winds, rain or thorns, and forms a splendid top garment for the coldest climates." Endorsement was given at the beginning of the century by both Roald Amundsen, first to the South Pole, who wrote from Hobart on 18 March 1912: "Heartiest thanks. Burberry overalls were made extensive use of during the sledge journey to the Pole and proved real good friends indeed," and Captain Scott, whose Burberry gabardine tent used on his sledge journey "Furthest South" was exhibited at the Bruton Galleries in that same year.

Burberry also produced menswear and womenswear for motoring from the earliest appearance of the motor car, or as their illustrated catalogues put it, "Burberry adapts itself to the exigencies of travel in either closed or open cars ... and at the same time satisfies every ideal of good taste and distinction."

The turn-of-the-century appeal to the buyer's ideal of "taste and distinction" has always proved a potent force in the appeal of Burberrys' designs. The traditional Burberry Check and the New House Checks are protected as part of the UK Trade Mark registration and are now used in a wide range of Burberry designs, from the

Burberrys.

traditional use as a lining for weathercoats to men's, women's, and children's outerwear, a range of accessories and luggage, toiletries, and several collections of Swiss-made watches featuring the Burberry Check and the trademark Prorsum Horse.

In the 1980s such distinctive goods satisfied the desire for label clothes in their appeal to young consumers as well as to traditional buyers both in Britain and abroad. In the 1990s the diversity of goods designed by Burberrys, from a countrywide home shopping and visiting tailor service in Great Britain, to an internationally available range of Fine Foods proved the efficacy of the Burberry tradition. Burberrys' power as an international household name signifying an instantly identifiable traditional Englishness is attested by the fact that "Burberry" and "Burberrys" and the device of an equestrian knight in armour are registered trademarks.

—Doreen Ehrlich

BURROWS, Stephen.

American designer

Born: Stephen Gerald Burrows in Newark, New Jersey, 15 September 1943. **Education:** Studied at Philadelphia Museum College of Art, 1961-62; studied fashion design, Fashion Institute of Technology, New York, 1964-66. **Career:** Designer, Weber Originals, New York, 1966-67; designer, Allen & Cole, c. 1967-68; co-founder, proprietor, "O" boutique, 1968; in-house designer for Stephen Burrows World boutique, Henri Bendel store, New York, 1969-73; founder-director, Burrows Inc., New York, 1973-82; also, designer, Henri Bendel, 1977-82, 1993; returned to ready-to-wear design, 1989, and to custom design, 1990; designed knitwear line for Tony Lambert Co., 1991. **Exhibitions:** Versailles Palace, 1973. **Awards:** Coty American Fashion Critics "Winnie" Award, 1973, 1977, and Special Award, 1974; Council of American Fashion Critics Award, 1975; Knitted Textile Association Crystal Ball Award, 1975.

Publications:

On BURROWS:

Books

Morris, Bernadine, and Barbara Walz, *The Fashion Makers,* New York 1978.
Milbank, Caroline Rennolds, *New York Fashion: The Evolution of American Style,* New York 1989.

Articles

Morris, Bernadine, "The Look of Fashions for the Seventies—In Colours that Can Dazzle," in the *New York Times,* 12 August 1970.
Fulman, Ricki, "Designer Has Last Laugh on His Critics," in the *New York Daily News,* 4 October 1971.
Klensch, Elsa, "Burrows: I Am Growing More," in *Women's Wear Daily* (New York), 6 April 1972.
Carter, M. R., "The Story of Stephen Burrows," in *Mademoiselle* (New York), March 1975.

Butler, J., "Burrows Is Back—With a Little Help from His Friends," in the *New York Times Magazine,* 5 June 1977.
Schiro, Anne-Marie, "Stephen Burrows, Sportswear Designer," in the *New York Times,* 3 September 1989.
Morris, Bernadine, "Color and Curves from Burrows," in the *New York Times,* 9 January 1990.
Morris, Bernadine, in the *New York Times,* 3 April 1990.
Morris, Bernadine, "The Rebirth of New York Couture," in the *New York Times,* 1 May 1990.
Morris, Bernadine, "The Return of an American Original," in the *New York Times,* 10 August 1993.

*   *   *

Phoenix and fire bird of New York fashion, Stephen Burrows is one of the most audacious and auspicious talents in contemporary fashion. As Bernadine Morris (*New York Times,* 3 April 1990) said of Burrows, he is "incapable of making banal clothes." When creating custom-made clothes in the 1990s, Burrows insisted he would make only one dress of a kind. He told Morris (*New York Times,* 1 May 1990), "Why not? I have plenty of ideas—I don't have to repeat myself."

With the Henri Bendel (New York) 1970 launch of Stephen Burrows' World, Burrows was recognized for his remarkable color-block, fluid, flirting with the *non-finito,* sexy separates that typified the assertive woman of the 1970s. Spectacularly successful in the 1970s, Burrows has enjoyed periods of triumph and quiescence in the subsequent years with forays into sportswear in the early 1990s, custom-made clothing in the 1980s, and eveningwear in 1993, again for Henri Bendel. He has come and gone and come again in the public gaze, partly for business reasons, but his design sensibility has been consistent. He sees bold color fields and tests color dissonance to achieve remarkable new harmony. His great mentor Geraldine Stutz, erstwhile president of Bendel's, commented (*New York Times,* 12 August 1970) that he "stretches a rainbow over the body." But Burrows's rainbow has never sought a Peter Max popularity; his rainbow is extraordinary and unexpected, juxtaposing the strongest colors.

Serviceable separates have always been a large part of Burrows' look. Even his flirtatious dresses of the 1970s, often with his characteristic lettuce edging, seem to be parts when broken by color blocks and zones. As a result, his clothing always seems unaffected and young in the tradition of American sportswear. Clinging jersey, curving lines, and off-setting of easy drape by tight cling make Burrows' clothing both comfortable and very sexy. Of his 1990 collections, the designer himself said: "The dresses are sexy. Women should have an escort when they wear them." (*New York Times,* 9 January 1990).

Like Giorgio di Sant'Angelo and, to a lesser degree, Halston, Burrows was the quintessential fashion expression of the 1970s in a disestablishment sensibility, young nonchalance, and unfailing insistence on looking beautiful. Native American themes (also explored by di Sant'Angelo in 1969 and 1970), bold color fields in jersey with exposed seams as edges, and the unfinished appearance of puckered lettuce edging seemed almost careless in 1969 and 1970 when invented by Burrows, but they can also be recognized as hallmarks of a truthful, youthful culture that demanded no deceit in dress and a return to basics. If Burrows never yielded the sensuality of the body, he again prefigured the last quarter of the century as the body becomes the inevitable discourse of a society of a century freed of Victorianism only at its end. His honesty in technique is an "infra-apparel" trait, betokening a strong feeling for clothing's process, not merely a superficial result. Ricki Fulman suggested in the *New York Daily News* (4 October 1971) that "you've got to have a sense of humor to understand Stephen Burrows' clothes."

If the clothing offers an immediacy and vivacity, Burrows himself and his recognition in his twenties are a comparable phenomenon. Emerging from among the Bendel's designers in 1969, Burrows was a world-class Coty-Award winning talent in the early-to mid-1970s and was one of the five designers selected to represent American fashion in the epochal showing at Versailles in November 1973. One of the first African-Americans after Ann Lowe to achieve stature as a designer, Burrows may have offered fresh ideas in palette and color combination, but he was also sustaining a sportswear ideal. Even his laced cords and snaps have affinity with Claire McCardell's germinal work. Many designers after Burrows have looked to African-American, African, and Latin styles for inspiration and especially to the sexy zest he found there for his designs.

Elsa Klensch argued that the name "Stephen Burrows' World" was more than a store sign. "It is his own world—a philosophy, a life style, an environment," one that is composed of astute street observation, a lively sense of contemporary living and its impatience with rules and convention, and of a non-verbal self-communication through clothing. As much as Halston and di Sant'Angelo, Burrows was the avatar of new styles accorded to a cultural transfiguration in the 1970s. Perhaps he so personifies the early 1970s that his later erratic career is inevitable: we have sacrificed our fullest appreciation of him to another sexy lady he dressed, Clio.

—Richard Martin

BYBLOS.

Italian fashion house

Founded in 1973 as a division of Genny SpA; independent company formed c. 1983; designers include Versace, 1975-76, and Guy Paulin. Principal designers, since 1981, Alan Cleaver and Keith Varty; collections include Byblos Uomo, 1983, Byblos USA, and Options Donna, 1985, Vis à Vis Byblos, 1986, and Options Uomo, 1988. **Address:** Via Maggini 126, 60127 Ancona, Italy.

Publications:

On BYBLOS:

Articles

Buckley, Richard, "Byblos: The Boys' Own Story," in *DNR: The Magazine* (New York), January 1985.

Haynes, Kevin, "Leave It to Byblos," in *Women's Wear Daily* (New York), 5 June 1985.

Elms, Robert, "Italian Fashion: The British Connection," in *Sunday Express Magazine* (London), 9 February 1986.

Frey, Nadine, "Varty and Cleaver: Revitalizing Byblos," in *Women's Wear Daily* (New York), 28 April 1987.

Harris, Lara, "La sera di Byblos," in *Donna* (Milan), October 1987.

Phillips, Kathy, "Men of the Cloth," in *You,* magazine of the *Mail on Sunday* (London), 8 November 1987.

Lomas, Jane, "Byblos Brits," in *The Observer* (London), 24 April 1988.

Cook, Cathy, "Boys Just Wanna Have Fun," in *Taxi* (New York), March 1989.

Racht, Tione, "Der Byblos Stil," in *Vogue* (Munich), March 1989.

Lobrano, Alexander, "Both Sides of Byblos," in the *Daily News Record* (New York), 19 June 1989.

*   *   *

Byblos takes its name from a hotel in St. Tropez, France. Since its inception in 1973, it has been a kind of international grand hotel of design, starting with a group of stylists, then engaging the Milanese Gianni Versace as designer 1975-76, then Frenchman Guy Paulin, and finally Keith Varty called from the Royal College of Art in London, via a period in Paris at Dorothée Bis, with Alan Cleaver. Varty and Cleaver have become the personification of Byblos objectives: a young line, international, with panache, and a carefree, optimistic nonchalance. In the 1980s the market-acute colorful palettes and relaxed resort-influenced informality of Cleaver and Varty for Byblos became a young *lingua franca* in fashion for the twenty-something and twenty-something generations. Together, Varty and Cleaver are as irresistible in person as their clothing design has proved to be: they seem to step out of a Somerset Maugham story, precocious and perspicacious English schoolboy adventurers travelling the world and absorbing ideas and visual design into an exuberant cultural colonialism at once laconic and vigorous, a passion about clothing evident in successive Byblos collections and manifest in the joy of the clothes, now available for women and men.

What Varty and Cleaver lack is any sense of the sinister or cynical: they are intent upon making clothing that is fun and exuberant. Varty described their design challenge to *Women's Wear Daily* in 1987, "Our product has to be salable, in the right fabrics with this young image and it's got to be fresh every season." The crux of the Cleaver-Varty achievement is color: they bring Matisse colors to clothing, can capture aubergines and gingers with a greengrocer's discrimination, and know the earth colors of every part of the globe with a geologist's imagination. *Daily News Record* (11 January 1989) rightly described the menswear: "Gold at the end of the rainbow. If anyone can make color successfully commercial, it's Keith Varty and Alan Cleaver for Byblos." They are to contemporary fashion what David Hockney is to contemporary art: British travel, observation, effervescence, and child-like delight in the world's bright colors. The American fashion press loves to call Varty and Cleaver "the Byblos boys" and they warrant the name in an irrepressible cheerfulness and delight that gives their clothing an upbeat mood that is its commercial success as well as its artistic signature.

Travel and exoticism is an important theme in Cleaver and Varty's work, reflecting their vacationing in Marrakech, their flirtations with Hawaii and the South Pacific, a recurring spirit of the American West (cowboys and Indian themes alike in womenswear, with cowboys especially applied in their menswear), menswear with the swagger of old-Havana *machismo,* and their love of tropical colors and refreshing prints inspired by southeast Asia, Oceania, and South America. In 1987 resort collections, the voyage was specific, with big skirts featuring postcards from the Bahamas and maps of islands. Fiesta brights are almost invariably featured in the spring and resort collections, with options for khaki, chocolates, mud, and tobacco brown. If the spring 1987 collections seemed like the British in India, their colonialism was mellowed by supple shapes, fluid lines, and khaki silk poplin. In 1988, the trek was to Russia in a savagely romantic display of fake fur, folkloric embroidery and motifs, and grand silhouettes that *Women's Wear Daily* (29 February 1988) called "Anna Karenina comes to Milan ...." Even their Russian collection, however, was no mere historicism or tourism: rich fabric combinations, pattern, and flamboyant shapes. It was as if all the extreme elements of peasant and Tsarist Russian fashion were distilled in select garments, redolent of the Russian novel, but also translated to the modern consumer in fake fur.

It seems unlikely that the sun will ever set on these two brilliant adventurers who have done so much to establish the Byblos style.

—Richard Martin

CACHAREL, Jean.

French designer

Born: Jean Louis Henri Bousquet in Nimes, 30 March 1932. **Education:** Studied at École Technique, Nimes, 1951-54. **Family:** Married Dominique Sarrut in 1956; children: Guillaume and Jessica. **Career:** Cutter and stylist, Jean Jourdan, Paris, 1955-57; founder and director, Société Jean Cacharel, women's ready-to-wear, from 1964; children's line added, early 1970s; perfume and jeans lines added, 1978; men's line added, 1994; fragrances: *Anais Anais*, 1978; *Loulou*, 1987; *Cacharel pour Homme*, 1991; *Eden*, 1994; cosmetics range introduced, 1991. **Awards:** Export Trade Oscar, Paris, 1969. **Address:** 3 Rue du Colisée, 30931 N mes, France.

Publications:

On CACHAREL:

Books

Lynam, Ruth, *Paris Fashion: The Great Designers and Their Creations,* London 1972.

Articles

Manser, José, "Cacharel's Rag Trade Riches," in *Design* (London), October 1969.
Contemporary Designers, London 1984.

*　　*　　*

Jean Cacharel became an established designer name in the mid-1960s when his fitted, printed, and striped shirts for women became fashion "must haves." So much so that by the end of the 1960s, French women did not go into a shop and ask for a shirt, they asked for a Cacharel. The reason for this was because until Cacharel began designing for women no one else had managed to produce a shirt that was flattering, comfortable and easy to wear.

Cacharel, Louis Henri Bousquet, came to Paris from Nimes in the mid-1950s, where he had apprenticed in men's tailoring. Adopting the name of Cacharel, which was taken from the Camargue's native wild duck, he moved into womenswear as a designer/cutter for Jean Jourdan, Paris. At that time womenswear was dominated by Parisian haute couture and the mass market took second place. Cacharel was one of the first designers to foresee a fashion future beyond the old monied clientèle and catered to an emerging new monied and fashion-conscious mass market. The strong emergence of youth culture in the 1950s and 1960s strengthened this vision.

Cacharel opened his own business at the end of the 1950s and employed Emmanuelle Khan as a stylist and designer. Together they created an image for the company that was very French, young, and sporty in fresh matching separates that were colourful, pretty and wearable.

Success was sealed in 1965 when Cacharel began working with Liberty of London. He rescaled and recoloured traditional floral prints so that they became softer and more flattering. Prints that had previously been scorned as frumpy and homely were transformed by Cacharel's cut and taste into snappy, feminine, and wearable clothes. Liberty of London has subsequently stocked and sold the Cacharel label for many years.

Further developments at Cacharel have included moves into licensing, mainly in jeans, socks, and bedlinen. Cacharel's sister-in-law, Corinne Grandval, joined the firm as designer in 1966. Continuing the feeling for young, trendy clothes, she also helped to introduce a successful mini couture line for children. This idea has since been widely copied and adapted by the mass market.

Jean Cacharel has the affable air of a country vet and enjoys spending much of his spare time at his country house. He is greatly inspired by travel and the cultures found in places like Japan, Mexico, Chile, and Paraguay. These cultural fusions are then softly moulded and filtered, to create his feminine, gentle yet sporty, looks. They are worn predominantly by a customer who is romantic and individual, who does not want to wear aggressive extremist fashion but adapts her Cacharel separates to express her individual taste and personality.

Cacharel is secure in his belief that his established customers recognize the essential classicism in his garments. When the fashion element has become superfluous, the ease and versatility of his clothes ensures a permanent place in any woman's wardrobe. This perhaps signifies Jean Cacharel's overriding contribution to fashion.

—Kevin Almond

CALUGI E GIANNELLI.

Italian design house

Founded in Florence, 1982, by Mauro Calugi (born 27 November 1941) and Danilo Giannelli (born 21 April 1957; *died 13 May 1987*). Incorporated, 1984; renamed Danilo Giannelli, SpA, c.1987. Principal designer, Mauro Calugi. **Exhibitions:** *Pitti Immagine Uoma,* Fortezza da Basso, Florence, 1985; *A Dress Beyond Fashion,* Palazzo Fortuny, Venicew, 1991. **Awards:** Ecco L'Italia (New York), 1985. **Address:** Via Catalani 28—Zona Industriale Bassa, 50050 Cerreto Guidi, Florence, Italy.

*　　*　　*

Calugi e Giannelli: Fall/Winter 1992/93.

Since beginning in 1982, Calugi e Giannelli has invented and re-invented clothing—menswear in particular—as if it were conceptual art. Arguably, Calugi e Giannelli clothing is an advanced art of the idea, often conveying avant-garde principles, frequently invoking and investing language and word play, and always bringing an edge to clothing. Formal properties matter, especially as they are developed from the properties of fabrics and fabric technology, most notably stretch, but the essence of a Calugi e Giannelli garment is its idea, or what 1993 press materials describe as "ironic temperament, a strong core and decisive taste." As playful as the Milanese Franco Moschino and as avant-gardist at the Parisian Jean-Paul Gaultier, Calugi e Giannelli's erudite conceptualism is accompanied by an equally strong sense of libido and sensuality. Transparency applied to textiles and the body becomes a *tour de force* of ideas for Calugi e Giannelli, but it also serves as a grand tour of erogenous zones. Pop Art is remembered, especially in the spring/summer 1991 collection, but when consumerism's systems and labels end up on tight swimwear and biker shorts, the equation of sex and consumption is only heightened. Both the Church and masculinity are special targets of Calugi e Giannelli satire and wit. A *leitmotif* of the collections is an interest in clerical dress subverted to secular clothing, with crosses and vestment details appearing again and again with schoolboy irreverence. Studded leather jackets are an over-the-top *machismo* that can only be interpreted as tongue-in-cheek. Calugi e Giannelli's work is always winning and not subject to the tiresome jokes of some sportswear: it is a fashion animated by fresh ideas and interpretive energy.

Learned and yet fun referencing to both dollar signs and hammer-and-sickle (spring/summer 1989), Arab motifs and script (spring/summer 1991), mocking motifs of ecclesiastical hats (fall/winter 1988-89), Tahiti and tattoos (spring/summer 1993), and tough biker leathers (fall/winter 1993-94) establish clothing as a widely referential, all-encompassing art. Singularly characteristic of the design's sartorial surrealism is the fall/winter 1988-89 anamorphic jacket with two lapels in which the exterior and interior, jacket and waistcoat, shell and marrow are purposely confused with resulting asymmetry and winsome disorder. A spring/summer 1988 double-collared shirt plays with the same uncertainties of the *doppelganger*. Art-like in its proposition, knowledgeable in its deliberate discords (snakeskin and lace together in spring/summer 1989), supremely sexy in its orientation, Calugi e Giannelli clothing sets a distinctive style in menswear.

While partner Danilo Giannelli died in 1987, the sensibility continued by Mauro Calugi has been seamless with the design duo's original objectives. Clothing is subject to aesthetic consideration. The fall/winter 1988-89 collection included a series of jackets with barbed wire motifs, introducing *faux* barbed wire at the shoulders or around the waist. In the seeming disparity of soft clothing and the fictive brutalism of barbed wire, Calugi e Giannelli displayed characteristic wit and irrepressible irony. In the same season, the "Violent Angels" leather jacket set metal plates with letters in continuous reading on a leather jacket: its diction is the continuous language of computer input; its effect is to put language onto the supposedly inarticulate form of the leather jacket. By such paradox, Calugi e Giannelli offers contradiction and incongruity about clothing, but also with an ideal of harmony and reconciliation. Even the language, redolent of Bruce Naumann and other artists, of the "Violent Angels" title, suggests the combination of the ferocious and the chaste.

Despite heady artistic purpose, Calugi e Giannelli clothing is well made and is never wearable art or craft. In fact, the interest in the basic templates of clothing arises in part from the preference in silhouettes for standard types, perfectly executed, and the knits and performance sportswear have the integrity of quality clothing. Detailing of embroidered suits, knit jackets with representational scenes, and sweaters with a range of illustration and image are consummately made; the lace T-shirts and jackets, and the tailored clothing with sudden apertures, have been copied in expensive and inferior versions, but the Calugi e Giannelli originals are beautifully made. The spring/summer 1988 block cutouts with sheer panels are a body peek-a-boo inflected with the design language of Piet Mondrian or Mark Rothko.

Menswear is the forum for Calugi e Giannelli ideas, though womenswear has also been produced. Perhaps menswear's accustomed reserve from fashion controversy and aggressive aesthetics lends itself to Calugi e Giannelli's definitive work in Mauro Calugi's insistence that fashion is an art of compelling dissent and dissonance that leads toward significant social and personal statement.

—Richard Martin

CAPELLINO, Ally. See **ALLY CAPELLINO.**

CAPUCCI, Roberto.

Italian designer

Born: Rome, 2 December 1930. **Education:** Attended Liceo Artistico and Accademia di Belle Arti, Rome, 1947-50. **Career:** Assisted designer Emilio Schuberth before opening first studio, Via Sistina, in Rome, 1950; opened Paris studio, in rue Cambon, 1962-68; returned to Rome and opened Via Gregoriana studio, 1968. Also costume designer for Pasolini's film *Teorema*, 1970, and for opera *Norma*, 1976, Verona. From 1982, designing only occasional fashion collections. **Exhibitions:** *Variété de la Mode 1786-1986*, Münchener Stadtmuseum, Munich, July 1986; *60 Years of Italian Cultural Life*, Columbia University, New York and Palazzo Venezia, Rome, 1986-87; *Fashion and Surrealism*, Victoria and Albert Museum, London, 1988; *Roberto Capucci: Art in Fashion—Volume, Colour and Method*, Palazzo Strozzi, Florence and Stadtmuseum, Munich, 1990; *Roben wie Rüstungen*, Kunsthistorisches Museum, Vienna, 1991. **Awards:** Medaglione d'Oro, Venice, 1956; Filene's Fashion Oscar, Boston, 1958; honoured by the Austrian Minister of Culture 1990. **Address:** Via Gregoriana 56, Rome, Italy.

Publications:

On CAPUCCI:

Books

Lambert, Eleanor, *World of Fashion: People, Places, Resources*, New York and London 1976.
Alfonsi, Maria-Vittoria, *Leaders in Fashion: i grandi personaggi della moda*, Bologna 1983.
Relang, Regina, *30 anni di moda*, Milan 1983.

Milbank, Caroline Rennolds, *Couture: The Great Designers,* New York 1985.

Buiazzi, Graziella, *La moda italiana,* Milan 1987.

Roberto Capucci: L'arte nella moda—colore, volume, metodo (exhibition catalogue), Fabbri Editore 1990.

Roberto Capucci: Roben wie Rüstungen (exhibition catalogue), Vienna 1991.

Articles

Pivano, Fernanda, "Roma alta moda: Roberto Capucci," in *Vogue* (Milan), September 1985.

"Roberto Capucci: Sontuose magie di un grande alchimista," in *Vogue* (Milan), March 1987.

Hume, Marion, "In Love with the Frill of It All," in *The Sunday Times* (London), 14 January 1990.

Gastell, Minnie, "A Solitary Artist," in *Donna* (Milan), March 1990.

Battaglia, Paolo, "Lo scenario per gli abiti scultura," in *Abitare con Arte* (Italy), May 1990.

Mölter, Veit, "Die Kunst der Mode," in *Parnassus* (Germany), July/August 1990.

Bertelli, "Quando la moda è arte," in *F.M.R.* (Italy), September 1990.

Celant, Germano, and Massimo Listri, "Roberto Capucci," in *Interview* (New York), September 1990.

Vergani, Guido, "Il sofà delle muse," in *Il Venerdì di Repubblica* (Rome), September 1990.

Hilderbrandt, Heike, "Florenze: Art and Fashion," in *Contemporanea* (Vienna), November 1990.

Plener, Doris, "Roben wie Rüstungen für Groâe Festlichkeiten," in *Die Presse* (Vienna), November 1990.

Kruntorad, Paul, "Drei Wiener Schaustücke Zur Gegenwart Von Harnischen," in *Der Standard* (Vienna), December 1990.

Morteo, Enrico, "Il lusso come ricerca," in *Domus* (Milan), February 1991.

Celant, Roberto, "Capucci," in *Interview* (New York), September 1991.

Wagner, Steven, "A Cut Above [Capucci]," *Town & Country* (New York), July 1994.

*

I first became curious about fashion as a child, when I observed, with a critical eye, the clothes worn by the women of my family. My talent for design and love of colour led me to art school, the Accademia delle Belle Arti, where I came into contact with art in its many forms.

Nature is my mentor. In my garden, quietly watching, with a child-like sense of fantasy, has helped to instill in me a sense of balance and a constant search for perfection, proportion, harmony, and colour. This has given me the strength to avoid being influenced by fashion trends.

Following my belief has enabled me to be true to myself, but this has meant renunciation. If my work lacks a commercial aspect, it is due not only to my desire for truth. For me, creating is a great experience and, while I would not have refused to diversify in my designs, the moment is not yet right.

Life is made up of encounters and I have had some memorable ones, although nothing that would significantly change my mind. In

this field, it is difficult to strike the right balance. To attempt a compromise between the will of the designer and that of the manufacturer inevitably leads to disappointment. On one side, industry takes a commercial stance; on the other the designer has an idealized view of fashion. Creating a design away from the reality of a woman, the dress has no form, it is merely a symbol.

The rock star, the television *soubrette,* everything comes down to appearance and show. Style and elegance have no place; they are merely seen as outdated rules. Today it is considered important to make an impact. The theatrical dress, the shocking dress, are simply following the trends. And the sexy dress—fashion has nothing to do with sexuality. Sexuality is something that belongs to the person, to one's body, but not with clothes.

Fashion today lacks culture. Newspapers, who should represent the means to transmit culture, often forget their responsibility to educate and inform. The role of the designer is not treated with respect. The photographer intrudes on the designer's creation with his own interpretation, wanting to modify and to change, forgetting that his own creativity is expressed through photography; the intensity of light, the composition, the setting. One must be able to recognize one's own ability to persevere. In my continuing quest for beauty and purity, I concentrate initially on the basic form. During this phase I do not want to be influenced by outside factors, and I think in black and white. Next comes colour, in all its intensity, blending with the pencil lines and producing the effect that I am looking for—faithful to my concept and to the women I am addressing. Only today is my work understood and accepted.

Because it is a work of luxury, it may be enjoyed by a few, but by those few who have a sense for luxury rather than the desire for ostentation and opulence. Luxury does not necessarily mean money. One can, perhaps, say that luxury is an art, like painting or sculpture, with its own scheme. To be inspired by art does not mean to imitate it, nor to establish a recognizable connection with it, but almost to fall in love with it. This is the feeling of culture for clothes and fashion which, as I said before, is sadly lacking today.

I am confident, nevertheless, that everyone wants to follow their own style rather than to conform.

—Roberto Capucci

*   *   *

One of Italy's most gifted and imaginative couturiers, Roberto Capucci has a select following of women who appreciate his architectural creations, and have the grand occasions on which to wear them. Having a Capucci wedding dress has long been the goal of fashionable brides looking for a special sense of shape and style. This is an uncommon couturier who shows infrequently, and produces only a few extraordinary designs for his clients.

The retrospective held at the Palazzo Strozzi in Florence in 1990 highlighted the variety of his genius and the sources of his art. The elegance of the 1950s shaped his concept of haute couture as an art form, and he has rigorously practiced it in that tradition. He has approached design as a form of architecture, building structures that the body can inhabit, and has rejected the arbitrary dictates of what might be momentarily fashionable. Instead, he deals with elements of design such as line, color, texture, and volume in a more abstract sense but always as they relate to the human body.

His sense of line can be found in the geometric planes imposed on the body and apparent both in his sketches and in the finished

Roberto Capucci: 1987; white satin dress bordered in black and green. *Photograph by Fiorenzo Niccoli.*

garments. The sketches show strong relationships with the work of the Italian Futurists, and some of his work has also been considered Surrealist. His second major source of inspiration draws from natural forms, where curvilinear volumes might refer to floral shapes while the linear, planar qualities might refer to crystalline structures. There can be no question of his mastery of the use of textiles. Crisp, lustrous silks are pleated and manipulated into moving, fluted sculptural forms; wools are cut and inlaid like mosaics. The care with which he works his materials into his humanly habitable structures ensures that they are wearable and that the finished garments are true to his original concepts. Many of the textiles are a combination of silk and wool, in fabrics with the weight and resilience needed to execute his complex volumes.

Capucci's sensitivity to color, or its absence, is equally impressive. In the black and white costumes, where the linear qualities are dominant, the absence of color is used for emphasis. One series of white silk crêpe dresses from 1980 have mask-like human faces sculpted into the structure of the sleeves, pockets, or bodice front. In combination, the use of black and white serves to make the spatial relationships even more effective. Instances of Capucci's dramatic use of color are to be found especially in the evening dresses of pleated silk taffeta. The brilliant colors, often juxtaposed in close harmonies, give added dimension to the linear effects.

The strength of Capucci's personality and his determination to remain true to his chosen art are obvious in his designs. His interest in seeking a variety of forums in which to display his work, for example the exhibition in Vienna that combined medieval armor with Capucci creations, demonstrates a creative approach to establishing a context for his work.

—Jean Druesedow

CARDIN, Pierre.

French designer

Born: Son of French parents, born in San Andrea da Barbara, Italy, 2 July 1922. **Education:** Studied architecture, Saint-Etienne, France. **Career:** Worked as a bookkeeper and as a tailor's cutter, Vichy, 1936-40; Apprentice, Manby men's tailor, Vichy, 1939; served in the Red Cross, World War II. Design assistant, working for the Madame Paquin and Elsa Schiaparelli fashion houses, Paris, 1945-46; head of workrooms, Christian Dior fashion house, Paris, 1946-50, helping to design "New Look" in 1947; founder-director and chief designer, Pierre Cardin fashion house, Paris, from 1950, presented first collection, 1951; opened up market in Japan, 1958; first ready-to-wear collection introduced, 1959; marketed own fabric, Cardine, 1968; children's collection introduced, 1969; holds more than 600 licenses. Also film costume designer from 1946; founder, Espace Cardin, 1970. **Exhibitions:** *Pierre Cardin: Past, Present and Future,* Victoria and Albert Museum, London, October-January 1990-91. **Awards:** *Sunday Times* International Fashion Award (London), 1963; Dé d'Or Award, 1977, 1979, 1982; named Chevalier de la Légion d'Honneur, 1983; Fashion Oscar, Paris, 1985; Foundation for Garment and Apparel Advancement Award, Tokyo, 1988; named Grand Officer, Order of Merit, Italy, 1988; named Honorary Ambassador to UNESCO, 1991. **Address:** 82 rue Faubourg Saint-Honoré, 75008 Paris, France.

Publications:

On CARDIN:

Books

Picken, Mary Brooks, and Dora L. Miller, *Dressmakers of France,* New York 1956.
Bender, Marylin, *The Beautiful People,* New York 1967.
Carter, Ernestine, *Magic Names of Fashion,* London 1980.
Pierre Cardin (exhibition catalogue), Tokyo 1982.
Milbank, Caroline Rennolds, *Couture: The Great Designers,* New York 1985.

Articles

d'Elme, Patrick. "Cardin: n'est il qu'un griffe?," in *La Galerie* (Paris), October 1971.
Sinclair, Serena, "Cardin," in Ruth Lynam, ed., *Couture: An Illustrated History of the Great Paris Designers and Their Creations,* New York 1972.
Parinaud, A., "Cardin Interviewed," in *Arts* (Paris), 11 September 1981.
Corbett, Patricia, "All About Cardin," in *Connoisseur* (London), January 1986.
Beurdley, Laurence, "Pierre Cardin fête ses quarante ans de création," in *L'Officiel* (Paris), May 1990.
Milbank, Caroline Rennolds, "Pierre Cardin," in *Vogue* (New York), September 1990.
Watt, Judith, "The World According to Pierre Cardin," in *The Guardian* (London), 24 September 1990.
Etherington-Smith, Meredith, "Pierre Pressure," in *The Correpondent Magazine* (London), 30 September 1990.
Bowles, Hamish, "Pierre the Great," in *Harpers & Queen* (London), October 1990.
McDowell, Colin, "The Pierre Show," in *The Daily Telegraph* (London), 6 October 1990.
Jeal, Nicola, "If the Suit Fits, Why Not Flog It?," in *The Observer* (London), 7 October 1990.
Rambali, Paul, "Pierre Cardin," in *Arena* (London), November 1990.
Niland, Seta, "Cardin Seeks to Widen Profile," in *Fashion Weekly* (London), 6 June 1991.
Pogoda, Dianne M., "Cardin Collection: Coming to America," in *Women's Wear Daily* (New York), 24 March 1992.

*   *   *

The shrewd entrepreneurial skills displayed by Pierre Cardin throughout his career have made him the world's richest fashion designer and a household name. A global phenomenon, he was the first designer to open up markets in Japan in 1958, China in 1978, and more recently Russia and Romania, applying the Cardin name to hundreds of products, from ties to alarm clocks and frying pans.

Cardin was the first designer to understand the potential of the business of fashion. His move into ready-to-wear in 1959 scandalized the Chambre Syndicale, the monitoring body of haute couture in Paris, and he was expelled from its ranks for what was essentially an attempt to make designer clothes more accessible, and also displaying an astute sense of where the real money to be made in fashion lay.

From his earliest work for the House of Dior up to the 1950s, Cardin displays an interest in the sculptural qualities of cut and construction that are still his trademarks in the 1990s. Cardin produces garments of a hard-edged minimalism, backed up by exquisite techniques of tailoring that he manipulates to produce sparse, geometric garments offset by huge collars and bizarre accessories such as the vinyl torso decoration he introduced in 1968.

His designs resist the rounded curves of the traditional female body, aided by his use of materials such as heavyweight wool and jersey rib, creating clothing that stands away from the body thereby producing its own structural outline. From the balloon dress of 1959 that delineated the body only at the pull of a drawstring at the hem, through the geometrically blocked shifts of the 1960s to his series of hooped dresses in the 1980s, Cardin describes the underlying form of the body obliquely, creating planes that intersect with, yet somehow remain disconnected from, the body itself.

Cardin's embrace of the romance of science and technology, together with the notion of progress that seemed so inherent in the two in the 1960s, was expressed in his 1964 Space Age Collection, which featured white knitted catsuits, tabards worn over leggings, and tubular dresses and more generally in his interest in man-made fibres. He created his own fabric, Cardine, in 1968, a bonded, uncrushable fibre incorporating raised geometric patterns.

Cardin's curiously asexual designs for women in the 1960s remained so even when making direct reference to the breast by the use of cones, outlines, cutouts, and moulding. Similarly, the exposure of the legs afforded by his minis was desexed by the models wearing thick opaque or patterned tights and thigh-high boots. Experiments with the application of paper cutout techniques to fabric with which Cardin was preoccupied in the 1960s were replaced in the 1970s by more fluid materials such as single angora jersey and the techniques of sunray and accordion pleating. A spiralling rather than geometric line began to be more noticeable and Cardin became renowned for his frothy evening dresses of layered, printed chiffon while continuing his experimentation with a series of unusual sleevehead designs.

Cardin was the first post-war designer to challenge London's Savile Row in the production of menswear. The high buttoned collarless jackets worn by the Beatles became *de rigueur* for the fashionable man in the 1960s and provided a relaxed yet elegant look when combined with a turtleneck sweater. Cardin, by paring away collars and relinquishing pockets, broke with tradition to create a new look for men realizing that the male suit, once a bastion of tradition, could be high fashion too.

Although merchandising and licensing his name may have overshadowed his influence as a fashion designer in recent years, Cardin's inventiveness and technical flair should not be underestimated.

—Caroline Cox

CARNEGIE, Hattie.

American designer

Born: Henrietta Kanengeiser in Vienna, 1889. **Family:** Married third husband, John Zanft, in 1928. **Career:** Left school at age 11 and moved with parents to New York, 1900; established as Carnegie—Ladies Hatter, 1909; opened custom dress-making salon, 1918; offered Paris models after first buying trip to Europe,

1919; opened East 49th St. building to sell own label, imports, and millinery, 1925; added ready-to-wear, 1928; Hattie Carnegie Originals carried in stores throughout the United States by 1934; custom salon closed, 1965. **Awards:** Neiman Marcus Award, 1939; Coty American Fashion Critics Award, 1948. *Died* (in New York City) *22 February 1956.*

Publications:

On CARNEGIE:

Books

New York and Hollywood Fashion: Costume Designs from the Brooklyn Museum Collection, New York 1986.
Milbank, Caroline Rennolds, *New York Fashion: The Evolution of American Style,* New York 1989.
Steele, Valerie, *Women of Fashion: Twentieth Century Design,* New York 1991.

Articles

"Luxury, Inc.," in *Vogue* (New York), 15 April 1928.
"Hattie Carnegie," in *Current Biography* (New York), October 1942.
Bauer, Hambla, "Hot Fashions by Hattie," in *Collier's* (Philadelphia), 16 April 1949.
"Hattie Carnegie" (obituary), in the *New York Times,* 23 February 1956.

*   *   *

For decades Hattie Carnegie's personal taste and fashion sense influenced the styles worn by countless American women. Whether they bought her imported Paris models, the custom designs, the ready-to-wear collections, or the mass market copies of her work, women welcomed Carnegie's discreet good taste as a guarantee of sophistication and propriety. Carnegie's business ability and fashion acumen enabled her to build a small millinery shop into a wholesale and retail clothing and accessory empire and made her name synonymous with American high fashion for almost half a century.

Carnegie's place in fashion history is assured not because of her own designs, but because of her talent for choosing or refining the designs of others. Between the World Wars, the list of couturiers whose models she imported included Lanvin, Vionnet, Molyneux, and Mainbocher—classic stylists—but also select creations for Chanel and Patou, Schiaparelli, and Charles James. In fact, Carnegie claimed in a *Collier's* article (16 April 1949) to have had a three-year unauthorized exclusive on selling Vionnet models in the early 1920s, a few years before Vionnet started selling "to the trade."

The Custom Salon was generally considered to be the heart of the Hattie Carnegie operation, since it was with made-to-order fashion that Carnegie began. The focus of her business was to interpret European style for American consumers, but the sense of dress that she chose to champion was not contained in the minutiae of design. It was instead an approach to fashion that emphasized consummate polish in every outfit. Norman Norell, who was with Carnegie from 1928 to 1940 (primarily as a ready-to-wear designer), remarked in *American Fashion* (Sarah Tomerlin Lee, ed., New York 1975) that he often worked from models that Miss Carnegie had brought back from Paris. He could legitimately claim, however, that he had imprinted his own signature on his designs for the firm, and it is often possible to make an informed attribution of Hattie Carnegie styles to her other designers. Certainly one gown featured in a 1939 magazine layout is recognizably the work of Claire McCardell, who spent two years with the firm. Others who worked for Carnegie were Emmett Joyce, Travis Banton, Pauline Trigère, Jean Louis, James Galanos, and Gustave Tassell.

Carnegie was already established as a taste-maker by the time she added the ready-to-wear division to her company in the 1920s. "Vogue points from Hattie Carnegie" contained her style tips and forecasts for *Vogue* readers. At the Hattie Carnegie salon, a customer could accessorize her day and evening ensembles with furs, hats, handbags, gloves, lingerie, jewelry, and even cosmetics and perfume, everything, in fact, but shoes.

The Carnegie customer, whatever her age, seems to have been neither girlish nor matronly, but possessed of a certain decorousness. Even the casual clothing in the Spectator Sportswear and Jeunes Filles ready-to-wear departments was elegant rather than playful. The Carnegie Suit, usually an ensemble with dressmaker details in luxury fabrics, traditionally opened her seasonal showings. She often stressed the importance of black as a wardrobe basic, both for day and evening, but was also famous for a shade known as "Carnegie blue." Perhaps Carnegie's preference for 18th-century furnishings in her home relates to the devotion of formality so clearly expressed in her business.

During World War II Carnegie was an impressive bearer of the standard of the haute couture. French style leadership was unavailable, and designs from her custom salon took pride of place in fashion magazines and on the stage, as in the original production of *State of the Union* by Lindsay and Crouse. Carnegie's leadership was also important to other fashion industries. She had always used fabrics from the best American textile companies, and continued to patronize specialty firms such as Hafner Associates and Onondaga Silks, which were not immersed in war work. She also used fabrics designed and hand printed by Brook Cadwallader, and continued to do so after French materials again became available. Only after Carnegie's death did the company claim to use exclusively imported fabrics.

Hattie Carnegie died in 1956. The fashion empire she had built survived into the 1970s, but in 1965 the custom salon was closed and the company concentrated on wholesale businesses. The informal youth culture of the 1960s and 1970s was ill suited to the type of clothing and client that had made Hattie Carnegie's reputation. The strength of her personal identification with the company made it difficult for the company to succeed without her at its head, and it quickly lost ground to the younger taste-makers who emerged in the 1960s.

—Madelyn Shaw

CARPENTIER, Suzie. See **MAD CARPENTIER.**

CARVEN.

French fashion house

Established by Mme Carven Mallet in Paris, 1945; Carven Scarves and Carven Junior lines launched, 1955; Kinglenes and Kisslenes

sweater collections introduced, 1956; neckwear collection introduced, 1957; swimwear collection introduced, 1965; fur collection introduced, 1966; jewelry collection, Ma Fille line for children and line of blouses introduced, 1968; Monsieur Carven boutique opened, Paris, 1985. Perfumes: *Ma Griffe,* 1948, *Robe d'un Soir,* 1948, *Chasse Gardée,* 1950, *Vetiver,* 1957, *Vert et Blanc,* 1958, *Madame,* 1980, and *Guirlandes,* 1982. Also designed uniforms for Air India, 1965, S.A.S., 1966, Aerolineas Argentinas, 1967, and Air France, 1978. **Exhibitions:** retrospective, Paris, 1986. **Awards:** Chevalier de la Légion d'Honneur, 1964, Grande Medaille des Arts et Lettres, 1978. **Address:** 6 rond-point des Champs-Elysées, 75008 Paris, France.

Publications:

On CARVEN:

Books

Perkins, Alice K., *Paris Couturiers and Milliners,* New York 1949.
Bertin, Celia, *Paris à la Mode,* London 1956.
Picken, Mary Brooks, *Dressmakers of France,* New York 1959.

Articles

"Carven Stages RTW Comeback with a Collection for Spring," in *Women's Wear Daily* (New York), 7 August 1989.
Aillaud, Charlotte, "Madame Carven: Eighteenth Century Splendor in Her Avenue Foch House," in *Architectural Digest* (Los Angeles), September 1989.

*   *   *

In 1949, when Jacqueline François sang of "Les robes de chez Carven" in her immortal song, *Mademoiselle de Paris,* the clothes of Madame Carven embodied all the charm, gaiety, and beauty of the city of Paris and its fabled women in the magical period after the war. The 1950s are seen as the Golden Age of the haute couture in Paris and Carven is regarded as having been one of its primary practitioners. She is still actively designing and while Carven's vast array of licensed products, from perfume to golfwear, have been distributed throughout the world, her name is not one that is immediately recognized in America. Perhaps this is because she has never sought to shock or create trends or to follow the whims of fashion. The single conceptual basis for her work has always been to create beautiful clothes for all women, but in particular women of petite size: "I felt that I was small, and the contemporary taste for tall mannequins combined with my own admiration for Hollywood stars ended up giving me a complex. At the age of 25 I was a *coquette.* France was learning to dance again after the war and I wanted to be slinky. This desire to be attractive inspired a few reflections. First I noticed that I wasn't the only petite woman I knew, and that the grand couturiers weren't very interested in us. But I had a feeling for proportion and volume. All that remained for me to do was to create, with the help of friends who were scarcely taller than I was, dresses that would allow us to be ourselves.... I'd found an opening where there was no competition and a moment when Paris was overflowing with happiness."

Carven's designs from the late 1940s through the early 1960s, while conforming to the prevailing stylistic tendencies of the period, are distinguished by the delicate decorative detail that flatters

Madame Carven.

the wearer without overwhelming her. Trims at collar and cuff are frequently executed in all variations of white lace and embroidery. Occasionally coolly plain white linen collar and cuffs assert the propriety of the wearer while enhancing an image of chic self-assurance. White on white is a recurring theme in Carven's designs as evident in an evening dress of 1950 in which an embroidery of white *fleurs de Mai* completely covers a white bustier and asymmetrical long skirt, supported by a white halter and pleated underskirt. A bouffant skirted afternoon dress with a closely fitted top from 1954 is executed in white linen subtly embroidered with white flowers, almost as if the dress were created from a fine tablecloth. Another recurring design motif is the use of fabrics and embroideries that shade from light to dark (*dégrader* in French), thus subtly enhancing the wearer's figure and stature.

Carven was one of the first designers to promote her clothes in foreign countries, presenting her collections in Brazil, Mexico, Egypt, Turkey, and Iran. These travels greatly influenced her designs. After a trip to Egypt she introduced a tightly gathered type of drapery to her evening designs which mimicked ancient Egyptian gowns: a design of 1952 shows a bodice of sinuous gathers closely outlining the body in white jersey that, under beaded fringe at the hip reminiscent of a belly dancer's jeweled belt, breaks loose into a long flowing skirt. Another dress of 1952 is covered with an all-over design of Aztec inspired motifs. An entire collection in 1959 was inspired by the beauties of Spain, as seen in paintings by Velazquez.

Today the Carven label can be found throughout the world as a result of extensive distribution of licensed products and especially Carven's perfume *Ma Griffe,* in its familiar white and green packag-

ing. Madame Carven always includes a signature white and green dress in her collections which, to this day, stand for a tasteful style of charm and beauty that complements the wearer no matter her proportions.

—Alan E. Rosenberg

CASAGRANDE, Adele. See FENDI.

CASELY-HAYFORD, Joe.

British designer

Born: Kent, England, 24 May 1956. **Education:** Trained at Tailor and Cutter Academy, London, 1974-75, St. Martin's School of Art, 1975-79, and history of art, Institute of Contemporary Arts, London, 1979-80. **Family:** Married Maria Casely-Hayford, 1 August 1980. **Career:** Designer of stage outfits for rock groups and stars including The Clash, Black Uhuru, Lou Reed, and U2, from 1984. Casely-Hayford designs appear in Derek Jarman's film *Edward II,* 1991. Designed hosiery range for Sock Shop chain, London, 1991. Commissioned to design clothes for ballet *Very,* by Jonathan Burrows, 1992. Established diffusion line, Hayford, 1992. Flagship boutique opened, 34 Tavistock Street, London, 1993. Also, freelance designer in Italy for Panchetti label, and Britain, for Joseph and Top Shop chain. **Exhibitions:** *Street Style,* Victoria and Albert Museum, London, November 1994-February 1995. **Address:** 128 Shoreditch High Street, London E1 6JE, England.

Publications:

By CASELY-HAYFORD:

Articles

Casely-Hayford, Joe, "Bovril Babes," *The Face* (London), June 1992.
Casely-Hayford, Joe, "Fashion," in *The Face* (London), December 1993.
Casely-Hayford, Joe, "Urban Nomad," *i-D* (London), The Urgent Issue.
Casely-Hayford, Joe, "A Question of Culture," in *i-D* (London), The Strength Issue.
"Year Review of Fashion," in *i-D* (London), January 1994.

On CASELY-HAYFORD:

Articles

"New Talent," in *Harpers & Queen,* September 1985.
"Da Londra, moda come provocazione: Eclectics," in *L'Uomo Vogue* (Milan), December 1985.
McCooey, Meriel, "East Side Story," in *The Sunday Times Magazine* (London), 27 April 1986.

Joe Casely-Hayford: Fall/Winter 1994/95.

DuCann, Charlotte, "Independent Style: Young British Design," in *Vogue* (London), November 1986.

"Shooting Stars," in *Women's Journal* (London), February 1988.

Bain, Sally, "British Designer Preview," in *Draper's Record* (London), 5 March 1988.

Yusuf, Nilgin, "The New Order of Nights," in *Elle* (London), December 1988.

Profile of Joe Casely-Hayford, in *Details Magazine,* February 1989.

Profile of Joe Casely-Hayford, in *The Observer,* 12 March 1989.

Samuel, Kathryn, "Designer of the Year," in *The Sunday Telegraph,* 15 October 1989.

Griggs, Barbara, "The Italian Connection," in *Vogue,* May 1990.

"Joe Casely-Hayford," in *Clothes Show* (London), March 1991.

Rodgers, Toni, "Double Vision," in *Elle* (London), March 1991.

Clarke, Adrian, "Black Panther," in *Fashion Weekly* (London), 14 March 1991.

Profile of Joe Casely-Hayford, in *The Guardian,* 22 April 1991.

"Five Cut Loose (And Ties Will Not Be Worn)," in *The Independent* (London), 22 August 1991.

Profile of Joe Casely-Hayford, in *The Glasgow Herald,* 9 October 1991.

"Fashion Warriors Set Sights on Impact," in *The Independent* (London), 17 February 1992.

"Joe Casely's Costume Karma," in *The Weekly Journal* (London), 23 May 1992.

Profile on Joe Casely-Hayford, in *Collezioni,* January/February 1993.

Tredre, Roger, "In the Black-White-Rock-Fashion World," in *The Independent Weekend* (London) 13 February 1993.

Schacknat, Karin, "Joe Casely-Hayford: Pure vormals ultieme doel," in *Kunsten de!* (Arnhem), May 1993.

Rawlinson, Richard, "Top Shop Signs Up Joe Casely-Hayford," in *Fashion Weekly* (London), 22 July 1993.

Alford, Lucinda, "Hey Joe!," in *The Observer Review* (London), 22 August 1993.

Profile of Joe Casely-Hayford, in *Manchester Evening News,* October 1993.

Tulloch, Carol, "Rebel without a Pause: Black Street Style and Black Designers," in Juliet Ash and Elizabeth Wilson (eds.), *Chic Thrills, A Fashion Reader,* Berkeley, California 1993.

Scott, Alexander, "Platform, Rusty New Ideas," in *The Ticket* (London), June 1994.

*   *   *

The traditional design tenets of quality fabric, attention to detail, and excellent cut underpin all of Joe Casely-Hayford's work. This is not to deny the surprise of his designs, which often have unusual details of decoration or spicy colour combinations to enliven them. His clothes are for the discerning customer, who wants styles to retain their appeal for more than one season. They are always very contemporary in feel, while rarely following fashion fads. Although returning to his skilful pleating and cutting of traditional wool fabrics for classic suits each season, his influences are wide ranging. He can just as stylishly redefine 1970s wide-collar coats as create American Indian-style soft leather jackets.

His menswear is perhaps his perennial *tour de force.* Always interesting and innovative, his collections are a combination of highly desirable good quality with witty detailing. His clean-cut wool suits will be given a stylish twist through pleating or cutout lapels with curling velvet inserts, making them more individual. His designs may reveal a certain amount of anarchic licence in their cut, but he is never cultish or unwearable, carefully balancing the elements in his work with his original vision to make clothes with a long lifespan. Even his more experimental garments, like the all-in-one suit he created in the late 1980s, which looked like a two-piece from the front but had a battledress back, still have a beauty in their fit and the refined finish that distinguishes all his work.

Having arrived on the wave of the exciting new art school-trained British designers that included John Richmond and John Galliano, he has remained dedicated to increasing Britain's fashion standing on the international market. Although he is part of "5th Circle," set up in August 1991 to showcase the menswear of five homegrown designers, he is equally committed to his womenswear collection. This has just the same strength of cut and clarity of design, often initiating ideas that are later taken up by others, as with the bra tops of his early shows that were later to flood the market, and the hot coloured patchwork suede wide-collar jackets, long coats, and hotpants he used that heralded the 1970s revival of the early 1990s.

His clothes for women have a sexy feel with sculpted leather waistcoats and neatly fitted suits alongside funky knitwear and simple yet sophisticated dresses, each with the usual Casely-Hayford twist marking out their design. His designs are complemented by the seasonal addition of interesting and unusual footwear created for the London shoeshop chain Shelly's.

Casely-Hayford has quietly built a niche for himself in British fashion as a master of cut. His clothes have a longevity of appeal, while maintaining style and well-balanced beauty through the combination of each element of design, providing carefully thought-out garments that flatter the wearer with their witty detail and consistently good fit.

—Rebecca Arnold

CASHIN, Bonnie.

American designer

Born: Oakland, California, 1915. **Education:** Studied at the Art Students League, New York, and also in Paris. **Career:** Costume designer, Roxy Theater, New York, 1934-37; designer, Adler and Adler sportswear, New York, 1937-43 and 1949-52; costume designer, 20th Century Fox, Los Angeles, California, 1943-49; designer, Bonnie Cashin Designs (with partner Phillip Sills), New York, 1953-77; established The Knittery, 1972; founder, Innovative Design Fund, c.1981. **Exhibitions:** Brooklyn Museum, 1962 (retrospective). **Awards:** Neiman Marcus Award, Dallas, Texas, 1950; Coty American Fashion Critics Award, New York, 1950, 1960, 1961, 1968, 1972; Sporting Look Award, 1958; Philadelphia Museum College of Art Citation, 1959; Woolknit Associates Design Award, 1959, 1961; Lighthouse Award, 1961; Sports Illustrated Award, 1963; Detroit Business Association, National Award, 1963; *The Sunday Times* International Fashion Award, London, 1964; Leather Industries American Handbag Designer Award, 1968, 1976; Kaufmann Fashion Award, Pittsburgh, 1968; Creator Citation, Saks Fifth Avenue, 1969; Mary Mount College Golden Needle Award, 1970; I. Magnin's Great American Award, 1974; The American Fashion Award for Furs, 1975; Drexel University Citation, Philadelphia, 1976.

Publications:

On CASHIN:

Books

Williams, Beryl, *Young Faces in Fashion,* Philadelphia, Pennsylvania 1956.

Levin, Phyllis Lee, *The Wheels of Fashion,* Garden City, New York 1965.

Carter, Ernestine, *The Changing World of Fashion: 1900 to the Present,* London 1977.

Milbank, Caroline Rennolds, *Couture: The Great Designers,* New York 1985.

New York and Hollywood Fashion: Costume Designs from the Brooklyn Museum Collection, New York 1986.

Maeder, Edward, et al., *Hollywood and History: Costume Design in Film,* New York 1987.

Milbank, Caroline Rennolds, *New York Style: The Evolution of Fashion,* New York 1989.

Leese, Elizabeth, *Costume Design in the Movies,* New York 1991.

Steele, Valerie, *Women of Fashion,* New York 1991.

Articles

"Bonnie Cashin: Trail Blazer in Fashion," in *American Fabrics* (New York) 1956.

Reily, Robert, "Bonnie Cashin Retrospective," in *American Fabrics and Fashions* (New York), No. 60, 1963.

"Bonnie Cashin," in *Current Biography* (New York), May 1970.

"Round Table: Bonnie Cashin," in *American Fabrics and Fashions* (Columbia, South Carolina), No. 133, 1985.

Elliott, Mary C. "Bonnie Cashin: Design for Living," in *Threads* (Newtown, Connecticut), Oct./Nov. 1990.

Weir, June, "Natural History," in *Mirabella* (New York), January 1995.

*   *   *

An awareness of the body in motion informs Bonnie Cashin's design style. Her earliest efforts were created for dancers: as a California high school student, Cashin costumed the local ballet troupe. Only two years later she became the house costumer for New York's famed Roxy Theater. There, her brief was to design three sets of costumes a week for the Roxy's chorus of 24 dancing showgirls. With minimal budgets, Cashin used her ingenuity, a little paint, and a knowledge of cut learned from her dressmaker mother to transform inexpensive fabrics into striking costumes that looked equally graceful in motion or in repose. Whether for stage or street, Cashin's work has always been styled for the active woman on the move, who prefers an easy, individual look with a minimum of fuss. The May 1970 issue of *Current Biography* (New York) quotes her: "All I want is to speak simply in my designing; I don't want the gilt and the glamor."

A 1937 production number, in which the Roxy dancers emerged smartly dressed from between the pages of a fashion magazine, sent Cashin in a new direction. Louis Adler, co-owner of the sportswear firm Adler and Adler, saw Cashin's designs and recognized her potential importance to the fashion industry. Wary of the garment district's regimentation, Cashin initially played it safe. She stayed on in the familiar collegial world of the theater and free-lanced for

Adler. Eventually she signed with the firm for whom she designed for approximately 12 years before and after World War II. In 1950, during her second stint at Adler and Adler, Cashin won both the Neiman Marcus Award and the first of five Coty Awards for a prototype of her signature *Noh* coat, an unlined, sleeved or sleeveless T-shaped coat with deeply cut armholes to wear singly, in combination, or under a poncho or cape.

Despite this success, Cashin sensed that she would never achieve her creative best working under contract in the profit oriented canyons of Seventh Avenue. In 1953 she began designing on a freelance basis from her studio. Unusual for the time, she worked on a royalty basis, creating complete coordinated wardrobes—accessories, knits, capes and coats, dresses and separates—to be combined in layers to suit the climate or the event.

Cashin typically worked years ahead of the market, pioneering clothing concepts which today seem part of fashion's essential vocabulary. In the 1950s, when most women's clothing was concerned with structure, the Cashin silhouette was based on the rectangle or the square and called for a minimum of darting and seaming. Bonnie Cashin showed layered dressing long before the concept became a universal option; she brought canvas boots and raincoats out of the show ring and into the street in 1952 and she introduced jumpsuits as early as 1956.

Signature pieces include her *Noh* coats, funnel-necked sweaters whose neck doubles as a hood, classic ponchos and such innovations as a bicycle sweater with roomy back pockets. Other Cashin hallmarks are her use of toggle closures and leather bindings. Indeed, Bonnie Cashin is often credited with having revived leather and suede as materials suitable for couture.

Very likely because of her early work in the theater, both color and especially texture play a starring role in Cashin's designs. An organza *Noh* coat may be trimmed with linen and shown over a sweater dress of cashmere. A jersey sheath may be paired with an apron-wrap skirt cut from a boisterous tweed. Her palette is both subtle and controlled: earth tones, sparked with vivid accents.

Bonnie Cashin worked to her own brief, forming a collaboration with women who were smart, active, and, like herself, of independent mind. She designed for the self-aware woman who asked that her clothes be practical, comfortable, and stylish.

—Whitney Blausen

CASSINI, Oleg.

American designer

Born: Oleg Loiewski in Paris of Russian parents, 11 April 1913; raised in Florence; adopted mother's family name, Cassini, in 1937. **Education:** Attended English Catholic School, Florence. Studied at Accademia delle Belle Arti, Florence, 1931-34; political science, University of Florence, 1932-34. **Military Service:** Served five years with U.S. Army Cavalry during World War II. **Family:** Married Merry Fahrney in 1938 (divorced); married the film actress Gene Tierney in 1941 (divorced, 1952); daughters: Daria and Christina. **Career:** After working in mother's Maison de Couture in Florence, opened own Maison de Couture in Rome; sketch artist, Patou, Paris, 1935; immigrated to the United States in 1936, naturalized, 1942; design assistant to couturier Jo Copeland, New York, 1936; designer, William Bass, New York, 1937, and James

Oleg Cassini: Floor-length sheath gown stitched with white sequins.

Rotherberg Inc., New York, 1938-39; New York salon, Oleg Inc., established, 1937-39; owner of Cassini fashion studio, New York, 1939-40; designer, Paramount Pictures, Los Angeles, 1939-42; designer under contract with Twentieth Century Fox, Los Angeles, 1940. Owner of Cassini Dardick fashion firm, New York, 1947-50: established Oleg Cassini Inc., New York, 1950; appointed official designer to U.S. First Lady Jackie Kennedy, early 1960s; established ready-to-wear business, Milan, mid-1963; returned to New York, designed tennis clothes for Munsingwear and swimwear for Waterclothes under own label, 1974; introduced new fragrance line, *A Love That Never Ends,* 1990. **Awards:** Has received numerous awards, including five first prizes, Mostra della Moda, Turin, 1934; Honorary Doctor of Fine Arts, International College of Fine Arts, Miami, 1989. **Address:** 3 West 57th Street, New York, New York 10019, USA.

Publications:

By CASSINI:

Books

Pay the Price, New York 1983.
In My Own Fashion, New York 1987.

On CASSINI:

Books

Bender, Marylin, *The Beautiful People,* New York 1967.
Milbank, Caroline Rennolds, *New York Fashion: The Evolution of American Style,* New York 1989.
Leese, Elizabeth, *Costume Design in the Movies,* New York 1991.

Articles

"Oleg Cassini," in *Current Biography* (New York), July 1961.
"Oleg Cassini, un couturier collectionneur de femmes," in *Elle* (Paris), 25 October 1987.
Tedeschi, Mark, "Cassini's Career—Straight Out of a Hemingway Novel," in *Footwear News* (New York), 17 December 1990.
"Oleg Cassini Comes to Town," in *Clothes Show* (London), December 1991.
"The Charm of First Lady's Man Oleg Cassini Shines On," in *Vogue* (London), December 1991.

*   *   *

Oleg Cassini has had an extremely varied, glamorous, and exotic career but is perhaps best known for the personal style and clothing he developed when official designer for the U.S. First Lady Jacqueline Kennedy in 1961. He worked closely with Mrs. Kennedy, a personal friend, and together they created many widely copied garments that have since become American fashion classics and that firmly established Kennedy as a style leader. She frequently wore a fawn wool two-piece outfit, a dress and a waist-length semi-fitted jacket or coat with a removable round neck collar of Russian sable, often topped by the famous pillbox hats created by Halston. Another outfit was a high-necked silk ottoman empire-line evening gown that gently flared in an A-line to the floor. Jacqueline Kennedy's vast public exposure proved a huge boost for Cassini's profile and brought worldwide attention to American fashion in general.

Cassini was born a count and was brought up by Italian/Russian parents in Florence, where his mother ran an exclusive dress shop. He began his career in 1934 by making small one-off designs sold through his mother's shop. He moved to New York in 1936 and worked for several Seventh Avenue manufacturers before joining Twentieth-Century Fox in Hollywood as a costume designer in 1940. He worked for several major film studios and created glamorous clothes for many film stars, even marrying one, Gene Tierney.

In 1950 the designer opened Oleg Cassini Inc., his ready-to-wear dress firm in New York, with 100 thousand dollars worth of backing. Femininity quickly became the keyword when describing his work. He produced dresses made from soft, romantic fabrics like lace, taffeta, point d'esprit, and chiffon. He popularized ladylike fashion innovations, such as the A line, the smart little white collared dress, the sheath, the knitted suit, and dresses with minute waistlines. Military details such as brass buttons and braid were also popular features. In the 1960s the Cassini look evolved to incorporate ease and simplicity. The straight, lined cocktail and evening dresses popularized by Jackie Kennedy were customer favourites, as were his plain and boxy jacket suits.

Retiring from his ready-to-wear and couture business in 1963, Cassini's next venture was a ready-to-wear business in partnership with his brother Igor. He presented a menswear collection for the first time, breaking tradition by introducing colour to shirts that had previously nearly always been white, and teaming them with traditional three-piece suits.

Today Cassini is president of a vast organization, exporting to over 20 countries. The company produces innumerable accessory products including cravats, luggage, children's clothes, make-up, shoes, umbrellas, and perfumes.

—Kevin Almond

CASTELBAJAC, Jean-Charles de
French designer

Born: Of French parents in Casablanca, Morocco, 28 November 1949. **Education:** Attended Catholic boarding schools in France, 1955-66; studied law, Faculté de Droit, Limoges, 1966-77. **Family:** Married Katherine Lee Chambers, 1979; children: two sons, Guillaume and Louis. **Career:** Founder and designer, with his mother Jeanne-Blanche de Castelbajac, of Ko and Co, ready-to-wear fashion company, Limoges, beginning in 1968; free-lanced for Pierre d'Alby, Max Mara, Jesus Jeans, Etam, Gadgling, Julie Latour, Fusano, Amaraggi, Carel Shoes, Ellesse, Hilton, Levi-Strauss, and Reynaud, beginning in 1968; director, Jean-Charles de Castelbajac label, Paris, 1970, and Societe Jean-Charles de Castelbajac SARL, Paris, 1978; established boutiques in Paris, New York, and Tokyo, 1975-76. Also designed for film and stage, including Elton John, Talking Heads, and Rod Stewart, beginning in 1976; interior and furniture designs, beginning in 1979. Member of Didier Grumbach's Les Createurs group of designers, Paris, 1974-77. **Exhibitions:** Centre Georges Pompidou, Paris, 1978; Forum Design, Linz, Austria, 1980; Laforet Museum, Belgium, 1984. **Collections:** Musée du Costume, Paris; Fashion Institute of Technology, New York. **Addresses:** 188 rue de Rivoli, 75001 Paris, France; 55 rue de Lisbonne, 75008 Paris, France.

Publications:

On CASTELBAJAC:

Books

Carter, Ernestine, *The Changing World of Fashion,* London 1977.
Who's Who in Fashion, Karl Strute and Theodor Doelken, ed.,
    Zurich 1982.
Delpais, Delbourg, *Le Chic et la Mode,* Paris 1982.
McDowell, Colin, *McDowell's Directory of Twentieth Century Fashion,* London 1984.
O'Hara, Georgina, *The Encyclopaedia of Fashion from 1940 to the 1980s,* London 1986.

Articles

"Un styliste bourree d'idees: Jean-Charles de Castelbajac," in *Gap*
    (Paris), October 1975.
"Jean-Charles de Castelbajac: French Revolutionary," in *GQ* (New
    York), April 1981.

*   *   *

If color produces optimism, then Jean-Charles de Castelbajac is
the most optimistic designer in existence. Void of lux rhinestones or
glitz, his collection features color to luxuriate the world. The designer will not only clothe people in color but create an environmental lifestyle, with everything from sofas, to crystal, to carpets.

Castelbajac is a man of passions—for form and function, for
color, for comfort and protection—and therein lies the basis of this
humanistic designer. Castelbajac began his obsession by cutting his
first garment out of a blanket from boarding school. Because the
material already existed, he was left to play only with the form.
Many times each year he returns to this first gesture, cutting the
cloth, so he remains close to its essence and function.

Recently titled Marquis, Castelbajac has erected the first monument to celebrate the living in Paris: one hundred and fifty thousand
names of young people are inscribed on a steel totem pole to support Castelbajac's project to give inspiration and a sense of worth
to a generation so used to growing up with war memorials celebrating the dead. Despite his interest in youth, he has always been
involved with heroes and heritage, but he is never archaic in his
designs. Castelbajac is a man of the future, but he does not make
futuristic clothing. His designs fulfill the need for practical and
unassuming fashion of maximum quality. While favoring natural
textures and fibers, Castelbajac creates designs that are innovative
but respectful of the classics; he has been called a modern traditionalist. And now, designing the collections of André Courrèges, the
futuristic designer who marked the 1960s, Castelbajac has managed
successfully to rejuvenate the original spirit of Courrèges clothes.

Castelbajac's fondness for architecture is apparent in the harmonious, architectonic shapes that flow through every collection. He
has a great affinity with painters, with whom he spends much time
to strengthen his creative impulses. Having a strong revulsion to
prints on garments, he humorously solved the predicament by using large scale motifs of Tom and Jerry, or phrases from Nerval or
Barbey d'Aurevilly inscribed on silk, for very simply shaped
dresses. At other times his garments are filled with angels, or medieval and heraldic motifs, or childlike inscriptions drawn with the
skill of an artistic adult but with the imagination of a child.

The inscription of Cervantes in Jean-Charles de Castelbajac's
book published in 1993 reads: "Always hold the hand of the child
you once were." His clothing and his art are identifiable by his
manner of being true to himself, that is, by being profoundly human
and knowing something that is not only style.

—Andrea Arsenault

CATALINA SPORTSWEAR.

American sportswear firm

Founded in 1907 by John C. Bentz as Bentz Knitting Mills, manufacturing underwear and sweaters. Renamed Pacific Knitting Mills,
1912, Catalina Knitting Mills, 1928, and Catalina, from 1955. Knitted swimwear introduced, 1912. Principal divisions include children's
and junior swimwear, misses' swimwear, misses' sportswear, and
men's swimwear and sportswear. Originated Miss Universe Pageant, 1952. Company purchased by Kayser-Roth apparel division
of Gulf and Western Company, 1975. **Awards:** Los Angeles Chamber of Commerce Golden 44 Award, 1979. **Address:** 6040 Bandini
Boulevard, Los Angeles, California 90040, USA.

Publications:

On CATALINA:

Books

Lencek, Lina, and Gideon Bosker, *Making Waves: Swimsuits and
    the Undressing of America,* San Francisco 1989.
Koda, Harold, and Richard Martin, *Splash! A History of Swimwear,*
    New York 1990.

Articles

Ross, Adele, "Catalina: A Giant Need Not Be Inflexible," in *Cali-
    fornia Apparel News* (Los Angeles), 1 October 1976.
"Catalina," in *Apparel Industry Magazine* (Atlanta, Georgia), De-
    cember 1984.
Shaffer, Gina, "Catalina Charts New Course," in *Man,* January
    1985.

*   *   *

Catalina Sportswear evolved from an obscure California knitting
mill into a world-leading swimwear manufacturer, reigning from the
1930s through the early 1990s.

The United States and Eastern Europe experienced a physical
fitness and sports craze in the 1920s and 1930s. Catalina, along
with Jantzen in Oregon, shrewdly and stylishly propelled West
Coast fashion into prominence as they filled the growing need for
active outdoor clothes, especially swimwear.

Their early wool knit suits, patterned after a simple one piece
style introduced to the United States by Australian swim star
Annette Kellerman, allowed women new freedom in the water. They
also challenged and broke down the Edwardian modesty codes. In
the 1920s, Catalina produced increasingly baring and fashionable as

well as functional swimwear, notably, the boldly striped Chicken Suit, men's Speed Suit, and Ribstitch S suits.

Catalina incorporated new fabrics into its products as fast as technology developed them. When Lastex, the rubber cored thread, appeared in the 1930s, Catalina advertised the LA or "Lastex Appeal" in men's swim trunks. Lastex and Spandex, and Vyrene Spandex in the 1960s, would provide the elasticity and shaping power under and in combination with knits, cotton, velour, Celanese Rayon, DuPont Antron, nylon, and Lycra fabrics.

Particularly in the 1930s and 1940s the company had a symbiotic relationship with Hollywood. Warner Bros costume designer Orry Kelly and film color consultant and make-up man Perc Westmore designed for Catalina. Starlets and stars like Ginger Rogers, Joan Crawford, Ronald Reagan, and Marilyn Monroe were photographed in Catalina sportswear for advertising and publicity purposes. Such shots boosted the stars, the California mystique, pool and beach business, and Catalina sales. Catalina's influence was also intertwined with the myth and icon of the Miss America Beauty Pageant. When the company sponsored the contest in the 1940s, contestants wore essentially off-the-rack Catalina suits, except that pageant suits had the flying fish logo on both hips instead of one. Catalina dropped sponsorship of Miss America in 1950 and went on to found the Miss USA, Miss Teen USA, and Miss Universe pageants and co-sponsored them until 1993. Since 1960 television beamed contestants wearing Catalina styles with gold embroidered flying fish to worldwide audiences. Catalina's participation in these two fashion and body conscious fixtures in American culture exemplifies an underlying *modus operandi* to design suits that allowed women and men to show off their bodies in a fashionable, abbreviated, yet socially acceptable garment.

In its long history, Catalina experienced bursts of innovative flair and attracted high profile design talent. Swimwear designer Elizabeth Stewart went on to found her own company. During Lee Hogan Cass's term as fashion director, specially commissioned patterns in European-inspired browns and innovative citrus batiks delighted consumers. Jacquard knit suits and casual wear in bright colors were a hit in Italy. Bikini-clad Europeans sought the maker of an innovative Grecian pleated suit seen on the Riviera.

Fashion editors of the better magazines paid close attention to Gustave Tassell's swimwear and coverups. After the boned and corseted 1950s suits, his natural styles without bra cups were a hit with the New York *cognoscenti,* including Diana Vreeland, as were the soft cup designs by Edith Stenbeck. Frank Smith, who went on to head Evan Picone for Saks Fifth Avenue, designed women's sportswear for Catalina. John Norman, later with Vogue and Butterick patterns, designed menswear. Menswear tended toward the country club look, at times showing influences of Pierre Cardin. The Sweethearts in Swimsuits line in the 1950s offered his and hers matching swimsuits and accessories.

Catalina successfully expanded its lines to appeal to the widest possible audience, offering knits, menswear, children's, Catalina Jr, sporting gear, and classic and trendy styles. The company had a knack of producing well-made mainstream fashions that sold in high volume and allowed average buyers to feel stylish and comfortable.

In recent decades many lines were conservative versions of revealing trendmakers. At times they went head to head with the competition, countering Body Glove's slick neons with Underwets while the slimming Contour Suit was the answer to Jantzen's 5 lbs Under line. Considering its ability to adapt, especially through many changes in ownership, perhaps its logo should have been the chameleon, rather than a fish.

Until its bankruptcy in 1993 Catalina was a keystone in the California swim and sportswear industry and sustained worldwide influence. It started as an early 20th-century swimwear pioneer and remained an important player in the American fashion industry. Finally, Catalina fashions significantly contributed to women's athletic liberation and the propagation of the Hollywood and California looks as well as molding and perpetuating beauty pageant culture.

—Debra Regan Cleveland

CAUMONT, Jean Baptiste.

French designer working in Italy

Born: Pau, France, 24 October 1932. **Education:** Studied fine art in Paris. **Career:** Design assistant, Balmain, Paris, and free-lance illustrator, *Vogue, Femina, Album du Figaro,* and *Marie-Claire,* late 1950s; textile consultant, Legler; design consultant, La Rinascente stores, Italy; designer and coordinator, Apem, 1960-63; design consultancies in Italy and France, including Christian Dior boutique, and others; moved to Milan, 1963; designed for Rosier, 1963-66; designed own ready-to-wear with own label, from 1965, and for Confezioni Amica, Treviso; first show in Milan, then New York, in 1966. Caumont S.r.L. founded with Paolo Russo in Treviso, Italy, 1968; knitwear line for men, then women, introduced, 1968-69; men's ready-to-wear collection, Monsieur Caumont introduced, 1970. Signed contract with Gruppo Finanziario Tessile, producing exclusive menswear line for Canada and U.S. In 1986, production of clothes and accessories began in Italy, for American market. Boutiques opened in Milan, Tokyo, and New York. Perfume line *Jib* launched. **Awards:** Oscar from Rome fashion school; Oscar from Store Palacio de Ierro, Mexico. **Address:** Corso Venezia 44, 20121 Milan, Italy.

Publications:

On CAUMONT:

Books

Mulassano, Adriana, *The Who's Who of Italian Fashion,* Florence 1979.
Khornak, Lucille, *Fashion 2001,* New York 1982.

Articles

de la Falaise, Maxime, "Right for the Moment: Jean Baptiste Caumont," in *Interview,* January 1980.
Moor, Jonathan, "Caumont: Classic Renegade," in *DNR: The Magazine* (New York), 28 January 1980.
"Champion a l'étranger," *Madame Figaro* (Paris), No. 12471.
Scio, Marie Louise, "Four Stars to Caumont and Missoni," *International Daily News.*

*   *   *

Throughout his long career, Jean Baptiste Caumont has never wavered from his original vision: classic, sophisticated ready-to-wear clothing and accessories for men and women. Beginning with his first women's collection in 1966, Caumont has consistently delivered stylish, refined sportswear, knits, leather, and evening clothes aimed at the well-bred customer who wants a look of elegance and ease devoid of affectation.

A Frenchman originally from the Basque country, Caumont is based in Italy. He was one of the original group of designers (Walter Albini, Cadette, Krizia, Missoni, and Ken Scott) who broke with the Italian fashion industry in Florence and brought Milan into the limelight. His first foray into womenswear was quickly followed by men's knits and then a complete menswear collection. As his reputation as a tastemaker grew, his business continued to expand, including luggage, handbags, shoes, jewelry, and other goods. But Caumont continued to adhere strictly to his notion of line, form, craftsmanship, and control, creating clothing and accessories using rich fabrics, elegance of cut and richness of color, never sacrificing quality to mass production no matter how fast his fortunes grew.

Caumont has often looked to the past for inspiration for his classic styles. He has been particularly drawn to the styles worn by the wealthy during the early twentieth century, clothes that might have been worn on Grand Tour holidays or at exclusive resorts. But these references are used only to conjure a mood—never for slavish revival. Some design sources, for example, have been the glamour of luxury travel on the Orient Express, the prim uniforms of English schoolgirls, and the natty men's silk smoking jacket. But instead of degenerating into clichés, in Caumont's capable hands these sources were translated into great sweeping fur and leather coats, classy traditional sportswear separates, and oversized quilted evening coats for women, respectively.

In keeping with his taste for clothes that suggest patrician nonchalance, Caumont's trench coats, suits, blazers, and other sporty looks for men and women are frequently fashioned of richly-textured tweeds, houndstooth, and glen plaids. His daytime looks often feature layering, using wools and cashmere for pullovers and sweaterjackets for colder weather, linen and silk for summer/resort wear. For evening he favors unabashed luxury, with soft silks and crepe de chine. Whatever the occasion, the telling Caumont signature is understatement—these are clothes that signal their high quality with quiet restraint.

Caumont's devotion to subdued luxury has also resulted in the use of a relatively pared-down palette. Early collections were nearly

Jean Baptiste Caumont.

monochromatic, with black, gray, and white punctuated very occasionally by a dash of red. Otherwise, he has shown a predilection for earth tones, marrying various camels, beiges, and tans to create subtly harmonious variations on a theme. It was only after many seasons that he began to experiment with brighter hues, tropical tones, and bolder prints, as fashion dictates in the 1970s began to loosen the notion of proper palettes for men and women.

Caumont places much more emphasis on style than fashion. "Fashion is a thing of the moment," he has said. "Fashion is a gimmick. Who can afford to pay for a gimmick?" During the 1980s, his design philosophy paid off, as the trend toward elegance and glamour placed Caumont yet again at the forefront. His menswear—combining his hybrid talent for Italian tailoring, French lines, and English coloring—was especially well-received as being fresh, comfortable, and eminently wearable. The Caumont look, a worldly and sophisticated one, was considered at once timeless and yet essentially Milanese, embodying the urbane chic for which that Italian center of fashion is known.

Jean Baptiste Caumont designs for himself and others of his kind: well-travelled, well-heeled clients who believe in a refined and understated way of life. Not a true fashion innovator, he has nonetheless found his niche as a designer: clothes that bespeak of elegance, gentility, and propriety, and are never out of style.

—Kathleen Paton

CERRUTI, Nino.

Italian designer

Born: Biella, Italy, in 1930. **Career:** General manager for family textile firm (founded 1881), Cerruti Brothers, Biella, from 1950. Hitman men's ready-to-wear line introduced, 1957; knitwear line introduced, 1963; first menswear collection presented in Paris, opened Cerruti 1881 boutique, Paris, and launched unisex clothing line, 1967; women's ready-to-wear added, 1976. Fragrances include *Nino Cerruti Pour Homme,* 1978, *Cerruti Fair Play,* 1984, *Nino Cerruti Pour Femme,* 1987, and *1881,* 1988. **Awards:** Bath Museum of Costume Dress of the Year Award, England 1978; Cutty Sark award, 1982, 1988; Pitti Uomo award, Italy, 1986. **Address:** 3 place de la Madeleine, 75008 Paris, France.

Publications:

On CERRUTI:

Books

Mulassano, Adriana, *The Who's Who of Italian Fashion,* Florence 1979.

Articles

Crome, Erica, "Nino Cerruti: Designers of Influence No. 2," in *Vogue* (London), December 1978.
Hicks, Sheila, and Barbara Grib, "Nino Cerruti," in *American Fabrics and Fashions* (New York), No. 127, 1982.
Menkes, Suzy, "King of the Supple Suit," in *The Times* (London), 11 November 1986.

"Buon Anniversario," in *Profession Textile,* 18 September 1987.
"Nino Cerruti Refined," in *Esquire* (New York), September 1987.
Watt, Judith, "By Design," in *For Him* (London), Autumn 1989.
Tredre, Roger, "Nino, the Wardrobe Master," in *The Independent* (London), 9 August 1990.
"Biella," supplement to *L'Uomo Vogue* (Milan), November 1990.
Fiedelholtz, Sara, "Escada Sees Good Year for Cerruti Collection," in *Women's Wear Daily* (New York), 13 May 1993.
Morche, Pascal, "Eleganze der Hoflichkelit," in *Manner Vogue* (Wesseling, Germany), August 1993.

                              *   *   *

Nino Cerruti's life could be the most dramatic narrative of the post-World War II Italian renaissance. *L'Uomo Vogue* (November 1990) declared: "Nino Cerruti, a name synonymous with modern restraint. Industrialist-designer, one of the founding fathers of Italian fashion...." Assuming control of his family's mills as a young man of 20, he transformed the staid business of textile mills that had been significant for generations in the textile-producing region of Biella, Italy. Cerruti saw the quiet revolutionary possibility of a vertical operation, a kind that other Italian textiles companies would later pursue with astounding success, following Cerruti's model. According to Adriana Mulassano (*The Who's Who of Italian Fashion,* 1979), in the 1950s "he earned the fame as a fashion madmam for his ventures and publicity in textiles and fashion denounced as cheap Americana." His sensibility was immediately for fashion, rather than for the traditionalism of textiles manufacturing. In fashion, Cerruti prefers the streamlined, near-industrial design in tailoring applied to richly textured fabrics.

Ironically, Cerruti's fashion madness was short-lived. His first men's ready-to-wear line Hitman was launched in 1957, he showed unisex clothing in 1967, and opened his Cerruti 1881 boutique in Paris on the Rue Royale, off the Place de la Madeleine, in 1967. His icons are distinguished dates and places; tradition abides in the stable factors of 1881 and his elective association with Paris. Mulassano argues for a kind of vanguard genius about Cerruti: "Among those working for him (and perhaps even outside) there might be those who still think he's crazy. Perhaps it is the fate of the avant-garde, of those who know that the mind guides the hand, to be perennially misunderstood." It is Mulassano, however, who misunderstands Cerruti. He is the businessman-designer, not the raw-talent creative; he displays the tempered intelligence of vertical operations and commercial acumen. He is involved today in the fragrances and advertising not out of unremitting creativity but out of the controlling perspicacity of business. The raging revolutionary of the 1950s and 1960s has mellowed into the judicious businessman of the 1980s and 1990s as his model has been so fully copied by others, both in menswear and in women's clothing. He reflected to *Esquire* (September 1987): "I like to describe my operation as a modern version of the handcraft *bodegas* of centuries ago. It is important to know each link in the chain. I consider myself still very close to the theory of industrial design: using modern technology to reach the market. It's a very modern challenge: the continuous harmonization between the rational or scientific world and the emotional or artistic world." Cerruti projects an impeccable harmony.

His fall-winter 1993-94 menswear collections were shown in Paris with none of the histrionics of some menswear presentations. He kept in his tailored clothing to his simple principle: "A man should look important when he wears a suit," allowing for the unconstricted jackets of the period, but rendering them with sufficient solidity to avoid being too limp for the office. He showed the prevailing elongated three-button single-breasted look of Giorgio Armani and others. One can always tell, however, that Cerruti is a man of cloth: his menswear fabrics are so textural, in pebbled and oatmeal grains, and so luxurious in their handling. The touch of history that the dates of the mills' foundations convey is one of traditional authority, one that is palpable in the clothing. Cerruti has experimented with dandies and even designed Jack Nicholson's costumes in the movie *The Witches of Eastwick* and costume for *Philadelphia* (1993), but anyone can experiment. Nonetheless, Cerruti has made his mark with the restraint of his clothes. His principal effort in menswear takes advantage of the thriving vertical operations that he commands from mills to clothing to advertising and promotion and related products. Mulassano is, in fact, much more on target when she recognizes Nino Cerruti is what is commonly known as an "enlightened businessman." To wit, there is Cerruti's 1987 statement to *Esquire:* "I think that innovation and fancy are essential to daily life. But my clothes are designed to be real. It's easy to indulge in decadence in fashion, but I don't think that's meaningful. The world has been full of enough of that."

If Cerruti exemplifies post-war Italy, perhaps in his judiciousness, cautious good taste, and reversion to his own basic values, he exemplifies Everyman. He foresaw menswear's future in *L'Uomo Vogue* in 1990: "A fashion that will be more refined and yet at the same time more everyday. In other words, a greater desire for authenticity, a traditionally elegant simplicity that doesn't smack too much of fashion."

—Richard Martin

CESARANI, Sal.

American designer

Born: New York, 25 September 1939. **Education:** Studied design at the Fashion Institute of Technology, New York, 1959-61. **Family:** Married Nancy Cesarani, 1961; children: Lisa, Christopher. **Career:** Junior designer, Bobby Brooks, New York, 1961-63; fashion display coordinator, Paul Stuart menswear store, New York, 1964-69; merchandising director, Polo by Ralph Lauren, 1970-72; designer, Country Britches, New York, 1973-75; designer, Stanley Blacker, New York, 1975-76; Cesarani Ltd., New York, formed, 1976, women's collection introduced, 1977; company closed, c.1978-80, reorganized, 1980-88, as Cesarani division for Jaymar Ruby; formed licensing agreements with Hartmarx, 1987-88, Corbin, 1989, Britches of Georgetowne, 1991, and Japan Toray Diplomode; leather bag collection for Ace Luggage launched, 1992; eyeglass collection for Nanamua Co. launched, 1992; designer, Cesarani and SJC Concepts Inc, from 1993; childrenswear collection for Matsuta Co. launched, 1993; menswear collection for Thomas Co. Inc. launched, 1994. Also: Designer of menswear and sportswear for Thomas Co. Inc., in Japan; Cesarani shops opened in Japanese retailers Matsuya, Seer and Tobu, 1972. **Exhibitions:** Institute of the Metropolitan Museum of Art, 1995. **Awards:** Special Coty Award for Menswear, 1974, 1975; Coty Award for Menswear, 1976; Fashion Group Award of Boston, 1977; Coty Return Award, 1982. **Address:** 40 East 80th Street, New York, New York 10021, USA.

Publications:

On CESARANI:

Articles

Guerin, Ann, "Spotlight on Sal Cesarani," in *Playbill,* November 1977.
"Sal Cesarani: Tradition Missing," in *GQ* (New York), January 1982.
Staetter, Suzanne, "Cesarani Collection Is Just for Certain Women," in the *Houston Chronicle* (Texas), 12 December 1984.
Lane, Dotty, "Cesarani Designs for the International Man," in *Record-Courier,* 20 August 1993.
Boies, Elaine, "Clothes for the Well-Dressed Man," in *Staten Island Advance,* 3 June 1994.

*   *   *

To the earthbound, Sal Cesarani's menswear might be traditional or even historicist. For the dreamer, the wanderer, or the imaginer, Cesarani's evocative and romantic apparel epitomizes and condenses the perfect past. Like a Cindy Sherman portrait, Cesarani's work is seldom a precise equivalent, but gains its power from its suggestive resemblance and its ultimate inability to be classified into the past, so powerful are its connections and so focused is its originality. Extracting a nonchalance from American style between the wars and an *élan* from English aristocracy in its palmier days, Cesarani possesses the transportative power of Merchant-Ivory film or the revery of Golden Age Hollywood, yearning and so nearly sublime. Were Cesarani merely offering history and a wardrobe inventory that is of grandfathers and imagined heroes, we would be respectful, but not, I think, captivated. Cesarani realizes that history in clothing is like the visual history that Walter Benjamin postulated: we gain enhanced historicity, the contingency and added valuing of history, from the new historical horizons of adaptations of the traditional with subtle change.

Cesarani refutes our 20th-century predisposition to think that menswear is mundane. Rather, he gives sentimental spirit to the classic templates of 20th-century menswear. Having worked both as a designer for Polo/Ralph Lauren and Stanley Blacker and for a while as a menswear coordinator at Paul Stuart, Cesarani has consistently emphasized styling and the adventuresome ensemble of clothing. Sportswear and tailored clothing, tennis separates, classic tuxedos with debonair slouches of the 1930s and 1940s, and the looser cuts and drape of Hollywood chic evoking Gary Cooper and Cary Grant characterize Cesarani's style. True, not every man realizes the harmony of proportions of C.S. Bull or Hurrell heroes, but each Cesarani client is capable of some aspiration to such pictorial grace.

When he re-initiated a tailored clothing line in 1993, Cesarani's Trans-Atlantic collection was not only Anglo-American, but as suggestive as a crossing on the *Normandie.* Redolent of the 1930s and 1940s, the collection employed separate vests with lapels, pattern mixes of herringbones, glen plaids, and other standard elements, and a very cool look with the amplitude of 1930s and 1940s styles. What is exceptional about Cesarani is his sense of the fashion composition and modification: the slight eccentricity of a peak lapel on a single-breasted jacket or tartan blazer paired with evening separates is enough to evoke memory, but also to jostle it, making the clothing fresh again.

Sal Cesarani: Spring 1994. *Photograph by Richard Reed.*

Key to Cesarani's sensibility, in addition to his Paul Stuart fashion styling, is his work as a design assistant to Ralph Lauren. If Lauren condenses nostalgia into an impacted sentiment more perfect than any real world that has ever existed, Cesarani creates a fictive, movie-star desire, the fantasy of men's clothing and nonchalant style. Like Lauren, his is a study in composition, offering some components perfectly regular, more than are at first sight conventional and only later are realized as extreme, and a few that suggest special flourish.

As a designer, Cesarani has displayed a special gift for understanding the market: in the 1990s, both his ties and his later tailored clothing came at the right moment for a renewed classicism, rejecting, for example, the earlier print ties of Armani and other designers for rep ties and tiny pattern. These more understated ties then were composed into imaginative ensemble dressing with the grand patterns of vests, mixed slacks, and jackets. "I perceive," said the designer, "each piece of the collection as a component of man's personal style, to be worn and combined according to his own needs." If Cesarani invents a menswear that is never tedious, it is because it is graphically conceived, understood as each element to be a consummate piece eventually to be coordinated in the man's wardrobe. His penchant for vintage perfection and superb, unerring editing and styling of collections of the wardrobe is akin to Ralph Lauren's, though Cesarani tends to greater fullness and drape as well as a greater informality, to say nothing of more congenial prices.

While Cesarani has also designed women's clothing, inspired by his success in menswear, his attainment as a designer is to project an image of men's informal grace in the tradition of Leyendecker, urbane Hollywood of the 1930s and 1940s, and of archetypal sportswear presented in luxurious fabrics. In choosing the most compelling images of modern menswear as his avatars, Cesarani realizes the inherent trait of menswear—even more than fashion for women—to honor the traditional and concomitantly to offer an involving, evolving renewal and refinement.

—Richard Martin

CHAMPION.

American sportswear manufacturer

Founded by Abe and Bill Fainbloom, 1919. **Address:** 3141 Monroe Avenue, Rochester, New York 14618, U.S.A.

Publications:

On CHAMPION:

Articles

Arlen, Jeffrey, "Champion Brands Overseas Markets," in *Daily News Record,* 18 April 1985.

Murray, Kathy, "Thanks for the Advice," in *Forbes,* 2 May 1988.

Robb, Gregory A., "Champion Products Accepts Bid," in *New York Times,* 14 February 1989.

Berger, Warren, "Champion Starts to Show Its True Colors Off the Field," in *Adweek's Marketing Week,* 23 April 1990.

Sterne, Hilary, "Honest Sweats: Champion's Cotton Shirts Are the Real McCoy," in *Gentlemen's Quarterly* (New York), May 1992.

Leibowitz, David S., "Two Cases Where Quality Will Out," in *Financial World,* 23 June 1992.

Phalon, Richard, "Walking Billboards," in *Forbes,* 7 December 1992.

*   *   *   *

Champion Products have always catered to the customer who wants to get an ease of movement out of their apparel. Since the company's inception in 1919, by brothers Abe and Bill Fainbloom, it has been supplying sweatshirts to students and athletes alike.

The company's utilitarian roots made it one of the largest suppliers of athletic and lifestyle apparel in the world. Champion has even evolved into a brand name that kids ask for in this age of generic designer sportswear. Along with such companies as British Knights, Reebok, Cross Colours, and Nautico, Champion shares the distinction of being the hottest, hip-hot name around.

It's the serious athlete who is the tried and true fan of Champion Products, however. The company's reverse weave sweatshirts and trousers, imprinted logo T-shirts and nylon mesh tanks, to name a few items, are supplied to hundreds of intercollegiate and high school level athletic programs to use as both practise and competition uniforms.

In 1992, the United States Olympic basketball team named Champion its official supplier of practise and game uniforms. It's quite a compliment to be included at the competition of some of the world's top athletes.

Another reason for the popularity of the Champion sweatshirts is the way they take wear and tear. Durability may be one main reason why the Champion name is so popular with the consumer. As these garments age, they become more comfortable and valued. It has been said that a Champion sweatshirt is at its best after it has been worn vigorously for about four years, even sported with holes and frayed areas, the sign of a vintage Champion. Its owner understands the value of time-worn traditions, especially when it comes to the blood, sweat, and tears it probably took to break in this particular athletic garment.

—Lisa Marsh

CHANEL, "Coco" Gabriel Bonheur.

French designer

Born: Saumur, the Auvergne, France, 19 August 1883. **Education:** Educated at convent orphanage, Aubazine, 1895-1900, and at convent school, Moulins, 1900-02. **Career:** Clerk, Au Sans Pareil hosiery shop, Moulins, 1902-04; café-concert singer, using nickname "Coco," in Moulins and Vichy, 1905-08; lived with Etienne Balsan, Château de Royalieu and in Paris, 1908-09; established millinery and women's fashion house with sponsorship of Arthur "Boy" Cappel, in Paris, 1913, later in rue Cambon, Paris, 1928; established fashion shops in Deauville, 1913, Biarritz, 1916; fragrance, *No. 5,* marketed from 1921; other fragrances include *No. 22,* 1921, *Cuir de Russie,* 1924, *No. 19,* 1970, and from House of Chanel, *Cristalle,* 1974, *Coco,* 1984, and *Egoïste* for men, 1990. Rue Cambon headquarters closed during World War II, re-opened, relaunching Chanel's work, 1954, and continued after her death. Also stage costume designer, 1912-37, and film costume designer, 1931-62. Lived as exile in Lausanne, 1945-53. **Exhibitions:** *Les*

Grands Couturiers Parisiens 1910-1939, Musée du Costume, Paris, 1965; *Fashion: An Anthology,* Victoria and Albert Museum, London, 1971; *The Tens, Twenties, Thirties,* Metropolitan Museum of Art, New York, 1977. **Awards:** Neiman Marcus Award, Dallas, 1957; *Sunday Times* International Fashion Award, London, 1963. *Died* (in Paris) *10 January 1971.* **Address:** 29-31 rue Cambon, 75001 Paris, France.

Publications:

On CHANEL:

Books

Crawford, M. D. C., *The Ways of Fashion,* New York 1948.

Baillen, Claude, *Chanel solitaire,* Paris 1971, London 1973.

Haedrich, Michael, *Coco Chanel secrète,* Paris 1971, published as *Coco Chanel: Her Life, Her Secrets,* Boston 1972.

Galante, Pierre, *Les années Chanel,* Paris 1972, published as *Mademoiselle Chanel,* Chicago 1973.

Charles-Roux, Edmonde, *L'irrégulière, ou mon itinéraire Chanel,* Paris 1974, published as *Chanel, Her Life, Her World,* New York 1975, London 1976.

Morand, Paul, *L'allure de Chanel,* Paris 1976.

Charles-Roux, Edmonde, *Chanel and Her World,* Paris 1979, London 1981.

Delay, Claude, *Chanel solitaire,* Paris 1983.

The Polytechnic, *Coco Chanel,* Brighton 1984.

Milbank, Caroline Rennolds, *Couture: The Great Designers,* New York 1985.

Haedrich, Marcel, *Coco Chanel,* Paris 1987.

Leymarie, Jean, *Chanel,* New York 1987.

Charles-Roux, Edmonde, *Chanel,* London 1989.

Kennett, Frances, *Coco: the Life and Loves of Gabrielle Chanel,* London 1989.

Grumbach, Lilian, *Chanel m'a dit,* Paris 1990.

Madsen, Axel, *Chanel, A Woman of Her Own,* New York 1990.

Steele, Valerie, *Women of Fashion: Twentieth-Century Designers,* New York 1991.

Mackrell, Alice, *Coco Chanel,* New York 1992.

Articles

"Obituary: Gabrielle Chanel," in *The Times* (London), 12 January 1971.

"Chanel No. 1," in *Time* (New York), 25 January 1971.

Asley, Iris, "Coco," in Ruth Lynam, ed., *Couture: An Illustrated History of the Great Paris Designers and Their Creations,* New York 1972.

Shaeffer, Claire, "The Comfortable Side of Couture," in *Threads* (Newtown, Connecticut), June/July 1989.

Kazanjian, Dodie, "Chanel Suit," in *Vogue* (New York), August 1990.

Fedii, Daniela, "Coco la ribelle," in *Elle* (Milan), November 1990.

Steele, Valerie, "Chanel in Context," in Juliet Ash and Elizabeth Wilson, eds., *Chic Thrills, A Fashion Reader,* Berkeley, California 1993.

Collins, Amy Fine, "Haute Coco," in *Vanity Fair* (New York), June 1994.

Menkes, Suzy, "Strong Chanel Holds Up Couture's Falling Walls," in *International Herald Tribune* (Paris), 21 March 1995.

Spindler, Amy M. "Lagerfeld Tones Down the Look at Chanel," in the *New York Times,* 21 March 1995.

"Chanel: The Naughty Professor," in *Women's Wear Daily* (New York), 21 March 1995.

* * *

A woman of ambition and determination, Gabrielle Chanel, nicknamed "Coco," rose from humble beginnings and an unhappy childhood to become one of this century's most prominent couturiers, prevailing for nearly half a century.

In contrast to the opulent elegance of the *belle époque,* Chanel's designs were based on simplicity and elegance. She introduced relaxed dressing expressing the aspirations of the 20th-century woman, replacing impractical clothing with functional styling.

Chanel's early years tend to be vague in detail, being full of inaccuracies and contradictions, due to her deliberate concealment of her deprived childhood. It is generally accepted that Chanel gained some dressmaking and millinery experience prior to working in a hat shop in Deauville, France. Using her skills as a milliner she opened shops in Paris, Deauville, and Biarritz with the financial assistance of a backer. Chanel was an astute businesswoman and skilful publicist, quickly expanding her work to include skirts, jerseys in stockinette jersey, and accessories.

Chanel, recognized as the designer of the 1920s, initiated an era of casual dressing, appropriate to the occasion, for relaxed outdoor clothing created to be worn in comfort and without constricting corsets, liberating women with loosely fitting garments. Her style is that of uncluttered simplicity, incorporating practical details. She dressed the modern woman in clothes for a lifestyle.

In 1916 Chanel introduced jersey, a soft elasticated knit previously only used for undergarments, as the new fashion fabric. Wool jersey produced softer, lighter clothing with uncluttered fluid lines. She made simple jersey dresses in navy and grey, cut to flatter the figure rather than to emphasize and distort the natural body shape. The demand for her new non-conformist designs by the wealthy was so great and the use of jersey so successful that Chanel extended her range, creating her own jersey fabric designs, which were manufactured by Rodier.

Highly original in her concept of design, Chanel ceaselessly borrowed ideas from the male wardrobe, combining masculine tailoring with women's clothing. Her suits are precise but remain untailored, with flowing lines, retaining considerable individuality and simple elegance. Riding breeches, wide-legged trousers, blazers, and sweaters were all taken and adapted.

A major force in introducing and establishing common sense and understated simplicity into womenswear, Chanel's coordination of the cardigan, worn with a classic straight skirt, has become a standard combination of wearable separates. Chanel produced the cardigan in tweed and jersey fabrics, initiating the perennially popular "Chanel suit." It usually consisted of two or three pieces: a cardigan-style jacket, weighted with her trademark gilt chain stitched around the inside hem, a simple easy-to-wear skirt, worn with a blouse, the blouse fabric coordinated with the jacket lining. Her work offered comfort and streamlined simplicity, creating clothes for the modern woman, whom she epitomized herself. The key to her design philosophy was construction, producing traditional classics outliving each season's new fashion trends and apparel. Whilst other designers presented new looks for each new season, Chanel adapted the refined detailing and style lines.

Her colours are predominantly grey, navy, and beige, incorporating highlights of a richer colour palette. Chanel introduced the ever popular "little black dress," created for daywear, eveningwear, and cocktail dressing and a firm fixture in the fashion world today.

Attentive to detail, adding to day and eveningwear, Chanel established a reputation for extensive uses of costume jewelery, with innovative combinations of real and imitation gems, crystal clusters, strings of pearls, and ornate jewelled cuff links, adding brilliant contrast to the stark simplicity of her designs. The successful development of *Chanel No. 5* perfume in 1922 assisted in the financing of her couture empire during difficult years. An interesting aspect of Chanel's career was the re-opening of her couture house, which was closed during World War II. After 15 years in retirement, Chanel relaunched her work in 1954 at the age of 71, re-introducing the "Chanel suit," which has formed the basis for many of her collections and become a hallmark. The look adopted shorter skirts and braid trimmed cardigan jackets.

Despite her work and individual style, Chanel craved personal and financial independence, and was ruthless in her search for success. She was unique in revolutionizing the fashion industry with dress reform and in promoting the emancipation of women.

Her influence has touched many American and European designers, who continue to reinforce her concept of uncomplicated classics that inspire many contemporary designers' ready-to-wear collections—a homage to Chanel's essential modernist styling and her legacy to the world of fashion.

—Carol Mary Brown

CHARLES, Caroline.

British designer

Born: Cairo, Egypt, c. 1943. **Education:** Attended boarding school in Harrogate, England; studied fashion at the Art School in Swindon. **Career:** Worked for couturier Michael Sherrard, and for Mary Quant, Knightsbridge; assisted fashion photographer Tony Rawlinson; returned to Mary Quant; established own business, 1963; moved to Beauchamp Place, 1966. Designed for a number of celebrities and musicians, 1960s; designed for British royalty, beginning in the 1980s; opened up new store on Bond Street, London, 1990s.

Publications:

On CHARLES:

Articles

"Designs for the Princess of Wales," in *Times,* 3 November 1981.

Brampton, Sally, "Showing the Rest of the World," in *The Observer,* 20 March 1983.

Kendall, Ena, "Caroline Charles: A Room of My Own," in *Observer Magazine,* 16 August 1987.

Lomas, Jane, "Staying Power," in *The Observer,* 16 August 1987.

Samuel, Kathryn, "A Feel for the Fabric of the Times," in *Daily Telegraph,* 16 May 1988.

Coleman, Alix, "Breaking New Ground," in *Sunday Express Magazine,* 22 October 1989.

Haggard, Claire, "The House that Caroline Built," in *Fashion Weekly* (London), 9 November 1989.

Haggard, Claire, "Setting the Style," in *Country Life* (London), 18 January 1990.

Nesbit, Jenny, "A Perfect Fit," in *Sunday Times Magazine,* 14 October 1990.

Bridgstock, Graham, "Me and My Health," in the *Evening Standard* (London), 19 July 1994.

Tyrrell, Rebecca, in the *Tattler* (London), November 1994.

*   *   *

"A child of the Sixties" is how Caroline Charles has described herself, and certainly she could be said to have been in the right place at the right time. Charles, born to an army family in Cairo, was sent to England to a boarding school in Harrogate where she claims to have "picked up a survival kit for life." She studied fashion at the Art School in Swindon, after which she worked for couturier Michael Sherrard and for Mary Quant at her Shop Bazaar in Knightsbridge. She then assisted fashion photographer Tony Rawlinson before returning to Mary Quant.

In 1963 she set up on her own and moved to Beauchamp Place in 1966. From there her business boomed, and with sound and sensible strategies she has expanded from London to the rest of Europe, Japan, and America. She has built an empire that takes in more than 40 top store accounts and licenses for wedding dresses, hosiery, bed linen, underwear, and menswear.

Armed with talent and ambition—"I do have tremendous drive," she has said—Charles admits to having in the early days a woeful lack of business acumen, a trait she was to acquire very quickly as the momentum of the "swinging" sixties launched her onto the fashion scene. 1965 found her jetting around the world and the subject of headlines in the United States. Americans loved her fresh, "Kinder, London Ladylike Look," and at the tender age of 22 she was feted by "trend" hungry New York audiences.

During these years she created Ringo Starr's wedding outfit, dressed Petula Clark, Madame George Pompidou, Barbra Streisand, Lulu, Marianne Faithfull, and Mick Jagger. "The sixties were totally celebrity driven," she said. "There was this mood and we got great press. The editors loved the mini-star designer who dressed the major-star pop singer." With singular inspiration she transformed a lace bedspread into a long empire-line dress and sold it to Cilla Black. When Cilla's record *Anyone Who Had a Heart* became a hit, Charles's dress became a best-seller. All this she took in stride and became one of London's "swinging set."

Quite a celebrity in her own right, she was a regular guest on *Juke Box Jury,* the popular "Teen Scene" program; was interviewed on the *Johnny Carson Show*; was a guest writer for the teen press; and modeled her own trendy designs. She was one of a myriad of talented young designers in the 1960s who made the clothes that she and her friends wanted, full of youthful energy and gaiety, invention and individuality; people seemed to want everyday clothing for the streets of London, Paris, or anywhere in Europe, a trend to be well marketed and exploited by the new young designers.

Charles is treated with reverence in the fashion industry as someone who "got it right." She is a business-like technician, straightforward, and in love with her craft. "I enjoy what I do now more than I ever have. Every day I do precisely what I want and I am not so anxious now." Despite 30 successful years in the industry, she admits to an irrational fear that she cannot design clothes. Her show is regularly chosen to launch London Fashion week, yet this anxiety pervades every waking moment up to the launch.

After such an auspicious start in the 1960s, she reflects that the 1970s were "a terrible time for fashion." But the 1980s saw her in full swing again, attiring the newly married Prince of Wales in a tartan suit for the Braemar games and an oatmeal wrap-around dressing-gown coat for a walkabout in Wales. She had become one of the exclusive breed of "Royal Designers." The exuberance of the swinging sixties had given way to a more classic, sensible look. Charles has an eye for lavish fabrics combined with easy wearability. Hers are beautifully made clothes with simple accessories (she hopes her clients would wear them to the supermarket).

Her many illustrious clients, Lady Lloyd Webber and Dame Diana Rigg among them, will attest to the beguiling quality of her fabrics: perennial velvets, rich wool paisleys and elegant brocades, and, in the 1990s, black leather mixed with flippy lace skirts (a slightly vampy departure for the designer) toned down into wearable sexy party clothes. The 1990s have seen yet another phase of extremely successful, well-thought-out business expansions. A new flagship shop in Bond Street, and with it an entirely new Bond Street customer, opens up a whole new market for Charles.

Charles is that rare commodity who has survived the vicissitudes of the fashion industry while retaining her own personal signature. After 30 years of quiet good sense, it's difficult to imagine Caroline Charles making a mistake now.

—Elian McCready

CHLOÉ.

French deluxe ready-to-wear house

Founded by Jacques Lenoir and Gaby Aghion, 1952; company acquired by Dunhill Holdings, plc, 1985, and by Vendome, 1993. Karl Lagerfeld, designer, 1965-83, and again from 1992; Martine Sitbon, designer, 1987-1991. **Address:** 54-56 rue du Faubourg St-Honoré, 75008 Paris, France.

Publications:

On CHLOE:

Articles

Gross, Michael, "Paris Originals: Chloé in the Afternoon," in *New York,* 15 May 1989.
Friedman, Arthur, "Chloé Reshapes Its Identity," in *Women's Wear Daily* (New York), 2 January 1991.

*   *   *

Style, modernity, and a strong sense of femininity have been the key elements of Chloé since its inception. It has maintained a quiet confidence among the Parisian ready-to-wear houses, relying on the abilities of various already-established designers to produce fresh and vibrant clothing which reflected and, in the high points of its history under Karl Lagerfeld, defined the *Zeitgeist*.

Riding the wave of prêt-à-porter companies set to challenge couture in the 1950s, Chloé was keen from the start to produce wearable clothes which conveyed the immediacy of modernism in clear, strong styles. The house's identity remains true to the design tenets of its early days, producing simple garments made from fluid fabrics. These promote a sense of elegant movement, enlivened by the artistic sense of colour which distinguishes French fashion; a constant feature at Chloé, despite the varied nationalities of its designers.

Chloé and its peers provided a lively, frequently directional alternative to haute couture, whose dictatorial status was diminishing. It was able to headhunt inspirational designers with the talent to translate the Chloé design image into clothing which would remain distinct to the label, while consistently evolving to embrace contemporary styles.

In the 1960s this meant keeping pace with the youth-orientated look in London, with clothes imbued with a futuristic vitality. In 1966 this sense of freedom through technology was assimilated into Jeanne Do's design for Chloé of the slim, straight-falling Empire line dress in stark white. This was decorated with metallic geometric shapes which marched down the dress, seeming to emanate from the slatted silver squares that made up the shimmering cropped bodice. This modern armour as eveningwear was a current fashion trend, picking up on the sci-fi trend of this early period of space exploration. The dress also pinpointed the introduction that year of maxi skirts, reinforcing Chloé's place at the cutting edge of fashion.

Indeed, it has continued to occupy this place, rarely absent from the fashion pages, despite temporary dips in status due to a loss of direction between designers. This reliance on different names to pursue Chloé's viability has, however, enabled a chameleon-like adaptability to the contemporary fashion temperature, calling upon such catalytic free-lancers as Karl Lagerfeld, at the height of his creative powers, to invigorate the house's image.

From the late 1960s Chloé's name became synonymous with Lagerfeld's, as he gave their line strongly conceived evening- and daywear of modernity and direction without compromising the supple femininity of the luxury fabrics employed.

The house style remained pared-down sheath dresses, hovering around the figure, adorned with minimal decoration, which distilled the late 1960s fashion directive. Under his guidance, the label moved with ease into the pluralistic 1970s, absorbing and refining the myriad of reference points with which fashion toyed. He was as adept at witty reinterpretations of the multi-ethnic gypsy look of pop festivals, referred to in patterned bordered skirts, as the more artistic classics popular the following year, when he turned two poster-paint bright patterned circles into versatile skirts and shawls which emphasized movement as they swirled onto the figure.

The success of his work for the label is indisputable, reinforcing its ready-to-wear dominance. It is unsurprising that Chloé languished after his departure. Having spent the previous decade pushing fashion forward, the label could only mark time until Martine Sitbon was chosen to reinject a sense of originality and verve in 1988.

Sitbon embodied facets of Chloé's style which had been established in the 1960s: uncluttered designed, which drew on popular culture to provide distinct themes for each collection, translated into classic shapes for women confident of their own identity.

Sitbon toned down the more overtly 1970s rock-influenced styles of her own named line to produce masculine tailored suits. These were softened by a dandyish swing to their cut and by delicately

Chloé: Fall/Winter 1994/95; violet flowered lace dress with lamp sleeves draped at the elbow. *Photograph by Karl Lagerfeld.*

coloured silk chiffon blouses which blossomed into curving frilled collars. She defined Chloé's look during the 1980s, rounding the edges of the decade's often over-extravagant silhouette with well placed decoration and rich fabrics that drew on the glamorous mood which spilled into the first years of the 1990s.

In fall/winter 1991, shortly before she left the label, this sense of feminine swagger was shaped into scarlet textured silk evening dresses, cut short to mid-thigh and standing out from the hips to add a mobile swing from the fitted high collar bodice. The bold impact of the dress was tempered by the tantalizing gold bead strands, which hung in a bunch from the back fastening zip.

The desire to remain in the forefront prompted the return of Lagerfeld in 1992, when he captured the mood for unstructured, easy-to-wear styles in his fluid slip dresses in faded prints which harked back to the heights of his Chloé collections of the 1970s and tapped the nostalgia for the flower child look upon which they drew. He adorned them with dressing-up-box flair, throwing long strings of beads around the models' necks and silk blooms in their hair. Although the initial reaction was uncertain, Chloé had judged the fashion moment for change well, and Lagerfeld continues to fit comfortably into their mould.

Chloé's place in prêt-à-porter history has been ensured by the house's ability to allow designers to flourish under its auspices. Lagerfeld, particularly, has encapsulated its ideals of femininity and sophistication through pure distinct designs which enhance the figure in a contemporary way.

—Rebecca Arnold

CLAIBORNE, Liz.

American designer

Born: Elizabeth Claiborne in Brussels, 31 March 1929, to American parents from New Orleans. Moved to New Orleans, 1939. **Education:** Studied art at Fine Arts School and Painters Studio, Belgium, 1947, and at the Nice Academy, 1948. Self-taught in design. **Family:** Married Ben Schultz in 1950 (divorced); son: Alexander. Married Arthur Ortenberg, 1957. **Career:** Sketch artist and model, Tina Lesser, 1950; design assistant to Omar Kiam for Ben Reig, Seventh Avenue, New York; designer, Youth Guild division of Jonathan Logan, 1960-76; founder and partner with Art Ortenberg, Liz Claiborne Inc., 1976; went public, 1981. Petite Sportswear line, 1981; dress division formed, 1982; shoes, 1983; purchased accessory firm Kaiser-Roth Corporation, 1985; Lizwear label featuring jeans, 1985; men's sportswear, Clairborne, 1985; *Liz Claiborne* perfume, 1986. Dana Buchman and Claiborne Furnishings inaugurated, 1987-88; larger-size line, Elizabeth, introduced, 1988; First Issue inaugurated, 1988, currently 38 stores throughout USA. Liz & Co. knitwear division formed, 1989; men's fragrance, *Claiborne,* launched, 1989; Elizabeth Dresses introduced, 1990; Sports Shoes and Suits, 1991; Sport Specific Activewear and Liz Sport Eyewear introduced, 1992; Russ and Crazy Horse labels purchased from Russ Toggs, 1992. **Awards:** Winner, *Harper's Bazaar* Jacques Heim national design contest, 1949; Hecht and Company Young Designer Award, Washington, D.C., 1967; Woolknit Association Award, 1973; Entrepreneurial Woman of the Year, 1980; Council of Fashion Designers of America Award, 1985; award from Barnard College, 1991; High School of Fashion Industries Award,

1990; award from Marymount Manhattan College, 1989. **Address:** 1441 Broadway, New York, New York 10018, USA.

Publications:

On CLAIBORNE:

Books

Milbank, Caroline Rennolds, *New York Fashion: The Evolution of American Style,* New York 1989.
Daria, Irene, *The Fashion Cycle,* New York, 1990.

Articles

Klensch, Elsa, "Dressing America: The Success of Liz Claiborne," in *Vogue* (New York), August 1986.
Stan, Adele-Marie, "Four Designing Women," in *Ms,* November 1986.
Sellers, Patricia, "The Rag Trade's Reluctant Revolutionary: Liz Claiborne," in *Fortune* (New York), 5 January 1987.
Gannes, Stuart, "American's Fastest-Growing Companies," in *Fortune,* 23 May 1988.
Morris, Michele, "The Wizard of the Working Woman's Wardrobe," in *Working Woman* (New York), June 1988.
Deveny, Kathleen, "Can Ms. Fashion Bounce Back?," in *Business Week* (New York), 16 January 1989.
"Liz Claiborne," in *Current Biography* (New York), June 1989.
Graham, Judith, "Clairborne Opens Its Own Sites," in *Advertising Age,* 5 June 1989.
Armstrong, Lisa, "Working Woman's Ally," in *Vogue* (London), February 1991.
Hass, Nancy, "Like a Rock," in *Financial World,* 4 February 1992.
Agins, Teri, "Liz Claiborne Seems to Be Losing Its Invincible Armor," in *Wall Street Journal,* July 1993.

*   *   *

Liz Claiborne is founder, president, and chief executive officer of Liz Claiborne Inc., by December 1991 a publicly held company posting sales increases of 17.6 percent to two billion dollars. With 19 divisions and three licensees, the company ranks fourth on *Fortune's* "America's Most Admired Corporations."

In 1976, after a 25-year career as a designer, Liz Claiborne founded her own company to provide innovative design in women's working clothes. By 1988 her designs for the new market needs of the rapidly expanding women's workforce earned her the title of "The Wizard of the Working Woman's Wardrobe" in the series "Women Who Have Changed the World" in the journal *Working Woman* (June 1988). Liz Claiborne views herself as her down-to-earth client, "the Liz Lady ... a working woman like myself," who now makes up 45 percent of the US workforce. Her original concept was, as she explained in a *Vogue* (New York) interview in August 1986, "to dress the women who didn't have to wear suits—the teachers, the doctors, the women working in southern California and Florida, the women in the fashion industry itself."

In 1980 her innovative designs were so successful that she became the first woman in the US fashion industry to be named Entrepreneurial Woman of the Year and in the following year her firm went public, prospering financially to such a degree that it has been described by Merrill Lynch as "a case history of success."

The phenomenal growth of the company has been spurred on by diversification from the two original basic lines—active sportswear and a slightly dressier collection—to include a dress division in 1982, and a unit for shoes in 1983. In 1985 Liz Claiborne Inc. bought the Kaiser-Roth Corporation, the company it had licensed to produce accessories, including handbags, scarves, belts, and hats. In the same year a collection of men's sportwear, Claiborne, was introduced and 1986 saw the launch of a perfume *Liz Claiborne,* described by its eponymous designer as appealing "to a woman's idealistic version of herself.... She's active, whatever her age. It's the same feeling we try to give in the clothes" (*Vogue,* New York, August 1986).

Claiborne's designs worked on the premise that what she needed, other American women needed, and the company's links with their consumers are strengthened by such devices as the questionnaires to encourage customers to express their views and provide accurate and timely customer feedback which are a feature of the 18 US stand-alone Claiborne shops. They provide Liz Claiborne Inc. with near-instantaneous information on market trends.

Liz Claiborne Inc., which already controls an estimated one-third of the two billion dollar US market for upmarket women's sportswear, sells through some 3,500 retailers in the United States alone. The company also sells products to stores in Great Britain, Spain, Ireland, and the Netherlands and has recently established its first free-standing retail licensee in Singapore.

—Doreen Ehrlich

CLARK, Ossie.

British designer

Born: Raymond Clark in Oswaldtwistle, Lancashire, 2 June 1942. **Education:** Studied fashion design, Manchester College of Art, 1957-61, and Royal College of Art, 1961-65. **Family:** Married Celia Birtwell in August 1969 (divorced); son: Albert. **Career:** Free-lance designer, selling to Quorum, London, and Henri Bendel, New York, 1964-74, and to Mendes, French ready-to-wear firm; designer, Quorum, 1965-74; designer, Radley, 1968, and 1983; business closed, 1981; business reorganized, 1983; signed contract with Evocative boutique for made-to-measure clothes, 1987. **Awards:** Bath Museum of Costume Dress of the Year Award, 1969. **Address:** 17D Penzance Street, London W11, England.

Publications:

On CLARK:

Books

Lambert, Eleanor, *World of Fashion: People, Places, Resources,* New York and London 1976.
Howell, Georgina, *Sultans of Style: 30 Years of Fashion and Passion 1960-1990,* London 1990.

Articles

Peters, Pauline, "Ossie and Alice in Wonderland," in *The Sunday Times Magazine* (London), 11 January 1970.

Roberts, Michael, "Michael Roberts Talks to Ossie Clark," in *The Sunday Times* (London), 16 November 1975.
"Ossie Clark Designs," in *The Times* (London), 27 January 1976.
"Ossie Clark Special," in *Ritz* (London), No. 5, 1977.
"Ossie Clark Goes Out of Business," in *The Times* (London), 5 February 1981.
"Peace in Our Time: Summer of Love Revisited," in *Elle* (London), June 1987.
Howell, Georgina, "The Dressmaker," in *The Sunday Times Magazine* (London), 12 July 1987.

*   *   *

Ossie Clark, described as the King of King's Road, rose to prominence as a fashion designer during the Swinging Sixties. Trained at Manchester College of Art, then at the Royal College of Art, London, he graduated at a time when London was entering a period of international prominence for its designs for the youth market. In a pre-Green era, variety and the ability to produce a fast turnover of styles were desirable qualities in a designer. Ossie Clark provided a great variety of images for both day and eveningwear.

From 1966 he was designing for Quorum, a London-based wholesale and boutique business, in partnership with Alice Pollock. His wife, Celia Birtwell, also an RCA graduate, provided many of the pattern designs for the printed textiles used by Clark. He designed both day and eveningwear, often using sensuous fabrics such as satin, chiffon, crêpe, and clinging jersey. Although, since he was so versatile and prolific, it is hard to characterize Ossie Clark's style, he was probably best known for clinging crêpe and jersey dresses with plunging necklines, figure-hugging waists, and swirling skirts, but he was equally capable of producing close-fitting crisp linen suits. Innovations in terms of cut included suits with elbow-length tight fitting sleeves over full long sleeved blouses. In the late 1960s he used exotic materials such as snakeskin, feathers, and metallic prints.

In 1968 Clark launched his menswear range which reflected the period's more relaxed attitude to male dressing. Examples from his first menswear range included a pink crêpe shirt with a fall of ruffles at the front diminishing in size and edged in white silk braid. His clothes for Quorum were in the medium to expensive price range, comparing with other contemporary designers such as Zandra Rhodes and Jean Muir. Quorum produced garments for direct sale as well as more specialized outfits to order. The company sold through its own retail outlets, through department stores such as the "Way In" section of the Harrods chain, and through individual boutiques such as Image in Bath. His clothes were sold in America and Europe, being stocked in Italy by Fiorucci. His clientèle in the 1960s and 1970s reads like a catalogue of rich and famous trendy dressers and includes Marianne Faithful, Mick and Bianca Jagger, Twiggy, Marie Helvin, Cathy McGowan, and Goldie Hawn. In 1972 Mick Jagger owned no less than ten Ossie Clark jumpsuits. Jagger wore a blue sequined stretch velour jumpsuit which unzipped down the front for his performance at Madison Square Garden, New York in 1972. Clark's clothes regularly featured in the fashion press and fashion editors reputedly fought for tickets for his shows in the early 1970s.

From 1970 Quorum was 65 per cent funded by Rady Fashions and Textiles who provided business premises. Alice Pollock dealt with day to day practicalities such as organizing staff, buying cloth, and having it dyed. From 1977 Ossie Clark had his own company using the design label Ossie Clark Ltd. However, in 1981 Clark's company succumbed to the economic recession, despite having been taken over in 1980 by MAK Industries who wished to gain control of the Ossie Clark label and attempted unsuccessfully to open an American branch. Ossie Clark Ltd went into voluntary liquidation in 1981 and Clark was declared bankrupt in 1983. Ossie Clark lasted longer than most designers who began in the late 1960s youth boom, which is a tribute to the enduring quality of his design stamina and the range and flexibility of his ideas.

Bankruptcy, however, was not the end of Clark's fashion career. He taught at the Royal College of Art and designed evening dresses for Radley Fashions and in 1986 HE launched a lingerie company in partnership with Gina Fratini, trading under the name Rustle. He made use of his skills in employing the bias cut to produce clinging lingerie in silk satin with lace trimmings and insertions.

In 1987 Evocative, the newly opened Grosvenor Street boutique, ordered one-off made-to-measure dresses from Ossie Clark for individual clients, with balldresses retailing for three thousand pounds. Despite his still evident international fame, in 1987 Clark was reduced to living by a barter system, for example, making a hat for dancer Wayne Sleep who, in exchange, paid for Clark's sewing machine to be mended. An enterprising solution all too many young designers today may identify with.

—Linda Coleing

CLEAVER, Alan. See BYBLOS.

COLE OF CALIFORNIA.

American swimwear company

Formed by Fred Cole from family knitwear firm in Los Angeles, 1923. Designers include Margit Fellegi (from 1936), Anne Cole (from 1982), Adrienne Vittadini (from 1990). Divisions include Cole, Hot Coles junior division (introduced, 1982), Sandcastle, Anne Cole (introduced, 1982), Adrienne Vittadini, and Juice junior division (introduced, 1990). Company purchased by Kayser-Roth, early 1960s; sold to the Wickes Company, purchased by Taren Holdings, 1989; taken over by Authentic Fitness, 1993. **Awards:** Los Angeles Chamber of Commerce Golden 44 Award, 1979. **Address:** Authentic Fitness, 6040 Bandini Boulevard, Los Angeles, California 90040, USA.

Publications:

On COLE OF CALIFORNIA:

Books

Lencek, Lena, and Gideon Bosker, *Making Waves: Swimsuits and the Undressing of America,* San Francisco 1989.
Martin, Richard, and Harold Koda, *Splash!: A History of Swimwear,* New York 1990.

Articles

Sajbel, Maureen O., "Sea Notes: Anne Cole Takes the Plunge," in *Women's Wear Daily* (New York), 28 July 1982.
Flint, Jerry, "Cover-up," in *Forbes* (New York), 2 May 1988.
Drizen, Ruth, "High Spirits at Cole," in *Apparel Industry Magazine* (Atlanta, Georgia), August 1990.

*   *   *

1964 was the high-water mark of swimwear exposure. Rudi Gernreich showed a topless bathing suit that achieved awestruck attention, but sold very few copies. *Sports Illustrated,* the New York magazine, began its annual swimsuit edition. Cole of California, in the same year, produced the three-item "scandal suit" collection that likewise plunged to new exposure with an astonishing commercial success, typifying the long tradition of Cole's being the most provocative, but commercial, swimwear manufacturer in America. Ever since Fred Cole had first hitched his company's wagon to the stars of Hollywood, Cole had been the style setter, P. T. Barnum style. Cole knew by unerring instinct, like his film-producer *confrères* how to be sensational and to sell to the American public without being overly salacious. As Lena Lencek and Gideon Bosker describe: "Cut extremely conservatively by mid-1960s standards, the Scandal suits put everything under wraps, at least theoretically. In practice, however, the vast expanses of see-through netting turned their wearers into sizzling sex goddesses"(*Making Waves: Swimsuits and the Undressing of America*). If black mesh only made a plunging *décolletage* or midriff transparency seem more radical and seductive in the tantalizing peek-a-boo of exposure or coverage, Cole encouraged the sensation in dramatic public events and publicity. A major American company was thus in the vanguard of what was already being described as a 1960s sexual revolution and seemed ready to bring all of its license to the beach. Fred Cole knew that going to the beach or pool was recreation, but that it was also spectator sport.

Fred Cole had three brilliant ideas that he put into action step by step. First, he transformed the family's prosaic knit underwear business into a swimsuit business. Second, he seized upon California and Hollywood to bring glamor to the swimwear industry and specifically to the imagery of Cole of California, Third, he knew that sex appeal would be determined in the middle and late years of the 20th century by public relations and popular opinion. The health and dress-reform issues of knitwear paled beside the excitement that Cole brought to the swimwear industry. His conjunction to Hollywood, working with the ingenious designer Margit Fellegi, who was to the Hollywood swimsuit what Edith Head was to every other Hollywood film garment, enshrined a public relations icon of the contract player or starlet appearing poolside or on the beach in a Cole swimsuit, demonstrating the figure and face that would draw crowds to the movies, but also set ideals for recreational swimwear. It was a cunningly American ideal: sexy without being smarmy, a pin-up excused by the sun-drenched healthy life of California and linked to another persuasive product, the movies. Cole in the trio of great American swimwear manufacturers went to Hollywood while Jantzen emphasized family fun and healthy sport and Catalina became associated with beauty pageants.

More than any other American company, Cole has connected fashion and swimwear. Fred Cole reshaped the wool knit swimsuit to define the bust and waist and introduced a sunny California palette of colors. With the popularity of tans in the 1930s, Cole progressively sheared away the bulk of the traditional swimsuit to provide more and more exposure. Margit Fellegi, a Hollywood costumer, began working with Cole in 1936 and, immediately utilizing rubberized and stretch possibilities of new fibers that could surpass the old wool knits, brought a body-clinging science to the sex appeal that Cole desired. When rubber was restricted in World War II, Cole created the "swoon suit," a two-piece suit that laced up the sides of the trunk and tied for the bra, still an enduring pin-up. After the war, Cole and Fellegi pursued fashion and Hollywood glamor with New Look-inspired dressmaker swimsuits and profligate details of sequins, gold-lamé jersey, and water resistant velvets. In 1950, Cole signed film/swimming star Esther Williams to a merchandising-design contract that created and promoted the most popular and glamorous swimwear of its time. In 1955, with the phenomenal success of Esther Williams secured in her film aquacades and romances, Cole entered into agreement to produce swimwear for Christian Dior, thus bringing the most famous fashion name of the moment to swimwear design.

More recently, Cole has produced a variety of lines addressed to the increasingly segmented (principally, age and body types) swimwear market. Since 1982, the Anne Cole Collection, designed by Fred Cole's daughter, sustains the designer swimwear ideal in a fashion-conscious image and product, supplemented by the variety of Cole swimwear. Anne Cole's sensibility is traditional elegance; her swimsuits often recall the 1930s, not only of the beach, but of Patou and the most elegant sportswear. The product's differentiation is always fashion and glamor. The quest of California is not merely for the water, but to be ever on the crest of the wave that defines bathing beauty.

—Richard Martin

COLEMAN, Nick.

British designer

Education: Graduated from St. Martins School of Art, London, mid-1980s. **Career:** Producer of such collections as "Kimota Returns"; operator of London night clubs, including Solaris. **Addresses:** 202 New North Road, London N1 7BJ, England; 66 Neal Street, London WC2H 9TA, England.

Publications:

On COLEMAN:

Articles

Flett, Kathryn, "Patsy Looks Perfect," in *The Sunday Times Magazine* (London), 12 April 1987.
"Model Interiors," in *The Sunday Express Magazine* (London), 25 October 1987.
"Shooting Stars," in *Women's Journal* (London), February 1988.
Hume, Marion, "The Italian Connection," in *The Sunday Times* (London), 14 May 1989.
Collen, Matthew, "Nick Coleman," in *i-D* (London), April 1990.

Carter, Charles, and Charlotte Du Cann, "Europe 1990: Designers to Watch," in *Vogue* (New York), August 1990.
Yusuf, Nilgin, "London Sport Deluxe," in *Elle* (New York), August 1990.
Rodgers, Toni, "Double Vision," in *Elle* (London), March 1991.

*   *   *

Nick Coleman's work has reflected the shift in mood that has taken fashion from the sleek tailoring and obvious luxury of the mid- to late 1980s into the more casual-based sports influence of the early 1990s.

Among the rash of London-based talent that heralded the designer boom, Coleman produced consistently strong silhouettes for women. His earlier work was based mainly on careful tailoring, dresses that fitted to the body and then flared into little full skirts, concentrating on charcoal and navy-blue pinstripes for daywear and branching into warmer shades for sharply balanced modern evening designs. In 1988 he showed a popular claret palazzo trouser all-in-one, which hugged the torso in gauzy georgette, with tucked silk forming a bustier section linked to the trousers by a strip of buttons that reached from the collar.

In the late 1980s his clothes encapsulated the confidence and streamlined modernity that dominated fashion. His menswear was equally well adapted to the smart tailored look that was aspired to, with, in 1986, black double-breasted trenchcoats and classic turn-up trousers. By the dawning of the 1990s, however, Coleman was immersed in the burgeoning rave scene with its more relaxed attitude to clothing. After taking a break from fashion to run his own club nights, his designs began to reflect the tribalism and body-conscious sports influence of the scene. The freer feel of young London clubbers led to the development of a more recognizable signature to his work.

The variations on the classic biker jackets that he designed in 1989, with fringing for sleeves and chain-trimmed bra tops, were obviously influenced by the music scene. Later versions were even teamed with punk-inspired tartans. These, however, were quickly surpassed by sexy, sporty, shaped separates that gave ease of movement and a recognizable image for the dance floor.

His strong advertising campaigns followed this mood, with models daubed with body paint to represent the shield emblem that adorns much of his diffusion range. He dressed ardent clubbers in the heavily padded puffa jackets that were obligatory at raves during the first two years of the decade, worn with his bodies, stretch skirts, and trousers with stripe trim that referred to school sportswear in its detailing. Although it is this clubwear that is most instantly recognizable, he continues to produce well-cut suiting (recently in velvet-collared slim-fitting Teddy Boy styles) for his main line, mixing classic shapes with more experimental elements. His involvement in the 5th Circle menswear collective underlines this dedication to innovative designs, and the attention to detail which is echoed in his consistently strong leather and denim lines. His work has continued to fall under the influence of the London club scene, but his ability to produce interesting tailored designs widens his appeal and prevents his clothes being too narrowly pigeon-holed. His popularity in London is based on his skill in producing clothing imbued with the *Zeitgeist,* as well as more classic garments that prolong the longevity of his appeal.

—Rebecca Arnold

COLONNA di CESARO, Simonetta. See **SIMONETTA.**

COMME DES GARÇONS. See **KAWAKUBO, Rei.**

CONRAN, Jasper.

British designer

Born: London, 12 December 1959. **Education:** Attended Bryanston School, Dorset; studied at Parsons School of Design, New York, 1975-77. **Family:** Married Jeanne Spaziani. **Career:** Worked for Fiorucci, New York, 1977, then for ICI and Courtaulds, London; design consultant, Wallis Fashion Group, 1977; showed first womenswear collection, 1978; opened boutique, Beauchamp Place, London, 1986; showed menswear from 1988. Also: theatre designer. Awards: British Fashion Council Designer of the Year Award, 1986; Fashion Group of America Award, New York, 1987. **Address:** 2 Berners Street, London W1P 4BA, England.

Publications:

On CONRAN:

Books

Coleridge, Nicholas, *The Fashion Conspiracy,* London 1988.
Stegemeyer, Anne, *Who's Who in Fashion* supplement, New York 1992.

Articles

"Lookout: A Guide to the Up and Coming," in *People,* 8 March 1982.
Search, Gay, "The Conran Clan: Jasper," in *Women's Journal* (London), April 1984.
Kendall, Ena, "Jasper Conran: A Room of My Own," in *The Observer* (London), 22 September 1985.
McDowell, Colin, "Jasper Conran," in *The Guardian* (London), 31 October 1985.
Powell, Fiona Russell, "Jasper Conran," in *Fashion '86* (London), 1985.
Soames, Emma, "British Style: The Impact of the Designer Star," in *Vogue* (London), February 1987.
Barron, Pattie, "24 Carat Jasper: Fashion's Brilliant Brat," in *Cosmopolitan* (London), April 1987.
Young, Russell, "Jasper," in *Blitz* (London), April 1987.
Allott, Serena, "Jasper Conran in Search of Something Perfectly Simple," in *The Sunday Telegraph Magazine* (London), 20 September 1987.
Menkes, Suzy, "Jasper and John," in *The Independent* (London), 9 October 1987.
Sinclair, Paul, and Lesley Jane Nonkin, "Designer, Client: The Modern Equation," in *Vogue* (New York), November 1987.

Nadelson, Regina, "Scion of the Times," in *Metropolitan Home* (New York), August 1988.
"Bon Magique," in *Elle* (London), November 1988.
"Jasper Conran," in *Fashion Weekly* (London), 16 August 1990.
Jeal, Nicola, "Conran's Comeback," in *The Observer Magazine* (London), 18 November 1990.

*   *   *

Dubbed the "Calvin Klein of London," Jasper Conran creates menswear and womenswear collections that epitomize urbane, classic lines. As British Fashion Council's Fashion Designer of the Year in 1986, Conran has balanced British imagination with international chic. His designs are inspired by early garments of Coco Chanel and the American look of Claire McCardell's monastic and "popover" dresses but the outcome reflecting modern sophistication, not retro style.

Conran attended Parsons School of Design in New York, and worked briefly for the British company Wallis as design consultant, producing the Special Label. He introduced his first independent womenswear collection in 1978 showing black cashmere trousers, coats and jackets lined with cream satin. This established his hallmark use of expensive fabrics such as silk, cashmere, taffeta, and lines with classic cuts. *Vogue* writer Emma Soames has observed that British fashion editors discovered Conran early, as the refined simplicity of his work contrasted sharply with other British designers of the time (for example Vivienne Westwood, Katherine Hamnett, and Rifat Ozbek). Main pieces from his collections change very little from season to season, allowing many of his garments to be regarded as long-term wardrobe investments.

Colour is an important factor in the overall look of Conran's collections: for example, the brightly coloured cashmere jackets in cerise, orange, chrome yellow, and mint green, produced for the 1992 collection, and earlier eveningwear in fuchsia, cobalt, and kelly green organza highlighting the clean lines of each garment. Silk separates have since been designed in ice blue, cocoa, bright red, and sorbet colours.

While in many collections Conran has produced undemanding and straightforward designs, he has occasionally incorporated elements characteristic of what might be expected of British fashion fantasy—fur-trimmed suits and wedding dresses, trumpet-hem jersey skirts, bold plaid toppers over leather jacketed pantsuits, and brightly coloured chevron-patterned sweaters with white flannel pleated skirts. *Breakfast at Tiffany's* and Grace Kelly 1950s nostalgia inspired Conran to design enormous bell-shaped coats, boxy cropped jackets, and little flirtatious minis with stiff, standaway backs in white cotton poplin for his 1986 collection. Recently the English seaside has set the background for a 1920s classic approach with oversized three-quarter-length wool tailored jackets and palazzo pants.

In 1988 Conran began his menswear line, maintaining the same classic designs as his women's collections. A black and white ticking stripe cotton jacket with matching high-buttoned waistcoat and tapered trousers depicts a quintessentially English style, while the importance of colour is maintained in Conran's intense red suede blazer and waistcoat. In addition to organizing the 1985 "Fashion Aid" charity evening for African famine relief, Conran has ventured into costume design for the ballet, Jean Anouilh's *The Rehearsal* and a London revival of *My Fair Lady.* His theatrical flair for colour and defined style readily translates to the stage. Conran's contribution to the British fashion scene is well recognized. He has a strong commercial sense positioning him solidly within the international arena, with clients who include The Princess of Wales. The timeless quality of his classic designs has ensured him a place alongside Calvin Klein, Karl Lagerfeld, and Perry Ellis.

—Teal Triggs

CORD, Barry Kieselstein. See **KIESELSTEIN-CORD, Barry.**

CORNELIANI SpA.

Italian menswear firm

Founded in Mantova, Italy, 1930s; subsequently modernized, 1958, by Carlalberto (born 1931) and Claudio Corneliani (born 1921). Sergio Corneliani (born 1959) became chief designer. Lines include "Via Ardigo, Styled by Corneliani," "Corneliani," "Corneliani Trend," and "Corneliani Sportswear"; trademarks include Nino Danieli, Browngreen, and Full Time; producers and manufacturers, beginning in 1984, for Daniel Hechter, Erreuno, Karl Lagerfeld, Krizia Uomo, Trussardi, and Renoma. Costume designers for various films, including *Little Women.* Carlalberto Corneliani president of Italy's fashion committee Comitato Moda, 1976; also president of Federtessile, Italian textile association, 1991. **Awards:** Pitti Immagine Prize, 1989; Carlalberto Corneliani named Cavaliere del Lavoro, 1991. **Address:** Via M. Panizza 5, 46100 Mantova, Italy.

Publications:

On CORNELIANI:

Books

Alfonsi, M., *Figli d'arte? No grazie,* Trento 1989.

Articles

Lobrano, Alexander, "Still Growing Corneliani," in *DNR: The Magazine* (New York), 4 January 1988.
"Dietro la griffe," in *L'Uomo Vogue* (Milan), February 1991.
"I Corneliani dell'Abital agli States," in *L'Arena* (Verona), 24 February 1991.
"Vestiremo all'americana," in *Il Mondo* (Milan), 29 April 1991.
"Corneliani," in *La Repubblica* (Rome), 12 June 1991.
"Corneliani—Hartmarx il Patto Atlantico," in *Uomo Harper's Bazaar* (Milan), 8 July 1991.
Gabbiano, M., "La quinta di Corneliani," in *La Repubblica* (Rome), 6 March 1992.
"I segreti di Corneliani," in *L'Arena* (Verona), 13 March 1992.
Perego, G., "Corneliani, 172 miliardi di vestiti," in *Italia Oggi* (Milan), 3 April 1992.

Forden, Sarah Gay, "The Corneliands of Mantova: A Family, a Company, a Label," in the *Daily News Record* (New York), 4 January 1993
Bagnoli, D., "Fratelli Corneliani, nuova organizzazione in Germania," in *Textil-Wirtschaft,* 3 March 1994.

*

Corneliani: a designer label, a company, a family. An important blend which embodies the secret of the Corneliani success.

The Corneliani company is run by the Corneliani family: quite different from the traditional stylist, and probably far superior, on today's scene.

Now that stylists work on an industrial level and the consumer is no longer prepared to accept something just because it carries a designer label, the winning card appears to be the entrepreneur-stylist. Capable of guaranteeing taste and creativity but first and foremost the quality of the product. This trend seems custom-made for the Corneliani, since this has always been our philosophy, the thinking that has made our company what it is today. Corporation styling, indicated by everyone as the true future of Italian fashion, has been practiced successfully for years at Corneliani by the Corneliani.

Corneliani style interprets the Italian culture of fine clothing. Corneliani quality is the technological version of the great Italian tailoring tradition.

—Corneliani

* * *

Corneliani is a high quality menswear design company based in Mantova, Italy. Seeking out the perfect balance between fashion content and classic style, the family company, now in its third generation, had its start in the tailoring business in the 1930s. By the late 1950s the group had established itself as producers of fine men's clothing, a tradition it upholds today.

Corneliani constitutes a company, a family, and a designer label, a blend that seals their success. The group does not promote itself as an individual designer-led label but as "Corporate Styling." Opposed to the idea that the consumer only purchases clothes because they carry a designer label, Corneliani believes that a group-led label guarantees not only creativity, taste, and style but also quality in the cut and manufacture of the product.

Elegance defines the look. Styles tend to denote the relaxed, classic taste of Hollywood stars like Cary Grant or George Sanders. The customer is style conscious, not necessarily fashion conscious, and his clothes need to be dependable, functional, and highly durable, yet also have a feeling of comfort and quality. Corneliani is also aware that its customer can have moments of extravagance: a man can suddenly be taken with a striking detail, like an unusual colour mix or an interesting fabric.

Corneliani develops most of its own fabrics from the initial selection of fibres, design, and colour to the final approval of ideas from amongst hundreds of samples. Natural fibres predominate: linens, cottons, pure woolen tweeds and herringbones, wool crepes, and wool venetians. Colours are simply and classically combined. Super fine, madras checked jackets in navy, beige, and cream are teamed with a sky blue checked shirt, navy trousers, and distinctive navy, beige, and cream striped tie. Beige on beige is a recurrent effect: a crepe beige suit with matching waistcoat is teamed with a brown

Corneliani SpA: "Corneliani Trend" collection; four-button overjackets with patch pockets.

checked tie and checked shirt. It's a tweedy English elegance, combined with slick Italian styling.

The company produces four main seasonal collections, which all adhere to the style principle of relaxed classicism. "Corneliani" is the flagship collection. Elegant and restrained, it is defined by the company as the point at which fashion and style meet. "Corneliani Trend" is a more fashion-oriented collection, designed for a customer who wants to follow fashion but retain a sense of good taste and intelligence. The "Corneliani Sportswear" collection is refined sportswear that combines both comfort and function. "Via Ardigo, Styled by Corneliani" is a more upbeat, fashion-conscious sportswear line, easy to wear but adhering to the company's trademark respect for quality and elegance.

Corneliani produces a wide range of men's apparel, from jackets and trousers to carcoats and overcoats. They rarely work to a design theme or make fashion trend statements; instead they produce an array of seasonal coordinates, within their four main seasonal collections, from which the customer can choose to put together his own look according to his own personal taste. The company's one aim and philosophy is to meet the clothing needs of contemporary, professional men who lead high gear lives that demand a wardrobe allowing them comfort and freedom.

—Kevin Almond

CORREGGIARI, Giorgio.

Italian designer

Born: Pieve di Cento, Bologna, Italy, 5 September 1943. **Education:** Studied political science, University of Bologna. **Career:** Apprenticed in textile companies in Lyon, France, 1967, and in England and Germany; free-lance designer with own boutique, Pam Pam, in Riccione, Italy, 1968; opened second boutique with brother Lamberto in Milan, 1969; designer for Fancy, New Delhi, 1972-73; designed UFO jeans for Gruppo Zanella, Italy, from 1974; designer for Daniel Hechter, Paris, 1975; Giorgio Correggiari SrL formed, 1975; designed Cadette collection, 1977; Giorgio Correggiari womenswear line launched, 1977. Also in 1970s designed menswear for Herno, leatherwear for IGI of Perugia, Reporter line of menswear in USA, Cleo and Pat knitwear, furs for Pellegrini (1970-73), Trifurs (1976), and Bencini (until 1985). Consultant to International Wool Secretariat, adviser to Cantoni on printed velvets, 1979; also adviser to International Cotton Institute, Brussels, Lana Gatto wool mill and Tessitura e Filature di Tollegno, Italy. Designer for Divi, 1986; produced line of leather coats for Robrik; young jackets and raincoats for Coral. **Exhibitions:** Museum of Modern Art, New York, 1976.

Publications:

On CORREGGIARI:

Books

McDowell, Colin, *McDowell's Directory of Twentieth Century Fashion,* London 1984.
Italian Fashion, Milan 1986.

Articles

Donna (Milan), April 1986.

*

Giorgio Correggiari can be regarded as an intellectual critic of top fashion designers. His philosophy is to offer customers a high degree of fashion at highly competitive prices without sacrificing quality. His design is simple, unsophisticated, but unquestionably fashionable and very avant-guard. He uses few accessories and avoids printed materials. He is not strong on colour and prefers to bring out the colour of the person.

—Giorgio Correggiari

*   *   *

Giorgio Correggiari is a spontaneous designer who loves his work. There is a constant feeling of improvisation about his designs and he thrives on the unexpected and the irregular. This open-minded approach keeps him on his toes, ready to face the uncertainties of the fashion business and maintaining his interest, essential for a man who declares that he would stop designing the moment it ceased to amuse him.

Born into a wealthy textile family (his father owned a textile mill near Bologna, Italy), Correggiari went on to study political science at the University of Bologna. He was 20 years old when a fire completely destroyed the textile mill, decimating the family fortunes. Correggiari then took off to travel through Germany, England, and France. An eight-month stint in a Lyon mill revived his interest in textiles, and on returning to Italy he ventured into business on his own. He opened a boutique in Riccione, christened Pam Pam, which he decorated in papier maché. Correggiari filled it with his own avant-garde designs, called Follies, which were made by a group of local outworkers. This first shop was successful but shortly after opening a second in Milan, the designer declared himself disillusioned with his profession and left to travel around India.

The lure of fashion proved irresistible, however, and Correggiari was soon back designing in Italy. A contract with the leather firm Zanella, in 1974, was an instant success. He created a collection of 12 styles in leather and introduced a new style called UFO jeans. The success was justified as the company took 1,500,000,000 lire in sales in the first season alone. At the same time Correggiari was also commissioned to work for Daniel Hechter in Paris, designing their men's, women's and childrenswear lines.

In 1976 he formed his own company, Giorgio Correggiari, to produce his own ready-to-wear collections. His frenzied, restless approach to his work rapidly made the company a success. His designs reflected his insatiable curiosity and thorough research into detail and themes. He has been known to pound the streets of Milan on foot trying to find someone who can replicate an original Liberty buckle, or stay up all night in his kitchen dyeing accessories to exactly the right shade to complement a collection. He also enjoys pillaging junk shops and second-hand shops for original buttons or old velvet fabrics that can be reproduced or incorporated into his designs.

If one word could be used to describe Giorgio Correggiari is should be prolific. Establishing his own company has not contained him. He also designs a knitwear line called Cleo and Pat, a men's line, Reporter, a leather collection for leather goods company IGI in

Giorgio Correggiari: Fall/Winter 1992/93. *Photograph by Bob Krieger.*

Perugia and a collection of velvets that returns him to his textile roots for Cantoni. He has also ventured into licensing, designing belts, scarves, handbags, ties, and raincoats under his own label. The Parisian branch of the International Wool Secretariat has also commissioned his services as a design consultant. Small wonder, therefore, that Correggiari declares a day has to be frenzied for him to feel alive.

—Kevin Almond

COSTA, Victor.

American designer

Born: Houston, Texas, 17 December 1935. **Education:** Studied fashion design at Pratt Institute, Brooklyn, New York, University of Houston, and École d'Chambre Syndicale de la Haute Couture, Paris, 1954-58. **Family:** Married Terry Costa, 1958; children: Kevin, Adrienne. **Career:** Bridal designer for Murray Hamberger, New York, 1959-61; bridal designer, Pandora, 1962-65; joined Suzy Perette, and became known for "line for line" copies of European couture, 1965-73; partner, Anne Murray Company, Dallas, 1973. Established Victor Costa, Inc., Dallas, Texas, 1975-present, and Victor Costa Bridal, Dallas, 1989; also produces five collections a year of day and eveningwear for the American market under a licensing agreement with Dior from 1990. **Awards:** May Company American Design Award, 1967; Stix, Baer & Fuller Golden Fashion Award, 1975; Wild Basin Award from the State of Texas, 1979, 1982; American Printed Fabrics Council Tommy Award, 1983, 1984, 1988, 1989; Dallas Fashion Award, 1980, 1987, 1991; University of Houston Distinguished Alumni Award, 1990; Fashion Group of San Antonio, Night of Stars Award, 1991. **Address:** 7600 Ambassador Row, Dallas, Texas 75427, USA.

Publications:

On COSTA:

Books

Fairchild, John, *Chic Savages,* New York 1989.
Milbank, Caroline Rennolds, *New York Fashion: The Evolution of American Style,* New York 1989.

Articles

Primeau, M., "Victor Costa," in the *Dallas Morning News* (Texas), 4 September 1983.
McCue, J., "Costa Lends Voice, Designs," in *The Plain Dealer* (Cleveland, Ohio), 10 September 1987.
Swartz, Mimi, "The Fantasy World of Victor Costa: Texas' Most Famous Dress Designer Had a Dream: He Would Copy His Way to the Top," in *Texas Monthly,* September 1987.
Foote, Jennifer, "King of the Copycats: Costa Cashes in on the Highest Form of Flattery," in *Newsweek* (New York), 4 April 1988.
Johnson, B., and L. Powell, "Copycat King Victor Costa Cuts the High Costa Designer Duds," in *People* (New York), 22 August 1988.
Cohen, R., "Hot Costa," in the *Baltimore Jewish Times* (Maryland), fall 1989.

Paul, M., "Victor Costa Threads History through High Fashion," in the *Dallas Morning News* (Texas), 25 March 1990.
Saenz, Harris J., "Victor Goes Legit," in the *Dallas Morning News* (Texas), 23 May 1990.
Bischoff, R., "Victor(ious) Costa Calls the Shots," in *Trends,* June 1990.
Charles, D., "Not Dior by Ferré, but Dior by Costa," in the *New York Times,* 12 June 1990.
Haber, H., "Victor Costa on Life with Dior," in *WWD: Best of Group III* (New York), August 1990.

*

"The word 'fashion' would not exist if there were no copying," Costa said in the *Baltimore Jewish Times* (fall 1989). "The mirroring of the highest standard has been the basis of our society from Day One. There's a Rolls Royce, a Tiffany, a Beluga caviar—and there's a customer who knows and wants what is considered the ultimate. It takes talent to look at the world and see what is in the wind for his customer so that she always looks pretty and feels provoked to buy."

I am in the business of dressing ladies when they are seen socially in the latest fashions. That basically has to do with social sameness. A lady goes to the same places and sees the same faces so she needs changes in social attire. Whether she is a career woman, housewife, or executive, each day she may go about her daily duties while her clothing is a secondary concern. When she is seen socially, she thinks about what she will wear and that is where I come into play. Social dressing has evolved into a "pay and play" occasion. Private parties have merged with charity events and new outfits are required frequently.

I have some customers that I have been dressing for 30 years and now I'm dressing their daughters and their granddaughters. So there are three generations of Victor Costa customers out there—it keeps you young because the younger girls, the granddaughters, have made a whole return to tradition. In the 1990s, with the Aids epidemic, a return to traditional values has put a new emphasis on the wedding and all of its attendant parties, teas, fêtes, and receptions.

Special occasion dresses have always been the hallmark of my business. My quest for what is new sends me around the world. It is a sense of pride and fulfilment that some of the most noted and important women in the world are wearing my clothes. But also a young girl of 13 may get a Victor Costa dress which will have name recognition and make her feel special. Women adore how they look in their Victor Costa dress.

—Victor Costa

*   *   *

Victor Costa has always loved fashion. Known as the "King of the copycats," his status in the design world is unique. Costa designed dresses for childhood friends in Houston and was entranced by Hollywood film stars and their glamour. He went on to study at the Pratt Institute, New York, and later spent a year at the School of the Chambre Syndicale de la Haute Couture in Paris. This early contact with the Paris fashion world as it existed in the days when Christian Dior reigned and before changes were ushered in by the 1960s had a great impact on Costa. His feeling for dressing women is based on a 1950s sense of style and formality.

New York's Seventh Avenue fashion business was built on copying Paris designs. Buyers and designers alike would flock to Paris to buy a model to "knock-off" or reinterpret. Hattie Carnegie built a respectable business doing this and nurtured several important designers, among them Norman Norell. Post-World War II saw the escalation of photographs from Paris couture shows being published in newspapers, but with a significant lag time. When Costa returned from Paris to New York in 1959 he was immediately charged with copying the latest Paris designs. Costa, who had a photographic memory and a quick hand at sketching, was able to translate what he saw on the Paris runways into successful designs for the Suzy Perette company during the 1960s.

Costa has parlayed his early training into a multimillion-dollar business. He travels to Europe frequently to attend the haute couture, prêt-à-porter fashion shows and Premier Vision fabrics. His ability to comprehend couture and ready-to-wear fashions is a complex and masterful talent. He is not content with only a quick sketch or photography but often goes so far as to purchase the original couture design to study the construction and fabric. He chooses many fabrics in Europe and the United States, but all of his construction is conducted on-site in Dallas so that Costa can oversee the work.

Victor Costa is openly doing what others often attempt to mask. Now that the world sees fashion changes so rapidly and shopping has become a recreational hobby, Costa must deliver new merchandise to five different markets a year. All of these dresses are not replicas but may represent a distillation of the most current fashion trends. Costa translates the essence of these trends in his work. There are loyal customers to whom he personally caters with the loving attention of a couture designer. Costa, whose client list reads like a "Who's Who?" of society and entertainment personalities, seeks to make all women feel beautiful.

—Myra Walker

COSTELLOE, Paul.

Irish designer

Born: Dublin, Ireland, 27 June 1945. **Education:** Studied at the École d'Chambre Syndicale de la Haute Couture, Paris, 1968-69. **Family:** Married Anne Cooper, December 1981; children: Justin, Paul-Emmet, Gavin, Jessica, Robert, William, Nicholas. **Career:** Worked with Jacques Esterel, Paris, c. 1967, and for the Rinascente Group in Italy for three years, 1970-73; moved to New York and worked on Seventh Avenue, also worked for Anne Fogarty, then moved back to Ireland, 1978; showed first collection, 1979; first men's collection 1981; introduced diffusion line, Dressage, 1989; introduced Studio Line 1992. **Address:** Castle House, 76 Wells Street, London W1P 4BN, England.

Publications:

On COSTELLOE:

Articles

"Paul Costelloe—Designer Profile," in *Vogue* (London), November 1981.

Buckley, Richard, "A Bit o'Costelloe," in *DNR: The Magazine* (New York), August 1984.
Eastoe, Jane, "The Tall Guy," in *Fashion Weekly* (London), 3 August 1989.
Jeal, Nicola, "A Profit in His Own Land," in *The Observer Magazine* (London), 17 September 1989.
Burgess, Robert, "Man of the Cloth," in *Country Living* (New York), May 1991.

*   *   *

In its time the fashion industry has been accused of being many things: flippant, bitchy, overly theatrical, or suffering from short-lived trends that are too wacky to sustain economic gain. Amid such hysteria and uncertainty, it is perhaps reassuring to find a designer like Paul Costelloe. Unpretentious and realistic, the Irish-born Costelloe is known as an ordinary man, level-headed and calm. Attributing his drive, ambition, and success to his wife and family in Dublin, he remains a popular figure in London fashion circles and is held in great affection by his employees.

Renowned for use of natural fibres and fabrics, the best quality wools and silks, and a particular bias towards traditional Irish linen, Costelloe clothes are one of the most subtle, understated, yet beautifully designed and manufactured collections available today. Acknowledging his love of Giorgio Armani's tailoring and the influence of Italian taste and style on the cut and flair of his collections, Costelloe always manages to fit an inspirational visit to Italy into his schedule, before commencing the design of a new collection.

Currently three collections are produced each season under the Costelloe label, including the main line range which is elegant, formal and quietly sexy and the diffusion range called Dressage, described as country, timeless, and more suited to weekend dressing. A third collection, Studio Line, was launched in 1992 and is described as investment tailoring, in neo-classic colours. The clothes are aimed at today's modern career woman who has a distinctive, quiet taste and understated sophistication.

Costelloe's spring-summer 1992 collection was an example of the designer at his peak. A series of sharp, sugary suits in pink, yellow, and green wool opened the collection. Teamed with short, flirty, polka dot skirts or blouses, and oversize double crown hats, they were perfect for summer events like Ascot or garden parties. Ladylike check cotton suits followed. Teamed with straw boaters and decorated with Costelloe's distinctive brass buttons, the look was demure and pristine, offset by soft kid gloves and gold jewellery. Like Armani, Costelloe loves beige and this colour, in various hues, features strongly in nearly all of his collections. For the Dressage spring-summer 1992 collection, long slim-line linen separates were shown teamed with an overscaled beige and cream lily print. The look was very Greta Scachi in the film *White Mischief,* accessorized with round dark glasses and panama hats.

Before starting his own label, Costelloe had a varied and well-travelled fashion career. Born in Dublin, he was from an early age fascinated by women: the way they dressed, talked, and acted. This inspired him to pursue a career in fashion and he enrolled at a local design college. He graduated in the early 1960s, and his sense of adventure directed him to Paris.

Armed with only a portfolio of design ideas, he followed the familiar route of knocking on fashion company doors, asking for work. The house of Jacques Esterel took him on. This was followed by work for an Italian manufacturer, then several positions in fashion houses on Seventh Avenue in New York. By this time Costelloe

Paul Costelloe: Autumn/Winter 1994.

had become experienced in fashion design, import, and export. Ever the opportunist entrepreneur, he realized that he should use his talent and knowledge for his own benefit, rather than someone else's, so he returned to Ireland to set up his own business.

He teamed up with Robert Eitel, a successful Irish businessman, to form the company Paul Costelloe and launched the first collection in 1979. The small fashion company has since grown into a multimillion-pound concern. Until recently the collections were shown seasonally at the British Designer Show at Olympia in London, where Costelloe was always a popular figure. Recently, following a trend established by several other London designers, he has opted to show at smaller, more distinctive venues.

Costelloe envisages the company expanding into other product areas and has ambitions to extend his love of cloth and colour into the creation of a Paul Costelloe lifestyle. He wants to surround his customer with the subtle Costelloe touch, incorporating accessories and an interior collection for the home as well as a line of clothes for men and women.

A keen member of the Chelsea Arts Club where he stays in London, Costelloe retains his down-to-earth Irish charm and wit, as exemplified when he met Bruce Oldfield in Paris. Forgetting his name he quipped, good naturedly, "Ah, the King of Fashion."

—Kevin Almond

COURRÈGES, André.

French designer

Born: Pau, Pyrenées Atlantiques, 9 March 1923. **Education:** Studied engineering at École des Pont et Chaussées; studied fashion in Pau and Paris. **Family:** Married Jacqueline (Coqueline) Barrière in 1967; daughter: Marie-Clafoutie-Ustoa. **Career:** Cutter, Cristobal Balenciaga, Paris, 1945-61; independent fashion designer, Paris, 1960-61; founded Courrèges fashion house, boulevard Kléber, Paris, 1961-65; first haute couture collection, 1965; business sold to l'Oréal, 1965; resumed designing, 1967, with Prototype custom line, Couture Future high priced ready-to-wear line introduced 1969; first fragrance line *Empreinte* introduced, 1971; men's ready-to-wear line and men's fragrance introduced, 1973; Hyperbole lower priced ready-to-wear line, 1980; company purchased by Itokin, 1983; produced collection with Jean-Charles de Castelbajac, spring-summer 1994 and 1995. Also: designed own boutiques from 1970, accessories, leather goods, watches, belts, bathrooms, furniture, stationery, automobiles, windsurfing equipment and others, from 1979. **Awards:** Couture Award, London, 1964. **Address:** 40 rue François Premier, 75008 Paris, France.

Publications:

On COURRÈGES:

Books

Halliday, Leonard, *The Fashion Makers,* London 1966.
Bender, Marylin, *The Beautiful People,* New York 1967.
Lambert, Eleanor, *World of Fashion: People, Places, Resources,* New York and London 1976.

André Courrèges: 1969.

Milbank, Caroline Rennolds, *Couture: The Great Designers,* New York 1985.

Articles

Ryan, Ann, "Courrèges," in Ruth Lynam, *Couture: An Illustrated History of the Great Paris Designers and Their Creations,* New York 1972.
Wolfe, David, "Courrèges," in *International Textiles* (London), April 1990.
Schneider, Karen, "Up, Up and Hooray! Designer André Courrèges Celebrates 25 Years of Miniskirt Fame," in *People,* 9 July 1990.
Betts, Katherine, "Courrèges: Back to the Future," in *Women's Wear Daily* (New York), 22 January 1991.
"Courrèges," special supplement of *L'Officiel* (Paris), 1994.

*   *   *

One of a generation of strikingly innovative designers working in Paris in the 1960s, André Courrèges was one of the first since Chanel to understand the potential for womenswear of using the items which make up the male wardrobe. His goal became to provide the same simple range of garments for women, not by mere appropriation of male adornment, but inventing a totally new modernistic aesthetic.

Courrèges regarded the 1950s silhouette of a tightly boned and wasp-waisted mannequin, teetering on impossibly high stiletto heels, as completely alien to the needs of the modern woman of the 1960s, even though he had worked for Balenciaga for 11 years, from 1950 to 1961, as chief cutter. Courrèges subsequently left to set up his own business with his wife Coqueline. Their first collection, using tweeds and soft wools, had yet to shake off Balenciaga's influence.

Ultimately Courrèges saw the male wardrobe as more logical and practical than a woman's because of its unadorned and reductionist nature, resulting from its being pared down to the barest essentials over the passage of time. Thus he responded as an engineer well versed in the functionalist aesthetics of architectural practitioners such as Le Corbusier and, utilizing the skills he had learned and finely honed at Balenciaga, and his own modernist tendencies, Courrèges conceived a new look of femininity entirely different from that of Balenciaga.

Cutting skills were used to free rather than contain the body, emphasized by short trapeze skirts for extra movement. By 1964 Courrèges was producing spare but not spirited ranges of clothing, such as his monochromatic pinafore dresses and suits with hemlines well above the knee, all in crisply tailored, squared-off shapes. Renouncing the stiletto as an item of clothing symbolizing women's subordination, Courrèges provided his models with flat-heeled white glacé boots and accessorized his honed-down clothes with extraordinary headgear such as futuristic helmets and strange baby bonnets.

Courrèges believed that the foundation of successful design was in understanding function; correct form would automatically follow. Aesthetics was only the wrapping. In fact, the only decoration to be found on Courrèges clothes is either directly allied to its construction, as in the use of welt seaming, or is minor such as the small half belt on the back of his coats. One decorative device he revels in and which was copied extensively within mass market fashion was his use of white daisies made out of every conceivable material such as sequins, lace, or used as patches.

It is still debated whether or not Courrèges invented the mini skirt, but he was indisputably responsible for making trousers and matching tunic tops *de rigueur* for every occasion, overturning the taboo of trouser wearing by women, creating versions slit at the seam to give an exaggerated elongation to the female body and emphasizing this clean streamlined look by using lean, well-muscled female models.

Courrèges displays his love of construction in his use of chevron stitching, such as that used in 1965 at the hips of dresses and trousers, and his use of devices such as the bib yoke, keyhole neckline, and patch pocket. Hip yokes and welted seams with top stitching emphasize the lines of the garment, the stitching occasionally deployed in contrasting colours, such as orange on white, to exaggerate the details of assembly.

Courrèges collections were copied and disseminated worldwide, although the taut outline of the originals was lost when cheaper materials were used. Consequently he refused to stage shows for the press or retail buyers and would only sell to private clients, biding his time until he was ready to produce his own ready-to-wear collection, entitled Couture Future, in 1969. However, by this time his hard-edged style had become dated in comparison with the hippie, ethnic style of the 1970s and his seminal structured A-line dresses with welt seams and square-cut coats on top seemed out of step with contemporary fashion.

By 1990 Courrèges was again designing successfully, spurred by a 1960s revival as the architectural lines of his short trapeze dresses were rediscovered by a new generation.

—Caroline Cox

COVERI, Enrico.

Italian designer

Born: Prato, Italy, 26 February 1952. **Education:** Studied stage design, Accademia delle Belle Arti, Florence, 1971-74. **Career:** Free-lance designer for Touché, Gentry, Tycos, Aquarius, Lux Sports, and Ilaria Knitwear, Milan, 1972-79. Formed Enrico Coveri, SpA, 1978; formed Enrico Coveri France S.A.R.L., 1983. Opened boutique in Milan, 1981, with subsequent shops in Genoa, Viareggio, Piacenza, Paris, Saint Tropez, Beirut, and New York. Launched perfumes *Paillettes,* 1982, and *Dollars,* 1983; introduced home furnishing line, 1984. **Exhibitions:** *Consequenze impreviste,* Prato, 1982; *Italian Re-Evolution,* La Jolla Museum of Art, California, 1982. **Awards:** Uomo Europeo Award, Rome, 1982; Fil d'Or Award, Munich, 1982. *Died* (in Florence, Italy) *6 December 1990.*

Publications:

On COVERI:

Books

Mulassano, Adriana, *The Who's Who of Italian Fashion,* Florence 1979.
Sartogo, Piero, ed., *Italian Re-Evolution: Design in Italian Society in the Eighties* (exhibition catalogue), La Jolla, California 1982.

Articles

Baldacci, Luisa, "Enrico Coveri: lo stilista del colore," in *Arbiter* (Milan), No. 2, 1982.
"Enrico Coveri illustra il segreto della sua moda," in *La Nazione* (Milan), 14 June 1983.
"Enrico Coveri: graffiti che corrono e ballano," in *Vogue* (Milan), January 1985.
"Parigi: spot su Enrico Coveri. Enorme o incollato, la moda degli opposti," in *Vogue* (Milan), February 1985.
"Enrico Coveri: nuovi schemi per il classico," in *L'Uomo Vogue* (Milan), July/August 1985.
Morera, Daniela, and Joe Dolce, " Enrico Coveri," in *Interview* (New York), February 1986.
"Enrico Coveri: uno stile all'inglese," in *Donna* (Milan), July/August 1987.
"Enrico Coveri: righe, quadri, forme base ...," in *Vogue* (Milan), January 1988.
"Enrico Coveri Dies in Italy of Stroke," in *Women's Wear Daily* (New York), 10 December 1990.

*   *   *

You Young is the name of one of the several seasonal Enrico Coveri collections. It is also perhaps the most succinct description for his bold, unpretentious, and fun loving fashion: strong, vibrant colours and striking, witty designs that have always been clear and intelligible, with zany prints and knits often incorporating Pop Art designs and cartoon characters.

Enrico Coveri was born in Prato, near Florence, Italy and studied at the Accademie delle Belle Arti in the city. He began his career as a free-lance designer, creating knitwear and sportswear lines for three collections, Touché, Gentry, and Tycos, making his mark by being one of the first designers to use soft pastel shades. After a brief move to Paris in 1978 to work for Espace Cardin, he returned to Italy and established his own namesake company.

Each season the company produces a ready-to-wear women's line and several less expensive boutique collections for men, women, teenagers, and children, as well as a vast array of subsidiary Coveri accessory products such as shoes, bags, hats, scarves, and gloves.

Although he excelled at casual clothing, even his eveningwear exuded a young, sporty, wearable feel. Coveri enjoyed shocking and going out on a limb with design. "I love the unexpected to the point of travelling everywhere without set itineraries," he declared when, after three seasons pursuing his ultra casual look, he suddenly produced a collection of extremely feminine tight skirts and high heels. "That certainly shattered the common belief of Coveri only doing things for 16-year-olds," he recalled.

Asked for his design inspiration, he replied that he never really gave it any serious intellectual thought, preferring spontaneous incidents that sparked off ideas and feelings. His ideal woman, he declared, was as indistinct and volatile as he, living for the present and spurning retrospectives or fashion revivals. He studied the contemporary woman in the street, her attitude, her clothes, movements, and accessories.

Perhaps Coveri's strongest and most recurrent theme was in his use of *paillettes* or sequins. Each collection produced a new garment in the fabric, a bright red skin-tight all-in-one, for instance, or a full-length evening dress, or it promoted a new development in the fabric, such as stretch sequin or mixtures of matte and shine. Other favourite fabrics included Lycra and stretch satin, superfine linen, silk, and cotton poplin.

The young, sporty Coveri woman's silhouette seemed always to fluctuate between cling or fluidity, with a recurrent ethnic theme interpreted in a fresh and contemporary way. This led journalist Hebe Dorsey to dub him the "Italian Kenzo" in the *Herald Tribune.*

In a 1978 interview Coveri declared that he had a disdain for the usual work methods of a fashion designer, adding that he hated to draw or do fittings. His approach was very immediate. Ideas would come in torrents during long, sleepless nights and were sketched out rapidly the next day. Models were also dressed and styled at the last minute, the outcome on the catwalk being directed by the type of mood he happened to be in at the time. "I probably make and will continue to make dreadful mistakes," he explained. However, his mistakes were obviously not serious enough to prevent his establishment as one of Italy's most famous and successful fashion names.

Although Enrico Coveri died in 1990, the business has been continued by his family under the direction of his sister and a chosen design team whose successive collections continue to evoke Coveri's acknowledged fashion legacy.

—Kevin Almond

COX, Patrick.

Canadian footwear designer working in London

Born: Edmonton, Canada, 19 March 1963. **Education:** Studied at Cordwainers College, Hackney, London, 1983-85. **Career:** Established firm in London and designed collections for Bodymap, Vivienne Westwood, John Galliano, and others, from 1987. London shop opened, 1991. **Address:** 8 Symons Street, London SW3 2TJ, England.

Publications:

On COX:

Books

McDowell, Colin, *Shoes: Fashion and Fantasy,* New York 1989.
Trasko, Mary, *Heavenly Soles: Extraordinary Twentieth Century Shoes,* New York 1989.

Articles

"Shoe Shines," in *Elle* (London), March 1987.
Rumbold, Judy, "The Last Shall Be First," in *The Guardian* (London), 21 September 1987.
Thackara, John, "Put Your Foot in It," in *The Observer Magazine* (London), 22 November 1987.
Lender, Heidi, "Foot Fetish: Patrick Cox's Wild and Woolly Shoes Have Come to Paris," in *W,* August, 1989.
"Best Foot Forward," in *The Guardian* (London), 10 June 1991.
"Patrick Cox," in *DR: The Fashion Business* (London), 2 November 1991.
"Shoe Shine Boy," in *Toronto Life Fashion,* December/January 1991-92.
"Shoe King," in *For Him* (London), April 1992.
"Taming of the Shoe," in the *Evening Standard* (London), 30 June 1992.

*   *   *

"My early shoes stick in people's minds," says Patrick Cox, "but things are getting more refined." Those who may remember him as the devoted nightclubber of the early 1980s might be surprised to find him, a decade later, presiding over the salon atmosphere of his shoeshop-cum-antiques emporium in London. Patrick Cox has grown up, but he has also gone beyond the image of the shoemaker with "street credibility," designing for Vivienne Westwood, John Galliano, *et al.* He has survived the designer decade of the 1980s and emerged with his ability to wittily re-interpret traditional styling, still constantly in tune with contemporary fashion.

Cox's fascination with the British fashion scene brought him to London, rather than the obvious footwear design centres of Italy. He enrolled at Cordwainers College, Hackney, London to study, but soon found that college life was less rewarding than meeting and making contacts within the London club world. His involvement with the music and fashion scene brought him the chance to design for Vivienne Westwood's first solo collection, whilst he was still at college. He recalls: "I used to shop at Westwood's quite a lot and my flatmate David was her assistant. Six weeks before the show someone realized that nothing had been done about shoes and David suggested that I could probably help ... my gold platform shoes with large knots went down a treat. Everyone noticed them—you couldn't miss them really—and my other commissions have followed from there."

Indeed they did. In no time at all he was designing shoes to accompany the collections of the young English designers who were then flavour of the month on the international fashion circuit. Cox shod the feet to fit the wilful perversities of Bodymap, the calculated eccentricity of John Galliano, and the ladies-who-lunch chic of Alistair Blair.

Cox went on to design his own label collections with such delightfully named styles as Chain Reaction, Rasta, and Crucifix Court. These were typical, hard-edged classic women's silhouettes given the Cox treatment—chain mesh, silk fringes and crucifixes suspended from the heels. Witty and amusing as these styles were, they had limited appeal and Cox would not have attained his current prominence had he not sought a larger audience.

The launch of his own London shop in 1991 gave him the opportunity to show his collections as a whole, displaying the brash alongside the sophisticated. His audience now came from both the devotees of the off-the-wall fashion experimentation of the King's Road and the classic chic of the Sloane Square debutante. Cleverly, his shop was geographically situated between the two.

Selling shoes alongside antiques was a novelty that appealed to the press and boosted Cox's profile. There was something delightful in the presentation of shoes balanced on the arms of Louis XVI gilt chairs or popping out of the drawers of beautiful old dressers. The shoes gained an aura of respectability; a sense of belonging to some tradition, which perfectly complemented Cox's re-interpretation of classic themes.

No longer is there a typical Cox customer. They include the young and not so young. Cox takes great delight when elderly ladies appreciate his now subtle styling and women's shoes now rival those of Manolo Blahnik in their sophistication; a calculated move.

In contrast, the development his men's footwear is less obvious. Cox has always loved traditional English styling, and says: "I believe that British men's shoes are the best in the world, so mine are just an evolution from those classic ideas." This evolution has kept him close to the spirit of British footwear, if not to the colourways. He reproduces the weight and proportions of the styles whilst exaggerating the soles and fastenings.

Patrick Cox is the shoe designer who admits that there is not a lot you can do with shoes. The very nature of footwear imposes constraints upon the designer, where there are fewer problems for the clothing designer. Cox sees shoes as more architectural than clothes; a free standing form with an inside and out. Yet these restrictions do not stop him producing fresh contemporary styles which still work within the perceived framework of what a classic silhouette should be.

—Chris Hill

C.P. COMPANY.

Italian design house

Based in Emilia-Romagna region of Italy, C.P. Company produces menswear fashions designed principally by Massimo Osti; women's

line introduced, mid-1990s; U.S. subsidiary called C.P. Company Sportswear Inc. **Address:** (U.S.) 156 Fifth Avenue, Number 134, New York, New York 10010, USA.

Publications:

On C.P. Company:

Articles

Bober, Joanna, "C.P. Co.'s City of Women," *Women's Wear Daily* (New York), 29 September 1994.

*   *   *

Massimo Osti is synonymous with C.P. Company and to know Massimo Osti is to know what C.P. Company stands for. He chooses to live and work in his native Bologna, Italy, a university town populated by a young, international set. C.P. Company's headquarters are situated in the Emilia-Romagna region of Italy, renowned for its cuisine and local produce. As such, it—and Massimo Osti—is far removed from the hustle and bustle of Milan.

With Italian fashion designers' propensity for generating myths around their collections, Massimo Osti's approach is in stark contrast to this prevailing trend. Osti has no myths and is proud of it. He fashions his collection not only from an aesthetic point of view but, first and foremost, from a functional one.

Osti feels close to his roots, and lives an understated lifestyle. Unlike some of his better-known counterparts, he is never in the limelight. He does not hold fashion shows, and his catalogues highlight only the clothes, with no glamorous models, or exotic locations, and no fancy studio lighting. Osti is against artifice in any form. He does not even consider himself to be a true designer, but occupies himself with mastering the technical challenge of the items in his line—specifically, the fabrics and finishes. He shows a new line twice a year, but never refers to his output as a collection; rather, they are "pieces." There is never any theme or story in the C.P. Company line.

This designer's working uniform consists of a navy C.P. silk shirt and a pair of navy Stone Island jeans, with perhaps a navy tie. Osti himself loves to sail and even has a soccer field on his property. Thus, as a sportsman, he understands the need for performance sportswear. All his woven fabrics are garment-washed, and he started using this process long before it was all the rage in the men's sportswear industry. He was also one of the first to use water-repellent coatings on his fabrics, a process that is now standard on outerwear. What would otherwise be a delicate item—such as a burlap linen raincoat—is coated with polyurethane to make it practically indestructible. An indigo denim shirt is garment-bleached and enzyme-washed to have the feel of silk.

That is the essence of Osti's philosophy, if he were willing to articulate one: to take fine, even luxury fabrics, and to treat them in such a way that they can be worn nonchalantly—or to take common fabrics and give them a luxury finish. C.P. Company is the essence of casual elegance and rugged versatility. It is stylish, never trendy, ideal for the man with good taste, a modicum of style, and a love of the finer things in life. Men who wear C.P. Company are averse to displaying designer labels, preferring instead to appear well-dressed in an unselfconscious way. They also have an intellectual bent and are not impressed with flashy things. In other words, Massimo Osti's customers are very much like himself. Indeed, Osti chose the Flatiron Building as the location for his New York store not only because of its architectural and historical significance, but because it is also slightly off the beaten path, setting C.P. Company apart from the pack.

For over 20 years, Osti has done for men's sportwear what, perhaps, Balenciaga did for women's couture. He has honed it almost to a science, becoming the standard against which many other sportswear firms measure themselves. There is a strong probability that any novelty in finishing or dyeing that one may encounter in the men's market has been tested—and probably developed—first by Massimo Osti. He is as thorough as they come in the area of fabric research, having at his disposal an archive of tens of thousands of items of used clothing, what he refers to as his "inspirational muse," and the "conscience" of the past. He has respect for styles of the past, but strives to perfect them for the future. While his fabrics may be novel, his silhouettes are consistently classic, with an appealing lived-in quality.

Underneath the C.P. Company label is the phrase "Ideas from Massimo Osti," and that in itself speaks volumes about the pragmatic approach of the line's designer. "We are selling a garment or product and not its label or name," Osti has said, refusing to take part in any self-promotion.

—Vicki Vasilopoulos

CRAHAY, Jules François.

French designer

Born: Liège, Belgium, 21 May 1917. **Education:** Studied fashion and art in Paris, 1934-35; worked in mother's dressmaking salon, Liège, 1936-39; salesman, Jane Regny, Paris, c.1939. **Military Service:** Performed military service, taken prisoner of war in Germany, 1940-44. **Career:** Opened own fashion house, Paris, 1951 (closed); designer, Nina Ricci, Paris, 1952-63; Joined Lanvin, Paris, 1963; head designer, 1964-84; formed ready-to-wear company, Japan, 1985. **Awards:** Neiman Marcus Award, Dallas, 1962; Maison Blanche Award, New Orleans, 1963; Dé d'Or Award, 1984. *Died* (in Monte Carlo) *5 January 1988.*

Publications:

On CRAHAY:

Articles

"Le Dé d'Or à Jules François Crahay: vingt ans de création," in *L'Officiel* (Paris), September 1984.
"Jules François Crahay Dead at 70," in *Women's Wear Daily* (New York), 7 January 1988.
"Jules François Crahay," obituary in *The Observer* (London), 31 January 1988.

*   *   *

Jules François Crahay made his name as a designer, not through the establishment of a label under his own name, but through his work for two of the more elegant Parisian haute couture houses, Nina Ricci and Lanvin. His polished, graceful eveningwear, young and unrestrained, was particularly sought out by many *soignée* French society ladies in the 1950s, 1960s, and 1970s.

Crahay is an interesting, well-known example of many designers who have worked for fashion houses in virtual anonymity. It should be remembered that many couture and ready-to-wear fashion houses have been supported by a vast retinue of designers and assistant designers, whose talent and vision have elevated the established name of a house into the annals of fashion history.

Crahay was born in Liège, France, in 1917, to a dressmaker mother and industrialist father. After attending university and a fashion design school in Paris, from 1934 to 1935, he returned to Liège and a position in his mother's dressmaking business, remaining there until 1951 when he was offered a position as salesman at the house of Jane Regny in Paris.

In 1952 Nina Ricci employed Crahay as a dress designer. Initially, he assisted Ricci with the collections and reorganized and rejuvenated the workshops. He was eventually entrusted with the ready-to-wear and presented his first collection in 1959. The range proved a peak in Crahay's design career. It featured low plunging necklines that foresaw the gypsy styles of the early 1960s. It also highlighted Crahay's unique understanding of pattern cutting, cloth, and garment construction.

In October 1963 Crahay succeeded Antonio del Castillo as the designer at Lanvin in Paris. Jeanne Lanvin had created her Maison de Couture in 1889 and since that date it had conveyed the prestige and traditional image of French elegance. Crahay did little to revolutionize this tradition; instead he emphasized and flattered it. His first collection for the house, spring/summer 1964, met with an enthusiastic response from both buyers and the international press, and verified his position as one of the top Parisian designers, even though he did not work under his own name.

Crahay was one of the first designers to glamorize trousers for eveningwear. Elegant slacks, in sequined or pleated silk, proved best sellers. He also innovated and reintroduced leg o' mutton sleeves in organdy, bejewelled leather gauchos, and alluring jumpsuits for evening.

When it came to his studio work he established a reputation as a demanding taskmaster. He adhered to the best haute couture traditions, where nothing was left to chance and original, fine details were researched and executed with the greatest care. When asked about his work he replied simply, "Look at my dresses; they are what I have created and they are much more important than anything I can say."

Crahay's achievements have been recognized with several important fashion awards. In the early 1970s he succeeded in seeing his own name on a label, when Arkins of New York commissioned him to design a ready-to-wear collection for their department store.

—Kevin Almond

DACHÉ, Lilly.

American millinery designer

Born: Bèigles, France, c.1904. **Education:** Left school at 13. **Family:** Married Jean Desprês in 1931; daughter: Suzanne. **Career:** In Paris, apprenticed with Reboux, later worked for Maison Talbot and Georgette. Immigrated to New York, 1924. Designer, Darlington's (Philadelphia); millinery saleswoman, Macy's, 1924; saleswoman, The Bonnet Shop, New York, 1924; purchased shop from owner and established own millinery business, 1924; expanded and moved business in 1925, 1928; built Lilly Daché Building, East 56th St., New York, 1937; added dresses and accessories, introduced fragrances, *Drifting* and *Dashing,* 1946; launched own clothing line, 1949; added coats, stockings, cosmetics, early 1950s; ready-to-wear millinery collections Mlle. Lilly and Dachettes introduced, early 1950s; closed business, 1968. **Awards:** Neiman Marcus Award, Dallas, 1940; Coty American Fashion Critics Award, 1943. *Died* (in Louvecienne, France) *31 December 1989.*

Publications:

By DACHÉ:

Books

Talking through My Hats, New York and London 1946.
Lilly Daché's Glamour Book, New York 1956.

On DACHÉ:

Books

Morris, Bernadine, and Barbara Walz, *The Fashion Makers,* New York 1978.
Milbank, Caroline Rennolds, *New York Fashion: The Evolution of American Style,* New York 1989.
McDowell, Colin, *Hats: Status, Style, Glamour,* London 1992.

Articles

"Lilly Daché," in *Current Biography* (New York), July 1941.
"Lilly Daché," obituary in the *New York Times,* 2/20 January 1990.

*   *   *

Lilly Daché was the archetypal flamboyant immigrant beloved of Americans and so often taken to their hearts. In approved rags-to-riches fashion, she arrived in New York with a few dollars in her pocket (13 henceforth her lucky number) in the heady days of the mid-1920s. Twenty years later, her name was as much a household word as any milliner's could be.

Daché's heyday coincided with a period in fashion history, the mid-1930s to the mid-1940s, during which one's hat—one always wore a hat—was often more important than one's frock. Great heights of chic and absurdity were achieved by the milliners of the day: tiny doll's hats perched over one eye, two-tone "Persian" turbans stuck with jewelled daggers, pom-poms of mink or marabout; Daché's hats were amongst the most outrageous of all. Her "complexion veil" was tinted green across the eyes, and blush-rose across the cheeks. For Beatrice Lillie, she made a "hands-across-the-sea" hat, with two clasped hands on the front, for the actress to wear both in England and America.

Daché's verve and skills attracted a high-profile clientele of stage and film stars: Marlene Dietrich, Carole Lombard, Joan Crawford, Marion Davies, Gertrude Lawrence—all the big names. She worked with Travis Banton on Hollywood films, providing the hats to top his costumes, as many as 50 for one star for one movie. Often it was she who stuck Carmen Miranda's towering turbans with birds and fruit, and yet more birds and more fruit.

At her New York headquarters, Daché created a setting for herself which now seems the essence of kitsch glamour. Her circular salon was lined with mirrors; she had a silver fitting-room for celebrity brunettes, and a golden one for blondes. For wholesale buyers, she had another circular room padded with tufted pink satin, where she reigned from a leopard-skin divan wearing a leopard-skin jacket and leopard-skin slippers with bells on (to warn her girls of her approach, a job later undertaken by her armful of jingling bangles).

Not an early riser, Daché conducted her morning's business from her bed, in the style of an 18th-century *levée,* dictating letters, buying supplies, designing, and interviewing employees whilst wrapped in a leopard-skin rug (she had a robe made from the skins of more of these unfortunate cats, lined with shocking-pink felt). Occasionally business would be conducted from the reasonably modest depths of a neck-high bubble-bath. But Daché, like so many fashionable New Yorkers of her day, professed herself never so happy as when digging around in the garden of her upstate Colonial home.

Daché was one of the so-called Big Three New York milliners of her day, the others being John Fredericks and Sally Victor, and as such exerted a powerful influence on the American millinery trade, designing for wholesale manufacturers as well as for personal clients. Her designs sold worldwide and she embarked enthusiastically on promotional tours, accompanied by mountainous luggage and concomitant publicity.

At the height of her fame, Lilly Daché had shops in Chicago and Miami Beach, Florida and employed 150 milliners at her flagship building off Park Avenue, New York. Daché was a great self-publicist and epitomized the kind of woman to whom her smart American customers aspired. She was chic, dressy, and flamboyant, and presented herself with self-assured bravado—"I like beautiful shoes

Lilly Daché: 1945. *Photograph courtesy of Costume Institute, Metropolitan Museum of Art.*

in gay colours, with thick platforms and high heels. I like splashy jewellery that clinks when I walk, and I like my ear-rings big. I am...Lilly Daché, milliner de luxe."

—Alan J. Flux

DAGWORTHY, Wendy.

British designer

Born: Gravesend, Kent, England, 4 March 1950. **Education:** Northfleet Secondary School; studied at Medway College of Design, 1966-68, and at Hornsey College of Art (now Middlesex University), London, 1968-71; first-class honours. **Family:** Married Jonathan Prew in August 1973. **Career:** Designer, Radley, 1971-72; founder, designer, Wendy Dagworthy Ltd, 1972-88; joined London Designer Collections, 1975; director, 1982-90. Lecturer in fashion from 1972, including Royal College of Art, London; course director on Fashion BA course at Central St Martin's College of Art and Design, London, 1989; free-lance designer and consultant, Laura Ashley, 1992. Exhibitor Victoria and Albert Museum, London; member of British Fashion Council management committee; speaker at The Fashion Conference, Lagos, Nigeria, 1992; participates in many charity fashion shows and awards. **Awards:** Fil D'Or International Linen Award, Monte Carlo, 1985. **Address:** 18 Melrose Terrace, London W6, England.

Publications:

On DAGWORTHY:

Articles

Polan, Brenda, "The Discreet Charms of a Dagworthy," in *The Guardian* (London), 12 November 1981.
"Influences: Wendy Dagworthy," in *Women's Journal* (London), April 1984.
Polan, Brenda, "British Open," in *The Guardian* (London), 21 March 1985.
Polan, Brenda, "Natural Leaders," in *The Guardian* (London), 25 April 1986.
"Face to Face," in *Creative Review* (London), June 1986.
"Dagworthy Goes Under," in *Fashion Weekly* (London), 24 November 1988.
"The Learning Curve," in *Drapers Record,* 29 May 1993.

*   *   *

For nearly 20 years Wendy Dagworthy produced bright, easy, wearable separates and established herself as one of the most successful British designers in the wacky world of 1980s fashion. Her style was always distinctive and colourful, incorporating cheerful mixtures of fabrics, colours, patterns, textures and an attention to fine detail; "You wear them, they don't wear you," was Dagworthy's fashion philosophy.

She formed her company in 1972 after one year as a designer for the wholesale firm Radley and a year after graduating from the Hornsey College of Art fashion course, with a first-class honours degree. There was an immediate consumer demand for Dagworthy's designs, and prestigious international stores soon placed orders. Italy, in particular, proved a lucrative outlet for her very English look and during the early 1980s she was exporting nearly half of her total output to that country.

Dagworthy loved to use vibrant colours and prints, embroidered Caribbean style *batiks,* mixed with stripes or swirling floral designs in fuchsia, scarlet, and orange. Favourite fabrics were mohairs, strongly textured woven wools, and wool baratheas. Her most popular, signature garments were oversize wool coats, back buttoning smocks, circular skirts, and gathered skirts with boldly tied waists, teamed with easy cardigans or wide cropped jackets. The menswear collections, introduced in the early 1980s, adhered to the same lively, colourful themes and quickly emulated the success of the womenswear, being comfortable and easy to wear.

Dagworthy has always been a strong supporter of British fashion design. In 1975 she joined the London Designer Collections, a prestigious collaboration of British designers, supporting and promoting their industry, and became a director in 1982. She has always been active in British fashion education, both as a lecturer and assessor, participating in design competitions like the Royal Society of Arts Awards and the British Fashion Awards. She has also appeared regularly as fashion consultant to television shows like *The Clothes Show, Frocks on the Box,* and *Good Morning America.*

Wendy Dagworthy Ltd exhibited their seasonal collections at trade shows in London, Milan, New York, and Paris. Her international reputation went from strength to strength each season and her work was recognized with several awards including the Fil d'Or

Wendy Dagworthy: Check short jacket with stripe classic shorts. *Photograph by Jon Prew.*

International Linen Award in 1985. The Victoria and Albert Museum in London display a Wendy Dagworthy outfit in their permanent costume collection.

Wendy Dagworthy closed her business in 1988 and in the following year became the course director for the BA fashion course at London's Central St Martin's College of Art and Design. Since then she has devoted herself to fashion education but has not completely forsaken commercial designing. She still accepts consultancies, her most recent being in 1992, as free-lance designer and consultant for Laura Ashley. She is also an active member of the British Fashion Council's Management Committee.

—Kevin Almond

DALLAS, Sarah.

British knitwear designer

Born: Bristol, England, 1 August 1951. **Education:** Studied at Middlesex Polytechnic, 1971-74; Royal College of Art, London, 1974-76. **Career:** Designed and produced women's knitwear collections under the Sarah Davis label, 1976-88; introduced men's knitwear line, 1987; free-lance design work, 1980—. Has also been a part-time teacher and visiting lecturer at various institutions; course leader, Royal College of Art, Fashion Knitwear, 1990—, Knitted Textiles, 1992—. **Awards:** British Design Council Award, 1987. **Address:** 13 Ranelagh Mansions, 319 New King's Road, London SW6 4RH, England.

Publications:

On DALLAS:

Books

Menkes, Susy, *The Knitwear Revolution,* 1983.
Sheard, Stephen, *Rowan: Designer Collection Summer and Winter Knitting,* 1987.
Sheard, S., *The Rowan/Brother Designer Machine Knitting Boor,* 1987.
The European Design Prize, 1988.

Articles

"Designer Knits for You," in *Pins and Needles,* Fall 1982.
Chubb, Ann, "Knitting it Together with the Skipton Factor," in *The Daily Telegraph,* August 1982.
"Sarah Dallas Knitwear Collection," in *Design,* February 1987.
Dodd, Celia, "Knit Wit in Bold Strokes," in *The Field,* April 1987.

*

I feel quite passionately that Knitwear should have an identity of its own and be an intrinsic part of fashion rather than an accessory to woven garments. This is something I have always striven to achieve with my own knitwear collections.

Starting with colour, yarn is spun and dyed to my specification so developing a unique group of colours and textures I can use in a subtle but witty way, reflecting the spirit of the season.

All the design work and sample knitting is done by myself, then I work closely with the factories to ensure that each garment is produced as I intend it to be. For me, this is one of the most fulfilling and exciting stages of designing a collection, working closely with highly skilled technicians to achieve the final products.

The clothes are new classics, timeless but with an injection of humour. For instance a contrasting coloured stripe on the back, but not on the front of the garment or an entirely different pattern on the sleeves or the back, an element of surprise.

Each piece stands on its own yet works with others as part of a fully co-ordinated collection of sweaters, skirts, dresses, jackets, shawls and scarves. The garments are simple and comfortable, can be styled in a classic, or modern contemporary way, sophisticated or casual. Knitwear is incredibly versatile, and is an ideal way of producing your own exclusive fabric, often engineered to suit each garment.

I endeavour to keep prices keen and so appeal to as wide an age range as possible. Nothing satisfies me more than to see someone of twenty and someone of sixty wearing the same garment but probably styled in quite a different way.

—Sarah Dallas

*   *   *

Sarah Dallas is a prominent fashion knitwear designer who has run her own company and now works as a consultant and an educator. It was while studying for a degree in woven textiles that she first became fascinated by the more spontaneous results made possible by hand knitting. At London's Royal College of Art she studied in the Textile School, but challenged established boundaries to create fashion knitwear.

When she graduated, fashion knitwear designers were still quite rare and the knitwear boom was yet to come. Many companies were very conservative in their approach and in order to get her designs into production, Sarah had to set up on her own. Initially she produced knitwear exclusively for the London-based, upmarket fashion shop Bombacha, creating designs which were made by outworkers on domestic knitting machines. This led to her first independent coordinated fabric and knitwear collection. Building up a market was very time consuming, particularly as it meant shattering preconceptions of the role and potential of knitted garments. Increasing demand for her work led to the decision to move away from hand knitting to full factory production. The change enabled Dallas to extend her range and output, but also affected the appearance of the fabrics and the finished garments. Dallas does not favour the chunky, earthy look which characterizes some hand knits. She is concerned with creating interesting fabrics suitable for a classic fashion look. For her, fashion knitwear is about style.

Dallas's fabrics were usually produced using natural yarns; pure wool for winter and cotton for summer. She had yarns specially spun and dyed in England to match her own specifications and to provide an exact colour palette. The basics were the classic neutrals, navy and black, but her talent was in enlivening them with current fashion tones. Black and white were combined in geometric patterns to create simple crew-necked sweaters which were highlighted by a bright coloured handkerchief in a breast pocket. This detail became a signature of her work. Her look consisted of bold classic shapes with a feel for current fashion. A concentration on detail and an accent on splashes of bright colour characterized each collection. Her ranges sold at the middle and upper ends of the market. The

Sarah Dallas.

customer profile was broad, covering ages 20 to 60. This was due to the versatility of the look and the uncomplicated styling. Described as "New Classics," they won a British Design Council award in 1987.

Since she ceased to work under her own label, Dallas has undertaken free-lance consultancy for British based companies and for those in other manufacturing centres such as Italy, Hong Kong, and China. She has designed hand and machine knit patterns for books and magazines. A lot of work has been for Rowan Yarns, of Holafirth, West Yorkshire, creating patterns for people to knit at home. Her emphasis is still on clean lines and interesting yarns. It is a minimalist approach which concentrates on using every element, yarn, colour, and shape to its fullest extent in each design.

Currently Dallas is course leader of a new M.A. course in Fashion Knitwear and Knitted Textile at the Royal College of Art. The intention is to develop the potential of knitted fabrics and fashion. The recession has badly affected knitwear sales. The future, in Sarah's view, lies in machine knitting and in the use of factory techniques. Hand knitting is too expensive for a depressed market and machines are becoming increasingly sophisticated. Dallas is biding her time. She has no intention of re-establishing her own company just yet. As a businesswoman she knows the importance of right timing. However, she continues to influence the direction of fashion knitwear through her teaching and her consultancy. They enable her to preserve high standards and to prepare the way for a revival of interest in knitwear and knitted fabrics.

—Hazel Clark

DANSKIN

American hosiery manufacturer

Danskin brand of hosiery and leotards introduced as Triumph Hosiery in New York City by Goodman Brothers, 1923; company incorporated as Triumph Hosiery, 1923; changed name to Danskin, Inc., early 1950s; acquired by International Playtex, Inc., 1980; bought by investor Esmark Group, 1986, and Danskin, Inc., became a wholly owned subisdiary of Esmark Inc. **Awards:** Coty Award, 1978. **Address:** 111 West 40th St, 18th floor, New York, NY 10018, USA.

Publications:

On DANSKIN:

Books

McGill, Leonard, *Disco Dressing,* Englewood Cliffs, New Jersey 1980.

Articles

de Ribere, Lisa, "Danskins Are For Dancers," in *Dancemagazine,* October 1983.
Grieves, Robert T., "Stretching the Image," in *Forbes,* 18 April 1988.
Moore, Lila, "Danskin Leaps Back from the Bunk," in *Apparel Industry Magazine,* January 1993.

*   *   *

In 1952 a small family-owned hosiery mill in York, Pennsylvania, quietly introduced a new concept in legwear that would transform the industry. The product was a pair of heavy, two-way-stretch nylon, waist-to-toe tights. They called them Danskins.

This new kind of stocking offered a more precise fit along with greater freedom of movement than did the standard product with limited stretch. Dancers, skaters, and other athletes were the intended market and they bought with enthusiasm. It was not until five years later than a 1957 feature article in American *Vogue* demonstrated the fashion possibilities of these bright, opaque leggings to a broader public. The first national consumer advertising campaign for Danskins followed in fall, 1958. By the end of the 1950s the York Hosiery Mill was the leading American manufacturer of tights and leotards. What had begun as a novelty became the most profitable and visible product for a company whose stock in trade had for decades been so-called "specialty items"—opera hose, long wearing service weight stockings, full fashioned extra longs and extra wides.

The company continued to prosper throughout the 1960s and 1970s under the leadership of third generation owner Peter Goodman. A ten year long advertising campaign advised that Danskins were "...not just for dancing." The versatile Danskin leotard easily made the transition to the beach, with the added benefit to the customer that its cost was less than half that of a purpose designed swimsuit. Danskin tights continued to make a strong fashion statement as hemlines rose in the 1960s and the leg became the focus of attention.

In the 1970s, Danskins moved easily into the discotheque and to the gym floor as Americans made a renewed commitment to fitness and health. Staff designer Bonnie August, who helped win a Coty award for the house in 1978, created disco outfits from a new generation of stretch fabrics which glittered or literally glowed under the black lights of the dance floor. With over 100 styles and almost as many colors to choose from, a Danskin garment existed for all tastes and any leisure time activity. They were easy to find, too. Points of purchase within a single store might include the swimwear, hosiery, and active sportswear departments, as well as special in-store dance or exercise shops.

Nor did the firm ignore professional and aspiring athletes and dancers. In the 1970s, the dazzling performances of Olympic gymnasts Olga Korbut and Nadia Comaneci inspired thousands of little girls to take to the balance beam. Danskin responded with a line of children's gymnast apparel and by sponsoring a universal skill rating test under which children could rate their progress using objective, standardized criteria. Sleeve patches, gold stars and certificates of achievement added to the incentive. Danskin has continued its sponsorship of athletic events in the 1990s. New lines for the 1990s include the Witt line, named for skater Katerina Witt, and the Martha Graham Couture Collection for dancewear, launched in 1993.

Danskin was the first apparel company to exploit the possibilities of synthetic stretch fabrics. From their earliest days, Danskin products combined practicality with innovative materials, imaginative styling, and down to earth prices. Contemporary designers' bodywear fashions may be seen as their upscale, linear descendants.

—Whitney Blausen

Danskin.

DAVIES, George. See **NEXT PLC.**

---

de CASTELBAJAC, Jean-Charles. See **CASTELBAJAC, Jean-Charles de.**

---

de GIVENCHY, Hubert. See **GIVENCHY, Hubert de.**

---

de la RENTA, Oscar.

Dominican designer working in New York

Born: Santo Domingo, 22 July 1932. **Education:** Studied art, National School of Art, Santo Domingo, 1950-52; Academia de San Fernando, Madrid, 1953-55. **Family:** Married Françoise de Langlade in 1967 (died, 1983); married Annette Reed in 1989; adopted son: Moises. **Career:** Staff designer under Balenciaga, Madrid, from 1949; assistant designer to Antonio Castillo, Lanvin-Castillo, Paris, 1961-63; designer, Elizabeth Arden couture and ready-to-wear, New York, 1963-65; partner, designer, Jane Derby Inc., New York, 1965-69; designer, chief executive, Oscar de la Renta Couture, Oscar de la Renta II, de la Renta Furs and Jewelry, Oscar de la Renta Ltd., from 1973; signature perfume introduced, 1977, followed by *Ruffles,* 1983, and *Volupté,* 1991; also owner, de la Renta specialty shop, Santo Domingo, from 1968; designer, couture collection for Balmain, from 1993. **Exhibitions:** *Versailles 1973: American Fashion on the World Stage,* Metropolitan Museum of Art, 1993. **Awards:** Coty American Fashion Critics Award, 1967, 1973; Coty Return Award, 1968; Neiman Marcus Award, 1968; Golden Tiberius Award, 1969; American Printed Fabrics Council "Tommy" Award, 1971; Fragrance Foundation Award, 1978; named Caballero of the Order of Juan Pablo Duarte, and Gran Comandante of the Order of Cristobal Colón, Dominican Republic, 1972. **Address:** 550 Seventh Avenue, New York, New York 10018, USA.

Publications:

On de la RENTA:

Books

Morris, Bernadine, and Barbara Walz, *The Fashion Makers,* New York 1978.
Diamonstein, Barbaralee, *Fashion: The Inside Story,* New York 1985.
Milbank, Caroline Rennolds, *Couture: The Great Designers,* New York 1985.
Perschetz, Lois, ed., *W, The Designing Life,* New York 1987.
Coleridge, Nicholas, *The Fashion Conspiracy,* London 1988.
Milbank, Caroline Rennolds, *New York Fashion: The Evolution of American Style,* New York 1989.

Martin, Richard, and Harold Koda, *Orientalism: Visions of the East in Western Dress* (exhibition catalogue), New York 1994.

Articles

"Everybody's Oscar," in *Time* (New York), 10 November 1967.
Greenstein, S., "The Business of Being Oscar," in *Vogue* (New York), May 1982.
McDowell, Colin, "How to Sniff Out the Right Kind of People," in *The Guardian* (London), 9 January 1986.
"Mr. Peeper's Nights: The Magic Kingdom," in *New York,* 24 November 1986.
Kornbluth, Jesse, "The Working Rich: The Real Slaves of New York," in *New York,* 24 November 1986.
Bentley, Vicci, "King of Ruffles," in *Woman's Journal* (London), November 1987.
Gross, Michael, "A Fitting with Oscar," in *New York,* 18 April 1988.
Hirshey, Gerri, "The Snooty Dame at the Block Party," in the *New York Times Magazine,* 24 October 1993.
Schiro, Anne-Marie, "'Tasteful' Comes in Many Colors," in the *New York Times,* 4 November 1994.
Beckett, Kathleen, "Runway Report: My One and Only Hue: Oscar de la Renta," in *New York Post,* 4 November 1994.
"New York: Oscar de la Renta," in *Women's Wear Daily* (New York), 4 November 1994.
"New York: Oscar de la Renta," in *Women's Wear Daily* (New York), 7 April 1995.

*   *   *

Although he was born in the Dominican Republic and moved to New York at the age of 30, Oscar de la Renta has become a great ambassador for American fashion. His recent appointment as designer to the French couture house of Pierre Balmain in early 1993 was an historic occasion; the first time an American designer had been commissioned by the French couture. This choice in many ways reflects the growing eminence of New York as a fashion force and the international status of American designers.

As a designer, de la Renta has inspired many international trends. During the 1960s his clothes were elaborate and witty parodies of experimental street fashion: jackets and coats of bandanna printed denim, embroidered hotpants under silk mini dresses, or caftans made out of silk chiffon and psychedelic silk saris. He was largely responsible for initiating the ethnic fashion of the 1970s with gypsy and Russian fashion themes incorporating fringed shawls, boleros, peasant blouses, and full skirts. In recent years, de la Renta has been popular for his romantic evening clothes, glamorous, elegant, and made from richly opulent fabrics such as brocade, transparent chiffon, fox fur, ermine, and embroidered *faille.*

All through his career de la Renta has concentrated on simple shapes and silhouettes that have created dramatic and flashy statements. He has an inherent feeling for women's femininity and has established fashion classics, such as variations of his portrait dresses in taffeta, chiffon, or velvet with ruffled necklines or cuffs, or his ornate luncheon suits, embroidered in costume jewellery and gold.

Since founding his own company in 1967 to produce luxury women's ready-to-wear, de la Renta has expanded to create jewellery, household linens, menswear, and perfumes. These products are marketed and sold all over Europe, the Orient, South and North America.

De la Renta had a well travelled international fashion pedigree before establishing his own label business. He studied art at the Academia de San Fernando in Madrid and began sketching for leading Spanish fashion houses, leading to a job at Balenciaga's Madrid couture house, Eisa. A move to Paris in 1961 brought him work as an assistant to Antonio De Castillo at Lanvin-Castillo. He moved with Castillo to New York in 1963 to design at Elizabeth Arden. Joining Jane Derby Inc. as a partner in 1965 he began operating as Oscar de la Renta Ltd. in 1973.

The designer's first marriage to the late Françoise de la Langlade, the editor-in-chief of French *Vogue*, in 1967 was an undoubted asset to his business. Together they created *soirées* that were the equivalent of 18th-century salons. This environment enhanced the wearing of an Oscar de la Renta creation and provided valuable publicity, with frequent mentions in society columns.

De la Renta has not forgotten his Dominican associations and has been honoured as its best known native son and one of its most distinguished citizens with the Orden de Merito de Juan Pablo Duarte. He also helped build a much needed school and day care centre in the republic for over 350.

De la Renta continues to design in New York today, redefining American elegance with his famous womenswear line, Signature, the couture line, Studio, the ready-to-wear line and a range of sophisticated dresses and suits known as Miss.

—Kevin Almond

DEMEULEMEESTER, Ann.

Belgian designer

Born: Kortrijk, Belgium, 29 December 1959. **Education:** Studied at the Royal Academy of Fine Arts, Antwerp, 1978-81. **Family:** Married Patrick Robyn; son: Victor. **Career:** Showed first collection of women's ready-to-wear, 1981; free-lance designer for international ready-to-wear men's and women's collections, 1981-87; has also designed shoes, handbags, sunglasses and accessories since 1987, outerwear since 1989, knitwear since 1991. Founded B.V.B.A. "32" company, with husband, 1985. Opened Paris showroom, 1992. **Exhibitions:** *La bienale de venise avec Rodney Graham,* Anvers, 1993. **Awards:** Golden Spindle Award, Belgium, 1983; Golden T Award, Spain, 1992. **Address:** B.V.B.A. "32," Populeerenlaan 34, B-2020 Antwerp, Belgium.

Publications:

On DEMEULEMEESTER:

Articles

Mower, Sarah, "Six Romp," in *The Guardian* (London), 12 February 1987.

Grauman, Brigid, "The Belgium Connection," in *Elle* (London), October 1987.

"Ann Demeulemeester en grande," in *Le Nouvel Observateur,* 15 November 1991.

Betts, Katherine, "La Nouvelle Vague," in *Vogue* (New York), September 1992.

Sepulchre, Cécile, "Ann Demeulemeester a mis le Hors-Mode a la Mode," in *Journal du Textile,* 12 October 1992.

Dombrowicz, Laurent, and Pascale Renaux, "Ann Demeulemeester, belle et rebelle," in *Jardin des Modes,* November 1992.

Spindler, Amy M., "3 Designers Thrive on Fashion's Unraveled Edge," in the *New York Times,* 15 March 1993.

Mair, Avril, "This is the New Vision," in *i-D* (London), 11 May 1993.

Spindler, Amy M., "Coming Apart," in the *New York Times,* 25 July 1993.

"Trois créateurs: Ann Demeulemeester," in *Arte Magazine,* 27 November-3 December 1993.

"La Cote des Createurs: Les 'baroques' sont plébiscites par les boutiques," in *Journal du Textile,* 28 February 1994.

Spindler, Amy M., "A Mature Mugler, Demeulemeester and Lang," in the *New York Times,* 18 March 1995.

"The Paris Collections: The Ideas of March: Ann Demeulemeester," in *Women's Wear Daily* (New York), 17 March 1995.

*   *   *

Linked to a group of designers to come out of Belgium in the mid-1980s, Demeulemeester's deconstructed style has come into its own as the 1990s have progressed. Her work, with its monochromatic colour schemes and matt layering onto the body of flowing columns of fabric, encapsulates the contemporary *Zeitgeist.*

The impact of this Belgian avant-garde designer's pared-down structure, combining rough edges with more traditionally cut suiting, has been comparable to that of Japanese designers Kawakubo and Yamamoto a decade earlier. Both superseded more overtly designed fashions in favour of purer silhouettes that combine references to antique clothing with the worn-in patina of their fabrics and a disregard for the more conventional notions of fit.

Demeulemeester's work represents (along with Margiela, Dries Van Noten *et al.*) a recognizable 1990s approach to clothing and designer style. It overtakes the often directionless attempts to integrate the sportswear styles of the late 1980s into a high fashion context and the myriad of 1970s reworkings in the early 1990s. Dedicated to this more experimental strain of fashion, Demeulemeester, having won early accolades for her designs while still at college, pays great attention to detail. From the start she used local craftsmen to make up her work. In the late 1980s her designs were more attuned to fashionable classic garments. In 1987 short black sunray pleated skirts were shown with cross-over braces and crisp white shirts, worn with stark gabardine coats. Even at this stage, however, she showed concern for proportion, constructing skirts and dresses with adjustable waistlines that could be worn high or low, altering the emphasis of the design to suit the figure of the wearer and give a different sense of balance to the overall outfit.

The appeal of designs which are at the cutting edge of fashion and yet ultimately still wearable has ensured Demeulemeester's success, and, as her work has grown in confidence, so have her sales. The strong lines of her signature long coats and dresses are punctuated by more deconstructed styles like the frayed-edged lacy knit top shoe showed in 1993. This, with its shrunken fit, married the resurgent punk ethos of rough, makeshift anti-fashion to the languorous swing of Gothic-inspired floor-skimming coats.

Her autumn-winter collection for 1993 continued in this vein. Shroud-like white dresses with overlong cuffs and black velvet and brocade coats were set against fitted crêpe sheaths, their differing textures giving a sense of shade and light to provide interest and

Ann Demeulemeester: Winter 1994.

definition to each outfit. The trumpet cuffs and jet crucifixes with which these were teamed gave a religious aspect to the show which was echoed amongst her contemporaries.

Although there will inevitably be a backlash against such austerity, Demeulemeester's work is strong enough to outlive short-term trends and consolidate her name as a designer of avant-garde independent styles, incorporating an artistic use of fabric and texture and an attention to detail.

—Rebecca Arnold

de PRÉMONVILLE, Myrène.

French designer

Born: Pays Basque region of France, 1949. **Career:** Assistant to Popy Moreni; free-lance designer; designer, Prémonville et Dewavrin, 1983—; also free-lance designer for Fiorucci. First boutique opened in Paris, 1990; New York boutique opened, 1991; Munich boutique opened, 1992. **Address:** 52 boulevard Richard Lenoir, 75001 Paris, France.

Publications:

On DE PRÉMONVILLE:

Articles

Joby, Liz, "Designing Women: Myrène de Prémonville," in *Vogue* (London), July 1987.

*   *   *

"Great feel, beautiful proportions, fantastic colour," declared Myrène de Prémonville stockist Carole Cruvellier, whose Manchester, England shop, De La Mode, stocks exclusively French designers. "I particularly remember a petrol blue trouser suit with a wine cuff, that seemed to sum up her meticulous research and use of colour," she said. Lucille Lewin of the Whistles shops in London, who backed the opening of Myrène de Prémonville's first British boutique in 1991, enthuses about her superb cut. She believes the clothes have a longevity that makes economic sense to the customer, always flattering, yet never trite. Not classic, they are collectable for their quirky individuality.

De Prémonville began her company in the mid-1980s, with Giles Dewavrin as partner. Backed by a large finance group, the Union Normand Investissement, her first designs were a response to what she felt was not available to women at that time: effervescent, young tailored suits in bright colours, often with witty contrasting colour trims or bright check details; unexpected coloured appliqués on bright white, translucent blouses; a huge, painted sunflower detail on a cream georgette mini tunic, teamed with black leggings. She even introduced her own stirrup trousers because, as she said at the time, "No one else's felt comfortable."

There is always a hint of 1950s couture in her work but never heavy or overly structured. She brings a younger, lighter, more modernistic feel to mini-skirted frock coats in yellow wool, with Balenciaga-style gathered sleeves. Full skirted jackets with huge belts, reminiscent of Doris Day shirtwaists, and a pastel, deckchair-striped trouser suit looked perfect for a 1950s into 1990s St. Tropez.

De Prémonville is very concerned with the practicalities of the fashion business. Positions at Hermès then at Fiorucci strengthened her appreciation of vivid colour and kitsch, both prominently combined in her designs today. She sees her customer as being practical yet artistically and intellectually aware, with a witty sense of fun, very much an extension of her own personality. This also explains why her designs are often a reaction to what she feels her wardrobe lacks.

De Prémonville believes that a designer's work should evolve, rather than change radically, each season. Gradual alterations in detailing, proportion, and silhouette are the key to her appeal. Today she looks to English eccentricity for inspiration. She feels that the French have become opposed to change and somewhat institutionalized in their dress sense.

Conclusively it is the suit that emerges as the signature Myrène de Prémonville garment. Sharp, quirky, and geometric, it has been restyled and restructured for the 1980s and 1990s woman.

—Kevin Almond

de RIBES, Jacqueline.

French designer

Born: Jacqueline de Beaumont in Paris in 1931. **Education:** Studied architecture. **Family:** Married Comte Edouard de Ribes in 1947; children: Elizabeth, Jean. **Career:** Free-lance fashion designer, Paris, from 1982; showed first collection, 1983; jewelry collection introduced, 1984. **Awards:** Rodeo Drive Award, Los Angeles, 1985. **Address:** 47 rue de la Bienfaisance, 75008 Paris, France.

Publications:

On DE RIBES:

Articles

"Parisienne," in *Holiday* (Philadelphia), January 1956.
Donovan, Carrie, "Social Graces," in the *New York Times Magazine,* 10 July 1983.
"De Ribes Style: Allure and Tradition," in *Vogue* (New York), May 1984.
Morris, Bernadine, "Jacqueline de Ribes Had a Design Suited to Success," in the *New York Times,* 30 September 1985.
Shapiro, Harriet, "Going from Riches to Rags, Designing Vicomtesse Jacqueline de Ribes Reaps as She Sews: Handsomely," in *People* (Chicago), 16 December 1985.
"Jacqueline de Ribes," in *Harper's Bazaar* (New York), April 1986.
Dryansky, G. Y., "Jacqueline de Ribes' Jewelry: Specially for the Upper Crust," in *Connoisseur* (New York), April 1988.
Bogart, Anne, "Regal Air," in *Harper's Bazaar* (New York), September 1989.
Menkes, Suzy, "Couture's Grand Ladies," in the *Illustrated London News,* Spring 1990.

*   *   *

When the January 1956 *Holiday* magazine featured Vicomtesse Jacqueline de Ribes in the series "The Most Fashionable Women" she was, at the age of 25, already recognized for her good taste in clothes. Even then she favored line and color over excessive detail. Growing up in privileged surroundings, she had worn couture all of her life, secretly harboring a desire to become a fashion designer herself, an occupation unsuitable for someone of her status. Throughout her life de Ribes had been making suggestions to the couturiers who dressed her, bringing sketches, making changes, so that when she took the plunge and produced a collection for fall 1983, she was using all of her years of exposure to haute couture, synthesizing with it her own carefully developed aesthetic taste. It helped that another society woman, Carolina Herrera, had successfully entered the fashion business two years before.

Known as a great beauty, with an aristocratic profile and demeanor, possessed of a tall, long-necked, slender figure, de Ribes designed what she knew best: evening dresses and sophisticated daytime suits. The gowns were long, slim, with shoulder interest consisting of dramatic ruffles, drapes, or simple bows. Tailored suits were detailed with black velvet. The clothes were expensive ready-to-wear, each suit or gown priced at several thousands of dollars. Clearly de Ribes was designing for herself, and for women with her money and physical elegance. The clothes were well received in Paris and especially by American buyers. Critics did point out that de Ribes's work showed the clear influence of Saint Laurent, Dior, Cardin, and Valentino. Nevertheless she knew how to distil the elements to focus on her own special "look."

Consistent with her emphasis on color and line, de Ribes continued to design plain, almost severe, dinner suits in bright pastel satins. Her gowns of unadorned bright or deep colours became the perfect background for de Ribes's next venture, jewelry. To maintain her own less-is-more philosophy, de Ribes turned to designing jewelry deliberately made of non-precious materials such as rhinestones, beads, fake pearls, even ceramics. Her clients had adequate supplies of real jewelry; de Ribes designs would be chunky, modern, dramatic, perfect adornment for her clothes.

Even lace could find an eye-catching use in a slim black de Ribes gown which featured V-shaped bodice and side insertions of the see-through fabric. Four years later, the highest compliment was paid to the designer when Carolyne Roehm, another socialite designer of the late 1980s, created a long black evening gown featuring sections of sheer black georgette in a similar fashion. By 1990, de Ribes had softened her look somewhat. Her evening gowns began to be made of gathered, draped bodices and yards of sherbet-hued chiffon. An even younger look evolved the next year with the introduction of above the knee cocktail dresses, with seductive side draping or flouncy layered organza. de Ribes continues to travel to show fashions at charity balls, and to sell to the wealthy in her boutiques in Japan and on Rodeo Drive, Beverly Hills.

—Therese Duzinkiewicz Baker

de SENNEVILLE, Elisabeth.

French fashion designer

Born: Paris, 16 October 1946. **Education:** Studied at Notre Dame des Oiseaux school in Paris. **Family:** (Children) Loup, Zoé. **Collections:** Musée Galliera, Paris; Musée de la Mode, Paris; Musée de Roubaix; Musée de la Mode de Marseille. **Exhibitions:** *Elisabeth de Senneville,* Musée des Arts Décoratifs, Paris, 1986; *Elisabeth de*

Senneville: une mode hors mode, Musée d'Art et d'Industrie, Roubaix, France; *Elisabeth de Senneville,* Musée de la Mode, Marseille, 1994. **Address:** 3 rue de Turbego, Paris, France.

Publications:

On de SENNEVILLE:

Books

Elisabeth de Senneville: une mode hors mode (monograph), Paris 1994.

*

I like to see myself as a designer of futurism and technology. Since 1979 I have been designing all my prints with computers and I have introduced futuristic fabrics into fashion, such as holographic material. I always try to think that my clothes can still be worn after the year 2000. I also like to design for children. I make very modern prints and shapes for them. My clothes have often been compared to Chinese clothes because they have simplicity.

—Elisabeth de Senneville

* * *

While Elisabeth de Senneville has been active in French fashion since the 1960s, she came to prominence in the late 1970s and 1980s with her collections of avant-garde contemporary sportswear, defining her design signature, a combination of functionalist and futuristic sensibilities.

De Senneville's look and inspirations have remained consistent since she founded her own line in 1975. Rather than following trends, de Senneville is primarily interested in new technological developments and constantly seeks to apply nonapparel industrial processes and materials to her clothes. Her vivid, often neon or fluorescent colored, prints are derived from computer generated images, using video technology and images from the mass media or art history that she appropriates and applies to her clothes. Unconventional and industrial materials she has used include plastic, Tyvek (an extremely strong, nonwoven fireproof material), canvas, knitted copper threads, rubber, and wool mattress padding. Among her most unusual innovations were the creation, in 1981, of plastic clothes imprinted with holograms. While many of her materials are unusual, the shapes of de Senneville's clothes are often basic and functional, inspired by athletic wear, work clothes such as jumpsuits, or the quilted clothes of the masses of China. Her signature Chinese inspired outerwear jacket is hip-length quilted canvas that snaps up to a bright plastic collar.

The de Senneville customer is young, adventurous, and intelligent. In her stores in Paris, customers can shop for avant-garde books as well as clothes and can see and hear the work of young artists and musicians. The designer not only has an affinity for contemporary art but has also actively participated in the intellectual discourses of current art practice by adopting theoretical techniques such as appropriation and reinterpretation and recycling of images. De Senneville's work is not meant, however, for an intellectual élite. She has consistently sought new means of exposing her clothes to a wider audience, through licensing agreements, mailorder, and worldwide distribution arrangements.

In 1994-95, de Senneville celebrated 20 years designing her own collection with an exhibition at the Musée de la Mode de Marseille. The exhibition title, *Une mode hors mode* (A Fashion Outside Fashion), aptly expresses de Senneville's design point of view which, though always stylish and contemporary, is a distinct manifestation of her individualistic concerns with materials and processes.

—Alan E. Rosenberg

DESSÈS, Jean.

French designer

Born: Jean Dimitre Verginie, in Alexandria, Egypt, 6 August 1904. **Education:** Studied law, then design, in Paris. **Career:** Designer, Mme. Jane in Paris, 1925-37; opened own house in Paris, 1937; launched Jean Dessès Diffusion line in America, 1950; in Paris, opened boutique Les Soeurs Hortenses, 1951, and made-to-measure dress shop, Bazaar, 1953; closed couture house, 1960; closed ready-to-wear house, 1965; free-lance designer in Greece, to 1970. *Died* (in Athens, Greece) *2 August 1970.*

Publications:

On DESSÈS:

Books

Bertin, Célia, *Paris à la Mode,* London 1956.
Carter, Ernestine, *With Tongue in Chic,* London 1974.
Lambert, Eleanor, *World of Fashion: People, Places, Resources,* New York and London 1976.
Carter, Ernestine, *The Changing World of Fashion: 1900 to the Present,* London 1977.

*   *   *

Jean Dessès belongs to the small group of couturiers, such as Vionnet, Balenciaga and Grès, whose clothing combines technical skill with sculptural aesthetic. Although he began as a designer for a small couture house in Paris in the 1920s, and opened his own house in 1937, it was not until the post-war years of the 1940s and 1950s that his work gained its greatest acclaim.

The hallmarks of his post-war fame are evident in his pre-war work. Draped and twisted sashes and bodices, cape or kimono sleeves, a fondness for asymmetry, and ornament derived from the architecture of the garment rather than applied as surface decoration, were all elements of both his day and evening wear in the late 1930s. Magazine coverage during that period suggests that he favored jerseys and crêpes, with the jersey dresses in particular anticipating the draping skill which Dessès would use to such advantage after 1945.

Immediately after the war Dessès began to explore his own heritage for design themes which would best use his cutting expertise. He showed a collection inspired by ancient Egyptian costume in 1946 and returned to that theme in the mid-1950s, while the costume of ancient Greece provided a continuous thread through his work. Today his reputation rests primarily on the pleated and draped silk chiffon evening dresses which most notably express Dessès's historical interests.

Dessès's transition from jersey to chiffon may have been mandated by the fuller silhouettes of the 1940s, or perhaps by the fact that Madame Grès was the acknowledged master of the draped jersey column, but the change set him on a path which made his name. In September 1951 New York *Vogue* lauded Dessès's chiffon gowns as the "Fords" of his collection, "good for a lifetime." By 1958 they were termed "classic." The variations on the theme seemed endless, but there are several important common factors. Appearances notwithstanding, the dresses were not always simple Grecian draperies. The understructures were formal and the cuts were complex, with swags, sashes, bows, and scarves twisted and pleated into shapes that seem effortless, and defy analysis. In lesser hands they might simply seem contrived. The dresses also show his sensitive, if somewhat conservative, color sense. Cream or ivory, always flattering, are constants, but Dessès often used two or three shades of one hue, or used three different hues, but of equal value, to maintain harmony. It is also worth noting that the garments are impeccably made; every yard of hem in the double- or triple-tiered chiffon skirts has a hand-rolled finished.

Dessès was equally deft with crisp silks, rough tweeds, and fine dress wools, and his most skilful and inventive draping and cutting techniques were often allied with these fabrics. Dropped shoulder lines, raglan or kimono sleeve variations, and draped collars softened voluminous mohair coats and tweed suit jackets. Tucks, godets, and intricate seaming molded crêpe and gabardine dresses to the contours of the figure. Skirt fullness was swept to the back, folded in at the side, or turned into tiers of flounces which spiraled from hem to hip—all through manipulation of the grain in one piece of cloth.

The most successful of his silhouettes, such as the Streamlined and Winged collections of 1949 and 1951, may not have set trends, but they interpreted the trend with elegance. He favored asymmetry and oblique lines, which gave the garments a sense of movement even in repose. Bold, architectural details such as stand-away pockets and cuffs were used like punctuation marks, adding drama and intensity to a silhouette. Dessès made clothes which were complex but not fussy, and, on occasion, did set the trend in 1950 when he introduced a one-sleeved stole.

Dessès made an easy transition to the 1960s. His stylistic talents were well suited to the cutting possibilities of the stiffer fabrics and simpler silhouettes in vogue at the time. He was also able to devote more of his attention to the ready-to-wear "Dessès Diffusion" line he had started in 1949, and licensed to two US manufacturers—one for suits and one for evening clothes. Dessès closed his couture operation in 1965, apparently due to poor health. His influence on fashion has outlived him, however, figuring even today in the work of Valentino, who was with Dessès's house for several years in the 1950s.

—Madelyn Shaw

DIOR, Christian.

French designer

Born: Granville, France, 21 January 1905. **Education:** Studied political science at École des Sciences Politiques, Paris, 1920-25.

Military Service: Served in the French Army, 1927-28, mobilized, 1939-40. **Career:** Art dealer, 1928-31; free-lance designer and sketch artist, 1934-37; assistant designer, Piguet, 1937-39; lived in Provence, 1940-42; designer, Lelong, 1941-46; Maison Dior opened, 1947; Christian Dior-New York opened, 1948; Miss Dior boutique opened, 1967; fragrances: *Miss Dior,* 1947, *Diorama,* 1949, *Diorissima,* 1956, *Diorling,* 1963. **Exhibitions:** *Christian Dior et le Cinéma,* Cinémathèque Francaise, Paris, 1983; *Dessins de Dior,* Musée des Arts de la Mode, Paris, 1987; *Gruau: Modes et publicité,* Musée de la Mode et du costume, 1989; *Réne Gruau pour Christian Dior,* Musee des Beaux Arts, 1990; *Christian Dior: The Magic of the Fashion,* Powerhouse Museum, 1994. **Awards:** Neiman Marcus Award, Dallas, 1947; Remise de la legion d'honneur a Christian Dior, 1950; Parsons School of Design Distinguished Achievement Award, New York, 1956; Fashion Industry Foundation Award, to the House of Dior, New York, 1990. *Died* (in Montecatini, Italy) *24 October 1957.* **Company address**: 30 avenue Montaigne, 75008 Paris, France.

Publications:

By DIOR:

Books

Talking about Fashion, with Alice Chavane and Elie Rabourdin, London 1954.
Dior by Dior, London 1957.

On DIOR:

Books

Keenan, Brigid, *Dior in Vogue,* London 1981.
Milbank, Caroline Rennolds, *Couture: The Great Designers,* New York 1985.
Musée des Arts de la Mode, *Homage à Christian Dior* (exhibition catalogue), Paris 1986.
Giroud, Françoise, *Dior: Christian Dior 1905-1957,* London 1987.
Pochna, Marie-France, *Christian Dior,* Paris 1994.

Articles

"Paris Forgets This Is 1947," in the *Picture Post* (London), 27 September 1947.
"Christian Dior Story," in *American Fabrics and Fashions* (New York), Summer 1964.
McCooey, Meriel, "The New Look," in *The Sunday Times Magazine* (London), 11 August 1968.
Sweetinburgh, Thelma, "Dior," in Ruth Lynam, editor, *Couture: An Illustrated History of the Great Paris Designers and Their Creations,* New York 1972.
"Dior Is Dior Is Dior," in *American Fabrics and Fashions,* No. 114 (New York), 1978.
McDowell, Colin, "Dior: The Myth, the Legend and Tragedy," in *The Guardian* (London), 12 February 1987.
Buck, Joan Juliet, "Dior's New Look, Then and Now," in *Vogue* (New York), March 1987.
"L'âge Dior," in *Elle,* March 1987.

Bricker, Charles, "Looking Back at the New Look," in *Connoisseur* (New York), April 1987.
Harbrecht, Ursula, "Hommage à Christian Dior," in *Textiles Suisses* (Lausanne), May 1987.
Snow, Carmel, "It's Quite a Revolution, Dear Christian. Your Dresses Have Such a New Look," in *The Independent* (London), 23 October 1987.
Schiro, Anne-Marie, "Color-Filled Chloé and Rarefied Dior," in the *New York Times,* 17 March 1995.

*   *   *

Although Christian Dior died in 1957, he is perhaps one of the most famous fashion designers of the 20th century. In the years after the debut of his first collection in 1947 he was a legendary figure and the world press developed an extraordinary love affair with him, increasing their enthusiasm with each new collection. Dior never disappointed them, constantly creating clothes that were newsworthy as well as beautiful.

Dior was middle-aged when he achieved fame. A sensitive and gentle personality, he had previously worked as a fashion illustrator, then as a design assistant for both Robert Piguet and Lucien Lélong in Paris. In 1946 the French textile magnate Marcel Boussac offered to finance the opening of Dior's own couture house and secured the lease on 30 avenue Montaigne, Paris.

The first collection was revolutionary, heralded as the "New Look" by the fashion press—Dior himself had christened it the "Corolle Line." It was a composition of rounded shoulders, shapely emphasis of the bust, cinched waist, and curvaceous bell-shaped skirt in luxurious fabric. The concept of the collection was not new, bearing a striking resemblance to French fashions of the 1860s. Dior himself attributed his inspiration to the pretty, elegant clothes he had remembered his mother wearing to the Deauville races in the 1900s.

Even though several other designers had experimented with or predicted the new silhouette, Dior's luxurious version reawakened the world to the importance of Parisian couture. At a standstill during World War II, Paris had lost its way as the world's fashion capital. Dior reestablished it as a centre of excellence, creating what Janey Ironside of the Royal College of Art in London described as "a new chance in life, a new love affair."

There were many criticisms of the New Look. Feminists have argued that it was an attempt to return women to an oppressed, decorative role with its emphasis on the restrictive padding, corset, and crinoline. Others were shocked by the extravagant use of ornament and fabric metreage when clothes were still being rationed. The New Look, however, rapidly became a postwar cultural symbol for what Dior himself described as "Youth, hope, and the future."

After creating a furor with his first collection, Dior established himself as a cautious, methodical designer. Each collection that followed was a continuation of the New Look theme of highly constructed clothes. They were christened with names that described their silhouettes, the Zig Zag Line, A Line, Y Line, Arrow Line, etc. All the collections were realized with the finest tailoring and the most sumptuous fabrics: satins, traditional suiting, fine wools, taffetas, and lavish embroideries.

Throughout Dior's ten years of fame, none of his collections failed, either critically or commercially. The only threat to his run of success occurred when Chanel made a fashion comeback in 1954 at the age of 71. Chanel's philosophy, that clothes should be re-

Christian Dior: Fall/Winter 1948/49. *Photograph by Maywald; copyright, A.D.A.G.P.*

laxed, ageless, dateless, and easy to wear, completely opposed Dior's philosophy. "Fifties Horrors," was how she described male couturiers, deploring them for torturing bodies into ridiculous shapes. Dior's reaction was to introduce his most unstructured collection, the "Lily of the Valley Line," was young, fresh, and unsophisticated. Relaxed, casual jackets with pleated skirts and sailor-collared blouses, clothes that "Couldn't be easier," described *Vogue*.

By the time Dior died his name had become synonymous with taste and luxury. The business had an estimated turnover of 20 million dollars a year, thanks in part to Dior's own shrewdness. Dior organized licence agreements to manufacture Dior accessories internationally. By the time Dior died, perfume, furs, scarves, corsetry, knitwear, lingerie, costume jewellery, and shoes were being produced.

Many of Dior's associates have said that his death was timely and that his work and fashion philosophy were entirely suited to his period. It would be interesting to speculate how Dior would have adapted to the excesses of fashion in the 1960s, 1970s and 1980s, because, as his former personal assistant, Madame Raymonde, once said, "If Dior had lived, fashion would not be in the state it is in now."

—Kevin Almond

di SANT'ANGELO, Giorgio.

American designer

Born: Count Giorgio Imperiale di Sant'Angelo in Florence, 5 May 1933. Raised in Argentina; immigrated to the United States, 1962. **Education:** Studied architecture in Florence, industrial design in Barcelona, and art at the Sorbonne. **Career:** Animator, Walt Disney Studios, Hollywood, 1962-63; textile and jewelry designer, 1963-67; designer, Sant'Angelo, New York, 1967-89; company incorporated, 1968. **Awards:** Coty American Fashion Critics Award, 1968, 1970; Inspiration Home Furnishings Award, New York, 1978; Knitted Textile Association Designer Award, New York, 1982; Council of Fashion Designers of America Award, 1987; Fashion Designers of America Award, 1988. **Address:** 611 Broadway, New York, New York 10012, USA. *Died* (in New York) *29 August 1989.*

Publications:

On di SANT'ANGELO:

Books

Morris, Bernadine, and Barbara Walz, *The Fashion Makers,* New York 1978.
Milbank, Caroline Rennolds, *New York Fashion: The Evolution of American Style,* New York 1989.

Articles

Mazzaraco, M., "Di Sant'Angelo's Head," in *Women's Wear Daily* (New York), 16 October 1968.
Nemy, Enid, "It Takes a Little Bit of Being Yourself." in the *New York Times,* 4 March 1969.

"Restless Count from Italy Who Took Picasso's Advice," in *Life* (New York), 7 March 1969.
Klensch, Elsa, "Sant'Angelo Superstar," in *Women's Wear Daily* (New York), 4 February 1972.
Haber, Holly, "Sant'Angelo, a Master of Fantasy, Dies," in *Women's Wear Daily* (New York), 31 August 1989.
Polan, Brenda, "Sant'Angelo: Lycra Looks," [obituary] in *The Guardian* (London), 1 September 1989.
Moore, Jackie, "Obituary: Giorgio Sant'Angelo," in *The Independent* (London), 4 September 1989.
"Giorgio di Sant'Angelo: 1933-1989," [obituary] in *Vogue* (New York), November 1989.

*   *   *

Giorgio di Sant'Angelo was a child of the 1960s. Unlike many of that decade's talented new designers—including Pierre Cardin, André Courrèges, and Rudi Gernreich—who suffered symptoms of career burn-out as the 1960s came to a close, di Sant'Angelo soared on a creative high. His formative years, leading up to his move to New York, included an education in the arts in Florence and a studio apprenticeship with Picasso who urged di Sant'Angelo to trust his own restless creativity and to keep trying new artistic ventures.

Di Sant'Angelo, who had an affinity for the new plastics developed with Space Age technology, designed lucite jewelry and accessories in colorful geometric shapes. Diana Vreeland, editor of *Vogue* from 1963-71, found di Sant'Angelo's designs to be in step with her own ideas and gave him carte blanche as a stylist. The results of their association during the late 1960s are stunning examples of the breadth of di Sant'Angelo's originality. His concoctions of colored Veruschka were the peak of fashion fantasy. This option of make-believe went beyond mere merchandise shown in a magazine layout. Di Sant'Angelo's work was theatrical, exotic, and on some level could be considered performance art. This taste for escapism through dress coincided with the escalation of the Vietnam War in 1968-69.

Inspired by hippie and street fashions, di Sant'Angelo also translated ideas that would fit the marketplace. His love of ethnic clothing was evident, and his gypsy looks included elements of romanticism. Introducing a modern component, di Sant'Angelo also incorporated Lycra body suits with these varied influences. He offered women a chance at self-expression through dress.

In 1972, di Sant'Angelo left behind his gypsy and American Indian inspirations and concentrated on body-conscious designs that combined knits and wovens. His collection of 33 pieces was shown at the Guggenheim Museum further emphasizing di Sant'Angelo's commitment to fashion design as an artform. Calling the group "Summer with Soul," Sant'Angelo stated: "To me, soul means freedom and inner confidence. I express it in happy, bright colors, and in simplicity of design." He presented matching knit shirts, tops, trousers, and bra that folded into an envelope for travel. These pieces were based around a body stocking and formed the 1970s American fashion silhouette.

A 1978 advertisement read: "Giorgio di Sant'Angelo Spoken Here." He saw his work as a new language in fashion. Di Sant'Angelo admired the ideas of Rudi Gernreich, whose work also contributed key elements to modern design. He also respected the work of Halston, Elsa Peretti, Betsey Johnson, Stephen Burrows, Oscar de la Renta, Yves Saint Laurent, Pierre Cardin, and Valentino. Throughout the 1980s' shifts in fashion, di Sant'Angelo worked on classical refinements of his own concepts. Poised for a timely re-emergence as a name in fashion, di Sant'Angelo died in 1989. A truly original free spirit was lost forever.

—Myra Walker

***

DKNY. See **KARAN, Donna.**

***

DOLCE & GABBANA.

Italian ready-to-wear firm

Established by Domenico Dolce and Stefano Gabbana, 1982. Dolce born in Palermo, Italy, 13 August 1958. Gabbana born in Venice, Italy, 14 November 1962; studied graphic design. Both designed in Milan, 1980-82. First major women's collection, 1985; knitwear collection first shown, 1987; lingerie and beachwear introduced, 1989; menswear collection first shown, 1990; signature fragrance line launched, 1992; lower priced D&G line introduced, 1993. Opened showrooms in Milan, 1987 and New York, 1990. Dolce & Gabbana Monogriffe shops opened in Tokyo, 1989, Milan, 1990, Hong Kong, 1991, and Milan shop for menswear, 1991. Consultants to Genny for Complice line, 1990. **Awards:** Woolmark Award, 1991. **Address:** Euroitalia, via Ghirlandaio 5, 20052 Monza, Italy.

Publications:

On DOLCE & GABBANA:

Books

Stegemeyer, Anne, *Who's Who in Fashion* supplement, New York 1992.

Articles

Hume, Marion, "La Dolce Vita," in *The Sunday Times* (London), 4 March 1990.
Spindler, Amy M., "Dolce & Gabbana: Salt-of-the-Earth Chic," in *Daily News Record* (New York), 26 September 1990.
Hume, Marion, "The Sicilian Connection," in *Elle* (London), March 1991.
"Italy Now: Dolce & Gabbana," in *Daily News Record* (New York), 14 January 1992.
"Day of the Dolce," in *Women's Wear Daily* (New York), 9 March 1992.
"La Dolce Vita and the Top Gabbana," in *Women's Wear Daily* (New York), 13 March 1992.
Orlean, Susan, "Breaking Away," in *Vogue* (New York), September 1992.
Costin, Glynis, "Dolce & Gabbana," in *W,* 14 May 1992.
Broome, Geoff, "Dynamic Duo," in *International Collections,* Spring/Summer 1992.
Koski, Lorna, "The Mod Couple," in *Women's Wear Daily* (New York), 16 November 1994.

Forden, Sara Gay, "Dolce and Gabbana Present Dolce & Gabbana," in *Daily News Record* (New York), 2 January 1995.
Menkes, Suzy, "A Manhattan Melody in Italian Shows," in *International Herald Tribune* (Paris), 7 March 1995.
"Distinctly Dolce," in *Elle* (London), April 1995.

*   *   *

Since their first womenswear collection in 1985, Dolce & Gabbana have evolved into perhaps the definitive purveyors of sexy clothes for women who want to revel in their voluptuous femininity. They have taken items like satin corset bodies, black hold-up stockings, fishnets, and maribou-trimmed babydolls out of their previous *demi-monde* existence and put them together in such a way that they have become classy outfits for the new glamorous image of the 1990s, an escape from the pervasive unisex sporty styles.

Loved by fashion magazines and film stars alike, this partnership revives the Southern Italian sex bomb look, inspired by the films of Roberto Rossellini, Luchino Visconti, and Federico Fellini which the pair grew up on, coupled with an adoration of the strongly romantic Mediterranean ideals of Sicily. They can take a large amount of credit for the rise in images of the fashionable woman empowering herself by reclaiming sexual stereotypes and using them to her own benefit.

They brush aside the preoccupations of other Milan-based designers with mix-and-match separates and revamp potent images previously deemed degrading to women—the *geisha,* the baby doll, the scantily clad starlet—and give them a new lease of life. Confidence and irony are key for Dolce & Gabbana: their women are very much in control, whether in one of their glittering rhinestone-covered bodices—notably chosen by that post-feminist icon Madonna to make an impact at the 1991 Cannes Film Festival and subsequently filtered down into every High Street chain—or a slightly more sober, but nonetheless sexy, stretch velvet Empire cut jacket and leggings.

Although originating from opposite ends of Italy, Dolce & Gabbana's shared interests and influences give a sense of unity to their collections and an instantly recognizable look. Their use of film imagery, and obvious love of the fiery beauty of stars like Sophia Loren and Gina Lollobrigida, has imbued their advertising with an unforgettably glamorous style of its own. They combine supermodels with screen stars to create images which ooze an earthy sexuality.

The same key elements of sexiness mixed with traditional elements are applied to the menswear range, first shown in January 1990 and designed to complement Dolce & Gabbana's women. Skilled Sicilian craftswomen and tailors, supervised by Dolce's father, are employed to produce the internationally acclaimed menswear collections which espouse a more laid-back, witty approach to the 1990s, after the brasher, more rigid styles of the previous decade. Muted shades of earthy browns are used alongside blacks with flashes of scarlet to produce modern-day versions of Sicilian bandits, with bandannas around their necks, and bikers in tattoo-covered leather jackets, lightened by the leggings used so widely by Dolce & Gabbana. Current fashion influences are often absorbed, the tie-dyed 1970s feel of their 1992 summer collection being a prime example, but there is always a more timeless selection of unstructured suits, often based on a 19th-century high-buttoning tighter cut style, and knitwear which explores all its textural possibilities to give it a very tactile appeal.

Dolce & Gabbana: Spring/Summer 1992.

Both Dolce & Gabbana's men's and womenswear are international bestsellers. Influential and innovative, the clothes express a confident, sexy glamour which, however potent, never over powers the wearer's personality, making them one of the most important design forces to emerge from Italy in recent years.

—Rebecca Arnold

DOLCI, Flora. See **MANDELLI, Mariuccia.**

DOMINGUEZ, Adolfo.

Spanish designer

Born: Orense, Spain. **Education:** Graduated with degree in philosophy, Universidad Santiago de Compostela, 1968; studied cinematography and aesthetics in Paris and London. **Career:** Formed men's ready-to-wear company, early 1970s; added women's line, opened first Dominguez shops, 1980s; with Jesús, Javier, María-José, Kerme and Ada Dominguez, established Adolfo Dominguez fashion company, Vigo; first womenswear collection, 1983; also designed jewellery, accessories, shoes, handbags. Dominguez Basico bridge line introduced, 1987; also designs Jeans line of casual sportswear. Licensing and distribution agreement in Japan with company Taka-Q. **Address:** Poligono San Ciprian de Vinas, Apartado 1160, 32080 Orense, Spain.

Publications:

On DOMINGUEZ:

Articles

Coad, Emma Dent, "Flamenco, Fabrics and Fun," in *Design* (London), January 1988.

*   *   *

Working from his native Galicia, Adolfo Dominguez represents the new wave of post-Franco Spanish design. His international corporation has helped to widen the influence of Spanish fashion around the world.

The Dominguez family business grew in 20 years from a small manufacturer of ready-to-wear men's clothing to a fashion house with more than 40 outlets worldwide plus their own shops in Spain, London, Paris, and Hong Kong. The rapid expansion of the business from the early 1970s was founded on the decision to emphasize design and image for the wealthy, urban consumers of the new Spain and also for a sophisticated international clientèle. The opening of the first Dominguez shop in Madrid marked the beginning in Spain of such chic establishments, presenting an appropriate ambience to support the image of the clothes on sale. The Madrid shop was quickly followed by another in Barcelona and

eight more opened from the home market. With Spain's entry into the European Common Market, shops were established in London and Paris. The appearance of Dominguez's women's collections in the early 1980s helped to assure his status in the international fashion world, and markets were consolidated in the United States and Japan, where a manufacturing operation was subsequently established.

His intellectual and cosmopolitan approach to design reflects Adolfo Dominguez's Parisian education in literature and philosophy. He likens fashion to industrial design, describing it as a response to need. Similarly, he rejects the wilfulness of much designer clothing and couture, asserting instead the designer's responsibility to the user. Dominguez's clothing is purposeful in the modernist idiom, providing a solution to a particular problem, and a solution which will stand the test of time. Like the Japanese designers from the generation of Yohji Yamamoto, his designs are essentially intellectual in character.

Dominguez's Apollonian view of design as an activity also extends to his sense of the human figure and his treatment of the form through tailoring. He concentrates on elegant contour rather than overt body consciousness; he accentuates stature and elegance of proportion to allure, rather than revealing flesh or emphasizing obvious sexual characteristics. Dominguez makes use of classic drapery patterns in his garments for women. His unstructured cuts

Adolfo Dominguez.

emphasize the drape of fine materials and the traditional Spanish skill of soft tailoring.

Through his ranges of high quality menswear and womenswear, a lower cost Basico line and Jeans, a casual line, Dominguez has developed a reputation for producing unpretentious and comfortable looking garments of the highest quality with regard to materials and construction. A characteristic of Dominguez designs is the elimination of superfluous detail. His clothes are not ornamented by applied decoration, and surface patterning is rare, yet austerity is relieved by soft drapery and the subtlety of colours used. Dominguez's rich, earthy palette of colours is reminiscent of the landscape of his native Galicia.

The Dominguez shops designed by Santiago Seara and Alfredo Freixedo, like the clothes sold in them, reflect a classic, modern simplicity, discreetly detailed and finished in high quality materials. Both the shops and the fashions mirror the elegant minimalism of much 1980s industrial and interior design.

Dominguez's work has presented the most sophisticated face of the new Spanish design to both a recently liberated and affluent home market and to an increasingly appreciative world market. His name is synonymous with minimalist perfection of form, material, and construction.

—Gregory Votolato

E

ELLIS, Perry.

American designer

Born: Perry Edwin Ellis in Portsmouth, Virginia, 30 March 1940.
Education: Bachelor of Arts, business, College of William and Mary, Williamsburg, Virginia, 1961; Master of Arts, retailing, New York University, New York City, 1963. **Family:** One daughter: Tyler Alexandra. **Military Service:** Served in the US Coast Guard, 1961-62. **Career:** Sportswear buyer, Miller and Rhodes department stores, Virginia, 1963-67; design director, John Meyer of Norwich, 1967-74; vice-president, sportswear division, 1974, and designer, Vera sportswear for Manhattan Industries, 1975-76; designer with own Portfolio label, Manhattan Industries, 1976-78; president and designer, Perry Ellis Sportswear, Inc., 1978-86; Perry Ellis International menswear line launched, 1980; Portfolio label, lower priced sportswear revived, 1984; fragrance collection launched, 1985. Licenses include furs, coats, shoes, bedlinens, household textiles, toiletries, and clothing patterns for Levi Strauss, Greif, Martex, Visions Stern, etc., from 1978. Council of Fashion Designers of America Perry Ellis Award established in memoriam, 1986. **Awards:** Coty American Fashion Critics Award, 1979, 1980, 1981, 1983, 1984; Neiman Marcus Award, Dallas, 1979; Council of Fashion Designers of America Award, 1981, 1982, 1983; Cutty Sark Award, 1983, 1984; California Men's Apparel Guild Hall of Fame Award, 1993. *Died* (in New York City) *30 May 1986.* **Address:** 575 Seventh Avenue, New York, New York 10018, USA.

Publications:

On ELLIS:

Books

Morris, Bernadine, and Barbara Walz, *The Fashion Makers,* New York 1978.
Diamonstein, Barbaralee, *Fashion: The Inside Story,* New York 1985.
Milbank, Caroline Rennolds, *Couture: The Great Designers,* New York 1985.
Perschetz, Lois, ed., *W, The Designing Life,* New York 1987.
Moor, Johnathan, *Perry Ellis,* New York 1988.
Milbank, Caroline Rennolds, *New York Fashion: The Evolution of American Style,* New York 1989.

Articles

Fressola, Peter, "Perry Ellis," in the *Daily News Record* (New York), 13 April 1987.
Parola, Robert, "At Ellis: Discord on Design and Direction," in the *Daily News Record* (New York), 24 July 1992.

*   *   *

The house of Perry Ellis has seen some tumultuous times. From the early days things had never been particularly easy, with Ellis continuously battling over finances with the parent company, Manhattan Industries. Problems with stability continued after Ellis's death in 1986, when Robert McDonald assumed the helm of Perry Ellis International, only to die four years later.

Recent problems have arisen from Salant's $100 million takeover of Manhattan Industries and its subsequent bankruptcy filing. Obstacles with direction, especially within the menswear divisions, with the death of designer Roger Forsythe in 1991 from AIDS, to the recent disjointed running of Perry Ellis Group and Perry Ellis International, have done nothing to remedy the company's disarray.

Through all the problems and despite the fickle nature of the fashion world, the fashions of Perry Ellis's men's and women's collections have remained relatively consistent, true to the tenets and goals in which, as a designer, Ellis believed and aspired to.

Perry Ellis was known as a flirtatious, fun-loving man with a great sense of humor. According to Claudia Thomas, former chair of Perry Ellis International, it is hard to characterize Ellis, except to describe him as whimsical. There was, however, an air of seriousness about him when it came to creating and fulfilling his objectives, as reflected in his personal philosophy of "never enough." It was the playful side of his personality, however, that was reflected in his fashions. When his company arrived on the scene in the 1970s, it was a time of increasing emphasis on American designers and designer name merchandise. Perry Ellis did his best to create a mystique about himself and his lifestyle that would attract fans.

The Perry Ellis look began as a playful, relaxed and comfortable look that was exclusively American in feeling and sportswear-like in its practicality. So playful and relaxed was it that at shows, the models would skip down the catwalk. As Ellis matured as a designer, his clothing occasionally took on a more serious tone, but even his most formidable collections were considered easy-dressing by fashion industry standards.

Inspiration came in many forms—California; the movie *Chariots of Fire;* artist Sonia Delaunay; the Broadway show *Dream Girls*— all retained the casual ease for which Americans are known internationally and the sense of proportion and freedom from fashion conformity which was the hallmark of Perry Ellis. The company's subsequent womenswear designer, Marc Jacobs, and menswear design director, Andrew Corrigan, appeared to create their collections with the feeling that Perry Ellis had tried to instil into a consumer's mind when buying clothing.

Ellis once said, "Always provide the clothes needed for daily life. Never be afraid to take risks and, most importantly, never take the clothes you wear too seriously." It is to this statement one should refer when trying to understand the essence of Perry Ellis designs.

—Lisa Marsh

EMANUEL, David and Elizabeth.

British designers

Born: *David*—Bridgend, Wales, 17 November 1952; *Elizabeth*—born Elizabeth Weiner in London, 5 July 1953. **Education:** *David*—Attended Cardiff School of Art, Wales, 1972-75, and Harrow School of Art, Middlesex, 1974-75; *Elizabeth*—Attended Harrow School of Art, 1974-75. Both David and Elizabeth studied fashion in postgraduate courses at the Royal College of Art, 1976-77. **Family:** Married in 1976; (divorced). Children: Oliver and Eloise. **Joint Career:** Partners and directors of Emanuel, in London, 1977-90; ready-to-wear line 1977-79; designed custom clothing only, 1979-90; established The Emanuel Shop, Beauchamp Place, London, 1987-90; collections also sold at Harrods and Harvey Nichols, London, and Bergdorf Goodman, Henri Bendell and Neiman Marcus, New York. Also: ballet and stage production designers, from 1985. Fellows of Chartered Society of Designers, London, 1984; Partnership dissolved, 1990. **Individual Careers:** *David*—Formed David Emanuel Couture, autumn 1990. Fellow of The Society of Industrial Artists and Designers. *Elizabeth*—Launched Elizabeth Emanuel Couture fashion label, 1991; designed complete range of Virgin Airways uniforms and accessories, 1991; Sew Forth productions established 1993; launched range of wedding dresses for Bridal Fashions, London, 1994. Also; costumes for Ballet Rambert, London Contemporary Dance Theatre, and Royal Ballet productions, London, 1990-94, and for musical theatre production of *Jean de Florette,* London, 1994-95. **Address:** David Emanuel Couture, 13 Regents Park Terrace, London, England; Elizabeth Emanuel, Sew Forth Productions, Studio 7, 44 Grove End Road, London, England.

Publications:

By the EMANUELS:

Books

Style for All Seasons, London 1982.
Emanuel, Elizabeth, Autobiography (title unknown), London c. 1994.

Articles

"Getting Going: David and Elizabeth Emanuel," in the *Designer,* July 1981.

On the EMANUELS:

Articles

Morris, B., "Couple's Design: Fit for a Queen," in the *New York Times Biographical Service,* vol. 12, November 1981.
Lynn, Frances, "The Amazing Emanuels," in *Women's Journal* (London), October 1983.
"Life with Elizabeth Emanuel," in *Living Magazine* (London), November 1985.
Staniland, Kay, "The Wedding Dresses of H.R.H. the Princess of Wales and H.R.H. the Duchess of York," in *Costume* (London), 1987.
"In, Out and In Again," in *People,* vol. 29, Spring 1988.

Fairley, Josephine, "The 10 Year Stitch," in the *Sunday Express Magazine* (London), 27 November 1988.
"The Emanuel Gallery," in *Vogue* (London), December 1988.
Dutt, Robin, "The Emanuels," in *Clothes Show* (London), April 1989.
Fernand, Deirdre, "Framing a Fashion Career Move," in *The Sunday Times* (London), 7 January 1990.
Lee, Vinny, "Cream Sequence," in *Sunday Express Magazine* (London), 31 March 1991.

* * *

The romantic Renaissance revival came to life in the early 1980s in the music world and in films. Nowhere, however, was it more apparent than in certain fashion circles.

The announcement of the engagement of Charles, the Prince of Wales, to Lady Diana Spencer made this an even bigger trend than it would normally have been. Lady Diana's penchant for ruffles created a need for this type of apparel, as she was already becoming a woman many wanted to emulate fashion-wise.

It is appropriate that she chose the design team of David and Elizabeth Emanuel to design her wedding dress as romance is the underlying theme to all they designed. Ruffles are the rule for the Emanuels, used on everything from gowns to pant suits and even swimwear.

This duo, the only married couple to be accepted at the Royal College of Art, had operated their dressmaking shop in London since 1977 and in 1979 took the unusual step of closing their ready-to-wear business to concentrate on the made-to-order business.

Although it was the Princess of Wales's ivory silk taffeta wedding dress that brought the Emanuels international fame, they had a firmly entrenched business catering to what Americans would call the carriage trade. It also enabled the Emanuels to enter into licensing agreements for items such as linens, sunglasses, and perfume.

Princess Anne and Princess Michael of Kent have both worn Emanuel designs for portraits. Her Royal Highness the Duchess of Kent joins these women and the Princess of Wales in their love of the Emanuels' work.

Each dress was created for each individual, taking into account where it would be worn and the style of the wearer. Next, a suitable reference in art would be determined and work would progress from there. Creations by artists from Botticelli to Renoir and Degas were used as influences, as were photographs of some of the more romantic women in history. The garments seen on Greta Garbo in *Camille,* Vivien Leigh in *Gone with the Wind,* and Marlene Dietrich in *The Scarlet Empress* were all recreated to some degree.

In this respect, David and Elizabeth Emanuel were more stylists than designers, recreating a mood or image. However, they usually reinterpreted the design rather than copied it, adding a fresh dimension through fabric or hidden detail. A wedding dress, for example, had subtly glittering mother-of-pearl sequins for a woman who was marrying in a dark church. The sequins picked up the light, allowing the bride to glow luminously. The Princess of Wales's veil also incorporated these sequins, drawing attention to the star of the show. David and Elizabeth Emanuel are nothing if not retrospectively romantic and all they do reflects this.

—Lisa Marsh

EMARY, John. See **AQUASCUTUM, LTD.**

EMILIA, Reggio. See **MARINA RINALDI SrL.**

ENGLISH ECCENTRICS.

British textile design and fashion company

Founded by Helen and Judy Littman, 1982. Helen Littman, born in Brighton, Sussex, 1955. Studied Brighton and Hove High School for Girls, 1966-72; Eastbourne College of Art and Design, 1972-74; Camberwell School of Arts and Crafts, 1974-77. Founded Personal Items design company with Judy Littman, 1979; began printing under name English Eccentrics, 1982. English Eccentrics made a limited company, 1984; Fulham Road, London shop opened, 1987; first catwalk show, London, 1985. Designed scarves for Royal Academy, London, 1989; Royal Pavilion, Brighton, 1990; Harvey Nichols, London, 1990; Girl Guides Association, 1990; scarf and clothing for Joseph, London, 1990. **Exhibitions:** *Mad Dogs and Englishmen,* Young Designer Show, London, October 1983; *London Goes to Tokyo,* Hanae Mori Building, Tokyo, November 1984; *Innovators in Fashion,* Pitti Palace, Florence, October 1985; *British Design,* Vienna, 1986; *British Scarves,* London, 1987; *British Design, New Traditions,* Boymans Museum, Rotterdam, 1989; *British Design,* Tokyo, 1990; *British Design 1790-1990,* Costa Mesa, California, 1990; *Collecting for the Future,* Victoria and Albert Museum, London 1990. **Awards:** *Avant Garde Designer Preis,* Munich, 1986. **Address:** 9/10 Charlotte Road, London EC2A 3DH, England.

Publications:

On ENGLISH ECCENTRICS:

Books

Johnson, L., ed., *The Fashion Year,* London 1985.
McDermott, Catherine, ed., *English Eccentrics: The Textile Designs of Helen Littman,* London 1992.

Articles

"Fabricated Fashion," in *You* magazine of the *Mail on Sunday* (London), 10 July 1983.
Brampton, Sally, "Still Crazy," in *The Observer* (London), 24 March 1985.
Polan, Brenda, "Eccentric Fantasy," in *The Guardian,* 20 June 1985.
Thorpe, Brendan, "English Eccentrics in Retail Adventure," in *Design Week* (London), 7 August 1987.
Bain, Sally, "British Designers Preview," in *Draper's Record* (London), 5 March 1988.
Fitzmaurice, Arabella, "Appearing in Print," in the *Sunday Times* (London), March 1992.

Gattemayer, Michela, "English Eccentrics: Moda Souvenir," in *Elle* (Italy), March 1992.
Menkes, Suzy, "From Cultural Symbols to Fabric Designs," in the *International Herald Tribune* (Italy), March 1992.
McHugh, Fionnuala, "Material Success," in *The Telegraph Magazine* (London), 14 March 1992.
Feron, Francesca, "The Eclectic Eccentrics Whose Designs Got to Your Head," in the *Glasgow Herald,* May 1992.

*

I believe that all women have their own beauty and that striving to look like the stereotyped images in our media can undermine this. However, I feel that there is no reason why we should not enjoy using beauty products and I think dressing well is a great pleasure. For me, make-up or high heels are not undesirable *a priori,* but I don't like to produce obviously sexually provocative clothes because I think that in most social situations they make women feel uncomfortable and look frivolous.

We dress to enhance our appearance, and my aim in designing is that the clothes and accessories we produce are fun to wear and help to make any woman look wonderful be she overweight, over-eighty, or a fashion model.

I am always conscious of the body as the final show-place for my designs.

—Helen Littman

*   *   *

Named after Edith Sitwell's book of the same title, English Eccentrics have established an international reputation for their distinct printed textiles since they first started selling at a stall in London's Kensington Market in 1984. The company was founded in 1982 by sisters Helen and Judy Littman, when they began printing their designs onto fabric on the floor of their studio in Wapping. Helen Littman, the creative inspiration behind the company, trained as a textile designer at Camberwell School of Art, while Judy, who studied painting, controls the business and promotions side. The Littman sisters and their quirky company name were timed perfectly with the emergence of London as the most happening fashion centre during the early 1980s, when the likes of John Galliano, Katharine Hamnett, and Vivienne Westwood were beginning to make their mark in international fashion. English Eccentrics were also mentioned in the famous article published by *Women's Wear Daily* (New York), when it announced in 1983 that "London Swings Again."

English Eccentrics are recognized for the use of extravagantly rich combinations of colour and unusual *trompe l'oeil* designs inspired by a myriad of subjects, including travel, ecology, architecture, costume, and nature, which are translated onto the highest quality silks. Helen Littman credits much of her inspiration from what she calls her own "Grand Tour" which was in fact a series of short trips abroad during which she used a sketch book and a camera to record ideas for future designs. It is, however, the way in which Littman uses the ideas that is the key to her success as a designer. She acknowledges that "obvious cultural piracy is boring" and thus reworks each idea in a thoroughly modern way. Littman's treatment of her inspiration is clearly illustrated by what has become one of English Eccentric's best-known designs, called *Hands.* On a visit to Manhattan, Littman was surprised by the number of palmistry parlours she saw which she found completely at odds

English Eccentrics: Spring/Summer 1995. *Photograph by Huggy.*

with her personal image of the powerful city. For the design, Littman combined a hand print with elements taken from New York graffiti and palmistry diagrams. Its spiral border pattern was inspired by Gustav Klimt's painting, *The Tree of Life*. The result is an abstract pattern printed in five colourways for scarf squares and which has also been adapted for gift wrap paper as well as designs for hosiery. The special qualities of silk have proved to be the ideal fabric medium for English Eccentrics since it enables very intense, vibrant colours as well as softer muted shades to be printed in accurate detail. Another feature of Littman's designs is that all printing is done by hand with acid dyes rather than pigment colours which do not have the same qualities of clarity. Between 1984 and 1988 English Eccentrics also produced ten clothing collections and translated their designs onto stationery, furnishing fabrics, and packaging. However, the ensuing financial climate of the late 1980s forced the company to tailor these activities and they began to concentrate solely upon producing the silk scarf squares for which they are now best recognized. These designs were also used to create a small range of classic garments such as shirts and waistcoats which incorporated the square scarf into their design. The company introduced *devore* velvet into their collection for winter 1993, with great success—their *devore* tunic becoming one of the season's key garments, worn by fashion editors, buyers, and film stars alike. That season English Eccentrics also enlarged the scarf range to include more than 60 colours, fabrics, and styles.

For spring/summer 1994 English Eccentrics introduced their first ready-to-wear collection since 1988 which included sarong skirts, trousers, shirts, and jackets in plain linens, silks and *devore* velvet combined with pieces featuring the season's new print designs on silk.

Unlike many of their designer counterparts who achieved notoriety during the early years of the 1980s, English Eccentrics have managed to build upon their success whilst remaining firmly based in Britain. They export all over the world from England, which is, after all, the only proper base for a company of that name.

—Catherine Woram

ERREUNO SCM SpA.

Italian ready-to-wear firm

Founded by Ermanno Ronchi (born 28 May 1947) and Graziella Ronchi Pezzutto (born 24 November 1945) in Milan, 1971. Added Donnaerre line of women's clothes, 1981; Erreuno Uomo line, 1985; Erreuno Jeans collection, 1986; Graziella Ronchi Cocktail line, 1986; Erreuno Golf lines, 1989; Erreuno J line, designed by Michael Kors, introduced in USA, 1990. **Address:** Via Bensi 6, 20152 Milan, Italy.

Publications:

On ERREUNO

Articles

Haber, Holly, "Erreuno J Makes U.S. Debut in Dallas," in *Women's Wear Daily* (New York), 15 August 1990.

*   *   *

Erreuno is the brainchild of Ermanno and Graziella Ronchi, who established the company in Milan in 1971. The company name is a combination of the pronunciation of the first letter of the Ronchi name R (Erre) and Uno, the Italian word for one, chosen because it was the couple's first business venture.

The Ronchis' aims were to create something influential and significant in the Italian fashion world, to establish a company that provided top quality ready-to-wear designs for the smart, modern, and discerning woman. Extremely positive in their approach, their success has been the result of hard work, commitment, and teamwork. Ermanno handles all the administrative and financial side of the business whilst Graziella oversees design and marketing.

Fabric is of prime importance in any Erreuno collection. Designing often appears to be a grouping together of expensive fibres, textures, plaids, prints, mattes, and shines, then coordinating these into wearable, sporty, classic clothes. Graziella Ronchi places great emphasis on fabric research and 70 per cent of the fabrics are developed in their Milan studios. Great care is given to the choice of fabrics used in each collection to ensure that, when made into garments and styled together, they give a strong visual impact and provide versatility of choice for a wide variety of women.

Never at the cutting edge of designer fashion, Erreuno instead evolves its own particular style each season. A feeling for softness combined with architectural design is reflected in each individual garment and, when incorporated as part of an outfit, adds its own contribution to the finished look.

Erreuno's initial success was in the design and manufacture of skirts. The range expanded and developed to include complete womenswear outfits and in 1975 led to a seasonal ready-to-wear collection, shown twice a year in Milan. Since then the company has steadily evolved to incorporate many other goods: leathers, wallets, foulards, key pouches, bags, hats, and gloves. Sold in worldwide boutiques, the products give customers the opportunity to coordinate an Erreuno outfit with top quality accessories, adding greater credence to the company's marketing strategy.

Today Erreuno collections provide a refreshing presence on the Milan catwalks. Perched midway between the extremes of Dolce & Gabbana's expensive vamps and Giorgio Armani's exquisite classicism, the Erreuno look is one of neutrality. A softly tailored tiny-check suit is teamed with a belted, collarless blouson, an oversize ankle-length, belted mackintosh is teamed with shorts, subtly playing on long and short, or an understated mix of stripes in an outfit comprised of four different types of stripe. Colour for Erreuno is soft and discerning; the beiges, browns, creams, lilacs, off-whites, or warm greys are never loud or unflattering.

The expression and imagination of Ermanno and Graziella Ronchi, combined with their flair for design, marketing, and manufacture, have found the perfect complement in their company. Erreuno stands on its own in the Italian fashion marketplace with a particular special identity for a particular woman.

—Kevin Almond

ESCADA.

German fashion house

Founded by Wolfgang and Margarethe Ley (*died 1992*), 1976. Lines include Laurel, Crisca, from 1984, Escada leather goods, from 1990,

Erreuno: Spring 1994.

and Apriori bridge line, from 1991. Escada Beauté company formed, 1990; fragrance, *Escada by Margarethe Ley,* introduced in USA, 1990, and in Germany and United Kingdom, 1991. Michael Stolzenburg named designer to succeed Ley, 1992. **Awards:** Fragrance Foundation Award, 1990. **Address:** Karl Hammerschmidt Strasse 23-29, Dornach, 80ll Munich, Dornach, Germany.

Publications:

On ESCADA:

Articles

Agins, Teri, "Despite the Recession, High Fashion Escada Expands World-Wide," in the *Wall Street Journal* (New York), 15 April 1992.
"Swede Success," in *Woman's Journal* (London), May 1992.
"Margarethe Ley, Co-founder of Escada AG Dead at 56," in *Women's Wear Daily* (New York), 8 June 1992.
White, Constance C. R., "Escada Evolves," in *Women's Wear Daily* (New York), 4 November 1992.

*   *   *

The Escada group was founded in 1976 by Wolfgang and Margarethe Ley and is currently based in Dornach, near Munich. The group designs, produces and distributes high quality women's fashion, marketed worldwide to leading fashion stores and own name boutiques. Apart from Escada by Margarethe Ley, which includes apparel, luggage, fragrance and accessories, the group's other labels are Cerruti 1881, Crisca, Kemper, Laurel, Apriori, Seasons, Natalie Acatrini, Marie Gray, Schneberger, and St John.

Margarethe Ley was the chief designer for the group until her death in 1992. She strongly adhered to the belief that a designer must never rely solely on creative talent to be a success; creativity must be balanced by a strong market appeal. Ley created a highly distinctive identity for Escada, clean, slick, and sophisticated. She also pioneered the development of exiciting new fabric combinations and colour schemes.

Ley was succeeded by Michael Stolzenburg who has brought a younger, more modern perspective to the company. Taking his influence from daily life, he believes that the balance of a collection relies on the mix of tried and true design and fresh new ideas. He is backed by a strong team of designers, chiefly from British and German fashion schools.

Bright, bold colour statements have always been integral to the Escada look: geometric blocks of colour that contrast with vibrant prints, embroideries, and appliqué. Stripes often appear, one season in sharp nautical blocks of navy and white, the next in black and gold, teamed with black and gold leather for a glitzy evening look. Other strong themes have included Animal Rustics—country gentry and pure nature; High Society—a colour cocktail of purple and pink. Overall, Escada provides a complete ready-to-wear look for a high-salaried, professional woman, sexy, sharp, and sometimes overstated.

As a design group all Escada operations share a common objective, to be market leaders producing fashions that set the highest quality standards in the fashion industry.

The company's commitment to quality production has resulted in the installation of advanced technology equipment. Computer-assisted pattern-making equipment, automated cutters, and state-of-the-art knitting machines contribute to continued development and leave the design team greater time to concentrate on the creative development of innovative collections, for their specific market segments.

The Escada group sees the whole world as its market place. The products are sold in over 55 countries with an overall objective to achieve the leading market share in each country in which the products are sold, as determined through market analysis into the disposable income available at the top of the market in each country. Escada's success relies on the canny entrepreneurial spirit first instilled into the business by Wolfgang and Margarethe Ley.

—Kevin Almond

ESPRIT.
American fashion design company

Co-founded as Plain Jane Dress Company by Susie and Doug Tompkins and Jane Tise in San Francisco, 1968; Susie and Doug Tompkins became sole owners, 1975; shares sold to Susie Tompkins, 1990; company incorporated and name changed to Esprit de Corp., 1970; worldwide sales reached more than $1 billion during 1977-1987; Esprit Men designed in Dusseldorf and launched in Europe, 1989; Ecollection, environmentally friendly line using organic fabrics and low impact fibres, launched, 1992; ready-to-wear in Japan, 1993; 240 retail stores worldwide, by 1994. Sub-lines include Esprit Footwear and Accessories, Esprit Kids, Suzie Tompkins, and Dr. Seuss; also sleep, bath, and lingerie collections. **Address:** 900 Minnesota Street, San Francisco, California 94107, USA.

Publications:

On ESPRIT:

Articles

Sudjic, Deyan, "Esprit: The Singular Multiple," *Blueprint* (London), June 1987.
Benson, Heidi, "Reinventing Esprit," in the *San Francisco Focus,* February 1991.
McGrath, Ellie, "Esprit, the Sequel," in *Working Woman* (New York), September 1991.
White, Constance, "Tompkins Gets Her Line," *Women's Wear Daily* (New York), 2 March 1992.
Zinn, Laura, "Will Politically Correct Sell Sweaters?," in *Business Week,* 16 March 1992.
Lawson, Skippy, "Esprit and the Rain Forests," in *Women's Wear Daily* (New York), 29 April 1992.
White, Constance C.R., "Susie Tompkins: Crossing a New Bridge," *Women's Wear Daily* (New York), 10 March 1993.
"Susie's New Spirit," in *W,* 10 May 1993.
Stodder, Gayle Sato, "A Perfect Fit," in *Entrepreneurial Woman* (New York), Summer 1993.

Articles also appear in *New York Times,* 6 April 1985; 4 April 1986; *Wall Street Journal* (New York), 11 June 1985; *Working Woman* (New York), October 1985; *View on Colour,* January 1992.

*

When we started the Plain Jane Dress Company in 1968, we never dreamed it would develop into a worldwide organization now known as Esprit, with operations in 40 countries. "Esprit de Corp.," our official corporate name, was intended to inspire the spirit of the organization and evoke a sense of cooperation, camaraderie and community.

When we started Esprit we had no previous experience whatsoever in the fashion business, in fact what business skills we might have possessed came from being in the mountain climbing equipment industry for a brief time, where any reference to fashion was an anathema. The idea of fashion, image, and image making was far from our minds. It was not, in fact, until 12 years after the founding of the company that any attempt to form an image and create a context for the product was made. In 1980 a radical shift in direction was undertaken. A mixed bag of seven different trade names was consolidated under one name, Esprit, and a new logo along with new labels, tags, packaging, and strong fashion photography was created.

As in all things that start modestly and by amateurs, progress, growth, expansion, and refinements come in steps and stages. Experience is gathered on the job and a process begins and evolves. Likewise, success leads to more opportunities and mistakes and to improvements and avoidance of repeating past errors, or hopefully so!

It has long been understood that the psycho graphic profile of target customers, or the idea of getting "into" the head of the customer, will lead you to the best understanding of what makes the customer respond to product, advertising, and services. Therefore, a thorough understanding of this profile makes design that much easier. In the fashion industry, where trends of status-related products are in a state of constant flux and evolution, the designer must be fast to respond to a changing marketplace.

Today, Esprit designs, manufactures, and distributes product lines four seasons per year, including infant, toddler, kids, womenswear, menswear, footwear, accessories, bath and bed, eyewear, and watches. This adds up to over 60 million garments and accessories annually. As a privately held network of companies, we employ more than 4,000 people. Because clothing is one of our most basic means of self expression, the fashion industry lends itself toward the communication of values, and offers us the challenge and opportunity to interpret the ongoing changes throughout the world. Our corporate mission statement is: "Be informed. Be involved. Make a difference." It may seem like an idealistic and unusual guiding philosophy for an international fashion company, but Esprit has never been "business as usual."

—Esprit

*   *   *

The Esprit label graces clothing, shoes, accessories—anything a woman can wear with comfort both at work and at play. As *W* magazine put it, Esprit is "part of that huge, growing category of well-priced clothes that range from the street-smart style of DKNY [Donna Karan New York] and CK Calvin Klein to the career-oriented mood of Ellen Tracy and Anne Klein II."

Perhaps the most distinguishing features of Esprit fashions are what the clothing *isn't*. Esprit labels may never appear on the clingy cocktail dress, the stifling "power suit," or the crippling high-heeled pump. Instead, a typical Esprit outfit shows a looser-fitting rayon vest or tunic over wide-legged pants or perhaps a flowing, calf-length skirt made of soft cotton.

According to the journal *View on Colour,* Esprit "has come to epitomize the Northern California lifestyle, an informative mix of a sunny climate, bold colors, outdoor sports, eternal youth, and social values. Esprit's saucy sportswear ... encouraged (if not triggered) the worldwide sportswear boom."

This success was the result of the personal vision of Esprit de Corp.'s co-founder, Susie Tompkins, who got her start, along with partner Jane Tise, in her native San Francisco in 1968, selling homemade frocks under the name Plain Jane.

For its first several years, the line was especially popular with teenagers. Eventually, Esprit clothing would represent both youthful style and career-minded fashion that might be found in grown-up settings, such as the casual office.

In the early 1980s, a poor business decision over shopping venues nearly caused the downfall of Esprit de Corp. Though it had its best success as a subsection of other retail outlets the company attempted to expand its base into individual outlets. This put Esprit into direct competition with such names as The Gap and The Limited. By the time Esprit had extricated itself from that marketing notion, the fashion line had, according to industry expert Allan Millstein, "missed the market for five years. They missed 20 seasons. That means they lost half a generation of kids."

Between 1975 and 1987, Esprit's worldwide sales approached $1 billion. But by 1987, after Tompkins and her husband and business partner Doug Tompkins disagreed on the company's direction, sales dropped. Doug offered to buy the company from under Susie; she considered the proposal until a meeting with another fashion entrepreneur, Bruce Katz of Rockport Shoes, persuaded her to stay with the company she had founded.

So the designer elected to buy out Doug instead, enlisting the financial support of Katz and several others. The estranged Doug and Susie met to work out the future of Esprit. They came to the decision that Susie would buy back the company, and Doug would bow out to the tune of $125 million.

Under Tompkins' direction, the company initiated the Ecollection line of clothing in the spring of 1992—"a big step, even for trendsetting Esprit," according to *View on Colour.* The Ecollection fashions are notable for being produced in the most environmentally friendly way possible.

Ecollection isn't the only Esprit subsection. Since the 1970s the company has initiated several product lines. Besides the regular Esprit-branded products, there are Esprit Footwear and Accessories, Esprit Kids, and the Susie Tompkins signature line. Considered more sophisticated, the latter bridge line is aimed at working women older than 25.

In the field of marketing, Esprit works hard to keep its brand name in chain department stores like T. J. Maxx and in various company-owned venues. Franchises range in location from Hawaii to Puerto Rico, and Esprit maintains outlet stores throughout the United States.

In March of 1993 Tompkins outlined Esprit's future for *Women's Wear Daily:* "Develop business with existing customers as well as with existing stores.... Esprit, like the entire junior market, is in the process of reevaluating the customer today, and I'm continuing to pursue this marketplace with consideration of the roots and culture of this company." And Tompkins wants to make sure that Esprit "isn't trendy," as she stated in a *San Francisco Focus* article. "We don't have to be doing what everybody else is doing. We just have to do *our* style, which is a kind of eclecticness and an integrity of design. Mixing old things with new things. Having a really nice way of presenting color. We try not to use the cliche teen colors. We

Esprit: Fall 1994.

wouldn't use a powder-pink, we'd use a dusty-pink, colors that are more sophisticated. Being young but still appropriate for an older customer."

—Susan Salter

ESTEREL, Jacques.

French designer

Born: Charles Martin, 1918. **Education:** Studied engineering. **Career:** Writer and composer. Couture house, Creations Jacques Esterel established, 1953. *Died in 1974.* **Address:** 124 rue du Faubourg St. Honore, 75008 Paris, France.

Publications:

On ESTEREL:

Articles

"L'univers de Jacques Esterel," in *Jardin des Arts* (Paris) May/June 1973.

*   *   *

Couturier Jacques Esterel liked to refer to himself as a "Parisian craftsman of dresses and songs." And in fact he was an entertainer as well as a designer, writing several plays and songs for the guitar in addition to running his many boutiques in France and throughout Europe. He brought his theatrical side into his clothing design, creating amusing novelties and employing outrageous styles and props, so much so that many of his admirers and critics considered him more of a showman than a serious couturier.

Esterel, whose real name was Charles Martin, was the son of a French industrialist and was originally educated as an engineer. He established his couture house, Jacques Esterel, in 1953. The first years were especially successful as Esterel contributed to a playful fashion spirit, illustrated by the "Vichy" bridal gown which he designed for French actress Brigitte Bardot. Esterel built up an international reputation for his couture house, travelling the world over to promote his collections, even appearing behind the Iron Curtain when the Soviet Union was off-limits to Westerners. But he always remained true to his love of the stage and his background as an engineer, claiming that the 72 patents he held on machine tools allowed him to support his fashion design career.

There was something of the carnival performer in Esterel's attitude toward fashion. His designs were often extremely fanciful—and often ridiculed by the fashion press. It was as if couture for Esterel was more about exploring his own sense of whimsical creativity rather than about designing clothes. In 1963 his show included tweed hats with small black veils and umbrellas with built-in lights. Prior to the 1964 show he declared that several of his top models would appear with shaved heads "to give a new importance to a woman's face." His 1965 collection was called "confused and complicated," and included striped bathing suits with long skintight legs described as looking like "something out of a Mack Sennett movie."

Jacques Esterel was not simply a jester at the court of fashion, however. He was often in the forefront of fashion trends in the 1960s and 1970s, taking *au courant* looks from stylish young "Mods and Rockers" on the streets and translating them into haute couture. His 1965 designs for men included a plaid suit with a kilt and a salmon-colored Nehru jacket in corduroy, worn over high yoked pants with zippers on front and back. For women he created dramatic evening wear, including an ensemble of overblouse, floor-length skirt and great hooded evening cape of matching velour.

Esterel's lively intelligence saw no creative boundaries, whether he was designing a garment, writing a song, making his own store fixtures, or sharing his vision with other designers. In the early seventies Esterel created his most well-known and talked-about collection, the "unisex" line, presenting clothes designed for both men and women. Ever the iconoclast, his first foray into the United States found him opening a couture shop in the New York suburbs, far from the fashion industry center in New York City. And the high-spirited, uninhibited house of Esterel attracted and fostered young talents, including future stars Anne Marie Beretta and Jean-Paul Gaultier.

Esterel's unfortunate and sudden death in 1974 did not signal the end of the house of Esterel. His widow and daughter strove to continue his spirit of fashion adventure, overseeing Creations Jacques Esterel. In the mid-1980s the company was involved in several highly-publicized lawsuits in regard to trademark copying against Chanel and also over the disputed purchase of the venerable house of Madame Alix Grés, but both suits were settled.

—Kathleen Paton

ESTEVEZ, Luis.

Cuban/American designer

Born: Luis Estevez de Galvez in Havana, Cuba, 5 December 1930. **Education:** Studied architecture, University of Havana, and fashion design, Traphagen School, New York. **Career:** Window display designer, Lord and Taylor; design assistant, Patou, 1953-55; founder, designer, Grenelle, 1955-68; also menswear designer, from 1967. Moved to California, 1968; designer, Eva Gabor collections, 1972-74, and Luis Estevez International line for Gabor, 1974-77; designer, Estevez for Neal and other free-lance work; own firm, from 1977, concentrated on couture from 1980s. **Awards:** Coty American Fashion Critics Award, 1956.

Publications:

On ESTEVEZ:

Books

Morris, Bernadine, and Barbara Walz, *The Fashion Makers,* New York 1978.
Milbank, Caroline Rennolds, *New York Fashion: The Evolution of American Style,* New York 1989.

Articles

Ginsberg, Steve, "Another Comeback for Luis Estevez," in *Women's Wear Daily* (New York), 17 October 1989.
Romano-Benner, Norma, "Shaping the 90's," in *America,* September/October 1990.

Vannett, Kasey, "He Likes Black Velvet," in *Hispanic,* January/February 1991.

*   *   *

Since 1977 when he opened his own company, Luis Estevez has produced elegant and restrained eveningwear for prestigious Californian clients, including Merle Oberon and Betty Ford. His style is well suited to the Californian lifestyle, with its emphasis on wealth, luxury, and success.

Born to a privileged background in Cuba in 1930, Estevez studied architecture in Havana but switched to fashion after spending a summer job as a window dresser for Lord and Taylor department store in New York. After study at the Traphagen School of Fashion, New York, he left for Paris and found work at the house of Jean Patou for two years. This experience in Parisian couture was to influence his creative approach to design for the rest of his life.

By 1955, Estevez was designing in his own name, for a company called Grenelle. Specializing in evening and cocktailwear, with occasional forays into daywear, Estevez was an immediate success and was honoured with the Coty American Fashion Critics Award in 1956. The clothes had an exclusive, individual look but were made from reasonably priced fabrics, selling well in the higher brackets of the mass market. Estevez attributed much of his inspiration to his wife, who liked to dress in sexy but tasteful clothes with sharp and uncluttered silhouettes.

In the 1950s and 1960s Estevez clothes were distinguished by his individual cutout neck designs; unusual angles like Os or Vs or in the shape of daisy petals, the edges of the fabric appearing jagged. Frequent use was made of stark black and white and of full, rustling skirts, or narrow lines with floating back panels. He also introduced less fitting clothes in the form of barrel-shaped ottoman coats and dresses in two versions; one with a narrow skirt, the other with a puffball skirt. Evening jumpsuits were late 1960s innovations, as was a foray into menswear which featured horizontally tucked evening shirts. He was fond of designing around a strong theme, as in his ethnic-African inspired collection of 1959, featuring oversize tiger and zebra stripe prints. Estevez was also know for his dramatic use of accessories and has designed swimwear and furs as a free-lance designer for other companies.

The designer has lived and worked in California since 1968. His name became established on the West Coast when actress Eva Gabor commissioned his talents as a glamorous eveningwear designer for her own label Eva Gabor Collections. This venture was so successful that in 1974 he signed a contract with her parent firm to design a line called Luis Estevez International. Since establishing his own firm in 1977 he has concentrated on the couture market and although less celebrated than in the 1950s and 1960s, his reliability and expertise are well respected by clients, who eagerly pour themselves into his sensual black velvet dresses and embroidered sheaths.

Luis Estevez looks set to continue designing in the couture mode into the next century, as recent press cuttings about the designer seem to confirm. *Women's Wear Daily*'s article "Another Comeback for Luis Estevez," and *America*'s article "Shaping the 90's," are indicative of his predicted longevity.

—Kevin Almond

———

ETTEDGUI, Joseph. See **JOSEPH.**

———

FABRICE.

Haitian-born American fashion designer

Born: Fabrice Simon in Port au Prince, Haiti, 29 January 1951. Moved to the United States, 1964. **Education:** Studied textile design and fashion illustration, Fashion Institute of Technology, New York, 1969-70. **Career:** Free-lance textile designer, 1971-76; formed own company producing hand painted and beaded gowns, 1976; menswear line introduced, 1985. **Awards:** Coty American Fashion Critics Award, 1981. **Address:** 24 West 57th St, New York, NY 10019, USA.

Publications:

On FABRICE:

Books

Milbank, Caroline Rennolds, *New York Fashion: The Evolution of American Style,* New York 1989.

Articles

Wihlborg, Lee Wohlfers, "Style," in *People* (New York), 25 April 1983.
Milbank, Caroline Rennolds, "Fabrice," in *Interview* (New York), December 1986.

* * *

Since founding his company in 1976, Haitian-born Fabrice has been known primarily for eveningwear targeted to the high end of the custom and ready-to-wear markets.

He trained as a textile designer. When he turned from textile to fashion design in 1975, not surprisingly he began to work in hand painted fabrics. His first significant sale was a small number of gowns purchased by the New York specialty shop Henri Bendel. Bendel's was instrumental in establishing the career of many young designers. This was the heyday of Bendel's "open house," where the store's buyers set aside a weekly time to view, sometimes to purchase, work from unknown artists. Typically, these unknowns lacked major financial backing and production resources. More than a few of them were also producing hand painted silks in limited quantity. It was a labor intensive, but otherwise relatively inexpensive way to enter the world of fashion.

Fabrice sought to distinguish his product from theirs and to expand his market. He found the way when he discovered a selection of beaded motifs originating in Haiti. Fabrice commissioned Haitian beaders and embroiderers to execute his designs, beginning in 1979. Although he still works at times with hand painted fabrics, today he is best known for his distinctive beaded gowns.

His work reflects a contemporary approach to the ancient craft. These are gowns with a modern sensibility, designed from within a frame of reference that suggests a response and asks for a second look. Fabrice's beaded squiggles invite comparison with the paintings of Joan Miró and with the graffiti found on public buildings. On a dark ground, his abstract designs seem suspended in space, like the lights of a far off bridge at night. More easily read patterns also startle and amuse when worked in bugle beads. Imagine, for example, a beaded gown patterned like an argyle sock, or one inspired by a woven *ikat.* Fabrice's references include cobwebs and comic strips; he acknowledges current street style without ignoring past traditions.

In his formal menswear collections, Fabrice offered alternatives to the traditional black tie ensemble. He showed silk T-shirts for evening, pairing them with houndstooth or floral damask dinner jackets, or with unstructured smoking jackets for an even more relaxed look.

Acknowledging the street influence on his work, Fabrice introduced a bridge collection in 1992 called Graffiti. His nylon, rayon, and Lycra Spandex dresses in stinging colors with contrasting insets or appliques were sleek and colorful wearable graphics. In his ready-to-wear and in his custom clothes, Fabrice's wit complements his artistry.

—Whitney Blausen

FAINBLOOM, Abe and Bill. See **CHAMPION.**

FARHI, Nicole.

British designer

Born: France, 25 July 1946. **Education:** Studied fashion illustration at Studio Bercot, Paris. **Career:** Free-lance designer for Pierre D'Alby, Bianchini-Férier, *Elle, Marie-Claire,* 1966-c.1973. Designer, French Connection, from 1973; own label introduced to coincide with first Nicole Farhi boutique, 1983; opened free-standing shops, London and New York, 1984, Norway, 1987; menswear collection introduced, 1989. Awards: British Fashion Award, 1989; British Design Council Award, 1991. **Address:** 16 Fouberts Place, London W1V 1HH, England.

Publications:

On FARHI:

Articles

Bloomfield, Judy, "Nicole Farhi Strengthens U.S. Connection," in *Women's Wear Daily* (New York), 28 September 1988.
"Din Adds Spice to French Dressing," in *Design Weekly* (London), 14 July 1989.
Martin, Rosie, "So Farhi, So Good," in *Vogue* (London), April 1991.

*

My clothes are for women like me who are active, either because they work or simply live life to the full. The designs are understated but with tremendous style ... never boring ... and even when it is a fun garment, I like to keep the shape very simple.

—Nicole Farhi

Nicole Farhi was born in France of Turkish parents, and trained in Paris to be a fashion illustrator, working first for Parisian fashion magazines illustrating the haute couture collections in Paris. When she was 20 she made the transition to fashion design when she was asked to design dresses by such magazines as *Marie-Claire* and *Elle*, which were sold as patterns for their readers to make up. She then met Stephen Marks and began designing for the company that soon became French Connection. "We went to India," she relates, "sourcing fabrics and designing textiles. This was 1973-74 and there was a demand for Eastern fabrics and embroidery." By 1983, when French Connection was floated on the London Stock Exchange, Farhi launched a company under her own name, backed by the now considerable resources of the larger label. In 1984 she wrote: "The clothes I was designing for French Connection were too constricting for me. They were very successful, but I wanted to design unstructured clothes for women."

Unstructured design is a distinctive feature of Farhi's work, as is the importance of understatement, attention to detail, and subtle colours and textures: "My collections over the years have become more and more feminine ... altogether softer, using layers of colour and texture. I think a woman should express her sexuality ... not in a blatant way, but subtly—perhaps just by using fabric that is pleasing to the touch." In winter 1989 Farhi launched her first collection for men, a move welcomed as a new development in British menswear. As Farhi explained at the time "... many of the fabrics and shapes I had used for women in the past had been quite simple and 'masculine,' so it was not too difficult to make the transition."

Both women's and men's collections express Nicole Farhi's Europe-based design philosophy. "Nowadays the way we live means less of a partition between day and evening clothes ... they need to be relaxed in the day yet sophisticated enough for the evening. We must mix them to suit ourselves ... at last there is no dictation."

In addition to the original shop in St Christopher's Place, London, there are now Nicole Farhi shops in Covent Garden, Knightsbridge, and Hampstead, as well as concessionary outlets in many major stores throughout the United Kingdom. In 1989, Nicole Farhi won the British Classics category at the British Fashion Awards and in 1991 was awarded the British Design Council Award

for Design Excellence for her spring-summer 1991 collection, the first time in five years that the award had been given to a fashion designer.

—Doreen Ehrlich

FASSETT, Kaffe.

American knitwear designer working in London

Born: San Francisco, California, 7 December 1937; educated Museum of Fine Arts School, Boston. Moved to Britain, 1964. **Career:** Created knitting patterns for Women's Home Industries, Browns of London, and Rowan Yarns of Yorkshire. Also creator of needlepoints. Television series *Glorious Colour*, for British Channel 4. **Exhibition:** *Kaffe Fassett at the V & A*, Victoria and Albert Museum, London, 1988. **Address:** c/o Ebury Press, 20 Vaux-Hall Bridge Road, London, SW1V 2SA, England.

Publications:

By FASSETT:

Articles

Glorious Knitting, London 1985.
Glorious Needlepoint, London 1987.
Kaffe Fassett at the V & A (exhibition catalogue), London 1988, published as *Glorious Colour*, USA.
Family Album, with Zoë Hunt, London 1989.
Glorious Inspiration, London 1991.
Kaffe's Classics, London 1993.
Glorious Interiors, London due 1995.

On FASSETT:

Books

Sutton, Alan, *British Craft Textiles*, London 1985.

Articles

Coleman, Marigold, in *Crafts* (London), March/April 1975.
"Craftsmen of Quality," Crafts Advisory Committee, 1976.
Green, William, "Kaffe Fassett the Colour Man," in *Vogue* (London), April 1980.
Innes, Jocasta, in *Cosmopolitan* (London), January 1984.
Polan, Brenda, in *The Guardian* (London), 21 March 1985.
Schneebeli, Heini, "Observatory," in *The Observer* (London), 9 November 1986.
Roberts, Glenys, in *The Sunday Telegraph Magazine* (London), 15 February 1987.
Kendall, Ena, "A Room of My Own," in *The Observer Magazine* (London), January 1988.
Interview in *New Pins and Needles* (London), May 1988.
Hilliard, Elizabeth, "A ***** in the Life of Kaffe Fassett," in the *Evening Standard* (London), 16 November 1988.
Campbell, Sylvia, "Kaffe Fassett Fiber Artist," in *Needlepoint Plus* (California), May/June 1989.

Molesworth, Melanie, "Table Manners," in *Woman's Journal* (London), January 1990.

*   *   *

Kaffe Fassett was born in 1937 in San Francisco. His family moved to the former home of the Aga Khan and Rita Hayworth in the wild and rocky Big Sur region of California. An unconventional childhood in an artistic household fostered a creative talent in the young Fassett, and schooldays spent at a school run by followers of the Indian guru Krishna Murti were also to be a lasting influence. A scholarship took him to study at the Museum of Fine Arts School in Boston but he stayed only briefly and left to make his way as a society painter. Arriving in Britain in this capacity on a three-month vacation in 1964, he met the newly graduated fashion student Bill Gibb. He accompanied Gibb on a trip to Scotland and fell in love with the colours of the landscape and the Shetland wools. A woman on the train home taught him how to knit "and that is all I've done in 20 years."

His first waistcoat sold for £100 in 1969 and earned a full page in *Vogue*. Thus began "a wonderful obsession," which was to ensure him a place in 20th-century fashion history. "I think knitting is just mysteriously, incredibly magic. I mean who would ever think that you could just take two sticks and rub them together with a bit of thread in between and out would come this incredible tapestry of colour."

Abandoning his paints but still with the painter's eye, he set about using yarns to explore the world of colour. He designs organically, learning techniques when necessary. He is simply not interested in rules or in a variety of stitches and claims to have arrived at non-*Angst* knitting. He abhors the hard and fast rules that have kept hand-knitters enslaved for so long. Fassett uses only stocking stitch and rib. "I wanted to make it elegant so there was no point in trying anything fancy which immediately goes wrong when you drop a stitch. If you make a mistake according to my method, it can be a positive benefit." He works with as many as 150 colours in a garment—"anything worth doing is worth overdoing," he claims. After a brief spell working in machine knits with dress designers—notably Bill Gibb—Fassett turned his back on the machine. The intricacy of pattern he sought was incompatible with the industrial process.

Fassett works impulsively and intuitively and at an astonishing pace. Using circular needles he sits cross-legged, barefoot, on his bed, the design emerging line by line. He seldom uses a graph. For him, colour and pattern are paramount, styling very much secondary. "The colouring is totally instinctive, a gut thing." He worships colour, uses it with great abandon and total assurance, seeing it everywhere even in the most inauspicious surroundings. He advocates "if in doubt, add twenty more."

His inspiration comes from the world of ethnic decorative arts: Turkish kilims, Islamic tiles, Chinese pots, Spanish brocades. For him knitting garments is about patterns, not pictures. He doesn't feel that large pictorial sweaters are really flattering to wear. Repeats and stylization render the figurative more appropriate for knitwear. Decoration follows through the entire garment, often using a contrasting tartan or stripe on the back. Favourite themes—circles, spots, squares—recur, transformed by a change in scale or colour.

As well as individual commissions, he began to design for Women's Home Industries and for Browns who made up the patterns and sent them out to home knitters. His early work used mainly small

Kaffe Fassett: Needlepoint waistcoat.

repeat geometric motifs inspired by oriental rugs. Next there were grand romantic coats like the Romeo and Juliet coat inspired by the Nureyev ballet, with extravagant gathered shoulders and floor-sweeping skirts, in stripes of mohair and bouclé with a tight jewelled bodice. A commission from the Aberdeen Art Gallery produced the huge "map coat," a landscape extravaganza.

Of enduring appeal have been his ballooning coats, large, simply cut, T-shaped garments gathered at mid-calf into horizontally striped ribs—loose, enveloping shapes sized to fit anyone. Vast canvases for oversize geometric pattern or stylized Chinese pots or autumn leaves—more than garments, more three-dimensional works of art, but very much intended to be worn, to swirl, to drape, to cling around the figure. He makes giant triangular shawls resplendent with a dazzling variety of dots and spots inspired by the Roman glass at the Victoria and Albert Museum, London.

In October 1988 the ultimate accolade in craft circles came with his exhibition at the Victoria and Albert Museum. It was the first by a contemporary textile designer.

High fashion has been influenced by Kaffe Fassett. At the London Fashion Week in 1985, in collaboration with Bill Gibb, he produced "simply-cut, richly-coloured, knitted suits and throws," and closed "with a series of fairy-tale exercises in the baroque, the beaded and the burnished"—all in "the glowing richness of Kaffe Fassett's colours." Bill Gibb's huge American-Indian style coat-sweaters came from Fassett's American past.

Missoni, the renowned Italian designers, invited Fassett to Milan to design knitwear for them. Fassett generously left the Italian fashion house with years of ideas.

In 1990 in Stockholm a ballet featuring flowing Fassett coats and shawls was staged at the Art and Industry Museum for the opening of his exhibition there. The queues were so long, the opening had to be restaged three times, and 107,000 people attended.

Extensive lecture tours and workshops have brought Kaffe Fassett's message to millions of people the world over. Students have described these talks as "electrifying." He has also starred in a series on colour on British television, in 1988. He freely shares all he knows with the hand-knitting public and has tirelessly campaigned to awaken that unexplored potential he believes lies in everyone.

His first book, *Glorious Knitting* (London 1985), sold 180,000 copies, and a string of knitting shops opened in its wake. Five books followed, and a sixth is due to be published in 1995.

Fassett's painterly approach has revolutionized the way we consider hand knitwear. He is a missionary for colour, prodigious, enthusiastic, unpretentious and, until recently, "never really did get around to owning furniture." He has been described as the man who brought knitting back from the dead. He has kept his work at a very personal level, resisting all entreaties to expand into big business. He decided very early on that for him it was essential to remain at the helm. His creations are put together with love and feeling far removed from the overworked designer product.

Fassett reflects on his success: "The British are not that ambitious for quick success. They'll put in the time. They made me patient enough to make something gorgeous instead of racing for a quick effect. It couldn't have happened that way in America—it would have been commercialized too soon."

—Elian McCready

FATH, Jacques.

French designer

Born: Lafitte, France, 12 September 1912. **Education:** Studied bookkeeping and law, Commercial Institute, Vincennes, France. **Family:** Married Geneviève Boucher de la Bruyère, 1939; son: Philippe. **Military Service:** Completed required military service and served again in the artillery during World War II. **Career:** Bookkeeper, then trader at the Paris Bourse, 1930-32. Showed first collection, Paris, 1937; reopened salon, 1940; designed ready-to-wear collection for American manufacturer Joseph Halpert, 1948; formed own company in the United States, 1951; developed ready-to-wear collection in Paris, 1954, including Fath scarves and hosiery. Business sold, 1957. **Exhibitions:** *Jacques Fath Création-Couture des Années 50* (retrospective), Palais Galliera, Paris, 1993. **Awards:** Neiman Marcus Award, Dallas, 1949. *Died* (in Paris) *13 November 1954.* **Address:** 3 rue du Boccador, 75008 Paris, France.

Publications:

On FATH:

Books

Bertin, Célia, *Paris à la Mode,* London 1956.

Ballard, Bettina, *In My Fashion,* New York 1960.

Milbank, Caroline Rennolds, *Couture: The Great Designers,* New York 1985.

Veillon, Dominique, *La mode sous l'occupation,* Paris 1990.

Guillaume, Valérie, *Jacques Fath* (exhibition catalogue), Paris 1993.

Articles

Coughlan, Robert, "Designer for Americans: Jacques Fath of Paris Sells U.S. Women Wearable Glamour," in *Life Magazine* (New York), October 1949.

"Jacques Fath," in *Current Biography* (New York), April 1951.

Roberts, Eleanor, "Fath Brings Paris Chi-Chi to Boston," in the *Boston Post,* 18 December 1953.

"Jacques Fath," [obituary] in the *New York Times,* 14 November 1954.

Oster, André, "Jacques Fath Recalled," in Ruth Lynam, ed., *Couture: An Illustrated History of the Great Paris Designers and Their Creations,* New York 1972.

Deeny, Godfrey, "A Revival of the House that Jacques Built," in *Women's Wear Daily* (New York), 26 February 1992.

Stern, Suzanne Pierrette, "Memories of a Parisian Seamstress: Tales and Techniques from the Workrooms of Couturier Jacques Fath," in *Threads* (Newtown, Connecticut), April/May 1992.

*   *   *

Jacques Fath had a short career—from 1937 until his death in 1954—and after he died his name fell into obscurity. In contrast to his great contemporaries, Christian Dior and Cristobal Balenciaga, Fath has been largely forgotten, but he deserves to be rediscovered as a talented creator.

Fath was born in 1912 into a Protestant family of Flemish and Alsatian origin. His great-grandmother had been a dressmaker to the empress Eugène and, from an early age, he showed an interest in designing clothes. He also toyed with the idea of becoming an actor, a craving that he later indulged in private theatricals and costume parties.

Fath had "the showy elegance of a character from a Cocteau play and the charm of an *enfant terrible,"* recalled Célia Bertin (*Paris à la Mode,* London 1956). But fashion editors like Bettina Ballard and Carmel Snow (of *Harper's Bazaar*) tended to dismiss him as "a good-looking child prodigy ... with slightly theatrical fashion ideas not worthy of the hallowed pages of *Vogue* or *Harper's Bazaar."*

His career was interrupted by the outbreak of World War II. Taken prisoner in 1940, he was, however, soon back in Paris, where he reopened his couture house with his wife Geneviève. A recent book on fashion during the Nazi Occupation notes that scruples of conscience did not embarrass Fath, who was closely associated with various Franco-German groups and whose clientèle consisted heavily of Germans, wealthy collaborators and black marketeers. Unlike Chanel, however, whose reputation as a Nazi sympathizer temporarily injured her post-war career, Fath's image emerged intact, and after the war, his international career took off.

His glove-fitted dresses glorified the female form, and some have said that he even inspired Dior's New Look. Certainly, Fath designed some of the sexiest and most glamorous dresses to come out of Paris. The typical Fath dress featured a fitted bodice that moulded a slender waistline and emphasized the swelling curves of bosom and hips. Sleeve and collar treatments were important to Fath, and he favored irregular necklines that drew attention to the breasts.

Skirts were either very slim or very full, characterized perhaps by a whirlpool of pleats or interesting draped effects.

If Dior and Balenciaga were known for the architectural beauty of their designs, Fath's style was praised for its glamour and vivacity. He often used diagonal lines, asymmetrical drapery, and floating panels to give a sense of movement. Nor was he afraid of color, even using such daring combinations as bright blue and green. (He himself liked to wear a red tartan jacket.) Whereas Dior's career was characterized by striking shifts of silhouette (the A-line, the H-line, etc.), Fath maintained an unswerving fidelity to the female form divine, focusing on sexy lines and novel decorative details, such as rows of nonfunctional buttons. Fath's style of wearable glamour had a wide appeal, and in 1948 he signed an agreement with the American manufacturer, Joseph Halpert. Henceforth, in addition to his own couture collections, Fath also produced a low-priced American line.

Fath was increasingly regarded as the "heir apparent to Dior's throne." As *Life Magazine* said in 1949: "Dior is still generally acknowledged to be the head man, so to speak, of the fashion world, but Fath has recently had a spectacular rise in prestige, and it now seems likely that the next look to confront and impoverish the U.S. male will be the Fath look." Carmel Snow, editor of *Harper's Bazaar*, revised her earlier opinion of Fath, and now declared that, "He makes you look like you have sex appeal—and believe me, that's important."

Fath himself had tremendous personal appeal, with his blond wavy hair and slender physique (a 28-inch waist, claimed one source). He was also very much a social personality; he and his pretty wife loved throwing lavish and imaginative parties, which had the pleasant side-effect of providing excellent publicity. "An atmosphere of glitter, chic, and perfumed excitement permeates both his personal and business affairs," observed *Life* (October 1949). Yet behind the scenes, Fath was struggling with illness. Only a year before his death in 1954, the American press had hailed him as the "fabulous young French designer who ... is out to make every woman look like a great beauty." Now that promise was cut short.

—Valerie Steele

FENDI.

Italian design firm

Established as a leather and fur workshop by Adele Casagrande (1897-1978), Rome, 1918; renamed Fendi with her marriage to Edoardo Fendi, 1925. Current principals are daughters Paola (born 1931), Anna (born 1933), Franca (born 1935), Carla (born 1937), Alda (born 1940), their husbands and children. The firm designs leather and fur clothing and accessories, a ready-to-wear line, knitwear and beachwear; bridge line introduced, 1990; jewelry line licensed, 1991; *Fendi Uomo* perfume introduced, 1988. Karl Lagerfeld has collaborated with Fendi for over 30 years. **Awards:** National Italian American Foundation Award to Paola Fendi, 1990. **Address:** Fendi Paola e S.lle S.A.S., Via Borgognona 7, 00187 Rome, Italy.

Publications:

On FENDI:

Books

Mulassano, Adriana, *Moda e modi,* Milan 1980.

Alfonsi, Maria-Vittoria, *Leaders in Fashion: I grandi personaggi della moda,* Bologna 1983.
Giocomoni, Silvia, *The Italian Look Reflected,* Milan 1984.
Soli, Pia, *Il geno antipatico,* Venice 1984.

Articles

Schiavi, Maria, "Che cosa di chi: Fendi," in *Vogue* (Milan), October 1984.
"Da Fendi: Lusso, classe e successo," in *Linea Italiana* (Milan), No. 157, 1985.
Acquarone, Lele, "Le incredibili pellicce Fendi," in *Vogue* (Milan), September 1985.
"La grande moda di Fendi," in *Vogue* (Milan), September 1986.
"Fendi: Stupore nel lusso," in *Donna* (Milan), July/August 1987.
"Le grandi pellicce Fendi," in *Vogue* (Milan), September 1987.
Bachrach, Judy, "The Roman Empire," in *Savvy,* December 1987.
Barron, Pattie, "La Famiglia Fendi," in *Cosmopolitan* (London), September 1988.
"Fendi Furs: Karl Goes on a Tear," in *Women's Wear Daily* (New York), 17 March 1992.

*   *   *

Like many Italian firms producing luxury goods, the Fendi company is a family dynasty that owes a great deal of its success to the strong blood links which are an intrinsic part of the business. Fendi is unique in that it is run not by male members of the family (of which there are none, except by marriage), but by five sisters, daughters of Adele and Edoardo Fendi, who became involved in the business after the death of their father in 1954. The firm of Fendi originally specialized in producing high quality furs and leather goods on the via del Plebiscito in Rome in 1925. It was at this point that the firm moved towards a more high fashion profile, with the first Fendi fashion show being staged in 1955.

Although Fendi produces a ready-to-wear sports line, the name is probably best known in the fashion arena for its dramatic fur collections, which have been designed by Karl Lagerfeld since 1962. It was the company's relationship with Lagerfeld that brought the name of Fendi to the attention of the fashion press, where it has since remained. Lagerfeld was also responsible for designing the double-F *griffe* that is almost as well-recognized among the fashion *cognoscenti* as the double-C and double-G symbols of Chanel and Gucci.

Lagerfeld's innovative treatment of fur is both witty and, at times, shocking and has kept the Fendi company at the forefront of this particular field. In Lagerfeld's capable hands, real fur has taken on the appearance of fake fur; it has been perforated with thousands of tiny holes to make the coats lighter to wear; it has been printed to look like damask and other similar fabrics. Denim coats are lined with mink by Lagerfeld, who has also employed unorthodox animal skins such as squirrel and ferret in his creations. More recently, Lagerfeld has covered an entire fur coat with woven mesh and created completely reversible fur coats as his stand against the anti-fur movement that has created great problems for the trade. Another design he produced for autumn-winter 1993-94 consisted of a small zipped bag that unfolded into a calf-length fur coat. Whatever one's personal beliefs regarding the wearing of animal furs, the partnership of Karl Lagerfeld and the Fendi company has undoubtedly broken barriers in the field of fur design. In Italy, the fur sales continue to constitute a major part of the company's

Fendi: 1993/94.

business—where the Fendi sisters claim to have changed the age-old tradition of fur as being a status symbol, to being a covetable high-fashion garment.

Like many luxury goods companies, Fendi has capitalized upon its name, with the usual plethora of accessories, gloves, lighters, pens, glasses and perfumes that have become a natural progression for a well-recognized label. However, in terms of design, the house of Fendi will be remembered for its innovative treatment and development of luxury furs that has occurred as a result of its successful working partnership with designer Karl Lagerfeld.

—Catherine Woram

FENG, Han.

Chinese designer

Born: Hangzhou, China. **Education:** Graduated from Zhejiang Art Academy, South-East China. **Career:** Began career designing scarves in the United States, in the 1980s. **Address:** 2109 Broadway, New York, NY 10023, USA.

Publications:

On FENG:

Books

Gumpert, Lynn and Richard Martin, *Material Dreams* (exhibition catalogue), New York 1995.

Articles

Goodman, Wendy, "Living with Style: Hang Feng Comes Round the World to Spin Heavenly Tales in Silk," in *House and Garden* (New York), June 1993.
Enfield, Susan, "Meditative Pose," in *Avenue* (New York), September 1993.
Spindler, Amy M., "Bringing New Life (and Bamboo Bra Tops) to the Party," in *New York Times,* 3 November 1993.
Staples, Kate, "Feng's Fashion: Smooth as Silk," in *Departures* (New York), March/April 1994.
"New York: Han Feng," in *Women's Wear Daily* (New York), 7 November 1994.
Schiro, Anne-Marie, "Designed for Retailers and Real Women," in the *New York Times,* 5 April 1995.

*   *   *

Amy Spindler has said of Han Feng that she "offers a few lines of the poetry of Romeo Gigli and Issey Miyake, but for much lower prices" (*New York Times,* 3 November 1993). Spindler rightly perceives the affinities of the gossamer pleated, yet practical, clothing and accessories that Feng designs, but it may be that a touch of poetry is just the levitating apparition we need in the midst of practical clothing. Feng creates unremittingly real clothing, wearable and practical, but with a concise, *haiku*-like hint of the historicist romance conveyed by Gigli and of the Cubist authority suggested by Miyake. There is something about Feng's inventiveness

that is so radical a disposition for clothing that, like Miyake's pleats, it will either be a significant historical interlude in reform dress for an avant-garde margin of the population or a revolution in the way in which all people dress. There is a poetry to Feng's minimal natural structures for clothing.

One wonders, however if clothing is the ultimate or exclusive goal of a designer who, growing up in Hangzhou, China, a great silk city, has become a devotee of the extraordinary organic materials that, with human intervention, yield even more possibilities of organic shapes. A graduate of the Zhejiang Art Academy in South-East China, Feng approaches her work as an artist. She began her work in the United States in the 1980s creating scarves, and the effect of the clothing is still a wondrous wrapping and veiling uncommon in the tailored West. Her clothing wraps the body as the clouds enclose a mountain; her "smoke rings" are wraps of the kind that Charles James and Halston made, allowing a gentle helix of cloth to fit from hand to hand and sheathe the shoulders in an arch out of nature. In as much as Feng is using materials that are, as Wendy Goodman described, "magic out of silk" (*House and Garden* New York, June 1993) the organic compositions are only reinforced by the pliant materials, diaphanous delicacy, and classic shapes, often defying clothing as ceremony. She all but ignores tailoring and, in fact, uses many of the same experiments in textiles for her home furnishings. Not bothering with tailoring and instead assembling the garment as a light sculpture on the body, Feng fulfils the most predicted expectations in the West of design from the East. Spindler notes, "Her most beautiful dresses were of organza, which was gathered in little puffs, as if filled with helium. Han Feng's vision is so romantic that the clothes look dreamily feminine even when draped over the tattooed form of the auto mechanic-cum-model Jenny Shimizu." The mystery of the clothing is that Feng is offering soft shells of body wrap and comfort that return us to the most primitive, pre-tailored sensibility for dress.

In delving into clothing at the fundamental principle of wrapping, Feng is offering an alternative to the evolved forms of Western dress. It would be unlikely that a relatively young, unknown designer will have the opportunity to transform so thoroughly and effectively the principles of fashion, yet Feng's work has the visionary impact to cast a wide and important influence. Even as her dresses and jackets gradually achieve acceptance, her work in home fashion, including table linens, pillows, and bed covers, is perhaps the most likely to be broadly accepted. Even in apparel, pleated, weightless ringlets do not seem to be the stuff of insurrection, but in this case they may be an anticipation for clothing of the 21st century. It is not surprising that Feng's work was prominently featured in the Christmas 1994 mail-order catalogue of the Museum of Modern Art (New York).

—Richard Martin

FENN WRIGHT AND MANSON.

British fashion house

Founded by Trevor Wright, Colin Fenn, and Glen Manson in London, 1974; American subsidiary formed in New York, 1977. **Addresses:** Moray House, 23-31 Great Tichfield St., London W1P 7FE, England; 500 Seventh Avenue, New York, NY 10018, USA.

Fenn Wright and Manson: Spring 1995.

the United States in 1978. It now employs some 300 people world-wide in such locations as New York, Melville (Long Island), Los Angeles, Hong Kong, and Korea. Fenn Wright and Manson sells to the better department stores internationally, the better specialty chains, and independent specialty stores. Sales in the US now account for nearly 90 percent of Fenn Wright and Manson's volume. A large proportion of these sales are made through the operation of retail outlets, most of which are situated in off-price malls in the US, primarily on the East Coast. The Company also has a show-room at the Dallas Mart which operates only during show weeks.

Fenn Wright and Manson womenswear draws on the themes of timeless classics, stylish and functional sportswear, and refined tailoring. The combination of styles creates a feeling of warmth, comfort, and easy dressing. In the most recent collections, longer lines are a marked feature, with softer tailoring, uncluttered shapes, and clean layers in soft and earthy colours: cream, mushroom, camel, tobacco, and chocolate. A variety of fabrics and knits include lambswool, angora, wool, cotton, as well as leather and Lycra.

The latest menswear collection has silk shirts as a major feature with sandwashed silk available in 30 different colours, and silk twill, as well as needlecord and cotton poplin shirts taking on the guise of the classic denim shirt, with top stitching detail and billow pockets.

Fenn Wright and Manson designs are directed towards upmarket department stores. The design focus of the company is one of producing understandable and wearable fashion with an emphasis on quality and value.

—Doreen Ehrlich

Publications:

On FENN WRIGHT AND MANSON:

Articles

"Cygne Inks Deal to Buy Fenn Wright and Manson," in *Daily News Record,* 14 December 1993.
"Cygne Designs Buys Fenn Wright and Manson," in *Women's Wear Daily* (New York), 8 April 1994.
Green, Roy E., "Cygne Designs, Inc. Announces Record Fourth Quarter and Year-End Results," in *Business Wire,* 14 April 1994.
Furman, Phyllis, "Apparel Maker's Star Waxing with Purchase," in *Crain's New York Business,* 8 August 1994.

*   *   *

The Fenn Wright and Manson Group was founded in 1974 by Trevor Wright, Colin Fenn, and Glen Manson, as a British-based company operating from London. Initially, all sales were to the United Kingdom market, and production was wholly in Hong Kong. The company designs, manufactures, and sells both women's and men's clothing, with by far the largest part of the business generated through the women's divisions.

An international market has been established since 1976, in which year the company also formed a buying office to oversee and control its production requirements in the Far East. The firm established its own American subsidiary in 1977, and began trading in

FÉRAUD, Louis.
French designer

Born: Arles, France, 13 February 1921. **Family:** Married Zizi Boivin in 1947 (divorced, 1963); married Mia Fonssagrièves in 1964 (divorced, 1972). **Military Service:** Served as lieutenant in the French Resistance. **Career:** Opened first couture boutique in Cannes, 1955; moved to Paris, entered ready-to-wear; first menswear line launched, 1975; costumer designer for films and television, has designed over 80 films; perfumes *Justine,* introduced, 1965, *Corrida,* 1975; *Fantasque,* introduced, 1980, *Fer,* 1982; *Jour de Féraud/Vivage,* introduced, 1984; sportswear line introduced, 1989; New York flagship store opened, 1990; accessories line introduced, 1992. Also painter. Also author of novels, *The Summer of the Penguin,* 1978, and *The Winter of the Mad.* **Exhibitions:** Exhibition of paintings in Paris, 1988, 1989, 1992, 1993, 1994, and in Japan, 1989; Gallery Urban, New York, 1990. **Awards:** Légion d'Honneur; Golden Thimble Award, 1984; Dé d'Or Award, 1978, 1984. **Address:** 88 rue Faubourg Saint-Honoré, 75008 Paris, France.

Publications:

By FÉRAUD:

Books

Louis Féraud, Paris 1985.
L'hiver des fous, Paris 1986.

Louis Féraud: Haute Couture collection, Fall/Winter 1994/95.

On FÉRAUD:

Articles

"Louis Féraud l'atout coeur," in *L'Officiel* (Paris), September 1984.
"Louis Féraud, mille facettes," unpaginated feature in *L'Officiel* (Paris), September 1985.
"Louis Féraud: le chic," in *Vogue* (New York), April 1986.
Smithers, T. S., "Fast Times with Louis Féraud," in *Women's Wear Daily* (New York), 20 October 1986.
"Louis Féraud: pour fêter l'Espagne," in *L'Officiel* (Paris), March 1987.
Guernsey, Diane, "The Other Féraud," in *Town and Country* (New York), October 1990.
Petkanas, Christopher, "French Accents," in *Harper's Bazaar* (New York), February 1991.
Bowles, Hamish, "Louis the Fun King," *Harpers & Queen,* December 1991.

*   *   *

It has been said of Louis Féraud that he is a man who loves women. Indeed, he describes himself as "Louis Féraud who adores women, Louis Féraud who admires women." This no doubt inspired this former lieutenant from the French Resistance to pursue a career in the rarefied worlds of French haute couture and ready-to-wear.

Féraud designs for a seductive woman who lives in harmony with life and herself, a woman looking for comfort and freedom. He declares himself fascinated by the different personalities of women and how this inspires him to create different moods and themes. For women, he says, "Fashion is an opportunity to be chic, to conspire between reality and desire."

Louis Féraud creates glamorous, luxurious clothes at ready-to-wear prices; he also designs for couture. Among his clients are Joan Collins, for whom he designed some of the clothes worn in the television series *Dynasty* and Madame Mitterand, wife of the French President. The collection is divided between the prêt-à-porter Louis Féraud Paris collections and the less expensive Louis Féraud set.

A strong team backs up the Féraud business. The creative team is led by Féraud himself and consists of ten international designers, colour specialists, and stylists who work together to form what he describes as a weather forecast that predicts trends. Féraud has also designed clothes for film and television. As well as suits and dresses for *Dynasty* and *Dallas,* he has designed clothes for Brigitte Bardot, 1955, Paulette Goddard, 1959, Kim Novak, 1963, Catherine Deneuve, 1965, Mireille Mathieu, 1970, and Sabina Anzema, 1983. However, when asked if, given the chance to design clothes for women from another era, which era he would choose he declared: "Tomorrow. I am often seriously asked what fashion will be doing next year. I am like an art medium for these people, who has the ability to look into the future."

Féraud lists painting as being amongst his passions; it inspires him to develop colour in his work. "Colours are fantasies of light," he claims. "However, all colours are diffused in black, memories of the sun, the indispensable, and the perfect that is beauty." He selects specific colour ranges each season, but declares himself unaffected by fashion trends. "The only thing that we must know in our business is what doesn't exist as yet." Colour is developed within the team, which also creates new ideas for fabric trims.

When asked how, out of the French Resistance in World War II, emerged one of the leading fashion designers of the world, Féraud replied: "Fashion does not separate people but holds them together. One can also describe fashion as the meeting place out of love."

—Kevin Almond

_____

FÉRIER, M. See **BIANCHINI-FÉRIER.**

_____

FERRAGAMO, Salvatore.
Italian footwear designer

Born: Bonito, near Naples, Italy, June 1898. **Family:** Married Wanda Miletti in 1949; children: Fiamma, Giovanna, Ferruccio, Fulvia, Leonardo, Massimo. **Career:** Apprentice shoemaker, Bonito, 1907-12; immigrated to the United States, 1914; with brothers, opened shoemaking and shoe repair shop, Santa Barbara, California and also created footwear for the American Film Company, 1914-23; relocated to Hollywood, 1923-27; returned to Italy, established business in Florence, from 1929; bankrupted in 1933; back in business by late 1930s. Business continues. **Exhibitions:** *Salvatore Ferragamo 1898-1960* (retrospective), Palazzo Strozzi, Florence, 1985; *The Art of the Shoe* (retrospective), Los Angeles County Museum, 1992. **Awards:** Neiman Marcus Award, 1947; *Footwear News* Hall of Fame Award, 1988 [Fiamma Ferragamo]. *Died* (in Fiumetto, Italy) *7 August 1960.* **Address:** Salvatore Ferragamo SpA, Palazzo Feroni, Via Tornabuoni 2, 50123 Florence, Italy.

Publications:

By FERRAGAMO:

Books

Shoemaker of Dreams: The Autobiography of Salvatore Ferragamo, London 1957.

On FERRAGAMO:

Books

Swann, June, *Shoes,* London 1982.
Alfonsi, Maria-Vittoria, *Leaders in Fashion: I grandi personaggi della moda,* Bologna 1983.
Palazzo Strozzi, *I protagonisti della moda: Salvatore Ferragamo (1898-1960)* (exhibition catalogue), Florence 1985.
McDowell, Colin, *Shoes: Fashion and Fantasy,* New York 1989.
Almansi, Guido, et. al., *Salvatore Ferragamo,* Milan 1990.
Ricci, Stefania, Edward Maeder, et al., eds., *Salvatore Ferragamo: The Art of the Shoe,* New York 1992.

Articles

Infantino, Vivian, "Salvatore Ferragamo (1898-1960): A Retrospective," in *Footwear News* (New York), July 1985.

Salvatore Ferragamo.

"The Flourishing Fashions of the Ferragamo Family of Florence," in *Vogue* (Paris), October 1985.

Harlow, Vanessa, "Sole Obsession," in *The Observer* (London), 27 September 1987.

Morrison, Patricia, "Feet Were Ferragamo's World," in *The Daily Telegraph* (London), 2 November 1987.

McDowell, Colin, "Wanda Ferragamo: A Woman of Destiny," in *Women's Journal* (London), December 1987.

Hope, Emma, "Designed to Last," in *Design* (London), January 1988.

"Salvatore Ferragamo: The Art of the Shoe, 1927-1960," in the *Arts Review* (London), 15 January 1988.

McKenzie, Janet, "Shoemaker of Dreams," in *Studio International* (London), No. 1020, 1988.

"Il calzolaio dei sogni: Palazzo Strozzi, Firenze," in *Domus* (Milan), No. 663, 1989.

Horovitz, Bruce, "Well-heeled Controversy," in the *Los Angeles Times,* 24 April 1992.

Stengel, Richard, "The Shoes of the Master," in *Time* (New York), 4 May 1992.

*   *   *

A master craftsman, Salvatore Ferragamo was known as one of the world's most innovative shoe designers, transforming the look and fit of the shoe. He broke away from conventional footwear designs, exploring not only innovative design, but also the technical structure of the shoe.

Ferragamo acquired the basic skills of shoe production whilst apprenticed to the local village cobbler in Bonito. Ambitious for success, he emigrated from his home town in Naples to America, where he studied mass production in shoe design. The years in the United States assisted him in fully understanding the technical procedures implemented in manufacturing his unique design. Owing to his excellent grounding in shoe design exploration and study, Ferragamo fully understood all the technical aspects of shoe production, the anatomy, and the balance of the foot. Eventually he set up in business in Santa Barbara, California, where his original, inventive designs caught the regard of many famous customers. Private commissions came from actors, actresses and celebrities including Sophia Loren, Gloria Swanson, the Duchess of Windsor, and Audrey Hepburn.

Initially a designer and creator of hand-made one-off shoes for individual customers, Ferragamo introduced the possibility of creating shoes that were exotic and beautiful, yet supportive to the foot and ankle. Function and comfort, together with an understanding of good design, were the essential elements behind his success.

His name is synonymous with style, glamour, ingenuity, and quality. Ferragamo diverged from the restrictions of conventional shoe design and manufacture, exploring the realms of fantasy and creating footwear well advanced of contemporary classic designs. Ferragamo produced shoes for every occasion; ankle boots, moccasins, laced shoes, Oxford brogues, stilettoes, shoes for evening and daywear, including classic traditional styles.

The shortage of leather and quality skins during the war years encouraged Ferragamo to explore new materials, continually searching beyond the realms of traditional materials for aesthetically attractive alternatives. Cork, crochet, crocheted cellophane, plaited raffia, rubber, fish skins, felt, and hemp were successful if unconventional alternatives.

His designs were brilliant in concept and craftsmanship, creating many unique and outrageous styles. He was inspired by past fashions, cultures, Hollywood, oriental clothing and classical styling. He created over 20,000 styles in his lifetime and registered 350 patents, including oriental mules with a unique pointed toe, patented by Ferragamo at the end of the 1930s. From the late 1930s his amusing, ambitious, and extreme designs involved the use of perforated leathers, raffia checks, elasticated silk yarns, appliqué motifs, needlepoint lace, sequined fabrics and patchwork.

In 1938 he launched the platform shoe which has re-emerged in varying forms ever since. His "invisible shoe," created in 1947, was produced with clear nylon uppers and a black suede heel and Ferragamo produced many variations on this design.

His innate sense of colour extended from traditional browns and beiges to vivid contrasting colours of ornate richness. The technical knowledge attained whilst developing new dyeing techniques assisted him in combining technical knowledge with his creative colour flair.

In 1927 Ferragamo returned to Italy, setting up a workshop in Florence, a city which was to become the fashion centre of Italy. He continued to produce custom-made shoes, many of his customers' individual lasts still being in existence today, maintained in collections in Feroni. Using modern production methods his made-to-measure shoes had quality, durability, and style. He was modern in his approach to design, taking advantage of new technology to improve his output, without jeopardizing standards. Through ambition and ingenuity his productivity and creativity improved greatly, leading to the industrialization of his work, producing 60 per cent hand crafted shoes and 40 percent mass production. Ferragamo maintained high standards by overseeing all aspects of production. The mass produced shoes were manufactured under the label Ferrina Shoes, produced in England.

After his death in 1960 his family continued to produce quality shoes. Ferragamo's biography, published in 1957, three years before his death, titled *Shoemaker of Dreams,* aptly describes his work. His innovative masterpieces in shoe design and his quality accessories contributed to and inspired the world of couture and introduced respectability to the craft of shoe making, raising its importance in the concept of fashion.

—Carol Mary Brown

FERRÉ, Gianfranco.

Italian designer

Born: Legnano, Italy, 15 August 1944. **Education:** Graduated in architecture from Politecnico, Milan, 1969. **Career:** Free-lance jewellery and accessory designer, Milan, 1969-73; designer, Baila, Milan, 1974; launched own label for women's fashions, Milan, 1978; introduced secondary Oaks by Ferré line, 1978; introduced men's collection, 1982; introduced perfume line, 1984; introduced watch collection, 1985; introduced glasses collection and perfume and bath line for men, 1986; introduced haute couture collection, 1986-88; introduced furs collection, 1987; signed agreement with Marzotto for the Studio 000.1 by Ferré lines for men and women, 1987; introduced Ferrejeans, 1989; introduced Forma O by GFF, 1989; introduced feminine fragrance, *Ferré by Ferré,* 1991; introduced household linens collection, 1992. Named artistic director for the House of Dior, 1989. **Exhibitions:** *Italian Re-Evolution,* La Jolla Museum of Art, California, 1982; *Intimate Architecture: Contemporary Clothing Design,* Massachusetts Institute of Technology, Cambridge, 1982; *Design Italian Society in the Eighties,* La Jolla Musuem of Contemporary Art, 1982; *Creators of Italian Fashion 1920-80,* Osaka and Tokyo, 1983; *Il Genio Antipatico: Creatività e tecnologia della Moda Italiana 1951-1983 (The Unpleasant Genius: Creativity and Technology of Italian Fashion 1951-1983),* Rome, 1984; *Tartan: A Grand Celebration of the Tradition of Tartan,* Fashion Institute of Technology, 1988; *Momenti del design italiano nell'industria e nella moda,* Seoul, 1990; *Japonism in Fashion,* National Museum of Modern Art, 1994. **Awards:** Tiberio d'Oro Award, 1976; Best Stylist of the Year Award by *Asahi Shimbun* and *Women's Wear Daily,* 1983; Modepreis for women's fashions, Monaco, 1985; Cutty Sark Men's Fashion Award, New York, 1985; Medal of Civic Merit, Milan, 1985; named Commendatore dell'Ordine al Merito della Repubblica Italiana, 1986; Dé d'Or prize for first haute couture collection for Dior, 1989; named "Milanese of the Year" by the Famiglia Meneghina, 1989; I Grandi Protagonisti prize from the Italian Furs Association, 1990; Lorenzo il Magnifico award from the Medicean Academy, Florence, 1990; Occhio d'Oro prize, 1983, 1983/84, 1985, 1986/87, 1987/88, 1989; Il Fiorino d'Oro Award, 1991; Pitti Immagine Uomo Award, 1993. **Address:** Via della Spiga 19a, 20121 Milan, Italy.

Publications:

By FERRÉ:

Articles

"Le ragioni del sentimento," in *L'Uomo Vogue* (Milan), October 1987.

On FERRÉ:

Books

Mulassano, Adriana, *I mass-moda: Fatti e personaggi dell'Italian Look,* Florence 1979.
Sartogo, Piero, ed., *Italian Re-Evolution* (exhibition catalogue), La Jolla, California 1982.
Alfonsi, Maria-Vittoria, *Leaders in Fashion: I grandi personaggi della moda,* Bologna 1983.
Giacomoni, Silvia, *The Italian Look Reflected,* Milan 1984.
Soli, Pia, ed., *Il genio antipatico* (exhibition catalogue), Milan 1984.
Perschetz, Lois, ed., *W, The Designing Life,* New York 1987.

various, *La moda italiana,* Milan 1987.

Aragno Giordani, Bonizza, ed., *Moda Italia* (exhibition catalogue), Milan 1988.

Howell, Georgina, *Sultans of Style: Thirty Years of Fashion and Passion 1960-90,* London 1990.

Howell, Georgina, *In Vogue,* London 1992.

Carloni, Maria Vittoria, "Bello & Brutto: Lo Stile Secondo Ferré, in *Panorama,* June 1994.

Articles

"New Architects of Fashion," in the *New York Times Magazine,* 16 August 1981.

"The New Architectural Approach to Fashion," in *Vogue* (New York), June 1982.

"Gianfranco Ferré: Expanding His Research," in *Women's Wear Daily* (New York), 5 April 1986.

"Gianfranco Ferré: Uniformi d'eccezione," in *Vogue* (Milan), July/August 1987.

"Roma alta moda: Gianfranco Ferré," in *Vogue* (Milan), September 1987.

Smith, Liz, "Architect of New Classics," in *The Times* (London), 8 December 1987.

"Gianfranco Ferré: Dà alla donna forma e slancio," in *Vogue* (Milan), January 1988.

"Who'll Pay the Ferré Man?," in *W* (London), 28 January 1988.

"Ferré's Blueprint for Men's Wear Is Surprisingly Realistic," in the *Daily News Record* (New York), 12 April 1988.

"Fashion by Ferré," in the *New York Times,* 19 July 1988.

Howell, Georgina, "Gianfranco Ferré Is the Nonconformist," in *Vogue* (New York), July 1988.

"Ferré and Gigli, Architects of Modern Style," in *Elle* (London), October 1988.

"Sinnliches Tuch," in *Der Spiegel,* 23 January 1989.

"Gianfranco Ferré," in *Donna* (Milan), March 1989.

Gastellier, Fabian, "Un Italien cousu Dior," in *Elle* (Paris), 29 May 1989.

Menkes, Suzy, "The Italian Connection," in the *Sunday Express Magazine* (London), 11 June 1989.

"Ferré's Debut at Dior: Much Too Serious," in *Women's Wear Daily* (New York), 25 July 1989.

Smith, Liz, "My Fair Ferré," in *The Times* (London), 25 July 1989.

"Back to the Future," in the *Sunday Times* (London), 30 July 1989.

Baudet, François, "Gianfranco Ferré," in *Vogue* (Paris), August 1989.

Mardore, Lucienne, "Du nouveau dans la mode," in *Marie Claire* (Paris), September 1989.

Menkes, Suzy, "Ferré Strikes Gold," in *Illustrated London News* (London), Autumn 1989.

"Dior for Ever," in *Elle* (New York), October 1989.

Mayer, Margit J., "O Dior mio!," in *Vogue* (Munich), October 1989.

Kleers, Paul, "Ferré in Focus," in *GQ* (London), March 1990.

Mattioni, Marina, "Thinking Big," in *Donna* (Milan), March 1990.

Mayle, Peter, "Ferré's a Jolly Good Fellow," in *GQ,* September 1990.

Boriou, Gisella, "Gianfranco Ferré: I Am a Mix of Sensitivity and Concreteness," in *Donna* (Milan), November 1990.

"Dior Sees Red," in *Elle* (New York), December 1990.

"Gianfranco Ferré," in *Current Biography,* July 1991.

Forden, Sara Gay, "Frankly Ferré," in the *Daily News Record,* 21 June 1993.

Dickson, E. Jane, "The Babar of Milan," in *The Independent Magazine,* October 1993.

Aspesi, Natalia, "Le Donne di Ferré," in *Il Venerdi' di Repubblica,* April 1994.

"La Parole est Dior," in *Vogue Paris,* May 1994.

Blanchard, Tamsin, "New-look Dior Fails to Suit Nineties Woman," in *The Independent* (London), 11 October 1994.

Spindler, Amy M., "Armani and Ferré: A Study in Contrast, in the *New York Times,* 11 March 1995.

La Ferla, Ruth, "The Gilda'd Age," in *Elle* (New York), June 1995.

*

Fashion is a reality connected with the changes of our society, of which it is an attentive interpreter.

Artistic trends, new expressive languages, individualistic or mass behaviour and any other event which marks our society or determines its choices, also determine trends or, at least, fashion changes. A fashion designer has to be an attentive interpreter of these events; he has to be able to prophecy, without forgetting the realities of industry and commerce.

Gianfranco Ferré: Fall/Winter 1994/95.

Gianfranco Ferré: Fall/Winter 1994/95.

My role as a fashion designer comes from a complex process, where creativity and imagination play an important role, but are supported by a firm rational analysis.

—Gianfranco Ferré

*   *   *

Gianfranco Ferré has been dubbed by *Women's Wear Daily* (New York) as the "Frank Lloyd Wright of Italian Fashion." Trained initially as an architect, his work bears many references to this early discipline. He draws up a plan for each collection based on a philosophy that his customer wants functional, classic yet powerful clothes, constructed in the highest quality materials. The clothes are then created with a distinct eye for dramatic proportion and purity of line.

There is nothing understated about Ferré's womenswear. His minimalist approach has often made opulent, theatrical statements on the catwalk, bearing many references to the film star glamour projected by Anita Ekberg in the film *La Dolce Vita.* The clothes reflect a glamorous, fantasy dressing, combined with architectural symmetry. Ferré often exaggerates proportions in tailoring and dressmaking. Classic shirt shapes often have extreme cuffs or collars; coats and jackets are always defined by silhouette. An extravagant use of luxury fabrics like fur on dresses or long evening coats, leather, and taffeta often in the distinctive, stark colours of red, black, white or gold reinforce this definition of modern glamour.

His menswear collections are less extravagant, based on tradition but designed with his characteristic modernist approach. Ferré sees his customer as a man who appreciates traditional cloth and a classic line. He has developed new tailoring techniques to create a more relaxed, expansive shape for men, a reaction to the hard-edged lines so prevalent in 1980s power dressing. Ferré often looks to London for inspiration, believing that the British capital is a key point in the world of fashion. As he explained to journalist Liz Smith, "There is an in-bred eccentricity in London which allows clothes to be worn in original and completely modern proportions."

Ferré has a reputation for being a realist, with a practical approach to projects. His assistant Airaghi confirmed this when she described the designer as going to work with everything in his head—market requirements, manufacturing schedules, financial limitations, development of themes, advertising. Brought up in a secure family environment, his mother instilled in him an obsessive sense of duty and responsibility; she was strict when it came to homework and passing exams. This level-headed approach even caused him to react with economic sense to Diana Vreeland's famous fashion quote, "Pink is the navy blue of India," made during the course of a conversation with Ferré. He replied judiciously, "Naturally pink is the navy blue of India because it's the cheapest of all dyes."

In 1989 Ferré was appointed as designer for Dior, with a brief to supply the house with an image for the 1990s. His first collection made no reference to Dior's illustrious past. Dior's extravagant and romantic tradition and the coquettish style of Marc Bohan, designer for the house since 1960, were ignored. Instead, Ferré introduced a refined, sober, and strict collection inspired by Cecil Beaton's black and white Ascot scene from the film *My Fair Lady.* Black and white herringbone and checked tweed suits, sprinkled with embroidered pearls, jet, and jewels, opened a show that ended with a series of evening dresses in russet red and grey, edged in fox, combined with lace stoles and rose corsages with sweeping trains.

Ferré is easily identifiable as an Italian designer. His clothes are well shaped, confident, and powerfully feminine or masculine. Through his own label collections, he has developed such hallmarks as the crisp white shirt with stand-up collar or in his signature colour, red. However, as a designer he has adapted to a variety of customers and markets from French haute couture to the larger-size jeans market. The Ferré product, whether it be prêt-à-porter or leather goods, glasses, furs, or shoes, has become synonymous with precision and elegance, an identity which he feels has strongly increased the cachet of "made in Italy."

—Kevin Almond

FEZZA, Andrew.

American designer

Born: New Haven, Connecticut, 1955. **Education:** Graduated from Boston College, 1976; traveled in Europe, summer, 1976; studied at the Fashion Institute of Technology, New York, 1976-77. **Family:** Married Marilyn Cousa Fezza in 1985; two children. **Career:** Assistant designer for womenswear, Schrader Sport, New York, 1977-78; free-lance designer, selling to Camouflage and other New York menswear stores, 1977-78; formed own company, Andrew Fezza, Ltd, 1979; also designer, Firma by Andrew Fezza for Gruppo GFT from 1986, and designer, Andrew Fezza Company, joint venture with Gruppo GFT, from 1990; maintained Assets by Andrew Fezza boutique to 1991. **Awards:** Chrysler Stargazer Award, 1981; Cutty Sark Award, 1982, 1984, 1985; Coty American Fashion Critics Award, 1984. **Address:** 300 Park Avenue, New York, New York 10022, USA.

Publications:

On FEZZA:

Articles

Buckley, Richard, "Andrew Fezza," in *DNR* (New York), 27 December 1982.
Fressola, Peter, "Andrew Fezza," in *DNR* (New York), 25 November 1987.
Morrisroe, Patricia, "Almost Famous: Turning Andrew Fezza into the 'American Armani,'" in *New York,* 24 October 1988.
Parola, Robert, "Andrew Fezza," in the *Daily News Record* (New York), 25 March 1992.

*   *   *

Andrew Fezza's design is based around unchanging elements that have characterized his men's clothing throughout changing labels and businesses: relaxed drape, soft silhouette in all garments but never at a loss of proportion, are combined with an interest in unusual materials, whether in leather or fabric, luxurious richness in fabric more often associated with womenswear and mellifluous color harmony in individual collections, always including neutrals and earthbound tones. Respect for American sportswear is challenged and complemented by a sensibility that is not provincially American or traditional, often with influences from Italy.

Andrew Fezza: Spring/Summer 1992.

In such intensity of conviction and integrity of sensibility, Fezza is unusual in menswear (while he trained for and has designed womenswear, he is chiefly a menswear designer) and has inevitably been called an "American Armani," so sincere and sustained are his design objectives. Menswear is seldom thought of as a profession for purists with distinct aesthetic marks, given the market-driven practicality of the field, but Fezza has flourished with an uncompromising crusade for male attire. He suffers, however, from the Armani characterization. So reminiscent is his style of the Milanese master that some have chosen, especially after he entered into production agreements in 1990 with Gruppo GFT, to call Fezza a poor man's Armani. In fact, almost all advanced menswear designers in the 1990s have been displacing collars, mutating jackets into longer and softer shapes, and watching the textile industry for both innovation and the most sumptuous materials to bring to men in that indeterminate arena between contemporary office and home. Similarly, Fezza has created tailored clothing with the unconstructed effects of the Armani-inspired contemporary jacket, for casual living as well as the conventional office, but so have almost all other menswear designers of the past decade.

Fezza's aesthetic, however close at times to Armani's, is nonetheless his own. That he began in knitwear and leather, as Armani had some five or six years earlier, is partly a matter of how designers can get started in small-scale production and partly an example of parallelism, but not of derivativeness. Points of differentiation include Fezza's deep colors, consistent in his collections, his reliance on sportswear, and a keen sense of comfort for the American male body, large and athletic.

Fezza brings his own style to each achievement, beginning with his first sweaters, made free-lance and delivered by hand to Camouflage when still working in womenswear at Schrader Sport, soon after graduating from the Fashion Institute of Technology, New York. Subsequently, his leathers, of which *DNR* wrote in 1981: "Andrew Fezza is a leather innovator. In his approach to color, silhouette, and texture, Fezza has consistently broadened the scope of American leather design, which is rapidly catching up with the European market," generated excitement and esteem for their directional colors, embossed treatments, and knowledgeable shapings: unconventional for leather, but not extreme. Fezza has likewise brought a lifetime interest in luxurious textiles and the traditional designs of textiles into menswear, often making a garment seem even softer and more costly by virtue of the fabric. Even his earliest collections, in the early 1980s, brought together linens, cotton, silk-wool blends, and knits with leather and suede. Arguably, Fezza brings elements of womenswear sensibility to menswear with such emphases as proportion and luxury in textiles. In such a characteristic, he indicates the great shift in menswear in the 1980s and 1990s.

Few menswear designers possess Fezza's unity and clarity of vision. Business shifts, which might have diverted or deflected most other designers in the big-business climate of menswear, have not deterred Fezza. In his second decade as a still-young designer, Fezza is pursuing the relaxed new look, acknowledging Europe but affirming America. When he says that he entered the menswear business because he was uninspired when looking for clothing for himself, he anticipates some characteristics of his designs: so purposeful they are elegant, so unassuming that they become the nonchalance of high style in menswear, and so luxuriously casual that they fit the lifestyles of men in the 1980s and 1990s. He has deliberately avoided, with one or two exceptions in the early 1980s (with some justice, Melissa Drier in *DNR* attacked his spring 1984

collection as overworked), any of the excesses of menswear, with extraneous detailing or extreme proportions, but he has insisted upon clothing with texture and an interest in color and shape. A 1983 press kit for Fezza reports: "Andrew's unique hand with fabric, shape, and color reflects a designing mind that is both thoughtful and provocative, without surrendering to fashion 'trends' either here or in Europe. But from the beginning, Andrew Fezza's trademark has been his individuality." In this instance, a press kit is true. In the fixed and fascinating domain of menswear, Andrew Fezza has offered a highly consistent and individual aesthetic in the 1980s and 1990s.

—Richard Martin

FIELDEN, David.

British fashion designer

Career: Studied theatre design, then choreographer, Ballet Rambert, in France. Also choreographed for Ballet Theatre Contemporain. Returned to London, specialized in fashion, concentrating on bridalwear and eveningwear. **Address:** 15 Lots Road, London SW10 0QD, UK.

Publications:

On FIELDEN:

Articles

"Fielden's Body English," in *Women's Wear Daily* (New York), 12 June 1991.

*   *   *

David Fielden is a small British fashion company that produces ladies' eveningwear and bridalwear, mainly ready-to-wear, although some pieces are made to measure. Fielden's designs are similar to those produced by Catherine Walker or Caroline Charles in London, but are perhaps less understated and sophisticated, more brash, bold, and glitzy.

Fielden uses a lot of traditional eveningwear fabrics in his collections, such as crêpe, velvet, chiffon, and georgette. Embroidered fabrics, fabrics using bugle beads, sequins, and fake stones are popular as is lace, especially imported from France. For a small company the collections are unusually large; the winter collection for 1993, for instance, contained over 130 pieces. This is advantageous from a selling point because many different themes and styles can be covered, catering to various different customers. Smart navy and white ballgowns head straight for Saks on Fifth Avenue, whilst short, brightly coloured halter neck dresses with net petticoats head for Italy.

Fielden built up a loyal band of followers when he had a shop on London's King's Road in the 1980s. Since the shop closed down, the clothes are sold through a number of distinctive stores throughout Britain such as Harrods in London, À La Mode, and Pollyanna. The clientèle is mainly international. Boutiques from Italy, Germany, the United States, Hong Kong, and Saudi Arabia all place orders.

David Fielden: Fall/Winter 1994/95.

A typical Fielden customer is a woman who needs a large amount of occasion wear in her wardrobe. She is not particularly fashion conscious but is involved in County or Society events and is an avid reader of society style bibles like *Harper's and Queen* and *The Tatler.* She probably aspires to buying a Valentino or an Yves Saint Laurent, but cannot quite afford it.

Fielden is often nominated for a glamour award by the British Fashion Council, acknowledging his undoubted contribution to this area of fashion. Popular styles include long, simple and elegant vest top dresses in velvet, enhanced by beaded belts; sharply tailored double-breasted coat dresses with satin lapels or velvet tuxedo-style jackets; short, sexy cocktail dresses with revealing back and side slits, and the romantic glamour evoked by embroidered, full skirted, tulle and taffeta ball dresses with matching stoles. Fielden is also noted for the recurrent use of brightly coloured satins in his eveningwear.

Fielden himself is the sole owner of his company. He oversees the production and design and is at the end of the day financially responsible. This is probably one reason why the company is so small and has not expanded into lucrative licensing areas like perfume and accessories. Fielden's decisions affect the entire business and a wrong move by him could close the company.

Fielden has a definitive niche within British fashion, producing distinctive clothes that often compete with the best of Italian and French eveningwear. The irony is that the clothes emerge from a culture that is still similar to a cottage industry. Teams of outworker specialists work on production, while the company itself is streamlined to be a small, cost effective unit. This is probably one of the strengths of British fashion and companies like David Fielden can acknowledge credit for this strength.

—Kevin Almond

FIORUCCI, Elio.

Italian designer and manufacturer

Born: Milan, 10 June 1935. **Career:** Founder, Fiorucci shoes, Milan, 1962-67; director, Fiorucci fashion shop, Galleria Passerella, Milan, selling clothes by Ossie Clark, Zandra Rhodes and others, from 1967; began wholesale production of jeans, fashion and home accessories, 1970; founder, Fiorucci SpA, 1974, and Fiorucci Inc., New York, 1976; first American boutique opened, New York, 1976, Boston and Los Angeles, 1978; stores opened throughout Europe, USA, Japan and Southeast Asia, from 1978. Also founder, Technical Design School, Milan, 1977. Contributor to *Donna* magazine, Milan. **Exhibition:** *Italian Re-Evolution,* La Jolla Museum of Art, California, 1982. **Address:** Fiorucci SpA, Galleria Passerella 2, 20122 Milan, Italy.

Publications:

On FIORUCCI:

Books

Mulassano, Adriana, *I mass-moda: fatti e personaggi dell'Italian Look,* Florence 1979.
Babitz, Eve, *Fiorucci: The Book,* Milan 1980.
Malossi, Giannino, *Liberi tutti: 20 anni di moda spettacolo,* Milan 1987.
Connikie, Yvonne, *Fashions of a Decade: The 1960s,* London 1990.

Articles

Neustatter, Angela, "Clown Prince," in *The Guardian* (London), 9 August 1978.
Besemer, H. C., "Fiorucci," in *Novum Gebrauchsgraphik* (Munich), No. 7, 1981.
Jones, Terry, "Mr Fiorucci: 20 Years of Global Pollution," in *i-D* (London), September 1987.
Mills, Simon, "Elio Fiorucci, 52, Comes of Age," in *The Observer* (London), 3 January 1988.
Alden, Tim, "The Key to the Door," in *Fashion Weekly* (London), 19 May 1988.
Tredre, Roger, "Fiorucci: Going Places Again," in *Fashion Weekly* (London), 28 July 1988.
Morozzi, Cristina, "Orfani di un mito," in *Moda* (Milan), August/ September 1988.

*   *   *

Visitors to Milan in Italy during the late 1960s could not fail to notice a constant crowd trying to enter a narrow fronted shop in the centre of the city. The birth of Elio Fiorucci's boutique caused consternation amongst the elders and delight in their offspring. Those who travelled the European city circuit in pursuit of fashion and footwear inspiration now ensured that this was one retailer who could not be missed.

Visiting manufacturers and designers fought over the limited stock with local customers. Italy, the accepted home of stylish clothing, had seen nothing like it. It was Fiorucci, more than any other single entrepreneur of the time, who possibly created a worldwide market for the youth culture that first expressed itself in music, then in clothing. In the mid-1960s it was the young people who were creating and dictating the fashions they wanted to wear. It was the skill of this man, who had his finger on the pulse and brought it into reality, that created the visual dreams and recognized the aspirations of this new and hitherto untapped market.

Fiorucci had inherited a shoe store from his father. In 1967, at the age of 32, he added mini skirts brought from the then "swinging" London. Designs by Ossie Clark, Zandra Rhodes, and other young English talents soon followed and the store was gradually enlarged to accommodate a vast range of assorted items. From this embryonic beginning grew a world famous chain of boutiques, culminating in outlets in New York, Boston, Beverly Hills, Rio de Janeiro, Tokyo, Hong Kong, Zurich, and London. Conceived for the youth culture, the stores were constantly filled with new ideas and exciting styles. The atmosphere was unique and the presentation always witty and original. Shopping for clothes was suddenly a different and stimulating experience. The sales assistants were teenagers, too, who helped the customer to put together the latest looks in fashion clothing, accessories, and even make-up.

Fiorucci was a constant traveller, collecting ideas from around the world, including the original hippie woven bags from Morocco which became so synonymous with the spirit of Flower Power. A team of designers translated ideas, seeming always to capture the moment, for example, recycling the themes of the 1950s with plastic shoes in riotous colours, fluorescent socks, or graffiti T-shirts. Possibly best remembered of all were the tightly cut, streamlined jeans which established Fiorucci as a label in the marketplace for many years. At one time they even replaced Levi's as the most desirable and fashionable shape of the moment.

Elio Fiorucci.

One of the company's greatest strengths and the reason for its place in fashion history was the ability to control all aspects of advertising, packaging, store design, and merchandising in a clever and original way. It should not be forgotten that Elio Fiorucci was the first to establish what has subsequently become an indispensable part of so many success stories, a Total Concept.

—Angela Pattison

FISHER, Donald and Doris. See **THE GAP.**

FLETT, John.
British designer

Born: 28 September 1963. **Education:** Received diploma in fashion, Worthing Polytechnic, West Sussex; graduated from St Martin's College of Art, 1985. **Career:** Formed own business, selling to Joseph Ettedgui, London, and Bergdorf Goodman, New York, 1985-

89; assistant designer, Claude Montana, Paris, and Enrico Coveri, Florence, 1989-91. *Died* (in Florence, Italy) *18 January 1991.*

Publications:

On FLETT:

Articles

"Alright John?," in the *Sunday Express Magazine* (London), 3 August 1986.
"Flett in Business Split," in *Fashion Weekly* (London), 16 February 1989.
"John Flett," obituary, in *The Daily Telegraph* (London), 28 January 1991.
"Style Victim," in *The Independent on Sunday* (London), 3 February 1991.

*   *   *

The story of John Flett is a short and sad one; an extreme example of the good and bad aspects of the British fashion industry. Flett graduated in 1985 from St Martin's College of Art, London, in a blaze of glory. His first collection was bought by Joseph Ettedgui for his Joseph shops in London and there was a prestigious order from Bergdorf Goodman in New York. By 1988 he was showing on the international catwalk at the British Designer Show, in company with John Galliano (a friend from St Martin's), Jasper Conran, and Betty Jackson. By 1989 money had run out and Flett parted company with his backer, Miles Gill. Short-lived positions followed, first as assistant to Claude Montana at Lanvin in Paris, then in the studio of the Enrico Coveri house in Florence, Italy. Whilst at Coveri he was approached by Zuccoli who proposed to sign him as their rainwear and knitwear designer, with the promise of his own label to come. Before signing, John Flett was found dead of a heart attack in his hotel room in Florence. He was 27.

Many of Flett's friends and contemporaries attributed his premature death to the strain of dealing with Britain's inadequate fashion system. Renowned for having the best fashion schools in the world, excellent breeding grounds for creative talent, British industry, at the ground level of production and mass market manufacture, is at a loss to know how to capitalize on this talent, employing merchandisers and selectors, who copy designs in the shops, rather than a designer to originate. As a result, many British fashion graduates have left to find work abroad. The Italian and French fashion industry is subsidized by governments who understand how to direct creativity towards financial gain.

Described as "wickedly talented" by John Galliano, much of Flett's skill was in his cutting, intricate and inventive, with which he developed clothes that seemed to cling to the body. In fact, many of his garments were difficult to understand on the hanger and needed to be worn to be appreciated. John Galliano declared that Flett could run up the "sexiest frocks in town," but this seems to generalize his often complex and avant-garde approach.

In his critically successful autumn/winter 1988-89 show, Flett presented sophisticated, opulent fabrics cut into lean, elongated shapes. Another success was a white transparent pleat dress that seemed to coil itself around the body like an asymmetric floral display. He wanted to redefine that much abused fashion adjective "chic" to designate an updated modernity.

Flett was an avid socialite during his time in London and participated in the thriving avant-garde club scene. Contemporaries like the designers Bodymap and performance artists Leigh Bowery and Trojan combined to create a flourishing atmosphere for designers, models, photographers, and artists to meet and relax, at their Thursday night club Taboo. Flett quickly gained a reputation as a wild boy who partied every night. However, he worked as hard as he played, recalled a friend who described his energy capacity as "enormous."

In an interview with fashion journalist Sally Brampton John Galliano recalled how Flett seldom allowed his creative temperament to affect his sound business acumen. "He had a passion for the business side of fashion as well as the creative," he said. This, perhaps, makes an even more tragic symbol of Flett, an original design talent whom fate and circumstances did not allow to realize his potential.

—Kevin Almond

FLUSSER, Alan.

American designer

Education: Studied at the University of Pennsylvania, Fashion Institute of Technology, and Parsons School of Design, New York. **Family:** Married Marilise Flusser; children: Morgan Skye and Kaitlin Piper. **Career:** Head designer, Pierre Cardin Relax Sportwear (six years); designer, Van Heusen Company, New York; formed own company; hosiery line introduced 1980; women's sweater collection introduced, 1983; custom tailored collection introduced, 1985; East 52nd Street shop opened, New York, 1987; Wall Street shop opened, New York, and Washington, D.C. shop opened, 1989; company reorganized, sold to Copley of Canada, 1993. **Awards:** Coty American Fashion Critics Award, 1983; Cutty Sark Award.

Publications:

By FLUSSER:

Books

Making the Man, the Insider's Guide to Buying and Wearing Men's Clothes, New York 1981.
Clothes and the Man, New York 1985.

Articles

"Hints on Hats," in the *New York Times Magazine,* 16 September 1990.

On FLUSSER:

Articles

Boyer, G. Bruce, "The Compleat Outfitter," in *Town and Country* (New York), November 1989.

Sterba, James P., "Style: Father of the [ED] Look," in the *Wall Street Journal* (New York), 18 May 1990.

* * *

There is a certain relaxed elegance about the way Alan Flusser designs and styles his tailored clothing. His sartorial skill is best known to those outside the fashion industry through his costuming work for Michael Douglas in the movie *Wall Street.* Flusser's Gordon Gekko dressed with the excessiveness of the 1980s. His wide, bead-striped single-breasted suits with peak lapels and turned-back rollback cuffs showed that he was a man of style, yet not one to follow the rules. Shirts continued the look with bold, heavy, and wide stripes, extra long spread white collars, French cuffs, braces, and ties. To flaunt oneself in this fashion was pure arrogance, not unlike the character Douglas played (remember, Gekko was the originator of the tenet "greed is good").

The commonly known Flusser style, however, is a more understated elegance. His influences run the gamut from the Duke of Windsor to the glamorous gentlemen of film in the 1930s and 1940s—including Douglas Fairbanks Jr, and Cary Grant—and stemmed from Flusser's own father, a successful industrial realtor in northern New Jersey, who had suits custom-made by Brooks Brothers, and shoes and shirts made in London.

Flusser's career as an influencer of fashion started when he was still in college at the University of Pennsylvania in Philadelphia. He was following his father's lead, already having his clothing custom-made at Brooks Brothers, and friends, recognizing the sartorial style which Flusser refers to as "relaxed elegance," would come to him for wardrobe advice. Advising his friends on what was appropriate was not enough for Flusser—he wanted to influence the direction of style and elegance.

The archetypal Flusser suit comes from his custom-made business. The environment of his shop is not unlike that of an old-world gentleman's club, and it is from there that the relaxed elegance is derived. A man coming in for a suit can choose between a ready-to-wear suit or one custom made to his size and specifications. It is the latter choice that allows Flusser to create what he is known for. The customer chooses a fabric from a finely edited group of swatches, followed by the style of the suit. Flusser generally tries to be on the scene, supervising and offering helpful suggestions, almost as if he were still advising his college friends.

Then begins the lengthy process of sewing and fitting the garment. More often than not, by the time a Flusser suit is finished, the customer has decided that he must also be fully outfitted with Flusser accoutrements. Flusser ties, shirts, braces, and pocket squares are as exquisitely made and as stylish as the suits they will accessorize.

It is unfortunate that Alan Flusser's attempts to introduce a line of sportswear, in fall 1992, failed. The offerings included tweed sports coats and trousers, rich cashmere sweaters, roomy car coats, and field jackets worthy of any gentleman farmer. The styling of this collection evoked weekends at the country estate. A victim of the economic climate, it offered the wearer of Flusser's formal suits a more casual alternative.

It is ironic that the man who created the look of excess for Gordon Gekko, "greed is good," faced bankruptcy in 1993. However, as with most things that are classic and timeless, like Alan Flusser's clothing, his style will continue to live on.

—Lisa Marsh

FOGARTY, Anne.

American designer

Born: Anne Whitney in Pittsburgh, Pennsylvania, 2 February 1919. **Education:** Attended Allegheny College, Meadville, Pennsylvania, 1936-37; studied drama at Carnegie Institute of Technology, Pittsburgh, 1937-38; studied design at East Hartman School of Design, 1939. **Family:** Married Thomas E. Fogarty in 1940 (divorced); children: Taf, Missy; married Richard Kollmar (widowed, 1971); married Wade O'Hara (divorced). **Career:** Worked as a fit model and copywriter in New York; designer for Sheila Lynn, New York; fashion stylist, Dorland International, New York, 1947-48; fashion designer, with the Youth Guild, New York, 1948-50, and with Margot Dresses Inc., New York, 1950-57; designer, Saks Fifth Avenue, 1957-62; managed own business, Anne Fogarty, Inc., New York, 1962-74; lines included Anne Fogarty Boutique, Clothes Circuit, Collector's Items; closed business, c.1974; free-lance designer to 1980; final collection designed for Shariella Fashion, 1980. **Awards:** Coty American Fashion Critics Award, 1951; Neiman Marcus Award, Dallas, 1952; Philadelphia Fashion Group Citation, 1953; International Silk Association Award, 1955; Cotton Fashion Award, New York, 1957. *Died* (in New York) *15 January 1980.*

Publications:

By FOGARTY:

Books

Wife Dressing: The Fine Art of Being a Well Dressed Wife, New York 1959.

On FOGARTY:

Books

Williams, Beryl, *Young Faces in Fashion,* Philadelphia 1956.
Roshco, Bernard, *The Rag Race,* New York 1963.
Milbank, Caroline Rennolds, *New York Fashion: The Evolution of American Style,* New York 1989.

Articles

"Fogarty Was Ahead of Dior," in *Life,* 31 August 1953.
"Anne Fogarty," in *Current Biography* (New York), October 1958.
"Anne Fogarty," [obituary] in the *New York Times,* 16 January 1980.
"Anne Fogarty," [obituary] in *Current Biography* (New York), March 1980.

*   *   *

Anne Whitney Fogarty designed the American look, creating clothes that were youthful, simple and stylish. Although Fogarty studied drama at the Carnegie Institute of Technology in Pittsburgh, Pennsylvania, her real love was for the costumes she wore. Moving to New York she worked as a fitting-model for Harvey Berin while looking for acting parts. When she received the offer of an acting job, Berin encouraged her to think about becoming a stylist instead and in 1948 Fogarty began designing clothes for Youth Guild. Youth Guild's market was teenagers, who were perfect for the narrow waist and full skirts of the "New Look," a style Fogarty used.

In 1950 Fogarty began designing junior-size clothing for Margot, Inc. She still favored the "paper-doll" silhouette for both day and evening wear, with its full skirt, narrow waist, and fitted bodice. To help create this shape, she adopted the idea of crinoline skirts from the Edwardian age. These stiffened petticoats made of nylon net, frilled or trimmed in lace, helped to hold out the skirt and Fogarty encouraged wearing two at a time to enhance the silhouette. She herself had an 18-inch waist.

Fogarty wrote a book called *Wife Dressing* in 1959, a guide for "the fine art of being a well-dressed wife with provocative notes for the patient husband who pays the bills." In the book she recognized that women led varied lives working, as students, wives, and mothers and she encouraged women to find their own style and color, recommending an understated, natural look that did not slavishly follow the fashion of the day.

Fogarty continued to design for Margot, Inc., and eventually for Saks Fifth Avenue. In 1962 she opened her own business, Anne Fogarty, Inc., and added misses' sizes to her line of clothes. Although she began with full skirts, and fitted bodices, she adapted her designs to suit the times. After the paper-doll silhouette came the tea cozy dress in which the full skirt fell from a dropped, rather than natural waist. She used a narrow silhouette without fullness, the Empire line, with its emphasis on the bust line, and she introduced the "camise," a chemise which falls from a high yoke. Fogarty designed separates and long dresses, quilted skirts over hot pants, and mini skirts. She produced designs in a peasant style, blouses with ruffles, long skirts with ruffled hems, and ethnic styling. Whatever the silhouette or fashion type, her interpretation was youthful, with details like puffed sleeves and round collars. She avoided the use of trims.

Fogarty produced different design collections under the names of A.F. Boutique, Clothes Circuit, and Collector's Items. In 1950 she was selected as one of the Young Women of the Year by the magazine *Mademoiselle.* In 1951 she received the Coty Award and in 1952 the Neiman Marcus Award.

Although she closed her own business in the 1970s, Fogarty continued to design. In 1980, she finished a collection for Shariella Fashion shortly before she died. During her career Fogarty worked with a variety of silhouettes and fabrics, in a broad range of sizes. She was a prolific designer who was able to adjust to a changing market, responding with designs that typified the all-American look.

—Nancy House

FOLEY, Brigid.

British knitwear designer

Born: Yorkshire, England, 9 December 1948. **Education:** Studied pre-diploma course, Sheffield College of Art, 1967-68; Nottingham College of Art, BA Hons Fashion and Design, 1968-71. **Family:** Married Kevin Keegan, photographer, 1973; children: Shelley, Peter, Jennifer. **Career:** While at art college began knitting and supplying shops with own designs. Part-time lecturer, Plymouth Col-

Brigid Foley: Rosebud Sweater, made of mohair with chenille rosebuds.

lege of Art, specializing in knitwear, 1971. Designed, manufactured and supplied shops with knitwear; joined Carr Jones designer group, London, 1973; first showed at London collections, 1975; went on to exhibit at international prêt-à-porter shows, including Milan, Paris, New York; introduced first hand-knits into collection, 1980. First Brigid Foley shop opened, Tavistock, Devon, 1991; second shop opened, Exeter, 1994. **Address:** Greenway, Harrowbeer Lane, Yelverton PL20 6DY, Devon, England.

*

I like women to look elegant and feminine. From classic simple shapes my clothes are often adorned on some way to make them special for the woman who wears them. One of my specialities is luxurious handknitted sweaters and jackets. Texture and colour play a large part in the intricate hand embroidery applied. My work has a typically English look about it—many of my designs are inspired from nature—flowers, wildlife, poppy fields, the Devon country-side where I live and work in. Other sources of inspiration are paintings, tapestries and Persian carpets.

I chose knitwear as my medium because it is such a challenge, creating the entire article—deciding on the colours, the texture, the weight and softness of the fibres, choosing the embroidery threads, seeing the sweater or jacket emerge stage by stage, after such a lot of painstaking handwork. I take great pride in endeavouring to repro-duce each design as closely to the original as possible. I am very proud of the people who work for me: such skill, patience and dedication.

Fashion today is gloriously diverse—with no direct style im-posed: such a variety of shapes, lengths, colours are available. Women can choose a style for themselves.

Of my designs I would say they are classic, timeless, wearable, comfortable and appealing. I like to think they are clothes to enjoy and treasure.

—Brigid Foley

*   *   *

Brigid Foley's first designs were mainly for sweaters for a young age group. She was experimenting with knitting machines, mixing geometric patterns with stripes and plains.

After joining the Carr Jones designer group in 1973, a more feminine style emerged, with calf-length flowing skirts, fitted to the hips and swirling around the hemline with inset panels of different texture or colour matched to sweaters with soft cowl necklines, and accompanied by plaited knitted belts in tones of the suit. These suits were among the first of their kind, attractive, feminine, com-fortable, and easy to wear.

In 1975 Brigid Foley was invited to join the London Collections and exhibited at the London fashion shows each season, building on her growing success by exhibiting later at the Paris Prêt-à-Porter, and in New York, Dusseldorf, and Copenhagen. The colours of the collections at this time were mainly soft, and often marled as sev-eral different fine yarns would be used through the machine at once. A distinctive feature was the gored skirt, where the swing of the skirt was emphasized by the different shades used in the gores. The ranges varied from heavier, sometimes tweedier suits for autumn, fine knits with a sheen and hints of gold for cocktail wear, and fine lacy knits for the spring. Commenting on her work, Brigid Foley explains, "fully fashioned knitwear is a very exciting medium. You start with nothing but cones of yarn, and mix textures, colour, and

mathematical skill to shape into lovely flattering outfits. These can suit many different shapes, ages, and types of women."

By 1980 Foley had brought a selection of hand-knits into the collection. Finding mohair a good medium, she introduced a range of soft fluffy sweaters which were highlighted with hand embroidery. Most notable were the designs featuring wildlife: "Hedgehog" is still selling to this day. Other designs featured wild flowers and landscapes, some of which were beautifully embroidered with a wide range of textured yarns and silks, bringing them to life. Brigid Foley lives in a village in the middle of Dartmoor, Devon and con-siders the distinctive Dartmoor landscape to be a constant source of inspiration for her designs. Recurring hand-knit designs include a range of landscape-inspired themes such as Cornfields and Mead-ows, as well as other wildlife scenes drawn from the countryside, including rabbits and hedgehogs.

Brigid Foley's designs are considered to be very English and are stocked by retailers worldwide, as well as at the two exclusive Brigid Foley shops in Devon, one in the traditional market town of Tavistock, opened in 1991, and another which opened three years later in the cathedral city of Exeter.

—Doreen Ehrlich

FONTANA.
Italian fashion house

Founded in Rome, 1944, by sisters Zoe (1911-78), Micol (1913—) and Giovanna (1915—) Fontana. The sisters began working in their mother's tailoring business. Zoe and Micol worked in Milan, early 1930s; Zoe moved to Paris after her marriage, returning to Italy, to work for Zecca in Rome, 1937; Nicol and Giovanna moved to Rome, 1940; Zoe, Micol and Giovanna open the Fontana studio in Palazzo Orsini, Rome, 1943, designing and producing gowns for the Roman aristocracy and many film stars; participate in first catwalk presen-tation of Italian Alta Moda, Florence 1951; studio moved to present address, 1957; designed first ready-to-wear collection, 1960. Incor-porated as Sorelle Fontana Alta Moda SrL by Micol Fontana, Rome, 1985. Also: Costume designers for many films, including *The Bare-foot Contessa,* 1954, *The Sun Also Rises,* 1957, *On The Beach,* 1959, and *La bibbia (The Bible),* 1966. **Exhibitions:** retrospective, University of Parma, 1984; evening dresses, Venice, 1985; Castel Sant'Angelo Museum, Rome, 1985; Munich, March 1986. **Collec-tions:** Metropolitan Museum of New York; Metropolitan Mu-seum of San Francisco; Museo Fortuny, Venice. **Awards:** Silver Scissors Award, Pittsburgh Fashion Group, 1956; Silver Mask Award, Rome, 1960; Fontana sisters named Cavaliere della Repubblica, Rome, 1965; Fashion Oscar Award, St Vincent, 1968; Stella di Michelangelo Award, Rome, 1985; Polifemo Prize, Sperlonga, Italy, 1985; Minerva Prize, Rome, 1985; Attraction 1986 Prize, Italy; Europe Plate, 1987; Europe Gold Plate, 1988. **Ad-dress:** Via San Sebastianello 6, 00187 Rome, Italy.

Publications:

By FONTANA:

Books

Fontana, Micol, *Specchio a tre luci,* Rome 1992.

Fontana: Sorelle Fontana collection, 1991.

On FONTANA:

Books

Sorelle Fontana, Parma 1984.
Alta Moda: grandi abiti da sera anni cinquanta-sessanta, Venice 1984.
Steele, Valerie, *Women of Fashion,* New York 1991.
Villa, Nora, *Le regine della moda,* n.p. n.d.

Articles

Da Riz, Oscar, "La via della seta parte da Roma e arriva in Cina," in *Paese Sera* (Rome), 20 June 1980.
"Le Sorelle Fontana hanno aperto la via alle grandi griffe," in *Sole 24 Ore* (Milan), 17 May 1988.
Mendia, Fabiana, "Via Zoe Fontana: Una strada da indossare," in *Il Messaggero* (Rome), 12 July 1988.
Pilolli, Carla, "Il matrimonia torna di moda," in *Il Messaggero* (Rome), 5 December 1990.
Pertica, Domenico, "Bianco vince: Micol Fontana, la regina dell'abito da sposa," in *Paese Sera* (Rome), 4 July 1991.
Tiezzi, Monica, "Quel successo appeso a un filo," in *Gazzetta di Parma* (Parma, Italy), 12 February 1992.

*   *   *

Fontana created fantasy dresses, wedding gowns, and ball gowns, and the glamor of movie stars. In the 1950s, in particular, the Fontana style was a rich excess and ideal of the sumptuous dress. For the client, these were the most flattering kinds of party dresses cognizant of the New Look, buoyant in full skirts, and attentive to the bust. To the observer, theatrical high-style 1950s was crystallized in the internationally known clientèle including Linda Christian for her wedding dress on marrying Tyrone Power, Audrey Hepburn, and preeminently Ava Gardner. Gardner, in particular, was the perfect Fontana client and model: unabashedly and voluptuously sexy and known for high-style glamour. Gardner wore Fontana for film roles in *The Barefoot Contessa* (1954), *The Sun Also Rises* (1957), and *On the Beach* (1959). Whereas American film had its own specialty costume designers such as Edith Head and Travis Banton, post-war Rome re-ignited its status as a glamor capital by the conflation of life and film. Sisters Zoe, Micol, and Giovanna Fontana had begun their business in 1936, but seized the public imagination when American films were made on location in Italy using their costumes and, to a lesser degree, with the Italian film industry. The popular appeal internationally of the Power/Christian wedding and Ava Gardner's paparazzi-trailing fame brought vast international visibility and recognition.

If waning Hollywood glamor found its ideal Trevi Fountain wardrobe in Fontana, Fontana came to Middle America and intellectual America with the demure but unequivocally rich lace wedding dress designed for the 1956 wedding of Margaret Truman, daughter of the ex-President of the United States, and Clifton Daniel, *New York Times* journalist and editor. Long-time celebrity Margaret Truman Daniel, famous as the apple of her father's eye and as a television performer, put the good-girl seal of approval on Fontana for America that Gardner's sultry glamor, Elizabeth Taylor's buxom beauty, or Loretta Young's dream-girl radiance had been unable to provide. Roman grace and opulence of materials were, for Americans, more accessible in many ways, including cost, than the couture of Paris.

By the late 1950s, the strong silhouettes of Balenciaga and Dior (under Yves Saint Laurent) were so immediately and carelessly processed into American clothing that Roman dress, with its conspicuous extravagance of lace and taffeta and aura of luxuriance, seemed ineffably richer than Paris design. The preference of the Fontana sisters for wedding dresses, eveningwear, and full-skirted cocktail dresses through the 1950s and 1960s, made their style seem especially colorful, a kind of pre-*La Dolce Vita* for Americans covetous of Italian flair.

So much a part of the Italian post-war renaissance that Rome designated one street Via Zoe Fontana, the work of the Fontana sisters testifies to Italy's command of magical aura, dressmaking skill, and international glamor in the 1950s. Later work assumes more tubular silhouettes of the 1960s and 1970s and some similarity to Princess Irene Galitzine, but the definitive work of the Fontana sisters is the bust-enhanced, narrow-waisted, full-skirted resplendence of their style in the 1950s. Their extravagance walked a fine line between vulgarity and richness, one to which Americans felt a keen affinity. The Fontana sisters created a Roman Empire of post-war fashion; they enjoyed an influential and unforgettable decade of style sovereignty.

—Richard Martin

———

FONTICOLI, Nazareno. See **BRIONI.**

———

FORTUNY (y MADRAZO), Mariano.
Spanish designer

Born: Granada, Spain, 1871. **Family:** Married Henriette Negrin, 1918. **Career:** Produced Knossos printed scarves from 1906; produced Delphos gowns, 1907-52; Delphos robe patented, 1909; method for pleating and undulating fabric patented, 1909; methods for printing fabrics patented, 1909, 1910; 18 other patents received, 1901-33. Opened showroom for sale of textiles and clothing, Venice, 1909; established Società Anonima Fortuny, factory for printed textiles, 1919; opened shops in Paris and Milan, 1920. Also: inventor, stage designer, painter, photographer. **Exhibitions:** *A Remembrance of Mariano Fortuny,* Los Angeles County Museum, 1967-68; *Mariano Fortuny (1871-1949),* Musée Historique des Tissus, Lyons, and Brighton Museum, 1980, Fashion Institute of Technology, New York, 1981, and Art Institute of Chicago, 1982; *Exposition Fortuny y Marsal y Fortuny y Madrazo* [etchings], Biblioteca Nacional, Madrid, 1952; *Mariano Fortuny y Madrazo* [drawings and paintings], Galeria Dedalo, Milan, 1935, Galerie Hector Brame, Paris, 1934. *Died* (in Venice, Italy) *2 May 1949.*

Publications:

By FORTUNY:

Books

Éclairage scénique: Système Fortuny, Paris 1904.
Fortuny 1838-1874, Bologna 1933.

On FORTUNY:

Books

Deschodt, Anne Marie, *Mariano Fortuny: Un magicien de Venise,*
    Paris 1979.
Brighton Museum, *Mariano Fortuny (1871-1949)* (exhibition cata-
    logue), Brighton 1980.
de Osma, Guillermo, *Mariano Fortuny: His Life and Work,* London
    1980.
Fashion Institute of Technology, *Fortuny* (exhibition catalogue),
    New York 1981.
Milbank, Caroline Rennolds, *Couture: The Great Designers,* New
    York 1985.

Articles

"The Beauty of Fortuny Is Brought to America," in *Vogue* (New
    York), 15 May 1923.
"Mariano Fortuny," in *La renaissance de l'art Français et des
    industries de luxe,* June 1924.
Malaguzzi Valeri, Francesco, "Le stoffe Fortuny," in *Cronache
    d'arte,* vol. 4, 1925.
"Fortuny of Venice," in the *Nomad,* April 1928.
de Cardona, Maria, "Mariano Fortuny y Madrazo," in *Arte Español,*
    Jan.-April 1950.
Sheppard, Eugenia, "The Fortuny Dress," in the New York *Herald
    Tribune,* 10 September 1962.
Hale, Sheila, "Fragments from the Fortuny Rainbow," in *The Daily
    Telegraph Magazine* (London), 27 October 1972.
Quennell, J. M., "Precious Stuff: Fortuny," in *Vogue* (London),
    December 1972.
Minola de Gallotti, Mariana, "El Museo Fortuny de Venecia," in
    Goya, Sept./Oct. 1975.
Deschodt, Anne Marie, "Seeking Your Fortuny," in *The Sunday
    Times Magazine* (London), 23 July 1978.
Blasi, Bruno, "Con la firma di Fortuny," in *Panorama* (Italy), 22
    August 1978.
Tosca, Marco, "Fortuny," in *Vogue* (Milan), July/August 1989.

*   *   *

Mariano Fortuny was an artistic genius with an insatiable curiosity. This led him to pursue a variety of disciplines, which evolved
through an interesting series of interconnections. Always a painter,
he turned to etching, sculpture, photography, lighting design, theatre direction, set design, architecture, and costume design, ultimately to be a creator of magnificent fabrics and clothing. Through
painting he learned the subtle uses of color that would enable him to
produce unequalled silks and velvets from which he made exquisite
gowns. Fortuny's work as a fabric and dress designer was determined by a combination of external and internal influences: exter-
nally by Modernism and the English Aesthetic movement, during
the early part of the 1900s, as well as Greek and Venetian antiquity;
internally by a love inherited from his father of everything Arabic
and oriental. During all these creative experiences he maintained a
keen artistic sense and the mind of an inventor.

Fashion, as we know it, did not interest Fortuny and he rejected
commercial fashion and the couture houses. First and foremost a
painter who happened to create stage scenery and lighting effects,
as well as clothes, Fortuny's initiation with fabrics and fashion was

through costumes for the theatre designed in conjunction with his
revolutionary lighting techniques. His first textile creations, known
as the "Knossos scarves," were silk veils, printed with geometric
motifs (inspired by Cycladic art) which were made in any number
of variations until the 1930s. This scarf was, essentially, a type of
clothing—a rectangular piece of cloth that could be wrapped, tied,
and used in a variety of ways—always allowing for freedom of
individual expression and movement. His sole interest was the woman
herself and her personal attributes, to which he had no wish to add
any ornamentation. These simple scarves allowed Fortuny to combine form and fabric as they adapted easily into every kind of
shape, from jackets to skirts, and tunics.

Fortuny's most famous garment was the Delphos gown. It was a
revolution for the corseted woman of 1907 in that it was of pleated
silk, simply cut, and hung loosely from the shoulders. Fortuny
regarded his new concept of dress as an invention, and patented it
in 1909. The dress was modern and original and numerous variations were produced—some with short sleeves, some with long,
wide sleeves tied at the wrist, and others that were sleeveless. The
original Delphos gowns had batwing sleeves. They usually had
wide *bateau* necklines and always, no matter what the shape, a cord
to allow for shoulder adjustments. They were invariably finished
with small Venetian glass beads that had a dual purpose: not only
did the beads serve as ornamentation, they also weighed the dress
down, allowing it to cling to the contours of the body rather than
float. The pleats of the Delphos were achieved through Fortuny's
secret, patented invention. However unconventional for the time,
these dresses were extremely popular for at-home women entertaining and considered primarily tea dresses. It was not until the
1920s that women dared to popularize them as clothing acceptable
to be worn outside the home. Fortuny's techniques were simple but
effective. Today the Delphos dress has pleats that are as tight and
crisp as when they were new. Storing them as rolled and twisted
balls makes them convenient for travel and eliminates the need for
ironing.

In addition to his work in silk, Fortuny began printing on velvet,
first with block prints followed by the development of a stencil
method that was a precursor of the rotary silk screen. The velvet
found its use in dresses, jackets, capes, and cloaks to cover the
Delphos gowns, as well as home furnishing fabrics, still available
today. Due to the fact that his work in silk and velvet never radically changed into anything different, it is almost impossible to
establish a chronology of his garments.

To Mariano Fortuny fashion was art, an unchanging fashion outside the world of fashion. Although many of his contemporaries
were innovative designers, their designs were created for a specific
time and season with built-in obsolescence. By contrast, Fortuny's
clothes are timeless. The elegant simplicity, perfection of cut, and
unusual sensuality of color is where their beauty lies. Perfectly
integrating these elements and placing them on the female figure
makes a Fortuny garment a work of art.

—Roberta H. Gruber

———

FOWLER, Grahame. See TIMNEY FOWLER LTD.

———

FRASER, Graham. See **WORKERS FOR FREEDOM.**

FREIS, Diane.

American fashion designer

Born: Los Angeles, California. **Education:** Studied Fine Art at the University of California, Los Angeles. **Career:** Opened first boutique, Hong Kong, 1978; established own design and manufacturing studio, 1982; launched diffusion line, Freis Spirit, 1994. **Awards:** Governor's Award for Industry for Export, Hong Kong, 1993. **Address:** 6a Picton Place, London W1, UK.

Publications:

On FREIS:

Articles

Block, Elizabeth J., "After a Rough Start, Designer Diane Freis Hopped Aboard the Orient Express to Success," in *People Weekly,* 18 July 1983.
Rourke, Mary, "Designer Diane Freis Oriented to Pace of Hong Kong," in the *Los Angeles Times,* 19 June 1987.
Wallace, Charles P., "A Rags and Riches Tale in Hong Kong," in the *Los Angeles Times,* 5 February 1991.

*   *   *

Diane Freis is one of the few Hong Kong based designers to have gained an international reputation. Hers is a typical Hong Kong success story, based on hard work and determination. Since arriving in the territory in 1973 she has built a commercially successful brand name which has become a role model for Hong Kong manufacturing.

The Freis signature is represented by multi-coloured prints applied to one-size, easy-care dresses, primarily designed in polyester georgette. Non-crushable and easy-to-pack, they present a travel solution for higher income, more mature women in search of a glamorous and feminine look. The fashion philosophy is pragmatic. Freis stresses the importance "of making a one-size dress that allows the freedom of fit in our daily schedules of health programmes one day and over-indulgence the next." With their hallmark elasticated waists and shirring, these dresses will cover imperfections, but can never be accused of being dowdy. The prints are usually exotic, the designs include pretty florals, dramatic geometrics, bold stripes, and plaids. Embroidery and beading are particular features of the look. Besides her traditional georgette, she has used silk, cotton, and wool coordinates, hand knits for casual daywear and chiffon and taffeta for grand evening ensembles.

Freis's eye for colour and design can be attributed to her Fine Art education at the University of California in her native Los Angeles. When a student, her sideline was to create elaborately beaded jackets which sold to media stars such as Diana Ross. It was a search for new, exotic materials and skilled embroiderers which first attracted her to the Far East. In Hong Kong she found the fabrics and the workmanship which have contributed to her distinctive fashion identity.

In 1978 Freis opened her first fashion boutique in Hong Kong; by 1986 she had six more. But her influence did not remain in the local market. International buyers from Europe and the United States soon took her work overseas. In the States her dresses came to adorn the bodies of society women who shopped at the likes of Neiman Marcus in Dallas or Bergdorf Goodman in New York. Suited more to the European figure than to the Asian, today the label can be found in over 20 countries. Her success has been based on locating a market niche, not by following international fashion trends. Falling somewhere between haute couture and prêt à porter the designs are produced in limited editions. No more than ten of any one design are distributed around the world. Basic shapes remain consistent; the variety is provided by new fabric designs and combinations. In order to retain exclusivity the company set up its own print design studio and manufacturing base in 1982. In recognition of her commercial achievement for Hong Kong, Freis was awarded the Governor's Award for Industry for Export in 1993.

Despite its established success, the company continues to develop new ranges and to target new markets. Her easy flowing garments have gradually gained some structure via shoulder pads, more tucking, and fitted pleat detail. In recognition of changing lifestyles Freis Spirit was launched in spring 1994 as a diffusion line aimed mainly at the South East Asian market. Featuring a pared down silhouette and more subdued designs, the collection offered mix-and-match coordinates in quality fabrics to a younger market.

The success of Diane Freis's labels is destined to continue. The company has its eye set cautiously on China. Almost 20 years of experience will serve them well. They have made their impression by creating for target markets. This provides a clear reminder of how, at the end of the 20th century, there is no longer one predominant international fashion formula.

—Hazel Clark

FRENCH CONNECTION.

British fashion house

Founded in London by Stephen Marks, 1969. French Connection label introduced, 1972; menswear collection launched, 1976; Nicole Farhi hired as designer, from 1978; Nicole Farhi label introduced, 1983. **Address:** 75 Fairfield Road, London E3 2QA, England.

Publications:

On FRENCH CONNECTION:

Articles

Bloomfield, Judy, "Nicole Farhi Strengthens U.S. Connection," in *Women's Wear Daily* (New York), 28 September 1988.
Gordon, Maryellen, "French Connection's Broadway Debut," in *Women's Wear Daily* (New York), 14 April 1993.

*   *   *

French Connection was founded in 1969 by Stephen Marks (who even today remains actively involved in all aspects of the company) with a range of tailored upmarket womenswear in traditional materials marketed under his own name. Marks recognized the need

Diane Fries.

at the time for a less expensive but carefully conceived womenswear collection for a broader market. Stephen Marks started the French Connection label in 1972.

Four years later the first menswear collection was shown. French Connection was one of the first British companies to address the market for well-designed, accessible men's casualwear, and now markets both formal and informal clothes for men, women, and children, a relatively new departure. The menswear division of the group has proceeded to grow at a rate of 25-50 percent each year.

The childrenswear range, for children aged six to 16, began as a scaled-down version of aspects of the main French Connection womenswear and menswear collections, using the same designs, fabrics and sources of manufacture and including everything from T-shirts to tailored clothing.

French Connection design studios are based at the company's headquarters at Bow, East London, and are led by Nicole Farhi who trained in Paris and worked for many major French and Italian companies before joining French Connection in 1978. She is the designer in charge of the company's entire range, as well as having her own label.

French Connection's design philosophy as stated by the company is to "always give its produce that extra fashion content and value; the clothes are remarkable for their comfort and reliability, their continuing anticipation of fashion trends in fabrics, shape, lengths, and styles and their attention to detail."

Women's and menswear collections are produced in four annual collections—two major collections in summer and winter and two mid-season ranges in between. These collections represent some one thousand new designs each year, in a wide variety of fabrics, cuts, and styles from formal clothes to leisurewear. A summer collection for women, for example, might include the extremes of "criss-cross strappy Lycra for minimalist style" and "the timeless combination of navy and white in plain and punchy prints." A winter menswear collection "translates a look of understated distinction, giving a whole new meaning to 'a man in a grey suit.'" The same collection includes "untraditional fabrics, colourful cables, and crunchy winter whites with primitive embroidery."

Within the fashion industry, French Connection is known for its injection of strong distinctive design content into High Street merchandise. Among its customers it has over the years established what might be described as a brand loyalty, for its witty sensitivity to fashion trends translated into well-made garments for a wide range of wearers.

—Doreen Ehrlich

FREUD, Bella.

British designer

Born: London, 17 April 1961. **Education:** Attended Michael Hall School, Forest Row, East Sussex. Left school at 16 to work as shop assistant to Vivienne Westwood, London, 1977. Studied at Accademia di Costume e di Moda, Rome, and tailoring at the Istituto Mariotti, Rome. **Career:** Design assistant to Vivienne Westwood, c.1980-83. Launched own label, 1989. Showed collection for first time at The London Designer Show, October 1991. Capsule collection for Stirling Cooper, Bella Freud for Stirling Cooper, 1994. Consultant designer to Dewhirst, manufacturers for Marks and Spencer plc, 1994. **Collections:** Victoria and Albert Museum, London. **Exhibitions:** Court Couture exhibition, Kensington Palace,

London, 1991. **Awards:** British Fashion Council Innovative Design New Generation Award, 1991. **Address:** 21 St Charles Square, London W10 6EF, England.

Publications:

On FREUD:

Articles

Casadio, Mariuccia, "Bella Freud," in *Interview* (New York), August 1991.
Baker, Lindsay, "Freud's World of Dreams," in *The Guardian* (London), 16 September 1991.
Tredre, Roger, "The Fears and Dreams of Bella Freud," in *The Independent* (London), 10 October 1991.
Brampton, Sally, "Joined by the Hip," in *The Times Magazine* (London), 28 December 1991.
Lender, Heidi, "A Freudian Clip," in *Women's Wear Daily* (New York), 8 January 1992.
Ferguson, Stephanie, "Living with Labels," in *The Sunday Times Magazine* (London), 5 April 1992.
Woram, Catherine, "Freudian Analysis," in *Australian Collections Magazine,* Autumn/Winter 1992.
Harris, Martyn, "The Art of Not Coming Apart at the Seams," in *The Daily Telegraph* (London), 8 October 1992.
Kay, Karen, "Me and My Style by Bella Freud," in the *Daily Mirror* (London), 20 October 1993.
Armstrong, Lisa, "Safe Sex," in *Vogue* (London), February 1994.

*   *   *

Bella Freud's involvement with British fashion began in 1977 when, at the age of 16, she was offered a job by Vivienne Westwood at her World's End shop, then called Seditionaries. Freud decided to study fashion in Rome and left Westwood's shop for Italy where, for the next three years, she studied fashion at the Accademia di Costume e di Moda, tailoring at the Istituto Mariotti, and designed shoes for private clients in her spare time. Freud completed her fashion training under Vivienne Westwood (who is also held in high regard for her tailoring technique) where she worked as an assistant in her design studio for four years.

It was in 1989 that Freud decided the time was right to launch her own label—a move many thought was foolhardy, with Britain in the midst of recession. Freud presented her first collection for fall/winter 1991 in March 1990, which consisted of tailored knitwear and accessories. Her "violin case" bags, typical of her slightly quirky style, were photographed by *Vogue* magazine in America. The following season the designer added tailored pieces to the collection which were manufactured for her in Italy. Knitwear continues to play an important role in Freud's collections and her tailored knitwear now appears to be the Freudian hallmark. She also designs the bags and shoes which make up the total Freud look.

Freud's designs are an interesting combination of tailored pieces which have a somewhat prim air about them, teamed with short skirts and ultra-high-heeled shoes—blending an air of innocence with provocative appeal. The designer cites the Edwardian period as being a major source of inspiration, with its formal silhouette and what Freud describes as its "suppressed-looking" style. Other important influences include designers Coco Chanel and Yves Saint Laurent and, not surprisingly, her mentor Vivienne Westwood.

Westwood's influence is evident in Freud's tailoring which has a decidedly English style, although it is somewhat less structured, which Freud admits she owes to the Italian influence during her fashion training: "Their tailoring is much more extravagant—and sexy—whereas English tailoring is much plainer." Eveningwear by Freud is more glamorous and has included floor-length satin sheaths and crêpe gowns with maribou cuffs with a distinctive 1940s-style air. Freud's little day dresses, which come in both stretch fabrics and as more tailored shapes, also possess the same balance of formality and quietly provocative sex appeal. Fashion journalist Lisa Armstrong succinctly describes Freud's style as being "... a bit like Sharon Stone wearing a St Trinian's uniform designed by a Paris couturier" (*Vogue* [London], February 1994).

In October 1991 Bella Freud launched her collection for the first time at an exhibition, The London Designer Show, and that month she was also named Young Innovative Fashion Designer of the Year at the British Fashion Awards ceremony.

For spring/summer 1993 Freud introduced a range of denim pieces which included a jeans-style dress, jacket, and trousers, and these have now become an established part of each collection, produced in different designs and coloured denims. Freud also works closely with milliner Philip Treacy who designs the hats for her collections. Bella Freud is typical of the new breed of young British designers who have emerged during the 1990s. They have concentrated upon building their businesses at a slower, more carefully-planned rate than their predecessors who, in the early 1980s, came and went at an alarming rate. Freud set up her business in what she describes as a now acceptable "humble way" and has gradually built up a reputation which has established her as a recognized name in British fashion.

—Catherine Woram

FUJIWARA, Giuliano.

Japanese designer working in Italy

Education: Studied law and oriental literature at Chuo University, and design at Bunka College of Fashion, Tokyo. **Career:** Designer, Van Jacket, Japan; immigrated to Italy, 1976; designer, Barbas, beginning 1976; designer, Giuliano Fujiwara, Srl, from 1986; women's collection introduced, 1988. **Address:** Via della Spiga 2, 20121 Milan, Italy.

Publications:

On FUJIWARA:

Articles

Lobrano, Alexander, "East Meets West in Giuliano Fujiwara," magazine supplement to the *Daily News Record* (New York), 29 June 1987.

*   *   *

It is paradoxical for Giuliano Fujiwara to be based in Milan, working as a part of the Italian fashion design community. Characteristically Japanese, Fujiwara seems antithetical to everything Italian. He is introverted while Italians are generally extroverted. He understates while Italians exaggerate. He is reserved while Italians

are expressive. Nevertheless, he seems comfortable in Milan where he has lived and worked since 1976, first as a designer for Barbas and then creating his own line of menswear. "If I stayed in Japan," Fujiwara muses, "my work might have followed the direction of Comme des Garçons and Yohji Yamamoto." Presumably he is talking about the Japanese fashion environment, which encourages avant-garde approaches to menswear.

The Fujiwara style is a curious mixture of American Ivy League, Japanese stark simplicity, and Italian sensitivity in fabrication and workmanship. Take a typical Fujiwara jacket. It has many similarities to the traditional American style—a straight-cut body, the high button stance, small lapels, the jacket length shorter that the Savile Row prototype. "The Ivy League style was my first love. I loved the way JFK looked," he says, remembering his college days when he organized a group to study the manner of dressing. His first job was with a company called Van Jacket. Although it has long been defunct, Van was a catalyst in propagating the Ivy League look in post-World War II Japan, and its influence is felt even today, as in Fujiwara's case.

"Traditional menswear is restricted with numerous rules. My clothes are based on the classic look, but I have eliminated inflexible rules," says Fujiwara. Such a method, however, is not Fujiwara's monopoly. Rather, it is the basic principle for most Milanese designers, with Giorgio Armani being the most notable example. What distinguishes the Fujiwara look from the others is its stoic cleanliness and serene simplicity. To paraphrase, his clothes are disciplined and refined, but lack carnal sexiness. Fujiwara readily agrees. He hates macho images, such as exposed hairy chests and brash exhibition of the male body. When he shows coarsely knit sweaters or open-neck shirts, his models always wear T-shirts under them. Nor does he like slouchy looks. His trousers are always cut at the top of the shoes, or above. He is quite definite about the choice of colors, too, eschewing dayglo brights or ice cream pastels.

These likes and dislikes reflect his concept of masculinity which derives from his nostalgia for old Japan. "I like the image of men from the *Meiji* and *Taisho* periods (1862-1926)," says Fujiwara. "They ware slightly rough around the edges and gutsy and robust inside." To supplement taciturn Fujiwara's statement, those men were taught not to show inner feelings and weaknesses. Excessive concern for one's appearance was looked down upon as a sign of shallowness or femininity. "At the same time," Fujiwara continues, "I also like the certain roguish charm of Italian men."

Since he launched his own business in 1986, Fujiwara's silhouette has changed little, but his clothes are refreshed each season with innovative details. Intricate inlays and patchwork, oddly placed extra pockets, decorative stitching and pipings, and many other clever ideas are delights for Fujiwara fans who are rather limited in number at this writing. "It takes much longer to build business on your convictions than on trendy fashions. But unless you stick to your guns, I see no reason to be in this business," says Fujiwara, who counts stubbornness as one of the essential qualities of a designer.

—Yoko Hamada

FURSTENBERG, Diane Von. See **VON FURSTENBERG, Diane.**

G

GABBANA, Stefano. See **DOLCE & GABBANA.**

GALANOS, James.

American designer

Born: Philadelphia, Pennsylvania, 20 September 1924. **Education:** Studied at the Traphagen School of Fashion, New York, 1942-43. **Career:** General assistant, Hattie Carnegie, New York, 1944-45; sketch artist for Jean Louis, Columbia Pictures, Hollywood, 1946-47; apprentice designer, Robert Piguet, Paris, 1947-48; designer, Davidow, New York, 1948-49; designer, Galanos Originals, from 1951; licenses include Galanos Furs, introduced in 1984, and Parfums Galanos, 1980. **Exhibitions:** *Galanos Retrospective, 1952-1974,* Costume Council of the Los Angeles County Museum of Art, 1975; *Galanos—25 Years,* Fashion Institute of Technology, New York, 1976; Smithsonian Institution; Metropolitan Museum; Brooklyn Museum; Philadelphia Museum; Ohio State University; Dallas Museum of Art. **Awards:** Coty American Fashion Critics Award, 1954, 1956; Neiman Marcus Award, Dallas, 1954; Filene's Young Talent Design Award, Boston, 1958; Cotton Fashion Award, 1958; Coty American Hall of Fame Award, 1959; *Sunday Times* International Fashion Award, London, 1965; Council of Fashion Designers of America Lifetime Achievement Award, 1985; Stanley Award, 1986. **Address:** 2254 South Sepulveda Boulevard, Los Angeles, California 90064, USA.

Publications:

On GALANOS:

Books

Bender, Marylin, *The Beautiful People,* New York 1967.
Waltz, Barbara, and Bernadine Morris, *The Fashion Makers,* New York 1978.
Diamonstein, Barbaralee, *Fashion: The Inside Story,* New York 1985.
Milbank, Caroline Rennolds, *Couture: The Great Designers,* New York 1985.
Milbank, Caroline Rennolds, *New York Fashion: The Evolution of American Style,* New York 1989.

Articles

Donovan, Carrie, "Good as Gold Clothes," in the *New York Times,* 23 November 1980.
Talley, André Leon, "A Certain Quality: Galanos," in *Vogue* (New York), April 1985.
Batterberry, Ariane and Michael, "The Loner," in *Connoisseur* (New York), May 1985.
Milbank, Caroline Rennolds, "James Galanos: Disciplined Elegance in the Hollywood Hills," in *Architectural Digest* (Los Angeles), September 1988.
Morris, Bernadine, "By Galanos, the Simplest of Splendors," in the *New York Times,* 27 February 1990.
"A Galanos ... Why Is It Worth It?," in *Harper's Bazaar* (New York), June 1991.
Morris, Bernadine, "Galanos Has the Last Word for Fall," in the *New York Times,* 24 August 1993.

* * *

Dedication to excellence, in craftsmanship and design, is the foundation of James Galanos's career. The quality of workmanship found in his clothing is unsurpassed in America today. It may seem a contradiction that his sophisticated, mature, and elegant clothing is designed and produced in southern California, traditionally the land of sportswear. But Galanos is satisfied to remain where he began his business in 1951, a continent away from New York and the center of the American fashion industry.

Galanos knew what he wanted to do early in life and he pursued his dream to design school, an internship in Paris and several design positions with companies in New York. When the opportunity arose for him to open his own company, he created a small collection, which was immediately ordered by Saks Fifth Avenue. From that first collection his clothing has been admired for its particularly high quality, especially considering that it is ready-to-wear, not custom-made. His chiffon dresses in particular made his reputation in the early 1950s, with their yards of meticulously hand-rolled edges.

Galanos had gathered some of the most talented craftspersons available in his workrooms; many were trained in Europe or in the costume studios of Hollywood. If his work is compared to that of anyone else, it is compared to the French haute couture. Indeed, his business is more comparable to a couture house than a ready-to-wear manufacturer; there is an astonishing amount of hand work in each garment and all of his famous beadwork and embroidery is done by his staff. Galanos chooses his fabrics and trimmings personally during several trips to Europe each year. It is acknowledged that he often lines dresses with silks that other designers use for dresses themselves. He is a firm believer in the importance of hidden details, such as exquisite silk linings. These details make a difference in the feel of the clothes on the body and the hang of the fabric, and his clients all over the world are happy to pay for them. Many of the world's most socially prominent women are Galanos customers. In the 1980s, he made national headlines as one of former First Lady Nancy Reagan's favorite designers. The fact that Mrs.

James Galanos.

Reagan wore a 14-year-old Galanos to her first state dinner at the White House attests to the timelessness and durability not only of his workmanship, but more importantly, of his design. This type of occurrence is commonplace among his faithful customers.

His silhouette has remained narrow with a fluid ease and he continues to refine his shapes. If his design has changed in more than 40 years of business, it has become more simple and refined. Not one to be satisfied with past success, he still relishes the challenge of creating the perfect black dress. But despite his fondness for black in design, he is also known for his brilliant and unusual combinations of darker shades. His masterful handling of chiffon and lace tends toward the softly tailored, staying away from excess fullness of any kind. Galanos is not necessarily synchronized with the rest of the fashion world; if the themes of his collections bear similarities to others from year to year, it is coincidental.

Galanos prefers to work somewhat in isolation, both geographically and ideologically. His goal has always been to make the most elegant clothing possible for a select group of the world's most sophisticated women. The number of women who are what he considers truly elegant may be smaller than it was when his career began, but he has certainly succeeded in his goal of providing the clothing that they require. His designs are collected by his customers, like other objects of artistic value, and they are represented in museum collections around the United States.

—Melinda Watt

GALITZINE, Irene.

Russian designer working in Rome

Born: Tiflis, Russia, 1916. **Education:** Studied art and design in Rome. **Family:** Married Silvio Medici. **Career:** Assistant, Fontana, c.1945-48; established own import business, Rome, 1949; first collection, 1959; business closed 1968; worked as free-lance designer, 1968-70; designer for own business, reopened as Princess Galitzine, from 1970. **Awards:** Filene Award for new talent, Boston, 1959; Designer of the Year Award, Italy, 1962; *Sunday Times* International Fashion Award, 1965; Isabella d'Este Award, Italy, 1965.

Publications:

On GALITZINE:

Books

Lambert, Eleanor, *World of Fashion: People, Places, Resources,* New York and London 1976.
Soli, Pia, *Il genio antipatico* (exhibition catalogue), Venice 1984.
Villa, Nora, *Le regine della moda,* Rizzoli, Milan 1985.

Articles

"Galitzine seta e lustrine: tutto scivola," in *Vogue* (Milan), September 1984.
"Roma Alta Moda: Irene Galitzine," in *Vogue* (Milan), September 1985.

Colen, Bruce, and Massimo Listri, "Princess Irene Galitzine: Rich Patterns in the Heart of Rome," in *Architectural Digest* (Los Angeles), September 1988.

*   *   *

Nathaniel Hawthorne and Henry James were Americans who dreamed of Italy; after World War II, the dream was a film, *Three Coins in a Fountain,* eventually superseded by the Italian-made *La Dolce Vita.* Italian freedom and innate style held romance; Italian nobility in the fashion and beauty industries such as Emilio Pucci, Princess Marcella Borghese, and Princess Irene Galitzine were fairy-tale heroes.

In the 1950s and 1960s (launching her business in 1949), Princess Irene Galitzine exemplified Roman high style and the princely life. Diana Vreeland, then of *Harper's Bazaar,* dubbed Galitzine's full, liquid trousers for at-home leisure (introduced to a standing ovation at the Palazzo Pitti fashion showing in 1960) "palazzo pajamas" and every aura of Renaissance and romantic (and erotic) Italy flooded the American imagination. Galitzine's palazzo pajamas were, in fact, not wholly an invention, but they became in Galitzine's countless versions of uncompromising luxury a silken reverie. The silks of Italy were a factor, but Galitzine was especially inventive in the elaboration of the palazzo pajamas, bringing to the leisure trousers expressions of *alta moda* embellishment. She treated the drapey silks as a scrim for attached necklaces in the manner of Mainbocher and created other illusions of encrusted ornament and articulated hems and sleeves with beads in a manner reminiscent of Fortuny's Murano bead edges, but even more of Renaissance paintings. Even with the comfort and casualness of palazzo pajamas, the wearer seemed to step out of a lustrous, bejewelled world of Renaissance art. Similarly, her decoration of hems, collars, and cuffs articulated countless Pierrots (often with long tops over either palazzo trousers or narrow trousers). Galitzine used these applied effects not only to establish the grandeur of what might otherwise lapse into a too casual mode, but also to apply a countervailing weight to the almost fly-away big cutting of her styles. Weight and the illusion of weight was an effective punctuation of the clothing. Likewise, in her signature toga top over trousers, the elaborate *fibula* at the shoulder not only secures, but gives a solid balance to the loose drape.

Roman grandeur led rather dramatically, in the 1960s, to the Cardin-like futurism in Galitzine's work. A quilted vinyl jumpsuit with matching helmet on the cover of the May 1966 *Harper's Bazaar* is *Brave New World* anticipation, but continues to observe Galitzine's dress rationalism. In the same era, she was converting her palazzo pajamas into ensembles with Empire-waisted tops and boxy jackets in reinforcement of the new geometry. In fact, her clothing had always understood lifestyle and the reductivism of the 1960s. After a brief hiatus in the late 1960s, Galitzine reopened to show for spring/summer 1970. In that collection, she used bold graphics for trousers and dresses to be worn with sleeveless tunics, again a device that could seem to step out of a Renaissance painting or step forward into fantasies of outer space.

For a fashion designer able to trace her Russian ancestry back to Catherine the Great and insistent on her Russian style even as much as her Roman, Galitzine became the epitome of Roman style. "I've always tried to design new outlines that feel good on the body.... I don't care for clothes that you have to think about after you've put them on. No elegant woman ever looks ill at ease." Galitzine's formula for easy and comfortable dressing managed to combine the avowed comfort of the clothing with an unmistakable pomp of Roman refinement and the abiding presence of Italian Renaissance lustre. Always adding to the aura of Galitzine's design was her remarkable client list, the best of Italy and an international clientèle that discovered Italian clothing in the 1950s and 1960s. *Architectural Digest* (September 1988) noted, "As Eleanor Lambert once remarked at a Galitzine showing: 'The audience is snob, not mob.'" Yet, the supreme evidence is Galitzine's clothing: luxurious and inventive high-style casualness with grace.

—Richard Martin

GALLIANO, John.

British designer

Born: Gibraltar, 1960. **Education:** Studied design at St Martin's School of Art, London. **Career:** Graduation collection, Les Incroyables, sold to Brown's. Free-lance designer, establishing John Galliano fashion house, London, from 1984. **Awards:** British Fashion Council Designer of the Year Award, 1987; Bath Costume Museum Dress of the Year Award, 1987. **Address:** Passage du Cheval Blanc, 2 rue de la Roquette, 75011 Paris, France.

Publications:

On GALLIANO:

Books

Coleridge, Nicholas, *The Fashion Conspiracy,* London 1988.

Articles

Brampton, Sally, "Still Crazy," in *The Observer* (London), 24 March 1985.
Mower, Sarah, "Loves Me, Loves Me Not," in *The Guardian* (London), 27 February 1986.
Brampton, Sally, "Capital Collections: John Galliano," in *Elle* (London), March 1987.
Hume, Marlon, "Boy's Own Story," in *Fashion Weekly* (London), 18 June 1987.
Menkes, Suzy, "Jasper and John," in *The Independent* (London), 9 October 1987.
Rumbold, Judy, "A Steal for Galliano," in *The Guardian* (London), 14 October 1987.
Mower, Sarah, "London Follows Galliano," in *The Observer* (London), 18 October 1987.
Coleman, Alix, "Viva Galliano!," in the *Sunday Express Magazine* (London), 8 November 1987.
Filmer, Deny, "Designer Focus: John Galliano," in *Cosmopolitan* (London), February 1988.
Jobey, Liz, "John Galliano: Romantic Hero," in *Vogue* (London), February 1988.
Brampton, Sally, "The Great Galliano," in *Elle* (London), March 1988.
Carpenter, Sue, "Could You Wear a Galliano?," in *You* magazine of the *Mail on Sunday,* 13 March 1988.
"Avant-garde to Vanguard Galliano," in *Harper's Bazaar* (New York), April 1988.

Irvine, Susan, "Galliano and Co.," in *Harrods Magazine* (London), Spring 1988.
Gasperini, Nicoletta, "John Galliano's Golden Year," in *Donna* (Milan), April 1988.
"Le asimmetre preziose di John Galliano," in *Elle* (Milan), August 1988.
"Five Go Wild," in *Elle* (London), September 1988.
Flatt, Kathryn, "Ahead for Business," in *Harper's Bazaar* (New York), September 1989.
Collin, Matthew, "The Boy Wonder: An Interview with John Galliano," in *i-D* (London), November 1989.
Rumbold, Judy, "Galliano Leaps onto Centre Stage," in *The Guardian* (London), 26 February 1990.
Dickson, Elizabeth, "A Life in the Day of John Galliano," in the *Sunday Times Magazine* (London), 1 March 1992.
Billen, Andrew, "Galliano: Can He Really Cut It?," in *The Observer Magazine* (London), 28 February 1993.
Reed, Julia, "Incurable Romantic," in *Vogue* (New York), March 1993.
Ingrassia, Michele, with Meggan Dissly, "Dior Meets Disney World," in *Newsweek* (New York), 26 December 1994/2 January 1995.
Mauriès, Patrick, "Ma Poulette, Quel Style," in *Vogue* (Paris), February 1995.
"Sei grande, grande, grande ... /Nobody Does It Better," in *Moda In* (Modena), January-March 1995.
Spindler, Amy M., "Four Who Have No Use for Trends," in the *New York Times,* 20 March 1995.
Menkes, Suzy, "Show, Not Clothes, Becomes the Message," in *International Herald Tribune* (Paris), 20 March 1995.
Kerwin, Jessica, "Galliano in Gotham," in *Women's Wear Daily* (New York), 23 May 1995.

*   *   *

Experimental and innovative, John Galliano has become internationally renowned as one of Britain's most exciting designers, acclaimed from the start for his brilliance in cut and magpie-like ability to take inspiration from diverse sources to create a completely new look. Although his clothes are often difficult to understand when on the hanger—with collars that seem to be bows or halter necks that actually fit over the shoulders—they are frequently ahead of the current fashion trends and eventually filter down the clothing chain to the High Street, as well as being picked up by other designers. A favourite among fashion aficionados, Galliano was spotted as soon as his first student collection was completed and has continued to develop since, despite repeated problems with backers that have hampered his career.

As part of a new breed of avant-garde British designers, Galliano led the way in the mid-1980s with his historically influenced designs. This fascination for period detail and adaptation of traditional styles into highly contemporary pieces has continued throughout his work. Studying surviving garments in museums to learn about construction methods and different ways to cut and drape fabric to create new shapes inspired his innovative 18th-century Incroyables collection for his degree show. He has suffused this knowledge with other diverse influences to produce collections always exciting and different. His great belief in the necessity to push fashion forward by learning from the past, coupled with his skill at balancing his designs with modern ideals, has earned him the reputation of a prodigy.

Every outfit is thought out to the last detail, producing a series of completely accessorized looks as he constantly strives for perfection. His love of bias cut gives added fluidity to the asymmetrical hemlines of many of his designs, with a taste of 18th-century dandyism thrown in, always with a surprise twist—often in his use of fabric, another area where Galliano loves to experiment and challenge. In one collection he presented Napoleon-style jackets in bright neoprene, in another, *devoré* velvet bias-cut dresses which clung to the body, giving the element of sexiness that pervades his work. His love of shock gave us the camped-up glamour of his "underwear as outer wear," with satin knickers worn with feathered bras and leather caps, tapping the trend for drag in the London clubs.

With Galliano's Girl and, perhaps to an even greater extent, the largely denim and Lycra-based line Galliano Genes, the designer demonstrates his ability to redefine existing subcultures to develop clothes for the younger, funkier sisters of his mainline buyers. Produced at a cheaper cost by using less exclusive fabrics, these designs are nonetheless inventive. Three-way jackets can be worn with attached waist-coats outside or inside, and there are more basic items that are more commercial, confronting occasional claims from his critics that his work is too avant-garde and less popular than other European names.

The sheer breadth of vision of Galliano's designs, which frequently rethink form and shape, and the great inventiveness of his cut surely earn him his reputation as one of the best of British designers. The research he does before forming a collection—bringing together influences and details from the French Revolution to Afghan bankers to Paul Poiret—and his experimentation with fabrics demonstrate his dedication to pushing fashion and dress forward, yielding excitement and surprise in every collection.

—Rebecca Arnold

THE GAP.

American casualwear company

Founded by Donald and Doris Fisher in San Francisco as a retail store specializing in Levi's jeans in 1969. Company expanded into activewear throughout the 1970s, adding more retail outlets; private label clothing consolidated under The Gap brand name, 1983; company purchased Banana Republic chain of stores, 1983; GapKids line of clothing and GapKids boutiques introduced, 1985; BabyGap clothing line introduced, 1990. Hemisphere chain of shops, selling European-styled clothing introduced, 1987, discontinued, 1989; Old Navy Clothing Company chain of shops introduced, 1994. **Awards:** *Sales and Marketing Management* magazine Marketing Achievement Award, 1991. **Address:** 1 Harrison Street, San Francisco, California 94105, USA.

Publications:

On THE GAP:

Books

Hoover, Gary, et. al., *Hoover's Handbook of American Business 1994,* Austin, Texas 1993.

Articles

Forman, Ellen, "Widening the Gap," in the *Daily News Record* (New York), 26 May 1987.

Conant, Jennet, "The Age of McFashion: Specialty Stores Are Selling Prepackaged Style for Busy Shoppers," in *Newsweek* (New York), 28 September 1987.

Callagher, Sue, and Ros Ormiston, "Filling the Gap," in *Fashion Weekly* (London), 16 November 1989.

Van Meter, Jonathan, "Fast Fashion," in *Vogue* (New York), June 1990.

Kantrowitz, Barbara, "Now, You Can Crawl into The Gap: A Retailer Proves that Style Knows No Age Barrier," in *Newsweek* (New York), 29 October 1990.

"Ready, Set, Gap!," in *Harper's Bazaar* (New York), February 1991.

Pogoda, Dianne M., and Thomas Ciampi, "Growing The Gap," in *Women's Wear Daily* (New York), 6 January 1992.

Mitchell, Russell, in *Business Week* (New York), 9 March 1992.

Tyrer, Kathy, "Back to Basics: Gap Too Hip for Its Britches in the Value-Oriented 90's," in *Adweek Western Advertising News,* 9 November 1992.

Ozzard, Janet, "Is The Gap Losing Its Fashion Edge?," in *Women's Wear Daily* (New York), 9 June 1993.

Strom, Stephanie, "How Gap Inc. Spells Revenge," in the *New York Times,* 24 April 1994.

"Who's Who in the American Sportswear Market 1995," in *Sportswear International* (New York), Vol. 13, May 1994.

Duff, Christina, "'Bobby Short Wore Khakis'—Who's He, and Who Cares?," in *Wall Street Journal* (New York), 16 February 1995.

*   *   *

The Gap, it could be argued, is one of the few (and enduring) good things to be remembered from the disturbed, disestablishment year of 1969. The Gap opened that year to sell jeans and records, one of countless head-shop, youth-oriented variations on grass-roots retailing in the period. Founder Donald Fisher and President Mickey Drexler (hired in 1983) burnished hippie capitalism and Levi's in quantity into an ethic and a chain of immaculate image and quality. As *Business Week* (9 March 1992) reported, "The result is a company that connects with consumers the way only a few other giant brands, such as Coca-Cola or McDonald's, manage to do. Buttressed by its acclaimed advertising, The Gap look is accepted equally by tots, teenagers, young adults, and graying baby boomers." In the fractious 1990s, The Gap is one of a few harmonious and homogenous entities to thrive in America, serving not only differences in age, but the wide American geography and even an international appetite for the casual, as well as the heterogenous American ethnicities of population.

It has become one of the prodigious survivors of the period, flourishing in the 1990s as the most profitable apparel retailer in America with sales in excess of $3 billion. Ironically, only Levi Strauss (whose jeans are no longer carried in The Gap) is a larger clothing brand in the United States. Fifteen hundred stores, including GapKids (begun in 1985), GapShoes (launched 1993), Banana Republic (acquired 1983), and Old Navy (launched 1994) operate out of the 1960s matrix of casual dress, but with the efficiency and style of the 1990s. So archetypal now to the American 1980s and 1990s that its advertising is epochal and continuously imitated, its ebullient sales staff regularly mocked on American television, and its clean white modernism inflected by neatly soft piles of color copied by many other retailers, The Gap is the quintessential late 20th-century American apparel retailer. It built in the 1980s and 1990s upon closeness between men's and women's clothing, some items selling across gender; it depends on rudimentary sizes and has been able to thrive in a time of oversizing and supple casualness. Of course, if there were any fears in The Gap's probable rosy future, they would have to be: revived formality, an emphasis on fit and size, and pronounced gender segregation, all quite unlikely.

Jeans entrepreneurs with loud rock music, Day-glo horror vacui, and beaded entryways were a dime a dozen in the era of hippie capitalism. The Gap realized a pathway into the contemporary imagination through jeans and casual clothing, emphasizing basics, staying clear of gimmicks (after a few fateful bad tries), and by displaying merchandise in color masses surrounded by pure, snowy white fixtures. What private-label merchandise had once identified for department stores became the Gap credo of the 1980s and 1990s as its franchise was built: a comfortable fashion security and dependable quality, purchased with confidence and convenience. Basics became cool not only in the purchasing environment, but culturally "cool" with some of the choicest advertising of the late 1980s and 1990s. Hip photographers caught "Individuals of Style," beginning in 1988, wearing Gap clothes, often with their own favored apparel. The informal basics worked with the personal style of creative individuals as diverse as k.d. lang, Ryuichi Sakamoto, Miles Davis, and Andrée Putman, and The Gap established its corporate philosophy of generic clothing or basics taken to be significant personal style. Choice is evident in a continually refreshed merchandise mix that allows the balance between selection and a predetermined range of color and style, and also serves to bring customers to the store on a regular basis.

Other advertising campaigns for The Gap have been equally successful in sustaining the stylish image of Gap basics, including BabyGap and GapKids, which are both wholesome and vigorous without being sensationalized. *Sportswear International* observed in 1994: "The Gap endures, staying hip when it could easily fall into a cliché. It's upgraded and broadened its assortments in response to the ebbing basics trends, providing it not only with a new fashion vitality, but also a means of differentiating it from its new mass-market cousin, Old Navy."

The Gap, in fact, is perhaps the most important new concept in mass retailing in the hundred years since department stores arrived with the steadfast promise of congenial and convenient shopping, established prices, and a quantity of reliable merchandise. The Gap is a condensed clothing retailer trading not only in informal clothing, but in the informal life of the late 20th century. Inasmuch as its faith to informality has proved to be culturally correct and bears every promise of sustained reason at least through the 1990s, this straightforward merchandising and appealing marketing is both the clothing retailing business at its basics and in its romantic future. Despite the distinctness of individual components of The Gap style, it is unpretentious, a style that declares and negates. One has the sense that an Amish farmer, a blue-collar worker, a best-dressed matron buying for weekends, and a high-fashion model would all be contented when shopping in The Gap—and self-confident in wearing the product. It is hard to describe the aura of The Gap (and its related aesthetic of Banana Republic), but The Gap does convey mood and a sense of presence, thus valorizing its garments in a very special way and enhancing the experience of shopping. The Gap is neither pause nor void; it is the future of retailing.

—Richard Martin

GARAVANI, Valentino. See VALENTINO.

GARRATT, Sandra.

American designer

Born: Sandra Harrower in Milwaukee, Wisconsin, 16 December 1951, to British parents. **Education:** Graduated from Fashion Institute of Design and Merchandising, Los Angeles, 1975. **Family:** Married Michael Garratt in 1977; one son: Wesley. **Career:** Design assistant to Ossie Clark, London, 1971-73; design assistant to Bob Mackie, Los Angeles, 1974-75; textile research/design assistant, Holly Harp, San Francisco, 1975; first design assistant, Dinallo, Beverly Hills, California, 1975; textile designer, Mary McFadden, New York, 1976; window and showroom display designer, Halston, New York, 1976; first design assistant, Zoran, New York, 1976; illustrator, Giorgio di Sant'Angelo, New York, 1976-77; textile design, CMS Spectrum, New York, 1976-77; director, Texas Developmental Group, Dallas, 1978-80; director and designer, Units, Dallas, 1981-86; sold to JCPenney, 1986; artistic/creative director responsible for all aspects of design including textile, packaging, marketing, fashion shows and videos, Multiples, Dallas, Texas 1987-89; designer, New Gotham and Moda Vida collections, Greaten Corporation, Los Angeles, 1990; director and designer, New Tee, Inc., original line of 100% organic materials, 1992-present. **Exhibitions:** Scott Theatre, Ft. Worth, Texas, 1980; 500X Gallery, Dallas, Texas, 1981; Milam St. Gallery, Houston, Texas, 1982; Wadsworth Atheneum Museum, Hartford, Connecticut, 1989; Musee des Arts decoratifs, Paris, 1990; Natural History Museum, Los Angeles, 1990. **Awards:** Bob Mackie Award for Outstanding Achievement in Design, Los Angeles, 1976; Female Entrepreneur of the Year, 1988. **Address:** 4216 Main Street, Dallas, Texas 75226 USA.

Publications:

On GARRATT:

Books

Milbank, Caroline Rennolds, *New York Fashion: The Evolution of American Style,* New York 1989.

Articles

"Sandra Garratt Jumps into the Dallas Designer Game," in "Fashion!Dallas," *The Dallas Morning News* (Texas), 4 April 1979.

Anderson, K., "Close to the Edge," in "Fashion!Dallas," *The Dallas Morning News* (Texas), 31 October 1979.

Brobston, Tracy, "Five Easy Pieces," in "Fashion!Dallas," *The Dallas Morning News* (Texas), 28 July 1982.

Ennis, M., "The Empress's New Clothes," in *Texas Monthly* (Austin, Texas), September 1982.

Zimmerman, A., "Bits and Pieces," in *Dallas City Magazine, The Dallas Times Herald* (Texas), 11 May 1986.

Sandra Garratt.

Herold, L., "Picking Up the Pieces," in *Dallas Life Magazine, The Dallas Morning News* (Texas), 1 February 1987.

Herold, L., "A Designer Is Reborn," in "Fashion!Dallas," *The Dallas Morning News* (Texas), 6 January 1988.

"Sandra Garratt," in *Detour* (Dallas, Texas), April 1988.

Herold, L., "No Hang-Ups," in *Texas Business* (Dallas, Texas), June 1988.

Shapiro, H., "Style: Success Comes in Many Forms for Mix and Match Designer Sandra Garratt," in *People* (New York), 20 June 1988.

Mangelsdorf, M., "Dressed for Success," in *Inc.* (Boston, Mass.), August 1988.

Hockswender, Woody, "Modular Clothes: Count the Ways," in the *New York Times,* 18 October 1988.

Mitchell, C., "Riches from Rags," in *The Wall Street Journal* (New York), 20 March 1989.

*

I see my original modular concept as a classic—like Levi's 501 jeans. The empty-canvas-like appearance begs for personal touches. I'm taking a flat, square architectural design in a soft, knit fabric, which makes it pliable, then putting it on a three-dimensional form so there are contradictions. It stirs up dynamics. Stiff clothes lack body awareness. Through my designs, I offer people a tiny opportunity at self-expression which everyone craves.

Both Jean Muir and Zandra Rhodes have influenced me throughout my career but my favourite designer of all times is Paul Poiret. He really created a new approach for all of 20th-century fashion. Other inspirations that can be seen in my work come from Rudi Gernreich, who was also trained as a dancer, and Giorgio di Sant'Angelo. Working with Halston in the 1970s gave me a new direction. Halston offered a basic way of dressing that seemed suited to Americans. His clothes were realistic in the sense that they worked for you instead of your having to adopt the characteristics of the clothes.

I think people relate to jeans and simple T-shirts because they are functional and authentic. The challenge is to offer good design in an average price range for people. It is easy to work with beautiful, fancy fabrics but not easy to create things that work out of simple, pure materials. That is why working with organically produced fabrics is a great challenge for me and is where I want to focus my designer energies for the rest of my career.

—Sandra Garratt

*   *   *

Sandra Garratt's career evolved from an early interest in dance and costume design. Forced to abandon her ballet studies that took her to Canada and Europe, Garratt ended up in London as a design assistant to Ossie Clark during the early 1970s. Returning to the United States in 1973, Garratt worked on elaborate clothing out of luxury fabrics as a design student at the Fashion Institute of Design and Merchandising, Los Angeles. As a senior, she was asked to design a line contrary to her then baroque interest in costume dressing. She created a collection of slim skirts and bright tunics out of silk that became the basis for her career.

After a series of design positions in New York, where she was influenced by designers such as Halston and Giorgio di Sant'Angelo, Garratt moved to Dallas, Texas. In 1978, her lifestyle as a busy

working mother made her realize that millions of women like herself were struggling with increasing demands on their time and resources. Most available clothing failed to address these issues so she began to cultivate ideas based on her senior show. Garratt pioneered the concept of modular one-size-fits-all cotton knits in basic shapes: T-shirts, leggings, tunics, bandeaux, and bikinis. The interchangeable, mix-and-match pieces were eventually called Units. Garratt marketed Units as "modular clothing for the masses expressing individuality through apparent uniformity."

Units were affordable, could be worn alone or layered, and made the customer feel both casual and fashionable. The early 1980s were swept by an aerobics and jogging craze. Units offered an appealing, comfortable alternative to sweatsuits and workout clothes. Garratt's early interest in dance contributed to her ability to respond to a woman's need for comfort and flexibility in her wardrobe. She eventually sold out her interest in Units in 1987 after a dispute with her financial partners. Units, which was later purchased by JCPenney, operates as a chain of stores in shopping malls.

Another company, called Multiples, was launched in 1987 with Garratt at the design helm. Described as a "system of dressing," Multiples was a collection of 20 knit separates that were sold in more than 350 department stores nationally. Garratt monitored the production by the Jerrell company and helped market and promote the line vigorously. Multiples were more sophisticated shapes than previous forms designed by Garratt. Cut out of square pattern pieces, the knit jackets often echoed Japanese design concepts that were pervasive in fashion of the late 1980s. Multiples offered a versatile group of tunics, skirts, jumpsuits, leggings, and tubular accessories that could be worn as a scarf, cowl, belt, etc. The boxy shapes were sold folded in practical plastic bags at a low price to a huge cross-section of women.

Multiples could be casual or sophisticated depending on the mood of the wearer. Claire McCardell, an American designer during the 1940s and early 1950s, designed comfortable jersey knits similar to Multiples but her timing was unfortunate. Garratt, who also formulated her own ideas ahead of the market, was fortunate enough to be in step with current times throughout the 1980s. Since 1989, Garratt has discontinued her relationship with the Jerrell company and Multiples.

Garratt also took time to explore her other love: romantic dressing. She introduced a line of one-of-a-kind, hand-sewn original confections of lace, tulle, and taffeta that were referred to as "Viennese pastry" dresses during the early 1980s. This specialist work was carried by specialist stores but is no long marketed as a separate line. However, Garratt has a devoted private clientèle for these special occasion creations. Since 1990, Garratt has opened her own business called New Tee which is focused on using organically grown cotton and nontoxic, water-based dyes. Garratt continues to design her body-wear-oriented clothing with hopes of effecting changes in marketing and manufacturing practices related to saving the environment.

—Myra Walker

GAULTIER, Jean-Paul.

French designer

Born: Arcueil, France, 24 April 1952. **Education:** Educated at the École Communale, the College d'Enseignement, and at the Lycée d'Arcueil, to 1969. **Career:** Design assistant, Pierre Cardin, 1972-74; also worked for Esterel and Patou; designer, Cardin United States Collection, working in the Philippines, 1974-75; designer, Majago, Paris, 1976-78; founder, Jean Paul Gaultier S.A., from 1978; menswear line introduced, 1984; Junior Gaultier line introduced, 1987; furniture line introduced, 1992; licenses include jewelry, from 1988, perfumes, from 1991, and jeans, from 1992. Awards: Fashion Oscar Award, Paris, 1987. **Address:** 70 Galerie Vivienne, 75002 Paris, France.

Publications:

By GAULTIER:

Books

À nous deux la mode, Paris 1990.

On GAULTIER:

Articles

"An Audience with Jean-Paul," in *Fashion Weekly* (London), 11 December 1986.
Drier, Deborah, "The Defiant Ones," in *Art in America* (New York), September 1987.
Arroyuelo, Janvier, "Gaultier: Tongue in Chic," in *Vogue* (New York), August 1988.
"Alaia e Gaultier, due stilisti a confronto," in *Vogue* (Milan), October 1988.
Martin, Richard, "An Oxymoranic Jacket by Jean-Paul Gaultier," *Textile and Text,* 13 March 1990.
Duka, John, "Gaultier," in *Vogue* (New York), January 1989.
Mower, Sarah, "Gaultier, Comic Genius," in *Metropolitan Home,* February 1991.
Howell, Georgina, "The Maestro of Mayhem," in *Vogue* (New York), March 1991.
Spindler, Amy, "Jean-Paul Gaultier: France's Homeboy," in the *Daily News Record* (New York), 22 July 1991.
Yarbrough, Jeff, "Jean-Paul Gaultier: Fashion's Main Man," in *The Advocate* (USA), 17 November 1992.
Martin, Richard, "Machismo in Trapunto: Jean-Paul Gaultier's 1991 Physique Sweater," *Textile and Text,* 14 March 1992.
Weldon, Fay, "Jean Paul the First," in *Tatler* (London), March 1995.
Spindler, Amy M., "Four Who Have No Use for Trends," in the *New York Times,* 20 March 1995.
Menkes Suzy, "Show, Not Clothes, Becomes the Message," in *International Herald Tribune* (Paris), 20 March 1995.

*   *   *

By injecting kitsch into couture, Gaultier has redefined the traditionally elegant trappings of Paris fashion. He is a playful, good-natured iconoclast, glamorizing street style and cleaning it up for the haute couture. By turns surreal but never completely bizarre, rebellious but always wearable, he produces seductive, witty clothes which redefine notions of taste and elegance in dress.

His eclectic source material, inherited from punk via the fleamarket, and an astute sense of the origins of style mean his clothes make constant historic and literary references, as opposed to the cool modernism of contemporaries such as Issey Miyake, displayed in his use of heraldic motifs in the late 1980s or a collection based on Toulouse-Lautrec in 1991.

Gaultier challenges orthodox notions of the presentation of gender through both male and female dress and ignores the stereotypical femininity normally paraded on the catwalks of traditional Parisian haute couture. During his employment at Jean Patou, Gaultier recognized how most couturiers ignored the female form at the expense of the construction of a particular line. He was, on one occasion, horrified to see a model having to wear heavy bandages to suppress her breasts in order for the dress she was modelling to hang properly. This impulse eventually culminated in a controversial series of negotiations of the corset, stemming from his interest in the exaggerated definition of the female form it produced. In the 1980s he redefined this usually private, hidden garment, whose traditional function is to provide a structure from which to hang the more important outerwear, by recreating it as outerwear itself. One of these, the Corset Dress of 1982, commented astutely on femininity, constructing the breast less as a soft malleable object of passive attraction and more as an object of power, a female weapon, whilst at the same time alluding to the conically stitched bras of the 1950s sweater girl—a particularly tacky glamour. These ideas achieved mass attention when Gaultier designed the costumes for Madonna's Blonde Ambition tour in 1990.

By 1984 Gaultier had decided to move more directly into menswear. Through personal experience he could find nothing he really wanted, particularly in terms of sizing, and even unstructured Armani jackets seemed too small. He noticed that men had been buying his women's jackets because of the unusual fabrics and cut, so he began his seminal reworking of the pin-striped suit for both men and women. He displayed a traditional male wardrobe by redesigning such classics as the navy blazer and Fair Isle jumper and dismantling clichés of masculine styling by producing skirts, corsets, and tutus for men. During one notorious catwalk show female models smoked pipes and men paraded in transparent lace skirts. This acknowledgement of male narcissism and interest in the creation of erotic clothing for men, as shown in the Man-Object Collection of 1982, has influenced designers such as Gianni Versace into the 1990s.

Gaultier is perhaps best associated with the rise of popular interest in designer clothing in the mid-1980s. His redefinitions of traditional male tailoring made his clothes instantly recognizable amongst so-called fashion victims in most of the major European capitals, using details such as metal tips on collars and extended shoulder lines. Structured, fitted garments like jackets were reworked, being cut long and slim over the hips to mid-thigh to give an hourglass shape to the wearer's physique.

Gaultier has always been interested in new developments in fabric and intrigued by the design possibilities of modern, artificial fibres, and is known for using unconventional fibres like neoprene. He uses fabrics outside of their usual context, such as chiffon for dungarees, resulting in a utilitarian garment being produced out of a delicate material traditionally associated with eveningwear. This juggling with expected practice directs him to produce items such as a willow pattern printed textile incorporating the head of Mickey Mouse and Aran sweaters elongated into dresses with the woollen bobbles taking the place of nipples.

Gaultier rebels against the old school of Parisian couture but, because of his years of training within its system under Pierre Cardin, Jacques Esterel and Jean Patou, he is a master craftsman. However avant-garde his collections may seem, they are always

Jean-Paul Gaultier: Corset evening dress, 1991. *Photograph courtesy of the Metropolitan Museum of Art; gift of Richard Martin, 1993.*

founded in a technical brilliance based inventive tailoring and are able to convince because of the technique.

—Caroline Cox

GENNY SpA.

Italian ready-to-wear manufacturer

Founded in Ancona by Arnoldo and Donatella Girombelli in 1961. Lines include Genny Moda, Complice, Byblos (introduced 1973, became independent company, 1983), Malisy (to 1993), Montana Donna and Montana Uomo (to c.1992). Chief designers for Complice include Gianni Versace, from 1975; Claude Montana, from 1980; Dolce e Gabbana, from 1990. Designers for Byblos include Versace, 1975-77; Guy Paulin, 1977-80; Keith Varty and Alan Cleaver, from 1980. **Address:** Strada Statale 16, 60131 Zona Pip (Ancona), Italy.

Publications:

On GENNY:

Articles

"Armonie a confronto," in *Linea Italiana,* October 1984.
Griggs, Barbara, "Lo stile Donatella," in *Vogue* (Milan), October 1988.
Rolfe, Gail, "The Winning Genny," in the *Daily Mail* (London), 6 March 1991.
Smith, Liz, "Polished Touch to Milan Line," in *The Times* (London), 6 March 1991.
"Snappy Dressing Italian-Style," in the *Daily Mail* (London), 12 March 1992.
Gordon, MaryEllen, "Varty, Cleaver in New York: High Spirits," in *Women's Wear Daily* (New York), 16 September 1992.
Levine, Joshua, "Italy's First Lady of the Factory," in *Forbes* (New York), 28 September 1992.
Forden, Sara Gay, "Versace, Genny, to End 19 Years Together with Spring Collection," in *Women's Wear Daily* (New York), 23 July 1993.

*   *   *

Named after their first-born child, Genny was the brainchild of Arnoldo and Donatella Girombelli, who founded the company in 1961. Genny Holding has since become one of Italy's foremost fashion companies, designing, manufacturing, and distributing its own ranges which include Genny, Genny Due, Complice, and Byblos among others. From relatively humble origins as a small clothing factory based in Ancona, Italy, the company was operating at an industrial scale by 1968. During the 1970s it experienced rapid growth when its founder made radical changes in the company structure, steering it towards a more fashionable product in terms of garment styling. These changes did not, however, alter the company's original commitment to the production of high quality, predominantly tailored garments. As an early protagonist of the "Made in Italy" label, Genny assumed a leading role during the 1970s when the Italian fashion industry took its first steps toward becoming a serious competitor with French ready-to-wear fashion.

Genny Holding is typical of a number of Italian fashion companies who manufacture high fashion lines designed for them by leading names in the industry, yet launched under the company's own label. Fashion writer Colin McDowell has described this very successful, as well as lucrative, format as a form of "moonlighting." Considerable financial reward, coupled with the high quality of the Italian ready-to-wear product, has meant that there is no shortage of well-known designers willing to supply their creative talent for such companies. Genny's earliest working relationship with an outside designer was with the young Gianni Versace (then relatively unknown) who designed his first collection for Genny in 1974. Versace was also responsible for designing the early Byblos collections, a younger range introduced in 1973 to complement the classic Genny image.

After the death of Arnoldo Girombelli in 1980, his wife, Donatella, assumed a leading role in the company and now chairs its board of directors. Described by fashion retail entrepreneur Roberto Devorik as "a rare catalyst for design talent," Donatella Girombelli has continued her husband's policy of employing top designers to create lines for the Genny labels. These include Dolce e Gabbana, who design for Complice, and Alan Cleaver and Keith Varty who have designed the Byblos collection since 1980.

The position of Genny and its other labels, including Complice and Byblos, is not a real cutting edge of fashion. They are not dramatically avant-garde or barrier-breaking, but rather producers of top quality ready-to-wear clothing with a strong design element. It is this that has led to the company's widespread success in the international market. In 1992 Genny Holding produced over 2,050,000 items under its different labels, which were distributed worldwide through the company's boutiques, and under carefully controlled licensing agreements.

—Catherine Woram

GERNREICH, Rudi.

American designer

Born: Vienna, 8 August 1922. Immigrated to the United States, 1938, naturalized, 1943. **Education:** Studied at Los Angeles City College, 1938-41; Los Angeles Art Center School, 1941-42. **Career:** Dancer, costume designer, Lester Horton Company, 1942-48; fabric salesman, Hoffman company, and free-lance clothing designer, Los Angeles and New York, 1948-51; designer, William Bass Inc., Beverly Hills, 1951-59; swimwear designer, Westwood Knitting Mills, Los Angeles, 1953-59; shoe designer, Genesco Corp., 1958-60; founder, GR Designs, Los Angeles, 1960-64; designer, Rudi Gernreich Inc., 1964-68. Designs featured in first fashion videotape, *Basic Black,* 1966. Designed furnishings for Fortress and Knoll International, 1970-71, lingerie for Lily of France, 1975, cosmetics for Redken, 1976. Also designed knitwear for Harmon Knitwear, kitchen accessories, ceramic bathroom accessories, and costumes for Bella Lewitzky Dance Company. **Exhibitions:** *Two Modern Artists of Dress: Elizabeth Hawes and Rudi Gernreich,* Fashion Institute of Technology, New York, 1967. **Awards:** *Sports Illustrated* Designer of the Year Award, 1956; Wool Knit Association Award, 1960; Coty American Fashion Critics Award, 1960, 1963, 1966, 1967; Neiman Marcus Award, Dallas, 1961; Sporting Look Award, 1963; *Sunday Times* International Fashion Award, London, 1965; Filene's Design Award, Boston, 1966; admitted to Coty American Fashion Critics' Hall of Fame, 1967; Knitted Textile Association Award, 1975; Council of Fashion Designers of America Special Tribute, 1985. *Died* (in Los Angeles) *21 April 1985.*

Publications:

On GERNREICH:

Books

Bender, Marylin, *The Beautiful People,* New York 1967.
Morris, Bernadine, and Barbara Walz, *The Fashion Makers,* New York 1978.
Milbank, Caroline Rennolds, *New York Fashion: The Evolution of American Style,* New York 1989.
Loebenthal, Joel, *Radical Rags: Fashions of the Sixties,* New York 1990.
Moffitt, Peggy, and William Claxton, *The Rudi Gernreich Book,* New York 1991, London 1992.

Articles

Steinem, G., "Gernreich's Progress; or, Eve Unbound," in the *New York Times Magazine,* 31 January 1965.
"Rudi Gernreich," in *Current Biography* (New York), December 1968.
"Fashion Will Go Out of Fashion," interview, in *Forbes* (New York), 15 September 1970.
Guerin, T., "Rudi Gernreich," in *Interview* (New York), May 1973.
"Head on Fashion," interview, in *Holiday* (New York), June 1975.
Lockwood, C., "The World of Rudi Gernreich," in *Architectural Digest* (Los Angeles), October 1980.
Kalter, S., "Remember Those Topless Swimsuits?," in *People Weekly* (New York), 25 May 1981.
"Rudi Gernreich," obituary, in *Current Biography* (New York), June 1985.
Timmons, Stuart, "Designer Rudi Gernreich Stayed in the Fashion Closet," in *The Advocate,* 25 September 1990.
Armstrong, Lisa, "Peggy and Rudi Go Topless," in *The Independent on Sunday Review* (London), 2 February 1992.

*   *   *

Son of a hosiery manufacturer, born into an intellectual Viennese family in the 1920s, Rudi Gernreich was to become one of the most revolutionary designers of the 20th century. After fleeing the Nazis in the late 1930s he settled in Los Angeles, becoming an American citizen in 1943. Perhaps because of this geographic detachment from the centres of fashion and the fact that he refused to show in Paris, Gernreich is a name which is not spoken in the same breath as Balenciaga, Dior, or even Courrèges, although Gernreich had just as much influence on women's appearance, especially during the 1960s and 1970s.

Gernreich studied dance before entering the world of fashion and, using as inspiration the practice clothes of dancers, particularly leotards and tights, he produced pared down body-clothes in the 1960s, aimed at what seemed to be the new woman of the era. To cater to this popular construction of femininity, Gernreich attempted to produce a new version of women's clothing, freed of all constraints.

Influenced by Bauhaus functionalism, Gernreich conceived a body-based dressing with coordinated underwear, celebrating the unfettered movement of the body based on his early involvement with Lester Horton's modern dance troupe. This interest in liberating the body from the limitations of clothing surfaced in his early swimwear designs of 1952 in which he eliminated the complicated boned and underpinned interior construction which had been obligatory in the 1950s. He revived the knitted swimsuit or *maillot* of the 1920s, which he elasticized to follow the shape of the body. These experiments were continued in his knitted tube dresses of 1953.

Gernreich was interested less in the details and decorations of clothes and more in how they looked in motion. In the 1950s he was designing relaxed, comfortable clothes fabricated out of wool, jersey, and other malleable materials, usually in solid colours or geometric shapes and checks. During the next decade he went on to use unusual fabrics and bold colour disharmonies such as orange and blue or red and purple.

In the early 1960s Rudi Gernreich opened a Seventh Avenue, New York, showroom where he showed his popular designs for Harmon knitwear and his own more expensive line of experimental garments. During the 1960s he acquired a reputation for being the most radical designer in America. His designs included the jacket with one notched and one rounded lapel, tuxedos made of white satin, and the topless bathing suit of 1964, which reflected the new vogue for topless sunbathing.

Gernreich's freeing of the breasts was a social statement, somehow part of the emancipation of women, and a portent of the unfettering of the breast by the women's movement in the 1970s. Gernreich invented the "no bra" bra in 1964, a soft nylon bra with no padding or boning in which breasts assumed their natural shape, rather than being moulded into an aesthetic ideal. He went on to display overtly his sympathy for women's liberation with his 1971 collection of military safari clothes accessorized with dogtags and machine guns.

Gernreich was also responsible for developing the concept of unisex, believing that as women achieved more freedom in the 1960s, male dress would emerge from the aesthetic exile into which it had been cast in the 19th century. He conceived of interchangeable clothes for men and women such as floor length kaftans or white knit bell-bottom trousers and matching black and white midriff tops, and even, in 1975, Y-front underwear for women. Other designs included the first chiffon T-shirt dress, see-through blouses, coordinated outfits of dresses, handbags, hats, and stockings, mini dresses inset with clear vinyl stripes, and the thong bathing suit, cut high to expose the buttocks. He experimented constantly with the potentials of different materials using cutouts, vinyl, and plastic, and mixing patterns such as checks with dots.

His clothing was part of a whole design philosophy which encompassed the designing of furniture, kitchen accessories, rugs, and quilts—even, in 1982, gourmet soups. His notion of freeing the body was taken to its logical extreme in his last design statement, the pubikini, which appeared in 1982, revealing the model's dyed and shaped pubic hair.

—Caroline Cox

GHOST.

British fashion house

Founded in 1984 by Tanya Sarne. **Awards:** British Apparel Export Award, 1992. **Address:** The Chapel, 263 Kensal Rd., London W10 5DB, England.

Publications:

On GHOST:

Articles

Fallon, James, "Ghost: Getting the U.S. Spirit," in *Women's Wear Daily* (New York), 11 January 1993.

Spindler, Amy M., "Color It with Silver and Spice," in the *New York Times*, 4 November 1993.

Women's Wear Daily (New York), 11 April 1994.

Orlean, Susan, "The Talk of the Town: Fashion Designers Uptown and Downtown Get Ready for This Week's Shows in Bryant Park," in *The New Yorker* (New York), 7 November 1994.

*   *   *

The British label Ghost was founded in 1984 by Tanya Sarne and has since become a firmly established name in the fashion industry. The company's signature use of flowing fabric, with its softly crinkled look cut in loose, flowing shapes, has always formed the basis of each collection. Ghost designs are not usually viewed as the cutting edge of fashion. This was particularly true during the power-dressing period of the 1980s, when strict tailoring and padded shoulders were a major element in fashion. A label such as Ghost offered an individual and alternative way of dressing.

Fabrics are the hallmark of each Ghost collection and 99 per cent of them are woven from viscose yarns derived from specially-grown soft wools that have a fluid, crêpe-like texture. An intricate process of washing, shrinking, and dyeing is applied to each garment, which is constructed from the unfinished material or "grey cloth" and dyed at the final stage. These "grey cloth" garments are cut several sizes bigger to allow for the ensuing process of shrinking that occurs when the viscose is boiled to the consistency of vintage crêpe fabric. The traditional process employed by Ghost of garment dyeing at the final stage is rarely used in production today, due to its cost and the fact that it is extremely time-consuming. Another feature of each Ghost collection is its richly varied use of colour, which can achieve great depth on the viscose fabric and changes each season from softest pastels and pale powdery shades to rich autumnal and spicy tones. The signature fabric is also treated with surface decoration such as heavy embroidery, cutwork, and *broderie anglaise* lace effects. Due to the soft, fluid nature of this fabric, Ghost was initially perceived as being primarily summerwear. However, over the past few seasons, new fabrics have been introduced, in particular to the autumn-winter collections, and which have included quilted satin, velours, and mohair wool mixes.

Like many of its British counterparts, more than 80 percent of Ghost's business is export, of which America and Japan represent around 50 percent of sales volume. This was one of the main reasons that prompted Sarne to start showing her collections in New York in 1993, where the company had been selling successfully since 1987. In 1992, Ghost was awarded the British Apparel Export Award when the company exports rose from 60 percent to over 70 percent of the company business. However, although Sarne has abandoned London as a base for her catwalk shows, her design studio and offices remain in Britain. While the United States remains the largest export market for Ghost, others markets include Japan, Europe, Australia, the Caribbean, and the Middle East.

According to Sarne, her philosophy of creating clothes, which she describes as "By Women, For Women," is the key to the con-siderable success of the Ghost label and its consequential appeal to a wide-ranging age group. Each new garment is tried on by the design team before it goes into production. The revolutionary nature of each Ghost collection, which means that existing pieces can be added to each season, is another appealing feature of the company's designs and may be the key to dressing in the 1990s. "It's a unique product and very feminine," says Sarne of the Ghost label. "It also has a very 'antipower dressing' stance—a look that I believe will only increase in importance as the decade progresses."

—Catherine Woram

———

GIANNELLI, Danilo. See **CALUGI E GIANNELLI.**

———

GIBB, Bill.

British designer

Born: William Elphinstone Gibb in Fraserburgh, Scotland, 23 January 1943. **Education:** Studied in Fraserburgh until 1960; studied at St Martin's School of Art, London, 1962-66, Royal College of Art, London, 1966-68. **Career:** Founder and partner of Alice Paul clothing boutique, London, 1967-69; free-lance designer, working for Baccarat, London, 1969-72; founder-chairman Bill Gibb Fashion Group, London, 1972-88; opened first shop, in Bond Street, London, 1975. **Exhibitions:** *British Design,* Musée du Louvre, Paris, 1971; *Fashion: An Anthology,* Victoria and Albert Museum, London, 1971; *Bill Gibb: 10 Years,* Albert Hall, London, 1977. **Collections**: Bath Costume Museum, Avon; Leeds Museum, Yorkshire; Victoria and Albert Museum, London; Royal Ontario Museum, Toronto. **Awards:** *Vogue* Designer of the Year, 1970; ITV Best Fashion Show Award, London, 1979. Also: Fellow, Society of Industrial Artists and Designers, London, 1975. *Died* (in London) *3 January 1988.*

Publications:

By GIBB:

Articles

"Getting Going Again," in *The Designer* (London), May 1981.

On GIBB:

Books

Howell, Georgina, ed., *In Vogue, Sixty Years of Celebrities and Fashion,* London 1975, 1978, New York 1976.

Carter, Ernestine, *The Changing World of Fashion,* London 1977.

Bond, David, *The Guinness Guide to 20th Century Fashion,* Enfield, Middlesex, 1981.

Glynn, Prudence, *Sixty Years of Faces and Fashion,* London 1983.

Sparke, Penny, et.al., *Design Source Book,* London 1986.

Articles

"Top of the Bill," in *The Sunday Times Magazine* (London), 8 May 1977.

Ebbetts, L., "The Fall and Rise of Bill Gibb," in the *Daily Mirror* (London), 12 October 1978.

Boyd, Ann, "Gibb's Comeback," in *The Observer* (London), 22 October 1978.

"Bill Gibb Comes Back with Flowers," in *Art & Design* (London), November 1985.

"Obituary: Bill Gibb," in *The Daily Telegraph* (London), 4 January 1988.

O'Dwyer, Tom, "Bill Gibb—An Appreciation," in *Fashion Weekly* (London), 14 January 1988.

Rancer, Katherine, "Bill Gibb: 1943-1988," in *Vogue* (London), March 1988.

*   *   *

Arriving in London at the age of 19 from northern Scotland, Gibb was already obsessed with the dream of a career in fashion. He trained at St Martin's School of Art, then at the Royal College under the aegis of Professor Janey Ironside. An unprecedented flow of new talent was to emerge from the college in the early 1960s. For the next three years he worked for Baccarat, the prestigious London fashion house, before setting up his own company in 1972 with a complete team, including designers, cutter, and business manager. By 1975 he was in retail.

In the early 1970s unconventionality was the order of the day and Gibb was one of several young designers in the British wholesale market whose work reflected this trend. He responded to the new predilection for romantic and ethnic clothes, inspired by the folk costumes of Europe or the Near East and displaying, too, a feeling of nostalgia for the dress of an earlier historical age, with his full length skirts and billowing slashed sleeves.

Gibb's was a career of considerable variety and change. "I strove for the top and achieved it within ten years," he said. He believed consummately in his "rare gift ... to design beautiful clothes" which would appeal to the sensuality of women. This talent led him through a series of outlets from the personal customer to department stores, from boutiques to newspaper and magazine fashion features, to the opening of his first shop in London's Bond Street in 1975, and was to earn him an international reputation for unique special occasion clothes.

Always an individualist, he was faithful to his own design principles, which relied on the enterprising and ingenious use of textures, weaves, and patterns in fabrics and knitting. Boldly inventive to the point of abandon at times, he mixed and matched materials and colours. His mood was romantic and way-out: the effects often larger than life and always unmistakably his own. "I feel rather than dictate. I create a mood," he said. He wanted to create coordinates that gave women choice and pleasure to assemble in the "Gibb style," and with homage to the ethnic feeling of the day, he mixed florals with geometrics, tartans with cheques, and produced sunray pleated, beaded and fringed separates, all of which became very popular during the decade.

Gibb's output during the 1970s was of such a consistently high standard, it verged on couture. He was probably best known for his evening gowns, fabulous concoctions in floaty and exotic fabrics embellished with appliqué or heavily embroidered nets and lace, silks, brocades, and chiffon panels. In this vein was his 1976 hooded cape, a favourite shape, and voluminous smocks, and kimonos with coloured braid trims.

He confessed to a strong feeling for knitwear, which he attributed to his Celtic roots, and certainly he did produce some very fine knitted garments, reflecting an interest in soft, thinner fabrics, layered upon themselves, which originated with the Italian school of designers, notably the Missoni family. He also made some beautifully elaborate outfits in printed wool, often Liberty fabrics. By the mid-1970s he was creating stunning leather clothes, using the softest of skins for coats and jackets with wide collars and peplums.

Through most of the 1970s he ran a small wholesale business, but was forced into liquidation. A brief period of financial support followed, but it is doubtful whether Bill Gibb enjoyed the restrictions and deadlines implicit in such an arrangement.

The mid-1980s saw a brief recovery and, with a renewed collaboration with the knitwear designer Kaffe Fassett, Gibb showed a collection at the London Fashion Week in 1985: "Bill Gibb, the master of the decorative, showed for the first time in many years, opening with simply cut, richly coloured knitted suits and throws"—"a series of fairy tale exercises in the baroque, the beaded, and the burnished."

Gibb will best be remembered for his flights of fancy, and they make a unique contribution to 20th-century fashion. As *Vogue* said in 1962, in a feature called "Fresh Air in the Rag Trade": "For the first time the young people who work in the rag trade are making clothes which are relevant to the way they live....ours is the first generation that can express itself on its own terms." Gibb was very much a product of that time, a free spirit.

In Britain the commercial reality of the 1980s distinguished many ascendant stars. Bill Gibb was among them. He died in 1988.

—Elian McCready

GIGLI, Romeo.
Italian designer

Born: Castelbolognese, Faenza, Italy, 12 December 1949. **Education:** Studied architecture. Travelled internationally for ten years. **Career:** First collection for Quickstep by Luciano Papini; small collection of handknits, 1972; designer, Dimitri Couture, New York, 1978; Romeo Gigli label, from 1981; designer, Romeo Gigli for Zamasport, from 1984; designer to 1989, then consultant, Callaghan for Zamasport; signature fragrance launched, 1991; lower priced G Gigli sportswear line introduced, 1990. **Address:** Via Marconi 3, 20129 Milan, Italy.

Publications:

On GIGLI:

Books

Martin, Richard, and Harold Koda, *Orientalism: Visions of the East in Western Dress* (exhibition catalogue), New York 1994.

Articles

Kellett, Caroline, "Cue: New Talent. Take Two: Romeo Gigli," in *Vogue* (London), March 1986.

Romeo Gigli: Summer 1995. *Photograph by Max Vadukul.*

"Ferre and Gigli: Architects of a Modern Style," in *Elle* (London), October 1986.

Morena, Daniela, "The Solitary Chic of Romeo Gigli," in *Interview* (New York), December 1987.

"In diretta da Milano: I virtuosi difetti di Gigli," in *Donna* (Milan), February 1988.

Brubach, Holly, "The Master of Understatement," in *Vogue* (New York), May 1988.

"Designer Focus: Romeo Gigli," in *Cosmopolitan* (London), August 1988.

"Opinions: Romeo Gigli—'I've Had Enough of These Women Executives,'" in *Donna* (Milan), September 1988.

Gross, Michael, "Romeo, Romeo: The Monk of Milan," in *New York,* 5 December 1988.

Thim, Dennis, "Romeo and Paris: A New Love Story," in *Women's Wear Daily* (New York), 22 March 1989.

"Gigli's Genius," in *International Textiles* (London), May 1989.

Rafferty, Diane, "The Empress's New Clothes," in *Connoisseur* (New York), July 1989.

Petkanas, Christopher, "Romeo, Romeo," in *Harper's Bazaar* (New York), August 1989.

Pringle, Colombe, "Au pays de Romeo," in *Vogue* (Paris), August 1989.

Alexander, Hilary, "Romeo's Affairs," in *Women's Journal* (London), October 1989.

"The Designers Talk Passion, Whimsy and Picassos," in *ARTnews* (New York), September 1990.

Lesser, Guy, "Milan: One Night Art Extravaganzas," in *ARTnews* (New York), September 1990.

Gerrie, Anthea, "Designer Profile: Romeo Gigli," in *Clothes Show* (London), March 1992.

Buckley, Richard, "Romeo's Imbroglio," in *Mirabella* (New York), March 1992.

Spindler, Amy M., "Lagerfeld Tones Down the Look at Chanel," in the *New York Times,* 21 March 1995.

*   *   *

Romeo Gigli produces clothes that are always subtle and sophisticated. He blends a spectrum of muted colours with a fluid sense of cut and drape to the body to give a feeling of balance and harmony to all his designs, perhaps as a result of his architectural training. His prime influences are fine art and travel, both apparent in the Renaissance luxury of the fabrics he uses in some of his pieces and the mix of cultural influences discernible in their shaping and decoration. A soft sculptural beauty pervades both his day and eveningwear, with a talent for shaping clothes to the body in an elegantly flattering way without ever clinging too tightly or restrictively.

His womenswear encapsulates these qualities and has been very influential, having taken its cue from the elastic fluidity of dancewear to produce garments that are soft and feminine. Although Gigli's clothes are obviously designed for the busy modern woman, they are never merely a series of mix-and-match separates, nor indeed are they as ostentatious as the work of some of his Italian counterparts. His use of stretch fabrics and rich warm woollen suiting have inspired many imitators with their purity of cut and sensuous, body-skimming fit. The classical virtues of the body which pervade Gigli's work give a feeling of an evolutionary process to fashion, rather than a slavish following of seasonal dictates, and it is perhaps this innate classicism that gives his clothes a timeless air.

Some garments, like his richly enveloping embroidered coats, seem destined to become treasured collectors' items, passed on like heirlooms rather than falling victim to the fickleness often associated with fashion. His use of detailing is subtle and uncluttered, as in the minimal silhouette of the Empire line dresses and ballet-style wrap tops he introduced and popularized during the mid-1980s. When decoration is used it follows his restrained ideals of iridescent beauty: golden thread embroidered around the edge of a soft bolero jacket, evoking a feeling of the East, dull amber gold beads making a shimmering glow of fringing from waist to floor, or thousands of glittering gunmetal blue beads on a cocoon-like evening dress.

If Gigli's strength is perhaps his gently romantic womenswear, his menswear is nonetheless notable for the same kind of muted colours and sinuous cut, giving it a feeling of luxury without any obvious show of wealth. Suiting is again unstructured, working with the shape of the body rather than against it. His jackets are often high-buttoned, with an extra sense of depth and texture given to their rich wools by the subtle range of mossy greens, dull aubergine and bitter chocolate browns used to stripe the fabric. It is this kind of colour sense which, combined with clever mixing of shiny and matt fabrics, marks out all his work. Even his most formal menswear has an effortless elegance, and a fluidity of cut, which has made it unfailingly popular with discerning male customers.

Gigli has followed the increasingly popular notion of the diffusion range with the more practical daywear basics of his Gigli line, launched in 1990. Here the silhouette is bulkier, with rich berry coloured chenilles and sage and golden corduroys being used to produce a collection of classic zip-style cardigans, hooded tops, trousers, and soft leggings for men and women. Although less ethereally beautiful than much of his main collection, there is still the same signature use of contrasting fabrics and muted colours to produce a very tactile appeal through texture and shade.

An intelligent balance of all elements of design and choice of textiles makes Gigli's work uniquely sophisticated and beautiful. His subtlety of touch and soft sculptural forms have influenced all levels of design from the High Street up, especially during the last half of the 1980s, when his elasticated wrapped styles and pure tailoring were seen in every fashion magazine. His work has continued to develop along his self-assigned tenets of harmony and balance, while always retaining a feeling of sensuous luxury.

—Rebecca Arnold

GIRBAUD, Marithé & François.

French design team

Born: Marithé Bachellerie born in Lyon, France, 1942. François Girbaud born in Mazamet, France, 1945. **Career:** Business formed in 1965; showed first collection, 1968, first boutique selling Girbaud-designed jeans opened, Paris, 1969; Halles Capone boutique opened in Paris, from 1972; first US shop opened, Nantucket Island, Massachusetts, 1984. Jeaneration 21 line introduced, 1993; HiTech/HiTouch line developed, 1993; other lines include Complements for women, Closed for men, Reproductions for children, Complete Look accessories, Kelian-Girbaud shoes, Maillaparty, Compagnie des Montagnes et des Forêts, 11342, and Millesimes. **Address:** 12 bis rue des Colonnes du Trône, 75008 Paris, France.

Publications:

On GIRBAUD:

Articles

La Ferla, Ruth, "François & Marithé Girbaud: Beyond Fashion," in the *Daily News Record* (New York), 20 September 1982.

Daria, Irene, "After the Switch: The Girbauds," in *Women's Wear Daily* (New York), 21 December 1984.

Walsleben, Elizabeth C., "The Girbauds' Design Is in Their Jeans," in *California Apparel News* (Los Angeles), 11-17 July 1986.

Daily News Record (New York), 11 February 1987.

Bloomfield, Judy, "Girbaud: Keeping It Simple," in *Women's Wear Daily* (New York), 3 February 1988.

Martin, Richard, "Wordrobe: The Messages of Word and Image in Textile and Apparel Design of the 1980s, *Textile and Text,* 12 January-February 1989.

Martin, Richard, "The Eleventh Little Middle Ages: Signs and Chivalry in the Reconstitution of Medieval Dress in the 1980s," *Textile and Text,* 12 March 1990.

Vasilopoulos, Vicki, "The World According to Marithé and François," in the *Daily News Record* (New York), 3 May 1993.

*   *   *

Marithé and François Girbaud have created fashion that emanates from the street; that revels in design problems of cylinders, mutation, and reversibility; and that brings high-style aspirations to casual materials and effects. Their proclivity to oversizing seems akin to Japanese design and Middle Eastern and East Asian peasant garb. Their futurist vocabulary of tubes and metamorphosis can seem a highly conceptual eventuality worthy of Marinetti or Balla, but it also functions as fluid streetwear. Their deconstructivist bent, exposing the elements of garment manufacture, parallels Karl Lagerfeld at Chanel, but their medium is a more accessible casual wear that is almost hip-hop homeboy style in New York and *insouciant* flair for the "week-end" in Paris. In the casual jeans-based "look that they almost invented" (*Daily News Record,* New York, 11 February 1987), the Girbauds have been consistently the most innovative, experimental, concept-driven designers.

They have, in fact, commanded the avant-garde position in casualwear, customarily characterized by stasis, in the manner of high-fashion designers such as Jean-Paul Gaultier or Issey Miyake, thriving on conceptual development and change, yet never failing to represent the irrefutable leadership position in the field. Ruth La Ferla (*Daily News Record,* 20 September 1982) called François Girbaud "three parts fashion technician, one part theoretician," yet the Girbauds are also savvy interpreters, bringing cascades of Ninja-inspired pantaloons to the contemporary wardrobe with the practical note of snaps to gather the trousers at the ankles, rugged survival wear for fall 1983, and sophisticated 1940s and 1950s revival for spring 1988. Beginning in retailing, the Girbauds are as street smart as they are conceptually witty and ingenious. François Girbaud told Irene Daria (*Women's Wear Daily,* 21 December 1984), "We design from the streets. We start at the bottom and move up."

Their streets are global. Roomy drawstring trousers, loose shirts worn over the waist, and other styles evade traditional European and American notions of fit. The Amerasian collection for summer 1984—featuring Moudjahadin outfits with drawstring jackets and wide tubular trousers inspired by the Middle East and Afghanistan as well as boxy jackets inspired by China—typifies the eclectic, globe-trotting ethos of the Girbauds' design. For summer 1985, the Jet Laggers collection showed no straggling or fatigue: trousers called "Kaboul/Champs Elysées" could be worn in the Middle East or in Paris in their amplitude, cargo pockets adding to the engorged size, with a rustic combination of buttons and drawstrings. For fall 1986, big *dhoti* trousers and exotic cummerbunds and kilto-pants with voluminous tops and tapered legs combined East and West, exercise and boudoir. Shirts and jackets can flow with the simple grace of Brancusi and sensuous volume of balloon shapes in the couture, but the virtuoso accomplishment of the Girbauds is their repertory of trousers options for men and women, international in possibilities and strikingly original and inventive in realization.

The Girbauds are also aware of the history of Western dress. In menswear, their high-waisted Hollywood style for fall 1987 evoked the glamour era of movies in the 1940s. Their interest is also in materials, the softness of fabrications that lend themselves to the tubes and cones of form that they prefer, including quilting, fabric-backed leather, and a soft stonewashed denim. Another conceptual element of the Girbaud style is the didactic display of the garment's construction, one Momento Due jacket revealing its pattern components, other garments inscribed with all their wearing options. In addition to the language of clothing, the Girbauds also play with language itself, vocabulary, hieroglyphs, and alphabets appearing again and again in the collection. In interview, the designers like to suggest that their work is a perfect synthesis of their childhood preoccupations, she with creating doll clothes, he with American pop culture, films, and military outfits. There is a truth to that proposition, yet it also is unlikely that these two designers who began as retailers are only pursuing personal desires. The casual clothing they have created is imbued with heritage, even if that legacy is working clothing, while brought to the present in technical and even futuristic ways. In the evident conceptualism of their clothing (and in their bridge lines), they have expanded the market of casual clothing beyond the young, so that their clothes are as appropriate to the market of persons in their 30s and 40s as they are to the primary market for jeans of teens and 20s. They face many competitors in stylish casual wear for the young; they command the market for an abiding casual style for an older market, ever-increasing. *California Apparel News* (11-17 July 1986) reported accurately, "In an industry where fashion changes with each season, the Girbauds' clothes have kept the image of comfort while growing in style and versatility to become 'concept dressing.'"

—Richard Martin

GIROMBELLI, Arnoldo and Donatella. See **GENNY SpA.**

GIVENCHY, Hubert de.
French designer

Born: Hubert James Marcel Taffin de Givenchy, in Beauvais, 21 February 1927. **Education:** Studied at the Collège Felix-Fauré,

Beauvais and Montalembert; École Nationale Supérieure des Beaux Arts, Paris; Faculty of Law, University of Paris. **Career:** Worked in Paris for Lucien Lelong, 1945-46; for Piguet, 1946-48; for Jacques Fath, 1948-49; for Schiaparelli, 1949-51; established Maison Givenchy, 1952; president, Société Givenchy Couture and Société des Parfums Givenchy, from 1954. Fragrances include *De,* 1957; *L'Interdit,* 1957; *Givenchy III,* 1970; *L'Eau de Givenchy,* 1980; *Vetyver; Ysatis,* 1984; *Xeryus,* 1986; *Amarige,* 1991. **Exhibitions:** *Givenchy: 30 Years,* Fashion Institute of Technology, New York, 1982; *Givenchy: 40 Years of Creation,* Palais Galliera, Paris, 1991. **Address:** 3 avenue George V, 75008 Paris, France.

Publications:

On GIVENCHY:

Books

Lynam, Ruth, ed., *Paris Fashion: The Great Designers and Their Creations,* London 1972.
Fashion Institute of Technology, *Givenchy: 30 Years* (exhibition catalogue), New York 1982.
Milbank, Caroline Rennolds, *Couture: The Great Designers,* New York 1985.
Leese, Elizabeth, *Costume Design in the Movies,* New York 1991.
Givenchy: 40 Years of Creation (exhibition catalogue), with texts by Catherine Join-Dieterle, Susan Train and Marie-Jose Lepicard, Paris 1991.
Martin, Richard, and Harold Koda, *Bloom,* New York, 1995.

Articles

"Givenchy: 30 ans de couture," in *Textile Suisses* (Lausanne), April 1982.
"Givenchy Bucol," in *Vogue* (Paris), February 1985.
Arroyuelo, Javier, "La haute couture: Givenchy," in *Vogue* (Paris), March 1985.
"Le point sur les collections: Givenchy," in *L'Officiel* (Paris), September 1986.
Menkes, Suzy, "Strong Chanel Holds Up Couture's Falling Walls," in *International Herald Tribune* (Paris), 21 March 1995.
Spindler, Amy M. "Lagerfeld Tones Down the Look at Chanel," in the *New York Times,* 21 March 1995.

*   *   *

In 1992 Hubert de Givenchy celebrated his 40th anniversary as a couturier. Givenchy chose his vocation at the age of ten, and as a youngster admired the designs of Elsa Schiaparelli and Madame Grès. Later, after stints with Jacques Fath, Robert Piguet, and Lucien Lelong, he spent four years working for Schiaparelli, during which he designed the clothes sold in her boutique, many of them separates, an American idea new to Paris in the early 1950s, for which Givenchy gained a following. Although he is now appropriately acclaimed as a classicist and traditionalist, it was as an *enfant terrible* of sorts that Givenchy burst upon the couture scene in 1952, just weeks before his 25th birthday, with a novel collection based on separates, in which even eveningwear was conceptualized as a series of interchangeable pieces. Also noteworthy in that first collection was his generous use of white cotton shirting, which had an economic as well as an aesthetic rationale: the shirting was as

inexpensive as it was fresh-looking. The Bettina blouse which Givenchy has recently used as his signature was part of that cotton group; it had a convertible stand-up collar and ruffled sleeves with scalloped black eyelet trim. A few years later the blouse reappeared, in white organdie without trimming, a metaphor for the direction Givenchy's work would take: Simplify and refine were the watchwords.

Again and again in Givenchy's early years as a couturier, the appeal of his designs to young women was remarked upon. The symbol of that youthful appeal was Audrey Hepburn, an actress whose rise to fame paralleled his. Givenchy created the clothes worn by Hepburn in several of her most beloved roles, starting with *Sabrina* (1954) for which Edith Head won the Oscar for costume design and Givenchy received no credit. Although Head designed some of Hepburn's *Sabrina* wardrobe, the very soigné black tailleur and hat in which Sabrina returned from Paris, and the strapless white organdie gown embroidered with black and white flowers which was the envy of every young woman who saw the film, were both from Givenchy's collection. Typically, these were clothes which transformed Hepburn from charming gamine to paragon of chic sophistication. Similar transformations were at the heart of *Love in the Afternoon* (1957), *Funny Face* (1957), and *Breakfast at Tiffany's* (1961). By 1963, when *Charade* appeared, the gamine had finally grown into the sophisticate, and "the world's youngest couturier" had become the most elegant of classical couturiers. Hepburn remained Givenchy's muse for almost 40 years, the quintessential Givenchy client, flying into Paris from Switzerland to sit in the front row for his collections until shortly before her death.

Givenchy shared the ideal of creating a perfect, simple dress from a single line with his idol, Balenciaga. When the two men finally met, by accident, in 1953, they developed a relationship that was perhaps unique in the annals of couture, with Balenciaga giving Givenchy unprecedented access not only to his sketches, but also to his fittings and his workrooms. Starting in 1959, after Givenchy moved to 3 avenue George V, almost across the street from Balenciaga, they conferred daily, critiquing each other's sketches and collections. Their aesthetic affinity was such that when Balenciaga closed his couture salon, he referred his most valued clients to Givenchy.

Because of the emphasis on line rather than decoration, Givenchy's designs were easy to adapt, endearing him to the many American manufacturers who interpreted them. Givenchy himself helped to make his clothes accessible to a much wider market in the early, pre-licensing years, designing junior sportswear to be made by American manufacturers with American fabrics, for *Seventeen* and *Glamour* magazines. The caption for *Glamour*'s December 1955 cover, featuring a Givenchy sweater, speaks directly to the appeal of his designs: "The Givenchy marks: its young chic, ... meant for long, lean people in pipestem skirts ... for when they want to look casual in a worldly way."

Today Givenchy continues to enjoy designing fashions that make a woman look beautiful; his oeuvre bespeaks restraint and refinement, with gradual transitions from one season and style to the next. Although Givenchy still designs cotton separates, including some with Matisse-inspired patterns in his 40th anniversary collection, his designs have matured along with his original clientèle. Givenchy's creations begin with the fabric; his forte is choosing or developing Europe's most luxurious, yet tasteful, fabrics and embroideries in an expansive range of colours. From these he creates exquisite couture clothes that complement the lifestyles of a clientèle which has included several of the world's most elegant women. He is known for deceptively simple day dresses, superbly tailored suits, coats that are marvels of line and volume, sumptuous cocktail dresses or suits, extravagant evening dresses that are nevertheless eminently wearable, and hats that reveal his sense of whimsy and fantasy.

—Arlene C. Cooper

GODLEY, Georgina.

British designer

Born: London, 11 April 1955. **Education:** Putney High School, London; Thames Valley Grammar School, London; Wimbledon School of Art; Brighton Polytechnic; Chelsea School of Art. **Career:** Worked as art restorer, illustrator, mannequin maker, freelance designer, late 1970s; designer, Brown's, London and Paris, 1979-80; designer and partner, with Scott Crolla, Crolla menswear boutique, London, 1980-85; women's collection added, 1984; director and sole designer, Georgina Godley Ltd, with own label collections, from 1986. Also, member of British Fashion Council Designer Committee. Visiting lecturer in fashion in London and United Kingdom. **Collections:** Victoria and Albert Museum, London; Bath Costume Museum, Bath, England. **Address:** Georgina Godley (London) Ltd, 19a All Saints Road, London W11, England.

Publications:

On GODLEY:

Books

McDermott, Catherine, *Street Style: British Design in the 80's* (exhibition catalogue), London 1987.

Articles

"Cue: Talking to New Designers," in *Vogue* (London), November 1981.
"Scott Crolla & Georgina Godley of Crolla," in *Vogue* (London), November 1982.
Buckley, Richard, "Crolla's Counter Couture," in *DNR The Magazine* (New York), January 1985.
Brampton, Sally, "Fashion Wallahs," in *Vanity Fair* (London), April 1985.
Reed, Paula, "Spirit of Godleyness," in *The Sunday Correspondent* (London), 8 October 1989.
Sharkey, Alix, "On the Trail of the Elusive 'X' Factor," in *The Guardian* (London), 30 April 1990.
MacSweeney, Eve, "London After Dark," in *Harper's Bazaar* (New York), November 1990.

*   *   *

High-minded, serious, and intellectual in her approach to fashion design, Georgina Godley began her fashion career in the early 1980s in partnership with designer Scott Crolla. They emerged in a period when most of the important designers were making unisex, androgynous clothing. Gender barriers were being broken down, as

the difference between clothing for men and women seemed old-fashioned and no longer relevant. The media had latched on to this trend with its enthusiastic hyping of role swapping pop stars like Annie Lennox and trendy male/female design partnerships like Bodymap and Richmond/Cornejo, who were making clothes that anybody could wear. In opposition Georgina Godley returned to the idea of womanliness and the female form. She used floral-patterned chintz or sections of transparent gauze over breasts and referred to female fertility symbols in her advertising, such as a bridal figure gazing adoringly at the male phallus. She also plundered a traditional female submissiveness and medieval imagery in her research.

In many ways Godley has worked against fashion but, rather than taking an aggressively feminist anti-fashion stance, she is aesthetic in her reaction. Her first collection without Crolla was entitled Body and Soul. Featuring a body dress, a soul dress and a muscle dress, the collection celebrated the female form by exaggerating its proportions. Using fabric to drape, pad, pull, and stretch over the body, the results were often distortive and faintly erotic. The aim was simply to exemplify the beauty of a woman's body.

Never a commercial designer, Godley is primitive yet sophisticated: primitive in that she emphasizes and magnifies the primary female form; sophisticated in the fact that the result is often desexed by a high seriousness. The clothing is usually impractical, designed to be collected rather than worn: clinging, thin white cotton jersey dress inset with organza panels for maximum bodily exposure and a curved wire hem; a shaped underwear dress in which elements of corsetry distort curvaceousness; a pregnancy dress, padded to make the wearer look pregnant; a pair of hoof-bottomed trousers; and an infamous wedding dress with cutouts for the breasts.

Godley is similar in context to her contemporary, Azzedine Alaia, but whereas Alaia's clothes are erotic and sexy in their contouring of the body, Godley's clothes are womanly. Alaia's clothes create a curvaceous shape by reacting with the body. Godley's clothes often have their exaggerated shapes constructed onto the clothes.

Whether Godley can be termed a fashion designer is arguable because her clothes have often reacted against contemporary trends. Her work is designed for the connoisseur of specialist clothing, rather than mass public acceptance.

—Kevin Almond

GRÈS, Madame.

French designer

Born: Germain "Alix" Barton in Paris, 30 November 1903. **Education:** Studied painting and sculpture, Paris. **Family:** Married Serge Czerefkov, late 1930s; daughter: Anne. **Career:** Served three-month apprenticeship with Premet, Paris, 1930; made and sold *toiles* using the name Alix Barton, Paris, 1930s; designer, Maison Alix (not her own house), 1934-40; sold rights to the name Alix and adopted Grès, from husband's surname, 1940; director, Grès Couture, from 1942; accessory line introduced, 1976; ready-to-wear line introduced, 1980; retired, 1988. Perfumes include *Cabochard,* 1959, *Grès pour Homme,* 1965, *Qui Pro Quo,* 1976, *Eau de Grès,* 1980, *Alix,* 1981, *Grès Nonsieu,* 1982, and *Cabotine de Grès,* 1990. **Exhibition:** Madame Grès, Metropolitan Museum of Art, New York, 1994. **Awards:** Named Chevalier de la Légion d'Honneur, 1947; Dé d'Or Award, 1976; New York University Creative Leadership in the Arts Award, 1978. *Died* (in the South of France) *24 November 1993* (death not made public until December 1994). **Address:** 422 rue du Faubourg Saint-Honoré, 75008 Paris, France.

Publications:

On GRÈS:

Books

Perkins, Alice K., *Paris Couturiers and Milliners,* New York 1949.

Lynam, Ruth, ed., *Couture: An Illustrated History of the Great Paris Designers and Their Creations,* New York 1972.

Milbank, Caroline Rennolds, *Couture: The Great Designers,* New York 1985.

Steele, Valerie, *Women of Fashion: Twentieth-Century Designers,* New York 1991.

Petit Précis de Mode: Collections du Musée de la Mode, Marseilles 1992.

Martin, Richard and Harold Koda, *Madame Grès,* Metropolitan Museum of Art (exhibition catalogue), New York 1994.

Articles

"Grès Grey Eminence," in *Realities* (San José, California), July 1965.

"Mme. Grès," in *Current Biography* (New York), January 1980.

"Mme. Grès, Hélène de Paris," in *Jardin des Modes* (Paris), December/January 1980-81.

Villiers le Moy, Pascale, "The Timeless Fashions of Madame Grès," in *Connoisseur,* August 1982.

Sciaky, Françoise, "Lovely Grès," in *American Fabrics and Fashions* (New York), No. 128, 1983.

"Mme. Grès for the People," in *Connoisseur,* January 1985.

Cooper, Arlene, "How Madame Grès Sculpts with Fabric," in *Threads* (Newtown, Connecticut), April/May 1987.

"The Ionic Woman," in *Harper's Bazaar* (New York), September 1994.

Auchincloss, Eve, "Eminence Grès," in *Town & Country* (New York), September 1994.

Bernasconi, Silvana, "Mme. Grès," in *Vogue* (Italy), March 1994.

"New York: Grès Gardens," in *Women's Wear Daily* (New York), 1 November 1994.

Benaim, Laurence, "La Mort confisquée de Madame Grès," in *Le Monde* (Paris), 13 December 1994.

Deeny, Godfrey, "The Strange, Secret Death of Madame Grès," in *Women's Wear Daily* (New York), 14 December 1994.

Spindler, Amy M., "Surprising the Fashion World, to the Last," in the *New York Times,* 14 December 1994.

Mulvagh, Jane, "Grès Eminence," in *Vogue* (London), May 1995.

*   *   *

According to many who attended, the Madame Grès showings were exquisite anguish. With emendations up to the last minute by the designer, models would be delayed, garments could appear trailing strings, and long intervals might occur between the display of individual garments. At the very end, a flurry of models in the flowing draped jersey evening dress would come out on the runway in rapid succession, an abrupt finale to a halting presentation. Known

for designing with the immediacy of draping with cloth, Grès was the self-committed and consummate artist, never the agreeable couturière. Her white salon bespoke her austerity in engineering and her clarity in grace.

Grès shunned the promotional grace and personal identification of many fashion designers, insisting instead on rigorous attention to the clothing. First a sculptor, Grès depended upon sculptural insight even as she, in her most famous and signature form, brought the Louvre's statue of the *Nike of Samothrace* to life in clothing form. Grès's draped and pleated silk jerseys flatter the body with the minimalist and rationalist radicalism of 1930s design, but provide a classical serenity as well. The real achievement of the draped dresses is not their idyllic evocation, but their integrity. They are a unified construction, composed of joined fabric panels continuously top to bottom, fullest in the swirling flutes of the skirt, tucked at the waist, elegantly pinched through the bodice, and surmounted at the neckline—often one-shouldered—with the same materials resolved into three-dimensional twists and baker's-like *volutes.* Thus, Grès was creating no mere look-alike to classical statuary, but a reasoning exercise in formal abbreviation and a characteristically modern enterprise in imparting the body within clothing.

Grès, however, was never a one-dress designer. Her 1934 black Cellophane dress with a black-seal-lined cape (photographed by Hoyningen-Heuné) is, as *Vogue* described, a scarab, but with the cling of bias cut. Following a trip to the Far East in 1936, Grès created a brocaded "Temple of Heaven" dress, inspired by Javanese dance costume. Throughout the 1930s, she took inspiration from North Africa and Egypt. An exuberant *chinoiserie* evening coat of the 1930s, in an exquisite reversible textile by Raoul Dufy with embroidered hummingbirds, flares into shaped pagoda extensions. In the 1940s, after managing to keep her business alive through most of the war, Grès became interested in tailoring and created some of the most disciplined tailoring of suits for day in the 1940s and 1950s. By the 1960s and 1970s, Grès was translating the planarity of regional costume into a simplified *origami* of flat planes, ingeniously manipulated on the body to achieve a minimalism akin to sportswear. Ironically, she who exemplified the persistence of the couture treated the great dress with the modernist lightness of sportswear, and she who held out so long against ready-to-wear turned with a convert's passion to the possibilities of ready-to-wear in the 1980s, when she was in her late 80s. The personalizing finesse of a plait or wrap to close or shape a garment is as characteristic of Grès as of Halston or McCardell; her ergodynamics can bring fullness to the chest simply by canting sleeves backward so that the wearer inevitably creates a swelling fullness in the front as arms force the sleeves forward, creating a pouch of air at the chest.

For evening, Grès practiced a continuous antithesis of disclosure of the body and hiding the body in cloth. Even the Grecian "slave" dress, as some of the clients called it, seemed to be as bare as possible with alarming apertures to flesh. But the Grès draped dress, despite its fluid exterior, was securely corseted and structured within, allowing for apertures of skins to seem revealing while at the same time giving the wearer the assurance that the dress would not shift on the body. Conversely, more or less unstructured caftans, clinging geometries of cloth, could cover the wearer so completely as to resemble dress of the Islamic world, but in these instances the softness of structure complemented the apparent suppleness. Never is a Grès garment, whether revealing or concealing, less than enchanting. The slight asymmetry of a wrap determined by one dart, the fall of a suit button to a seaming line, or the

Madame Grès: Fall/Winter 1994/95. *Photograph by Jean Claude Lussier.*

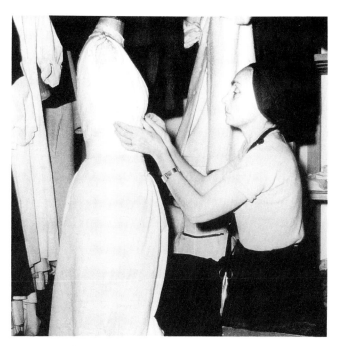

Madame Grès.

wrap of a draped dress to a torque of shaping through the torso, is an invention and an enchantment in Grès's inventive sculptural vocabulary.

History, most notably through photographers such as Hoyningen-Heuné and Willy Maywald, has recorded Grès's sensuous skills chiefly in memorable black-and-white images, but the truth of Grès's achievement comes in garden and painterly colors of aubergine, magenta, cerise, and royal blue, along with a spectrum of fertile browns. Her draped Grecian slaves and goddesses were often in a white of neo-classicism, but an optical white that has tended, with exposure to light, to yellow over time. Grès's streamlined architecture of clothing reminds us of the optimism of pure white dreaming, languorous physical beauty, and apparel that is perfect in comfort and image.

—Richard Martin

GRIFFE, Jacques.

French designer

Born: Near Carcassonne, France, in 1917. **Education:** Apprenticed with local tailor at age 16, later with the dressmaker Mirra, in Toulouse. **Military Service:** Completed required military service, 1936; served in World War II and was imprisoned for 18 months. **Career:** Employed at the house of Vionnet, 1936-39; opened own salon in rue Gaillon, 1941; with backing from Robert Perrier, opened Jacques Griffe Evaluation, in rue du Faubourg Saint-Honoré, 1947; contributed styles to Vogue Patterns, 1950-68. Fragrances: *Enthusiasme, Griffonnage, Mistigri.* Retired in 1968. **Exhibitions:** *Elégance and Création: 1945-1977,* Musée de la Mode et du Costume, Palais Galliera, Paris, 1977. **Collections:** Fashion Institute

of Technology, New York; The Costume Institute of the Metropolitan Museum of Art, New York; Musée de la Mode et du Costume, Palais Galliera, Paris.

Publications:

On GRIFFE:

Books

Perkins, Alice K., *Paris Couturiers and Milliners,* New York 1949.
Bertin, Célia, *Haute Couture,* Paris 1956 (as *Paris à la Mode,* New York and London 1956).
Pickens, Mary Brooks, and Dora Loues Miller, *Dressmakers of France,* New York 1956.
Delpierre, Madeleine, *Elegance and Creation: 1945-77* (exhibition catalogue), Paris 1977.
Milbank, Caroline Rennolds, *Couture: The Great Designers,* New York 1985.

*   *   *

One of the few designers capable of taking an idea from concept to realization, Jacques Griffe can sketch, drape, cut, and sew. He was taught sewing and encouraged towards haute couture by his mother, who placed him with the local tailor. Although he found the work tedious, he later recognized that it was the foundation for perfecting his craft. His skills were expanded when learning dressmaking at the house of Mirra, and he came to Paris with the proficiency needed for haute couture. His placement at the house of Vionnet exposed him to unique ways of cutting, and the belief that through draping, cloth would relate to and enhance the female body. He would adapt this philosophy for his own creativity. Temporarily delayed by World War II, he was at its end prepared to open his own house.

Vionnet gave him one of her dolls as encouragement solely to drape new models. Since he was equally able to sketch, he did both. Unlike his mentor, he was more of a colourist. He chose conservative colours—grey, brown, black, and checks in alpaca, wool jersey, crêpe, and broadcloth for suits and coats. Seen in them is the hand of a creative tailor. He was the first to introduce the boxy jacket, tunic, and cone-shaped coat in the 1950s. Aesthetically pleasing lines were imposed by his cut onto darts and seams used for fitting between the waist and shoulders. Decorative curved welt seams ending in an arrow were often used.

His day and afternoon dresses were softer than his suits. Sleeves were often kimono cut; bodices often blouson. Asymmetrical clothing ended in drapes, scarves, or bows at neck or hips. Pleating was used for insets of sunburst panels or for entire dresses. Polka dots were his favourite print. Evening dresses were also soft, supple, and feminine. Colours were pink, mauve, apricot, chartreuse, yellow, bright blue, navy, or black in chiffon, lamé, moiré, faille, satin, tulle, lace, taffeta, velvet, or brocade. High waisted or camisole bodices had halter, strapless, or shepherdess necklines. Gowns were sheaths, or had extremely elaborate full skirts, floor or ballet length that ended in harem or flounced hems. Skirt decorations were either shirred, bands graduated in size, repeated swirled ruffles, or petal-like panels of pleating.

—Betty Kirke

GRUPPO GFT.

Italian fashion manufacturer

Established in Turin, 1887, as Donato Levi e Figli for production of men's off-the-rack clothing. Company purchased in 1925 by the Rivetti family who formed Gruppo Finanziario Tessile in 1930. GFT USA established, 1971, GFT Mode Canada established, 1983. Manufacturers for Armani, Valentino, Ungaro, Montana, Dior, Abboud, and others. Also publisher or co-publisher: *Il libro del sarto,* 1987; *L'abito della rivoluzione,* 1987; *Giornale delle nuove mode di Francia e d'Inghilterra,* 1988; *Apparel Arts,* 1989; *Ready Made Fashion: An Historical Profile of the Clothing Industry in Great Britain, France and Germany,* 1990; *Women and Modernity: Fashions, Images, Female Strategies in Germany from the Beginning of the Century to the 1930's,* 1991; *Pagine e tavole del costume antico e moderno,* 1992; company sold, 1994. **Address:** Corso Emilia 6, 10152 Turin, Italy.

Publications:

On GRUPPO GFT:

Articles

Rosenbaum, Andrew, "Italy's Fashion Trillionaire," in *Avenue* (New York), September 1988.
Nardoza, Edward, "GFT Gets Set for the 90's," in the *Daily News Record* (New York), 31 May 1991.
Howard, Robert, "The Designer Organization: Italy's GFT Goes Global," in *Harvard Business Review* (Massachusetts) September/October 1991.
Bannon, Lisa, "Apparel Maker for Top Labels to Sell Big Stake," in the *Wall Street Journal* (New York), 6 April 1993.

*   *   *

Before being sold in 1994, Gruppo GFT (Gruppo Finanziario Tessile, or Textile Financial Group) had been the world's largest manufacturer of designer clothing, competing at the highest end of the fashion business—ready-to-wear designer collections, one step below made-to-order haute couture. Its success is rooted in its unparalleled history, its cutting edge technologies, well-organized labour practices and thorough understanding of fashion as an expression of contemporary culture. Innovative and flexible in an ever changing market, GFT has single-handedly revolutionized the way artistic clothing is conceived, manufactured, marketed, and distributed. Its heart is on the pulse of social trends and needs, keeping it way ahead of its competitors.

GFT's involvement in contemporary fashion goes beyond the business world. They are deeply committed to publishing rare treatises on the history of costume, organizing exhibitions with accompanying catalogues, and working with major contemporary artists. The exhibitions organized by Gruppo GFT, usually in conjunction with international events such as the Florentine Pitti Uomo shows, are a symbolic expression of this world and of GFT's relationship with contemporary creativity. For example, Pitti Uomo exhibitions have featured the work of Frank O. Gehry (1986); Arata Isozaki (1986-87); and Giulio Paolini (1988); for Moda Italia they collaborated with Haim Steinbach; and they sponsored major exhibitions of the work of Claes Oldenburg, Coosje van Bruggen, and Aldo

Rossi, who also designed their headquarters in Turin, Italy. In the 1990s, GFT helped to support the Rebecca Horn show at the Guggenheim Museum in New York.

Before 1887, most clothing was produced by cottage industry tailors who produced a small range of styles for local clients. In that year, however, in the Piedmont region of Italy, Donato Levi e Figli produced one of the first prototypes of a suit made to standardized measurements. In 1925 the Rivetti family purchased Donato Levi and Sons and created Finanziario Tessile (Fites), and by 1930 Gruppo Finanziario Tessile (GFT) was established as an organization to produce and market ready-made clothing. The company flourished in the period after World War II. While the rest of the world was still producing clothes in small cottage industry workshops, GFT laid the foundations for product-ready-made, mass-produced clothing and created a vast new market for this product.

The democratic, mass-market and homogeneous styles of the 1960s gave way in the 1970s to a new era of increased individualization to which GFT responded immediately. GFT entered the more upscale market by catering to a stable of looks and adding to its mass production activities exclusive prêt-à-porter collections by some of Europe's leading fashion designers. Today its core group consists of Valentino, Armani, Ungaro, and Claude Montana. GFT grew intellectually in their craft through their exchanges with these designers. Marco Rivetti, chief executive officer of GFT until 1994, has commented that the company learned much from its fashion artists: "From Armani, a great deal about the construction of jackets, from Valentino, the design of shirts and the use of silk." These designers were, in turn, drawn to GFT's commitment to quality workmanship, openness to new systems of production, and superb distribution system.

It is GFT's ability to operate in a global market that benefits the designers. Armani's classicism is less classic and more sporty for the GFT-USA lines. Giorgio Armani, Mani by Giorgio Armani, Valentino Boutique, Valentino Night, Valentino Uomo and others are adaptations of the European lines produced and marketed by the American division.

Since 1987 GFT has collaborated with American designer Joseph Abboud, recognizing his world market appeal. In 1988 they signed Andrew Fezza and in 1991 Calvin Klein—two other American designers who are truly of our time, with the artistic sensibility of understated elegance that is accessible to a variety of markets.

In 1993 GFT had 46 companies worldwide, 18 manufacturing plants, and some 10,000 employees. Before GFT was sold in 1994, the company's mandate and goals had remained the same as they were in 1887—to create fashion for the truly contemporary world, to pay attention to detail, to produce it efficiently, and to create the market and deliver the goods on time. The company met its goals by immersing itself in the history of the fashion arts and in the interrelation of the genre and other contemporary artforms. Such vision changed the way designers work, without disturbing the integrity or soul of their creations.

—Marianne Carlano

GUCCI.

Italian fashion and accessory house

Founded in Florence, Italy, as saddlery shop by Guccio Gucci (1881-1953), 1906, after family millinery business failed; became retailer of accessories, 1923. Subsequently became Società Anonima Guccio Gucci, 1939, Guccio Gucci srl, 1945, and Guccio Gucci SpA, 1982. Component companies include Gucci Shops, Inc. (USA), from 1953; Guccio Ltd, (UK), from 1961; Gucci et cie (France) and Gucci Boutique, from 1963; Gucci Ltd (Hong Kong), from 1974; Gucci Parfums, formed 1975, became Gucci Parfums SpA, 1982. Gucci shops opened in Florence, 1923; Rome, 1938; Milan, 1951; New York, 1953; Paris, 1963; Hong Kong, 1975. Sons: Aldo, Ugo, Vasco, and Rodolfo part of Gucci firm; Aldo Gucci (1909-90) head of firm, from 1960s; Maurizio Gucci (1948-1995) president of Gucci shops, beginning in 1989. Design/creative director: Dawn Mello, from 1990-91; Richard Lambertson, 1989-92; Tom Ford, 1994; firm acquired by Investcorp, 1993. **Exhibitions:** Costume Archive, Metropolitan Museum, New York. **Address:** 73 Via Tornabuoni, Florence, Italy.

Publications:

On GUCCI:

Books

Swann, June, *Shoes,* London 1982.
Alfonsi, Maria-Vittoria, *Leaders in Fashion: I grandi personaggi della moda,* Bologna 1983.
McKnight, Gerald, *Gucci: A House Divided,* New York 1987.

Articles

Crittendon, Ann, "Knock-Offs Aside, Gucci's Blooming," in *New York Times,* 25 June 1978.
"Artisans & Art: Gucci," in *Fortune,* 23 July 1984.
"Gucci, Taking Control," in *Women's Wear Daily,* 9 January 1987.
McKnight, Gerald, "Gucci: Hell for Leather," in *The Sunday Times Magazine* (London), 6 September 1987.

Gucci: The company's famous loafers.

Wolman, Karen, "Can an Outsider Fill Aldo Gucci's Loafers?," in *Business Week,* 30 November 1987.
Bernier, Linda, "Crazy for European Luxury," in *International Management,* December 1987.
"Gucci's Empire Splits a Seam," in *Time* (New York), 20 June 1988.
"Aldo Gucci," in the *New York Times,* 21 January 1989.
McKnight, Gerald, "Obituary: Aldo Gucci," in *The Independent* (London), 23 January 1990.
Rossant, John, "Can Maurizio Gucci Bring the Glamor Back?," in *Business Week,* 5 February 1990.
Beurdley, Laurance, "Gucci: La nouvelle génération," in *L'Officiel* (Paris), May 1990.
Jereski, Laura, "Watch Your Step, Cousin Paolo," in *Forbes* (New York), 15 October 1990.
Howell, Georgina, "Gucci Again," in *Vogue* (New York), December 1990.
"Gucci to Go," in *Harper's Bazaar,* February 1991.
Dudar, Helen, "Reversal of Fortune: Dawn Mello Gets Gucci Back on Its Feet," in *Working Woman,* April 1991.
Friedman, Arthur, "Aldo Gucci Dies at 84," in *Women's Wear Daily,* 29 May 1992.
Costin, Glyn, "Dawn Mello Revamping Gucci," in *Women's Wear Daily,* 29 May 1992.
Spindler, Amy M., "A Retreat from Retro Glamour," in the *New York Times,* 7 March 1995.

*   *   *

The illustrious name of Gucci began as a mark on leather goods produced in Florentine workshops for the young Guccio Gucci. Inspired by the grandiose luggage transported by wealthy guests to the Ritz Hotel in London, where Gucci worked in the kitchens, the young Italian returned to his native country where he began making leather luggage.

The characteristic double-G motif printed on the canvas that was introduced after World War II due to a shortage of leather—with its bold red and green bands on suitcases, bags, satchels, wallets, and purses—has become one of the most copied trademarks in the world, along with France's Louis Vuitton. The Florence-based company grew to international proportions in the post-war period, expanding its range to include clothing, perfume, household items such as decanters and glasses painted with the distinctive red and green bands, scarves, and other accessories. It was this indiscriminate expansion that ultimately proved to be detrimental to the name of Gucci for, as Yves Saint Laurent's director Pierre Bergé once said, "A name is like a cigarette—the more you puff on it the less you have left." Added to this, the proliferation of Gucci imitations which reputedly cost the company a fortune in legal fees, along with infamous conflicts between the volatile members of the Gucci clan, were detrimental to the high profile image the company needed to maintain. However, there were many Gucci items that became status symbols in their own right—namely, the Gucci loafer with its unmistakeable gilt snaffle trim which, according to the *New York Times,* was what carried the company to fortune. Biographer Gerald McKnight notes in his book *Gucci* (New York 1987) that the loafer even became the subject of well-worn jokes in the 1970s, when the name Gucci became as well known as household items such as the Hoover and Sellotape.

Having lost a great deal of the prestigious aura that is a vital element to the success of a luxury brand, the house of Gucci suffered bad press during the 1980s, as journalists hungered after stories of bitter rivalry between family members and their legal battles. It was an American woman, Dawn Mello, who would restore the luxurious image of Gucci when, in 1989, she was appointed executive vice-president and creative director of the company. Under control, the existing Gucci lines have been edited and refined and new items have been introduced. A clever combination of just the right balance of historical relevance (essential to a status name brand) with a real sense of modernity has restored Gucci to its former glory as a "must have" name. The Gucci clog was a sell-out item among the fashion *cognoscenti* in the summer of 1993. This became the most copied shoe style that season, and established the Gucci name not only as a purveyor of luxury goods but also as a serious contender in the high fashion stakes. In 1994, Gucci relocated all officers from Milan to Florence in another sign of renewal of tradition; Mello left to rejoin Bergdorf Gordman in New York.

—Catherine Woram

GUESS, INC.
American fashion house

Founded by Paul, Georges, Maurice and Armand Marciano, 1981. Eyewear line added, 1992. **Address:** 1444 South Alameda St, Los Angeles, California 90021, USA.

Publications:

On GUESS:

Books

Byron, Christopher, *Skin Tight: The Bizarre Story of Guess v. Jordache—Glamour, Greed, and Dirty Tricks in the Fashion Industry.*

Articles

Behar, Richard, "Does Guess Have a Friend in the IRS?," in *Forbes* (New York), 16 November 1987.
Byron, Christopher, "The Great Jeans War," in *New York,* 24 July 1989.
Welles, Chris, "A 'Blood War' in the Jeans Trade," in *Business Week* (New York), 13 November 1989.
"Blue Jeans," in *Consumer Reports,* July 1991.
Marlow, Michael, "Guess at 10: $550 Million and Growing," in *Women's Wear Daily* (New York), 20 December 1991.
Appelbaum, Cara, "Recession Killers," in *Adweek's Marketing Week,* 10 February 1992.
Marlow, Michael, "Guess on Rodeo: The Beverly Hills Cowboy," in *Women's Wear Daily,* 24 November 1992.
Wilson, Marianne, "Guess Ranch Lassos Rodeo Drive," in *Chain Store Age Executive,* January 1993.
"Guess? Solving Fashion Formula," in *Sporting Goods Business,* March 1993.
Ryan, Thomas J., "Marchianos Buy a Piece of Gitano," in *Women's Wear Daily,* 17 March 1993.
Strom, Stephanie, "Guess Names Specialty Store Chief to Lead its Retail Unit," in *New York Times,* 31 August 1993.

*   *   *

It is sometimes hard to see beyond the sexy image projected by Guess, Inc., co-created by Paul Marciano, to appreciate the fashions created by his brother, Georges; strong, denim-driven collections that belie the glossy images, for men, women, and children.

Criticized for being demeaning to women, the Guess advertisements have created such response that most American men or women can name at least one Guess girl. Supermodels Claudia Schiffer and Shana Zadrick are among the small group who can claim that being a Guess model has boosted them to celebrity status.

The line evokes a playful, body-conscious attitude. When Guess appeared on the scene in 1981, the designer jeans craze was all but over. However, the Marciano brothers created enough of a stir through their powerful advertising to induce a new trend in designer denims.

There is usually a seasonal theme to the Guess collections from year to year, but more often a Western tone will have been adapted in some shape or form.

It has taken more than a simple image and basic denim line to make this company so successful. Guess works hard to develop innovative treatments and washes for denim, all the while experimenting with colors other than indigo. This company pioneered the use of acid and enzyme washes for their textiles, abrading and brushing denims and twills and using different types of denims, such as ring-spun.

Businesswise, the company went through a bit of a shake-up in the mid-1980s, when the Nakash brothers of Jordache Enterprises challenged the Marciano brothers in a long legal battle over ownership of Guess. A stronger Guess, Inc. emerged from the fight, larger and more successful than ever before, with forceful entries into the men's and children's areas as well as a foray into a more sophisticated category for women, the Georges Marciano signature line.

The Marciano line offers more tailored dressing in the form of skirts, trousers, jackets, and related coordinates. Again, however, this is no ordinary power dressing line: the clothes are cut and fitted closer to the figure of a woman's body. Although these are clothes that can be worn in a work environment, the wearer must be a supremely confident woman—confident in her sensuality and in her position. These clothes are not for the meek.

The creative efforts of the Marciano brothers are based on an instinctive appreciation of the female form and an understanding of her sex-appeal, capitalizing on this knowledge in a business that is never far from fantasy.

—Lisa Marsh

GUILLEMIN, Olivier.
French fashion designer

Born: Paris, France, 10 July 1961. **Education:** Studied art history at Sorbonne, Paris, 1978-80, and Studio Bercot, 1979-80. **Career:** Assistant to Thierry Mugler, 1981; assistant to Azzedine Alaïa, 1982; consultant and free-lance designer for Woolmark, Claude Montana menswear, 1987-88. Launched own line, P.A.P. for women, 1987; label produced under Paco Rabanne, 1991. Specialises in ready-to-wear, accessories, fibers and yarns, and fabrics. Président du Comité Français de la Couleur, 1994. **Exhibitions:** *Fashion and*

Surrealism, Fashion Institute of Technology, New York, and Victoria and Albert Museum, London, 1984; *La Fée Electricité,* Musée d'Art Moderne, Paris, 1985; *Les Créateurs,* Villa Noaille, Hyères, France, 1992; *Mode et Liberty,* Musée des Arts Decoratifs, Paris, 1993; *CONTREX,* Musée des Arts Decoratifs, Paris, 1994; *Mode et Gitane,* Carousel du Louvre, Paris, 1994; *Voyage dans la Matière,* Grand Palais, Paris, 1994. **Collections:** Union Francaise des Arts du Costume, Paris; Musée de la Mode à Marseille, France. **Awards:** Bourse pour la Création, Ministère de la Culture, 1990; 1er Prix de la Création Woolmark, 1990. **Address:** 177 rue du Temple, 75003 Paris, France.

Publications:

On GUILLEMIN:

Articles

Hood, Frederique, "Fantastic Meteor," in *Elle* (New York), March 1992.
Valmont, Martine, "Les fils de l'été 1995," in *Journal du Textile,* 29 November 1993.
Hepple, Keith, "The Young and the Fun," in *DR: The Fashion Business* (London), 1 December 1990.
Voight, Rebecca, "Vanity Fairs," in *Paris Passion* (Paris), October 1990.
Molin Corvo, Roberta, "Vive la recherche!," in *Trends: Collezioni* (Modena, Italy), Spring/Summer 1995.

*

I chose the profession of fashion designer because it was for me the catalyst for my various creative aspirations—commercial, sociological, and technical. I consider myself an experimentalist and it is for this reason that my path is very varied. The way my career is developing leads me increasingly towards a more forward way of looking at clothes, in unusual fibers, threads, and fabrics, but also at the process of distribution and consumption. I think that we are at a turning point in our Western society and that in future years other codes of fashion are going to appear. It is with this in mind that I see my collections, which were elitist at the beginning of my career, becoming increasingly creatively democratic.

—Olivier Guillemin

*   *   *

Olivier Guillemin designs wearable art for the fashion follower who is looking ahead to the twenty-first century. One of a group of hot young Parisian stars, including Sophie Sitbon and Corinne Cobson, Guillemin frequently uses unusual and novel fabrics to surprising effect. His modern, futuristic designs often appear to signal a world where high technology will triumph over nature and the human body. Not unlike the 1960s science fiction looks of Paco Rabanne, with whom Guillemin is associated, these are designs which address today's postindustrial, satellite-linked global society head-on.

Guillemin demonstrated his stubborn individuality from the beginning by premiering his collections in odd and diverse places, from a gloomy medieval church, to an old-fashioned hotel ballroom, to the French Institute of Fashion. In accord with the spirit of his times, he has been allied with other fashion Deconstructivists; his

designs have been called "absurd and enchanting." He has created garments which seem to have been literally torn apart and then patched back together, or merely draped over the figure, or left ragged and unfinished. One collection included a frock made from pieces of a dress pattern secured haphazardly with strips of black tape, exposing bits of the model's skin. Other designs have appeared to be exploding, as in his dress of woven paper fabric covered with forbidding spiky cones radiating from the bodice. A backless, gathered, knee-length shift looked like a paint-spattered drop cloth picked up off an atelier floor and draped around an artist's model. He created a jumpsuit that had one leg missing; other garments have been shorn into bandage-like strips. As these examples show, Guillemin is not timid about exploiting the limits of what constitutes "clothing" within the fashion arena.

Unusual shapes, materials, and accessories are a Guillemin trademark, such as his black plastic jewelry designs coiling in arabesques around the model's face and body. One collection was comprised mainly of metallic fabrics, including metallic indigo toile suits and long, metallic toile coats. He has toyed with neon-colored fake fur, transparent plastics, and stretch Lycra. His fascination with industrial materials has resulted in long, rubberized apron dresses and black plastic luggage closures used as jacket fasteners. His clothes often seem to refer to a nonspecific, postapocalyptic era, where body covering will be cobbled together from the remains of urban destruction. But his fantastic designs have also been prescient; his use of neon colored fabrics easily predated the trend for those materials by several seasons.

When Guillemin was named ready-to-wear designer for Paco Rabanne in 1991, he expressed the desire to continue working on his own line and to keep the two collections separate. His own lines continued to display the inventiveness, unusual fabrics, and devotion to experimental fiber technologies for which he was already known. And, lest the impression be given that he is only a provocateur, he has also made quite wearable, (though still playful) clothing, showing that, both before and during his association with Paco Rabanne, Guillemin has not been entirely unwilling to create realistic styles.

Like many of his contemporaries, Guillemin revels in the exposure of the human form. The body is to be peeked at through a red plastic raincoat, peered at through slashed fabric, or simply left starkly nude. One example of his penchant for peekaboo styles was a most surrealist-inspired selection of garments resembling hedges in a topiary garden. Models paraded in clingy dresses and bodysuits covered with tightly-cut net and tulle patches, giving the impression of a group of cartoonish, mobile shrubbery. In the same show, ruffs of stiff tulle were positioned around the figure like fur, with bare portions of the midriff showing through, creating a look somewhat akin to an oversized poodle. (The finale to this event was a bare-breasted stilt-walker.)

For Paco Rabanne, Guillemin has drawn upon the famous looks of the 1960s with their references to space travel and their use of metallic stretch fabrics. He has even revived Rabanne's famed silvery plastic and metal disk garments. But Guillemin is not simply paying homage to the past, and has brought his unique vision to Rabanne with dramatic, well-cut modern garments that utilize the latest advances in microfiber technology and seem poised for the future. Whether creating his own phantasmagorical styles or updating the venerable but forward-looking designs of Paco Rabanne, Guillemin remains on the cutting edge.

—Kathleen Paton

Olivier Guilleman: Spring/Summer 1993.

HALSTON.

American designer

Born: Roy Halston Frowick in Des Moines, Iowa, 23 April 1932. **Education:** Studied at Indiana University, Bloomington, and at the Art Institute of Chicago to 1953. **Career:** Free-lance milliner, Chicago, 1952-53; window dresser, Carson-Pirie-Scott, Chicago, 1954-57; designer and hats division manager, Lilly Daché, New York, 1958-59; millinery and clothing designer, Bergdorf Goodman, New York, 1959-68; founder, designer, Halston Ltd, couture, New York, 1962-73; with Henry Pollack Inc, established Halston International, ready-to-wear, 1970; established Halston Originals ready-to-wear with Ben Shaw, 1972; Halston Ltd renamed Halston Enterprises, 1973, and company, design services and trademark sold to Norton Simon; menswear and signature fragrance introduced 1975; company sold to Esmark, Inc, and Halston III collection initiated for JCPenney Company, 1983; company sold to Revlon, 1986; company has been owned by Halston Borghese Inc. since 1992. **Exhibitions:** Fashion Institute of Technology, New York, 1991 (retrospective). **Awards:** Coty American Fashion Critics Award, 1962, 1969, 1971, 1972, 1974. *Died* (in San Francisco, California) *26 March 1990.* **Address:** Halston Borghese Inc., 767 Fifth Ave., 49th Floor, New York, New York 10153, USA.

Publications:

On HALSTON:

Books

Morris, Bernadine, and Barbara Walz, *The Fashion Makers,* New York 1978.
Milbank, Caroline Rennolds, *Couture: The Great Designers,* New York 1985.
Milbank, Caroline Rennolds, *New York Fashion: The Evolution of American Style,* New York 1989.
Gaines, Steven, *Simply Halston: The Untold Story,* New York 1991.

Articles

Newsweek (New York), 21 August 1972; 7 August 1989; 9 April 1990.
"The Private World of Halston," in *Harper's Bazaar* (New York), February 1973.
Sheppard, Eugenia, in the *New York Post,* 7 February 1973.
"Couturier's Coup," in *Time* (New York), 22 October 1973.
Bowles, J., "Will Halston Take Over the World?," in *Esquire* (New York), August 1975.
Lemann, N., "Halstonization of America," in *Washington Monthly* (Washington, D.C.), July 1978.

Belkin, Lisa, "The Prisoner of Seventh Avenue," in the *New York Times Magazine,* 15 March 1987.
Darnton, Nina, "The Inimitable Halston: The Legendary Designer Breaks the Silence on his Current Dilemma," in *Newsweek* (New York), 7 August 1989.
Morris, Bernadine, "Halston, Symbol of Fashion in America in the 70s," [obituary] in the *New York Times,* 28 March 1990.
"Halston: An American Original," [obituary] in *Women's Wear Daily* (New York), 28 March 1990.
Los Angeles Times, 28 March 1990.
Mulvagh, Jane, "Obituary: Halston," in *The Independent* (London), 29 March 1990.
People (Chicago), 9 April 1990.
Brady, James, "A Prince of the Captivity," in *Advertising Age,* 16 April 1990.
"Halston," [obituary] in *Current Biography* (New York), May 1990.
Minnelli, Liza, and Polly Mellen, "Halston: 1932-1990," in *Vogue* (New York), July 1990.
Martin, Richard, and Harold Koda, "Some Modernist Principles in Presenting *Halston: Absolute Modernism,*" *Textile & Text* (New York), 14 January 1991.
Gaines, Steven, "The Man Who Sold His Name," in *Vanity Fair,* September 1991.
"Halston: Modernist Master," in *Connoisseur* (New York), November 1991.

*   *   *

The life of Roy Halston Frowick was marked by deeply American directness. He became one name known internationally. But it was, after all, his name in a concise form. In a nonchalant elegance that stripped away all that was superfluous in his life and art, Halston was the creation of his own obsessive, workaholic achievements. In the markedly public world of fashion and in his own dialectic between gregarious social extrovertism and sincere, almost hermetic, privacy, Halston provided a personal contradiction. Gatsby in fashion sovereignty, laconic but inexorable personal charisma, and tragic acumen to cultural need and moment, Halston was in the 1970s and early 1980s not only the supreme American fashion designer, but the quintessential one.

Again and again, Halston would say to the press, as he told Eugenia Sheppard in the *New York Post* (7 February 1973), "Women make fashion. Designers suggest, but it's what women do with the clothes that does the trick." While this modest disavowal is, in part, canny public relations, granting to the client or potential client the creativity of dress, Halston believed his statement. He recognized and accounted for the women who would wear the clothing as much as for his own creation and acknowledged a partnership between designer and wearer. One aspect of the partnership was Halston's continuous synergy with important clients, beginning with his millinery work which, after all, started from the top to reconcile per-

213

Halston.

sonal attitude and physiognomy with apparel. Later, even as the "total designer" he strove to be and so successfully became, Halston's personal affection for and connections to clients in show business, design, dance, and public life gave him an intimate and abiding affiliation with the wearer. And when he sought to dress every woman, there was a grounded, natural aspect to Halston that readily reminded the wearer that this cryptically simple, *soigné* designer was born in Des Moines, Iowa and raised in Evansville, Indiana.

If Halston ascribed the social function to the wearer, he himself was the consummate creator of the garment in formal terms and his work corresponds to the taciturn discourse of minimalism in American arts. His geometry of design, employing bias as the three-dimensional element that causes the geometry to drape splendidly on the body, was as conceptual as that of Vionnet, if even more abstemious. Some design problems were played out in paper origami, as he created twisted forms in white paper on a black lacquer tray. Discovering such form, Halston projected it onto the body with absolute integrity, cutting as little as possible, and allowing the simplicity of the two-dimensional design to be felt, even as it assumes form on the body.

Likewise, Halston's colours were as selective as Mondrian's, preferring ivory, black, and red, but knowing that fuchsia, electric blue, or deep burgundy could provide accent and emphasis. Of textiles, he worked with cashmere, silk and rayon jerseys, double-faced wools, and Ultrasuede as chosen aesthetic media. His Ultrasuede shirtwaist, which sold 60,000 copies, was one of the most popular dresses in America in the 1970s: in its utmost simplicity, the same dress could be worn in a multitude of ways (collar up or down, sleeves down or rolled, front buttoned or unbuttoned) to allow each woman to wear it in her own personal style. Its success was in that *tabula rasa* plainness and the attraction of contributing one's own style to the garment, as well as the probity of Halston's colour choices and the putative convenience of Ultrasuede, even to its claim of being able to be tossed into the washing machine. His rich double-faced wool coats were the luxury of colour fields, an art brought to apparel; his athletic looks in bodysuits and sports-inspired dressing were as much an ancipation of the late 1980s American fashion as they were renewals of 1940s and 1950s Claire McCardell. He could dress a Martha Graham dancer as readily as he could create a mass-market dress.

Halston's eveningwear was acclaimed for its glittery, gossamer shimmer, but often unacknowledged for the same principles of simplicity. Working on the bias, Halston caressed the body with spiralling scarfs of form. His one-piece, held-at-the-shoulder "orange-peel" dress was the product of a deft hand, like that of the fruit peeler. His evening jackets were often nothing more than rings of material twisted into cocoon fantasies. As Liza Minnelli has said of Halston, he made one feel comfortable and feel beautiful.

Merging the special chic of a custom business and a vast ambition to dress everyone in the world was Halston's high goal, briefly achieved in the late 1970s and early 1980s. But business changes ignited the American Icarus's wings and he plummeted to earth, a loss and an angel ahead of his time to all who might later reconcile high fashion and mass marketing.

—Richard Martin

HAMNETT, Katharine.

British designer

Born: Gravesend, 1948. **Education:** Studied at Cheltenham Ladies College and at St Martin's School of Art, London, 1965-69. **Family:** Children: Samuel and William. **Career:** Co-founder, Tuttabanken Sportswear, London, 1970; free-lance designer, London, Paris, Rome and Hong Kong, 1970-79; Katharine Hamnett, Ltd founded, London, 1979; menswear line introduced, 1982; launched "Choose Life" shirts, 1983; flagship London shop and three others opened, 1986. **Awards:** International Institute for Cotton Designer of the Year Award, 1982; British Fashion Industry Designer of the Year Award, 1984; Bath Museum of Costume Dress of the Year Award, 1984; Menswear Designer of the Year Award, 1984; British Knitting and Clothing Export Council Award, 1988. **Address:** 202 New North Road, London N1 7BJ, England.

Publications:

On HAMNETT:

Books

Coleridge, Nicholas, *The Fashion Conspiracy,* London 1988.

Articles

Hall, Dinah, "Streets Ahead," in *You* magazine of the *Mail on Sunday* (London), 21 August 1983.

Katharine Hamnett: 1994/95. *Photograph by A. Albertone.*

Katharine Hamnett: 1984.

Warner, Marina, "Counter-couture," in *Connoisseur* (London), May 1984.

"Katharine Hamnett: La mode pour sauver le monde," in *Elle* (Paris), September 1984.

Etharington-Smith, Meredith, "New Guard/Old Guard: Fashion Designers Katharine Hamnett and Jean Muir," in *Ultra,* December 1984.

Buckley, Richard, "Katharine the Great: Miss Hamnett Talks," in *DNR: The Magazine* (New York), February 1985.

Polan, Brenda, "Under the Hamnett Influence: 12 Pages of Key Looks for Summer," in *Cosmopolitan* (London), March 1985.

Roberts, Yvonne, "The Queen of Radical Chic," in the *Sunday Express Magazine* (London), 9 March 1986.

"Designer Reports. Summer 87. London: Katharine Hamnett," in *International Textiles* (London), December 1986.

"Katharine Hamnett Interview," in *Art and Design* (London), December, 1980; December 1986.

Franklin, Caryn, "Power Dressing," in *i-D* (London), February 1987.

"Be Bardot Says Hamnett," in *The Sunday Times Magazine* (London), 1 February 1987.

Mower, Sarah, "British Style: The Designer Star Katharine Hamnett," in *Vogue* (London), February 1987.

Cottam, Francis, "Katharine Hamnett," in *Unique* (Bridgeview, Illinois), No. 3, 1987.

Rowe, Gillian, "Katharine Hamnett," in *The Observer* (London), 31 January 1988.

"Katharine Hamnett Goes It Alone in London," in *Fashion Weekly* (London), 24 March 1988.

"Hamnett: Retailing Push for '89," in *Fashion Weekly* (London), 5 May 1988.

"Bertelson Sued by Hamnett," in *Fashion Weekly* (London), 30 June 1988.

"Blair Quits Beleaguered Bertelson as Hamnett Sues," in *The Independent* (London), 8 July 1988.

Filmer, Deny, "Katharine Hamnett," in *Cosmopolitan* (London), July 1988.

Cottam, Francis, "Katharine Hamnett," in *Clothes Show* (London), November 1988.

"Perspectives," in *Blueprint* (London), November 1988.

Manser, José, "Nigel's Fishing Trip," in *Designers' Journal* (London), January 1989.

Hume, Marion, "Hamnett Soars to Designer Stardom," in *The Sunday Times* (London), 5 March 1989.

"Euro Hamnett," in *Cosmopolitan* (London), October 1989.

"Sex, Money and Golden Oldies: Profile: Katharine Hamnett, Fashion's Fireball," in *The Independent* (London), 14 October 1989.

Mathur, Paul, "Hamnett," in *Blitz* (London), November 1989.

Mills, Simon, "Katharine Hamnett," in *Sky* (London), February 1990.

Polan, Brenda, "Katharine's Cutting Edge," in *The Independent* (London), 10 March 1991.

Goodkin, Judy, "Fashion Rebel with a Cause," in *The Sunday Times* (London), 5 May 1991.

*   *   *

A British designer as much recognized for her political and environmental beliefs as she is for her catwalk collections, Katharine Hamnett designed some of the most plagiarized fashion ideas in the 1980s. Hamnett set up her own company in 1979 after freelancing for various European companies for ten years. Although the designer claims she never intended to become involved in the manufacturing side of the fashion industry, preferring to concentrate solely on design, she was often, as a free-lancer, badly treated. In 1979 she produced her own collection under the Katharine Hamnett Ltd label, of which six jackets were taken by the London fashion retailer, Joseph Ettedgui, and which subsequently sold out. Hamnett's early collections utilized parachute silk, cotton jersey, and drill, which she cut as functional unisex styles, based on traditional workwear that became her hallmark and, like many of her designs, spawned a thousand imitations.

Her nomination as British Fashion Industry Designer of the Year in 1984 testifies to her influence in the early years of that decade. One of Hamnett's most influential designs was the idea of the slogan T-shirt bearing statements about political and environmental issues in bold print on plain white backgrounds. Perhaps the most famous is the one which read "58% Don't Want Pershing" that Hamnett wore when she met Margaret Thatcher at a Downing Street reception in 1984. Like Coco Chanel before her, Hamnett sees imitation as a form of flattery—particularly in the case of her slogan T-shirts which, she says, were meant to be copied to help promote her cause. Another example of Hamnett's obsession with politics was seen in the launch of her own magazine, *Tomorrow*, in 1985, in which the designer attempted to portray both fashion and political views. Unfortunately this combination was not a great success and the magazine folded after the first issue.

By 1986 a change was evident in Hamnett's design as she embraced the theme of sex as power with her Power Dressing collection aimed at the post-feminist woman. Since that time her collections have become decidedly less workwear-oriented, to which critical reactions have been somewhat mixed.

Although the slogan T-shirts are no longer part of her collection, Hamnett's devotion to environmental issues continues to play an important role in her approach to fashion design. One project in which Hamnett became involved is the Green Cotton 2000 campaign, launched in conjunction with the Pesticides Trust in 1990, which aims to reduce the harmful waste and discharged effluent produced by the textile industry. The power of the media is seen by Hamnett as a vital instrument in her personal campaign for the protection of the environment, and her fashion has provided an ideal vehicle. Hamnett admits that she has more publicity than she needs to sell the clothes themselves, and can afford to use her influence as a designer to promote her own causes. However, while undoubtedly a major force in British fashion during the 1980s, along with John Galliano and Vivienne Westwood, her influence as a designer has declined in recent years.

Hamnett's most important contribution to fashion, and the one for which she will best be remembered, is her use of clothing as a vehicle for political and environmental concerns. Her success as a fashion designer has enabled her ultimately to pursue her commitment to these issues.

—Catherine Woram

HARDWICK, Cathy.

American designer

Born: Cathaline Kaesuk Sur, in Seoul, Korea, 30 December 1933. **Education:** Studied music in Korea and Japan. Immigrated to the United States, 1952; naturalized, 1959. **Family:** Married Anthony Hardwick in 1966 (divorced); four children. **Career:** Free-lance designer and boutique owner, San Francisco, c.1966-70; knitwear designer, Alvin Duskin, San Francisco, 1960s, and Dranella, Copenhagen; moved to New York, 1960s; sportswear designer, Pranx, New York; designer, Cathy Hardwick 'n' Friends, New York, 1972; president, designer, Cathy Hardwick Ltd., New York, 1975-81, and Cathy Hardwick Design Studio, New York, from 1977; company reorganized, 1988; also, sportswear designer for Sears Roebuck and Co., from 1990. **Awards:** Coty American Fashion Critics Award, 1975. **Address:** 215 West 40th Street, New York, New York 10018, USA.

Publications:

On HARDWICK:

Books

Morris, Bernadine, and Barbara Walz, *The Fashion Makers,* New York 1978.
Milbank, Caroline Rennolds, *New York Fashion: The Evolution of American Style,* New York 1989.

Articles

O'Sullivan, Joan, "She's a Natural," in *Living Today* (Wheaton, Illinois), 16 September 1977.
Colborn, Marge, "East Village with Seoul: A Hands On Approach to Fall," in the *Detroit News* (Michigan), 4 May 1986.
Daria, Irene, "Cathy Hardwick: Craft, Compromise and Creation," in *Women's Wear Daily* (New York), 3 August 1987.
Klensch, Elsa, "Cathy Harwick—Success with Style," in *Vogue* (New York), June 1988.

*   *   *

Cathy Hardwick designs ready-to-wear for the audience she knows best—the modern career woman with an active lifestyle. There is a certain spirit and success about Hardwick's designs that come from this defining relationship to the clothing and its purpose. Hardwick's collections consistently offer women clothing with ease and simplicity, appealing to the young and young-minded spirit of the confident, self-assured businesswoman. Her clothing is not merely a somber uniform, but rather it has an air of wit and sophistication that makes it fun, worn by the stylish young woman who is secure with her life and is moving in a positive direction.

Cathy Hardwick was recognized early in her career as a talented young designer involved in creating simplistic, modern clothing. In the late 1960s she began designing knitwear for Alvin Duskin in San Francisco. The designs were well received and commercially successful. Soon after, she developed her own company and continued to design knitwear as a part of her collections throughout the 1970s and 1980s. She continues to design under her own label in New York, using natural fibers almost exclusively.

"Know your physical type and personal style, and be true to it. Any current look can be adapted in silhouette, scale and color so it's right for you. You have to feel comfortable. The most fabulous clothes won't work if you're self-conscious," says Cathy Hardwick (*Harper's Bazaar,* February 1978).

Hardwick's design success is a result of the masterful execution of her pure and basic principles—neutral colors and simplicity of form. By centering her collections around basic, neutral colors and relating the colors of current collections to previous ones, the wearer can develop a wardrobe of pieces that work together. Her designs recognize fashion trends but always retain a clean, simplistic style that is distinctly her own. Hardwick's clothing is associated with the modern woman's ability to go from an effective day at work to an evening out with minimal changes.

A 1980 advertisement for B. Altman and Co. shows her collection coordinating in different ways to suit the style of the potential wearer. The ad reads: "Hardwick's done a forward looking collection that lets you choose the new length you like, a little or a whole lot shorter. Another fine fashion point you should notice: These separates are all cut and colored (in magenta and black) so you can build your own new-decade pants-set." The philosophy of personal style and selection is one that is apparent in Hardwick's collections throughout her career.

Hardwick's collections are based on strong, simple shapes reminiscent of traditional Korean clothing. She was born to a Korean family of diplomats and financiers including her grandfather, who was ambassador to France. Hardwick's clothing reflects her lifelong exposure to and depth of understanding of the fusion of Eastern and Western styles. The *chinoiserie* elements in the designs seem to be a part of the total vision and philosophy that she has about clothing rather than a motif that is applied on Western fashion. In her first formal show in New York in 1974, Hardwick showed *obi* style wrapping in the closures of her skirts and trousers along with oriental prints and accessories. In 1975, she showed the effectiveness of shaping a "Big Dress" with an *obi*-inspired tie. Earlier Hardwick incorporated frog closures in her mandarin collared jacket for a more direct use of the Eastern look. The mandarin collar and frog closures are used again in her spring 1994 collection on light and easy shaped tops.

—Dennita Sewell

HARP, Holly.

American designer

Born: Buffalo, New York, 24 October 1939. **Education:** Attended Radcliffe College; studied art and fashion design, North Texas State University. **Family:** Married Jim Harp, 1965 (divorced, 1975); son: Tommy. **Career:** Opened first boutique on Sunset Strip, Los Angeles, 1968; opened in-store boutique, Henri Bendel, New York, 1972; developed wholesale collection, 1973. Also: designed for Simplicity Patterns, Fieldcrest Linens, and Hollywood films including *Cabaret, Sleeper,* and *She Devils. Died April 1995.* **Address:** 8924 Lindblade Street, Culver City, California 90232, USA.

Publications:

On HARP:

Books

Milinaire, C., and C. Troy, *Cheap Chic,* New York 1975.
Morris, Bernadine, and Barbara Walz, *The Fashion Makers,* New York 1978.
Stegemeyer, Anne, *Who's Who in Fashion,* New York 1980.
Lobenthal, Joel, *Radical Rags: Fashions of the Sixties,* New York 1990.

Articles

"Holly's Harp," in *Women's Wear Daily* (New York), 7 November 1974.
"Rainy Day Women?," in *People* (New York), 21 February 1977.
Sajbel, Maureen, "The Unsinkable Holly Harp," in *Women's Wear Daily* (New York), 6 January 1987.
"Holly Harp" [obituary], in *Women's Wear Daily* (New York), 26 April 1995.

*

I have been designing clothes since the late 1960s. I always try to remind myself that I am dressing a woman's soul as well as her body. Souls and bodies do best when they are relaxed, fluid, and comfortable. They love to play "dress-up." They love a good laugh as well as perfect quiet and softness. I hope my clothes reflect a woman's soul.

—Holly Harp

*   *   *

Many students are torn between the glamour of stage or film design and high fashion. Holly Harp was able to merge both her love of costume and fashion into a professional career that has been stable and successful for more than 25 years. Harp went with an early instinct after designing sandals on a whim, and returned to college with her sights set on becoming a designer. She studied in the theatre department and worked on her fashion degree. Her style is dramatic, feminine, and refined.

Harp moved to the West Coast during the height of hippiedom in 1966. San Francisco hippies tended to borrow street styles and recycle clothing salvaged from the local Goodwill, while Los Angeles, where Harp set up shop, was more interested in marketing styles and trends in the form of new designs. This was more of a "rich hippie" look. Harp was inspired by the youthful street fashions and was referred to by the *Los Angeles Times* as the city's "doyenne of feathers and fringe" (Lobenthal, New York, 1990). Her rock star clients included Janis Joplin and Grace Slick, who loved Harp's wonderful batiks, feathers and hand-dyed fabrics. Harp's clothes suited the tastes of the youthful population who loved psychedelic colors and melodramatic effects.

It was more than being in the right place at the right time. Harp began to distil her designs into her own personal expression. During the 1970s there was more emphasis on the body. The soft matte jersey Harp experimented with became a signature fabric along with chiffon. There was a continuation of using beadwork, flowers, feathers, and airbrushed designs but with a softer, refined touch. Harp used complicated draping techniques to emphasize feminine qualities rather than the prevailing minimal approach.

Harp became known for making fabulous dresses that attracted the attention of the Hollywood élite. Her customer list reads like a Who's Who: Liza Minelli, Jane Seymour, Lauren Hutton, Bette Midler, Diana Ross, Jane Pauley, and Sally Field are just a few. Her clients also include a long list of famous male customers such as Ryan O'Neal, Jon Voight, and Jack Nicholson, who select Harp's clothing for the women in their lives. Some Harp originals have appeared in Hollywood films as well. Harp successfully challenged the glitzy Hollywood image with nostalgically beautiful designs.

The ability to create clothing with both romantic and classic qualities has carried Harp through the 1980s into the 1990s, and her work continues to be in demand. By limiting her production and not overextending herself, Harp survived with her design integrity intact.

—Myra Walker

HARTNELL, Norman.

British designer

Born: London, 12 June 1901. **Education:** Studied at Magdalen College, Cambridge, 1921-23. **Career:** Assistant to Court Dressmaker, Mme. Désiré, 1923; opened own dressmaking studio, London, 1923; first Paris showing, 1927; appointed dressmaker to the Royal Family, 1938; designed women's uniforms for the Royal Army Corps and the Red Cross; introduced ready-to-wear lines, from 1942; also designed for Berkertex, from the late 1940s, for *Women's Illustrated* magazine, 1950-60s, and lingerie line for Saks Fifth Avenue, 1950s; theatrical designer, 1923-60s. **Exhibitions:** *Norman Hartnell, 1901-1979* (retrospective), London, 1985; *Norman Hartnell* (retrospective), Brighton, 1985; *Hartnell: Clothes* *by the Royal Couturier, 1930s-1960s* (retrospective), Bath, 1985-86. **Awards:** Officier d'Academie, France, 1939; first Royal Warrant received, 1940; Neiman Marcus Award, 1947; appointed Member of the Royal Victorian Order, 1953; appointed Knight Commander of the Royal Victorian Order, 1977. *Died* (in Windsor, Berkshire), *8 June 1979.*

Publications:

By HARTNELL:

Books

Silver and Gold, London 1955.
Royal Courts of Fashion, London 1971.

On HARTNELL:

Books

Brighton Art Gallery, *Norman Hartnell* (exhibition catalogue), Brighton 1985.
Kennett, Frances, et al., *Norman Hartnell, 1901-1979* (exhibition catalogue), London 1985.
McDowell, Colin, *A Hundred Years of Royal Style,* London 1985.
Milbank, Caroline Rennolds, *Couture: The Great Designers,* New York 1985.

Articles

Wyndham, Francis, "The Pearly King," in *Vogue* (London), September 1960.
Glynn, Prudence, "Hartnell: The Norman Conquest," in *The Times* (London), 6 January 1977.
Sinclair, Serena, "For Sir Norman, At Last, a Royal Reward," in *The Daily Telegraph* (London), 10 January 1977.
Hassian, Nicky, "Sir Norman Hartnell," in *Ritz* (London), No. 3, 1977.
Laurance, Robin, "But Will Sir Norman Arise?," in *The Guardian* (London), 2 March 1977.
Scroggle, Jean, "The Norman Conquests," in *Homes and Gardens* (London), June 1985.
Hoare, Sarajane, "Relaunch of Ready-to-Wear at Hartnell," in *The Observer* (London), 9 March 1986.
McDowell, Colin, "The Rise of the House of Hartnell," in *The Guardian* (London), 13 March 1986.
Williams, Antonia, "Hartnell Then and Now," in *Vogue* (London), August 1986.
Hume, Marion, "Heart to Hartnell," in *Fashion Weekly* (London), 15 January 1987.

*   *   *

Norman Hartnell began his fashion career working as an assistant to the extravagant society couturière Lucile. Through his exposure to this rarefied world of fashion, gossip, decoration, and illicit romance, he was inspired to open his own dressmaking business in 1923, establishing what has become one of the best-known and longest-running couture houses in Britain. Situated in the heart of London's Mayfair, the house on Bruton Street has always had an

air of splendour. A graceful staircase, panelled with mirrors, leads up to the splendid salon where gilt mirrors and two giant crystal chandeliers create an air of tranquillity. Seated on their gilt-encrusted chairs, society hostesses, actresses, film stars, debutantes, and royalty have watched countless collections float elegantly by.

The early collections shown in both London and Paris quickly established Hartnell's reputation for lavishly embroidered ballgowns in satin and tulle, fur trimmed suits, and elegantly tailored tweed day ensembles. His first wedding dress fashioned from silver and gold net was a showstopping finale to an early collection and was described as "the eighth wonder of the world" when worn by the bride of Lord Weymouth. Other early commissions included a 1927 wedding dress for romantic novelist and socialite Barbara Cartland, and informal clothes for actress Tallulah Bankhead who scandalized 1920s London with performances both on and off-stage.

Hartnell's clothes often stood apart from fashion, owing a greater allegiance to costume. This was no doubt fuelled by his early experience designing theatrical productions whilst at Cambridge University. He drew inspiration from the saucy French paintings of Watteau and Boucher, purity of line from Italian masters like Botticelli and painters such as Renoir and Tissot for what he described as a touch of "chi chi." Summoned to Buckingham Palace on the succession of King George VI to discuss designs for the coronation dresses of the maids of honour, the King led them through the hall of Winterhalter portraits. This gave him the inspiration for the crinoline dresses that would later become a symbolic royal look for the two monarchs—Queen Elizabeth the Queen Mother and Queen Elizabeth II. The dresses also influenced the silhouette of Dior's New Look of 1947, a line that came to epitomize a post-war return to femininity.

Hartnell was officially appointed dressmaker to the royal family in 1938 and subsequently designed for various royal occasions, eventually being acknowledged for creating a stylistic royal image that remains today. He was responsible for both the wedding dresses of Queen Elizabeth II and Princess Margaret. In 1953 he created the Queen's historic coronation dress, embroidered with the emblems of Great Britain and the Commonwealth. The House of Hartnell is today still responsible for the personal wardrobe of Queen Elizabeth the Queen Mother.

It could be argued that Hartnell limited himself as a designer by his work for British royalty and aristocracy. He created to promote and protect an establishment, encasing it in a grandiose aura of ornament and glamour, a service that was honoured by a knighthood in 1977. However, it should be remembered that Hartnell also produced ready-to-wear collections, sold through department stores from 1942 onwards. He also designed for Berkertex and created the uniforms of the British Red Cross and the Women's Royal Army Corps during World War II.

Although Norman Hartnell died in 1979 his legacy is continued today by the French couturier Marc Bohan, who is responsible for the design of the haute couture collections and maintaining the Hartnell name as a major force in contemporary fashion.

—Kevin Almond

HAWES, Elizabeth.

American designer

Born: Ridgewood, New Jersey, 16 December 1903. **Education:** Studied at Vassar College, Poughkeepsie, New York, 1921-25. **Fam-**

ily: Married Ralph Jester in 1930 (divorced, 1934); married Joseph Losey in 1937 (divorced, 1944); son: Gavrik Losey. **Career:** Worked in Paris as fashion copyist, stylist, journalist, then designed for Nicole Groult, 1925-28; designer and partner, Hawes-Harden, New York, 1928-30; designer, Hawes, Inc., New York, 1930-40; designer, Elizabeth Hawes, Inc., New York, 1948-49; occasional freelance designer, New York and California, 1950-68. Also: author, union organizer, political activist. **Exhibitions:** *Two Modern Artists of Dress: Elizabeth Hawes & Rudi Gernreich,* Fashion Institute of Technology, New York, 1967; Brooklyn Museum (retrospective), 1985. *Died* (in New York) *6 September 1971.*

Publications:

By HAWES:

Books

Fashion Is Spinach, New York 1938.
Men Can Take It, New York 1939.
Why Is a Dress?, New York 1942.
Good Grooming, Boston 1942.
Why Women Cry, or Wenches with Wrenches, New York 1943.
Hurry Up Please, It's Time, New York 1946.
Anything But Love, New York 1948.
But Say It Politely, Boston 1954.
It's Still Spinach, Boston 1954.

Articles

Writing as "Parasite," fashion items in *The New Yorker,* 1927-28.
Columns in *PM* magazine, 1940-42.

On HAWES:

Books

New York and Hollywood Fashion: Costume Designs from the Brooklyn Museum Collection, New York 1986.
Berch, Bettina, *Radical by Design,* New York 1988.
Milbank, Caroline Rennolds, *New York Fashion: The Evolution of American Style,* New York 1989.
Steele, Valerie, *Women of Fashion,* New York 1991.

Articles

Obituary in the *New York Times,* 8 September 1971.
Mahoney, Patrick R., "Elizabeth Hawes," in *Notable American Women,* New York 1980.
Mahoney, Patrick R., "In and Out of Style," in *Vassar Quarterly* (New York), Spring 1986.

*   *   *

Brainy and articulate, Elizabeth Hawes challenged the fashion industry's dictum that stylish clothing must originate only in the salons of a handful of French couturiers, to be worn by a privileged few. Hawes was trained in the French system and from 1928 to 1940 her studio in New York provided custom-made clothing and accessories for a distinguished clientèle. A gifted publicist with a knack for self-promotion, Hawes successfully debunked the myth

that beautiful clothes could only be created in Paris and became one of the first American designers to achieve national recognition.

She saw no reason, however, why mass-produced clothing should not be equally as distinctive and she became increasingly interested in designing for the wholesale market. It was an unhappy collaboration: Hawes's clothes were both too simple and too forward looking for most manufacturers. She found her ideas compromised time and time again in the finished product.

In her best-selling autobiography *Fashion Is Spinach* (New York, 1938), Elizabeth Hawes called fashion and the fashion industry parasites on true style. Style, she said, gives the feeling of the period, and changes only as there is a real change in point of view. Fashion, by contrast, changes not in response to events or to public taste or need, but because industry payrolls must be met, magazines published, a myth perpetuated.

Hawes despaired that most men and women were clothing conformists. In her view, clothes should be the expression of personality, of fantasy and above all of individuality. If a woman occasionally wanted trousers to wear, or a man ruffles, she argued provocatively, why shouldn't they have them? The important thing was to dress to please yourself.

Hawes's iconoclastic theories about clothing were supported by solid academic and practical training. As an undergraduate she studied anatomy and economics before apprenticing herself to the workrooms of Bergdorf Goodman and Nicole Groult, among others. Her fluid, bias-cut clothes moved with the body, revealing its natural curves. She believed that a successful dress must fuse with the wearer, that line, in relationship to anatomy, was the basis for a beautiful dress. Not surprisingly, the designer Hawes most admired was Madeleine Vionnet.

Those who might not have been familiar with Hawes as a designer knew her as an author and journalist, a witty and astute critic of the fashion system. In her writing Hawes incited men and women to rebel against the *status quo,* to speak up for clothing that suited the way they lived. She explained how the system worked against the consumer, producing shabbily made clothes that fit poorly and which were certainly not intended to last beyond a single season. Hawes disliked seeing women in unbecoming, uncomfortable clothes which cost more than they were worth, all in the name of fashion.

In 1940 Elizabeth Hawes turned her business over to her staff in order to concentrate on applying her theories about design to mass production. In *Why Is a Dress?* (New York, 1942), Hawes said that she had come to regret the Paris training which prepared her for the past when the future clearly lay in ready-to-wear. However Hawes once again found herself at moral and philosophical odds with the wholesale garment manufacturers. She did not return to designing until 1948, and then only briefly.

Elizabeth Hawes was a visionary and an iconoclast. She was a designer of inventive clothing and a fashion writer whose analytic prose still illuminates the world of Seventh Avenue.

—Whitney Blausen

HEAD, Edith.
American film costume designer

Born: Edith Claire Poesner in San Bernadino, California, 28 October 1897. **Education:** B.A., University of California at Los Angeles; M.A., Stanford University, Palo Alto, California; also studied at the Otis Art Institute and Chouinard School, Los Angeles. **Family:** Married Charles Head in 1923 (divorced, 1923); married Wiard Ihnen in 1940 (died, 1979). **Career:** Instructor in French, Spanish and art, The Bishop School for Girls, La Jolla, California and at Hollywood School for Girls, 1923; sketch artist, Paramount Pictures, 1924-27; assistant to Travis Banton, Paramount, 1927-38; Head of Design, Paramount Studios, Hollywood, 1938-66; chief costume designer, Universal Studios, Hollywood, 1967-81. Also author, radio and television commentator; lecturer, University of Southern California, 1949-51, 1973; fashion editor, *Holliday* magazine, 1973. **Exhibitions:** *Romantic and Glamorous Hollywood Design,* Metropolitan Museum of Art, New York, 1974; *Hollywood Film Costume,* Whitworth Art Gallery, Manchester, 1977. **Awards:** Academy Award, 1949, 1950, 1951, 1953, 1954, 1960, 1973; Film Designer of the Year Award, Mannequins Association, Los Angeles, 1962; Costume Designers Guild Award, 1967. *Died* (in Los Angeles, California) *26 October 1981.*

Publications:

By HEAD:

Books

The Dress Doctor, with Jane Ardmore, Boston 1959.
How to Dress for Success, with Joe Hyams, New York 1967.
Edith Head's Hollywood, with Paddy Calistro, New York 1983.

Articles

in *Silver Screen* (New York), September 1946, January 1948.
in *Hollywood Quarterly* (Los Angeles), October 1946.
in *Photoplay* (New York), October 1948.
in *Good Housekeeping* (New York), March 1959.
in *Holiday* (New York), January and July 1973, September and November 1974, January, March and September 1975, March 1976.
in *Inter/View* (New York), January 1974.
in *Take One* (Montreal), October 1976.
in *American Film* (Washington, D.C.), May 1978.
in *Cine Revue* (Paris), 19 April 1979.

On HEAD:

Books

Williams, Beryl, *Fashion Is Our Business,* Philadelphia 1945, London 1947.
Steen, Mike, *Hollywood Speaks: An Oral History,* New York 1974.
Vreeland, Diana, *Romantic and Glamorous Hollywood Design* (exhibition catalogue), New York 1974.
Chierichetti, David, *Hollywood Costume Design,* New York and London 1976.
McConathy, Dale, *Hollywood Costume,* New York 1976.
Regan, Michael, *Hollywood Film Costume* (exhibition catalogue), Manchester 1977.
Morris, Bernadine, and Barbara Walz, *The Fashion Makers,* New York 1978.
La Vine, W. Robert, *In a Glamorous Fashion: The Fabulous Years of Costume Design,* New York 1980, Boston and London 1981.

Pritchard, Susan, *Film Costume: An Annotated Bibliography,* New Jersey and London 1981.
New York and Hollywood Fashion: Costume Designs from the Brooklyn Museum Collection, New York 1986.
Acker, Ally, *Reel Women: Pioneers of the Cinema,* New York 1991.

Articles

Hollywood, Molly, "Film Colony, New York Battle to Set Styles," in the *Los Angeles Examiner,* 21 September 1941.
Scallion, Virginia, "Meet the Woman Who Dresses the Stars," in the *California Stylist,* July 1954.
"Dialogue on Film: Edith Head," in *American Film,* May 1978.
"Edith Head, Designer of Hollywood Glamour," in the *Los Angeles Times,* 27 October 1981.
Dolan, Judith, "A Head for Design," in *Stanford Magazine* (Stanford, California), 1991.

*   *   *

As head of design for Paramount Pictures, Edith Head was the last great designer to work under contract to a major film studio. Head's first significant assignment was to create the wardrobe for silent film star Clara Bow in *Wings* (1927). Her last was costuming Steve Martin as a 1940s *femme fatale* for the 1982 release *Dead Men Don't Wear Plaid.* In a career that spanned 60 years, Head was responsible for the on-screen persona of such stars as Mae West, Dorothy Lamour, Bob Hope, Barbara Stanwyck, Ginger Rogers, Olivia de Haviland, Gloria Swanson, Grace Kelly, and Elizabeth Taylor.

Head had no formal training in design and she took care to work within what she saw as her limitations. She might never be considered a couturier, but she could—and did—become a taste-maker. Thus, while contemporaries Erté and Adrian came to be known for gowns which epitomized fantasy and glamour, Edith Head made herself known for designing beautiful and flattering clothes which the movie-going public could easily imagine wearing.

Head's wardrobe for Barbara Stanwyck in *The Lady Eve* (1941) advanced her growing reputation as a designer particularly attuned to the psyche of the average woman. Stanwyck had most often been cast in roles which required that she look plain. Her on-screen transformation to a woman of style thrilled audiences as much as it thrilled Stanwyck herself. The star had Edith Head written into her contract, and the studio publicity department saw to it that the name Edith Head became synonymous with home-grown American fashion.

Beginning in 1945, Head had a featured spot on Art Linkletter's radio programme "House Party," giving advice on matters of dress to the listening audience. When the show moved to television in 1952, Head moved with it. On live television, she would perform an impromptu verbal and visual make-over on members of the studio audience, sometimes using some element of her own clothing to suggest a more effective personal presentation. Head had a keen intellect, and when she brought her gift of analysis to the human figure, she created a look that flattered the wearer and fitted the occasion. This was one of her great strengths as a costumier and it was a skill which could benefit anyone.

In her film work, Head was known as a "director's designer" whose interpretation of a character became the visual embodiment of the directorial thought process. Olivia de Haviland's subtly ill-fitting costumes for the opening scenes of *The Heiress,* or Gloria

Swanson's clothes for *Sunset Boulevard,* with their simultaneous references to the 1920s and the 1950s, remain superb examples of characterization. Head often said that, even without a sound track, the story of *The Heiress* could be understood through its costumes.

One of the most challenging problems for any theatrical designer is so-called "modern dress." A motion picture may be shot up to two years before it is shown to the public but clothing must not betray that fact by seeming dated. If so versatile a designer may be said to have a trademark, Head's would be a clean and simple line with a minimum of detail, in a subdued palette. Head produced timeless classics which never competed with the performer and never took focus from the story-line. It was all, she said, "a matter of camouflage and magic."

—Whitney Blausen

HECHTER, Daniel.

French designer

Born: Paris, 30 July 1938. **Education:** Completed trade school education, 1956. **Family:** Married first to Marika Hechter, then to Jennifer Chambon in 1980; daughter: Carinne. **Military Service:** Served in the French Army, 1958-60. **Career:** Delivery boy, Paris ready-to-wear firm, 1956; formed own design studio, 1956; salesman, then designer, Pierre d'Alby, Paris, 1960-62; founder and designer, the Hechter Group, from 1962; added children's line, 1965; introduced menswear, 1968; active sportswear and home furnishings lines introduced, 1970; furniture collection launched, 1983. **Address:** 4 ter, avenue Hoche, 75008 Paris, France.

Publications:

On HECHTER:

Articles

Moor, Johnathan, "The Americanization of Daniel Hechter," in the *Daily News Record* (New York), 21 January 1980.
Moor, Johnathan, "Daniel Hechter: Taking it Easy ... With Enthusiasm," in the *Daily News Record* (New York), 18 August 1980.
Wood, Mary Ann, "Daniel Hecter: Bringing High Fashion Down to Earth," in *Fashion Retailer N.E.,* November 1980.
Highe, Jackie, "Decision Makers: The Fashion Dictators," in *Living* (London), 13 July 1983.
"Court Orders Removal of Anti-Hechter Posters," in *Women's Wear Daily* (New York), 4 December 1988.
d'Aulnay, Sophie, "Daniel Hechter: Coming to America—Again," in the *Daily News Record* (New York), 12 July 1993.

*   *   *

Daniel Hechter was one of the first designers to recognize the commercial viability of lifestyle dressing and has marketed the concept with enormous success, today exporting to some 47 countries and licensing goods in the United States, South America, Europe, Australia, and Canada. In many ways he provided the inspiration for the 1980s explosion of lifestyle concepts in retailing.

Hechter identified his particular market as including the young, sometimes married with children, upwardly mobile twenty- to thirty-somethings, who may not have the income to finance the designer lifestyle and fashionable appearance to which they aspire. As a mass market designer it is essential to be able to perceive what is right for the moment, particularly when dealing with the fickle youth-orientated market. Hechter's taste and style are often directed by the unpredictable forces of pop, club, and street culture, and his business has rapidly prospered owing to his ability to adapt speedily to the sense of what is wanted now at the price his identified customer can afford.

Born into a family who owned a ready-to-wear company, Hechter was brought up in an environment sympathetic to fashion. He worked for the designer Pierre d'Alby from 1958 before opening his own house in 1962, together with a friend, Armand Orustein. The company opened with a womenswear collection that captured the developing need of the 1960s—young, fun, and sometimes throw-away. He produced sweaters, maxi coats, trouser suits, smoking jackets, gabardine raincoats and boot-top-length divided skirts. His casual jersey and ribbed duffle coats and greatcoats emphasized his skills for sophisticated unisex outerwear, sporty yet wearable and stylish.

The business has grown to incorporate many areas of fashion and clothing design, producing shoes, sunglasses, school uniforms, corporate wear, and tennis and ski clothes. He has also moved into designing for the home, broadening his lifestyle concepts by producing household linen and furniture. The company is a regular employer of fashion design graduates from all over the world. Hechter believes that this inserts a continual flow of fresh ideas and invigorates the Daniel Hechter image.

As well as exporting goods, the company has a chain of boutiques and own label stores throughout Europe, the United States, and Canada. Hechter attributes this success to his practical, matter-of-fact approach to design. He displays none of the airs or temperament associated with the personality of the fashion designer. Fashion is regarded as a down-to-earth business which perhaps explains why he describes his ideal customer as being a strong-willed woman, sure of what she likes, and how she should wear what she likes!

—Kevin Almond

HEIM, Jacques.

French designer

Born: Paris, 8 May 1899. **Family:** Married; one son: Philippe. **Career:** Manager, Isadore and Jeanne Heim fur fashion house, from c.1920; initiated couture department for coats, suits and gowns, c.1925; opened own couture house, 1930; Heim Jeunes Filles collection introduced, 1936; Heim sportswear boutiques established in Biarritz and Cannes, from 1937; Heim-Actualité girlswear collection introduced, 1950; fragrances include *Alambie,* 1947, *J'Aime,* 1958, *Shandoah,* 1966; house closed, 1969. President, Chambre Syndicale de la Couture Parisienne, 1958-62. Also: owner and publisher, *Revue Heim,* 1950s. *Died* (in Paris) *8 January 1967.*

Publications:

On HEIM:

Books

Milbank, Caroline Rennolds, *Couture: The Great Designers,* New York 1985.

Daniel Hechter: Fall/Winter 1995/96. *Photograph by Fréderique Dumoulin.*

Articles

Peterson, Patricia, "Heim Drops Hemline and Ban on Photographs," in the *New York Times,* 23 July 1962.
Obituary, in the *New York Times,* 9 January 1967.

*   *   *

"An innovator by nature," says Caroline Rennolds Milbank of Jacques Heim (*Couture: The Great Designers,* New York 1985). Few would agree. The *New York Times* obituary (9 January 1967) read: "Mr Heim's fashion house designed and made clothes of a modest style. He was never in the front ranks of the big houses that radically changed the looks of women by offering new silhouettes in the manner of Balenciaga, Chanel or Saint Laurent." Perhaps the median truth was expressed in *Women's Wear Daily*'s obituary (9 January 1967): "Heim was basically an innovator in business. He didn't want to be called a designer, but rather an editor of clothes." He was aggressive in conceiving of ways in which the couture might be vital to new audiences (his Heim Jeunes Filles brought garments to a young audience, even before the boutiques of other couture designers, and engendered early client loyalty) and an impeccable (until he broke with the couture schedule for delayed photographs in summer 1962) spokesman for the fashion industry of France. He was an editor of many design ideas, beginning with the possibilities of fur, continuing through beach and play outfits, even the two-piece swimsuit, and the plane and planar simplifications of design in the youth-conscious 1960s.

If he was not driven by the market, he was at least keenly sensitive to it. In *Femina* in April 1928, spring Heim fashions are casual and sportswear-inspired, with low waists and combinations of fur and textile. In autumn 1950, day suits swing out from the waist with Balenciaga equilibrium; spring 1950 evening gowns and a two-piece shantung suit are indebted to Dior. Heim was a smart, eclectic designer of many styles. In that consistent sales sensitivity he had transformed the fur business of his parents Isadore and Jeanne Heim, founded in 1898, and persevered and prospered as a designer for nearly four decades. But his commerce was clearly his passion and his *métier,* not the design itself. The *New York Times* obituary said, "Jacques Heim, a tall good-looking man with a cheery disposition, seemed more like a businessman or banker than a couturier. He exhibited none of the flamboyance or temperament of competitors like Yves Saint Laurent or Christian Dior." But, of course, design is made by acumen as well as by inspiration.

Heim's fashion breakthrough was to realize that fur could be worked as a fabric. Wool and fur combinations, geometries of fur and textiles, and fur accents became hallmarks of the Heim fashion in the 1930s. At the same time, along with Chanel and Patou and others, Heim was alert to the possibilities of elegant sportswear and observed bathing and sports costumes as inspiration. According to Milbank, Heim was inspired by the Tahitian exhibits in the Paris colonial exhibition of 1931 to create *pareos* and sarongs. Later, his 1950 two-piece swimsuit Atome came considerably after the bikini incident and invention, but addressed a broader public.

Through the 1950s, Heim addressed American needs for sportswear in innovative and utilitarian fabrics, while still remaining, in the vocabulary of the day, very ladylike. Moreover, his Heim *Actualité* diffusion line, launched in 1950, extended his influence into ready-to-wear along with the young styles of Heim Jeunes Filles. From 1958 to 1962 he was President of the Chambre Syndicale de la Couture Parisienne, "probably the last effective president of the couture's professional body," according to *Women's Wear Daily.* When, however, he permitted immediate release of collection photographs to the press in July 1962, in advance of the agreed-upon delayed release, he precipitated a furor among designers still eager, in the old way, to preserve the design's secret until their slow dissemination. Heim was steadfastly modern and business-oriented. In this decision, he anticipated the couture's gradual *détente* in the 1960s, but did it so abruptly that he lost the confidence of his colleagues. Patricia Peterson reported, "Photographs were not to have been published in the United States until August 26. For Europe the release date was to have been August 27. When Heim allowed photographs to run even before the opening, the chase was on to find photographers. Men used to shooting wars, riots, and dignitaries were suddenly faced with swirling models. Other couture houses were besieged with queries." (*New York Times,* 23 July 1962). Perhaps it always takes an insider to bring the certain news of change, but Heim was as wounded as any messenger with the apparent bad tidings that couture's control was over and the camera and the press held sway.

Favored by Mme. Charles de Gaulle and a designer for Mrs Dwight D. Eisenhower, Heim would have understood the expression "old soldiers never die." He had never married a style or become one form's advocate. Instead, he had insisted on the business principle that fashion would thrive in change and adaptation. "The life of a couturier is a magnificent and continuous torture," Heim said. But he was probably only expressing a businessman's shrewd romanticism and a leader's quixotic belief in fashion's anguish.

—Richard Martin

HEISEL, Sylvia.

American fashion designer

Born: Princeton, New Jersey, 22 June 1963. **Education:** Barnard College, New York, 1980-81. **Career:** Designed and sold costume jewelry, 1981-82; designed collection of coats for Henri Bendel, New York, 1982, and exclusive line of womenswear for Barney's, New York, 1987; first full catwalk collection shown, 1988. Also film costume designer mid-1980s. **Awards:** Chicago Gold Coast Award, 1993. **Address:** 580 Broadway, New York, New York 10012, U.S.A.

Publications:

On HEISEL:

Articles

"Fashion," in *Interview* (New York), July 1987.
Washington, Roxanne, "Designer Heisel Guided by the Feel, Not the Look," in *The Ann Arbor News* (Michigan), 10 September 1991.
Pandiscio, Richard, "Sylvia Heisel: Gun Control Fashion," in *Interview* (New York), January 1993.
Siroto, Janet, "Evening Star," in *Vogue* (New York), February 1993.

*

I think fashion is about who you are right now. What you're wearing says who you are at that moment in time. It's the first thing you communicate to another person.

My favorite clothes are easy, comfortable, creative, and beautiful because that's what I'm attracted to in people. What we wear is a combination of reality and what is in our minds. The reality is where we have to go, what we have to do, and what we can afford. The dream is who we want to be, what's beautiful and exciting to us, and what we desire. I try to design clothes with a combination of these qualities: wearability in the real world with an aesthetic of dreams.

Inspiration comes from everything in the world, more often from the *Zeitgeist* than from other pieces of clothing or designed items. Historically, fashion is interesting because of what it says about any particular moment in history. What looks good, new, and exciting one day looks old and tired the next. It is the most transient of art and design fields.

The clothes I design combine skills of construction and manufacturing with the communication of my ideas.

—Sylvia Heisel

*   *   *

Sophisticated elegance is perhaps the most distinguishing characteristic of Sylvia Heisel's collections. Heisel's use of exquisite fabrics, colors and the simplicity of cuts have assured her favorable recognition by fashion buyers and critics alike. As one of New York's young contemporary fashion designers, Heisel has instinctively avoided catering to recent trends. Her approach to fashion combines an "aesthetic of dreams" with the reality of modern wearability and affordability.

Heisel studied art history briefly at Barnard, leaving college eventually to pursue a free-lance career designing costume jewelry, theatre costuming, and fashion display. With no formal training in fashion design, Heisel launched her first coat collection for Henri Bendel in New York, followed by an exclusive line for Barney's first women's store in New York in 1987. Her first independent collection appeared in the spring of 1988.

Heisel is interested in communicating ideas intrinsic to particular moments in history. The 1980s emphasis on body consciousness led Heisel to embrace the notion of executing a controlled draping of her now signature slip and tank dresses. Constructed in fabrics such as jersey, mesh, and silk, these dresses are contoured, accentuating the body with deep cut backs and high slits. They are simultaneously wearable and feminine.

The growth of professional American women in the job market highlighted the fashion designers' need to accommodate this new status with garments both practical and timeless. Heisel addressed these needs with small, tightly edited collections, including "sportswear inspired suits, separates for day and sophisticated dresses and coats for evening." Her jackets range from waist-length to sleek over-the-hip styles. The selected fabrics, such as silk and wool crêpe, are comfortable and travel well. Her garments are architectural, employing both body-fitting silhouettes and a boxy construction in her coats and jackets. Heisel's color selection is based on instinct rather than forecasts and she often uses black for balance. The use of solids highlights the minimalist cut, drape, and texture of each garment. At the same time, simplicity allows for a variety of ways of wearing each piece.

Sylvia Heisel.

Heisel's awareness of contemporary culture was successfully transferred into costume designs for the 1985 film *Parting Glances*. In 1985 Heisel was included by the *New York Times* in the list of young designers—including Carol Horn, Cathy Hardwick, and Mary Jane Marcasiano—who are "currying favours with American women and retailers." Heisel has on several occasions deviated from collections based on minimalist constructions—fake pony-fur coats, lizard prints, and McFaddenesque dresses. She still maintains a consistent approach, stressing that how a woman feels in her clothes is as much a part as how the clothes look.

—Teal Triggs

———

HELPERN, Joan and David. See **JOAN & DAVID.**

———

HEMMINGWAY, Wayne and Geraldine. See **RED OR DEAD.**

———

HENDERSON, Gordon.

American designer

Born: Berkeley, California, 19 March 1957. **Education:** Studied medicine, University of California; studied fashion design, Parsons School of Design, New York, 1981-83. **Career:** Assistant designer, Calvin Klein, 1984; formed own company, 1985; launched lower priced But, Gordon line, 1990; signed exclusive contract with Saks Fifth Avenue, 1992. **Awards:** Council of Fashion Designers of America Perry Ellis Award, 1989. **Address:** 450 West 15th Street, New York, New York 10011, USA.

Publications:

On HENDERSON:

Books

Stegemeyer, Anne, *Who's Who in Fashion* supplement, New York 1992.

Articles

Darnton, Nina, "At What Price Young Success?," in *Newsweek* (New York), 20 November 1989.
Haynes, Kevin, "Gordon Henderson: All the Rage," in *Women's Wear Daily* (New York), 22 November 1989.
Hochswender, Woody, "Realism Takes Henderson to Top," in the *New York Times,* 28 November 1989.
Duffy, Martha, "But Gordon, I Want It All," in *Time* (New York), 26 February 1990.
"Flash! Gordon Has Designs on You," in *Mademoiselle* (New York), March 1990.
Shapiro, Harriet, "Gordon Henderson's Affordable Designs Are Making Him Fashion's Man for the Woman Who Works," in *People* (Chicago), 19 March 1990.
Shapiro, Harriet, "Designer Clothes at a Lower Price," in the *New York Times,* 16 September 1990.
Agins, Teri, "In Fashion, the Talent and His Money Man Make Promising Team," in the *Wall Street Journal* (New York), 18 September 1990.
Washington, Elsie B., "Now: Brothers on Seventh Avenue," in *Essence,* November 1991.

*   *   *

Versatile separates. Dressing with ease. These American sportswear tenets are the meat and potatoes of Gordon Henderson's fashion. Although young, he has the discipline of engaging in no design that is superfluous and of giving the customer what she wants—garments that can be multipurpose and mixable in a wardrobe, favoring fashion that is neither flamboyant nor expensive. Henderson is anomalous among designers making a mark in the late 1980s in adhering so intensely to the sportswear ethos, never succumbing to the glamour of high-priced fashion. His penchant for vegetable and earth colors seems even politically correct in the ecology-aware 1990s. He is, as Woody Hochswender said, "a real-

ist" (*New York Times,* 28 November 1989). Such sportswear orthodoxy and awareness to design's realization in sales has made Henderson the "hottest new designer" on Seventh Avenue, New York, according to the *Wall Street Journal* (18 September 1990). As there is a pragmatism to Henderson's view of fashion, there is a corresponding restraint in the designer. Photogenic enough to pose for a Gap advertisement (wearing denim) and for selection as one of *People* magazine's beautiful people, Henderson provides a beguiling and handsome personal accompaniment to his plain message of fashion modesty. For Hochswender, Henderson is "a designer many are calling the first important new talent of the 1990s." He told Kevin Haynes, "People identify me as doing classics with a twist—it sounds like a drink to me. But there's beauty in using relatively inexpensive fabrics and treating them like they're very expensive. I don't like people getting uptight with clothes."

The ideal Henderson client would be a woman who shops for other labels and perhaps even buys basics at The Gap or other retailers, allowing the Henderson separates to work as accent pieces. "You can take the clothes and put them together for career women," Henderson told Nina Darnton, "or combine them for weekend or evening. That's what the nineties are about—servicing your customer in the way she needs." Even beyond his eponymous line, Henderson created But, Gordon, an even more responsive, inexpensive line with its name coming from stores who liked certain garments, but wanted them at lesser prices, whining, "but, Gordon..." again and again until the designer acquiesced with a secondary line.

When one examines Henderson's work, one realizes its appeal as fashion basics, from simple dresses to halter tops, beautifully cut trousers, and other wardrobe-building elements. Inevitably, one designer he acknowledges as a favorite is Claire McCardell, whose ingenuity with materials and with basic sportswear elements is recapitulated in Henderson's imagination with materials and flair for a simple, uncluttered style. Henderson's lyrical summer dresses, bandeaux, and capelet jackets reflect that spirit of McCardell. His slightly off-beat colors—occasioned in part by necessity and in part by a commitment to the earth—and his love of plaids and checks also align Henderson with McCardell. But Henderson also admires Chanel, an admiration evident in his very serviceable boxy jackets. Yet, McCardell works better as a model for Henderson as she realized the sensibility of suburbs and country (Henderson was brought up in California.) There is something so unabashedly price-conscious and trend-avoiding about Henderson's clothing that it becomes almost anti-urban. And it may be precisely the gleeful suburban, campus, low-pressure calm that makes his work so attractive to a broad audience. After all, the working woman is no longer an exclusive phenomenon of the big city, but a staple of suburban lifestyle as well. Henderson also says of his work at Calvin Klein, "I learned everything there. He gives you consistency, and he's so clean and precise it's almost ridiculous. He can take a good idea and go on with it forever."

Gordon Henderson has a promising prospect of his own "forever" in a consistent and compelling vision of sportswear separates kept at a reasonable price for the American (and international) customer. Fashion has always had a tendency to drift upward, even among designers who start out with the intention of serving the broadest public. Henderson gives every sign of being different: reaching the top of his field by adamantly and effectively staying at the bottom of the price ranges.

—Richard Martin

HERMÈS.

French design house

Founded in Paris, 1837. Began accessories, including silk scarves, 1926. Founder's grandson, Emile Hermès, established luggage and couture clothing in 1930s. **Address:** 13/15 rue Sadi Carnot, Rambouillet, 78120 France.

Publications:

By HERMÈS:

Books

Hermès Handbook, New York n.d.
How to Wear Your Hermès Scarf, Paris 1988.
Baseman, Andrew, *The Scarf,* New York 1989.
Hermès: Le Monde d'Hermès 1992, Paris 1991.

On HERMÈS:

Books

Hermès Handbook, New York n.d.

Articles

"A Boutique Where You Don't Just Buy—You Invest," in *Vogue,* October 1974.
Van Dyke, Grace, "Hermès: Old World Luxury in the New World," in *USA Today,* July 1984.
Dryansky, G. Y., "Hermès: Quality with a Kick," in *Harper's Bazaar,* April 1986.
Berman, Phyllis, "Mass Production? Yech!," in *Forbes* (New York), 22 September 1986.
"Scarves Everywhere," in *The New Yorker,* 30 January 1989.
Aillaud, Charlotte, "The Hermès Museum: Inspiration for the Celebrated Family Firm," in *Architectural Digest* (Los Angeles), January 1989.
Beckett-Young, Kathleen, "Signature in the Social Register," in *Connoisseur* (New York), June 1989.
Tompkins, Mimi, "Sweatshop of the Stars," in *U.S. News and World Report,* 12 February 1990.
Gandee, Charles, "Jean-Louis Dumas-Hermès Is Flying High," in *House & Garden* (New York), August 1990.
Hornblower, Margaret, "As Luxe As It Gets," in *Time* (New York), 6 August 1990.
"The Handbag to Have," in the *New York Times,* 14 April 1991.
"Hermès: Still in the Saddle," in *Women's Wear Daily* (New York), 25 September 1991.
"Hermès of Paris, Inc.," in the *New York Times,* 5 October 1991.
Slesin, Susan, "Ah, the Horse," in the *New York Times,* 21 May 1992.

*　　*　　*

"Leather, sport, and a tradition of refined elegance." That is how Emile-Maurice Hermès, grandson of founder Thierry Hermès, summed up the philosophy of his family's celebrated firm in the 1920s. Passed down over generations, the House of Hermès has been committed to quality in design and production for over 150 years. At the close of the twentieth century, the name Hermès represents the ultimate in French luxury.

Hermès began as a Parisian harness shop in 1837, making finely wrought harnesses and bridles for the carriage trade. As early as 1855 Hermès was earning accolades, winning first prize in its class at the 1855 Paris Exposition. Thierry Hermès' son Emile-Charles established the current flagship store at 24 rue du Faubourg Saint-Honoré, where he introduced saddlery and began retail sales. With the advent of the automobile, the firm adapted its careful saddle stitching techniques to the production of wallets, luggage, handbags, watchbands, and accessories for golfing, hunting, and polo playing, and began to design couture sportswear. All were made with the same fine materials and attention to detail as the original leather wares, and the firm continued to build on its reputation for quality. Hermès made fashion news in the 1920s by designing one of the first leather garments of the 20th century, a zippered golfing jacket, for the Prince of Wales. For a time the zipper was called the *fermature Hermès.*

The fourth generation of proprietors were two sons-in-law, Jean Guerrand and Robert Dumas. Guerrand and Dumas added perfume and scarves to the line, while the leather artisans remained loyal, often staying on for decades. Into the 1960s the company continued to expand, with the introduction of new styles and fragrances. Jean-Louis Dumas-Hermès, Robert Dumas's son, became président-directeur général in 1978.

The 1980s were a period of unprecedented growth for the firm. Hermès benefited from the revival of status dressing. Women sported the Kelly bag, the Constance clutch, brightly colored leathers, sensuous cashmeres, bold jewelry, tri-colored spectator shoes and silk ballet slippers. For men, Hermès made leather jackets with sherpa lining and trim, gabardine blazers and dashing greatcoats, and richly patterned silk ties. Dumas-Hermès introduced new materials like porcelain and crystal, expanding the line to 30,000 items. It is to the firm's credit that they have never licensed any of their products, but keep tight controls over the design and manufacture of this vast range of goods. Thus, every leather bound datebook, porcelain teapot, silk waistcoat, and custom saddle is made under Hermès' watchful eye.

One of the most visible—and bestselling—items in the Hermès line is the scarf, or *carré* as they are called. The carefully printed, heavy silk scarves are coveted for the air of Parisian style they impart. Many of the *carrés* feature equestrian motifs, as well as other symbols of prestige, like coats of arms, banners, and military insignia. Women boast of how many they own, and hand them down through generations; some of the scarves end up as framed wall-hangings or are made into pillows. The firm corresponds regularly with Hermès addicts trying to collect every scarf on the books, and reports that, during the holiday season in the Paris store, a scarf is sold every 20 seconds. Queen Elizabeth II was pictured on an English postage stamp with an Hermès scarf wrapped around her royal head. Each scarf could be considered a small symbol of all of the carefully made luxury goods that Hermès has produced for generations.

Hermès has always kept pace with trends in contemporary fashion, but the clothing and accessories remain essentially timeless. The Hermès look relies not on the vagaries of fashion but on the finest materials, exquisite construction, and the instinctively casual chic of French style. Thus, over the course of the 20th century, the cut of the clothing or the palettes may have changed, but the classic quality of Hermès designs has remained constant. Beyond mere status symbols, the firm's goods are the embodiment of simplicity and elegance in extremely well made and durable products. Whether it be a jacket of meltingly soft leather, a paisley silk dressing gown, a Kelly bag, a valise, or a *carré*, an Hermès purchase comes with the assurance that it will be stylish and appropriate for a lifetime.

—Kathleen Paton

HERRERA, Carolina.

Venezuelan designer working in New York

Born: Maria Carolina Josefina Pacanins y Nino in Caracas, Venezuela, 8 January 1939. **Education:** El Carmen School, Venezuela. **Family:** Married Reinaldo Herrera in 1957; children: Mercedes, Ana Luisa, Carolina, Patricia. **Career:** Showed first couture collection, 1981; introduced fur collection for Revillion, 1984; launched CH diffusion line, 1986, Couture Bridal collection, 1987, Carolina Herrera Collection II sportswear line, 1989, Herrera for Men, Herrera Studio bridge line and W by Carolina Herrera, 1992; Carolina Herrera fragrances introduced, 1988; jewelry collections introduced, 1990, 1991; **Awards:** Pratt Institute Award, 1990. **Address:** 501 Seventh Avenue, New York, NY 10018, USA.

Publications:

On HERRERA:

Books

Diamonstein, Barbaralee, *Fashion: The Inside Story,* New York 1985.
Steele, Valerie, *Women of Fashion: Twentieth-Century Designers,* New York 1991.

Articles

Shapiro, Harriet, "From Venezuela to Seventh Avenue, Carolina Herrera's Fashions Cast a Long Shadow," in *People* (New York), 3 May 1982.
Rayner, William and Chesbrough Rayner, "An Evening with Carolina and Reinaldo Herrera: Strong Opinions, European Style," in *Vogue* (New York), March 1987.
Daria, Irene, "Carolina Herrera: A Personal Evolution," in *Women's Wear Daily* (New York), 2 March 1987.
Daria, Irene, "Designers on Designing: Carolina Herrera," in *Women's Wear Daily* (New York), 2 March 1987.
Estrada, Mary Batts, "Carolina Herrera Talks about Fashion," in *Hispanic,* March 1989.
Reed, Julia, "Talking Fashion: Carolina Herrera Is the Undisputed Queen of Seventh Avenue," in *Vogue* (New York), June 1990.
Koski, Lorna, "Carolina's Prime Time," in *Women's Wear Daily* (New York), 18 June 1991.
Struensee, Chuck, "Carolina Herrera's New Horizons," in *Women's Wear Daily* (New York), 20 October 1992.
"New York: Carolina Herrera," in *Women's Wear Daily* (New York), 1 November 1994.
"New York: Carolina Herrera," in *Women's Wear Daily* (New York), 4 April 1995.

*   *   *

When Carolina Herrera introduced her first fashion collection in 1981, *Women's Wear Daily,* New York dubbed her "Our Lady of the Sleeve." Her early interest in the shoulder area has remained constant throughout her many lines and seasons. The Herrera look is characterized by strong, fitted shoulders, tight bodices, straight lines and slightly pushed-up sleeves.

Though she has often been referred to as a socialite turned designer, her contributions to the industry are many. Prior to beginning her career as a designer, Carolina Herrera was on the International Best Dressed List for over ten years and was then nominated to the Best Dressed Hall of Fame. Her personal style influenced how women dressed around the world. Her affluent, South American background exposed her to the work of the best couturiers and dressmakers in the world. She cites Balenciaga as her greatest influence. It was a natural transition from socialite to fashion designer, as Herrera is a member of the world for which she designs. She understands her customer's lifestyles and needs because she is one of them. Her friends, impressed with her design quality, fabric selection, attention to detail, construction and drape, also became her clients.

Herrera's designs have been described as being for the "quintessential woman of the 1980s who has consummate style and taste as well as an active lifestyle." Her clothes have a couture element, feminine detail, and genuine ease. Herrera herself believes that her clothes are feminine, elegant and, most importantly, comfortable. Though she loves to mix and match expensive Italian and French fabrics, she maintains the importance of the cut of the clothes. Herrera states, "You don't have to buy very expensive materials if the clothes are well cut." In terms of color, Herrera favors the combination of black and white and black and brown.

Becoming a designer seemed a logical evolution in Herrera's life. She married and had four children. She came to symbolize the upper-class South American lifestyle. When her children were grown, she decided, with the financial backing of a wealthy South American publisher, to open a design house in New York.

Like many designers, Herrera expanded her business to include other lines. The CH Collections, introduced in 1986, are less expensive versions of her high-fashion lines, similar silhouettes in cut and finish but made of different fabrics. Herrera also launched a successful bridal line in 1987 after designing Caroline Kennedy's wedding gown. A perfume for both women (1988) and men (1991) also followed.

In the early collections, Herrera's strengths were in her day dresses and luncheon suits. They expressed femininity through their beautifully tailored hour-glass design. In more recent collections, Herrera has ventured into the downtown New York scene for inspiration, showing chiffon split skirts topped with satin motorcycle jackets, thus illustrating her ability to interpret and combine the surrounding culture with her own design sense. Most importantly Carolina Herrera's clothes are about style and elegance achieved by her trademark of shoulders, sleeves, line, and construction.

—Margo Seaman

HILFIGER, Tommy.

American designer

Born: 1952. **Career:** Owner and designer, People's Places, New York, until 1979; founder, designer and vice-chairman, Tommy

Hilfiger Corporation, New York; company floated on Stock Exchange, 1992. Member of Council of Fashion Designers of America. **Address:** 25 West 39th St, New York, NY 10018, USA.

Publications:

On HILFIGER:

Articles

La Ferla, Ruth, "Hilfiger Re-emerges," in the *New York Times,* 31 July 1990.
Younger, Joseph D., "The Man Makes the Clothes," in *Amtrak Express* (Washington, D.C.), September/October 1993.
"Throwing Down the Trousers," in *Newsweek* (New York), 11 July 1994.
Mather, John, "Tommy Hilfiger's Great Leap," in *Esquire* (New York), August 1994.

*   *   *

In an article titled "Throwing Down the Trousers" (*Newsweek,* 11 July 1994), Calvin Klein and Tommy Hilfiger are rendered in a showdown over men's underwear, the former having long occupied Times Square (New York) billboard space with provocative underwear ads. Hilfiger, seen standing on Broadway and 44th Street with his boxer-clad male models, meekly states, "My image is all about good, clean fun. I think Calvin's image is about maybe something different." Hilfiger is smart. He juxtaposes his hunky models in boxers in flag and stripe designs at surfer jam length with the implied enemy in bawdy, black, sopping promiscuity. Hilfiger has been right—in design and business—in promising "good, clean fun" in an unabashed American style that has achieved phenomenal success. America has wanted a menswear mainstream, neither aristocratic nor licentious. Emerging first in the 1980s with a clever campaign announcing himself among established designers, he has come to fulfil his own declaration to become one of the leading names in American design, certainly in menswear.

Acknowledging "I'm both a designer and a businessman" (*Amtrak Express,* September-October 1993), Hilfiger divides his own successful role into its two components that he himself has rendered indivisible. Hilfiger has indubitably learned from older American designers Ralph Lauren and Calvin Klein that fashion is a synergy of business, aspiration, and classic design—with the image and craving that constitute aspiration perhaps the most important element. Hilfiger has shrewdly and wonderfully chosen a particular place for himself in American menswear imagery. Whereas Lauren has pre-empted old-money WASP styles and Klein has successfully created a sexy vivacity, Hilfiger has come closer to Main Street, a colorful Americana that still waves flags, that still loves button-down collars, that appreciates classics, that adores his "good, clean fun" along with family values and may even abhor pretence or promiscuity, that strives for college and collegiate looks but would never rebel too much even on campus, and that dresses a little more modestly and traditionally than those who prefer his designer-commerce confreres. His closest kinship (or competitor) in the market is David Chu's similarly brilliant work for Nautica, likewise reaching into the small-town, cautious American sensibility for roots and imagination.

The "real people" effectiveness of Hilfiger is, of course, both real and illusory: he is stirring the deep-felt American conservative sensibilities of the late 20th century at the very moment at which culture is annulling any vestigial *Our Town* sentimentalities. The "feel good" ethos of Hilfiger's design is not image alone, for his intense commitment to value-for-price and quality materials confirms the joy in his design. His colorful, sporty, comfortable clothing appealed preeminently in the 1980s to the middle-class in America. By the 1990s, Hilfiger was a clothing symbol of African-American and Hispanic urban youth, engendering immense street-smart urban loyalty along with his classic Main-Street constituency. Hilfiger's clothing is readily identified, with logo crest on shirttails, pockets, or even boxer waistband center-front; green "eyes" (green-lined buttonhole on the breast pocket flap near the heart) on pockets; and contrasting linings within collars.

Hilfiger has associated himself with two other popular American images, both with special appeal to youth: sports teams and rock music. He has captured a 30-something client who is ageing into his 40s, and yet Hilfiger is also building his young following. Hilfiger's great success has defied much élitist fashion skepticism. Ruth La Ferla reported unforgivingly, "As a 'name' designer Mr Hilfiger sprang full grown from the mind of his sponsor, Mohan Murjani, in the mid-80s. Explicitly promoted as a successor to Perry Ellis or Calvin Klein or Ralph Lauren, Mr Hilfiger achieved a degree of fame, or notoriety. But the stunt never came off; Mr Hilfiger's fashions and image did not gel" (*New York Times,* 31 July 1990). Of course, American enterprise is full of "stunts," from P. T. Barnum to Henry Ford to Dr Kellogg, all with origins in harmless chicanery and old-fashioned *chutzpah*. Despite detractors, Hilfiger has consistently created his own dynamic and vigorous vision. After Murjani's backing, Hilfiger took his business public on the New York Stock Exchange in 1992, a rare instance of a designer name business trading with success.

In 1994, Hilfiger added tailored clothing to his line, confident that the men who have already associated him with comfort and clean-cut exuberance would carry those same ideals to a full-cut American suit or jacket for business. In 1988, Hilfiger had spoken in his own advertising, "The clothes I design are relaxed, comfortable, somewhat traditional, affordable and ... simple. They are the classic American clothes we've always worn, but I've reinterpreted them so that they fit more easily into the lives we live today." His sensitivity to casual wear (and his sympathetic American ethos of inclusiveness) can be brought to the business side of the male wardrobe, especially as it is already inflected by casual and sports-influenced notes. Part of his business acumen and pragmatism is expressed in his statement to Joseph Younger that he wants to dress men from head to toe before beginning to dress women (though his full-bodied shirts and oversized trousers are often borrowed). But, of course, there is no end to a wish as empowered and desirable as Tommy Hilfiger's distinct and determined American dream.

—Richard Martin

HOBBS LTD.

British fashion company

Founded in 1981 by Marilyn and Yoram Anselm. Marilyn Anselm studied sculpture, Central School of Art, London. Married Yoram Anselm; children: Kate and Amy. Began career retailing leading English design labels before turning to shoe and clothing design. Developed idea of "capsule wardrobes," coordinated clothes, shoe, and accessory design for women, 1980s. **Address:** 122 Gloucester Ave, London NW1 8HX, UK.

Publications:

On HOBBS:

Articles

Garrett, Pat, "Hobb's Choice," in *Homes & Antiques.*

*   *   *

A family business based in London, Hobbs is a successful clothing and footwear chain owned by designer Marilyn Anselm, with her husband Yoram in charge of finance, Kate Anselm as footwear designer and Amy Anselm the merchandise director in charge of shoes, clothes, and accessories. The targeted customer is perceived as an ABC1 woman between the ages of 20 and 40 who is interested in clothing "designed by mothers and daughters for mothers and daughters," which displays an understated yet unmistakeably English sense of style.

The origins of the business are with clothing retail, although it is footwear which has made the company's name. This success is possibly due to the fact that Marilyn Anselm has a background in sculpture, having studied at London's Central School of Art, and can render three-dimensional forms in a convincing manner. "A shoe designer should be a sculptor rather than a painter," she points out. Her fine art training is used in sculpting the company's heels and lasts.

The popularity of the footwear ranges can be explained by Marilyn Anselm's goal—to produce shoes of the same quality, style, and above all, with the comfort usually found in men's shoes. In women's footwear design the emphasis is often put on fashion, above all other considerations, the traditional idea being that the shoes are meant to be quickly phased out owing to rapidly changing trends in the women's retail market. Hobbs, however, produces classic, albeit slightly quirky designs which attempt to provide quality and style at an affordable price. An emphasis on good craftsmanship in production has led to the majority of Anselm's shoe and knitwear designs having to be manufactured in Italy. This achieves the desired quality of finish which she believes is unavailable in Britain for the same manufacturing costs.

Originally based in Hampstead in the early 1970s, the business concentrated on the retailing of leading English design labels until Anselm visited a shoe fair in Italy and was bowled over by what she saw. She began designing her own collection of shoes and clothes which led in turn to the setting up of the name company and its first shop in South Molton Street, London.

Hobbs's success is ultimately due to an emphasis on redesigning traditional British styles, using luxury natural fibres alongside newly developed fabrics such as Lycra for stretch or drape, and the notion

Hobbs Ltd.

of the capsule wardrobe, a coordinated approach to women's fashionwear. Anselm believes in designing a top-to-toe look, with every garment following a specific theme or fashion story; an idea later popularized on a massive scale by the lifestyle marketing campaigns of companies such as Next.

The name Hobbs makes direct reference to a particular kind of Britishness, as created and espoused by magazines such as *Country Living,* having been filched from an advertisement in *Horse and Hound* for George Hobb's Horseboxes. The imagery Hobbs plays on, from the design of the shops' interiors with their fruitwood shelves and wardrobes, wrought iron brackets, abundance of plants, and tapestry woven stools to the classic court shoes, cashmere reefers, jodhpurs, and linen trousers, is that of an ineffable and timeless Englishness, reflective of country houses, horses, and herbaceous borders—all this mediated through the gaze of a 20th-century businesswoman trading on the type of associations that Paul Smith has so successfully conjured up for men.

—Caroline Cox

HOGG, Pam.

British fashion designer

Born: Paisley, Scotland; grew up in Glasgow. **Education:** Studied Fine Art at Glasgow School of Art; switched to printed textiles course, winning two medals and two scholarships; MA in Textiles at Royal College of Art, London. **Career:** Lectured in Derby, England, and Glasgow while selling paper designs to New York and Paris. First collection Psychedelic Jungle, 1981. Singer in rock band, from 1987; current band Doll, from 1993. **Exhibitions:** Art Gallery Museum, Glasgow, June-August 1991. **Address:** 5 Newburgh St., London W1V 1LH, UK.

Publications:

On HOGG:

Articles

Franklin, Caryn, "Hogg in the Limelight," in *Clothes Show* (London), April 1989.
Godfrey, John, "Warrior Queen," in *i-D* (London), August 1989.
Niland, Seta, "Hogging the Spotlight," in *Fashion Weekly* (London), 22 March 1990.
Rodgers, Toni, "Double Vision," in *Elle* (London), March 1991.
Godfrey, John, "Pam Hogg," in *Elle* (London), June 1994.

*   *   *

Drawing on influences as diverse as sportswear, S&M rubberwear and 15th-century armour, Pam Hogg produces distinctive clubwear with a punk feel. Exploring similar routes to those charted by Vivienne Westwood, she has developed her own niche in the London fashion scene, while vehemently retaining elements of her native Scotland in her designs.

Riding the wave of British talent which swept to the forefront in the mid-1980s, Hogg, in common with John Richmond, represents the coming together of popular culture and fashion. She uses rock and roll as a constant source of visual ideas, to create strong images

for womenswear in PVC and studded leather. In a sense her clothes reflect her own lifestyle, her aspirations to pop stardom, which sometimes take precedence over her designing, and her enthusiastic involvement in London clubland. This close contact with street life enables her work to remain in tune with shifts in focus among the generation of clubbers and pop stars she has dressed.

Hogg's work is infused with the desire to create fashion as a series of costumes, first for the early 1980s New Romantic nightlife, with heady silver-printed velvets which drew upon her training in textiles, and later, as she began to establish a more coherent and distinctive look, in sporty stretch jersey with leather. Her clothes promote strong, often provocative images for women that dabble in the confrontational sexual and tribal motifs of punk, and respond to her own uncompromising personality.

In 1990, this interest in raw sexual statements was crystallized in a collection that included shiny black rubber front-laced catsuits and thigh-high spike heeled platform boots, which toyed with fetishism. The stark, anarchic personae created by such clothes are tempered by a sense of humour and frequent references to another strong look from the 1970s: glam rock. Hogg often uses sparkling gold lurex for leggings or bell bottoms that flout convention, to back fake cowhide chaps, or clashed with red tartan panels and fringing.

Her silver leather minikilts and studded biker jackets equally exemplified her mixing of imagery. In characteristic style, in the autumn to winter of 1989-90, she combined references to Joan of Arc with Hell's Angels and go-go dancers, dubbed the Warrior Queen collection. It was typical of her work; shiny corsets were worn with jersey separates with puffed shoulder and elbow sections that referred to slashed 15th-century styles and seemingly castellated cutout hems, and leather crowns-cum-helmets providing a nocturnal urban armour. Her work clearly runs parallel with Westwood's, yet Hogg is more concerned to explore subcultures and historical inspirations for strong imagery than for overriding philosophies.

The ability to combine shock tactics with wearable clothes continues in her menswear. This derives its distinctive style from similar sources, with punkish overtones and an overblown humour, combining macho leather with lace, gold trimmings, and the obligatory tartan. It challenges notions of what is acceptable as menswear and sets Hogg within the movement from the late 1980s to broaden the horizons of this area of design. Her own line was developed in response to the success of unisex garments within her women's range, with male customers keen to adopt Hogg's upbeat style and sport her flaming heart logo.

Despite having shifted her interest from clothing to music in 1992, her last collection continues to sell well, having become as close to a classic style as clubwear can do. Her encapsulation of the traits of British city street life—music, sex, rebellion, and a perverse sense of its own heritage—ensures a continued popularity. Hogg's success in Britain is complemented by the appeal of such witty, indigenous imagery to foreign buyers, who can quickly recognize her cult status.

—Rebecca Arnold

PETER HOGGARD.

British design firm

Founded by Michelle Hoggard (born in West Yorkshire, England, 1962), and Peter Leathers (born in Tyneside, England, 1962), in

Tyneside, 1983, selling clothes to local retail outlets; opened own outlet in Hyper Hyper store, London, 1985; first catwalk collection presented at British Fashion Week, London, 1986; opened shop in Rupert Court, London, 1987; established small factory in Yorkshire, England, to manufacture own label, 1987; established retail chain selling own label and other small designer labels, with shops in Leeds and Manchester, England, 1992. **Awards:** Yorkshire Television Young Business Entrepreneur of the Year, 1985; Fil d'Or Linen Award, Paris, 1991. **Address:** 32 Queen Victoria St, Victoria Quarter, Leeds, West Yorkshire, England.

*   *   *

When Oscar Wilde wrote "One should either wear a work of art or be a work of art," little did he imagine it would one day appear embroidered on the sleeve of a Peter Hoggard jacket. Ideas such as this, not to mention coats made from a Bayeux Tapestry print or Peter Rabbit appliqués on skirts, have been a staple of Peter Hoggard collections since their inception at the beginning of the 1980s. This was the age of Do It Yourself fashion, street credibility being the latest in media hypes, with style bibles such as *i-D* and *The Face* eagerly documenting the wild and outrageous sartorial antics of British youth.

Amid this heady atmosphere and fuelled by their joint passion for clothes and dressing up, Peter Leathers and Michelle Hoggard formed their fashion company. Hoggard explained, "We were both very visual people—I think that's why we were attracted to each other—I made my own clothes while Peter customized his."

Their first collection of clothes was inspired by Leather's innovative idea of making couture one-offs from hotel laundry, which were then sold to friends. Big, baggy shirts, each one sprayed with an individual pattern, were customized with *de rigueur* designer rips and tears. The skirts were spotted by television presenter Leslie Ash, when the duo appeared suitably attired on the set of pop music show *The Tube*. She promptly placed an order, as did guest artist Gary Glitter.

Encouraged, the duo decided to take the bull by the horns and approach the fashion world in a serious and business-like way. Becoming their own agents, they sold clothes to various retailers through a trunk show; this success led in turn to the opening of their own retail outlets and a stall in Hyper Hyper, the thriving and bustling centre for London's young and avant-garde designers in Kensington High Street.

Concentrating on womenswear with strong yet eclectic themes that were both interesting and inspirational to research, Peter Hoggard collections have evolved to embody a sophisticated designer interpretation of street fashion, in tune with the 1990s customer who demands quality and superb cut. Working in fabrics that often oppose and contradict—linen and raffia, venetian wool and plastic, waxed cotton piping and rayon—themes have included prints based on dollar and pound signs and ships' rigging, which incorporated jackets and sheath dresses with waxed cotton piped sleeves or inserts. Bomber jackets in plastic with Dada-inspired imagery are appliquéd and reembroidered to create a cornucopia of reference. and crushed velvet mini dresses and jackets are trimmed in New Age crystal.

Peter Hoggard are part of a similar breed of talented British designers and design duos to emerge in the early 1980s, Bodymap, Richmond/Cornejo, and Mark and Syrie being contemporaries. Compared to the vast success of international designers such as Gianni Versace or Calvin Klein, Peter Hoggard and company run the risk of being shackled by what Michelle Hoggard calls "the great British disease," that being the traditional difficulties that small designers have with production. This in a British industry that is geared up to the medium quality mass market yet fails in the mainstream to appreciate and comprehend designer clothing, except perhaps as a source for ideas and reference. When public relations officer Richard Titchner described Peter Hoggard as being "the best kept secret in fashion," his ironic statement served only as a reminder that many talented individuals have had to go abroad to be taken seriously as creative designers. Peter Hoggard view themselves as an endangered species, determined to retain their design integrity and a very English look to their product.

—Kevin Almond

HOLAH, David. See **BODYMAP.**

HOPE, Emma.
British footwear designer

Born: Portsmouth, England, 11 July 1962. **Education:** Studied at Cordwainers College, Hackney, London, 1981-84. **Career:** Business established in London, 1984, first collection sold to Whistles, Joseph and Jones, London; designed and manufactured six collections for Laura Ashley, 1985-87; also designed for, among others, The Chelsea Design Co., Betty Jackson, Jean Muir, English Eccentrics, 1985-87; opened first London store, 1987; designed for Harel, Paris, 1988, for Arabella Pollen, 1989, and for Nicole Farhi, from 1989. Also footwear fashion critic, from 1988. **Awards:** Five Design Council Awards, 1987-88; Martini Style Award, 1988; *Harper's and Queen* Award, 1989. **Address:** 33 Amwell St., London EC1R 1UR, England.

Publications:

By HOPE:

Articles

"Shoe Design: Tiptoeing into Industry," in *Design* (London), November 1988.

On HOPE:

Books

Debrett's *People of Today,* London 1991.

Articles

Callen, Kerena, and Liz Freemantle, "Bit Parts," in *Elle* (London), May 1987.
Lott, Jane, and Charity Durant, "Hoofers to the Nation," in *The Observer* (London), 30 August 1987.

Rumbold, Judy, "The Last Shall Be First," in *The Guardian* (London), 21 September 1987.

"Brave New Heels," in *Connoisseur* (London), October 1987.

Thackara, John, "Put Your Foot in It," in *The Observer Magazine* (London), 22 November 1987.

Allott, Serena, "A Foot in Every Door," in *The Daily Telegraph,* 20 November 1989.

"A Life in the Day of Emma Hope," in *The Sunday Times* (London), November 1991.

Sharpe, Antonia, "Frivolity with Discipline," in *The Financial Times* Saturday edition (London), June 1992.

*   *   *

Emma Hope was part of the flowering of talent in British shoe design in the late 1980s. She trained at Cordwainers Technical College in London's Hackney along with successful contemporaries Christine Ahrens, Elizabeth Stuart-Smith, and Patrick Cox; there, she received a thorough technical grounding which has enabled her to design free, fanciful shoes which are also practical and comfortable to wear. Her first collection was sold to shops in London and America in 1984 and she has produced shoes for leading fashion designers including Jean Muir, Bill Gibb, John Flett, Betty Jackson, and Joe Caseley-Hayford. From 1987 she began to exhibit collections under her own name. In the same year her work was featured in the 22 different styles of boots and shoes accepted by the Design Council for their Footwear Selection.

The opening of Hope's own shop in London in 1987 marked a new phase. She acknowledged that it caused her to produce designs which were more straightforward and wearable. She has described her shoes as "regalia for feet," decorative and distinctive but with comfort being an important feature. Inspiration comes from historical sources studied in the collections of the Victoria and Albert Museum in London and the Shoe Museum in Northampton. Paintings and Greek and Roman statues are explored for source material as well. Louis heels and elongated toes are often to be seen in her work. Emma Hope's shoes feature in the style pages of fashionable magazines such as *Vogue, Cosmopolitan,* and *Harper's and Queen.* The regular appearance of her shoes in more specialized publications such as *Wedding and Home* reflects her prominence in the field of decorative special occasion shoes. For example, a pair of white shoes sprigged with coloured embroidered flowers, simple in outline and with pointed toes, appearing in *Wedding and Home* magazine in April/May 1992. They retailed at £239.

Her shoes are made up to her specification in London, where she has access to skilled craftspeople who can embroider the fabric uppers she favours. The existence of a network of individual craftspeople supports the revival of handcrafted shoes designed by Emma Hope and her contemporaries, operating in the gap between custom-made and High Street shoe manufacture. However, all of the new young designers acknowledge the difficulty of finding enough skilled workers to carry out their designs. Relationships with suppliers and craftspeople are carefully built up and jealously guarded. Emma Hope's success at the designer end of the shoe trade is indicated by her winning two design prizes, the Martini Style Award in 1988 and the Smirnoff Award in 1989.

Mary Bentham of Russell and Bromley writing in *The Guardian* in 1987 suggested that the products of the new breed of shoe designers were not a commercial proposition and wondered whether they would still be around in five years' time. Emma Hope has certainly proved that she is here to stay and that it is possible to sell interesting, stylish, handcrafted shoes in Britain.

—Linda Coleing

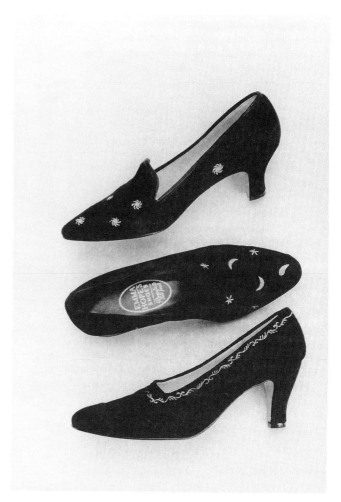

Emma Hope.

HOWELL, Margaret.

British fashion designer

Born: Tadworth, Surrey, 1946. **Education:** Studied Fine Art at Goldsmiths' College, London. **Collections:** Museum of Costume, Bath; Victoria & Albert Museum, London. **Address:** 5 Garden House, 8 Battersea Pk Rd, London SW8 4BG, UK.

Publications:

On HOWELL:

Books

Mulvagh, Jane, *Vogue History of 20th Century Fashion,* London 1988.

Rothstein, Natalie, *400 Years of Fashion,* London 1984.

Articles

Rumbold, Judy, "A Howell of Triumph," in *The Guardian* (London), 26 October 1987.

"Designs on Men," in *Elle* (London), February 1990.

Armstrong, Lisa, "Fashioned for Life as Women Live It," in *The Independent* (London), 2 April 1992.

Reed, Paula, "Out of the Woods," in *The Sunday Times* (London), 13 September, 1992.

*

From an early age I remember having an awareness of clothes and a response to those of my parents; the softness of my Father's well-worn cotton shirts and raincoat, the slim hang of a pleated chiffon dress my Mother used for ballroom dancing. She made her children's clothes. I loved the smell of new cotton as it was cut. I had fun making my school uniform stylish in the early '60s. We wore our skirts long with ankle socks. We bought men's cardigans from Marks and Spencer. I enjoyed the androgynous character of the white shirt, the duffle coat and the double breasted gaberdine raincoats. In fact, I was styling the basics which I think is what I do now. I take a classic and reinterpret it by cut, detailing and the choice of fabric to make it modern and enjoyable to wear.

I am interested in the selection and then the editing process that goes on in design and in the grouping of things together to make a statement as a result of their selection. I am more interested in styling, quality and workmanship than in the impact of fashion, but the styling has to run parallel with a current fashion that is determined by lifestyle and the needs of today.

—Margaret Howell

*   *   *

An established name in British fashion design, Margaret Howell originally trained as a fine artist at Goldsmiths' College of Art in London in the 1960s. Although having no formal training in fashion, in 1971 she produced her first range of accessories, the success of which led to the creation of a small business, printing and selling scarves to boutiques. Later she began designing men's shirts, which were sold in South Molton Street by Joseph.

Her clothes for both men and women, designed from the early 1970s onwards, are based on a typically English look, using vernacular materials such as Melton cloth, tweed, and wool. The clothing makes references to what are considered to be traditional approaches to dressing—the British traditions of cashmere and tweeds but twisted into a more relaxed image which is particularly appealing to Americans. Howell has a shop in New York. Her reinterpretations of classic English clothes—a style dubbed "preppy" in the United States and equally successfully interpreted in Ralph Lauren's Polo range—negotiate a series of experiments around standard garments such as the striped cotton shirt, box pleated skirt, Fair Isle sweater, or archetypal cardigan as in the 1994 cashmere version with tiny pearl buttons worn with silk pyjama bottoms. The clothes themselves seem hardly to alter from season to season and it seems ironic that Howell, a designer noted for timeless classics, is involved in the fashion world which operates on the notion of novelty for novelty's sake rather than being allied to any improved functionality. However, "timelessness" and "classic" are a staple part of fashion terminology used to describe and market looks which connote notions of wealth and taste through good tailoring and the use of traditional materials. The classic look signifies affluence through the wearing of clothes which fit within the parameters of understated elegance and sophisticated taste; an emphasis on the texture of the materials used and the expertise of tailoring rather than more obviously conceptual ideas like grunge or punk. This concept has been successfully utilised in the design and marketing of Armani, say, or Hermès.

Howell's clothes also operate successfully on the notion of nostalgia. Past eras such as the 1930s are referenced in women's eveningwear, particularly the 1950s in daywear, an evocation of an Enid Blyton world where boys wear cricket flannels or knee-length shorts and girls wear cotton frocks, short socks, and cardies. In the early 1980s British style guru Peter York dubbed Howell the designer for Babytimers, those who wore archaic children's clothes particularly from their own childhoods, clothes with a children's book feel as worn by the Famous Five or Just William. Striped blazers, Fairisle slipovers, macintoshes, and flannel trousers in archaic cuts are all staples of Margaret Howell's collections. With the demise of the Babytime era, however, and the assertion of the tougher 1980s power look, Howell's clothes were later bought for their comfort and "classic" qualities by the more "aesthetically aware" consumer who considers yarns, dyes, and reworkings of conventional clothing forms before the vagaries of high fashion.

The contemporary Howell look is praised for its pared-down line and simple silhouettes, the controlled restraint of shape and colour, the workmanship and quality of cloth and cut. By the mid-1990s she was concentrating on women's clothing, particularly trouser suits which have always been an integral part of her collections. The 1994 autumn-winter version featured masculine suiting feminized with soft chiffon scarves. Her designs for jackets, eveningwear, and nightwear still have a feel for styles of the past—such as her 1994 white handkerchief linen pyjamas. These styles evoke memories of her own childhood, such as her father's gardening raincoat which hung on the back door, her mother's cotton dresses, and an English sporting look popularized by designers from Chanel onwards and seen in Howell's nautical navy cotton cardigans with brass buttons and linen jodhpurs, worn with a white linen shawl-collared shirt.

—Caroline Cox

HULANICKI, Barbara.
British designer

Born: Warsaw, Poland, 8 December 1936. Raised in Palestine, immigrated to England in 1948. **Education:** Studied fashion and fashion illustration at Brighton College, 1954-56; winner in the *Evening Standard* Design Competition, beachwear division, 1955. **Family:** Married Stephen Fitz-Simon in 1961; one son: Witwold. **Career:** Illustrator for Helen Jardine Artists, London, c.1956-59; free-lance fashion illustrator, 1961-64; opened Biba's Postal Boutique, 1963; established first Biba emporium, Abingdon Road, London, 1964; moved and expanded to Church Street, London, 1965; opened branch location in Brighton, 1966; launched mail order catalogue, 1968; moved Biba to High Street, Kensington, London, 1969; introduced line of Biba cosmetics, 1969; cosmetics distributed nationally through Dorothy Perkins shops, 1969; introduced line of footwear, 1969; 75% interest in company sold to consortium of investors, 1969; Biba boutique established at Bergdorf Goodman, New York, 1970; purchased Derry and Toms Department Store for "Big Biba," 1972; control of firm passed to British Land, 1972; Big Biba opened, 1973, closed, 1975; firm declared bankruptcy, 1976. Fashion designer in Brazil, 1976-80; relocated to Miami Beach, Florida, 1987;

Margaret Howell.

designer of hotel and club interiors, videos, ready-to-wear children's clothes, theatre costumes, from 1988. **Exhibitions:** Retrospective, Newarke Houses Museum, Leicester, England, 1993. **Awards:** Bath Museum of Costume Dress of the Year Award, 1972. **Address:** 1300 Collins Avenue, Suite 205, Miami Beach, Florida 35139, USA.

Publications:

By HULANICKI:

Books

From A to Biba, London 1983.
Disgrace, London 1990.

Articles

"The Dedicated Modeller of Fashion," in *The Times* (London), 15 August 1983.
"When Big Becomes Beautiful," in *The Times* (London), 16 August 1983.
"The Shattering of a Dream," in *The Times* (London), 17 August 1983.

On HULANICKI:

Books

Bernard, Barbara, *Fashion in the 60's,* London 1978.
Harris, Jennifer, Sarah Hyde and Greg Smith, *1966 and All That: Design and the Consumer in Britain, 1960-1969,* London 1986.
Whiteley, Nigel, *Pop Design: Modernism to Mod,* London 1987.
Loebenthal, Joel, *Radical Rags: Fashions of the Sixties,* New York 1990.

Articles

"Twiggy in Bibaland," in *Vogue* (London), December 1973.
"Biba: What Went Wrong?," in *Drapers Record* (London), 30 August 1975.
"Biba," in *The Times* (London), 1 April 1976.
"Biba Is Back: A 'Paradise' in London," in *Drapers Record* (London), 2 December 1978.
"Bye-bye Biba—Hello Hulanicki," in *Women's Journal* (London), March 1981.
Brampton, Sally, "Bringing Up Baby," in *The Observer* (London), 4 September 1983.
Neustatter, Angela, "Biba and Son," in *The Sunday Times Magazine* (London), 18 May 1986.
Samuel, Kathryn, "Biba Goes Back to the Drawing Board," in *The Daily Telegraph* (London), 19 June 1986.
Neustatter, Angela, "Life No. 3 for the Biba Girl," in *The Daily Telegraph* (London), 21 January 1987.
Cuccio, Angela, "Mini Rock Rolls," in *Women's Wear Daily* (New York), 10 October 1988.
Brampton, Sally, "Barbara Hulanicki and *Disgrace,*" in *The Correspondent Magazine* (London), 25 March 1990.
McRobbie, Angela, *"Disgrace,"* [book review] in *New Statesman and Society,* 30 March 1990.
Fallon, James, "Barbara Hulanicki, Biba and Beyond," in *Women's Wear Daily* (New York), 14 May 1990.

Gandee, Charles, "Barbara Hulanicki Is Hot for Miami," in *House & Garden* (New York), June 1992.
Webb, Michael, "Island Fantasy," in *Hospitality Design,* July/August 1992.
Tredre, Roger, "Heaven Was a Place Called Biba," in *The Independent* (London), 12 February 1993.
Godley, Georgina, "The Importance of Biba," in *Blueprint* (London), No. 96, April 1993.

*   *   *

In the decade from 1964 to 1974, Barbara Hulanicki's design and entrepreneurial skills contributed to the development of an entirely new ethos in British fashion which responded to ideas generated by the rising youth culture of the period. Hulanicki and her husband Stephen Fitz-Simon created a series of fashion businesses, under the name of Biba, perfectly suited to the spirit of change and adventure which characterized the Mod movement originating in London during the early 1960s. Unlike the English establishment rag trade, Hulanicki understood that fashion ideas would, henceforth, originate in the streets of British cities, rather than in couture houses across the Channel. She styled her shop as a meeting spot and a place of entertainment for those interested in a lifestyle represented by the clothes and other goods designed by Hulanicki.

Following a year at art school, Hulanicki set up Biba's Postal Boutique in the early 1960s, with herself as designer and Fitz-Simon as business manager. The success of their business was assured when an early design for a simple smock dress was worn by Cathy McGowan, "Queen of the Mods," on the popular television programme *Ready, Steady, Go.* The first Biba shop was opened in 1964 in a small, old-fashioned chemist's shop on a corner of Abingdon Road, Kensington, London. Hulanicki concentrated on generating a unique atmosphere through décor, music, and the glamour of the young shop assistants—all of which turned her shop into an instant "scene," a gathering place for a hip, young clientèle who knew where to go for the latest ideas in clothing, without even the benefit of a sign over the shop-front.

Hulanicki's early clothes were short, simple dresses, the "Biba smock" which became the uniform for an era. Her little girl look was given a major boost when Julie Christie selected her wardrobe for the film *Darling* from the Biba shop. Other early customers included Sonny and Cher, Twiggy, and Mick Jagger. The typical Biba dolly girl would have a slim, boyish figure, huge eyes and a childlike pout, updating the Audrey Hepburn gamine look of the 1950s. She would wear a simple mini dress selected from a wide range of muted colours, blueberry, rust, plum, which Hulanicki called Auntie colours, as they had previously been associated with the wardrobes of old ladies. At this time, she also introduced the first fashion T-shirts, distinguished from their ordinary equivalent by the range of Auntie colours in which they were dyed. The T-shirts initiated the unisex appeal of Biba goods.

In 1966, the shop moved to larger premises in Kensington Church Street. The new shop sported a black and gold art nouveau logo and was decorated in an eclectic mix of late 19th-century decadent motifs, Victoriana and art deco. Hulanicki expanded her range of clothing to include fashion accessories, including bangles and feather boas displayed on old-fashioned bentwood hatstands, cosmetics, menswear, and household accessories. The Church Street Biba became an internationally known symbol of Swinging London in the mid-1960s.

In the early 1970s, the Biba style developed in the direction of retro glamour and glitter. Hulanicki introduced a line of children's clothing which followed the styles and colours of the adult ranges. She featured items such as straw hats with veils and artificial flowers, velvet and lace, all enhanced by a new element of innocent eroticism and un-childlike glamour. Her cosmetics had, by the late 1960s, become big business, the range of colours corresponding to the Auntie colours of her clothing and including bizarre hues such as blue, green, purple, and black lipstick, eye-shadow and powder.

Rapidly increasing sales forced Biba to move again, in 1969, to a larger shop in Kensington High Street where art nouveau and art deco fused into a single style which became Biba's own. During the early 1970s, Hulanicki and Fitz-Simon expanded their operations to the United States through New York's Bergdorf Goodman, which set up a Biba boutique in its flagship store.

The final phase of expansion came in 1973 when Hulanicki opened the Biba department store in the former Derry and Toms premises in Kensington High Street, London. This enormous art deco building housed a huge enterprise which provided a complete setting, including an all-day restaurant and nightly entertainment in the glamorous Rainbow Room, exotic roof gardens, and a kasbah for the elegant and exotic retro style clothes, all designed by Hulanicki. The Biba store was, for a short time, a mecca for fashionable young Londoners looking for a setting in which to parade the elegant and eclectic clothing of the period. Management difficulties forced Hulanicki to leave Biba in the mid-1970s. She eventually moved to Brazil and thence to Florida, where she began to design under the Hulanicki name.

—Gregory Votolato

IJ

I. MAGNIN. See under **MAGNIN.**

IRIÉ, Sueo.

Japanese designer working in France

Born: Osaka, Japan, 23 December 1946. **Education:** Graduated from Osaka Sogo Fukoso Gakium, 1970. **Career:** Assistant to Hiroko Koshino, 1968. Moved to Paris, 1970; assistant designer, Kenzo, 1970-79; presented first collection as designer for Studio V, 1980. Set up own shop, 1983. **Exhibitions:** *Technology and Design,* Victoria & Albert Museum, London. **Address:** 8, rue du Pre-aux-Clercs, 75007 Paris, France.

Publications:

On IRIÉ:

Books

The Tokyo Collection, Tokyo 1986.

Articles

de L'Homme, F., "Irié ou l'art de la simplicity," in *Dépèche Mode* (Paris), March 1987.
Betts, K., "The Next Wave," in *Women's Wear Daily* (New York), April 1990.
Carter, Charles, "Europe 1990: Designers to Watch," in *Vogue* (New York), August 1990.
Risbourg, P., "View: European Designers to Watch," in *Vogue* (New York), August 1990.
Hochswender, Woody, "Clothes of Irié: Stylish, But Not Stuffy," in the *New York Times,* September 1990.
Bailhache, P., "Créateurs: Leur monde secret," in *Marie-Claire* (Paris), October 1992.
Menkes, Suzy, "On Paris's Left Bank," in *International Herald Tribune* (Neuilly, France), May 1993.
Coppet, A., "Irié, le succès merité," in *Marie-Claire Bis* (Paris), Autumn 1993.
Zamelly, C., "Irié a l'affiche de St Germain-des-Pres," in *Elle* (Paris), Autumn 1993.
Ronaldson, F., "Designer Inspiration Focus Irié," in *Joyce* (Hong Kong), Autumn 1993.

*

I wish to continue creating, inspired by the air of the present.

—Sueo Irié

*　　*　　*

Irié is the name of a Japanese-born designer who first travelled to Europe in the 1970s. Over the last 20 years, he has built a life and career in fashion, based in St. Germain des Prés, Paris. With his clothes available from boutiques across France, and outlets in Munich and Milan, Irié is a craftsman-artist of contemporary fashion.

Arriving in Paris, on the Trans-Siberian Express, with little money and no firm plans, Irié worked for the Japanese designer Kenzo before opening his own shop and launching his own collection in 1983. Irié claims that opening his first outlet would never have happened, except that, on the spur of the moment, he bought a Corinthian column from a Paris flea market and decided he needed a boutique in which to house it. By the mid-1990s the company remained very small. Irié oversees everything himself: stock, manufacture, sales, and customer satisfaction. Though he plans to open a new shop in Rome, there is a feeling that for Irié, one could be enough.

The style of Irié's collections is simplicity paired with casual chic. Irié likes to design for women, all women, across the spectrum of age and profession. He keeps his clothes simple and believes they form a base upon which women can build; the raw components of a wardrobe to which a woman can add personal touches as required. The clothes adapt to let the wearer's identity shine through. Irié's early innovations included the use of Lycra to increase comfort of short skirts. He also designed colourful leotards as underclothes, long before they became an established and popular fashion.

Irié excludes no colours from his designs. The 1990s collections include splashes of brighter acid toned, fluorescent hues. Irié also makes extensive use of patterned fabrics, some of which he designs himself. Patterns range from romantic florals to wild fantasy, and here we find the one recurring theme of Irié's collections: animal-skin prints. The materials and fabrics he uses are dictated by his professed preference for comfort and convenience: natural cotton, wool, and silk, as well as synthetics, polyester, vinyl, and fake fur. He uses stretch fabrics everywhere.

Irié's essential idea is cheap chic. His ideal woman would wear a Chanel jacket with cheap trainers. He defines elegance as an expensive shirt worn with old jeans and Tiffany earrings to a black-tie dinner. He claims to be motivated to create clothes that allow a woman to share lunch with her banker in *Paris 16e* then drink a *café noisette* with some friends on the *Rive Gauche*.

Irié's influences are all French: café life-styles and black-and-white French films. There is nothing of the Far East in his clothes; no hint of Asian heritage. *Champagne* or *Coca Cola,* Irié is Westernized through and through. His originality is his presentation. For

Sueo Irié: Fall/Winter 1994/95; wool scarf top with bias skirt.
Photograph courtesy of Vague 7.

a small design company he has big designer pretensions. His Paris boutique, all chrome and mirrors, houses a stuffed zebra, a grand piano, and the enduring Corinthian column. Another stuffed lion is kept in his flat. Though he may head a small-scale company, he does not act like a small player. The clothes he sells are the best quality at affordable prices.

The Irié collection is really too small to influence a larger fashion world, apart from one essential way. Irié's influence is his choice to live in a small flat, two minutes from his shop, to keep his business small, and to enjoy a full life in Paris. His is neither the great fame nor associated wealth and power problems of the large designers. Daytimes, he creates fabrics, designs and sells clothes to pay his bills and fuel his moped. At night he loses himself in a Parisian nightlife that might be a long night of philosophical conversation over *pastis,* or a concert by Vanessa Paradis.

—Sally Ann Melia

ISANI.

Korean design team working in America

Isani comprised of Jun Kim (born in Korea, 1966) and Soyon Kim (born in Korea, 1968). Trained in their family's Sao Paulo, Brazil,

clothing firm, Anderson, Ltd. Jun Kim studied marketing, Pace University, New York, B.A., 1988, and fashion design for one semester, Parsons School of Design, New York. Soyon Kim studied fashion design, Parsons School of Design, B.F.A., 1989. Designer sportswear line shown, 1988-93; Isani Studio bridge line introduced; Christina line introduced, 1990; Isani Shirts blouse collection introduced, 1992.

Publications:

On ISANI:

Articles

"Great Expectations," in *Women's Wear Daily* (New York), 12 June 1991.
White, Constance C. R., "Isani's Busy Signals: A Hot Line," in *Women's Wear Daily* (New York), 4 September 1991.
White, Constance C. R., "Isani: Facing Reality," in *Women's Wear Daily* (New York), 2 June 1993.

*   *   *

Cosmopolitan, discreet, stylish clothing created by Jun and Soyon Kim for Isani bespeaks a worldly grace and a reserved, sensible approach to clothing rarely associated with young designers. But the Kim pair (brother Jun and sister Soyon) purposefully spare themselves the excesses more commonly seen in young designers to practice the calculations of the most stylish, creating clothes in the scrupulous heritage of Mainbocher and Halston as an American tailoring for a sophisticated client. The design propensity is modernist, but there is often a picturesque charm to the garments, whether in their Jackie O dresses in suave 1960s revival in 1991 or the fall-winter 1992 accommodations of menswear to the most delicate details and accentuated femininity of fit. Jun Kim avers: "Our clothes are directed at American women, but they're not typical American sportswear. They reflect an approach to fashion that looks right anywhere in the world." In this avowal and attribute, Isani represents the possibility of clothing in the 1990s to surpass parochial sense of nationhood and even global regionalism to seek a style that would be right and reasonable in any major city of the world. The designers, who were born in Korea but grew up chiefly in Brazil followed by higher education and the launch of their professional careers in New York, chose Isani as the firm's name from the Italian for "healthy." As one of the most urbane design teams in fashion today, Isani offers easy translation in one language, but it also offers a sweet euphony that equally characterizes their worldly, elegant style.

There is a secure sense of anachronism about Isani. It eschews the aggressiveness of much young design; its bashful and absolute discretion and its predilection for exquisite refinement are hallmarks of fashion design before World War II. No such historicism exists in the work, but there is an ethos, a point of view that is distinctly and positively old-fashioned, a one-world global optimism, a woman-assuming-working-power pragmatism, and an elegance in self-confident subtlety. While Isani clothing is directed toward a middle-class consumer, the design recalls the couture in its suppressed, cultivated aplomb.

Isani has achieved a distinctiveness in the marketplace even in its first collections, so refined is the sensibility and so subtle are the plays in the fabrication and proportions. Even the spring-summer

1992 collection, inspired in its color by some aspects of the Brazilian carnival, was characterized by the same simplicity and reserve of other Isani collections. The inspiration of Jacqueline Kennedy Onassis and the 1960s was, as the designers admit, a "very fresh way of interpreting" the period by two designers too young to remember the 1960s directly. But their recollection was not the hyperbole and exaggeration offered by some other young designers: it was instead a kind of elegant, reductive modernism with the chic that Mrs Onassis has epitomized in the time. Their historical memory of the 1950s and 1960s is, they admit, largely through the movies and their immediate reference to Audrey Hepburn suggests the romance of their interpretation of clothes. Citing their love of trimmings and buttons, the Kims use these details in elegant understatement, sparingly and in proportion. The Kims love suits, recognize the suit as a wardrobe builder, especially for the working woman, and perfect the suit the way a composer creates *concerti,* an inexorable and fascinating pursuit of perfection through finesse.

The Kims propose that the most important aspect of fashion design is that clothes have to be real, with the prospective client able to associate herself with the vision of the designer. Isani reconciles this plausibility and wearability with a romantic imagination about clothing, coming from movie images and a strong sense of a ladylike but practical presence in dress. In saying that the client is dressed "not to be the center of attention," the designers describe the woman of impeccable taste, but of reserve and charm. It is this elusive woman, whom others have abandoned in the 1990s, that the Isani team chooses to define and dress. They make clothing that is always smart-looking and appropriate, but never ostentatious. The "lady" still exists, as dressed in the contemporary but decidedly decorous manner of Isani.

—Richard Martin

JACKSON, Betty.

British designer

Born: Bacup, Lancashire, 24 June 1949. **Education:** Studied at Birmingham College of Art, 1968-71. **Family:** Married David Cohen in 1985; children: Pascale and Oliver. **Career:** Free-lance fashion illustrator, London, 1971-73; design assistant to Wendy Dagworthy, London, 1973-75; chief designer, Quorum, London, 1975-81. Director and chief designer, Betty Jackson Ltd., London, from 1981; Betty Jackson for Men collection introduced, 1986; opened flagship shop in the Brompton Road, London, 1991. **Awards:** *Woman* Magazine Separates Designer of the Year Award, London, 1981, 1983; Cotton Institute Cotton Designer of the Year Award, 1983; Bath Museum of Costume Dress of the Year Award, 1984; British Designer of the Year Award, 1985; Harvey Nichols Award, 1985; International Linen Council Fil d'Or Award, 1985, 1989; Viyella Award, 1987; Honorary Fellow, Royal College of Art, London, 1989; Fellow, Birmingham Polytechnic, 1989; Honorary Fellow, University of Central Lancashire, 1992; Member of the British Empire, 1987. **Address:** 33 Tottenham Street, London W1P 9PE, England.

Publications:

On JACKSON:

Articles

Spankie, Sarah, "First Sight: The Chiller Thriller from the Jackson File," in *The Sunday Times Magazine* (London), 6 May 1984.

Dodd, C., "Betty Jackson: Seeing Through to the Street," in *Design* (London), November 1984.

"Influences: Betty Jackson," in *Woman's Journal* (London), April 1985.

Brampton, Sally, "The Elle-Shaped Room: A Fine Collection," in *Elle* (London), April 1986.

"Designer Reports. Summer '87. London: Betty Jackson," in *International Textiles* (London), December 1986.

Rumbold, Judy, "Jackson Heights," in *The Guardian* (London), 28 September 1987.

Fremantle, Liz, "Designer Focus: Betty Jackson," in *Cosmopolitan* (London), November 1988.

"Betty Jackson," in *DR: The Fashion Business* (London), 3 December 1988.

*

My work is understated and easy. I do not like formal dressing and I always try to achieve a relaxed and casual look. The mix of texture and pattern is very important and we work with many textile designers to have specialness and exclusivity on fabrics. Unexpected fabrics are often used in simple, classic shapes.

—Betty Jackson

*   *   *

"What makes you most depressed?," Betty Jackson was once asked by a fashion editor. Her reply was that it was only when work was going badly and that in such situations strength of character and conviction became important assets. It comes as no surprise therefore to find that she admires strong women, "Bold and casual like Lauren Bacall." A stoic, no-nonsense fashion approach underpins a business that Jackson declares began in a recession only to find itself in one again when the company celebrated its tenth anniversary in 1991.

Betty Jackson began her career at Birmingham College of Art in 1968, working in London as a free-lance fashion illustrator until 1973 when she joined Wendy Dagworthy as her design assistant. She moved to further positions at Quorum, then Coopers, before setting up her own design company with husband David Cohen in 1981. Success was quick to come, culminating in several awards including The Cotton Institute Designer of the Year in 1983 and the Fil d'or Award from the International Linen Council in 1985, the year she was also named British Designer of the Year; two years later she was awarded the MBE in the Queen's Birthday Honours list for services to British industry and export as well as becoming an elected member of The British Fashion Council.

Betty Jackson has gained an international reputation as a designer of young, up-to-the-minute clothes. "I've never liked prettiness much," she is quoted as saying, and this is reflected in her designs. She rescales separates into larger and unstructured proportions. Loose, uncomplicated shapes with no awkward cuts are often made up in boldly coloured and patterned fabrics. Jackson loves bright prints and knits, often working in conjunction with the textile designers Timney Fowler in colours that complement the warm, smoky, and earthy base colours of the collections. The oversized printed shirts and hand knit sweaters are always popular and usually the first garments to sell out. Previous print and knit themes have been inspired by Sonia Delauney, oversized paisleys or abstract painterly shapes and textures reminiscent of Matisse or Braque.

Betty Jackson: Fall/Winter 1994.

The rescaled sporty shapes give the clothes an androgynous feeling which was reflected when the menswear collection was launched in 1986. However Jackson never uses androgyny to shock or alienate her established customer or to make a fashion statement. Instead her themes evolve each season, incorporating the newest shapes, lengths, and fabrics. She tends to favour expensive, supple fabrics like linen, suede, or viscose mixes, crêpes, chenilles, and soft jerseys.

She has said that she prefers not to follow trends set by other designers or predictions from fashion forecasters. Instead she prefers to source her own ides for inspiration; ideas that are relevant to her and her own design philosophies. "There's nothing like taking a colour you love, making something wonderful, and seeing a beautiful girl wearing it. I think if you ever tire of that feeling, then it's time to think again," she says.

The most recent developments at Betty Jackson Ltd have been the opening of a shop which she describes as her greatest extravagance. She was quick, however, to deny that extravagance implied recklessness "... and it's certainly not reckless as it's part of a well laid plan." She has also turned her talents to accessories; chunky jewellery in bright colours encased in bronze and silver, soft suede gloves, belts, bags, and printed scarves.

Jackson declares that the single thing that would most improve the quality of her life would be more time. "I organize myself badly and never have enough time to do anything." It is the dilemma of many creative people, forced to sacrifice precious creative time to the day-to-day practicalities of running a business. However, lack of time has not halted Betty Jackson's achievements; her business is thriving and she has recently been made honorary fellow of both the Royal College of Art, London, and the University of Central Lancashire.

—Kevin Almond

JACOBS, Marc.

American designer

Born: New York City, 1964. **Education:** Graduated from Parsons School of Design, New York, 1984. **Career:** Designer, Sketchbook label, for Ruben Thomas Inc., New York, 1984-85; managed own firm, 1986-88; named vice-president for womenswear, Perry Ellis, 1988; head designer, Perry Ellis, New York, 1989-93, Marc Jacobs, 1994-. **Awards:** Parsons School of Design Perry Ellis Golden Thimble Award, 1984; Council of Fashion Designers of America Perry Ellis Award, 1988; Womenswear Designer of the Year Award, 1992. **Address:** 113 Spring Street, New York, New York 10012, USA.

Publications:

On JACOBS:

Articles

Badum, John, and Kurt Kilgus, "So Good They Named It Twice: A Second Bite at the Big Apple," in *Fashion '86* (London), 1985.

Boyes, Kathleen, "Marc Jacobs: Getting Focused, Staying Passionate," in *Women's Wear Daily* (New York), 4 April 1988.

Allis, Tim, "At 25, Whimsy-Loving Designer Marc Jacobs Has Been Up, Down, and Everywhere in Between," in *People* (Chicago), 2 May 1988.

Young, Lucie, "Corporate Greed: A Fashionable Vice," in *Design* (London), August 1988.

Lockwood, Lisa, "Jacobs Is In, Pastor Is Out at Perry Ellis," in *Women's Wear Daily* (New York), 23 November 1988.

DeCaro, Frank, "A Very-Perry New Boss," in *Newsday* (Long Island, New York), 6 December 1988.

Edersheim, Peggy, "The Comeback Kid," in *Manhattan, Inc.* (New York), February 1989.

Gooch, Brad, "Jacobs Makes His Mark," in *Vanity Fair,* April 1989.

Wayne, George, "Verry Jacobs," in *Paper,* May 1989.

Worthington, Christa, "The Three Choicest Dudes in the USA," in *The Sunday Times Magazine* (London), 26 August 1990.

Martin, Richard, "Double Entendres: Art, Decorative Arts, and Fashion Discourse in Marc Jacobs for Perry Ellis, 1991," in *Textile and Text* (New York), 13/4, 1991.

Postner, Caryl, "Jacobs Ladder: Climbing to the Top," in *Footwear News* (New York), 3 June 1991.

Orlean, Susan, "Breaking Away," in *Vogue* (New York), September 1992.

Boehlert, Bart, "12 Minutes: Marc Jacobs," *QW* (New York), 8 November 1992.

James, Laurie, "On the Marc," in *Harper's Bazaar* (New York), January 1993.

"Designer Dish," in *Women's Wear Daily* (New York), 29 March 1993.

Norwich, William, "As Retail Shrinks, Jacobs Thinks," in the *New York Observer,* 24 January 1994.

Foley, Bridget, "Hard Acts to Follow: Marc Jacobs," in *Women's Wear Daily* (New York), 24 October 1994.

Spindler, Amy M., "Lots of Sugar, With Some Pinches of Spice," in the *New York Times,* 31 October 1994.

"New York: Marc Jacobs," in *Women's Wear Daily* (New York), 31 October 1994.

Menkes, Suzy, "Amid the Trashy Glamour, the Ladies Have Their Day," in *International Herald Tribune* (Paris), 1 November 1994.

Davis, Peter, "Men à la Mode," in *Genre* (Hollywood, California), March 1995.

Spindler, Amy M., "Mod Look Returns, à la Jacobs," in the *New York Times,* 5 April 1995.

"New York: Marc Jacobs," in *Women's Wear Daily* (New York), 5 April 1995.

*   *   *

Marc Jacobs was from the start a fashion legend, a prodigy of mythical talent, tribulation, and triumph who attains unequivocal success and authority. The legend is indisputably true, but the clothing tells a similar and instructive story in which a special genius is realized in clothing—encyclopedic in its sources, poignantly romantic, remarkably sophisticated, and yet imperturbably impudent and joyous. Through a succession of labels and collections, Jacobs has consistently demonstrated a strong personal sensibility of the kind that marks clothing definably and, in his case, the history of clothing forever.

Jacobs's first collection was hand-knit sweaters produced by Charivari, the New York clothing store where he worked as stock boy. Fatefully, those sweaters earned him the Perry Ellis Golden Thimble Award at Parsons. Upon graduation in 1984, he designed Sketchbook for Ruben Thomas through fall 1985. There, he created a memorable collection based on the film *Amadeus.* In 1986, he began designing his own label, first with backing from Jack Atkins and later from Onward Kashiyama. In fall 1988, Jacobs was named vice-president for womenswear at Perry Ellis, succeeding Patricia Pastor who had worked with and succeeded Ellis. Along the way, there were Homeric afflictions and distress, ranging from a major theft at the Ruben Thomas showroom to a fire that gutted his Kashiyama studio and destroyed his fall 1988 collection and fabrics two months before showings. The appointment at Perry Ellis was, of course, only another trial for a then-25-year-old designer. As Peggy Edersheim wrote in *Manhattan, Inc.,* "Instead of staying one step ahead of the bill collector, he now has to worry about keeping up with Calvin Klein," a prodigious challenge in leadership for one of the principal sportswear houses in America. However, Jacobs made a great critical success of Perry Ellis, re-instilling the firm with the bountiful energy and excitement of its founder.

Significantly, Jacobs's works reflect Ellis's design. Jacobs did not perpetuate Ellis, but expanded on fundamental traits. For example, Ellis's imaginative, imagistic, even painterly palette was hauntingly revived in Jacobs's work, including extraordinary colors of fall in ocher, pumpkin, plum, camel, and rust, renewing the vitality of the Ellis spectrum. In fall 1991, Jacobs showed a grape princess coat over a brown cardigan, and a tangerine car coat with a butterscotch sweater and trousers with complete coloristic self-confidence. Ellis's sensuous fabrics are transmuted into Jacobs's hallmark sophistication: cashmere, camel, wool and angora, and mohair are soft, sumptuous materials. Moreover, Jacobs returns again and again to a basic vocabulary of design, treating each new interpretation of stripes, American flag, tartan, or gingham with a renewing luxury. His tailoring is also refined, returning to such classics as a Norfolk jacket or the eight-button double-breasted camel wool flannel suit for fall 1990 that appeared on the front page of *Women's Wear Daily.*

Jacobs's special interests include homages to designers he admires. His "hugs" sequined dress of 1985 remembers Schiaparelli and his spring 1990 English sycamore sequined short sheath "for Perry Ellis" was a touching condensation of the workroom and showroom environment of Perry Ellis, with its silver accents on a blond sycamore. Jacobs loves the 1960s and returns not only in the early sweaters with happy faces, but also in his voluminous mohair balloon sweaters for fall 1989. Suzy Menkes, reviewing his first collection at Perry Ellis, noted "Jacobs's own-label collections have also been all-American, but much less innocent—celebrations of Miami Beach kitsch, sendups of the 1960s hippies and wacky versions of patchwork and down-home gingham." New York-bred and unquestionably street-smart, Jacobs knows so much and is so nimbly, naturally witty that some cynicism blends with the joy in his clothing. A spring 1990 red-and-white tablecloth cotton shirt and jacket is accompanied by embroidered and beaded black ants. His early "Freudian slip" was a simple dress imprinted with the face of the Viennese master, a play on words. In fall 1991, Jacobs showed sweaters with aphorisms borrowed from the tart embroideries of Elsie de Wolfe. Language crops up even in Jacobs's fall 1990 "fresh berries and cream" collection that included blueberry herring-bone patterns on a cream field in wool jackets and the same design in short chiffon flirt skirts. His spring 1992 collection, focused on the Wild West and southern California, was a smart synthesis of Hollywood glamour (including an Oscar dress with the Academy Award statue) and boot-stomping country-and-western cowgirls, a perfect combination of rodeo and Rodeo Drive.

The legend of fashion prodigy is probably inseparably attached to Jacobs; that he has performed prodigiously as a leading master of American style in an immediate and seamless transition from child prodigy is indeed a marvel.

—Richard Martin

———

JACOBSON, Jacqueline and Elie. See **DOROTHÉE BIS.**

———

JAEGER.
British fashion house

Founded in London in 1884 by Lewis Tomalin based on the principles of Dr. Gustav Jaeger; sole purveyor of Dr. Jaeger's Sanitary Woollens to the 1920s; Tomalin obtained the rights, patents and Jaeger name; began manufacturing undergarments in 1884; added cardigans, dressing gowns, jumpers, shawls, and, by the early 1900s, coats, skirts, suits, etc. Designers associated with Jaeger, primarily with Regent Street, London branch, include Jean Muir, from 1956, Sheridan Barnett, and Alistair Blair. **Address:** 57 Broadwick Street, London W1, England.

Publications:

On JAEGER:

Books

Wilson, E., and L. Taylor, *Through the Looking Glass,* London 1989.

Articles

"The Jaeger Story," in *American Fabrics and Fashion* (New York), No. 100, Spring 1974.
"Quiet, Classic Jaeger," in *The Sunday Times* (London), 25 May 1980.
Alexander, Hilary, "Mrs Roache (and Jaeger) Go to Court," in *The Daily Telegraph* (London), 2 November 1991.
"Suits Are Getting a Kinder Cut," in the *Eastern Daily Press* (Norwich, Norfolk), 22 April 1992.
"Jaeger Variation," in the *Watford Free Observer* (Watford, Hertfordshire), 28 May 1992.

*   *   *

Jaeger is a British retail fashion company producing distinctive clothes for both men and women. Its origins lie in Germany over a century ago—a period when theories of rational dress abounded throughout Europe and the United States. In 1880 Dr. Gustav Jaeger of Stuttgart, a zoologist and physiologist, expounded his belief that only clothes made of animal fibres (principally wool) were conducive to one's health. Jaeger's theories were translated into English by Lewis Tomalin and taken up by *The Times* which devoted a leading article to Dr. Jaeger's ideas on 4 October 1884, on the occasion of the London International Health Exhibition in South

Kensington. Tomalin obtained Dr. Jaeger's permission to use his name and opened a shop to sell the "Sanitary Woollen System" of clothing in Fore Street, in the city of London, where two of the earliest and most famous customers were Oscar Wilde and George Bernard Shaw. The latter heartily endorsed the product and wore Jaeger clothing for much of his long life.

The clothes were remarkable not only for their material: extraordinarily fine machine-knit wool jersey, cashmere, alpaca, and vicuna ("the woollen stuffs which are microscopically tested for adulteration with vegetable fibre can be supplied by the yard" runs an advertisement of 1884) but for their unrestrictive construction. This made both underwear and outerwear particularly suitable for travelling. "Day and night—prevents chill—a necessity to all who value health" claimed an 1898 advertisement for "lovely and luxurious dressing gowns." Famous British expeditions were kitted out in Jaeger, from Scott and Shackleton in the Arctic to Stanley on his search for Dr. Livingstone in Africa and later. Before the First World War, Jaeger's functional, mobile approach gave the firm much of its impetus in what was to prove a rapidly expanding market from its new purpose-built shops, such as those in Regent Street, London, and Edinburgh, and its wholesale company supplying agents as far afield as Shanghai.

By the 1930s, however, Jaeger had greatly extended its range from the early emphasis on "sanitary wear" as exemplified in turn-of-the-century exhortations to "Wear wool to South Africa—khaki drill spells chill." Under the founder's son, H. F. Tomalin, the emphasis turned from functionalism to fashionability, all a woman (or man) needed for work and leisure, from country tweeds and twinsets and stylish coats to swimsuits and slacks.

Jaeger still exported its goods to such diverse locales as Beirut and Buenos Aires, upholding Tomalin's now-dated dictum, "Wherever you go among white people you will find that Jaeger is known." Jaeger's continuing attention to the actual fabric of their clothes gave them an honoured place in the British post-war export market, while the emphasis on durability which was part of the original design ethos continues to the present. The original ethos of health clothing, however, has long been superseded by one of cool, timeless elegance, albeit still in fine materials. This image is aided by the high calibre of Jaeger design. Jean Muir is but one British designer whose distinctive talents developed under Jaeger's aegis: she spent seven years designing for the company from 1956.

Jaeger is one of the few fashion companies able to produce a complete package, from sourcing exclusive fabrics and producing original designs through to manufacturing extensive ranges of tailoring and knitwear. These ranges are sold throughout the world: exporting the Jaeger product has always been a prime part of the business. Jaeger Ladieswear and Jaeger Man are as distinctive as the firm's witty "straw" logo and today reach markets undreamed of by Dr. Jaeger and his English translator.

—Doreen Ehrlich

JAMES, Charles.

American designer

Born: Camberley, England, of Anglo-American parentage, 18 July 1906. **Education:** Self-taught in design. **Family:** Married Nancy Lee Gregory in 1954 (separated, 1961); children: Charles, Louise.

Career: Moved to United States, established as Charles Boucheron, milliner, Chicago, 1924-28; milliner and custom dressmaker, New York, 1928-29; custom dressmaker, using the name E. Haweis James, London and Paris, 1929-c.1939; also sold designs to wholesale manufacturers in New York, 1930s; relocated to New York, 1939; established as Charles James, Inc., primarily for custom designs, from 1940; became permanent resident of the United States, 1942; designer, couture collection, Elizabeth Arden salon, New York, 1943-45; worked as independent designer, 1945-78. Charles James Services, Inc., licensing company established, 1949; Charles James Associates, limited partnership for manufacture of custom clothes, established, 1954, then merged with Charles James Services; Charles James Manufacturers Company established, 1955. **Exhibitions:** *A Decade of Design,* Brooklyn Museum, 1948; *A Total Life Involvement* (retrospective), Everson Museum, Syracuse, New York, 1975; *The Genius of Charles James* (retrospective), Brooklyn Museum and Art Institute of Chicago, 1982-83; *Charles James, Architect of Fashion,* Fashion Institute of Technology, New York, 1993. **Awards:** Coty American Fashion Critics Award, 1950, 1954; Neiman Marcus Award, Dallas, 1953; Woolens and Worsteds of America Industry Award, 1962; John Simon Guggenheim fellowship, 1975. *Died* (in New York) *23 September 1978.*

Publications:

By JAMES:

Articles

"Portrait of a Genius by a Genius," in *Nova* (London), July 1974.

On JAMES:

Books

Morris, Bernadine, and Barbara Walz, *The Fashion Makers,* New York 1978.
Coleman, Elizabeth A., *The Genius of Charles James,* New York 1982.
Milbank, Caroline Rennolds, *Couture: The Great Designers,* New York 1985.
New York and Hollywood Fashion: Costume Designs from the Brooklyn Museum Collection, New York 1986.
Milbank, Caroline Rennolds, *New York Fashion: The Evolution of American Style,* New York 1989.

Articles

Riley, Robert, "Advise without Consent," in *Harpers* (New York), September 1963.
Bosworth, Patricia, "Who Killed High Fashion?," in *Esquire* (New York), May 1973.
"Charles James, the Majority of One," in *American Fabrics and Fashions* (New York), No. 98, 1973.
Cunningham, Bill, "Is the New Subculture Getting You Down?," in the *New York Daily News,* 3 February 1975.
Barr, Jeffrey, "Charles James, Master of Couture," in *Fashion World Daily,* August 1978.
Duka, John, "Ghost of Seventh Avenue," in *New York,* 16 October 1978.

Bryant, Gay, "Charles James, 1906-1978," in *Harper's & Queen* (London), September 1979.

Taki, "Arbiter of Chic," in *Esquire* (New York), May 1981.

Coleman, Elizabeth A., "Abstracting the 'Abstract Gown,'" in *Dress* (Earleville, Maryland), 1982.

Campbell, Lawrence, "Fashion Shapes by Charles James," in *Art in America* (New York), May 1983.

Turner, Florence, "Remembering Charles," in *Vogue* (London), May 1983.

Coleman, Elizabeth A., "Charles James at the Brooklyn Museum," in *American Fabrics and Fashions* (New York), No. 128, November 1983.

Tobias, Tobi, "A Man of the Cloth," in *Dance Ink* (New York), Winter 1994-95.

*   *   *

"Charles James is not only the greatest American couturier, but the world's best and only dressmaker who has raised it from an applied art form to a pure art form." From anyone other than their author, and James's closest professional equal, Cristobal Balenciaga, these words would seem potentially pretentious and inflated. Instead they constitute a balanced and deserved evaluation.

Charles Wilson Brega James was of Anglo-American parentage and possessed an incredibly sharp mind. He could have excelled in any number of fields but a foray into millinery in Chicago of the 1920s led to a career devising intellectually refined and devastatingly beautiful women's garments. James's lifetime career was devoted not to producing quantities of either designs or products but rather to refining and evolving concepts. His clièntele in Britain, France, and the United States was dedicated: they put up with his unpredictability and his inflated costs. When they ordered a garment there was no guarantee of its delivery, or its permanence in their wardrobe as the designer would freely play roulette with his clients' clothes.

Why did clients remain loyal? Why is the word "genius" applied so frequently in describing James? Because James saw the female form as an armature on which to fashion sculpture, not just cover with clothes. He did not just sketch or drape a model. He approached the craft of dressmaking with the science of an engineer, often studying the weight distribution of a garment. Like an artist he analyzed the interacting elements of proportion, line, color, and texture. Construction details were not merely important, they were an obsession. He spent a vast sum on perfecting a sleeve. He turned a four-leaf-clover hat into the hemline of a ballgown which he then built up into the garment he designated as his thesis in dressmaking.

A cruciform became a circular skirt. An evening dress (with matching cape of antique ribbons) which made its debut in 1937 was still offered 20 years later, the finesse of the ribbon replaced by other yardgoods of silk, but the detailing to infinity remaining. James was such a perfectionist that clients never banked on wearing either a new or old James to a function. Even his well-known quilted jacket designed in 1937, and now in the Victoria and Albert Museum, London, bears witness to his challenge to perfect. One can follow his tortured, ghost-like tracts of stitching and restitching.

As brilliant as his design sense is James's subtle sensibility of color. Open a coat or jacket of subdued hues and be confronted with a lining of an unexpected range. Follow his curvilinear pattern configurations and note that inset sleeves and darts are not part of either his design or construction vocabulary. His lines are seductive and intellectually intriguing. Rarely did he employ patterned mate-

rials, relying rather on the most revealing, unforgiving plain goods. While he is perhaps best remembered for his spectacular eveningwear his tailored daywear was equally original. It was with his coats that he attempted to enter what he perceived to be the more lucrative ready-to-wear market. However, this didn't suit his temperament or methods of working.

James dressed many of America's best-dressed women of the generation. They patronized the couture salons of Paris and could easily have been dressed abroad. Instead they had the courage and determination to support a unique creator of fashion: Charles James.

—Elizabeth A. Coleman

JANSEN, Jan.

Dutch shoe designer

Career: Worked originally under the Jeannot label; became known for his original and often extreme footwear designs; eventually designed under his own label; collections shown at European trade fairs; shop based in Amsterdam.

Publications:

On JANSEN:

Books

McDowell, Colin, *Shoes, Fashion and Fantasy,* London 1989.

*   *   *

Little known to the public but highly regarded by fellow professionals, Jan Jansen, the Dutch shoe designer, is one of the most inventive and original translators in his chosen field. Unlike those designers who produce cosmetic updates of existing styles, Jansen conceives the item in a truly unique and conceptual way. An original and gifted man, his work inspires great admiration from those who recognize his quite individual style. His footwear is different, often extreme, unexpected with verve and daring. It can visually arrest you in a way that the work of few other shoe designers can and seems to push the boundaries of one's expectations of what a shoe should be.

Jansen worked originally under the Jeannot label, pouring out thousands of highly successful designs. His ability to translate his prototypes into commercially acceptable shoes is legendary, and the mass multiple footwear retailer and many factories, in particular those in Brazil—at the time one of the leading supply sources in the world—had reason to be grateful for his undoubted skills. His work was also widely copied, although many organizations subsequently turned their backs on the traditional reasons for success, failing to understand the crucial importance of creativity within a collection. Commercially this proved to be a disaster. Plagiarism has never reaped great rewards and ultimately the use of innovative stylists with independent minds and the freedom to explore and experiment for the customer will always pay dividends. Jan Jansen was such a person and must be heartened that once again there are signs that the trade is resurrecting the delights of individual interpretations and promoting the work of a new generation of shoe designers.

In the 1990s Jansen designed under his own label, and these collections, shown at the European trade fairs, are viewed eagerly by devotees who also visit his tiny shop in Amsterdam. Liberated in his thinking, and a true entertainer, his ideas are visually stunning at times, and quite beautiful. His great affection for suede, whether of the finest quality or rougher and more casual, and his dramatic use of colour, ensure that brilliant red, peacock blue, saffron yellow, or even the density of black will be an integral part of each season's handwriting. No matter how extreme, the shoes always look as if they could be worn. Indeed they can, should one have the courage. They are extravagant, with a certain eroticism in the curves and silhouettes that this artist so easily draws. Seldom understated in shape, with unusual use of texture and a modernistic approach to materials—plexiglass, bamboo, cork, etc.—or the latest development to catch his eye, they are frequently a mystery, a surprise, like an unexpected and breathtaking gift as you take the lid off the black and white box that is Jansen's trademark. His skills cover a wide range of disciplines. He can make by hand, in addition to designing collections for some of the most famous fashion designers in the world, and he can adapt his most inventive styles for quantity production to satisfy the mass market. Truly a colossus of the modern footwear world, Jansen can stand easily alongside any of the familiar and respected names in the trade.

—Angela Pattison

JANTZEN, INC.

American knitwear company

Founded in Portland, Oregon, as the Portland Knitting Company by John A. Zentbauer, C. Ray Zehntbauer, and Carl C. Jantzen, 1910; renamed Jantzen Knitting Mills, 1916, and Jantzen, Inc., beginning in 1949; first rib stitch swimsuit introduced 1913; North American sales extended to Mexico and Canada, beginning in 1920; company went public, 1921; diving girl logo introduced, 1923; knitwear and foundation lines added, 1938; separate men's and women's divisions established, mid-1960s; company became a wholly owned subsidiary of Blue Bell, Inc., Greensboro, North Carolina, 1979-86, and a division of VF Corporation, 1986; first retail store opened, Portland, 1992. **Awards:** 6 Woolknit Awards for men's sweater design 1965-80. **Address:** 411 N.E. 19th St., Portland, OR. 97232.

Publications:

On JANTZEN:

Books

Wallace, Don, *Shaping America's Products,* New York 1956.
Wallis, Dorothy, *The Jantzen Story,* New York 1959.
Cleary, David P., *Great American Brands,* New York 1981.
Morgan, Hal, *Symbols of America,* Penguin, 1986.
Lencek, Lena, and Gideon Bosker, *Making Waves: Swimsuits and the Undressing of America,* San Francisco, 1989.
Martin, Richard, and Harold Koda, *Splash! A History of Swimwear,* New York 1990.
Jantzen: A Brief History, Jantzen Inc., Portland, Oregon 1992.

Articles

Magiera, Marcy, "Swimwear Makers Aim for 'Older' Women," in *Advertising Age,* 21 April 1986.
Bloomfield, Judy, "Jantzen Turning the Tide," in *Women's Wear Daily* (New York), 19 September 1990.
"Accounts," in the *New York Times,* 4 September 1991.
Smith, Matthew, "Jantzen Slimming Down to Fit Into New Corporate Suit," in *Business Journal,* 23 September 1991.
Parola, Robert, "Keep the Environment in Fashion," in the *Daily News Record* (New York), 20 April 1992.
Van Dang, Kim, "Vintage Power," in *Women's Wear Daily* (New York), 10 February 1992.
Hartlein, Robert, "On the Comeback Trail," in *Women's Wear Daily* (New York), July 1992 (swimwear supplement).
Walsh, Peter, "Jantzen Aims for Bigger Chunk of Sweater Biz," in the *Daily News Record* (New York), 16 March 1993.

*　　*　　*

Eight decades ago the struggling Portland Knitting Company developed "the suit that changed bathing to swimming." Due to a burgeoning fitness craze, their new knit swimwear found a ready audience. The renamed Jantzen company quickly became an international name and gained a commanding position in the leisure wear industry by expanding its markets and manufacturing sites overseas.

Jantzen's success story and long-term fashion influence spring from their innovative merchandising and promotional programs as well as their appealing apparel. They led the way in creative, comprehensive marketing campaigns aimed at the mainstream market. The initial springboard product was a one-piece wool bathing suit in an elasticized rib stitch. It was made on knitting equipment used to make sweater cuffs. Like the improvised suit that Australian swimming celebrity Annette Kellerman wore in 1907, the Jantzen suit eliminated the encumbering yardage of the standard bathing costume of the late Edwardian era. Men and women who wanted to swim, not just dunk and splash, embraced it.

Jantzen's subsequent designs combined fashion and function. New cutting and patented assembly methods achieved a better fit for ease of swimming movement and figure enhancement. The basic style—the so-called California style—of long shorts attached to a sleeveless clinging skirted top—came in vibrant colors with accent stripes for all members of the family. Jantzen soon offered new styles, colors, and novelty knits. The company fostered swimming (and swimsuit sales) with its "Learn to Swim" campaigns.

Jantzen's clinging and increasingly abbreviated swimwear at first outraged local moral authorities and helped crumble recreational dress restrictions. This coincided with the evolving corsetless streetwear of the twenties. Jantzen's swimwear lines tended toward the sporty, athletic look while adapting to technological and sociological changes. An advertising campaign with catchy phrases heralded each new style.

The eight-ounce "Molded-Fit" swimming suits knitted from "Miracle Yarn elastic in all directions" were "the answer to nude bathing." Famed illustrator George Petty's 1940 "Petty Girl" suit was made in "new superb-fitting Sea-Ripple with live all-way elasticity." Lastex fabric of rubber-cored thread made possible suits "with the figure control qualities of a foundation garment." French designer Fernald Lafitte designed textured knits "with a Paris flavor."

In the annals of fashion, Jantzen's Red Diving Girl symbol is notable as one of America's first pin-up girls and first memorable apparel logo. She leaped from the cover of a 1920 catalog to make a sensational splash on ground-breaking billboard advertisements and as a sometimes-banned decal on millions of car windshields. Jantzen hired artists like Alberto Varga to update her figure periodically. The Red Diving Girl graced all advertising and countless advertising giveaways and gadgets. She was embroidered or sewn on Jantzen swimsuits for over sixty years.

Like the other major West Coast sportswear companies, Catalina and Cole of California, Jantzen created advertising featuring Hollywood celebrities. Collaborative promotions with First National and Warner Brothers included Loretta Young as Miss Jantzen in 1931. In 1947 independent campaigns used a teenage "Mr. Jantzen," actor James Garner to model "Savage" and Lastex swim trunks, while a young Marilyn Monroe modeled the "Double-Dare" two-piece suit with peek-a-boo cut-outs on the hips.

Jantzen often emphasized color coordination in their ads and in-store merchandising. For a smart fashion-conscious beach look, in 1928 customers turned to authority Hazel Adler's "Jantzen Color Harmony Guide." In the 1950s Jantzen went in with Revlon for a "Love that Red" campaign and based a swimwear collection on a bright red line of lipstick and nail polish.

Jantzen expanded its lines to include bras and foundation garments as well as a wide range of men's and women's leisure wear in interchangeable parts of coordinating and contrasting colors and fabrics. The "Darlings from Jantzen," traveling fashion consultants, prepared personalized color charts to encourage customers to buy flattering color-coded Jantzen wardrobes.

At times Jantzen provided suits and sponsorship of both the Miss America and Miss Universe beauty pageants. Two modified suits gained mystique as lucky "supersuits," because whoever wore them won the swimsuit competition and often the Miss America crown or runner-up status.

Jantzen's pioneering merchandising programs as well as fashion innovations put it into the forefront of influential American apparel manufacturers. Through its overseas operations it exported American West Coast- and Hollywood-inspired fashions to a worldwide audience. The Red Diving Girl logo, involvement in major beauty pageants, and "Learn to Swim" and recent "Clean Water Campaign" programs significantly contributed to American recreational and popular culture.

Today Jantzen is the leading brand of swimwear in over 100 countries. It continues to make leisure clothes that their Executive Vice-President Mitchell Heinemann said "look best on the greatest number of people, and which make them look good at the things they like to do."

—Debra Regan Cleveland

JAVITS, Eric.

American milliner

Born: New York, 24 May 1956. **Education:** Choate School, 1970-74; graduated from Rhode Island School of Design, 1978. **Career:** Co-founded company, Whittall and Javits, Inc., 1978, creating women's hats and later separates and T-shirts. Sold out to partner, 1985. Founded Eric Javits, Inc., specializing in women's hats and

occasionally hair accessories, 1985. Licenses include Maximilian Furs, 1991-93, and Kato International, Japan. Also designs hats for films, including *Bonfire of the Vanities,* for television shows, including *Dynasty* and *Dallas,* for many advertising campaigns and for runway collections of other designers, including Carolina Herrera, 1984-93, Caroline Roehm, 1988, Mary McFadden, 1988-93, Pauline Trigère, 1990-93, Adolfo, 1990-91, Louis Féraud, 1989-90, and Donna Karan, 1991-92. **Exhibitions:** *Mad Hatters,* Women's Guild of the New Orleans Opera Association, 1989; *Current Trends in Millinery,* Fashion Institute of Technology, New York, 1990; *The Art of Millinery—20th Century Hat Design,* Philadelphia Museum of Art, 1993. **Collections:** Metropolitan Museum of Art Costume Institute, Fashion Institute of Technology, New York. **Awards:** "Millie" Award, Hat Designer of the Year, 1991, 1992. **Address:** 406 West 31st St, 3rd Floor West, New York, NY 10001, USA.

Publications:

On JAVITS:

Articles

Hochswender, Woody, "Designers Find Fashionable Ways of Talking through Their Hats," in the *New York Times,* 14 June 1988.
Stevenson, Peter M., "Crown Prince," in *Manhattan, inc.* (New York), August 1989.
Newman, Jill, "Many Hats of Eric Javits," *Women's Wear Daily* (New York), 2 March 1990.
Sherman, Jean, "Top Hatter," *New York Magazine,* 16 September 1991.
"Hats are Back," *The Kansas City Star,* 4 April 1993.

*

My design work is only one aspect of involvement with owning my own hat company, and it remains the only part where I am not relying on the team's abilities but on my own.

Whenever an inspiration hits me, I make a note of the idea by sketching a small diagram. This provides a springboard from which many things can later develop. Using this method, I can have the concepts for an entire collection outlined within a few days. Sometime later in the process, when the designs are actually being fabricated, I will consider them from a production and marketing viewpoint. Those issues are quite complex given today's woman's varied needs, and the ever-changing nature of the fashion business.

Many of my ideas are the result of an evolution, synthesizing and reworking bits and pieces of my most effective ideas and occasionally going off to test a completely new direction which, if successful, could eventually become part of the line's core.

When a design arrives successfully, most of my developmental energy is not evident. What remains, seemingly, is an object which has its own logic and which appears to have been plucked effortlessly from our collective subconscious.

—Eric Javits

*   *   *

Eric Javits is, as *New York Magazine* (16 September 1991) assessed, "quite simply, tops." In an era in which the hat is a style anachronism and a definite statement of individuality, if not idio-

Eric Javits: Summer 1994; "Pagoda Planter" hat: two-tone milan braid, woven chin ties with clay beads.

syncrasy and exhibitionism, Javits has created hats of distinct and discreet identity, the designer's and the potential wearer's.

Upon graduation as a painter and sculptor from the Rhode Island School of Design in 1978, Javits began his millinery career as a sculptural improvisation. Javits creates a wide range of hats: United Airlines flight attendant caps, private-label millinery for many American department stores and specialty chains, Louis Féraud hats, his own label, and its diffusion line, Lily J., named for his grandmother. But even as he is dubbed "crown prince" by Peter Stevenson in *Manhattan, inc.* (August 1989), Javits is not making hats for grandmothers. He is almost Spartan in millinery adornment and has concentrated on hats that are not agglomerations and concoctions, but are modest one-statement sculptures for the head. Javits's restraint is his focus on one important statement in each hat, seldom adding secondary elements. Often the interest is, in fact, in the shape as he has searched the past for a wondrous array of traditional shapes to frame the face. Yet, even as shape is of critical importance to Javits, one of the millinery myths is he or the archetypal hat designer whips a perfect hat out of his pocket, as Javits is said to have done for Carolina Herrera. The legerdemain of the hat in his pocket notwithstanding, Javits plays with a softening of shape so that even his military inspirations and his menswear derivations work as softer versions of the source, though never collapsing into Oldenburg flaccidity.

Defending his decision to enter millinery, as he did somewhat serendipitously, Javits describes the early hat-making as a relief from painting and sculpture. "Hatmaking was playful, there was no pressure. A weight was taken off, and it snowballed into something more serious." Javits's play is quite serious, a *Bauhausian* caprice rather than Carmen Miranda theatrics. While some of Javits's hats can compete at the races and in the evening sweepstakes, his most important contribution is hats that can serve for day and cocktail hours. He makes one of the most convincing arguments for the possible return of millinery to daily attire in dealing with classic shapes, giving a velour beret, for example, a luxury, or offering a most refined form of basic derby. His red tophat with poinsettia photographed on the cover of *Town & Country,* New York (December 1990) is indicative: Dickensian tradition is manifest in a time-honored silhouette, but made fresh with a feminine and flattering red as well as the single note of the white poinsettia adornment. Javits excels in such distilled grace notes, projecting the hat as a deliberate statement for and upon the wearer.

Simple enough for the working day, special at the cocktail hour, and still splendid for evening, Javits's hats afford the contemporary woman a *raison d'être* and repertory for returning to the systematic wearing of hats. Fantasy and special-occasion hats will probably never serve to revive the custom of wearing hats; Javits's reasoned, history-invoking hats may, in the same manner in which American (and subsequently Italian) luxurious minimalism in the 1970s and 1980s restored the faith of women in elegant dress. Moreover, in the late 1980s and 1990s, Javits has also designed headpieces and hair accessories that extend the possibility of millinery.

Fred Miller Robinson argues for the bowler hat as a salient sign of the modern spirit (*The Man in the Bowler Hat,* Chapel Hill, 1993). He points out that it is ever and increasingly filled with the semantics of its origin. What happens in an Eric Javits hat? Customarily, saving most of the over-the-top extravagance for the Louis Féraud line, the Javits hats have the snappy stateliness of a wonderful tradition fittingly renewed. Without succumbing either to arid art or to a conceptual base alone, Javits's fundamentals of

hatmaking likewise give the hat its historical function and purpose and offer it as a basic vessel adaptable to modern lives. Few milliners have been as conscientious as Javits in reconfiguring the hat in accordance with its historical templates and modern comforts. Few milliners have taken a modernist sculptural responsibility and talent in honing in one element of the hat to make it converse with the apparel to give presence to the face of its wearer.

—Richard Martin

JOAN & DAVID.
American footwear and fashion firm

Begun by Joan and David Helpern in Cambridge, Massachusetts, 1967; Joan & David label introduced, 1977; David & Joan menswear division launched, 1982; Joan & David Too lower priced line of shoes and accessories introduced, 1987; first women's apparel collection produced by Sir for Her, 1983-85; second women's ready-to-wear collection produced by Gruppo GFT, from 1988. Maintained licensing agreement with Ann Taylor chain of fashion shops, 1967-92; producer and distributor, Calvin Klein Footwear, from 1990, and Calvin Klein accessories, 1990-91. New York flagship shop opened, 1985; in-store boutiques opened at Harvey Nichols, London, and Ogilvey's, Montreal, 1987; freestanding Paris and Hong Kong boutiques opened, 1988. **Awards:** American Fashion Critics Coty Award, 1978; Footwear News Designer of the Year Award, 1986; Cutty Sark Award, 1986; Fashion Footwear Association of New York Award, 1990; Michelangelo Award, 1993. **Address:** 4 West 58th Street, New York, New York 10019, USA.

Publications:

On JOAN & DAVID:

Books

McDowell, Colin, *Shoes: Fashion and Fantasy,* New York 1989.
Trasko, Mary, *Heavenly Soles,* New York 1989.

Articles

Bethany, Marilyn, "Sole Sister," in *New York Magazine,* 10 March 1986.
"Joan and David: Less Is More," in *Vogue* (Paris), October 1986.
Infantino, Vivian, "Designer of the Year: Joan Helpern," in *Footwear News Magazine* (New York), December 1986.
Williams, Lisa, "Uniquely Joan and David," in *Footwear News Magazine* (New York), March 1989.
Huffman, Frances, "Role Model," in *Entrepreneurial Woman* (Irvine, California), March 1992.
Furman, Phyllis, "Putting New Foot Forward: Joan and David Rebuilds After Ann Taylor Rift," in *Crain's New York Business,* 23 March 1992.
Quinn, Colleen, "The Many Dimensions of Joan Helpern," in *Footwear News* (New York), 1 June 1992.

Joan & David: Spring/Summer 1995.

Infantino, Vivian, "World Class Performances: Joan and David—It Ain't Just Shoes," in *Footwear News* (New York), 30 November 1992.

Moin, David, "Joan's New Platforms: Not Just Shoes," in *Women's Wear Daily* (New York), 23 August 1993.

*   *   *

Joan & David, Inc. is responsible for making flat shoes for women fashionable. The company developed because Joan Helpern wanted a comfortable, stylish shoe that would not become dated through its design. When Joan married David Helpern in the 1960s, she was a student in child psychology working on her PhD at Harvard University. In her multiple roles of wife, mother, teacher, and student, Joan wanted a shoe that was not a gym shoe, loafer, or stiletto, the only readily available styles for women at the time. She needed a shoe that would look stylish, yet allow her to get about the city in comfort. The solution was to design the shoe she needed herself, an oxford style which is still available in a modified form today.

While editing academic manuscripts, Joan created footwear designs for department stores and private labels, including Harvard Square and Foreign Affairs. She began designing under the name of Joan & David in 1977. Today, Joan serves as president and David is the chairman of the company.

Joan & David designs are found throughout the world. The shoes are manufactured in Italy, because it was there that Joan found craftsmen willing to produce limited editions of her designs, numbering from 12 to 120, to her specifications. Joan & David, Inc. produce shoes specifically for women under the name Joan & David, Joan & David Too, and Joan & David Couture. Men's footwear is designed under the names David & Joan and David & Joan Couture. Through the years the product line has expanded to include purses and other accessories, as well as women's ready-to-wear.

Helpern's entry into the design field was not planned and she had no formal design training. However, she knew what she wanted in a shoe, so she researched the market and technology involved in their manufacture. She was able to produce footwear which met the needs of active women like herself, who race through the day serving in many different roles: women who are not self-consciously fashionable, but value good quality and style. Joan has a less-is-more philosophy when it comes to design. She concentrates on classic, usable styles such as oxfords and patent pumps with designs that evolve from year to year. The colors she uses are subtle, and the emphasis in on interesting textures. Comfort is essential. Neither flat shoes nor shoes with low heels have extraneous details or extreme designs. In 1978 she was given the Coty Award for her designs.

Joan Helpern has been influential in the field of shoe design. By successfully creating shoes that were both stylish and comfortable, she helped open up a new way of thinking about shoe design for women. Women who work as professionals wanted what Joan herself originally searched for: a stylish, yet comfortable shoe that would not be an obsolete design the next season. They needed a shoe more stylish than sneakers, and more comfortable than stilettos. By providing herself with a comfortable shoe to wear, Joan Helpern was able, with her husband David, to fill this need and develop the successful business named Joan & David.

—Nancy House

JOHN, John P.

American milliner

Born: John Pico Harberger in Munich, 14 March 1906. Immigrated to the United States, 1919. **Education:** Studied medicine, University of Lucerne, and art at the Sorbonne and l'École des Beaux Arts, Paris. **Career:** Milliner, Mme Laurel, dressmaker, New York, 1926; partner (with Fred Fredericks), John Fredericks, milliners, 1929-48, with shops in New York, Hollywood, Miami and Palm Beach; formed independent company, Mr John, Inc., New York, 1948-70; designed for private clients, from 1970. **Awards:** Coty American Fashion Critics Award, 1943; Neiman Marcus Award, 1950; Millinery Institute of America Award, 1956. *Died* (in New York) *25 June 1993.*

Publications:

By JOHN:

Articles

"It Had to Be Hats," with Nanette Kutner, in *Good Housekeeping* (New York), June 1957.

On JOHN:

Books

Lambert, Eleanor, *World of Fashion: People, Places, Resources,* New York and London 1976.
Morris, Bernadine, and Barbara Walz, *The Fashion Makers,* New York 1978.
McDowell, Colin, *Hats: Status, Style, Glamour,* London 1992.

Articles

Fredericks, Pierce G., "Mad Hatter," in *Cosmopolitan* (New York), April 1951.
"John P(ico) John," in *Current Biography* (New York), October 1956.
Morris, Bernadine, "Fashion's Mad Hatter Turns Conservative for Spring," in the *New York Times,* 7 January 1966.
Schiro, Anne-Marie, "Mr. John, 91, Hat Designer for Stars and Society," [obituary] in the *New York Times,* 29 June 1993.
"John P. John," [obituary] in *Current Biography* (New York), September 1993.

*   *   *

"My business," John P. John told *Good Housekeeping* (June 1957), "is strictly an individual business. When I go, there will be no more Mr John. I have only one worry. When I do go, should I reach heaven, what will I do? I know I cannot improve on the halo." Ironically, John, who had made almost every kind of head covering other than a halo, saw the demise of his kind of milliner on earth; by the time of his death in 1993, perhaps even the halo was obsolete. As early as 1957, he was already on the defensive, arguing, "A hat cannot actually give one golden curls if the hair is mouse-colored and stringy; it cannot lift a face, pay overdue bills, subtract ten years from one's age, or transform a plain soul into a reigning princess. But it *can* lend practically any woman a temporary out-of-herself feeling. For *the right hat creates a desired mood,* and that isn't fiction or fancy, but fact, fact, fact."

Like his contemporary Lilly Daché and Halston who would follow later (translating the concept to apparel, but retaining John's contradictory modes of shape reductivism and theatrical sparkle), John successfully combined the glamor of a custom business with a wide-reaching appeal. He could create extraordinary hats for exceptional women. At the same time, he was a hero to countless middle-class women who copied his styles or had them copied by local milliners. John's hats were on the cover of *Vogue* many times, including 15 June 1943, 15 October 1944, 15 January 1946, 1 August 1946, and 15 February 1953.

From the opening of his own business in the 1920s, after apprenticing with his mother, through the 1960s, John was an important milliner, never fixed in one style but producing eclectic variations of romantic picture hats, snoods, subdued cloches, and other forms. Indeed, it was form that was essential to John: his hats were sculptural, shaped to flatter the face, outfit, and presence. His historicist pieces, in particular, could use surface decoration, but the effect of a Mr John hat nonetheless always resided in the shape. As Anne-Marie Schiro (*New York Times,* 29 June 1993) described, "In the 1940s and 1950s, the name Mr John was as famous in the world of hats as Christian Dior was in the realm of haute couture. At a time when other milliners were piling on flowers, feathers, and tulle, Mr John was stripping hats naked, relying on pure shape for effect." Turbans, berets, and snoods, a specialty, were supple shapes in favor with John and were often shown in the fashion magazines with American fashion. He could, however, also cut crisp shapes and bow a brim to flatter the face and forehead to accompany Dior, Schiaparelli, and Balenciaga. For all the flamboyance of his own life and all the drama that he could vest in a suite of picture hats that ever seemed to belong at Tara, John could also create what *Vogue* (15 October 1951) called a "strict" black hat of utmost simplicity. Even at their most whimsical and wild, John's hats were flattering to the wearer and to the ensemble of dress.

Eugenia Sheppard (New York *Herald Tribune,* 2 July 1956) called him "the artist among milliners" and he self-consciously courted the rubric of art, including collections with the themes of modern art and style history, and a sense of the avant-garde. However, it was one piece of historical recreation that made John most famous: his millinery for Vivien Leigh in *Gone with the Wind.* Widely copied, the *Gone with the Wind* hats confirmed John's long-time association with Hollywood and women of style, including Mary Pickford, Greta Garbo, Gloria Vanderbilt, Gloria Swanson, Jacqueline Kennedy Onassis, and the Duchess of Windsor. His hats were also worn in films by Marilyn Monroe in *Gentlemen Prefer Blondes* and Marlene Dietrich in *Shanghai Express.* By the time Mr John closed in 1970, hats were largely *démodé.*

Custom-made millinery is a matter of extreme co-dependency between client and milliner. If it is the purpose of the hat to flatter, the milliner, too, must practice a psychology of intervention and flattery. When Pierce Fredericks dubbed John the "Mad Hatter" in *Cosmopolitan* (April 1951), the madness was only of energy; rather, clients enjoyed John's "diplomatic manner." John used only one house model, a Miss Lynn, for many years: she was his type for countless hats, many of which he made directly on her head. He was also famous for his miniature hat collection, prototypes for his own hats and historical recreations based upon his study in museums and historical references. John lived in and defined the golden age of millinery. Once, in the 1950s when I was a child, my mother

and I were on train from Philadelphia to New York. John walked by and complimented my mother on the picture hat she was wearing. She never forgot Mr John's approval.

—Richard Martin

JOHNSON, Betsey.

American designer

Born: Weathersfield, Connecticut, 10 August 1942. **Education:** Studied at Pratt Institute, Brooklyn, New York, 1960-61; B.A., Phi Beta Kappa, Syracuse University, Syracuse, New York, 1964. **Family:** Married John Cale in 1966 (divorced); daughter: Lulu; married Jeffrey Oliviere in 1981. **Career:** Guest Editor, *Mademoiselle,* New York, 1964-65; designer, Paraphernalia boutiques, New York, 1965-69; partner in boutique Betsey, Bunky & Nini, New York, from 1969; designer, Alvin Duskin Co., San Francisco, 1970; designer in New York for Butterick patterns, 1971 and 1975; Alley Cat, 1970-74; Jeanette Maternities, 1974-75; Gant, 1974-75; Betsey Johnson's Kidswear division of Shutterbug, 1974-77; Tric-Trac by Betsey Johnson, 1974-76; Star Ferry by Betsey Johnson and Michael Miles, 1975-77; head designer, President and Treasurer, B. J. Vines, from 1978; owner, Betsey Johnson stores, from 1979. **Awards:** *Mademoiselle* Merit Award, 1970; Coty American Fashion Critics Award, 1971; American Printed Fabrics Council Tommy Award, 1971, 1990. **Address:** 209 West 38th Street, New York, New York 10018, USA.

Publications:

On JOHNSON:

Books

Milinaire, Caterine, and Carol Troy, *Cheap Chic,* New York 1975.
Morris, Bernadine, and Barbara Walz, *The Fashion Makers,* New York 1978.
Milbank, Caroline Rennolds, *New York Fashion: The Evolution of American Style,* New York 1989.
Lobenthal, Joel, *Radical Rags: Fashions of the Sixties,* New York 1990.
Steele, Valerie, *Women of Fashion,* New York 1991.

Articles

"We Orbit Around ... Betsey Johnson," in *Mademoiselle* (New York), August 1966.
Fraser, Kennedy, "On and Off the Avenue: Feminine Fashions," in *The New Yorker,* 1 April 1972.
Comer, Nancy, "Betsey Johnson," in *Mademoiselle* (New York), August 1972.
Kaiser, Diane, "Profile on People," in *Fashion Accessories Magazine,* March 1979.
Burggraf, Helen, "Betsey Johnson: Alive and Well and Designing in New York," in *Apparel News,* 1981.
"Sweet and Tough," in *Soho News* (New York), 23 February 1982.
Bloomfield, Judy, "Happy Partners: Bacon and Johnson," in *Women's Wear Daily* (New York), 7 September 1988.
Haistreiter, Kim, "Earth to Betsey," in *Paper* (New York), April 1989.

Benatar, Giselle, "Betsey Johnson," in *Mademoiselle* (New York), February 1993.

*   *   *

For the youthquake generation, the names Betsey Johnson and Paraphernalia symbolized the hip, young fashions of mid-1960s America just as Mary Quant and Biba did for the equivalent age group in Great Britain. In the early 1970s, a second wave of young women with a taste for affordable style discovered the flippant body-conscious clothes Johnson designed for the ready-to-wear firm Alley Cat. Throughout the 1980s and into the 1990s Johnson's clothes have been characterized by her sense of humor and an innocent, tongue-in-cheek sexiness. Wearing a Betsey Johnson dress is like putting on a good mood.

After graduating Phi Beta Kappa, magna cum laude from Syracuse University, Syracuse, New York, Johnson won a guest editorship at *Mademoiselle* magazine. There, colleagues put her name forward to Paul Young who was scouting out fresh new design talent to launch his Paraphernalia boutiques. It was a good match. Young encouraged experimentation and Johnson had begun to develop what was to be a long-standing interest in such unorthodox materials as vinyl, sequin sheeting, and the then new stretch fabrics. Her "kit" dress, for example, was of clear vinyl with a trim-it-yourself package of stars, dots and ellipses cut from reflective adhesive foil. The "noise" dress had a hem fringed with loose grommets.

Johnson's approach to clothing is very much influenced by her early days as a dancer. "I am basically about a ballerina torso and a full skirt," she told a reporter for the *Soho News* (New York), in 1982, "a dancing school dress-up craziness." Johnson's emphasis on tight, stretch bodices also grows out of her dancing school background. Not surprisingly the shift in the 1970s to a subdued, tailored look was incompatible with Betsey Johnson's style as a designer. She continued to have her own label with a variety of manufacturers, but it was not until the end of that decade that Johnson's real *joie de vivre* emerged again, this time for her own company.

—Whitney Blausen

JONES, Stephen.

British millinery designer

Born: West Kirby, Cheshire, England, 31 May 1957. **Education:** Studied at High Wycombe School of Art, 1975-76; B.A. (with honors) in fashion from St Martin's School of Art, London, 1979. **Military Service:** Served as chief petty officer in the Royal Navy, 1974-76. **Career:** Chairman and designer, Stephen Jones Millinery, from 1981; S.J. Scarves and Miss Jones lines introduced, from 1988; Jonesboy and S.J. Handkerchieves, from 1990; S.J. Kimonos, from 1991; handbag line introduced, 1993. Also colour creator, Shiseido Cosmetics, 1988. **Exhibitions:** *Headspace by Stephen Jones,* Isetan Museum, Tokyo, 1984; *Fashion and Surrealism,* Victoria and Albert Museum, London and Fashion Institute of Technology, New York, 1988; *Mad Hatter,* Australian National Gallery, Canberra, Sydney, 1992; *Hats: Status, Style, Glamour,* The Collection, London, 1993; *Rococo Futura,* Ginza Artspace, Tokyo, 1994. **Address:** 29 Heddon St, London W1R 7LL, England.

Publications:

By JONES:

Articles

"Heads You Win," in *You* magazine of the *Mail on Sunday* (London), 29 May 1983.

On JONES:

Books

Polan, Brenda, *The Fashion Year,* London 1983.
McDowell, Colin, *Twentieth Century Fashion,* London 1984.
Damase, Jacques, *L'histoire du chapeaux,* Paris 1987.
Martin, Richard, *Fashion and Surrealism,* New York 1987.
Mulvagh, Jane, *Vogue History of Twentieth Century Fashion,* London 1988.
Ginsburg, Madeleine, *The Hat,* London 1990.
McDowell, Colin, *Hats: Status, Style, Glamour,* London 1992.

Articles

Jagger, Harriett, "Making Up Is Art to Do," in *The Observer Magazine* (London), 11 December 1983.
"Stephen Jones: un toque de chapeaux," in *Elle* (Paris), September 1984.
Smith, Liz, "Mad as a Hatter," in the *Standard* (London), 23 October 1984.
"Jones the Hat," in *You* magazine of the *Mail on Sunday,* 2 December 1984.
Grieve, Amanda, "Hat Check Job," in *Harpers & Queen* (London), December 1984.
"Hats to Turn Heads," in *The Observer* (London), 2 June 1985.
"Stephen Jones: un idea per cappello," in *L'Uomo Vogue* (Milan), December 1985.
Gessner, Liz, "Thoroughly Modern Millinery," in *Women's Wear Daily* (New York), 26 June 1987.
DuCann, Charlotte, "Keeping Ahead of Jones," in *Elle* (London), September 1987.
Barron, Patti, "Thoroughly Modern Millinery," in the *Standard* (London), 6 October 1987.
Ranson, Geraldine, "The Hatter Who Flatters," in *The Sunday Telegraph* (London), 24 April 1988.
Brampton, Sally, "Just a Trifle Over the Top," in *The Observer* (London), 3 October 1992.
McDowell, Colin, "Crown Jewels," in *The Sunday Telegraph* (London), 8 November 1992.
Davidson, John, "Crowning Glory," in *The Scotsman* (Edinburgh), 11 May 1994.

*

Hats for me are an expression of the spirit. They can parallel the whole range of human emotions and may exaggerate them to dramatic effect. The expression of an eye can be enhanced by the particular line of a brim, a Roman profile concealed or enhanced by twists of fabric, or the wearer can be veiled with mystery. Whatever effect my hats achieve, they must have, as Diana Vreeland would have said, "Pizazz." Therefore the balance between them and the

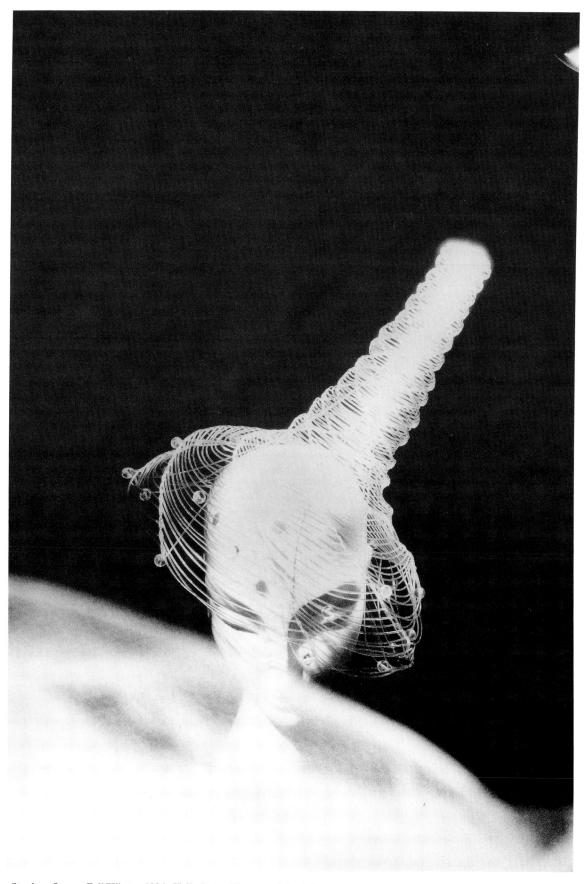

Stephen Jones: Fall/Winter 1994; Helix hat. *Photograph by Ashworth.*

wearer is all-important; too much emotion in the curl of a feather or the glint of a *paillette* is vulgar and dominating, too little and the exercise is pointless.

Unlike clothing, novelty is the *raison d'être* of millinery. I must rewrite the score in every hat I make. Making a hat should be like dancing; as one's body follows the beat, so must one's hands be in rhythm with the tempo of the particular hat. Hats make themselves, I merely help them along.

—Stephen Jones

*   *   *

When Stephen Jones left St Martin's School of Art, London in 1979 hats were yet to become high fashion news for the young. Ethnic styles had spread from the mid-1970s onwards, drably cloaking the fashion-buying public with Serious Good Taste and leaving little room for wit or fantasy.

In the late 1970s, however, there was a glimmer of change. Waists, hips, and padded shoulders were beginning to emerge from shapeless chemises and sloppy knits. What better to complete this new silhouette than an amusing and frivolous piece of headgear. Many of London's young clubgoers had first appeared on the scene wearing the spikily aggressive trappings of punk. They were new to this glamour born of Hollywood retro-kitsch and embraced it wholeheartedly; and Jones entered right on cue.

Jones was a champion of the eccentric, the stylish, and the innovative. He could be seen emerging from the morning train at Paddington, dressed like the other commuters in smart pinstriped suiting, but with black patent stilettos emerging from his immaculate turn-ups. He was a great ornament to the clubs and parties of the era, usually wearing one of his own asymmetric and intriguing hats, perched on his bald head. An enthusiastic self-publicist, his charm and good humour endeared him to many.

Jones's salons—the first in Covent Garden's P.X.—were unique environments, swathed in lush fabric and dripping with gilt cupids, where one might gaze leisurely at his always astonishing and delightful creations. He re-interpreted the chic and quirky styles of the past, cleverly draping, moulding and trimming his hats in a way so personal as to be entirely of its own time. Moreover, Jones's hats are well-crafted—a reflection of early work at the traditional couture house of Lachasse.

Jones was soon a fast-rising star in the heady London galaxy of the early 1980s; his talent, and that of his peers—Bodymap, Stephen Linard—burst on the scene like a vivid firework display, drawing the world's fashion buyers and press as moths to the British flame.

During the following decade, Jones's esoterically titled collections—Sunset on Suburbia, Ole' Steamy, Passport to Pleasure—have continued to delight and inspire; and he must take due credit for the current popularity of hats amongst the young. Millinery is once more a popular subject on fashion course timetables, whereas a decade or so ago it was fast becoming an endangered species.

Jones's talents have naturally taken him abroad; he continuously designs for top French fashion houses—Gaultier, Montana, Mugler—and enjoys much success in Japan, where genuinely innovative design skills allied with Western charisma are justly lauded. Other young milliners have arisen, some to stay and some to go; but Stephen Jones was the first of this new breed, and remains one of its most influential and quixotic practitioners.

—Alan J. Flux

JOOP, Wolfgang.

German designer

Born: Potsdam, Germany, 18 November 1944. **Family:** Married Karin Bernatzky; children: Henriette, Florentine. **Career:** Journalist, *Neue Mode;* free-lance designer for Christian Aujard, Brecco and others. Showed first fur collection under own label, 1978; Joop! ready-to-wear line added, 1981; menswear line added, 1985; Joop! boutiques opened, Hamburg and Munich, 1986; fragrances introduced, 1987; Joop jeans added, 1989; ready-to-wear fur collection introduced, 1990. **Address:** Harvestehuder Weg 22, 2000 Hamburg 13, Germany.

Publications:

On JOOP:

Articles

Morais, Richard, "Who Is First in the Market, Sells," in *Forbes,* 16 September 1991.
Morris, Belinda, "Talking Fashion," in *FHM* (London), September 1993.

*   *   *

Photogenic Wolfgang Joop is at least as recognizable as his fashion and fragrance products. Along with Jil Sander, one of the major figures of German fashion in the 1990s, Joop is as much a national anomaly as he is an international celebrity. Until Sander and Joop, Germany had few designers of sexy clothing achieving world-class status: suddenly, after years in Germany, both came into international recognition in the early 1990s.

Joop, the design identity with an exclamation point, is the hyperreal, hyperbolic badge of the designer. He has brought the American concept of the designer to Germany, with its strong sense of personal identification and the projection of style. Again and again, he appears charismatically, if a little too prominently, in his own imagery. Further, as he describes in a 1993 press release, "When it comes to designing the men's collection, the man I have in mind for the clothes is myself." When Joop bought an apartment in New York in 1993, it was the former apartment of Bill Blass, for Joop has cleverly understood the impulse of contemporary fashion marketing to personification and projection. He has expressed his admiration for the work of American minimalists and marketing prodigies Donna Karan and Calvin Klein. Like Blass, Joop projects utmost self-confidence in style, an aplomb that allows him the polymath aptitude to design for menswear, women's apparel, and fragrance. In examining himself, he gives some surety in the ambiguous realms of style.

In telling his own story in a 1993 press release, with a merchant's beguiling fluency, Joop cites as an important influence growing up on a farm near Potsdam: "As the city of Philip the Great it was one of the poorest of the European courts, but the one with the most style," thus enjoying both a simple life and a proximity to high style. His statements on fashion lean to the populist though his clothing is always on the well-mannered side of democracy (he called a fragrance *Joop! Berlin* after the fall of the Berlin Wall in 1989). He avers: "Fashion should not just be a blatant expression of money. It should be humorous and give dignity to the individual wearing the clothes."

Wolfgang Joop: Winter 1995.

Among his greatest successes have been jeanswear, likewise in the optimistic spirit of American style and ready-to-wear populism. But the Joop denim collections are not standard: fit, size, and style distinctions bring to the lowly subject of jeans at least a rudiment of tailoring and individuation. Joop's principle is that the ready-to-wear client, even in denim, must be served with a kind of customized distinction and satisfaction, again very much in the ethos of traditional American sportswear. Contending that "jeans are fashion's *alter ego,*" Joop adumbrates his view of fashion as an alien force and his conviction in jeans and other products that are wholly part of a daily life. The effect is both real and marketing strategy. A denial of fashion, thus avoiding any purport of excess or exploitation, is fashionable in the 1990s for reasons of economics and lifestyle, but Joop has consistently been a lifestyle designer. Joop attributes to his upbringing in circumstances both rustic and stylish his range of occasion. Thus, the collections work for both casual dress and contemporary high style.

—Richard Martin

JOSEPH.

British retailer and fashion entrepreneur

Born: Joseph Ettedgui in Casablanca, 1938. **Family:** Married twice; two children. **Career:** Immigrated to England, 1965; hairdresser, Joseph Salon 33, London, 1969-72; proprietor, Coco boutique, 1974; established chain of shops including Joseph, from 1977, Joseph Tricot and Joseph pour la Maison, from 1985, Joseph pour la Ville, from 1986, and Joseph Bis; Joseph *Parfum de Jour* introduced, 1985; opened Joe's Café restaurant, 1985; open Paris boutique, 1993. **Awards:** *Woman* Magazine Award, London, 1985; Knitwear Designer of the Year Award, 1990, 1992. **Address:** 88 Peterborough Road, London SW6 3HH, England.

Publications:

On JOSEPH:

Books

Coleridge, Nicholas, *The Fashion Conspiracy,* London 1988.

Articles

Cleave, Maureen, "Makers of Modern Fashion: Joseph," in *The Observer Magazine* (London), 5 October 1980.
Miller, Sarah, "Joseph: Where Fashion Meets Design," in *Blueprint* (London), June 1984.
White, Lesley, "Saint Joseph," in *The Face* (London), June 1984.
Brampton, Sally, "Still Crazy," in *The Observer* (London), 24 March 1985.
Miller, Sarah, "Stainless Reputation," in *Elle* (London), 29 September 1985.
Appleyard, Bryan, "Co-ordinated Style of a Clone Prince," in *The Times* (London), 4 June 1986.
Verdier, Rosy, "Joseph: Un homme de mode," in *L'Officiel* (Paris), August 1986.
Jaffe, Michele, "Ragtrade to Riches: My First Million: Joseph," in *The Observer Magazine* (London), 25 October 1987.

"Joe's Public," in *Fashion Weekly* (London), 7 January 1988.
De Gramont, Laurie, "Joseph le lutin," in *Vogue* (Paris), September 1988.
Filmer, Denny, "The Story of Joseph," in *Cosmopolitan* (London), December 1988.
Gandee, Charles, "The Merchant of Style," in *House and Garden* (New York), April 1989.
Brampton, Sally, "Joe Cool," in *Elle* (London), October 1989.

*			*			*

A love of precision and a good eye for detail underpin Joseph Ettedgui's skills as an entrepreneur, enabling him to build up a group of shops that bring together a selection of the best and most innovative contemporary designer fashion alongside his own strong self-named lines, all aimed at a modern and confident audience.

The endless black and chrome of his London stores defined the stark monochromatic obsession of the 1980s and spawned endless concrete-floored imitators, eager to espouse the same sense of sophisticated style but unable to match his unfaltering mix of carefully chosen labels. Wise enough not to buy entire collections, he prefers to select the most streamlined and well designed pieces. His constant search for perfection, combined with convincingly structured in-store and window displays, has brought many designers to the fore. So influential is his choice of names that his favour can raise a designer's status overnight. Having overseen the careers of many, including Kenzo, Katharine Hamnett, and Bodymap, he continues to purvey a mixture of new and established names.

The omnipresent black that he favoured during the 1980s spread throughout the fashion world, as endless stretch-fit Azzedine Alaia dresses hung from his rails, mingling with the bold suiting that ruled the decade. His power as a buyer is huge, backing avant-garde designers and hand-picking new talents who would otherwise find such support or retail space difficult to secure. The slick image of his emporia is underlined by the stark black and white minimalism of his advertising, as sympathetic to the promotion of the clothes as his stylized shops.

His own name lines complement the other labels he sells. They provide classic garments to be mixed with other designer wear, or constitute carefully designed and coordinated outfits themselves. Joseph pour la Ville provides smart suiting and witty, easy to wear casuals. Alongside the bright, bold, striped trouser suits with shiny gilt buttons that he produced in 1989 were more relaxed and feminine sheer georgette skirts and multi-coloured waistcoats, the subtle shades of which added a twist to the more pervasive dark colours. His ranges always contain clothes for every occasion, directed at the sophisticated metropolitan. The silhouette is usually well defined, to enhance the wearer with its simple chic, like the matt violet and beige column dresses side split to the waist for the evening in 1991, with three buttons at the top of each slash adding definition to the plain line.

Running alongside these classic garments is the Joseph Tricot collection, filled with thick rib woollens to layer with softer leggings and strikingly patterned cardigans and tube skirts, as well as subtle-toned wrap tops and fine jersey T-shirts. In 1987, chunky cream cardigans with little gold buttons were given bold black decoration, one of his perennial basic designs. These complement more fashion-led shapes and yarns, like the claret chenille belted jackets of 1992 and the huge rose off-the-shoulder jumper with wide fold-over collar shown in 1991.

Joseph. *Photograph by Michael Roberts.*

Joseph's ability to act as a catalyst, bringing together the work of innovative designers in a suitably stylish environment, has been very influential on fashion retailing, providing the clothing and accessories for a whole lifestyle. These skills are rivalled in London only by Browns of South Molton Street. His success is undeniable, as is his talent, which has enabled him to ride out the designer-led 1980s and to continue his influence into the 1990s, recognizing and adapting to a more relaxed approach to fashion.

—Rebecca Arnold

JOURDAN, Charles.

French shoe designer

Born: 1883. **Career:** Foreman at Établissements Grenier, shoe leather cutters, 1917; independent shoe manufacturer, 1919. Seducta, a luxury range, introduced in Romans sur Isère, France, 1921. In the 1930s, extended distribution to all of France; other shoe lines introduced. After World War II, sons Rene, Charles, and Roland took over factory, adding shoe lines in the mid-1940s. First Charles Jourdan women's boutique in Paris launched, 1957, launched in London, 1959. Dior contract with international distribution of shoes under Dior label, 1959. Perugia began designing for Jourdan in early 1960s. First New York boutique launched, 1968. Bags and ready-to-wear clothing line launched in 1970s. By 1975 there were 21 franchises. Firm continued after Jourdan's death; sons launched menswear and *Un Homme* fragrance in early 1980s. Company bought over by Portland Cement Werke in 1981. Chief designer: Bernard Sucheras. Outside designers are commissioned, including Hervé Leger for accessories. Company specializes in shoes, leather goods, accessories, jewelry, scarves. **Exhibitions:** *Charles Jourdan: 70 Years,* Galeries Lafayette, Paris and The Space, Tokyo, both 1991. **Collections:** Musée de la Chaussure, Romans sur Isère, France; Charles Jourdan Museum, Paris, including 2000 creations by André Perugia. **Address:** 28, Avenue de New York, 75116 Paris, France. *Died in 1976.*

Publications:

On JOURDAN:

Books

Swann, June, *Shoes,* London 1982.
Benaim, L., *L'année de la mode,* Paris 1987.
McDowell, Colin, *Shoes, Fashion and Fantasy,* London 1989.
Grumbach, D., *Histoires de la mode,* Paris 1994.

Articles

"Dateline Paris," *Footwear News* (New York), 15 April 1985.
"The Added Essence of Elegance: Charles Jourdan," *Elle* (London), September 1987.
"Flirtations of a High-Heeled Pump," *Vogue* (London), September 1987.
Pringle, C., "Quoi de neuf?," *Vogue* (Paris), October 1987.
"La couture a quatre mains," *Vogue* (Paris), August 1992.
Anniss, Elisa, "French Connection," *Shoe and Leather News,* November 1992.

"Le jeux de la métière," *Liberation* (Paris), March 1993.

*   *   *

Charles Jourdan, a shoe manufacturer, made the name Jourdan synonymous with couture by licensing and diversifying in the manner of the Paris haute couture houses. No other footwear company has so successfully marketed its image, and 75 years later Jourdan still symbolizes luxury, international fashion, and the best of couture.

The founder of the company, Charles Jourdan, was both a skilled craftsman and creative businessman. His aim was to produce shoes of quality, made with the best materials and the traditional skills of a *bottier.* He also recognized that many of these bespoke skills could be translated into the much larger ready-to-wear market, producing affordable luxury shoes. Jourdan believed in the power of advertising. As his business expanded during the 1930s he used a network of commercial travellers to introduce his brands across the whole of France, backing up this sales force with advertisement in popular magazines—a new concept at the time.

His styles were not trendsetting, but their classic luxurious look succeeded. He produced perfectly hand-crafted ladies shoes that could be worn in harmony with elegant outfits. Not that these first simple styles were influenced by the direction of Parisian fashion. The only thing that Jourdan had in common with his contemporaries Poiret, Schiaparelli, and Chanel was that he also used only the finest materials. He did, however, benefit from the new higher hemline which raised the visibility of shoes, making them a much more important accessory in the modern woman's wardrobe.

The economic crisis of the 1930s followed by the war, drastically affected the couture market, which could not cheapen its products. Jourdan, ever ready to diversify, recognized that price was an important selling factor at all levels of the market, and he introduced new lines at lower prices. He sold to the newly emerging chain stores, and the Jourdan empire grew.

In the 1950s Jourdan's three sons began managing the business. The youngest son, Roland Jourdan, who was responsible for design and development, has been described as "the most able man in the shoe industry." He was fully aware that it was simplicity and quality, not wild innovation, that sold Jourdan shoes. When Jourdan's first boutique opened in Paris in 1957, Roland Jourdan only offered a small range of styles. But each style was available in 20 colours, all sizes, and three widths. At Jourdan, not only would the shoe fit, but it would also perfectly accessorize any shade of outfit.

The ultimate connection of the luxury shoe brand to haute couture came with the contract between Jourdan and the house of Christian Dior in 1959. Jourdan created, manufactured, and distributed shoe models for Dior worldwide. It was the ultimate seal of approval. The next two decades saw Jourdan at their most successful and creative. They launched a series of seminal advertising campaigns that profoundly influenced both fashion and advertising. In the 1960s they commissioned Guy Bourdin, a young Parisian photographer who produced a series of surreal, witty, and often visually stunning advertising photographs. The images usually had nothing to do with shoes, and the name "Charles Jourdan" appeared as a small caption in one corner. It is difficult now to imagine the impact of this campaign, but its success was such that for a time the brand became associated with a sense of innovation and modernity that the shoes themselves, perfect creations though they were, did not really possess.

Charles Jourdan: Autumn/Winter 1992/93.

The Jourdan shop design helped to perpetuate this innovate image. The ultra modern interiors and striking window displays of the first Paris boutique became a blueprint for a chain in every fashion capital of the world. It was the environment that created the Jourdan look, that extended at its peak in 1979 from neckties to sunglasses, allowing the dedicated customer to be completely Jourdan accessorized.

Jourdan achieved a level of product diversification unsurpassed in the footwear industry. Borrowing the haute couture strategies of licensing and franchising, and creating a global presence, Jourdan became the couture accessory. This success attracted competition. New names such as Bruno Magli and Robert Clergerie were concentrating solely on footwear. The diversity that had made Jourdan so big now threatened to dilute the brand names exclusivity. Finally, the loyal customer base was growing older, and a new generation of women found alternative designers outside the classic couture mould.

In 1981 the family's dynastic control of the empire ended with the retirement of Roland Jourdan. The name survives, confident in the knowledge that a luxury brand will never be out of fashion. New and younger lines have been launched. Charles Jourdan remains an important name because its enduring strength is the recognition that all a woman really wants in a shoe is the perfect accessory, with the perfect fit. Simple.

—Chris Hill

JULIAN, Alexander.

American designer

Born: Chapel Hill, North Carolina, 8 February 1948. **Education:** Graduated from the University of North Carolina, Chapel Hill, North Carolina, 1969; self-taught in design. **Family:** Married wife Lynn (divorced); daughter: Alystyre; married wife Megan in 1987; son: Will. **Career:** Worked in his father's Chapel Hill menswear store to 1969; menswear designer and retailer with own store, Alexander's Ambition, Chapel Hill, 1969-75; founder and designer, Alexander Julian company, New York, from 1975; showed first collection, 1975; popular priced Colors by Alexander Julian line introduced, 1981; womenswear line introduced, 1983; Colors by Alexander Julian for Boys line and Watercolors by Alexander Julian swimwear line introduced, 1984; Colors by Alexander Julian girlswear and hosiery collection introduced, 1984; home furnishing line introduced, 1985; Alexander Julian Enterprises men's couture line and Colors by Alexander Julian luggage line introduced, 1988; fragrance for women introduced, 1991. Also designed uniforms for the Charlotte (North Carolina) Hornets professional basketball team, 1988, the Charlotte Knights semi-professional baseball team, 1990, and the Knights Stadium, 1990. **Awards:** Coty American Fashion Critics Award, 1977, 1979, 1980, 1983, 1984; Cutty Sark Award, 1980, 1985, 1988; Men's Woolknit Design Award, 1981; Council of Fashion Designers of America Award, 1982. **Address:** 63 Coppo Hill Road, Ridgefield, CT 06877, USA.

Publications:

On JULIAN:

Articles

Burggraf, Helen, "Profile: Alexander Julian," in *Men's Apparel News,* 6 January 1981.

Boyagian, Paula, "Alexander Julian," in *Fashion Retailer,* October 1983.

Fressola, Peter, "Alexander Julian," in the *Daily News Record* (New York), 1 March 1988.

Barol, Bill, "Pastels on the Hardwood: High Fashion in the NBA," in *Newsweek* (New York), 3 October 1988.

"The Americans: Alexander Julian," in the *Daily News Record* (New York), 15 August 1989.

*   *   *

Alexander Julian states his philosophy on his most recent Colors collection, first launched in 1981: "I believe in men who want to dress in their own image and not according to any singular vision that would have all men appear alike."

Alexander Julian was born in Chapel Hill, North Carolina and grew up in the retail environment of his father's shop, which he managed from the age of 16. He moved to New York in 1975, winning the prestigious fashion Coty Award for the first time in 1977, and thus became the youngest designer to be included in the Coty Hall of Fame. Alexander Julian has had citations on the U.S. International Best Dressed List for nine consecutive years, and has won nearly all the most prestigious fashion design awards in the United States. Julian was one of the first U.S. men's clothing designers to create his own exclusive fabrics by working with Euro-

pean mills and exploring a broad range of colour with a special eye for innovative and unusual colour effects.

Since the launch of Colors by Alexander Julian in 1981, a well-priced collection that reflected the use of colour and texture that had become Julian's signature on his Couture Menswear Collection, the Colors range has expanded beyond menswear in the United States to include outerwear, furnishings, sleepwear, leather goods, belts, bedlinen, eyewear, and women's and men's fragrances. Today the collections are a multi-million-dollar business worldwide with licensees in Japan, Mexico, Canada, and in the UK, where the imaginative colour palette, changing each season, is a novelty in British menswear.

Julian has designed uniforms for sports teams, such as the Charlotte Hornets and North Carolina University Tar Heels basketball teams, and the uniforms, car colours, and crew clothes for the Newman Haas racing team, which is co-owned by Paul Newman. His clothes are worn by entertainment personalities such as Bill Cosby, Paul Newman, Tim Robbins, and jazz singer Harry Connick, Jr.

In 1992 Julian designed the clothes for all the male leads in Robert Altman's critically acclaimed movie *The Player,* creating a complex series of variations on the dress codes prevalent in the film industry. "What exists with most movie studios is that everyone tries to emulate the boss," states Julian, "and that's exactly what we did here." The personality of each character is played out in the colour of his clothes: the style of jacket worn by all the male executives is identical, and as the narrative becomes more complex, the colours of the clothing worn by the main protagonist, played by Tim Robbins, change from green and gold to darker and darker colours as his situation changes.

Alex Julian believes that creative thinking in education should play a more significant role in children's learning development and to this end he has set up the Alexander Julian Foundation for Aesthetic Understanding and Appreciation, which is helping to pioneer an experimental learning centre in the United States.

—Doreen Ehrlich

KAHNG, Gemma.

American designer

Born: Masan, Korea, 21 May 1954. **Education:** Immigrated to the United States, 1969. Graduated from the Art Institute of Chicago, 1979. **Family:** Married Charles Chang-Lima in 1984 (divorced in 1994). **Career:** Design assistant, Cathy Hardwick, New York, 1981-84; designed free-lance before establishing own business in1989. **Address:** 550 Seventh Avenue, New York, New York 10018, USA.

Publications:

On KAHNG:

Articles

Bizer, Karen, "A Designing Couple," in *Women's Wear Daily* (New York), 22 July 1988.

Hartlein, Robert, "Gemma Kahng Emerges on Her Own," in *Women's Wear Daily* (New York), 23 August 1989.

Staples, Kate, "The Kahng Formation," in *Women's Wear Daily* (New York), 1 April 1991.

Darnton, Nina, "The New York Brat Pack: Their Clothes Are Coming Soon to a Closet Near You," in *Newsweek* (New York), 29 April 1991.

Schiro, Anne-Marie, "With Help, Gemma Kahng's Star Soars," in the *New York Times,* 5 May 1991.

Saeks, Diane Dorrans, "Gemma's Jewels," in *West,* 16 June 1991.

Phillips, Barbara D., "Gemma Kahng: Paper Dolls to Haute Couture," in the *Wall Street Journal* (New York), 6 August 1991.

Servin, James, "How I Got That Look: The Exotic Route," in *Allure,* June 1993.

"New York: Gemma Kahng," in *Women's Wear Daily* (New York), 4 November 1994.

*

The inspiration for each of my collections comes from my desire to create clothing that is sexy, witty, glamorous, comfortable, and most importantly, practical. I reflect on my own personality and lifestyle and think of things I would like to wear and what I need to expand my wardrobe.

Each of my collections begins with high quality fabrics, an important tool for good design. Mostly I choose wools, silks, cottons, and linens that are luxurious yet basic, so that my design aesthetic becomes more prominent than the fabric itself. The details of clothing from the historical past are a good influence for my ideas. I am fascinated by the cultures of different time periods, especially the Victorian era, and find it challenging to combine them with the look of today.

This design sensibility appeals to my customer, a consistently busy woman who doesn't have the time to experiment with her image. She is a person who has enough confidence to incorporate a sense of humor in her style and can rely on my clothing and accessories for a complete look. Over the past five years, my image has become a recognizable one throughout the United States and is rapidly growing in foreign markets, especially in Hong Kong and Taipei where I have freestanding boutiques.

My goal is to perfect upon what it is that my customers like about my clothing and create something new. Design is a growing process and each season I experiment further by bringing more of my self-expression to a collection. What makes it exciting for me is the challenge and risk involved in taking the next step. No one can tell me what to bring to the future. I just have to be aware of the everyday world we live in.

—Gemma Kahng

*   *   *

"She's a lot like her designs—a winning mix of playfulness and practicality, forthrightness and charm," said Barbara Phillips of Gemma Kahng (*Wall Street Journal,* 6 August 1991). Kahng's fashion design is practical and tries hard to meet price points appropriate for a relatively new designer, while at the same time the chief trait of her work is to render a classic idea slightly askew or fresh with a theme of whimsy, exaggeration, or notice. The charm of the work is its perturbed normality: it is all just right, but for that one eccentricity or detail that seems gloriously juvenile or marvelously anomalous in the template of a traditional garment.

Kahng's clothing is undeniably serious, addressed paramountly to an American working woman of some means, but always with a note of self-expression. Buttons can be almost as whimsical as those of Schiaparelli; pockets are unexpectedly given colorful flaps in accent colors; and pockets bounce with asymmetry. Schiaparelli is Kahng's soul-mate in fashion history, not for the flamboyant garment, but rather for those most restrained tailored suits that Schiaparelli created with nuanced absurdities and minor amazements. Kahng's identifying style resides in such quirky twists on classics, attention inevitably being drawn to the garment by an outstanding detail, but restrained in every other aspect of the composition.

Kahng, who collaborates with her former husband Charles Chang-Lima, oversees production in a new, yet traditional, way employing the resources of the Seventh Avenue garment district in New York. Rather than seeking large-scale production elsewhere, Kahng has preferred to do all her production in the garment-district neighborhood of Manhattan. It is a matter for Kahng of quality and control, not flag-waving. After all, Kahng was born Shin Kyong in Korea; Chang-Lima was born in Venezuela of Chinese parents. Instead, they are attempting to guarantee production standards by watching

Gemma Kahng: Fall 1994.

the process, an old tradition of the garment industry now abandoned by many bigger companies. Of course, there may be reason in a designer and her partner, neither born in the United States, appraising American traditions and Western dress with a reasoning, potentially ironic, eye. Kahng recalls that in her Korean childhood there were no store-bought dolls and that she had to fantasize and create clothing for her paper dolls.

"Classic with a twist" is a conventional goal of many young designers who take a minimal risk in construction and allow one lovely or bizarre note to make a memorable difference. In fact, the concept is difficult to carry out as one disturbance from the norm can seem to be an unwelcome aberration, especially in clothing that depends upon our sense of recognition of formality. Kahng has demonstrated an unusually sure and decisive sense of distorting or contributing enough in the gesture of discrepancy, but without destroying the practical validity of the garment. When a tweed jacket is trimmed with red, the effect is at first of the most diabolically arresting house-painting on the block, but the combination settles into a rather winsome palette of clothing for the hunt. A pea jacket that is modified by horses on the pockets and jeweled buttons on the front assures that it will not be worn by Popeye, but deliberately softens the military regimen into a feminine and whimsical jacket. The anomaly for Kahng is never mere kitsch or cuteness: it is a feature that alters our perception (whether color or content) of the entire garment, an abnormality that makes us see the normal in a wholly new way.

Kahng described her collaboration with Chang-Lima to Barbara Phillips in a way that may show the matched capacities of Kahng's clothing: "Most lines we design together. He thinks women should be glamorous and sexy. And I think women should be charming and practical. We make, together, a combination." The combination is, in fact, very effective: never unduly impulsive, the design is nonetheless different and enchantingly whimsical: Kahng honors the great traditions in dress and yet gives a happy surprise with each garment.

—Richard Martin

KAISERMAN, Bill.

American designer

Born: Brooklyn, New York, 8 September 1942. **Education:** Studied drama, no formal training in design. **Family:** Married wife Millie, 1971. **Career:** Millinery designer under the label Rafael; formed joint venture with Onward Kashiyama Co., 1989-92; launched independent label, WJK, to show menswear collection, 1992. **Awards:** Coty American Fashion Critics Award, 1974, 1975, 1976, 1978. Elected to Coty Hall of Fame, 1976. Hall of Fame citation, 1978. **Address:** Via Manzoni 43, Milan, Italy.

Publications:

On KAISERMAN:

Books

Lambert, Eleanor, *World of Fashion,* New York 1976.

Morris, Bernadine, and Barbara Walz, *The Fashion Makers,* New York 1978.
Khornak, Lucille, *Fashion 2001,* New York 1982.

*   *   *

Bill Kaiserman has had success in the fields of menswear and womenswear. With no formal design training, he began his career as a salesman in a men's clothing shop. Whilst there he started designing hats and sold them under the label Rafael. He was soon producing suede and leatherwear to complement the millinery. Cashmere sweaters and silk shirts were added, together with the safari suit— a revolutionary new shape in menswear establishing the concept of the leisure suit and leisure dressing for men.

His menswear success led him to produce ranges of womenswear, still under the label of Rafael. Beginning with tailored clothes, his look gradually became softer and more casual, evolving into a sophisticated daywear look, made to high standards in luxurious, discerning fabrics and colours. Produced in Italy, Kaiserman's clothes came to represent the best standards in American fashion.

Kaiserman cited his customers as being between 30 and 45, who wanted to look young and well dressed, without resorting to the extremes of teenage fashion. As a men's and womenswear designer he has noted the marked difference in designing for both sexes. With womenswear the approach is more creative and free. An idea can often be realized to its full potential, whereas with menswear an imaginative idea has often to be restrained. "There are just a few shapes that are acceptable, there is less room for fantasy," he said. He believes that men should not look too formal, styled, or contrived. Women, on the other hand, look fabulous when the body shape is emphasized and exaggerated.

Kaiserman has been amply recognized for his contribution to American fashion, with several Coty Awards and a Hall of Fame citation for his contribution to menswear. He and his wife Millie both declared themselves fitness and health fanatics. Kaiserman confessed that he often gets design ideas when lifting weights and has joked that if he never made it as the world's biggest international designer, he would certainly be the strongest.

It is ultimately his menswear concept that has been Bill Kaiserman's greatest contribution to fashion. His leisurewear opened up greater boundaries for menswear design as a whole and his leisure suit became a liberated classic for many men. Kaiserman chose the name Rafael because he thought it would look better in print than his own. Ironically his name as a designer has eclipsed the label he chose to represent his product.

—Kevin Almond

KAMALI, Norma.

American designer

Born: Norma Arraes in New York City, 27 June 1945. **Education:** Studied fashion illustration at Fashion Institute of Technology, New York, 1961-64. **Family:** Married Mohammed (Eddie) Houssein Kamali in 1967 (divorced, 1972). **Career:** Free-lance fashion illustrator, New York, 1965-66; airlines reservation clerk, 1966-67; free-lance fashion designer and partner, with Eddie Kamali, Kamali Fashion Imports, New York, 1967-78; opened first retail store, Kamali, in New York, 1968; established OMO (On My Own) Norma Kamali boutiques in New York, from 1978; ready-to-wear line introduced, 1981; also produced sportswear for Jones Apparel Group, 1981, children's sportswear for Empire Shield Group, 1982, sportswear for Renown Corporation, Japan, 1983, bags and footwear for Vittorio Ricci, 1983-84, headwear for Stetson, 1983, and belts for Raymon Ridless, 1985; signature fragrance collection introduced, 1985; OMO home collection introduced, 1988; 1-800-8-KAMALI line of casual wear introduced, 1993; cosmetics line introduced, 1994. Also: Designer of costumes for the Emerald City in film, *The Wiz;* designed and opened Norma Kamali Building, New York, 1983; producer and director of video, *Fall Fantasy;* designer of costumes for the Twla Tharp dance in *The Upper Room.* **Exhibitions:** Parachute designs displayed at Metropolitan Museum of Art, New York, 1977. **Awards:** Coty American Fashion Critics Award, 1981, 1982, 1983; Council of Fashion Designers of America Award, 1982, 1985; Fashion Institute of Design and Merchandising Award, Los Angeles, 1984; Fashion Group Award, 1986; Distinguished Architecture Award from New York Chapter of American Institute of Architects; Outstanding Graduate Award from the Public Education Association of New York; Award of Merit, Video Culture International Competition; American Success Award from the Fashion Institute of Technology in New York, 1989. **Address:** Norma Kamali Building, 11 West 56th Street, New York, New York 10019, USA.

Publications:

By KAMALI:

Articles

"Fashion," in the *New York Times,* 1 January 1989.

On KAMALI:

Books

Diamonstein, Barbaralee, *Fashion: The Inside Story,* New York 1985.
Milbank, Caroline Rennolds, *Couture: The Great Designers,* New York 1985.
Perschetz, Lois, ed., *W, The Designing Life,* New York 1987.
Milbank, Caroline Rennolds, *New York Fashion: The Evolution of American Style,* New York 1989.

Articles

"Norma Kamali Talks to Sarah Montague," in *Ritz* (London), No. 25, 1978.
"The Kamali Effect," in *Vogue* (New York), June 1982.
Krupp, C. "Reluctant Fashion Guru," in *Glamour* (New York), September 1982.
"Working Seventh Avenue Has Been No Sweat for Fashion's Greta Garbo," in *People* (New York), 27 December 1982.
Radakovich, Anka, "Hot Kamali's 'Kicky' Clothes," in *Apparel News* (New York), April 1984.
Talley, André Leon, "True Wit: The Zany World of Norma Kamali," in *Vogue* (New York), November 1984.
"Norma Kamali: An Interview with the Fashion Video Pioneer," in *Back Stage,* 14 November 1986.
"Shirting the Issue: Norma Kamali," in *Self* (New York), November 1988.

Hamilton, William L., "The State of the Shape: Va-va-voom," in *Metropolitan Home* (New York), April 1989.
Schiro, Anne-Marie, "Pastels at the Plaza, Cowgirls in the Park," in the *New York Times,* 31 October 1989.
"The Designers Talk Passion, Whimsy and Picassos," in *ARTnews* (New York), September 1990.
Schiro, Anne-Marie, "A Spectrum for Spring, Hot to Cool," in the *New York Times,* 31 October 1990.
Brubach, Holly, "In Fashion: On the Beach," in *The New Yorker,* 2 September 1991.
Schiro, Anne-Marie, "Patterns," in the *New York Times,* 4 August 1992.
Schiro, Anne-Marie, "For Evening Wear, Various Degrees of Retro," in the *New York Times,* 31 March 1993.
Gandee, Charles, "Hot Kamali," in *Vogue* (New York), April 1993.
"That Vargas Vamp," in *American Photo* (New York), March/April 1993.
La Ferla, Ruth, "Mode: Norma Kamali," in *Elle* (Paris), July 1993.

*   *   *

In a highly original way, Norma Kamali has been designing with uncanny foresight for the modern woman's multifaceted lifestyle. The sensational success of her sweatshirt fleece fabric line in 1981 brought Kamali clothes into the mainstream, while she continued to design experimental, one-of-a-kind fashions for wealthier clients. The mass produced sweats offered good design in comfortable clothes, with a touch of the eye-catching elements that distinguish Kamali. Inspired by the late 1960s British clothes she brought back from England to sell in the New York Norma Kamali boutique, the retro Biba clothing of Barbara Hulanicki in particular, Kamali began offering her own designs to keep up with the demand. When she opened her New York OMO (On My Own) boutique in 1978 after her divorce, Kamali symbolized all newly independent women.

As early as 1972 Kamali designed bathing suits according to her own vision: gold lamé *maillots,* structured or spare bikinis, decorated or plain, introducing the then-startling high-thigh styles with cutouts to show off a well-toned body—beach fashions that have become mainstream as the 1980s progressed. In the late 1960s Kamali was credited with the hot pants craze. A sense of playfulness combined rhinestones with stretch leotard material, pleasing the celebrities who patronized the Madison Avenue store. In 1974 Kamali changed to a more refined look, lacy and delicate, specializing in well-made suits and dresses.

It was in the West Side OMO store that Kamali came into her own. Cosy down-filled coats became popular after she introduced them, spurred by the necessity of sleeping in a sleeping bag after her divorce. Drawstringed jumpsuits made of colorful parachute material resulted in her inclusion in the *Vanity Fair* Exhibition at the Costume Institute of the Metropolitan Museum of Art. She showed draped 1930s-styled jerseys, and exaggerated broad shoulders on garments from coats to sweatshirt dresses to evening gowns, always a little before her time. She also utilized suede in bright colors before it became trendy. Kamali 1950s-style "Ethel Mertz" dresses were fabricated in plaid flannel, certainly different than anything else on the streets in the early 1980s. Her short cheerleader skirts were the first popular mini skirts in a decade. Dramatic lamé accents appeared on special occasion sweats and she designed sweatshirting for children.

Kamali epitomizes the shy person who allows her clothes to speak for her, yet there is an inner strength that has led to successful business enterprise and the willingness to take risks. Using her boutique as an *atelier,* Kamali has been producing one-of-a-kind garments from unusual fabrics in versatile shapes that could be worn in a number of ways. She was one of the first to present unitards or bodysuits as serious fashion staples. As in French couture, Kamali listens to her customers, on whom she has waited in person in her boutique, to get their honest opinions. She has described herself as relying upon intuition, taking inspiration from the street, but making it her own result as if in a creative trance. Her credo has been to make attractive the functional aspects of clothing, taking inspiration from the unique qualities of each fabric, always designing for the woman who will wear the clothes.

Throughout her career Kamali has inspired other designers, and has been considered one of the most original designers in New York. She has brought the inventiveness that used to be allowed only in couture salons to versions affordable to working women, although many of her more exclusive designs remain high priced. Kamali has also introduced revolutionary marketing techniques to fashion merchandising. Twenty-four hours a day, fashion videos play in the windows of OMO. Unlike ordinary catwalk videotapes, Kamali videos are actually mini-movies, often as long as 30 minutes, with story lines and character development, showing various situations in which Kamali fashions might be worn. Kamali also advertised through the use of billboards and by staging fashion shows in New York's Central Park. By 1993 she was offering a toll-free number for ordering her new lower priced label, while retaining the OMO Norma Kamali label for her expensive line. Plans for expansion to Los Angeles, Europe, and Japan as well as 1-800-8-KAMALI shops all over the country attest to her mission to bring well-designed fashion to all women.

Kamali clothes continue to be timeless in evoking past fashion eras while representing a modern outlook in interpretation, use of new materials and technology. The newest innovation has been a non-perishable fiber, soft yet impervious to wrinkling and staining, to create an entire wardrobe of interchangeable pieces. In 1991 Kamali presented bell-bottomed trousers, then scoffed at by the fashion press, which have now become standard in the revival of the 1970s. She herself revived her own fake leopard print coats to combine in the eclectic individualistic mood of the 1990s with other garments having vintage and ethnic overtones. Soft flowing floral tunics, Edwardian and 1930s detailing, hip-huggers, lace dresses all in spirit with the times denote the experimentation that has always been the hallmark of Kamali's style and has at last caught up with her fashion forward attitude. Shiny Lurex bathing suits feature underwire cups and a direction toward a more covered-up look in response to the new consciousness about the dangers of sunlight. Her own best model, Kamali epitomizes the 1940s vamp that is a characteristic classic expression of her aesthetic. She has made self-expression seductive.

—Therese Duzinkiewicz Baker

Publications:

On KAPLAN:

Articles

Richardson, John, "Fauve Country," in *House & Garden,* February 1992.

*   *   *

"One of the few means of self expression left today is fashion," Jacques Kaplan told Grace Glueck of the *New York Times* in the 1960s, and in many ways Kaplan has used fashion as a canvas to express many innovative new ideas.

Kaplan's business had originated with his grandparents who founded a fur business in Paris in 1889. The business moved to New York in 1942 and Kaplan eventually became the chairman and chief designer for the house. His exuberant, lively personality soon elevated the company to its status as the biggest volume fur business in the United States.

Fur coats had long established themselves as a luxury item in fashion. Stylistically their image was somewhat stately, grand, and status conscious. Kaplan pioneered the concept of "fun furs" in unusual pelts, or fake fur, fur dresses, skirts, boots and hoods, all of which helped attract a younger, more fashion-conscious clientèle. He introduced stencilled and coloured furs, and for a 1963 promotional campaign, he commissioned five avant-garde artists to paint fur coats. Marisol painted a pink nude, whilst Richard Auszkiewicz did an Op Art arrangement on calfskin.

Kaplan's philosophy was that bizarre or arty antics help to promote and sell furs. With his ranch mink coats retailing at a highly profitable $4,500 in the mid-1960s this entrepreneurial attitude certainly helped. However, he also found ways to bring down the price of fur. In 1961 he produced a cheaper version of a black dyed ranch mink, made famous by Jackie Kennedy. In a similar stylish, yet spare silhouette, with horizontally worked pelts, made from Japanese mink, the coats sold for $1,000 a piece. Kaplan was also known to stage fun fur shows in art galleries and was the first to admit that he drove to work on a Honda motor scooter and underwent psychoanalysis that helped him come to terms with the idiosyncrasies of the fashion business.

In acknowledgement of the growing anti-fur movements in the socially aware 1960s, the company was one of the first to take a stand against the use of fur from endangered species. Kaplan has himself said, "Twenty years ago I used to hate to be a furrier, I thought it was the lowest degree socially." However, he learned to love the trade and acquired a great deal of creative fulfillment from his role.

In the late 1960s the company was bought by the Kenton Corporation, and when they wished to sell it in the 1970s Kaplan decided to leave fashion and pursue his interests in art and painting.

—Kevin Almond

KAPLAN, Jacques.

French fur designer

Born: Paris, 1924. **Career:** Joined father's furrier business (founded in Paris, 1889) on its move to New York, 1942. Retired, 1971.

KARAN, Donna.

American designer

Born: Donna Faske in Forest Hills, New York, 2 October 1948. **Education:** Studied at Parsons School of Design, New York. **Fam-**

Donna Karan: Fall 1994; flint doubleface crepe side-tie wideneck wrap dress.

ily: Married Mark Karan in 1973 (divorced); daughter: Gabrielle; married Stephen Weiss in 1977; stepchildren: Lisa, Cory. **Career:** Assistant designer, Anne Klein & Co., and Addenda Company, New York, 1967-68; designer, Anne Klein, 1968-71; designer and director of design in association with Louis Dell'Olio, Anne Klein & Co., 1974-84; launched Anne Klein II diffusion line, 1982. Designer, Donna Karan New York (DKNY), from 1985; added swimwear line, 1986; hosiery collection, 1987; DKNY bridge line, 1988; DKNY menswear collection, 1991; founded Donna Karan Beauty Company, fragrance and cosmetic division, New York, 1992; lingerie, and children's line, DKNY Kids, from 1992. **Awards:** Coty American Fashion Critics Award, 1977, 1981, 1984, 1985; Fashion Footwear Association of New York Award, 1988; Council of Fashion Designers of America Award, 1985, 1986, 1990, 1992; Woolmark Award, 1992; Honorary Degree, Bachelor of Fine Arts, Parsons School of Design, 1987. **Address:** 550 Seventh Avenue, New York, New York 10018, USA.

Publications:

On KARAN:

Books

Millinaire, Caterine, and Carol Troy, *Cheap Chic Update,* New York 1978.
Morris, Bernadine, and Barbara Walz, *The Fashion Makers,* New York 1978.
Diamonstein, Barbaralee, *Fashion: The Inside Story,* New York 1985.
Perschetz, Lois, ed., *W, The Designing Life,* New York 1987.
Coleridge, Nicholas, *The Fashion Conspiracy,* London 1988.
Steele, Valerie, *Women of Fashion: Twentieth-Century Designers,* New York 1991.

Articles

Wahlfert-Wihlborg, L., "The Label Is Anne Klein, but the Name that Keeps It Going Is Donna Karan," in *People Weekly* (Chicago), 29 March 1982.
"Cue: Designing Women—Donna Karan," in *Vogue* (London), September 1985.
Pedrix, "The Making of New York Fashion," in *Connoisseur* (New York), February 1986.
Donovan, Carrie, "How a Fashion Star Is Born," in the *New York Times Magazine,* 4 May 1986.
Infantino, Vivian, "Interview: Donna Karan," in *Footwear News Magazine* (London), July 1986.
Gottfried, Carolyn, "In Conversation: Donna Karan and Joan Burstein ...," in *Vogue* (London), October 1986.
"Seventh Avenue Sweetheart," in *Fashion Weekly* (London), 5 May 1987.
Jobey, Liz, "Designing Women," in *Vogue* (London), July 1987.
Chubb, Ann, "Action Packed," in *Country Life* (London), 12 May 1988.
Lebowitz, Lisa, and Patrick Pacheco, "New Working Class," in *Harper's Bazaar* (New York), March 1989.
Mansfield, Stephanie, "Prima Donna," in *Vogue* (New York), August 1989.
Conant, Jennet, "The New Queen of New York," in *Manhattan, inc.* (New York), October 1989.

Donna Karan: Men's collection, Fall 1994; black drawstring collar coat and black wool crepe three-piece suit.

Mulvagh, Jane, "Donna è Mobile," in *The Sunday Times Magazine* (London), 4 March 1990.
Chubb, Ann, "Donna Karan," in *Options* (London), August 1990.
"Donna Karan," in *Current Biography* (New York), August 1990.
Weisman, Katherine, "Designing Woman," in *Forbes* (New York), 1 October 1990.
Alderson, Maggie, "Donna Karan: USA Today," in *Elle* (New York), October 1990.
Howell, Georgina, "Putting on the Style," in *The Sunday Times Magazine* (London), 7 April 1991.
Cihlar, Kimberly, "Donna's Man," in the *Daily News Record* (New York), 12 April 1991.
Mesdon, Randall, "The Empress's New Clothes," in *Esquire* (New York), September 1991.
White, Constance C. R., "Donna Karan: Talking Bridge," in *Women's Wear Daily* (New York), 11 September 1991.
White, Constance C. R., "DKNY: a Home of Its Own," in *Women's Wear Daily* (New York), 12 February 1992.
Born, Pete, "Karan Fashions a Fragrance," in *Women's Wear Daily* (New York), 1 May 1992.
Howell, Georgina, "Donna's Prime Time," in *Vogue* (New York), August 1992.

Weinfeld-Berg, Adrienne, "DKNY Kids the Real," in *Earnshaws,* October 1992.

Ducas, June, "Prima Donna," in *Women's Journal* (London), November 1992.

Brampton, Sally, "Queen D.," in *Vogue* (London), December 1992.

Rudolph, Barbara, "Donna Inc.," in *Time* (New York), 21 December 1992.

Spindler, Amy M., "The Power Suit Chills Out," in the *New York Times,* 29 July 1993.

Myerson, Allen R., "Partners at Odds, Donna Karan to Go Public," in the *New York Times,* 14 August 1993.

Spindler, Amy M., "Piety on Parade: Fashion Seeks Inspiration," in the *New York Times,* 5 September 1993.

Cosgrave, Bronwyn, "Donna Karan Crosses the Atlantic," in *Élan* magazine of *The European* (London), 12-14 August 1994.

Lubow, Arthur, "The Mega Mom-and-Pop Shop," in *The New Yorker* (New York), 7 November 1994.

Beckett, Kathleen, "Slip-sliding to a Close: Donna Karan," in the *New York Post,* 5 November 1994.

Spindler, Amy M., "Klein and Karan: Clothes that Do the Job," in the *New York Times,* 5 November 1994.

"New York: Donna's Underworld," in *Women's Wear Daily* (New York), 7 November 1994.

Spindler, Amy M., "Luxurious Armor by Karan, Klein, Mizrahi," in the *New York Times,* 8 April 1995.

"Donna Krishna," in *Women's Wear Daily* (New York), 10 April 1995.

*   *   *

Donna Karan can be considered the designer who has made it fashionable to be voluptuous. She has based her corporate philosophy on clothes that are designed to hug a woman but also hide bodily imperfections. "You've gotta accent your positive, delete your negative," she declared in a press release, emphasizing the fact that if you're pulled together underneath, you can build on top of that. Karan firmly relates designing to herself and her role as a woman. She sees design as a personal expression of the many roles she has had to balance, being a wife, mother, friend and business person. She believes that her sex has given her greater insight into solving problems that women have with fashion, fulfilling their needs, simplifying dress to make life easier and to add comfort, luxury, and durability. Originating as a womenswear label, the company now also produces menswear, childrenswear, accessories, beauty products, and a perfume that perpetrate the lifestyle and philosophy instigated by the womenswear line. Donna Karan stresses that she has not drawn the line there. "There's so much to be done. DKNY underwear, swimwear, home furnishings....the designs are already in my head, it's just a matter of getting them executed."

Karan was born and raised on Long Island, New York. Both her mother and father were involved in fashion careers so it seemed inevitable that Donna should follow in their footsteps. After two years studying fashion at Parsons School of Design in New York she was hired by Anne Klein for a summer job. She later became an associate designer until Anne Klein died in 1974. Her next lucky break was to shape the rest of her career. She was named successor to Anne Klein and together with Louis Dell'Olio, who joined the company a year later, designed the collection.

Shortly after the launch of the diffusion line, Anne Klein II, in 1982, Karan felt ready to go it alone. Together with her husband,

Stephen Weiss, she launched the first Donna Karan collection in 1985 and since then the company has grown at a dizzying pace. Karan is inspired by New York. She believes that its energy, pace, and vibrance attracts the most sophisticated and artistic people in the world, the type of people and lifestyle for whom she has always designed. Her principle is that clothes should be interchangeable and flexible enough to go from day to evening, summer to winter. Fashion should be a multi-cultural language, easy, sensuous, and functional, a modern security blanket. This explains perhaps why her fundamental trademark items, the bodysuits, unitards, black cashmere, stretch fabrics and sensuous bodywrap styles, owe great allegiance to the innate style and taste of the artist.

There is a great sense of urgency about Donna Karan; to say that there are not enough hours in a day would be an understatement. Her interviews are always frenetic, emotionally charged yet human and blatantly honest. When asked by journalist Sally Brampton to describe her life, she replied, "It's chaos, C.H.A.O.S."

Karan's magic touch is a combination of creative flair and marketing know-how. She designs for human needs, people who live, work, and play. She conceptualizes a customer and wardrobe and can then merchandise a line, applying her designer's eye for colour, proportion, and fit. In many ways she is like a contemporary American Chanel in that she analyses women's needs with a question to herself: "What do I need? How can I make life easier? How can dressing be simplified so that I can get on with my own life?"

—Kevin Almond

KASPER, Herbert.

American designer

Born: New York City, 12 December 1926. **Education:** Studied English at New York University, 1949-53; studied fashion at Parsons School of Design, New York, 1951-53, and l'École de la Chambre Syndicale de la Couture Parisienne, 1953. **Family:** Married Betsey Pickering in 1955 (divorced, 1958); married Jondar Conning in 1979. **Military Service:** Served in the United States Army. **Career:** Spent two years in Paris working for Fath, Rochas, and at *Elle;* designer, Arnold and Fox, New York, 1954-64; designer, Kasper for Joan Leslie division of Leslie Fay, New York, 1964-85; designer, J.L. Sport, and Kasper for Weatherscope, 1970-85; vice-president, Leslie Fay; designer, Kasper for ASL, from 1980. **Awards:** Coty American Fashion Critics Award, 1955, 1970, 1976; Cotton Fashion Award, 1972; Maas Brothers Pavilion Design Award, 1983; Cystic Fibrosis Foundation, Governor of Alabama Award, 1984; Ronald MacDonald House Award, 1984. **Address:** 32 East 64th Street, New York, New York 10021, USA.

Publications:

On KASPER:

Books

Morris, Bernadine, and Barbara Walz, *The Fashion Makers,* New York 1978.

Diamonstein, Barbaralee, *Fashion: The Inside Story,* New York 1985.

Stegemeyer, Anne, *Who's Who in Fashion,* New York 1988.

Herbert Kasper.

Milbank, Caroline Rennolds, *New York Fashion: The Evolution of American Style,* New York 1989.

*

Over a lifetime of designing I've evolved a philosophy that comes from creating clothes for a particular kind of American woman. (Who, by the way, I very much admire.) This woman is adventurous and vital with a lifestyle that demands she play many different roles throughout the day. It's the confident spirit of this kind of woman that inspires me most.

Whatever she's doing, running a home, a career, entertaining, mothering, traveling, I deeply believe that this woman remains an individual. No one is going to tell her exactly what she has to wear, no matter what's currently in style. She wants and needs high style, high quality, fashion-conscious clothes that can last for more than one season. That's what I believe I offer her. And because I think I have an exceptional ability to anticipate trends, my clothes always have a "today" spirit. They're high fashion ... in the mood of the moment. I'm constantly refining, improving, interpreting ... trying to capture the essence of the times without being trendy.

I design sophisticated clothes for women who are spirited and young ... whatever their age. And I believe in the concept of wardrobe dressing—being able to mix clothes—which is the basis of American sportswear, so my pieces are often mixable. A jacket from one suit may work wonderfully with the skirt of another, or look great with an odd pair of trousers.

In fact, interesting mixes of color and fabric have become my signature ... it's what gives them their individuality. My inspiration comes from many sources. Ideas come from the streets, museums, from my own way of twisting an idea around. I remember once being at a beach in the south of Italy and seeing a woman wearing a long black tunic. This inspired me to do a resort collection based on black and gold which at the time was very different from the more traditional navy for beachwear.

Another time I went to a Matisse exhibition in Paris and built an entire collection using Matisse prints on many different kinds of fabrics. But from whatever source my ideas come from, I always keep in mind that lively, energetic, smart looking woman who is my customer. She's my motivation and my ultimate inspiration.

—Herbert Kasper

*   *   *

Herbert Kasper has made his name as a designer by working predominantly for one company, Joan Leslie in New York, whom he joined in 1963. In 1980 he became vice-president of the company as well as designer, creating high fashion looks that reflect trends but are commercial and wearable. A private customer, Joanne Carson (then the wife of talk-show host Johnny) described his clothes as being both feminine and sexy: "He's got a totally female concept," she enthused, adding that he knew how to put together the perfect interchangeable wardrobe for her various excursions abroad.

Kasper is a designer who really cares about his customer. He wants the person who buys a dress to enjoy it and return for more. His satisfaction comes from seeing a woman look and feel good in his clothes. His reputation has always been that of a respectable craftsman who honours all levels of production involved in creating fashion, from design to manufacture.

After military service in World War II, where he designed costumes for the troupe shows in which he took part as a chorus boy, Kasper enrolled at Parsons School of Design in New York. He then spent two years in Paris perfecting his skills, with a short period at l'École de la Chambre Syndicale de la Couture, Paris and positions at Jacques Fath and Marcel Rochas. Returning to the United States he worked for the milliner Mr. Fred, where his reputation grew. In his next position as dress designer for a company called Penart, the department store Lord and Taylor in New York, who were promoting American designers, said they wanted to feature his work; he became known as Kasper of Penart. His talent was for making inexpensive clothes look exquisite and expensive, which endeared him to several other Seventh Avenue manufacturers in the 1950s.

Kasper's forte has always been dresses, but a designer's job involves adapting to the demands of the market and in the early 1970s he opened a sportswear division for Joan Leslie, J. L. Sport. Part of his fashion philosophy has been that clothes should always work together, so he often found it difficult to differentiate between these two lines when designing. A coat for Joan Leslie Dresses, he once declared, could work equally well with the less expensive separates line for J. L. Sport.

While working in Paris, Kasper noted that women spent a lot of money on custom-made clothes, ordering several outfits for different occasions. He formed a philosophy based on these observations that individual garments can be mixed and matched with many others to create an outfit, a sportswear concept that has become a way of life in the United States today.

Kasper has always been a great socialite. His social life inspires his work because it gives him an insight into how people live, their attitudes, and changing tastes. As a designer he is happy with his work, regarding each creation as one of his own children, which in a way justifies his devotion to his craft.

—Kevin Almond

KAWAKUBO, Rei.

Japanese designer

Born: Tokyo, 1942. **Education:** Graduated in fine arts, Keio University, Tokyo, 1964. **Career:** Worked in advertising department, Asahi Kasei textile firm, 1964-66; free-lance designer, 1967-69; founder-designer, Comme des Garçons, 1969, firm incorporated, 1973; menswear line Homme introduced, 1978; Tricot knitwear and Robe de Chambre lines introduced, 1981; first Paris boutique opened, 1981; Comme des Garçons, S.A. ready-to-wear subsidiary formed, 1982, New York subsidiary formed, 1986; furniture collection launched, 1983; Homme Plus collection introduced, 1984; men's Paris boutique opened, 1986; Homme Deux and Noir collections introduced, 1987; Comme des Garçons *Six* magazine published, from 1988; Tokyo flagship store opened, 1989. **Exhibitions:** *A New Wave in Fashion: Three Japanese Designers,* Phoenix, Arizona, Art Museum, 1983; *Mode et Photo, Comme des Garçons,* Centre Georges Pompidou, Paris, 1986; *Three Women: Madeleine Vionnet, Claire McCardell and Rei Kawakubo,* Fashion Institute of Technology, New York, 1987; *Essence of Quality,* Kyoto Costume Institute, Tokyo, 1993. **Awards:** Mainichi Newspaper Fashion Award, 1983, 1988; Fashion Group Night of the Stars Award, New York, 1986; Chevalier de L'Ordre des Arts et des Lettres, Paris,

1993. **Address:** Comme des Garçons, 5-11-5 Minamiaoyama, Minato-ku Tokyo 107, Japan.

Publications:

On KAWAKUBO:

Books

Phoenix Art Museum, *A New Wave in Fashion: Three Japanese Designers* (exhibition catalogue), Phoenix, Arizona 1983.

Koren, Leonard, *New Fashion Japan,* Tokyo 1984.

Comme des Garçons (exhibition catalogue), Tokyo 1986.

Koda, Harold, Richard Martin and Laura Sinderbrand, *Three Women: Madeleine Vionnet, Claire McCardell, and Rei Kawakubo* (exhibition catalogue), New York 1987.

Sparke, Penny, *Japanese Design,* London 1987.

Sudjic, Deyan, *Rei Kawakubo and Comme des Garçons,* New York 1990.

Steele, Valerie, *Women of Fashion: Twentieth-Century Designers,* New York 1991.

Hiesinger, Kathryn B., and Felice Fischer, *Japanese Design: A Survey since 1950,* New York 1995.

Articles

Cocks, Jay, "Into the Soul of the Fabric," in *Time* (New York), 1 August 1983.

Saint-Leon, Rhoda Marcus de, "Comme des Garçons: Rei Kawakubo Makes Magic," in *American Fabrics and Fashions* (Newtown, Connecticut), Fall 1983.

Koda, Harold, "Rei Kawakubo and the Aesthetic of Poverty," in *Dress* (Earlville, Maryland), No. 11, 1985.

"New Products," in *Architectural Record* (New York), January 1985.

Mower, Sarah, "The Kimono with Added Cut and Thrust," in *The Guardian* (London), 6 March 1986.

Sudjic, Deyan, "All the Way Back to Zero," in *The Sunday Times* (London), 20 April 1986.

Stetser, Maggie, "Future Shock, with the Brilliant Innovators of Japanese Fashion," in *Connoisseur* (London), September 1986.

Conant, Jennet, "The Monk and the Nun: The Shock Value of Two Japanese Designers," in *Newsweek* (New York), 2 February 1987.

Martin, Richard, "Aesthetic Dress: The Art of Rei Kawakubo," in *Arts Magazine* (New York), March 1987.

Weinstein, Jeff, "Vionnet, McCardell, Kawakubo: Why There Are Three Great Women Artists," in the *Village Voice* (New York), 31 March 1987.

Withers, Jane, "Black: The Zero Option," in *The Face* (London), March 1987.

Drier, Deborah, "Designing Women," in *Art in America* (New York), May 1987.

Klensch, Elsa, "Another World of Style ... Rei Kawakubo," in *Vogue* (New York), August 1987.

Delmar, Michael, "Avec Rei Kawakubo," in *Jardin des Modes,* September 1987.

Filmer, Deny, "Designer Focus: Rei Kawakubo," in *Cosmopolitan* (London), May 1988.

Popham, Peter, "Modern Art by the Yard," in *The Sunday Times* (London), 16 April 1989.

Redman, Susan, "Art for Fashion's Sake," in *Studio Collections,* October/November 1989.

Jeal, Nicola, "Mistress of Monochrome," in *The Observer* (London), 22 October 1989.

Livingston, David, "New Decade for Kawakubo," in the *Globe and Mail,* 26 October 1989.

"Back from Zero," in *Blueprint* (London), November 1990.

Morozzi, Christina, "Partire da zero," in *Moda* (Milan), April 1991.

Yusuf, Nilgin, "My Criterion Is Beauty: Rei Kawakubo of Comme des Garçons," in *Marie Claire* (London), April 1992.

Bowles, Hamish, "Fashion's Visionary," in *Vogue* (New York), March 1993.

Menkes, Suzy, "'Auschwitz' Fashions Draw Jewish Rebuke," in *International Herald Tribune* (Paris), 4-5 February 1995.

Martin, Richard, "The Shock(ing) Value at Fashion's Cutting Edge," in *Los Angeles Times,* 19 Feburary 1995.

Spindler, Amy M., "Beyond Sweet, Beyond Black, Beyond 2001," in the *New York Times,* 17 March 1995.

*

My approach to fashion design is influenced by my daily life .... my search for new means of expression.

I feel that recently there has been a little more of an interest towards those who look for new ideas and who are searching for a new sense of values. My wish is to be able to continue my search for the new.

—Rei Kawakubo

*   *   *

Rei Kawakubo's work is both paradox and ideological imperative. Minimal, monochromatic and modernist, her approach to fashion design challenges conventional beauty without forgoing stylish cloth, cut, and color. Her clothing is not so much about the body as the space around the body and the metaphor of self. Architectonic in conception and decidedly abstract, the clothing nevertheless derives from Japanese traditional wear.

Kawakubo emerged as a clothing designer by an indirect route, from both a training in fine art at Keio University in Tokyo and work in advertising for Asahi Kasei, a major chemical company that produced acrylic fibres—promoted through fashionable clothing. In 1967 she became a free-lance stylist, a rarity in Japan at the time. Kawakubo's dissatisfaction with available clothes for the fashion shoots provided the impetus for designing her own garments. She launched the Comme des Garçons women's collection in Tokyo in 1975 with her first shop in Minami-Aoyama and her first catalog the same year. It was an especially fertile period for Japanese fashion design, with the concurrent rise of Issey Miyake and Yohji Yamamoto.

Kawakubo's themes combine the essence of Japanese traditional work-end streetwear, its simplicity of style, fabric, and color, with an admiration for modern architecture, especially the purism of Le Corbusier and Tadao Ando. Translated into clothing's rational construction, these affinities emphasize the idea of garment—the garment as a construction in space, essentially a structure to live in. The tradition of the kimono, with its architectural silhouette off the body and its many-layered complexity of body wrappings, combines with a graphic approach that is flat and abstract. It is a disarming look that requires a cognitive leap in wearability and social function.

Rei Kawakubo: Comme des Garçons, Fall/Winter 1984/85. *Photograph by Peter Lindbergh.*

The building block of Kawakubo's design is the fabric, the thread that produces the clothing structure. Her long-standing collaboration with specialty weaver Hiroshi Matsushita has allowed her to reformulate the actual fabric on the loom, the complexities of the weave, the imperfections, the texture of the fabric. Her 1981 launch of the Comme des Garçons line in Paris marked her first international exposure and the introduction of her loom-distressed weaves. What have been referred to as "rag-picker" clothes, a homage to the spontaneity and inventiveness of street people, was based on fabric innovation—cloth that crumpled and wrapped, that draped coarsely as layers, folded and buttoned at random. Most notable of these was her so-called "lace" knitwear of 1982, where sweaters were purposely knitted to incorporate various-sized holes that appear as rips and tears or intentionally intricate webs. This was an attack on lingering Victorianism in fashion, on the conventional, the precise and the tight-laced. It offered a rational argument for anti-form at a time when minimalism had lapsed into decorativeness.

Kawakubo's use of monochromatic black as her signature is analytical and subtle rather than sensual and brash. Black, which is often perceived as flattering, assumes the status of a non-color—an absence rather than a presence. Her intent is to reject clothes as mere decoration for the body. Even with the later introduction of saturated color in the late 1980s lines, in which her clothes became slimmer. Black was still a basic—evident in the Noir line, as well as in Homme and Homme Plus, her menswear collections.

Her control of the presentation of Comme des Garçons in photography, catwalk shows, the design of store interiors, catalogs, and most recently a magazine, is integral to the design concept that extends from the clothing. Kawakubo was the first to use non-professional models, art world personalities, and film celebrities, both in photography for catalogs and in catwalk shows. Her early catalogs from the 1970s featured noted figures from Japanese art and literature. The 1988 introduction of the quarto-sized biannual magazine *Six* (for sixth sense) replaced the Comme des Garçons catalogs and pushed Kawakubo's anti-fashion ideas to extreme. These photographic essays became enigmatic vehicles for stream-of-consciousness, surrealism, exoticism, and Zen, that which informs Kawakubo's sensibility and, ultimately, in a semiotic way, is imbued in her fashion designs. Rei Kawakubo's ideas have explored the realm of possibilities associated with the production and selling of clothing. Her control of the environment of her stores from the sparse design of the interiors, on which she collaborates with architect Takao Kawasaki, to the industrial racks and shelves, to the way the sales people act and dress, even now to the furnishings, which she designs and sells, is total and defining. Kawakubo's art is one of extending the boundaries of self-presentation and self-awareness into an environment of multivalent signs. It is an extension of fashion design into the realism of metaphysic, of "self in landscape," of which the clothing is a bare trace.

—Sarah Bodine

KELLY, Patrick.

American designer working in Paris

Born: Vicksburg, Mississippi, 24 September 1954. **Education:** Studied art history and black history at Jackson State University, Jackson, Mississippi, and fashion design at Parsons School of De-

sign, New York. **Career:** Held various jobs in Atlanta, Georgia, including window dresser, Rive Gauche boutique, instructor, Barbizon School of Modeling, vintage clothing store proprietor, mid-1970s. Moved to Paris, 1980; costume designer, Le Palais club, c.1980-81, also free-lance designer, 1980-90; Patrick Kelly, Paris, formed, and first ready-to-wear collection introduced, 1985; also free-lance sportswear designer, Benetton, 1986; opened first boutique in Paris, produced first couture collection, sold worldwide rights to ready-to-wear collections, 1987. *Died* (in Paris) *1 January 1990.*

Publications:

On KELLY:

Articles

Bain, Sally, "The King of Cling," in the *Drapers Record* (London), 16 May 1987.

Johnson, Bonnie, "In Paris, His Slinky Dresses Have Made Mississippi-born Designer Patrick Kelly the New King of Cling," in *People,* 15 June 1987.

George, Leslie, "Patrick Kelly: An American in Paris," in *Women's Wear Daily* (New York), 15 January 1988.

Gross, Michael, "Kelly's Blackout," in *New York,* 23 May 1988.

Conant, Jennet, "Buttons and Billiard Balls: A Designer from the Deep South Captures Paris," in *Newsweek* (New York), 27 June 1988.

"Meet Patrick Kelly," in *Vogue Patterns* (New York and London), July 1988.

Dissly, Megan, in *Christian Science Monitor,* 25 August 1988.

Hornblower, Margot, "An Original American in Paris," in *Time* (New York), 3 April 1989.

Goodwin, Betty, "Maverick and Mastermind," in the *Los Angeles Times,* 7 April 1989.

Johnson, Pamela, "Patrick Kelly: Prince of Paris," in *Essence,* May 1989.

"Glitz Tips: Do-it-Yourself Ideas from Glitzmeister Patrick Kelly," in *Chatelaine* (Toronto), September 1989.

Gross, Michael, "Patrick Kelly: Exuberant Style Animates the American Designer's Paris Atelier," in *Architectural Digest* (Los Angeles), September 1989.

"Patrick Kelly," in *Current Biography* (New York), September 1989.

"Patrick Kelly" (obituary), in the *New York Times,* 2 January 1990.

Moore, Jackie, "Patrick Kelly" (obituary), in *The Independent* (London), 11 January 1990.

"Designer Dies," in *DR, The Fashion Business* (London), 13 January 1990.

"Mississippi Couturier," in *US News and World Report* (Washington), 15 January 1990.

"Designer Patrick Kelly Dies of Bone Marrow Disease," in *Jet* (New York), 22 January 1990.

Articles also in *Women's Wear Daily* (New York), 3 January 1990 and 2 April 1990.

*　　*　　*

A published "Love List" for designer Patrick Kelly included "fried chicken," "foie gras," and "pearls" (*Women's Wear Daily,* 1 March 1990). Kelly's designs celebrated pride in his spiritual upbringing in the American South and a tourist-like adoration of Paris.

Not for the faint-hearted, his specialty was form-fitting knits irreverently decorated with oversized and mismatched buttons, watermelons, black baby dolls, and huge rhinestones densely silhouetting the Eiffel Tower.

Wearing too-big overalls and a biker's cap emblazoned "Paris," Kelly engendered folklore as important as the clothing he designed. Growing up in Mississippi, taught sewing by his grandmother, selling vintage clothing in Atlanta, failing to be hired on New York's Seventh Avenue ... a one-way ticket to Paris from a model/friend resulted in his being discovered while selling his own designs in a Paris flea market.

Kelly was exotic and different. He and his clothing charmed the French and the rest of the world, and he was the first American ever admitted to the elite Chambre Syndicale de la Couture Parisienne, the group of Paris-based designers permitted to show collections in the Louvre. Exuberantly witty, his first show at the Louvre began with Kelly spray painting a large red heart on a white canvas, and included dresses entitled "Jungle Lisa Loves Tarzan," a spoof of Mona Lisa featuring leopard-print gowns.

Kelly's designs remained unpretentious yet sexy, affordable while glamorous. Dresses were fun and uncontrived, yet Kelly paid great attention to design details. Bold, theatrical details such as white topstitching on black, low necklines, and dice buttons on a pinstriped business dress, silver fringe on a western skirt, and vibrant color combinations make one want to shimmy just looking at them. Kelly's art was in embellishment of women, young and old. Trims become jewelry; collars and hemlines become frames. Frills are exaggerated, enlarged, unexpected, and re-thought, saucily decorating what would otherwise be rather simple designs.

A love-in atmosphere prevailed at an April 1989 show and lecture for students at New York's Fashion Institute of Technology. A standing-room-only crowd screamed, laughed, and applauded Kelly—his effervescence and his happiness were contagious. He showed a sassy and smart collection, including a tight black mini dress with shiny multicolored buttons outlining a perfect heart on the buttocks; wide, notched, off-the-shoulder collars; leopard-print trench coats and turtlenecked body suits; multicolored scarves suspended from the hip, swaying below abbreviated hemlines; and a *trompe l'oeil* bustier of buttons on a fitted mini dress. Kelly's models danced, even smiled, down the catwalk, delighted to be wearing his clothing (they modeled this show for free). The audience was delighted to be there: the clothing and designer seemed to be welcoming everyone to a good party, and everyone had a good time.

Kelly's personal attention to detail, his love of design, his spirit, sold his clothing. He stated "the ultimate goal is selling," but he did more than just sell. Wearing a Patrick Kelly dress meant embracing one's past, doing the best with what you have, triumphing over failure, and laughing at one self. One could be part of Patrick Kelly's fairy tale and celebrate his *joie de vivre.*

—Jane Burns

KENZO.
Japanese designer working in Paris

Born: Kenzo Takada in Tokyo, 27 February 1939. **Education:** Studied at the Bunka College of Fashion. **Career:** Designer for

Kenzo. *Photograph by Peter Lindbergh.*

Sanai department store; pattern designer *Soen* magazine, Tokyo, 1960-64; free-lance designer, Paris, from 1965, selling to Féraud, Rodier and several department stores; designer for Pisanti; established Jungle Jap boutique in Paris, 1970; Rue Cherche Midi Boutique opened, 1972; Kenzo-Paris boutique established, New York, 1983; menswear line launched, 1983; boutiques opened in Paris, Aix en Provence, Bordeaux, Lille, Lyon, Saint-Tropez, Copenhagen, London, Milano, and Tokyo, 1984-85; menswear and womenswear lines, Kenzo Jeans, and junior line, Kenzo Jungle, both launched, 1986; Kenzo Bed Linen and Bath Wear line launched, 1987; boutiques opened in Rome, New York, 1987; established childrenswear, line, 1987; womenswear line, Kenzo City launched, 1988; boutique opened in Brussels, 1989, and in Stockholm, 1990; line of bath products line Le Bain launched, 1990; boutique opened in Hong Kong, 1990, Bangkok, 1991, and Singapore, 1991; Kenzo Maison line launched, 1992; Bambou line launched, 1994. Perfumes: *Kenzo,* 1988; *Parfum d'Été,* 1992. Also: costume designer for opera, film director. **Awards:** Soen Prize, 1960; Fashion Editors Club of Japan Prize, 1972; Bath Museum of Costume Dress of the Year Award, 1976, 1977;Chevalier de l'Ordre des Arts et des Lettres, 1984. **Address:** 54 rue Étienne Marcel, 75001 Paris, France.

Publications:

On KENZO:

Books

Milbank, Caroline Rennolds, *Couture: The Great Designers,* New York 1985.
Sparke, Penny, *Japanese Design,* London 1987.
Sainderichin, Ginette, *Kenzo,* Paris 1989.

On KENZO:

Articles

"The JAP Designer," in *Newsweek* (New York), 1 May 1972.
Morris, Bernadine, "Designer Does What He Likes—And It's Liked," in the *New York Times,* 12 July 1972.
Morris, Bernadine, "Kenzo Displays His Imagination," in the *New York Times,* 4 April 1973.
"Lively Influence on Dull Paris Scene," in *The Times* (London), 1 September 1976.
"Mini Redux," in *Newsweek* (New York), 8 November 1976.
Dorsey, Hebe, "Kenzo Grows Up," in the *New York Times Magazine,* 14 November 1976.
Talley, André Leon, "Kenzo: One Needs Folly to Work in Fashion," in *Women's Wear Daily* (New York), 17 February 1978.
Tucker, Priscilla, "Designer Becomes a Superstar: Kenzo Marches to Different Tunes; All of Them Are Hits," in the *New York Daily News,* 11 April 1978.
McEvoy, Marian, "Kenzo Barges Up the Nile," in *Women's Wear Daily* (New York), 20 October 1978.
Cleave, Maureen, "Makers of Modern Fashion: Kenzo," in *The Observer Magazine* (London), 14 December 1980.
"L'oeil de Vogue: l'anniversaire de Kenzo," in *Vogue* (Paris) October 1985.
Salvy, Gerard-Julien, "L'art d'être soi l-même," in *Vogue* (Paris), February 1986.
Boyd, Ann, "Cap by Denny, So Why Buy Kenzo?," in *The Observer* (London), 8 January 1987.
"Kenzo: créations tous azimuts," in *Profession Textile* (Paris), 5 February 1988.
Boriolli, Gisella, "Kenzo Back Home in Japan," in *Donna* (Milan), July/August 1989.
"Kenzo Modern Folklore," in *Elle* (New York), September 1989.
Baudot, Francois, "Le pélerinage de Kenzo," in *Elle* (Paris), 5 September 1989.

*   *   *

In 1986, Kenzo [Takada] called his menswear collection "Around the World in Eighty Days," but that expedition had long been underway in Kenzo's clothes for women and men. Significantly, for more than 20 years, Kenzo has been the most prominent traveller in fashion, but also the most multicultural and the most syncretistic, insisting on the diversity and compatibility of ethnic styles and cultural options from all parts of the world. Kenzo has steadfastly mixed styles. This Japanese tourist has rightly perceived and selected from all cultures and styles. In 1978, he told *Women's Wear Daily* (17 February 1978), "I like to use African patterns and Japanese patterns together." Kenzo interprets style and specific cos-

tume elements of various parts of the world, assimilating them into a peaceful internationalism more radical than other designers. Thus, the spring-summer 1975 Chinese coolie look was combined with Portuguese purses, copious Riviera awning-striped beach shirts, and T-shirt dresses for full cultural diversity. In 1973, Romanian peasant skirts became his inspiration, as did Mexican *rebozos* and heavy Scandinavian sweaters. In fall 1976, he was inspired by Native Americans in a highly textural, colorful, and feather-inflected collection. In spring-summer 1984, his collection was based chiefly on North Africa, with elements of an excursion to India for a modified Nehru suit. For spring-summer 1979, the Egyptian look became the front-page headline of *Women's Wear Daily,* "Kenzo barges up the Nile." *Wunderkind* and celebrity in 1970s fashion, Kenzo never fixed on one look, but has preferred to view fashion as a creative, continuous adventure. Shyly, Kenzo said in 1978: "It pleases me when people say I have influence. But I am influenced by the world that says I influence it. The world I live in is my influence."

Other influences include American popular culture: Chinese tunics and wrappings, especially at the low-swung waist, batiks of East Asia, European peasant aprons and smocks, and Japanese woven textiles. For his 40th birthday, the designer became Minnie Mouse; his spring-summer 1988 menswear collection was a homage to Al Capone. Asked by Joan Quinn about travels and ethnic clothing, Kenzo replied: "I prefer to travel only for vacations. I don't go around looking for influences. The energy arrives." In fact, Kenzo serves as "the prototype of the young designer, the designer with a sense of humor about fashion, culture, and life, as well as a lively curiosity about clothing itself," as Caroline Milbank described, precisely because his theme collections and almost volcanic change imply a continuous stream of ideas. Kenzo, after all, emerged first as a designer of poor-boy-style skinny sweaters. Like Elsa Schiaparelli who likewise began with ingenious knits, he has become a prodigious continuing talent. His fashion references seem never to be imposed upon clothing, but are reasonable as a consequence of his design exploration: the low-slung waist returned Kenzo to casual, boyish styles of the skirt even as he acknowledged ethnic sources. Military and ecclesiastical looks in 1978 simply streamlined and simplified his style.

In addition, Kenzo has been fascinated by painting, drawing upon Wassily Kandinsky and David Hockney for inspiration, as well as calligraphy. His pallet has always been internationally vibrant, filled with the ethnic eruption of Fauvism, play of pattern, and unorthodox color combinations.

Is the work of this influential Japanese designer, born in Japan in 1939 and living in France since 1965, merely a kind of ethic parade in which the designer as a kind of latter-day Haliburton plunders the vocabularies of regional styles to remain exciting and innovative? Or, is there in Kenzo's synthesis of many aesthetics a creative mix, synergy, and energy that we might understand as the best product of multicultural awareness? After all, there were many fashion designers in the 1970s who used ethnic expressions merely to be hip.

Kenzo's work, in fact, argues strongly for the harmony of cultural influences, the most disparate and distinct expressions of dress coming together in the styles of a designer who has himself raised barbed issues of ethnicity in insisting upon "Jap" for his early collections, encouraging a racist pejorative to be converted into a positive identity.

Kenzo demonstrates a sustained aesthetic of absorption, assimilating many global influences into an integrated and wholly modern style of his own. The flamboyance of Kenzo's art and life captured the popular imagination of fashion in the 1970s, but his abiding and exemplary contribution is his ability to digest many style traits and to achieve a powerful composite. In 1978, Kenzo told André Leon Tally, "One needs a lot of folly to work in fashion" (*Women's Wear Daily*, New York, 17 February 1978). It is that sense of exuberance, creative excitement, and caprice that has marked Kenzo's work for more than two decades. Claude Montana once commented, "Kenzo gives much more to fashion than all the couturiers lumped together." Indubitably, Kenzo epitomized fashion energy and imagination in the 1970s: his brilliant creative assimilation brought street initiative and global creativity to fashion.

—Richard Martin

KHANH, Emmanuelle.

French designer

Born: Renée Mezière in Paris, 12 September 1937. **Family:** Married the designer Quasar Khanh (Manh Khanh Nguyen) in 1957; children: Othello, Atlantique-Venus. **Career:** Mannequin for the Balenciaga and Givenchy fashion houses, Paris, 1957-63; began creating own designs, 1962; created collections for Belletête, Missoni, Dorothée Bis, Laura, Cacharel, Pierre d'Alby, Krizia, Max Mara, and Le Bistrot du Tricot, 1963-69; founder, director, Emmanuelle Khanh label and fashion garment and accessory company, from 1971; opened first Paris boutique, 1977; President, Emmanuelle Khanh International, 1987. **Awards:** Named Chevalier des Arts et des Lettres, Paris, 1986. **Address:** Emmanuelle Khanh International, 39 avenue Victor Hugo, 75116 Paris, France.

Publications:

On KHANH:

Books

Lynam, Ruth, ed., *Paris Fashion: The Great Designers and their Creations,* London 1972.
Carter, Ernestine, *With Tongue in Chic,* London 1974.
Carter, Ernestine, *The Changing World of Fashion: 1900 to the Present,* London 1977.
Mulvagh, Jane, *Vogue History of 20th-century Fashion,* London 1988.
Loebenthal, Joel, *Radical Rags: Fashions of the Sixties,* New York 1990.

Articles

"The Drop," in *Vogue* (London), February 1963.
Gabbey, Regine, "The Ready-to-Dare Designers," in *Réalités* (Paris), January 1969.
"Living in Heavenly Blue Blow-up Space in Paris," in *Vogue* (London), February 1969.
Toll, Marie-Pierre, "Where Beauty Is Not a Luxury," in *House and Garden* (New York), September 1984.

*

Women inspire me—fashions bore me.
A model made with love will skip off to the person who will live with it.
My strength is to make clothes which are timeless. To create clothes for me is a wonderful way to participate and belong to my era.

—Emmanuelle Khanh

*   *   *

While Mary Quant was revolutionizing fashion in England at the beginning of the 1960s, Emmanuelle Khanh was at the vanguard of the young French ready-to-wear movement. From the French pronunciation of the Beatles' "yeah, yeah, yeah," the emerging clothes were known as "yé yé" fashion. Having modelled for Balenciaga and Givenchy in the late 1950s, Khanh believed the time was right for rebellion against the strictures of haute couture and to begin making attractive clothing for the masses. Her individuality quickly caught on in France, where she modelled and sold the clothes herself. Soon her modern fashions reached the United States and were in demand in major department stores. The clothes Khanh had been making for herself, with the help of her husband, Quasar Khanh, were noticed by *Elle* magazine. This exposure led to Khanh's collaboration with another ex-Balenciaga model to design the groundbreaking "Emmachristie" collection in 1962. Khanh criticized haute couture for hiding the beauty of the body. For her own designs, she emphasized femininity by cutting clothes along the body's curves, to follow the movement of the body, unlike Balenciaga's gowns, which could practically stand alone, regardless of the woman's body within them.

Khanh created an architecturally classic mode with a twist: careful seaming, narrow armholes, a slim, close to the body "droop" silhouette. Her suits had the surprise element of skirts that were actually culottes. Innovations included dog-eared collars, long, fitted jackets with droopy collars, blouses and dresses with collars consisting of overlapping petal-like shapes along a U-shaped opening. Khanh also had a democratic approach to fabric. She used denim and tie-dyeing, chenille, and plastic. A characteristic evening top in 1965 was made of crêpe appliquéd with fluorescent plastic circles. Khanh often used the Shetland wools and Harris tweeds that had long been favored by middle-class Frenchwomen. In the late 1960s she introduced ready-to-wear furs, and tulle and lace lingerie. In cooperation with the Missonis, Khanh made fashions from Italian knit fabrics. The results of her work for the Paris ready-to-wear house of Cacharel, and her work with designer Dorothée Bis, resulted in dresses with a long, slim, flowing 1930s feeling. The use of Romanian hand embroidery became a hallmark of the clothes which Khanh produced under her own label. Keeping pace with the ethnic trend of the 1970s, Khanh created short, loose, peasant-style dresses out of colorful Indian gauze fabrics. Feminine blouses would be trimmed with scalloped embroidered edges, short skirts would be frilled, and lace would be used to trim soft linen in her designs of that period.

Later, during the 1970s, Khanh turned to designing knitwear and skiwear. A casual summer look consisted of a wide, striped cotton skirt, buttoned down the front, worn with a matching halter top and wedged-heeled shoes of matching fabric. The matching shoes were a couture touch for ready-to-wear. During the next decade Khanh continued to free-lance, making soft, individualistic fashions, bouncing creative ideas off her engineer, inventor, and interior-designer husband.

Emmanuelle Khanh: Winter 1994. *Photograph by H. Meister.*

Khanh's signature boldly-rimmed glasses have been successfully marketed, as have the clear plastic umbrellas she designed. One hundred and fifty boutiques around the world attest to her lasting popularity. In the 1980s her clothes had a retro feeling about them, with extended shoulders and cinched waistlines that flattered the figure. One outfit featured a very long, very loose camel hair coat falling freely from the shoulders, caught about the waist by a narrow leather belt, worn over a soft dark-brown wool jersey jumpsuit. For Jet Lag Showroom in 1990, Khanh designed a suit consisting of a waist-length tightly fitting jacket, worn with a long full flannel skirt. She continued in the 1990s to create comfortable, simple jackets and coats for special orders from the firm.

—Therese Duzinkiewicz Baker

KIESELSTEIN-CORD, Barry.

American jewelry and accessories designer

Born: New York, 6 November 1948. **Education:** Studied at Parsons School of Design, New York University, and the American Craft Institute. **Family:** Married Elizabeth Anne (CeCe) Eddy in 1974 (divorced); daughter: Elizabeth. **Career:** Worked as art director/producer for various advertising agencies, 1966-70; founded company, 1972; divisions include jewelry, belts, handbags (from 1991), gloves, and home furnishings and accessories. Opened instore boutiques at Bergdorf Goodman, New York, 1985; Neiman Marcus, Beverly Hills, 1990, and Mitsukishi, Tokyo, 1990; has also opened shops in Italy, Germany, and Switzerland. Also: Artist; Director of Council of Fashion Designers of America, 1987. **Collections:** Metropolitan Museum of Art, New York; Louisiana State Museum. **Awards:** Hollywood Radio & Television Society Award, 1965; two Art Directors Club Awards, New York, late 1960s; Illustrators Society Award, New York, c.1967; Coty American Fashion Critics Award, 1979, 1984; Council of Fashion Designers of America Award, 1981. **Address:** 119 West 40th Street, New York, New York 10018, USA.

Publications:

On KIESELSTEIN-CORD:

Articles

Talley, André Leon, "Double Jointed," in *Women's Wear Daily* (New York), 14 November 1975.
Crowley, Susan, "Jewelry's New Dazzle," in *Newsweek* (New York), 4 April 1977.
Grossman, Karen, "Barry Kieselstein-Cord, Artist and Designer," in *People* (Chicago), September 1978.
Duka, John, "Postmodern Belt Buckles," in the *New York Times,* 11 October 1980.
Talley, André Leon, "Barry Kieselstein-Cord," in *Interview* (New York), November 1981.
Kingstone, Barbara, "New Status for Jewelry," in the *Toronto Globe and Mail,* March 1985.
Goodwin, Betty, "Designer Takes Artist's Tact with Buckles," in the *Los Angeles Times,* 10 May 1985.
Masse, Cheryl, "Moving Pieces," in *Beverly Hills 213* (Beverly Hills, California), 15 May 1985.
Tsutagawa, K., "The Sculptor as Jeweler: Interview with Barry Kieselstein-Cord," in *New York Style* (Japan), July 1985.
Allen, Jennifer, "Barry and CeCe Kieselstein-Cord," in *Architectural Digest* (Los Angeles), September 1988.
"Creative Collaborators," in *Harper's Bazaar* (New York), June 1989.
Ravel, Margo, "Barry Kieselstein-Cord: Pure Inspiration," in *Beverly Hills 213* (Beverly Hills, California), 20 September 1989.
Menkes, Suzy, "Kieselstein-Cord: Anthropomorphic Chic," in the *International Herald Tribune* (Neuilly, France), 14 November 1989.
Newman, Jill, "Kieselstein-Cord: Keeping It Tried and True," in *Women's Wear Daily Accessories Magazine* (New York), January 1990.
Newman, Jill, "Kieselstein-Cord's Newest Luxury: Handbags," in *Women's Wear Daily Accessories Magazine* (New York), 16 August 1991.
Newman, Jill, "A Bergdorf's Ace: Kieselstein-Cord," in *Women's Wear Daily* (New York), 15 November 1991.
Beard, Patricia, "To Have and to Hold," in *Mirabella* (New York), April 1992.
Van Gelder, Lindsy, "Promenade Purse," in the *New York Times,* 7 June 1992.

*

My life as an artist started when I was about eight. My primary interest at that moment was directed toward North American Indian art. This was my first influence between the ages of eight and 14. I produced large-scale carvings and effigies and interpretations. Between 14 and 22 my focus had switched to painting and metalwork. At 14 I had also started to bury objects and metal in the ground to observe color and patina changes. From the earliest moments I can recall fascination with all past cultures and an intense attraction to art and architecture, not surprising as in their youth my mother had been an illustrator and father an architect. I still hold these fascinations and occasionally some recall slips into my work. I have rarely ever looked at the ornamentation of other artists; my primary influences come from entire cultures and periods.

I am not influenced by fashion, preferring to be an influencer. Some of my most successful collections took three to five years to create the impact needed to make them commercially successful— really my most successful pieces I could not give away until people developed a new appreciation for my directions. Naturally this has produced my greatest reward (influencing direction) as an artist. My intent is to capture the illusive mental image—a single example is if you are riding in a car down a country road at a good speed, and think you see something wonderful. You stop your car and back up to discover what it was, only to find a jumble that your mind saw as a completed image. That is my creative process: to capture the illusive image that was the correlation between the speed, your mind's eye, and what you thought you'd seen; to make it three-dimensional; and to fill space with something new that was not there before this creation. As to contemporary fashion, the present mode of "anything goes" is quite wonderful. One can live out one's fantasy, bring it out of the closet and, if in good taste, be really very chic. I do like black ties on men and sexy elegant evening gowns on beautiful women. It quickens the pulse....

—Barry Kieselstein-Cord

*   *   *

Barry Kieselstein-Cord: 1993.

In his affirmation "I don't make jewelry; I do sculptures for the body," Barry Kieselstein-Cord has described the independence and the ambition of his work. Like Elsa Peretti and other contemporary designers of jewelry, Kieselstein-Cord has sought to define an art that is autonomous from fashion, boldly sculptural in a way that makes a clear distinction from the wondrous but miniaturized repertory of a designer like Miriam Haskell, and historically aware without being subservient to past styles. His scarab *minaudiere,* for example, is indebted to ancient Egypt, as well as to the art deco Egyptian revival, but with the curtly reduced modernism that characterizes his work. His landmark—in law as in art, as their copyright was legally upheld from accessories pirates—belt buckles, the Vaquero, and the Winchester, are both of the Old West, but transmitted through art nouveau curvilinear interpretation. In fact, it is hard not to call Kieselstein-Cord's work jewelry, even as he avoids the term with "bodywork" or "sculpture," but the feeling is undeniably different from that of most jewelry. The designer argues that it comes from all the sculpture having as its Platonic ideal some large, even monumental form, surpassing its role on the human body.

Kieselstein-Cord has been one of the critical designers who, from the 1970s, has offered a jewelry that aspires to the condition of sculpture, allowing shapes to reclaim their ancient expressive, even spiritual/prophylactic, aspect in allowing jewelry to become something more than trivial adornment. After expressing his admiration for Easter Island statues, the designer told André Leon Talley, "I also like things which are sophisticated in an innately primitive way. Things that are transformed into a past and present that you can't identify. I like some of Miró's giant sculptures, some by Lipchitz, Noguchi, and Brancusi. The last thing I look at for inspiration is jewelry of any kind or period." Peretti, Robert Lee Morris, and Tina Chow would all probably adhere to the same spiritual striving and monumental desire for jewelry. Kieselstein-Cord had liberated jewelry from being paltry and precious in scale.

Similarly, Kieselstein-Cord disavows fashion as an influence, maintaining that jewelry must hold its separate aesthetic and power. While wife and partner CeCe also produced jewelry for Perry Ellis and was a model and muse for the fashion designer, Kieselstein-Cord's work has never bent to specific demands of fashion. "My accessories are not meant to be fashion," he told Jill Newman (*Women's Wear Daily Accessories Magazine,* January 1990). "They are designed to augment fashion. Things made of precious metal are meant to last forever and a day." Indeed, many of Kieselstein-Cord's designs have been of such enduring interest that they continue to be produced, while some collectors wait for each new sculptural edition in the manner of collecting any other artistic production. The Winchester belt buckle first produced in 1976 is still produced. In the early 1980s, he produced accessories for the home. Kieselstein-Cord's work has recently expanded in a line of high-quality handbags.

If Kieselstein-Cord takes his art seriously enough to declare it sculpture and not jewelry, he is nonetheless playful enough to realize diverse properties of materials and to bring some elements of non-western culture to the vocabulary of jewelry. In 1976, for example, a coiled choker of silk cord was accented with a gold orb; gold was used with tortoise-shell hair combs. In the same year, he created a splendidly reeling art nouveau antelope *minaudiere* that he sand-blasted on the gold body to give the feeling of fur. A 1981 duck bandolier was a little Pancho Villa, a little nursery frieze for a fantastic equivocation in jewelry. John Duka declared his spring 1981 belt buckles "postmodern," perhaps the first time that appel-lation was used for accessories. Bold concha belts, Celtic interlace, and Gauguin-inspired shapes have been featured in his collections.

Kieselstein-Cord began his work in the 1970s, when American alternative culture might have convinced almost any marijuana-smoking hippie of the probity of body sculpture—and he even used cowboys and Indians to prove the point. What Kieselstein-Cord has done is more important and far-reaching: he has convinced all of us of the probity of body sculpture, spiritual and symbolic; he has enlarged the tradition of jewelry, giving it a chunky, palpable integrity; he has declared jewelry sovereign from fashion; and he has given jewelry and related accessories a standard of luxury along with a contemporary vocabulary.

—Richard Martin

KIM, Jun and Soyon. See **ISANI.**

KLEIN, Anne.

American designer

Born: Hannah Golofsky in Brooklyn, New York, 7 June 1923. **Education:** Studied art at Girls' Commercial High School, New York, and fashion at Traphagen School, New York, 1937-38. **Family:** Married Ben Klein (divorced, 1958); married Matthew Rubenstein in 1963. **Career:** Designer, Varden Petites, New York, 1938-40; designer, women's fashions for Maurice Rentner, 1940-47; founder and partner with Ben Klein, Junior Sophisticates, 1948-66; Anne Klein and Co., and Anne Klein Studio design firms established, c.1965. **Exhibitions:** Versailles, 1973; *American Fashion on the World Stage,* Metropolitan Museum of Art, New York, 1993. **Awards:** *Mademoiselle* Merit Award, 1954; Coty American Fashion Critics Award, 1955, 1969, 1971; Neiman Marcus Award, 1959, 1969; Lord and Taylor Award, 1964; National Cotton Council Award, 1965. *Died* (in New York) *19 March 1974.* Firm continued after her death with designers Donna Karan (to 1984), Louis Dell'Olio (to 1993), and Richard Tyler (from 1993). **Address:** 205 West 39th St, New York, New York, 10018, USA.

Publications:

On KLEIN:

Books

New York and Hollywood Fashion: Costume Designs from the Brooklyn Museum Collection, New York 1986.
Milbank, Caroline Rennolds, *New York Fashion: The Evolution of American Style,* New York 1989.

Articles

"Designers Who Are Making News," in *American Fabrics and Fashion* (New York), No. 38, 1956.

Beckett, Kathleen, "Runway Report: In-Kleined to Wow Fans: Anne Klein," in the *New York Post,* 1 November 1994.

"New York: Anne Klein," in *Women's Wear Daily* (New York), 1 November 1994.

Ozzard, Janet, "Anne Klein: The Next Act," in *Women's Wear Daily* (New York), 1 March 1995.

Wadyka, Sally, "New Kid in Town," *Vogue* (New York), April 1995.

Schiro, Anne-Marie, "Ralph Lauren Does What He Does Best," in the *New York Times,* 6 April 1995.

* * *

Known as an American designer, Anne Klein often bragged that she had never seen a European collection. Klein's philosophy was "not with what clothes might be but what they must be." Anne Klein's career spanned three decades and her contributions to the industry were many. Like Claire McCardell before her, Anne Klein helped to establish casual but elegant sportswear as defining American fashion.

Most notably, Klein transformed the junior-sized market from little-girl clothes designed with buttons and bows to clothes with a more sophisticated adult look. She also recognized that clothes for juniors should be designed for size rather than age. By analyzing the lifestyles of young women, Klein realized that the fashions offered to them did not reflect their needs. In 1948, Klein and her first husband, Ben Klein, opened Junior Sophisticates, a company dedicated to this market, thus expanding the industry. Her first collection for Junior Sophisticates featured the skimmer dress with jacket; full, longer skirts; small waists; and pleated plaid skirts with blazers.

During the mid-1960s, Klein free-lanced for Mallory Leathers, where she established leather as a reputable dress fabric in the ready-to-wear market. She designed leather separates in bright colors and smartly styled silhouettes.

In 1968 Anne Klein and Company and Anne Klein Studio were opened by Klein and her second husband, Chip Rubenstein. Focusing on sportswear with elegant styling, Klein established the concept of separates dressing. In doing this, she was teaching women a new way to dress. Klein proclaimed: "Do not buy haphazardly, but rather with a theme of coordination." In the showing of the collections as well as in the stores, Klein emphasized how interchangeable the clothes were. Her designs were sold in boutiques called Anne Klein Corners, which were in major department stores. This marked the beginnings of the individual designer shops within retail environments. Accessories also became an important part of the overall look. Klein designed belts, chains, shoes, and scarves which complemented her clothes.

Anne Klein focused on the needs of the American business woman in many of her collections for Anne Klein and Company. She relied on her own instincts to understand the diverse needs of the 1960s woman. By simplifying clothing, and showing women how to coordinate separates and accessorize, Klein taught the American woman how to dress with a minimum amount of fuss. The result was a finished, sophisticated look. The classic blazer was the central garment with shirtdresses, long midis and trousers introduced as well.

Anne Klein died in 1974. Designers Donna Karan, Louis Dell'Olio, and Richard Tyler continued as the designers at Anne Klein & Co. Anne Klein reformed the junior market and expanded the concept of separates dressing to define sportswear and the American Look.

—Margo Seaman

KLEIN, Calvin.

American designer

Born: Bronx, New York, 19 November 1942. **Education:** Studied at Fashion Institute of Technology, New York, 1959-62. **Family:** Married Jayne Centre in 1964 (divorced); daughter: Marci; married Kelly Rector in 1986. **Career:** Assistant designer, Dan Millstein, New York, 1962-64; free-lance designer, New York, 1964-68; Calvin Klein Co. formed in partnership with Barry Schwartz, 1968, company reorganized, 1991. Fragrances include *Obsession,* 1985, and *Eternity,* 1988. **Awards:** Coty American Fashion Critics Award, 1973, 1974, 1975; Bath Museum of Costume Dress of the Year Award, 1980; Council of Fashion Designers of America Award, 1993. **Address:** 205 West 39th St, New York, New York 10018, USA.

Publications:

On KLEIN:

Books

Morris, Bernadine, and Barbara Walz, *The Fashion Makers,* New York 1978.

Perschetz, Lois, ed., *W, The Designing Life,* New York 1987.

Coleridge, Nicholas, *The Fashion Conspiracy,* London 1988.

Milbank, Caroline Rennolds, *New York Fashion: The Evolution of American Style,* New York 1989.

Howell, Georgina, *Sultans of Style: 30 Years of Fashion and Passion 1960-1990,* London 1990.

Gaines, Steven, and Sharon Churcher, *Obsession: The Lives and Times of Calvin Klein,* New York 1994.

McDowell, Colin, *The Designer Scam,* London 1994.

Articles

Peer, Elizabeth, "Stylish Calvinism," in *Newsweek,* 3 November 1975.

Brown, Erica, "The Rag Trade to Riches Rise of Calvin Klein," in *The Sunday Times Magazine* (London), 29 April 1980.

Cleave, Maureen, "Calvin Klein," in *The Observer* (London), 7 December 1980.

Alter, Jonathan, and Ann Hughey, "Calvin and the Family Firm," in *Newsweek,* 12 December 1983.

Sherrid, Pamela, "Ragman," in *Forbes,* 15 February 1982.

Trachtenberg, Jeffrey A., "Between Me and My Calvins," in *Forbes,* 9 April 1984.

Morris, Bernadine, "Calvin Klein Keeps It Smart and Simple," in the *New York Times,* 1 May 1985.

Brady, James, "In Step with Calvin Klein," in *Parade Magazine* (New York), 26 October 1986.

Hume, Marion, "The Secret of My Success," in *Fashion Weekly* (London), 27 August 1987.

Brampton, Sally, "Drawing a Klein Line," in *Elle* (London), January 1988.

Gross, Michael, "The Latest Calvin: From the Bronx to Eternity," in *New York,* 8 August 1988.

Orth, Maureen, "A Star Is Reborn," in *Vogue,* September 1988.

Howell, Georgina, "Mr Klein Comes Clean," in *The Sunday Times Magazine* (London), 10 September 1989.

"Calvin Klein's Obsession," in *Cosmopolitan,* May 1991.

"Calvin Klein's Bold Strategy in U.S., Europe," in *Women's Wear Daily,* 19 June 1991.

Behbehani, Mandy, "Nothing Between Success and Calvin," in *San Francisco Examiner,* 30 January 1992.

Grant, Linda, "Can Calvin Klein Escape," in *Los Angeles Times,* 23 February 1992.

Sloan, Pat, "'I Don't Have Long-Term Plans. I Just Act Instinctively,'" in *Advertising Age,* 18 May 1992.

Mower, Sarah, "Calvin in Control," in *Harper's Bazaar,* 11 November 1992.

Hirshey, Gerri, "The Snooty Dame at the Block Party," in the *New York Times Magazine*, 24 October 1993.

Morris, Bernadine, "Master of Ease," in the *New York Times,* 6 February 1994.

Brampton, Sally, "Calvin Clean," in *Marie Claire* (London), August 1994.

Reed, Julia, "Calvin's Clean Sweep," in *Vogue* (New York), August 1994.

Beckett, Kathleen, "Slip-sliding to a Close: Calvin Klein," in the *New York Post,* 5 November 1994.

Spindler, Amy M., "Klein and Karan: Clothes that Do the Job," in the *New York Times,* 5 November 1994.

"New York: Calvin's Minimal Magnetism," in *Women's Wear Daily* (New York), 7 November 1994.

Spindler, Amy M., "Luxurious Armor by Karan, Klein, Mizrahi," in the *New York Times,* 8 April 1995.

"Calvin Cool Edge," in *Women's Wear Daily* (New York), 10 April 1995.

*   *   *

Indisputable genius in marketing, recognized wizard in fashion financing, charismatic image-maker and image himself, Calvin Klein is the quintessential American fashion expression of the last quarter of the 20th century. The energy of his identification with jeans in the late 1970s and early 1980s, his later frontiers of underwear, and his consistent edge and eye in advertising image in print and media have rendered him a vivid figure in the landscape of American cultural life. A sleazy, potboiler biography of Klein in 1994 was titled *Obsession: The Lives and Times of Calvin Klein* (New York, 1994), taking its title from one of his fragrance and beauty products; its reference to "lives" sprung from lurid insinuations, but also testified to Klein's professional daring in being chameleon and index to American needs and desires. Years before, Michael Gross had already described Klein's life in *New York* magazine (8 August 1988) as "an extraordinary odyssey—a sort of one-man pilgrimage through the social history of modern America." Klein is home-grown hero to young America, the elusive image of the creator as mega-power and carnal charmer, the recurrent American worship of a tragic grandeur in those few who achieve absolute power in a democracy and who practice sexual thrall in a Puritan ethic. In 25 years as a top designer, Klein has established himself as a veritable

obsession. He has only intensified that stature in spiralling success that challenges, yet flourishes in, the very visible arenas of fashion's dilation into culture.

Is Klein a designer? Suffused with aura and surrounded by negotiation—commercial and social—Klein might seem to have sacrificed his essential métier as a designer. Significantly, he has not. His sensibility for minimalist aesthetics, in an active lifestyle configuration with the ethos of sportswear, is as evident today as it ever was. Klein's clothing is as judicious as his marketing is advanced: streamlined pattern to be worn with ease prevails, even as he has looked at Madeleine Vionnet in the 1990s as assiduously as he considered, modulated Halston's and Giorgio di Sant'Angelo's radical innovations in the 1970s, and absorbed Armani's sober luxury in the 1980s. Klein's best eveningwear gives a first impression of delicacy and refinement, but the chaste construction—characteristically avoiding linings and complications—and the more durable and accommodating fabrics than one had imagined come into play as the wearer enjoys an unexpected freedom and mobility. Klein has made a virtue of all the cost-cutting, production-saving emendations that Seventh Avenue always wanted to make to save money; he has put the few high expenses in fabric at a conspicuous level of visibility and tactility, thus maximizing the economic effect.

Klein's fashion is the quintessence of American fashion expression and taste: his minimal construction promotes mass manufacturing; his ease allows comfortable dressing in all sizes and shapes; his penchant for quality wool, cashmere, cotton, and other feel-good textile luxuries affirms a sense of luxury in clothes otherwise so undistinguished in their simplicity as to pass unnoticed. While in a 1994 press statement Klein avows that "Everything begins with the cut," one knows that we are not thinking of cut and construction in the traditional fashion measure of Vionnet or Madame Grès. Klein's spare cut is not truly architectural; it is unobtrusive, or, in Bernadine Morris's words, "without frills" (*New York Times,* 1 May 1985). When the Council of Fashion Designers of America honored Katherine Hepburn in 1986, Klein made the presentation, one of true affinity, speaking to her traits of the "hard-working and independent woman who was never afraid to be comfortable" and whose penchant for trousers went from "scandalous" in the 1930s to "sensational" style in the 1980s.

Arguably, even Klein's marketing of jeans, underwear, and fragrance has been consistent in its aggressive, even opportunistic, address to gender and sexuality. Beginning with 1980 television advertising conceived by Richard Avedon and Klein using young model Brooke Shields, Klein has steadily set and stretched the parameters of American acceptance of overt sensuality in promotion of fashion and in public display ranging from national television campaigns to Times Square (New York) billboards to print media. Significantly, Klein's campaigns have been progressive, seeming in each instance to build upon and move beyond the first provocation and the inevitable acceptance of the prior campaign. Defining the public protocols of the 1980s and 1990s, Klein has made a distinct cultural contribution in advertising alone. Transporting fashion sensibility to clothing classifications prodigiously latent in sexuality such as jeans and underwear, Klein has likewise established the possibility of assertive sensuality and its designer personification in heretofore undeclared dominions of apparel. Cleaving gender needs and identities in fragrances in the 1980s through his Escape lines introduced in 1991-92, Klein launched the first major campaign for a shared gender fragrance in 1994.

James Brady wrote of Klein (*Parade,* 26 October 1986): "His success is so enormous, his income so vast, his lifestyle so lavish, that we tend to forget that in life there are no free rides." America distrusts its creative artists; America denies its geniuses in marketing and promotion; America violates its tokens of sexual license; America devours its heroes with zoological exigency. Controversy surrounds Klein as much as does celebrity. But it is incontrovertible that Klein has altered the landscape of modern American fashion and its perception as only a genius and a giant can. In an epoch of uncertainty and recriminations, Klein's imperfect, but ever-upward course of design actions has prompted dispute and jealousy, but there can be no contest to his incorporation of our time in his cleanly minimalist clothing and in the bodies that he has instinctively defined in media imagery to inhabit the clothes.

—Richard Martin

KLOSS, John.

American designer

Born: John Klosowski in Detroit, Michigan, 13 June 1937. **Education:** Studied architecture at Cass Technical High School, Detroit; studied fashion at Traphagen School of Fashion, New York. **Career:** Worked for couturier Bob Bugnand, Paris, 1957-58; own business established with signature boutique at Henri Bendel, New York, 1959; designer, Lily of France, New York, 1970s; designer, John Kloss for CIRA division of SLC Fashion Corporation, 1970s. **Awards:** Coty American Fashion Critics Award, 1971, 1974; Knitted Textile Association Crystal Ball Award, 1974. *Died* (in Stamford, Connecticut) *25 March 1987.*

Publications:

On KLOSS:

Books

Milbank, Caroline Rennolds, *New York Fashion: The Evolution of American Style,* New York 1989.

Articles

Molli, Jeanne, "Designer Works in Loft Amid Art and Greenery," in the *New York Times,* 19 March 1962.
Taylor, Angela, "The Kloss Style: Modern Art and Jigsaw Puzzles," in the *New York Times,* 30 March 1966.
"Inspiration Comes from People," in *Intimate Apparel,* August/September 1971.
Shelton, P., "Fashion's Constant Nostalgia Kick Bores John Kloss," in *Biography News,* January 1974.
"John Kloss, Designer, Dies," in *Women's Wear Daily,* 30 March 1987.

*   *   *

Dress and lingerie designer John Kloss (John Klosowski) was born in Detroit, Michigan, where he studied architecture at Cass Technical High School. He moved to New York and worked for Irving Trust Co. on Wall Street. Kloss ultimately gained his fashion training when he attended the Traphagen School of Fashion in New York. At age 20, he apprenticed with American-born couturier Bob

Bugnand in Paris and went on to work for Serge Matta. In 1959, Kloss turned down an offer to work with Nina Ricci and instead began to co-design with Lisa Fonssagrives and later worked on his own, designing collections for wholesale manufacturers. Some of his designs were manufactured and distributed by Bendel's Studio, a part of Henri Bendel of New York, a store noted for discovering and supporting young fashion designers.

In the early 1960s, Kloss designed dresses that were sculptural shapes, constructed from fabrics such as cotton brocades, that could be formed and molded to enclose the body. By the late 1960s he was using chiffon, matte jersey, and crêpe de chine; fluid materials that moved gracefully with the wearer. Simple dress shapes were formed without darts that did not fit tightly to the body, but flowed seductively over its curves.

Kloss used vivid colors like lemon yellows, greens, amethyst, and ruby in abstract shapes that were reminiscent of abstract expressionist paintings. Sophisticated, simple, clean designs were detailed with top stitching, tiny rows of buttons, simple edge trims, or tie closures.

These non-structured designs were adapted for lingerie and loungewear marketed by Lily of France and CIRA. Included were designs for nightgowns and bras, both seamless and underwired, again without superfluous lace trimmings.

The most revolutionary clothing design Kloss is responsible for came about as a reaction to the "ban the bra" movement in the 1970s. In 1974, for Lily of France, he designed a bra that appeared not to exist. Called the "glossie" this bra was made from stretchy, sheer, glittery material. The design was seamless, and unconstructed, but underwired, so it provided support for those women who needed it, yet wanted the braless look. The "glossie" came in solid-colors such as amethyst, indigo, ruby, and mocha.

Kloss received two Coty Awards, one in 1971 and another in 1974, for his lingerie designs. His nightgowns were cut from nylon in non-boudoir colors, in sophisticated, seductive cuts that emulated some of his eveningwear. Leotards, pajamas, swimwear, and sportswear were also designed by Kloss. Under license he designed foundation garments, lingerie, loungewear, hosiery, tenniswear, and home sewing patterns. He was affiliated with the Kreisler Group of young designers under the management of Stuart Kreisler.

Whether designing dresses or loungewear, John Kloss was aware of the fashion trends, moving from sculptural, molded forms, to the free flowing more casual looks of the late 1960s and 1970s. He avoided unnecessary details, relying instead on the cut of the garment, and the materials used to provide the design. The garments moved and flowed with the wearer. His designs were simple, clean, and seductive.

John Kloss committed suicide in 1987.

—Nancy House

KNECHT, Gabriele.

American designer

Born: Munich, Germany, 8 January 1938. **Education:** Studied fine arts, majoring in fashion design at Washington University, St Louis, Missouri, USA, 1956-60; synergetics, cosmology, physics at New School for Social Research, New York, 1977-80; Hayden Planetarium, New York, reflective theory; Museum of Natural History,

Gabriele Knecht.

New York, insect kinematics. **Career:** Bra designer, Formfit Co., Chicago, 1959; dress designer, Carlye Dress Co., St Louis, Mo., 1960-61; designer of boyswear, Hummelsheim, Murnau, West Germany, 1961-62, junior dresses, Big Ben Modelle, West Berlin, 1962, childrenswear collection for Bill Atkinson, Glen of Michigan, New York, 1963-67; designed Sally Forth childrenswear for Boe Jests Inc., New York, 1967-68; S.W.A.K. children and pre-teen sportswear for Villager, New York, 1968-69; women's sportswear for Boe Jests Inc., 1969-70; owner/designer operating mail-order hand-knit kits, I Did It Myself Mother, New York, 1970-73; designed children's sportswear under Gabriele Knecht label for Suntogs, Miami, Florida, 1971-73; author and designer, *Learn to Crochet* and *Learn to Knit,* booklets, leaflets and yarn kits, Columbia Minerva Corp., New York, 1973-77; free-lance designer, junior and children's knitwear for firms including Bago Ltd, Aperitif, Kiffe and Baby Togs, 1977-82; designs, markets and produces for G. K. Forward Inc., New York, from 1982. United States patent awarded for garments constructed with forward sleeves, 1984. Lectures, Fashion Institute of Technology and Parsons School of Design, New York; Washington University; North Carolina State University; University of Cincinnati School of Design; The Fashion Group of St Louis; The American Association of University Women; Fashion's Inner Circle. **Collections:** Fashion Institute of Technology, New York. **Exhibitions:** *More Fashion Award Grand Prize-Winning Designs,* Henderson Gallery, Yellow Springs, Ohio, 1985; *Her Works Praise Her: Women as Inventors,* Goldstein Gallery, University of Minnesota, St Paul, Minnesota, 1988; *A Woman's Place Is in the Patent Office,* US Patent and Trademark Office, Washington, 1990. **Awards:** Outstanding Women in America, listing, 1966; Best New Designer in women's clothing field, *More Fashion Award,* New York City, 1984; National Endowment for the Arts grant, 1986. **Address:** G. K. Forward Inc., 264 West 35th St, New York, NY 10001, USA.

Publications:

On KNECHT:

Articles

Peterson, Patricia, "The No-Waistline Set," in the *New York Times Magazine,* February 1966.
Peacock, Mary, "Gabriele Knecht's Patented Patterns and Other Fashion Breakthroughs," in *Ms* (New York), March 1985.
Harte, Susan, "Patterned for Perfection," in *Atlanta Journal and Constitution* (Atlanta, Georgia), 4 August 1985.
Engelken, "Rethinking Sleeves," in *Washington University Alumni News,* March 1986.
Sayers, Donna, "Armed Revolution," in *The Cincinnati Enquirer,* October 1988.
Friedman, Arthur, "Knecht Steps Forward," in *Women's Wear Daily* (New York), September 1991.
Van Horne, Gladys, "Maestra's New Suit Stitched Just in Time," in *Wheeling News-Register,* September 1992.

*

I started my own company of designer sportswear and coats after spending several years developing an original clothing concept which relates the structure of clothing to the unique way the human body moves. The technology for this concept has been fully documented in a United States patent.

Unlike clothing which fits a body at rest or standing still, I base my designs on an underlying construction which anticipates the forward direction the body takes in movement, producing new fashion shapes.

I achieve my designs from a pattern-making system based on squares, working out the technical construction in miniature first, then enlarging the squares for the life-size version.

My "K" trademark illustrates the difference between conventional construction and my forward-sleeve construction: the left part of the logo showing the top view of the body with sleeve direction of conventional garments; the right part of the logo showing the top view of the body with sleeve direction of garments based on my patented forward sleeve.

—Gabriele Knecht

*   *   *

New York designer Gabriele Knecht believes that if you want to change fashion, and achieve new shapes, you must change the underlying foundation. So she did. Conventional construction methods used in the making of garments today are hundreds of years old and based on the T-shape or *kimono* pattern. This method assumes that our arms and legs have an equal range of movement around the anterior and posterior of the body. She states that while the arms have a large range of movement around the body, this freedom is not equal in all directions. "We can hug ourselves and move our legs forward but there is a limited or different movement toward the back of the body." Knecht has, possibly for the first time in history, looked at the real differences between the body's front and back range of movement, and how these differences impact fashion design, pattern making, and garment construction. The result is her "forward-sleeve" design.

Knecht's one-piece and multi-piece forward-sleeve pattern brings the axis of the sleeve substantially forward of the body's lateral plane and into the arm's center range of movement. This can be accomplished by moving the low point of the armhole forward, while leaving the high point in the lateral plane of the body. By doing this Knecht has put a larger degree of ease and mobility in the side front area of her garments, where it is needed, yet with a closer body fit. The forward-sleeve design is an evolution in pattern making and construction, a process developed over a ten year period, that has earned Knecht a United States patent in 1984 and foreign patents in Canada and Japan.

Using the forward-sleeve orientation as the basis for all of her work Knecht designs a line of chic, well-cut, and excellently proportioned sportswear. The range of movement achieved with her forward-sleeve design allows for a fitted, even tailored garment to have the movement and comfort of a much less constructed piece. Knecht's work, like that of American sportswear designer Claire McCardell, is simplified, reductive, and appeals to our human nature. Using geometrical shapes, diagonals to break or eliminate side seams, and when possible only one pattern piece, she creates a design aesthetic and spirit all her own. While Knecht will not bow to the mandates of changing trends, her innate ability to design and her integrity of cut and construction are evident in every garment with the Gabriele Knecht label. The Gabriele Knecht line has been sold in a number of major retail and specialty stores such as Saks

Fifth Avenue (exclusively for one season), Bonwit Teller, Macy's, Bergdorf Goodman in New York, and Neiman Marcus, Dallas. A new customer finding their way to Gabriele Knecht is the orchestral conductor, looking for the Conductor Coat she has designed. Maestra Rachel Worby of the Wheeling Symphony, in West Virginia, states: "The best feature is that the sleeves are attached in such a way that when I move my arms up and down as I am conducting, the jacket does not hike up too."

Knecht's undeniable spirit and singleness of purpose were best expressed when Susan Harte wrote in the *Atlanta Journal and Constitution* 4 August 1985), "There is unlimited direction open to her now that she has set her fundamental precepts. She will design human clothes, not necessarily 'with-it' ones, and will do it autonomously, not deferentially."

—Fred Dennis

KOBAYASHI, Yukio.

Japanese designer

Career: Designer, menswear line, Monsieur Nicole line, for Matsuda. **Address:** (Matsuda) 3-13-11 Higashi, Shibuya-ku, Tokyo 150, Japan.

Publications:

On KOBAYASHI:

Articles

Fressola, Peter, in *DNR,* 5 November 1986.
DNR, 5 February 1992.

*   *   *

Memory, both in the collective and crystalline form of analytical history and in the most vaporous ether of personal recollection, is the primary concern of Yukio Kobayashi's menswear for Matsuda. Memory mingles in Kobayashi's work with a desire for literary expression. Language blurts out irrepressibly in the work in frequent words, letters, and numbers. A lapel, for instance, may vanish into linear design or letters may become a surrealist free-fall of pattern. Literature abides in another way: the clothing is laden with an evocative knowledge of the tangible literary past, as if sartorial costuming for a Merchant-Ivory film (Kobayashi's 1984 collections had reflected movie-star elegance from the 1940s).

Kobayashi builds his clothing on the dandy's proposition that all clothing is to be seen in a self-conscious spectatorship. Tailored clothing explores a repertory of early 20th-century menswear with erudition; sportswear is supple and minimal, sometimes suggesting the Renaissance, Beau Brummel languor, or anticipating Utopia. Without contradiction to his historicism, Kobayashi is an apostle of advanced technology in synthetic fibers, often in startling juxtaposition with traditional materials and craft-domain handwork. The knowledge that manifestly animates Kobayashi's aesthetic has made Matsuda menswear favored apparel for artists and intellectuals; the *boulevardier* dandyism of the clothing is due to its intellectual edge.

Peter Fressola characterized Kobayashi's work for Matsuda Men almost as an acquired, special taste in *DNR* (5 November 1986): "If you have never liked Matsuda, chances are good that you never will. But this designer has inspired the loyalty of a great many who willingly suspend judgment in favor of the rich, romantic, almost decadent aesthetic that is the world of his design." In literary traits and propensities, audacious style eclecticism, and dandy-like exactness, Kobayashi is creating the most romantic menswear of our time. Kobayashi's clothing is like learned, earnest, university discourse. Language specifically plays a role in meandering letters and in the adaptations of Matsuda's interest in speaking vestments. But design is also used ontologically: shapes, design standards, and menswear paradigms are acknowledged as principles in Kobayashi's work.

Kobayashi's aesthetic is invariably elegant, but he achieves his elegance not solely through refined materials, but through the tactile satisfactions of fabric and pattern. A Norfolk jacket, a favorite template of Kobayashi's design, is transformed by blocks of pattern at differing scale; robust outerwear becomes luxurious by the swelled proportions of the collar; in the 1990s, trousers are transfigured by their uninflected plainness, flat-front and cropped just above the ankle. Kobayashi mediates between the inherent elegance of his style and a simple sincerity of the design: he treats the basics of clothing, allows jackets to move with loose fit, explores soft velvety and corduroy materials, gives the gentle irony of tweed and houndstooth and plaids at all scales, and even in fall/winter 1992 uses a patchwork theme derived from childhood memories of his mother sewing patches on his play-worn trousers. *DNR* (5 February 1992) called the Kobayashi fall 1992 menswear "a modern, down-to-earth, *very* Matsuda look," capturing its unpretentiousness. Even argyle pattern, Donegal tweeds, jackets with suppressed waists, and other usurpations of the aristocracy seem common, comfortable, and friendly again. Thus, Kobayashi achieves the dandy's grace with none of the dandy's disdain or arrogance: rugged materials, comfort and vernacular borrowings are essential to his design. England and Scotland are the motherland of Kobayashi's historicist vision.

In brilliant command of menswear history, Kobayashi favors early 20th-century clothing, the time of menswear codification. Nonetheless, he is capable of reflecting with *bravura* elegance on Victorian *tartanitis* and in creating revelers from a Venetian masked carnival in modern form. Responding to a question in *Details,* Kobayashi said: "The early part of the century was a time when the way people thought about clothes was radically changing. But the period I enjoy speculating about most is the future." Without such a sense of late-modern invention and adventure, the components of Kobayashi's style might seem to fall into clever, but tiring, eclecticism. Instead, he keeps a sharp analytical edge and an unremitting sense of the new and vanguard about his clothing. After all, almost all other menswear designers have recourse to the same body of Anglophilic and Edwardian styles that inspire Kobayashi, but his energy is quicker, more intellectual, and more transforming. He does not succumb to the British Empire: he takes a sense of history and invests it in his personal memories and choices. In this, he divests the clothing of its colonialism: Kobayashi makes the tradition his own.

Few designers, especially in menswear, possess Kobayashi's consistency and intensity of vision. In this work the past becomes the present. He practises a cognitive historicism of styles, but insists on the freshness of the new garment. He functions with aesthetic opinion and conviction in the market of menswear. His

Yukio Kobayashi: For Matsuda, Fall/Winter 1993. *Photograph by Guy Marineau.*

style makes use of memory, even nostalgia, but he is creating advanced, manifestly modern clothing in the romantic tradition.

—Richard Martin

KONISHI, Yoshiyuki.

Japanese knitwear designer

Born: 1950 in Tsu, Japan. **Career:** Established Ficce Uomo Co. Ltd. and introduced men's wear line, Ficce Uomo, 1981; introduced men's wear line, Yoshiyuki Konishi, 1987; introduced men's wear line, Ficce Jeans, 1988; introduced ladie's wear line, Ficce Donna, and ski wear line, Ficce Sport, 1993. **Awards:** Mainichi Fashion Grand Prix, 1991. **Address:** Ficce Uomo Co. Ltd., 4-3-11 Minami Azabu, Minato-Ku, Tokyo 106, Japan.

Publications:

On KONISHI:

Books

Tokyo Collection, Tokyo 1986.
Yoshiyuki Konishi's Knits, Tokyo 1986.
Takeshi Beat Wears Knits of Yoshiyuki Konishi, Tokyo 1992.

*

The yarns I design are the vital essences of my finished products and the finished products are the radiators of my energy.

The clothes I design—the multi-coloured, multi-textured products—are the results of numerous experiments and challenges made and built up in the years I have lived and worked.

The productions—yarn making, dying, knitting and weaving, and construction of the final product—all need to attain a level of equilibrium that must be maintained throughout the entire process.

In order to sustain originality, my designs begin from the productions of the single yarns and I do not to believe in rationalization. Most of my handmade products require time consuming and complicated procedures but when artisan and spirit unite, a new world is introduced.

The finished product—well designed wearable clothes that include fantastic colours, materials, silhouettes, and shapes—function as comfortable clothes with evidenceof my identity in every aspect of the product.

I hope to establish and stablise my styles and at the same time I wish to analyze the world changes and affairs and translate them into my work.

—Yoshiyuki Konishi

*   *   *

Yoshiyuki Konishi is categorized as a men's sweater designer, but his sweater is not a sweater in the conventional sense. It may be called an *objet d'art,* an intricate tapestry, or a Jackson Pollock in three dimensions, but hardly an everyday variety. Not a few people see a similarity between Konishi's sweaters and Gaudi's architecture. A Japanese critic even had Konishi's sweaters photographed in front of Gaudi's buildings in Barcelona to prove the point.

"Until I saw those photos, I hadn't known anything about Gaudi. Later I looked at Gaudi's work and realized that some of my sweaters had a lot in common with Gaudi's baroque structures," says Konishi. He wonders if Gaudi shared his creative process. "I don't plan anything. I don't leaf through art books looking for an inspiration. An idea often comes to me while I stare vacantly at an empty wall," Konishi explains. "Once I get going, more ideas spring up, and I constantly add and change even after the production process has started. My production people think I am hopelessly disorganized."

Every aspect of his sweater is unusual and excessive. An average of 30 different colors are knit into a sweater. Konishi has used as many as 60 colors for a particularly elaborate one. He is obsessed with the quest for new materials. He has experimented with baling ropes, leather strips, vinyl tubes, and many other odd materials, and still complains, "I wish I weren't making sweaters. The requirement for comfort prohibits the use of interesting materials." His staff processes and dyes raw materials such as silk, alpaca, angora, instead of buying already processed yarns. Konishi's knitting methods are as varied as his materials: machine knit, hand crochet, macramé, to name a few. Almost every season he comes up with new stitch patterns.

Obviously Konishi is a black sheep in the fashion industry, albeit a cheerful and genial one. He does not mind being labelled a renegade or a rebel. "Actually," he confesses, "I feel embarrassed every time people call me a fashion designer. I am not sure if what I am making is fashion." But he was peeved when a French journalist called his work un-Japanese. "This person thought that black was a 'Japanese' color," he fumes. "But black is not traditionally Japanese. Look at *kimonos* and *obis.* Japanese have always loved a riot of radiant colors."

He should know. He grew up in Japan in an old feudal castle town called Tsu, where his maternal family had operated a *kimono* store for generations. "My childhood memories are all about *kimonos,"* Konishi recalls. "A trip for me meant accompanying my mother on her buying trip, to Kyoto to select gorgeous *obis,* or to a trade show to look at hundreds of *kimono* fabrics."

Konishi's penchant for color was probably nurtured by early experiences, but his design motifs are anything but traditionally Japanese, ranging from American cartoon characters to the Amazon jungle, and to mythical ancient India. You cannot stay neutral about his sweaters. You either passionately love them, or passionately hate them, which is fine with Konishi. He has a sizeable following among Japan's creative and professional circles. One ardent collector of Konishi sweaters asked Konishi to design his garden. Owning dozens of Konishi sweaters was not enough for him. He wanted even his house to enjoy a touch of Konishi.

As long as he has such enthusiastic supporters, Konishi would happily consume his energies in pursuit of the perfect sweater.

—Yoko Hamada

KORS, Michael.

American designer

Born: Long Island, New York, 9 August 1959. **Education:** Studied fashion design at Fashion Institute of Technology, New York, 1977. **Career:** Sales assistant, at Lothar's boutique, New York, 1977-78 (whilst studying at FIT), then designer and display director, 1978-

Yoshiyuki Konishi.

80; established own label for women's sportswear, 1981; also designer for Lyle & Scott, 1989; lower priced "Kors" line and menswear collection introduced, 1990; designer, womenswear collection for Erreuno J, from 1990; bridge line discontinued, company reorganized, 1993. **Awards:** Dupont American Original Award, 1983. **Address:** 119 West 24th Street, New York, New York 10011, USA.

Publications:

On KORS:

Articles

Sinclaire, Paul, and Lesley Jane Nonkin, "Designer, Client: The Modern Equation," in *Vogue* (New York), November 1987.

Boehlert, Bart, "On Kors," in *Connoisseur* (New York), August 1988.

Hochswender, Woody, "Designers on a Quiet Road to Success," in the *New York Times,* 1 November 1988.

Reiger, Nancy, "Michael Kors Keeps It Cool," in *Footwear News* (New York), 30 July 1990.

Worthington, Christa, "The Three Choicest Dudes in the USA," in *The Sunday Times Magazine* (London), 26 August 1990.

Hochswender, Woody, "Casual, for the Car Pool (or Whatever)," in the *New York Times,* 9 September 1990.

Hochswender, Woody, "Amid the Scramble of the Style Race, Individuality Lives," in the *New York Times,* 1 November 1990.

Darnton, Nina, "Acclaim for a New Mister Clean: Move Over, Calvin, and Make Room for Kors," in *Newsweek* (New York), 3 December 1990.

Baker, Martha, "Of Kors," in *New York* magazine 17 December 1990.

Goodman, Wendy, "Upper-Deck Accommodations," in *HG* (New York), October 1991.

Rudolph, Barbara, "Why Chic Is Now Cheaper," in *Time* (New York), 11 November 1991.

Smith, Liz, "Just the Way Mother Likes It," in *The Times* (London), 13 April 1992.

Morris, Bernadine, "The Evolution of Leather's Gentler Image," in the *New York Times,* 28 April 1992.

"New York: Michael Kors," in *Women's Wear Daily* (New York), 7 November 1994.

Lockwood, Lisa, "Kors Designing Bridge Line for Onward Kashiyama," in *Women's Wear Daily* (New York), 7 February 1995.

*   *   *

Perhaps the best summary of Michael Kors was offered by Woody Hochswender (*New York Times,* 1 November 1988) when he said, "Mr Kors showed that simple doesn't have to be zero." Kors is inherently a minimalist working within a sportswear tradition. In this, he perpetuates and advances ideas of Halston, including a strong sexuality. He particularly flatters the gym-toned body of the late 1980s and early 1990s in stretchy, simple dresses that call attention to the body within. Minimalists in art and architecture might seem to remove themselves from the figure and human proportion; the irony is that a fashion minimalist like Kors draws attention to the figure within.

Moreover, while he has shown pattern, Kors prefers neutral color fields and emphasizes the apparel of the fabric with luxurious wools and cashmere for fall-winter and stretch and cotton for spring-summer. Leather in shirts, skirts, and jackets is essential for any Kors fall-winter collection; trousers are critical in all collections; and layering is important, even light layers in spring-summer collections. Kors spoke the language of separates in arguing to Bernadine Morris (*New York Times,* 28 April 1992), "Store buyers are zeroing in on the idea that women will probably not be shopping for entire new wardrobes. A single piece or two that will enliven everything else is what they will be searching for. And leather fills the bill—suede for times they are in a softer mood, smooth leather when they feel more aggressive." Kors's distinctive position as a leading minimalist in late-20th-century sportswear is achieved by his precise harmonics of color and fabrications in separates. In this, he predicts a reduced as well as reductive wardrobe, but one that has its own correlations and unanimity.

There is some affinity between Kors and Donna Karan, both creating innovative body suits, sensual stretch skirts and tops, and other sportswear elements, as well as borrowings from menswear. In fact, Karan and Kors are somewhat similar in their menswear collections as well. They share the dubious distinction of both offering bodyshirts (underpants attached to shirts) in menswear collections for fall 1992. If anything, Kors's minimalism is a little more referential than Karan's: he has deliberately evoked the glamour and sportiness of the 1930s, the "Belafonte" shirt of the 1950s, or vinyl late-1960s clothing. Despite his proclivity to the most simple in shapes, he produces clothes that are undeniably romantic (and Kors admits to loving the movies, telling Wendy Goodman (in *HG,* October 1991) that he had only two choices in life, movie star or fashion designer).

Of Claire McCardell, Kors acknowledges that he looked at her clothes in old magazines. "They were timeless. And she was the first designer to look not to Paris for inspiration but to the needs of the American woman." A spring-summer silk shantung scarf blazer by Kors reminds one of the McCardell twists and ties, but with all the sleek romance of a Noel Coward drawing room. Like the other sportswear designers, he learns from and responds to his clients and potential customers. He told Bart Boehlert (in *Connoisseur,* August 1988) that he likes to talk with women from his office, customers, and his mother, and ask what they most want in clothing.

His sportswear-based pragmatism is particularly effective as a monitor to the sexuality of his clothing. A bare Kors dress or jumpsuit may be audaciously sexy, but toned down with a neutral jacket or other cover-up, it can become suitable for the office. Conversely, Kors can take a simple skirt and blouse from the office setting into hot evening life with the addition of a leather jacket and a satin swing jacket. Only partly facetiously, he told Woody Hochswender (*New York Times,* 9 September 1990) of his comfortable and chic Kors line, "In Texas they call it carpool couture. They all want to wear something pretty for the carpool." Kors creates the pretty, the sexy, and the highly practical, a mastery in the harmonic balance of American sportswear.

—Richard Martin

KOSHINO, Hiroko.

Japanese designer

Born: 15 January 1937 in Osaka. **Education:** Graduated from the Department of Design of Bunka Fashion College, Tokyo, 1961.

Family: Married in 1960 (divorced, 1976); children: Yuka and Yuma.
Career: Designer, Komatsu Department Store, Tokyo, 1961-63; owner and designer, Hiroko Koshino haute-couture, textile, prêt-á-porter, children's clothing, nightie accessories and objects, boutique, Tokyo, from 1964; chairman, Hiroko Koshino International Koshinocorporation, Tokyo, from 1982; president, Hiroko Koshino Design Office, Tokyo, from 1988; created branch lines Hiroko Koshino Resort, Hiroko Koshino, Hiroko Bis, Hiroko Homme, Hiroko Koshino Golf. **Exhibitions:** Roma Alta Moda Collection, 1978; *Three Sisters,* Osaka, 1982; Shanghai, 1984; with Borek Sípek and Bambi Uden, Prague, 1994. **Awards:** Osaka City Award for Cultural Merit, 1989. **Address:** #502 Palais Royal, 3-12-1 Sendagaya, Shibuya-ku, Tokyo 151, Japan.

Publications:

On KOSHINO:

Books

The Tokyo Collection, Tokyo 1986.

Articles

"Japan's Master Strokes," in *The Guardian* (London), 28 April 1988.
"Architecture du Silence," in Special Japon on *Vogue,* September 1994.

*

I love Japan and have been attracted to traditional Japanese culture. I'm trying to express oriental sensitivities in a modern, Western framework.

What I think, What I feel, My lifestyle—These are the starting points for my designs. They give me confidence in and a sense of identity with my creations.

—Hiroko Koshino

*   *   *

An established designer based in Japan, Hiroko Koshino first showed in Paris after the breakthrough of the more avant-garde Japanese group in 1983. A member of a very old and established Japanese family which spawned two other successful women designers, Junko and Michiko, Koshino was brought up to respect the past and grew to love traditional *kabuki* theatre. Her designs are based on the traditional clothing idiom of the Japanese *kimono,* following its aesthetics of volume and layering, an area of focus for other designers such as Kenzo Takada. Koshino's clothes explore the tension between Western influences and Japanese values—a notion which still has currency, as a Western conception of fashion has only been in existence in Japan since 1945. The encroaching influence of the West has meant that many traditional Japanese aesthetic concepts have been explored and brought into the present by designers attempting to unite the modern with a strong sense of their own cultural continuity and concerns.

Tradition and Westernized ideas of progress were historically separated in Japanese culture; for example, in the 19th century, modern Japanese painting (*nihonga*) and modern painting display-

Hiroko Koshino.

ing a Western influence (*yosa*) were shown in different rooms—the dualism was made physically apparent. However, since the Meiji period (1868-1912), Japan's former cultural isolation vanished and increasingly there were concerted efforts to overcome the dichotomy of East and West to achieve what was hoped to be a more unified cultural pattern. Koshino's attempts to overcome cultural duality can be deduced in her endeavours to remove the *kimono* from its 20th-century function as formal wear for weddings and other ceremonial occasions and to introduce more current ideas of fashion terminology into its traditional form—a concerted effort to reintroduce the *kimono* as a form of everyday dress.

The tradition of the *kimono* within which Koshino intervenes is essentially a rectilinear two-dimensional one, which could be considered shapeless in comparison with Western female clothing, which tends to fit the body and emphasize its shape. In traditional Japanese clothing, padding and quilting are used to create a space between the body and the wearer, a concept which can clearly be seen in the explorations in contemporary ready-to-wear of Rei Kawakubo's designs for Comme des Garçons. The patterns of the *kimono* follow equally strict rules, being derived from nature; yet nature is then stylized and made graphic. These traditions can be discerned in the work of Koshino, who employs bird or bamboo prints to counteract the uniformity of her garment's more modular construction. Koshino's overlarge tops, dresses, and trousers of silk, cotton, and linen look back to the traditions of the Japanese court where styles became so exaggerated that enormous amounts of material were used to signify status. Large amounts of material and many layered undergarments led to a stiffened style where the body all but disappeared. Koshino retains this volume but by the use of natural fibres brings this traditional styling into the 20th century and makes clothing more fitted to the demands of contemporary women. Her modular units are more voluminous and asymmetrical than tradition allows and she is renowned for utilizing bright colours for decoration, whereas within traditional Japanese colour symbolism, brights are reserved for the young.

With the fashion media's focus on the more obviously radical side of Japanese fashion—Miyake, Yamamoto et al—Hiroko Koshino's more understated experimentation has been somewhat ignored. Her popularity among European women in particular testifies to the wearability of her designs.

—Caroline Cox

KOSHINO, Junko.

Japanese designer

Born: Osaka, Japan, 1939. **Education:** Studied fashion design, Bunka Fashion College, Tokyo, to 1961. **Family:** Married Hiroyuki Suzuki; son: Yoriyuki Suzuki. **Career:** Showed first ready-to-wear collection, Paris, 1978; couture collection introduced, from 1978; Mr Junko menswear collection launched, 1980; home furnishings line introduced, 1988. Opened first boutique in Tokyo, 1966; opened Boutique Junko Koshino, Tokyo, 1970, renewal, 1994; opened boutiques in China, 1985 and 1987; Paris boutique opened, 1989; New York boutique opened, 1992; Singapore boutique opened, 1993. Has also designed costumes for opera productions, uniforms for sports teams, and corporations. **Exhibitions:** *Three Sisters,* Osaka, 1982; Metropolitan Museum of Art, New York, 1990; *Junko Koshino Design Exhibition,* National Museum of Chinese History, Beijing, 1992; *Modes Gitanes,* Carrousel du Louvre, Paris, 1994. **Awards:** Soen Prize, Bunka College, Japan, 1960; Fashion Editors Club Prize, Paris, 1978. **Address:** 6-5-36 Minami-Aoyama, Minato-Ku, Tokyo, Japan.

Publications:

On KOSHINO:

Books

Tokyo Collection, Tokyo 1986.
Modes Gitanes: Exposition de 50 Createurs, Paris 1994.

Articles

Bernstein, Fred A., "Junko Koshino: Style that Translates," in *Metropolitan Home* (Des Moines, Iowa), March 1990.
Berman, Phyllis, "Not for Everyone," in *Forbes* (New York), 15 October 1990.
"'Art Futur' Designer Coming to Manila," in *Manila Bulletin,* 12 January 1994.
"Japan's Junko Koshino: Imagining the 21st Century," in *Business World,* 14 March 1994.

*   *   *

Sleek color-blocked sports uniforms, distinctive forward-looking corporate and exposition uniforms, costumes of opera fantasy and grandiloquence, and future-aimed clothing characterize the work of Junko Koshino. While producing a fashion and lifestyle line for men and women, Koshino's notable strength derives from her strong play between the individual and the group. Ironically—at least to a conventional view of fashion as self-expression—Koshino's best works are her uniforms, collective vestments, not the elective garments of individuals. Her sports *samurai* are elegant and reductive, almost a kind of refashioned nudity streamlined by fashion as a shell. In outfitting sports teams she has excelled, noting the aerodynamics of sports and applying those principles to her technology-aware garments. Koshino's sports uniforms realize Marinetti's visionary comparison toward "new beauty" in his 1909 Futurist Manifesto of the racing car and the Victory of Samothrace. But she has also sought the individual identity of Futurism, a clothing inspired by the 20th-century dynamic of projecting oneself into an even more technologically-intense outlook. Cocoons and spirals, concentric circles, ribbed construction, and materials from plastic to metal to cloth are typical of Koshino's exploring mind.

Graduating from the Bunka Fashion School in Tokyo in 1961, Koshino chose not to go abroad with Kenzo and Matsuda and other Japanese designers of her generation, but to create design in Tokyo where she opened her first boutique in 1966. Helmeted figures, sculptural forms, and biomorphic Futurism suggest that Koshino is inspired in part by Cardin and the tradition of Futurist design, though Koshino remains distinctive. Her uniforms for the 1990 Beijing Asian Games and Japanese 1992 Olympic volleyball team have a Flash Gordon Futurism about them, but they are also serviceable, sport-specific outfits creating a flag and semaphore-like reading on the competitive field. Corporate uniforms for many clients include Asahi Brewing, Mitsubishi Chemical, and Seibu Department Stores. A paradox of humankind's future expectation is that often we dream of—or, conversely, fear—the role of the collective in the future. Koshino gives garb to that vision: her work fosters an easy and elegant collective character. Its inherent rationalism about clothing and its propensity to see design coherence around the body promotes the sense of common traits. The first generation Futurism of Balla or Thayatt seems to be fulfilled in such work. To be sure, that Futurism led to armies; Koshino's future is Utopian.

Individual pieces are likewise Utopian in vision. "Taikyoku" is the guiding philosophy of the work, signifying contrast and balance or harmony. Mystically and philosophically, the circle is most important to Koshino, who sees the form as complete and eternal, both ancient and futuristic. This symbolic approach to form animates not only Koshino's view of apparel, but the outreach of her work to lifestyle and environmental design. As a designer, she has convened an Art-Futur Committee of various artists, designers, and thinkers, but she has also gone back into history to provide costumes for Mozart's *Magic Flute* and has shown her work in the Museum of History in Beijing. Moreover, Koshino has played a major role, in the late 1980s and 1990s, in introducing fashion ideas to China.

Each of the foreign headquarters is designated a gallery, and Koshino insists upon the identity of these establishments as more than mere boutiques or retail establishments. Perceiving globalism as a necessary function of her Utopian outlook, Koshino sees each international site—Paris (established 1989), New York (established 1992), and Singapore (established 1993)—as a missionary outpost, but also as a listening post, an opportunity to absorb and draw back

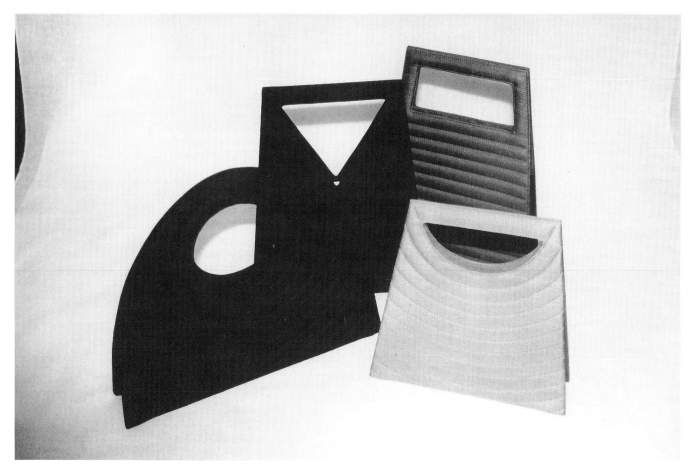

Junko Koshino: Silk cocktail bags.

to her design center the forces of international thinking and lifestyle.

Koshino challenges almost every preconception about fashion from the materials available for clothing to the way in which clothing serves the commonweal and the individual. Philosophically (and she requires such thought), she is cognizant of the past, but straining with Futurist and Utopian vision. She brings fashion into fuller and more fulfilled discourse with the other arts of design. It is the area of attainment that gives Koshino a distinctive and enduring place in the history of design.

—Richard Martin

KOSHINO, Michiko.

Japanese designer working in London

Born: Osaka, Japan, 1950. **Education:** Graduated from Bunka Fashion College, Tokyo, 1974. **Career:** Showed first collection, London, 1976; opened flagship store in Neal Street, London, closed 1994; knitwear, luggage, denim, children's clothes lines introduced. **Exhibitions:** *Three Sisters* [Hiroko, Junko, Michiko Koshino], Osaka, 1982. **Address:** 2E MacFarlane Road, Shepherd's Bush, London W12 7JZ, England.

Publications:

On KOSHINO:

Articles

Hatfield, Julie, "The Bottom Line," in the *Boston Globe* (Massachusetts), 14 May 1990.
"Take Five Designers," in *Clothes Show* (London), February 1991.

*   *   *

Michiko Koshino has come into her own since the switch in gear in the fashion world that began in the late 1980s. As sportswear became the major imperative of design, Koshino was one of the most successful in responding to customers' new needs, producing tightly thought-out collections that bridged the gap between sportswear and clubwear to appeal to a young streetwise consumer. Indeed, it seems to have been her aim to create a series of uniforms for the various London clubs with which she linked her name, and the logos she emblazoned them with had the same kind of recognizable impact as the established sports companies that were also increasingly popular.

Although Japanese by birth, Koshino eschews the more philosophical approach to fashion favoured by her often more prominent counterparts, seeming to lean towards the quirkier modern side of the Japanese national character rather than its solemn traditions of harmony and balance. It was this which led Koshino to produce the infamous and much-copied inflatable rain jacket in the mid-1980s. This was itself based on the thickly quilted B-boy "goose" jackets so popular with clubbers at the time, and clearly showed her ability to combine elements of both fun and functionalism.

In the 1990s, however, Koshino has shown that her design abilities can go much further than the witty garment for which she was most widely known. She has consistently shown how closely attuned she is to the shifting sands of London's extensive club scene. Her past collections have responded to the growing wish for clothes that reflect a certain aspect of this scene, making the wearer an instant initiate. They give a kind of streetwise credibility that has as much to do with the tribalism of London's nightlife as with fashion itself. The need to feel and look good is enhanced by Koshino's use of stretch fabrics, comfortable to move in as well as being sexy, clingy but not restrictive.

Although she has embraced London culture as her own, she has not limited the appeal of her clothes. The very English "Pukka Clobba" tag she borrowed from the rave scene has merely given her designs a kind of brand-name authenticity which sells, albeit quietly, across the world and has enabled her to diversify. She produces funky accessories to complement each collection, from the sequin disco ball earrings to the ubiquitous ski hats so popular with ravers in the winter. There are also Koshino bags, umbrellas, shoes, and towels, all spreading her name by their very presence and adding to the brand-name feel of her very contemporary styles.

Koshino's collections also offer a selection of different types of clothes, to provide a whole wardrobe for her customers. Her flagship store in Covent Garden, London, with its DJ mixing-tables providing a direct link with the clubs, always shows her full range, spanning the biker-inspired Motor King collection, its title often emblazoned on the stark contrast leathers, the designer name T- and sweatshirts popular with tourists, the sharp, brightly coloured suits, and the sexier, more overtly clubby Lycra, viscose and leather of the Michiko London range.

Koshino's greatest talent is undoubtedly her ability to absorb changing emphasis in fashion and respond with sexy sports-based clothing that can be targeted at the waiting customers of the club scene by clever marketing ploys like fashion shows in clubs and promotional wear for companies like Vidal Sassoon. Using her clever eye for striking designs and sexy styles, coupled with the kind of marketing skills that are anathema to many more traditional designers, she has developed an instantly recognizable style and loyal customer base among the often fickle younger fashion customer.

—Rebecca Arnold

KOUYATÉ, Lamine (for XÜLY BET).

Malian fashion designer working in Paris

Born: Bamako, Mali, c. 1963, son of a diplomat and a doctor. Moved to Paris, c.1986. **Education:** Studied architecture at Architecture School of Strasbourg, France, and at La Villette, Paris. **Career:** Designs under Xüly Bet label, based in Kouyaté's Funkin' Fashion Factory, Paris; became known for recycled, patched-to-

gether clothing. **Address:** L'Hôpital Ephémère, 2, rue Carpeaux, 18e Paris, France.

Publications:

On KOUYATÉ:

Articles

Donovan, Carrie, "Paris Report," in the *New York Times Magazine,* 9 May 1993.
Spindler, Amy M., "Prince of Pieces," in the *New York Times,* 2 May 1993.
Hume, Marion, "Coming Unstitched, or Just a Stitch-up?," in *The Independent* (London), 30 September 1993.
Martin, Richard, "A Sweater as Quasi-surreal Composition," in *The Independent* (London), 30 September 1993.
Talley, Andre Leon, "Piecing It Together," in *Vogue,* October 1993.
"The Last Word," in *Women's Wear Daily* (New York), 14 March 1994.
Jacobs, Patricia, "Xüly Bet," in *Essence,* May 1994.

*   *   *

In a Paris collections report under the rubric "The Last Word," *Women's Wear Daily* (14 March 1994) recounted: "Deadly heat, a grating live band and groupies lounging on the floor.... But it wasn't a Grateful Dead concert—just Xüly Bet's *défilé* at La Samaritaine department store." Lamine Kouyaté, designing for his label Xüly Bet, has all the characteristics of an avant-garde and disestablishment fashion, but one that at least assumes a fashion system and that even shows good likelihood of becoming a positive and lasting element of the fashion system.

Recycling, collage, rags to riches economics, exposed seams and construction, a profoundly African sensibility and artistic temperament all seem at odds with Establishment fashion, but have, in fact, brought Xüly Bet to the mainstream and major recognition. Lauded as a fashion post-modernist and deconstructivist, Kouyaté's fashion coincides only with the intellectual postulation; his design creativity is more intuitive and personal, founded in his childhood in Mali, Africa, and the necessarily pastiched view of the world that he perceived in a former French colony. The 1993 Xüly Bet collection was based on torn, dismembered, and reassembled surplus and flea-market clothing, each a one-of-a-kind invention from the "given" of a distressed or discarded fashion object. His urban picturesque includes cropped jackets, bold African prints, graphics, and graffiti lacerated and reassembled, and long dresses that defy their own length in haphazard apertures, visible seaming, and a charming sense of coming apart. Kouyaté's dilapidated dresses and clothes are a romantic, enchanted vision.

As Kouyaté told Amy Spindler (*New York Times,* 2 May 1993), "At home, all the products come from foreign places. They're imported from everywhere, made for a different world, with another culture in mind. A sweater arrives in one of the hottest moments of the year. So you cut the sleeves off it to make it cooler. Or a woman will get a magazine with a Chanel suit in it, and she'll ask a tailor to make it out of African fabric. It completely redirects the look." Adaptation and alteration are paramount in Xüly Bet's work, beginning with the patchwork of distressed, repaired, and patched garments of 1993 and his 1994 compounds of cultures and fabrics. Like the Futurist demand that sculpture relinquish its pedestal, material unity, and high-art status, Kouyaté's fashion demands that high fashion come to the streets, flea markets, and collage medium to renew itself. It is, of course, a demolition for the purpose or rejuvenation, but an extreme of ruin that some find difficult to accept. Yet few could deny the beauty of Kouyaté's vision: sensuous patchwork, often skintight, gives the dress a sense of tattoo or body decoration more than of party dressing; his 1993 show sent African models out in Caucasian-colored "skin-tone" Band-Aids to reinforce the impression of scarification and the necessary politics of adornment. If Kouyaté's oeuvre shares principles with Martin Margiela's pensive and poetic deconstruction in fashion and both owe some debt to Rei Kawakubo's pioneering deconstructions of the early 1980s and again in the late 1980s, Kouyaté's African roots and sensibility set him apart, mingling rich pattern mix with the concept of collage. Kouyaté requires different eyes—the Xüly Bet name means the equivalent of "keep your eyes open," as with alertness and wonderment—and a Western willingness to accept an African aesthetic.

The reluctance to accept fully Kouyaté's innovative work resides less in its *épater les bourgeois* scorn for tradition and deliberate inversion of the economic order, for both of these are standard gambits of fashion novelty. The greater difficulty is probably in seeing improvised and aesthetically coarse (in Western terms and fashion's propensity to refinement) creation of fashion. But what Kouyaté proves is that the colonial disadvantage that he might supposedly have begun with is an opportunity and offers its own aesthetic. The lesson to old imperialisms is obvious; and fashion must know better than to be one of the ruined empires. A few tatters, some exposed junctures, and disheveled first impressions may be tonic and certainly far more interesting than an inflexible and rarefied status for fashion. Like Jean-Michel Basquiat's brilliant and lasting impact on American art, Kouyaté is showing the "real thing" of an African taste rendered in his own meeting with Western terms, not merely rich peasants or tourist views of a third world pageantry. Kouyaté's aesthetic is irrefutably an eye-opener for fashion.

—Richard Martin

———

KRIZIA. See MANDELLI, Mariuccia.

———

LACHASSE.

British fashion house

Founded as couture sportswear branch of Gray, Paulette and Shingleton, 1928; company incorporated as Lachasse Ltd, 1946. Chief designers include Digby Morton, 1928-33; Hardy Amies, 1934-39; Michael Donellan, 1941-52. Peter Lewis-Crown (born, 1930) joined Lachasse as apprentice, 1948; became director in 1964; later became designer and sole owner. Lachasse has also made clothes for theatre, film and television productions. **Collections:** Victoria and Albert Museum, London; Costume Gallery, Castle Howard, York; Costume Museum, Bath, England. **Address:** 29 Thurloe Place, London SW7 2HQ, England.

Publications:

On LACHASSE:

Books

Ewing, Elizabeth, *History of 20th Century Fashion,* London 1974.
McDowell, Colin, *McDowell's Directory of 20th Century Fashion,* London 1984.

*   *   *

Lachasse was often referred to as London's tailoring stable and it saw a succession of British designers who completed their training there after Digby Morton established the couture house in 1928. The house of Lachasse was renowned primarily for its tailored suits which, in the tradition of British tailoring, were said to mature like vintage wine. Lachasse was representative of the distinctive type of British tailoring which evolved from the masculine style as opposed to the softer dressmaker tailoring employed in Paris. The early success of Lachasse owed much to the popularity of sportswear during the 1920s, as advocated by Coco Chanel who also promoted the use of British wools and tweeds for these clothes. Certain other factors played a significant role in establishing Lachasse: Digby Morton presented his first collection there in 1929, the year of the Wall Street Crash, which saw a dramatic fall in the number of American buyers at the Paris couture houses. Many overseas buyers turned to London, attracted by the new generation of couturiers and the lower prices.

According to Peter Lewis-Crown, who joined Lachasse in 1949 and now owns the couture house, its three main designers, all of whom left their mark, were Digby Morton, who popularized Donegal tweed for womenswear; Hardy Amies, who gave the tailored suit a geometrical approach by using the fabric selvedge around the body instead of downwards, and Michael Donellan, who made the tai-

lored suit an acceptable mode of dress from morning through to evening.

Hardy Amies joined the house of Lachasse after Digby Morton's departure in 1934, learning about the construction of tailored suits by examining copies of Morton's models. Michael Donellan followed Hardy Amies to Lachasse where he trained until he established his own house in 1953. Originally a milliner, Michael was the only designer to have his name on the label, which read "Michael at Lachasse." The Irish-born designer was also likened to Balenciaga because of his strong, uncompromising signature. In the post-war period Lachasse enjoyed a sizeable export trade, particularly with America. The firm used to send a doll called Virginia around the world, dressed in the latest models by Lachasse, and took orders for her couture outfits. As a member of the Incorporated Society of London Fashion Designers, the house also partook in the export and publicity ventures organized by the Inc. Soc. as it was known.

Lachasse was exclusively a couture house until 1981 when Peter Lewis-Crown opened a mini-boutique on the premises. He is also responsible for introducing more dresses and feminine clothes to the house which was once famed principally for its tailored suits. Former attempts to introduce eveningwear had been unsuccessful. Hardy Amies describes Lachasse's La Soirée department as "un-epoch-making" and it was closed down, with many of the evening gowns unsold. While Lachasse can make no claims to breaking any fashion barriers, it is one of the longest-surviving couture houses and continues to attract an international clientèle to its Kensington premises.

—Catherine Woram

LACOSTE SPORTSWEAR.

French sportswear company

Founded Paris, 1933 by Rene Lacoste (born 2 July 1904). Son Bernard Lacoste (born 22 June 1931), Chairman and Managing Director since 1963. Manufacture tennis, golf and leisure clothing; technical products for tennis and golf. Launch of first Lacoste shirts, 1933; first exports to Italy and addition of colour range to shirts, 1951; first exports to United States, 1952; first collection for children, 1959; first steel racket invented by Rene Lacoste, 1963; first exports to Japan, 1964. Jean Patou licensed for Lacoste Eau de Toilette, 1968. L'Amy S.A. licensed for Lacoste sunglasses and frames. New line of men's toiletries launched with Patou, 1984. Lacoste tennis shoes developed, 1985. *Land* and *Eau de Sport* fragrances, with Patou license, developed, 1991 and 1994 respectively. Lacoste boutiques open in New Delhi, Madras, and Bombay, 1993; Lacoste corners open at Saks and Barney's in New York, Neiman Marcus, Dallas. Lacoste includes, as manufacture and sales partners, Jean Patou for toiletries, Dunlop France for tennis and golf equipment, Roventa-Henex and Vimont for watches. **Exhibitions:** *L'art de vivre en France,* Teien Museum, Tokyo, 1985, Haus der Kunst, Munich, 1987; *De main de maitre,* Grand Palais, Paris, 1988; *Vraiment faux,* Fondation Cartier, Paris, 1988; *Decorative Art and Design in France,* Cooper Hewitt Museum, New York, 1989; *Veramente falso,* Rotonda di via Besona, Milan, and Villa Stuck, Munich, 1991. **Collections:** Tennis Hall of Fame, Newport, Connecticut; Museum of Modern Art, New York; Musée de la Mode, Paris; Musée du Sport, Paris. **Awards:** Design award, 1984; Innovation award, 1988. Also: Rene Lacoste: Officier de la Legion d'Honneur, France. Bernard Lacoste: Chevalier de l'Ordre National de la Legion d'Honneur; Chevalier de l'Ordre National du Merite. **Address:** 8 rue de Castiglione, 75001 Paris, France.

Publications:

By LACOSTE:

Books

Tennis, France 1928.
Plaisir du Tennis, France 1981.

On LACOSTE:

Books

Cornfeld, B., and O. Edwards, *Quintessence: the Quality of Having It,* USA 1983.
Chapais, B., and E. Herscher, *Qualité, objets d'en France,* France 1989.
Koda, Harold, and Richard Martin, *Jocks and Nerds: Men's Style in the Twentieth Century,* New York 1989.
Labels and Tags, France 1990.
Duhamel, J., *Grand inventaire du genie français en 365 objets,* France 1993.
A Historic Look at Izod Lacoste Sportswear, Southport, Connecticut 1993.
The Story Behind Izod, Southport, Connecticut 1993.
Le dictionnaire de la mode au vingtieme siecle, France 1994
International Directory of Company Histories, London 1994.

Articles

"Le 'crocodile', dieu des loisirs," in *Le Figaro* (Paris), 5 July 1991.
Hartlein, Robert, "Izod Women's Changes and Drops Croc," in *Women's Wear Daily,* 29 April 1992.
"Real Men, Real Style, René Lacoste," in *Esquire* (Japan), October 1992.
"Les Mousquetaires: Down to Two, Still Riding High," in *International Herald Tribune* (Neuilly, France), 21 May 1993.
"Bon Anniversaire Monsieur Lacoste," in *Figaro Madame* (Paris), 5 June 1993.
"La chemise Lacoste," in *Marie-France* (Paris), June 1993.
"Lacoste, Retour de Chine," in *Le Figaro* (Paris), 30 May 1994.

*   *

The only way we consider fashion is colour. Beyond fashion trends, because of our historic roots in tennis and golf, because we design activewear which must be comfortable, we try to provide the consumer with basics he can wear for many years as our products are durable.

Our marketing strategy is clear-cut: keep your markets hungry, so that they want you to sell more and more. But don't starve them. After all, you need to sell.

A brand remains powerful if it has a strong concept and it adds on new lines of products solely when it has something new and worthwhile to offer to its existing consumers.

The quality of our products and the optimum price to quality ratio is the result of the quality of the men who create, manufacture and sell and, moreover, the quality of teams prepared to work together in the same spirit. Quality is not controlling but manufacturing.

Even if I assume the final responsibility in the Company, I believe we form a true team, and it is this point which I am especially proud of, that allows us to be what we are today.

—Bernard Lacoste

*   *   *

Lacoste's seminal fashion impact rests on the cotton knit tennis shirt with alligator symbol developed in the 1920s by Jean René Lacoste. Lacoste, a popular French tennis player in a sports-mad and style-conscious era, was nicknamed "Le Crocodile" for his aggressive play and long nose. Then, spectators and fashion editors eagerly noted what sports stars and celebrities wore to and from the matches. On the courts players wore the unexciting standard tennis whites of flannel trousers and woven buttoned shirts with their long sleeves rolled up.

Lacoste challenged this traditional uniform by playing in shortsleeve knit shirts with a crocodile monogrammed on them. He designed his shirts for comfort and good looks during the rigors of the court. The short cuffed sleeve ended the problem of sleeves rolling down. The soft turned down collar loosened easily via the buttoned placket. The pullover cotton knit breathed, while the longer shirt tail prevented the shirt from pulling out.

Not content merely to introduce the style for his own use, Lacoste turned to producing and marketing them, following his retirement in the early 1930s. The shirts he commissioned from friends in the textile industry included an embroidered crocodile on the left breast at a time when few clothes had symbols. Lacoste's renown and photos of Riviera and Palm Beach notables in this type of shirt popularized the style for recreational wear, especially in the United States.

While white remained traditional on tennis courts, the Lacoste shirt went Technicolor on the American golf links in the 1950s. The same characteristics that made it comfortable for tennis, especially the longer shirt tail, made it the sought-after style. Licensed to American manufacturer David Crystal, Inc., the crocodile swam on colored piqué knit versions of the original model. Munsingwear came out with a comparable style, dubbed the Grand Slam golf shirt.

As memories of René Lacoste faded, the crocodile trademark was increasingly referred to as an "alligator." The alligator symbol, like the country clubs at which it was seen, acquired an upscale reputation. David Crystal further enhanced this image by melding the Lacoste and Izod names. Izod derived from a British tailor who outfitted the British Royal Family. To update and increase its appeal in the late 1960s, Crystal made the shirt in double knit easy

Lacoste: The classic chemise, 1986. *Photograph by Irving Penn.*

LACROIX, Christian.

French fashion designer

Born: Christian Marie Marc Lacroix in Arles, France, 16 May 1951. **Education:** Studied art history at Paul Valéry University, Montpellier, and museum studies at the Sorbonne, Paris, 1973-76. **Family:** Married Françoise Rosensthiel in 1974. **Career:** Freelance fashion sketcher, 1976-78; assistant at Hermès, Paris, 1978-80; assistant to Guy Paulin, 1980; designer and Artistic Director, house of Patou, 1981-87. Opened own couture and ready-to-wear house, 1987; Christian Lacroix haute couture and Boutique salons established in Paris, 1987; cruise collection developed, 1988; ready-to-wear collection designed for Genny, 1988; followed by menswear collection and boutique; seven accessory lines introduced, from 1989; line of ties and hosiery introduced, 1992; perfume, *C'est la Vie!* launched, 1990. Also designed costumes for American Ballet Theater's *Gaieté Parisienne,* New York, 1988. **Awards:** Dé d'Or Award, 1986, 1988; Council of Fashion Designers of America Award, 1987. **Address:** 73 rue du Faubourg St Honoré, 75008 Paris, France.

Publications:

By LACROIX:

Books

Pieces of a Pattern, Lacroix by Lacroix, with Patrick Mauries, London 1992.

On LACROIX:

Books

Coleridge, Nicholas, *The Fashion Conspiracy,* London 1988.
Mulvagh, Jane, *Vogue History of Twentieth Century Fashion,* London 1988.
Wilson, Elizabeth, and Lou Taylor, *Through the Looking Glass,* London 1988.
Howell, Georgina, *Sultans of Style: Thirty Years of Fashion and Passion, 1960-90,* London 1990.
Martin, Richard, and Harold Koda, *Bloom,* Metropolitan Museum of Art, 1995.

Articles

Verdier, Rosy, "Jean Patou et Christian Lacroix," in *L'Officiel* (Paris), November 1984.
"Lacroix: The New Paris Star," in *Women's Wear Daily* (New York), 31 July 1986.
McEvoy, Marian, "Blithe Spirit," in *Connoisseur* (London), November 1986.
Harbrecht, Ursula, "Christian Lacroix: nouvelle étoile au firmament de Paris," in *Textiles Suisses* (Lausanne), March 1987.
Baumgold, Julie, "Dancing on the Lip of the Volcano: Christian Lacroix's Crash Chic," in *New York,* 30 April 1987.
Baudet, François, "Christian Lacroix: la nouvelle couture," in *Elle* (Paris), August 1987.
Brampton, Sally, "Lacroix's Grand Entrance," in the *Sunday Express Magazine* (London), 30 August 1987.

care Dacron polyester but cotton had perennial appeal. The colors followed current fashion's whimsy, including the worn and faded look. As the shirt settled into an enduring style for sport and casual wear, other companies, including US mass-merchandiser Sears, Roebuck, and Co., brought out their own variations with two to four button plackets and their own symbols. Ralph Lauren's polo shirt is a notable successful upscale rendition.

The preppy look of the 1970s ignited the alligator shirt's popularity and sales and gave it cachet among men, teenagers, and children. They wore the shirt differently—shirt tails were out and the ribbed collars open and flipped up. In the 1980s, collars went back down and all buttons were buttoned. Women sported feminine versions or wore their partner's. The alligator appeared on related garments with the name Izod Lacoste. At times the symbol was revamped or removed. The shirt, or a facsimile, was a staple of the American middle class wardrobe. The phrase "Lacoste shirt" came to be a generic alternative term for a tennis or polo style shirt.

Ultimately the shirt and its trademark were hurt by overmarketing, copies, and caricature in the form of a satiric upside down "dead alligator" symbol. In recent years, as the license for making Lacoste brand garments bounced from corporation to corporation, the licensees worked to return the shirt to its former successful niche. The current producer has returned to basics: a well-made cotton piqué shift for the upscale market. After 60 years and near extinction, Jean René Lacoste's crocodile is returning to the élite waters that spawned it.

—Debra Regan Cleveland

Christian Lacroix: Fall/Winter 1994/95.

Paquin, Paquita, and Francis Dorleans, "Christian Lacroix: fièvre inaugurale," in *L'Officiel* (Paris), September 1987.

Howell, Georgina, "How Lacroix Took Paris by Storm," in *The Sunday Times Magazine* (London), 4 October 1987.

"The Heir to Yves Saint Laurent," in *The Observer* (London), 18 October 1987.

Mestiri, Mohand, "Christian Lacroix: portrait chinois d'un provincial cosmopolite," in *Connaissance des Arts* (Paris), October 1987.

"Lacroix Designs for Us," in *Connoisseur,* October 1987.

Brubach, Holly, "Lacroix Goes to the Ballet," in *Vogue* (New York), February 1988.

Garmaise, Freda, "Chic Frills," in *Ms* (New York), February 1988.

"Christian Lacroix," in *Current Biography* (New York), April 1988.

"Les trésors de Christian Lacroix," in *L'Officiel* (Paris), March 1989.

Colchester, Chloe, "Paris soie," in *Crafts* (London), March/April 1989.

Grossman, Lloyd, "The Wider Side of Paris," in *Harpers & Queen* (London), May 1989.

Donovan, Carrie, "The Three Who Are Key: Couture's Future," in the *New York Times Magazine,* 27 August 1989.

"A Day in the Life of Christian Lacroix," in *The Sunday Times Magazine* (London), 27 August 1989.

Gerrie, Anthea, "Lacroix's Business Scents," in the *Sunday Express Magazine* (London), 18 March 1990.

Rafferty, Diane, "Christian Lacroix: The Art of Sensuality," in *Connoisseur,* June 1990.

"Lacroix's Fan Club," in *Women's Wear Daily* (New York), 18 December 1990.

Levin, Angela, "Christian Lacroix," in *You* magazine of the *Mail on Sunday* (London), 10 February 1991.

Rolf, Gail, "Racy and Lacy ... A Perfect Paris Match from Lacroix," in the *Daily Mail* (London), 20 July 1993.

Menkes, Suzy, "Sweetness and Light by Lacroix," in *International Herald Tribune* (Paris), 27 January 1995.

Spindler, Amy M., "Olé: Lacroix Conquers the Couture," in the *New York Times,* 27 January 1995.

Schiro, Anne-Marie, "Lacroix and Rykiel: Classics," in the *New York Times,* 18 March 1995.

*   *   *

There is a prevalent myth in French haute couture that only once every decade does a new star emerge. Writer Nicholas Coleridge traced this path of succession from Paul Poiret, to Chanel, to Balenciaga, to Saint Laurent, then Lagerfeld (*The Fashion Conspiracy,* London 1988). Judging by the buzz and excitement that preceded the launch of his first collection in the Salon Impérial Suite of the Hotel Intercontinental in July 1987, there could be no doubt that the new star was Christian Lacroix.

Quite why Lacroix became the new star of couture is debatable but his timing was definitely right. There had been no opening of a couture house since 1961 with Saint Laurent. (Karl Lagerfeld became a star

by resuscitating the established house of Chanel.) As the chairman and financial director of the new house, Paul Audrain was to declare, "We had a very strong presentiment that the climate was right for a new couture house." New social and cultural changes had reversed the values of the 1970s; the jeans and T-shirt dressing, so prevalent during that decade, had changed. A new sexual identity had emerged. The entrepreneurial spirit of the 1980s created new money and Lacroix's debut was in time to capitalize on this trend.

Christian Lacroix had begun his career with an aspiration to be a museum curator. After moving to Paris from Arles in the early 1970s he met his future wife Françoise Rosensthiel who encouraged his interest in fashion which led to his taking positions at Hermès and Guy Paulin. He became the designer for Jean Patou in 1981, revitalizing the flagging couture house and upping sales from 30 dresses a season to a hundred. He seduced the fashion press with spectacular shows, reviving fashion staples such as the frou-frou petticoat and the puffball skirt. It was in 1987, with the backing of five million francs from the textile conglomerate Financière Agache, that Lacroix opened his new couture house.

As a designer Lacroix throws caution to the wind, providing the sort of luxurious product that, at first, justified the amount of "new money" spent on him. His collections are always an exotic, lavish cornucopia of influences, ranging from the primitive, rough naïveté of the paintings of the Cobra movement, to a homage to Lady Diana Cooper, to modern gypsies, travellers, and nomads. He uses the most luxurious fabrics in often unexpected mixes or even patchwork, embroidered brocades, fur, re-embroidered lace, ethnic prints and embroideries, even gold embroidery. Nothing is considered too expensive or too *outré* to be included in the clothes.

An extravagant technicolour musical from the golden age of Hollywood would perhaps be an understatement when describing the impact of a Lacroix collection. As an artist he is not afraid to plunder junk shops, museums, the theatre and opera, or the glamour of the bullfight to create designs that astound, yet are always stylish in their eclectic clutter.

There are many strong retrospective 1950s, 1960s and 1970s references in a Lacroix collection: the detached hauteur or waif-like gestures of fashion models from the period. The unapproachable allure of movie stars like Tippi Hedren or Capucine, or real-life personalities who embody these qualities, all inspire his designs, often resulting in eccentric accessories, colours, and poses.

Lacroix recognizes that contemporary couture is often only a public relations exercise for money-spinning ventures such as perfume or licensing deals that use a designer name to sell a product. However, Lacroix is fully aware of the value couture has in pushing fashion, projecting a dream, and making dramatically important fashion statements. This is essential if fashion is to survive commercially because the ready-to-wear and mass-market manufacturers always see designers as the inspirations that direct the movement of fashion. Before his first show Lacroix seemed to synthesize this point of view when he said, "I want to get back to the position where the couture becomes a kind of laboratory of ideas, the way it was with Schiaparelli 40 years ago."

—Kevin Almond

LADICORBIC, Zoran. See **ZORAN.**

LAGERFELD, Karl.

German designer

Born: Hamburg, 10 September 1938. Immigrated to Paris in 1952.
Career: Design assistant at Balmain, 1955-58; art director, Patou, 1958-63; free-lance designer for Chloë, Krizia, Ballantyne, Timwear, Charles Jourdan, Valentino, Fendi, Cadette, Max Mara and others, from 1964; director of collections and ready-to-wear, Chanel, from 1983; Karl Lagerfeld and KL ready-to-wear firms established in Paris and Germany, 1984; Karl Lagerfeld, S.A., acquired by Chloë parent company, Dunhill, 1992; created fragrances *Lagerfeld,* for Elizabeth Arden, 1975, *Chloé-Lagerfeld* for men, 1978, *KL* for women, 1983, *KL* for men, 1984. Also photographer and stage designer. **Exhibitions:** *Karl Lagerfeld: Fotografien,* Galerie Hans Mayer, Dusseldorf, 1989. **Awards:** Second prize, International Wool Secretariat design contest, 1954; Neiman Marcus Award, 1980; Bath Museum of Costume Dress of the Year Award, 1981; Council of Fashion Designers of America Award, 1991; Fashion Footwear Association of New York Award, 1991. **Address:** 14 Boulevard de la Madeleine, 75008 Paris, France.

Publications:

On LAGERFELD:

Books

Lynam, Ruth, ed., *Paris Fashion: Designers and Their Creations,* London 1972.

Milbank, Caroline Rennolds, *Couture: The Great Designers,* New York 1985.

Piaggi, Anna, *Karl Lagerfeld: A Fashion Journal,* London 1986.

Perschetz, Lois, ed., *W, The Designing Life,* New York 1987.

Coleridge, Nicholas, *The Fashion Conspiracy,* London 1988.

Howell, Georgina, *Sultans of Style: 30 Years of Fashion and Passion 1960-1990,* London 1990.

Articles

"Karl's Classics," in *Women's Wear Daily* (New York), 11 April 1972.

Buck, J., "How Karl Lagerfeld Changed Some Lives," in *Interview* (New York), March 1973.

"In Focus—Karl Lagerfeld," in *International Textiles* (London), Winter 1974/75.

"Great Designers of the World: Karl Lagerfeld," in *Vogue* (London), 1 March 1975.

"Edna O'Brien Meets Karl Lagerfeld," in *Over 21* (London), February 1979.

Menkes, Suzy, "The Man Who Takes Over from Chanel," in *The Times* (London), 31 January 1983.

"A Certain Style: Karl Lagerfeld," in *Vogue* (London), July 1984.

Moore, Jackie, "Karl Lagerfeld, the Devil of a Designer," in *Women's Journal* (London), April 1985.

"Karl Lagerfeld: militaresco o sexy, semplicemente nero," in *Vogue* (Milan), October 1985.

"Karl Lagerfeld: The Many Faceted Man," in *Vogue* (Paris), October 1985.

Dryansky, G. Y. "Baroque to His Bones," in *Connoisseur,* December 1985.

Pringle, Colombe, "Karl Lagerfeld, une collection de talents," in *Elle* (Paris), 7 April 1986.

Barron, Pattie, "Playing Court to Kaiser Karl," in *Cosmopolitan* (London), October 1986.

"A Diary of Dress," in *Du* (Zurich), No. 5, 1987.

"Le film d'un film par Karl Lagerfeld," in *Vogue* (Paris), March 1987.

Green, Peter S., "Shaping Up," in *Connoisseur,* October 1987.

"A Life in the Day of Karl Lagerfeld," in *The Sunday Times Magazine* (London), 8 November 1987.

Barker, Rafaella, "Karlsberg," in *House & Garden* (New York), December 1987.

Lobrany, Alexander, "Lagerfeld Logs On: At 50, King Karl Makes a Foray into Men's Wear," in the *Daily News Record* (New York), 6 April 1988.

Brook, Danae, "King Karl," in the *Sunday Express Magazine* (London), 15 May 1988.

"Karl Lagerfeld: Don't Talk to Me About Hemlines," in *Donna* (Milan), June 1988.

Jodidio, Philippe, "Pleins feux sur Jack Lang," in *Connaissance des Arts* (Paris), December 1988.

Talley, André Leon, "Petit Palais," in *Vogue* (New York), April 1989.

Howell, Georgina, "Royalist Leanings," in *Vogue* (New York), April 1989.

Ciavarella, Michele, "Karl Lagerfeld: A Burst of Genius," in *Maglieria Italiana* (Modena), April/June 1989.

Levin, Angela, "At Home with Karl Lagerfeld," in *You* magazine of the *Mail on Sunday* (London), 14 May 1989.

Bowles, Hamish, "Reviving the Past," in *Harpers & Queen* (London), September 1989.

"A Lagerfeld Extravagance," in *The Independent* (London), 28 September 1989.

Falconer, Karen, "King Karl," in *Fashion Weekly* (London), 14 December 1989.

Farrah, Leilah, "Of Shoes and Candlewax," in *The Sunday Times* (London), 13 May 1990.

Mynott, Lawrence, "Kaiser Karl: The Darling Dictator," in *The Independent* (London), 24 May 1990.

Etherington-Smith, Meredith, "He Came, He Drew, He Conquered," in *Harpers & Queen* (London), September 1990.

"The Designers Talk Passion, Whimsy and Picassos," in *ARTnews* (New York), September 1990.

Mower, Sarah, "Karl Lagerfeld," in *Vogue* (London), April 1991.

Spindler, Amy M., "Karl Lagerfeld: Hartmarx's New European Connection," in the *Daily News Record* (New York), 30 May 1991.

Kramer, Jane, "The Chanel Obsession," in *Vogue* (New York), September 1991.

Mayer, Margit, "King Karl," in *Women's Wear Daily* (New York), 20 November 1991.

Orth, Maureen, "Kaiser Karl: Behind the Mask," in *Vanity Fair* (New York), February 1992.

"The Kaiser's Empire," in *Women's Wear Daily* (New York), 2 June 1992.

Lane, Anthony, "The Last Emperor," in the *New Yorker,* 7 November 1994.

Menkes, Suzy, "Chanel: Beauty without Gimmicks," in the *International Herald Tribune* (Paris), 25 January 1995.

Spindler, Amy M., "Four Who Have No Use for Trends," in the *New York Times,* 20 March 1995.

Menkes, Suzy, "Show, Not Clothes, Becomes the Message," in *International Herald Tribune* (Paris), 20 March 1995.

*   *   *

Universally recognized as one of the most prolific and high-profile designers of the last 20 years, Karl Lagerfeld has maintained his reputation through consistently strong work for the numerous lines he produces every year. Each label has its own distinct look, while clearly bearing the bold, uncompromising Lagerfeld signature that guarantees the success of everything he produces.

Moving between the six main collections he designs with consummate ease, he displays the skills he learned from his couture background in his fine tailoring and flashes of surreal detailing. He functions best as a catalyst, re-invigorating labels and broadening their customer base. Since 1983 he has most spectacularly demonstrated this capability at Chanel, where, despite some criticism, Lagerfeld has brought the label to the pinnacle of high fashion. He has produced endless innovative variations on the signature tweed suits that often mix street style references, for example, teaming the traditional jacket with denim mini skirts (1991), with the signature Chanel gilt buttons and chains. He stretches the look to embrace younger customers' tastes, with club-influenced black fishnet bodystockings, the traditional Chanel camellia placed cheekily over the breasts, and hefty lace-up boots set against flowing georgette skirts and leather jackets. This combination of wit with recognizable Chanel symbols has rejuvenated the house, making Lagerfeld's fashion word an aspirational message to a new generation. His experiments are at their most fantastic in the vibrant lines of the couture show, made more accessible in the ready-to-wear range. Only Lagerfeld could put the Chanel label on underpants (1993) and camellia-trimmed cotton vests (1992) to make them the most talked-about elements of the Paris collections. This quirkiness is underpinned by the quality of his designs and the mix of classic separates that are always an undercurrent in his work.

His own name label KL highlights these skills. Bold tailoring, easy-to-wear cardigan jackets in his favourite bright colours, combined with softly shaped knitwear, show the breadth of his talents and ensure the longevity of his appeal. If his more outrageous combinations of references at Chanel have enabled him to outlive the excesses of the 1970s that trapped some of his contemporaries, then his clever manipulation of fabric and colour prolongs the life of his clothes still further.

During the 1970s his work for Chloë was equally influential, his love of eveningwear coming to the fore, albeit in a more restrained form than at Chanel. The main look of this period was flowing pastel chiffon draped onto the body to give a highly feminine feel and trimmed with silk flowers. He recreated this style for his return to the label in spring-summer 1993, complete with Afro-wig-wearing models. At first coolly received by the fashion press, it went on to inspire many with its floaty silhouette and flower-child air, reviving ethereal dresses with no linings, unnecessary seams, or extraneous detail.

While he continues to move from label to label, never quite losing the free-lance mentality of his early days, it is only the occasional lack of editing in his collections that betrays how widely his talents are spread. Idea follows idea, frequently inspired by his current model muse as he re-interprets garments to create very modern styles. At Fendi this desire to continually push forward to greater modernity, absorbing the influences around him and seeking greater perfection in his work, led to his taking the furriers' trade a step

further. The lightness of touch that had established his name as early as 1970 led him to strip the Fendi sisters' signature fur coats to the thinnest possible layer. He removed the need for heavy linings by treating the pelts to produce supple lightweight coats shown in 1973 with raglan sleeves and tie belts, which complemented the sporty feel of the knitwear he also produces for the company.

Lagerfeld's position in fashion history is assured. He is equally skilled in his bold strokes at Chanel as in his delicate shaping at Fendi and Chloë, or in the vibrant classics of his own lines. His skill as a designer has enabled him to push the discipline further by combining the immediacy of ready-to-wear with the splendour and elegance of couture.

—Rebecca Arnold

LAM, Ragence.

British fashion designer

Born: Lam Kwok Fai in Hong Kong, 24 January 1951. **Education:** Harrow School of Art, London, 1971-74, and at the Royal College of Art, London, 1974-76. **Career:** Designer for Fiorucci, Milan, 1976. Designer and owner, Ragence Lam, London, 1977-83; Ragence, Hong Kong, 1980-83; Ragence Lam Ltd, Hong Kong, from 1983. Also: founder member of Hong Kong Fashion Designers Association, 1984, chairman, 1985-88. **Exhibitions:** *Ragence Lam Fashion Design Exhibition,* Hong Kong Arts Center, 1985. **Awards:** Hong Kong Artist Guild Fashion Designer of the Year Award, 1988; China Fashion Exhibition Competition Gold Prize, 1990. **Address:** 83085 Wongnei Chong Road, 17th Floor, Linden Court, Happy Valley, Hong Kong.

Publications:

On LAM:

Articles

Kivestu, Pat, "Best of Hong Kong Fashions: The New Fashion Generation," in *Women's Wear Daily* (Hong Kong supplement), 1 December 1986.

*

Growing up in a Chinese family in the British Colony of Hong Kong at the tip of south China, I have always felt the need to define my identity. Western culture was pervasive in my daily life. European art and history were part of my education and training. And so I had no difficulty adapting when I went to study at the Royal College of Art in London and then to work as a designer in Italy. But, paradoxically, it was when I was enjoying my first early success in the Western world, particularly in London where I had my own label, that I became keenly aware of my Chinese origins. I am not only modern and Western, but also Chinese, and I felt that unless my designs could capture my identity, they will never be entirely satisfying to me.

My work in the 1980s, when I returned to Hong Kong and opened my own shop with my own label, covered a wide diversity of styles. I frequently used unusual materials such as fishnet, or rattan mats. But in a way they were just random experiments, without my knowing exactly what I wanted. As designs they had merit and originality, but as self-expression they were to me lacking and uncertain.

Then followed a period of contemplation and reassessment. I began to examine a tremendous amount of Chinese art forms—architecture, painting, sculpture, ceramics, textiles, furniture—whatever I could lay hands on, from all historical periods of China. Not only did their immense richness astonish me, but I discovered I felt instinctively towards them an affinity, such as I never felt about Western art. It is as if I appreciate the Western sense of beauty only intellectually through my training, but the Chinese sense of beauty is in my blood.

I also travelled to China. The vibrancy of the people and the often bold and witty way in which they seek expression in fashion struck me as entirely encouraging.

It became perfectly clear to me that what I wanted as a designer was to express the Chinese sense of beauty in contemporary and international fashion language. It must be contemporary. I want not historical revival but development, to carry into the 20th century the great Chinese tradition of art and costume truncated by traumatic events in China's recent history. It must be international, because only then can it enter the mainstream and have real impact. Above all it must have depth and meaning, and not just superficial borrowings here and there from folk or court art or theatre or whatever. It must be truly new.

I see this as my life's work. In the exploration of the Chinese sense of beauty, I have an inexhaustible source of infinite variety, from the floating lines of elegant Sung-style robes to the elaborate bejewelled and embroidered Q'ing artefacts. Then there is something religious or ceremonial in this beauty—in Buddhist statues, in a monk's habit—an austerity and tranquillity that deeply appeals to me.

In addition, there are China's traditional fabrics and craftsmanship, the numerous techniques of embroidery, tapestry, ornamentation which could be put to exciting new use and create a totally new look.

In a way, I had stumbled on to this dimension being caught up in Hong Kong's fate as a city. In the second half of the 1980s, Hong Kong was plunged into the great anxiety of facing a fundamental change. British rule was to end and Chinese sovereignty was to be resumed in 1997. As a result of the Sino-British Joint Declaration, the China link came more and more to dominate Hong Kong life. Like others I, too, was anxious. Like others I, too, became drawn more and more to China. The Tiananmen Square tragedy of 4 June 1989 had a great impact on me: it reaffirmed my Chinese identity. Instead of being frightened into emigration I want more than ever to stay.

Myself, my artistic aim, the identity I have sought to express are all bound up with the history and the unique society of Hong Kong, and with its future. As Hong Kong's link with China grows in the coming years, I see my work growing with a strong sense of direction and inner purpose.

—Ragence Lam

* * *

In his native Hong Kong he has been referred to as the "Little Giant." He is one of the few local designers to have achieved an international reputation. It is well-deserved. For over 15 years, Ragence Lam has been developing his own lines and helping to promote the status of his fellow designers.

His interest in fashion began as a child, but he never seriously considered it as a career. He became a fashion student at Harrow School of Art and the Royal College of Art, having never studied art. In fact he went to London originally to study law, but became bored. At the Royal College of Art, his talent developed quickly and led to him winning a number of student competitions. After graduating he spent a short time in Milan, designing for Fiorucci, before setting up his own label in London and then in Hong Kong. During the 1980s he evolved a look characterized by well-defined shapes and cut which revealed his passion for structure and three-dimensional forms. He highlighted his collections with quality fabrics, often from Italy or Japan, to provide an individual look. Frequently he experimented with unusual materials such as fishnet and rattan mats to create unique statements. He was never afraid of being experimental, even outrageous. Pure commercialism was not his goal, he was much more a provider of ideas. Ragence Lam became known, and loved by the press, as an innovator.

Towards the end of the 1980s he began to change direction. The look became more minimal, with fewer dramatic details. The clothes were simpler but more versatile; customers appreciated the opportunity to be able to dress them up or down. He was moving away from the avant-garde to create something more stylish and lasting. For autumn-winter 1989-90 he featured knots and ties on simple silhouettes, interpreted in wool, Lycra and jersey, using a subtle palette of textures and patterns. In the same collection he created eveningwear and cocktail dresses in taffeta and lace. His designs have sold in Europe, south-east Asia, and Japan. For a time his collections, including both womenswear and menswear, were available in his own exclusive boutique in Hong Kong.

A testament to his achievement came in 1989 when he was invited to contribute to an international symposium as part of the World Fashion Fair in Japan. He formed part of a prestigious panel which included Issey Miyake, Sybilla, and Romeo Gigli. Lam has acted as a consultant to fashion design education in Hong Kong. As a founder and one-time chairman of the Hong Kong Fashion Designers Association, he has helped to support and encourage young designers. However he is not a natural committee person; designing is his major interest and motivation.

At the beginning of the 1990s Lam underwent a period of reassessment. Original though his work was, it did not provide the means of self-expression which he found he was seeking. To try and establish his fundamental identity, he began to examine his Chinese roots. He found a genuine affinity for Chinese art and culture and wanted to reflect this in his own work. A totally new direction began to evolve. This was not a mere pastiche of Chinese traditional dress, but a more fundamental attempt to carry the great traditions of Chinese art into the late 20th century. Lam wants to create an international fashion look which reflects his own Chinese identity. He is aware that this will not be easy, but he is committed to his future direction. Ragence Lam's personal integrity is striking. It is born of maturity, but also of an overwhelming belief in what he is doing. With his experience, talent, and determination he remains a name to watch on the international fashion scene.

—Hazel Clark

Ragence Lam: Resort collection in 100% cotton knit trimmed with net.

LANE, Kenneth Jay.

American jewelry and accessories designer

Born: Detroit, Michigan, 22 April 1932. **Education:** Studied at the University of Michigan, 1950-52, and at Rhode Island School of Design, Providence, 1953-54. **Family:** Married Nicola Samuel Waymouth in 1975 (divorced, 1977). **Career:** Art staff member, *Vogue* (New York), 1954-55; assistant designer, Delman Shoes, New York, 1956-58; associate designer, Christian Dior Shoes, New York, 1958-63; founder, designer, Kenneth Jay Lane, New York, from 1963. Kenneth Jay Lane shops located in the United States, Great Britain, France, and Austria. Awards: Coty American Fashion Critics Award, 1967; *Harper's Bazaar* International Award, 1967; Tobé Coburn Award, 1966; Maremodo di Capri-Tiberio d'Oro Award, 1967; Neiman Marcus Award, 1968; Swarovski Award, 1969; *Brides* Magazine Award, 1990. **Address:** 20 West 37th Street, New York, New York 10018, USA.

Publications:

On LANE:

Books

Bender, Marylin, *The Beautiful People,* New York 1967.
Morris, Bernadine, and Barbara Walz, *The Fashion Makers,* New York 1978.
Shields, Jody, *All that Glitters,* New York 1987.
Becker, Vivienne, *Fabulous Fakes,* London 1988.
Ball, Joanne Dubbs, *Costume Jewelry: The Golden Age of Design,* Schiffer, Pennsylvania 1990.

Articles

Lynden, Patricia, "Kenneth Jay Lane: Faking It with Style," in *Northwestern,* November 1986.
Lane, Jane F., "Ballad of Kenny Lane," in *W* (New York), August 1987.
Mehta, Gita, "The Fast Lane at Home," in *Vanity Fair* (New York), November 1988.
Hawkins, Timothy, "Excellent Adventure," in *Egg,* March 1991.
Rubin, Robert H., "Kenneth Jay Lane," in *Night,* March 1991.
Shaw, Daniel, "Confessions of an Extra Man," in *Avenue* (New York), November 1991.
Nemy, Enid, "The King of Junque," in the *New York Times,* 27 June 1993.
Espen, Hal, "Portrait of a Dress," in the *New Yorker,* 7 November 1994.
Spindler, Amy M., "A Mature Mugler, Demeulemeester and Lang," in the *New York Times,* 18 March 1995.

*   *   *

Acclaimed by *Time* Magazine as "the undisputed King of Costume jewelry" and called "one of the three great costume jewelers of the 20th century" by *Women's Wear Daily,* Kenneth Jay Lane transformed a previously undistinguished field into the height of fashion.

"I believe that every woman has the right to be glamorous and have always believed that a woman can be just as glamorous in costume jewelry as million dollar bangles and beads," he once said.

"Style has little to do with money and expensive possessions; attitude and flair make all the difference."

Born in Detroit, Kenneth Jay Lane attended the University of Michigan for two years, then came east to earn a degree in advertising design from the Rhode Island School of Design. After a brief stint in the art department at *Vogue* in New York, he went on to become the fashion coordinator at Delman Shoes, New York. Later, while working as an associate designer for Christian Dior Shoes, he spent part of each summer in Paris under the tutelage of the preeminent French shoe designer, Roger Vivier. He also designed a shoe collection for Arnold Scaasi in New York. In 1963, while adorning shoes with rhinestones and jeweled ornaments, he began to experiment with making jewelry.

"A whole new group of beautiful people began to exist," Lane said. "They started dressing up and costume jewelry was rather dull. I believed it didn't have to be." The thought that fake jewelry could be as beautiful as the real thing grew on Lane. He bought some plastic bangles at the dime store, covered them with rhinestones, crystals, leopard and zebra patterns and stripes, and a new era in costume jewelry was born.

In 1963, while still designing shoes, he worked nights and weekends, creating jewelry. "I started moonlighting jewelry," he said. Since he was being paid by Genesco, Delman's parent firm, to design shoes, "I thought it would be in better taste to use my own initials and not my name for jewelry." His work was enthusiastically received, written about and photographed by the fashion magazines. Neiman Marcus in Dallas and Bonwit Teller, New York placed orders for rhinestone earrings. Within a year, his jewelry was bringing in 2000 dollars a month wholesale, and by June 1964, sales had risen to 10,000 dollars a month wholesale. His part-time jewelry business became a full-time career. In 1969 Kenneth Jay Lane Inc. became part of Kenton Corporation, an organization that includes Cartier, Valentino, Mark Cross, and other well known names in fashion. Lane repurchased the company in 1972.

Lane considers himself a fine jeweler, and eschews the traditional methods of making costume jewelry. First, he fabricates his designs in wax by carving or twisting the metal. He often sets the designs with opulent stones highlighted by their cut and rich colors. Many of these stones, particularly the larger ones, he has created for himself. "I want to make real jewelry with not-real materials," he noted. He sees plastic as the modern medium: lightweight, available in every color, and perfect for simulating real gems. He likes to see his jewelry intermixed with the real gems worn by his international roster of celebrity customers. Lane is proud of the fidelity of his reproductions and claims that some of "faque" stones look better than the real ones.

"I work in less commercial ways than most manufacturers of costume jewelry," says Lane. He is realistic about the source of his designs. "My designs are all original—original from someone," he said. "There are original ideas, but a lot of good designing is editorial, choosing what is available idea-wise and applying these ideas practically. I think it's called 'having the eye'. It isn't necessarily reinventing the wheel."

Lane is as much a showman as talented designer. In addition to receiving numerous fashion awards, his jewelry was regularly featured on several soap operas, including *Another World, The Guiding Light,* and *Days of Our Lives.* He has also created jewelry for the Costume Institute exhibitions at the Metropolitan Museum of Art, New York.

In addition to being a fixture on the social circuit, Lane is frequently named on the International Best Dressed Men's List. "All

Kenneth Jay Lane.

Helmut Lang: 1994/95; reflecting jeans and cowboy boots painted with red nail polish. *Photograph by Jürgen Teller.*

you need is one person and you can meet the world," he said. Dinner-partner and friend to some of the world's most fashionable women, his clients have included Jacqueline Kennedy Onassis, Princess Margaret, the Duchess of Windsor, Elizabeth Taylor, Audrey Hepburn, Nancy Reagan, Joan Collins, Babe Paley, Brooke Astor, and Lee Radziwill Ross. Ex-First Lady Barbara Bush wore his "pearls" to her husband's inauguration, and that triple-strand has become an integral part of her signature style. Recently, he sent his 21-dollar saxophone pin to First Lady Hillary Rodham Clinton, to whom he wrote: "Looking forward to eight years of sweet music."

In 1993 Kenneth Jay Lane celebrated his 30th anniversary in business. The *New York Times* called him "the man who made costume jewelry chic and, more important to his bank account, readily available to what is loosely referred to as the masses. Chanel had done it earlier, but to a more affluent clientèle" (27 June 1993). Lane now has 20 stores in the United States, Canada, and Europe and recently celebrated his second year selling fashion on QVC, the cable television home-shopping network.

—Janet Markarian

LANG, Helmut.

Austrian designer

Born: Vienna, Austria, 10 March 1956, of Czechoslovakian/Polish and Hungarian/Yugoslavian descent. **Career:** Grew up in Austrian Alps and Vienna; became acquainted with Viennese art scene; established own fashion studio in Vienna, 1977; made-to-measure shop opened in Vienna, 1979; developed ready-to-wear collections, 1984-86. Presented Helmut Lang womenswear, 1986, and Helmut Lang menswear, 1987, as part of Paris Fashion Week. Established license business, 1988. Moved several times between Paris and Vienna, 1988-93. Professor of Fashion Masterclass, University of Applied Arts, Vienna, since 1993. Other lines include Helmut Lang Underwear, 1994, and Helmut Lang Protective Eyewear, 1995. **Collection:** Museum of Applied Arts, Vienna. **Addresses:** P.O. Box 133, A-1013 Vienna, Austria. Press Office, c/o Michele Montagne, 184 rue St Maur, F-75010 Paris, France.

Publications:

On LANG:

Articles

Cressole, Michel, "Une lancinante variation en jersey zippé," in *Libération* (Paris), 24 March 1986.

Kaupp, Katia D., Une manif pour Helmut Lang," in *Le nouvel Observateur* (Paris), 29 March 1990.

Blumenberg, H. C., "Der Retter des Einfachen," in *Zeit Magazin* (Hamburg, Germany), 1 March 1991.

Tredre, Roger, "The Maker's Culture: The Wearer's Imprint," in *The Independent* (London), 9 September 1993.

Mair, Avril, "Designs of the Times," in *i-D* (London), December 1993.

Mower, Sarah, "Brilliant," in *Harper's Bazaar* (New York), February 1994.

Spindler, Amy M., "Lang Points the Way to a New Elegance," in the *New York Times,* 7 March 1994.

Brampton, Sally, "Langevity," in *The Guardian* (London), 20 August 1994.

Watson, Shane, "Cool Hand Lang," in *Elle* (London), September 1994.

Espen, Hal, "Portrait of a Dress," *New Yorker* (New York), 7 November 1994.

*

At a moment of conflicting demands, people want modernity and identity, street style and savviness. Fashion now is fast, downbeat, and relentlessly urban. Because of that, I have been developing a particular vision; what I call a non-referential view of fashion. It is all about today. It has to do with my personality, with my life and with the idea that quality doesn't go out of style every six months. Working effectively with fashion means adding pieces to a continuing story, evolving fluently year after year. The basis of really effortless style is found in minimal exaggeration. A perfect economy of cut and exacting attention to finish is sometimes lost to the careless eye, which gives it precisely the sort of anonymous status that the truly knowing admire. If you have to ask, you don't get it, in either sense. Downbeat elegance is founded in precise proportions and clean tailoring; balancing hi-tech fabrics with real clothing. The result is fashion put into a different context to become something known, unknown.

—Helmut Lang

*   *   *

An attenuated, urban aesthetic, embodied by subtle mixes of luxury fabrics and post-punk synthetics, dominates Helmut Lang's confident designs. Both his men's and womenswear is uncompromisingly modern: stark minimalist pieces in sombre city shades are combined with harsh metallics and slippery transparent layers, questioning the restrictions of traditional tailored clothing.

Although Lang's work is avant-garde, he is unafraid to use sharply cut suiting, lending it an etiolated androgyny; with a punk-like disregard for accepted fabric use, as cigarette trousers and three buttoned jackets come in shiny PVC with clingy net T-shirts worn beneath. He enjoys the surprise of such cheap fabrics being lent a certain chic through their combination with their more luxurious counterparts, and often backs silk with nylon to give a liquid, shifting opacity to column dresses and spaghetti-strapped slips.

For all the deconstructed glamour of his clothes, they remain essentially understated, drawing their interest from the layering of opaques and transparents in sinuous strong lines, rather than unnecessary details which might dull their impact. Even the sexuality of his figure-hugging womenswear is tempered by a nonchalance and apparent disregard for the impact the clothes have. This parallels the growing sense of independence and confidence of women over the 15 years Lang has been designing.

If his stylistic reference points originated touching the past, then his distillation of them is always utterly contemporary. In line with, and often ahead of, current trends, he honed his skills during the 1980s, contradicting the decade's often overblown characteristics and charming first the Parisian, then the international fashion scene, which was impressed by the modernity of his work. He remains a hero of the *cognoscenti,* influencing mainstream fashion.

The simplicity of the cut of his garments is deceptive though. The slim mannish-shaped trousers he favours for women may be timeless enough, but the surprise of rendering them in hot red stretch synthetic in 1992 and creating an urban warrior look with halter top and toning boned breast-plate meant they appealed to the stylishly lanvinunconventional, who were unafraid to slip from day to night, informal to formal, disregarding the normal restrictions of what is appropriate to wear.

His emphasis on the importance of the innovative use of textiles is as prevalent in his menswear. He has been at the forefront of the shift of feeling in this area, which has gathered momentum during the 1990s. He has pushed for a crossover of fabrics from womenswear and a narrower line, shown in 19th-century cut three-piece single breasted suits, more attuned to the times than the big triangular silhouette of the 1980s. His deconstructed closefit tops with visible seaming and layered angora tank tops over untucked shirts increased his popularity as fashion became tired of its own overpowering dogma in the early 1990s.

Lang's work continues to maintain a high profile in fashion magazines. The deceptive simplicity of his clothes, complicated by his constant comparisons of clear and opaque, matt and shiny, silk-smooth and plastic-hard, has carried him successfully into the 1990s and, indeed, has enabled him to be part of a movement in fashion towards a redefinition of glamour and beauty. This revelling in texture and surface effect with raw dark and bright colours brings together the confrontation of the emaciated punk aesthetic with sophisticated restrained tailoring, producing a mature sense of negligent chic.

—Rebecca Arnold

LANVIN.

French fashion house

Founded in Paris in 1890 by Jeanne Lanvin (1867-1946) offering custom children's clothing; women's clothing offered, from 1909, men's clothing, from 1926, and women's sportswear, furs and accessories; women's ready-to-wear, from 1982. Fragrances: *My Sin,* 1925; *Arpège,* 1927; *Scandal,* 1931; *Runeur,* 1934; *Pretexts,* 1937; *Crescendo,* 1960. Products also included women's toiletries and cosmetics. Designers for the House of Lanvin have included Antonio del Castillo (active, 1950-62), Jules-François Crahay (active, 1963-85), Maryll Lanvin (from 1982), Claude Montana (1990), and Dominique Morlotti (from 1992). **Exhibitions:** *Paris Couture—Années Trente,* Musée de la Mode et du Costume, Palais Galliera, Paris. **Collections:** Victoria and Albert Museum, London; Fashion Institute of Technology, New York; Costume Institute of the Metropolitan Museum of Art, New York; Musée de la Mode et du Costume, Paris; Musée des Arts de la Mode, Paris. Jeanne Lanvin, **recipient:** Chevalier de la Légion d'Honneur, 1926; Officier de la Légion d'Honneur, 1938. **Address:** 15, 22 rue du Faubourg St.-Honoré, 75008 Paris, France.

Publications:

On LANVIN:

Books

Bourdet, Denise, *Art et style: les fées,* Paris 1946.

Bertin, Celia, *Paris à la mode,* London 1956.
Pickens, Mary Brooks, and Dora Loues Miller, *Dressmakers of France,* New York 1956.
Contini, Mila, *Fashion from Ancient Egypt to the Present Day,* Milan 1965; New York 1965.
Lynam, Ruth, *Couture,* Garden City, New York 1972.
Milbank, Caroline Rennolds, *Couture: The Great Designers,* New York 1985.
Garnier, Guillaume, *Paris Couture—Années Trente* (exhibition catalogue), Paris 1987.
Martin, Richard, and Harold Koda, *The Historical Mode: Fashion and Art in the 1980s,* New York 1989.

Articles

"Magic by Lanvin-Castillo," in *American Fabrics and Fashions* (New York), No. 41, 1957.
Mulvagh, Jane, "Lanvin, c'est moi," in *The Sunday Times Magazine* (London), 4 November 1990.
Deeny, Godfrey, "Lanvin Gets It All Together," in *Women's Wear Daily* (New York), 19 February 1992.
Spindler, Amy M., "A 'Real' Look at Lanvin's New Designer," in *Women's Wear Daily* (New York), 26 February 1992.

*   *   *

The youthful look identified with Lanvin came from her earliest couture, children's dresses; the many decorations were inspired by a trip to Spain during her childhood. The memory of the play on shadows and light would influence her choice of embroidery, such as multi-needle sewing machines stitching and quilting. She had three embroidery *ateliers.* Beading and appliqué were also applied. With dyes she ombréed textiles. She had her own dye works—Lanvin Blue inspired by stained glass was developed there. These decorations were applied to all categories: millinery, couture, menswear, and accessories.

Lanvin did not drape or sketch, but gave verbal instructions to the sketchers. Approved drawings were sent to *ateliers* for execution. Although Art Déco-style embroideries continued well into the 1930s, ideas come from all periods of art. She found inspiration everywhere—from her painting collection containing Vuillard, Renoir, Fantin-Latour, and Odilon Redon—from books, fruit, gardens, museums, travel, and costume collections. She had her own costume archives dating 1848-1925. Nothing was taken literally but interpreted. The chemise as women's dress was introduced in 1913. Her best known innovation, the *robe de style,* was an adaptation of the 18th-century pannier. Introduced in the 1920s, repeated in a variety of fabrics: silk taffeta, velvet, metallic lace with organdy, chiffon, and net. New models were presented for two decades.

She showed tea gowns, dinner pajamas, dolman wraps, hooded capes, and Zouave bloomer skirts that were either youthful, classic, or romantic. Her clear colors were subtle and feminine: begonia, fuchsia, cerise, almond green, periwinkle blue, cornflower blue. Silver was combined with black or white.

Adjusting to World War II, she created the split coat for bicycling and bright colored felt gas-mask cases. During the Liberation, she presented showings for American soldiers. Her family continued the business after her death. Antonio del Castillo, arriving in 1950, attempted to adapt to the house image. His Spanish background influenced his choice of brighter colors, light and heavy combinations of fabrics, and more severe sophisticated styles. His successor, Jules-François Crahay, returned to the collections the youthful quality which remains today.

—Betty Kirke

LAROCHE, Guy.

French designer

Born: La Rochelle, France, 16 July 1923. **Career:** Began working as a milliner, Paris; free-lance designer, New York, c.1947-50; designer, Jean Dessès, 1950-57; established first Paris salon, 1957; opened Guy Laroche couture house and introduced ready-to-wear collection, Paris, 1961; added menswear line, 1966; designed last collection, 1989. Fragrances include *Fidji,* 1967; *Eau Folle,* 1970; *J'ai Osé,* 1977; *Drakkar,* 1972; *Drakkar Noir,* 1982; *Clandestine,* 1986. Fragrance company sold to L'Oréal. **Awards:** Macy's Outstanding Creativity Award, New York, 1963; Dé d'Or Award, Paris, 1986, 1989; Chevalier de la Légion d'Honneur, 1987. *Died* (in Paris) *17 February 1989.* **Address:** 29 avenue Montaigne, 75008 Paris, France.

Publications:

On LAROCHE:

Articles

Parinaud, A. ed., "La Haute Couture intéresse-t-elle les peintres?," in *Galerie des Arts,* March 1979.
"A chacon son Dé d'Or," in *Vogue* (Paris), February 1986.
"Guy Laroche à Bordeaux: le style de l'élégance," in *Vogue* (Paris), May 1987.
[Obituary] in *The Daily Telegraph* (London), 18 February 1989.
[Obituary] in *The Independent* (London), 18 February 1989.
"Couturier Guy Laroche Dead at 67," in *Women's Wear Daily* (New York), 21 February 1989.
"Un Dé d'Or au doigt de Guy Laroche," in *Vogue* (Paris), March 1989.
Benaim, Laurence, "Une griffe demeure: Guy Laroche un grand couturier," in *Elle* (Paris), 6 March 1989.
"Guy Laroche: l'album sur mesure," in *Vogue* (Paris), April 1989.
Premoli, Francesca, "The Realm of Illusion," in *Casa Vogue* (Milan), November 1989.
Beurdeley, Laurence, "Guy Laroche: l'esprit de la Renaissance," in *L'Officiel* (Paris), August 1990.

*   *   *

Before entering the industry in the 1940s, Guy Laroche had no formal training in fashion design. He soon, however, built up a varied portfolio of experience, beginning with styling and millinery in New York followed by work in fashion and merchandising on Seventh Avenue. Returning to Paris he was offered a job as design assistant at the fashion house of Jean Dessès. Dessès was famous for designing the stole and distinctive, draped chiffon evening gowns in striking colours. He also designed one of the first diffusion lines in 1950 and this marked the beginning of ready-to-wear in French

Guy Laroche: Prêt-à-Porter Fall/Winter 1994/95; kimono-sleeved red herringbone wool pea-jacket over stretch wool suit. *Photograph by William Laxton.*

haute couture. Guy Laroche was involved in these innovations and in 1955 travelled to the United States to study new fabrication methods for ready-to wear.

He opened his own couture house in 1957 at the age of 34. The first collection, shown in his apartment, was one of subtle sophistication, reminiscent of Balenciaga's restrained elegance: simple tops that spread into huge bouffant skirts with baroque inspired, twisted drapes, or relaxed short evening dresses in black silk chiffon, with elegant capes bordered in satin ribbon. Later collections were more feminine, fun, and younger in feel: short puffed hems and schoolgirl dresses or delicate gathered drapes and scallop-effect necklines. Guy Laroche clothes were particularly noted for their skilful cutting and tailoring.

By the early 1960s Laroche had launched a ready-to-wear line and opened a boutique. His reputation as a creative but shrewd businessman grew as his company expanded. Capitalizing on his following amongst actresses and socialites, the company moved swiftly into licensing and perfumes. The major perfume, *Fidji,* was introduced in 1967 to immediate success and the men's aftershave *Drakkar Noir* was introduced in 1982, to complement the previously established men's ready-to-wear clothing.

Licensed goods promoted the reputation of the Guy Laroche name internationally, particularly in the lucrative Middle Eastern markets where the allure of Paris on a label sells goods. Lingerie, nightwear, hats, ties, bags, scarves, and jersey knits are exported, or sold today through around boutiques opened by the company worldwide.

During the late 1960s, Guy Laroche sold a large amount of shares in his business to Bernard Cornfeld and to L'Oréal, the hair and beauty product manufacturers. The perfume side of the business then became a division of the L'Oréal beauty company. The company has also developed over 250 worldwide licences throughout Europe, Asia, and South America.

—Kevin Almond

LARS, Byron.
American designer

Born: Oakland, California, 19 January 1965. **Education:** Studied at the Brooks Fashion Institute, Long Beach, California, 1983-85, and at the Fashion Institute of Technology, New York, 1986-87; selected to represent USA at the International Concours des Jeunes Créateurs de Mode, Paris, 1986, and at the Festival du Lin, Monte Carlo, 1989. **Career:** Free-lance sketcher and pattern maker, Kevan Hall, Gary Gatyas, Ronaldus Shamask, Nancy Crystal Blouse Co., New York, 1986-91. Showed first collection, 1991; also designer, En Vogue fashion collection, from 1993. **Exhibitions:** *Byron Lars' Illustrations,* Ambassador Gallery, New York, 1992. **Awards:** *Vogue* Cecil Beaton Award for illustration, London, 1990. **Address:** 202 West 40th Street, New York, New York 10018, USA.

Publications:

On LARS:

Articles

White, Constance C. R., "Rookie of the Year," in *Women's Wear Daily* (New York), 24 April 1991.
"Great Expectations," in *Women's Wear Daily* (New York), 12 June 1991.
Washington, Elsie B., "Now: Brothers on Seventh Avenue," in *Essence,* November 1991.
Gerber, Robert, "Byron Lars: Elmer Fudd Fab," in *Interview* (New York), December 1991.
"Byron Takes Off," in *Women's Wear Daily* (New York), 15 April 1992.
Schiro, Anne-Marie, "The Sweet Smile of Success," in the *New York Times,* 7 June 1992.
Walt, Vivienne, "From Rags to Riches," in the *San Francisco Examiner,* 9 August 1992.
Piaggi, Anna, "By Air," in *Vogue* (Milan), August 1992.
Jaffe, Deborah, "Great Style," in *Elle* (New York), September 1992.
Baker, Martha, "(Byronic) Poses," in *New York,* 12 October 1992.
"Designer Dish," in *Women's Wear Daily* (New York), 29 March 1993.
"New York: Bryon Lars," in *Women's Wear Daily* (New York), 4 April 1995.

Byron Lars.

*   *   *

The career of Byron Lars took wing with his fall 1992 collection inspired by legendary aviatrix Amelia Earhart, but Lars had already been for several years one of the most closely watched and praised newcomers in New York. If the fall 1992 collection consolidated his reputation (and not coincidentally his business circumstances, including backing from C. Itoh & Company), it was built on the same strengths that had characterized his earlier work. Appropriating from menswear, with a special interest in the man's dress shirt and in stripes and patterns especially associated with menswear, melding isolated elements of exaggeration with conventional dress in a dry irony, and responding concomitantly to high fashion and street influences, Lars has developed a signature style while still in his twenties. According to Anne-Marie Schiro (*New York Times,* 7 June 1992), stores "love his clothes, which can be quirky yet classic, streetwise but never vulgar. His inspiration may come from baseball or aviation, from rappers or schoolgirls. And the accessories are outrageous: caps with oversize crowns and two-foot-long peaks, lunch boxes or boom boxes as handbags. They make you smile." The references of Lars's clothing are easily identified and wholly likable in a quintessentially American mix of the orthodox and heretical, a flip view of fashion history and sources that can take the most wonderful plaids of the north woods and bring them into urban baseball-cap insouciance. A fall 1992 greatcoat with airplanes and parachutes bespeaks East Asia in the simplicity of its design and in the integrity of its shaping into the trajectories of the planes.

The designer Jeffrey Banks called Lars "the African-American Christian Francis Roth," relating Lars's visual resolution of content incongruity to Roth's paradoxes of sophisticated innocence in clothing. Roth and Lars share yet another characteristic: they are both consummate masters of the cut, enjoying the construction of the garment almost in the manner of the couture. Lars is not making a mere joke of the man's shirt cross-dressed for a woman, but takes the shirt tail as a constructive element, reshapes the bust, and deconstructs, as it were, the man's shirt to be worn by a woman. It is as much a *tour de force* in construction as it is an apt idea of 1990s gender transaction. If Byron Lars's clothes were merely facetious, they would succeed as great fun. But they succeed as great fashion because they are beautifully cut.

In adapting menswear, Lars is attentive to feminine outcomes, offering a kind of enhanced sensuality in the presence of male and female in one garment. In many instances, peplums emphasize waist and hips (but not with the 1980s power look) and the sartorial nuancing of shirt and jacket for women directs attention to a broadened expanse of the bust. Often including even the man's tie, the result is unequivocally feminine when Lars includes a built-in bra for shaping. Even as he used airplane motifs in textiles in his epochal fall 1992 collection, his fantasy was not a little boy's: aviator jackets had a curvaceous femininity approximating Azzedine Alaia (also taking advantage of exposed seams as force lines and body-hugging allure); shorts, short skirts, and leggings emphasized the female. A duck hunter's outfit in plaid (with a duck decoy made into a handbag), seemingly destined for the L.L. Bean catalog before a perverse, savvy drollery rendered it chic, was featured in the "Tribute to the Black Fashion Museum" exhibition at the Fashion Institute of Technology, New York, in spring 1992.

Even before the Earhart collection, Lars was influenced by the 1940s. His twists of menswear in the best Rosie-the-Riveter tradition, and his fascination with the sarong, recall the period. Both shirts and sarongs depend upon tying, a sense of the improvised wrap, that the designer builds into the garment, but may read for the viewer as a kind of improvisation. In this, Lars also has a great antecedent in Claire McCardell, whose lifelong interest in casual wraps is similar to Lars's fascination with the shaping and informality afforded by tying.

If still a prodigy today, Lars began as a fashion designer in tenth grade when he designed the baggy pants he wanted for himself. Little more than a decade later, Lars is making clever yet important clothes, wearable ideas, wondrous social transplants and mutations, and some of the most sensitively and sensuously cut garments in America.

—Richard Martin

LAUG, André.

French designer working in Italy

Born: Alsace, France, 29 December 1931. **Career:** Moved to Paris, 1958, to begin working for Raphäel fashion house; designer, Nina Ricci, Paris, early 1960s. Worked free-lance, from 1962, selling designs to Venet; also collaborating with Courrèges until 1963, when he moved to Rome. Designed nine collections of haute couture and five of ready-to-wear for Maria Antonelli, 1964-68; opened own couture house and showed own collection, Rome, 1968. *Died* (in Rome) *December 1984.* House continued after his death. **Address:** 81 Piazza di Spagna, 00187 Rome, Italy.

Publications:

On LAUG:

Books

Lambert, Eleanor, *World of Fashion: People, Places, Resources,* New York 1976.
Soli, Pia, *Il genio antipatico,* Milan 1984.

Articles

McEvoy, Marian, "Rome Laurels to Laug, Valentino," in *Women's Wear Daily* (New York), 20 July 1978.
Talley, André Leon, "André Laug," in *Vogue* (Paris), December/January 1980-81.
Morris, Bernadine, "André Laug, Stylist ...," [obituary] in the *New York Times,* 18 December 1984.
"André Laug: chiaro, lieve con quel preciso stile," in *Vogue* (Milan), March 1987.
"Roma alta moda: André Laug," in *Vogue* (Milan), March 1988.

*   *   *

Women's Wear Daily (20 July 1978) reported on a retailer's response to André Laug's couture collection: "The suits, the suits, the suits. His suits are divine. I love everything in black and black with gray—and there's a lot of it. These clothes are so neat, so technically perfect, so sharp. I could not be happier." For the client of keenest interest in impeccable tailoring along with a kind of restraint and temperate elegance about her style, Laug was the perfect expression of the Roman couture. From the 1960s until his death in 1984, Laug produced definitive collections of Roman style combining expertise in tailoring and the richest materials with a sober moderation.

For the American clientèle in particular, his suits held a *Daisy Miller* enchantment in an equilibrium between European sensuality and luxury and American simplicity. Americans may have, in general, expected the fireworks of extravagant Roman couture in the 1970s, but Laug provided an aesthetic closer to *Roman Holiday,* a reserved beauty. Moreover, the designer's success in the couture occasioned a lively, if somewhat less characteristic, ready-to-wear business in the late 1970s and 1980s.

Tailored clothing by Laug was sufficiently elegant to move from cocktails to evening. A simple Laug black jacket with mushroom-like shoulders could have worked for daywear, but clearly would pass as evening dress. In his final collection, a charcoal quilted wool and silk evening jacket with black velvet trousers could have sufficed for an elegant day as much as for evening. Laug knew the ethos of casual clothing in the 1970s and created an eveningwear that accommodated the social change of the period toward informality. His American clientèle was typically old-guard and even conservative, the high-quality and high-comfort sense of the Philadelphia

Main Line (his discreet good taste sold especially well at Nan Duskin in Philadelphia). As Bernadine Morris noted, "His designs were not the spectacular kind that change the shape of fashion. They were conservative day and evening clothes, which made women feel comfortable. They reflected the way Mr. Laug himself dressed, like a banker."

Trustworthy chic of Laug's kind has often been compared to men's wear in opposition to the fluctuations of women's fashion in the 1970s. By avoiding excess, in allowing for a mix of day and evening elements, Laug allowed his clients to develop a sensible, abiding wardrobe. Like menswear, trousers and jackets were basic for both day and evening. Jackets were clearly tailored for women with a defined waist. Ironically, Laug's design interests and his personal sense of forbearance were pursued by many other designers by the time of Laug's death at the age of 53. His love of black was almost the same as the prevalence of fashion black in the 1980s. The swanky luxury of Laug's understated garments began with the textiles, lining jackets with rich and vivid textiles that inflect the relative moderation of the exterior. Further, the abstemious chic of a Laug suit would assume apparent luxury as accompanied by its silk blouse.

In the subtle distinctions among those designers who influence their colleagues and establish wardrobes for the most stylish women, as opposed to the most flamboyant and visible, André Laug represents the achievement of fashion as a well-bred, well-made design art. His catwalk shows were extravagant and showy, but not so the clothing. He sought no vanguard and claimed no new invention, but he made undeniably beautiful clothing for the most selective clients practicing a lifestyle of utmost urbanity and discretion.

—Richard Martin

LAUREN, Ralph.

American designer

Born: Ralph Lifschitz, in the Bronx, New York, 14 October 1939. **Education:** Studied business science, City College of New York, late 1950s. **Military Service:** Served in the U.S. Army, 1962-64. **Family:** Married Ricky Low-Beer, c. 1964; children: Andrew, David, and Dylan. **Career:** Part-time sales assistant, Alexanders stores, New York, 1956-57; assistant menswear buyer, Allied Stores, New York, 1958-61; salesman, Bloomingdale's and Brooks Brothers, New York, 1962; road salesman in New England for A. Rivetz neckwear manufacturer, Boston, c.1964-66; designer, Polo Neckwear Division, Beau Brummel, New York, 1967; founder, designer and chairman, Polo Fashions, New York, from 1968; Ralph Lauren Womenswear, from 1971; Polo Leather Goods, from 1979; Polo/Ralph Lauren Luggage, from 1982; Polo Ralph Lauren Corp., from 1986; diffusion line, Chaps, introduced 1972; Ralph, Double RL, and Polo Sport lines introduced, 1993; established Polo/Ralph Lauren stores in Beverly Hills, 1971, Lawrence, Massachusetts, 1983, Paris, 1986, flagship store in New York, 1986, Costa Mesa, California, 1987, East Hampton, New York, 1989; Polo Sport, New York, 1993; launched fragrances *Polo* and *Lauren*, 1978, *Chaps* and *Tuxedo*, 1979, *Safari*, 1990, *Polo Crest*, 1991. **Exhibitions:** Retrospective, Denver Art Museum, Colorado, 1983. **Collection:** Fashion Institute of Technology, New York. **Awards:** Coty American Fashion Critics Award, 1970, 1973, 1974, 1976, 1977, 1981, 1984;

Neiman Marcus Distinguished Service Award, 1971; American Printed Fabrics Council "Tommy" Award, 1977; Council of Fashion Designers of America Award, 1981; Coty Hall of Fame Award, 1981; Retailer of the Year Award, 1986, 1992; Museum of American Folk Art Pioneering Excellence Award, 1988; Council of Fashion Designers of America Lifetime Achievement Award, 1992; Woolmark Award, 1992. **Address:** 650 Madison Avenue, New York, New York 10022, USA.

Publications:

On LAUREN:

Books

Morris, Bernadine, and Barbara Walz, *The Fashion Makers,* New York 1978.
Diamondstein, Barbaralee, *Fashion: The Inside Story,* New York 1985.
Milbank, Caroline Rennolds, *Couture: The Great Designers,* New York 1985.
Perschetz, Lois, ed., *W, The Designing Life,* New York 1987.
Coleridge, Nicholas, *The Fashion Conspiracy,* London 1988.
Milbank, Caroline Rennolds, *New York Fashion: The Evolution of American Style,* New York 1989.

Articles

Wohlfert, Lee, "What Do Woody, Bob and Diane Have in Common?
Money, Yes, But Designer Ralph Lauren Too," in *People,* 6 February 1978.
Ling, F., "Ralph Lauren's Polo Game," in *Forbes* (New York), 26 June 1978.
"Profile of a Designer: Ralph Lauren," in *The Sunday Times* (London), 13 September 1981.
Langway, L. and L. R. Prout, "Lauren's Frontier Chic," in *Newsweek* (New York), 21 September 1981.
Ettorre, Barbara, "'Give Ralph Lauren All the Jets He Wants,'" in *Forbes,* 28 February 1983.
"Beyond the Name Game: New Design World from Halston and Ralph Lauren," in *Vogue,* September 1983.
Feretti, Fred, "The Business of Being Ralph Lauren," in the *New York Times Magazine,* 18 September 1983.
Trachtenberg, Jeffrey A., "You Are What You Wear," in *Forbes,* 21 April 1986.
Cocks, Jay, "Born and Worn in the U.S.A.," in *Time,* 16 June 1986.
Infantino, Vivian, "Interview: Ralph Lauren," in *Footwear News* (New York), July 1986.
Koepp, Stephen, "Selling a Dream of Elegance and the Good Life," in *Time,* 1 September 1986.
Skenazy, Lenore, "Lauren Gets Honorable Mansion," in *Advertising Age,* 20 October 1986.
Tornabene, Lyn, "The World According to Ralph Lauren," in *Cosmopolitan,* February 1987.
Brubach, Holly, "Ralph Lauren's Achievement," in *Atlantic Monthly* (Boston), August 1987.
"Ralph Lauren: The Dream Maker," in *U.S. News & World Report,* 8 February 1988.
"Ralph Lauren à la coquete du vrai," in *Vogue* (Paris), October 1988.

Aronson, Steven M. L., "High Style in Jamaica," in *House & Garden,* October 1988.

Dowling, Claudia Glenn, "Ralph Lauren," in *Life,* May 1989.

Agins, Terry, "Clothing Makers Don Retailers' Garb, Manufacturers Open Stores, Irk Main Oulets," in *Wall Street Journal,* 13 July 1989.

"A Big Time Safari for Ralph Lauren," in *Women's Wear Daily,* 27 October 1989.

Mower, Sarah, "The Unspeakable Chic of Summer," in *The Independent* (London), 19 April 1990.

Hume, Marion, "In the Swing," in *The Sunday Times* (London), 29 April 1990.

Parola, Robert, "Polo/Ralph Lauren," in *Daily News Record,* 17 October 1990.

Parola, Robert, "Polo/Ralph Lauren: At the Crossroads," in *Daily News Record,* 29 October 1990.

Buck, Joan Juliet, "Everybody's All-American," in *Vogue* (New York), February 1991.

"Reed & Barton/Ralph Lauren Ties: Flatware from Resource to Add New Dimension to Noted Designer's Home Collection," in *HFD,* 18 February 1991.

Spevack, Rachel, "Polo and Izod: Adding New Luster to Knit Logos," in *Daily News Record,* 12 March 1991.

Agins, Terry, "Izod Lacoste Gets Restyled and Repriced," in *Wall Street Journal,* 22 July 1991.

Born, Pete, "Polo Crest Takes Fashion Approach to Fragrance," in *Daily News Record,* 26 July 1991.

Forbes, Malcolm S., Jr., "Dressing Us with His Dreams," in *Forbes* (New York), 2 September 1991.

Slonim, Jeffrey, "Ralph Lauren: October 14," in *Interview* (New York), October 1991.

Talley, Andre Leon, "Everybody's All-American," in *Vogue,* February 1992.

Born, Pete, "New Men's Lauren Fragrance to Debut," in *Daily News Record,* 6 March 1992.

Siroto, Janet, "Ralph Lauren—Looking Back," in *Mademoiselle,* May 1992.

Born, Pete, "Lauren Hits TV Trail for Men's Safari," in *Women's Wear Daily,* 21 August 1992.

Mander, Lois, "Safari for Men by Ralph Lauren Off to a Powerful Start," in *PR Newswire,* 18 September 1992.

Moin, David, "Ralph Lauren Is Back at Saks in a Big Way," in *Women's Wear Daily,* 14 October 1992.

Donaton, Scott, and Pat Sloan, "Ralph Lauren Sets Magazine Test," in *Advertising Age,* 2 November 1992.

Gross, Michael, "The American Dream," in *New York,* 21 December 1992.

Goldman, Kevin, "More Made-in-the-USA Claims, Surprisingly, Are Showing Up," in *Wall Street Journal,* 15 January 1993.

Gross, Michael, "Ralph's World," in *New York,* 20 September 1993.

Mower, Sarah, "Ralph Lauren's New World of Sport," in *Harper's Bazaar* (New York), October 1993.

Hirshey, Gerri, "The Snooty Dame at the Block Party," in the *New York Times Magazine,* 24 October 1993.

Rutberg, Sidney, "Goldman, Sachs buys into Ralph," in *Women's Wear Daily,* 24 August 1994.

Gill, Brendan, "Lauren's Home Movies," in *The New Yorker,* 7 November 1994.

Schiro, Anne-Marie, "Ralph Lauren Does What He Does Best," in the *New York Times,* 6 April 1995.

Menkes, Suzy, "Lauren: An Oscar for Polish," in the *International Herald Tribune,* 8-9 April 1995.

"Einer fur alle: Ralph Lauren, der Lifestyle-Spezialist," in *Vogue Manner* (Munich), April 1995.

*   *   *

Style, as opposed to fashion, is the major imperative underlying Ralph Lauren's work. Initially a designer of the high-quality ties that started the Polo label, Lauren soon directed his talents to menswear. Inspired by such notable dressers as the Duke of Windsor, Cary Grant, and Fred Astaire, he began to produce classic lines derivative of the elegant man-about-town or the country squire of a bygone age. A love of the fashions of the F. Scott Fitzgerald era led him to introduce wide neckties and bold shirt patterns. In 1974 he achieved world acclaim as the designer of the men's fashions in the film version of F. Scott Fitzgerald's novel *The Great Gatsby.*

When he turned to womenswear, he applied the same qualities of timeless elegance to his designs. By using uniformly high-quality tweeds, by tailoring down men's trousers and jackets, and by producing shirts in finer cottons, Lauren created clothes for the active woman of the 1970s, as epitomized in the Annie Hall look. These classic, tailored garments have changed little since they were first introduced but continue to epitomize long-lasting quality and style.

Another side of Ralph Lauren is seen in his Roughwear. Directly inspired by the tradition of America's past, this takes the form of long tweed or plain skirts combined with colorful, hand-knitted, Fair Isle or sampler sweaters, tartan scarves, trilby hats, and lumberjack's wind cheaters and brushed cotton shirts. The origins are easy to trace, but the result is an updated, truly American style. Romantic touches of Edwardian and Victorian times occur in lace-trimmed jabots and large collars delicately held together with aging cameo brooches. Shades of the classic English riding costume appear in his tailored tweed jackets. Lauren's contribution to fashion can perhaps best be summed up on the names that he gave to his cosmetics introduced in 1981: "Day," "Night," and "Active."

In the 1990s he continued to tune into contemporary life. The Double RL label featured new, high quality clothes that looked old as a response to the craze for the vintage and second hand. For increasingly fitness-conscious women he produced informal clothes with a strong fashion input.

His skill and experience has enabled him to design for women and men, their children, and their homes. The Rhinelander store on Madison Avenue, New York City, reflects his total lifestyle approach. As a native New Yorker, Lauren has promoted a truly American casual style in his prairie look, while developing classic, uncluttered lines that have brought him international fame along with his colleagues Calvin Klein and Perry Ellis. For Ralph Lauren, fashion is something that lasts for more than one season. It is this timelessness, abetted by inspirations deep in the soil of America's past, that distinguishes his work and won him a Lifetime Achievement award from the Council of Fashion Designers of America in 1992.

—Hazel Clark

———

LAURENT, Yves Saint. See **SAINT LAURENT, Yves.**

———

LEATHERS, Peter. See **PETER HOGGARD.**

———

LEE, Mickey.

Chinese designer

Education: Graduated in Commercial and Industrial Design from the Hong Kong Polytechnic, 1973, Interior Design from Leeds Polytechnic, England, 1976, and Advanced Fashion and Illustration, at St. Martin's School of Art and Design, London, 1977. **Career:** Fashion designer for various Hong Kong garment manufacturers, 1978-83. Established own design studio, mainly providing fashion design and illustrations for promotional projects, 1983. Fashion Consultant, then Head of Design and Merchandise, for Hwa Kay Thai Development Company, managing design, merchandising, and promotion of company's Puma projects, and graphic and interior designer of Puma boutiques. Director and Fashion Consultant of own company Highmax International Ltd; launched fashion and lifestyle product range for young people, Living Basic. **Address:** Highmax International Ltd, 13/F Zoroastrian Building, 101 Leighton Road, Hong Kong.

Publications:

On PUMA:

Articles

"The Puma Suede," in the *New York Times,* 21 February 1993.
"Doyle Swaps Sneaker Accounts," in the *New York Times,* 29 April 1994.
"Puma AG: Pretax Profit Is Reported for Year's First Five Months," in the *Wall Street Journal* (New York), 21 June 1994.

*   *   *

In 1983 Hwa Kay Thai (Hong Kong) Limited bought the design and merchandising licence for Puma Hong Kong from the German parent body. Mickey Lee was employed as their design consultant and so began a design success story. The business has expanded geographically to encompass Thailand, Singapore, and China and the product range has developed likewise. Mickey Lee has taken Puma from basic sportswear into a complete range of leisurewear and accessories. He has created the concept of a healthy and energetic lifestyle especially for Hong Kong young people. "Live the Puma life" is the slogan which represents the direction.

Mickey Lee became director, in charge of the design of the products, their merchandising, and the window display of the Puma shops. He had five assistants to help him with fashion. For the greater part of his time with the company he did most of the designing, consisting of two annual fashion collections and an accessory collection, plus promotional material. He spearheaded the creation of a market-oriented image which is very different from the German original. Germany now controls only the quality of the workmanship and influences technological aspects, like the composition of sports shoes.

From the original tracksuits and swimsuits, the range developed to include jeans and other forms of leisurewear. The clothes are medium priced and mass-market; functional, but enlivened with fashion details and up-to-date cutting. The original tennis bags gave way to lively accessories suited to the particular demands of Hong Kong. Backpacks and weekend bags in bright colours or sensible black are much in demand in a place where people tend to go away for short trips, perhaps to nearby Macau or China. Eighty per cent of the merchandise is for men. Black and white are the staple colours, with sprinklings of the seasonal colour trends. The image is masculine and sporty and the womenswear aims to project a feminine, but equally healthy look. Mickey Lee pays attention to international design directions, but does not consciously follow trends. His strongest inspiration comes from Japan, whose young people provide style models for Hong Kong.

Puma offers a totally coordinated image—everything relates. The garments and accessories have their own colour scheme, characterized by brights. Hong Kong was the first place to open the Puma boutiques. Here one experiences the full impact of Mickey Lee's total design image. He was also responsible for the promotional material. The television commercials and brochures have an annual theme; set in far away locations such as Kenya, Egypt, or Moscow, they are exciting and create an impact. Mickey Lee has complete artistic control. His varied background before coming to the company, in graphic, interior, and fashion designs has served Puma well. He credits himself with developing the swimsuit, jeans, and accessory ranges, but this is under-playing his influence. Mickey Lee has developed the company's profits by creating a lively design image. It has proved just right for its target market, but it is strong enough to be equally successful further afield.

—Hazel Clark

LÉGER, Hervé.

French fashion designer

Born: Bapaume, Pas de Calais, France, 1957. **Education:** Studied Arts Plastiques in Paris until 1975. **Career:** Designed hats for Venus et Neptune, Pablo Delia, Dick Brandsma, 1975-77; assistant for Tan Giudicelli, couture and ready-to-wear, 1977-80; assistant to Karl Lagerfeld, furs, ready-to-wear, swimsuits and accessories at Fendi, Rome, 1980-82; designer Chanel, 1982-83; designer for Cadette, Milan, 1983-85; founded own company, MCH Diffusion, 1985; opened boutique in rue Pelican, Paris, assistant at Lanvin for couture and ready-to-wear, and assistant to Dianne von Furstenberg, 1985; designed fur collection for Chloé, 1987; designed accessory collection for Swarovski (Vattens, Austria), 1988-92; same year designed ready-to-wear collections for Charles Jourdan; partnership with Mumm, 1992; first ready-to-wear collection for Hervé Léger SA, 1993. Also: designed theatre costumes for *The Troyens,* Milan, 1992, and *Trois Ballets,* Opéra de Paris, 1994. **Address:** 29, rue de Faubourg Saint-Honoré, 75008 Paris, France.

Publications:

On LÉGER:

Articles

Elle (New York), July 1990.

Hervé Léger.

"Day for Night Body Dresses Make All the Right Moves," in *Elle* (New York), May 1991.

Frankfurt Allemein, 15 October 1993.

Elle (Paris), 30 November 1993.

Deitch, Brian, "Herve's Legerdemain," in *Women's Fashion Europe,* December/January 1993-94.

Quick, Harriet, "Leger Wear," in *Elle* (London), April 1994.

Doe, Tamasin, "Splashing Out on That Curvy Feeling," in the *Evening Standard* (London), 21 June 1994.

*

In interviews I try systematically to dodge the connotation "artist, designer." The French word *créateur* seems to me particularly bombastic. I usually avoid theories on fashion in terms of "art" and I hate definitions on style. On the other hand I always insist on the quality of my work. People will always appreciate quality. Quoting Madeleine Vionnet, to her niece, I used to say, "we are not rich enough to buy cheap."

The quality "hand-sewn," "good investment," "good value," is a rather original attitude when one thinks about it. The dissertation on fashion has a tendency to glorify the short-lived, the novel, the whim, ostentatious consumption rather than the everlasting. I think it's a pity.

Two consumer types exist for me: the first, "crazy about fashion," "fashion victim," will irrevocably conform to the fashion of the designers and systematically adopt their outlook.

The second type of woman, the one I prefer, is fed up with the vagaries of fashion. She will not act as a guinea pig for the designer's "experiments." She does not give a damn about the trends, she refuses to be a feminine clothes hanger.

My fashion is made for that woman, to help her to express herself. I do not use woman to express my world vision.

—Hervé Léger

*   *   *

If any designer heralded the shift away from the deconstructed, loose, long shapes of the early 1990s it was Hervé Léger. His clothes, based on the deceptively simple principles of Lycra and Spandex-rich fabrics pulling the body into the desired hourglass shape, have made him the darling of the fashion world. Tired of the austerity of recession dressing and eager for a contrary style which would revive a sense of glamour and flatter the wearer with its overblown femininity, Léger's work has been warmly embraced both by fashion opinion makers and the rock stars, models and minor royalty who are his most publicized clients.

He takes the 1980s cliché of "underwear as outerwear" to its logical conclusion by imbuing his dresses with the properties formally associated with foundation garments: the ability to mould the body and keep it in place. They enhance the figure, metamorphosing the wearer into cartoon-like proportions with full bust and hips. If this exaggeratedly feminine image is in direct contradiction to the narrow adolescent silhouette which had preceded and, indeed, runs in parallel with Léger's vision, it has nevertheless struck a chord with women wishing to relish their sexuality and unafraid to display their redefined body in the late 20th-century equivalent to tight laced corsetry.

Chiming in with the post-feminist doctrine of Naomi Wolf and Camille Paglia, which promotes the reclaiming of the right to en-hance and emphasize the figure, this trend, labelled new glamour, is unashamed in its devotion to the female form. It is the latter which undoubtedly inspires Léger, his creations geared towards maximizing the purity of the curving lines of his models.

His most obvious predecessor is the Algerian designer Azzedine Alaia, who rose to fame in the late 1980s with his clingy Lycra creations, which Léger so clearly refers to in the overt sexiness of his own work. Léger, however, has developed the style further, exploiting the stretchy qualities of Lycra and Spandex to the full, so that the dresses are more restrictive and better able to maintain the desired shape. His signature outfits, known as "bender" dresses, are composed of narrow strips of these elastic materials combined with rayon, which are sewn horizontally like bandages to form the whole shape of the garment, sometimes with extra bands curving over the hips and across the bust to add emphasis. Even on the hanger, therefore, they have a three-dimensional quality, so reliant are they on the Olympian figure they at once create and emulate.

He produces innumerable variations of this style, all equally flattering, the fabric eliminating any faults in the figure to produce smooth hourglasses. For all their glamour his clothes avoid brashness through their lack of any unnecessary detail or decoration; their interest is in their shaping and the subtle Parisian tones in which they are produced. He concentrates on classic black, navy, white, and cream, tempered by stripes of burnt orange on halter dresses reminiscent of 1930s swimwear and delicate pastels with dark bodices.

Transforming women into Amazonian figures or goddess-like nymphs, his name has gained importance as the 1990s have progressed, especially as in the middle of the decade there is an increasing desire to express rather than obscure the potential sexuality of clothing. His dresses (and his work is predominantly the shapely one-piece) blur distinctions of day or eveningwear, since his designs are all equally glamorous.

Even when not using his moulding Lycra strips, his clothing still aspires to a feminine ideal. Full-length coats were given subtle emphasis in his autumn-winter 1994 collection—coats with curved satin inserts stretching from bust to waist set into their matt silhouettes to draw the eye to this area, held together with two tiny hooks to enable flashes of bare skin and fluid satin floor length skirts as the wearer moved. Grecian-inspired halter neck dresses with little floating chiffon skirts were also sculpted with tiny pleats to produce a similar effect.

Léger's concentration on the ability of clothing to create the desired flattering silhouette, through manipulation of fabrics and eye-arresting details, owes its legacy to his couture background. His time at great houses like Chanel, Fendi, and Chloé enabled him to witness the power of a thoughtfully-cut ensemble to transform the wearer. His homage to the goddess-like form has touched on the 1990s desire to demonstrate beauty through strong, clear lines and sexually-changed imagery which his clinging dresses so literally embody.

—Rebecca Arnold

LEHL, Jürgen.

German designer working in Japan

Born: Poland, 1944. **Education:** Trained as textile designer, 1962-66; free-lance designer in France, 1967-69; moved to New York,

1969; moved to Japan, 1971. **Career:** Textile designer, 1970-74; formed Jürgen Lehl Co., Ltd, 1973; first ready-to-wear collection, shown 1974; also designer, bed and bath Tint collection. **Exhibitions:** *Contemporary Fabric Exhibition,* Kyoto International Conference Center, 1992; *Seasonal Exhibition,* Tokyo; Cooper-Hewitt Museum, New York. **Awards:** Creative Prize, 1991; Best Advertisement Award, 1993. **Address:** 3-1-7 Kiyosumi, Koto-ku, Tokyo 135, Japan.

Publications:

On LEHL:

Books

Tadanori, Yokoo, *Made in Japan—The Textiles of Jürgen Lehl,* Tokyo 1983.
Koren, Leonard, *New Fashion Japan,* Tokyo 1984.
Martin, Richard, and Harold Koda, *Flair: Fashion Collected by Tima Chow,* New York 1992.

*   *   *

Jürgen Lehl represents a cultural amalgam that is reflected in his design philosophy. Born in Poland of German nationality, he has lived in Japan since 1970. He founded his textile design company, Jürgen Lehl Co., Ltd, in 1972, producing a ready-to-wear line of clothing in 1974.

His clothes convey united elements of both Eastern and Western fashion. In 1982 his contemporaries Yohji Yamamoto and Rei Kawakubo of Comme des Garçons founded a fashion revolution when they showed their respective collections in Paris, introducing clothes that were Asian in origin and inspiration, with few concessions to traditional Western ideas of dressing. The clothes presented a design theory that contradicted established Western modes, yet immediately became essential dressing for any serious follower of 1980s fashion.

The Japanese invasion permanently altered concepts of fashion in the West. Their clothes seemed to owe nothing to trend, reaction, or retrospection, rather a constantly evolving and refined version of the traditional *kimono* shape. Multi-layered and elaborate in its simplicity the *kimono* represents the basis of all Japanese fashion thinking.

Lehl's clothing married Eastern and Western fashion. A man's jacket in black wool from 1986 combines the notion of Western tailoring with the band neckline of a *kimono* jacket. His radical minimalism is reflected with a single button that fastens the jacket, with a simplistic buttonhole that is created logically between the band and the body of the jacket. Lehl is intellectually reductive in his approach to design, reexamining and reducing details to produce unpretentious simplicity.

Lehl is also culturally eclectic in his textile designs, introducing concepts from high art or native idioms in both Western and Asian customs. He is inspired by the unexpected. Chance discoveries of old shop signs or even an upturned shoe are applied to his design mechanism of refinement and reduction.

Japanese designers often seem subtle when compared with their Western contemporaries. Their logical, controlled approach has a mathematical precision, a calculation accurately solved. Fabric, texture, and proportion are of supreme importance to the designer. Kansai Yamamoto admits to spending as much as 70 per cent of his

Jürgen Lehl.

time working with textiles, which explains perhaps why Lehl's career expanded into clothing from his textile design origins.

When a major assessment is made of the influence of Japanese designers on contemporary fashion, it should be remembered that the East to West design passage is not all one way. Lehl represents the rare phenomenon of a Western designer working in the East.

—Kevin Almond

LEIBER, Judith.

American handbag and accessories designer

Born: Judith Peto in Budapest, 11 January 1921. **Education:** Educated in England, 1938-39; apprenticed with Hungarian Handbag Guild, 1939, became journeyman and first woman Meister. **Family:** Married Gerson Leiber in 1946. **Career:** Immigrated to the United States and moved to New York, 1947. **Exhibitions:** Designer in New York for Nettie Rosenstein, 1948-60, Richard Kort, 1960-61, and Morris Moskowitz Co., 1961-62; launched own firm, 1963. **Exhibition:** *The Artist and Artisan: Gerson and Judith Leiber,* Fine Arts Museum of Long Island, 1991. **Awards:** Swarovski Great Designer Award; Coty American Fashion Critics Award, 1973; Neiman Marcus Award, Dallas, 1980; Foundation for the Fashion Industries Award, New York, 1991; Silver Slipper Award, Houston Museum of Fine Arts Costume Institute, 1991; Handbag Designer

Judith Leiber: Alligator handbags.

of the Year Award, 1992; Council of Fashion Designers of America Award, 1993; Council of Fashion Designers of America Lifetime Achievement Award, 1994. **Address:** 20 West 33rd Street, New York, New York 10001, USA.

Publications:

On LEIBER:

Books

Martin, Richard, *The Artist & Artisan: Gerson and Judith Leiber* (exhibition catalogue), Hempstead, New York 1991.
Nemy, Enid, *Judith Leiber* (exhibition catalogue), New York 1994.

Articles

Jakobson, Cathryn, "Clutch Play: In Judith Leiber's Line of Work, the Fun Is in the Bag," in *Manhattan, Inc.* (New York), February 1986.
Newman, Jill, "Judith Leiber: The Art of the Handbag," in *Women's Wear Daily* (New York), accessories supplement, August 1986.
Harris, Leon, and Matthew Klein, "Judith's Jewels," in *Town and Country* (New York), December 1988.
Van Gelder, Lindsey, "It's in the Bag," in *Connoisseur* (New York), April 1990.
Morris, Bernadine, "Flights of Fancy Take Shape in Lush Evening Bags," in the *New York Times,* 18 December 1990.
"Houston Costume Museum to Honor Leiber Saturday," in *Women's Wear Daily* (New York), 25 January 1991.
Peacock, Mary, "The Whimsy of Judith Leiber's Handbag Designs Comes Through in the Clutch," in *Departures,* December/January 1991/92.
"Splurge," in *The New Yorker,* 25 May 1992.
Newman, Jill, "Judith Leiber; Leader in Luxury," in *Women's Wear Daily* (New York), 6 November 1992.
Newman, Jill, "British Watch Giant Buys Judith Leiber," in *Women's Wear Daily* (New York), 8 March 1993.
Menkes, Suzy, "Just a Handful of Art," in the *International Herald Tribune* (Paris), 22 November 1994.

*

I love to design beautiful objects that can be worn of course, whether it is made of alligator, ostrich, lizard or silk, or a great metal box/*minaudière* that can be held in the lady's hand. Top quality is a great concern and it pleases me greatly to keep that paramount.

Today's fashions really cry out for beautiful accessories, be they belts, handbags or great jewelry.

—Judith Leiber

*   *   *

Judith Leiber talks of herself as a technician and prides herself on the Budapest-trained craft tradition that she exemplifies and continues. But her skill and the consummate perfection of her workshop are only one aspect of the recognition of her work. She is steadfast in advancing the artistic possibility of the handbag and she is unceasing in her own artistic pursuit of the handbag. Yet, as Mary Peacock averred, "a sense of whimsy is integral to Leiber's vision" and the committed pursuit of craft is matched with a stylish wit and the cultural cleverness that is akin to craft's creativity. A Leiber handbag is aN item of expert handwork and engineering, but it is also a charm, a potent amulet, and a beguiling object of beauty.

Technique is central to the Leiber concept. A Leiber *minaudière,* for example, might seem at first glance like a Christmas tree ornament, but in technique is more like an ecclesiastical censer, an object of perfection intended for long-lasting use. Her watermelon and citrus slices are farm fresh in their juicy hand-set rhinestone design, but these are fruits that will never perish. As Cathryn Jakobson describes the sound and impeccable impact of closing a Leiber handbag, "The engineering is perfect: it is like closing the door on an excellent automobile" (*Manhattan Inc.,* February 1986). Leiber's product may be jewel-like and ladylike in scale, but Leiber collectors are rightly as proud and avid about these small objects as any possessor of a Rolls Royce. There is perhaps one drawback to the Leiber evening bags: they hold very little. But Leiber's aesthetic more than mitigates the possible problem. If going out is a matter of saddlebags and gross excess, then Leiber's sweet purses and precious objects are not the answer. But if there is any truthful measure that the best things come in small packages, Leiber's beautiful clutches make the maxim true. In fact, Leiber's characteristic evening bags compound their delicacy in scale with their solid form: these hardly seem, despite their elegance, to be places of cash and chattel. Leiber has achieved a carrier that is neither wallet nor winnings: it is something intimate and personal. Indeed, many collectors of Leiber's evening bags present them as sculptural display when they are not in service as eveningwear.

The ideas for the bags come from a variety of sources. Arguably, little is invented *ex nihilo* in Leiber's work, but is instead understood and applied from other arts to the bag. Leiber acknowledges that she loves finding objects in museums and even the objects in paintings that lend themselves to her imaginative formation as the handbag, realizing the capability of an object to serve as a container. Leiber's version of Fabergé eggs at substantial, but less than Romanov, prices are inherently about containment, but her inventions of the three-dimensional bunch of grapes or the frogs that open up or Chinese Foo dogs with hollow insides are her own invention. Leiber has also looked to the arts of the East, especially *netsuke* purse toggles, for their wondrous world of invented objects and miniatures from nature. Leiber's first jeweled evening bag was a metal teardrop purse, an ironic play on the soft shape of the purse or moneybag converted into a hard form.

Handbags by Leiber for the day employ beautiful reptile and ostrich skins, antique Japanese *obis,* and extraordinary embroider-

ies. In the daytime bags, Leiber uses not only the softest materials and a colorist's palette, even in skins, but lightens the touch with supple pleats, braid, and whimsical trims and closings. Leiber makes elegantly simple envelope bags accented by a single point or line of decoration.

Bernadine Morris says of Leiber's evening bags, "Women with an awareness of fashion consider them the finishing touch when they dress up for big evenings." (*New York Times,* 18 December 1990). The importance of Morris's observation is that the handbag is not thereby subsumed into an ensemble, but perceived as the accessory that fulfils all that has gone before in *maquillage* and dress: the finishing touch is the independent object that realizes the potential of all the preceding elements. Leiber never makes a subservient bag, but the autonomous object that, whether egg, *minaudière,* or piggy is the finality and *finesse* of style. In this, Leiber observes fashion as critically and cognizantly as she scours art for her selection of objects, but she never creates a tartan to be coordinated to a textile or a frog or other animal to fit into an established environment of garments. Rather, she creates commodities that enhance dress and create style because they are self-sufficient. Leiber creates objects that are undeniably, despite the creator's modesty, sculptures on a small scale, style at its finale, ultimate objects.

—Richard Martin

LELONG, Lucien.

French designer

Born: Paris, 11 October 1889. **Education:** Studied business, Hautes Études des Commerciales, Paris, 1911-13. **Military Service:** Performed military service, 1914-17, awarded Croix de Guerre. **Family:** Married Princess Natalie Paley (second wife). **Career:** Designed first collection, 1914; joined father's dressmaking firm, 1918; house of Lelong established, 1919; showed designs under own name, from 1923; Parfums Lucien Lelong established, 1926; Éditions Lucien Lelong ready-to-wear established, 1933; served as President of the Chambre Syndicale de la Couture, 1937-1947; retired from couture, 1948. *Died* (in Anglet, France) *10 May 1958.*

Publications:

On LELONG:

Books

Picken, Mary Brooks, and Dora L. Miller, *Dressmakers of France,* New York 1956.
Latour, Anny, *Kings of Fashion,* London 1958.
Lynam, Ruth, ed., *Couture,* Garden City, New York 1972.
Ewing, Elizabeth, *History of Twentieth Century Fashion,* New York 1974.
Howell, Georgina, *In Vogue,* Middlesex, England 1975.
Glynn, Prudence, *In Fashion,* New York 1978.
Carter, Ernestine, *Magic Names of Fashion,* Englewood Cliffs, New Jersey 1980.
Garnier, Guillaume, *Paris couture années trente,* Paris 1987.

*   *   *

While Lucien Lelong dressed many a fashionable lady during the 1920s and 1930s, he is most remembered for his heroic diplomatic efforts to sustain Parisian couture during World War II. He was, in every respect, a hero of both world wars fought during this century.

He received his call to serve during World War I two days short of showing his first collection at his father's already established dressmaker shop. He served from 1914 until 1917 when he was severely wounded. He was one of the first seven Frenchmen to be decorated with the Croix de Guerre for his heroism.

In 1918, after recuperating, he rejoined his father's firm. By 1923 he was designing under his own name. As a contemporary of such designers as Chanel, Vionnet, Molyneux, Lanvin, and Patou, he designed for café society during the 1920s and 1930s. His designs were characterized by classic lines which followed the major silhouettes of each period. He was not particularly innovative, choosing rather to concentrate on fine workmanship and fabrication. He was, however, the first designer to introduce a lower priced line—he called it Édition—to cater to less wealthy clients in 1933. During the height of his career he employed 1,200 workers.

His election as president of the Chambre Syndicale de la Couture in 1937 proved to be his greatest challenge and contribution to fashion. Faced with threats to move the entire couture to Berlin and Vienna, Lelong negotiated, cajoled, and lied to the Germans throughout the occupation of Paris. "One of the first things the Germans did was break into the Syndicate offices and seize all documents pertaining to the French export trade. I told them that *la couture* was not a transportable industry, such as bricklaying."

When not one foreign buyer appeared in Paris after war was declared, Lelong sent an emissary to New York with gowns and models to prove that couture was still a viable industry. In January 1940, despite having to be routed through Italy, 150 buyers appeared for the showings. By 1941 the Germans had issued textile cards which followed a point system to every design house. It was obvious that compliance with these regulations would spell the end of Paris couture. Lelong, through difficult negotiations, obtained exemptions for 12 houses. "Unfortunately the Germans noticed at the end of six months that 92 houses were operating, which led to more discussions. Finally we succeeded in keeping 60." Madame Grès and Balenciaga both exceeded their yardage requirements one season and were ordered to close for two weeks. Banding together in a show of unity and force, the remaining houses finished these two collections so they could be shown on time.

Lelong is credited with saving over 12,000 workers from deportation into German war industries. "Over a period of four years, we had 14 official conferences with the Germans ... at four of them they announced that *la couture* was to be entirely suppressed, and each time we avoided the catastrophe." Paris couture had won its own, private war.

Lelong, much as Hattie Carnegie did in the United States, employed talented young designers and gave them the opportunity to grow professionally. Christian Dior, Pierre Balmain, Hubert de Givenchy, Jean Ebel, Serge Kogan, and Jean Schlumberger were all employed by Lelong at one time or another. "It was from Lucien Lelong that I learned that fabrics have personality, a behavior as varied as that of a temperamental woman," said Christian Dior.

Exhausted from his efforts during the war and his earlier wounds, Lelong retired in 1948. He showed a total of 110 collections during his career. While Lucien Lelong's clothes were elegantly conceived and executed, he will be remembered as fashion's leading diplomat during the German siege on Parisian couture.

—Mary C. Elliott

LEMPICKA, Lolita.
French fashion designer

Family: (Daughter) Elisa. **Career:** Showed first collection, 1984; Lolita Bis junior line introduced, 1987; signature leather collection and lines of knitwear, jewelry, glasses introduced. Ready-to-wear designer, Cacharel. **Address:** c/o Leonor International, 78 Avenue Marceau, 75008 Paris, France.

Publications:

On LEMPICKA:

Articles

Hochswender, Woody, "Young French Designers Stretch Fashion's Rules," in the *New York Times,* 19 October 1990.

* * *

Pert, gamine, nostalgic, playful, these are just some of the words that can be used to describe Lolita Lempicka collections. Since her debut in 1984, she has reintroduced a discarded Parisian elegance to fashion. Although her look is of the moment, young and modern, it has often echoed 1940s themes and styling: turbans, pearl chokers, tiny floral prints on viscose crêpes, piping, polka dots teamed with tiny stripes, contrast trims, pearl trims, and wedged shoes. Even the sepia-coloured tones used in a distinctive promotional booklet for her 1991 spring-summer collection suggest the discovery of a utility frock, produced to the British government's austere guidelines for goods in World War II, in grandmother's attic and the subsequent restyling and alteration of the garment to give it a naughtier, more risqué 1990s feel.

Lempicka places greatest importance on the use of meticulous detailing and the finest materials from international textile manufacturers. She is renowned for her precise and exquisitely cut tailored suits that are never hard-edged and gently flatter the customer. Her look is very French and she was the first of a new generation of female designers to emerge in Paris during the 1980s. Myrène De Premonville, Martine Sitbon, and Sophie Sitbon were others who promoted a fresh Parisian femininity with a classical base.

Lempicka's business has expanded into several areas since its inception. She created a junior diffusion line, Lolita Bis, in 1987, designed for nice and naughty young girls. She dedicated the line to her daughter, Elisa, whom she described as both "cute and feminine," like Lolita Bis.

The company has expanded rapidly in the international marketplace, aided by two agreements for fabrication and distribution; one with the Guy Laroche group for the main line collection and the other with the CGP group for Lolita Bis. There are also contracts with the Rinel group for Lolita Lempicka leather collections and the Italian company Alma for knitwear. Her other lines of jewellery and eyewear are licensed by Kashiyama, which directs Lolita Lempicka boutiques in Japan.

Lempicka sees her customers as ranging from schoolgirls through to students, their mothers and grandmothers. Her clothes need to be interesting and accessible for all ages. She dresses women gently and does not compromise characteristically clever detailing and sculptured cuts to fashion's whims.

—Kevin Almond

LENOIR, Jacques. See **CHLOÉ.**

LESER, Tina.

American designer

Born: Christine Wetherill Shillard-Smith in Philadelphia, Pennsylvania, 12 December 1910. **Education:** Studied art at the Pennsylvania Academy of Fine Arts, the School of Industrial Arts, Philadelphia, and at the Sorbonne. **Family:** Married Curtin Leser in 1931 (divorced, 1936); married James J. Howley in 1948; daughter: Georgina. **Career:** Sold designs through her own shop in Honolulu, Hawaii, 1935-42; also formed a company in New York, 1941-43; designer, Edwin H. Foreman Company, New York, 1943-53; designer, Tina Leser, Inc., New York, 1953-64; designed Signet men's ties, 1949, Stafford Wear men's sportswear, 1950, and industrial uniforms for Ramsey Sportswear Company, 1953; retired briefly, 1964-66; retired permanently, 1982. **Awards:** Fashion Critics Award, New York, 1944; Neiman Marcus Award, Dallas, 1945; Coty American Fashion Critics Award, 1945; *Sports Illustrated* Sportswear Design Award, 1956, 1957; US Chamber of Commerce Citation, 1957; Philadelphia Festival of the Arts Fashion Award, 1962. Member, National Society of Arts and Letters Fashion Group. *Died* (in Sands Point, New York) *24 January 1986.*

Publications:

On LESER:

Books

Stuart, Jessie, *The American Fashion Industry,* New York 1951.
New York and Hollywood Fashion: Costume Designs from the Brooklyn Museum Collection, New York 1986.
Milbank, Caroline Rennolds, *New York Fashion: The Evolution of American Style,* New York 1989.
Steele, Valerie, *Women of Fashion,* New York 1991.

Articles

"Southern Resort Fashions," in *Life* (New York), 14 January 1946.
"Women Designers Set New Fashions," in *Life* (New York), 14 January 1946.
Robin, Toni, "Global Fashions," in *Holiday* (New York), November 1949.
"Industrial Uniforms Get Beauty Treatment," in *American Fabrics* (New York), Summer 1953.
"Tina Leser," in *Current Biography* (New York), June 1957.
"Designer Tina Leser Dies; Services Will Be Held Today," [obituary] in *Women's Wear Daily* (New York), 27 January 1986.
"Tina Leser, a Designer, Dies," [obituary] in the *New York Times,* 27 January 1986.

*   *   *

Tina Leser was an early and very successful proponent of an American design aesthetic inspired by textiles and clothing from non-Western cultures. She travelled through Asia, India, and Africa as a child, and lived in Hawaii after her first marriage in 1931, which may explain the ease with which she later adapted influences from those areas into her designs. Although she is remembered today primarily for that gift, her success was not confined to that genre, but also encompassed references to other folk and historical traditions.

Her earliest work was done in Hawaii, where she opened a shop in 1935 selling high quality ready-to-wear and playclothes of her own design. She used Hawaiian and Filipino fabrics, and even hand block-printed sailcloth. In 1940 she brought her work to New York where she was to open her own firm, but only began to be a force in fashion in 1943, when she joined the Edwin H. Foreman sportswear firm as designer.

Leser's work during World War II reflected the fabric scarcities of the wartime economy, and the limits of wartime travel. From Mexico she derived a printed flannel jacket with sequined trim; from Guatemala a strapless dress made from a handwoven blanket. Sarong-styled dresses and wrap skirts were an important part of her design vocabulary at this time, possibly stemming from her years in Hawaii. She varied these with less exotic styles, such as a tartan cotton playsuit with a matching shawl and kilted skirt, and wonderful wool flannel calf-length overalls—offspring of a very American idiom.

From the first Leser emphasized an uncluttered mode, and by the end of the war she had won awards from both Neiman Marcus and Coty for her contributions to American fashion. She had also widened her horizons to include India—very much in the news in the immediate post-war years—with her *dhoti* pants-dress, available in several versions for a variety of occasions. The facility with which she could adapt one model into many styles can be attributed to her artist's eye for proportion, and clean balance between line and form.

What was, in theory, an around-the-world honeymoon trip with her second husband in 1949 became, in practice, a way for Leser to collect fabrics, clothing, and antiques from a multitude of cultures. She based designs on objects as varied as an English game table, Siamese priests' robes, an Italian peasant's vest, and a Manchu coat. Her mature work, from this date on, displayed a consistent sense of humour and intelligence in her choice of references.

Her collections included many "play" pieces but also contained relaxed day and evening clothes eminently suited to the needs and budgets of many post-war American women. Her variation on the ubiquitous 1950s sweater twinset was a halter with an embellished cardigan, and she is also credited with introducing the cashmere sweater dress. Sensitivity to the realities of life for working women induced her, in 1953, to design a line of industrial uniforms for Ramsey Sportswear Co. The trim fitting separates included a skirt to be worn over uniform slacks on the way to or from work.

Her fabric choices as well as her fashion inspirations were wide-ranging. Indian sari silks, Pringle woollens, Boussac floral prints, and embroidered Moygashel linens shared her stage with cottons from Fuller fabrics' "Modern Masters" print series, Hope Skillman wovens, Galey & Lord ginghams, and Wesley Simpson prints. She championed denim as a fashion fabric, using it in 1945 for a two-piece swimsuit trimmed with chenille "bedspread flowers," in 1949 for coolie trousers and sleeveless jacket, and in the mid-1950s for a strapless bodice and wide cuffed pants. American bandanna prints or tablecloth fabrics were as likely to show up in her work as copies of Persian brocades, and they might equally be used for playsuits or cocktail dresses. One butterfly patterned batik print turned up as a swimsuit and cover-up skirt, capri trousers and strapless top, a sarong dress, and even as binding on a cardigan sweater.

Leser remained active throughout the 1960s and into the 1970s, maintaining her flair for sportswear, loungewear, and bathing suits. Some of her best pieces from this period were slim toreador or stirrup trousers worn with long, boxy sweaters or baby-doll tunics, and her coordinated bathing suits and cover-ups remained strong. The details of her designs, however, are rather less important than the spirit she brought to them. Many young American designers carry on the referential style Leser helped establish, creating, as she did, something uniquely American from a melting-pot of cultural sources.

—Madelyn Shaw

LEVI-STRAUSS & CO.

American clothing company

Founded by Levi Strauss (born in 1829). Strauss arrived in San Francisco in 1853, and began selling dry goods to gold prospectors. He made and sold "waist-high overalls" out of material originally intended for sale as tent canvas. Rivets to reinforce seams and pockets introduced, 1873. "White Levi's," jeans made of beige twill introduced, 1960s; corduroy jeans introduced, 1961; stretch jeans and Sta-Prest® slacks introduced, 1964; womenswear introduced, 1968; began manufacturing and marketing in Hong Kong, early 1970s. Company floated on stock market, 1971, with family members retaining controlling interest. Official outfitters of US Winter and Summer Olympic teams, and Los Angeles Olympic Games staff, 1984. In 1985 publicly held shares repurchased by family members. World's largest apparel manufacturer, marketing jeans, jeans-related products and casual sportswear for men, women and children in over 70 countries. **Collections:** Smithsonian Institution, Washington, DC. **Awards:** Coty Special Award, 1971. **Address:** 1155 Battery St., San Francisco, California 94111, USA. *Died in 1902.*

Publications:

On LEVI-STRAUSS & CO.:

Articles

Kurtz, Irma, "Levis: Not So Much a Pair of Pants, More a Nation's Heirloom," in *Nova* (London), September 1970.
"The F T C Gets into Levis," in *The Economist* (London), 15 May 1976.
Willat, N., "The Levitation of Levi Strauss," in *Management Today* (London), January 1977.
"Levi Strauss & Co.," in *American Fabrics & Fashions* (New York), No. 109, 1977.
"Market Manipulation: The Levis 501 Experience," in *International Textiles* (London), July 1987.
"Denim: Is the Party Over?," in *Fashion Weekly* (London), 14 January 1988.
Bradley, Lisa, "A Modest Success," in *Fashion Weekly* (London), 14 January 1988.

Simpson, Blaise, "Levi's Makes Push in Women's Wear," in *Women's Wear Daily,* 2 March 1988.
Rowlands, Penelope, "Vintage Power: Levi's," in *Women's Wear Daily* (London), 10 February 1992.
Elliott, Stuart, "The Media Business: Levi's Two New Campaigns Aim at Who Fits the Jeans," in *New York Times,* 27 July 1992.
Magiera, Marcy, and Pat Sloan, "Levi's, Lee Loosen Up for Baby Boomers," in *Advertising Age,* 3 August 1992.
"Fashion Statement," in *San Francisco Business Magazine,* October 1992.
Elliott, Stuart, "The Media Business: Going Beyond Campaigns and into Sales and Marketing," in *New York Times,* 18 November 1992.

*   *   *

Levi's are an American icon. People of all ages, from countries as diverse as Japan, Russia, and the United States wear Levi's, buying them new or used. They are valued for both their quality and design.

Levi Strauss & Co. was established in the 1850s in San Francisco, California, to sell the finest domestic and foreign dry goods, clothing, and household furnishings. Levi and his brothers Jonas

Levi-Strauss & Co.: A "classic" pair of jeans.

and Louis as well as two brothers-in-law, William Sahlein and David Stern, ran the company. They had a ready market for their wares in the goldminers, cowboys, and lumbermen, who had moved west to make their fortunes. Especially popular were their sturdy pants that stood up to the rugged work.

The pants were further improved thanks to Jacob W. Davis, a tailor who lived in Reno, Nevada. Davis sewed horse blankets, wagon covers, and tents from an off-white duck cloth bought from Levi Strauss & Co. Davis also made work clothes, though the miners and cowboys complained about pockets ripping off. As a result he tried riveting the pockets on the pants with the same copper rivets he used to attach straps to horse blankets. Using a 10 oz. duck twill Davis made more riveted trousers and, by word-of-mouth advertising, a steady business grew.

Davis could not finance the patent necessary to protect his idea so he offered Levi Strauss & Co. half the right to sell all such riveted clothing in exchange for the $68.00 patent fee. The patent was for a "fastening for pocket-openings whereby the sewed seams are prevented from ripping or starting from frequent pressure ... by the place of the hands in the pockets." It was granted to Davis and Levi Strauss & Co. of San Francisco, on 20 May 1873.

Levi Strauss & Co. made and marketed trousers, vests, and jackets using the rivets at stress points. White and brown duck twill and denim were used in the trousers Strauss called waist pantaloons or overalls, not "jeans." The term jeans referred to trousers constructed from a fabric woven in Genoa, Italy, called Genoese cloth. Denim, is derived from *serge de Nimes,* cloth of Nimes, France; the fabrics all shrunk to fit. A snug fit was desirable because wrinkles caused blisters when riding in a saddle. Suspender buttons, two in back, and four in front were used. There were no belt loops, though cinch straps and a buckle were sewn onto the back of the trousers to tighten the waist.

Strict price and quality standards were established by Levi Strauss & Co. Amoskeag, a New England mill, furnished the fabric. Orange linen thread was used for stitching because it matched copper color rivets. Two curving v's were stitched on back pockets to distinguish these pants from those of competitors. In 1942 this arcuate row of stitches became a registered clothing trademark. An oilcloth guarantee with the "Two Horse Brand" was tacked to the seat of the trousers. It had an engraving of two teamsters whipping a pair of dray horses trying to pull apart riveted trousers. In 1886 a leather label with the two horse logo was permanently affixed with orange linen thread. Due to the quality of manufacture and fabric, Strauss was able to charge 25 percent more than competitors. The original double X 10 oz. denim trousers were known as the 501, and became the hallmark to be measured against. Levi's were functional, simple and above all durable.

The company grew and evolved to meet changing economic and societal needs brought about by world wars, the Depression, and unionization of the labor force. Clothing was sized to specifically fit children as well as women; linen thread was replaced with a fine gauge version of the cord used to stitch shoes to make seams stronger; belt loops replaced suspender buttons on the original 501 design; the cinch belt was removed; 13 1/2 oz. denim was used; a zipper fly was introduced; pre-shrunk fabric was used; and the red tag Levi label was added to further distinguish the jeans from the competition. New lines of more dressy yet casual clothes were introduced. The company went public in 1971.

The mystique and marketability of Levi's received a boost when they were worn by James Dean in the movie *Rebel Without a Cause* and Marlon Brando in the *Wild One.* These pants, originally in-

tended for use by goldminers and cowboys, have become an integral part of the American way of life and are sought after by people around the world.

—Nancy House

LEWIN, Lucille. See WHISTLES.

LEY, Wolfgang and Margarethe. See ESCADA.

RENÉ LEZARD.
German fashion company

René Lezard Mode GmbH founded in 1978, Schwarzach, Wurzburg, by Thomas Schaefer. Managing directors: Schaefer and Winifred Wagner. Managing director of René Lezard womenswear, Gunter Eschemann; specialises in womenswear, sportswear, and menswear. Main lines are Classic, Excess, Sophisticated, plus Denim House. Licensee products, include shirts (Asoni), ties (Albisetti), belts (Condor), and leather accessories (Traveller). Exports to Europe, USA, and Asia. **Address:** Industriestrasse 2, D-97359 Schwarzach, Germany.

Publications:

On RENÉ LEZARD:

Articles

Erlick, June C., "René Lezard Establishes U.S. Group," in *Daily News Record* (New York), 13 August 1991.
"Jennifer Nichols Joins René Lezard Fashion Group Inc. as Director of Sales and Marketing," in *Daily News Record* (New York), 8 January 1992.
Gellers, Stan, "Suit Makers Doubling Up for Fall," in *Daily News Record* (New York), 15 April 1993.

*

Company philosophy—planned growth, team work and strong relationships with our clients are our top priorities. Product philosophy—offering a unique collection, using the highest quality fabrics available, the prerequisite for a smart mix of fashion.

—René Lezard

*   *   *

René Lezard is a medium-sized German fashion group making clothes for men and women. Neither high fashion nor cheap mass-market, René Lezard makes quality outfits and separates for High Street shops throughout Germany. Ranked 69 out of the top 100 European Fashion companies, René Lezard is a top German fash-

M0502/W2101

H0803

F1101

MODERNE
ZEITEN

René Lezard.

ion brand and company. It makes quality, everyday clothes for normal, practical lives.

The clothes have a very practical, Northern European look and feel: thick, warm, heavy-duty office, leisure, and outdoor wear, distinctively German or middle-European. The accent is on tailoring, not cut; fabrics are expensive but not flashy. The look is smart-sombre, like a Northern European city in the rain or snow.

Fabrics used include soft fleeces and refined leathers, warm corduroys and smooth velvets, thick tweeds, heavy lambswool and cashmere. Colours include all the darker shades of brown, grey, green, and blue, some dark mustard, some burgundy. The occasional item or outfit shines out in mother-of-pearl or cream. Though the styles are very classical, René Lezard does not seem particularly influenced by either English or French fashion. The overall composition is pure German, with home-grown lines and styles. Shoulders are soft; upper parts are unrestricted and loose. There are lots of buttons and buttonholes, turn-ups, dark linings, high collars. The overall look is soft and loose, dry and warm. The clothes tend to be long; jackets, coats, and waistcoats reach below the hips to half-way down the thighs. Multiple layers of comfortable clothes are de rigueur; blouson, jacket, jumper, shirt, and T-shirt for men. Outer coats, flowing waistcoat, blouse, and undershirt for women. The smart chic of the clothes comes through the choice of refined colour and fine fabric.

The range is comprehensive. For men, there are suits, jackets, vests, trousers, coats, sport jackets, shirts, neckties, belts, knitwear, T-shirt, polo-neck sweaters, and leathers. These are split into three lines: Classic, the basic elements of the collection; Excess, the young, approachable, commercial range; and Sophisticated, the fashionwear and experimental items. Similarly for women the range covers suits, trousers, skirts, blazers, coats, leatherwear, knitwear, blousons, and belts. Denim House is a mass-market brand, with jeans, shirts, jackets, and waistcoats clearly aimed at the High Street and a young adult market that buys one or more items to build or expand an existing wardrobe. In addition to the above, René Lezard uses licensee products within the collection: Asoni shirts, Albisetti ties, Condor belts, Traveller leather accessories.

René Lezard is a mass-market brand. It has some of its fabrics made in Italy, but buys in the bulk of its raw materials and creates the clothes in factories across the world. There are some shops, showcases for the collection, but no chain of boutiques. Only 30 per cent of sales in 1993 were outside of Germany, mostly to other North European countries and the United States.

Leafing through images of the collection, examining the corporate information, one is aware of dealing with a large company. No creative spark shines through the corporate press releases; charisma, flair, and imagination seem lost, as if smothered by bureaucracy, in the same way that René Lezard models are smothered in layers of clothes.

—Sally Anne Melia

LIBERTY OF LONDON.

British department store

Founded by Arthur Lazenby Liberty (1843-1917), as oriental import emporium, "East India House," 218A Regent Street, London,

1875; expanded, 1876, 1878, 1883, 1924. Liberty Art Fabrics produced, from 1878; Umritza Cashmere introduced, 1879; opened furnishing and decoration department, 1883; opened costume department, 1884; opened jewellery and metalwork department, 1899; opened Birmingham branch, 1887; opened Paris branch, 1890; became public company, 1894; Manchester branch opened, 1924; Liberty and Company, Ltd., wholesale company established, 1939; acquired Dutch firm, Metz and Company, 1973. **Exhibitions:** *Liberty's, 1875-1975,* Victoria and Albert Museum, London, 1975. Awards: Silver Medal, Rational Dress Exhibition, 1883; Gold Medal, Amsterdam Exhibition of 1883; Arthur Lazenby Liberty received knighthood, 1913. **Address:** Regent Street, London W1R 6AH, England.

Publications:

By LIBERTY

Periodicals

Aglaia (journal of the Healthy and Artistic Dress Union), 1894.
Liberty Lamp (in-house magazine), 1925-1932.

On LIBERTY:

Books

Laver, James, *The Liberty Story,* London 1959.
Adburgham, Alison, *Liberty's: A Biography of a Shop,* London 1975.
Liberty's 1875-1975 (exhibition catalogue), London 1975.
The Liberty Style, London 1979.
Milbank, Caroline Rennolds, *Couture: The Great Designers,* New York 1985.
Levy, Mervyn, *Liberty Style, The Classic Years: 1898-1910,* London 1986.
Morris, Barbara, *Liberty Design, 1874-1914,* London 1989.
Calloway, Stephen, ed., *The House of Liberty. Masters of Style and Decoration,* London 1992.

Articles

Amaya, Victor, "Liberty and the Modern Style," in *Apollo* (London), February 1963.
Boyd, A., and P. Radford, "The Draper Who Made History," in *The Observer Magazine* (London), 6 April 1975.
Williams, Antonia, "Liberty Quality Centenary: At the Sign of the Purple Feather," in *Vogue* (London), June 1975.
Banham, Reyner, "A Dead Liberty," in *New Society* (London), 7 August 1975.
Nichols, Sarah, "Arthur Lazenby Liberty: A Mere Adjective?," in the *Journal of Decorative and Propaganda Arts* (Miami, Florida), Summer 1989.

*   *   *

Sir Arthur Lazenby Liberty, the founder of Liberty of London, contributed in 1894 to the Healthy and Artistic Dress Union's journal *Aglaia,* which stated clearly that his declared aim was to "promote improvements in dress that would make it consistent with health, comfort and healthy appearance, but [dress] should not obviously depart from the conventional mode." Lazenby Liberty had left the Oriental Warehouse of Messrs Farmer and Rogers, famous among the leading artists and aesthetes of the day for its collections of blue and white porcelain and oriental fabrics in 1874 to set up on his own in half a shop in London's Regent Street. Lazenby Liberty presided over the shop's transformation from an Eastern bazaar to a department store which commissioned and sold modern design of all kinds.

"Liberty art fabrics" in subtle tones which soon became known worldwide as "Liberty colours" (produced in collaboration from 1878 with the dyers and printers Thomas Wardle) were the first step towards the creation of the shop's new image and, by the end of the century, *Stile Liberty* was synonymous in Italy with art nouveau. The quintessential fabric of the Aesthetic Movement was Liberty or Art silk and, aided by such popular successes as the Gilbert and Sullivan opera *Patience* (where the clothes were made from Liberty fabrics and Liberty artistic silks were advertised in the programme), and the cartoons of George du Maurier, Liberty was soon to become a household name.

In 1884 Arthur Lazenby Liberty opened the Costume Department, appointing as its first director the celebrated architect E. W. E. Godwin, whom Oscar Wilde once described as being "the greatest aesthete of us all." Godwin had made a study of historic dress and approached his task with almost missionary zeal, aiming to "establish the of dressmaking fame hygienic, intelligible and progressive basis."

Godwin's death three years later did not mean the end of his influence on Liberty dress, and the catalogues show a wide range of Liberty Art Costumes, ranging from a Grecian costume in Arabian Cotton, to a peasant dress in thin Umritza Cashmere, embroidered and smocked (a skill revived by Liberty and used on the finest materials). Smocking was also a striking feature of the Kate Greenaway-influenced Artistic Dress for Children, a range of clothes hugely popular with Liberty's customers from the late 1880s onwards.

In the present century Liberty fabrics have been used by the best known designers of each decade, from Paul Poiret to Yves Saint Laurent, from Cacharel to Jean Muir. The famous Liberty silk scarves and ties are sold all over the world, and the distinctive fabrics are still used by home-dressmakers to create their own "Liberty style" in a fashion familiar from the time of their 19th-century forebears. Liberty has also recently relaunched its own clothing collections. Liberty describes the new collections as "contemporary yet classic. Simply yet beautifully styled, they could be worn by the modern girl or she of between the wars era alike."

Of all the major London department stores, the character of Liberty's Regent Street flagship store and the quality and range of the goods it offers have changed least in recent years. In fashion terms, Liberty's offers a unique combination of its own entirely distinctive and yet ever-changing fabric and clothing designs for womenswear and menswear and the fashion collections of such distinctive contemporary designers as Nicole Farhi, Kenzo, Issey Miyake, and Paul Smith.

—Doreen Ehrlich

LINARD, Stephen.

British designer

Born: London, 1959. **Education:** Studied at Southend College of Technology, 1975-78, and at St. Martin's School of Art, London, 1978-81. **Career:** Designer, Notre Dame X, 1981-82; showed first womenswear collection, 1982; menswear line introduced, 1983; designer, Bigi, Japan; designer, Georges Sand Range for Jun Co., Japan; designer, Beyond Stephen Linard range for Bazaar; designer for Powder Blue, 1986; assistant designer, Drakes.

Publications:

On LINARD:

Articles

"Cue: Future Talent," in *Vogue* (London), October 1981.
Grieve, Amanda, "Quids In," in *Harper's and Queen* (London), April 1983.
"Da Londra: moda come provocazione eclettica," in *L'Uomo Vogue* (Milan), December 1985.

*   *   *

It would be difficult to exaggerate the impact of Stephen Linard's degree collection when his models appeared on the catwalk at St Martin's School of Art in London in the summer of 1981.

Linard was a menswear student, and his models were real men, with real muscle, stubble, tattoos, and the demeanour of East End toughs about to enter the boxing ring. The Reluctant Emigrés collection was a subtle mix of solid and transparent, the safely known and the unpredictable. Traditional pinstripe trousers had contrast patches at the *derriére;* solid dark waistcoat fronts and shadowy organza backs. Striped city shirts were seen to have curious underarm patches, and all was concealed beneath swirling black greatcoats. The clothes were instantly covetable, thoroughly masculine in an entirely new way, and electrifying in the way that only the truly innovative can be.

Linard was famous overnight, and his charisma and photogenic air ensured him an enthusiastic press. He joined a leading young design team known as Notre Dame X, with Richard Ostell and Darlajane Gilroy amongst others. When he split from this group, backers set him up in a City studio where he produced sought-after garments in esoterically-titled collections—Angels with Dirty Faces, and Les Enfants du Chemin de Fer. He was an early revivalist of bias cutting, and showed underwear as outerwear: he continued with an anarchic mix of fabrics and influences which appealed to the glam-sex clubbers always in search of new heroes, and labels with cachet. These were great days of club couture, with punters in fierce competition over their evening toilettes. New heights of sartorial extravagance were scaled, with Linard and art-world personality Leigh Bowery in the running for chief mountaineer.

British rag-trade backing is notoriously fickle, however, and when Linard's company collapsed he went to Japan to join the stable of eccentric models at Men's Bigi. The Japanese are always swiftly attracted to high-profile talent with high-profile personality, and Linard was soon designing the prestigious Georges Sand range for Jun Company selling in Japan, the Far East, and the United States. At home, he designed the Beyond Stephen Linard ranges for Bazaar in South Molton Street, London. Starting Powder Blue in 1986, he designed the Chess and Innocents Abroad collections, the latter an eclectic mix of leopard-skin, broderie Anglaise and Edwardian schoolgirls. Since teaching at Southend, his former college, and Middlesex, he has been the Assistant Designer at Drakes, producing exclusive menswear accessories in silk and cashmere.

Linard has long been involved in the fashion/music mix, designing for singers David Bowie and Boy George, and for pop groups such as Fun Boy 3, Spandau Ballet, and the Pet Shop Boys; he hosted the "Total Fashion Victims" theme nights at the Wag club, introducing Sadé and Swing Out Sister, with John Maybury's light installations. He has styled for *The Face* and interviewed for *Blitz,* two top London style magazines: in short, for more than a decade he has lived and worked a life of glamour and style.

We are now used to real men on the catwalk; some agencies—So Dam' Tuf, for example—deal in nothing else; we are used to traditional menswear with a twist, and underwear worn as outerwear. But in the early 1980s all this was new, and therein lies Linard's contribution to his time: with all the above and more, he did it first.

—Alan J. Flux

LITTMAN, Helen and Judy. See **ENGLISH ECCENTRICS.**

L.L. BEAN. See under **BEAN.**

LLOYD, Alison. See **ALLY CAPELLINO.**

LORCAN MULLANY. See **BELLVILLE SASSOON-LORCAN MULLANY.**

MA, Walter.

British designer

Born: Hong Kong, 28 August 1951. **Education:** Graduated from Hong Kong Institute of Design, 1975. **Career:** Worked for a fashion company for eight months before opening his own first boutique, Vee Boutique; now has line of seven boutiques. Labels are Gee, womenswear coordinates; Vee, classic style womenswear; Front First, young mens- and womenswear; Walter Ma, designer collection. **Address:** Gee Boutique Fashion Ltd, Room 11, 8/F, Tower 1, Harbour Centre, Hok Cheung Street, Hunghom, Kowloon, Hong Kong.

*   *   *

Walter Ma is very much a home-grown designer. Born and educated in Hong Kong, he now dresses its young and fashion conscious. One of the first graduates from Hong Kong's Institute of Fashion Design, Ma has worked consistently to establish himself as one of the foremost local designers. When he left college it was usual for graduates to work in the industry or to go abroad for further training. After a short stint working for an export company, Ma took the risky step of opening his own shop. It paid off: his boutiques, Gee and Vee, are now found in major shopping locations and his workshops employ over a hundred people.

Ma designs for three labels, Gee, Vee, and Front First. Each offers a distinct look. Vee is the most upmarket and offers sophisticated party and daywear. The clothes are feminine, detailed and dressy. Gee is an easy to wear, middle priced range aimed at the career woman. The emphasis here is on quality fabric and neutral shades which mix and match. His most recent look, Front First, is his most outrageous. It is a casual, fun line providing mainly separates for fashionable young men and women. Together they cater to the needs of Hong Kong people, from leisurewear to clothes for special occasions such as graduate parties and the annual Chinese New Year celebrations. As a consequence, Walter describes himself as being client-led. His regular customers are women whose ages range from 20 to 40 plus. "She is a career woman who knows what she wants," he says. He also designs one-off eveningwear for regular customers, who include local film stars, pop singers, and society figures.

Designing for the Hong Kong market is no easy task. It is small in scale and quite difficult to please. There is a regular demand for new items. Ma designs around a dozen basics which are produced in very small quantities, on average from six to 24 pieces per design. Comfort is always an important consideration in his work, but the clothes are not safe or dowdy. Ma's look is distinctive. The inspiration comes from European fashion capitals like Paris and Milan, modified for the local market. Pinstripes and checks are popular fabrics. Suits are a staple. Unusual cutting reveals unexpected parts of the body. His "two in one" look coalesces the ease of a single garment with the appearance of two. Combinations of black and white have become another part of his signature. This is applied, somewhat unusually, to jumpsuits and other leisurewear, rather than for business. Embroidery and beading are other constant features. Locally he has become so influential that others are mimicking his look. He regards this both as an irritation and a compliment. Copyists can threaten a designer's reputation, but they also represent the success of a look or a direction.

Ma creates fashionable clothing for a market he knows and understands. He strictly controls the quality of each garment and has a sensitivity for fabrics—his favourites are jerseys and knits which drape well. Fabrics influence the overall style and he keeps a close watch on the whole process from design to production. Others may imitate his look, but his professionalism sets him apart.

—Hazel Clark

MACKIE, Bob.

American designer

Born: Robert Gordon Mackie in Monterey Park, California, 24 March 1940. **Education:** Studied advertising and illustration at Pasadena City College, c.1957-58, and costume design at Chouinard Art Institute, Los Angeles, 1958-60. **Family:** Married Marianne Wolford in 1960 (divorced, 1963); son: Robin. **Career:** Sketch artist for film designers Frank Thompson, Jean Louis and Edith Head, 1960-63; worked in television as assistant designer to Ray Aghayan, receiving his first screen credit for *The Judy Garland Show,* 1963; designer for *The King Family Show,* 1965, Mitzi Gaynor's night club acts, from 1966, *The Carol Burnett Show,* 1967-78, *The Sonny and Cher Comedy Hour,* 1971-74, and *The Sonny and Cher Show,* 1976-77; designed swimwear for Cole of California, 1976; independent designer of ready-to-wear fashions, with own label Bob Mackie Originals, New York, from 1982. **Awards:** Emmy Award, 1967 (with Ray Aghayan), 1969, 1976, 1978, 1985; Costume Designers Guild Award, 1968; American Fashion Award, 1975. **Address:** Bob Mackie Originals, 225 West 29, New York, New York 10001, U.S.A.

Publications:

By MACKIE:

Books

Dressing for Glamor (with Gerry Brenner), New York 1979.

Walter Ma: Spring/Summer 1995.

On MACKIE:

Books

Morris, Bernadine, and Barbara Walz, *The Fashion Makers,* New York 1978.
Maeder, Edward, et al., *Hollywood and History: Costume Design in Film,* New York 1987.
Pecktal, Lynn, *Costume Design: Techniques of Modern Masters,* New York 1993.

Articles

Thomas, Kay, "Spotlighting Two Designers Who Took Broadway by Storm," in the *New York Daily News,* 28 November 1971.
"Bob and Ray," in *Newsweek* (New York), 11 June 1973.
Moore, Didi, "Designing Man," in *Us* (New York), 19 January 1982.
Rittersporn, Liz, "Bob Mackie: The World's Most Visible Designer," in the *New York Daily News,* 5 May 1985.
Oney, Steve, "Bob Mackie: Daring, Dazzling Designer to the Stars," in *Cosmopolitan* (London), April 1986.
Milbank, Caroline Rennolds, "Bob Mackie," in *Interview* (New York), December 1986.
Michaels, Debra, "Bob Mackie: Cashing in on the Glamor," in *Women's Wear Daily* (New York), 19 April 1988.
"Bob Mackie," in *Current Biography* (New York), October 1988.
Mansfield, Stephanie, "Bob Mackie, the Boogie-Woogie Bugle Bead Boy of Seventh Avenue, Wants to Be Taken Seriously," in *Vogue* (New York), February 1990.
Finke, Nikki, "Trouble in the House of Mackie," in *Vanity Fair* (New York), June 1993.

*   *   *

Bob Mackie is one of a handful of designers to work with success in the related but disparate fields of theater and fashion design. Mackie is probably best known for the wittily revealing, glamorous beaded and feathered ensembles he has designed for the actress and singer Cher since the early 1970s. This collaborative image remains so strong that to visualize Cher is to see her dressed by Mackie. His true genius as an interpretative designer, however, can best be seen in his work for comedienne Carol Burnett. For 11 years Mackie designed costumes and wigs for Burnett's weekly variety show, including full-scale production numbers to showcase guest artists: elaborate parodies of such classic cult films as *Sunset Boulevard* or *Mildred Pierce.* These character sketches were written for Burnett's company of regular performers and on-going stories starring Burnett as one of her various alter egos. In Mrs Wiggins, for example, Mackie and Burnett created the archetypal "keep busy while doing nothing" secretary, complete with over-long fingernails, brass spittoon-colored perm, stiletto heels and a skirt so tight that walking seemed doubtful and sitting impossible. In this case the costume first defined the character and thus gave direction to the ensuing scripts. Visually, audiences were led away from the personality of the performer and towards that of the character portrayed. By contrast, Bob Mackie's designs for guest artists always enhanced their visual trademarks, so that the personalities remained the focus, supported by wig and costume, even when they played comic or character roles.

When he turned to ready-to-wear in 1982, Mackie's name had been before the television viewing public for 15 years. Women who had admired the casual but elegant tailored outfits Carol Burnett wore to open and close her show or the dramatic allure of Cher's gowns formed an eager and ready market for the first designs from Bob Mackie Originals. The fashion press took rather longer to convince that the aptly dubbed "sultan of sequins, rajah of rhinestones" had the necessary seriousness of purpose to sustain a career on Seventh Avenue. In fact, Mackie has always designed day and evening clothing in addition to his theatrical work. As early as 1969 he and partners Ray Aghayan and Elizabeth Courtney established their Beverly Hills boutique, Elizabeth the First, which in turn spawned the short-lived wholesale firm Ray Aghayan/Bob Mackie.

In his 1979 book, *Dressing for Glamor,* Mackie states his belief that glamor is "... a state of mind, a feeling of self-confidence." His strength as a designer is an intuitive understanding of what makes a woman feel self-confident and well dressed: solid craftsmanship, attention to detail, clothes which combine wit and artistry with a sense of flair and drama.

—Whitney Blausen

MAD CARPENTIER.

American design house

Founded by Mad Maltezos and Suzie Carpentier in Paris, January 1939 (taking over from Vionnet after her retirement). House closed, 1957.

Publications:

On MAD CARPENTIER:

Books

Perkins, Alice K., *Paris Couturiers and Milliners,* New York 1949.
Picken, Mary Brooks, and Dora Loues Miller, *Dressmakers of France: The Who, How and Why of the French Couture,* New York 1956.

Articles

"Carpentier Likes to Work with Folds," *Women's Wear Daily* (New York), 14 April 1948.

*   *   *

There were many diaspora far more urgent and desperate in the late 1930s than that which led to the creation of the house of Mad Carpentier in January 1940. The firm's two partners—Mad Maltezos and Suzie Carpentier—banded together when Madeleine Vionnet, their former employer, closed in 1939. In the unexamined cliché in fashion history and for a number of clients, the two women represented a continuation of Vionnet's bias cut and elegance in fashion combined with a discreet social model, always proper. Twins seized from a most inspired rib, two women balanced to equal one, and perseverance through the war years established an inexorable mythology around Mad Carpentier. Picken and Miller write passionately, "When it was almost impossible to think of luxury, of the richness of colors, of the beauty of fabrics, in a city without joy and without light, of deserted nights when there was no life except that of hope, these two talented women carried on" (New York, 1956).

Like Antoine de Saint-Exupéry heroines, Maltezos, designer and creative spirit, and Carpentier, refined and cordial proprietress, formerly a Vionnet *vendeuse,* sustained some of the ideas of Vionnet in soft evening clothes, but there were two special and autonomous distinctions for Mad Carpentier. In the late 1940s, Mad Carpentier created evening dresses of extraordinary historical fantasy, attenuating the body with *faux* bustles and creating the new sumptuousness of post-war evening clothes determined chiefly by silhouette. If these gowns did not achieve the flamboyant success of Fath and Dior in the same years, it is because the Mad Carpentier gowns are too redolent of the past and failed to capture the spirit of the "new" that was necessary to the marketing and imagination of the post-war era. Though Fath and Dior were both influenced by the past, the Belle Epoque could scarcely be revived in this era without, at least, the veneer of the newest and most extravagant. A Mad Carpentier gown photographed in *L'Officiel* (Christmas 1947) has New Look traits, but maintains the aura of a Victorian past.

The other hallmark of the house of Mad Carpentier was its most remarkable coats, long surpassing the Vionnet tradition. The bravura shapes of Mad Carpentier coats in robust textures were immensely popular in the 1940s and 1950s independent of the Vionnet tradition. In particular, the coats were much imitated by Seventh Avenue, New York manufacturers, often rivalling the ever-popular Balenciaga coats for copying. B. Altman & Co., New York, for example, advertised a Romantically sweeping long coat with high collar as "Mad Carpentier's famous coat ... beautifully copied in all-wool fleece" in *Vogue,* January 1947. Amplitude, rugged materials, and the swaggering grandeur of riding coats gave both assertiveness and grace to the Mad Carpentier coats.

Indubitably, the Vionnet tradition was maintained in ease, a desire for easy shaping and even for tying. In the dresses, the full three-dimensionality emphasized by Vionnet was often compromised by an interest in details at the side, as if to reinstate planarity, but in the coats, the effect was to create soft, large volumes. It was the negligent, comfortable ease that made the coats so eminently susceptible to copying by the American manufacturers who avoided the greatest refinements of tailoring to duplicate pieces that could be mass-marketed. *Women's Wear Daily* (14 April 1948) reported that "the firm has gone its quiet way, and now ranks as a house for clothes of distinctive character rather than one taking an active or publicized role in the general development of the Paris couture. Carpentier clothes have the handmade air of Vionnet, but do not always follow the bias technique of that school of dressmaking."

Linked to Vionnet's innovations in dressmaking, but in fact functioning with little inclination to their inventiveness, Mad Carpentier turned out to be a house of the most traditional dresses, genteel tailoring, and of sensational coats. Its understated, highly proper sensibility was at odds with advanced and aggressive post-war fashion and only in the exuberance of its sculptural coats did the imagination and reputation soar.

—Richard Martin

MADRAZO, Mariano Fortuny y. See **FORTUNY (y MADRAZO), Mariano.**

I. MAGNIN.
American department store chain

Founded by Mary Ann Magnin in San Francisco, 1876. First branch opened in Santa Barbara, 1912; Los Angeles store opened, 1938, flagship San Francisco store opened, 1948. Sold to Bullock's, 1943, to Federated Department Stores, 1964, to Campeau Corporation, mid-1980s; acquired by R. H. Macy Corporation, 1988. **Address:** Union Square, San Francisco, California 94108, USA.

Publications:

On I. MAGNIN:

Books

Crawford, M. D. C., *The Ways of Fashion,* New York 1948.
Riley, Robert, *Fashion Makers,* New York 1968.
Birmingham, Nan Tillson, *Store,* New York 1978.
Hendrickson, Robert, *The Grand Emporiums,* Briarcliff Manor, New York 1979.
Dresner, Susan, *Shopping on the Inside Track,* Salt Lake City, Utah, 1988.

Articles

Stabiner, Karen, "Store Wars," in *Savvy* (New York), July 1988.
Ginsberg, Steve, "I. Magnin: Seeking Solutions in the '90's," in *Women's Wear Daily* (New York), 9 October 1990.
Also articles in *Women's Wear Daily* (New York), 27 September 1989 and 19 June 1991.

*   *   *

Founded by Mary Ann Magnin in 1876, I. Magnin and Co. has always stood for beautiful designs of a high quality. They were responsible for making women in San Francisco, California among the best dressed in the world.

Mary Ann and Isaac Magnin were married in London, England, though both were originally from Holland. They moved to San Francisco in the 1870s, travelling by boat around Cape Horn. They had eight children. Mary Ann did not want her husband working on ceilings as a wood carver, because he might fall and be crippled, leaving her with a large family to support. As a result she used her skills as an accomplished seamstress to make babies' clothes which Isaac sold, carrying the items in a pack on his back. Before long they were able to open the first I. Magnin in San Francisco, selling needles, thread, and notions. This store expanded to include the fashions Mary Ann made, including trousseau, and exquisite lingerie which she made for the fashion-starved ladies of Nob Hill, San Francisco. She made nightgowns, chemises and drawers, bridal gowns, and baby clothes, ordering her lace and linen from Europe. Owing to transportation costs, these items were expensive. Nevertheless, the orders increased and she was able to hire helpers. Her four sons— John, Grover, Joseph, and Sam—were encouraged to learn about fabrics and, most importantly, quality.

Magnin's moved to a larger store, but the 1906 earthquake destroyed it. Mary Ann and Isaac operated their business from their own home until they could rebuild. San Francisco was a thriving community of people who had money to spend and was an excellent market for the luxury goods available at I. Magnin and Co.

Eventually one son, John, moved to New York where he opened a buying office. While on a visit there, Mary Ann was so impressed with a marble floor she saw at B. Altman's store that she had one put into her own store. Magnin's store was elegant and designed as a stage for their fashions. Marble, crystal, and gold leaf were used extensively throughout. Just as Mary Ann emphasized the best quality in fashion, she also demanded the best for the setting.

I. Magnin and Co. showcased the work of the major designers of the times, Jeanne Lanvin, Hattie Carnegie, and Christian Dior. Here they would introduce their new designs to the West Coast and the United States. The customers were wealthy: the Magnin woman purchased the best of everything, with price never a problem. Magnin's was noted for fine apparel and having fashion firsts sometimes a year before they reached other stores. Quality, as Mary Ann impressed on her sons at an early age, was always an important ingredient in the operation of I. Magnin and Co.

In her book *Store* (New York, 1978) Nan Tillson Birmingham describes I. Magnin's doorman who would greet the car as customers arrived to shop for their school clothes. These would be selected by a personal shopper who would have them hanging in the dressing rooms, waiting for their approval. Service to the customer is another aspect of the Magnin shopping experience.

Today, I. Magnin and Co. is part of R. H. Macy Corporation. Though they are based on the West Coast, they have stores in the major cosmopolitan areas of the United States. Their customer base is still counted among the wealthy. They sell women's, men's, and children's fashions as well as home accessories, with Donna Karan, Anne Klein II, Yves St Laurent, and Emanuel Ungaro boutiques in the stores. The setting for the merchandise is still important, and updated as needed. Customer service is emphasized.

—Nancy House

MAINBOCHER.

American designer

Born: Main Rousseau Bocher in Chicago, Illinois, 24 October 1890. Adopted name Mainbocher, c.1929. **Education:** Studied at the Lewis Institute, Chicago, 1907; studied design, Chicago Academy of Fine Arts, 1908-09, and at the Art Students' League, New York, 1909-11; attended University of Chicago, 1911, and Königliche Kunstgewerbemuseum, Munich, 1911-12; studied painting with E. A. Taylor, Paris, 1913-14; also studied piano and opera. **Military Service:** In the American Ambulance Corps, and Intelligence Corps, Paris, 1917-18. **Career:** Lithographer, part-time, New York, 1909-11; sketch artist for clothing manufacturer E. L. Mayer, New York, 1914-17; illustrator, *Harper's Bazaar,* Paris, 1917-21; fashion correspondent, then editor, French *Vogue,* 1922-29; established cou-

turier firm, Paris, 1930-39, and New York, 1939-71; also designed stage costumes, from 1932, and uniforms for American WAVES (US Navy), 1942; American Girl Scouts, 1946; American Red Cross, 1948; US Women's Marine Corps, 1951. **Collections:** Mainbocher sketchbooks, Costume Institute, Metropolitan Museum of Art. *Died* (in New York) *27 December 1976.*

Publications:

On MAINBOCHER:

Books

Levin, Phyllis Lee, *The Wheels of Fashion,* New York 1965.
Lee, Sarah Tomerlin, ed., *American Fashion: The Life and Lines of Adrian, Mainbocher, McCardell, Norell, Trigère,* New York 1975.
Milbank, Caroline Rennolds, *Couture: The Great Designers,* New York 1985.
Milbank, Caroline Rennolds, *New York Fashion: The Evolution of American Style,* New York 1989.

Articles

"Mainbocher," in *Current Biography* (New York), February 1942.
"Mainbocher," special monograph issue of *Harper's Bazaar* (New York), July 1967.
"Mainbocher: Great Gentleman of Fashion," in *Harper's Bazaar* (New York), June 1971.
[obituary], *The Times* (London), 5 January 1977.
"The Career of Mainbocher Discussed," in *The Times* (London), 14 January 1977.
Lawford, Valentine, "A Look Back in Fashion," in *Architectural Digest* (Los Angeles), September 1988.

*   *   *

The snob appeal of patronizing an American couturier with a French sounding name, extremely successful in Paris for a decade before his arrival in the United States, appealed to the socially élite trade in 1940 New York. No less appealing was the fact that Mainbocher had designed the Duchess of Windsor's trousseau upon her marriage in 1937. In 1930, after several years as editor of French *Vogue,* Mainbocher suddenly decided to channel his artistic sensibilities into the establishment of a couture salon in Paris. Editorial experience enabled him to sense what would become fashionable, and to package himself as an exclusive designer to the wealthy and the titled. From the start, he specialized in simple, conservative, elegant, and extremely expensive fashions, the luxury of cut, materials, and workmanship that could only be recognized by those in the know. Most importantly, the clothes, exquisitely finished inside and out, gave self-confidence to the women who wore them.

Mainbocher considered his contemporary Chanel too plebeian, and Schiaparelli too avant-garde. Instead, he admired Vionnet and borrowed her bias-cut technique for his own simple slip evening dresses in the 1930s. A very similar slip design was employed by Mainbocher, as he was known in New York, 20 years later, produced in a signature elegant silk velvet fabric. From Augustabernard, another 1920s French dress designer, Mainbocher was inspired not only to form his name, but to use godets in skirts, and shoulder bows to catch the folds of draped bodices. Frequent Mainbocher suit treatments in the 1930s included short capelet effects or dropped shoulders widening into full sleeves. The designer knew his clientèle personally and designed for the lives they led, specializing in evening clothes. For resort wear he ventured into a mix-and-match ensemble consisting of matching top, skirt, bathing suit, and hat. Slim, demure black wool dresses for daytime would sport white chiffon interest at the throat. While Mainbocher did use some Japanese-like kimonos as eveningwear during this period, his hallmark was non-aggressive, not exaggerated or period dressing. A touch of labor-intensive luxury would be bestowed by all-over sequins on an evening jacket or on a bare top worn discreetly under a jacket. The grayish-blue, "Wallis blue," of the Duchess of Windsor's wedding dress, as well as the long, fluid crêpe dress itself, was widely copied. The simple, conservative elegance of Mainbocher's style, feminine but not fussy, suited perfectly the slim, severe good looks of the Duchess and wealthy women like her. Additionally, she was honoring a fellow American.

In 1934, Mainbocher introduced the boned strapless bodice, and, just before the war that forced him to leave Paris, a waist cincher, forming tiny waisted, pleated skirted dresses that presaged Dior's post-war New Look. Mainbocher's arrival in New York coincided perfectly with the city's élite's love for French couture, for he epitomized that, yet satisfied their patriotism because he was actually an American. Society matrons such as C. Z. Guest and the Vanderbilts, stage actresses such as Mary Martin, avidly patronized this "most expensive custom dressmaker" who made women look and feel exquisitely well-bred. Accedance to wartime economies resulted in Mainbocher's short evening dresses, and versatile cashmere sweaters, beaded, lined in silk, and closed by jeweled buttons, designed to keep women warm in their bare evening gowns. Another practical wartime innovation, the "glamor belt," an apron-like, sequined or bead-encrusted accessory, could be added to embellish any plain costume. Practically gratis, Mainbocher designed uniforms for the US Women's Marine Corps, the WAVES (Navy), the American Red Cross, and the Girl Scouts.

As the years progressed, Mainbocher continued to design exclusively on a made-to-order basis, refusing to license his name. La Galerie, a department in his salon, did make to order clothes in standard sizes, a compromise for busy women without time for lengthy fittings. The reverse snobbery of the humble pastel gingham or cotton piqué used for fancy dresses appealed to Mainbocher's clientèle, as did refined tweed suits with subtle dressmaker touches: curved bands or self fabric appliqués, worn with coordinating bare-armed blouses. A Mainbocher standby was the little black "nothing" sheath dress. By the 1950s and 1960s, Old Guard Mainbocher customers enjoyed wearing impeccably made classic coats and suits of wool, often fur-lined, in the midst of nouveau-riche ostentation. The typical ladylike daytime Mainbocher look was accessorized by a plain velvet bow in the hair instead of a hat, a choker of several strands of real pearls, white gloves, and plain pumps with matching handbag. The integrity of luxurious fabrics, intricate cut, quality workmanship and materials, elegance and classicism, were cherished and worn for years by Mainbocher's upper crust customers.

—Therese Duzinkiewicz Baker

————

MALTEZOS, Mad. See **MAD CARPENTIER.**

————

MANDELLI, Mariuccia (for KRIZIA).

Italian fashion designer

Born: Bergamo, Italy, 1933. **Family:** Married Aldo Pinto. **Career:** Worked as a teacher, Milan, 1952-54, designer and founder with Flora Dolci, of Krizia fashion firm, Milan, from 1954: founded Kriziamaglia knitwear, 1966, and Kriziababy children's clothes, 1968: subsequently established Krizia boutiques, in Milan, Tokyo, London, New York, Detroit, Houston, etc. **Exhibitions:** Italian Revolution, La Jolla Museum of Art, California, 1982; *40 Years of Italian Fashion,* Trump Tower, New York, 1983. **Awards:** Fashion Press Award, Florence, 1964. **Address:** Via Agnelli 12, 20100 Milan, Italy.

Publications:

On MANDELLI:

Books

Aragno, B. G., compiler, *40 Years of Italian Fashion* (exhibition catalogue), Rome 1983.

Black, J. Anderson, and Madge Garland, *A History of Fashion,* London 1975, 1980.

Kennett, Frances, *The Collector's Book of Twentieth Century Fashion,* London and New York 1983.

Lambert, Eleanor, *The World of Fashion: People, Places, Resources,* New York and London 1976.

McDowell, Colin, *McDowell's Directory of Twentieth Century Fashion,* London 1984.

Mulassano, Adrianna, *I Mass-Moda: Fatti e Personaggi dell'Italian Look,* Florence 1979.

O'Hara, Georgia, *Encyclopedia of Fashion from 1840 to the 1980's,* London 1986.

Sparke, Penny, and others, *The Design Source Book,* London 1986.

Stegemeyer, Ann, *Fairchild's Who's Who in Fashion,* New York 1980.

Strute, Karl, and Theodore Doelken, editors, *Who's Who in Fashion,* Zurich 1982.

Articles

Menkes, Suzy, "Berets Are Off to Krizia," in *International Herald Tribune* (Paris), 7 March 1995.

Alhadeff, Gini, "La Beauté platonicienne de Krizia," in *Vogue* (Paris), April 1995.

Muritti, Elizabetta, "A Roaring Forty," in *Mondo Uomo* (Milan), May-June 1995.

* * *

The success of the Milanese boutique called Krizia, and, in fact, the prominence of Milanese fashion that has occurred during the 1980s and 1990s, are both largely due to the efforts of Krizia's founder and designer, Mariuccia Mandelli. Mandelli is one of the originators of the major contrast trend of Milan in which a simple, classic tailoring is punctuated with original and amusing accents to create a new face for stylish ready-to-wear fashion that is both eminently wearable and exuberantly youthful.

Among Krizia's early, important presentations was a showing at Orsini's on the invitation of Jean Rosenberg, vice-president of Bendel's. It was on this occasion that Mandelli was labeled "Crazy Krizia" by the fashion press for her combinations of simple shapes with madcap details. In 1976 Bergdorf Goodman featured stock by Krizia and other Milanese designers, providing the final step necessary for the Italians' rise to the forefront.

Representative of what has been called Krizia's "rough and sweet" look are Mandelli's 1977 outfittings consisting of nylon undershirts topped by matching rose-colored or dove-gray mohair bedjackets or cardigans in open-knit weaves and worn with dropped-waist ballerina skirts of scalloped lace. Mandelli's daywear tends toward the practical; she has, for example, put elastic waistbands on her skirts for comfortable ease of movement, and her 1982 group of sport suits of loose tweeds and checks are plain, loose, and stylized. Mandelli's use of her signature "improbable contrasts," however, abound most openly in her evening clothes, such as the mixes of satin skirts with sporty Angora sweaters that appeared in 1978. In that same year, she also presented her simple slip dress accompanied by characteristic touches of humourous flamboyance such as a long, feathered stole or quilted jacket of satin faced in a different shade of the same color.

Mandelli has often used jodhpur pants. One 1977 outfit consisted of loose, draping jodhpurs in silk charmeuse worn with a lacy, mohair camisole, the whole enlivened by the glowing berry colors she featured that year. Also among Mandelli's original fashion accomplishments is her development of what she named "harmonica pleats," which combine vertical and horizontal pleatings.

Outstanding among Mandelli's designs are her knits, which include items such as her 1977 lacy, mushroom-colored evening sweater teamed with double-scarf of silk taffeta and eyelet taffeta and jodhpur pants. In 1981 she showed subtly sophisticated shiny knits and white angoras bedecked with yokes of pearls. Often appearing on Mandelli's knitwear are her signature animal motifs. In 1978 there was a jacquard crepe blouse with the front view of a tiger on its front and rear-tiger-view on its back. In her 1980 collection, there were colorful knits featuring parrots and toucans; short knit dresses included a one-piece version sporting the front half of a leopard and a two-piece style revealing the leopard's rear half. Not limiting herself to knitwear, Mandelli also put highly colorful birds and parrots on that season's summer tote bags and shoulder purses. For 1984, it's the dalmatian, sharing the scene with more streamlined suits and double-dresses such as a back-buttoned flare over a little bit longer slim skirt.

From the start, Krizia's Mariuccia Mandelli has continuously based her highly original designs on nervy eccentricity and wit that have earned her a prominent place in the recent Milanese force that has successfully nudged ready-to-wear fashion in a new direction.

—Barbara Cavaliere

MANN, Judy.

Chinese designer

Born: Mann Lai-Yin in Hong Kong, 13 August 1946. **Education:** Good Hope School, Hong Kong, 1962-65. **Family:** Married David Hsu Kin in 1974. **Career:** For Thayer International New York (Hong Kong), fashion coordinator and merchandiser, 1972, and junior stylist, 1973, and designed for Roncelli and R-2 labels, 1974-77. Formed own company, Cheetah Management, 1977 with Judy Mann, J.M. Diffusion, and Cheetah labels. Showed first collection in London and Paris, 1979. First boutique opened in Taipei, Taiwan, 1983; co-founder of Hong Kong Fashion Designers Association, 1984, chair 1984-85 and 1989-94. *Judy Mann* perfume introduced, 1985. Established company in Beijing, Charisma, 1994, in partnership with Chinese government-owned enterprise; outlets in Beijing and Shanghai and production factory in Canton. Also: Marketing, advertising and promotion consultant for Continental Jewellery Ltd, Hong Kong, 1989-91; Chief Editor *Videofashion* (Chinese version), Hong Kong, 1990-91; Fashion Consultant to the Romano Group, Hong Kong, 1991-92. **Exhibitions:** Hong Kong Design Gallery (permanent collection). **Awards:** Ten Best Dressed Personalities Award, 1977. **Address:** Cheetah Management Co. Ltd, 51 Conduit Road, Block J 10/Fl., Hong Kong.

Publications:

On MANN:

Articles

Russell, Tara, "Judy Mann Builds on Her Reputation," in *Style,* July 1987.

Cheung, Raymond, "Sketches of Designers: Judy Mann," in *New Wave,* June 1988.

"Hong Kong Designers: Perseverance Is Paying Off," in *Women's Wear Daily Asia,* 22 July 1988.

Gopinath, Sharmila, "Vanity under the Rose, Vanity on the Go," in *Lifestyle Asia,* September 1988.

"Winter Fashion: Back to Classics," in *The Bulletin* (Hong Kong), September 1989.

Chen, Kent, "Cultural Obstacles Block Local Talent," in *South China Morning Post,* 22 April 1990.

Bartlett, Frances, "Settings for Love: Judy Mann," in *Beautiful Home,* October 1990.

Allemann, Angela, "Hong Kong: Frauen Ganz Oben. Fünf mal Erfolg," in *Annabelle,* 13 November 1990.

Bourke, Marion, "Designs on Hong Kong," in *Eve Magazine* (Hong Kong), January 1991.

Stravinsky, Sonya, "Judy Mann: Designing," in *Boutique,* Summer 1991.

Chu, Kennis, "Top Designer Prepares for Fashion Week," in *Sunday Morning Post* (Hong Kong), 13 January 1991.

*

I design for young executive women who are alert to fashion trends, but by no means a slave to them; who know what suits them and want to look presentable and efficient, yet stylish and sophisticated. My objective is to offer quality clothes at affordable prices.

My designs have to reach most women, not just a limited number. Most women are not built like catwalk models, so I believe in workable styles, easy to make and easy to wear. My collection very much reflects my own lifestyle, a working woman of the modern days. I like very simple silhouettes with perfect cut, quality fabric, and good colour coordination. I prefer separates and coordinates to dresses, as they give customers more flexibility; colours that you don't easily get tired of, which will last more than

Judy Mann: Winter 1992.

one season, and still look elegant and stylish; clothes that you can always change the look of by adding different accessories.

I don't believe that only intricately designed clothes can make a woman look outstanding. A well coordinated, simple outfit can achieve the same effect, or better.

I believe that, as a designer, it is important to know your clientèle, to know how to put a collection together—concept, sampling, fabrication, colouring—and make sure it can be put into production. We are not from the tailoring era. We are the age of mass- or semimass production.

My design inspiration comes mainly from the lifestyle of modern women, things happening around me, and the culture of my own race and that of others.

—Judy Mann

*   *   *

Judy Mann is an influential figure in Hong Kong fashion. As a designer, fashion merchandiser, and coordinator, a founder and chair of the Hong Kong Fashion Designers Association, she knows her business very well. Beginning as a fashion model, she became a designer by learning through the trade. This has instilled in her the importance of market awareness. Mann knows her clients. They are young executive women who want to appear efficient, yet stylish. She specializes in coordinated daywear, separates, and informal eveningwear. It is a young, sophisticated look which she calls "casual chic." The image reflects her own way of dressing. Simple silhouettes, quality fabrics, and colours which can mix and match are her trademark. While her collections reflect seasonal trends and colours, 50 per cent are classics, in neutral, easy to match colours, which are guaranteed to sell. Judy Mann is a businesswoman; sales are her motivation. "Every sketch I make has to be thought out, rethought and then designed with a view to selling."

Mann works for export, chiefly to Europe, where she is fast gaining a reputation. Japan, Australia, and the Middle East are other major foreign markets where her garments can be found in specialty boutiques and stores. She designs a little for the United States, but only in silk, a fabric not subject to quota restrictions. For the same reason, her first European collection under her own label, Cheetah, was also in silk. Nowadays she likes working in jersey, Swiss cotton, and Italian linens and wools; fabrics which are comfortable and travel well. Designing for export poses creative challenges. Colours have to be chosen carefully to complement different skin tones. A neutral palette provides the basis for each season. In winter, black dominates and in summer white is heightened by brighter shades.

Designing fashion garments has not been the only focus of Judy's career. She was the first Hong Kong designer to have her own perfume, *Judy Mann,* produced for her in Switzerland. She spent two years with a jewellery company, as a part-time consultant responsible for marketing, advertising, and promotion. Recently she started her own fashion consultancy with the Romano Group which owns 17 retail outlets in Hong Kong specializing in European men and women's wear. At the same time she has licensed her label to a local garment manufacturer who produces three collections a year.

Ideally Mann would like to trade closer to home, in Hong Kong or China. Having had her own boutique, JM Diffusion in Hong Kong, she seeks a partner or sponsor to help set up a similar venture. She has worked hard to help promote Hong Kong as a

creative fashion centre. In 1984 she was a founder member of the Hong Kong Fashion Designers Association, which she currently chairs. It has attempted to dispel the image of Hong Kong as a production base by encouraging and promoting local fashion designers. Annual fashion shows, its "Young Talent Award," Hong Kong Fashion Week, and regular contact between members have helped to strengthen the designer's position in the industry. Mann stresses that more support is needed. "Being a designer in Hong Kong is not easy—you have to struggle and struggle." Greater encouragement by the local media and increased financial backing are needed. Hong Kong fashion has come a long way in a short time. With Judy Mann as a role model and a champion, much more can be achieved.

—Hazel Clark

———

MANSON, Glen. See **FENN WRIGHT AND MANSON.**

———

MARA, Max. See **MAX MARA SpA.**

———

MARAMOTTI, Achille. See **MAX MARA SpA.**

———

MARCASIANO, Mary Jane.
American designer

Born: Morristown, New Jersey, 23 September 1955. **Education:** Attended Montclair State College, Montclair, New Jersey; graduated from Parsons School of Design, New York, 1978. **Career:** Showed first collection, 1979; launched Mary Jane Marcasiano Company, New York, from 1980; introduced menswear line, 1982; licenses from 1985 include shoes, jewelry. **Exhibitions:** *All American: A Sportswear Tradition,* Fashion Institute of Technology, April-June 1985. **Collections:** Fashion Institute of Technology, New York City. **Awards:** Cartier Stargazer Award, 1981; Wool Knit Association Award, 1983; Dupont Award, 1983; Cutty Sark Award, 1984. **Address:** 138 Spring St, New York, NY 10018, USA.

Publications:

On MARCASIANO:

Articles

"Making It Big in Prime Time," in *Harper's Bazaar* (New York), April 1988.
Boyes, Kathleen, "Mary Jane Marcasiano: Staying in the Arts," in *Women's Wear Daily* (New York), 6 June 1988.
Starzinger, Page Hill, "Smart Women, Smart Clothes," in *Vogue* (New York), September 1988.

Mary Jane Marcasiano. *Photograph by Jean Michel Cazabat.*

Matousek, Mark, "Mary Jane Marcasiano," in *Harper's Bazaar* (New York), October 1988.

*

My design philosophy and how I want to look as a woman have always been intertwined.

My first collection came out of a desire to wear something that didn't exist yet. There is always a dual purpose when I design—the aesthetics of the line and color have to coexist with wearability. Therefore, I test all the yarns and fabrics first on myself.

Color is where I start when I'm working on a new collection, simultaneously matching color with the surface of the yarn or fabric to enhance the color impact. My goal is to create a wearable surface of color, texture and light. My shapes are simple. I like the ease of knitwear, giving enough room for the garment to move around the body, both covering and revealing it. Necklines are very important to my designs. I use simple geometric shapes to create a presentation of the face, neck, and decolleté.

I am designing for the lifestyle of the modern woman who needs clothes that can take her from day into evening, cold to warm weather, sexy to serious.

I want a woman to be as comfortable in all of my designs as she is wearing her favorite sweater. Complete knitwear dressing combined with Lycra blend stretch fabrics are how I achieve this.

I don't impose a "look" on my customer—my customer has her own style or I help her to discover her own. This is one of the great satisfactions in designing.

—Mary Jane Marcasiano

*　*　*

Mary Jane Marcasiano began her business as primarily a sweater knit house, a focus she has maintained throughout her years in business. The company, which is located in the Soho district of New York, has grown and now includes woven fabrics as well as knits. When beginning a new collection, Marcasiano starts with color, simultaneously matching the color with the yarn or fabric to enhance the impact of the completed look. The yarns she prefers are rayon, cotton, silk, linen, and blends of these fibers. In woven fabrics, rayons and silks are favored owing to their lightness and drapeability. At a more experimental level she also utilizes yarns and fabrics with Lycra and superior uses of polyester and nylon. Her ultimate goal is to create a wearable surface of color, texture, and light. Shapes are always simple, as required by the needs of her specific knitwear designs. Beginning with the neckline, Marcasiano uses a variety of geometric shapes to create a pleasing presentation of the face, neck, and decolleté. The ease of wearing her knitwear as well as the woven elements of the collection allow the garments to flow around the body, both covering and revealing it.

Throughout the years Marcasiano's designs have been influenced by a wide variety of historical and artistic movements. The ancient cultures of Egypt, North Africa, Greece, and Rome, with clothes that were the ultimate in simplicity, are an obvious influence on her minimalist designs. Etruscan and Roman jewelry and the Neo-Etruscan movement in Europe have also influenced her designs.

Her target market is women who buy designer price clothing, appreciate quality, comfort, and ease in their garments. Many professional women, women in the arts as well as women involved in the fashion industry, wear the Marcasiano label. Exclusive depart-

ment stores such as Bergdorf Goodman in New York and Neiman Marcus, Dallas, have recognized Marcasiano's talent for understanding and designing for the American woman.

In her desire to create beautiful and wearable knitwear, Marcasiano follows in the footsteps of women designers such as Coco Chanel, Sonia Rykiel, and Dorothy Bis; typical of women designers in Europe who have influenced her work. Her personal innovations in the advancement of knit dressing in America through the use of unusual yarns, stitches, and simplification of the shape of sweaters, is an inspiration to a new generation of young independent designers working on their own.

—Roberta Hochberger Gruber

MARCIANO, Paul, Georges, Maurice, and Armand. See **GUESS, INC.**

MARGIELA, Martin.

Belgian designer

Born: Louvain, Belgium, 9 April 1957. **Education:** Royale Académie of Fine Art, Antwerp, 1977-80. **Career:** Free-lance designer, Milan, 1980-81; free-lance fashion stylist, Antwerp, 1982-85; design assistant to Gaultier, 1985-87; showed first major collection under own label in Paris, 1988; knitwear line manufactured by Miss Deanna SpA, Italy, launched 1992. **Exhibitions:** *Le monde selon ses créateurs,* Musée de la Mode et du Costume, Palais Galliera, Paris, 1991; *Infra-Apparel,* Metropolitan Museum of Art, 1993. **Address:** 13 Boulevard St Denis, 75002 Paris, France.

Publications:

On MARGIELA:

Books

Le monde selon ses créateurs (exhibition catalogue), Paris 1991.
Martin, Richard and Harold Koda, *Infra-Apparel* (exhibition catalogue), New York, 1993.

Articles

Allen, Elizabeth, "Marvelous Martin," in *Women's Wear Daily* (New York), 22 March 1989.
Cunningham, Bill, "The Collections," in *Details* (New York), March 1989.
Paz, Ricardo Martinez, "Los margenes de Margiela," in *Impar* (Spain), No. 3, 1991.
Voight, Rebecca, "Martin Margiela Champions the Seamy Side of French Fashion," in *Blitz* (London), March 1991.
O'Shea, Stephen, "Recycling: An All-New Fabrication of Style," in *Elle* (London), April 1991.

"La mode Destroy," in *Vogue* (Paris), May 1992.

Betts, Katherine, "La Nouvelle Vague," in *Vogue* (New York), September 1992.

Spindler, Amy M., "Coming Apart," in the *New York Times,* 25 July 1993.

Spindler, Amy M., "Four Designers in the Vanguard Hold the Line," in the *New York Times,* 11 October 1993.

Zahm, Olivier, "Before and After Fashion," in *Artforum* (New York), March 1995.

Spindler, Amy M., "Beyond Sweet, Beyond Black, Beyond 2001," in the *New York Times,* 17 March 1995.

*

a creativity : unfailing and inexhaustible (force) where everything fits

an energy : that makes things move

an extremity : that calls into question again

an action : carried out and provoking reactions

a force : that every time again provokes emotions

a fantasy : that makes one dream

a sensitivity : that makes you want to be part of it

a proposal : everyone has the choice to interpret

a subtlety : that makes everything possible

a sensuality : that makes everything acceptable

an authenticity : that restores the true or right values of things again

a professionalism : that makes one interested, curious, and inquisitive

a positivity : that gives hope for the future.

—Jenny Meirens for Martin Margiela

*   *   *

Martin Margiela is a powerful new talent in avant-garde fashion. Formerly an assistant to Jean-Paul Gaultier, the Belgian-born Margiela showed his first collection in 1989 and immediately achieved cult status. He was heralded as fashion's latest "bad boy" genius and the most notorious exponent of *la mode destroy.* He dislikes the term "destroy fashion" and has insisted that he does not regard it as destructive when he slashes old clothes. On the contrary, he told *Elle* (April 1991), it is his way of "bringing them back to life in a different form."

The idea of cutting up clothes goes back to the ripped T-shirts of the Punks and the subsequent street style of slicing jeans with razor blades. But the new deconstruction goes much further. Margiela has unravelled old army socks and made them into sweaters, transformed tulle ballgowns into jackets, recut second-hand black leather coats in the form of dresses, even made plastic laundry bags into clothes. He has designed jackets—beautifully tailored and lined with three different kinds of fabrics—with the sleeves ripped off.

Although conservative members of the fashion industry cringed, young trend-setters enthusiastically embraced the radical new look, which has nothing to do with traditional forms of ostentatious elegance and everything to do with creativity and what Margiela calls "authenticity." Exposed linings and frayed threads testify to the internal construction of the garments, while the deliberate deconstruction of garments implicitly raises questions about our assumptions regarding fashion. Detached sleeves, for example, hark back to the way clothes were made in the Middle Ages, when mercenaries first slashed their silken garments. A cloven-toed boot-

shoe and fingers laced in ribbons are rebellious statements in a world of high fashion orthodoxy.

The freedom of Margiela's imagination also evokes the sartorial liberty of the 1970s (a decade that Margiela views in a positive light), especially in contrast to the opulent and conservative 1980s. Like the hippies who pillaged flea-markets, Margiela gives a second life to old and rejected garments, recycling them, and giving a priority to individual creativity rather than consumerism. Opposed to the status-hungry cult of the designer, so ubiquitous in the 1980s, Margiela chose for his label a blank piece of white fabric and he resists talking to the press about what his clothes "mean."

Clothing per se interests him less than how styles are created and interpreted. In this respect, he is very much a conceptual and postmodern designer. Yet, like his former mentor, Gaultier, Margiela is an excellent tailor who really knows how to sew, and his clothes, although undeniably strange, are beautifully (de)constructed.

Margiela's aesthetic also extends to his fashion shows. He staged one show in an abandoned lot in a poor immigrant neighborhood of Paris, with local children dancing down the improvised catwalk along with the models. Another show was held at a Salvation Army hall, at the edge of the city, so that an international crew of fashion journalists found themselves wandering around, hopelessly lost, trying to read the hand-drawn map—and when they finally made it there, having to perch on second-hand furniture and drink wine in plastic cups. More recently, he held two simultaneous shows (one of all black clothes, the other white) at the edge of a cemetery, with crowds of admirers fighting to get in.

Symbolically powerful colors like black, white, and red dominate Margiela's palette. In his *atelier* are posted dictionary definitions of these colors, with red, for example, being associated with wine, blood, and rubies. His *atelier* itself, on the Boulevard Saint Denis, is near the red-light district of Paris. Like his clothes, his studio is a masterpiece of *bricolage*. Graffiti decorate the walls and the floors are covered with xeroxes of old magazine and newspaper articles, which on close inspection turn out to be reviews of his collections.

Margiela was one of six avant-garde designers to be featured in the 1991 exhibition *Le monde selon ses créateurs* [*The World according to its Creators*] at the Musée de la Mode et du Costume, Paris. Like Jean-Paul Gaultier, Vivienne Westwood, and Rei Kawakubo, Martin Margiela boldly moves fashion forward towards an unknown future.

—Valerie Steele

MARIMEKKO.

Finnish textile and clothing design firm

Founded by Armi Ratia (1912-79) and Viljo Ratia in Helsinki, 1951. Fabrics introduced in the United States by Design Research stores, from 1951; Marimekko bedlinens produced by Dan River company, 1976; Marimekko wallpapers and home furnishing lines introduced, 1978; licensees include CIT, France, for bedding and accessories, Decor Home Fashions, USA, for table linens, John Ritzenthaler, USA, for kitchen textiles; firm acquired by Amergroup, Finland, 1985, sold to Kristi Paakkanen, in 1991; new Helsinki flagship shop opened, 1993; 21 additional shops and in-store boutiques exist throughout Europe. **Address:** Marimekko Oy, Puusepankatu 4, Helsinki 00810, Finland.

Publications:

On MARIMEKKO:

Books

Marimekko-Printex Oy, *The Marimekko Story,* Helsinki 1964.
Beer, Eileene Harrison, *Scandinavian Design: Objects of a Life Style,* New York 1975.
Lambert, Eleanor, *World of Fashion: People, Places, Resources,* New York and London 1976.

Articles

Davies, David, "Fabrics by Marimekko," in *Design* (London), August 1968.
Lintman, Jaako, "Finland Marches Forward," in *Design* (London), No. 245, May 1969.
"Bright Spell Forecast," in *Design* (London), October 1973.
Tulberg, Diana, "That Old Marimekko Magic," in *Designed in Finland 1975* (Helsinki), 1975.
Holm, Aase, "Marimekko," in *Mobilia* (Amsterdam), No. 284, 1979.
Apple, R. W., "Finland's Spirited Designer," in the *New York Times,* 2 August 1979.
Slesin, Suzanne, "Finnish and Muted," in the *New York Times,* 16 September 1979.
"Armi Ratia, Marimekko Founder and Innovator in Printed Fabrics," [obituary] in the *New York Times,* 4 October 1979.
Furman, Phyllis, "Marimekko's Designs on a Turnaround," in *Crain's New York Business,* 5 September 1988.
Fraser, Mark, "Marimekko on the Move in America," in *HFD— The Weekly Home Furnishings Newspaper* (New York), 20 November 1989.
Schwartz, Donna Boyle, "Thoroughly Modern Marimekko," in *HFD—The Weekly Home Furnishings Newspaper* (New York), 26 July 1993.

*   *   *

A strong Finnish design movement emerged in the postwar period and was given decisive impetus by the International Triennales of 1951 and 1954 which defined the concept of "Finish design." By formally integrating design into manufacturing, the textile from Marimekko acquired international attention through its identification of an exclusive market responsive to the strong Finnish design aesthetic.

Marimekko was founded by Armi and Viljo Ratia in 1951 and has since established a reputation for producing quality furnishing and clothing textiles. The Finland-based company began in 1949 by acquiring Printex OY—an oilcloth factory in the suburbs of Helsinki. After a refit, the factory reintroduced the craft-based technique of hand silk-screen printing on cotton sheeting. The technique, which is recognized by resulting irregularities and repeat lines, evokes a human feel to each design. Although production techniques at Marimekko have been long since mechanized, the company maintains hand-crafted quality in its printing. Its use of decorative designs and natural fibres has strengthened its commitment to the Scandinavian affinity to nature.

Under the design direction of Armi Ratia, the company broke ranks with conventional Finnish textile designers and implemented a range of non-figurative patterns, using abstract graphic designs of

art colleagues. The first collection of simply cut dresses, introduced in 1951 in Helsinki, originated as a promotional vehicle for the company's printed cotton fabrics. Wrap-around and front-buttoned garments were included which accentuated the textiles rather than the styling of the garments. The collection was called Marimekko, combining the old-fashioned Finnish girl's name of Maria and the term *mekko* which described a tow shirt, open at the back and worn like a pinafore. Since then "Mari's little dress" has expanded into home furnishing textiles, with overseas licensing agreements (initiated in 1968) for wall coverings, infant bedding, decorative fabrics, paper products, table linens, kitchenware, ceramics, and glassware.

The textile patterns have maintained Marimekko's unique identity throughout, inspired by elements, forms, and colours taken from Finland's landscape and national heritage. At the same time however, Marimekko's textile designs embrace experimental ideas and contemporary graphic thinking, often resulting in bold patterns and saturated colours. The attitude is based on an understanding of modernity rather than sole concern with contemporary fashion trends.

The design of Marimekko's garments continues to incorporate functionalist ideas. Comfort and timelessness are evident in the design of the fabrics themselves. Designs produced in the 1950s by Maiha Isola and Vuokko Nurmesniemi (founder of Vuokko in 1964) included small, simple stripes and nature-inspired graphic prints in black and white. By the 1960s, though, oversized decorative graphics, flowers, and Op-Art-inspired prints were introduced, reflecting the playful and opulent mood of the period. By the end of the 1970s stripes were rendered primarily in bold primary colours as exemplified by the Peltomies series (1975-79). Similar designs continued to be produced through the next decade, with geometric patterns scaled for furniture in shades including mauve, opal, and midnight.

Marimekko's design has come full circle in the 1990s collections. Fujiwo Ishimoto (prints in celebration of the 75th anniversary of Finnish Independence), Jukka Rintala (womenswear), and Elina Helenius and Jatta Salonen (prints and patterns) have returned to the natural patterns and coloured world of Finland's seasons and landscape, which inspired original designs of the 1950s. Marimekko's commitment to the use of natural fibres, their continued use of bold, simple, classic shapes in garment cuts, their unconventional textile print designs, and their characteristic use of colour have established a permanently recognizable identity that remains to this day highly individualistic.

—Teal Triggs

MARINA RINALDI SrL. See under **Rinaldi.**

MARINO, Manuel Roberto. See **VERINO, Roberto.**

MARKS, Stephen. See **FRENCH CONNECTION.**

MARMOTTI, Achille. See **MARINA RINALDI SrL.**

MARONGIU, Marcel.

French designer

Born: Paris, 9 February 1962. **Education:** Studied economics and fashion design in Stockholm, Sweden. **Career:** Fashion illustrator for newspapers and magazines, 1980-82; assistant to France Andrevie, Paris, 1982-88; first own-name collection, 1988; first catwalk show, Paris, 1989; founded company Permanent Vacation, Paris, 1989; collection shown at Cour Carré du Louvre, October 1991. **Awards:** "Venus" Best Young Designer Award for spring/summer collection 1993. **Address:** 3 passage Saint Sebastien, 75011 Paris, France.

Publications:

On MARONGIU:

Articles

Nilard, Sita, "Sita Nilard Meets Fashion Upstart," in *Fashion Weekly* (London), 28 February 1991.
Baker, Lynsey, "Glad Rags to Riches," in *The Guardian* (London), 13 January 1992.
Menkes, Suzy, "The North Wind Doth Blow," in the *International Herald Tribune* (Neuilly, France), 13 March 1993.
Gordon, Mary Ellen, "Marongiu's Spare Shapes," in *Women's Wear Daily* (New York), 13 September 1993.

*

I believe that the 1980s was all about appearance, money and "power dressing." The consumer was suddenly unimportant as media, photographers and stylists went too far in seeking to shock and surprise each other through unreal super-models.

We are facing a new era where a designer has once more to contact the consumer and make them feel that fashion can be fun and easy. Therefore I try to do interesting, personal clothes—easy to mix and at affordable prices.

There is a new generation of women with a completely new attitude towards fashion. I believe that clothes are an important and interesting way of communicating. Therefore it is important to make the "user" comfortable and secure, to bring out the best in them.

Silhouette is my main preoccupation and everything is in the cut and the fabric. Details are secondary and should be avoided as much as possible.

—Marcel Marongiu

*   *   *

Marcel Marongiu sees fashion design as a genuine means of communication. He wants people to be able to live out their fantasies by wearing his clothes and to discover what he terms "La Vie Plus Belle," the beautiful life.

He designs clothes that are classically elegant yet also up-to-date, sexy, and carefree. His style is always strong and pronounced, the cut always clean and streamlined, emphasizing the contours and shape of the human body. Stretch fabrics and natural classic fabrics, often with a small Lycra percentage, help him achieve these silhouettes.

His customer is a young, modern women, slightly tongue-in-cheek and sexy, who refuses to dress expensively. Marongiu targets this clientèle in a logical, businesslike way and, in the short time since the company's inception in 1991, the clothes are now sold in many boutiques throughout Sweden, Great Britain, Italy, France, Japan, and the United States.

Marongiu draws his inspiration from various sources. His favourite fashion designers are Jacques Fath and Christian Dior, two designers who had a huge influence on 1940s and 1950s fashion, a period to which Marcel particularly adheres when designing. He adores Hard Rock music and in 1991 even named his company after the title of an Aerosmith album, *Permanent Vacation.* Other favourite muses are painter Nicholas de Stael, writer Graham Greene, and film makers Martin Scorsese and Peter Greenaway.

Comparing two Marongiu collections perhaps gives an indication of the essence of the designer's style. The spring/summer 1994

Marcel Marongiu. *Photograph by Magnus Reed.*

collection is a mixture of three styles: Renaissance in the fluidity and lightness of the materials; Baroque in its generous volume; and Classical in its Greek and Roman influences. Constructed mainly around a basic dress shape, Marcel wanted to create a collection that was soft, serene, and human, in colours that made reference to nature, reds and chestnuts, the blues of dusk and twilight and the colours of sand, beige and white.

The fall/winter collection for 1994-95 moved on from the ruralistic feeling of spring/summer. It was inspired by the lifestyle and atmosphere of European cities between World War I and World War II and contrasted with shapes inspired by the Ottoman Empire. Using lots of striped fabrics, Prince of Wales checks, mock astrakhan, and pleats, Marongiu created baggy silhouettes and distinctively superimposed tunics, smocks, or waistcoats on dresses or trousers. He also introduced colours of orange, green and saffron yellow to his usual palette of burgundies, aubergines, and greys.

Marongiu prides himself on the fact that his clothes are 100 percent French in production. The sample collection is produced in his Paris studio but is manufactured in the Vendée. Retail prices are very reasonable for a designer label.

As well as clothes, the company has diversified by producing a small line of accessories, shoes, necklaces, belts, boots, bags, and hats, all in the distinctive Marongiu style. As Paris is the base of Marcel Marongiu's activities, he is now established as one of the city's leading young designers. He looks set to expand his business further from this base because Paris, as he describes it, is a present-day city, full of energy and romance.

—Kevin Almond

MATSUDA, Mitsuhiro.

Japanese designer

Born: Tokyo, 1934. **Education:** Graduated from Waseda University, 1958; graduated with degree in fashion design from Bunka College of Fashion, 1961. **Career:** Ready-to-wear designer, Sanai Company, Japan, 1961-67; traveled to Paris and the USA, 1965; free-lance designer; formed own company, Nicole, Ltd., Tokyo, 1971; introduced divisions Monsieur Nicole, 1974, Madame Nicole, 1976, Chambre de Nicole, 1978, Nicole Club, 1982, Nicole Club for Men, 1984, Séduction de Nicole, 1986; cosmetics line introduced, 1987; formed Matsuda, USA, and opened boutiques, New York, 1982, Hong Kong, 1982, and Paris, 1987. Also worked in planning room of San-Ai Co., Ltd and publisher of *Nicole Times*. **Awards:** So-en Prize. **Address:** 3-13-11 Higashi, Shibuya-ku, Tokyo 150, Japan.

Publications:

On MATSUDA:

Articles

Kidd, J. D., "Matsuda Collects His Dues," in the *Daily News Record* (New York), 1 November 1982.

Morris, Bernadine, "From Japan, New Faces, New Shapes," in the *New York Times,* 14 December 1982.

Trucco, Terry, "Behind the Japanese Look," in *Across the Board* (New York), December 1983.

Kidd, J. D., "Matsuda: The Other Japanese," in *Women's Wear Daily* (New York), 10 April 1984.

"Matsuda," in *Women's Wear Daily* (New York), 29 November 1989.

*   *   *

Mitsuhiro Matsuda's design is picturesque, evoking historical passages and a profound sense of connection with the past and place, but at the same time a transformation through Matsuda's personal style. *Women's Wear Daily* (29 November 1989) commented, "Few can tread the fine line between sophistication and adventure the way Mitsuhiro Matsuda does." In fact, the comparable designer is probably Romeo Gigli who brings a like erudition, yet transfiguration to his clothing. Matsuda, of course, precedes Gigli and also differs from him in an essential way: despite the whimsical romance of his clothing which could seem to suit a Brontë heroine, Matsuda observes a stern rule of practicality borrowed from menswear. His basic canon of separate elements, the signature Matsuda silk blouse, jackets (generally elongated), trousers of various kinds, vests, and sweater often elaborated with embroidery or other textural play, affords a versatile set of components in the sportswear tradition. Eminently pragmatic, but irrepressibly romantic and sensuous (even in appropriations of menswear to womenswear). Matsuda has defined a kind of practical aesthetic dress of the late 20th century.

In the mid-1960s, Matsuda and Kenzo sailed from Japan to Europe to make their way to Paris, the great beacon of fashion. After some six months, Matsuda returned to Japan with no money, while Kenzo stayed. Matsuda's aesthetic and cultural allegiance outside of Japan is not to Paris, but to England and America. His first company outside of Nicole Co. in Japan was Matsuda USA which opened a Madison Avenue boutique in 1982. Matsuda has delved into the Anglo-American sportswear traditions as ardently as any designer, even as much as Ralph Lauren. What differentiates Matsuda from Lauren, though, is his critical, slightly adverse, edge on examining the traditions. His famous fall 1982 collections showed the impeccable tailoring of the English jackets, heavy trousers, layering, and indulgent textiles of the English countryside for men now adapted to women, but with the almost impish heterogeneity of canvas aprons that served both as working-class signs and as reminders of the transference from male to female, female to male. That is, the apron customarily signifies the female; Matsuda both breaks and then re-employs the customary index of apron to female. In this scholarly and mischievous transgression, Matsuda declared his clothing to be free of mere continuation; he is one who interprets and alters, not merely observes. In this, Matsuda may be said to express his position as one of the foremost among the first generation of Japanese designers to function in the international arena of fashion. But Western critics would be myopic to believe that Matsuda, or any other Japanese designer of his era, creates an Asian international design out of late acquaintance or foreign feeling from Western clothing which had been present in Japan since the Meiji period. Matsuda, for example, knows and feels Anglo-American dress viscerally and intellectually (though his initial intention was to design textiles for *kimonos*). He has allowed himself critical revision, not mere continuity.

In fall-winter 1984, Matsuda's collections were seemingly inspired by Edwardian England; in fall-winter 1985, the collections

Mitsuhiro Matsuda: Fall/Winter 1992/93. *Photograph by Guy Marineau.*

seemed to step out of Burne-Jones's paintings; while the Moroccan embroideries of 1989 could costume a Paul Bowles novel. Matsuda's inherent picture-making of the garment, his ability to see it as a spectator as much as creator, is most evident in his propensity to fashion-illustration elongated forms, often seeming more like the Barbier illustrations of style than the garments Barbier, fashion illustrator of the 1920s, depicted. There is a further literary aspect to Matsuda's work in his preoccupation with words and letters. Matsuda's work has been favoured by artists, writers, and other creatives who have recognized a kinship with this most literary image-making style and who enjoy the practicality of clothing that mixes so easily, even improvisationally, with other separates.

There is a synaesthesia about Matsuda's work. In fall-winter 1992, he created a homage to jazz saxophonist Miles Davis. His collections are regularly presented as performance and are often affiliated with dance or visual arts. His advertising and photography have been collaborative art, often presenting the clothing in secondary status to the picture. His boutiques project the absolute austerity of the design and yet showcase the lasciviousness of Matsuda's details. Matsuda's work is unmistakable; his clients are ardently loyal; his work is profoundly progressive. In such characteristics, there is the sureness of the artist, uncompromising and singular in style.

—Richard Martin

MAXFIELD PARRISH.

British design firm

Founded by designer Nigel Preston, 1972. Preston born in Reading, Berkshire, 1946. Studied painting and graphic art at Dartington Hall, then interior design. By late 1960s designed for such pop musicians as Suzi Quatro and Emerson, Lake and Palmer. Maxfield Parrish cloth collection launched, 1983. **Address:** 5 Congreve St., London SE17 1TJ, England.

Publications:

On MAXFIELD PARRISH:

Books

McDowell, Colin, *McDowell's Directory of Twentieth Century Fashion,* Englewood Cliffs, New Jersey 1985.

*   *   *

For centuries it was believed that by adorning the body with the skin of an animal, the wearer was thereby encouraged to develop its attributes. Accordingly, a lion denoted strength and courage, while a rabbit implied a rather inferior metamorphosis. In time certain types of fur, especially those more difficult to find such as ermine, became symbols of wealth, power, and privilege and—ultimately—in Western culture, eroticism. The history of the meanings of the wearing of animal skin is varied and responses to it differ from culture to culture and change with time. In contemporary Western culture, for instance, there is still a certain amount of prestige attached to the sporting of an animal skin on one's shoulders; less so fur, as a result of the 1980s campaigns by pressure groups such as Lynx and the Green movement.

Leather, however, and its more "well-bred" counterpart suede, are still generally acceptable; in fact a whole mythology exists for the rebellious black leather jacket. These seemingly arbitrary distinctions and distortions can be set against the continuing success of the company Maxfield Parrish, whose name for some brings to mind the production of well cut and crafted suede, sheepskin, and leather garments. The company was founded over ten years ago by designer Nigel Hayter Preston who was born in Reading, Berkshire in 1946. After studying painting and graphic design at Dartington Hall, Devon, Hayter Preston moved into interior design, toyed for a time with music, and in turn began designing clothes for his friends in the record industry. This low-key venture took off so successfully that by the end of the 1960s Hayter Preston was producing stage outfits for names such as Suzy Quatro and Emerson, Lake and Palmer. From these humble beginnings Maxfield Parrish was to become an international label, synonymous in womenswear with the design and production of suede, leather, and sheepskin clothing which displayed unusual combinations of colour—thanks to Hayter Preston's studies in fine art—and classic relaxed styles whose defined cutting betrays the discipline of a training in graphic design.

During the production cycle of the company's definitive garments it is the choosing of the skins which is of the utmost importance for the designer. Those of the softest, supplest kind are picked so they can be cut into and shaped like cloth, one of the company's trademarks. Hayter Preston handles skins confidently, using the same methods that other designers would utilize with more malleable wool, seen in classically styled outerwear such as the 1982 voluminous loose coats and jackets in soft blues, faded rose or beige, worn over softly draped skirts and cropped trousers. One of his more innovative methods is to overlap several skins so as to produce a montaged patchwork textured effect. This is used as a bolt of cloth from which he cuts various garments such as tubular or sarong skirts and tops.

Working in a design studio based in a Normandy chateau, with his partner Brenda Knight, Hayter Preston creates sample collections of elegant, easy to wear garments which are then manufactured and distributed from the company's administrative base in London. Today Maxfield Parrish is an international brand name in retail; the goods bearing the name are available in boutiques and stores in Europe and the United States. Despite the fragmented nature of fashion for women in the 1980s and 1990s with its changing styles and alternative looks, there have always been designers who have a lower profile being more interested in producing elegant styles out of quality materials for a client less interested in the avant-garde and looking for wearability and longevity in dress, from high quality materials. The directional nature of Maxfield Parrish comes from the development of new techniques in the cut and construction of leather, suede, and sheepskin; the use of expensive materials and the continuing popularity amongst a certain section of society for the notion of luxury attached to the adornment of the body with the finest skins.

—Caroline Cox

MAX MARA SpA.

Italian fashion design company

Founded in 1951 by Achille Maramotti. Launched Commerciale Abbigliamento Company, 1976, and Marina Rinaldi Company, 1980.

Max Mara: Spring/Summer 1995; black dress with net back.

In 1990 Max Mara comprised five companies. Registered trademarks are Max Mara, Sport Max, Marina Rinaldi, Penny Black, I.Blues, and Pianoforte. Lines produced by the Maramotti group have been designed by Emanuelle Khanh, Jacques Delaye, Karl Lagerfeld, Castelbajac, and Anne Marie Beretta. **Address:** Via Fratelli Cervi 66, 42100 Reggio Emilia, Italy.

Publications:

On MAX MARA:

Books

Alfonsi, Maria Vittoria, *Leaders in Fashion,* Bologna 1983.
Soli, Pia, *Il genio antipatico,* Venice 1984.

Articles

"Che cosa di chi: MaxMara," in *Vogue* (Milan), October 1984.
"Pianoforte di MaxMara: giunco e sabbia da turismo coloniale," in *Vogue* (Milan), February 1986.
Mower, Sarah, "Chasing the Wise Monet," in *The Guardian* (London), 3 July 1986.
Rumbold, Judy, "Grey Cells: Bright Ideas," in *The Guardian* (London), 7 September 1987.
"Altre scelte da MaxMara," in *Vogue* (Milan), October 1987.
Armstrong, Lisa, "The Max Factor," in *Vogue* (London), October 1988.
Tredre, Roger, "A Piece of Cake," in *Fashion Weekly* (London), 1 December 1988.

*   *   *

The brainchild of Achille Maramotti, Max Mara was founded in 1951 and has since become one of Italy's most successful fashion companies. Like many Italian firms, Max Mara remains a family company although, interestingly, no member of the family is a fashion designer. Instead, Max Mara operates by the highly successful formula of employing well-known fashion designers to create their collections—a method described by fashion critic Colin McDowell as a form of designer "moonlighting" and which is characteristic of a number of Italian ready-to-wear companies. Designers who have created collections for Max Mara include Anne Marie Beretta, Karl Lagerfeld, Emanuelle Khanh, Luciano Soprani, Guy Paulin, and Jean Charles de Castelbajac. However, the identity of Max Mara's current designers is a jealously-guarded secret and they are always acknowledged in retrospect.

The first Max Mara shop was opened in Reggio Emilia in northern Italy in 1951 and the first collection consisted of two coats and a suit which were copies of Paris couture designs. Although Achille Maramotti was officially trained as a lawyer, his family background was firmly entrenched in dressmaking since his mother had founded a tailoring school in 1923. Maramotti's vision to produce designer fashion from the mass market was remarkably farsighted at a time when haute couture still dominated fashion and high fashion ready-to-wear clothing did not exist. Like the whole fashion industry at that time during the early 1950s, Maxmara looked to Paris as inspiration for its designs and produced garments which with combined Parisian designs with their quality manufacturing techniques.

By 1969, Maramotti introduced a new line called Sport Max to cater for its younger customers which was an early forerunner of diffusion lines which are not an established part of most major fashion companies. The company has 16 lines today which include Marella, Weekend, Penny Black, Newpenny, I. Blues, Blues Club, Prisma, Marina Rinaldi, Marina Sport, and Persona.

Max Mara proved to be as astute in its attitude towards the importance of advertising its product as it was in the early production of fashionable ready-to-wear. As early as 1970 the company commissioned photographer Sarah Moon to capture the mood of their collections for a series of advertisements. Since that time the essence of Max Mara has been captured by prominent fashion photographers including Paolo Roversi, Oliviero Toscani, Steven Meisel, and Peter Lindbergh.

The basis of the Max Mara design philosophy is understated clothes that are easy to wear, in luxury fabrics, with an emphasis placed on quality of cut and make. The company consistently emphasizes the requirements of the Max Mara customer and the importance of innovation is always carefully balanced by wearability. Luigi Maramotti, managing director of the Max Mara group, maintains that "Our customers are led by fashion, but are never its slaves." Tailoring is one of the company's strong points, although in the softer Italian mode as opposed to the stiff British style of tailoring. Max Mara is perhaps best recognized for its coats and it is this garment that best illustrates the latter—often described as a dressing gown or kimono which indicates their simplicity of style, cut in soft wools or cashmere mixes.

According to Dr. Luigi Maramotti, managing director of the Max Mara group: "Clothes must be designed with an understanding of the women who wear them and the demands of their life. Max Mara's highly successful policy of employing design consultants results in clothes which serve an international demand within an Italian design concept. It has always been Max Mara's aim to give the consumer a worthy product with a high ratio of content, price, and quality."

—Catherine Woram

MAXWELL, Vera.

American designer

Born: Vera Huppe in New York, 22 April 1903. **Family:** Married Raymond J. Maxwell in 1924 (divorced, 1937); son: R. John Maxwell; married Carlisle H. Johnson (divorced, 1945). **Career:** Danced with the Metropolitan Opera Ballet, 1919-24; studied tailoring in London and worked as a fitting model before beginning to design in 1929; designed for New York wholesale firms, including Adler & Adler, Max Milstein, Glenhurst, 1930s and 1940s; designer of sports and tailored clothes, Brows, Jacobson & Linde, from 1937; launched firm, Vera Maxwell Originals, New York, 1947; closed firm, 1985; designed collection for Peter Lynne division, Gulf Enterprises, 1986. **Exhibitions:** Smithsonian Institution, Washington, D.C., 1970 (retrospective); Museum of the City of New York, 1978 (retrospective). **Awards:** Coty American Fashion Critics Award, 1951; Neiman Marcus Award, Dallas, 1955.

Publications:

On MAXWELL:

Books

Milbank, Caroline Rennolds, *Couture: The Great Designers,* New York 1985.

New York and Hollywood Fashion: Costume Designs from the Brooklyn Museum Collection, New York 1986.
Milbank, Caroline Rennolds, *New York Fashion: The Evolution of American Style,* New York 1989.

Articles

Curtis, Charlotte, "Vera Maxwell: The Designer with Many Interests," in the *New York Times,* 1 June 1961.
Morris, Bernadine, "Fashion Retrospective at the Smithsonian for Vera Maxwell," in the *New York Times,* 2 March 1970.
"Vera Maxwell," in *Current Biography* (New York), July 1977.
Morris, Bernadine, "Timeless Fashions at Vera Maxwell Retrospective," in the *New York Times,* 12 December 1980.
Shapiro, Susan, "A Classic on Seventh Avenue," in the *New York Times Magazine,* 2 December 1984.

*   *   *

Throughout her long career, Vera Maxwell held steadfastly to her belief that good design is timeless. Decade after decade her collections bore the fruit of this philosophy. In 1935 her career was launched with the goal of achieving softer tailoring in women's suits. The silhouette of those early designs would be quite fashionable today. In 1937 she joined Brows, Jacobson & Linde as a designer of sports and tailored clothes. Active sportswear was her specialty with emphasis on skiing, riding, and the shorts, jackets, slacks, and skirts that are the foundation of American sportswear separates and the staple of the industry. She was most famous for her suits and topcoats, worn for both the city and the country, and characterized by excellent tailoring, choice fabrics, beautiful colors, and pragmatism. One suit, designed under her own label in 1948, a year after she opened her own business, was designed for travelling. Called "the original flight suit," it consisted of a brown and white Irish tweed coat with a plastic lined pocket for carrying a washcloth and toothbrush, worn over slacks and blouse of a coordinating cocoa wool jersey. Ease of movement and comfort while travelling were of great importance, but the effectiveness of the design, with the close fitting jersey and the fingertip length full coat, have given this particular costume a timeless modernity.

Influences on Vera Maxwell's designs have come from many sources. One of her early memories is of a visit to Vienna with her father, an *aide-de-camp* to the Emperor Franz Joseph, where she was impressed with the beautifully dressed military officers. She herself has said that Chanel was an important influence. Long considered a classicist by the industry, her clothes are usually described as "handsome, interesting, and eminently wearable," as they were in a *New York Times* article on 25 November 1964. In 1960, on the occasion of the 25th anniversary of her entry into the fashion business, she pulled together her favorite designs of the past and discovered that she had trouble identifying them by year, an indication of what she has called the "constant" element in her work. In 1935 she visited Albert Einstein and was inspired by his Harris tweed jacket which she adapted and paired with a gray flannel skirt and pants, giving an important boost to the concept of separates and what she called the "weekend wardrobe." During the 1940s she designed a coverall, which she considered the first jumpsuit, for the women doing war work at the Sperry Gyroscope Corporation. In 1951 she was honored with a Coty Special Award, and in 1955 the Neiman Marcus Award, both during one of her most prolific decades. In 1970 she was given a retrospective at the Smithsonian

Institution. Ever concerned with attractive and convenient clothes and wardrobes that could travel well, and ever on the lookout for new means to achieve them, in 1971 she took a significant risk to purchase 30,000 yards of a new fabric called Ultrasuede produced by a company in Japan. Initially buyers were afraid to purchase clothes made of the new material, but time proved Maxwell right and the fabric became identified with her designs.

Until the day she closed her business, early in 1985, Vera Maxwell had a loyal following of fashion conscious women who sought the timeless wearability of her clothes. She ranks among the top of the group of craftspeople-designers who flourished during the 1930s and 1940s in New York and who created the well-tailored but casual look long associated with American fashion.

—Jean Druesedow

McCARDELL, Claire.
American designer

Born: Frederick, Maryland, 24 May 1905. **Education:** Attended Hood College, Maryland, 1923-25, and Parsons School of Design, New York and Paris, 1926-29. **Family:** Married Irving D. Harris in 1943. **Career:** Fashion model, knitwear designer, Robert Turk, Inc., New York, 1929-31; designer, Townley Frocks, New York, 1931-38; designer, Hattie Carnegie, New York, 1938-40; designer, Claire McCardell for Townley Frocks, New York, 1940-58; children's line, Baby McCardells, introduced, 1956. **Exhibitions:** Retrospective, Frank Perls Gallery, Beverly Hills, California, 1953; *Innovative Contemporary Fashion: Adri and McCardell,* Smithsonian Institution, Washington, D.C., 1971; *Three Women: Madeleine Vionnet, Claire McCardell and Rei Kawakubo,* Fashion Institute of Technology, New York, 1987. **Awards:** *Mademoiselle* Merit Award, 1943; Coty American Fashion Critics Award, 1944, 1958; Neiman Marcus Award, 1948; Women's National Press Club Award, 1950; Parsons Medal for Distinguished Achievement, 1956. *Died* (in New York) *22 March 1958.*

Publications:

By McCARDELL:

Books

What Shall I Wear? The What, Where, When and How Much of Fashion, New York 1956.

On McCARDELL:

Books

Williams, Beryl, *Fashion Is Our Business,* Philadelphia 1945.
Lee, Sarah Tomerlin, editor, *American Fashion: The Life and Lines of Adrian, Mainbocher, McCardell, Norell, Trigere,* New York 1975.
Milbank, Caroline Rennolds, *Couture: The Great Designers,* New York 1985.
New York and Hollywood Fashion: Costume Designs from the Brooklyn Museum Collection, New York 1986.

Koda, Harold, Richard Martin and Laura Sinderbrand, *Three Women: Madeleine Vionnet, Claire McCardell and Rei Kawakubo* (exhibition catalogue), New York 1987.

Milbank, Caroline Rennolds, *New York Fashion: The Evolution of American Style,* New York 1989.

Steele, Valerie, *Women of Fashion: Twentieth Century Designers,* New York 1991.

Articles

"Claire McCardell," in *Current Biography* (New York), November 1954.

"Designers Who Are Making News," in *American Fabrics and Fashions* (New York), No. 38, 1956.

"Claire McCardell," obituary in the *New York Times,* 23 March 1958.

Morris, Bernadine, "Looking Back at McCardell: It's a Lot Like Looking at Today," in the *New York Times,* 24 May 1972.

Beckett, Kathleen, "Designing Women," in *Vogue* (New York), March 1987.

Weinstein, Jeff, "Vionnet, McCardell, Kawakubo: Why There Are Three Great Women Artists," in *Village Voice* (New York), 31 March 1987.

Drier, Deborah, "Designing Women," in *Art in America* (New York), May 1987.

Yusuf, Nilgin, "Form and Function," in *Elle,* June 1990.

Als, Hilton, "Suited for Leisure," in *Artforum* (New York), 4 November 1994.

*   *   *

Claire McCardell was the founder of American ready-to-wear fashion, and in doing so defined what has become known as the American Look. She created casual, but sophisticated clothes with a functional design, which reflected the lifestyles of the American woman. McCardell's design philosophy was that clothes should be practical, comfortable, and feminine. Capitalizing on the World War II restrictions on the availability of French fashions and fabrics, McCardell designed simple, inexpensive clothes under the label Townley Frocks by Claire McCardell and later Claire McCardell Clothes by Townley.

The first successful silhouette McCardell designed was the Monastic, a dartless, waistless, bias-cut, tent style dress that could be worn with or without a belt. McCardell had several other successful designs which stayed in her collections, with slight changes, for years. In 1942, McCardell introduced the Popover, a wrap around, unstructured, utilitarian denim dress to be worn over smarter clothes. This garment was made in response to a request by *Harper's Bazaar* for clothing for those women whose hired help had left for wartime factory work. The Popover evolved, in later collections, into dresses, coats, beach wraps, and hostess dresses.

McCardell was known for many other innovations and she experimented with unconventional fabrics for various silhouettes. Her wool jersey bathing suits and cotton diaper swimsuit are examples of non-traditional fabric use. Madras cotton halter-style full-length hostess gowns were shown for evening. Her design trademarks were double top-stitching, brass hardware replacing buttons with decorative hooks, spaghetti ties, large patch pockets, and Empire waists. McCardell also brought denim to the fashion forefront as a dress fabric, as well as mattress ticking, calicos, and wool fleece. Manmade fibers, too, were a source of innovation. She also loved leotards, hoods, pedal pushers, and dirndl skirts. Surprising color combinations were indicative of McCardell's work.

Ever resourceful, McCardell viewed the 1940s wartime restrictions as challenging. Shoes were heavily rationed, so McCardell promoted the ballet slipper as street wear, often covered in coordinating or matching fabrics to her clothing ensembles.

The inspirations for McCardell's designs were many. She relied primarily on her own intuition as a woman, believing that many other women had the same needs for their wardrobes. "Most of my ideas," stated McCardell, "come from trying to solve my own problems." She sought to find solutions by analyzing the various needs of women, concluding that essentially clothes must be functional. While skiing she found her head became quite cold and thus designed winter playclothes with hoods. She recognized that cars and airplanes had changed the American travel lifestyle dramatically. Women needed clothes which would travel well. Accordingly, McCardell designed a six-piece interchangeable, coordinated wardrobe of separates which would enable the woman who traveled to produce many combinations from just a few garments.

McCardell rarely looked to contemporary French fashion for inspiration, as many other American designers did before and after World War II. She recognized the differing needs of the American woman from the European couture client and the potential of the larger ready-to-wear market in the United States. In this way she was able to define the American style of casual elegance. In 1926, during her sophomore year at Parsons School of Design, New York, McCardell studied in Paris. Whilst there she was able to buy samples from the French couturier Madeleine Vionnet and study the pattern and cut of her garments. Vionnet's influence is evident in McCardell's work; though McCardell did not work in the couture tradition, she was able to create ready-to-wear by simplifying Vionnet's cut. She incorporated the bias cut into her designs, both for aesthetic as well as functional effects. From Vionnet, McCardell said she learned "the way clothes worked, the way they felt."

The beauty of McCardell's clothes lay in the cut which then produced a clean, functional garment. Her clothes accentuated the female form without artificial understructures and padding. Rather than use shoulder pads, McCardell used the cut of the sleeve to enhance the shoulder. Relying on the bias cut, she created fitted bodices and swimsuits which flattered the wearer. Full circle skirts, neatly belted or sashed at the waist without crinolines underneath, a mandatory accessory for the New Look, created the illusion of the wasp waist. McCardell clothes often had adjustable components, such as drawstring necklines and waists, to accommodate many different body types.

Claire McCardell's greatest contribution to fashion history was in creating and defining the American Look. Her inspiration is evident in the work of many contemporary fashion designers.

—Margo Seaman

McCLINTOCK, Jessica.

American designer

Born: Jessica Gagnon in Frenchville, Maine, 19 June 1930. **Education:** Studied at Boston University, c.1947-49; received Bachelor of Arts degree, San Jose State University, California, 1963; no formal training in design. **Family:** Married Al Staples in 1949 (died,

1964); married Fred McClintock (divorced, 1967); son: Scott. **Career:** School teacher, Marblehead, Massachusetts, 1966-68, Long Island, New York, 1968, and Sunnyvale, California, 1964-65 and 1968-69. Partner and designer, Gunne Sax Company, San Francisco, from 1969, company renamed Jessica McClintock, 1986. Girl's line and Jessica McClintock Contemporary line introduced, 1979; Romantic Renaissance bridal collection introduced, 1980; Scott McClintock line of women's clothes introduced 1982; first sleepwear collection presented, 1985; Scott McClintock sportswear line introduced, 1986; Jessica McClintock Collection introduced, 1987. First boutique opened, San Francisco, 1980; second shop opened, Costa Mesa, California, 1986; Beverly Hills retail store opened, 1991. Signature fragrance introduced, 1987. **Awards:** Ernie Award, 1981; California Designers Award, 1985; American Printed Fabrics Council Tommy Award, 1986; Press Appreciation Award, 1986; Dallas Fashion Award, 1988; Merit Award in Design, 1989. **Address:** 1400 16th Street, San Francisco, California 94103, USA.

Publications:

On McCLINTOCK:

Articles

Wilhelm, Maria, "Jessica McClintock Weaves a Romantic Fashion," in *People Weekly* (New York), 17 September 1984.
Mercer, Marilyn, "Space to Dream," in *Working Woman* (New York), May 1986.
Evans, Karen, "Meet Designer Jessica McClintock," in *Seventeen* (New York), April 1987.
Simpson, Blaise, "Jessica McClintock: Marketing Romance," in *Women's Wear Daily* (New York), 5 January 1988.
Dunhill, Priscilla, "Jessica McClintock: An Endearing Quality," in *Victoria* (New York), August 1989.

*   *   *

At the height of the hippie movement, Jessica McClintock joined the San Franciscan Gunne Sax Company to design their long, calico, lace trimmed dresses, very popular with the young. Besides "granny" dresses, McClintock also designed lace trimmed denim clothes and combined lace with linen. By the 1970s she had added prom dresses and wedding gowns, continuing to use lavish lace trim, which had become her trademark. When the more contemporary Jessica McClintock line was introduced in 1979, Gunne Sax became the little girls' division, for which the calico, ruffled lace trimmed dresses were eminently suitable. In her San Francisco shop McClintock sold accessories, cosmetics, and her higher-priced designs, but it was for her feminine alternative to the hard-edged emerging high tech trends in fashion that she became known. A moderately priced Scott McClintock line specialized in misses' dresses and sportswear, all with the romantic McClintock look, but more sophisticated than Gunne Sax.

Gunne Sax dresses for teenagers featured ribbons, ruffles, Victorian lace collars, ballerina length skirts. In the mid-1980s, McClintock drew her inspiration for misses' dresses from the 1920s, combining straight silhouettes, loose enough for maternity wear, with Victorian details of lace insertions, peplums, or high collars. McClintock designed 2500 outfits per year, each with her unique romantic touches and femininity. The Jessica McClintock label, aimed at

women in their 20s and 30s, offered special occasion ready-to-wear at relatively moderate designer label prices. The use of man-made materials (polyester, acetate, nylon, rayon) made possible the lavishly decorated heirloom looks at a lower price. Cotton and linen are also used by McClintock, resulting in tea-gown-length Edwardian-inspired dresses in ecru, suitable not only for attendance at weddings, but for wear by the bride for a second or third, less formal, occasion. McClintock expanded into sleepwear, also romantic and nostalgic.

McClintock studies what teenagers wear to incorporate new trends, such as sundresses or the can-can skirts of 1987, and interprets them in her own manner. Unlike Jeanne Lanvin's matching mother-daughter outfits, McClintock designs coordinating little girl-mother or older sister dresses. The fabrics, colors, and trims may be the same, but the styling and placement of trimmings will differ. In keeping with mainstream fashion's more opulent evening looks, McClintock began adding deep colored and black velvets into her collection, creating long, unabashedly romantic gowns. Tight *décolleté* bodices edged with heavy white or metallic gold Venetian lace contrasting with lush velvets falling to the floor, sometimes with a bustle effect, would be more demurely echoed in little girls' dresses reminiscent of "The Little Princess."

The mother of the bride could select a Jessica McClintock tapestry brocade with leg o'mutton sleeves and peplumed top over a mid-calf slim skirt, all balanced by an overlay of lace at the neckline and caps of the sleeves. Emphasis upon tucking, braid, satin panels as well as lace lend a classicism to McClintock's style. Her dresses are the sort that might be taken out of a trunk to be worn over and over again when a woman tires of her mundane everyday clothes. For juniors, the Scott McClintock line has even offered short black velvet halter dresses, without any lace, paired with black velvet jackets. Additional sophistication has been developed by the use of velvets brocaded with metallic, stiff bouffant taffeta skirts topped by metallic floral brocade jackets. Most recently Jessica McClintock added a short sexy strapless black lace dress sparkling with all-over *paillettes*. McClintock continues to interpret special occasion dressing with her own vision, looking to the past to create nostalgic looks with a sense of mystery to appeal to the women—and their daughters—of today.

—Therese Duzinkiewicz Baker

McFADDEN, Mary.

American designer

Born: New York City, 1 October 1938. **Education:** Studied at the École Lubec, 1955-56, and at the Sorbonne, Paris, 1956-57; studied fashion at the Traphagen School of Design, New York, summer 1956; studied sociology at Columbia University and at the New School for Social Research, New York, 1958-60. **Family:** Married Philip Harari in 1965 (divorced); daughter: Justine; married Frank McEwan in 1968 (divorced, 1970); married Armin Schmidt in 1981 (divorced); married Kohle Yohannan in 1988 (divorced). **Career:** Director of Public Relations, Dior New York, 1962-64; merchandising editor, *Vogue,* South Africa, 1964-65; travel and political columnist, *Rand Daily Mail,* South Africa, 1965-68; founder, Vukutu sculpture workshop, Rhodesia, 1968-70; also free-lance editor for *My Fair Lady,* Cape Town, and *Vogue,* Paris, 1968-70; special projects editor, American *Vogue,* New York, 1970; free-lance fashion and jewelry designer, New York, from 1973; Marii pleated fabric patented, 1975; president, Mary McFadden Inc., from 1976; home furnishings line introduced, 1978; lower priced line manufactured by Jack Mulqueen, from 1980; Mary McFadden Knitwear Company, launched 1981. Also film costume designer for *Zooni,* 1993. **Exhibitions:** *A Passion for Fashion: The Mortimer Collection,* Wadsworth Atheneum, Hartford, Connecticut, 1993. **Awards:** Coty American Fashion Critics Award, 1976, 1978, 1979; Audemars Piquet Fashion Award, 1976; Rex Award, 1977; Moore College of Art Award, Philadelphia, 1977; Pennsylvania Governor's Award, 1977; Roscoe Award, 1978; Presidential Fellows Award, Rhode Island School of Design, 1979; Neiman Marcus Award, 1979; Doctor of Fine Arts, Miami International Fine Arts College, 1984; American Printed Fabrics Council Tommy Award, 1991. **Address:** 240 West 35th St., New York, New York 10001, USA.

Publications:

On McFADDEN:

Books

Morris, Bernadine, and Barbara Walz, *The Fashion Makers,* New York 1978.
Diamonstein, Barbaralee, *Fashion: The Inside Story,* New York 1985.
Milbank, Caroline Rennolds, *Couture: The Great Designers,* New York 1985.
Milbank, Caroline Rennolds, *New York Fashion: The Evolution of American Style,* New York 1989.

Articles

Tucker, Priscilla, "Mary Had a Little Dress," in the *New York Daily News,* 6 April 1980.
Foley, Bridget, "Mary McFadden: A New Type of Tycoon," in *New York Apparel News,* March 1983.
"Mary McFadden," in *Current Biography* (New York), April 1983.
Rafferty, Diane, "Beyond Fashion," in *Connoisseur* (New York), October 1988.
Thurman, Judith, "Power Gives You an Aura, Says Mary McFadden," in *Mirabella* (New York), September 1989.
Gross, Michael, "Mary, Mary, Quite Contrary: The Life and Loves of Mary McFadden," in *New York,* 26 March 1990.
"The Designers Talk Passion, Whimsy and Picassos," in *ARTnews* (New York), September 1990.
Horyn, Cathy, "A Mary-Tale Romance," in the *Washington Post,* 9 June 1991.
New York: Mary McFadden," in *Women's Wear Daily,* 4 November 1994.

*   *   *

With an artist's sensitivity to color, harmony, and proportion, Mary McFadden has been successfully designing decidedly original clothing for nearly 20 years. Her distinctive garments reflect an avid study of ancient and ethnic cultures. Inspired by the art and artifacts of Greece, Byzantium, South America and China, among others, as well as the distant cultures encountered during her own travels around the world, McFadden has built a foundation of pure,

timeless silhouettes to which she adds exotic details, decorations, in stunning fabrics, to culminate in elegant and flattering results.

When *Vogue* featured McFadden's simple tunics made of African prints and Oriental silks, clothes she had fashioned for herself out of necessity during her years spent in South Africa, the effect created sensation. While trousers had become accepted as daytime workwear during the 1970s, women were resigned to spongy polyester double-knits in mundane sherbet colors. McFadden's tunics, worn over silk Chinese pants, offered the comfort of natural fabrics and the eye appeal of vibrant colors and patterns. McFadden's first collection included quilted *kimono*-shaped jackets, flowing silk or chiffon trousers topped by loose togas made of stylized batik prints depicting Indonesian flowers and dragons, themes she was to repeat in a more luxurious manner in the fall of 1992. Bold, chunky, African-inspired jewelry made from various metals, plastic, and coral accented the eclectic mix.

Shimmering tunics resembling the shapes and patterns of butterfly wings followed, as McFadden developed her famous *"marii"* pleating, recalling Fortuny's silk pleated fabrics, which were, in turn, based upon ancient Greek and Egyptian pleating. McFadden's pleated evening gowns were ideal for her wealthy, jet-setting clientèle because, being made of satin-backed polyester, they could retain their pleats through hand washing and travel. McFadden's awareness of modern technology had succeeded in making the pleats permanent.

Even her less expensive clothes, offered in the late 1970s, maintained an exotic feeling through the use of hand-painting on challis and suede, macramé yokes, quilting, and grosgrain ribbon binding. Herself a striking model for her creations, McFadden presented some black and white outfits in every collection, echoing her own straight black hair and very pale skin. Drama was created by the contrast, texture, and richness of fabric. The same sense of sophistication was imbued into McFadden's bedding and table linen licensing. During the late 1970s her more expensive line of dresses included chiffon embroidered in gold, silver, and gold lamé, gold washed silks, foreshadowing the opulence of the 1980s. McFadden continued to design bold sculptured jewelry and braided belts to tie her gowns closer to the body or to use as edgings. Bolero jackets featured details from Portuguese tiles, an example of McFadden's ability to focus on a detail of a work of art, enlarge the motif, and incorporate it into her design.

Ever sensitive to the interplay of textures, the designer punctuates her columns of fine vertical pleating with beaded cuffs and collars, jewel encrusted panels, draped diagonals. Many of her garments come close to the surface richness of the art-to-wear movement but, eschewing the social statements inherent in the movement, her work is instead wearable art, to be collected and taken out to wear as one might precious jewelry. As evocative of the past as some of McFadden's designs may be, they stop short of looking like costumes. Pattern-upon-pattern mosaics of gold embroidery on sheer silk may highlight a Gustav Klimt-inspired collection, but the clothes are always modern.

Despite the vagaries of fashion, McFadden has maintained a consistent aesthetic. Her clothes offer something for almost everyone who can afford them. They are pretty and always have some interesting detail that will cause comment when the self-assured woman who wears them makes an entrance. McFadden herself has recommended "chiffons for the heavy figures, the pleats for the thin ones, the velvets for everyone." By the end of the 1980s, McFadden had experimented with showing slits of bare skin in between swaths of pleated strips composing the bodices of her gowns. The columns closely outlined the curves of fit figures, for the cult of the body was in full swing. The designer shortened her skirts to above the knees, flippy skirts of rows of layered pleats dancing beneath sequined tops. A striking short dress in the spring of 1992 had a skirt encrusted with beads forming a panel from a Tiffany wisteria window, belted with a beaded belt beneath a diagonally "*marii*" pleated sleeveless bodice. Her Japanese collection followed, the mystery of the Orient conveyed through embroidered snakes and sinuous blossoms.

It may well be said about Mary McFadden that "she walks in beauty" as she continues to wear her own designs. She was recently seen in a luminous cascading white Ionic *chiton,* delicately bordered with glitter, in which she appeared to be the most glamorous caryatid of all.

—Therese Duzinkiewicz Baker

MEDINA del CORRAL, José Luis. See VICTORIO Y LUCCHINO.

METT, Madame Torrente. See TORRENTE.

MILLER, Nicole.

American designer

Born: Lenox, Massachusetts, 1952. **Education:** Graduated from Rhode Island School of Design, Providence, Rhode Island attended École de la Chambre Syndicale Parisienne as a third-year student at RISD. **Career:** Designer, Rain Cheetahs, New York, 1975; head designer for Bud Konheim, P.J. Walsh women's fashion company, New York, 1975-82; in partnership with Konheim, company renamed Nicole Miller, 1982; launched line of men's accessories, c.1987, footwear, 1992; fragrance and cosmetics collection introduced, 1993; licenses include socks and tights, from 1991, jeans, from 1992, also handbags and men's formal wear; opened boutiques in New York, 1987, Mexico City and Naples, Florida, 1991, Barcelona, Tokyo and Osaka, 1992, Seville, 1992, Los Angeles, 1993. **Awards:** Dallas Fashion Award, 1991; Girl Scouts of America Award, New York, 1994. **Address:** 525 Seventh Avenue, New York, NY 10018, USA.

Publications:

On MILLER:

Articles

Schulte, Lucy, "A Real Fashion Outlaw," in *New York,* 16 February 1987.
Hochswender, Woody, "A First Show with the Right Flair," in the *New York Times,* 3 November 1990.
"Nicole Miller: Fashion's Wittiest High Roller," in *People,* 29 April 1991.
Shand, Gayle, "Miller's Crossing," in *Footwear News* (New York), 3 February 1992.
Ball, Aimee Lee, "Thoroughly Modern Miller," in *New York,* 8 March 1993.
Drake, Laurie, "Can Nicole Eat Lunch in This Town?," in *Los Angeles Magazine,* May 1993.

*   *   *

Immense talent as a designer, fun, and an astute sense of fashion are the key to Nicole Miller's success. Miller is a hands-on designer, who pays particular attention to clothing construction throughout the entire design process. Her studies at a haute couture school in Paris taught her the importance of a well engineered and well fitting garment. Realizing that few women have perfect bodies, she makes certain the body looks its best, camouflaging problem areas. Because of simple but unique details and superior cut, a woman wearing a Nicole Miller garment is assured of always looking her best.

Nicole Miller has had her own women's line of clothing for over ten years. The company is primarily known for her great looking dresses in both solid and printed fabrics. However, due to an overabundance of leftover fabric from a line of unsuccessful dresses, she opted to make the conversational black silk print, featuring colored ticket stubs in the foreground, into the Nicole Miller necktie sensation. Thus, the Nicole Miller line of men's accessories was born. This dark cloud turned out to have a platinum lining and Miller has blossomed into a leading men's accessory manufacturer. Presently the Miller ties, shirts, boxer shorts and robes account for 20 percent of its business. Men choose flashy tie patterns because they want to feel good. That is the whole reason for the fashion.

Inspiration for her prints can come from anywhere. After seeing the off-Broadway hit *Song of Singapore,* Miller decided to create a special silk print in honor of the show. Nicole Miller presently employs 40 artists who develop graphics to please consumers from all walks of life. Designs incorporate everything from assorted candy, animals or vegetables, to the sports collection, featuring basketballs, footballs, or baseballs. These prints have become so influential that knockoffs can be found at every level of the marketplace.

Miller has been prolific in other areas of design as well. She was involved in designing costumes for the Brooklyn Academy of Music's New Wave festival tribute to the late Carmen Miranda. Inspiration for the costumes was the peasant clothing of the Bahia region of Brazil that Miller had visited.

Although she has received a great deal of publicity for her prints, Nicole Miller's reputation has actually been built with her dramatic pared-down silhouettes and her striking use of graphics. Some examples are her curvy, strapless pale linen chambray dresses, and her short white rompers and dresses stitched in red like a baseball. Flattering fit and drop-dead designs are not Miller's only strong points. She is one of the few American designers with fashion's sixth sense for setting the trends without resorting to fads. Nicole Miller's clothes are young and fresh. In a time where many of the baby boomers have become more conservative, the Miller customer remains forever young.

—Roberta H. Gruber

Nicole Miller: Fall 1995. *Photograph by Dan Lecca.*

MISCHKA, James. See BADGLEY MISCHKA.

MISSONI.

Italian knitwear and fashion house

Founded in Gallarate, Varese, Italy, 1953, by Ottavio Missoni (born in Dalmatia, 11 February 1921) and Rosita (Jelmini) Missoni (born in Lombardy, 20 November 1931). First collection produced for Rinascente Stores, 1954; Missoni label introduced, from 1958; first Paris showing, 1967; Missoni SpA workshop and factory established, Sumirago, 1968; first New York showing, 1969; first boutiques opened, Milan and New York, 1976; fragrance line introduced, 1981; Missoni Uomo and Missoni Sport lines introduced, 1985. **Exhibitions:** Solo exhibition, Il Naviglio Gallery, Venice, 1975; retrospective, La Rotonda Gallery, Milan, and the Whitney Museum, New York, 1978; solo exhibition, Galleria del Naviglio, Milan, and the University of California, Berkeley, 1981; retrospective, Ridotto/Pergola Theatre, Pitti Immagine Filati, Florence, 1994. **Awards:** Neiman Marcus Award, 1973; Bath Museum of Costume Dress of the Year Award, 1974; American Printed Fabric Council Tommy Award, 1976; Gold Medal of Civic Merit Award, Milan, 1979; Fragrance Foundation Award, 1982; Tai Missoni given Arancia Award, 1986; Rosita Missoni named Commendatore al Merito della Repubblica Italiana, 1986; Fashion Group International Design Award, 1991; Munich Mode-Woche Award, 1992. **Address:** Via Luigi Rossi 52, 21040 Sumirago (Varese), Italy.

Publications:

On MISSONI:

Books

Ballo, Guido, *Missoni and the Magician-Machine* (exhibition catalogue), Gallery Naviglio, Venice 1975.
Mulassano, Adriana, *The Who's Who of Italian Fashion,* Florence 1979.
Alfonsi, Maria Vittoria, *Leaders in Fashion: I grandi personaggi della moda,* Bologna 1983.
Aragno, Bonizza Giordani, *Moda Italia: Creativity and Technology in the Italian Fashion System,* Milan 1988.
Giacomozzi, Silvia, *The Italian Look Reflected,* Milan 1984.
Tutino Vercelloni, Isa, editor, *Missonologia: The World of Missoni,* Milan 1994.

Articles

Buck, Joan Juliet, "The Missoni Way," in *Women's Wear Daily* (New York), 12 March 1975.
Klensch, Elsa, "Knit Together for 25 Years," in the *New York Post,* 24 May 1978.
Morris, Bernadine, "Missoni's Clothes a Hit As Milan Showings Open," in the *New York Times,* 26 March 1979.
Buckley, Richard, "Tai and Rosita: Designing Missoni for the Future," in the *Daily News Record* (New York), 4 January 1984.
"Missoni: i colori sul tappeto," in *Donna* (Milan), July/August 1987.
Piaggi, Anna, "Ottavio e Rosita Missoni: legati a doppio filo," in *L'Uomo Vogue* (Milan), October 1987.
"Missoni in mostra: freschi di stampa," in *Donna* (Milan), February 1988.
"In diretta da Milano: l'energia concentrata di Missoni," in *Donna* (Milan), October 1988.
"Missoni Story," in *Donna* supplement (Milan), October 1988.
Menkes, Suzy, "Missoni: First Family of Knits," *International Herald Tribune,* 12 July 1994.

* * *

Missoni exemplifies success in a specific fashion area, knitwear for men and women. In the knitwear business since 1953, the business begun by Ottavio (Tai) and Rosita Missoni took off with recognition by Anna Piaggi in 1965 and was through the 1960s and 1970s one of the landmark enterprises of the Italian renaissance in post-war fashion products. In 1968 and 1969, Missoni garnered worldwide attention for knit dresses, coats, and sweaters that revived the sensational appeal of knits in the 1920s. From a start in producing the finest knits at a moment when both the Establishment and anti-Establishment were looking for poor-boy sweaters and the liquid ease of knits, the Missoni repertory now includes pullovers, long coats, chemises, and knit trousers and skirts. Even more, in the 1970s, the Missonis' deliberate allegiance to Milan heralded that city's eminence as a fashion center and helped create Milan fashion week. In spring 1967, at the Pitti collections in Florence, Rosita had been discouraged by the visibility of the models' bras under the thin knit dresses; she had the models remove their bras for the Missoni show. Stage lights made the clothes seem transparent and the showing became a *cause célèbre* in Italy. While it does not seem that the Missonis were banned from the Pitti showings thereafter, they defected to Milan and took with them a certain sense of Milan's most worldly view of fashion.

Primarily creators of exceptional knitwear, Missoni has been noted as an art as much as a business. Technology provides a range of fluid knits and special effects, but the identifying and indescribable aspect of the Missoni knits is color, the affinity to art. Most importantly, Missoni brought a vivid sense of imagination to knits, rescuing them from the heirlooms and old-fashioned aspects of handknits and from the conventional sameness of many machine-knitted products. Like many Italian products of the post-war period, the value of the product was not in its handwork, but in the unquestioned supremacy of design attained through machine. Today computers and sophisticated machines make the Missoni knits that are thought of as artisan production, so exceptional are their colors, so extraordinary do such knits seem to be in texture as in color. Today, Missoni knits seem as intrinsic to Italian style as Ravenna mosaics, likewise brilliant in elements and creative of color fields beyond their discrete *tesserae* or components. The knits have also proved as successful in menswear, sweaters in particular, as in women's apparel.

Tai Missoni's introduction to the knitwear business was as an athlete. Knitwear was for active sports, but by 1958 a striped Missoni knit shirtdress was produced and the crossover from sports to casual living was underway. The sports heritage remains in some graphic boldness, including stripes and zig-zags and even patchwork, that read with distinctness across a room. What enhances Missoni for daywear and even for evening (especially with Lurex)

Missoni: Fall/Winter 1992/93.

is the subtleties within. In fact, the Missonis have often pointed out that they deny fashion. Rosita told Elsa Klensch: "Our philosophy since we went into business has been that a piece of clothing should be like a work of art. It should not be bought for a special occasion or because it's in fashion, but because a woman likes it ... and feels she could wear it forever" (*New York Post,* 24 May 1978). Little the Missonis have produced depends upon fashion. Instead their knits seem perennial. Their color multivalence works to the same effect: a Missoni design might be worn with a favored color one season and still be compatible with other colors in other seasons. Moreover, the color partakes of a convention of abstract painting and satisfies for many a sense of being modern through abstract pattern. Thus, Bernadine Morris's declaration that the Missonis "have elevated knitted clothes to a form of art" is not as startling as it might seem. (*New York Times,* 26 March, 1979). If they have done so, they have made that advancement because they realized that modern design is a synergy between machine and art. In fact, Missoni knits became in the 1970s and 1980s such visible status symbols that they might easily have become telling symbols of the time. Continued change has kept Missoni a vital force in the field of fashion that they self-consciously ignore to create enduring clothes.

—Richard Martin

MIYAKE, Issey.

Japanese designer

Born: Kazumaru Miyake in Hiroshima, 22 April 1938. **Education:** Studied at Tama Art University, Tokyo, 1959-63, and at École de la Chambre Syndicale de la Couture Parisienne, 1965. **Career:** Design assistant, Guy Laroche, 1966-68, and Givenchy, 1968-69; designer, Geoffrey Beene in New York, 1969-70; established Miyake Design Studio in Tokyo, 1970; also director, Issey Miyake International, Issey Miyake and Associates, Issey Miyake Europe, Issey Miyake USA, and Issey Miyake On Limits. Lines include Issey Sport, Plantation, and Pleats Please (introduced, 1993); fragrances: *L'Eau de Missey,* introduced, 1993, *L'Eau d'Issey pour Homme,* introduced, 1995; first US boutique opened in New York, 1988. Also theater designer, from 1980. **Exhibitions:** *Issey Miyake in the Museum,* Seibu Musem, Tokyo, 1977; *Les Tissus Imprimés d'Issey Miyake,* Musée de l'Impression sur Étoffes, Mulhouse, 1979; *Intimate Architecture: Contemporary Clothing,* Massachusetts Institute of Technology, 1982; *Bodyworks,* international touring exhibition, 1983; *A New Wave in Fashion: Three Japanese Designers,* Phoenix Art Museum, Arizona, 1983; *À Un,* Musée des Arts Decoratifs, Paris, 1988: *Issey Miyake Pleats Please,* Touko Museum of Contemporary Art, Tokyo, 1990; *Twist,* Naoshima Contemporary Art Museum, 1992. **Awards:** Japan Fashion Editors Club Award, 1974; Mainichi Newspaper Fashion Award, 1976, 1984; Pratt Institute Design Excellence Award, New York, 1979; Council of Fashion Designers of America Award, 1983; Neiman Marcus Award, 1984; Officier de l'Ordre des Arts et Lettres, France, 1989; Honorary Doctorate, Royal College of Art, London, 1993; Hiroshima Art Prize, 1991; Chevalier de l'Ordre National de la Legion d'Honneur, Paris, 1993. **Address:** 1-23 Ohyamacho, Shibuya-ku, Tokyo 151, Japan.

Publications:

By MIYAKE:

Books

Issey Miyake, East Meets West, Kazuko Koide and Ikko Tanaka, editors, Tokyo 1978.
Issey Miyake Bodyworks, Shozo Tsurumoto, editor, Tokyo 1983.
Issey Miyake and Miyake Design Studio 1970-1985, Tokyo 1985.
Issey Miyake PLEATS PLEASE, Touko Museum of Contemporary Art and Miyake Design Studio, Tokyo 1990.

Books

Deslandres, Yvonne, *Les Tissus Imprimés d'Issey Miyake* (exhibition catalogue), Mulhouse 1979.
Hayden Gallery, Massachusetts Institute of Technology, *Intimate Architecture: Contemporary Clothing Design* (exhibition catalogue), Cambridge, Mass. 1982.
Phoenix Art Museum, *A New Wave in Fashion: Three Japanese Designers* (exhibition catalogue), Phoenix, Arizona 1983.
Koren, Leonard, *New Fashion Japan,* Tokyo and New York 1984.
Milbank, Caroline Rennolds, *Couture: The Great Designers,* New York 1985.
Fraser, Kennedy, *Scenes from the Fashionable World,* New York 1987.
Sparke, Penny, *Japanese Design,* London 1987.
Calloway, Nicholas, editor, *Issey Miyake: Photographs by Irving Penn,* Boston 1988.
Coleridge, Nicholas, *The Fashion Conspiracy,* London 1988.
Howell, Georgina, *Sultans of Style: 30 Years of Fashion and Passion 1960-1990,* London 1990.
Miyake Design Studio, editors, *Ten Sen Men,* Hiroshima City Museum of Contemporary Art, Tokyo 1990.
Miyake Design Studio, editors, *Issey Miyake by Irving Penn 1991-1992,* Toyko 1992.
Miyake Design Studio, editors, *Issey Miyake by Irving Penn 1993-1995,* Tokyo 1995.
Hiesinger, Kathryn B., and Felice Fischer, *Japanese Design: A Survey since 1950,* Harry N. Abrams, 1995.

Articles

Bancou, M., "Issey Miyake," in *American Fabrics and Fashions* (Columbia, South Carolina), No. 106, Winter 1976.
Takahashi, M., "Issey Miyake," in *Idea* (Concord, New Hampshire), No. 144, 1977.
"Issey Miyake, Clothes Designer," in *Zoom* (New York/Milan), Dec./Jan. 1978-79.
Lewis, J., "The Man Who Put Show in Fashion Shows," in *Far East Economic Review* (Hong Kong), 22 January 1979.
Bancou, M., "Issey Miyake Revisited," in *American Fabrics and Fashions* (Columbia, South Carolina), No. 115, Spring 1979.
"Issey Miyake," in *The New Yorker,* 8 and 15 November 1982.
"Issey Miyake," in *Art and Design* (London), March 1985.
Popham, Peter, "The Emperor's New Clothes," in *Blueprint* (London), March 1985.
"Issey Miyake's *Bodyworks,*" in *Domus* (Milan), May 1985.
White, Lesley, "Miyake's Marvelous But Issey Art," in *Cosmopolitan* (London), August 1985.

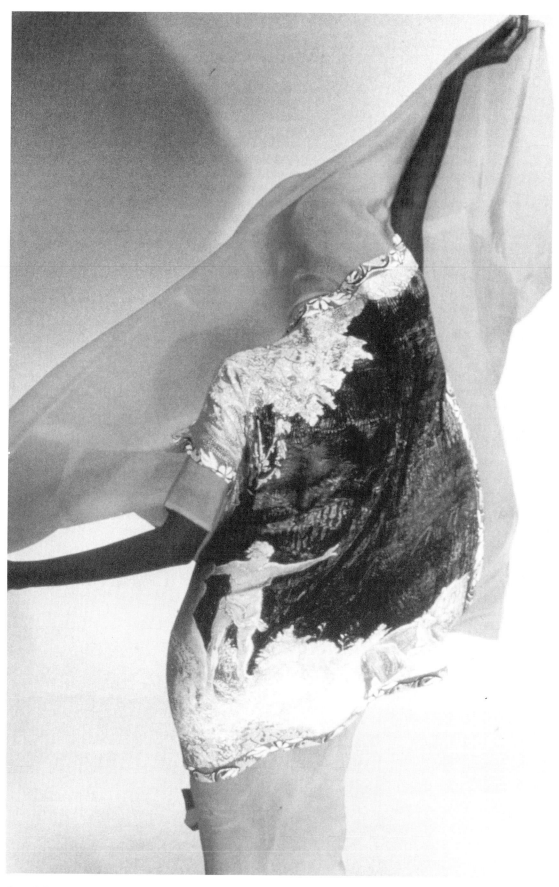

Issey Miyake: "Paradise Lost," Spring/Summer 1977. *Photograph by Noriaki Yokosuka.*

Issey Miyake.

Cocks, Jay, "The Man Who's Changing Clothes," in *Time* (New York), 21 October 1985.

"1970-1986: le phénomène Issey Miyake," in *Elle* (Paris), 3 February 1986.

"Issey Miyake: Dateless Fashion," in *Art and Design* (London), October 1986.

Neret, Gilles, "Issey Miyake: le plus sculpteur des couturiers," in *Connaissance des Arts* (Paris), March 1987.

Angel, Sally, "Zen and the Art of Fashion," in *Blueprint* (London), October 1987.

Knafo, Robert, "Issey Miyake Is Changing the Way Men View Clothes," in *Connoisseur* (New York), March 1988.

"Eye of the Artists: Issey Miyake," in *Vogue* (New York), October 1988.

Holborn, Mark, "Image of Second Skin," in *Artforum* (New York), November 1988.

Brampton, Sally, "Modern Master," in *Elle* (London), June 1989.

Martin, Richard, "The Cubism of Issey Miyake," in *Textile & Text* (New York), 12/4, 1990.

Penn, Irving, and Ingrid Sischy, "Pleats Please," in *Interview* (New York), September 1990.

Tilton, Mary, "Issey Miyake: Designer for the Millennium," in *Threads* (Newtown, Connecticut), June/July 1991.

Gross, Michael, "Issey Does It," in *New York,* 22 July 1991.

Bucks, Suzy, "Clothes that Grow on You," in *The Independent on Sunday* (London), 3 July 1994.

Spindler, Amy M., "Art or Vanity?: Fashion's Ambiguity," in the *New York Times,* 13 December 1994.

Schiro, Anne-Marie, "Photogenic, But Out of Focus," in the *New York Times,* 20 March 1995.

Menkes, Suzy, "Show, Not Clothes, Becomes the Message," in the *International Herald Tribune* (Paris), 20 March 1995.

*   *   *

Architect Arata Isozaki begins his essay in Issey Miyake's *East Meets West* with the question, "What are clothes?" The question, perhaps too fundamental and unnecessary for most designers, is the matrix of Issey Miyake's clothing. More, possibly, than any other designer of the century, Miyake has inquired into the nature of apparel, investigating adornment and dress functions from all parts of the world and from all uses and in all forms, to speculate about clothing. Aroused to question fashion's viability in the social revolution he observed in Paris in 1968, Miyake has sought a clothing of particular lifestyle utility, of renewed coalition with textile integrity, and of wholly reconsidered form. In exploring ideas that emanate from the technology of cloth, Miyake has created great geometries that surpass the body, the most effortless play of drapery on the bias and accommodating the body in motion since his paragon Madeleine Vionnet, and the folds and waffles of a first-phase cubism followed by a crushed, irregular form of fluid dressing. His highly successful "Windcoats" wrap the wearer in an abundance of cloth, but also generate marvelously transformative shapes when compressed, or billowing and extended. In these efforts, Miyake has created garments redolent of human history, but largely unprecedented in the history of dress, so committed is he to fashion that expresses and realizes life in the latter years of the 20th century. He is, without question, aesthetically the most visionary fashion designer of the second half of this period, often seeming to abandon commercial ideas of dress for the more extravagantly new and ideal experiments.

Characteristic examples demonstrate the designer's incomparable sense of experiment and innovation. In 1976, a knit square with sleeves becomes, as if by a magician's transmogrification, a coat with matching bikini. His 1982 rattan body sculpture is an ironically externalized cage of the body for which it serves instead as an ideal pattern of ribs and structural lines. Yet he also returns to kimono textiles as the basis for new textile design and fabrication and even experiments with paper and other materials to find the right medium for apparel. His fall/winter 1989-90 pleated collection partakes of a radical Cubist vision of the human body and of its movement, whereas the 1990s commitment to irregularly pleated fabric suggests a fashion possibility in disparity to any existing idea of dress. Is Miyake's insight so thoroughly Utopian and visionary as to defy a current fashion use? Despite idealist propensity and a highly original and conceptual nature, Miyake has appealed to a clientèle of forward thinkers and designers who wear the clothing with a zeal and identity of the creative enterprise and energy with which they are vested.

Miyake transcends the garments. Like Duchamp, he gives to his work interpretative issues and contexts that contribute to their meaning, acknowledging the garments as prolific signs. Thus, his books *East Meets West* (Tokyo, 1978) and *Bodyworks* (Tokyo, 1983), accompanied by these and other museum exhibitions, have placed a reading and meaning on the works that become inextricably involved with the sign-value of the garment. Miyake can be anthropologically basic; again and again, he returns to tattooing as a basic body adornment, rendered in clothing and tights and bodysuits. He relishes the juxtaposition between the most rustic and basic and the most advanced, almost to prove human history a circle rather a linear progression. But he is also the theorist ascribing to his clothing a plethora of signifying and significant thoughts. No other designer—with the possible exception of the more laconic Geoffrey Beene, for whom Miyake worked briefly and with whom he maintains a mutual admiration—interprets his work as deliberately and thoughtfully as Miyake.

Such allusiveness and context would have little value were it not for the abiding principles of Miyake's work. He relies upon the body as unerringly as a dancer might. He demands a freedom of motion that reveals its genesis in 1968. The experiments, then, of materials and design cannot impede motion, but can only enhance it, as do the aerodynamic works of the 1980s and 1990s. If Miyake's concept of the body is the root of all of his thinking, it is a highly conceptual, reasoned body. His books have customarily shown friends and clients—young and old-wearing the clothing. They come from East and West; they do not possess the perfect anatomy and streamlined physique of body sculptures and bustiers, but they are in some way ideals to Miyake. He intends clothing to be the dress of the intellectually and emotionally peerless. His is an uncommon, even unprecedented fashion idealism. In *Couture: The Great Designers,* Caroline Rennolds Milbank classifies Miyake among "Realists": he is no realist; he is our most compelling dreamer and visionary.

—Richard Martin

MIZRAHI, Isaac.

American designer

Born: New York City, 14 October 1961. **Education:** Graduated from Parsons School of Design, New York, 1982. **Career:** Assistant designer, Perry Ellis, New York, 1982-83; womenswear designer, Jeffrey Banks, New York, 1984; designer, Calvin Klein, New York, 1985-87; formed own company, 1987; menswear collection introduced, 1990; added accessories line, 1992, and handbags, 1993. **Awards:** Council of Fashion Designers of America Award, 1988, 1989; Fashion Industry Foundation Award, 1990; Michaelangelo Shoe Award, New York, 1993. **Address:** 104 Wooster Street, New York, New York 10012, USA.

Publications:

On MIZRAHI:

Martin, Richard, and Harold Koda, *Bloom,* Metropolitan Museum of Art, 1995.

Articles

"Mr. Clean: New Designer Isaac Mizrahi," in *Vogue* (New York), February 1988.
Slonim, Jeffrey J., and Torkil Gudnason, "Retro-active: Back to the '60's with Isaac Mizrahi," in *Interview* (New York), March 1988.
Foley, Bridget, "Isaac Mizrahi: Setting Out for Stardom," in *Women's Wear Daily* (New York), 18 April 1988.
"Color Me Chic," in *Connoisseur* (New York), October 1988.
Hoare, Sarajane, "Vogue's Spy: Isaac Mizrahi," in *Vogue* (London), November 1988.
Bender, Karen, "Isaac Mizrahi," in *Taxi* (New York), February 1989.
Mansfield, Stephanie, "Nobody Beats the Miz," in *Vogue* (New York), February 1989.
Mower, Sarah, "Isaac Mizrahi," in *Vogue* (London), September 1989.

Jeal, Nicola, "The Divine Mr. M.," in *The Observer Magazine* (London), 1 April 1990.
Hepple, Keith, "Plum in the Middle of the Pomegranate," in *The Independent* (London), 12 April 1990.
Menkes, Suzy, "Mizrahi: The Shooting Star," in the *International Herald Tribune* (Neuilly, France), 17 April 1990.
Wayne, George, "Brooklyn Kid K.O.'s Couturiers," in *Interview* (New York), June 1990.
Talley, André Leon, "The Kings of Color," in *Vogue* (New York), September 1990.
Gross, Michael, "Slaves of Fashion: Isaac Mizrahi, the Great Hip Hope," in *New York Magazine,* 1 October 1990.
DeCaro, Frank, "Mizrahi Loves Company," in *Mademoiselle* (New York), January 1991.
"Isaac Mizrahi," in *Current Biography* (New York), January 1991.
Bernhardt, Sandra, "I and Me," in *Harper's Bazaar* (New York), March 1993.
"Designer Dish," in *Women's Wear Daily* (New York), 29 March 1993.
Foley, Bridget, "Hard Acts to Follow: Isaac Mizrahi," in *Women's Wear Daily,* 24 October 1994.
Spindler, Amy M., "Cocktails, Anyone? Clothes that Strut," in the *New York Times,* 2 November 1994.
Menkes, Suzy, "Mizrahi's All-American Swirls," in the *International Herald Tribune* (Paris), 3 November 1994.
Ezesky, Lauren, "Isaac Unbound," in *Paper* (New York), March 1995.
Spindler, Amy M., "Luxurious Armor by Karan, Klein, Mizrahi," in the *New York Times,* 8 April 1995.
"Dueling Isaacs," in *Women's Wear Daily* (New York), 10 April 1995.

*   *   *

Isaac Mizrahi worked, upon graduation from Parsons School of Design, for Perry Ellis, Jeffrey Banks, and Calvin Klein. When he started his own business in 1987, he knew intimately the world of American sportswear at its best, but his work refines the sportswear model by a special sense of sophistication and glamor. His ideals, beyond those he worked for, are such American purists as Norell, Halston, Beene, and McCardell, each a designer of utmost sophistication. Suzy Menkes analyzed in 1990: "The clean colors and Ivy League image of Perry Ellis sportswear might seem to be the seminal influence on Mizrahi. But he himself claims inspiration from his mother's wardrobe of all-American designers, especially the glamorous simplicity of Norman Norell." (*International Herald Tribune,* 17 April 1990).

It is as if Mizrahi is most challenged by distilling the most well-bred form of each garment to an understated glamor, whether tartan taken to a sensuous evening gown but still buckled as if Balmoral livery; pocketbooks and luggage ingeniously incorporated into clothing with the practical pocket panache of McCardell; or versions of high style in adaptations of men's bathrobes or sweatshirting used for evening. While Mizrahi is often commended for the youthfulness of his clothing, the praise is properly for the freshness of his perception, his ability to recalculate a classic, not just a market for young women. His interest in the Empire waistline; his practicality of wardrobe separates in combination; and his leaps between day and evening address all women equally. In the 1990s, many designers and manufacturers have seen the value in simplification: Mizrahi seeks the pure in tandem with the cosmopolitan.

When Sarah Mower described Mizrahi as "that rare thing in contemporary design: a life-enhancing intelligence on the loose," she rightly characterized his revisionist, rational, distilling, pure vision ("Isaac Mizrahi," *Vogue* [London], September 1989). With his fall 1988 collection Mizrahi was immediately recognized by the *New York Times* as "this year's hottest new designer" in combinations of color (for example, rust and mustard and orange-peel and pink) that were unusual, alpaca and other luxury materials, and the diversity of silhouettes from baby-doll dresses to evening jumpsuits to long dresses. Mizrahi had immediately demonstrated the range of a commercially viable designer while at the same time demonstrating his simplifying glamor and the cool, nonchalant charm of his smart (intellectually and aesthetically) clothing. The spa collection of 1988 included rompers and baseball jackets and playsuits as well as the debonair excess of trousers with paperbag waist. His spring 1989 collection assembled sources from all over the fashion spectrum to create a unified vision of elegance and appeal. The fall 1989 collection featured tartan (later developed by Mizrahi for costumes for a Twyla Tharp production for the American Ballet Theater in 1990) with most extraordinary accompaniment. In a notable instance, *New York* (21 August 1989) showed Mizrahi's tartan dress with his raccoon-trimmed silk taffeta parka in a perfect assembly of wild and urbane.

In 1990, Mizrahi showed a short-lived menswear line and sustained his color studies, creating double-faced wools and sportswear elements in watercolor-like colors, delicate yet deliberate. Spring 1990 was a typical Mizrahi transmogrification. Black and white pattern recalling both art déco and the 1960s was, in fact, derived from costume for the Ballets Russes. In 1991, Mizrahi's themes were American, creating a kind of Puritan revival in dresses with collars and bows in spring/summer 1991—like Norell in the early 1970s, but with more Massachusetts Bay Colony (American orthodoxy) than Norell's more demure version—and an American ethnic parade in fall 1991, including Native American dress and a notable totem-pole dress inspired by Native American art.

Mizrahi's drive to find the most sophisticated version of each concept he develops is the *leitmotif* of his work. His spring 1991 collection examined motifs of the 1960s, but with a clever sharpness not observed in other designers of the same year looking back to the period. In 1991, his tube dresses with flounces were inspired by Norell, but manifestly given proportion by Mizrahi. McCardell's audacious applications of cotton piqué are extended by Mizrahi's love of the same material and Halston's radical simplicity is inevitably a source for any designer longing to return to essential form. Mizrahi's color fields owe their consciousness to Perry Ellis, but the particular color sensibility is Mizrahi's. Mizrahi's immaculate, ingenious modernism is as clearly aware of sources as it is pushed toward the clarification of form.

Mizrahi has referred to his style as a "classic New York look," which presumably means a casual American idiom, but inflected with big-city reserve and refinement. Indeed, Mizrahi captures something of Manhattan chic and glamor of the 1940s and 1950s. It is perhaps the best description for fashion which is otherwise often indescribably beautiful in subtlety and sophistication.

—Richard Martin

MOLINARI, Anna. See **BLUMARINE.**

MOLYNEUX, Edward H.

British designer

Born: Hampstead, London, 5 September 1891. **Military Service:** Served as captain in the British Army during World War I. **Career:** Worked for the couturier Lucile in London and the USA, 1911-14; opened own house, Paris, 1919; added branches in Monte Carlo, 1925, Cannes, 1927, and London, 1932; moved business to London, 1939-1946; returned to Paris, added furs, perfume, lingerie and millinery, 1946-49; turned business over to Jacques Griffe and retired, 1950; reopened as Studio Molyneux, Paris, 1965; retired permanently soon thereafter. Fragrances include *Numéro Cinq,* 1926, *Vivre,* 1930, and *Rue Royale,* 1943. *Died* (in Monte Carlo), *23 March 1974.*

Publications:

On MOLYNEUX:

Books

Balmain, Pierre, *My Years and Seasons,* London 1964.
Carter, Ernestine, *Magic Names of Fashion,* New York 1980.
Milbank, Caroline Rennolds, *Couture: The Great Designers,* New York 1985.
de Marly, Diana, *The History of Haute Couture,* London 1988.

Articles

"Captain Edward Molyneux," obituary in *The Times* (London), 25 March 1974.

*   *   *

Captain Edward Molyneux embodied the style he created in the 1920s and 1930s, an idle, slim ("never too rich or too thin"), elegant style on the verge of dissipation, at the edge of the outrageous, and always refined. His friendship with Noel Coward was *kismet,* two personifications of the elegant style that made both drawing-room comedy and its grace. Caroline Milbank describes, "Molyneux was the designer to whom a fashionable woman would turn if she wanted to be absolutely 'right' without being utterly predictable in the Twenties and Thirties" (*Couture: The Great Designers,* New York 1985). Indeed, Molyneux's ineffable decorum had come as a privilege of his own style liberation from Lucile, Lady Duff Gordon. Lucile's trademark was her rich proliferation of fine details and adornment. One would not characterize Lucile as florid, but one would certainly characterize Molyneux as chaste. (In fact, his military self-presentation and English background made him seem even more Spartan in the world of French couture.) Molyneux banned all superfluous decoration in an early and intuited version of modernist International Style akin to the architecture of the period. He was a "modern" in his adoration of line and avoidance of excessive decoration. He was a "modern," not only in his engaging manner, but in his identification with style simplicity, his love of luxurious materials, and his embrace of modern circumstances, including the automobile. While his work is most often in black, navy blue, beige, and grey, he had the sophistication as an art collector to collect late Impressionist and Post-Impressionist paintings, shown in 1952 at the National Gallery of Art in Washington, D.C. and subsequently sold to Ailsa Mellon Bruce and later bequeathed to the National Gallery. He could love those bourgeois scenes of beauty. But he also created motoring outfits and easy-to-wear slip-like evening dresses for the leisure class of his time and superbly cut evening pajamas that could have costumed any Noel Coward comedy. Molyneux would be a designer successful at designing for and determining the lifestyle of his own social class, participant-observer in what Pierre Balmain called Molyneux's international set. His curious Franco-English snobbism belonged to a time and place. Indeed, Molyneux's two post-World War II business enterprises were of limited success, so fully was he the product and model of a world already forgotten.

The modern charm of Molyneux's creation was appreciated by Pierre Balmain who apprenticed with Molyneux in Paris. Balmain writes of his regret on departing that first job in the late 1930s and "that temple of subdued elegance. For if the magazines were filled with photographs of Schiaparelli's eccentricities, the world's well-dressed women wore the inimitable two-pieces, and tailored suits with pleated skirts, bearing the label of Molyneux" (*My Years and Seasons,* London 1964). Indeed, there is always a schism between the fashion that claims public attention and even the attention of the élite and that couture clothing that is so consistent, reserved, even understated that it is barely noticed by the fashion press, yet is the manifestation of a conservative, continuous style. Molyneux designed for the theater and was a friend of Gertrude Lawrence who wore his clothing with a West End and Broadway panache, but the costumes never subsumed the actress. Molyneux's international set wore his tailored suits by day, but also could be seen at night in one or both nightclubs owned by Molyneux in partnership with hostess Elsa Maxwell wearing furs, long gowns, beaded chemises, and other elegant outfits by the designer.

Today the designer who mingles with his clients is often criticized for social climbing. There is no evidence that such charges were placed against Molyneux as he moved so effortlessly and with *soigné* flair among the ladies that he dressed. Ernestine Carter called him "dashing and debonair," comparing him to Fred Astaire (*Magic Names of Fashion,* New York 1980). Further, that he dressed women of the greatest propriety and restraint made it clear that, in dwelling among them, he was of like sensibility and shared spirit. It was Molyneux's place in international café-society that allowed him to cavort with Noel Coward and that gave the sobriety of his design its sense of belonging. Given that fashion went through so many changes and excesses in the 1920s and 1930s, Molyneux was a constant model of cool elegance.

—Richard Martin

MONDI TEXTILE GmbH.

German fashion and accessory firm

Founded in Munich by Herwig Zahm, 1967; accessory collections added, 1970s; fashion lines, mainly women's ready-to-wear, in-clude Elementi, Mondi, Portara, Patrizia S, Braun and Chris (by Christa Zahm); opened free-standing shops in Budapest, 1989, and New York, 1993. Company purchased by Investcorp, 1993. **Awards:** Forum prize of the textile industry, 1986; Igedo's International Fashion Marketing Award, 1988; Fashion Oscar, Munich, 1991. **Address:** Nawiaskystrasse 11, D-81735 Munich, Germany.

Publications:

On MONDI:

Articles

Morais, Richard, "Who Is First in the Market, Sells," in *Forbes,* 16 September 1991.
"Investcorp Buys Stake in Mondi, and Pushes Ahead with Circle K.," in *Middle East Economic Digest,* 8 January 1993.
Dreier, Melissa, "Mondi Making Major Revamp," in *Women's Wear Daily* (New York), 5 January 1995.

*   *   *

The fashion house of Mondi was established in Munich in 1968 by Herwig Zahm. The company now sells exclusive coordinating fashion and accessory goods in over 54 countries worldwide, through 2300 independent speciality stores, 95 company owned stores and 200 franchised stores, including a capsule collection on the prestigious cruise liner *Queen Elizabeth 2.*

The group incorporates six labels: Portara (sophisticated fashion); Mondi (the main label); Chris by Christa Zahm (designer collection); Patrizia S by Mondi (large size fashion) and Braun (sport and golf wear). The overall appeal is cosmopolitan, designed for American, European, and Asian markets. The Mondi woman herself is difficult to categorize. She is undoubtably strong, individual, and successful but she is also ageless. "We know of customers aged 16 years and we know of others who are probably into their 60s," said Paul Peake, director of UK operations, in an interview in *Fashion Buyer* magazine.

There is a multicultural feel to all Mondi collections that is intentional. The design team at the Munich headquarters is as strong and individual as the Mondi customer, yet it is also diverse. The designers' varied backgrounds and experience combine to create a look that is cosmopolitan, formal and informal, adapting to the demands of city and country.

Mondi collections can be mixed and matched. Different fashion themes are explored in each collection, then combined with each other. The customer has the freedom to interpret each look according to her own personality or the occasion for which she is dressing. The company's goal is to ensure that the customer is in control and will feel confident, yet individual, in her Mondi outfit.

In an expanding but unstable fashion market, Mondi maintains its belief in strong design, bold colour, and fashionability. Their wide appeal and distinctive multicultural approach are repeated in each collection, when at least six strong yet interrelated themes are presented to the buyer. Spring/summer 1991 was an example. Pure Paris presented fresh summer elegance, with a distinctive Coco Chanel influence: bouclé and knitted cream and white coordinates with gold and pearl embroidery and chain accessories; Neo Geo, a graphic, chic black and white look combining lace, dogtooth check, and severe geometric lines; Colorissima, a street-smart city silhouette in primary colours, sharp tailored jackets with Ungaro-inspired

Mondi Textile: Spring/Summer 1995.

knee-length floral dresses; Polo Club, a nautical, sporty look in water colours, with embroidered polo emblems, shirts with hoods, skirts and trousers in all lengths, and edge-striped blazers and jackets. Modern classics meet traditional basics in every design theme to create casual elegance, yet sporty and wearable fashion style.

Germany has produced few fashion houses to have made their mark on international fashion but Mondi is an exception. Strategically clever marketing, innovation and creativity, combined with the classic German virtues of good workmanship and reliability, ensure their continuing worldwide success.

—Kevin Almond

MONTANA, Claude.

French designer

Born: Paris, 29 June 1949. **Education:** Studied chemistry and law. **Family:** Married Wallis Franken in 1993. **Career:** Free-lance jewelry designer, London, 1971-72; designer, with Michelle Costas, ready-to-wear and accessories line for Idéal-Cuir, Paris, 1973; assistant designer, 1973, and head designer, 1974, MacDouglas Leathers, Paris; free-lance designer, Complice, Ferrer y Sentis Knitwear, Paris, from 1975; founded own company, 1979; Hommes Montana presented, 1981; first boutique opened, Paris, 1983; *Montana Pour Femme* fragrance introduced, 1986; *Parfum d'Homme* introduced, 1989; *Parfum d'Elle* introduced, 1990; designer in charge of haute couture, Lanvin, 1989-92; continues ready-to-wear collections under own name: diffusion line introduced, 1991. **Exhibitions:** *Intimate Architecture: Contemporary Clothing Design,* Hayden Gallery, Massachusetts Institute of Technology, 1982. **Awards:** Prix Medicis, 1989; Fragrance Foundation Award, 1990; Golden Thimble Award, 1990, 1991. **Address:** 131 rue St Denis, 75001 Paris, France.

Publications:

On MONTANA:

Books

Hayden Gallery, Massachusetts Institute of Technology, *Intimate Architecture: Contemporary Clothing Design* (exhibition catalogue), Cambridge, Massachusetts 1982.
Perschetz, Lois, ed., *W, The Designing Life,* New York 1987.

Articles

Talley, André Leon, "The State of Montana," in *Women's Wear Daily* (New York), 13 March 1978.
McCarthy, Patrick, "Claude Reigns," in *Women's Wear Daily* (New York), 4 September 1979.
"Paris Advance: Claude Montana," in *Women's Wear Daily* (New York), 2 October 1980.
Brantley, Ben, "I, Claude," in *Women's Wear Daily* (New York), 18 May 1984.
Brampton, Sally, "La règle du jeu," in *The Observer* (London), 5 May 1985.
Filmer, Denny, "Claude Montana," in *Cosmopolitan* (London), October 1988.

Knafo, Robert, "Claude Montana," in *Connoisseur,* November 1988.
Brubach, Holly, "Selling Montana," in *The New Yorker,* 23 January 1989.
Petkanas, Christopher, "Chez Claude," in *Harper's Bazaar* (New York), June 1989.
Gross, Michael, "The Great State of Montana," in *New York,* 31 July 1989.
"Montana: Then and Now," in *Women's Wear Daily* (New York), 19 October 1989.
Thim, Dennis, "The New State of Montana," in *Women's Wear Daily* (New York), 29 May 1990.
Vernesse, Francine, "Viva Montana," in *Elle* (Paris), 13 August 1990.
Mulvagh, Jane, "Lanvin c'est moi," in *The Sunday Times Magazine* (London), 4 November 1990.
"Claude Montana," in *Current Biography* (New York), January 1992.
Spindler, Amy M., "Claude's New Adventure," in *Women's Wear Daily* (New York), 26 February 1992.
James, Laurie, "The State of Montana," in *Harper's Bazaar* (New York), October 1992.
Schiro, Anne-Marie, "Photogenic, But Out of Focus," in the *New York Times,* 20 March 1995.

*   *   *

In the late 1970s and 1980s Claude Montana was known for an *outré* silhouette and commanding sense of aggression that made him both *enfant terrible* in a cultural sense and yet fashion's most devoted adherent in design. Padded shoulders and leathers seemed to some observers a misogynist's view of women in the manner of a cartoon. To others, however, the same style renewed the shoulder-accented horizontal of Constructivism, or even the influence of Balenciaga's surgically acute cut. Little wonder, then, that Montana said in an interview in 1989, "I'm like a battlefield inside, a mass of contradictions." More than ever, Montana has proved in the late 1980s and 1990s how contradictory and how complex his style is, incapable of the kinds of knee-jerk reactions that many critics had initially. Few designers have been as virulently attacked as Montana has, sometimes for "gay-clone" proclivities to leather, for supposed misogyny, for impractical clothing, for excessive accoutrements. Leather jackets borrowed from menswear—bikers and the military—caused strong controversy in the American press and market in the 1980s when Montana appropriated them. A decade later, Ralph Lauren, Donna Karan, Calvin Klein, and Byron Lars were working with similar looks to no protest (and Saint Laurent had long borrowed from the male wardrobe to only mild demurral).

Few designers today can be equally admired for the surety of cut, the sensuousness of appearance, the femininity that is beneath the bold forms, the luxurious seductions of fabrics more varied than leather alone, and the continuous and consummate mastery of a fashion design that always plays between the abstract forms of art and the conventions of clothing. Indeed, Constructivism is a strong influence on Montana's work. Top-heavy geometry twirling into a narrow skirt or pencil-thin trousers was not commonplace until Montana offered the option. Reductive by nature, Montana has vacillated in terms of accessorizing, particularly in the mid-1980s, but by the 1990s he clearly preferred an austerity about clothing, approximating the linear probity and arc-based sculptural form. Like Constructivist drawings for the stage, Montana's designs come to life in the animation of gyrating proportions, often with exaggerated shoulders or collars, almost invariably with a very narrow waist, and the spin of a peplum over a narrow skirt. Cocoon coats could seem to be the nimbus of abstraction; spiralling line, alternately clinging to the body and spinning away, seemed a gesture of whole cloth, unpieced.

Montana's principal aesthetic contribution is silhouette; nonetheless, his materials, beginning historically with leather, and his color palette are beautiful and sensuous. What became the power look in women's clothing in the mid-1980s is derived from Montana's aesthetic, so persuasive was it as an option for assertive presence without sacrifice of the female form. Based on circuiting spirals and a few strong lines realized on the body, Montana's aesthetic was described by some critics as being too Space Age or futuristic, but recognized by its advocates for its invocation of the principles of Futurist abstraction. Moreover, after a signal collection for fall-winter 1984, in which Montana toned down the most extreme aspects of his style, he remained true to his aesthetic principles and interests, demonstrating that they were not merely the radical forms they had seemed at first, but the fundamental forms that fashion had known since Thayatt and Exter, Adrian and Balenciaga. As early as 1979, when many might have dismissed him as an iconoclast, Montana admitted to André Leon Talley of his admiration for

Vionnet and Madame Grès, likewise two designers of utmost simplicity of form (*Women's Wear Daily,* 13 March 1978).

What had been extreme now seems pure. Even in that convention, Montana has emulated avant-garde art. As an artist-designer, he sustains his own predilections. For example, the gargantuan shoulders are reduced in the late 1980s and great, oversized collars keep the outspoken gesture to the top. Robert Knafo (*Connoisseur,* November 1988) describes that transition: "casting out the sharp-shouldered, fearsomely assertive Montana woman, installing in her place a mellower, softer-edged, more romantic figure, although no less self-assured." Indeed, it is some of the referentiality of fashion—association we make with clothing types and image— that has attributed the controversial profile to Montana as a designer. More importantly, he has been a steadfast practitioner of a kind of isolated, non-referential abstraction, obdurately and passionately and compellingly exploring fashion at its most distinct cut. Montana's design survival as a classic figure and a model with lasting impact on other advanced designers in modern fashion attests to that design primacy and perseverance.

—Richard Martin

MORENI, Popy.

French designer

Born: Annalisa Moreni in Turin, Italy, 3 December 1947. **Education:** Istituto Statale d'Arte, Moda e Costume, Turin, 1961-64. **Family:** Children: Amour, Aimée. **Career:** Moved to Paris, 1964. Design assistant to Maïmé Arnaudin, 1964; designer in Arnaudin's Mafia design studio, Paris, 1965-67, and in Promostyl, Paris, 1967-73; designer, Timmi, 1972; established own design and consulting office (working for Rhone-Poulenc Textile and Rasurel), from 1973; first boutique opened, Paris, 1976; first fashion collection, 1980; first creations for catalogues 3 Suisses, 1981; ready-to-wear licensed, from 1982; childrenswear licensed, from 1987. **Exhibitions:** *Popy Moreni, Collerettes x 13,* Galerie des Femmes, Paris, 1985; *Les Années 80,* Musée des Arts de la Mode, Paris, 1989-90; *Mode et Liberté,* Musée des Arts de la Mode, Paris, 1992. **Awards:** named Chevalier de l'Ordre des Arts et des Lettres, 1986. **Address:** 170 rue du Temple, 75003 Paris, France.

Publications:

On MORENI:

Books

Deslandres, Yvonne, *Histoire de la mode au XXme siècle,* Paris 1986.
Benaim, Laurence, *L'Année de la mode,* France, 1987-88.

Articles

Godard, Colette, "La mode comme le souvenir d'un bonheur," in *Le Monde* (Paris), April 1986.
Seraglini, Marie, "Carte noire et blanche à Popy Moreni," in *Maison Française* (Paris), July 1986.

Popy Moreni: Winter 1990/91. *Photograph by Jean Paul LeLievre.*

Perrier, M. J., "Designer Close Up," in *Interior* (London), March 1987.

Mont Servan, N., "Les 100 poids lourds de la mode," in *Passion* (Paris), February 1990.

*

I hope to love everything, unfortunately I cannot yet do so. In fact, I tell myself that what I do not love is simply what I do not understand.

So, potentially, I love everything: the real and the false, the authentic and the copied, the straight line and the curve, elegance and vulgarity, the good and the bad, the law-abiding and the outlaw.

I would like to do everything! Not necessarily in order to do but in order to search ...

I'm rather inquisitive and dissatisfied on the whole ... so I persevere!

I am active because the unknown is so potent ...

For my work I like silence, white and black, open countryside, concrete, the morning, thick pencils ... the ideas are in the pencil ... it is through drawing a lot that one makes discoveries ... You rarely get surprising results early on ...

The main thing depends on time, the moment, and on the eye ... so it can always change ... what is essential?

At times the desire to simplify ...

At others the desire to complicate ...

Does the sky not have clouds?

Work keeps me busy and prevents me asking myself too many questions. I am short of time to do everything I would like to ... but you have to sleep, too, an indispensable condition for carrying on ...

When I am tired I am unable to stand back, the mere fact of doing gives me a restful sleep.

No one is indispensable ... you have to be egocentric to think you are needed ...

Every day I invent stories for myself and pretend to believe them otherwise what would I do?

I have thought about sitting down in front of a white space and moving no more ... it would be identical to what I am doing ... the white space, at any moment, would give me something new ...

So it is just a matter of choice and chance ...

—Popy Moreni

*   *   *

Popy Moreni is an Italian designer working in Paris, who manages to combine distinctive style elements from both countries: a strong Italian sense of colour and coordination, with a chic French practicality. She was born into an artistic family in Turin, Italy. Her mother is a sculptor and her father a painter. She studied costume and design in Italy at L'Istituto Statale d'Arte, Moda e Costume, then moved to Paris at 17 to pursue a career in fashion. Her first job was at Mafia, the design studio of Maïmé Arnaudin; next she worked for the Promostyl Organization and the Italian firm Timmi until 1972.

She opened her own design studio in 1973 and worked on consultancies with a range of clients that included Rhone-Poulenc Textile and Rasurel. In 1980 she showed her first collection on the catwalk. She quickly became known for her witty, carefree clothes. A taste for theatricality and the baroque gave her collections the recurrent theme of *commedia dell'arte* with harlequin prints and jagged-cut details, satin capes and Pierrot collars, all translated into inventive sportswear shapes. She also takes a great deal of inspiration from her artistic heritage, looking to abstract painters like Jackson Pollock and Hans Hartung when designing and choosing prints.

By 1985 the collections had grown in size and breadth, incorporating such details as petal shapes, corollas, and plush velvets. Recent innovations have been oversize crisp white cotton shirts decorated with ruffled cuffs and necklines. Cheeky sleeveless striped suits again decorated with a huge ruff collar of satin, plus fun linen suits, printed with an asymmetric leaf detail. Her most recent collection for autumn-winter 1993-94 showed a stark paring down of her carefree theatricality, with severe charcoal and black fit-and-flare dresses with unusual details like tiny cap sleeves or asymmetrical seaming. Accessory details like fingerless gloves, black nail polish, and a no-make-up look contribute to the austerity.

Expansion of the Popy Moreni business began with the opening of her first boutique in the Les Halles district of Paris in 1976. In 1980 she began a joint collaboration with a French mail order firm, Les Trois Suisses, to design children's and women's clothes. She also developed a distinctive eveningwear line, plus hat, shoe, and jewellery ranges. Of particular interest is her innovation of plastic shoes dyed to bright colours. A licensee agreement with Mitsukoshi Ltd. in Japan ensures a lucrative Oriental exposure and marketing of her name and products.

—Kevin Almond

MORI, Hanae.

Japanese designer

Born: Tokyo, 8 January 1926. **Education:** Graduated in literature from Tokyo Christian Women's University, 1947. **Family:** Married Kei Mori; children: Akira and Kei. **Career:** First atelier in Shinjuko, Tokyo, 1951; costume designer for films, 1954-c.1961; first New York fashion show, 1965; showed in Monaco and Paris, 1975; haute couture collection and haute couture house established in Paris and member of Le Chambre Syndicale de la Haute Couture Parisienne, 1977; Hanae Mori Boutique in Faubourg St. Honor, Paris, 1985; designer of costumes for La Scala, Milan; designer of costumes for Paris Opera Ballet, 1986; Hanae Mori Boutique launched, Monte Carlo, 1989. Shows in Paris, Budapest, Moscow and Kuala Lumpur, 1990; shows in Lausanne and Taipei, and member of Japan Olympic Committee and chairman of Cultural Affairs Promotion Committee of Tokyo Chamber of Commerce and Industry, 1991. **Exhibitions:** *Avant-garde Japon,* Centre Pompidou, Paris, 1986; *Hanae Mori: 35 Years in Fashion,* Tokyo, 1989, Monte Carlo, 1990, and Paris, 1990; *Diana Vreeland: Immoderate Style,* Metropolitan Museum of Art, New York, 1993-94; *Japonism in Fashion,* Kyoto Costume Institute, 1994; *Japanese Design: A Survey Since 1950,* Philadelphia Museum of Art, 1994; *Orientalism,* Metropolitan Museum of Art, New York, 1994-95. **Awards:** Neiman Marcus Award, 1973; Medaille d'Argent, City of Paris, 1978; The Symbol of Man Award, Minnesota Museum, 1978; Croix de Chevalier des Arts et Lettres, 1984; Purple Ribbon Decoration, Japan, 1988; Asahi Prize as pioneer of Japanese Fashion, 1988; named Chevalier de la Légion d'Honneur, 1989; Person of Cultural Merit, Japan, 1989. **Address:** 6-1, 3 Chome, Kita-Aoyama, Minato-ku, Tokyo, Japan.

Publications:

By MORI:

Books

Designing for Tomorrow, Tokyo 1979.
A Glass Butterfly, Tokyo 1984.
Hanae Mori 1960-1989, Tokyo 1989.
Fashion—A Butterfly Crosses the Border, Tokyo 1993.

On MORI:

Books

Marcus, Stanley, *Quest for the Best,* New York 1979.
Koren, Leonard, *New Fashion Japan,* Tokyo 1984.
Sparke, Penny, *Japanese Design,* London 1987.
Fairchild, John, *Chic Savages,* New York 1989.

Articles

"Hanae Mori: Legend in Her Own Time," in *American Fabrics and Fashions* (Colombia, South Carolina), Spring 1974.
Whitehead, Ron, "Japan's Queen of Haute Couture," in *Femina,* May 1979.
Lohse, Marianne, "Hanae Mori," in *Madame Figaro* (Paris), April 1987.
Lalanne, Dorothee, "Hanae Mori première!," in *Vogue* (Paris), March 1989.
Beurdeley, Laurence, "Hanae Mori," in *L'Officiel* (Paris), June 1989.
Menkes, Suzy, "Hanae Mori: Fashion that Fuses the East and West," in *International Herald Tribune* (Neuilly, France), June 1989.
Bumiller, Elizabeth, "Japan's Madame Couturier," in the *Washington Post,* February 1990.
Davy, Philippe, "Un souffle nouveau," in *L'Officiel* (Paris), February 1990.
Davidson, Monique, "Univers Hanae Mori: un empire au soleil levant," in *Joyce,* March/April 1991.

*

I design primarily to enhance our lifestyle and make it richer and more enjoyable. Expression changes with the times. But the essence does not change. The history of the world is the story of men and women—how men relate to women and how they live. I would like to express that great sense of existence in clothing. I have been in pursuit of that all through my life. For women, something that encompasses truly valuable things have elegance at their core. This is something I have been trying to find out.

I am true to my identity. I keep trying to be myself. I am Japanese. In Japan there is this beauty by itself which has been nurtured by tradition—fashion is an international language. What I have been trying to do is to express the wonderful beauty of Japan using international language.

—Hanae Mori

*   *   *

A delicate sense of feminine beauty, stemming from Hanae Mori's Japanese heritage, is married to an artistic use of colour and fabric in all her work. She treads a careful line, balancing Eastern influences with Western ideals to produce consistently successful couture and ready-to-wear lines with international customers. If her clothes lack the more outrageous, attention grabbing qualities of some of her couture counterparts, they compensate with the economy of their cut and base their appeal on the practical needs of the wealthy metropolitan women who wear them.

By stepping outside current trends and concentrating on conservative, but always feminine daywear, Mori has established a niche for herself in the Parisian fashion arena. Integral to this is the sense of the longevity of her easy to wear separates, which even in the ready-to-wear line retain a delicacy of touch through the textiles used. Floating silk dresses, in simple shirtwaist shapes, were shown for spring-summer 1989, covered in powdery pastel flowers standing out from a black background and coupled with abbreviated blossom pink jackets. They encapsulated Mori's design principles by conveying femininity and practicality.

Mori elaborates on the basic tenets of combining fine fabrics and flattering cut, adding her own feel for the dramatic to her eye-catching eveningwear. For this Mori makes optimum use of the lustrous printed textiles produced by her husband, and designed especially for her work. Although there is an air of restrained elegance to much of her design, symbolized by the fragile butterfly motif by which she is known, her eveningwear often breaks into more vibrant realms. In 1981 she produced a languorous silk mousseline dress, the vampish leopard print and deep *décolleté* of which were balanced by the soft, sinuous fall of the fabric. Other examples use bright hot colours, juxtaposed in one ensemble to provide interest, bringing a strong Japanese feel to their narrow hues, which frequently hark back to the kimono for their silhouette and cut. It is in this area that her work is most inspired, bringing together European tailoring and Japanese colour and ideals of beauty. She uses the Japanese love of asymmetry to further develop her style and the linear patterns she prints on to her distinctive silks. She exploits the natural appeal of such fabrics with a well defined sense of cut to illuminate her realistic styles. By doing so, Mori is providing both an alternative to and a definite rejection of the type of elaborate couture confections which mould the female form into fantastical shapes, ignoring the woman beneath the fabric.

The other main strand to her design is her close involvement in the arts. Her early costuming of innumerable Japanese films enabled her sense of colour to evolve, using each primary hued textile to represent a different emotion, and sharpened her sense of the dramatic effect of dress. This has grown in her work for opera and ballet, her clothing for which has drawn on her love of delicacy and poise counterpointed with strong coloration and arresting mixes of the two worlds her design principles straddle.

A firm grasp of the value of these cross cultural reference points has enabled Mori to establish herself in Paris couture and therefore develop an international market. Her understanding of the needs of contemporary women has lent a practical slant to her simple shaped, wearable clothes, while her theatrical preoccupations and Japanese background have inspired her love of rich, tactile fabrics in vibrant prints and colours which are the hallmark of her design.

—Rebecca Arnold

Hanae Mori.

MORRIS, Robert Lee.

American jewelry and accessories designer

Born: Nuremburg, Germany, 7 July 1947. **Education:** Graduated from Beloit College, Beloit, Wisconsin. **Career:** Showed first collection in 1972; owner and manager, Artwear Gallery, 1977-93; Robert Lee Morris Necessities mail order catalogue introduced, 1993. Also: packaging designer, Elizabeth Arden, New York, from 1992. **Exhibitions:** Artwear Gallery, New York, 1992; *Good as Gold: Alternative Materials in American Jewelry,* 1981-85 (Smithsonian Institution international touring exhibition); retrospective, Fashion Institute of Technology, New York, 1995. **Awards:** Coty American Fashion Critics Award, 1981; Council of Fashion Designers of America Award, 1985; International Gold Council Award, 1987; Woolmark Award, 1992; American Accessories Achievement Award, 1992. **Address:** 161 Sixth Avenue, New York, New York 10013, USA.

Publications:

On MORRIS:

Books

Untracht, Oppi, *Jewelry Concepts and Technology,* Garden City, New York 1982.
Cartlidge, Barbara, *Twentieth Century Jewelry,* New York 1985.
Shields, Jody, *All that Glitters,* New York 1987.
Mulvagh, Jane, *Costume Jewelry in Vogue,* London 1988.
Blauer, Ettagale, *Contemporary American Jewelry Design,* New York 1991.
Cera, Deanne Farneti, *Jewels of Fantasy: Costume Jewelry of the 20th Century,* New York 1992.

Articles

"Artwear: Redefining Jewelry with a Modern Style," in *Vogue* (New York), January 1984.
Greendorfer, Tere, "Going for the Bold," in the *Sunday Star Ledger* (London), 2 July 1989.
Newman, Jill, "On the Cutting Edge with Robert Lee Morris," in *Women's Wear Daily* (New York), 19 August 1989.
Myers, Coco, "Icon Maker," in *Mirabella* (New York), October 1990.
Greco, Monica, "Portrait of the Artist," in *Sportswear International* (New York), 1991.
Mower, Sarah, "Robert Lee Morris: A Multi-faceted New York Jeweller Finds Inspiration in the British Isles," in *Vogue* (London), November 1991.
Schiro, Ann-Marie, "Paying Tribute to a Wearable Art," in the *New York Times,* 26 April 1992.
Spindler, Amy M., "Piety on Parade: Fashion Seeks Inspiration," in the *New York Times,* 5 September 1993.
Menkes, Suzy, "A Jeweler's Creed: Value Is in the Design," in the *International Herald Tribune* (Paris), 17 April 1995.

*

My jewelry is a distant cousin of ancient armor (those smooth, sensual body-conscious constructions that employ ingenious me-

Robert Lee Morris: Fall 1993; Flaming Halo Cross Choker.
Photograph by Teresa Misagal.

chanics to allow for fluid movement). My inspiration has never been clothing or fashion trends, but rather, the human need for personal intimacy, with tokens of spiritual potential that amulets and talismans provide.

I constantly seek to fine-tune, focus, purify, and strengthen my style, to make it more clear, more recognizable, and more understandable by people of any and all cultures. Mass fashion jewelry, in my mind, is purely decorative, employing a cacophony of glittery values to achieve a dazzling effect. This is as much a part of human culture as the bright plumage of birds, and will remain with us, as it should. But, it has always been against this world that I design my work; placing value on classicism and heirloom status over the thrill of temporary trends. My forms and shapes lead my concepts. My concepts are generally anthropological and my attitude is "less is more."

—Robert Lee Morris

*   *   *

"Wearable art" as created by Robert Lee Morris has become a symbol of style among young, modern, rebellious, sexy, and chic individuals. Morris has redefined the way people perceive jewelry. Morris entered the fashion scene some 20 years ago and has transformed the contemporary jewelry industry by drawing on symbols from antiquity in ways that underscore their relevance to our lives today. He remains fascinated by the meaning of art, the role of jewelry as a talisman of the spirit. Morris maintains a keen appreciation of a pure, powerful aesthetic.

Morris is more like a student of culture than a fashion trend setter. He originally planned a career in anthropology, but recognizing his artistic talents, combined his favorite disciplines through the craft of jewelry making. As a self-taught artist, Morris developed his distinctive "Etruscan" gold finish by layering pure 24-carat gold over brass. As opposed to the high shine of 18-carat gold jewelry, the matt yellow gold has an unusual muted glow. Along the same lines Morris created a green patina—a crude finish with the look of weathered stone. These creations not only established his style but filled a gap between costume jewelry and the "really real stuff." His bold, minimalistic, sculptural forms quickly became popular in the early 1970s, where he was initially represented by the Sculpture to Wear Gallery at the Plaza Hotel in New York. Sales of his designs immediately outpaced such masters as Picasso, Braque, Calder, Max Ernst and Man Ray. His Celtic crosses, cuffs, collars, disc belts, and heart shaped brooches are treasured by the stylish glitterati. This list includes Hollywood celebrities, heavy metal rock stars, rich urban bikers, as well as businessmen and women who are eager to express their individuality.

In 1977, Morris launched an entire modern jewelry movement when he opened Artwear. At Artwear, Morris created a showcase "for artists focusing on jewelry as their prime medium," and attracted public interest through merchandising techniques that were as unique as the gallery's overall concept. The jewelry was displayed on dramatic plaster body-casts resembling sculptural relics of ancient civilizations. This concept was based on his belief that jewelry "comes alive on the body." He also developed an image catalog, featuring models covered in mud, sand, and flour, which instantly became a collectors' item.

In addition to being a successful jewelry designer and businessman, Morris designs handbags, belts, scarves, amulets, sconces, candlesticks, picture frames, packaging for beauty products (the latter for Elizabeth Arden) as well as his own fragrance, *Verdigris,* named for the ancient color which has become a signature of his mythic style.

Robert Lee Morris has continually sought out new avenues for expression, collaborating with such designers and contemporaries as Calvin Klein, Geoffrey Beene, Karl Lagerfeld, and Donna Karan. In his own collections, he has invented a clean, pure, uniquely American style—launching such trends as "bold gold" and the green patina verdigris—while as founder of the gallery Artwear, he has fostered an entire generation of modern jewelry makers.

—Roberta H. Gruber

MORTON, Digby.

Irish designer

Born: Digby (Henry) Morton in Dublin, 27 November 1906. **Education:** Studied architecture at the Metropolitan School of Art and Architecture, Dublin, 1923; London Polytechnic. **Family:** Married Phyllis May Painting in 1936. **Career:** Worked as sketch artist, Jay's fashion store, Oxford Street, London, 1928. Founded tailoring firm of Lachasse in Farm St, Mayfair, London, 1928; own house established, 1934; closed, 1957; founded Reldan-Digby Morton, 1958; founder member of the Incorporated Society of London Fashion Designers, 1942; designer of Utility clothing for British government, 1942; film costume designer in Hollywood during World War II; established Digby Morton (Exports) Ltd for marketing British womenswear to USA, 1947; Digby Morton for Jacqmar collection, 1950; designer, and vice-president, 1955-58, Hathaway Shirt Company, New York; designer-director, Reldan-Digby Morton, 1958-73; designed Women's Voluntary Services

uniform, 1939. **Awards:** Aberfoyle International Fashion Award, New York, 1956. *Died* (in London) *1983.*

Publications:

On MORTON:

Books

Amies, Hardy, *Just So Far,* London 1954.
Carter, Ernestine, *Tongue in Chic,* London 1974.
Lambert, Eleanor, *World of Fashion: People, Places, Resources,* New York and London 1976.
Ginsburg, Madeleine, and Prudence Glynn, *In Fashion,* London 1977.
Amies, Hardy, *Still Here,* London 1984.
Mulvagh, Jane, *Vogue History of 20th Century Fashion,* London 1988.

*   *   *

The fashion for sportswear during the 1920s was the ideal environment for Digby Morton to establish the London house of Lachasse, which specialized in the tailored sporting suit for women. Morton was brought in as chief designer of the sportswear department of a dress establishment owned by a businessman, Fred Singleton. Morton later claimed that his decision to call the new house Lachasse was because at that time British women would not consider anything but French labels in their wardrobes.

Digby Morton transformed the classic tweed suit into a fashionable garment through the carefully planned placing of seams that gave a more decorative line to the native Irish tweeds he used. Sir Hardy Amies acknowledges that Morton's intricate cutting technique and designs made the ordinary country tweed suit into a fashionable garment that could be worn confidently in town as well as the country. Morton's first collection of 1929 featured Ardara tweeds, large herringbone wools, and diagonal stripes and checks in then unusual colour combinations such as pale lime green and duck egg blue with dark brown. Morton used French printed silks by Rodier for blouses and linings which were clean cut and spare for detail, and far removed from what he called "postmistress blouses."

Morton's belief that British women could not successfully wear conspicuous clothes was evident in designs where he endeavoured to "translate the trends of feminine fashion into the masculine medium of tailoring." His theory was that it was more difficult to eliminate details than to decorate garments, which resulted in simple lines that relied for effect upon his use of fabrics. Digby Morton's preference for uncluttered designs was also reflected in his dislike of designing eveningwear, which he referred to as debutante clothes. When he began to introduce eveningwear into his collections in the late 1940s his designs were based upon the tailored evening dress. After five years at Lachasse, Morton established his own couture house in 1934. In 1939 he was invited to design the Women's Voluntary Service uniform and during World War II he was an active member of the Incorporated Society of London Fashion Designers, established in 1942 to promote exports of British fashion. Morton also designed a collection of garments for the British government's Utility clothing scheme (no-trims standards for wartime clothing and household goods), which went into production anonymously in 1942.

Morton became more closely involved in the field of ready-to-wear clothing in the postwar period and enjoyed particular success in the American market during the 1950s. In 1953 he was asked to design the Lady Hathaway shirt collection for the Hathaway shirt company—a manufacturer of top quality men's shirts. By copying the cut of men's shirts, with slight adjustments for the female form, Morton created the collection in brilliant colours and patterns with contrasting bow ties. The success of this venture earned him the title of *Daring Digby* by *Time* Magazine. It was this that may have prompted Morton to close his couture house in 1957 and enter the field of ready-to-wear on a full-time basis. Morton always acknowledged that he felt constrained by couture and that his real design career began when he started designing clothes for the average woman.

In 1958 Morton formed the company Reldan-Digby Morton with Nadler, a large fashion producer owned by Cyril Kern. Morton's ready-to-wear designs for the company Reldan-Digby Morton introduced ready-made garments with a couture image to the British public. The collection of separates was renamed Togethers and produced at the company's High Wycombe, Buckinghamshire factory. They were also successful in America where some of the more adventurous designs such as bright yellow and black stripe suits and jet black towelling beach coats appealed to the particular market. In 1963 Morton began designing menswear, an area that had always appealed to him—he had personally adopted the neo-Edwardian style that was fashionable for men in the 1950s. Morton designed his first menswear collection in Trevira cloth for the Cologne Fair, one of the most widely publicized garments of which was the *Mesh over Flesh Vestshirt* which featured string vest fabric with formal shirting. Other designs played on the traditional image of the male suit, with unusual features such as curved side slits on formal trousers.

Primarily a designer of tailored clothes, Digby Morton was recognized for his use of traditional fabrics in unusual colour combinations. His couture designs for womenswear reflected his belief that the British couture customer required unobtrusive suits in good tweeds that were wearable rather than dramatic.

—Catherine Woram

MOSCHINO, Franco.

Italian designer

Born: Abbiategrasso, 1950. **Education:** Studied fine art, Accademia delle Belle Arti, Milan, 1968-71. **Career:** Free-lance designer and illustrator, Milan, 1969-70; sketcher for Versace, 1971-77; designer for Italian company Cadette, 1977-82. Founded own company Moonshadow in 1983; launched Moschino COUTURE!, 1983; introduced diffusion line, CHEAP & CHIC, 1988; launched UOMO, menswear collection, 1986, and CHEAP & CHIC UOMO, 1991; also lines of underwear, swimwear, jeans, children's clothes, accessories; fragrance for women *Moschino* introduced, 1987, and *OKKO* men's fragrance, 1991. **Exhibitions:** *X Years of Kaos!* (retrospective), Museo della Permanente, Milan, 1993-94. *Died 18 September 1994.* **Address:** Moonshadow SpA, Via Ceradini 11/A, 20129 Milan, Italy.

Publications:

By MOSCHINO:

Books

X Anni di Kaos!, 1983-1993 (exhibition catalogue), with Lida Castelli, Milan 1993.

On MOSCHINO:

Books

Martin, Richard, and Harold Koda, *Jocks and Nerds: Men's Style in the Twentieth Century,* New York 1989.

Articles

Webb, Iain R., "Il Cattivo: Franco Moschino Is the 'Bad Boy' of Italian Fashion," in *Blitz* (London), August 1987.
Eastoe, Jane, "Designer Chaos," in *Fashion Weekly* (London), 23 February 1989.
"Franco Moschino," in *i-D* (London), May 1989.
Mower, Sarah, "Dressing Down with the Joker," in *The Independent* (London), 16 November 1989.
Ducas, Jane, "An Italian in Love with All Things English," in *The Sunday Times* (London), 29 April 1990.
Born, Pete, "Frankly Franco," in *Women's Wear Daily* (New York), 14 June 1991.
Casadio, Mariuccia, Jean-Baptiste Mondino, and Marguerite Shore, "I Am Proud of the Odor of Garlic and Tomato in My Clothes," in *Interview* (New York), September 1991.
Goodman, Wendy, "Surrealist at Work," in *House and Garden* (New York), March 1993.
Hochswender, Woody, "Pins and Needles," in *Harper's Bazaar* (New York), October 1993.
"Moschino," in *Mondo Vomo,* July-August 1994.
Talley, André Leon, "Franco Moschino, 1950-1994," in *Vogue* (New York), December 1994.
"Florence: Moschino," in the *Daily News Record* (New York), 18 January 1995.
Menkes, Suzy, "A Manhattan Melody in Italian Shows," in the *International Herald Tribune* (Paris),7 March 1995.

*   *   *

"Fashion is full of chic" believes Franco Moschino, an ironic statement coming from one of Europe's most successful designers.

Based in Milan, Moschino originally studied fine art, with ambitions to be a painter, but came to see that tailoring and fabrics could be just as valid a means of expression as paint and canvas. Consequently, his first job in fashion was with the Cadette label, for whom in 1977 he produced a simple range of stylish clothes.

Starting his own label in 1982, Moschino used his experience in the Italian fashion industry as a source for his philosophical ideas evolving a set of tactics designed to shake the fashion establishment out of its complacency. Much to his amazement, he was embraced with open arms as a new iconoclast by the very people he despised.

Essentially Moschino was picking up where Schiaparelli had left off, displaying an interest in the Surrealist tactic of displacement—he has for a long time professed a love of Magritte's use of the

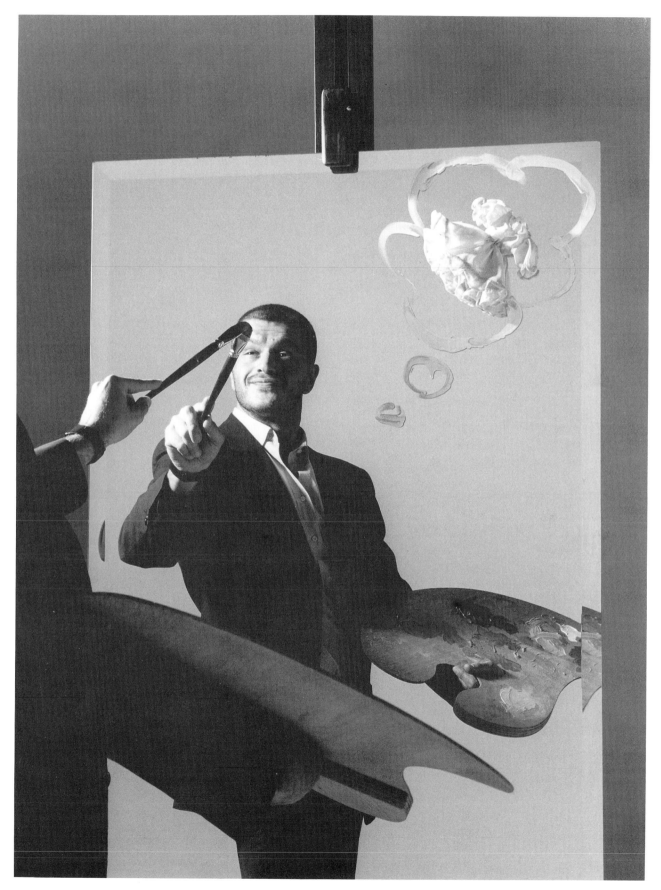

Franco Moschino: "Self portrait."

juxtaposition of incongruous imagery to produce a surreality. This is aptly shown in designs such as his quilted black denim mini with plastic fried eggs decorating the hemline, quilted jacket decorated with bottle tops, plug-socket drop earrings, and bodices made out of safety pins. Moschino's 1989 fun fur collection included a winter coat of stitched together teddybear pelts and a scorch-mark printed silk shirt saying "too much ironing."

Although dubbed the Gaultier of Italian fashion, Moschino responds to fashion differently. Unlike Jean-Paul Gaultier who is interested in playing around with the shapes and the fabrics of fashion, Moschino uses basic forms and traditional methods of construction to produce wearable, sexy clothes, cut to flatter and beautifully made. Dismissing his approach as visual and superficial, Moschino stresses that he is a decorator, completely disinterested in clothing construction.

Believing he can criticize the business more effectively from the inside, the underlying theme of his oeuvre is the parodying of so-called fashion victims, those prepared to be seen in the most ridiculous clothes if they are the latest style, and a general protest against the materialism of capitalism. He does this with visual gags like a triple pearl choker with attached croissant or the Rolex necklace—the pearls and Rolex being traditional ways of displaying wealth—and by mixing cheap plastics with expensive fur.

This parodying of the conspicuous consumers of fashion was continued in 1990 with his use of jokey logos on a series of garments like the cashmere jacket with the words "Expensive jacket" embroidered in gold across its back, or "Bull chic" on a matador style outfit. Designs such as these were supposed to make the wearer feel duped into spending vast amounts of money on designer clothing, but after achieving a vast amount of publicity, the people he was attacking flocked to buy his clothes. The iconoclasm of Moschino was destined to become the choicest thing on the catwalk.

Calling for a "Stop to the Fashion System" through his advertising in high fashion magazines, Moschino displays a classic Dada stance, for an end to the fashion system would mean the destruction of his own empire which now encompasses not just Moschino Couture! but the successful Cheap and Chic range—a diffusion line which is not actually all that cheap—and ranges of underwear, swimwear, jeans, children's clothes, accessories, and fragrances, the men's sold in a double-ended bottle so it can't stand up and the women's advertised with a model drinking it through a straw rather than dabbing it behind her ears.

Known for his theatrical fashion shows (in the past his models have impersonated Tina Turner and Princess Margaret), Moschino mixes up and twists classic styles and wrenches them into the present by using humour, for example a Chanel-type suit is restyled with gold clothes pegs for buttons. It will be interesting to see how far he can go before his insults are taken seriously. At one collection he pointedly mocked the top fashion editors by leaving moo-boxes on their seats, implying they were dull bovines with not an original thought in their heads, but they applauded all the more.

Moschino's ambition is to destroy the dictates of fashion so that people can please themselves with what they choose to wear, and to begin producing more anonymous clothes once he has finished with engineering the downfall of the industry. The irony is that the irony of Moschino has become its own status symbol, but his belief that fashion should be fun is valid and allows people to break the rules, if only in a way that is acceptable.

—Caroline Cox

MUGLER, Thierry.

French designer

Born: Strasbourg, Alsace, 1948. **Education:** Studied at the Lycée Fustel de Coulange, 1960-65, and at the School of Fine Arts, Strasbourg, 1966-67. **Career:** Dancer, Opéra de Rhin, Strasbourg, 1965-66; assistant designer, Gudule boutique, Paris, 1966-67; designer, André Peters, London, 1968-69; free-lance designer, Milan, Paris, 1970-73; created Café de Paris fashion collection, Paris, 1973; founder, Thierry Mugler, 1974, owner from 1986; Thierry Mugler Perfumes created, 1990, *Angel* fragrance introduced, 1992; first couture collection shown, 1992. Also professional photographer, from 1967. **Address:** 130 rue du Faubourg St. Honoré, 75008 Paris, France.

Publications:

By MUGLER:

Books

Thierry Mugler, Photographer, Paris and London 1988.

On MUGLER:

Books

Polhemus, Ted, and Lynn Proctor, *Fashion and Anti-Fashion,* London 1978.
Martin, Richard, *Fashion and Surrealism,* New York 1987.
Martin, Ricahrd, and Harold Koda, *Infra-Apparel,* New York, 1993.

Articles

LaLanne, Dorothee, "Thierry Mugler et Macbeth," in *Vogue* (Paris), November 1985.
Trittoleno, Martine, "Thierry Mugler: l'homme qui aimait les légendes," in *L'Officiel* (Paris), November 1986.
Gasperini, Nicoletta, "Travelling Goddesses," in *Joyce* (Hong Kong), March 1988.
Mory, Frederique, "De la mode à la photo," in *Madame Figaro* (Paris), 2 July 1988.
Baudot, François, "Double objectif de Thierry Mugler," in *Elle* (Paris), 7 November 1988.
Gross, Michael, "The Wild One," in *New York Magazine,* 4 June 1990.
Wrobel, Catherine, "Mugler à Moscou," in *France-Soir* (Paris), 26 June 1990.
"Mugler, Clarins Link for a Scent," in *Women's Wear Daily* (New York), 28 September 1990.
Forestier, Nadège, "Thierry Mugler: l'art de se faire une griffe," in *Le Figaro* (Paris), 6 October 1990.
Polan, Brenda, "Mugler," in *Elle* (Paris), December 1990.
von Unwerth, Ellen, "How to Look Good in Thierry Mugler," in *Interview* (New York), March 1991.
Martin, Richard, "Fashion License: Clothing and the Car," *Textile and Text,* 13 April 1991.
"Mugler's Monster Show," in *Elle* (New York), November 1991.
Yarbrough, Jeff, "Thierry Mugler Talks Trends," in *The Advocate* (USA), 21 April 1992.

Spindler, Amy, "Monsieur Mugler," in *Women's Wear Daily* (New York), 22 July 1992.

Spindler, Amy M., "A Mature Mugler, Demeulemeester and Lang," in the *New York Times,* 18 March 1995.

"The Paris Collections: The Ideas of March: Thierry Mugler," in *Women's Wear Daily* (New York), 17 March 1995.

Gaudoin, Tina, "Very Thierry," in *Elle* (London), April 1995.

*   *   *

Rich in iconography, the work of Thierry Mugler has, since 1974, exploited wit and drama to convey an imaginary narrative which is at once erotic, amusing, and unsettling. His clothing spans the spectrum from vulgar ornamentalism to the most rigorous minimalism, denying the possibility of defining a Mugler style.

It is Mugler's imagery which most clearly identifies him within high fashion. His sources include Hollywood glamour, science-fiction, sexual fetishism, political history, Detroit car styling of the 1950s, and various periods in the history of art and decoration. In this way, his work reflects the eclecticism of the art world during the 1970s and 1980s. Mugler has taken a particular delight in industrial styling which he displayed in the precise geometries of ornamental detail and through his vocabulary of thematic references, which have included the jet age forms used in the fantastic automobiles devised by Harley Earl for General Motors during the 1950s.

Clothing designs which operate as costumes in a dramatic narrative have reinforced the importance of Mugler's link with the cinema, and particularly with the American film costumes of designers such as Edith Head, Travis Banton, and Adrian. A love of glamour was evident in his extravagant 1992 collection, redolent of 1950s fashion at its most lavish, and photographed among the Baroque roof sculptures of the old city of Prague.

His interest in romance and the bizarre has often run counter to political ideologies. Against a backdrop of feminist reinterpretation of the female image, Mugler has adopted an ironic, post-modern stance and exploited an array of erotic icons as themes for his collections. Difficult to characterize and appearing to work in opposition to current fashion and intellectual trends, Mugler has remained a controversial figure on the fashion scene.

Mugler's photographic talent may prove to be as important as his fashion designs. A book of his photographs, *Thierry Mugler, Photographer,* published in 1988, contained images comparable in their artifice, explosive glamour, and formal control to the cinematic images of Peter Greenaway. His photographs exploit grand vistas, deep interior spaces, and heroic monuments as settings upon which models perch like tiny ornaments, strongly defined by the extravagant outline of their costumes and asserting their presence through dramatic pose and gesture. His fashion photographs provide a narrative framework for Mugler's clothes while relegating them to the role of costume within a larger dramatic context. The broad-shouldered Russian collection of 1986, for example, was presented against backgrounds of heroic Soviet monuments or sweeping landscapes reminiscent of earlier 20th-century Social Realist painting and poster art.

Mugler has also made photographic collages repeating and emphasizing the formal elements of his clothes in kaleidoscopic compositions which revealed his interest in abstract aesthetics. These images were conceived as pure works of art, in which the clothing became an element of the creative whole.

Mugler's clothes are designed to be performed in. His major catwalk shows are choreographed like the great Hollywood musi-

Thierry Mugler: Spring/Summer 1992.

cals of Busby Berkeley. Later exhibitions have been held in huge sports stadia, emulating the highly charged atmosphere of rock concerts. Mugler designs the off-stage wardrobes of rock celebrities such as Madonna, as well as dressing famous women, like Danielle Mitterand, who require a more dignified appearance.

Whether aggressively vulgar or caricatures of sobriety, Mugler's designs are consistently body conscious. His clothes can be read as essays in the aesthetic potential of extreme proportions; shoulder widths three times head height, wasp waists, and panniered hips are among the repertoire of distortions and exaggerations of the human figure to be found among his designs. Mugler's eight annual collections, for both women and men, consistently aim to provoke through their challenging themes and flamboyant formal qualities.

—Gregory Votolato

MUIR, Jean.
British designer

Born: Jean Elizabeth Muir in London, c.1933. **Education:** Dame Harper School, Bedford. **Family:** Married actor Harry Leuckert.

Career: Sales assistant in lingerie and made-to-measure departments, Liberty, London, 1950-55; studied fashion drawing, and also modelled, at evening classes, St Martin's School of Art, London. Joined Jacqmar. Joined Jaeger, 1956-63. Sent to study knitwear design and manufacture, especially jersey. Visited Paris collections. Joined Courtaulds, 1966-69. Formed own label, Jane & Jane, 1967. Formed, with husband co-director, Jean Muir Ltd, 1986. Sold majority interest to Coats Paton group; bought back 75% stake in company, 1989. Jean Muir department in Jaeger's flagship store, Regent Street, London. **Awards:** British Fashion Writers Group Dress of the Year Award, 1964; *Harper's Bazaar* Trophy; Ambassador Award for Achievement, 1965; Maison Blanche Rex Awards, 1967, 1968, 1974, 1976; Churchman's Fashion Designer of the Year Award, 1970; Royal Society of Arts Royal Designer for Industry, 1972; elected fellow of RSA; Neiman Marcus Award, 1973; elected Fellow of Chartered Society of Designers, 1978; Bath Museum of Costume Dress of the Year Award, 1979; named Honorary Doctor, Royal College of Art, 1981; appointed to the Design Council, London, 1983; made a Commander of the Order of the British Empire, 1984; Honorary Degree, Doctor of Literature, University of Newcastle; awarded Hommage de la Mode, Fédération Française du Prêt-à-Porter Féminin; British Fashion Council Award for Services to Industry, 1985; Chartered Society of Designers Medal; Textile Institute Design Medal, 1987; Australian Bicentennial Award, 1988; The Ford Award, 1989. *Died* (in London) *28 May 1995.* **Address:** 59-61 Farringdon Street, London EC1M 3HD, England.

Publications:

By MUIR:

Books

Jean Muir, London 1981.

Articles

"Getting Going," in *The Designer* (London), October 1979.

On MUIR:

Books

MacCarthy, Fiona, and Patrick Nuttgens, *Eye for Industry: Royal Designers for Industry, 1936-1986,* exhibition catalogue, London 1986.

Articles

"Jean Muir Designs," in *The Times* (London), 4 November 1971.
"1979 Design for Bath Museum," in *The Sunday Times,* 2 September 1979.
"Great British Design: Jean Muir," in *Vogue* (London), August 1981.
Green, Felicity, "The Gospel According to St Muir," in *The Sunday Telegraph Magazine* (London), 8 March 1987.
"Designers Take Two," in *Good Housekeeping* (London), March 1988.
Maitliss, Nicky, "A Day in the Life of Jean Muir," in *The Sunday Times Magazine* (London), 13 November 1988.

Dutt, Robin, "Jean Muir Interview," in *Clothes Show* (London), February 1989.
"Winter '89," in *DR: The Fashion Business* (London), 4 March 1989.
McCooey, Meriel, "The Prime of Miss Jean Muir," in *The Sunday Times Magazine* (London), 13 January 1991.
Webb, Ian R., "Secure with Miss Muir," in *Harpers & Queen* (London), March 1991.
van der Post, Lucia, "The Queen of Simple Chic," in *The Financial Times* (London), 9 March 1991.
Rawlinson, Richard, "Pure Miss Muir," in *DR: The Fashion Business* (London), 11 May 1991.
Menkes, Suzy, "25 Years of Disciplined Design," in the *International Herald Tribune* (Paris), 21 May 1991.
Menkes, Suzy, "Muir's Classical Rigor," in the *International Herald Tribune* (Paris), 30 May 1995.
Fallon, James, "UK Designer Jean Muir Dead at 66," in *Women's Wear Daily* (New York), 30 May 1995.

*   *   *

Jean Muir was noted for simple, flattering, and extremely feminine clothes that were sophisticated yet retain a hand crafted look with diligent attention to detail. Her favourite fabrics, jersey, angora, wool crêpe, suede, and soft leather, reappeared time after time, regardless of trends. Her more famous clients included the actresses Joanna Lumley and Patricia Hodge and writers and artists such as Lady Antonia Fraser and Bridget Riley.

Muir was renowned for being a designer who produces clothes women really want to wear and feel comfortable in. She achieved this by modelling all the clothes and toiles herself at fittings, an advantage she believed she had over male designers. "If you are going to make clothes, the first thing you have to understand is the female anatomy. When I try on a dress I can feel if something is wrong, I can tell if it's not sitting properly on the shoulders or the bust or the hip. I could not tell these things if I saw it on a stand," she explained.

There was an air of the fashion headmistress in Jean Muir's approach; her steadfast opinions could not be budged. Her tone was unrelenting when she stressed a need to restore a sense of pride in the technique of making clothes and her passion for "art, craft and design and the upholding of standards and quality, maintaining them and setting new ones." She believed fashion was not art but industry. The word fashion, she said, suggested the "transient and the superficial," hardly the best attributes for a commercial business.

Jean Muir described her work as being based on intuition, aesthetic appreciation, and mathematical technical expertise. Never at the cutting edge of fashion, the clothes were timeless, understated, and often dateless. Like Fortuny or Chanel, the company based its look on the evolution of a singular theme, a soft, supple fluidity of cut that creates the form of a garment.

In person Jean Muir epitomized the type of woman for whom she likes to design. The writer Antonia Fraser described her as a "Modish Puck." A white, powdered face with a mouth slashed in crimson lipstick. A wiry, bird-like frame always dressed in navy calf-length jersey dresses, with black stockings and Granny shoes. In her studio Muir had a reputation for perfectionism and exacting standards in all aspects of production. "There are tremendous activities involved in the making of clothes," she declared in a television interview, with such conviction that the viewer is left in no doubt about her sincerity.

In the annals of fashion history Jean Muir should be remembered as a designer who liberated the body. While many designers have forced bodies into structured tailoring, boning, or restrictive interfaced fabrics, Muir's fluid and easy clothes have always provided an emancipated alternative; devoid of structure and underpinning, the clothes remain womanly and melodious.

—Kevin Almond

MUJI.
Japanese design firm

Founded, 1983, by retail conglomerate Seiyu. Opened first European outlet, London, 1991. **Awards:** D and AD Silver Award, 1994; *Design Week*'s award for retail design, 1994. **Address:** Nikko Ikebukuro Building, 4-26-3 Higashi-Ikebukuro, Toshima-ku, Tokyo, Japan 170.

Publications:

On MUJI:

Articles

Glancey, Jonathan, "No Labels, No Brand Names, No Nonsense," in *The Independent,* July 1991.
Nakamoto, Michiyo, "Life with Liberty in the Pursuit of Happiness and Joint Profits," in *The Financial Times,* July 1991.
Furness, Janine, "The Brand with No Name," in *Interior Design* (London), September 1991.
Louiek Elaine, "If You Want to Make an Understatement," in *The New York Times,* Novemeber 1991.
van der Post, Lucia, "New Worshippers for Japan's Muji Cult," in *Financial Times,* June 1992.
Thompson, Elspeh, "Selling a Lifestyle without a Label," in *The Guardian,* July 1992.

*   *   *

The company name signals its policy. Muji, short for Mujirushi Ryohin, is represented by four characters meaning "no-brand quality goods." The concept is Japanese; its success is international. Muji is proving a workable design formula for the 1990s.

In providing an antidote to the 1980s designer label obsession, Muji is consciously self-effacing. The policy is to sell quality products at reasonable prices. Clothes, household goods, food, and stationery are the staples. The emphasis is on necessity, not superfluity: Muji caters for needs, not wants. The Muji concept is about lifestyle. "Kanketsu," the belief in simplicity which forms the heart of the Japanese art of living, guides the design and retail of the products. Packaging is in simple brown paper bags. Swing tags are made of recycled paper and clearly describe the product, in Japanese. The shops are strictly utilitarian: each one is different, but most of the materials and objects used in the construction are taken from local sources, such as scrapyards. The interiors, like the products, have been pared down and are intended to survive. Typical

Muji.

merchandise includes strongly woven undyed towels, notebooks made from unbleached paper, reusable storage bottles, rice crackers sold in plain see-through packaging. Each item is the result of a philosophy which is echoed in the clothes.

Muji garments have been described as an "alternative to fashion." Elegant and classic, they are, in the company language, "meant to be worn, not to adorn." White cotton shirts, West Point trousers, Californian cotton rugger shirts, tracksuit bottoms, polo shirts, and Peruvian cotton socks are representative of the range. Clothes which are designed to feel comfortable, to be easy to wear, pleasant to the touch and convenient to launder, sound almost anathema to fashion. The company does not use the term: "We would not call them fashion because they might make you think they are expensively designed with bits here and there thrown in for good measure," they say. In Tokyo they have become an acceptable alternative to fashion; increasingly this is happening elsewhere.

Since 1983, when it was founded by the Japanese retail giant Seiyu, Muji has achieved cult status. When the first London shop opened in the summer of 1991, at the back of Liberty's of Regent Street, consumer response was instantaneous. Items sold too rapidly to be immediately restocked from Japan. The next summer a second, bigger store followed. That season Muji clothing featured a strong development in "one mile wear." They are the comfortable clothes you wear at home, or within a mile radius, for leisure or for popping out to the local shop. Traditional Japanese workwear inspired relaxed, deconstructed coordinates in comfortable, natural fabrics. Muji clothes are sensible, but not boring, austere but not dull. They mix well with other labels. And their no-brand clothes *do* have a designer: Masuro Amano, who trained at St Martin's School of Art in London.

Ten years of trading in Japan have provided Muji with a firm base and an established design philosophy. The emphasis on tradition, longevity, and preservation of resources is completely in tune with global concern for ecology and the environment. Quality at reasonable prices is appealing to recession-hit markets. The message, like the products, has international appeal. Muji poses a healthy challenge to established preconceptions of fashion. Ironically, no-brand is becoming *the* brand of the 1990s.

—Hazel Clark

MULBERRY.

British fashion and accessory firm

Founded by Joan and Roger Saul, producing leather accessories, 1971; 16 workers employed by end of first year; opened factory, Chilcompton, Bath, England, and set up wholesale operation in Australia, 1973. Mulberry Ltd formed, 1974. London and New York showrooms open, and clothing line introduced, 1976; three-year contract signed with Sisheido, Japan, and first women's ready-to-wear clothing collection introduced, 1978; free-standing shop opened in Place des Victoires, Paris, and first men's shoe collection, 1982; men's ready-to-wear collection introduced, 1985; men's toiletry range introduced, 1989; added home furnishing collection, 1991; Mulberry shops opened in Tamagawa and Hankyu Osaka, Japan, 1991, and in Russia, 1992. First edition *Muberry Life* magazine, 1993. **Awards:** Queen's Award to Industry and Export, 1979; Queen's Award for Export, 1987, 1989; British Knitting and Clothing Export Council Award for Export, 1988, 1991; Business in Europe "Best Consumer Company" Award, 1989; Classic Designer of the Year, 1992, 1993. **Address:** 11-12 Gees Court, St Christopher's Place, London W1M 5HQ, England.

Publications:

On MULBERRY:

Articles

McDougall, Mary, "Rich and Romantic," in *Connoisseur* (London), March 1991.
"Fashion into Furniture," in *Elle Decoration* (London), September/October 1991.

*   *   *

Mulberry's foundation dates from 1971. Roger Saul, the co-founder of the company, had begun by selling his own designs for leather chokers and belts to such high fashion shops as Biba in London. His first collection of high fashion belts in suede and calf leather demonstrated the influence of saddlery techniques and traditional English crafts, and were worked to Saul's designs by local craftsmen in a building which was once an old forge in his parent's garden in Chilcompton, near Bath. The following year Saul made Mulberry's first significant export: an order of one thousand belts from the Paris department store Au Printemps, while at home he designed a belt collection for Jean Muir. By 1975, Mulberry had expanded into Europe, with handbag designs for Kenzo in Paris and a special range for Bloomingdale's, New York.

The definitive English "hunting, shooting and fishing" look which is the hallmark of Mulberry's style was enhanced the following year by an expansion from accessories to clothes, with the first jacket design: a cotton blouson with leather collar, which was a worldwide success. The first woman's ready-to-wear collection followed in 1978. By 1988 Mulberry was the largest manufacturer of designer quality leather accessories in Britain, with exports accounting for 80 per cent of production, and holder of the Queen's Award for Export 1987 and 1989. In 1991 a new At Home collection of home furnishings was launched at Harvey Nichols, in Knightsbridge London, and new shops opened in Tamagawa and Hankyu Osaka, Japan. In 1992 a shop opened in Russia.

Mulberry's worldwide success in its 21-year existence is defined by its founder, Roger Saul, in the following terms: "The spirit of Mulberry, with its witty English nostalgia, amusing eccentricity and uncompromising devotion to quality, is held in esteem and affection. 'Le style Mulberry' ... has been heralded as an experience, an outlook ... we take pleasure in reviving individual styles and in honouring ancient traditions of craftsmanship whilst constantly introducing the most exciting elements of current design and fashion. It is a romantic but robust lifestyle."

—Doreen Ehrlich

MULLANY, Lorcan. See **BELLVILLE SASSOON-LORCAN MULLANY.**

—————

MUSCARIELLO, Rocco. See **BAROCCO, Rocco.**

—————

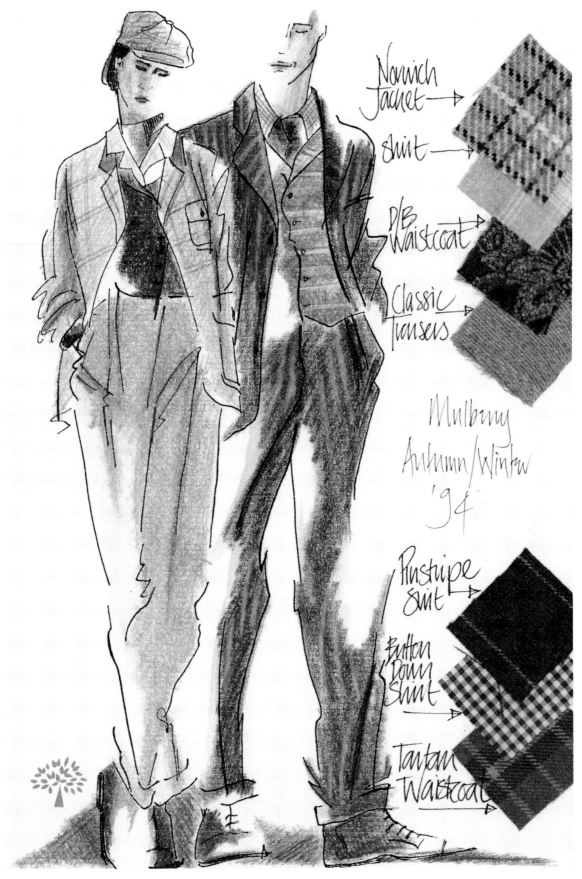

Norwich Jacket →

Shirt →

D/B Waistcoat

Classic Trousers →

Mulberry Autumn/Winter '94

Pinstripe Suit →

Button Down Shirt →

Tartan Waistcoat →

Mulberry: Fall/Winter 1994.

NATORI, Josie Cruz.

American designer

Born: Josie Cruz in Manila, 9 May 1947. **Education:** Studied at Manhattanville College, Bronxville, New York, 1964-68, B.A., economics. **Family:** Married Ken Natori in 1971; son: Kenneth. **Career:** Stockbroker, Bache Securities, New York and the Philippines, 1968-71; investment banker, vice-president, Merrill Lynch, New York, 1971-77; founder, designer, Natori Company, women's lingerie and daywear, from 1977; at-homewear introduced, 1983; boudoir accessories and footwear lines introduced, 1984; bed and bath collections introduced, 1991. **Awards:** Harriet Alger Award, 1987; Girls' Clubs of America Award, 1990; Laboratory Institute of Merchandising Award, 1990; National Organization of Women Legal Defense and Education Fund Buddy Award, 1990. **Address:** 40 East 34th Street, New York, New York 10016, USA.

Publications:

On NATORI:

Books

Martin, Richard, and Harold Koda, *Infra Apparel* (exhibition catalogue), New York 1993.

Articles

Ballen, Kate, "Josie Cruz Natori," in *Fortune* (New York), 2 February 1987.
Haynes, Kevin, "Three SA Women: How They Built Their Business Niches," in *Women's Wear Daily* (New York), 10 April 1987.
Hochswender, Woody, "Lounge Wear for Cocooning," in the *New York Times,* 3 January 1989.
Klein, Fasy, "Beyond the Paycheck," in *Dun & Bradstreet Reports* (New York), March/April 1989.
Morris, Bernadine, "Lingerie is Visible: So Are Its Designers," in the *New York Times,* 5 June 1990.
Goodman, Wendy, "Paris Ensemble," in *HG* (New York), September 1990.
Hofmann, Deborah, "Movie Star Pajamas for a VCR Public," in the *New York Times,* 21 October 1990.
Retter, Nancy Marx, "The Pajama Game," in *Savvy Woman* (New York), February 1991.
Monroe, Valerie, "The Natori Story," in *Mirabella* (New York), March 1991.
"A Touch of Lingerie in Outerwear," in the *New York Times,* 28 April 1991.

"Josie Natori: Queen of the Nightgown," in *Cosmopolitan,* December 1991.
Dohrzynski, Judith H., "The Metropolitan's Natori-ous Display," in *Business Week* (New York), 5 April 1993.
Hassan, Wendy, "The Mark of Natori," in *Women's Wear Daily* (New York), 23 April 1993.

*   *   *

Josie Natori provides a new model of the business of fashion. She presides (along with her husband Ken) over a business, but disavows the designation "designer." But that is a practice like traditional American post-war fashion production. What is unprecedented about Natori as a person and businesswoman is the degree of her vision and tenacity: Natori has taken lingerie from a barely visible inner layer of fashion to the entirety of fashion, including many major international licenses. As a visionary, she purports simply to answer the client's question of "how or where should I wear this?" with "wherever you want," granting lingerie an opportunity to enter into every aspect of attire. Recognizing that, in the 1980s, her lingerie was being increasingly exposed by the women who purchased it, she created garments that are lingerie inspired for public clothing.

Realizing that lingerie by the 1990s was the visible and wide foundation of the clothing pyramid, Natori was involved in almost every aspect of fashion. To build a major fashion house from the base of lingerie is unparalleled, visionary, and a sign of the very late 20th century in its ambition and success. The resulting neologist crossover category "innerwear-as-outerwear" has never been the corporate slogan, though it might serve. Natori has brought boudoir apparel out of the bedroom, perhaps inevitably so at a moment in culture when all heretofore-privileged and private matters of the bedroom have become the public discourse.

Perhaps Puritanism and body reticence have fought the concept of fashion developing from the inside out, but contemporary culture has taken to Natori's vision of the beautiful details of lingerie being exposed within a fashion vocabulary largely denied ornamentation. Natori has brought back to apparel a richness of detail that she herself remembered from Philippine embroideries and appliqués. That is, contemporary ready-to-wear had so eschewed ornamentation as a function of expense (and technical capability) and modernist streamlining that contemporary fashion may seem stark. Lingerie's abiding interest in ornament returns techniques, but also provides the connection to detailing and ornament. In fact, Natori had first approached a Bloomingdale's buyer about making shirts; Natori's destiny was set when the buyer recommended that she make them longer to be sold as nightshirts. Further, Natori shrewdly assesses the culture of the body, bringing stretch and bodysuits to the realm of lingerie and back to playwear, as well as the possibilities of feminine self-expression to dress for public circumstances.

Josie Cruz Natori.

Josie Natori neither supposes nor proposes that the clothing she designs be mistaken for career wear, the operative description for much apparel of the 1980s. Instead, she realizes the affiliation between private clothing, body expression, and eveningwear, all manifesting the body and all committed to comfort and to some degree of seduction and sensual pleasure. To some, Natori might seem anti-feminist; she argues, of course, that she is the true feminist in delighting in and extending the category endemic to feminine traits and the female body. Woody Hochswender quotes Josie Natori as exculpating her clothing from the male fantasies of lingerie, saying: "It's really a way for the woman to express herself. We've made women feel good without feeling sleazy" (*New York Times,* 3 January 1989). Indeed, all apparel addresses wearer and spectator; Natori's reassessment of the innerwear category is as viable as any patriarchal paradigm of male spectatorship.

"Think of Katherine Hepburn, answering her doorbell," Natori offered to Deborah Hofmann, giving evocative pedigree to the ease-without-sleaze that she makes of her innerwear-as-outerwear. Natori is a perfect exemplar for the woman who asserts authority in contemporary fashion: her first career was in investment banking; she herself wears couture (generally a tailored jacket and skirt) in impeccable taste; she makes her way and her company's way in the fashion market with unmistakable respect for the woman who wears her clothing, even more than for the grizzled, outmoded categories and classes of retailing. Natori's business acumen and design sensibility seem unerringly and culturally right: she is creating a fashion that satisfies women's feelings and practical needs in a culture and era of precious privacy and of women's expression of themselves.

—Richard Martin

NAVARRO, Sara.

Spanish fashion designer

Born: Elda, Alicante, Spain, 17 August 1957. **Education:** Studied psychology at University of Valencia, Spain, 1974; shoe styling at Ars Sutoria Institute, Milan, 1978; fashion design, under Gianfranco Ferre at Domus Academy, Milan, 1987; business management at Escuela de Organizacion Industrial, Madrid; classical art at Dante Alighiere School, Florence. **Career:** Director of fashion, Kurhapies Group. Head stylist, Sara Navarro Company, Alicante. First Sara Navarro shop in Madrid launched, 1979. Specialises in footwear, handbags, belts, and ready-to-wear in leather. Collaborates with Fernandez, Vittorio y Luccino, and Robert Verino for footwear. First international collection, 1988; Official designer for Expo-92, 1991-92, and V-Centenario, 1991. Launched shoe collection in Paris with Martine Sitbon, 1992. Director of fashion team for Creaciones Exclusivas, S.A. and Komfort Spain, SL. Lines introduced are Pretty Shoes and Via Sara Navarro. **Awards:** Fashion Oscar for footwear, 1978; Alipac de Oro award, 1979; Catalog-81 Prize, 1981; Master International Award, 1985; Premio Valencia Innovacion Award, 1989. **Exhibitions:** GDS Show, Dusseldorf, 1985; Premiere Classe Show, Paris, 1987; Expo Universal, Seville, 1992; *Luz Blanca* Collection, Galeria Nieves Fernandez, Madrid, 1992. **Collection:** Museu del Calzado de Elda, Alicante, Spain. **Address:** La Cruz 23, 03600 Elda (Alicante), Spain; or Poligono Campo Alto, Gran Bretana s.n. PO Box 464, 03600 Elda Alicante, Spain.

Publications:

On NAVARRO:

Books

Coad-Dent, Elizabeth, *Spanish Design and Architecture,* London 1990.
Fashion International Guide, Inc., *The Fashion Guide,* Paris 1990.

Articles

"10 anni vissuti intensamente," *Vogue Pelle* (Milan), May-June 1991.
"Pasos decivos," *Vogue* (Madrid), June 1991.
Marie France, September 1992.
Marie Claire Bis (Paris), Winter, 1992.
"Identità di gusto," *Vogue Pelle,* (Milan), July/August 1993
Barker, Barbara, "Sara Navarro: Profile of a Professional," in *Footwear News* (New York), 9 August 1993.

*

I view creating with an outlook onto the future, spending a great deal of time researching cultural trends to gather information for the

Sara Navarro: Summer 1994.

purpose of finding an underlying concept or thread tying together each collection that will reflect society's current cultural scene, so that my designs may serve as a response to the questions, desires, or needs of those purchasing these items, but will also be a response, reaching them by getting over a message that is never void of content. I like to play with the imagination, to create a story told through my designs, to have them include playful aspects with a certain touch of irony (hence my collaboration in Almodovar's film, *Mutant Effect*). I place a great deal of importance on quality and comfort.

—Sara Navarro

*　　*　　*

Sara Navarro comes from the third generation of shoemakers in her family. She is conscious of her Mediterranean heritage, incorporating the Spanish tradition of fine leatherwork, and hand-crafted finishes into her design work.

Dedication to hard work and craftsmanship were central to the family philosophy. Navarro's father, Juan Navarro Busquier, believed that in business, whilst the ultimate might be impossible, the "fervent desire for perfection" can lead to the greatest success. Juan's company, Kurhapies, was founded on the meagre savings of his father, a modest artisan shoemaker. Forty-five years later the company is an empirical leader in volume Spanish footwear.

Sara Navarro joined the design department of Kurhapies in 1979. She was only 21, but had already majored in industrial psychology, studied classical ballet, fine arts, and languages. She studied design at the Arts Sutoria and obtained a BA in business and clinical psychology. Clearly, her decision to join the family business was not motivated by any lack of career choices. Her broad ranging interests—from literature to piloting aircraft—typifies her dedication to study and work, in her own words: "There are few geniuses, only professionals. I've risked much with some pretty surprising collections."

Study of her work reveals an equal commercial versatility. The Sara Navarro collections are non-risk styling for the domestic market. Pretty Shoes are an everyday leisure line for "the woman who does not want to grow up." To find Navarro at her most creative and surprising, it is best to look at the Via Sara Navarro lines. Launched in 1988, the Via styles were designed and targeted at the export fashion market. This wider market brief has given Navarro the opportunity to explore and develop her own ideas about materials and techniques. The result is the emergence of a very personal design signature as the Via lines have become stronger over the years.

The trend of fashion in the 1990s to embrace recycled looks, distressed textures, and hand rendered natural finishes, is perfectly in harmony with Navarro's interest in her native Mediterranean heritage. She has explored derivatives of traditional constructions, such as clogs, espadrille shoes, and boots. The silhouettes are strong, often irregular, echoing the clean classic lines of early Via collections; but the use of materials and chaotic colour combinations is often surprising. This has attracted the interest of other designers, for example, John Galliano and Martine Sitbon, who find Navarro's styling in harmony with their own ideas.

It is a fortunate designer who can explore her interests and generate international acclaim for her work, and it is tempting to assume that the fashion climate is simply in tune with this designer. This would ignore the simpler truth that Navarro is a professional who

can react to the fashion demands of both her domestic and export market. She incorporates traditional Spanish craft skills, such as hand stitching, into her work, making the Sara Navarro style instantly recognizable.

—Chris Hill

NEW REPUBLIC.
American fashion firm

Founded in 1981 by Thomas Oatman (born 1953); established as a vintage clothing trading company and opened first store on Greene Street, Soho, New York; store moved to Spring Street, New York, 1986; company produces two collections per year; clothing sold to better department stores and specialty stores throughout the United States, Europe, and Japan. **Address:** 93 Spring Street, New York, NY 10012, USA.

Publications:

On NEW REPUBLIC:

Articles

Shields, Jody, "Everything Old Is New Again," in *Vogue,* April 1989.

*　　*　　*

Long before the current vogue for retro fashion, New Republic—founded by Thomas Oatman—has kept alive the flame of American menswear design that burned bright from the 1930s through the 1960s. However, New Republic is not about promoting any particular era. Oatman added a few different styles to the line's roster every season, changing only the fabrics and colors, and updating the sizing. What the company does manage is to always be in style, because the premise of New Republic is simply about good style.

Thomas Oatman has said: "The difference is that I'm downdating, not updating. I'm not interested in classics with a twist. I want to remain true to the real classics, not the modern knockoffs." New Republic's interpretations are exacting, dealing with more than just the images from those eras that other designers rely on. The company is able to appeal simultaneously to both an avant-garde audience as well as to a more conservative customer. Thus a 1950s Ivy League sack suit exists alongside a pair of 1960s plain-front pegged trousers. Fashion icons are, after all, in the eye of the beholder. New Republic manifests a postmodern sensibility, mixing clothes from different eras in their presentations, which, ultimately, only make fashion sense in an era that coincides with the end of the century.

Oatman is the utmost connoisseur of fine vintage men's clothing. As such, he designs by accessing the index cards in his memory. Every item in the collection can be placed in an elaborate mental stage set that recalls its glory days. And so, a belted leather jacket—as worn by Marlon Brando in the movie *On the Waterfront*—is endearingly called The Strikebreaker. A 1950s-inspired cabana shirt recalls one's parents' honeymoon photos in Havana.

New Republic weaves romantic dreams that span the decades: a khaki bellows-pocket jacket in Palm Beach cloth conjures up the

New Republic: Fall 1995. *Photograph by Corina Lecca.*

image of a gentleman on safari in the 1930s. A linen-blend three-button plaid jacket with solid sleeves recalls the look that American soldiers sported when they returned from World War II.

During their leisure time, men in this period wore a pajama-collar rayon gabardine shirt with flap pockets—which happens to be New Republic's trademark, and one of its first styles. Then later, when those soldiers went on vacation, they would wear clamdiggers and cabana shirts at the shore—just like the ones that New Republic designed in Creamsicle colors.

The late 1950s and early 1960s are also alive and well at New Republic in a natural-shoulder three-button madras sport coat with a hooked center vent and full lap seaming that could have come straight out of Brooks Brothers or J. Press.

America's icons are inextricably tied with Hollywood, and so it should be. For Hollywood has supplied us with countless images from which to draw, as New Republic has supplied menswear with a treasure trove of classic American looks.

—Vicki Vasilopoulos

NEXT PLC.

British fashion company

Established May 1981 by George Davies in conjunction with Hepworth; first womenswear chain opened, 1982; first dual Next/Hepworth store in Reading, Berkshire, 1984; Next for Men launched, 1984; first Next mini department store, Edinburgh, 1984; Next household furnishings range, Next Interior store, Regent Street, London, 1985; name change to Next plc, 1986; Next Cosmetics, 1986; merged with Grattans mail order company, 1986; womenswear divided into Next Too and Next Collection, 1986; lingerie introduced, 1986; boys- and girlswear launched, 1987; Next Directory mail order and Next Originals, 1988; jewellery stores opened, 1988; Department X stores in London and Glasgow, August 1988; David Jones appointed Chief Executive, 1988; retail and mail order merged, 1993; first US Next store, Boston, 1993. **Exhibitions:** *All Dressed Up: British Fashion in the 1980s,* British Council Touring Exhibition, 1990. **Address:** Next plc, Desford Road, Enderby, Leicester LE9 5AT, England.

Publications:

On NEXT PLC:

Books

Davies, George, *What Next?,* London 1989.
Huygen, Frédérique, *British Design: Image & Identity,* London 1989.
Wilson, Elizabeth, and Lou Taylor, *Through the Looking Glass: A History of Dress from 1860 to the Present Day,* London 1989.

Articles

"The Rise and Fall of Next," in *The Daily Telegraph* (London), 14 December 1990.
Gilchrist, Susan, "Next Fights Recession with 88% Profits Rise," in *The Times* (London), 30 March 1994.
"Buying British Pays Off for Fashion Firm," in the *Daily Mirror* (London), 30 March 1994.
Bethell, James, "Next Goes Streets Ahead of Its Rivals," in *The Sunday Times* (London), 3 April 1994.
Reed, Paula, "Good Value Ousts Designer Gloss," in *The Sunday Times* (London), 3 April 1994.

*   *   *

The brainchild of retail entrepreneur George Davies, the initial success of the British chain of Next shops during the 1980s is credited with having prompted greater awareness of the importance of good design in both clothing and fashion retailing on the High Street by travelling around the country to check out the existing competition. It is interesting to note that the two concepts he most admired were the upmarket German brand, Mondi, and the Italian company, Benetton. Elsewhere he found a lack of inspiration with what he described as the "buy it all approach to stock ... in the hope that something would sell" (London 1989).

Davies's vision of what the High Street required was firstly, a strong store identity and, secondly, a high level of quality control over the garments, from raw materials to finished product. Davies maintained that the tailored jacket was the garment that could establish Next, so long as it represented high quality and fantastic value for the price. The first seven Next shops opened on 12 February 1982 and the sales were two and a half times what the company had originally estimated. Davies's philosophy of providing what he called "affordable collectables" found a ready market for his merchandise, which represented good design at affordable prices. Next offered the "power suit" at an accessible price when that was what its female customers desired. Authors Elizabeth Wilson and Lou Taylor maintain that during the 1980s, Next brought together "... a fantasy of old-time shopping and 'aspirational buying'—the desire of newly affluent members of the 25 to 35 age group to wear an approximation of designer clothes" (London 1989). Textile expert Brenda Azario explains the success of Next thus: "Quality is what a customer expects or desires at any price point. This expectation has to be met. Next came in very strongly in this aspect, giving the public a better product. It wasn't a particularly expensive one but it was better—the designing was better and it was certainly better presented to the customer." There followed Next for Men, Next shoes, Next Interior (household furnishings), Next Two, Next Collection, lingerie, Next Boys & Girls, and Next Directory. The latter represented what was perhaps the most significant achievement of Next, for it was the first company to try to raise the rather downmarket image of the mail order business. The catalogue itself was a beautifully-produced book with a matt black cover, featuring well-recognized faces from the model world, photographed by established photographers in great locations. The early numbers even included fabric swatches of certain garments, all of which contributed to the widespread media coverage attracted by the launch of the Directory which revolutionized home shopping in January 1988.

The story of Next during the latter years of the 1980s to the early 1990s is renowned—a victim of over-zealous expansion that became answerable to analysts and institutional investors, not to mention the recession that hit Britain during that period. Another factor that is said to have contributed to the company's demise is the failure of Next Directory to achieve the success predicted by Davies who invested £24.1 million into its launch. The fall of Next was as dramatic as its meteoric rise—a profit warning came in December 1988 and within two weeks there followed the unceremonious sacking of George Davies.

Next: Fall/Winter 1994; wool brown and ecru semi-fitted jacket with matching skirt.

A dramatic rationalization programme ensued under the guidance of the newly-appointed chief executive of Next, David Jones. A large number of stores were sold off and the company also sold off the Grattan mail-order business to raise cash. However, these changes were not enough to fuel the relatively rapid rise of Next to its astounding profits, which doubled from £38.9m in 1992 to £73.5m in 1993. Improved customer service, new clothes displays, and larger fitting rooms are not enough to entice the customer to buy—it is the clothes themselves. It was in this area that Next succeeded in recapturing the British customer of the 1990s. In April 1994 Next owned 306 stores across Britain and counted more than 450,000 customers who bought from the Next Directory. According to journalist Paula Reed, "Now you get basic, honest merchandise without pretension to status or glamour. What makes Next sexy these days is not a glossy image but a quick response to catwalk trends and a canny anticipation of what is next in style."

—Catherine Woram

NIKOS.

Greek designer working in France

Born: Nikos Apostolopoulos in Patras, Greece. **Education:** Studied at the Sorbonne, Paris, diploma in political science, doctorate in international law. **Career:** Designed first collection of intimate wear for men, 1985; line expanded to include intimate wear for women, swimwear, and men's and women's ready-to-wear, 1987. Designer for coustumes for theater and opera, including Monsigny's *Cadi Dupe,* Paris Spring Festival, 1989, and Richard Strauss's *Salome,* Montpellier Festival, 1990. Perfume, "Sculpture," introduced, 1994. **Address:** 6 rue de Braque, Paris 75003, France.

Publications:

On NIKOS:

Books

Pronger, Brian, *The Arena of Masculinity,* New York 1990.

Articles

"Paris Now," in *Daily News Record* (New York), 7 February 1990.
"Nikos Eyes U.S. Market," in *Daily News Record* (New York), 26 June 1990.
Spindler, Amy M., "Tarlazzi, Nikos Cancel Paris Men's Showings," in *Daily News Record* (New York), 29 January 1991.
Deschamps, Mary, "Le retour de Nikos," in *Vogue Hommes International* (Paris), extra-series 16, fall/winter 1992-93.
"Lancaster to Try on New Scents," in *Advertising Age* (New York), 4 July 1994.

*   *   *

Homoerotic masculinity is the motive of Nikos's fashion. Invoking an idealism of gods and demi-gods, stretching and flexing on Olympus wearing versions of jock straps, ergonomic T-shirts and tank tops, and some street clothing, Nikos projects a similar image of apparel. Unmistakably, much contemporary menswear and even related fragrance advertising has exploited the possibilities of the homoerotic. The conventional packaging and presentation of men's athletic wear and underwear always ameliorates the image of the clothing, offering a better-than-average ideal (a male fashion plate). Beginning with his first collection in 1985, Nikos has employed cotton and Lycra for the stretchy, minimalist, erotic clothing of the callipygian gods and all who aspire to their condition of pumped-up muscles and physique divinity. An aesthetic out of Leni Riefenstahl heroes and Mr. Universe proportions informs Nikos's work. In 1988, he worked with American photographer Victor Skrebneski in an ideal collaboration of like-minded fashion erotics. Denizens of South Beach and Venice, California are logical candidates for this self-assured, body-flaunting clothing driven by heat, narcissism, and sexuality. Men who might dress for the evening in Gianni Versace might choose Nikos for activewear. While the line has diversified to some street clothing for men and swimwear and exercise wear for women, Nikos addresses primarily the homoerotic male.

Nikos's clothing template is the jock strap. He customarily provides a band (including many in the late 1980s that, like the underwear of competitors, included the designer name) around the waist from which an extended cod-piece or pouch distends. Brian Pronger argues in *The Arena of Masculinity* of this type, "And the jock strap, no doubt *the* garment of homoerotic athleticism, consisting as it does of an ample purse on one side and straps that highlight

Nikos: Summer 1995. *Photograph by F. Dumoulin.*

posterior potential on the other, epitomizes the twofold nature of Apollo. The jock strap, as the vestment of fluent anal and phallic aspirations, highlighting Apollonian versatility, draws us to the homoerotic paradox." Nikos's phallic primacy is complemented by bared sides and minimal coverage of buttocks, offering voyeurism (and implied accessibility) front and rear to the male. His tanks stress angularity almost as if to clothe men of granitic triangulation, rather than the ordinary soft body.

Further, two devices frequent in Nikos's work exacerbate the homoerotic content. In effectively using stretch materials, Nikos often opens apertures in the briefs and tops, allowing a peek-a-boo spectatorship more often associated with female undergarments. In addition, Nikos relishes piecing and visible seams, the stretchy activewear taking on something of the aspect of a virile Vionnet or an Azzedine Alaïa transferred to Muscle Beach. The effect, of course, is to promote even further the sense of the garment as strapping, swaddling, a bare covering for muscles and body movement. In instances when Nikos uses stripes, his only pattern, line enhances the verticality and size of the phallic pouch.

Recent seasons have emphasized more moderate clothing for the street, including the graphically strong spring/summer 1993 collection with outfits in black-and-white for exercise wear and shirts with bold design inspired by the Matisse cutouts. The spring/summer 1994 collection stressed sportswear for the street and offered a repertoire of loose, long knits and colorful shorts and white and black oversized trousers. When Nikos had shown streetwear in the late 1980s and 1990s, the look was still of a tacky Fire Island extremism, with see-through tank tops, *faux* leopard skins, and tailored clothing with zoot suit bravado. In the street clothes, Nikos has not abandoned fetishes, but has moved in the 1990s toward mainstream menswear, ironically leaving many other designers from Dirk Bikkembergs to Gianni Versace to fill his gap on the wild side.

One can either dismiss Nikos as another International Male or Parr of Arizona specialized marketing of the most blatant homoerotic clothing, of which probably a considerable portion is purchased but seldom worn, or worn only for the private circumstance. Or one can understand that Nikos stands, with many designers of men's underwear and related athletic wear, as one who cultivates specific and definable traits of the homoerotic to develop garments that possess their beauty when shown on the gods and buff quasi-gods, but further identify the longing and desire inherent in any garment.

—Richard Martin

NORELL, Norman.

American designer

Born: Norman David Levinson in Noblesville, Indiana, 20 April 1900. **Education:** Studied illustration at Parsons School of Design, New York, 1919; fashion design at Pratt Institute, Brooklyn, New York, 1920-22. **Career:** Costume designer, Paramount Pictures, Long Island, New York, 1922-23; theatrical costume designer, 1924-28; designer, Hattie Carnegie, New York, 1928-40; partner, designer, Traina-Norell company, New York, 1941-60; director, Norman Norell, New York, 1960-72. **Exhibitions:** Norman Norell retrospective, Metropolitan Museum of Art, New York, 1972. **Awards:** Neiman Marcus Award, Dallas, Texas, 1942; Coty Ameri-

can Fashion Critics Award, 1943, 1951, 1956, 1958, 1966; Parsons Medal for Distinguished Achievement, 1956; *Sunday Times* International Fashion Award, London, 1963; City of New York Bronze Medallion, 1972; honorary Doctor of Fine Arts, Pratt Institute, 1962. *Died* (in New York) 25 October 1972.

Publications:

On NORELL:

Books

Ballard, Bettina, *In My Fashion,* New York 1960.
Roshco, Bernard, *The Rag Race,* New York 1963.
Fairchild, John, *The Fashionable Savages,* New York 1965.
Morris, Bernadine, "Norman Norell," in Sarah Tomerlin Lee, editor, *American Fashion: The Life and Lines of Adrian, Mainbocher, McCardell, Norell, and Trigere,* New York 1975.
Glynn, Prudence, *In Fashion,* New York 1978.
Milbank, Caroline Rennolds, *Couture: The Great Designers,* New York 1985.
New York and Hollywood Fashion: Costume Designs from the Brooklyn Museum Collection, New York 1986.
Mulvagh, Jane, *Vogue History of 20th Century Fashion,* London 1988.
Milbank, Caroline Rennolds, *New York Fashion: The Evolution of American Style,* New York 1989.

Articles

"Designer Honoured by Fashion Critics," in the *New York Times,* 23 January 1943.
Pope, Virginia, "Designer Stresses Simple Silhouette," in the *New York Times,* 24 January 1944.
"Laurels Anew for Norell," in *Life* (New York), 8 October 1956.
Cushman, Wilhela, "American Designers," in *Ladies' Home Journal* (New York), March 1957.
Levin, Phyllis Lee, "Paris Sets Pace but Creative Talent, Critics Agree, Exists in US," in the *New York Times,* 19 June 1958.
"Four Inside Views of Fashion," in the *New York Times Magazine,* 19 June 1960.
Donovan, Carrie, "Stylist Gives Detailed Aid to Imitators," in the *New York Times,* 21 July 1960.
"Norell Styles Raise Ruckus All Their Own," in *Life* (New York), 26 September 1960.
Donovan, Carrie, "Norman Norell: Fashion Is His Life," in the *New York Times,* 28 June 1961.
"American Collections: Norell Shows Tailored and Femme-Fatale Designs," in the *New York Times,* 11 July 1962.
"Where the Shape Lies," in *Newsweek* (New York), 23 July 1962.
Frank, Stanley, "Style King of Ready-to-Wear," in *Saturday Evening Post* (New York), 20 October 1962.
"The Socko American Pair," in *Life* (New York), 1 March 1963.
"Backstage Notes at Norell," in *Vogue* (New York), March 1963.
"The Great Norell," in *Vogue* (New York), 1 October 1963.
Taylor, Angela, "Everything from Coats to Pants Cheered at Norman Norell Show," in the *New York Times,* 1 July 1964.
"Norman the Conqueror," in *Time* (New York), 10 July 1964.
"He's a Fashion Purist with the Golden Touch," in *Business Week* (New York), 12 September 1964.
"Norman Norell," in *Current Biography,* New York 1964.

Morris, Bernadine, "Parsons Honors Celebrated Dropout," in the *New York Times,* 30 April 1965.

Tucker, Priscilla, "Norman Norell," in The Metropolitan Museum of Art *Bulletin* (New York), November 1967.

Morris, Bernadine, "A Talk with Norman Norell," in the *New York Times,* 15 October 1972.

Morris, Bernadine, "At Retrospective Hundreds Salute an Ailing Norell," in the *New York Times,* 17 October 1972.

Morris, Bernadine, "Norman Norell Dies; Made 7th Avenue the Rival of Paris," in the *New York Times,* 26 October 1972.

"Homage to Norell," in *Newsweek* (New York), 30 October 1972.

Morris, Bernadine, "Recollections: Norell in Kansas City," in the *New York Times,* 23 September 1986.

Elliott, Mary C., "Norman Norell: Class All the Way," in *Threads* (Newtown, Connecticut), October/November 1989.

*   *   *

Simple, well-made clothes that would last and remain fashionable for many years became the hallmark of Norman Norell, the first American designer to win the respect of Parisian couturiers. He gained a reputation for flattering design while Traina, whose well-heeled clientèle appreciated the snob appeal of pared down day clothes and dramatic eveningwear. From his early years with Hattie Carnegie, Norell learned all about meticulous cut, fit, and quality fabrics. Regular trips to Paris exposed him to the standards of couture that made French clothes the epitome of high fashion. Norell had the unique ability to translate the characteristics of couture into American ready-to-wear. He did inspect each model garment individually, carefully, in the tradition of a couturier, and was just as demanding in proper fabrication and finish. The prices of "Norells," especially after he went into business on his own, easily rivalled those of Paris creations, but they were worth it. The clothes lasted, and their classicism made them timeless.

Certain characteristics of Norell's designs were developed early on and remained constant throughout his career. Wool jersey shirtwaist dresses with demure bowed collars were a radical departure from splashy floral daydresses of the 1940s. World War II restrictions on yardages and materials coincided with Norell's penchant for spare silhouettes, echoing his favourite period, the 1920s. Long before Paris was promoting the chemise in the 1950s, Norell was offering short, straight, low-waisted shapes during the war years. For evening, Norell looked to the flashy glamor of his days designing costumes for vaudeville. Glittering *paillettes,* which were not rationed, would be splashed on evening skirts—paired with sweater tops for comfort in unheated rooms—or on coats. Later, the lavish use of all-out glamor sequins evolved into Norell's signature shimmering "mermaid" evening dresses, form-fitting, round-necked and short sleeved. The round neckline, plain instead of the then popular draped, became one of the features of Norell's designs of which he was most proud. "I hope I have helped women dress more simply," was his goal. He used revealing bathing suit necklines for evening as well, with sable trim or jeweled buttons for contrast. Variations on these themes continued throughout the years, even after trousersuits became a regular part of Norell's repertoire.

Striking in their simplicity, Norell suits would skim the body, making the wearer the focus of attention rather than the clothes. Daytime drama came from bold, clear colors such as red, black, beige, bright orange or pale blue, punctuated by large, plain contrasting buttons. Stripes, dots, and checks were the only patterns, although Norell was credited with introducing leopard prints in the 1940s, again, years before they became widespread in use. Norell's faithful clients hailed his clothes as some of the most comfortable they had ever worn.

Early exposure to men's clothing in Norell's father's haberdashery business no doubt led to the adaptation of the menswear practicality. An outstanding example was the sleeveless jacket over a bowed blouse and slim woolen skirt, developed after Norell became aware of the comfort of his own sleeveless vest worn for work. As in men's clothing, pockets and buttons were always functional. Norell created a sensation with the culotte-skirted wool flannel day suit with which he launched his own independent label in 1960. His sophisticated clientèle welcomed the ease of movement allowed by this daring design. As the 1960s progressed, Norell presented another masculine-influenced garment, the jumpsuit, but in soft or luxurious fabrics for evening. Just as durability and excellent workmanship were integral to the best menswear, so they were to Norell's. Men's dress was traditionally slow to change; Norell stayed with his same basic designs, continually refining them over the years. He developed the idea that there should be only one center of interest in an outfit, and designed only what he liked.

What he liked was frequently copied, both domestically and overseas. The short, flippy, gored, ice-skater skirt was copied by Paris. Aware of piracy in the fashion business, Norell offered working sketches of the culotte suit free of charge to the trade to ensure that at least his design would be copied correctly. This integrity earned him a place as the foremost American designer of his time. Unlike most ready-to-wear that would be altered at the last moment for ease of manufacture, no changes were allowed after Norell had approved a garment. His impeccable taste was evident not only in the clothes, but in his simple life: meals at Schrafft's and Hamburger Heaven, quiet evenings at home, sketching in his modern duplex apartment, unpublicized daily visits to assist fashion design students at Parsons School of Design.

As the designer whose reputation gained new respect for the Seventh Avenue garment industry, Norell was the first designer to receive the Coty Award, and the first to be elected to the Coty Award Hall of Fame. True to his innate integrity, he attempted to return his third Winnie award when he learned that judging was done without judges having actually seen designers' collections. Norell promoted American fashion as founder and president of the Council of Fashion Designers of America, but also by giving fledgling milliners their start in his black-tie, special event fashion shows. Halston and Adolfo designed hats for Norell, for, as in couture, Norell insisted upon unity of costume to include accessories.

As the "Dean of American Fashion," Norell was the first to have his name on a dress label, and the first to produce a successful American fragrance, *Norell,* with a designer name. Some of his clothes can be seen in the films *That Touch of Mink* and *The Wheeler Dealers.* Show business personalities and social leaders throughout the country treasured their "Norells" for years.

—Therese Duzinkiewicz Baker

———

NOTT, Richard. See WORKERS FOR FREEDOM.

———

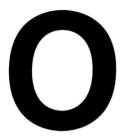

OATMAN, Thomas. See **NEW REPUBLIC.**

OLDFIELD, Bruce.

British designer

Born: London, 14 July 1950. **Education:** Ripon Grammar School, Yorkshire, 1961-67; studied at Sheffield City Polytechnic, Yorkshire; studied fashion design at Ravensbourne College of Art, Kent, 1968-71; St. Martin's School of Art, London, 1972-73. **Career:** Designed free-lance from 1973-75, including capsule collections for Liberty and Browns, London, and collection for Henri Bendel store, New York, 1974; established own fashion house, Bruce Oldfield, Ltd, London, from 1975; couture division established, 1978; opened flagship store in Beauchamp Place, Knightsbridge, London, 1984; reintroduced ready-to-wear line, 1984; produced first diffusion collection, 1988. Also: visiting lecturer at the Fashion Institute of Technology, New York, 1977, Los Angeles County Museum of Art, 1983, Aspen Design Conference, Colorado, 1986; columnist, *Welt am Sonntag* (Hamburg), 1987-91. **Exhibitions:** Metropolitan Museum of Art, New York; Victoria and Albert Museum; Bath Museum. **Awards:** Bath Museum of Costume Dress of the Year Award, 1985; *The Times* Designer of the Year award, London, 1985; named Honorary Fellow, Sheffield City Polytechnic, 1987; Honorary Fellow, Royal College of Art, London, 1990; Honorary Fellow, Hatfield College, Durham University, 1990; OBE, 1990. **Address:** 27 Beauchamp Place, London SW3 1NJ, England.

Publications:

By OLDFIELD:

Books

Bruce Oldfield's Season, with Georgina Howell, London 1987.

Articles

articles for *Welt am Sonntag* (Hamburg), 1987-91.
"Nothing to Do with Greed or Vanity," in *The Independent* (London), 9 September 1989.

On OLDFIELD:

Books

Coleridge, Nicholas, *The Fashion Conspiracy,* London 1988.

Articles

Tuohy, William, "Chic Guru of European Society," in the *Los Angeles Times,* July 1983.
Scobie, W., "Star Dresser," in *The Observer colour supplement* (London), 19 February 1984.
Cleave, Maureen, "Designs on the Famous," in *The Observer* (London), March 1985.
Polan, Brenda, "Life's Rich Pattern," in *The Guardian* (London), March 1985.
Moore, Jackie, "Men about Town: Bruce Oldfield," in *Women's Journal* (London), April 1985.
Kendall, Ena, "A Room of my Own," in *The Observer Magazine* (London), 8 June 1986.
Thackara, John, "With Euclid's Eye and the Patience of Percy," in *The Guardian* (London), 9 April 1987.
"Bruce Oldfield Makes Clothes for (Future) Queen," in *People Weekly* (New York), April 1987.
Lasson, Sally Ann, "A Life in the Day of Bruce Oldfield," in *The Sunday Times Magazine* (London), 10 May 1987.
Nadelson, Regina, "Bruce Oldfield—A Profile," in *European Travel and Life,* September 1987.
Gross, Michael, "A London Designer Leaves Poverty Behind," in the *New York Times,* 9 October 1987.
Stead, Kate, "Couturier to the Stars," in the *Morning Herald* (Sydney), January 1988.
Dutt, Robin, "G'day Bruce," in *Clothes Show* (London), Spring 1988.
Lomas, Jane, "The Essential Wardrobe," in *Arena* (London), August 1988.
Lambert, Elizabeth, "Modern Glamour for his London Flat," in *Architectural Digest* (Los Angeles), September 1988.
Samuel, Kathryn, "Rags to Rag-trade Riches and Home Again," in *The Daily Telegraph* (London), 31 October 1988.
Leston, Kimberley, "Oldfield's New Pastures," in the *Daily Express DX Magazine* (London), May 1989.
Eyers, Anthony, "The Conversion of St. Bruce," in *Isis* (Oxford University), 1989.
D'Silva, Beverly, "The Affordable Essence of Oldfield," in *The Daily Telegraph* (London), 18 January 1990.
Tredre, Roger, "Bruce Stoops to Conquer," in *The Independent* (London), 18 January 1990.
D'Silva, Beverly, "A Middle-class Man of the Cloth," in *The Sunday Times* (London), 21 January 1990.
D'Silva, Beverly, "The Bruce Oldfield Show," in *The Telegraph Magazine* (London), 3 March 1990.
"Oldfield Aims High," in *Fashion Weekly* (London), 16 August 1990.
Falconer, Karen, "Designs on the Future," in *Fashion Weekly* (London), 30 August 1990.
Deane, April, "Bruce Oldfield: An All Round Touch of Quality," in *The Journal,* 17 April 1991.

Bruce Oldfield: Spring/Summer 1994; black taffeta opera coat.

Reed, Paula, "Bruce Is Back," in *The Sunday Times,* 14 February 1993.

Rahim, JoAnna, "Charity Begins at Lunch," in *The Sunday Times,* 19 September 1993.

Himes, Winsome, "Guru of High Style," in *The Voice,* 19 October 1993.

"Bruce Oldfield: 20 Years at the Top," in *Hello Magazine,* November 1993.

Tyrrel, Rebecca, "Bruce Oldfield: 20 Years of Fashion Success," in *Tatler,* November 1993.

*

My approach to fashion is, and always has been, through couture-orientated technique in cut and detail. I like the idea of producing a garment where the actual technique and the cut are the integral design elements. For me, this approach in designing clothes allows a greater scope for developing ideas from season to season. I am not enamoured of *ad hoc* superfluous detailing and would always prefer to use a good quality plain fabric over a print, because if I should need to have a surface detail, I would rather create it myself.

I love quality and finesse and continuity and am horrified by the concept of "in one season and out the next." It seems to devalue the whole creative process. This is not to say that fashion could or should stand still, we need new ideas and a rolling out of attitudes to the way that we see ourselves, but the speed of change and the polarization of successive trends show an insecurity that to me is quite undesirable.

It would make me very happy if, in 2050, someone came across a Bruce Oldfield dress in a thrift shop and simply had to buy it.

—Bruce Oldfield

*   *   *

In an interview with journalist and writer Georgina Howell, Bruce Oldfield said, "It would have been better for me to have lived at an earlier period because I care about the technique of making clothes" (*Bruce Oldfield's Season,* London 1987). During the 1970s and 1980s there was an increasing disregard for quality and workmanship in dress manufacturing. It was this very sloppiness, readily accepted by retailers and customers alike, that Oldfield reacted against. He was attracted to the traditional high standards and technical workmanship of couture and the private client.

In the 1970s and 1980s, crazy fashion was very popular but Oldfield declared he could never create such fantasy clothes. To him they were totally unconvincing. He recognized that there was an established market for understated, flattering clothes and targeted an identifiable, timeless look towards this customer, someone he described as being expensive, sexy, body-conscious, a great looking woman in a flattering dress. Avoiding the need to make seasonal fashion statements he remains a staunchly classic designer. "There have been times when I have been in fashion and times when I have been out of fashion but I have always had six pages a year in *Vogue,* sometimes 15," he once declared.

After leaving St. Martin's School of Art with a fashion degree in 1973, Oldfield worked as a free-lance designer for several high-profile fashion companies, ranging from an exclusive collection for Henri Bendel in New York to selling shoe designs to Yves Saint Laurent in Paris. He established his own company in 1975 with a bank loan and a grant from Dr. Barnardo's, the children's home where Oldfield grew up. The business began as a ready-to-wear operation that produced two seasonal collections a year. Concentrating on occasion clothing, the range was available at prestigious stores such as Harvey Nichols in London, Bergdorf Goodman, Saks Fifth Avenue, and Bloomingdale's in New York. He also worked on specialist commissions, such as designing the film wardrobe for Charlotte Rampling in *Le Taxi Mauve* and Joan Collins in *The Bitch.*

The success of the business led to an increasing emphasis on the private customer, resulting in the decision to provide an exclusively couture service by 1983, producing unique and glamorous evening and wedding dresses. In 1984 the first Bruce Oldfield shop opened at 27 Beauchamp Place, London, selling a total look, both to the ready-to-wear and the couture customer.

Oldfield is perhaps best known for his couture and ready-to-wear evening dresses, often worn by high-profile clients such as the Princess of Wales or actresses Joan Collins and Anjelica Huston. Sumptuous fabrics like ruched and crushed velvets, taffeta, mink, printed sequins, crêpe, chiffon and lamé are used to design traditional sculpted shapes that are exquisitely manufactured. A ruched bodiced dress in velvet, with a huge *fischou* collar, is completed with a vast swathed taffeta bow on the hip. A velvet double-breasted coat dress is enhanced by an exaggerated mink collar. Particularly distinctive is Oldfield's use of colour blocking; simple jersey dresses are slashed asymmetrically and blocked in various vivid colour combinations. His tailoring is always curvaceous and womanly, with seams and darts significantly placed to flatter the feminine physique, in soft leathers and wool crêpes.

Oldfield's career has covered a wide span of activities and he has recently received awards that acknowledge his contribution to fashion. In 1990 he was awarded the OBE and made an honorary fellow of both the Royal College of Art and Durham University. That same year he was also the subject of a television documentary on his life and career, *A Journey into Fashion,* which was subsequently sold to television companies around the world.

If success can be measured by public recognition, then Bruce Oldfield has achieved it. His name is synonymous with style and he is universally acknowledged as having a unique understanding of how to make a woman look and feel her best.

—Kevin Almond

OLDHAM, Todd.

American designer

Born: Corpus Christi, Texas, 1961. **Education:** No formal training in design. **Career:** Worked in the alterations department, Polo/Ralph Lauren, Dallas, Texas, 1980; showed first collection, in Dallas, 1981; partner and designer, L-7 company, New York, incorporating Times 7 women's shirt collection, from 1988; signature Todd Oldham collection reintroduced with backing from Onward Kashiyama Company, 1989; line of handbags introduced, 1991; Todd Oldham patterns produced for *Vogue Patterns,* 1992; footwear line introduced, 1993. **Awards:** Council of Fashion Designers of America Perry Ellis Award, 1991. **Address:** 120 Wooster St. #3FL-SF, New York, New York 10012-5200, USA.

Publications:

On OLDHAM:

Articles

Robinson, Rob, "Todd Oldham," in *Interview* (New York), October 1982.

Badhum, John, and Kurt Kilgus, "So Good They Named It Twice: A Second Look at the Big Apple," in *Fashion '86* (London), 1985.

Morris, Bernadine, "2 Young Designers Decorate Their Clothes with Wit," in the *New York Times,* 27 November 1990.

Hochswender, Woody, "Flights of Fancy: Todd Oldham's Magic Carpet Ride," in the *New York Times,* 11 April 1991.

Darnton, Nina, "The New York Brat Pack," in *Newsweek* (New York), 29 April 1991.

"Great Expectations," in *Women's Wear Daily* (New York), 12 June 1991.

Schiro, Anne-Marie, "The 3-Year Leap of Todd Oldham," in the *New York Times,* 29 December 1991.

Lender, Heidi, "Hot Toddy," in *Women's Wear Daily* (New York), 8 May 1992.

Servin, Jim, "Todd Oldham: This Year's 'It,'" in the *New York Times,* 10 May 1992.

"Hot Designer: Todd Oldham," in *Rolling Stone* (New York), 14 May 1992.

James, Laurie, "Hot on the Trail," in *Harper's Bazaar* (New York), August 1992.

Orlean, Susan, "Breaking Away," in *Vogue* (New York), September 1992.

"Designer Dish," in *Women's Wear Daily* (New York), 29 March 1993.

Mower, Sarah, "How Does Todd Do It?," in *Harper's Bazaar* (New York), December 1994.

Ferguson, Sarah, "Natural Force," in *Elle* (New York), March 1995.

Spindler, Amy M., "Oldham and Tyler Look Super," in *Women's Wear Daily* (New York), 6 April 1995.

*   *   *

Todd Oldham's eclectic and electric fashion ties a traditional avant-garde premise of initial dissonance dissolving into resolved forms with an abiding love of the crafts. Acknowledging in *Women's Wear Daily* in 1992 that his "total hero" is Christian Lacroix, Oldham indicates his wild sense of rich pastiche and cultural mix. At the time of his show for fall 1991, Woody Hochswender wrote, "The young Texas-born designer is on his own strange trip, and Tuesday afternoon he whisked editors and buyers on a whirlwind round-the-world tour—by plane, flying carpet and Greyhound" (*New York Times,* 11 April 1991).

Nonetheless, Oldham's irrepressibly mischievous design takes fashion very seriously, bringing to dress a range of visual references. In 1990, in a collection called Garage Sale, he showed a black satin suit embroidered with items that might be found at a garage sale, including a lamp with its electrical cord, a clock, and crossed knife and fork. For fall 1992, he showed a coy "Old Masters—New Mistress" skirt with a beaded Mona Lisa on the front and a Picasso on the back. In between he showed a black silk shantung trousers suit with sequined and embroidered travel patches, African-inspired embroidered tops, and Lamontage (synthetic-fiber felting) designs akin to Byzantine mosaics. His vernacular references have strayed to the backyard for a 1991 hammock dress and to the kitchen for what he described to *People Magazine* as "embroidered shirts that look like they've been iced by cake decorators" (*People Magazine,* 1991) and his memorable 1991 "potholder suits" with pockets resembling the potholders of elementary crafts. In such gestures, Oldham gives literal meaning to "everything but the kitchen sink," but never with desperation, only with a charming surrealism. Another art-for-art's sake suit for 1990 used the motif of paint-by-numbers for its beaded pockets. Oldham's ever present sense of ornament is not, however, for resplendence alone, although the decoration plays an undeniable role, but for its contribution to the narrative, the ironic information dispatched in each garment.

Oldham disavows kitsch, an almost inescapable epithet for his idiosyncratic talent, but his enthusiasm for naïve crafts and his juxtapositions of good and highly uncertain taste encourage the description, however inadequate. Kitsch implies, however, no intervention or interpretation, only laconic appropriation. Oldham's aesthetic power is a wilful perversity, a zest for twisting and changing the original source, whether kitsch or Mediterranean mosaic. His buttons are curious and quirky; his well-tailored suits are saved from conformity by their odd pockets; and his canny and broad knowledge of fashion sources is saved from being scholastic by his whimsical juxtapositions. For all of its personal taste, Oldham's fashion extends the tradition of Schiaparelli in its bold thematic development, delicate equilibrium between propriety and aesthetic anarchy, propensity to decoration, weird fancy and fantasy in buttons, and annexation of related arts (including theater and film, a design studio with painted walls, and such street-inspired elements as using drag queen Billy Erb and the rock group B-52's Kate Pierson in his catwalk shows). Oldham's 1992 mirror dress pursues a Schiaparelli idea, as does his preoccupation with the unexpected and seemingly autonomous pockets of suits.

Big-city, high-style *savoir-faire* is key to Oldham's chic tongue in cheek, as it was for Schiaparelli. But Oldham's Texas roots and his family-based manufacturing give the work roots in the American mid-West as well as in the dry wit of capital cities. Born in Corpus Christi, Texas in 1961, Oldham began his fashion business 20 years later, following a brief stint in alterations at the Polo/Ralph Lauren boutique in Dallas. He moved to New York in 1988 and started the women's shirt collections Times 7 at the time.

Spring 1992 headlines for Oldham as "Hot Toddy" in *Women's Wear Daily* (8 May 1992) and "Todd Oldham: 'This Year's It'" in the *New York Times* (10 May 1992) might for some designers be the kiss of death from journalistic hyperbole, but Oldham possesses the characteristics of lasting, needed style, however *outré* or idiosyncratic it may seem. His persistent technical investigation—he was, for example, unique in experimenting with Lamontage as an apparel fabric—gives added meaning to his comment to the *New York Times* in 1991: "I haven't had any formal training, but that's worked to my advantage. People don't know what to expect." If cool whimsy is ever unexpected, so is the technology of the clothing endemic to Oldham's interest in the crafts. Likewise, his keen interest and perceptions in contemporary culture, beyond fashion, have provided him with a wealth of images for the work. Oldham's aesthetic is bold and self-assured, but far less transitory than it might initially seem. Rather, his strongly referential fashion pertains to popular culture and its resonance for apparel. Oldham's creativity is in tune with fashion's constant striving to achieve ironic involvement in matters outside of dress and attempts, with irony, to understand the phenomena of clothing and contemporary life.

—Richard Martin

ONG, Benny.

Singaporean/British designer working in London

Born: Singapore, 1949 (one source says 1956). Moved to London, 1968. **Education:** Graduated in fashion from St. Martin's School of Art, London. **Career:** Formed own company, Benny Ong Ltd., 1977; represented Britain in the Fashion Extravaganza in Milan, 1978; lectured in fashion at St Martin's School of Art and Newcastle Polytechnic, England, 1979; introduced Private Label business designs for Austin Reed, London, 1983; Sunday and Ong by Benny Ong lines introduced, 1988; private label designs for House of Fraser stores introduced, 1988; International Collection diffusion line, ONG, introduced, 1989; third label, Bene, introduced, 1992; opened two Benny Ong boutiques in Singapore, 1992. Also corporate uniform designer from 1986 with clients including BAA and British Telecom. **Address:** 3A Moreton Terrace, London SW1V 2NS, England.

Publications:

On ONG:

Books

Mulvagh, Jane, *Vogue History of Twentieth Century Fashion,* London 1988.

Articles

Freedman, Lisa, and Barbara Griggs, "Secrets of Diana's Wardrobe," in the *Sunday Express Magazine* (London), 12 June 1983.

*   *   *

Benny Ong is a designer of pretty, relaxed clothes that are charming and flattering to wear. Born in Singapore of Chinese descent, he moved to London in 1968 to study fashion design at St. Martin's School of Art. Today he retains his Singaporean connections with twice yearly visits that consolidate his successful design combination of Eastern philosophy with Western glamour.

He formed Benny Ong Ltd. in 1977 and presented a well received debut collection that was quickly snapped up by two of London's top stores, Harrods and Selfridges. The collection set the tone for Ong's later work, with exquisite loose fitting, hand sprayed silk chiffons and jerseys. That successful debut year also saw Ong becoming a founder member of the prestigious London Designer Collections, which now represents the cream of British designers.

Expansion of the business has proved no problem owing to the avid press interest and acclaim for the label since its inception. Today, in addition to the designer range the company produces several diffusion lines for the middle price market. The first, in 1980, the International Collection, featured predominantly silk spe-

cial occasion clothes. This was followed by Sunday, which presented less formal occasion clothes. The Ong by Benny Ong range was produced in 1988 and sells throughout Europe.

Fabrics for Ong are always classical, traditional, and stylish. As well as glamorous silk eveningwear fabrics there are easy handkerchief linens, plain or in tiny checks; crisp white cottons and voiles for pretty, oversize shirts, or stonewashed crêpes for simple jackets. In 1983 the company began promotions for the European Silk Commission, with major fashion shows and wide coverage in international fashion magazines. Simple and graceful knitwear and cashmere ranges were added to the collection in 1985 and were immediately snapped up in huge quantities by the New York retailer Barney's.

The Princess of Wales is a frequent Ong customer. She commissioned dresses and suits for her first official visit to Australia in 1985. The exposure generated by having possibly the most prestigious customer in the United Kingdom led to an invitation to participate in a fashion show on the BBC television programme *Pebble Mill at One,* that same year.

As well as producing ranges of clothes for the more glamorous end of the fashion market, Ong has worked on several corporate clothing commissions. In 1986 he was invited, alongside five other eminent British designers, to tender for the British Airports Authority corporate clothing project. He won the contract. This led to further invitations to tender for a new corporate clothing image for British Telecom and a prestigious clothing design contract for the reopening of the internationally famous Raffles Hotel in Singapore.

Ong's other activities have included guest lecture programmes in fashion design at St. Martin's College of Art and invitations to speak at various fashion forums for students and the trade, covering a range of topics from design to management. After the presentation of a first full fashion show to top buyers and press in 1979, the company has also expanded into the private label business, designing a young and well-made range for Austin Reed in 1983 and branded merchandise for the designer section of the popular catalogue for Great Universal Stores, alongside designers like Roland Klein, Jasper Conran, and Jean Muir.

Ultimately, Benny Ong is best known for his eveningwear. He can handle beautiful fabrics in a sensitive and refined manner, producing conventional yet becoming garments for a wealthy clientèle.

—Kevin Almond

OSTI, Massimo. See **C.P. COMPANY.**

OZBEK, Rifat.

British designer

Born: Istanbul, 11 July 1953. **Education:** Studied architecture at Liverpool University, 1970-72; studied fashion design at St. Martin's School of Art, London, 1974-77. **Military Service:** Performed national military service in Turkey, 1977. **Career:** Worked

Benny Ong.

with Walter Albini for Trell, Milan, 1978-80; designer for Monsoon, London, 1980-84; established own firm, Ozbek, 1984; second line, O, renamed Future Ozbek, established, 1987. Production under licence by Aeffe SpA, Italy, from 1988; launched New Age collection, 1989. **Exhibitions:** *Fellini: I Costumi e le Mode,* Pecci Museum, Prato, Italy, and Stedeligk Museum, Amsterdam, both 1994; *V & A: Street Style; From Sidewalk to Catwalk, 1940 to Tomorrow,* 1994-95; *Customised Levi's Denim Jacket for Benefit for Diffa/Dallas Collection,* 1990, 1991, 1992. **Awards:** *Woman* Magazine Designer Award, 1986; British Fashion Council Designer of the Year Award, London, 1988, 1992; British Glamour Award, 1989. **Address:** 18 Haunch of Venison Yard, London W1Y 1AF, England.

Publications:

On OZBEK:

Books

Coleridge, Nicholas, *The Fashion Conspiracy,* London 1988.

Articles

Brampton, Sally, "Wizard of Ozbek," in *The Observer* (London), 12 May 1985.

Hoae, S., "Out of the Playpen," in *The Observer* (London), 23 March 1986.

Thackara, J., "Hooked on Classics," in *Creative Review* (London), June 1986.

Etherington-Smith, Meredith, "Street Smart," in *The Observer* (London), 21 September 1986.

"Designer of the Year," in *DR: The Fashion Business* (London), 15 October 1986.

Jeal, Nicola, "The Wizard of Ozbek," in *The Observer* (London), 16 October 1986.

"Designer of the Year: Rifat Ozbek," in *Woman* (London), 8 November 1986.

Aitken, Lee, "Designer Rifat Ozbek, London's Young Turk, Dazzles the Rag Trade with a Theme for All Seasons," in *People,* 17 November 1986.

Ducann, Charlotte, "The Designer Star: Rifat Ozbek," in *Vogue* (London), February 1987.

"Rifat Ozbek," in *The Sunday Times Magazine* (London), 22 November 1987.

"View: London's Young Turk," in *Vogue* (New York), June 1988.

Rumbold, Judy, "Ozbek out on Top," in *The Guardian* (London), 11 October 1988.

"Ozbek on Top," in *DR: The Fashion Business,* 15 October 1988.

Jeal, Nicola, "The Wizard of Ozbek," in *The Observer Magazine* (London), 16 October 1988.

"Rifat Ozbek," in *Vogue* (London), December 1988.

Gross, Michael, "The Wizard of Ozbek," in *New York,* 23 January 1989.

Campbell, Lisa, "Ozbek on the Fringe," in *Vogue* (New York), January 1989.

Jobey, Liza, "Rifat Madness," in *Vanity Fair* (London), February 1989.

Brampton, Sally, "Aspects of Ozbek," in *Elle* (London), May 1989.

Perry, Beverly, "The Rifat Ozbek Collection," in *Marie Claire* (London), July 1989.

Bakjer, Caroline, "Beyond the Veil," in *The Sunday Times Magazine* (London), 26 November 1989.

Reed, Paula, "Ozbek: The Movie," in the *Correspondent Magazine* (London), 11 March 1990.

"The Designers Talk Passion, Whimsy and Picassos," in *ARTnews* (New York), September 1990.

Alderson, Maggie, "Rifat Ozbek's Hot Stuff," in *Elle* (New York), October 1990.

Daspin, Eileen, "Rifat Ozbek, Milan's New Turk," in *Women's Wear Daily* (New York), 16 October 1991.

Orlean, Susan, "Breaking Away," in *Vogue* (New York), September 1992.

McSweeney, Eve, "The Story of Ozbek," *Vogue UK,* August 1993.

Reed, Paula, "The Sultan of Style," *Sunday Times Magazine,* 5 June 1994.

"The Paris Collections; The Ideas of March: Rifat Ozbek," in *Women's Wear Daily* (New York), 17 March 1995.

                                        *

My collections always have an element of ethnic and modern feeling.

                                                        —Rifat Ozbek

                        *   *   *

One of Britain's few truly international designers, Rifat Ozbek draws on London street style and his own Turkish origins to produce sophisticated clothes which successfully amalgamate diverse sources and keep him at the forefront of new developments in style. Ozbek restyles the classic shapes of Western couture, using multi-cultural decorative references like the traditional stitching of the *djellabah* and kaftan to outline garments such as A-line linen dresses. He became renowned in the 1980s for a series of lavishly embroidered black cocktail suits which appeared with different themes each season, such as gold bows and tassels or Daliesque lips.

After leaving Turkey at the age of 17, Ozbek trained as an architect at Liverpool University, cutting his studies short after deciding he was more interested in decorating the surfaces of buildings than learning the methods of construction needed in order for his architectural projects to remain standing. This interest in the decoration of classic shapes, rather than breaking the barriers of garment construction, was expressed in his first clothing designs which appeared in 1984.

Ozbek graduated from St. Martin's School of Art, London, in 1977 and went on to work for three years at Monsoon, a company known for creating popular styles based on non-Western originals. Ozbek assimilated all these ideas and became known in the mid-1980s for his combinations of motifs and shapes from different cultures and juxtapositions of unusual fabrics, creating not just a straight pastiche of ethnic, but an arresting amalgamation of eclectic sources such as Africa, the Far East, ballet, and the Ottoman Empire.

At this time his skillfully tailored clothes were fashioned out of luxurious fabrics like moiré silks and taffeta, with an amazing palette of colours of turquoise, purples, and fuchsia. His sophisticated and understated designs developed into an easily recognizable style, using heavy fabrics like gabardine or cashmere to structure the top half of an outfit combined with lighter materials below, like silks or jersey. This elegant look was supplanted by a more overtly sexy one in 1988, where the multi-cultural aesthetic was taken to new levels with the use of a diverse array of eclectic material. His confidence in dealing with a number of different non-Western sources was displayed in this significant collection with garments showing their origins in Senegal, Tibet, and Afghanistan, an ethnic look made urbane for the fashion consumer. The collection included sarong skirts and gold chain belts, midriff tops, and boleros embroidered with crescent moons and stars, hipster trousers, and tasselled bras worn on the catwalk by models who resembled Turkish belly dancers.

In the 1990s Ozbek has become more heavily influenced by the club scene and his White Collection of 1990 caught the mood of the times. Acknowledging the New Age and Green consumerist tendencies of his audience, Ozbek created a range of easy to wear separates based on tracksuits and other sports clothing to be worn as club gear. This collection was in complete antithesis to the hard metropolitan chic of 1980s power dressing and paved the way for

hooded sweatshirt tops and trainers appearing in the catwalk collections of other designers that year. The clothes were a stark bright white, displaying New Age slogans like "Nirvana." Unlike designers who have used white before, such as the "yé yé" designers of the 1960s who employed white to glorify science and technology, Ozbek used the colour, without irony, to profess a faith in the concept of a New Age and a belief that a return to the spiritual would improve the quality of life in the city and save the planet.

This was an anti-fashion which became the fashionable look of the early 1990s. Casual, baggy clothes, making reference to sports and black youth subcultures, were worn with sequined money belts and baseball caps and Ozbek was lauded as a designer in touch with the street.

His popularity has continued in the 1990s with the Urban Cowgirl look of fringed suede tops, hotpants, and North American Indian jewellery, his mock bone fronts on waistcoats and evening gowns, and the Confederate look incorporating tailed or cropped military jackets.

—Caroline Cox

Rifat Ozbek: Autumn/Winter 1992.

PACKHAM, Jenny.

British designer

Born: Southampton, England, 3 November 1965. **Education:** Studied at Southampton Art College, 1982-84; studied textile and fashion design at St. Martin's College of Art, London, 1984-88 (1st class honours). **Career:** Designer and director, Packham Anderson Ltd., from 1988. **Address:** The Courtyard, 44 Gloucester Ave., London NW1 8JD, England.

Publications:

On PACKHAM:

Articles

Hepple, Keith, "Jenny Packham," in *DR* (London), September 1991.
Yusuf, Nilgin, "Designer's Inspirations," in *Joyce* (Hong Kong), 1991 Holiday Issue.

*   *   *

Jenny Packham's training as a textile designer is an important influence in her designs for eveningwear which bear the Jenny Packham label. Her first collection of 12 short evening gowns was created entirely in black and white silk, with a bold print of musical instruments designed by Packham. The short evening dress has continued to be the principal style in her collections, although full length dresses were introduced in 1992.

While the shapes of Packham's dresses remain essentially simple, their construction is complex and owes much to Christian Dior's designs of the 1950s which featured intricate seaming, linings, and boning. Dress panels are lined with stiff organdie to create fullness, while bodices have boned seams for a corsetted effect and full skirts are created with layer upon layer of stiff netting. A typical example of Packham's short evening dresses is the model with fitted torso, full skirt, and fichu neckline or short sleeves. Her theory that women want to look glamorous by night, with emphasis placed on the bustline and waist, is a recurring feature of Packham's designs. She also places emphasis on comfort, which she believes is vital for eveningwear.

While the styling of Packham's designs evolves gradually from one season to the next, the colours and textiles change dramatically. The designer acknowledges that eveningwear by tradition is less susceptible to major changes in fashion and thus unusual colours and fabric combinations play a central role in her designs. The works of artists are often drawn upon by Packham as inspiration for her use of colour and these have included Gaudi, Miro, and Van Gogh. Bold prints decorate the full skirts of her gowns, with designs based on such themes as harlequin checks, suits of playing cards, and giant florals. Packham's use of rich fabrics and colours has been likened to that of Parisian designer Christian Lacroix, and costly fabrics such as embroidered brocades, silk taffetas, satins, and silk gazars feature heavily in her collections.

Traditional styling married with contemporary prints and colour combinations is the essence of Jenny Packham's design formula, and this theme is continued through to the Jenny Packham Sequel collection of less expensive dresses which echo the shapes and colours of the mainline collection. Like the latter collection, Jenny Packham Sequel is also produced in the United Kingdom by a small factory and out-workers. The Sequel collection has opened up a new market for Jenny Packham's designs in the United States, already one of her principal export markets, where her collection is sold through prestigious stores such as Neimann Marcus and Bergdorf Goodman.

Packham's success in the American market, where her collections are widely sold, proves her theory that there was a gap in the middle market for eveningwear which is sophisticated yet still youthful, and sexy in a humorous way.

—Catherine Woram

PARNIS, Mollie.

American designer

Born: Sara Rosen Parnis, in Brooklyn, New York, 18 March 1902. **Education:** Briefly studied law, Hunter College, New York. **Family:** Married Leon Livingston (originally Levinson) in 1930. **Career:** After high school, worked in sales for a blouse manufacturer, then as stylist for David Westheim Company, New York, c.1928-30. Parnis-Livingston ready-to-wear established, New York, 1933; launched own label, 1940s; boutique line added, 1970; Mollie Parnis Studio Collection ready-to-wear line added, 1979; firm closed, 1984; first loungewear collection, Mollie Parnis at Home, designed for Chevette, New York, 1985. Molly Parnis Livingston Foundation established, 1984. *Died* (in New York), *18 July 1992*.

Publications:

On PARNIS:

Books

Levin, Phyllis Lee, *The Wheels of Fashion,* Garden City, New York 1965.
Bender, Marylin, *The Beautiful People,* New York 1967.
Morris, Bernadine, and Barbara Walz, *The Fashion Makers,* New York 1978.

Diamonstein, Barbaralee, *Fashion: The Inside Story,* New York 1985.

New York and Hollywood Fashion: Costume Designs from the Brooklyn Museum Collection, New York 1986.

Milbank, Caroline Rennolds, *New York Fashion: The Evolution of American Style,* New York 1989.

Articles

"It Can Happen to the President's Wife," in the *New York Times,* 1 April 1955.

"Blue-Green on the National Scene," in *Life* (New York), 25 April 1955.

"Molly Parnis," in *Current Biography* (New York), May 1956.

"Molly Parnis, Designer, Dies in Her Nineties," in the *New York Times,* 19 July 1992.

"A Woman of Many Modes: Mollie Parnis Dead at 93," in *Women's Wear Daily* (New York), 20 July 1992.

"Died, Mollie Parnis," in *Time* (New York), 3 August 1992.

Friedman, Arthur, "Memories for Mollie Parnis," in *Women's Wear Daily* (New York), 16 September 1992.

*   *   *

Mollie Parnis belongs to the first generation of American fashion designers to be known to the public by name rather than by affiliation to a department store. Her clothing became standard in the wardrobes of conservative businesswomen and socialites of the mid-20th century. Parnis herself was one of these women; she understood what women wanted to wear and what they required to appear appropriately dressed, yet feminine.

Mollie Parnis was a success in the fashion industry from the start. During her first job as a salesperson for a blouse manufacturer, she showed a keen interest in design details, as well as a good sense of what might sell. She was promoted to a design position with the firm in a short period of time. Her ability to determine what fashion would be successful served her throughout her career, spanning over 50 years in the industry. When she and her husband, Leon Livingston, started their own business just prior to World War II, the prospects for any new clothing wholesaler seemed dim. However, they knew that one of the keys to success is specialization, so Parnis-Livingston limited its line to women's dresses and suits which were immediately successful.

The look of Mollie Parnis clothes was conservative and classic. In the 1950s she was known for her shirtwaist dresses and suits in luxurious-looking fabrics that spanned seasons and made the transition from office to dinner. She also employed whimsical, all-American combinations such as menswear wool with silk fringe in some of her evening dresses. Though not always a design innovator, she was a consistent provider of well-made, highly wearable clothes. She interpreted the contemporary silhouette with her conservative good taste and her sensibility to the busy American woman's desires and needs.

United States First Ladies, from Mamie Eisenhower to Rosalyn Carter, were customers of Mollie Parnis's. One dress in particular received national attention in April 1955 when Mrs. Eisenhower arrived at a Washington reception wearing a Mollie Parnis shirtwaist of blue and green printed taffeta, only to be greeted by another woman in the same dress. Parnis expressed her embarrassment over the situation, but explained to the *New York Times:* "I do not sell directly to any wearer, nor do I usually make one of a kind; that is what makes this country a great democracy. But I do feel that the First Lady should have something special." (1 April 1955). There had been minor variations made to Mrs. Eisenhower's dress alone, but approximately 90 dresses of the similar style were shipped to stores around the United States.

Though other designers were hired by the firm eventually, Parnis remained the originator of themes and ideas, and the final editor of her design staff's creations. Eleanor Lambert described her as having "an architect's eye for proportion" and the ability to endow mass-produced clothing with a custom-made look. Like many designers who are successful in the long run, she avoided trendy looks in the service of her customers who came to expect from her clothing what was fashionable for more than one season. Mollie Parnis used her own life as inspiration and guide for her work. She stated her design philosophy in *Fashion: The Inside Story:* "Being a designer is being a personality. It's creating a look that you like, that your friends like, that belongs to the life that you know." (Barbaralee Diamonstein, New York 1985). Parnis's life exemplified the successful and civic-minded businesswoman in New York. In addition to her career as an award-winning fashion designer, she founded several philanthropic organizations. Through her design work and her membership in such organizations as the Council of Fashion Designers of America, she played a role in the promotion and success of the American fashion industry.

—Melinda Watt

PARRISH, Maxfield. See **MAXFIELD PARRISH.**

PATOU, Jean.

French designer/company

Company founded by Jean Patou (1887-1936). Patou worked in small dressmaking business, Parry, before World War I, producing first collection, 1914. Captain of Zouaves during World War I. Returned to fashion, launching first couture collection, 1919; moved to rue St Florentin, Paris, 1922; visited USA, brought back six American models, 1924; dressed tennis star Suzanne Lenglen; opened sports shop; created perfume house, 1925; introduced Princess line, 1929. Perfumes include *Amour Amour, que sais-je, Adieu Sagesse,* 1925, *Chaldée,* 1927, *Moment Suprême,* 1929, *Joy,* 1930, *Divine Folie,* 1933, *Normandie,* 1935, *Vacances,* 1936, *Colony,* 1938, *l'Heure Attendue,* 1946, *Caline,* 1964, *1000,* 1972, *Eau de Patou,* 1976, *Patou pour Homme,* 1980, and *Sublime,* 1992; Parfums Patou established in London, Milan, Geneva, Hong Kong, and Australasia, by 1982. Brother-in-law, Raymond Barbas, took over business on death of Patou, 1936. Designers for the house have included Bohan (1954-56), Lagerfeld (1960-63), Goma (1963-73), Tarlazzi (1973-77), Gonzalès (1977-82), and Lacroix (1982-87). **Address:** 7 rue St. Florentin, Paris, 75008 France.

Jean Patou: Fall/Winter 1954 Haute Couture collection.

Publications:

On PATOU:

Books

Who's Who in Fashion, 1st edition, New York 1980.
Etherington-Smith, Meredith, *Patou,* London 1983.
McDowell, Colin, *McDowell's Directory of Twentieth Century Fashion,* Englewood Cliffs, New Jersey 1985.
Milbank, Caroline Rennolds, *Couture: The Great Designers,* New York 1985.
Ewing, Elizabeth, *History of Twentieth Century Fashion,* Totowa, New Jersey 1986.
Milbank, Caroline Rennolds, *New York Fashion: The Evolution of American Style,* New York 1989.
Steele, Valerie, *Women of Fashion: Twentieth-Century Designers,* New York 1991.
Stegemeyer, Anne, *Who's Who in Fashion,* 2nd edition, New York 1992.

Articles

"Patou with a New Spirit," in *Vogue,* May 1985.
"Paris/Rome...Couture Superlative," in *Vogue,* October 1985.
Donovan, Carrie, "The Two Sides of Paris Couture," in *The New York Times Magazine,* 23 February 1986.
Everett, Patty, "After half a century, Joy adds bath, body line," in *Women's Wear Daily,* 9 January 1987.
Koselka, Rita, "Affordable Luxury," in *Forbes,* 4 May 1987.

*

Since its origin, the House of Jean Patou has always associated fashion (1919) and perfumery (1925) activities. I think that there are numerous similarities in the care given to these two industries, notably in the domaine of know-how, innovation, the constant research for quality and in the intervention of a highly qualified work-force.

Forever the forerunner, Jean Patou has always understood the tastes and aspirations of his contemporaries. Whilst he was the primary influence in women's sportswear and creator of the first knitted bathing-suits, he was also the first Couturier to use his monogram as a design feature. For Jean Patou, "the modern woman leads an active life, and the creator must therefore dress her accordingly, in the most simple way, whilst maintaining her charm and femininity."

It is in this sense that the stylists that have succeeded Jean Patou have worked. They have created original and striking collections, with no limits, maintaining the label's prestigious aura, its liberty and quality. I think that fashion should reflect a woman's desires, should not constrain her but allow her to live with her epoch.

—Jean de Moüy

*   *   *

Fashion history records that Jean Patou is best known for *Joy,* the world's most expensive perfume, and for his famous Cubist sweaters. His contributions to fashion were, however, much more substantial and far reaching. His genius was his ability to interpret the times in which he lived and translate the ideals of that era into fashion. In Paris, during the 1920s, couture was evolving from serving a few wealthy clients into a huge autonomous industry and Patou recognized couture's tremendous potential, both in France and in the United States. Patou helped expand the industry by introducing sportswear, expanding his business into the American market, emphasizing accessories and, like Paul Poiret, offering his customers a signature perfume.

The 1920s ideal woman was youthful, physically fit, and healthy looking. The truly athletic woman was realized in Suzanne Lenglen, the 1921 Wimbledon tennis star, who wore Patou clothes both on and off the court. The benefits gained by the sports stars and other celebrities publicizing Patou's designs were many. Patou also provided a complete wardrobe for the American female aviator, Ruth Elder, as well as many well-known stage stars. The Patou customers, most of whom did not play sports, sought to emulate this new look. Patou recognized the need for clothes for the sports participant, the spectator, and for those wishing to appear athletic, both in Europe and in the United States. In 1925, he opened a Paris boutique called Le Coin des Sports where he devoted, in the House of Patou, a series of rooms each to an individual sport. The complete, accessorized outfit was available for aviation, riding, fishing, tennis, golf, and yachting, among others. Also, recognizing the importance of leisure and travel to his customers, Patou opened salons in the resort areas, Deauville and Biarritz, where off-the-rack items such as sweater sets, swimsuits, and accessories were available.

After expanding his business in France, Patou realized the potential for the fashion industry in the United States. Patou admired the long, lean lines of the American silhouette. In 1925 he travelled to New York and hired six women to return to Paris with him and work as mannequins. This well-publicized action made the couture more accessible to the Americans, thus improving his overall market share and profits. The French sought to emulate this silhouette as well, making Patou one of the best-known names in fashion.

Patou's design philosophy was influenced by sportswear, continuing the theme of casual elegance into day and evening ensembles. He believed in beautiful but functional clothes which reflected the personality of the wearer. Patou never felt that fashion should dictate. The cut of the clothes was simple, often accented with architectural seam lines, embroidery detail, and attention to fabric, trims, and finishings. By collaborating with textile mills on design and color, Patou was able to create exclusive colors through thread-dyeing methods, thus eliminating exact copies by lesser competitors. Patou also developed a swimsuit fabric which resisted shrinkage and fading, pleasing both swimmer and sun worshipper. Design inspirations included Russian embroideries, antique textiles, and modern art.

By interpreting the surrounding art movements and cultural ideas into his designs, Patou created such classics as the Cubist sweaters. The sweater sets figured prominently in his business. By adding coordinating skirts, scarves, hats, and other accessories, he increased his overall sales. Patou revolutionized the knitting industry with machine production, which meant greater productivity and greater profits. The casual fit of sweater and sportswear, in general, was financially beneficial as it required fewer fittings and less overall production time. Patou also applied his own monogram to his sportswear designs—the first visible designer label.

The rivalry between Patou and Chanel is by now well known. It was intense and perhaps fueled both of their successful careers. Their visions for the modern woman were quite similar, and although it is Chanel that fashion history has credited with many of the silhouette and conceptual changes of 1920s fashions, it was Patou who, in 1929, dropped the hemline and raised the waistline. Chanel quickly followed suit.

The House of Patou prospered during the Depression but Patou himself was unable to interpret the 1930s as he had so successfully captured the 1920s. He died in 1936, a relatively young man. Patou had demonstrated a brilliant business sense which was ultimately undermined by his destructive gambling tendencies. The company is still in family hands and is now headed by the grand-nephew of Jean Patou.

—Margo Seaman

PAULIN, Guy.

French designer

Born: Lorraine, France in 1946 (one source says 1945). **Career:** Free-lance designer for Prisunic, Jimper, Dorothée Bis, Paraphernalia, Mic Mac, Byblos, and others, prior to establishing own house, 1970s-84, and 1986-89; designer, Chloé, 1984-86; designer, Tiktiner, 1990. *Died* (in Paris), *1990.*

Publications

On PAULIN:

Articles

"Designer Guy Paulin Dies in Paris at Age 44," in *Women's Wear Daily* (New York), 15 June 1990.

*   *   *

Guy Paulin began his career as a free-lance designer of women's ready-to-wear in Paris. Though he had no formal training he was hired as a design assistant to Jacqueline Jacobson at Dorothée Bis, where he first worked with knits. He then signed a contract with Paraphernalia, a chain of franchised stores in New York, where he rubbed shoulders with other young designers of the time: Mary Quant, Betsey Johnson, Emmanuelle Khanh, and Lison Bonfils. A shy, quick-witted conversationalist and lover of 1950s American Abstract Expressionist paintings, Paulin believed fashion to be part of life, an essential component of the French l'art de vivre. He claimed to be most inspired by Katherine Hepburn—a mature, free-spirited soul who eschewed fashion trends and projected her own sense of personal style, and his clothing designs were often acclaimed for their gentle and unpretentious lines, reminiscent of classic American sportswear.

On returning to Paris after his New York sojourn, Guy Paulin received an enthusiastic press response for the simple, feminine clothes he designed for various clients. He worked for the next two decades in France and Italy, designing for Bercher, Biga, P. Blume, Byblos, Sport Max for Max Mara, Mic-Mac, PEP and Rodier. Before establishing his own business, he was known to juggle as many as 13 different ready-to-wear collections, designed anonymously, in a single season. His designs were marked by simplicity of line, softness of color, and ease of movement—from loose sportswear separates to classic suits and cocktail dresses.

In 1984, he succeeded Karl Lagerfeld as director of design at Chloé, claiming that his appointment was "a dream." At Chloé he adapted his unerring fashion sense into a look he called "as French as French cuisine—an image of a young couture, of ready-to-wear with the finesse of couture but with a very young spirit behind it." But his casual, relaxed, and individualistic styles were not completely welcomed by Chloé's tradition-minded customers, and he resigned after overseeing only a few collections.

The disappointment he experienced at Chloé did not deter him: between 1985 and 1990 he created S.A. Guy Paulin design studio, the principal clients being Byblos and Mic-Mac; took back the direction of his own house and signed two licensing contracts with the groups Kanematsu Gosho and Yoshida, establishing himself in Japan; and signed on as part-time artistic director of Tiktiner, a French ready to-wear manufacturer. During this period he designed a range of classic garments, including clingy knit dresses, feminine pin-striped suits, pretty floral 18th-century-inspired dresses, and simple one- and two-piece swimsuits. His clothes never strove for shock value, but remained reserved and feminine, with only the occasional theatrical accessory for emphasis, such as a "waistcoat" of multicolored cords draped across the breasts, or an oversized fringed straw hat.

Though not strictly an avant garde designer, Paulin considered himself one of a creative generation of createurs that included Thierry Mugler, Claude Montana, and the younger Jean-Paul Gaultier. Towards the end of his career he was investigating retro looks, such as 1940s-inspired tweed suits and neo-Baroque velvet gowns strewn with embroidery. His death in 1990 at the young age of 44 prompted waves of regret among his peers at the loss of such a talented, industrious, and benevolent designer and colleague.

—Kathleen Paton

PEDLAR, Sylvia.

American designer

Born: Sylvia Schlang in New York, 1901. **Education:** Studied art and fashion illustration, Cooper Union school, and the Art Students' League, New York City. **Family:** Married William A. Pedlar. **Career:** Founder and designer, Iris Lingerie, 1929-70. **Awards:** Coty American Fashion Critics Award, 1951, 1964; Neiman Marcus Award, 1960. *Died* (in New York) *26 February 1972.*

Publications:

On PEDLAR:

Books

Lambert, Eleanor, *World of Fashion: People, Places, Resources,* New York and London 1976.
The Undercover Story (exhibition catalogue), Fashion Institute of Technology, New York 1982.

Articles

Bender, Marylin, "Lingerie Can Be Sensibly Elegant," in the *New York Times,* 17 December 1963.

*   *   *

For 41 years American women relied on Sylvia Pedlar for sleep and loungewear to suit their every mood. Fine fabrics, careful workmanship, and imaginative styling distinguished the Pedlar gown. Some of her designs were based on traditional favorites. Others were strikingly original, sometimes pleasingly provocative, but always in good taste.

Pedlar designed to suit many scenarios. She understood that a woman might prefer to dress in a certain way for the street, yet play a wider variety of roles in the privacy of her own home. She saw no reason why a wardrobe for sleeping should not be as versatile as one for day.

Pedlar was the co-founder and designer of Iris Lingerie, from its inception in 1929 until she closed the business in 1970. In all that time, according to Marylin Bender, writing in the *New York Times* in December 1963, the company employed no salesmen and bought no paid advertising. The product spoke for itself.

She is said to have created the baby-doll look, a phrase she disliked and did not use herself, as a response to the wartime fabric shortages of 1942. She interpreted the classic flannel Mother Hubbard nightgown in sheer cotton batiste, giving it a more sophisticated, bateau neckline and open, flowing sleeves. Deep borders of Cluny lace finished the neck, sleeves, and hem. For women who preferred to sleep in the nude, Pedlar offered the "bedside toga," a column of crêpe slit entirely up one side which fastened with a single tie at the shoulder and one at the waist. Originally designed as a novelty item for friends, the bedside toga was photographed for the cover of *Life* magazine in 1962 and became a bestseller.

Although she was trained as an illustrator, Pedlar preferred draping directly the form to sketching her ideas. Many of her designs rely on simple, bias cut shapes with a minimum of seaming, cut from solid shades of crêpe or chiffon. A trio of Iris gowns from the mid-1960s pictured in *The Undercover Story,* the catalogue for an exhibition held in 1982-83 at the Fashion Institute of Technology, New York and the Kyoto Costume Institute in Japan illustrate Pedlar's gift as a cutter. An asymmetrical layered gown in turquoise georgette both conceals and reveals. An off-white one shouldered gown in crêpe charmeuse evokes the pre-war years with its diaper hem and bias cut. A pair of coral lounging pajamas have trousers cut wide like a *dhoti*. Each is as wearable today as when they were first produced.

A winner of two Coty awards, Pedlar was cited by the American Fashion Critics committee for "her talent in combining luxury, beauty, and femininity with modern fabric developments and contemporary silhouettes."

—Whitney Blausen

PEPE.

British jeans/casualwear manufacturer

Pepe brand jeans began on London's Portobello Road market; lines include Basic, and the BSCO, Hardcore, and Buffalo labels. Maurice Marciano, Lawrence Stroll, and Silas Chou became owners of Pepe Group PLC, 1993; Jay Margolis became chairman and chief operating officer of Pepe Jeans U.S.A., early 1994; Edwin Lewis became vice-chairman/chairman and chief operating officer of Pepe Jeans U.S.A., April, 1994; LeAnn Nealz, director of design. **Address:** Pepe House, 11 Lower Square, Old Isleworth-on-Thames, Middlesex TW7 6HN, UK.

Publications:

On PEPE:

Articles

Lippert, Barbara, "Clean Jeans, Dirty War," in the *Chicago Tribune,* 16 December 1988.
Wall Street Journal (New York), 10 April 1989.
Bidlake, Suzanne, "Pepe Strides Upmarket with Branding U-Turn," in *Marketing,* 11 April 1991.
Fallon, James, "Maurice Marciano Seeks Interest in Pepe Group," in *Daily News Record* (New York), 6 January 1993.
Fallon, James, "Restructuring Done, Pepe Group Is Set to Go," in *Women's Wear Daily* (New York), 3 February 1993.
Gordon, Maryellen, "New Owners, New Power for Pepe," in *Women's Wear Daily* (New York), 10 February 1993.
Ozzard, Janet, "Margolis Cuts a New Pattern at Pepe," in *Women's Wear Daily* (New York), 19 January 1994.
Walsh, Peter, "Margolis Joins Hilfiger as Vice-Chairman, President; Succeeded at Pepe by Lewis," in *Daily News Record* (New York), 10 March 1994.
Lockwood, Lisa, "More Suitors Seen Pitching for CK Jeans," in *Women's Wear Daily* (New York), 14 April 1994.
Moore, M. H., "Pepe Jeans May Be Loose, Seeking Fit," in *Adweek,* 22 August 1994.

*   *   *

In the notoriously competitive denim sales market, Pepe has been able to maintain its profile as much through witty and eclectic marketing as through design details. The company and its various casualwear lines have carved a niche by concentrating on prompting a contemporary, directional image. This has enabled them to establish an identity which is distinct from the nostalgia-led promotional strategy of many jeans companies.

A potent mix of references has marked out Pepe and its sister ranges as fashionable and different. The attention to detailing, with double stitched seams and copper rivets, so important to serious denim wearers, has underpinned their success and enabled Pepe to prosper. The range of different denims they produce has also been significant. They have maintained a reputation for quality, both in their staple Basic line, which established Pepe's classic straight-cut shapes for jeans and jackets, and their production of a changing array of washes and colour dyes which pick up on current fashion trends, particularly in their BSCO, Hardcore, and Buffalo labels.

Having started life in London's Portobello Road market, Pepe has always had an affinity with street fashion and urban life, and it is this ability to chime in with the *Zeitgeist* which brought them to the fore in the 1980s. After the dip in denim's popularity at the start of that decade, the slick advertising of the market leader, Levi's, dominated by retro 1950s cool, sent jeans sales rocketing, partly triggered by the obsession with so-called design classics and media hype. If Pepe was lacking the long history of the main American labels, it certainly made up for it with its originality of approach.

Pepe recognized its own strengths as a British-based name and employed strong, innovative advertising to promote their ranges. They understood that it was just as important to generate an aura of streetwise cool about their product, as to keep up with trends in fabric washes and design details.

From 1986, they sidestepped the traditional American imagery associated with jeans and produced a series of adverts which ultimately led to an almost complete brand awareness by the end of the decade. Their advertising achieved cult status; two of their most successful campaigns produced a soundtrack of contemporary music fitted together with well-known clubland images with which the resistant younger market could identify. The "Wears Pepe" series cut images of the avant-garde nightclub figure Leigh Bowery with shots of natural-looking models in Pepe denims and increased Pepe's status as a company which could both encapsulate and define the times.

Along with the memorable "Raindance" advert, which also brought together maverick elements, looking more like a clip from a film than a piece of marketing, and "Laughter," which simply showed a group of people smiling and talking in a park, again in the now much-discussed Pepe line, they created a precedent. Pepe had recognized a crucial element of the 1990s youth market; they saw that the video generation was not taken in by straightforward name-plugging, but wanted to feel in on the joke, as though they were part of the street culture which Pepe represented.

This image has maintained momentum, shifting key with the more laid back post-rave scene, while continuing to tap into images of cool, more recently by using photographers like Bruce Weber to create a moody storyboard series of stills with actor Jason Priestly, and, in their latest campaign, a witty montage of shots of traditional London and soft-porn photographs set against black and white hotel room scenes with a punkish edge, featuring Donovan Leitch, Ione Skye, and other young models semi-clad on the bed.

Pepe has defined its role within the denim market and built on its strengths by clever advertising and an empathy with street fashion. If never quite in the same league as the biggest names in denim, it has chosen to strike out in a different direction, leaning on the contemporary rather than exploiting its own history to promote its ideals. This approach has since been mimicked by other British casualwear names, but never with Pepe's originality and quality of research, in marketing or design.

—Rebecca Arnold

PERETTI, Elsa.

Italian designer working in New York

Born: Florence, 1 May 1940. **Career:** Language teacher in Gstaad, Switzerland, 1961; studied interior design in Rome; modeled in London, Paris, New York, mid-1960s; began designing jewelry for Halston and Sant'Angelo, New York, 1969; designer, Tiffany and Co., New York, from 1974; also packaging designer, Halston fragrances and cosmetics. **Exhibitions:** *Fifteen of My Fifty with Tiffany,* Fashion Institute of Technology, New York, 1990. **Awards:** Coty American Fashion Critics Award, 1971; President's Fellow Award, Rhode Island School of Design, 1981; Fashion Group "Night of the Stars" Award, 1986; Cultured Pearl Industry Award, 1987. **Address:** 727 Fifth Avenue, New York, New York 10022, USA.

Publications:

By PERETTI:

Books

Fifteen of My Fifty with Tiffany (exhibition catalogue), New York 1990.

On PERETTI:

Books

Morris, Bernadine, and Barbara Walz, *The Fashion Makers,* New York 1978.

Articles

Kent, Rosemary, "Elsa Peretti ... Real Things with a Thought," in *Women's Wear Daily* (New York), 29 December 1971.
Talley, André Leon, "Elsa Peretti: Style Is to Be Simple," in *Women's Wear Daily* (New York), 11 June 1976.
"Jewelry's New Dazzle," in *Newsweek* (New York), 4 April 1977.
"The Peretti Obsession," in the *New York Times Magazine,* 26 February 1978.
Blair, Gwenda, "Elsa Peretti at 40," in *Attenzione,* August 1980.
McAlpin, Heller, "Designing Women," in *Savvy* (New York), October 1981.
Seebohm, Caroline, "All that Glitters," in *Savvy* (New York), May 1988.
"A Look at Peretti's Work and Life," in *Women's Wear Daily* (New York), 27 April 1990.
Sones, Melissa, "Jewelry: New Facets of 1991," in *Mirabella* (New York), December 1990.

*   *   *

"Style," Elsa Peretti says, "is to be simple." Peretti can deliver a brusque maxim in her husky voice with a Chanel imperiousness and a Montesquieu-like incisiveness. Her knowledge of style is perhaps so vivid because it comes intuitively from a career in modeling, friendships with fashion designers, interest in sculptural adornment, and a fascination with the crafts that go into jewelry. Her quest is for expressive, perfect form, even if it happens to look imperfect at first. Touch—the hand of making and of holding—is foremost. She has brilliantly expanded the materials and repertory of jewelry, assuring that it is a modern tradition, but also guaranteeing that it preserves special crafts of the past. Her art evades any particular place in the world, drawing upon Japanese traditions, Surrealism, and modernist design; it is an art so vagrant its only home is in the heart.

Peretti explores nature with a biologist's acumen and an artist's discrimination. The simplicity of her forms resides in the fact that she selects the quintessential form from among those found in nature, never settling on the median or most familiar, but striving for the essence. Her hearts, for instance, are never of a trite Valentine's Day familiarity; rather, they cleave to the hand with shaped, hand-held warmth. That the heart necklace hangs from its chain in asymmetry as the chain passes through the middle, gives it the quirk of love and the aberration of art that Peretti admires.

Reminding us that Chanel never forgot that she was a peasant, Peretti, too, never forgets the simple things of life. Her suite of beans is ineffably ordinary, yet they are extraordinary in their craft, in their scaling to hand, and in their finest materials. Her bottles are common; Peretti transfigures the crude practicality into an elegant simplicity. "The design," said Peretti, "is full of common sense. Of course I'm slow, I have to crystallize a form, find the essence."

In the 1990 catalogue *Fifteen of My Fifty with Tiffany,* I wrote: "A transcendental aspect haunts Peretti's work; she hints at our affinity to nature even as she plucks the perfect form from the cartload of nature's abundance and art's options. Peretti returns us in her absolute objects to a Garden of Paradise. There, all form has its lingering memory and every shape is the definitive best." (Richard Martin, Tiffany/Fashion Institute of Technology, New York 1990).

Peretti's sensibility is deeply touched by her professional and personal friendships with Halston and Giorgio di Sant'Angelo, no less so after the death of both designers. As a model, Peretti had known both. Halston's minimalism is a touchstone for Peretti, not only in the opportunity for her demonstrative forms to stand out in the ensemble of such simple luxury in dress, but also in the obdurate minimalism of her own design. From Giorgio di Sant'Angelo, Peretti's spirit is of incorporating regional materials in an aggregate at once a composite of many sources and a refinement of them in modern terms.

Generous in acknowledging such designers and in expressing her pleasure in cooperating with craftspeople in the fulfilment of her work, Peretti cannot disguise her own remarkable ability, which she sometimes passes off as craft, to distil form and ideas. The sabotage of her belts is that their sources are in the stable, not in haberdashery: Peretti's attention in 1969 to a leather horse girth inspired a belt without mechanisms, working by the unadorned looping to fulfil the function of the belt. Her tableware is fit for a peasant table, before chopsticks or other utensils: she has created the perfect setting for Picasso's *Blind Man's Meal* to transform it to Tiffany grace without ever compromising its rudimentary, manual presence.

Characteristically, when Peretti confronted the precious materials of diamonds, she flouted convention and offered the affordable—and revolutionary—"Diamonds by the Yard," giving even the desired stone a degree of access and of animation. Of that insouciant success, a landmark of 1970s design, Peretti says modestly, "My objective is to design according to one's financial possibilities." Few would earlier have imagined a leading jewelry designer to coming up with such a frank and sensitive view of the product or the consumer. In fact, it is one of Peretti's triumphs to restore to jewelry a vitality it had lost in the 1960s and early 1970s.

"My love for bones has nothing macabre about it," Peretti says. Indeed, Peretti's sensibility is one of unmitigated joy. Her fruits are prime produce; her sea life is a miracle of abundance; her scorpions and snakes are never scary, but seem instead to be mementoes of exhilaration; her handbags long to be clutched; even her teardrops adapted for earrings, pendants, and even pen-clips are never melancholic. They are tears of joy created by a designer who zealously celebrates life.

—Richard Martin

PERRIS, Bernard.

French designer

Born: Millau, France, 5 October 1936. **Education:** Studied fashion design at Cours Bazot School. **Career:** Assistant to Marc Bohan, assistant designer, Guy Laroche, 1960-61; designer, Jacques Heim, 1961-63; designer, Dior, 1963; designer, Paul Bon, 1964-69. Opened ready-to-wear firm, Bernard Perris Nouvelle Couture, 1969; New York shop opened, 1986; two Paris shops opened, 1988; introduced bridge line, 1989; business closed briefly, reopened, 1992. Specialities are haute couture and deluxe ready-to-wear. **Exhibitions:** Musée des Arts Decoratifs, Paris, 1988; Musée de la Mode,

Marseille, 1994. **Awards:** Best Fashion Designer, Houston Texas, 1988; Best Fashion Designer, Tokyo, 1988. **Address:** 5 rue de Magdebourg, 75116 Paris, France.

Publications:

On PERRIS:

Articles

"International Ethnic Is the Big News from Paris," in *Women's Wear Daily* (New York), 19 March 1990.
"Bernard Perris Liquidates Two Main Holding Companies," in *Women's Wear Daily* (New York), 12 July 1991.
"Perris to Reopen with New Partners," in *Women's Wear Daily* (New York), 13 October 1992.
Godfrey, Deeny "House of Scherrer Names Perris Couture, Ready-to-Wear Designer," in *Women's Wear Daily* (New York), 7 September 1994.
Articles on Perris also apppear in *Vogue, L'Officiel, Joyce* (Japan), *Elle, Figaro, Madame, Town & Country, Harper's Bazaar,* and *Mode x Mode* (Japan).

*

What has been mainly distinctive of my work during more than 25 years is an atmosphere of high standard elegance with a glance to independence of mind and fun toward "les ideés reçues."

I have been many times called the most "couturier" of the "createurs," probably because my line was more a "nouvelle couture" than a deluxe RTW.

As everyone, I have a double personality and am reflecting the influence of the "austerité" and "grandeur" of a Balenciaga, as well as the "glamour" and "sexy touch" and "joie de vivre" of a Jacques Fath.

—Bernard Perris

*   *   *

It has been said that the women's ready-to-wear designs by Parisian Bernard Perris embody the philosophy "more is more." From the moment he opened his own Paris showroom in 1969, Perris has favored dramatic, almost theatrical fare, incorporating luxurious fabrics, intricate construction, and extravagant trim into his creations. Indeed, he has been accused of cramming enough ideas for a dozen dresses into one garment, loading his designs with high voltage, eye-popping details.

As a young boy in the south of France, Perris was strongly influenced by the women's fashions he saw in his mother's ready-to-wear clothing boutique. At age 16 he ventured to Paris, where he eventually was hired as a couture assistant for Guy Laroche. He then went on to design debutante and wedding dresses under the Jacques Heim and Paul Bon labels where he learned ready-to-wear techniques. After a short stay at Dior, Perris opened his own house and showed his first collection of "Nouvelle Couture," a collection based on techniques which allowed him the creative freedom of haute couture, but whose prices were accessible to more women.

The designer's fortunes rose and fell precipitously, causing him to suffer bouts of nervous exhaustion, and from about 1971-77 he remained out of the fashion spotlight. But as the interest in ethnic revivals and the "hippy look" waned and a renewed taste for glamor-

Bernard Perris: Fall/Winter 1992/93. *Photograph by Brazil.*

ous dressing arose toward the end of the 1970s, Perris again re-emerged, promoting his special brand of opulent pret-a-porter deluxe. His fur-trimmed and embroidered velvets, gathered capes and evening gowns, tiered and ruffled cocktail dresses and appliqued resort wear garnered a newly appreciative audience, and he opened his own Paris boutique in 1985. He became particularly popular in America, appealing as he did to the big-spending, flashy customer who wanted to be seen in his bold yet high-quality clothing, and he established a Madison Avenue shop in New York. Perris did not shrink from personally promoting his clothes in the States, presenting trunk shows for wealthy buyers from Beverly Hills to Las Vegas, and often appearing at in-store events and charity dinners.

Chosen in 1985 by the "Best" committee as one of the ten most elegant men in the world, Bernard Perris created clothing for a high-profile, international clientele, including several film stars. He designed all the women's costumes for the 1986 film "Max, My Love," in which actress Charlotte Rampling wore ten different Bernard Perris ensembles. Clothing from the 1980s stressed strong lines, saturated color, and a kind of dazzling, urban chic—these were powerful clothes made for grand entrances, completely in step with the period's emphasis on wealth and conspicuous consumption.

Later styles found the designer embracing less show-stopping ideas without sacrificing his essential devotion to luxury or glamour, as in his wool daytime suits trimmed with sheared beaver, drapey silk georgette lounging ensembles, cashmere separates, and extravagant accessories. He remained true to his reputation for fabulous evening wear, however, as seen in his sumptuous 1988 all black-white-and-red collection featuring swaths of fur, rustling silks and liberal lace trim.

His acceptance into the Chambre Syndicale du Pret-a-Porter des Couturiers and des Createurs de Mode finally validated Bernard Perris' long and fruitful, if uneven, career. Recently his business has again experienced difficulty, but with new backers the designer hoped to change his focus from opulent evening wear to ready-to-wear lines for working women.

—Kathleen Paton

PER SPOOK. See **SPOOK, Per.**

PETER HOGGARD. See under **HOGGARD.**

PEZZUTTO, Graziella Ronchi. See **ERREUNO SCM SpA.**

PFISTER, Andrea.
Italian footwear designer working in Paris

Born: Pesaro, Italy, 30 August 1942. **Education:** Studied art and languages at University of Florence 1960-62, shoe design at Ars

Sutoria, Milan, 1962. **Career:** Designed collections for Lanvin, Patou in Paris, 1963; showed first collection under own label, 1965; opened first shop, Paris, 1967, and began production of own line, 1968; collaborated with Anne Klein, 1973-94; own shoe factory and introduced accessory line—belts, bags, scarves and jewelry, 1974; ready-to-wear line introduced, 1976; lower priced shoe range introduced, 1990. Invents colours and new finishings or prints for the Italian tannery Stefania, from 1990. Artistic Director of Bruno Magli Shoes since 1993. **Exhibitions:** *Mostra d'epoca della calzatura,* Vigevano, Italy; *Andrea Pfister: Trente ans de création,* Musée International de la Chaussure, Romans, France, 23 October 1993-6 February 1994 (travelling exhibition); UBS-Brugg, Switzerland, 9 September-10 October 1994; Palazzo degli Affari, Milan 9 December 1994-15 January 1995. **Collection:** Metropolitan Museum, New York. **Awards:** Fashion Footwear Association of New York gold medal of honor designer of the year, 1988; Designer of the Year, 1990 (for Anne Klein); First Prize, shoe designer international competition, Amsterdam. **Address:** Viale dei Mille, 47, Vigevano 27029 (PV), Italy.

Publications:

On PFISTER:

Books

Liu, Aimee, and Rottman, Meg, *Shoe Time,* New York 1986.
Trasko, Mary, *Heavenly Soles,* London 1989.
McDowell, Colin, *Shoes: Fashion and Fantasy,* New York and London 1989.
Hirmer, S., *Schuhe,* Munich 1992.
Andrea Pfister: Trente ans de création (exhibition catalogue), Romans, France 1993.

Articles

"Dateline Milan," in *Footwear News* (New York), 25 March 1985.
"Andrea Pfister," in *Footwear News* (New York), 11 February 1991.
Also: in *Donna* (Milan), October 1993;
Grazia (Italy), October 1993;
Panorama (Milan), October 1993;
Ars Sutoria (Italy), December 1993;
Moda Pelle (Milan), January 1994;
Bazaar Italy, February 1994.

*

My shoes are feminine, sexy, full of humour and perfectly made. But a shoe cannot only be pretty—it has also to fit, not hurt. Colours, materials and clear lines are very important to me. I love flat heels and very high heels.

—Andrea Pfister

*   *   *

"If a beautiful woman's feet hurt, she becomes ugly."
A typically robust statement from a designer whose opulent creations have been variously described as frivolous, witty, and even in dubious taste. Yet the success of his creations depends upon the combination of proportion and line with comfort: "I al-

ways think shoes should be very feminine and sexy. Compromises are often necessary. It's easy to make wonderful looking shoes, but they also have to fit and be comfortable."

Pfister's shoes are essentially Italian in their craftsmanship and attention to detail. Yet there is an element of lightness and irreverence about his creations not usually associated with the traditional shoemaker. He improvises on themes—starry skies, the sea, music, circuses and Las Vegas. Designing shoes such as Martini Dry, with cocktail glass heels supporting slices of lemon. He uses applique motifs, so that when a sandal is called Jazz, it really does have a snakeskin saxophone on the upper.

Another reason for the originality of his work may be that unlike most footwear designers, Pfister is a colourist. Twice a year he retreats for two months to prepare new collections. The starting point is always colour, then he works on shape, proportion, and styling. He is involved with several tanneries, creating seasonal colour charts and matching colours in diverse materials such as reptile and suede as a basis for his collections.

Pfister's commitment to colour also explains his copious use of ornamentation. Jewels, sequins, and glitter catch the light bouncing colour off upper and heel as the shoes trip light along. The fullest ranges of materials are used to create the desired effects. He will use sumptuous hand-crafted embroidery and silks and yet is equally at home with plastics and paste stones.

Despite the occasional jokiness of his themes, the shoes are true couture creations. Pfister has always been a couturier. He began his career at the top with Lanvin and Jean Patou at the age of 21. Today he creates shoes for Italian dress designer Mariuccia Mandelli, whose Krizia collections are also often quirky.

Like all original designers, his ideas were plundered by others. Snakeskin, a favourite material, was used in multicolored patches over white kidskin on a court shoe entitled Mosaique. This style, from the early 1980s, is instantly recognizable because it has been copied so often. His most famous style must be the Birdcage shoe of 1979. This was a closed-back opened toed flat pump, with the main body constructed in an open latticework of thin leather straps. It spawned millions of copies. Its final form, far removed from the finely crafted snakeskin original, is as a moulded plastic beach shoe.

Pfister has diversified into handbags, scarves, and leatherwear, but remains committed to producing beautiful shoes. His attitude towards fashion is relaxed. Pfister styles complement current trends but can also stand alone. He looks for this independence in his customers, including stars from Elizabeth Taylor to Madonna. For him the client is: "The woman who mixes different pieces—an Armani top, for instance, with a Donna Karan skirt, and a jacket by Ferre. My shoes work best on the woman who's sure enough of herself to create her own combination."

Andrea Pfister: Summer 1992.

Andrea Pfister creates truly original footwear. It may not be fashionable in a trendsetting sense. It may not always appeal to the mainstream idea of good taste, but the styles are extraordinary, often eccentric and frequently enchanting, making him one of the most innovative designers of the shoe.

—Chris Hill

PICASSO, Paloma.

French designer

Born: Paris, 19 April 1949, daughter of Pablo Picasso and Françoise Gilot. **Education:** Attended University of Paris, Sorbonne, and University of Nanterre; studied jewelry design and fabrication. **Family:** Married Rafael Lopez-Cambil (aka Lopez-Sanchez), 1978. **Career:** Fashion jewelry designer for Yves Saint Laurent, 1969; jewelry for Zolotas, 1971; designed costumes and sets for Lopez-Cambil's Parisian productions *L'Interprétation,* 1975, *Success,* 1978. Teamed with Mr. Lopez-Cambil to create Paloma Picasso brand, including jewelry for Tiffany & Co., 1980; introduced fragrance *Paloma* and cosmetics *Mes Jours, Mes Nuits,* 1984, *Minataure,* 1992; designed men's and women's accessories for Lopez-Cambil, Ltd., 1987; hosiery for Grupo Synkro; eyewear for Carrera; bone china, crystal, silverware, and tiles for Villeroy & Boch; household linens for KBC; fabrics and wall coverings for Motif. Paloma Picasso boutiques opened in Japan and Hong Kong. **Address:** Lopez-Cambil Ltd., 37 West 57th Street, New York, NY 10019, USA.

Publications:

On PICASSO:

Books

Mulvagh, Jane, *Costume Jewelry in Vogue,* London 1988.

Articles

Fischer, Daniela, "Incontri: Paloma Picasso," in *Bolaffiarte* (Turin), March 1972.
Sanesi, R., "Paloma Picasso," in *D'arts* (Milan), July 1973.
Capia, R., "Paloma: Portrait de la fille d'un peintre," in *Elle* (Paris), 17 June 1974.
Blond, S., "Paloma Picasso and Nicola Weymouth," in *Interview* (New York), August 1974.
"Paloma Picasso," in *Current Biography* (New York), April 1986.
"Women Facing Women," in *Vogue* (New York), August 1987.
Irvine, Susan, "Paloma's Pink Period," in the *Sunday Express* magazine (London), 7 August 1988.
Fusco, Ann Castronovo, "Paloma's Classic Touch," in *House Beautiful* (London), February 1989.
"The First Year: Striving for Status," in *Women's Wear Daily* (New York), 28 April 1989.
Lowry, Suzanne, "Living Up to Father's Fame," in *The Daily Telegraph* (London), 7 September 1989.
Samuel, Kathryn, "The Look that Says Picasso," in *The Daily Telegraph* (London), 7 September 1989.
Grove, Valerie, "The Red Revolutionary: My Style," in *The Sunday Times* (London), 17 September 1989.

Hoban, Pheobe, "Design of the Dove," in *Harper's Bazaar* (New York), December 1989.
Beckett-Young, Kathleen, "Design for Living," in *Working Woman* (New York), October 1990.
Gandee, Charles, "Paloma Picasso Has Mass Appeal," in *House and Garden,* November 1990.
Stern, Ellen, "The Prolific Paloma," in *House Beautiful* (London), March 1992.
Landis, Dylan, "Paloma Picasso's Signature Style," in *Metropolitan Home* (New York), September/October 1993.

*   *   *

With such a name, one could hardly fail to be noticed. And since her marriage, her name has an even more exotic ring—Paloma Picasso Lopez-Sanchez. The daughter of Pablo Picasso, however, is undoubtedly a personality and exciting talent in her own right. Visually arresting with striking features, she consistently wears her signature red lipstick to emphasize her white skin and thick, black hair. She is a newsworthy and photogenic participator in the world's fashion circuit. This, combined with her creative talent, makes her ideally suited to the needs of the modern world where a high profile and excellent social and professional contacts can be an integral part of success.

Paloma Picasso is truly international. Placed in the front row of the Paris and Milan couture collections, she visits the smartest restaurants, the interior decorations of her apartments are publicized, and her choice of garments is recorded in society publications throughout the world. Social gatherings are considered incomplete without her, and she numbers many celebrities amongst her circle.

Professionally, she is an individual designer who uses her assets to great effect in marketing and promoting her ideas. Her jewelry and perfume are particularly noteworthy, demonstrating a modernity and panache that single them out as something special. Her name and the colour red are used as essential ingredients of her work. Her name, meaning "dove," is distinctive, and when used skillfully, a good name has always been an advantage if cleverly exploited.

Paloma Picasso was born and educated in Paris. Formally trained as a jewelry designer, her interest was possibly kindled by childhood memories of the glass beads seen on the island of Murano in Venice and an early fascination with sparkling colours. Initially she was involved in costume design for the theatre, where her originality and exotic pieces attracted much attention. An invitation from Yves Saint Laurent to create a collection of jewelry for his couture house ensured that her work was widely seen, and in 1972 her gold designs for the Greek company Zolotas achieved further recognition and acclaim.

Tiffany and Co. of New York, founded in 1837 as a fancy goods store, has built an international reputation as a high class jeweler, specializing in gemstones and precious metals. In 1980 Paloma created the first of several imaginative and vibrant collections for the company. The signature pieces are unusual in their colour combinations and use of polished surfaces. The shapes are bold and vigorous and enhanced the clothing with which they may be worn. Striking and exciting, her jewelry, although always of the moment, seems to have the timeless quality that sets apart true creativity.

Paloma Picasso's other notable creative contribution to fashion appeals to another sense. The highly successful and distinctive fragrance *Paloma,* with its dynamic red and black packaging and strikingly shaped bottle, is a lingering and suitable evocative tribute to this individual and intriguing personality.

—Margo Seaman

PIGUET, Robert.

Swiss/French designer

Born: Yverdon, Switzerland, 1901. Immigrated to France, 1918. **Education:** Trained to be a banker; studied fashion design under Redfern and Paul Poiret, 1918-28. **Career:** Founded own fashion house, 1933; sold designs by Dior, Balmain, Bohan, Givenchy, and Galanos; introduced perfume, "Bandit," 1944; retired, 1951. *Died in 1953.*

Publications:

On PIGUET:

Books

Who's Who in Fashion, 1st edition, New York 1980.
McDowell, Colin, *McDowell's Directory of Twentieth Century Fashion,* Englewood Cliffs, New Jersey 1985.
O'Hara, Georgina, *The Encyclopaedia of Fashion,* New York 1986.
Stegemeyer, Anne, *Who's Who in Fashion,* 2nd edition, New York 1992.

*   *   *

The 18 years that Robert Piguet spent as head of his own couture house were the culmination and not the sum of his career in fashion. He learned his craft in two of the more important houses of the early 20th century, Poiret and Redfern. Both houses were fashionable and influential, but they espoused widely divergent philosophies of fashion and appeal to very different customers. In developing his own style, Piguet combined the imagination and awareness of Poiret to his peak with the quality and stability of Redfern. The resulting look was youthful but not girlish; the clothes echoed, flattered, and enhanced the body beneath them. There was an essential effortless wearability to garments from Piguet, which the vantage point of half a century has neither diminished nor obscured.

Like Poiret, Piguet understood and employed the links between high fashion and the arts. His collections often reflected his sensitivity to the cultural environment of the moment. An example is his response to the historical romanticism of the 1930s, an important movement fed by theatrical and motion picture costume dramas. These provided Piguet with inspiration for everything from suits to evening gowns. Particularly notable was the spring 1936 collection, which featured high, gathered sleeve caps, bold up-flaring collars, or wide shoulder yokes based on 16th century modes used in the hit play *Margot.*

Just a short time later, during the early years of World War II, Piguet produced collections with a different, darker mood, influenced by political circumstances. In these, models were accessorized with such wartime essentials as gas masks, or given topical names referring to the realities and hardships of wartime life. Even his fabric choices reflected his surroundings. In 1945, Piguet joined many fellow Paris designers in the Théâtre de la Mode. With an eye

to the scarcities and rationing of the immediate post-war years he used synthetics for several of his models. No matter what Piguet's mood or inspiration, however, the clothes themselves always remained clothing, and never descended into costume—or they would now be camp, not classic. Some of Piguet's most timeless designs are the post-New Look evening dresses which harkened back to the romantic silhouettes he used in the 1930s. These were in sync with his contemporaries, but, in a way, cleaner, with less ornamentation.

Since several different designers worked for Piguet, it is difficult to isolate elements of cut or construction as hallmarks of his house. There is, instead, an overarching impression of ease, comfort, and femininity. Piguet models, however fitted, do not seem to constrict or restrict the wearer. Allowance is made for movement: a narrow waist expands into pleats or gathers above or below, a sheath skirt is topped by a dolman-sleeved bodice. Tailored garments are rarely hard-edged. The severity of a pleated shirtwaist dress is mitigated by a short, cascading bolero top. Slim suit-skirts might be side draped sarong-style, or pegged with a gathered waistline. Jackets might have rounded peak lapels, or tulip hems. Even a post-liberation suit, styled on the lines of an Allied forces military police uniform, had a shawl collar, long gloves crushed around the wrists, and white detailing to lift the khaki linen outfit out of the masculine realm.

It might be said that Piguet's most lasting contributions to post-war fashion were the designers he employed and encouraged. Dior, Givenchy, and Balmain each worked for or sold designs to Piguet in the 1930s and 1940s, and went on to open houses of their own. Whether Piguet hired them because an inherent romanticism in their work agreed with his fashion sense, or they learned from him that trait which each would use to advantage in his own business is not yet a matter of record. However, Piguet's wisdom in choosing able designers was more than matched by his skill in maintaining the identity of his house and collections, no matter who had produced the actual sketches.

All Piguet's clothes provide distinction without constraint, and comfort without disorder. The fashions he fostered bespeak a mature editorial talent, ranging freely with his times and of his times.

—Madelyn Shaw

PIPART, Gerard.

French fashion designer

Born: Paris, 1933. **Education:** Studied at the École de la Chambre Syndicale de la Couture Parisienne. **Career:** Began selling sketches to Balmain and Jacques Fath; sketched for Marc Bohan and Givenchy. Became chief designer for Nina Ricci in 1963. Freelanced for London's Germaine et Jane, Jean Baillie-Itemcey and Chloe.

Publications:

On PIPART:

Books

Lambert, Eleanor, *World of Fashion: People, Places, Resources,* New York 1976.

Gerard Pipart: For Nina Ricci; Spring/Summer 1992 Haute Couture collection.

McDowell, Colin, *McDowell's Directory of Twentieth Century Fashion,* Englewood Cliffs, New Jersey 1985.

O'Hara, Georgina, *The Encyclopaedia of Fashion,* New York 1986.

Stegemeyer, Anne, *Who's Who in Fashion,* 2nd edition, New York 1992.

*   *   *

In 1963, before the age of thirty, Gerard Pipart had become the most vital women's ready-to-wear designer in Paris. His clothes were already great sellers abroad. He made his mark with snappy, colorful sportswear, well-tailored, detailed, and with a deceptively casual simplicity that only good seams and a fine cut can guarantee. He became known for his inspired use of fabrics, as he skillfully manipulated every material he chose into amusing, wearable chic. His work as a free-lancer at Chloe and other houses gained him widespread visibility, and he was hired by Nina Ricci in 1964. His move to Nina Ricci's Haute Couture Studio was closely watched, and indeed, the young, fresh-faced designer brought new life to Ricci with his lively, youthful designs.

As a young designer Pipart considered Balenciaga an important influence, and greatly admired the designs of Norell. His background as an assistant at Balmain, Fath, and with Marc Bohan at Patou gave him a solid grounding in haute couture before he became a bright young star in ready-to-wear and then back again to couture. His couture collections have included elegant daytime wear, sumptuous coats, extravagant evening looks, furs, and bridal wear. Early collections focused on supple lines and a fit close to the body without being overly confining, and his clothes were praised as "never, never too Haute." Later collections investigated the long, languid lines of the bias cut dress; played with loose, theatrical capes; feminized the culotte for daytime wear; and toyed with 1940s and 1950s retro looks.

His penchant for no-holds-barred glamour can be seen in evening dresses of frothy chiffon and bright, opulent taffeta, long-waisted and cinched, with high trumpet sleeves and luxuriant folds billowing to the floor, or exquisite embroideries requiring hundreds of hours of work. He dared to defy the "bride-wore-white" norm with his design for a Provencal-printed, multi-colored melange of a bridal dress, wrapped at the waist with a wide cummerbund, topped with a short jacket splashed with rhinestones. Fur trim, feathered hats, ruffles, lace, long gloves—Pipart has never shied away from a certain feminine, Parisian elegance in his designs and use of accessories.

1990s collections have included bright, crisp cruise wear, including short skirts and swimsuits with matching floor-length skirts in shades of hot orange, fuschia, and kelly green. Fabrics range from cotton pique and satin to embroidered linen and cotton jersey, affording comfortable and cheerful warm-weather looks. Other collections have highlighted pleats, with pastel skirts under pleated safari jackets for day and long iridescent taffeta dresses for evening. Pipart also received praise for his white linen suits and two-tone, draped crepe dresses.

Not really an innovator, Pipart's strength at Ricci has been his ability to take stock of fashion trends throughout each season and then to imbue them with freshness and youthfulness without sacrificing his unerring sense of French good taste.

—Kathleen Paton

_____

PLATT, Jonathan. See ALLY CAPELLINO.

_____

POLLEN, Arabella.

British designer

Born: London, 21 June 1961. **Education:** Self-taught in design. **Family:** Married Giacomo Algranti in 1985 (separated, 1992); children: Jesse and Sam. **Career:** Worked as a personal assistant in advertising and on film scripts in France, 1979-81. Established own business, Arabella Pollen, Inc., 1981; introduced Pollen B diffusion range, 1992; ceased trading, 1993. Free-lance designer, Courtaulds Textiles, from 1993. **Address:** 8 Canham Mews, Canham Road, London W3 7SR, England.

Publications:

On POLLEN:

Articles

Wansell, Geoffrey, "Buzz about Miss Pollen," in *The Sunday Telegraph Magazine* (London), 5 June 1983.

Modlinger, Jackie, "Bella la Bella," in the *Daily Express* (London), 14 July 1985.

Jobey, Liz, "Designing Women," in *Vogue* (London), July 1987.

Samuel, Kathryn, "Pollen: a Success Story Not to Be Sneezed At," in *The Daily Telegraph* (London), 14 December 1987.

"Soul Sister," in *The Sunday Times Magazine* (London), 6 May 1990.

Haggard, Claire, "Getting an Education in the Borders," in *The Independent* (London), 26 May 1990.

Smith, Liz, "In Her Own Image," in *The Times* (London), 3 July 1990.

Tredre, Roger, "A Designer Prepared to Meet Her Maker," in *The Independent* (London), 11 August 1990.

Collier, Andrew, "Pollen's Body English: A British Designer Puts Her Own Twist on the Classics," in *Women's Wear Daily* (New York), 4 September 1990.

Smith, Liz, "Putting New Faith in Pollen," in *The Times* (London) Saturday Review, 27 October 1990.

Armstrong, Lisa, "Stuff the Purple Satin Tabards! It's Pollen B, Honey!," in *The Independent* (London), 20 February 1992.

Flett, Scarth, "Arabella Pollen," in *The Observer Magazine* (London), 23 February 1993.

"Textiles Giant Axes Designer Fashion Firm," in *The Independent* (London), 20 May 1993.

Samuel, Kathryn, "From Cheers to Tears for Arabella Pollen Label," in *The Daily Telegraph* (London), 20 May 1993.

*   *   *

Arabella Pollen established a reputation as the bold colourist of British fashion. She became known for her snappy, classic, and wearable suits that were always trimmed with witty and unexpected touches—braid, velvet, or combinations of vivid orange, turquoise, and pink on a black jacket shape. Her special occasion wear was described by Harvey Nichols' buying director Amanda Verdan as "brilliant, perfect and never fuddy duddy." Traditional gold laces were made into slinky, long-sleeved tunics teamed with matching hotpants; short shifts of scarlet sequins were edged with pink velvet and wrapped in hooded velvet robes.

Pollen entered the world of fashion without formal training in design. She had hated drawing and sewing as a child but started making clothes for herself and friends at the age of 19. She found that she could survive on the money her clothes were making and began to expand. After designing and making a collection of clothes based on the hunting styles of the early 1900s, she showed the clothes to the wealthy publisher Naim Attallah who was impressed by her enthusiasm and talent and agreed to provide financial backing.

Pollen's customers have tended to be like herself: young, energetic, with a relaxed style. She realized quickly that in order to survive she had to find an identifiable look that was innovative but not too daring. She recognized that there was a niche for chic elegant sportswear, stating, "I try to do clothes that you can more or less slum around in, but that look elegant at the same time" (*The Sunday Telegraph Magazine* [London], 5 June 1983). The look instantly appealed to a particular group of upper class women and their daughters christened by the press as "Sloane Rangers." The Princess of Wales became one of Pollen's first customers, wearing a number of her well-cut tweeds and dresses from her first collections. This proved a great publicity coup for the young designer, convincing Attallah that he had made a wise investment.

Pollen was often her own best advert for the clothes, inspiring an affinity between designer and customer by incorporating many of her designs into her own personal wardrobe. This image was strengthened when she agreed to be photographed in the clothes she designed for fashion manufacturers, Windsmoor. The company recognized in Pollen a designer with a strong identity who could adapt her style to updating the Windsmoor image. Whereas Windsmoor suffered from its overly genteel reputation in the early 1980s, Pollen's youthful styles sharpened the company's identity and boosted sales.

In 1990 Courtaulds Textiles bought a minority stake in Pollen's business, a link that gave her the resources to make a huge international impact. Unfortunately, whilst sales grew rapidly in the UK, this was not the case in other parts of the world. After reviewing the situation both parties concluded it inappropriate at this stage to provide further resources and Arabella Pollen Ltd. announced that it had ceased trading in May 1993, though Pollen retained her link with Courtaulds as a design consultant.

As a woman designing for women Pollen proved that she had no preconceived ideas about what women wanted to wear. Wearing the clothes herself gave her insight into how women actually felt about them, their likes and dislikes; a major contribution to fashion that was accompanied by close attention to detail, quality, cut, and fit.

—Kevin Almond

POLO. See **LAUREN, Ralph.**

POMODORO, Carmelo.

American designer

Born: New York, 20 March 1956. **Education:** Studied painting, then fashion design at Parsons School of Design, New York, graduated in 1978. **Career:** Assistant to designers Ralph Lauren, Stan Herman and Bill Haire, c.1978-81; showed first collection, working from home, 1981; designer, Betty Hanson company, New York, 1982-86; established Carmelo Pomodoro Design Studio, Inc. for free-lance work, 1985; formed Carmelo Pomodoro Sportswear, Ltd., 1986; introduced lower priced line, 1987, and line of bodywear, 1991; licenses included jewelry, from 1989, furs, from 1990, and Toyota sportswear line, from 1990. First of seven Carmelo Pomodoro boutiques, joint ventures with Takashima Company, opened in Tokyo, 1989. *Died* (in New York) *1 October 1992.*

Publications:

On POMODORO:

Books

Milbank, Caroline Rennolds, *New York Fashion: The Evolution of American Style,* New York 1989.
Ewing, Elizabeth, *History of Twentieth Century Fashion,* New York 1992.

Articles

Behbehani, Mandy, "Young, Hip Believers in Affordable Fashion," in the *San Francisco Examiner,* 26 June 1990.
Hayes, Tracy Achor, "Young Designers with Big Potential," in *The Dallas Morning News,* 3 October 1990.
Hix, Charles, "The 'Hot Tomato' of Cornwall Hollow: Fashion Designer Carmelo Pomodoro Carves High-Profile Niche with His Forward Fashions," in *The Litchfield County Times* (Connecticut), 22 February 1991.
Morra, Bernadette, "Even Ivana Is Cutting Back," in *The Toronto Star,* 2 May 1991.
Hix, Charles, "Carmelo Pomodoro," in *Collections Tokyo-New York,* Spring/Summer 1991.
White, Constance C. R., "Sportswear Report SCOOP," in *Women's Wear Daily* (New York), 25 September 1991.
Blissard, Mardi, "Autumn Fashions on the Runway at Bolo Bash IV—New York Designer Carmelo Pomodoro," in the *Arkansas Times,* 11 June 1992.
Lambert, Bruce, "Carmelo Pomodoro, 37, Designer Who Led New York Fashion Firm," obituary in the *New York Times,* 2 October 1992.
White, Constance C.R., "Carmelo Pomodoro Dead at 37: Energetic and Talented, He Helped Lead SA's Young Designer Pack," in *Women's Wear Daily* (New York), 2 October 1992.

*   *   *

The November 1992 cover of *Harper's Bazaar* was redesigned at the last moment to pay homage to one of the most promising fashion designers of his generation, Carmelo Pomodoro. The cover speaks gently of Pomodoro's oeuvre: an elegant neo-1930s-type woman wears an ivory colored chenille open-work gridded robe. The words that describe this image are soft, sensual, and just a little bit Hollywood. From his first independent collection in 1987, it was clear that Pomodoro had an unclassifiable sense of style that was at once romantic, yet ruthlessly contemporary.

Pomodoro had thought of becoming an actor, an architect, and a painter, before discovering his natural affinity for the fashion arts through the guidance of Frank Rizzo, chairman of the fashion design department at Parsons School of Design, New York. After stints with Stan Herman, Ralph Lauren, Bill Haire, and Betty Hanson, Pomodoro established his own design studio in 1985 where he carried out free-lance projects. With characteristic good energy and optimism he started Carmelo Pomodoro Sportswear Ltd., and produced a collection in 1986. His business partner John P. Axelrod supported Pomodoro's career, even after it received substantial Japanese backing.

His first signature collection was memorable and indicative of his greatest strengths as a designer. What could be called "the white collection" resort 1987, featured drapy fabric, simple lines, and virtually no color. Akin to the paintings of Agnes Martin, the fabrics of Pomodoro's collection revealed subtle and delicate details at close range. The textures of his unusual fabric blends, or the quiet wit of an almost surreal self-scarf sweater, characterized his ability to balance artistic self-consciousness with a paradoxical sense of reverence and fun. This blend resulted in perhaps the best-ever designed trapeze tunic from the same collection, which seemingly floated over a tight tube skirt.

Throughout his all too brief career, Carmelo Pomodoro continued to develop this series of women in white, and these were arguably his most successful artistic and commercial fashions. From the eggshell cotton crochet cover-up, both a tribute to the 1960s and an avant-garde prefiguration of the 1993 crochet craze, from his resort 1990 collection, to virginal white cotton organza overshirts and cotton silk lace tank dresses that also appeared that year, Pomodoro brought forth inspirational designs that made women feel and thus project their most beautiful selves. Whether or not his attraction to monochromatic compositions came from his skills as a black-and-white photographer (he did much of the photography for his company's advertising campaigns himself), it is clear that this propensity distinguishes him among other artists of his generation such as Charlotte Neuville, Zang Toi, Jennifer George, and Rebecca Moses.

If white was his best non-color, knitted fabric was his best medium for making art (dresses). A master technician, he understood not only pattern making and construction but also his materials. In knitting, with its ability to hold a shape, to drape, to cling, and to stretch, he gave his designs a comfort quotient not possible from any other technique. What made his knits extraordinary was the mixture of mostly natural fibers, with a minuscule amount of the newest microfibers developed for him in Japan.

Softness permeated Pomodoro's oeuvre, even his much heralded leather designs. His use of leather, which he considered a very modern no-fuss fabric, was at times biker-chic but usually tempered when paired with flowing double layered georgette short skirts or pastel leggings. The fall 1992 line featured a leather bathrobe coat mixed with fake fur, and jackets that gracefully followed the natural contour of the torso.

Menswear collections developed as adjunct to the women's lines, but the intellectually savvy androgyny of his men's sleeveless undershirt with sequined evening skirt of 1992 reminds us that Carmelo Pomodoro was a gifted thinker with a lot to say about out sartorial lives.

Pomodoro's last collection was inspired by one of the world's most alluring women, Sophia Loren. A blend of camel hair and velvet pieces, the tailored glamor was eroticized by the leopard prints in the form of scarves, vests, and blouses. The look conjured up images of Rome, and the *dolce vita* of Federico Fellini. The formal elements, however, the colors, lines, and fabrics, were of-the-moment and Pomodoro world view.

Carmelo Pomodoro's love of the female was paramount. He demonstrated an uncanny knack for knowing how to interpret the ideal dress for his clients, women 25 to 45, part girl, part *femme fatale,* self-assured. The power of his clothing was its emotional connection to its designer. Early in his career he said, "If women wear my fashions and smile, I'll be happy." Mission accomplished *summa cum laude.*

—Marianne T. Carlano

PORTER, Thea.

British designer

Born: Dorothea Naomi Seale in Jerusalem, 24 December 1927. Raised in Damascus, Syria. **Education:** Studied French and Old English at London University, 1949-50; studied art at Royal Holloway College, Egham, Surrey. **Family:** Married Robert Porter in 1953 (divorced, 1967); daughter: Venetia. **Career:** Lived in Beirut, 1953-c.1962; established Greek Street, Soho, boutique selling textiles from the Near East and clothing of her own design, 1967-69; also maintained a shop in Paris, 1976-79; in-store Thea Porter boutique created at Henri Bendel specialty store, New York, 1969. Free-lance fashion, textile and interior designer, London, from 1969. **Awards:** English Fashion Designer of the Year Award, 1972. **Address:** 13 Bolton St., London W1Y 7PA, England.

Publications:

On PORTER:

Articles

"Thea Porter to Design Knitwear," in *The Times* (London), 1 April 1973.
"Back to Bakst," in *The Times* (London), 18 December 1973.
"Dressed to Vote," in *The Times* (London), 8 September 1974.
"Porterama," in *The Times* (London), 21 September 1975.
McColl, Patricia, "Couture Arabesque," in *Aramco World* (New York), March/April 1977.
Shapiro, Harriet, "In Style: Porter," in *People,* 9 January 1978.
Gibb, Frances, "Top Fashion Designers to Go Out of Business," in *The Times* (London), 5 February 1981.
"Thea Porter is Back," in *The Times* (London), 18 July 1982.

*   *   *

Having lived in the Middle East as a child, Thea Porter based her fashion aesthetic upon the ethnic clothing she encountered there. During the late 1960s, fashion revolutions of many kinds were taking place, one of which was the new romanticism mirroring the romantic view of the East common to Victorian England. Hippie types went to Porter's store in Greek Street, Soho, London, to purchase Middle Eastern imports to decorate their homes, true to the spirit of 19th-century artists who created a complete atmosphere in their immediate environment that included loose aesthetic robes echoing distant lands and other time periods. Porter's shop offered pillows and cushions made from fancy Middle Eastern textiles as well as antique caftans. These dresses sold so well that Porter began to design them herself to meet the demand.

An ancient, loosely cut ankle length garment, the caftan lent itself to opulent decoration and luxurious fabrics. Porter's evening gowns were made from silks, brocades, velvets, even crêpe de chine and filmy chiffon, embellished with metallic embroidery and spangles or braid. While not strictly native costume reproductions, the caftans captured the spirit of mysterious harem allure. Wealthy international clients like Elizabeth Taylor, Barbra Streisand, and the Empress of Iran comprised Porter's clientèle, as much for the exoticism of the clothes, as no doubt for the comfort. Porter had long admired Arabic clothing, entranced by the rich embroideries and fabrics, in shapes that produced a protected and secure feeling of being able to hide in one's clothes while feeling like a princess, in the richness of execution of her romantic fantasies.

Porter's nostalgic sensibilities also extended toward the Renaissance and the Edwardian periods. During the 1970s she offered high-waisted midi- or maxi-dresses with voluminous sleeves. These simple historic shapes also lent themselves to luxurious brocades, tapestries, velvets, and embroidery. Her Edwardian looks featured vintage trimmings, and sailor-collared or lacy dresses recalling the last days of the Imperial Russian Grand Duchesses. Porter claimed Chekhov as an influence as well as art déco. Gypsy dresses with their full-flounced skirts allowed for romantic play of colorful patterned fabrics. Again, the shapes were easy, flattering.

Much as Poiret brought Eastern exoticism to a turbulent era, so Porter reflected rapid fashion change toward individuality, coupled with comforting escapism. Even her knit collection, developed for the chilly English climate, included caftan-type dresses, skirt and cardigan sets, and culottes in bright, cheerful colors. By the 1980s Porter had dressed many well-known personalities in her couture and expensive ready-to-wear, including the Beatles, Donovan, Princess Margaret, and Jessye Norman. Her designs allowed the expression of artistic inclinations, while allowing the wearer a shield from the too-scrutinizing eyes of the public.

—Therese Duzinkiewicz Baker

Thea Porter. *Photograph by Ken Howard.*

Publications:

On PRADA:

Articles

Alford, Lucinda, "Modern De Luxe," in *The Independent* (London), 19 June 1994.
"New York: Miu Miu," in *Women's Wear Daily* (New York), 31 October 1994.
Spindler, Amy M., "Cool Rises to Intimidating Heights," in the *New York Times* (New York), 7 April 1995.

*   *   *

PRADA.

Italian fashion house

Luxury leather goods company founded by Mario Prada and brother. Mario Prada born in Milan, Italy in 1913. Taken over by granddaughter Miuccia Bianchi Prada. Studied political science, earning Ph.D.; studied mime at Piccolo Teatro di Milano. Worked briefly for the Communist Party. Began designing for company, early 1980s. First London boutique launched, 1994.

Fratelli Prada was established as a purveyor of fine quality leather goods and imported items in Milan, Italy in 1913, by Mario Prada and his brother. For most of this century, affluent clients have been offered the requirements of fine living, in an atmosphere immersed in the refined opulence of Milan's Galleria Vittorio Emmanuele boutique. The *oggetti di lusso* or luxury items have included steamer trunks, Hartman luggage made in America, handbags from Austria, silver objects from London, crystal, tortoise, and shell accessories as well as now obsolete articles made from exquisite materials. Mario Prada traveled throughout Europe in order to familiarize himself with those materials and elements which would build his essential concepts of style and luxury.

Attracted to these same aspects but integrating her own design philosophy, his granddaughter, Miuccia Bianchi Prada, proceeded to enrich and expand this inherited legacy in 1978. Initially she had dismissed any involvement with the family business as less important than the goals she had set for herself. She received a degree in political science, followed by a period of study in mime at the Piccolo Teatro di Milano in preparation for a career in acting. By her mid-20s she was a committed participant in the political activities of the 1970s in Milan. Though one who had always drawn inspiration from history, "she also refused to reject that part of herself." She was taught to value quality materials and craftsmanship, in a city noted for traditional tailor's *ateliers* and elegant fabric showrooms.

Her personal convictions and this serious aspect of her education probably attributed to her belief that women are successful designers because clothing today must express what many women deeply feel. This philosophy has resulted in clothing not preoccupied with sex appeal. What appears to be restrained design quite surprisingly feels exceptional on the body. There has continued to be a nonconforming aspect of beauty in all her collections. This was important to the continuance of Mario Prada's vision of fashion in a full and creative context, capable of making the artisan's qualities come alive in a contemporary spirit.

In 1978 Miuccia Prada, with her distinctive regard for clothing, accessories, and footwear, began to develop and market an innovative line of fashion accessories eventually followed by a line of ready-to-wear clothes and footwear. In a magazine article, she was quoted as saying that her designs had freedom of movement, freedom from definition, and freedom from constriction. Bohemians, the avant-garde, the beatniks had been constant motifs in her designs. Many of her designs are based on the northern Italian tradition of having clothes beautifully made by local tailors and seamstresses. Her philosophy of dress also includes aspects developed and influenced by her own free spirited personality. In fact, a recent and approving magazine writer remarked that "her clothes don't necessarily have misfit connotations, nor are particularly for young women, they're like uniforms for the slightly disenfranchised." In the 1970s she was among the first to produce a practical, lightweight, nylon backpack and other hand-held bags of the same waterproof material. Disregarding season and occasion, the metal stamped Prada logo and brilliant palette combined tassels and leather trim. Black was, without a doubt, the stylish choice. She states that she does not focus on inventing but rethinks the company's traditions in a different fashion, "I believe that every form is an archetype of the past."

In their Milanese headquarters, Miuccia Prada and her husband, business partner Patrizio Bertelli, oversee all aspects of the company. Collections are presented there as well as the occasional cultural event. In their Tuscan factory, near Arezzo, prototypes are sampled and all stages of design and technology are controlled. The firm, I Pelletieri D'Italia S.A. (IPI), produces and distributes the various lines. It was to this Bertelli-owned factory that Miuccia Prada was originally attracted when she researched improved manufacturing techniques. The firm continues to research all possible methods to make an industrial product look like the unique work of an artisan. The company Fratelli Prada continues to manufacture leather goods; suede trimmed with *passementerie* and silk tassels,

leather wallets embossed with constructivist motifs, jewelry rolls in suede-lined calf skin, boxy pigskin suitcases, and key rings with leather medallions. Beginning with autumn/winter 1989, ready-to-wear was presented in the calm and stately atmosphere of the Palazzo Manusardi headquarters. Admittedly inspirational to her first collections of black and white dresses and sportswear, were the predominantly stylish and lonely characters in films by Michelangelo Antonioni. "Prada is a reflection of Miuccia's taste, about being a connoisseur rather than a consumer," is an excerpt from a magazine interview. Her first footwear collections combined classicism with elements of the avant-garde in such styles as spectator oxfords and embroidered and bejeweled suede slippers.

Signora Prada begins developing her seasonal repertory with the concept that no single style is appropriate for one occasion. She offers her international clientele an open minded regard for style. In 1994 there were 45 Fratelli Prada retail stores worldwide and two Miu Miu stores. In the Fratelli Prada store in the Galleria, the original mahogany and brass fittings reflect luxury and tradition. On two floors, garments, accessories, footwear, and the recent addition of menswear, express refinement, grace and gentility as they fuse the past with the modern present. In one of her statements on design she confesses that combining opposites in unconventional ways such as refinement with primitive, and natural with machine made helped to produce the collections in her name-sake store Miu Miu. In 1992, inspired by items in her own wardrobe closet, she created this bohemian, artsy-craftsy collection of patchwork and crocheted garments, saddle bags, and sheepskin jackets, clogs, and boots. She based the new and fresh line on rough finishes, natural colors, and materials reflecting the artisan's craft, stylish in the small boutiques of the 1960s. Her choices of fabrics usually associated with haute couture have been cut into streamlined sportswear such as silk *faille* trenchcoats, double faced cashmere suits, and nylon parkas trimmed in mink. "In the end," she says, "fabric is fabric. What is really new is the way you treat it and put the pieces together."

—Gillion Skellenger

PRÉMONVILLE, Myrène de. See de PRÉMONVILLE, **Myrène.**

PRESTON, Nigel. See **MAXFIELD PARRISH.**

PRICE, Anthony.

British designer

Born: Bradford, 1945. **Education:** Studied at Bradford School of Art and at the Royal College of Art, 1965-68. **Career:** Designer, Stirling Cooper, 1968-74; Che Guevera; Plaza, 1974-79; formed own company incorporating Plaza, 1979. **Address:** 15 Cranmer Road, London SW9 6JE, England.

Publications:

On PRICE:

Articles

Yates, Paula, "Glamour at A. Price," in *Cosmopolitan* (London), April 1981.
Eggar, Robin, "Style at Any Price," in *You* magazine of the *Mail on Sunday* (London), 11 March 1984.
Webb, Ian R., "Price," in *Blitz* (London), April 1987.
Coleman, Alix, "The Frock Prince," in the *Sunday Express Magazine* (London), 10 April 1988.
"The Price of Stardom," in *Vogue* (London), August 1988.
Bell, Jaki, "Anthony Price," in *DR: The Fashion Business* (London), 10 February 1990.
Mower, Sarah, "Leader of the Glam," in *Vogue* (London), March 1990.
DiSilva, Beverly, "Adam on Eve," in *Mirabella* (New York), November 1990.

*   *   *

Antony Price, who designs glamorous clothes for glamorous people, was born during the swansong of Hollywood's star struck years. The last great screen goddesses loomed large in suburban Odeons, with scarlet lips and arched eyebrows under pompadour hairstyles: their square shoulders emphasized wasp waists and shapely hips swathed in pleated lamé.

By the time Price was attending the fashion course at London's Royal College of Art in the mid-1960s, these celluloid masterpieces of noir sex-kitsch were daytime television oddities. The shapely heroines gliding across the screen could not have been further removed from the London Twiggies in their flared Courrèges-style minidresses. It was the old-style glamour of these magical, sassy sirens—as embodied by Rita Hayworth—which inspired Price then, and continues to do so today.

Soon the golden boy at Stirling Cooper, Price designed clothes to fit and flatter: skin-tight snakeskin tailoring found its way on to the backs of the Mick Jaggers and Dave Clarks. A fortuitous association with Roxy Music, and their elegant front man, Bryan Ferry, led Price to design their stage sets and costumes, and to dress their stylish album covers, now identified as classics of their time.

Producing successful commercial ranges for Che Guevara and Plaza, icon fashion labels of their time, Price lays claim to inventing the ubiquitous cap-sleeved T-shirt, flatteringly cut for muscle appeal; and suggestively revealing trousers. Whilst designing largely for men at this time, Price's clothes had a contemporary unisex attraction.

Price's personal style emerged in his King's Road, Chelsea, shop— a starlet's fitting room of celestial blue and gold, with scalloped 1930s-style vases spilling luxuriant flowers. No clothes rails here: garments were displayed on boards like sculptures in a gallery. In the South Molton Street shop, the Price style came to a baroque climax in a crescendo of dove grey velvet drapes, gilt-framed mirrors, crystal chandeliers, and golden scallop-shell *fauteuils*.

Now a couturier, Price has a client list which reads like a who's who of current pop and fashion stars: Duran Duran, Annie Lennox, Paula Yates, Lucy Ferry, Joan Collins, Jerry Hall. He also effected a foray into royal territory, designing for the Duchess of York's Canadian tour. Price's love of camp cabaret culminated in unfor-

gettable party-shows, each a stunning revue of set pieces staged in front of his own gold monogrammed velvet cinema curtains.

Price's gowns are remarkable, not just for the way they look, but for the way they are made. Attaining the Hollywood hour-glass silhouette in these uncorseted days necessitates built-in structure, and his clothes are intricate masterpieces of boning and interfacing beneath the silks and taffetas. His wide-shouldered men's suits, with their narrow waists and snake-like hips, are equally flattering, whatever one's own shape beneath, and equally apt to attract and allure: "result" wear, to use the designer's own phrase.

Only a true craftsman could produce such collectable apparel for his devoted clients. Price once told a student audience that his pattern-cutting skills stem from his days as a dry-stone waller in his native Yorkshire. Certainly, he is that rare animal, a designer of unparalleled flair who can also cut, drape, and sew. He cuts his own patterns, piecing together mathematically intricate *toiles* on his secret system of client-shaped dummies. Practical in many ways, Price is as likely to be found rewiring his studio or laying down the law on the cultivation of the exotic *Gunnera Manicata* as cutting an evening gown.

Price has remained true to his early vision of a glamorous world populated with sex-exuding deities. He himself moves in glittering social circles, frequently staying on Barbados or Mustique, with their concomitant populations of nomadic *merveilleuses*. His clients, transformed by sculptured curves into beings from a higher plane, may walk with the well-postured assurance which springs only from the knowledge that one is clothed by a master of his craft.

—Alan J. Flux

PRINGLE OF SCOTLAND.

Scottish design house.

Established by Robert Pringle in Cross Wynd, Hawick, Scotland in 1815; known worldwide for quality cashmere sweaters. **Address:** Victoria Mill, Hawick, Scotland TD9 7AL.

Publications:

On PRINGLE OF SCOTLAND:

Books

Houck, Catherine, *The Fashion Encyclopedia,* New York, 1982.
O'Hara, Georgina, *The Encyclopaedia of Fashion,* New York 1986.

*   *   *

Founded in Cross Wynd, Hawick, Scotland in 1815 by Robert Pringle as a family business making hosiery, Pringle of Scotland is now known throughout the world as an established brand leader in fine cashmere and other high quality knitwear and sportswear, and a pioneer of modern knitwear technology and systems.

Although its origins lie in the production of hosiery and underwear, Pringle is well known today for its particular emphasis on leisurewear and sportswear. The emphasis on knitwear as outerwear is a comparatively recent one, dating from the earlier years of this century, when its use by sportsmen, particularly in golf, as nonconstricting, yet striking-style garments made it fashionable. Up until 1934 Pringle was known primarily as a company producing fine quality undergarments and a limited selection of knitted outerwear. In June 1934, the appointment of Otto Weisz, an Austrian refugee, as the first full-time professional designer to work within the British knitwear industry, brought a revolutionary attitude to the importance of design and a flair for colour to an insular industry. Weisz's designs include the concept of the twinset, which became a classic. It has been said that few industries did more than Scottish whisky and the Hawick knitwear industry to earn dollars for Britain.

Many Scottish crafts families have worked for generations in the Pringle mills and a substantial investment programme has resulted in these factories being equipped with the latest state of the art technology and machinery, employing over 1,700 works, and ranking with the most up-to-date production units in Scotland.

Some of the finest fibers in the world are used: cashmere from the mountains of East Asia, lambswool and the best quality Geelong from Australia, and the native Scottish wools, such as those from the Shetland Isles. The twice yearly collections of men's and womenswear take their inspiration from the wools themselves, current colour trends, lifestyles, and their surroundings. These collections include patterned, textured, plain, and highly styled garments in the latest shades to meet the requirements of an ever-changing fashion scene, and complementary woven accessories for both men and women, mainly in natural fibers. Active and leisure sportswear are particularly important Pringle of Scotland products. The Nick Faldo Collection of knitwear and coordinates has sold well over two million garments in the United Kingdom, Europe, Japan, and the United States, and with the Ladies Golf and sports Classic collections.

Since 1967 Pringle of Scotland has been part of Joseph Dawson (Holdings) Limited, now Dawson International PLC. The strong international style of the company's products ensures that an average of 60 percent of all sales have been exported for many years, and the name of Pringle of Scotland is established in over 45 countries throughout the world. The recent expansion of retailing activity means that Pringle shops and corners can be found in many European outlets, and in Japan as well as in South America.

Pringle of Scotland holds two Royal Warrants, as Manufacturers of Knitted Garments to both Her Majesty the Queen and Her Majesty Queen Elizabeth the Queen Mother. Regarded today as one of the world's leading international quality knitwear names, Pringle of Scotland's coordinating associated products for the leisure and sports market complement and complete the ranges for a total look that is distinctively stylish and relaxed.

—Doreen Ehrlich

PUCCI, Emilio.

Italian designer

Born: Marchese Emilio Pucci di Barsento in Naples, 20 November 1914. **Education:** Educated at the University of Milan, 1933-35, University of Georgia, 1935-36, Reed College, Portland, Oregon, 1936-37; M.A., 1937; Ph.D., University of Florence, 1941. **Family:** Married Cristina Nannini di Casabianca in 1959; children: Alessandro, Laudomia. **Military Service:** Bomber pilot in the Ital-

ian Air Force, 1938-42. **Career:** Women's skiwear designer, White Stag, for Lord and Taylor department store, 1948; free-lance fashion designer, from 1949; first Pucci shop established in Capri, 1949, and Rome, Elba, Montecatini, from 1950; President, Emilio Pucci SrL, Florence, and Emilio Pucci, New York, from 1950; vice-president for design and merchandising, Formfit International, 1960s. Also Olympic skier, 1934. **Awards:** Neiman Marcus Award, 1954, 1967; *Sports Illustrated Award,* 1955, 1961; Burdine Fashion Award, 1955; *The Sunday Times* Award, London, 1963; Association of Industrial Design Award, Milan, 1968; Drexel University Award, Philadelphia, 1975; Italy-Austria Award, 1977; Knighthood, Rome, 1982; Medaille de la Ville de Paris, 1985; Council of Fashion Designers of America Award, 1990. *Died* (in Florence, Italy) *29 November 1992.* **Address:** Palazzo Pucci, via dei Pucci 6, Florence, Italy.

Publications:

On PUCCI:

Books

Mulassano, Adriana, *I mass-moda: fatti e personaggi dell'Italian Look,* Florence 1979.
Aragno, B. G., editor, *40 Years of Italian Fashion* (exhibition catalogue), Rome 1983.
Kennedy, Shirley, *Pucci: A Renaissance in Fashion,* New York 1991.

On PUCCI:

Articles

"Emilio Pucci," in *Current Biography* (New York), February 1961.
Schiff, F., "If You Knew Pucci," in *Interview* (New York), September 1974.
"Founding Father of the Signature Print," in *The Times* (London), 1 September 1976.
Shields, Jody, "Pucci," in *Vogue* (New York), May 1990.
Porti, Anna Gloria, "Mai come adesso è Pucci," in *Vogue* (Milan), September 1990.
"Pucci Superstar," in *Elle,* October 1990.
Young, Lucie, "The New Pucci Coup: Psychedelic Swirls Back," in *Metropolitan Home* (London), December/January 1990- 91.
"Emilio Pucci Dead at 78," in *Women's Wear Daily* (New York), 1 December 1992.
"Prince of Prints," in *People,* 14 December 1992.
"Emilio Pucci," obituary in *Current Biography* (New York), January 1993.

*   *   *

Rising out of the ashes of European fashion after World War II, Emilio Pucci brought a spectrum of carefree colours to the rationed continent. His sportswear beginnings lent a casual air to his work, a welcome relief from recent austerity and a new meaning to the term "resort wear." The swirling freestyle patterns and fluid fabrics he used became internationally recognized and desired, copied by many but rivalled by few.

American Tina Lesser may have been earlier with her hand-painted silks, but Pucci quickly made them his own, covering the fine lus-

Emilio Pucci: Spring/Summer 1992.

trous fabric with optical fantasies of geometric shapes. His colour range came straight from an Aegean horizon, turquoise and ultramarine set against sea green and lime, or hot fuchsia and sunflower yellow. Pucci swept away the repetitive sailor styles and tailored linens of cruisewear and brought in a new air of ease and luxury with his breezy separates. He capitalized on the lull in British and French couture after the war that benefitted many American and Italian designers, and dressed the fashionable *mondaine* in bold ready-to-wear.

The government-backed presentations of Italian designers of the late 1940s provided an aristocratic Florentine backdrop for Pucci's collections, which were soon popular internationally, and he became increasingly aware of the importance of the American market to his success. His characteristic style was best seen in slim-legged trousers in fruity shades, which provided a sexy foil to loose-hanging tunics and classic shirts left to hang outside the waistband.

His collections encompassed more than just stylish but jaunty daywear. In 1961 he showed simple evening dresses with deep V-shape panels set into their sophisticated bias cut silhouette. The 1960s was the decade that saw his greatest success, his psychedelic pattern printed silks being seen everywhere. They were, and continue to be, worn by celebrities, from Marilyn Monroe, to Jackie Kennedy, and to Madonna, all seduced by the light touch of his designs.

As his reputation grew, his distinctive patterns were aspired to by many; a Pucci scarf or vivid silk handbag providing the cachet of luxury. His name was seen on everything from gloves to small ornaments. However, by the 1970s his work, like that of other big fashion houses, seemed less in tune with the times. During the 1980s, Pucci ranges seemed irrelevant to the weighty tailored severity that preoccupied the fashion world. It was not until the start of the 1990s that the pure whirling colours of the Pucci label (by then directed by his daughter, Laudomia) were again universally embraced. His signature shapes and vivid patterns had already inspired a generation of Italian designers, notably Gianni Versace and Franco Moschino, and in 1991 the reinvigorated Pucci look was everywhere. It had been translated into the modern essentials: clingy leggings, catsuits, and stretch polo necks which continued the sexy feel of his work and contrasted perfectly with his airy shirts. His clothes sold out across the world as a new, younger audience took up the label, perpetuating its popularity, albeit on a less high profile level after the initial Pucci mania of that year.

The eclectic use of surface pattern and innovative colour combinations that distinguish Pucci's work have been widely emulated throughout the fashion strata. His use of colour adds a feeling of movement to his clothes, while the quality fabrics he uses enhance the fluid line. The classic separates he designed continue to be successful, while the addition of newer styles ensures that the label will continue to provide a vibrant note to fashion in the 1990s.

—Rebecca Arnold

PULITZER, Lilly.

American designer

Born: Lillian McKim in Roslyn, New York. **Family:** Married Herbert (Pete) Pulitzer; children: Minnie, Liza; married Enrigue Rousseau. **Career:** Formed business in Palm Beach, Florida, for sale of women's shifts, 1959; president, Lilly Pulitzer, Inc., 1961-84; children's dresses, called "Minnies," introduced, 1962; Pulitzer Jeans introduced, 1963; Men's Stuff line introduced, 1969; business closed, 1984; rights to women's line purchased by Sugartown Worldwide, 1993.

Publications:

On PULITZER:

Books

Fairchild, John, *The Fashionable Savages,* Garden City, New York 1965.
Bender, Marylin, *The Beautiful People,* New York 1967.
Lambert, Eleanor, *World of Fashion: People, Places, Resources,* New York and London 1976.

Articles

Moin, David, "Lilly Pulitzer's Prizes: A 'Shift' into the Eighties," in *New York Apparel News,* February 1984.
Reed, Susan, "Lilly Pulitzer's Preppy Prints to Get a Second Life," in *People* (New York), 23 June 1986.
Staples, Kate, "Pulitzer's Prizes," in *Mademoiselle* (New York), May 1993.
Koski, Lorna, "The Return of Lilly," in *W,* October 1993.

*   *   *

According to the legend, it all began with an orange juice stand begun by a bored (and rich) housewife in October 1959. The boss brought a dozen dresses she made (actually her dressmaker made them, but that's not so Horatio Alger) from fabric bought at Woolworth's down to the stand and sold them off a pipe-rack. "I started it as a lark," Pulitzer remembered years later to Lorna Koski of *W,* "I just knew what I liked." Within five years, it seemed as if every woman in America had at least one "Lilly" and more or less lived in the comfortable lifestyle of the "Lilly."

Fashion—design and business—respects quintessence. For many, fashion is a business of knock-offs and copying, but there are gestures that epitomize and that captivate for their ability to distil a fashion idea. The "Lilly," designed by Lilly Pulitzer, is the fashion cipher for the shift or chemise, an unarticulated little dress, that may better serve to represent the chemise than its Balenciaga invention, its countless couture permutations, or its striving variations in the mass market. Publisher John Fairchild wrote in 1965, "Watch the chemise make a comeback with the masses. The élite have never given it up. Just look at the Lilly, those chemises designed by Lilly Pulitzer, who has a gold mine in those little nothing, beautiful print chemises which she turns out by the carloads in her Miami, Florida, factory. All the top stores clamor for them—the same fashion they had on their markdown racks a few years back. The only difference is the "Lilly" is lined and the shape controlled" (*The Fashionable Savages,* New York). There is, however, always a big difference between the uncomplicated Diane Von Furstenberg wrap dress, the Halston Ultrasuede shirtwaist or other icons of style, and all the competition. Pulitzer invented nothing; she is hardly a designer;

Fairchild is right to call them "little nothing" dresses; but she gave a uniform to the early-to-mid-1960s.

The barren non-design of the "Lilly" was its allure. A perky, bright, and unpretentious shift in polished cotton chintz met an American need for personal style amidst homogenous culture. Eleanor Lambert describes its evolution, "first a 'snob' uniform, then a general fashion craze" (*World of Fashion,* New York, 1976). Pulitzer is a powerful family name in America and the associations with Palm Beach's largely vestigial grandeur made vague allusion to wealth and aristocracy, but the dress was eminently accessible. In fact, one of the elements of its popularity was that it appealed not only across class lines, but across all ages of women, serving young women who might aspire to more than "Laugh-In" shifts and style and to women of a certain age who found the simplified form a kind of chaste elegance, especially in an era influenced by the easy and unadorned grace of First Lady Jacqueline Kennedy. As Marylin Bender reports, "the fact that Jacqueline, Ethel and Joan Kennedy were Lilly-fans didn't hurt at all" (*The Beautiful People,* New York, 1976). In fact, the history of the Lilly must be seen in the context of Jacqueline Kennedy's allure in American style, allowing high style to become an acceptable middle-class American grace, whether in décor or clothes and personal style.

Bender quotes Pulitzer as saying, "The great thing about the Lilly is that you wear practically nothing underneath." In this inner simplicity as well as the outward simplicity in silhouette and bold tropical print, Pulitzer understood her time as much as she understood herself. Reportedly, Pulitzer had worked with her dressmaker to come up with an alternative to trousers for the leisure life of Palm Beach, as she felt she did not look good in trousers. The alternative arrived at was nothing more than the classic housedress, sanctioned a little by Balenciaga's 1950s chemise, brightened by the tropical palette, and rarefied by the connection to grand lifestyle.

While Pulitzer diversified her business founded in such serendipity, especially with success in a girl's version known as the Minnie, the essential garment of the business was always the "Lilly," its basic design modulated three times a year to ensure a freshness—akin to the principles of the orange-juice stand—in the product. But the "Lilly" was treated by designer and consumer alike as a classic, not something to be significantly tampered with. In 1993, Pulitzer re-established the business, backed by Sugartown International, after a ten-year hiatus.

Only in America could the "Lilly" have happened as it did: a triumph of non-design; an aristocratic aura bestowed on a distinctly non-aristocratic idea; a dress that at a modest $30 to $75 retail exemplified its time. In fact, the mid-1960s youth-quake, with its extreme mini-dresses followed by paper dresses and other experiments and social temperaments, made the "Lilly" recede with accustomed dignity quite rapidly into its historical moment of the first half of the 1960s, where it abides, an icon.

—Richard Martin

PUMA. See **LEE, Mickey.**

QUANT, Mary.

British designer

Born: London, 11 February 1934. **Education:** Studied art and design at Goldsmith's College of Art, London University, 1952-55. **Family:** Married Alexander Plunket Greene in 1957 (died, 1990); son: Orlando. **Career:** Fashion designer, from 1955; established Bazaar boutique and Alexander's restaurant, London, 1955; founder, director, Mary Quant Ginger Group wholesale design and manufacturing firm, 1963, and Mary Quant, Ltd., 1963; cosmetics line introduced, 1966; Mary Quant Japan franchise shops established, 1983; has designed for JC Penney, Puritan Fashions, Alligator Rainwear, Kangol, Dupont Europe, Staffordshire Potteries, etc. Member, Design Council, London, from 1971. **Exhibitions:** *Mary Quant's London,* Museum of London, 1973. **Awards:** Woman of the Year Award, London, 1963; *The Sunday Times* International Fashion Award, London, 1963; Bath Museum of Costume Dress of the Year Award, 1963; Maison Blanche Rex Award, New Orleans, 1964; Piavola d'Oro Award, 1966; Chartered Society of Designers Medal, 1966; Officer, Order of the British Empire, 1966; Fellow, Chartered Society of Designers, 1967; Royal Designer for Industry, Royal Society of Arts, 1969; British Fashion Council Hall of Fame Award, 1990; Senior Fellow, Royal College of Art, London, 1991. **Address:** 3 Ives St., London SW3 2NE, England.

Publications:

By QUANT:

Books

Quant by Quant, London 1966.
Colour by Quant, with Felicity Greene, London 1984.
Quant on Makeup, with Vicci Bentley, London 1986.

Articles

"A Personal Design for Living," in the *Listener* (London), 19-26 December 1974.
"Things I Wish I'd Known at 19," in the *Sunday Express Magazine* (London), 21 June 1982.

On QUANT:

Books

Halliday, Leonard, *The Fashion Makers,* London 1966.
Bender, Marylin, *The Beautiful People,* New York 1967.
Morris, Brian, and Ernestine Carter, *Mary Quant's London* (exhibition catalogue), London 1973.
Bernard, Barbara, *Fashion in the 60's,* London 1978.
Carter, Ernestine, *Magic Names of Fashion,* 1980.
MacCarthy, Fiona, and Patrick Nugent, *Eye for Industry: Royal Designers for Industry 1936-1986* (exhibition catalogue), London 1986.
Whiteley, Nigel, *Pop Design: Modernism to Mod* (exhibition catalogue), The Design Council, London 1987.
Lobenthal, Joel, *Radical Rags: Fashions of the Sixties,* New York 1990.

Articles

"British Couple Kooky Styles," in *Life* (New York), 5 December
1960.

"Brash New Breed of British Designers," in *Life* (New York), 8
October 1963.

Davis, John, "Mary, Mary, Quite Contrary, How Does Your Money
Grow?," in *The Observer* (London), 19 August 1973.

De'Ath, Wilfred, "The Middle Age of Mary Quant," in the *Illustrated London News,* February 1974.

Kingsley, H., "How Does Her Empire Grow?," in the *Sunday Telegraph Magazine* (London), 29 March 1981.

Jackson, Jan, "Interview with Mary Quant," in the *Leicester Mercury* (England), 12 November 1984.

Lowe, Shirley, "Mary's Quantum Leap into the Eighties," in *The
Sunday Times Magazine* (London), 10 August 1986.

Savage, Percy, "Mary Quant," in *Art and Design* (London), September 1986.

Orr, Deborah, "Minis to the Masses," in *New Statesman & Society*
(London), 19 October 1990.

Kay, Helen, "Uppers and Downers: British Entrepreneurs of the
Past 25 Years," in *Management Today* (London), 9 October 1991.

*   *   *

The name Mary Quant is synonymous with 1960s fashion.
Quant's designs initiated a look for the newly emerging teen and
twenty market enabling young women to establish their own identity and put Britain on the international fashion map.

Quant did not study fashion. Following parental advice she enrolled in an Art Teacher's Diploma course at Goldsmith's College,
London University, but she was not committed to teaching. In the
evenings she went to pattern cutting classes. Her fashion career
began in 1955, in the workrooms of the London milliner, Erik. Also
that year she opened her boutique, Bazaar in the King's Road,
Chelsea, in partnership with her future husband, Alexander Plunket-
Greene. The idea was to give the so-called Chelsea Set "a *bouilla-
baisse* of clothes and accessories." Mary was the buyer, but she
soon found that what she wanted was not available. The solution
was obvious, but not easy. Twenty-one years old, with little fashion experience, Quant started manufacturing from her bedsit. Using
revamped Butterick patterns and fabrics bought retail at Harrods,
she created a look for the Chelsea girl. Her customers were hardly
younger than herself and she knew what they wanted. Her ideas
took off in a big way, on both sides of the Atlantic.

The Americans loved the London Look. So much so that in 1957
Quant signed a contract with JC Penney to create clothes and underwear for the wholesale market. American coordinates convinced
her that separates were versatile and ideal for the young. To reach
more of the British market in 1958 she launched the Ginger Group,
a mass-produced version of the look, with US manufacturer
Steinberg's. In the same year she was nominated Woman of the Year
in Britain and *The Sunday Times* in London gave her their International Fashion Award.

Quant created a total look based on simple shapes and bold
fashion statements. She hijacked the beatnik style of the late 1950s:
dark stockings, flat shoes, and polo necks became obligatory for the
girl in the street. The pinafore dress, based on the traditional British
school tunic, was transformed as one of the most useful garments of
the early 1960s. Hemlines rose higher and higher. Quant's mini
skirts reached thigh level, in 1965, and everyone followed. Courrèges
confirmed that the time was right by launching his couture version
in Paris but Quant needed no confirmation: 1965 was the year of
her whistlestop tour to the United States. With 30 outfits and her
own models, she showed in 12 cities in 14 days. Sporting mini
skirts and Vidal Sassoon's five-point geometric haircuts, the models
ran and danced down the catwalk. It was the epitome of Swinging
London and it took America by storm.

Quant's talents did not go unnoticed in higher places. In 1966 she
was awarded the OBE for services to fashion and went to
Buckingham Palace wearing a mini skirt. Her cosmetics range was
launched that year. Recognizable by the familiar daisy logo, Quant
cosmetics were an international success. Later taken over by Max
Factor, they were retailed in 90 countries. She also experimented
with new materials including PVC and nylon, to create outerwear,
shoes, tights, and swimwear.

In the early 1970s Quant moved out of the mass market and
began to work for a wider age group, chiefly for export to the
United States and Europe. Her range of merchandise expanded to
include household goods, toys, and furnishings. Mary Quant at
Home, launched on the US market in 1983, included franchised
home furnishings and even wine. By the end of the 1980s her
designs were again reaching the British mass market, through the
pages of the Great Universal Stores/Kays mail order catalogues.

Mary Quant remains a genuine fashion innovator. She has ad-
justed to change. The 1960s designer for the youth explosion became a creator for the 1980s lifestyle boom. Her market had grown
up with her and she was able to anticipate its demands. Quant is
truly a designer of her time.

—Hazel Clark

RABANNE, Paco.

French designer

Born: Francisco Rabaneda Cuervo in San Sebastian, Spain, 18 February 1934; raised in France. **Education:** Studied architecture at l'École Nationale des Beaux-Arts, Paris, 1952-55. **Career:** Presented first haute couture collection, 12 Experimental Dresses, Paris, 1964; home furnishing and tableware lines introduced, 1981; men's ready-to-ear line introduced, 1983; women's ready-to-wear line introduced, 1990; leather goods line introduced, 1991. Opened first shop in Paris, 1990. Fragrances include *Calandre,* c. late 1960s, *Paco Rabanne pour Homme,* 1973, *Metal,* 1979, *La Nuit,* 1985, *Sport,* 1985, *Tenere,* 1988; men's skin care line launched, 1984. Holds over 140 licenses. **Exhibitions:** *Body Covering,* Museum of Contemporary Crafts, New York, 1968. **Awards:** Beauty Products Industry Award, 1969; Fragrance Foundation Recognition Award, 1974; L'Aiguille d'Or Award, 1977; Dé d'Or Award, 1990; made Chevalier de la Légion d'Honneur, 1989; made Officier de l'Ordre d'Isabelle la Catholique (Spain), 1989. **Address:** 23 rue du Cherche-Midi, 75006 Paris, France.

Publications:

By RABANNE:

Books

Trajectory, Paris 1991.

On RABANNE:

Books

Bender, Marylin, *The Beautiful People,* New York 1967.
Clemmer, Jean, *Canned Candies: The Exotic Women and Clothes of Paco Rabanne,* Paris and London 1969.
Loebenthal, Joel, *Radical Rags: Fashions of the Sixties,* New York 1990.

Articles

Sharp, Joy, "Fashion Foibles of 1967," in *Costume,* No. 2, 1968.
Tretiak, Philippe, "Paco le visionnaire," in *Elle* (Paris), 24 October 1988.
Dutt, Robin, "Metal Guru," in *Clothes Show* (London), December/January 1989-90.
Bourdley, Laurence, "Paco Rabanne," in *L'Officiel* (Paris), February 1990.

* * *

It comes as no surprise, on viewing the designs of Paco Rabanne, to hear that he prefers to be described as an engineer rather than a couturier. Son of the chief seamstress at Balenciaga (a designer famed for his intricate techniques of construction), Rabanne, after studying architecture, made his name in the 1960s with a series of bizarre, futuristic garments made out of incongruous materials. When viewed on the catwalk they seemed space-age prototypes rather than high fashion garments.

Believing that the only new frontier left in fashion was the discovery and utilization of new materials, rather than the old couture method of changing lines from season to season, Rabanne totally broke with tradition, experimenting with plastic and aluminium, to create some of the most eccentric yet influential garments of the 1960s.

It was estimated that by 1966 Rabanne was using 30 thousand metres of Rhodoid plastic per month in such designs as bib necklaces made of phosphorescent plastic discs strung together with fine wire and whole dresses of the same material linked by metal chains. When he had exhausted the possibilities of plastic, Rabanne created a contemporary version of chainmail using tiny triangles of aluminium and leather held together with flexible wire rings to construct a series of simple shift mini dresses.

The delight of his designs comes in the use of disparate materials not previously considered appropriate for use in clothing, or the displacing of traditional materials in order to produce strange juxtapositions of colour and texture. For instance, he was one of the first designers to combine knits, leather, and fur, using combinations like a cape made of triangles of matte silver leather with black ponyskin or a coat teaming curly white lamb and white leather.

It could be said that in the 1970s and 1980s the name Paco Rabanne became associated with male toiletries rather than for the intriguing experimentation he had been carrying out. In fact, Rabanne relies on the sales of his successful line of skinscents—including *Calandre, Paco,* and *Metal*—in order to finance his more technological projects. In 1971 he collaborated with Louis Giffard, an authority on flow-moulding techniques, to produce a raincoat moulded entirely in one piece of plastic. Even the buttons were part of the same process, moulded directly into the garment and fitting into pressed-out pieces on the other side of the coat.

In the 1990s, with a 1960s renaissance in full swing, the inventive calibre of Paco Rabanne has been rediscovered. His latest collections are concentrating on stretch jersey, cotton and viscose fabrics in metallic hues, still accessorized by enormous pieces of jewellery.

The high modernism of his 1960s designs seems touchingly innocent when viewed through the jaded eyes of the 1990s. Science and technology in contemporary culture signify something far removed from the faith and hope in the future that Rabanne was expressing with his self-consciously space age materials. His designs give less a sense of the future than imbue us with feelings of nostalgia for the optimism in new technology embraced in the aesthetics of 1960s design.

—Caroline Cox

————————

RATIA, Armi and Viljo. See **MARIMEKKO.**

————————

RAYNE, Sir Edward.

British footwear designer and manufacturer

Born: London, 19 August 1922. **Education:** Studied at Harrow School. **Family:** Married Phyllis Court in 1952; children: Edward, Nicholas. **Career:** Trainee in family shoemaking firm, H & M Rayne (founded 1889), 1940-50; managing director, 1951-87. Purchased half share in Delman, formed Rayne-Delman Shoes, Inc., 1961, president, 1961-72, and executive chairman, 1972-86; Paris shop opened, 1970; firm acquired by Debenhams, 1973, director, Debenhams, London, 1975-88; chairman, Harvey Nichols Stores, London, 1978-88. Also Chairman British Fashion Council, c.1990. **Awards:** *Harper's Bazaar* Trophy, London, 1963; Fellow, Royal Society of Arts, London, 1971; Commander of the Victorian Order, 1977; Chevalier, l'Ordre National du Mérite, France, 1984; received Knighthood, 1988. *Died* (in London) *7 February 1992.*

Publications:

On RAYNE:

Books

Lambert, Eleanor, *World of Fashion: People, Places, Resources,* New York and London 1976.
Swan, June, *Shoes,* London 1982.
McDowell, Colin, *Shoes: Fashion and Fantasy,* London 1989.

Articles

Tyrrel, Rebecca, "The Face of British Fashion," in *The Sunday Times Magazine* (London), 16 October 1989.
Obituary in *The Guardian,* 8 February 1992.
McDowell, Colin, appreciation in *The Guardian* (London), 10 February 1992.
Obituary in *The Times* (London), 10 February 1992.
Obituary in *The Independent,* 11 February 1992.
Fallon, James, "Britain's Rayne, 69, Dies in Fire at Home," in *Footwear News* (New York), 17 February 1992.

*   *   *

In 1918, when the second generation of Raynes took over the family firm, the idea of shoes as an article of fashion was a novel one. "The only people who bought stylish footwear were actresses and ladies of easy virtue," said Edward Rayne of the type of customer to patronize the first New Bond Street, London shop. This changed rapidly as the flapper age of the 1920s produced a breed of

liberated and fashion conscious women who demanded shoes like those worn by their idols of stage and screen. An H & M Rayne advertisement of the time used the popular actress Lily Langtry to promote the Langtry Shoe and the company won fashion credibility in a 1920s issue of *Vogue* when their button boots were described as the "smartest footwear in town."

Long before stars of stage and screen were fashion leaders, trends were set by monarchs and aristocracy in the courts of Europe. When H & M Rayne received its first royal warrant from Queen Mary it was a sign that the company had shed its *risqué* theatrical past and had become respectable within the fashion world. Other royal warrants followed and a new generation of rich, famous, and aristocratic women patronized the company. These ladies were indeed well heeled, as H & M Rayne was the first British firm to introduce machinery from the United States to make the sole of the shoe more flexible. With American-style multiple fittings and sizes, a Raynes shoe had the comfort and fit found previously only in bespoke shoes. H & M Rayne's success as a British footwear fashion house to rival those of Charles Jourdan, Bally, and Miller came about in the 1950s. At 28, Edward Rayne was still a young man when he took control of the family firm, and he led a hectic social life in Paris, enjoying night clubs and the company of fashion editors and glamorous diplomatic socialites. French and Italian design led the field in the 1950s and Rayne, from early on in his career, took an interest in promoting British design. In the 1950s, when the buyers from important U.S. department stores came increasingly less often to London, Rayne courted them in the Paris couture houses and the fashionable night spots.

Edward Rayne became Chairman of the Incorporated Society of London Fashion Designers in 1960 and within two years *Vogue* was hailing his remarkable success in persuading American press and buyers to view British collections. Other members of the ISLFD included Hardy Amies, John Cavanagh, and Norman Hartnell, who all designed shoes for Rayne.

During the 1950s H & M Rayne produced classic styling that perfectly matched the rigid dress codes of the day. However, times were changing; the 1960s saw a fashion revolution in clothes, music, and dance. Edward Rayne called dancing the "language of the legs" and knew full well that what a woman wore to dance, and how she danced, would influence her choice of footwear. In response to the changing trends he contracted new British designers to contribute to the Miss Rayne range.

Mary Quant designed her first leather stacked stiletto heels and Shirley Temple-style ankle-straps for Rayne in 1960. Later she was commissioned to design her own range, along with other young British designers such as Jean Muir and Gerald McCann, to produce collections in synch with the Swinging Sixties. Rayne made sure that alongside the sophisticated styling for one generation there was sufficient fashion and frivolity for the next.

The quality of the footwear designs was matched by their production. Rayne was a shoemaker himself, having served an 11-year apprenticeship. He was, said Jean Muir, the "best British shoemaker of his age. He worked to a quality that matched anything from abroad." It is not surprising that in 1963 shoes by Roger Vivier were being made and sold exclusively by Rayne. In the 1970s shoes by Rayne were being used by leading French couturiers including Lanvin and Nina Ricci. The 1970s saw the fulfilment of one of Edward Rayne's personal ambitions, his first shop in Paris. It was the first British shoe-shop to open in Paris since John Lobb, which specialized in bespoke footwear. By 1985 H & M Rayne had some 70 retail outlets throughout the world.

Georges Rech: Spring/Summer 1994; black crepe suit.

It was the Americans, Rayne claimed, who taught him to sell shoes, and he used his transatlantic talents to promote fashion design at the same time. Fashion writer Colin McDowell described Rayne as "a mover and a shaker to whom the British fashion industry owes a permanent debt" (*Shoes: Fashion and Fantasy,* London 1989). Before the Incorporated Society of London Fashion Designers was formed, the idea that one could sell a fashion industry to a world market was unheard of but Edward Rayne changed that. For over 40 years, first through the ISLFD and then the British Fashion Council, he was involved in any scheme that would improve the image of British fashion. He used his contacts with royalty and governments to stage fashion shows, banquets, and receptions to promote British collections. British Fashion Week became a glamorous affair which helped persuade overseas buyers and press to visit London. In launching the British Fashion Awards in 1989, he brought catwalk shows to the public and, through television coverage, brought fashion to the attention of millions.

Edward Rayne's contribution to the development of the British Fashion Council was the culmination of a lifetime's diplomatic pioneering—and partying—in aid of British design. He did more than any other businessman to persuade overseas buyers and press to take British fashion design seriously. By the time he retired as Chairman of the British Fashion Council in 1990, the Council had success and recognition worldwide as a promotional body, and Edward Rayne had received a well deserved knighthood for his services to the industry.

—Chris Hill

RECH, Georges.

French designer/company

Georges Rech designer collection established in Paris, 1960; Synonyme separates division established, 1973; Unanyme division of coordinated knitwear and woven separates established, 1981; Georges Rech Group accessories division founded, 1983; licensing department established, 1983; Georges Rech Homme men's ready-to-wear established, 1987. Georges Rech group joined Courtaulds textile division, London, in 1989; renamed Courtaulds Textiles PLC in 1990 as part of their clothing brands division. Thirty franchised or wholly-owned Georges Rech around the world, including Paris, London, Brussels, Montreal, and Hong Kong; Unanyme distributed through 25 stores in France; group lines also found in 1,000 multi-brand retailers throughout the world. Firm continued after his death. **Address:** 112 rue Reaumur, 75002 Paris, France.

Publications:

On RECH:

Articles

Mower, Sara, "Anglo-French Mix of Aggression and Chic," in *The Independent* (London), 23 November 1989.

*   *   *

When asked once to sum up his style philosophy, French ready-to-wear designer Georges Rech replied with a single word, "balance." His fashion house aims to create a synthesis of ideas, design-

ing not for any one woman or type of person, but for an ever-changing, contemporary ideal. His simple, relaxed, well-made, and affordable coats, suits, dresses, and separates project an easy-going accessibility, without compromising on creativity or style, and his name has become synonymous with casual chic. As Rech put it early in his career: "Sportswear corresponds to the way people live. I don't like to shut a woman up in fabric."

Georges Rech first emerged in the 1960s as one of the pioneers of Parisian ready-to-wear for women. He became known as a leading French manufacturer of tailored coats and suits, before branching out into raincoats. The early coat and suit collections were rather structured and masculine in feeling, but into the 1970s his styles broadened and loosened, with easy jackets over trousers, bloused windbreakers, billowing dresses, and both short and long skirts.

Rech was interested in bringing the comfort of leisure wear and sportswear into focus at a time when the fashion majority still upheld notions of clothing propriety, whether it was dressing for city/country, or day/evening. He looked to the youth movements of his day for inspiration, noticing how the young defied adult conventions in their clothing, and he began to experiment with work and leisure fabrics for daytime. He declared that denim was the "perfect" fabric, and transformed the humble, working class cloth into several sophisticated and urbane looks, such as a short, black-and-white striped denim pantsuit with witty elbow patches.

In 1973 he created Synonyme, a collection of coordinating basic separates. The line was an immediate success, gaining special notice for an elegant black panne velvet sweatshirt over black crepe flare-leg pants. Rech also designed a best-selling "sweatshirt dress" for day, and adapted other sportswear styles in his loosely-draped Qiana top and skirt for evening. One observer referred to these dressing up/dressing down crossover ideas in fabric and cut as "le Style Americaine," and the designer's clever takes on casual sportswear were indeed well-received in the United States when he opened a boutique there in 1978.

The Unanyme junior line, combining knitwear with woven and tailored pieces, was premiered in 1981, emphasizing lower-priced compatible separates that could be freely mixed and matched. The next expansion was into a line of accessories, and then came the establishment of Georges Rech Homme, creating for men the clean-cut yet stylish look for which Rech's womenswear had become known. The fourth arm of the house remained the high-end Georges Rech designer line offering structured, sophisticated coats, suits, and dresses for women, with a timeless style independent of ephemeral fashion trends. Though each group has a separate identity, the pieces designed for each division continue to embody the basic Rech philosophy of creativity mitigated by realism and wearability.

The company was bought out in 1989 by Courtauld's Textiles of London, and Georges Rech relinquished his personal interests in the house. Since that time Danielle Jagot, who worked for the company for over 20 years, took over designing the Georges Rech top-range label, while Fumihiko Harada designs the Synonyme line.

—Kathleen Paton

RED OR DEAD.

British footwear and clothing design firm

Founded in London, 1982, by Wayne and Geraldine Hemmingway (both born 1961); incorporated in 1983; specialize in customized

Red or Dead: Spring/Summer 1993.

second-hand clothing and Dr. Marten shoes and boots. **Address:** 17-19 Popin Commercial Centre, South Way, Wembley, Middlesex HA9 OHB, England.

Publications:

On RED OR DEAD:

Articles

Collier, Andrew, "Red or Dead Becomes London Cult Happening," in the *Daily News Record* (New York), 7 November 1988.
Collier, Andrew, "2 UK Retailers Refuse to Sell Acid House Clothing," in *Footwear News* (New York), 5 December 1988.
Collier, Andrew, "Red or Dead: This British Chain Is Red Hot," in the *Daily News Record* (New York), 6 March 1989.
Haggard, Claire, "Alive and Kicking," in *Sportswear International* (New York), July 1990.
Heath, Ashley, "Sole Survivors," in *The Face* (London), March 1992.
Tredre, Roger, "What's Red, Dead, Alive and Kicking?," in *The Independent* (London), 15 March 1992.
Warren, Rachael, "My First Break," in the *Evening Standard* (London), 25 March 1992.
"Fashion, Fascism and Dead Old Doc," in *Management Today* (London), April 1992.
Fallon, James, "Red or Dead Finds 'Easy Does It' Works," in *Footwear News* (New York), 17 August 1992.
"The Doctor Is In," in *Daily News Record* (New York), 28 May 1993.

*

Red or Dead is a London based design company producing innovative clothing and footwear at affordable prices. Consisting of a dynamic group of young talent, the Red or Dead team work closely to create fashion with a refreshing sense of humour and individuality. In the space of ten years, Red or Dead has grown into an internationally known design label with eight shops in England, one in Copenhagen, and others planned for Amsterdam and Hong Kong. There is an extensive wholesale network selling to shops worldwide and a thriving mail order service with a bi-annual catalogue.

—Red or Dead

*   *   *

There are those who have described Wayne Hemmingway as the shrewdest man in fashion. In the 1980s, whilst other British footwear companies were closing or retreating into safely classic styling, Hemmingway, with his keen market trader's sense of street fashion, launched Red or Dead.

In the mid-1980s, formative years for Red or Dead, the well tailored young executive look dominated the London High Street stores. This was power dressing, clothes to make money in, the yuppie uniform. In contrast to the serious adult dressing there was a "hard times" student style, sometimes dubbed recession chic. The poverty stricken but style conscious dressed in jumble sale bargains and 1940s or 1950s cheap secondhand clothes. Heavy fabrics combined with a long layered look evoked the workwear of a proletariat still engaged in a class war.

This was a street fashion which seemed to be suggesting some hidden socialist agenda within a mode of dress. Suddenly, politics and fashion could be mixed. The first designer T-shirt by Katherine Hammett proclaimed "58% Don't Want Pershing"; a fashion label was named Workers for Freedom. Yuppies really were conservative and socialists were chic.

The footwear of choice for the young, idealistic, and working class at heart was the classic steel-toe boot originally aimed at postmen and construction workers. The Dr. Marten boot was desinged for those who wanted to make an anti-fashion statement, and it quickly became popular with punk rock devotees.

Hemmingway introduced the basic DM through his Camden Market stalls and shop. They were immediately taken up by young men and women and customized by cutting in metal toe-caps, putting safety pins through them, sewing on beads and threading them with brightly coloured laces. The basic black DM was sprayed in a multitude of colours and could be made as individual as the owner.

The DM boot was the only footwear available at that time with the heaviness of silhouette required to make a woman's foot look really weighty. This went against all the traditional ideas of dainty feminine footwear for ladies who wanted their feet to look smaller, not bigger. The idea of a heavy, functional shoe for women was not initially a fashion statement; it came out of the whole recession chic concept, but it soon became an obligatory accessory for those who would never have bought secondhand.

Red or Dead produced styles with jagged soles, platform soles, bigger and heavier than the basic DM. They made boots in perspex, bright orange patent, silver, and other colors. Hemmingway had found a winning formula and could have continued selling chunky shoes from his now rapidly expanding retail empire. However, he was, in his own words, easily bored. Moving into clothing was an obvious progression.

The Red or Dead clothing collections were as anti-fashion establishment as the footwear. Not for Hemmingway the traditional middle-class, middle-aged values of made to last quality. The idea behind Red or Dead was, he states, "to wear the stuff for a few months, and then it either drops to bits or becomes unfashionable."

Hemmingway recognizes that fashion changes very quickly for young people and does not believe in taking it terribly seriously. His collections have become somewhat more tailored since the Space Baby or Kaleidoscope days and more professional than the notorious Animals collection, where the prints simply dropped off the garments. But as Hemmingway refuses to court, as he sees them, the "la-di-da" fashion editors and stylists, his catwalk collections are not currently reviewed in the mainstream fashion bibles.

What the fashion editors think of Red or Dead is irrelevant. More than a third of the company's now international business comes from clothing, and Hemmingway's reputation as a shrewd businessman has earned him an invitation to sit on the British Fashion Council. His legacy to the fashion world, however, will always be firmly based in footwear. Red or Dead has changed the silhouette of women's feet, along with our preconception of how they should look.

—Chris Hill

———

RENÉ LEZARD. See under **LEZARD.**

———

RENTNER, Maurice.

American designer and manufacturer

Born: Warsaw, Poland, 3 March 1889. Immigrated to the United States in 1902. **Family:** Married Dorothy Fineberg; two daughters. **Career:** Worked as an errand boy, traveling salesman and jobber, 1902-12; partner, M. & H. Rentner, 1912-23; owner, Maurice Rentner, Inc., 1923-58. *Died* (in New York) *7 July 1958.*

Publications:

On RENTNER:

Books

Ballard, Bettina, *In My Fashion,* New York 1960.
Milbank, Caroline Rennolds, *New York Fashion: The Evolution of American Style,* New York 1989.

Articles

"Dress War," in *Time* (New York), 23 March 1936.
Article in *N.Y. World Telegram* (New York), 11 May 1945.
"Maurice Rentner," in *National Cyclopaedia of American Biography,* 1957.
"Maurice Rentner is Dead at 69; Noted as Dress Manufacturer," [obituary] in the *New York Times,* 8 July 1958.

*   *   *

According to Bettina Ballard's *In My Fashion,* Maurice Rentner styled himself the "King of Fashion." It is perhaps more accurate to call him a prince of American ready-to-wear. In his boyhood he worked briefly for his father's button-making company, then advanced from errand boy to salesman for a shirtwaist manufacturer by 1906. As ready-made clothing became more respectable, Rentner perceived its potential for growth, and began to develop the higher priced end of the emerging industry.

Between 1912 and 1923 he was associated with his brother in M. & H. Rentner, establishing his own company under his own name after that partnership was dissolved. From the very first, Rentner was careful to establish an air of exclusivity around his company. Advertisements were discreet but not inconspicuous, with text declaring that Maurice Rentner gowns were only to be seen in the finest shops. He offered high quality merchandise at prices to match, setting standards of excellence for other ready-to-wear manufacturers.

Suits and daydresses made up most of the company's output, but eveningwear was also produced. Rentner said that he could not "sketch, sew, drape, pin or cut" and counted on design assistants to realize his ideas, which were rooted in the belief that "clothes should never decorate, but should always frame" (*N.Y. World Telegram,* 11 May 1945). As a result, silhouettes were generally uncomplicated, with spare detailing which was often innovative and sometimes unexpected. A narrow ruffle down the placket of a suit jacket resolved into a pocket flap at the hipline, or a smooth wool sheath dress was paired with a shirt-jacket having a hand-crocheted body. Fabrics were generally kept simple but sumptuous: wool or silk crêpes and jerseys, fine Rodier tweeds, silk prints. And, at least for a while, Rentner published and wrote "most of the descriptive copy for his own little fashion magazine, *Quality Street*" (*Time,* 23 March 1936).

The prevailing theme was femininity, expressed in soft suits and graceful dresses. Rentner also claimed to have pioneered the use of casual styling in formal clothing, introduced in the 1930s with a gold lamé shirtwaist-styled dinner gown. His efforts to meld style with comfort helped to establish an American fashion identity, in which casual need not mean unkempt, nor formal signify stuffy. At his level of workmanship, detail, and fabric quality, ready-made clothing was not for the working girl, but for the society or business woman who did not care to spend much of her free time in fittings. Garments by Maurice Rentner, Inc. were available as exclusives at stores like Bonwit Teller, I. Magnin, Rich's, Lord & Taylor, and Kaufmann's.

As one of the upmarket manufacturers who supported an in-house design staff, Rentner was very aware of the plague of design piracy. In 1933 he formed the Fashion Originator's Guild, which established a design registration bureau for its members. The Guild grew from 12 original members to 60 by the end of its first year. Cooperating retailers agreed to refrain from buying or selling copies of garments created by Guild members. It seems to have been a laudable experiment, but consensus on the terms of the agreements rapidly broke down, and by 1936 the Guild was being sued by several retailers for restraint of trade. It was disbanded in 1941.

Rentner tried always to foster the interests of the garment industry, as a member of the New York Dress Institute Couture Group and other garment center organizations, and by serving on the advisory board of the Fashion Institute of Technology in New York. His company was among those that profited, in terms of consumer recognition, by the isolation of American fashion during World War II. It may be that his success with high quality name ready-to-wear inspired the rush of European couturiers to lend their own names to that market in the late 1940s.

Although Rentner died in 1958, his business does, in a way, live on. Maurice Rentner, Inc. merged with Anna Miller & Co., owned by Rentner's sister, in 1958, with Miller's head designer, Bill Blass, maintaining that position in the joined company. Bill Blass for Maurice Rentner was successful through the 1960s, while Blass became vice-president and then owner of the firm. He organized the company under his own name in 1970. It is a tribute to Rentner's achievement in making his name synonymous with quality and style that, even through the turbulent 1960s, his name endured.

—Madelyn Shaw

RESTIVO, Mary Ann.

American designer

Born: South Orange, New Jersey, 28 September 1940. **Education:** Studied retailing at College of St. Elizabeth, Morristown, New Jersey, 1958-60, and design at Fashion Institute of Technology, New York, 1960-61, with associate degree in Applied Arts. **Family:** Married Saul Rosen in 1978. **Career:** Trainee, Abby Michael junior sportswear house, New York, 1961; designer for New York firms Bernard Levine, Petti for Jack Winter, Something Special, Sports Sophisticates, and Mary Ann Restivo for Genre, 1962-74; for Cisco Casuals, head designer, women's blouse division, Dior New York, 1974-80; launched own firm, Mary Ann Restivo, Inc.,

Zandra Rhodes: "Unfinished Symphony," Fall/Winter 1995.   *Photograph by Rose Beddington.*

1980; sold company to Leslie Fay Corporation, 1988; designer, Mary Ann Restivo division, Leslie Fay Corporation, 1988-92; independent design consultant, from 1993. **Awards:** Hecht Company Young Designers Award, Washington, D.C., 1968; Mortimer C. Ritter Award, Fashion Institute of Technology, 1973; awarded Honorary Doctor of Humanities, College of Saint Elizabeth, 1986; Alumnus of the Year Award, American Association of Community and Junior Colleges, 1992; Ellis Island Medal of Honor Award, 1993.

Publications:

On RESTIVO:

Books

Milbank, Caroline Rennolds, *New York Fashion: The Evolution of American Style,* New York 1989.

Articles

Larkin, Kathy, "Meet Two Designers Who Are Changing Establishment Fashions," in the *New York Daily News,* 14 January 1973.

Foley, Bridget, "Mary Ann Restivo Marches to Her Own Drummer," in *New York Apparel News,* April 1983.

Morris, Bernadine, "Working Women: A Designer's Focus," in the *New York Times,* 30 June 1987.

Daria, Irene, "Mary Ann Restivo: Targeting the Working Woman and Herself," in *Women's Wear Daily* (New York), 26 October 1987.

Vespa, Mary, "Designer Mary Ann Restivo Walks on Fashion's Mild Side, Which Suits Her Working Women Fans Just Fine," in *People,* 23 November 1987.

Michals, Debra, "Dresses from Sportswear Firms: Plusses and Problems," in *Women's Wear Daily* (New York), 28 February 1989.

Schiro, Anne-Marie, "From Restivo, a New Look of Softness," in the *New York Times,* 3 November 1989.

Morris, Bernadine, "Building Wardrobes around Jackets," in the *New York Times,* 8 May 1990.

*   *   *

"People need fashionably sensible clothes," asserted Mary Ann Restivo to *People* magazine in the midst of the era of late 1980s excesses. *People* replied that Restivo is "emerging ... as the saviour of the stylish but sane professional woman." Career and professional dressing are the appropriate context for Restivo's work, not only in terms of her clientéle, but in terms of the clothing's emphasis on good fit, excellent materials and manufacture, personal luxury without ostentation, and wearable good taste.

Bernadine Morris, a likely champion of Restivo's work in her commitment to American sportswear, wrote of Restivo that she "tries to walk the tightrope between clothes that are subdued and those that attract attention." The attention that a Restivo garment attracts is primarily for its flattering image to the client. Restivo emphasizes fit, with some camouflage to the hips, appealing to women in sizes six, eight, and ten. As the designer argues in the

tradition of sportswear, no woman should feel squeezed into the clothing, but should have mobility for her own sense of elegance and self-confidence, as well as the functions of dressing for careers in which one outfit may suffice from home to office to evening. In the 1980s, Restivo's work directly coincided with the perceived need of women of middle- and upper-management to wear clothing that was sufficiently sensible to the office without merely adapting menswear. Other American designers came to the same conviction in the 1980s, but Restivo was one of the first to create stylish career dressing and to establish it as the cornerstone of her business.

In a 1993 lecture at the Italian Trade Commission in New York, Restivo spoke passionately of her love of textile resourcing, finding the best materials for her garments and permitting the textiles to determine the clothes. Arguing that every collection begins with its textile resources, Restivo uses wool jersey, cashmere, and other luxuries of texture and vision throughout her collections.

Through the 1980s, jackets were an important element of all Restivo collections, even for resort. Like most designers of the period, Restivo made her jackets softer and softer, choosing the textiles for unconstructed jackets still capable of the fresh self-confidence required by women in the place of business. Dresses play an important part in Restivo's ideal of the career wardrobe, but resort collections also permit trousers and her jackets in elegant proportions work as part of tailored suits or as separates. Restivo told Morris (*New York Times,* 8 May 1990) at the apogee of the well-tailored business jacket: "The jacket is the key. When you start to develop your collection, you begin with the jacket then build everything else around it. You work out the skirts or the pants and the blouses and sweaters." Restivo added: "It is interesting to me that when store buyers come to buy the collection, they follow the same procedure. When customers go shopping for their fall clothes, they will probably do the same thing."

Restivo's acuity to the customer has always been an essential part of her business, begun in 1981. The loyalty of her clients is legendary. When the Restivo line was abruptly dropped by Leslie Fay in the early 1990s, clients pursued the designer herself to be sure that they would not be cut off from their favorite clothing. Restivo's client empathy is undeniably important in the success of a woman designer creating for like-minded sensible women of business and style.

Gloria Steinem once said of Restivo's clothes that they are "the kind of clothes that, after you've died, another woman would find in a thrift shop and like." Such enduring good taste and clothing recycling may thwart the image of fashion as a place of excess and fickle change. Indeed, Restivo's clothing fosters another, more sensible, more purposeful, undeniably beautiful concept of fashion.

—Richard Martin

RHODES, Zandra.

British designer

Born: Zandra Lindsey Rhodes in Chatham, Kent, 19 September 1940. **Education:** Studied textile design, Medway College of Art, 1959-61, and Royal College of Art, 1961-64. **Career:** Established dressmaking firm with Sylvia Ayton, London, 1964, and textile design studio with Alexander McIntyre, 1965; partner, designer,

Fulham Clothes Shop, 1967-68; free-lance designer, 1968-75; director, Zandra Rhodes UK Ltd, and Zandra Rhodes Shops Ltd, from 1975; launched ready-to-wear collections, in Australia, 1979, and in Britain, 1984. Has also designed bedlinens and household textiles. **Exhibitions:** *Zandra Rhodes: A Retrospective with Artworks,* Art Museum of Santa Cruz, California, 1983. **Awards:** English Fashion Designer of the Year Award, 1972; Moore College of Art Award, Philadelphia, 1978; DFA, International Fine Arts College of Miami, 1977; Royal Designer for Industry, Royal Society of Arts, 1977. **Address:** 87 Richforth Street, London W6 7HJ, England.

Publications:

By RHODES:

Books

The Art of Zandra Rhodes (with Anne Knight), London 1984, New York 1985.

Articles

"A Life in the Day of Zandra Rhodes" (with Anne Whitehouse), in *The Sunday Times Magazine* (London), 24 January 1982.
"My Country, Right or Wrong," in the *Sunday Telegraph Magazine* (London), 10 May 1987.

On RHODES:

Books

Santa Cruz Art Museum, *Zandra Rhodes: A Retrospective with Artworks,* Santa Cruz, California 1983.
Milbank, Caroline Rennolds, *Couture: The Great Fashion Designers,* London 1985.
McCarthy, Fiona, and Patrick Nuttgens, *Eye for Industry: Royal Designers for Industry, 1936-1986,* exhibition catalogue, London 1986.
Loebenthal, Joel, *Radical Rags: Fashions of the Sixties,* New York 1990.
Mendes, Valerie, and Claire Wilcox, *Modern Fashion in Detail,* London 1991.
Steele, Valerie, *Women of Fashion,* New York 1991.

Articles

"Zandra's Fantasies," in *Viva* (New York), February 1974.
Perschetz, Lois, "On the Rhodes," in *Women's Wear Daily* (New York), 26 April 1974.
Kavanagh, Julie, "All Rhodes Lead to Zandra," in *Women's Wear Daily* (New York), 31 December 1975.
Walkley, Christina, "Zandra Rhodes," in *Costume* (London), 1976.
"British New Style," in *Vogue* (London), 15 March 1976.
Howell, Georgina, "The Zandra Rhodes Dossier," in *Vogue* (London), July 1978.
Bakewell, Joan, "Zandra Rhodes: A Profile," in the *Illustrated London News,* October 1978.
"Schooldays," in *Vogue* (London), October 1981.

"Zandra Rhodes at Home," in *Connoisseur* (London), December 1981.
Williams, Antonia, "Zandra, the Non-stop Rhodes Show," in *Vogue* (London), August 1982.
Fallon, James, "At Long Last Friends: Dress Designer Zandra Rhodes and Her Sister Beverly," in *The Sunday Times Magazine* (London), 8 May 1983.
"Zandra Rhodes," in *Art and Design* (London), February 1985.
Burnie, Joan, "We'll tak' the High Rhodes," in *You* magazine of the *Mail on Sunday* (London), 28 February 1988.
"The Fashion Fatigue of Zandra Rhodes," in *Design Week* (London), 11 March 1988.
Niesseward, Nonie, "Ware-ability," in *Connoisseur,* June 1988.
"Zandra Rhodes," in *Pins and Needles* (London), July 1988.
"The Correspondent Questionnaire: Zandra Rhodes," in *The Correspondent Magazine* (London), 21 October 1990.
Schaeffer, Claire B., "Zandra Rhodes Couture," in *Threads* (Newtown, Connecticut), June/July 1990.
O'Kelly, Alan, "The London Home of Zandra Rhodes," in *House Beautiful* (London), November 1990.

*   *   *

Zandra Rhodes is an artist whose medium is printed textiles. Working in a calligraphic style uniquely her own, she designs airy prints from which she produces floating, romantic garments whose cut evolves from the logic and placement of the print itself. Rhodes has no imitators; her work is instantly recognizable.

In a field where novelty is prized, Rhodes's work over the years is remarkable for its consistency. Because the shapes of her garments are fanciful and fantastical, using volume to display the textile to its best advantage, her clothes do not date. Rhodes's references are timeless: T-shaped gowns of printed chiffon belted in satin; the full pleated skirts and long gathered sleeves of Ukrainian festival dress; off-the-shoulder tabards finished with a fringe of dagging; children's smocking re-interpreted in silk jersey. Zandra Rhodes's clothes are extravagantly feminine, delicate, and mysterious, created, as one writer has observed, for "contemporary Titanias."

Each collection of prints evolves as a thoughtful response to a personal vision. Drawing on traditional historic sources, on images from nature, from popular culture, and from her own past, Rhodes sketches an object over and again, entering into a dialogue with it as the sketches become increasingly abstract and a personal statement emerges. Only at that point are a series of these personal images combined until the right composition presents itself to be translated into the final screen print. The print determines how the garment will be cut. Rhodes was not trained as a draper or cutter and she has not been bound by the concept of symmetry, conventional seam placement, or internal shaping. Many of Rhodes's dresses are cut flat or with minimal shaping, sometimes incorporating floating panels which follow the undulations of the patterned textile. She favours large repeats on silk chiffon or silk net and as the garment falls in on itself against the body it creates mysterious shapes and soft, misty layers not easily known. Rhodes is without doubt one of the most gifted and original designers of the late 20th century.

—Whitney Blausen

RIBES, Jacqueline de. See de RIBES, Jacqueline de.

RICCI, Nina.

French designer/company

Couture house founded by Nina Ricci (1883-1970) and son Robert Ricci (1905-88) in Paris, 1932. First ready-to-wear collection shown, 1964; men's collection introduced, 1986; first boutique opened, Paris, 1979; men's boutique, Ricci-Club, opened, Paris, 1986; cosmetics line, *Le Teint Ricci,* introduced, 1992. Fragrances include *Coeur de Joie,* 1945, *L'Air du Temps,* 1948, *Capricci,* 1961, *Farouche,* 1974, *Signoricci,* 1975, *Fleur de Fleurs,* 1980, *Nina,* 1987, *Ricci-Club,* 1989. **Awards:** Mme. Ricci awarded Chevalier de la Légion d'Honneur; Fragrance Foundation Hall of Fame Award, 1982; Fragrance Foundation Perennial Success Award, 1988; Dé d'Or Award, 1987; Bijorca d'Or Award, 1987, 1988; Vénus de la Beauté, 1990; Trophée International Pardum/Couture, 1991; Prix d'Excellence "Créativité" 92, 1992; Trophée de la Beauté de Dépêche Mode, 1992; Prix Européen de la P.L.V., 1992; l'Oscar du Mécénat d'Entreprises, 1993. **Address:** 39, avenue Montaigne, 75008 Paris, France.

Publications:

On RICCI:

Books

Milbank, Caroline Rennolds, *Couture: The Great Designers,* New York 1985.
Pochna, Marie-France, *Nina Ricci,* Paris 1992.

Articles

Carter, Ernestine, "The New Boys at Nina Ricci," in *The Sunday Times Magazine* (London), 15 December 1963.
Davy, Philippe, "Le charme romantique des succès de Nina Ricci," in *L'Officiel* (Paris), February 1990.

*

To make women beautiful, to bring out the charm of each one's personality. But also to make life more beautiful ... that has always been my ambition, and that is the underlying philosophy of NINA RICCI.

—Robert Ricci

*   *   *

Nina Ricci is established as one of the longest running Parisian couture houses. Unlike her peers, Elsa Schiaparelli and Chanel, Ricci's reputation does not rest on a revolutionary fashion state-ment. Instead, she was successful because she provided an understated, chic look for elegant and wealthy society women, always classic, yet intoxicatingly feminine.

When it came to designing clothes, Nina Ricci relied greatly on her feminine intuition. She worked directly on to the model and designed by draping the actual fabric, which she felt gave her the answer to what the dress would become. Creating clothes was simply a matter of solving problems and in the 1930s she described several of them; she had to find an extra special, elegant detail that would render a dress a client's favourite and achieve a maximum ease and lightness that did not encumber the wearer when moving or dancing.

Much of the detailing in Nina Ricci's clothes reflected her ultra-feminine approach, the flattering effects of gathers, tucks, and drapery and an attention to décolleté and figure-hugging details like fitting dresses below the waist. She was clever and original in her use of fabric, cutting plaids and tartans on the bias for evening dresses and a black silk border print fabric so that the print was avidly displayed over the bust, leaving the rest of the dress to become a straight column of fabric.

Ricci had been a successful designer for other houses before she decided to open her own house with her son Robert in 1932. At the age of 49, this could have been a risky venture but the gamble paid off as the company rapidly grew in size and stature during its first decade. By 1939 they occupied eleven floors in three buildings, a stark contrast to their humble beginnings in one room at 20 boulevard des Capucines, Paris.

Nina Ricci retired from the business in the early 1950s, leaving the field open to her son Robert who has since pursued his own ambitious plans for the house. An excellent businessman, Robert Ricci has established many divisions and licensees for the Ricci name. A fragrance, *Coeur de Joie,* was introduced in 1945, followed by the now classic *L'Air du Temps.* Later such fragrances as *Coeur de Joie, L'Air du Temps, Fleur de Fleurs,* and *Nina* were successively marketed. Sunglasses alone were reported to be grossing six million dollars in the late 1970s and by 1979 the house had become firmly established in the former Kodak Mansion, opposite the House of Dior on avenue Montaigne, Paris.

Robert Ricci has also been successful in his choice of recent designers for the house. The Belgian designer Jules François Crahay was named Head Designer in 1954 and made his debut with a collection that paid homage to Nina Ricci's trademark feminine look. Carrie Donovan from *The New York Times* described it as "a collection that was feminine in the extreme—beautiful of coloring and fabric, unbizarre and elegant." Crahay was succeeded in 1963 by Gérard Pipart, who remains today as designer of both the couture and boutique collections, turning out typically Ricci clothes in the most beautiful laces, tailored fabrics, appliqué, and natural fibres.

—Kevin Almond

RICHMOND, John.

British designer

Born: Manchester, England, 1960. **Education:** Graduated from Kingston Polytechnic, 1982. **Family:** Married Angie Hill; son: Harley D; daughter: Phoenix. **Career:** Free-lance designer in England for Lano Lano, Ursula Hudson, Fiorucci, Joseph Tricot, and Pin Up for Deni Cler, 1982-84; designer and partner with Maria

Nina Ricci: Fall/Winter 1994/95 Haute Couture collection. *Photograph by Fayçal.*

Cornejo, Richmond-Cornejo, London, 1984-87; John Richmod Man and John Richmond Woman collections introduced, 1987; lower priced Destroy collection introduced, 1990; Destroy Denim collection introduced 1991; first London boutique opened, 1992. **Address:** Proudheights Ltd, 25 Battersea Bridge Road, London SW11 3BA, England.

Publications:

On RICHMOND:

Books

Thackara, John, ed., *New British Design,* London 1986.
McDermott, Catherine, *Street Style: British Design in the 80s,* London 1987.

Articles

"All Right John?," in the *Sunday Express Magazine* (London), 3 August 1986.
"Design Duo Separate," in *Fashion Weekly* (London), 12 November 1987.
"Richmond/Cornejo," in *The Sunday Times Magazine* (London), 22 November 1987.
Scott-Gray, Chris, "Designing Contradictions," in *Fashion Weekly* (London), 6 October 1988.
Collen, Matthew, "Maximum Impact," in *i-D* (London), December/January 1989-90.
Ferguson, Sarah, "Cyclist," in *Elle* (New York), April 1991.
"John Richmond," in *The Face* (London), September 1991.
Fallon, James, "Richmond the Destroyer," in the *Daily News Record* (New York), 6 July 1992.
Gordon, Mary Ellen, "Rock 'n' Roll Control," in *Women's Wear Daily* (New York), 18 November 1992.
Clemente, Alba, "Limelighting John Richmond," in *Interview* (New York), January 1993.

*   *   *

The twin icons of popular rebellion, rock music, and biker chic, are combined with good tailoring and attention to detail to make John Richmond's designs a success, commercially and critically. He is one of the most business-minded of his British counterparts, steadily building up his clothing range while others have fallen prey to financial and production problems. His designs have developed along the lines initiated during his partnership with Maria Cornejo, with certain motifs being carried through. These make his work instantly recognizable and, he says, justify the use of the Destroy slogan as a brand name for his cheaper lines, instead of promoting it as a diffusion range.

His womenswear shows the use of sharp tailoring with subversive twists which carry out the motto of "Destroy, Disorientate, Disorder," so often emblazoned on his garments, as he tries to challenge accepted design conventions and expectations. Richmond's clothes are always sexy and brazen, leading many stylists and pop stars to reach for his styles when wanting to create an image that is striking and memorable. Well-cut jackets, often in hot fruity colours, are combined with fetish motifs. Bondage chains, zips, and leather inserts hark back to punk, although the sophistication of the style and the quality of the fabric make the overall look far more contemporary. His Tattoo sleeve tops and biker jackets were seen everywhere, even inspiring a vogue for the real thing among some London clubbers.

These design details also highlighted another side of his more subversive work. The macho tattoos he juxtaposed with transparent georgette wrap tops in the late 1980s questioned sexual stereotypes, something he continues in his menswear, where bright shiny fabrics are used for long-jacketed suits, and net is set against hard leather. These are perhaps a reflection of the vulnerable, slightly camp edge possessed by many of the rock 'n' roll heroes that inspire him, impossibly masculine images at the same time tempered by a glam-rock glitziness, or the feminine twist of a soft shiny fabric. Although the anarchy symbols he so often uses challenge, they never lead to his creating clothes that are unwearable or unsellable. A suit may be made with bondage trousers as a witty edge to a traditional design, but the fine Prince of Wales check of the fabric still makes it seem stylish and desirable.

Richmond's Destroy and Destroy Denim labels have the same pop star/rock chic feel, yet retain the quality of design of his main line, relying mainly on Lycra, denim, and splashes of leatherette to produce a sportswear influence and clubby feel. Jeans in denim and biker jackets form the basis of this collection, although sharp suits also feature, with 1970s glam rock again an influence: feather boa-like trim around coats and jackets and tight sequin tops for both men and women. Later collections have shown a growing maturity in style and widening of influences, in couture-inspired jackets with gilt buttons and quilted linings and sleek slit skirts, still with the distinctive Richmond elements like shiny leggings and the contrast platform heels of the boots designed for Shelly's, the popular London footwear chain.

John Richmond is undoubtedly one of the forerunners of contemporary British fashion, a dedication to which is shown in the part he takes in "5th Circle" with four other menswear designers who want to build on and develop Britain's innovative talents. His slick marketing techniques and his ability to reflect contemporary moods in his designs make him one of the most exciting and prominent of his country's designers. Many believe his business sense will ensure his future success, something which is often as important for survival as the production of consistently good designs.

—Rebecca Arnold

MARINA RINALDI SrL.

Italian fashion company

Founded by Achille Marmotti, Reggio Emilia, Italy, within the Max Mara Group, 1980. Launched first collection of larger size fashion, 1980; Persona line introduced, 1985; Marina Sport launched, 1986; knitwear line, 1987. **Address:** Via Mazzacurati 4, 42100 Reggio Emilia, Italy.

Publications:

On MARINA RINALDI/MAX MARA:

Books

Alfonsi, Maria Vittoria, *Leaders in Fashion,* Bologna 1983.
Soli, Pia, *Il genio antipatico,* Venice 1984.

Marina Rinaldi.

Articles

"Che cosa di chi: MaxMara," in *Vogue* (Milan), October 1984.
"Pianoforte di MaxMara: giunco e sabbia da turismo coloniale," in *Vogue* (Milan), February 1986.
Mower, Sarah, "Chasing the Wise Monet," in *The Guardian* (London), 3 July 1986.
Rumbold, Judy, "Grey Cells: Bright Ideas," in *The Guardian* (London), 7 September 1987.
"Altre scelte da MaxMara," in *Vogue* (Milan), October 1987.
Armstrong, Lisa, "The Max Factor," in *Vogue* (London), October 1988.
Tredre, Roger, "A Piece of Cake," in *Fashion Weekly* (London), 1 December 1988.

*   *   *

Marina Rinaldi originated as part of the Max Mara group, answering the needs of 40 percent of Italian women of size 46 and over. The group's other ranges, including Weekend and Penny Black, already catered for larger sizes, until it was recognized by the company that there was a significant gap in the market for a separate label that specialized in large sizes.

The aim was and is to produce a range that has the same fashion content as other Max Mara ranges. It has the same quality of cut, manufacture, fabric, and colour but is available only from size 16 upwards. Established as a separate company, there are now three labels under its umbrella, Marina Rinaldi, Marina Sport (launched to target a younger clientèle) and Persona. The label serves 400 points of sale worldwide, 100 of these are franchised, 80 being in Italy and 20 abroad (Paris, Tokyo, Brussels, and Amsterdam).

Marina Rinaldi have an ongoing Image Project that aims to establish a thorough understanding of their product, their customer, and the company's relationship to that customer. The large customer was identified as someone with very classic tastes, who is too afraid or too timid to try younger styles and modern silhouettes. The sales personnel are recognized as an important link. By establishing a trustworthy relationship with the customer, the important first hurdle is tackled. It should, after all, be understood that for some women, to wear a pair of jeans with a large cotton shirt and rib cardigan is a big fashion step forward. The moment a customer recognizes that she is looking younger and more up to date is the moment Marina Rinaldi know they have won a faithful new customer.

Marina Rinaldi try to combine looks that will flatter a heavier figure. For instance, tight trousers worn with a large shirt is a more slimming silhouette than a straight skirt worn with a shorter jumper. The company tries to incorporate as many fashion trends and styles as possible, but always includes classic items such as a sheepskin jacket, a cowboy style suede jacket, overcoats in pure cashmere, round turtleneck bodies in stretch jersey, brushed flannel suits, leather jackets, and jeans in many colours. An eveningwear look is always included with elegant smoking jackets and lounging suits, embroidered wraps and white evening shirts with gold cufflinks. A summer beachwear collection incorporates essentials from the swimming costume to the towelling bath robe.

The company also produces a twice yearly catalogue, *MR,* designed to accompany the customer throughout the fashion season and intended as an introductory guide to a fashion lifestyle for women not entirely used to fashion. As well as advice on how to interpret High Street trends with the Marina Rinaldi look, it gives advice on cookery, personal problems, and travel.

Glancing through a Marina Rinaldi sales brochure or browsing through their rails of clothes, it becomes difficult to distinguish much difference in style from any other Max Mara range. The quality of workmanship, styling, and fabrics are all there; the only real difference is in the sizing and the slightly rounder (but no less stunning) model used in the advertising. From a consumer point of view this is a measure of their success. Figure-hugging basques and fitted strapless dresses are not included in the range, but then sexy, revealing dressing has never been part of the Max Mara look. Marina Rinaldi represents a breakthrough in accessible fashion for all sizes, a business concept that many other companies now recognize.

—Kevin Almond

ROBERTS, Patricia.

British designer

Born: At Barnard Castle, County Durham, England, 2 January 1945. **Education:** Studied at Queen Mary's School, Lytham St Anne's, Lancashire, 1961-63; Fashion Diploma, Leicester College of Art, 1963-67. **Family:** Married John Christopher Heffernan, 1982; daughter: Amy. **Career:** Knitting editor, IPC Magazines, 1967-71; director and designer, Patricia Roberts Knitting, Ltd, from 1971, and, through *Vogue,* supplied knitwear for London shops. Designer, Patricia Roberts Yarns and Woollybear Yarns, from 1976; director and designer, Patricia Roberts shops, from 1976; *Patricia Roberts* perfume, 1990. **Exhibitions:** *Knit One, Purl One,* Victoria and Albert Museum, London, 1986. **Collections:** Victoria and Albert Museum, London; Whitworth Museum, Manchester. **Awards:** Duke of Edinburgh's Designer's Prize, 1986; Design Council Award, 1986. **Address:** 60 Kinnerton St, London SW1X 8ES, England.

Publications:

By ROBERTS:

Books

Patricia Roberts Knitting Patterns, London 1977.
Patricia Roberts Knitting Book, London 1981.
Patricia Roberts Second Knitting Book, London 1983.
Patricia Roberts Collection, London 1985.
Patricia Roberts Style, London 1988.
Patricia Roberts Variations, London 1991; New York 1992.

On ROBERTS:

Books

O'Hara, Georgina, *Encyclopedia of Fashion from 1840 to 1980s,* London 1986.

Sutton, Ann, *British Craft Textiles,* London 1991.

Articles

Raven, Susan, "Patterns for Patricia," in *The Sunday Times Magazine* (London), 8 December 1984.
Brampton, Sally, "A Priceless Pearl among the Plain Set," in *The Times* (London), 31 March 1986.
McDowell, Colin, "Never Out of Fashion," in *Crafts* (London), May/June 1986.

*

My knitwear is identifiable by its sophisticated stitchcraft. I love to push the technical limits of hand knitting into new areas, but always within the context of casual, easy to wear fashion. I am inspired by the creative possibilities of hand knitting and enjoy inventing new stitches and amalgamating them with colours, textures and form.

For each collection I think of a theme and then imagine ways of interpreting it into colour, Aran or lace work, or a combination of these. There is often something completely new about the way they are worked. The inspiration comes from anywhere and anything—holidays, nature, the sea, art exhibitions, bric-a-brac, etc. I work in natural fibres, often luxury ones, like cashmere and angora. We have developed our own range of cottons, specially for hand knitting, in a myriad of colours.

I want people to feel comfortable and enjoy wearing my sweaters at almost any time and anywhere from the city office, to the country, the sea, or the fashionable ski resort.

—Patricia Roberts

*   *   *

This century saw a revolution take place in hand knitwear and this fresh interpretation of knitting tradition was made by a small number of designers. The home-spun 1970s provided just the environment for this designer-led boom.

Foremost in the field was Patricia Roberts who had trained in fashion at Leicester College of Art. On leaving college as an enthusiastic hand knitter in the early 1960s, she worked for a group of women's magazines making up patterns, and quickly learned the value of technical accuracy. Frustrated by the general outlook of hand knitting for economy's sake and magazines wanting Marks and Spencer copies, she realized that knitwear had to go in a different direction to justify knitting by hand at all.

At the age of 26 she launched herself as a free-lance designer and put together a collection of entirely fresh-looking handknits which were sold to Browns of London and Bloomingdales in the United States. A few years later, in 1976, she opened her first shop in London's Knightsbridge, selling both made up garments and knitting kits for the home knitter. Noting the lack of quality and limited colour of available yarns, she set to and began selling her own range wholesale. Meanwhile, she had a thriving mail order business and had produced the first of her annual pattern books. To date ten have been published in paperback and three in hardback. She designs the books herself, stylish volumes of glamorous sophistication. The initial 30,000 print run of the most recent paperback sold out almost overnight.

Patricia Roberts.

Today she shows two collections each year to buyers in Paris, Milan, and London. Three retail shops have been opened in London and franchise shops in Hong Kong, Cyprus, and Melbourne. About 75 per cent of her garments are exported, mainly to Italy.

Patricia Roberts was probably the first to see the commercial possibilities in what had started in the early 1960s as a fairly obscure craft revival. She is seemingly untouched by her success: "I've always been a worker," she says, "a plodder. I tend to think I'm not ambitious but I must be. Other people seem to think I am." She has progressed steadily from designing knitting patterns to masterminding an internationally acclaimed empire of "haute couture and design."

Her knitwear is distinguished by its sophisticated stitchcraft, pushing the technical limits of hand knitting into new realms—comfortable, casual styling that can be worn anywhere. Her greatest satisfaction comes from creating new stitches, and she claims to have created hundreds over the years.

Texture and colour are dominant features of her work—she was one of the first to make the British Spinning Industry confront the challenge for more creative yarns for the burgeoning talents among British knitwear designers. Roberts skilfully explores new techniques to achieve textural bobbles and bas relief, taking images from nature like bunches of grapes and cherries or, more mundanely, novelties like children's sweets or even a Scrabble board. Her grapes and cherries were an all-time bestseller. Contrasting textural effect is created from stitches as diverse as the knobbly blackberry stitch or the smooth open work of lace. Aran castes thin as trellis intersect areas full of different pattern, colour, and stitchery. The yarns themselves further increase surface interest with fluffy mohair, smooth silks, and other luxury yarns like cashmere and angora. She uses only natural fibres and has designed her own range of cottons. Her plainer garments make use of thick linens, tweeds, and marls. These highly textured, one-colour designs vie for attention with the more dramatic multi-coloured intricately patterned garments in bright primaries or jewel colours. For the home knitter these are not garments for the faint hearted.

She designs on the needles: "I keep knitting it up," she says, "and unravelling it because I keep changing my mind." It is then written down and sent to outworkers to be made up. Ready made garments are definitely at the top end of the market and customers include stars of stage and screen.

The designer Jean Muir, who chairs the Knitting Committee of the Design Council, compares Roberts's work to that of a painter or sculptor, calling her "a craftsman who has made her work commercial.... I regard her as being a leader in the resurgence of artists and craftsmen who are bringing about the most exciting movement that has happened in this country for a century."

Roberts regards herself as primarily a designer, very interested in the product design, and claims to be not at all "arty crafty." She could be said to be the most commercial of Britain's hand knitters. With no loss of originality and quality, her ready-made collections, patterns, and yarns are available to a wide international public.

In 1986 she was awarded the Design Council Award and subsequently the supreme accolade, The Duke of Edinburgh's Designer's Prize of the year, never before awarded to a clothing designer. The Design Council described her achievement as "an outstanding example of British design success," and added that "despite a considerable growth of sales, the best design standards had been maintained throughout the growth of the company." Her work was included in exhibitions at the Victoria and Albert Museum twice in

that same year, and her work is to be seen in the museum's permanent collection.

Patricia Roberts has raised handknitting to an art form and pioneered a way for others to follow. Although self-effacing by nature, she is matter of fact about her success: "I'm not surprised because nothing has happened overnight. It's all been just one stage after another."

—Elian McCready

ROBINSON, Bill.

American designer

Born: c. 1948. **Education:** Graduated from Parsons School of Design, New York. **Career:** Chief designer of menswear collection, Calvin Klein, 1977-c.1983; Yves Saint Laurent, updated men's collection, beginning c.1983; premiered own collection, fall, 1986; introduced complete suit, dress shirt, and neckwear collections, 1988; signed deal with Kindwear Company of Tokyo for the distribution of the Bill Robinson collection in Japan, 1987. **Awards:** Student of the Year Award, Parsons School of Design, 1969; Cutty Sark menswear award nomination, 1987; Most Promising U.S. Designer Award, 1987. *Died 16 December 1993.*

Publications

On ROBINSON:

Articles

Dallas Morning News, 4 December 1985.
Daily New Record (New York), 3 January 1986.
New York Newsday, 12 January 1986.
The Globe and Mail (Toronto), 8 April 1986.
The Philadelphia Inquirer, 15 June 1986.
The Record (New Jersey), 26 September 1986.
USA Today, 8 September 1986.
Manhattan, Inc., October 1986.
Daily News Record (New York), 17 November 1986.
The Globe and Mail (Toronto), 25 November 1986.
New York Times Magazine, 18 April 1990.
Wall Street Journal (New York), 29 May 1990.
Daily News Record (New York), 1-2 August 1990.
Details, August 1990.
MR (Japan), September 1990.
New York Times Magazine, 17 March 1991.
Esquire, May 1991.
Crain's New York Business, 15 July 1991.
GQ, November 1991.
Rolling Stone: Fashion Issue, fall 1991.
New York Times Magazine, 13 September 1992.

*   *   *

Bill Robinson was a rare breed of designer—articulate, modest, and enormously intuitive. He was one of the few American menswear designers to achieve a worldwide reputation in the 1980s. His clothes had their roots in classic American styles but also reflected a tradition of European design. They were an amalgam of fashion basics and sophisticated, elegant sportswear.

Robinson was inspired mainly by the period of the 1930s through the 1950s, considered the golden age of American sportswear. Yet he always strived to be "up-to-date, contemporary, modern," in his own words. The innate American character of his philosophy was expressed in a quote regarding his spring/summer 1991 collection, "My summer collection tells little stories, from Main to Florida. Very Route 1" (*Esquire,* May 1991).

Ironically enough, having once designed uniforms for Avis and TWA, Robinson set his sights on eradicating uniforms for men and opening up the horizons of menswear design. Wearing an unconstructed suit to work is OK, he seemed to say. And rather than donning a run-of-the-mill denim shirt and jacket, one could wear an indigo washed silk shirt and blazer—a casual yet eminently sophisticated ensemble that sacrifices nothing to comfort. Taking the classics as his starting point, he designed modern clothes for forward-thinking, creative men who were unafraid of their sensuality.

His formative years were spent working on the menswear collection for Calvin Klein. "Somehow, by fate, when I moved into menswear, I really took off," he said. Robinson made his reputation with his sleek leather jackets and body-conscious knits, setting the standard against which other menswear designers were judged in these categories. He himself wore one of his signature looks, a black turtleneck, and managed to look chic yet down-to-earth, setting the tone for his collection.

He put his individual stamp on schoolboy ties, CPO shirts, regatta striped blazers, and mackinaw jackets. He was a master of subtlety and a superb colorist, qualities that were brilliantly expressed in a seminal show staged at New York's Plaza Hotel for the fall 1989 season, when he launched his Japanese license with Kindwear.

A velvet corduroy suit from the fall 1991 collection is among the best examples of his work, combining the utilitarian quality of a common fabric with the plush and rich color associated with luxury clothing. The collection was also the start of a new direction for the designer, who adopted a softened approach that cast aside the excesses and "Power looks" of the 1980s.

Having brought American design to a world-class level, he also collaborated on advertising campaigns with such equally renowned figures as photographers Steven Meisel, Kurt Markus, and Guzman, raising the level of fashion photography in the United States.

His fall 1992 collection included such classic as pea coats, slim, flat-front pants, a host of knits, short overcoats, and a generally slimmer silhouette. He combined the rugged with the urbane in a mackinaw jacket shown over a one-button business suit and a mock turtleneck. As he has said, "The lines between work and play are blurring."

With his backer, Bidermann Industries Corp., Robinson was also forward thinking in his pricing structure, making the collection accessible to a wide range of customers and emphasizing the value-price relationship way before it was in vogue in the post-Ronald Reagan era.

Bill Robinson's modesty was reflected in the fact that the pieces he designed could easily be incorporated into any man's wardrobe. They were not blockbuster looks with a limited shelf life but modern classics that would not go out of style.

—Vicki Vasilopoulos

ROCCOBAROCCO. See **BAROCCO, Rocco.**

ROCHAS, Marcel.

French designer

Born: Paris, 1902. **Career:** Opened fashion house in rue Faubourg St-Honoré, Paris, 1924. Moved to avenue Matignon, 1931. Perfumes include: *Femme,* 1945, *Madame Rochas,* 1960, and *Mystère,* 1978. *Died* (in Paris) *1955.*

Publications:

By ROCHAS:

Books

Twenty-Five Years of Paris Elegance 1925-50, n.d.

On ROCHAS:

Books

Picken, Mary Brooks, and Dora Loues Miller, *Dressmakers of France: The Who, How and Why of the French Couture,* New York 1956.
Garland, Madge, *Changing Face of Fashion,* London 1970.
Kennett, Frances, *Collector's Book of Twentieth Century Fashion,* London 1983.
Mohrt, Françoise, *Marcel Rochas: 30 ans d'élégance et de créations, 1925-1955,* Paris 1983.
Milbank, Caroline Rennolds, *Couture: the Great Designers,* New York 1985.

Articles

Noel, Lucie, "Marcel Rochas Stresses Youth in New Styles," in the *New York Herald Tribune,* 3 August 1948.
Alexander, Hilary, "The Face that Relaunched Rochas," in *The Daily Telegraph* (London), 16 November 1989.

*   *   *

In the sometimes indeterminate world of fashion, Marcel Rochas was determined and decisive. He operated with a business acumen and cultural strategy (including the fashion designer as a conspicuous social mixer) that caused him in the post-war period to doubt the continued vitality and interest of the couture and to turn resolutely to his boutique operation and lucrative fragrance business. His motto was "Youth, Simplicity, and Personality," alternatively reported in the *New York Herald Tribune* (3 August 1948) as "elegance, simplicity, and youth," but it was in many ways the characteristic of personality that differentiated Rochas from other designers of his era. Rochas's initial fame came in the 1920s and rested on his *tailleur,* accompanied with supple skirts with the fullness and articulation of godets. In 1942, five years before the Dior New Look, Rochas had offered a new corset to create the *guépière,* or wasp waist, anticipating the return of the extreme femininity that enchanted him. Caroline Rennolds Milbank describes, "The Rochas output is characterized by a calculated originality" (New York, 1985). This reserved encomium is perhaps just for a designer of obsession with feminine beauty, but also with a commercial perspicacity.

Originality was, however, important for Rochas, if only as a sign of rights and attribute of value rather than of real creative initiative. In the 1930s, he was already selling ready-to-wear and made-to-order clothes in his New York store. He claimed to have invented the word "slacks" in the early 1930s, along with originating the idea to include gray flannel slacks as part of a suit. In an era when women's trousers were limited to extreme informality or recreation, Rochas's trousers suit was highly advanced if not revolutionary. His clothing was not cautious, but it was in its way circumspect, even the vaunted "inventions" coming with a social justification. For Rochas, "original" and "invention" were key words in the vocabulary of fashion selling.

The wide shoulders of the 1930s were created by several designers more or less simultaneously. He continuously played on the shoulders as a sign of the feminine: a fall/winter 1947 evening gown, for instance, invents broad shoulders through a capelet-like scarf attached to the bodice. Bolero jackets of the 1940s are lighter in construction than Balenciaga's inspirations direct from Spain; rather, Rochas is interested in the effect of the enhanced shoulders to pad and to frame. Likewise, a 1949 *robe du soir* dips to a bouquet of silk camellias at the bust, but caps the shoulders and frames the face with a flaring lightness. Shoulders look like the soaring roof of Le Corbusier's architecture at Ronchamp. In other instances, grand white collars perform the same role of dilating the impression of the shoulders and in providing a sweet, portrait-like framing for the face. The *New York Herald Tribune* described in 1948, "white collars in Queen Cristina [sic] and Louis XIII manner with points on shoulders are shown on many dresses for every occasion." *Women's Wear Daily* (29 January 1948) reported of Rochas, "this house is very modern but with the modernity which carries with it a tradition linking it with the fashion picture of the day. There is always an air of excitement in his collections which are designed to enhance the charm of women." Rochas claimed his *robe Bali,* with pronounced shoulders, to have been inspired by the Balinese dance costumes he had seen at the 1931 *Exposition Coloniale:* what he learned from Asian dress was the light float of a prominent shoulder, but he reinforced the idea with constant recourse to portrait collars and cognate enhancement of the head and shoulders.

If Rochas's anatomical obsession was the shoulder, his second favorite was the arm. He often embellished the sleeves in suits and coats, and his coats from the 1940s, which tended to be voluminous and drapey, were characterized by large sleeves. Loose blouson effects were more than carried over into the excess of sleeves as well as an interest in full backs.

Picken and Miller record, "Conscious of the changes in fashion, Rochas was the first to give up his heavy burden of the haute couture collections and to restrict his present activities to his boutique which specializes not only in accessories, but also in separates." Lace used in packaging affirmed the luxury textiles and laces that Rochas used in his couture, especially the corset. In fact, Rochas's accessories tended toward a chic wit, less self-conscious than Schiaparelli, but similarly inventive and imaginative. Anticipating Cardin and the marketing orientation of fashion and beauty,

Rochas was a visionary. His feminine designs still conformed to a traditional fashion ideal, but Rochas's eye was on the future. At his death in 1954, he had not fully achieved the synthesis of design and marketing that would become the dynamic of late 20th-century fashion, but he was definitely a believer and a pioneer.

—Richard Martin

RODIER.

French fashion house

Founded by Eugene Rodier, 1848; entered ready-to-wear knit wear, 1956; U.S. subsidiary, Rodier USA. **Address:** 149 rue Oran, F-59061 Roubaix, France.

Publications:

On RODIER:

Articles

"French Clothier Picks Chief for Its Assault on the U.S.," in the *New York Times,* 28 March 1988.
Edelson, Sharon, "Rodier Spices Up Lines with New Looks, and Plans for More Stores," in *Women's Wear Daily* (New York), 22 November 1994.

*   *   *

Known today for fine knits and woolen clothes, the House of Rodier continues a tradition which began when Eugene Rodier was commended by the Comte de Montaliner, Minister of the Interior under Napoleon. Rodier's distinction was won by reinterpreting the shawls of Kashmir for the contemporary woman of the 1800s at home and abroad, thus making his contribution to French commerce as well as to the nascent fashion industry.

Eugene Rodier formally established the house in 1848. Under his direction, and later under the direction of his son Paul and grandson Jacques, the firm continued to produce inventive and experimental textiles, informed by a study of past traditions.

A collection introduced in the early 1920s was inspired by the decorative arts of French colonial territories shown at the 1922 *Exposition Nationale Coloniale de Marseilles.* Rodier adapted and edited motifs from French Indo-China (Vietnam, Cambodia, and Laos) and from French Equatorial Africa (Tunisia, Algeria, and Morocco). These were woven into a series of soft, winter white cloths of wool and cashmere in such a way that when the dress was made up, the motifs formed a border or band of trimming.

In the early part of this century the Rodier mills developed such new fabrics as *senellic,* an early experiment in spun rayon, and the copyrighted Kasha, which remains a staple in their line. Perhaps the best known fabric developed by Rodier is the knitted jersey which Coco Chanel rescued from its warehouse oblivion in 1916. The combined visions of Jacques Rodier and Gabrielle Chanel transformed a humble fabric, intended primarily for men's underwear, into a textile inextricably linked with 20th-century style.

During the 1920s and 1930s, Rodier was also associated with such couturiers as Jean Patou, for whom the firm produced new textures and distinctive colors of unusual depth and subtlety. According to his biographer Meredith Etherington Smith, Patou's expansion in the mid-1920s was partially financed by the Rodier family. It was also during the mid-1920s that the house expanded its range to include fabrics for interiors designed by such luminaries as Pablo Picasso.

For Rodier, the first function of the mill was to act as a laboratory for the production of new yarns, new textures, and above all inventive designs that reflected the spirit of their age. Paul Rodier and his family were not only master weavers, but artists and editors. As such, they naturally studied the arts of the past and kept current with contemporary movements in painting, ballet, and anything else which might provide inspiration for their hand-operated looms.

Rodier entered the ready-to-wear field in 1956 with a collection of fine knitwear. Today's collections center around color-related separates which allow women to combine pieces to suit their individual needs and style. Distinctive patterns, rich colors, and fine details continue the tradition of excellence for which the house has long been known.

—Whitney Blausen

RODRÍGUEZ, José Victor. See **VICTORIO Y LUCCHINO.**

ROEHM, Carolyne.

American designer

Born: Jane Carolyne Smith in Kirksville, Missouri, 7 May 1951. **Education:** Graduated from Washington University, St Louis, 1973. **Family:** Married Axel Roehm in 1978 (divorced, 1981); married Henry Kravis, in 1985 (divorced). **Career:** Designer, Mrs sportswear by Kellwood Co. for Sears, Roebuck & Co., c.1973; designer, Oscar de la Renta licensees, including Miss "O" line, New York, 1974-84; launched own deluxe ready-to-wear firm, New York, 1985; added couture line, 1988, and footwear, 1989; closed house, 1991-93; launched mail order clothing, accessories and gift collection, 1993, with related in-store boutiques at Saks Fifth Avenue. Also: President, Council of Fashion Designers of America, 1989. **Awards:** Pratt Institute Award, 1991. **Address:** 550 7th Avenue, New York, New York 10018, USA.

Publications:

On ROEHM:

Books

Milbank, Caroline Rennolds, *New York Fashion: The Evolution of American Style,* New York 1989.
Steele, Valerie, *Women of Fashion: Twentieth Century Designers,* New York 1991.

Articles

Kornbluth, Jesse, "The Working Rich," in *New York,* January 1986.
Jobey, Liz, "Vogue's Spy: Carolyne Roehm," in *Vogue* (London), September 1987.
Menkes, Suzy, "Couture's Grand Ladies," in the *Illustrated London News,* Spring 1990.
"Those Gilded Moments ...," in *Esquire* (New York), June 1990.
Howell, Georgina, "Roehm's Empire," in *Vogue* (New York), August 1990.
"The Designers Talk Passion, Whimsy and Picassos," in *ARTnews* (New York), September 1990.
"End of a Dream," in *Time* (New York), 23 September 1991.
"Carolyne Roehm," in *Current Biography* (New York), February 1992.
Ginsberg, Merle, "Henry and Carolyne Hit Hollywood," in *Women's Wear Daily* (New York), 28 May 1992.

*   *   *

Carolyne Roehm is an American designer who creates clothes for men to love and women to find flattering. She is a person with a passion for designing beautiful, feminine clothes in luxurious materials, who takes great care with the details. She opened the doors of her own ready-to-wear and couture design firm in 1985, only to close them six years later.

Designing clothes was a lifelong passion for Jane Carolyne Smith Roehm. After studying fashion design at Washington University, she spent a year designing polyester sportswear for Kellwood Co., a company that supplied Sears, before working for Oscar de la Renta, holding pins and serving as his fitting model. She learned the details of classic couture from him, and later designed the Miss "O" line. After ten years with de la Renta, she formed her own design firm known as Carolyne Roehm, Inc.

She designs for women, like herself, who have money and who live an active life, involved with benefits and social events, but who might also work. She is known for well-detailed, finely constructed, feminine clothes which are created to make women feel elegant. Fabrics are rich: cashmere, satin, velvet, and suede. Details might include *trapunto* stitching, embroidery, or leather trim. Roehm's eveningwear is glamorous, fairy tale-like, to be seen in at social occasions and photographed in at charity events. The dresses could be cut full and made of rich fabrics, reminiscent of those worn in the aristocratic portraits of the artist Franz Winterhalter, or sleek, sensuous columns that recall John Singer Sargent's *Madame X.* Although best known for her glamorous eveningwear, half of her design work is in everyday wear. She creates sporty separates, dresses, coats, hats, and shoes. In all circumstances, Roehm's design work is known for quality and fit.

Carolyne Roehm can be numbered among the working rich. Her former husband, Henry Kravis, financed her design firm before they were married. After she was married she did not have to work, but she was driven. She designed her collections and used her organizational skills to support charity events. As president of the Council of Fashion Designers of America, Roehm guided the organization as they became a major supporter of AIDS research. She served as her own fitting model and appeared in her own advertising campaigns.

In 1991, for personal reasons, Carolyne Roehm closed her design business, Carolyne Roehm, Inc. From 1991 to 1994, she maintained a small office and staff, created a mail-order business, and produced clothes for private customers only. It remains to be seen whether Roehm returns on a larger scale to the field she graced with her feminine, glamorous designs.

—Nancy House

RONCHI, Ermanno. See **ERREUNO SCM SpA.**

ROTH, Christian Francis.

American designer

Born: New York City, 12 February 1969. **Education:** Special student, Fashion Institute of Technology, New York, 1986-87; studied fashion design at Parsons School of Design, New York, 1987-88. **Career:** Apprentice, later employee, of Koos Van den Akker; produced first small collection in Van den Akker's studio, 1988; showed first full collection, 1990. **Awards:** Council of Fashion Designers of America Perry Ellis Award, 1990. **Address:** 18 East 17th Street, New York, New York 10003, USA.

Publications:

On ROTH:

Books

Stegemeyer, Anne, *Who's Who in Fashion* supplement, New York 1992.
Martin, Richard and Harold Koda, *Infra-Apparel,* New York 1993.

Articles

Chua, Lawrence, "Christian Francis Roth," in *Women's Wear Daily* (New York), 27 June 1989.
Brubach, Holly, [fashion column] in *The New Yorker,* 29 January 1990.
Starzinger, Page Hill, "New Faces," in *Vogue* (New York), March 1990.
"Word is Out: SA [Seventh Avenue] Has a New Boy Wonder," in *Women's Wear Daily* (New York), 10 April 1990.
Boucher, Vincent, "The New Youthquake," in *Vogue* (New York), September 1990.
Shaw, Daniel, "New Kid on the Block," in *Avenue* (New York), September 1990.
Morris, Bernadine, "2 Young Designers Decorate Their Clothes with Wit," in the *New York Times,* 27 November 1990.
"Great Expectations," in *Women's Wear Daily* (New York), 12 June 1991.
Coffin, David Page, "Stitching Fabric Puzzles," in *Threads* (Newtown, Connecticut), June/July 1992.
"Arts and Crafts," in *Women's Wear Daily* (New York), 1 September 1992.

*   *   *

In 1990, a week after his first show and at the young age of 21, Christian Francis Roth was heralded by *Women's Wear Daily* as Seventh Avenue's latest boy wonder. Acclaim came stiflingly early for Roth. *Vanity Fair* had already photographed Roth with his ingenious dress-form dress (now in the collection of the Metropolitan Museum of Art) in August 1989 and in *The New Yorker* of 29 January 1990, Holly Brubach proclaimed of Roth's designs, "These clothes would look first-rate in Paris or Milan or Timbuktu. It is already too late to call him promising. There is, in his clothes, nothing more to wait for." Such immoderate and unanimous praise could only be withering to many young artists, but Christian Francis Roth earned the adulation and has only gone on to warrant further accolades. Yet, after the last hurrah and congratulations, there is the designer who works as a consummate technician in a tightly circumscribed aesthetic. He reaches not for the gold ring of commercial success and recognition like other designers, but instead for a level of virtuosity and quiet quality in his work.

Roth is an artist as evidenced by his vocabulary of forms conversant with such artistic elements as Surrealist *trompe l'oeil,* used in the dress-form dress (1989) and his wool jersey dress with illusionistic inset collar, cuffs, and belt (1991). Pop Art-derived concepts from consumer culture are represented in the spring 1990 Cartoon collection featuring daffy squiggles and suits with buttons that look as though they were spilled out of M & M candy bags. His breakfast suit (1990) breaks some eggs and prepares them sunny-side up, while his Rothola crayon outfits play with the children's toy for making art, and his scribbles and pencil shaving skirt and jacket provide the means for artistic delineation. His 1990-91 wrought-iron (or, as he says, "Roth-iron") fence dress (also a jacket and jumpsuit) is partly indebted to the artist Jim Dine, while the dollar bill dress, which wraps the body in oversized bills, owes more than a buck to Andy Warhol. His spring-summer 1991 collection included a suite of brilliantly colored dresses inspired by Matisse's *découpages.*

Admitting such debts does not diminish Roth's luster and originality, however, for each artistic enterprise is different, and Roth has scrupulously chosen to take from art only that which he accommodates to the construction of clothing. His inlaid panels, sometimes compared to the finest marquetry, are a skilled fabrication in the pattern of the garment. While some fashion designers have sought to poach on art's prestige and to steal some aesthetic thunder, Roth has committed only the most discriminating, transmogrifying larceny, flattering both art and fashion. In fact, his concern in integrating the scribbles into the form of the garment is more integral to his medium than the cartoon appropriations of Pop Art. When he brings Matisse's cutouts to dressmaking, he does so not as surface decoration, but as pattern pieces to create the three-dimensional shape of the garment.

Roth's small collections are likewise developed with the concentration and formal intensity of musical form. His fall 1992 collection studied menswear. The lyrical spring 1992 collections included cocktail dresses that set up a 1950s bar and became the drinks themselves as well as a black cotton sateen dress with a diamond ring homage to Marilyn Monroe. In fall-winter 1991, his principal studies were Amish quilts which Roth translated from the spiral concentricity of flat quilt patterns into the piecing of dresses and circle skirts. Combining some techniques of color blocks with the rich harmonies of American quilts, the collection emphasized Roth's handmade warmth and beauty. Accompanying the quilt patterns, Roth provided a congenial coterie of hoboes in a trickle-up theory of fashion, the hoboes' improvisations of patches becoming Roth's elegant and equally affable piecing for clients not accustomed to a trackside way of life.

Like Geoffrey Beene, whom he admires, Christian Francis Roth is an American designer of extravagant gift who has chosen the almost scholastic life of precious technician and exacting artist. With the unceasing patience and quest of an artist, Roth has achieved in measure and modesty what others cannot attain in magnitude.

—Richard Martin

ROUF, Maggy.

French designer

Born: Maggie Besançon de Wagner in Paris, 1896. **Career:** Designer for company owned by parents, Drécoll; own house opened, 1929, specializing in sportswear and lingerie; retired, 1948; daughter, Anne-Marie, took over; retired, 1960; house turned briefly to ready-to-wear; closed, 1960s. **Awards:** Chevalier de la Légion d'Honneur; Conseilleuse du Commerce Exterieur. *Died* (in Paris) 7 *August 1971.*

Publications:

By ROUFF:

Books

Ce que j'ai vu en chiffonnant la clientèle, Paris 1938.
La philosophie de l'elegance, Paris 1942.
L'Amérique vue au microscope, Paris n.d.

On ROUFF:

Books

Latour, Anny, *Kings of Fashion,* London 1958.
Milbank, Caroline Rennolds, *Couture: The Great Designers,* New York 1980.
Steele, Valerie, *Women of Fashion,* New York 1991.

*   *   *

Harmony and simplicity were cornerstones of Maggy Rouff's belief in elegance as a way of life, and the way of fashion. A truly elegant woman was in harmony with her environment, and herself, and to Rouff this meant being properly dressed for every occasion. Even in her early work at Drécoll in Paris, Rouff addressed a basic longing in the relationship between many women and their clothes. Patrons of her salon were secure in the knowledge that they would emerge with the right clothes, clothes that were fashionable, flattering, and appropriate.

This did not mean she was conservative. Rather, she believed that novelty, and even surprise, were good for fashion. She said that novelty, when allied with taste, yielded chic, but novelty without taste was only eccentric.

As a result, a Maggy Rouff design that is just "too much" is very rare. She took care to establish a focal point in every costume. An evening gown in which the skirt was trimmed with a crossover hip

wrap and little side puffs had simply-cut sleeves and bodice. Afternoon dresses with plain skirts might have an asymmetrical cowl neckline with a jeweled clip at one side, or a platter collar and shaped belt in a contrasting color. She would enrich some surfaces with shirring, quilting, or trapunto, as in her 1936 "plus four" playsuit and 1938 button-quilted evening dress, but very lush fabrics and furs were handled in accordance with her "less is more" philosophy.

Common themes run through Rouff's designs, always enhancing the underlying sense of femininity. She had a fondness for draped details, whether the sarong-like side drape of a skirt panel or soft cowl folds at the neckline. Rouff often highlighted the upper body, drawing attention toward the face with a few favorite devices such as wrapped and tied surplice fronts, unusual necklines, and dramatic sleeves. Accents were important: belts and sashes were wide, buttons were bold, silk flowers were substantial, yet somehow they were always in proportion. Contrasts of color, texture, or luster were also used as accents, and with the same sense of balance.

Historical allusions were frequent, but, true to her beliefs, she used historicism as a tool and not a crutch. The Directoire collection she showed in 1936 was striking for its theme, with variations on cutaway and frock coats turning up in corduroy with a bias-cut plaid skirt, in printed floral shantung with a black crêpe skirt, and in velvet with a wool skirt and an oversized watch chain pocket detail. Usually her references to the past were less direct, perhaps expressed in *gigot* sleeves, or apron and bustle effects.

In 1942, while Paris was occupied by German troops, Rouff wrote *La Philosophie de L'Elégance.* Her justification for what might have been considered, in such circumstances, a frivolous topic, was her belief that even in dark times there must be faith in the future. An intelligent woman who had already lived through one world war, she could not help but understand that a different world than the one she had known would emerge from the second. Her book was, in a sense, an affirmation of the value and substance which the arts of elegance had given to her life and her success. Within the framework of her expertise—fashion—Rouff gave her readers a thread to tie the future to the past.

Rouff's daughter, Anne-Marie Besançon de Wagner, took over the designing upon her mother's retirement in 1948. The house maintained the attitudes toward dress it had always expressed, and the clothes were still elegant and feminine. For the first few years she was inclined to overdo, and some models seem to have been fussy or hard-edged. However, as the 1950s progressed, she found her own sense of focus and greater sureness of line. Particularly beautiful were her full-skirted organdy evening and cocktail dresses from 1952 and a group of short, bouffant gowns with floor-length trains from 1959. Engaging day ensembles included, from 1953, a sleek tweed sheath with standaway cornucopia-shaped pockets at the bust and from 1952, a fur-trimmed swing coat worn over a pleated wool dress belted at the waist.

The house of Maggy Rouff did not survive the make-or-break period of the 1960s. Three designers worked for the house in the 1960s, during which time the business was transformed into a ready-to-wear house. The collections seem to have been aimed at a younger customer, but the original precepts of the house may have made it difficult to become established with a clientèle more interested in the pursuit of youth than the pursuit of elegance. The company was closed before Rouff's death in 1971.

—Madelyn Shaw

ROWLEY, Cynthia.

American designer

Born: Barrington, Illinois, 29 July 1958. **Education:** Studied art at Arizona State University, graduated from the Art Institute of Chicago, 1981. **Family:** Married Tom Sullivan, 1988 (died, 1994). **Career:** Senior at the Art Institute when she sold an 18-piece collection to Marshall Fields. Moved to New York, 1983, business incorporated, 1988. Designed costumes for dance troupes and films (including *Three of Hearts* and *Dream Lover*). Produces shoes, ready-to-wear, sportswear, dresses. Introduced line of girl's dresses, 1991. Taught at Parsons School of Design, New York, 1992-93; critic at Fashion Institute of Technology, New York City, 1992-94, and at Marist College, New York, 1994. **Exhibitions:** *Objects of their Appreciation,* Interart Center, New York City, 1993; Linen exhibition, Fashion Institute of Technology, New York, 1993; Dupont/Lycra exhibition, Fashion Institute of Technology, New York 1994. **Collections:** Metropolitan Museum of Art Fashion Video Library, New York; Fashion Institute of Technology Permanent Collection, New York; Fashion Resource Center, Chicago Art Institute. **Awards:** New York Finalist, "Entrepreneur of the Year," *Forbes* magazine, 1994. **Address:** 550 Seventh Avenue, 19th Floor, New York, New York, USA.

Publications:

On ROWLEY:

Books

McBride, Mary, *Wedding Dress,* New York 1993.
Bartlett, L., *Feast for Life,* Chicago 1994.

Articles

Finkelstein, Anita J., "Rowley Revs Up," in *Women's Wear Daily* (New York), 6 January 1992.
"Cynthia Rowley Rises and Shines," in *Mademoiselle* (New York), March 1992.
Goodman, Wendy, "Living with Style," in *HG* (New York), May 1992.
Levine, Lisbeth, "A Sense of Whimsy," in *Chicago Sun-Times,* 3 May 1992.
Goodman, Wendy, "Fashion Designer Cynthia Rowley Serves Up 1940's Tablecloths. More Vegetables Please ...," in *HG* (New York), May 1993.
Spindler, Amy M., "Fresh Talents Dish Up Tasty Design," in *New York Times,* 5 November 1993.
Cawley, Janet, "Designer Makes Splash in New York," in the *Chicago Tribune,* January 1994.
Infantino, Vivian, "Rowley's Big Adventure," in *Footwear News* (New York), January 1994.
Trebay, Guy, "FTV," in *Harper's Bazaar* (New York), August 1994.

*

The underlying thing about my clothing is that I always think about a woman's shape. Sometimes it's a basic shape that everyone understands, but I try to make it a bit more fun. I definitely have a sense of whimsy with everything. I like clothes that are very femi-

Cynthia Rowley.

nine, but with an added twist. I also think that a woman shouldn't have to spend a lot for great clothes. Maybe it's my Midwestern practicality coming through, but I feel there's always a need for great dresses at good prices.

For me, inspiration is very personal. A lot of what I design is inspired by where I grew up. I often do a play on the classics: tiny crop twin sets, mixed-match plaids, and polo dresses. Like everyone growing up in the suburbs, television was my link to fashion coolness—it's where I got my first sense of glamour. My clothing reflects these classics but with wit and originality.

—Cynthia Rowley

*   *   *

Cynthia Rowley does not think that clothes should be taken too seriously; nor does she believe that style and individuality must necessarily go hand in hand with a high price tag. Rowley is known for a line of dresses which are charming, easily affordable, and utterly distinctive. This winning combination has enabled her sales to double twice within the past three years, while some of her better known colleagues have had to retrench.

Rowley's clothes reflect her well-developed sense of play. Drawing on shared and familiar elements of popular American culture, she elevates the mundane, rethinking and transforming the cliché to produce garments which arrest and amuse. Yet she is careful not to push a joke too far. These are clothes with a sense of humor for daily use, not novelty items to be quickly discarded.

For fall 1992, Rowley showed a long, snap fronted sleeveless dress of quilted rayon and acetate satin worn over a matching ribbed cotton turtleneck. The reference to the classic hunter's vest was simultaneously reinforced and subverted by a six-pack of Budweiser slung low on the model's hip.

To commemorate the 100th anniversary of the bottle cap, Rowley scattered them across the front of a sleeveless cotton sweater, one half of a twin set with an eye catching twist. Her spring 1993 collection included sundresses of classic red and white tablecloth checks, supported by straps made from plastic fruits and vegetables. "I definitely like to have a little sense of whimsy with everything," she said in a 1992 interview with the *Chicago Sun-Times.*

Rowley's more traditional dresses also incorporate styling elements not often seen at her end of the market. A halter dress becomes suitable for the office when cut from classic pinstripes and paired with a white shirt. She understands that the basics need not bore and that an imaginative dialogue between cut and fabric can produce distinctive clothing in any price range.

—Whitney Blausen

RUGGERI, Cinzia.

Italian designer

Born: Milan, 1 February 1945. **Education:** Studied design at Accademia delle Arti Applicate, Milan, 1963-65. **Career:** Freelance designer in Milan, from 1966. **Exhibitions:** Galleria del Prisma, Milan, 1963; Venice Biennale, 1981; *Italian Re-Evolution,* La Jolla Museum of Contemporary Art, La Jolla, California, 1982; *Per un vestire organico,* Palazzo Fortuny, Venice, 1983; *Italia: The Genius of Fashion,* Fashion Institute of Technology, New York, 1985; *Dopo Gondrand: Cinzia Ruggeri\Denis Santachiara,* Il Luogo di Corrado Levi, Milan, 1986; *Extra vacanze di Cinzia Ruggeri,* Galleria Tucci Russo, Turin, 1986; *Internationale Mobel Messe,* Cologne, 1987; *Fashion and Surrealism,* Fashion Institute of Technology, New York, 1987 (toured); *Pianeta Italia,* Kaufhof Stores, Cologne, 1988; Salon del Mobile, Milan, 1988. **Collection**: Museo della Moda, Parma. **Awards:** Fil d'Or Award, Confederation Internationale du lin, 1981, 1982, 1983. **Address:** Via Crocefisso 21, 20122 Milan, Italy.

Publications:

By RUGGERI:

Articles

In *Casa Vogue* (Milan), April 1980.

On RUGGERI:

Books

Amendola, Paola, *Vestire italiano,* Rome 1983.

Branzi, Andrea, *The Hot House: Italian New Wave Design,* London 1984.

Soli, Pia, *Il genio antipatico,* Milan 1984.

Manzini, Ezio, *La materia dell'invenzione,* Milan 1986.

Martin, Richard, *Fashion and Surrealism,* New York and London 1987.

Soli, Pia, *Pranzo alle 8,* Milan 1988.

Yajima, Isao, *Fashion Illustrators of Europe,* Tokyo 1989.

*   *   *

Following her studies in the applied arts at the Accademia delle Arti Applicate in Milan, Cinzia Ruggeri obtained a position in the *atelier* of Carven in Paris. On her return to Italy, she served as director of design for the ready-to-wear firm of Unimac SpA, owned by her father Guido Ruggeri.

The Milanese firm was founded in 1963 and ceased operations in 1975. It had been controlled by the family and, under the label Guido Ruggeri, produced women's suits and coats. Unimac SpA was one of the foremost manufacturers in the booming Italian ready-to-wear industry of the 1960s. Signor Ruggeri and his daughter integrated the artisan's aesthetics and sartorial traditions with new techniques of production and distribution. During the 1960s, radical changes were occurring in the Italian garment industry. Good design, improved manufacturing methods and competition, together diminished the pervasive antipathy to mass production. New ideas and reorganization were fused in collaborative efforts between manufacturer and small, but specialized companies. Around 1966 Unimac SpA began investigating alternatives, such as synthetic fur detailing and novelty fasteners. It was possibly Signorina Ruggeri's developing sense of design that was responsible for linking diverse fashion elements with the new manufacturing methods.

During the 1970s, when Milanese designers were involved more than usual with "things English," Cinzia Ruggeri worked for the manufacturer Bumblebee which produced a line of women's blouses labelled Bloom. On the Via Gandino in 1977 she proceeded to build her own line, labelled Bloom SpA, and presented her first collection to the press in 1978. In 1979 the *atelier* was moved to the Via Crocefisso where it remains today. From 1980 through 1984 Ruggeri presented her singular, thematic ready-to-wear collections with other Milanese designers at the Fiera di Milano. On one occasion, outside the seasonal venue, her 1985 collection was presented in a building formerly used for religious services. The lighting installation was designed by the English musician Brian Eno. In 1982 she added the label Cinzia Ruggeri to her existing Bloom SpA line, and in 1986 she introduced menswear.

Throughout the 1980s Cinzia Ruggeri continued to apply thematic appliqués to traditional styling employing contemporary fabrics. One 1981 winter ensemble included a jacket of synthetic fur strips, ornamented with a fabric appliqué of three pigs covering the entire back of the garment. At an early stage in her career, Ruggeri established her sense of global responsibility by rrefusing to use animal fur, and both the wool trousers and the crêpe de chine blouse also featured the threesome appliqué. On the blouse, the suspended metal chain joining two animals was recalled by the chain stitching as top stitch. The *pièce de résistance* in this case was a perfectly constructed three dimensional shoulder bag in the shape of a pig.

Ziggurat 1984-85 was a two-piece synthetic evening dress. The garment was appliquéd with scattered two dimensional fabric bows, knotted as if clutching the three dimensional feathers. The ruffle-edged jacket was traditional in design, while the floor length skirt was three tiered, recalling the stepped towers of ancient civilizations. Subsequent garments have included these ziz-zag elements and structuring to form a volume independent of the wearer's body. She refers the stepped pattern to a personal symbol which she has also repeated in other artistic expressions. *Artform Magazine* featured an illustration of a glass container which incorporated the pattern at right angles to each other. "What art imagined, fashion also depicts," wrote Richard Martin in *Fashion and Surrealism* (New York 1987).

The fantasy of nature itself was compelling to the Surrealists and to Cinzia Ruggeri. Her 1983 Surrealist vision of marine life was titled Dress with Octopus. The long-sleeved, boxy jacket was the surface for randomly placed cascading square fabric forms, while the straight shift worn underneath involved the same protrusions, including a neckline cut as an ocean's horizon. Her broken ground print dress, quite traditional in style and fit, was pierced with oversized blossoms and crawling with three dimensional lizards. Most recently, in her Milanese studio, she proceeded to design prototypes for various projects that combined fashion with photography, anthropology, geology, and ecology by incorporating photographs of grass, cobblestones and marble in her textile designs.

Ruggeri has developed "behavioral" garments, printed with material that changes color according to body heat, and designed a "rain coat" with images of lightning and wind. A fitted dress, printed with Scottie dogs and edged with a cantilevered structure from which the dogs appear to be running is, of course, not surprisingly featured in a magazine accompanied by a set of three dimensional Scottie dog suitcases. "*Abito Tovaglia,*" tablecloth gown, illustrates a seated woman wearing a floor-length gown. She wears a collar as napkin, at first rolled up to the waist and attached at the sides of the garment. When unrolled, the panel reveals a cloth set with the utensils of an entire meal. For the Milanese firm Poltrona Frau, she designed a chair ornamented with whiskered cats and illuminated eyes. A shower head is illustrated in the shape of a human hand with water spraying out from the ringer tips.

As an artist, Cinzia Ruggeri has challenged herself in designing theatrical productions, ballets and artistic events and has ventured into interior and furniture design. She has exhibited at the Triennale di Milano and the Biennale di Venezia. Performances involving her fantastical costumes have clearly reflected her poetic tendencies when given such titles as *Performance Adanamica* (Performance without Movement), *La Casa Onirica* (The House Where I Dream), and *Per Vestire Organico* (To Dress Organically), all from 1983. "*La Neo Merce, Il Design dell'Intensione e dell'Estasi Artificiale,*" new products design and artificial ecstasy in 1985 and *Vestiti al Video,* video-wear, 1986. Also presented in 1994 were *Verona Neo Eclettismo,* Verona new eclecticism, and an exhibit at the Bacini Meridionale Museo Nuova Era.

—Gillion Skellenger

RYKIEL, Sonia.

French designer

Born: Sonia Flis in Paris, 25 May 1930. **Education:** Attended high school in Neuilly sur Seine. **Family:** Married Sam Rykiel in 1953; children: Nathalie and Jean-Philippe. **Career:** Free-lance designer for Laura boutique, Paris, 1962; first Paris boutique opened, 1968; household linens boutique opened, Paris, 1975; Sonia Rykiel Enfant boutique opened, Paris, 1987; cosmetics line introduced in Japan, 1987; Rykiel Homme boutique opened, Paris, 1989; Inscription Rykiel collection, designed by Nathalie Rykiel, introduced, 1989; new flagship boutique opened, Paris, 1990; menswear collection, Rykiel Homme introduced, 1990; second Inscription Rykiel boutique opened, Paris, 1990; Rykiel Homme boutique opened, Paris, 1992; footwear collection launched, 1992; Sonia Rykiel fragrance introduced 1993. Also columnist for *Femme* from 1983. **Exhibitions:** *Sonia Rykiel, 20 Ans de Mode* (retrospective), Galeries Lafayette, Paris, and Seibo Shibuya department store, Tokyo, 1987; retrospective, the Orangerie, Palais du Luxembourg, 1993. **Awards:** French Ministry of Culture Croix des Arts et des Lettres, 1983; named Chevalier de la Légion d'Honneur, 1985; Fashion Oscar, Paris, 1985; Officier de l'Ordre de Arts et des Lettres, 1993. **Address:** 175 boulevard Saint Germain, 75006 Paris, France.

Publications:

By RYKIEL:

Books

Et je la voudrais nue, Paris 1979.
Rykiel, Paris 1985.
Célébrations, Paris 1988.
La collection, Paris 1989, Tokyo 1989.
Colette et la mode, Paris 1991.
Collection Terminée, Collection Interminable, Paris, 1993.
Tatiana Acacia, Paris 1993.

On RYKIEL:

Books

Fraser, Kennedy, *The Fashionable Mind. Reflections on Fashion 1970-1981,* New York 1981.
Chapsal, Madeleine, Hélène Cixous and Sonia Rykiel, *Rykiel,* Paris 1985.
Milbank, Caroline Rennolds, *Couture: The Great Designers,* New York 1985.

Articles

"Sonia Rykiel, ambigue, célèbre et solitaire," in *Elle* (Paris), 25 October 1976.
Tournier, Françoise, "Sonia Rykiel sa vie, de fil," in *Elle* (Paris), 17 June 1985.
Schoonejans, Sonia, "Autour de l'album Rykiel," in *Vogue* (Paris), August 1985.
Menkes, Suzy, "Sonia Rykiel—Winning at Life," in the *International Herald Tribune* (Neuilly, France), 18 October 1988.
Sacase, Christiane, "Sonia Rykiel, les 20 ans de la dame en noir," in *Biba,* November 1988.
de Turckheim, Hélène, "Mes rendez-vous," in *Madame Figaro* (Paris), 11 February 1989.
Chapsal, Madeleine, "Les vingt ans de Sonia Rykiel," in *Elle* (Paris), 20 February 1989.
Tredre, Roger, "Touch of the Grande Dame," in *The Independent on Sunday* (London), 25 February 1990.
"Sonia Rykiel," in *Current Biography* (New York), May 1990.

Nolin, Dominique, "En visite chez Sonia Rykiel," in *Marie-France* (Paris), March 1991.

Raulet, Sylvie, "Sonia Rykiel: une femme d'atmosphère," in *Vogue* (Japan), March 1991.

Lender, Heidi, "Rapping with Rykiel," in *Women's Wear Daily* (New York), 18 November 1991.

Schwarm, Barbara, "Sonia Rykiel, la compil," in *L'Officiel* (Paris), June 1993.

Lender, Heidi, and Godfrey Deeny, "Sex, Sweaters and Sonia Rykiel," in *Women's Wear Daily* (New York), 7 July 1993.

Menkes, Suzy, "Rykiel in Retrospect: The Unfinished Work of a Designer," in the *International Herald Tribune* (Neuilly, France), 13 July 1993.

Webb, Ian, "Capital Elle," in *The Times Magazine,* 1994.

Rafferty, Jean Bond, "The Leading Lady of the Left Bank," in *Town & Country* (New York), December 1994.

Ozzard, Janet, "Rykiel Sips Tea, Seeks N.Y. Store," in *Women's Wear Daily* (New York), 28 December 1994.

Schiro, Anne-Marie, "Lacroix and Rykiel: Classics," in the *New York Times* (New York), 18 March 1995.

*

First I destroyed, undid what I had made. I wasn't satisfied with it. It wasn't me. It didn't relate to me. It was fashion, but it wasn't my fashion. I wanted to abolish the laws, the rules. I wanted to undo, overflow, exceed fashion. I wanted to unfold, unwind it. I wanted a lifestyle appropriate to the woman I was ... this woman-symphony who was living the life of a woman mingled with the life of a worker.

I wanted airplane-style, travel-style, luggage-style. I saw myself as a woman on the go, surrounded by bags and children ... so I imagined "kangaroo-clothes," stackable, collapsible, movable, with no right side, no wrong side, and no hem. Clothes to be worn in the daytime that I could refine at night. I put "fashion" aside to create "non-fashion."

—Sonia Rykiel

*   *   *

The French ready-to-wear designer Sonia Rykiel is a compelling presence whose intellect and individuality are apparent in her clothes. With her small bones and trademark mane of hair, she is probably her own best model, projecting assurance and energy. She began designing with no previous experience when, as the pregnant wife of the owner of *Laura,* a fashionable boutique, she was unable to find maternity clothes she liked. Continuing to design knitwear for *Laura,* she soon carved a niche for herself designing for well-to-do and sophisticated modern French women.

By 1964, she had been nicknamed "The Queen of Knitwear" in the United States, where an ardent following developed for her knits, which were sold in trend-setting stores like Henri Bendel and Bloomingdale's in New York. For those women who were rich and thin enough to wear them, these skinny sweaters, with their high armholes, imparted instant chic. Part of their appeal lay in their distinctive colors and striped patterns. Black, navy, gray, and beige are still standards, but there was also a unique Rykiel palette of muted tones; for example, stripes of grayed seafoam green and grayed teal. Although she herself does not wear red (she wears

black, considering it a uniform), Rykiel still uses it consistently, with the shade changing from season to season.

Today, Sonia Rykiel continues to design a complete range of clothes and accessories for women, drawn from her experience and her fantasies, which she encourages women to appropriate and adapt whilst inventing and re-inventing themselves. In addition to knits and jerseys, she uses crêpe for soft clothes, and woven tweeds and plaids for a more structured day look. Evening fantasies are best expressed in lightweight black luxury fabrics, often combined with sequins, metallic thread, embroidery, or elaborate combinations incorporating velvet.

Physical fitness is implicit in Sonia Rykiel's idea of modern femininity, so it is no surprise that the innermost layers of the knitted or jersey separates at the heart of her collections continue to be body conscious, if not figure hugging. They range in style from skimpy, narrow-shouldered pullovers with recognizable Rykiel detailing, to drop-shouldered tunics, to cardigans both short and boxy, and long and flowing. The detailing itself can be as soft as ruffles and bows, or as hard as nail heads. Although certain themes like cropped wide-leg trousers recur, the skirts and trousers that accompany the sweaters sometimes reflect the fashion of the moment, as in the short skirt worn with a classic Rykiel sweater which was featured by the *New York Times Magazine* in Patricia McColl's Spring 1988 Fashion Preview, subtitled "The Byword Is Short." The sweater is a fine example of another important facet of her work: the dress, sweater, or accessory as bulletin board. As befits the author of four books, Sonia Rykiel began in the 1970s to incorporate words into her art. Across the stomach of a slinky 1977 dress is emblazoned the word "MODE." The next year saw the fronts or backs of sweaters variously inscribed "2," "TOI," "MOI" and "NU," "FÊTE," and "PLAISIR," among others. Nor has English been slighted: "ARTIST," "READY," "TRADITIONS," "BLACK TIE," and "BLACK IS THE BEST" are among the many examples. Not even eveningwear is sacrosanct: a 1983 ensemble with a sheer black lace bodice and black crêpe sleeves and skirt is encircled with a rhinestone studded belt which reads "SPECIAL EDITION EVENING DREAMS." Nonetheless, the most frequent words to appear are "Sonia Rykiel," and simply "Rykiel."

Rykiel was an early exponent of deconstruction. Made of the finest quality wool yarns, sometimes mixed with angora, her knits are frequently designed with reverse seams. She also innovated the use of lockstitched hems. Since the early 1980s Sonia Rykiel has also produced at least two casual lines a year in cotton velours, a fluid, sensual fabric well suited to uncluttered silhouettes. Each season there is at least one dress, in addition to trousers, pullovers, cardigans, and jackets, many of which have reverse seams. They are offered in several solid colors, in stripes and, occasionally, in prints. Like other clothes of illusory simplicity, they have often been unsuccessfully copied.

Another Rykiel specialty is outerwear. Her coats, whether in fine woolens, or in highly coveted fake fur, tend to be voluminous. Along with these and her accessories line, other Rykiel enterprises include children's and menswear lines and perfumes. The entire Rykiel design output is available in the lifestyle boutique on Boulevard Saint Germain which opened in 1990. Sonia Rykiel is a worthy successor to the Chanel tradition: a strong, ultra-feminine, articulate intellectual with a flair for simplicity and self-promotion, who has shown herself capable of both refined innovation and commercial success.

—Arlene C. Cooper

Sonia Rykiel: Spring/Summer 1994. *Photograph by Graziano Ferrari.*

SACHS, Gloria.

American designer

Born: Gloria Harris in Scarsdale, New York, c.1927. **Education:** Graduated in fine arts, Skidmore College, Saratoga Springs, New York, 1947; studied textile design, Cranbrook Academy of Art, Michigan, 1947; studied painting with Fernand Léger, Paris, 1949; studied architecture with Giò Ponti and Franco Albini, Italy. **Family:** Married Irwin Sachs in 1953; children: Nancy, Charles. **Career:** Worked as a model for Balenciaga and Balmain, Paris, 1949; textile designer, Hans Knoll, Herman Miller, 1948-49; apprentice, *Domus* magazine, Milan, 1949-50; executive trainee, assistant buyer, then fashion coordinator, Bloomingdale's department store, New York, 1951-56; pre-teen clothing designer, Gloria Sachs Red Barn company, 1958-60; fashion director for children's wear, Bloomingdale's, 1960-62; pre-teen clothing designer, Saks Fifth Avenue, New York, 1962-65; formed own sportswear company, Gloria Sachs Designs, Ltd, 1970; showed first evening collection, 1983; private label introduced, 1986. Also painter, sculptor, weaver. **Exhibitions:** paintings and sculpture shown at Pratt Institute, Brooklyn, New York, 1949, Art Alliance of Philadelphia, 1950, Art Institute of Chicago, 1950, Museum of Modern Art, New York, 1951. **Awards:** Saks Fifth Avenue Creator Award, 1969; Woolknit Design Award, 1974, 1976. **Address:** 117 East 57th Street, New York, New York 10022, USA.

Publications:

On SACHS:

Books

Milbank, Caroline Rennolds, *New York Fashion: The Evolution of American Style,* New York 1989.

Articles

Green, Wendy, "Gloria Sachs: Designing Her Own Business," in *Women's Wear Daily* (New York), 14 July 1986.

*   *   *

Gloria Sachs's intensive artistic education has played a major part in her fashion work and its development. A fine arts graduate of the Skidmore College, she went on, in 1947, to study textiles at the Cranbrook Academy of Art in Michigan. Her first job was as a textile designer, noted for designing her own yarns in distinctive and individual colour combinations. She used her earnings from this job to finance a cultural year in Europe. She was lucky enough to study painting at the *atelier* of Fernand Léger in Paris and architecture with both Giò Ponti and Franco Albini in Italy, which further developed her sense of colour and proportion.

Returning to New York, she worked in textiles at Bloomingdale's department store, eventually becoming their fashion coordinator. She later joined Saks Fifth Avenue as an in-house designer and her success there gave her the confidence to establish her own business on Seventh Avenue in 1970.

Her first designs established her as a smart, casual separates designer. Her mix-and-match pleated skirts, jackets, and coats, teamed with tailored shirts, were particularly distinctive. A glamorous, sporty evening look was another favourite with buyers. She later made glossy ensembles of colour-blocked sweaters, teamed with uncoordinated skirts and trousers. Alongside other New York designers, including John Antony and Calvin Klein, she pioneered the New York look for casual sportswear shapes in supple and expensive fabrics.

Gloria Sachs is famous for her clever development of textile designs in her fashion. She worked very closely with the mills that produced her fabrics and even opened her own mill in Scotland to produce contrast trim and embroidered cashmere sweaters. She often used classic and antique patterns, developed with her own particular twist. Paisleys and plaids were reworked in unusual colour combinations to be fresh and unexpected, always subtle and never brash. Experimentation with English gentlemen's neck-tie prints allowed Sachs to originate and rescale exciting new patterns and shapes. In turn the fabrics served as inspiration for the creation of new clothing designs.

In her later work in the 1980s Gloria Sachs continued her development of signature, revamped textiles in beautiful fabrics. She also introduced looser, more unstructured clothing. Supple, fluid shapes that were simply cut and well balanced were very flattering to wear and proved extremely popular. She sold her work through many such top retail outlets as Saks Fifth Avenue.

Gloria Sachs's major contribution to fashion is her easy, glamorous sportswear, dressed up for the evening or down for the day. These are clothes for the professional, executive woman who wants to retain her femininity in the boardroom with taste and style. More relaxed than power dressing, it is dressing for success with dash and individuality.

—Kevin Almond

SAINT LAURENT, Yves.

French designer

Born: Yves Henri Donat Mathieu Saint Laurent in Oran, Algeria, 1 August 1936. **Education:** Studied at L'École de la Chambre Syndicale de la Couture, 1954. **Career:** Independent clothing stylist, Paris,

1953-54; designer and partner, 1954-57, chief designer, Dior, Paris, 1957-60; founder, designer, Yves Saint Laurent, Paris, from 1962; Rive Gauche ready-to-wear line introduced, 1966; menswear line introduced, 1974; fragrances: *Y* (1965), *Rive Gauche, Opium, Paris;* firm purchased by Elf-Sanofi SA, 1993. Also film and theatre designer from 1959. **Exhibitions:** *Yves Saint Laurent,* Metropolitan Museum of Art, 1983; *Yves Saint Laurent et le Théâtre,* Musée des Arts de la Mode, Paris, 1986; *Yves Saint Laurent, 28 Ans de Création,* Musée des Arts de la Mode, 1986; retrospective, Art Gallery of New South Wales, Sydney, Australia, 1987. **Awards:** International Wool Secretariat Award, 1954; Neiman Marcus Award, 1958; *Harper's Bazaar* Award, 1966; Council of Fashion Designers of America Award, 1981. **Address:** 5 avenue Marceau, 75116 Paris, France.

Publications:

By SAINT LAURENT:

Books

Yves Saint Laurent, New York and London 1984.
Yves Saint Laurent par Yves Saint Laurent, Paris 1986.

On SAINT LAURENT:

Books

Lynam, Ruth, ed., *Couture: An Illustrated History of the Great Paris Designers and Their Creations,* New York 1972.
Madsen, Axel, *Living for Design: The Yves Saint Laurent Story,* New York 1979.
Milbank, Caroline Rennolds, *Couture: The Great Designers,* New York 1985.
Musée des Arts Décoratifs, *Yves Saint Laurent et le Théâtre* (exhibition catalogue), Paris 1986.
Art Gallery of New South Wales, *Yves Saint Laurent, Retrospectives* (exhibition catalogue), Sydney, New South Wales 1987.
Perschetz, Lois, ed., *W, The Designing Life,* New York 1987.
Yves Saint Laurent: Images of Design (exhibition catalogue), New York 1988.
Howell, Georgina, *Sultans of Style: 30 Years of Fashion and Passion 1960-1990,* London 1990.
Benaïm, Laurence, *Yves St Laurent,* Paris 1993.
Martin, Richard, and Harold Koda, *Orientalism: Visions of the East in Western Dress* (exhibition catalogue), Metropolitan Museum of Art, 1994.

Articles

"YSL Models *Rive Gauche* for Men in His Marrakesh Home," in *Vogue* (London), 1 October 1969.
"Yves Saint Laurent: His Very Special World," in *McCall's* (New York), January 1970.
"Mary Russell Interviews Saint Laurent," in *Vogue* (New York), 1 November 1972.
"Yves Saint Laurent Talks to Bianca Jagger," in *Interview* (New York), January 1973.
Julian, P., "Les années 20 revues dans les années 70 chez Yves Saint Laurent," in *Connaissance des Arts* (Paris), December 1973.
Heilpern, John, and Yves Saint Laurent, "Yves Saint Laurent Lives," in *The Observer Magazine* (London), 5 June 1977.

"Designers of Influence: Yves Saint Laurent, the Great Educator," in *Vogue* (London), June 1978.
"Bravo: 20 Years of Saint Laurent," in *Vogue* (London), April 1982.
"A Salute to Yves Saint Laurent," in the *New York Times Magazine,* 4 December 1983.
Brubach, Holly, "The Truth in Fiction," in *The Atlantic Monthly* (Boston, Massachusetts), May 1984.
Savage, Percy, "Yves Saint Laurent," in *Art and Design* (London), August 1985.
Berge, P., "Yves Saint Laurent der Modezeichner," in *Du* (Zurich), No. 10, 1986.
"Un équilibre définitif: Saint Laurent *Rive Gauche,"* in *Vogue* (Paris), February 1986.
Griggs, Barbara, "All About Yves," in *The Observer* (London), 25 May 1986.
Mauries, Patrick, "Yves," in *Vogue* (Paris), June 1986.
"Le triomphe de Saint Laurent," in *L'Officiel* (Paris), June 1986.
Pringle, Colombe, "Saint Laurent: sanctifié il entre au musée," in *Elle* (Paris), June 1986.
Worthington, Christa, "Saint Laurent: Life as a Legend," in *Women's Wear Daily* (New York), 18 July 1986.
"Yves Only," in *Vogue* (London), September 1987.
"Prince Charmant. Bernard Sanz: L'homme de Saint Laurent," in *Profession Textile* (Paris), 27 May 1988.
"Saint Laurent pour toujours," in *Profession Textile* (Paris), 30 September 1988.
Duras, Marguerite, "Saint Laurent par Duras," in *Elle* (Paris), 31 October 1988.
Hyde, Nina, and Albert Allart, "The Business of Chic," in the *National Geographic* (Washington, D.C.), July 1989.
Howell, Georgina, "The Secrets of Saint Laurent," in *The Sunday Times Magazine* (London), 2 July 1989.
Howell, Georgina, "Best Couturier: Yves Saint Laurent," in *The Sunday Times Magazine* (London), 16 July 1989.
Rafferty, Diane, Charles van Rensselaer and Thomas Cunneen, "The Many Faces of Yves: The Designer of the Half Century," in *Connoisseur,* February 1990.
Menkes, Suzy, "Yves of the Revolution," in the *Sunday Express Magazine* (London), 22 April 1990.
Germain, Stephanie, "All About Yves," in *Paris Passion* (Paris), October 1990.
Roberts, Michael, and André Leon Talley, "Unveiling Saint Laurent," in *Interview* (New York), June 1991.
Smith, Liz, "Thirty Years at Fashion's Cutting Edge," in *The Times* (London), 27 January 1992.
"Yves Saint Laurent, King of Couture," interview, in *Elle* (New York), February 1992.
Brubach, Holly, "Fanfare in a Minor Key," in *The New Yorker,* 24 February 1992.
White, Lesley, "The Saint," in *Vogue* (London), November 1994.
Kramer, Jane, "The Impresario's Last Act, in the *New Yorker* (New York), 21 November 1994.
Schiro, Anne-Marie, "Yves Saint Laurent's Shocking New Color: Black," in the *New York Times* (New York), 22 March 1995.
Menkes, Suzy, "YSL Plays Safe While Valentino Shines at Night," in the *International Herald Tribune* (Paris), 22 March 1995.
"Saint Laurent: A Fitting End," in *Women's Wear Daily* (New York), 22 March 1995.

*   *   *

Yves Saint Laurent: Fall/Winter 1987/88 Haute Couture collection.

A great adaptor, Yves Saint Laurent responds in his designs to history, art, and literature. Vast ranges of themes are incorporated into his work, from the Ballet Russes to the writings of Marcel Proust, who inspired his taffeta gowns of 1971; the paintings of Picasso to the minimalist work of Mondrian and the de Stijl movement, shown in the primary colours of his geometrically blocked wool jersey dresses of 1965.

Saint Laurent has a great love of the theatre. He has designed costumes for many stage productions during his long career and the theatre is an important source of ideas for his couture collections. Flamboyant ensembles, such as the Shakespeare wedding dress of brocade and damask of 1980 and his extravagant series of garments inspired by a romantic vision of Russian dress, reflect his passion for theatrical costume.

Less successful have been his attempts to engage with countercultural movements such as the 1960 collection based on the bohemian Left Bank look. The criticism levelled by the press on being confronted with the avant garde on the couture catwalk led to Saint Laurent's replacement as head designer for Dior, even though his 1958 trapeze line had been an enormous success and he had been fêted as the saviour of Parisian couture. At this time the House of Dior was responsible for nearly 50 per cent of France's fashion exports, so there was a heavy burden of financial responsibility on Saint Laurent's shoulders.

The 1960 collection appropriated the Left Bank style with knitted turtlenecks and black leather jackets, crocodile jackets with mink collars, and—a design which was to crop up again and again in his repertoire—the fur jacket with knitted sleeves. In 1968 Saint Laurent produced a tailored trouser collection reflecting his sympathy with the cause of the student marchers who had brought the streets of Paris to a standstill. The clothes were black and accessorized with headbands and Indian fringes. The use of politics as a decorative device hung uneasily on garments such as the fur duffle coat with gold toggles, giving the designs a paradoxical quality that was later expressed in such collections as the Rich Fantasy Peasant of 1976, which helped in internationalizing a sanitized ethnic look.

Where Saint Laurent sets the standards for world fashion is in his feminizing of the basic shapes of the male wardrobe. Like Chanel before him, he responded to the subtleties of masculine tailoring, seeking to provide a similar sort of style for women, and produced a whole series of elegant day clothes, such as the shirt dress, which became a staple of the sophisticated woman's wardrobe of the 1970s. Saint Laurent is justly acclaimed for his sharply tailored suits with skirts or trousers, le smoking (a simple black suit with satin lapels based on the male tuxedo, which became an alternative to the frothily feminine evening gown), safari jackets, brass buttoned pea jackets, flying suits—in fact many of the chic classics of post-war women's style.

Saint Laurent's designs contain no rigid shaping or over-elaborate cutting but depend on a perfection of line and a masterful understanding of printed textiles and the use of luxurious materials. He works with the silk printers Abraham to produce glowing fabric designs which incorporate a brilliant palette of clashing colours such as hot pink, violet, and sapphire blue. A sharp contrast is produced with his simple, practical daywear and romantic, exotic eveningwear, which is more obviously seductive with its extensive beadwork, embroidery, satin, and sheer fabrics such as silk chiffon.

Less interested in fashion than in style, Saint Laurent is a classicist, designing elegant, tasteful, and sophisticated dress, perfectly hand-crafted in the manner of the old couturiers. He is, however,

prepared to use industrial methods to produce his Rive Gauche ready-to-wear line, created in 1966, and sold in his own franchised chain of boutiques. He acknowledges in ready-to-wear that mechanically produced garments could never achieve the same standards of fit and tailoring so must be designed differently—a realistic approach which accounts for the success of the range.

There has been a radical change in the small company founded by Yves Saint Laurent and his business partner Pierre Bergé in 1961. It has become a massive financial conglomerate with a stock market listing on the Paris Bourse, the result of valuable licensing deals Yves Saint Laurent has negotiated to allow his signature to grace such items as designer perfume. His is a name that has become a symbol of classic design.

—Caroline Cox

SANCHEZ, Fernando.

Spanish designer working in New York

Born: Spain, 1934. **Education:** Studied fashion, École de la Chambre Syndicale de la Couture Parisienne, 1951-53. **Career:** Assistant designer, Maggy Rouff, Paris, 1953-56; designer, Hirsh of Brussels, c.1956-58; designer for Dior boutiques, and Dior lingerie and knitwear licensees, Paris, Germany, Denmark and the United States, 1960s; designer, Revillon, New York and Paris, 1961-73 and 1984-85; established own lingerie firm, New York, 1973; introduced ready-to-wear line, 1980; also designer for *Vanity Fair,* from 1984. **Awards:** Winner, International Wool Secretariat Competition, 1954; Coty American Fashion Critics Award, 1975, 1981; Coty Special Award for Lingerie, 1974, 1977; Council of Fashion Designers of America Award, 1981. **Address:** 5 West 19th Street, New York, New York 10011, USA.

Publications:

On SANCHEZ:

Books

Milbank, Caroline Rennolds, *New York Fashion: The Evolution of American Style,* New York 1989.

Articles

Krenke, Mary, "Frivolous Fernando," in *Women's Wear Daily* (New York), 16 September 1965.
Gross, Michael, "Glamour Guys," in *New York,* 23 May 1988.
McDowell, Colin, "Origin of the Species," in *The Guardian* (London), 18 October 1988.
Urquhart, Rachel, "Minimalism with a Flourish: Spanish Austerity and Oriental Fantasy Merge in Fernando Sanchez's Style," in *Vogue* (New York), January 1989.
Romano-Benner, Norma, "Shaping the '90's," in *Americas,* September/October 1990.
Morris, Bernadine, "A Touch of Lingerie in Outerwear," in the *New York Times,* 28 April 1991.
Koski, Lorna, "The Survivor: Designer Fernando Sanchez Has Seen, Done—Or Outlived—It All," in *W* (New York), July 1994.

*   *   *

Born of a Spanish father and a Flemish mother, Sanchez began his career in high fashion ready-to-wear in Paris after studying at the École de la Chambre Syndicale de la Couture. He started out at the house of Dior, where he produced knitwear, lingerie, and accessories for the prestigious company's chain of boutiques. From there he moved to design assistant at Yves Saint Laurent before starting up his own company in 1974, after a period of working in both New York and Paris. With a name already established for extravagant and exotic fur designs for Revillon, he rapidly built on his reputation through the creation of elegant, easy separates with an ambiguous functionality—they had no obvious place in the formal etiquette of dress. Such clothes as his soft, fluid camisoles with matching pyjama trousers and wrapped jackets or overshirts could be worn just as easily to bed as to dinner at an upmarket restaurant. He was quickly assimilated into the circle of New York fashion designers, which at the time included Halston, Calvin Klein, and Mary McFadden.

Sanchez's experimentation with separates dressing struck a chord amongst affluent American women in the 1970s and seemed to fit the notion of independent femininity which had filtered into fashion imagery and marketing. The ideal of self-reliant womanhood was superficially acknowledged in the whole concept of separates—the idea of putting together garments in one's own individual way, rather than being dictated into sporting a designer look from head to toe. However, Sanchez's separates, like those of other American designers, were always created with an organic whole in mind.

In the 1980s Sanchez was recognized for his use of lace appliqué which appeared extensively on his nightwear, and the fan motif became his trademark as was the bold use of synthetics and vibrant colour. His more contemporary forays into the high fashion ready-to-wear market follow the same lines as his original, understated and elegant look with its basis in the language of lingerie, for which he received a Coty Special Award in 1974 and 1977. The whole concept of underwear as outerwear, so current since the mid-1980s, seems especially suited to Sanchez who has been experimenting within precisely those parameters since the early 1970s, although in a less obvious fashion than Jean-Paul Gaultier or Dolce e Gabbana. His latest designs are sleek, flirty slip dresses for the same sort of fashionably wealthy woman who, like her counterpart in the 1970s, does not want to stand out from the crowd.

—Caroline Cox

SANDER, Jil.

German designer

Born: Heidemarie Jiline Sander in Wesselburen, Germany, 1943. **Education:** Graduated from Krefeld School of Textiles, near Düsseldorf, 1963; foreign exchange student, University of Los Angeles, 1963-64. **Career:** Fashion journalist, *McCall's,* Los Angeles, and for *Constanze* and *Petra* magazines, Hamburg (Director of Promotions for the latter), 1964-68; free-lance clothing designer, 1968-73; opened first Jil Sander boutique, Hamburg, 1968; founded Jil Sander Moden, Hamburg, 1969; showed first women's collection, 1973; founded Jil Sander GmbH, 1978; introduced fragrance and cosmetics line, 1979; Jil Sander furs introduced, 1982; leather and eyewear collections introduced, 1984; Jil Sander GmbH converted to public corporation, Jil Sander AG, 1989; opened Paris

boutique, 1993; showed first menswear collection, 1993. Perfumes include *Woman Pure, Woman II, Woman III, Man Pure, Man II, Man III,* and *Man IV.* **Awards:** Fil d'Or Award, 1980, 1981, 1982, 1983, 1984, 1985; City of Munich Fashion Award, 1983; Vif-Journal Silberne Eule, 1983; Fédération Française du Prêt à Porter Feminin Award, 1985; Aguja de Oro Award, Madrid, 1986; Forum Preis, 1989. **Address:** Osterfeldstrasse 32-34, 2000 Hamburg 54, Germany.

Publications:

On SANDER:

Articles

Mayer, Margit J., "Soft und Sander," in *Deutsch Vogue* (Munich), January 1990.
Gomez, Edward, "Less Is More Luxurious," in *Time* (New York), 25 June 1990.
Drier, Melissa, "Jil Sander," in *Mirabella* (New York), June 1991.
Mayer, Margit J., "Jil Sander: Ganz Privat," in *Marie Claire* (German), August 1991.
Mayer, Margit J., "A Walk with Jil Sander," in *W* (New York), 30 September-7 October 1991.
Livingston, David, "A Vision of Strength: Jil Sander," in *The Globe and Mail* (Toronto), 2 January 1992.
Miller, Annetta, "The Selling of Jil Sander," in *Newsweek* (New York), 16 November 1992.
Schaenen, Eve, "Minimalist No More," in *Harper's Bazaar* (New York), March 1993.
Rubenstein, Hal, "The Glorious Haunting of Jil Sander," in *Interview* (New York), September 1993.
La Ferla, Ruth, "Pure Style: Jil Sander Talks About Clothes with Soul, Fashion with Morals and Stars with Taste," in *Elle* (New York), February 1994.
Bellafante, Ginia, "Lessons in Lessness," in the *Time* (New York), 7 November 1994.
Spindler, Amy M., "Luminous Design from Jil Sander," in the *New York Times* (New York), 8 March 1995.
"Jil Sander: Coming on Strong," in *Women's Wear Daily* (New York), 8 March 1995.
Ozzard, Janet, "Jil Power," in *Women's Wear Daily,* 17 May 1995.

*   *   *

Jil Sander has often been described as the Queen of German fashion, but her style and ambitions are international. Her company headquarters are in the north German city of Hamburg, but her clothes are manufactured in Milan, were she showed for almost a decade before changing her venue to Paris. A self-made success story, Sander designs for independent, intelligent women around the world. She produces fragrances for both men and women, and since 1993, she has also produced a men's line.

Sander has a strong, modern sensibility, and her style may be described as luxurious minimalism, on the edge of forward. There are no frills or fads in Sander's world. Everything irrelevant is eliminated. Like Giorgio Armani, she is one of the fashion world's most austere purists, a creator of designs that are so clean they seem stripped down to the bone. Yet it is not entirely accurate to describe her clothes as classic, because this would imply that they are static, and Sander has never repeated a best-selling design from the previous season's collection.

"I find 'timeless' classic terribly boring," Sander told German *Vogue* (January 1990). "A classic is an excuse, because one is too lazy to confront the spirit of the time." Her own style of classicism always has a modern edge, and the woman who wears Sander's clothes "knows perfectly well what is 'in' this season, and has consciously reduced [it] to suit herself." Sander loves fashion and change, and believes that other women feel the same way. "We don't buy a new coat because we are cold. We buy things that animate, that give us a good feeling."

Sander is one of the most important women designers working in the world today, and she believes that there are definitely differences between the male and female design sensibilities. Male designers, Sander told *Mirabella* (June 1991), tend to "see things more decoratively—more from the outside. I want to know how I feel in my clothes." She tries on all the clothes in her women's collection herself, to ensure that they look and feel exactly right. They have the high quality of the best menswear; they are beautifully tailored, and made from menswear-derived fabrics, often her own luxury fiber blends, such as wool-silk or linen-silk. Yet her palette tends towards pale neutrals, which read as both strong and feminine.

Sander's combination of masculine and feminine design elements results in clothes that feel comfortable and look powerful, but are also sexy in a subtle way. Her version of understated chic is not cheap, however. "If you want quality, it costs," she bluntly told *Mirabella*'s journalist. (Her women's suits range from $1,500 to $6,500.) Think more and buy less, she advised. "People have already consumed too much." But, as journalist Melissa Drier observed, Sander's clothes give women the same confidence that a hand-tailored suit gives a man.

The words "strong" and "powerful" occur frequently in Sander's conversation, revealing something of her own personality, as well as her design aesthetic and her ideal customer. "A powerful women, a woman who knows who she is—I would say that is more interesting than a doll with the most beautiful nose in the world," she told *Marie Claire* (August 1991). Meanwhile, as if to complement the strong modern woman, Sander has called her men's fragrance *Feeling Man*.

Sander has no sympathy for the old-fashioned concept of woman as sex kitten or status symbol. "It is possible to have a very sexy feeling without looking like a sex kitten," she told *W* (30 September-7 October 1991). A woman wearing an austere, brown wool trouser-suit can look and feel sexy, she believes. The typical *alta-moda* woman might not be happy in Sander's clothes, but many women today do want clothes that express a liberated sensibility and a modern sensuality.

What is important, Sander emphasizes, is that fashion should underline the wearer's personality. Her own best model, Sander often appears in her advertisements, looking like what she is: an attractive and intelligent adult.

—Valerie Steele

SARNE, Tanya. See **GHOST.**

SARVEA, Jimmy. See **TRANSPORT.**

SASSOON, David. See **BELLVILLE SASSOON-LORCAN MULLANY.**

SAUL, Joan and Roger. See **MULBERRY.**

SAVINI, Gaetano. See **BRIONI.**

SCAASI, Arnold.
American designer

Born: Arnold Isaacs in Montreal, 8 May 1931. **Education:** Studied fashion design at École Cotnoir Capponi, Montreal, 1953, and at the École de la Chambre Syndicale de la Haute Couture Parisienne, 1954-55; apprenticed one year with Paquin. **Career:** Moved to New York and worked with Charles James, 1951-53; free-lance designer in New York working for Dressmaker Casuals and Lilly Daché, 1955-57; opened own business, 1957; president and designer, Arnold Scaasi, Inc., from 1962; designer, Scaasi couture collections, from 1962; designer, ready-to-wear collections, 1962-63, 1969, and from 1984. Signature fragrance introduced, 1989. **Exhibitions:** Retrospective, 1975, New York State Theater, Lincoln Center, New York. **Awards:** Coty American Fashion Critics Award, 1958; Neiman Marcus Award, 1959; Council of Fashion Designers of America Award, 1987; Pratt Institute Design Award, 1989; Dallas International Apparel Fashion Excellence Award, 1992. **Address:** 681 Fifth Ave., New York, New York 10022-4209, USA.

Publications:

On SCAASI:

Books

Morris, Bernadine, and Barbara Walz, *The Fashion Makers,* New York 1978.
Diamonstein, Barbaralee, *Fashion: The Inside Story,* New York 1985.
Milbank, Caroline Rennolds, *New York Fashion: The Evolution of American Style,* New York 1989.
Daria, Irene, *The Fashion Cycle,* New York, 1990.

Articles

Schwartzbaum, Lisa, "The Dramatist of Elegance," in *Connoisseur* (New York), July 1984.
Reed, Julia, "Little Big Man," in *Vogue* (New York), April 1989.
Milbank, Caroline Rennolds, "Scaasi's New Stars," in *Connoisseur* (New York), June 1989.
Sporkin, Elizabeth, "Scaasi," in *People* (New York), 23 April 1990.

Arnold Scaasi.

Shaeffer, Claire, "American Haute Couture," in *Threads* (Newtown, Connecticut), December/January 1991-92.

Goodman, Wendy, "Palm Beach Story," in *House and Garden* (New York), August 1992.

*

Clothes should be worn to make one feel good, to flatter and as a statement of personality. The overall effect should always be a well-groomed look, not sloppy.

Even if someone is not a great beauty or has some bad features, one should always try to look the best one can—at all times.

This is not a matter of self-indulgence. When you know you look your best, you face the day and the world with great self-assurance.

It's most important that one chooses clothes that work for their lifestyle, both financially and psychologically. Obviously, do not choose a dance dress if you don't go to dances but choose the best fitting trousers if they work into your lifestyle.

I try to design clothes that will flatter the female form. I create clothes that are pretty, usually with an interesting mix of fabrics. I like luxurious fabrics, great quality for day, opulence for evening dresses. I AM DEFINITELY NOT A MINIMALIST DESIGNER! Clothes with some adornment are more interesting to look at and more fun to wear.

I believe that clothes should touch and define the body at least in one spot. Most of my clothes have a defined waist and hipline, with some movement below the hip. Bustlines are always defined and I prefer, and am known for low decolletage—either off-the-shoulder, strapless or simply scooped-out necklines. Sweetheart necklines are also flattering and I use them constantly.

Throughout my career I have dressed many celebrities—Barbra Streisand, Claudette Colbert, Elizabeth Taylor, Dame Margot Fonteyn, Mary Tyler Moore, Joan Sutherland, Aretha Franklin, and Barbara Bush to name a few. I believe it is more graceful to wear a long evening dress for "public" appearances than a short one, especially on stage. Evening pajamas are sometimes interesting and accomplish the same graceful movement.

I prefer using color to black and white though sometimes black and/or white are most dramatic. Shades of red, pink, turquoise, violet and sapphire blue can be more flattering and exciting to look at.

At one point in my career I used an enormous amount of printed fabrics and found them wonderful to work with. However, in recent seasons my eye has changed and the prints seemed to have faded from fashion. Before long, the print craze will probably return as women—and designers—get bored with solid fabrics. In place of prints we are using more embroideries to give texture and life to the fabrics.

Lastly, clothes should be fun with a dash of fantasy. Scaasi creations are the champagne and caviar of the fashion world, as a very prominent Queen once said, "Let them eat cake!" I do hope I won't have my head chopped off for these thoughts!

—Arnold Scaasi

*   *   *

As a young apprentice to Charles James during the early 1950s, Scaasi was imprinted by James's concentration on "building" an evening dress as a sculpture. This early training led Scaasi to construct dresses in the round and to approach design as three-dimen- sional form. The influence of Charles James has been a life-long inspiration for Scaasi. Another stimulus for Scaasi was the richness of the fabrics and furs used during the 1950s, when the prerequisite for women was to be perfectly dressed from head to toe.

Scaasi began rethink his objectives after juggling a career during the late 1950s and early 1960s that included menswear, children's wear, and costume jewelry, in addition to ladies' ready-to-wear and custom designs. He decided to focus strategically on couture dress-making at a time when Paris couture was beginning to suffer. It was 1964 when Scaasi debuted his collection of eveningwear. He was able to take the freedom of the youth-obsessed 1960s and channel the energy into designs that featured keen attention to details and the workmanship of couture dressing.

Scaasi emphasized sequins, fringe, and feathers as trims, substituting new fabrics to create an ostentatious signature style that included mini dresses, trouser suits, and the use of transparency. Barbra Streisand wore a memorable Scaasi creation to the 1969 Academy Awards. His customers are often the celebrated rich and famous—Elizabeth Taylor, Ivana Trump, Blaine Trump, Joan Rivers, Barbara Walters, and many other glamorous clients favor Scaasi.

During the 1970s, styles changed to a more body-conscious, pared-down way of dressing. Scaasi, true to form, turned to dressing women who still loved to be noticed, such as the artist Louise Nevelson. It made sense to Scaasi to continue to create what he was known for and what he loved to do. The basis of his work is a combination of cut, color sensibility, and fabric selections that recall a past elegance yet speak to his clients' most current desires.

The 1980s, the Reagan era, ushered in a renaissance of upscale dressing which was perfect for the Scaasi touch. He dressed First Lady Barbara Bush for the Inaugural Ball and designed her wardrobe for the week of festivities. Never one to concern himself with everyday dressing, Scaasi dresses the urban woman who attends parties, galas, charity balls, and elaborate dinners. His customer is of a certain affluence and has a personality that enables her to wear a Scaasi creation. Often described as lavish, sumptuous, and magical, Scaasi's evening gowns are worn for making a sensational entrance.

—Myra Walker

———

SCHAEFER, Thomas. See **RENÉ LEZARD.**

———

SCHERRER, Jean-Louis.

French designer

Born: Paris c. 1936. **Education:** Studied ballet, Conservatoire de Danse Classique, Paris, and fashion, Chambre Syndicale de la Couture Parisienne. **Career:** Assistant at Christian Dior, 1955-57, and to Saint Laurent at Dior after Dior's death, 1957-59. Left to design for Louis Féraud, 1959-61. Founded Jean Louis Scherrer label, 1962 (left company in 1992); ready-to-wear collection and Scherrer Boutique ready-to-wear lines introduced, 1971; signature fragrance, 1979;

Scherrer 2 perfume, 1986; bath line, 1981; diffusion line, Scherrer City, 1992. **Awards:** Dé d'Or Award, Paris, 1980. **Address:** 51 avenue Montaigne, 75008 Paris, France.

Publications:

On SCHERRER:

Books

Lambert, Eleanor, *World of Fashion: People, Places, Resources,* New York, 1976.
McDowell, Colin, *Directory of 20th Century Fashion,* London 1984.

Articles

Morris, Bernadine, in the *New York Times,* 24 July 1973; 29 January 1974; 29 July 1975; 23 October 1975; 25 January 1977; 26 July 1977; 24 January 1978; 29 January 1980; 2 April 1980; 29 July 1980; 27 January 1981; 9 April 1981; 28 July 1981; 24 January 1984; 24 July 1984; 29 July 1986; 27 January 1987; 28 July 1987; 26 July 1988; 20 March 1991; 25 March 1992.
"In Paris, a Squabble over M. Scherrer's Good Name," in *The Times* (London), 24 June 1969.
"Scherrer: Third Time Round, But No Revolution," in *The Times* (London), 26 January 1971.
"... And Why Haute Couture Is Still Fun," in *The Sunday Times* (London), 28 July 1974.
"Le point sur les collections: Jean-Louis Scherrer," in *L'Officiel* (Paris), March and September 1986.
"Beauty: Daughters with Dash: Laetitia Scherrer," in *Vogue* (New York), September 1988.
Petkanes, Christopher, "Flair à la Scherrer," in *Harper's Bazaar* (New York), December 1988.
"Hearing in Scherrer v. Scherrer Delayed," in *WWD* (New York), 23 March 1994.
"Jean Louis Scherrer SA," in *Daily News Record* (New York), 18 May 1994.

*   *   *

His early training as a dancer exposed Jean-Louis Scherrer to theatrical costumes and prepared him to later design clothes that would suit the public roles of women connected with politics, theatre, and the arts, as well as the more private roles lived by the wives of wealthy Arabs, whose patronage accounted for 30 per cent of the income of the House of Scherrer.

From an early apprenticeship with Christian Dior in Paris, Scherrer learned the basics of cutting and draping, alongside young Yves Saint Laurent. When Saint Laurent inherited the house of Dior, Scherrer successfully started his own haute couture establishment during a period when critics foretold the demise of traditional couture. He quickly became known for designs described as classic, restrained, sophisticated, and sexy but not vulgar. His customers read like a roster of the world's wealthiest women: Mme Anne-Aymone Giscard d'Estaing, wife of the then President of France, as well as his daughter, Valerie-Anne Montassier; Baronness Thyssen; Olympia and Nadine de Rothschild; Queen Noor, the wife of the King of Jordan; Patricia Kennedy Lawford; Isabelle d'Ornano; Ann Getty; Nan Kempner; Françoise Sagan; Michèle Morgan; Raquel Welch; and Sophia Loren.

In the mid-1970s over a hundred American stores, including Bergdorf Goodman in New York, carried Scherrer. Chiffon evening dresses, often accented with sequinned embroideries, have long been a staple. De luxe ready-to-wear was often in the Scherrer Boutique line. These were simpler clothes, more moderately priced than the thousands of dollars of the couture, but still expensive-looking. One such boutique outfit, modeled by Scherrer's daughter Laetitia, featured a leopard print shaped blazer jacket with matching leopard *cloche* hat, worn with a slim black leather skirt.

Scherrer was not a maker of trends, but of refined de luxe versions of trends. When everyone was showing tiered flounced skirts during the 1980s, Scherrer made a restrained version that just grazed the knee and was topped by a long-sleeved, shirt-collared bodice, in luxurious silk. A prime example of Scherrer's hallmark "exotically pampered appearance" was a lavishly embroidered coat in mink-bordered beige cashmere, hooded, reminiscent of Anna Karenina and following in the footsteps of Saint Laurent's revolutionary Russian-inspired looks of the late 1970s. In fact, Scherrer often borrowed exotic details from the East. Chinoiserie and Mongolian-inspired coats and jackets frequently appeared in his collections. At the apex of 1980s opulence in couture, Scherrer indulged in pearl-decorated rajah jackets, tunics, and trousers. In a spirit of Arabian Nights fantasy much like Paul Poiret's, jeweled and feathered turbans completed the ensembles. Other evening looks included beaded taffeta ballgowns or paisley patterned lamé dresses topped with jewel-embroidered jackets. The old-fashioned grand couture hand-worked and hand-embroidered traditions were preserved. Beading was by Lesage.

Even day clothes featured opulent touches: velvet appliqués on wool, or gold piping on trenchcoats. Chiffon and silk were used for dresses and skirts; leathers and furs decorated coats. While hemlines rose during the remainder of the decade, Scherrer continued to show calf-length skirts. For him, surface texture and sumptuous workmanship were more important than innovative lines. The longer, covered-up fashions satisfied his customers' modesty requirements, dictated by Islamic law, while also proclaiming their wealth and status.

Into the 1990s Scherrer continued to employ luxury materials and to explore a variety of trends: long, short, bright colors (a departure from conservative beiges, grays, and white), patchwork prints, plaids, jumpsuits, feminine versions of men's suits and hunting attire. The Scherrer boutique continued to offer sleek, toned down versions of the high fashion items in over a hundred markets in 25 countries. In Europe and Japan men's and women's Jean-Louis Scherrer accessories could be obtained. A bestselling signature perfume launched in 1979 was followed by a spicy floral haute couture perfume, *Scherrer 2,* in 1986.

Despite financial difficulties that resulted in the 1992 firing of Scherrer from the firm he founded, Jean-Louis Scherrer SA plans a menswear collection, Jean-Louis Scherrer Monsieur, for spring/summer, consistent with the designer's high quality image.

—Therese Duzinkiewicz Baker

SCHIAPARELLI, Elsa.

French designer

Born: Rome, 10 September 1890. **Family:** Married Comte William de Wendt de Kerlor in 1914 (separated); daughter: Yvonne ("Gogo").

Career: Lived in New York working as scriptwriter and translator, 1919-22 and 1941-44; immigrated to Paris, 1923. Showed first collection, 1925; house of Schiaparelli operated, 1928-54; London branch opened, 1933, girls debutante department added, 1935; Schiaparelli Paris boutique opened, 1935. Fragrances include *Salut, Soucis,* and *Schiap,* 1934, *Shocking,* 1937, *Sleeping,* 1938, *Snuff* for men, 1939, *Le Roi Soleil,* 1946, *Zut,* 1948, *Succès Fou,* 1953, *Si,* 1957, and *S,* 1961. Also lecturer on fashion, 1940, and volunteer in the USA for French war effort, 1941-43. **Exhibitions:** *Hommage à Elsa Schiaparelli,* Pavillon des Arts, Paris, 1984; *Fashion and Surrealism,* Fashion Institute of Technology, New York, and Victoria and Albert Museum, London, 1987-88. **Awards:** Neiman Marcus Award, 1940. *Died* (in Paris) *14 November 1973.*

Publications:

By SCHIAPARELLI:

Books

Shocking Life, London 1954.

On SCHIAPARELLI:

Books

Flanner, Janet, *An American in Paris,* New York 1940.
Bertin, Celia, *Paris à la Mode: A Voyage of Discovery,* London 1956.
Latour, Anny, *Kings of Fashion,* London 1958.
Hommage à Elsa Schiaparelli (exhibition catalogue), Paris 1984.
Milbank, Caroline Rennolds, *Couture: The Great Designers,* New York 1985.
White, Palmer, *Elsa Schiaparelli,* New York 1986.
Martin, Richard, *Fashion and Surrealism,* New York 1987.
Leese, Elizabeth, *Costume Design in the Movies,* New York 1991.
Steele, Valerie, *Women of Fashion: Twentieth Century Designers,* New York 1991.

Articles

Wilson, Bettina, "Back to Paris with Elsa Schiaparelli," in *Vogue* (London), October 1945.
"Schiaparelli the Shocker," in *Newsweek* (New York), 26 September 1949.
Sheppard, Eugenia, "Schiaparelli's Dim View of Today," in *The Guardian* (London), 11 August 1971.
"Elsa Schiaparelli," obituary in the *New York Times,* 15 November 1973.
"Berry—We Called Her Schiap," in *American Fabrics and Fashions* (New York), No. 100, Spring 1974.
"Schiaparelli sa vie en rose—shocking," in *Elle* (Paris), 6 August 1984.
Moutet, Anne Elizabeth, "A Shocking Affair," in *Elle* (London), October 1986.
McCooey, Meriel, "Strung Along," in *The Sunday Times Magazine* (London), 21 April 1991.

*   *   *

Elsa Schiaparelli considered designing an art rather than a profession, making the unconventional acceptable. Born into a high ranking Italian family, her creativity was influenced by accepting the visually rich and rebelling against her extremely regulatory and proper upbringing. Much of her extravagance was inspired by the proper yet dramatic vestments of the priests and nuns remembered from her youth in Rome, combined with the city's architecture and the magnificent medieval manuscripts and ancient Greco-Roman mythology available to her in the library where her father worked and the family lived. The opulent and fanciful beadwork and embroidery that she later produced in Paris was reminiscent of stained glass windows and had its roots in her youth in Italy. Other influences in her work were Futurists, Fauves, Cubists, New York Dada, the Surrealists of Paris, and Art Déco.

Schiaparelli began designing gowns for herself and friends in 1915, with great help and influence from Paul Poiret. She was an inventor of clothes. Her clothes were immediately considered avant-garde, individualistic, eccentric, yet easy to wear. Sportswear, coordinated beachwear, and matching bags and shoes characterized her early work. Unusual fabrics such as upholstery material and terry cloth for beachwear and zippers on ski ensembles were characteristic.

Schiaparelli was a contemporary of Chanel; they worked during the same period and both started out designing sweaters—these are the only similarities they share. Schiaparelli's initial success came with her *tromp l'oeil* sweater which featured a knitted-in bow at the neckline. So influential were these sweaters that additional designs followed, which included belts, handkerchiefs, and men's ties, all utilizing Armenian knitters' unique method of knitting. The immediate success of these sweaters allowed her to open her shop on the rue de la Paix, the most fashionable street in Paris in 1927. An amazing success, it was estimated that by 1930 her company's income was approximately 120 million francs per year and her workrooms employed more than two thousand people. She introduced good working-class clothes into polite society and understood how snob appeal worked through pricing.

After the Great Depression, fashion was in desperate need of excitement. Schiaparelli was to answer this call. She shocked as well as entertained the public, believing that good taste was less important than creativeness, outrageousness, and fun. It was her belief that women should dare to be different, that by wearing attention-seeking clothes, a woman became chic. Utilizing wit and shock tactics to arm modern women, Schiaparelli believed they would gain equality and independence. The extraordinary and unusual were expected of her. She was the primary couturier to show brightly colored zippers. She used them initially on sportswear, beginning in 1930, and reintroduced them in 1935 on evening dresses. She collaborated with fabric houses to develop unusual novelty prints and unique materials. When Rhodophane, a cellophane material, was invented, she made glass-like tunics. Schiaparelli is known for such fabrics as "anthracite," a coal-like rayon; "treebark," a matte crêpe crinkled in deep folds to look like bark; and fabric that was printed with newsprint.

Her commissions of contemporary artists are famous—they include Christian Bérard, Jean Cocteau, and Salvador Dali. Their collaborations led to such eccentric designs as the lamb-cutlet hat, the brain hat, the shoe hat, and the suit with pockets that simulate a chest of drawers. She also incorporated outrageous, oversized buttons in the shape of peanuts, bumblebees, and rams' heads. The basic silhouettes were often simple and easy-to-wear, but through witty embellishments on a variety of themes such as the military, the zodiac, and the circus, they became unique. Through the study of Tunisian methods of sewing, draping, and veil twisting, Schiaparelli brought to Paris fashion Arab breeches, embroidered shirts, and wrapped turbans in addition to huge pompom-rimmed hats, barbaric belts, jewelry, and the "wedgie"—a two-inch-soled shoe that would be a trend throughout the century.

There was also a more cautious side to Schiaparelli, which appealed to the somewhat more conservative woman. For this woman, her severe suits and plain black dresses were appealing. To her tailored ensembles she added trousers and unconsciously influenced the mix-and-match sportswear concept that was not to be fully recognized for some 40 to 50 years. She showed her trousers suits for every occasion—travel, citywear, evening, and sports. After the acceptance of these slimmer, more slender divided skirts as they were called, she took the next step and shortened them, thus creating the culotte.

Black and the combination of black with white were favorites of Schiaparelli. In 1936 shocking pink, a brilliant pink somewhere between fuchsia and red, was launched. It became the hallmark of the couture house. Schiaparelli's influence can be seen today in the masculine chic looks, the surrealistic accessories, and ornate buttons. She broke down the walls that divide art and fashion and anticipated today's eclectic approach to designing. Elsa Schiaparelli remains an everlasting influence on contemporary fashion.

—Roberta H. Gruber

SCHNURER, Carolyn.

American designer

Born: Carolyn Goldsand in New York City, 5 January 1908. **Education:** Studied at the New York Training School for Teachers; received B.S. from New York University, 1941; studied fashion at the Traphagen School of Design, New York, 1939-40. **Family:** Married Harold Teller (Burt) Schnurer in 1930 (divorced, c. late 1950s); son: Anthony. **Career:** Taught music and art before turning to sportwear design in 1940; clothes originally manufactured by Burt Schnurer Cabana Co., sold only at Best and Co., New York; company renamed for Carolyn Schnurer, 1946; left fashion design, became textile consultant to J.P. Stevens Co., c.1956. **Awards:** New Orleans Fashion Group Award, 1950.

Publications:

On SCHNURER:

Books

Milbank, Caroline Rennolds, *New York Fashion: The Evolution of American Style,* New York 1989.
Steele, Valerie, *Women of Fashion: Twentieth-Century Designers,* New York 1991.

Articles

"Southern Resort Fashions," in *Life* (New York), 14 January 1946.
"Women Designers Set New Fashions," in *Life* (New York), 14 January 1946.
Carlyle, Cora, "Carolyn Schnurer's Flight to Japan," in *American Fabrics* (New York), No. 20, Winter 1951-52.
Carlyle, Cora, "Carolyn Schnurer's African Trip," in *American Fabrics* (New York), No. 24, Winter 1952-53.
"From Natives to Natives," in *Time* (New York), 11 January 1954.
"Carolyn Schnurer," in *Current Biography* (New York), March 1955.

* * *

Carolyn Schnurer was a rather late bloomer in the field of fashion design. After teaching for a time in the state school system, she attended the Traphagen School of Design in New York and began working for her husband's bathing suit company, Burt Schnurer, Inc., in 1940. Her timing was perfect. As one of a handful of American designers whose creativity filled the vacuum left by the war-enforced absence of European fashion, Schnurer capitalized on her Traphagen training in methods of adaptive design. She became so well known for her casual clothes that in 1946 the company name was changed to Carolyn Schnurer, Inc.

Schnurer was a product of a persistent theme in American design between the World Wars: the need for freedom from the dictates of Europe. To that end, fabric and garment designers were encouraged to do original research in museum collections. Schnurer embraced this practice, picking a country on which to base a collection and then examining relevant objects at the Brooklyn Museum or Metropolitan Museum of Art in New York.

She enjoyed an advantage over her predecessors in that as air travel became more common, the countries she studied became readily accessible. In 1944 she made her first trip, to the Andes Mountains, returning with the theme for her Serrano collection, and her first enormous success, the Cholo coat. So strongly did she become associated with the idea of foreign inspiration that it overshadowed the real diversity in her work.

American Fabrics magazine, founded in 1946, was one of Schnurer's biggest boosters. The magazine's editors denounced what they perceived as a fundamental lack—and fear—of originality within most of the North American textile industry. Praise and publicity were lavished upon the few innovators. Each issue included a survey of some textile or decorative arts tradition, to educate and inspire subscribers. Schnurer's methods were in accord with the *American Fabrics* editorial policy, and her trips abroad, together with the designs they inspired, received substantial coverage.

Her career travel included visits to Brittany and Normandy, Ireland, Portugal, Greece, India, Japan, South Africa and the (then) Gold Coast, Turkey, and Norway. Many of these were sponsored by stores such as Peck & Peck or Franklin Simon, with some secondary support coming from textile companies who then produced Schnurer's designs.

She differed from some of her contemporaries in the way she made use of the references she chose for garments. Schnurer preferred to graft an element or two of an ethnic style onto an otherwise Western silhouette. The Japanese-inspired collection, for instance, featured kimono sleeves, padded hems or wide, *obi*-like sashes on conventional full skirted dresses, pagoda-shaped shoulder and hem details on a bathing suit, beach coat, and shorts, and necklines which left the nape bare in virtually every outfit. The African collection of a year later showed cropped jackets with Hausa style embroidery and dress-bodices styled along the lines of tops worn by native women.

However, the African-inspired work depended much more on the fabrics she derived from native sources than on the shapes of native costume. Earlier, Schnurer had originated a wrinkle-resistant cotton tweed as a result of the trip to Ireland. Dan River, Fuller, Bates, Arthur Beir, and Hollander were among the companies she worked with to develop textiles based on the motifs which filled her travel notebooks. A love of texture is apparent in all her fabric choices. Print designs came from Japanese ink paintings, African wood carvings, and Islamic architecture. A knotted-fiber rain cloak from Japan and an African mud cloth were translated into all-over embroidery patterns. Supple fibers such as linen, cotton, cashmere, and alpaca, as well as fabrics with character, including glazed chintz, sueded jersey, or velvet, distinguish her work. Schnurer's most creative fabric designs and developments adapted the look of the original into a form better suited to the American environment and lifestyle.

It is not surprising that when Schnurer left fashion design after her divorce in the late 1950s, she spent some time as a consultant with the J.P. Stevens textile company. Although she had a relatively short career in fashion, Schnurer left a considerable legacy. With others of her generation who gained prominence in the 1940s, she gave credibility to American design, even at the level of "popular" pricing. Her casual wear enhanced the leisure time of the average woman, while the fabrics and styles she introduced opened the minds of both consumers and those in the industry to the variety awaiting them outside the borders of the nation.

—Madelyn Shaw

SCHÖN, Mila.

Yugoslavian designer working in Italy

Born: Maria Carmen Nutrizio Schön in Trau, Dalmatia, Yugoslavia, 1919. Raised in Trieste and Milan, Italy. **Career:** Opened atelier, Milan, 1958; first showed own custom designs, 1965; first boutique for womenswear opened, at No. 2, via Montenapoleone, Milan, 1966; launched Linea Uomo line of menswear, alongside opening of new boutique, Mila Schön Uomo, at No. 6, via Montenapoleone, 1972; Mila Schön 2, second company, set up in 1973 to produce and distribute Alta Moda Pronta, Miss Schön, and Mila Schön Uomo lines; launched perfume, *Mila Schön,* 1978; established Mila Schön Japan, company for distribution of products in Japan; took over running of company in Como, Italy, for the manufacture and distribution of textiles for all Mila Schön lines, 1983; Aqua Schön swimwear collection introduced, 1984; opened first U.S. shop, Beverly Hills, 1986. Also produced shoes, stockings, furnishings, eyewear. Long-standing collaboration with Mantuan goldsmith Loris Abate, who designed jewellery and buttons for Mila Schön collections from 1959; Moved to Florence. **Address:** Via Montenapoleone, Milan.

Publications:

On SCHÖN:

Books

Lambert, Eleanor, *World of Fashion: People, Places, Resources,* New York 1976.

Alfonsi, Maria Vittoria, *Leaders in Fashion: i grandi personaggi della moda,* Bologna 1983.

Soli, Pia, *Il genio antipatico* (exhibition catalogue), Venice 1984.

Articles

Pertile, Marina, "Roma: la primavera di Mila Schön," in *Vogue* (Milan), March 1985.

"Rigorosamente femminile: grande moda a Roma: Mila Schön," in *Vogue* (Milan), September 1986.

"Mila Schön, lo chic," in *Donna* (Milan), July/August 1987.

*   *   *

Mila Schön's interest in high fashion began when she became a personal client of Balenciaga. Her family were wealthy Yugoslav aristocrats who had fled to Italy to escape the communist regime. Living the life of a wealthy Italian demanded an elegant wardrobe and Schön's natural grace and good taste made her an excellent couture client. She must have studied the business thoroughly during her fittings because, when the family fortunes were lost, she turned to the fashion industry in order to make a living.

Business began in 1959 when Schön was 35, with a small atelier in Milan, where Parisian models were basically adapted and copied, combining Balenciaga's austerity of cut with Dior's versatility, plus a hint of Schiaparelli's wit. By the mid-1960s Schön was showing more original work at trade fairs in Florence and Rome, establishing a reputation as a perfectionist who worked within the constraints of a classic design structure. Her tailoring is particularly distinctive, executed with faultless attention to detail and cut in her favourite double-faced wools. The resultant clothes were and are highly sophisticated and sold at the top end of ready-to-wear or in the Mila Schön boutiques in Rome, Florence, and Milan. Small wonder that clients have included wealthy socialites like Jacqueline Kennedy Onassis, her sister Lee Radziwill Ross, and Babe Paley.

Mila Schön describes her company slogan as being "Not how much, but how." This is reflective of her attitude towards high quality and taste. The company decided to translate the DOC (controlled origin denomination), a quality mark used in the wine business, for use on their clothes, denoting the company's attitude towards perfection. Mila Schön is also very selective when it comes to choosing clients in order to retain quality. She trades on what she describes as a "medium circulation basis," so that when any side of her business is seen to make a marked profit, therefore operating beyond its limits, she starts a new company to accommodate it.

There have been several diffusion lines and licensees since the company's inception. In line with the Mila Schön business philosophy, all these products are marketed and sold through separately formed companies. Mila Schön Due is a less expensive ready-to-wear line; Mila Schön Uomo is the men's range. There is also a swimwear range, Aqua Schön, and a sunglasses range, Schön Ottica. Ties, scarves, fabrics, handbags, belts, and the perfume *Mila Schön,* are also produced.

Mila Schön is one of the most respected and established names in Italian fashion. She represents faultless design standards that are classic, flattering, and sometimes highly imaginative, and she ranks alongside Genny, Fendi, and Valentino in clientèle and prestige.

—Kevin Almond

Mila Schön: Fall/Winter 1994/95.

SENNEVILLE, Elisabeth de. See de SENNEVILLE, **Elisabeth.**

SHAMASK, Ronaldus.

Dutch designer working in New York

Born: Amsterdam, 24 November 1945. Raised in Australia. **Education:** Trained as an architect, self-taught in fashion design. **Career:** Window display designer, Melbourne, Australia, 1963-66; fashion illustrator for *The Times* and *The Observer,* London, 1967-68; theatrical designer, Company of Man performance group, Buffalo, New York, 1968-71; free-lance interior and clothing designer, New York, 1971-77; designer, Moss Shamask fashion company, New York, 1978-90; opened Moss on Madison Avenue boutique, New York, 1979, closed, 1986; introduced first menswear collection, 1985; showed new collection under his own name, and formed new company, SUSA (Shamask USA), 1990. **Exhibitions:** *Intimate Architecture: Contemporary Clothing Design,* Massachusetts Institute of Technology, Cambridge, Mass., 1982; *Infra-Apparel,* Metropolitan Museum of Art, New York, 1993. **Awards:** American Fashion Critics Coty Award, 1981; Council of Fashion Designers of America Award, 1987; Confédération Internationale du Lin Fil d'Or Award, 1987, 1989; Woolmark Award, 1989. **Address:** c/o Revlon, 625 Madison Avenue, New York 10022, USA.

Publications:

By SHAMASK:

Articles

"Commentary," in *Details* (New York), April 1989.

On SHAMASK:

Books

Massachusetts Institute of Technology, *Intimate Architecture: Contemporary Clothing Design* (exhibition catalogue), Cambridge, Massachusetts 1982.
Diamonstein, Barbaralee, *Fashion: The Inside Story,* New York 1985.
Milbank, Caroline Rennolds, *New York Fashion: The Evolution of American Style,* New York 1989.

Articles

"Shamask: High Technique," in *Women's Wear Daily* (New York), 3 November 1980.
Duka, John, "New Architects of Fashion," in the *New York Times Magazine,* 16 August 1981.
Shapiro, Harriet, "Ronaldus Shamask's Wearable Architecture," in *People Weekly* (Chicago), 24 August 1981.
Carlsen, Peter, "Ronaldus Shamask," in *Contemporary Designers,* ed. Ann Lee Morgan, Detroit 1984.
Sturdza, Marina, "Ronaldus Shamask," in *Fashion 85* (New York), ed. Emily White, 1984.

Sinclaire, Paul, and Lesley Jane Nonkin, "Designer, Client: The Modern Equation," in *Vogue* (New York), November 1987.
Boehlert, Bart, "Who's That Shamasked Man?," in *New York,* 8 February 1988.
Parola, Robert, "Cultural Influences," in the *Daily News Record* (New York), 3 October 1988.
Parola, Robert, "The Anatomy of Design," in the *Daily News Record* (New York), 17 October 1988.
Schiro, Anne-Marie, "Three US Designers, Less or More in the Mainstream," in the *New York Times,* 4 November 1988.
Chua, Lawrence, "Ronaldus Shamask Enjoying a Sense of Pleasure," in *Women's Wear Daily: Best of New York* (New York), March 1989.
"Designing Men," in *GQ* (New York), July 1989.
Boucher, Vincent, "The Two Mr Shamasks," in *Seven Days* (New York), 7 March 1990.
"The Word to Men: Hang Looser," in *People Weekly* (Chicago), Spring 1990.
Fenichell, Stephen, "The Look of the Nineties: Four Designers Lead the Way," in *Connoisseur* (New York), March 1991.

*   *   *

Peter Carlsen perceived Ronaldus Shamask's design in a most interesting and prophetic way. Carlsen claimed, "Shamask dresses an élite—the largely self-appointed élite comprising the devotees of high style. Certainly, his work is part of a way of life that is bound up with living in Manhattan; his clothes are meant to be worn in lofts, to downtown openings, are meant to signal to other members of what might be called the esthetic establishment their wearers' good standing in its ranks.... What Charles James was to 1940s New York, Shamask was to the late 1970s and early 1980s." (*Contemporary Designers,* Detroit 1984). Shamask creates intellectual/esthetic dress and therefore dresses, perhaps inescapably, intellectuals and esthetically minded individuals.

Recognized initially in a feature article by John Duka in the *New York Times Magazine* (16 August 1981) and subsequently in an exhibition, *Intimate Architecture: Contemporary Clothing Design* at the Massachusetts Institute of Technology in May-June 1982, Shamask was *wunderkind* of the architectural rubric. But people do not wear buildings. Nor is Shamask's design genuinely analogous to architecture. Rather, he is an immensely idiosyncratic and adventuresome designer with a sensibility for minimalism, a cant to the East, and a depth of conviction about fashion that often makes his work seem more utopian than commercially viable. And he denies the classification of architecture with every inventive fold and has enough folds and tucks to be a perfect master of origami creasing and gathering. He dispenses with the non-essential as a rigorous architect might, but he also enjoys the body as only the most Vitruvian builder would; and he mingles international traditions and possibilities with the inventiveness of a Lafcadio Hearn.

Shamask seeks a purity in fashion that others would not even warrant: his pursuit can seem too severe to some and austerely perfect to others. Anne-Marie Schiro wrote (*New York Times,* 4 November 1988), "At a time when many American designers are sticking to the classics, Mr. Shamask went a different route, showing styles that most women do not already have in their closets. Of course, they are not clothes for most women but for those with a flair for fashion and a desire to look different." His design is deliberate, but its visual rewards can be equally deliberate as well.

His fall 1981 two-piece coat with a visible spiraling seam may be more sophisticated in construction than most wearers or viewers would wish to know, though others such as Balenciaga and Geoffrey Beene have similarly designed to the utmost chastity of form. His 1979 linen ensemble literally unbuttons pockets down their sides to become part of the fold of the garment. In such gestures, Shamask stands in synthesis of two traditions: reductivism and the complications of details that constitute many multi-layered, multivalent cultures of clothing. His Japanese-inspired *hakima* trousers were featured in the "Japonisme" exhibition of the Kyoto Costume Institute at the Kyoto National Museum in 1994; his sensibility is shaped by Japanese esthetics. Shamask participates in a rarefied international culture that recognizes fashion as an art and seeks its participation with dance, theater, architecture, and all visual arts. He creates fashion worthy of such a status.

In the 1990s, Shamask has devoted himself to menswear where his talent for the building of clothing has been shown to advantage. Ruth Gilbert in *New York Magazine* (24 February 1992) acclaimed his tailored clothing "perfect fits." Earlier, Shamask had told *Esquire* (September 1987) "men are less interested in applied decoration than in the logical engineering of clothes."

Even in menswear, it may always be that Shamask has ardent admirers and a circle of devoted wearers without having vast commercial impact. His may not be an easily likable esthetic, but it definitely is a high art of dress, one highly informed by intelligence.

—Richard Martin

SHILLING, David.

British milliner and designer

Born: London, 27 June 1956. **Education:** St Paul's School, Hammersmith, London. **Career:** Underwriter, Lloyd's of London, 1973-75; established millinery business, 1974; own shop for couture hats established, from 1976; women's ready-to-wear collection introduced, 1984; other lines include menswear collection, 1986-89, and hand-painted ties, 1988-90. Also: fashion correspondent, Radio London, 1982-86; Senior Consultant on Design and Product Adaptation, United Nations, from 1990. **Exhibitions:** *David Shilling—The Hats,* toured the United Kingdom, 1981-84; Edinburgh College of Art, 1982; *David Shilling, A Decade of Design,* Chester Museum, England, 1991; exhibition of paintings, Richard Demarco Gallery, Edinburgh, 1991. **Awards:** President for Life of Valdivia, Ecuador. **Address:** 5 Homer Street, London W1H 1HN, England.

Publications:

By SHILLING:

Books

Thinking Rich, London 1986.

On SHILLING:

Books

Hickey, Ted, and Elizabeth McCrumb, *David Shilling: The Hats* (exhibition catalogue), Belfast 1981.

Polan, Brenda, ed., *The Fashion Year,* London 1983.
Ginsburg, Madeleine, *The Hat,* Hauppauge, New York 1990.
McDowell, Colin, *Hats: Status, Style, Glamour,* London 1992.

Articles

Neustatter, Angela, "Cheeky Chapeaux," in *The Guardian* (London), 15 March 1978.
Glynn, Prudence, "A Sense of Occasion," in *The Times* (London), 16 March 1978.
"The Shilling Hat Man," in *The Observer,* 30 April 1978.
Cleave, Maureen, "Over 21," in *Woman's Day,* June 1979.
"Simply Shilling, My Dear," in *Woman's Day,* 23 July 1979.
Clemeneigh, Mirella, "Capelli in mostra," in *Casa Vogue,* December 1980.
McKay, Peter, "Man with a Head for Hats," in *Woman's Journal* (London), December 1980.
Heron, Marianne, "Shilling, The Man Who Makes Headlines," in *Irish Independent,* Summer 1981.
Blume, Mary, "David Shilling, Wild Hatter of Ascot," in *International Herald Tribune* (Neuilly, France), 5 June 1982.
Webster, Valerie, "A Shilling's Worth of Extravagance," in *The Scotsman,* 15 February 1984.
Mercer, Tim, "A Room of My Own: David Shilling," in *The Observer Magazine* (London), 18 March 1984.
Benchy, Maeve, "Not Like the Ones He Used to Make for His Mother," in *The Irish Times,* 15 May 1984.
"Hats Off to Shilling," in *World of Interiors* (London), August 1984.
Hillier, Bevis, "David Shilling Hat Trick," in the *Los Angeles Times,* 13 October 1985.
"Haute Hats," in *Cosmopolitan* (London), November 1986.
"Who Needs Money to Be a Millionaire," in *The Sunday Express,* 2 November 1986.
"A Head for Hats," in *Woman's Journal* (London), February 1987.
Weber, Bruce, "The Milliner's Tale," in the *New York Times Magazine,* 24 April 1988.
"David Shilling, Hatmaker to the Rich and Famous," in *Hello* (London), 22 April 1989.
"A Hat Man's Day at the Races," *Herald-Sun,* 9 September 1990.
Smith, Liz, "David Shilling," in *The Times* (London), 6 February 1991.
Kuandika, Giyil, "David Shilling," in *Business Times* (Dar-Es-Salaam), May 1991.
Owens, Susan, "The Item to Top It All Off," in *Sydney Morning Herald,* 25 August 1992.
Gibbs, Warren, "The Mad Hatter," in *New Idea,* 24 October 1992.
Cawthorne, Zelda, "Hats That Are Ahead of the Rest," in *South China Morning Post,* 28 November 1992.
Bunoan, Vladamir S., "Hats Off to David," in *Philippine Business World,* 2 February 1993.
Gusman, Susan A., "Hats Off," in *Philippine Daily Enquirer,* 14 February 1993.

*

I have chosen to communicate not in words but in shapes and tones. In the catalogue to the 1981 Ulster Museum exhibition of my hats, I was quoted as saying that the work should speak for itself, that words about it are superfluous. I still believe this is true. If I thought I could express in words any meaningful essays or insights

David Shilling.

into my work, I might be able to save myself all the hard work that goes into creating whatever it may be that I am creating in all its glorious colour and form.

The passion has always been there. As a child I knew what I wanted to be. I redesigned my room constantly but I didn't earn a penny from my designing until I sold soft toys to my local toyshop at 13. From then on I was hooked on fashion.

I am very motivated by the challenges of my work, whether in art or design, and I always want to do better than before. I challenge myself; I love what I'm doing, and I guess if I find that much pleasure in it, so will my clients. I knew that my work would change over the years. What I had not expected was that enormous changes would occur at the heart of fashion itself. When I first started, you thought of fashion as clothes. Now, in every consumer purchase there is an element of fashion.

Success has not been an end in itself but the key to other things. Although I received no formal art education, it has enabled me to work in all sorts of areas, from interior design to working with the United Nations in developing countries.

I particularly enjoy innovation, but novelty alone is never enough. One of the keys of successful designing is getting your timing right. When I started designing hats commercially, I never dreamed they would have the global and continuing influence they have, but I knew I was on the right track. I knew that women should enjoy again the pure indulgence of wearing hats. What I didn't foresee were the generations of young people who would imitate my success. Luckily, I still love making hats.

The deeper messages of my work I express in my paintings, examining conflicts and relationships. The message when I design is simply that to be alive is a gift, so every day should be a celebration.

—David Shilling

*   *   *

David Shilling's interest in millinery was first inspired by a visit to his mother's hatmaker at the age of 12. He resolved to design a hat for his mother to wear to that year's Royal Ascot. Mrs. Gertrude Shilling, who was already noted for her eccentric and flamboyant taste in occasion dressing, caused a stir. The press adored her and have since made her annual appearance at Ascot into a national institution. "Once my mother had got into the papers, she was determined to be in each subsequent year," David later recalled. In order to gratify his mother's determination David was faced with the task of creating gimmick after gimmick, a process that led him to establish his own millinery business in 1974.

In contrast to his extravagant creations, David Shilling has a vulnerable and sensitive approach to his work. This attitude led him to anonymously send his first collection of millinery to the London department stores Liberty and Fortnum and Mason. He opened his first shop in Marylebone High Street, London, where everything was designed and made on the premises. Noted for always looking in on his shop to see the results of his efforts and to advise anyone unaccustomed to wearing hats, he has the eye for detail and design flair that ensures many of his devoted clients return each season.

Actress Susan George declared, "I only wear hats if it is a hat occasion, otherwise I tend to feel rather self-conscious." She was so overwhelmed by her choice of a David Shilling wide-brimmed, veiled hat for Ascot that her self-consciousness quickly gave way to en-

thusiasm. As David Shilling himself acknowledged, "I love women to look beautiful and could never let a woman walk out of my shop wearing a hat that I didn't think suited her."

In contrast, another customer, journalist and painter Molly Parkin, admits to being a hat fetishist. "I wear hats all the time, even in bed," she said, "in fact I can't do anything without a hat on." Shilling saw this as an ideal creative opportunity to encourage Parkin's idea that her hair is an accessory to his hats.

Shilling works with a variety of fabrics and trimmings in his creations: black lacquered straw hats filled with plastic apples and cherries, lacquered feathers, felting, antique velvets, silk veiling, tulle, and artificial flowers. His basic design philosophy is simple. He wants to flatter a customer, believing that a hat needs to be thought about equally from initial design to finishing touch.

When he began his company, David Shilling wanted to change the image people had of the English hat. "They've always been so boring," he declared. In many ways he created a niche in the British millinery market for fantasy, fashion hats that were witty yet stylish. He was the forerunner to milliners like Stephen Jones and Philip Treacy who have paved a path in the public's imagination for the chic tongue-in-cheek escapism of the hat.

"I'm the best hatmaker there is," Shilling once declared, but added modestly, "I don't know whether it is a good thing or not."

—Kevin Almond

———

SIMON, Fabrice. See **FABRICE.**

———

SIMONETTA.
Italian designer

Born: Duchess Simonetta Colonna di Cesaro in Rome, 10 April 1922. **Family:** Married Count Galaezzo Visconti in 1944 (divorced); daughter: Verde; married Alberto Fabiani in 1953 (divorced); son: Bardo. **Career:** Design studio opened, Rome, 1946-62 and 1965; partner, designer, Simonetta et Fabiani, Paris, 1962-65; *Incanto* fragrance introduced, 1955; traveled in India, in the 1960s and 1970s, establishing a colony for the care of lepers and a craft training program, 1973-76. **Address:** 8 via Cadore, 41012 Caroi (MO), Italy.

Publications:

On SIMONETTA:

Books

Lambert, Eleanor, *World of Fashion: People, Places, Resources,* New York and London 1976.
Steele, Valerie, *Women of Fashion: Twentieth Century Designers,* New York 1991.
Vergani, Guido, *The Sala Bianca: The Birth of Italian Fashion,* Milan 1992.

Articles

Sheppard, Eugenina, article in *New York Herald Tribune,* 14 November 1951.
"Simonetta," in *Current Biography* (New York), December 1955.
"Bonjour Paris, Addio Rome," in *Women's Wear Daily* (New York), 3 April 1962.
Forti, Anna Gloria, "La Lady dell'alta moda: Simonetta," in *Vogue* (Milan), December 1991 supplement.

                                    *   *   *

Eugenia Sheppard (*New York Herald Tribune,* 14 November 1951) called Simonetta the "youngest, liveliest member of the up and coming Italian Couture," commending the breadth of her collection from a two-part playsuit with cummerbund and bloomer shorts to a silk shantung dress-suit with tiered collar to her short and long eveningwear. By 1951, with ardent advocacy from American *Vogue* and Bergdorf Goodman, Simonetta was one of the best-known names in America for the new Italian post-war fashion.

Simonetta had presented her first collection in Rome in 1946. An aristocrat, she had been interned by the Mussolini government for anti-Fascist activities; the further pluckiness of starting up her couture business so immediately after the war was a sign of Simonetta's dauntless determination. A press release for her 1946 collection read in part: "To understand how difficult it was to open a *maison de couture* and have a show with 14 models just after the liberation of Rome by the Allies, one must remember the general situation at that time. Materials and trimmings were very scarce. The most surprising and common materials had to be used to make the extraordinary collection—dish cloths, gardeners' aprons, butlers' uniforms, strings and ribbons, and everything that could be found on the market." It was a humble beginning for an aristocrat dreaming of a high style.

The glamor of a politically-correct aristocrat improvising an Italian post-war renaissance was of hypnotic charm to the American market. Moreover, Simonetta's youthful style held a special appeal, especially in buoyant silk cocktail dresses and her elegant débutante dresses and ball gowns of the 1950s, with their emphasis on the bust. Equally popular were the daywear, sportswear, and coats, with coats in particular providing a favored inspiration for Seventh Avenue copying. She could rival Balenciaga in coats and suits of robust materials, cut with precision and minimal detailing to draw attention to one salient feature. Like Balenciaga, she favored cape-like sleeve treatments that gave the coats a dramatic sense of volume, especially in photographs. Further, she shared with Balenciaga a preference for the seven-eighths sleeve in coats, allowing for the display of gloves and jewelry. For the American market, these popular attributes constituted an idea of ease and mobility, but they also lent themselves to facile imitation and copying. In 1962, when Simonetta and her husband Alberto Fabiani moved to Paris and established Simonetta et Fabiani, the enterprise was less successful.

Her distinguished international clientèle included Audrey Hepburn, Clare Booth Luce, Eleanor Lambert, Lauren Bacall, and Jacqueline Kennedy Onassis. As Aurora Fiorentini Capitani and Stefania Ricci observed in *The Sala Bianca,* "the collections by Simonetta were invariably met with success, in terms of the public and in terms of sales, because they translated the image of a naturally chic woman, with essential lines, elevated by one simple feature, a knot or a raised neck, and corresponded in every way to the personality of the Roman designer" (Milan 1992). Simonetta was often photographed in her clothing and served in some ways as her own best model. She lived the life Americans dreamed of as portrayed in such movies as *Roman Holiday.* If Simonetta was the ideal model for her clothing in the 1940s and 1950s, exemplifying practicality and young elegance, she later epitomized another cultural transformation as she forsook fashion to devote herself to philanthropy and spirituality, working with lepers in India in the 1970s and 1980s. In the 1990s, she returned to Rome, interested in reviewing and collecting her fashion work for a museum.

Simonetta's life seems to have been, more than most, culturally keyed. If it was in any way a destiny granted with privilege, it was also a destiny seized. Her fashion recognized the possibility of renewed elegance in post-war Italian and American life as well as the practicality of designing for distinctly modern women.

                                                                —Richard Martin

SIMPSON, Adele.

American fashion designer

Born: Adele Smithline, in New York City, 28 December 1904. **Education:** Studied dressmaking at Pratt Institute of Design, Brooklyn, New York, 1921-22. **Family:** Married textile manufacturer Wesley William Simpson, 1930 (deceased); children: Jeffrey and Joan. **Career:** Assistant designer, 1922, then head dress designer, 1923-26, Ben Gershel's ready-to-wear fashion house, New York; chief designer, William Bass, New York, 1927-28; designer of Adele Simpson fashions, at Mary Lee Fashions, New York, 1929-49; president and director of Adele Simpson Inc. (bought out Mary Lee Fashions), New York, beginning in 1949. Member of the New York Couture Group; treasurer and board member, Fashion Group, New York; co-founder and board member, Fashion Designers of America. **Collections:** Brooklyn Museum, New York; Metropolitan Museum of Art, New York; Dallas Public Library, Texas. **Awards:** Neiman-Marcus Award, 1946; Coty American Fashion Critics Winnie Award, New York, 1947. **Address:** 530 Seventh Avenue, New York, New York 10018, USA.

Publications:

On SIMPSON:

Books

Celebrity Register, New York 1963.
Moritz, Charles, ed., *Current Biography Yearbook 1970,* New York 1970.
Watkins, Josephine Ellis, *Fairchild's Who's Who in Fashion,* New York 1975.
Babbitt, Marcy, *Living Christian Science: Fourteen Lives,* Englewood Cliffs, New Jersey 1975.
Walz, Barbra, and Morris, Bernadine, *The Fashion Makers,* New York 1978.
Stegemeyer, Anne, *Who's Who in Fashion,* New York 1980.
Houck, Catherine, *The Fashion Encyclopedia,* New York 1982.

O'Hara, Georgina, *The Encyclopaedia of Fashion,* New York 1986.

Stegemeyer, Anne, *Who's Who in Fashion, 2nd. ed.,* New York 1988.

Calasibetta, Charlotte Mankey, *Fairchild's Dictionary of Fashion, 2nd, ed.,* New York 1988.

Milbank, Caroline Rennolds, *New York Fashion: The Evolution of American Style,* New York 1989.

Articles

"First Lady Selects Spring Wardrobe," in the *New York Times,* 25 March 1966.

"Mrs. Johnson to Wear Slim Tunic for Easter," in the *New York Times,* 9 April 1966.

Morris, Bernadine, "Mrs. Nixon's One Midiskirt: She Bought It 'Just For Fun,'" in the *New York Times,* 14 March 1970.

Morris, Bernadine, "Beene's Surprise: Not Only Elegance, But Humor As Well," in the *New York Times,* 1 November 1973.

Morris, Bernadine, "Cheerful Designs for Winter Sun," in the *New York Times,* 27 August 1975.

Morris, Bernadine, "Joyful Fashions with a Folkloric Flavor," in the *New York Times,* 6 November 1976.

Bancou, Marielle, "Adele Simpson," in *American Fabrics and Fashions* (New York), Fall 1978.

Morris, Bernadine, "Designers Softly Changing the Way Women Will Dress," in the *New York Times,* 23 April 1977.

Morris, Bernadine, "Fashion: Serious About Summer," in the *New York Times,* 18 January 1978.

Anster, Linda, "Simsoniana on Display," in the *New York Times,* 15 November 1978.

Morris, Bernadine, "For Resort Wear: Trousers Are Shorter and Waistlines Easier," in the *New York Times,* 19 August 1978.

Morris, Bernadine, "Long Reach of the Reagan Style," in the *New York Times,* 24 February 1981.

Morris, Bernadine, "4 Designers Present Easy-to-Wear Clothes," in the *New York Times,* 29 October 1982.

Morris, Bernadine, "7th Ave. Winners: Coat Dresses, Suits," in the *New York Times,* 1 March 1983.

Morris, Bernadine, "Short Gowns Shine for Night," in the *New York Times,* 17 May 1983.

Morris, Bernadine, "Klein's Spring Look: Fluid and Flattering," in the *New York Times,* 7 November 1984.

Morris, Bernadine, "Perry Ellis Returns to Sportswear Look," in the *New York Times,* 6 November 1985.

*　　*　　*

The longevity of Adele Simpson's fashion business might be attributed to her acute awareness of the needs of her clientele: busy women who were frequently in the public eye and travel quite a bit, and who required practical, well-made clothes to please not only them, but also their husbands and their observers. Avant garde or bizarre fashions would not do for these women. Simpson consistently offered conservative, yet pretty and feminine versions of current trends. The garments were made of ordinary fabrics such as cotton—Simpson was the first American designer to treat cotton seriously as a fashion fabric—or sumptuous fabrics inspired by the textiles she saw and collected on her frequent world travels. Her inspiration might have come from close to home as well, as in her adaptation of a New York City public school child's drawing of a cityscape at dusk, which Simpson interpreted in a silk dress and jacket ensemble that was later displayed at the Fashion Institute of Technology.

From the beginning of her career, Simpson dedicated herself to what she described as "realistic" fashion. During a time when women's dresses were developing a radically simpler silhouette, Simpson went even further and devised clothing that could be stepped into rather than pulled over the head. She concentrated on creating dresses and coats, blouses and suits, or dress and jacket combinations, all of which could coordinate and allow the wearer to be well dressed from daytime into the evening with a minimum of effort. An ingenious design consisted of a woolen cape and skirt teamed with a luxurious brocade blouse, and a separate underskirt made of the brocaded blouse material. When the cape and outerskirt were removed for evening, the resulting costume would be an elegant two-piece dinner dress. Politicians' wives with busy itineraries and traveling schedules, and international performers such as Dame Margot Fonteyn, appreciated the practicality of Simpson's clothes, as well as their quality and artistic merits. As if to compensate for the basic conservatism of the styles, Simpson would render them in unusual, often sensuous fabrics.

Credited with "taking cotton out of the kitchen" during the 1940s, Simpson proved the fiber's suitability for street dresses and full-skirted evening gowns. Although known for her pretty prints in delicate colors, Simpson often used black for spring or summer, and made unusual pairings of fabrics, such as velvet over gingham. Silhouettes would generally be modified versions of prevailing shapes. There would usually be a defined waist and gentle overall curvaceousness that proved flattering to her somewhat more mature customers. Even the Simpson version of the chemise in the 1950s came with an adjustable tie belt.

Simpson often looked to the East for exotic touches to her designs. In the early 1960s, one collection featured day and evening clothes for summer that were made of linen and silk embroidered with Turkish patterns or printed in Byzantine mosaic motifs. Simpson also employed authentic Indian cotton sari fabrics, some embroidered in gold, for a dress collection that was exhibited at the New York World's Fair. Japanese silk prints would also be elegant and feminine sources of inspiration.

Drawing from the collection of foreign costumes she amassed during world travels, Simpson might conceive a fabric design from a single decoration, color scheme, or detail to create fashion that she would then display next to the original native piece. A printed evening gown might be inspired by a delicately embroidered Chinese jacket, or a vested outfit by a South American gaucho costume. Clothes such as these would appeal to clients who traveled, or merely wished to enliven their wardrobes with a touch of the exotic.

Adele Simpson, Inc. has long been one of the most successful manufacturers of women's better ready-to-wear. Prices of the designs ranged from about $100 in the 1940s, through $200 for a dress or suit in the 1960s, and from $400 to $1,000 in the 1980s, although a simple "ladylike dinner dress" could be had for $325. In 1990 Gump's catalogue (San Francisco, California) offered two versions of such "little black dresses" for around $400 each. First ladies Mrs. Eisenhower, Mrs. Johnson, Mrs. Nixon, and Mrs. Carter included Simpson designs in their public and private wardrobes. When Mrs. Johnson selected a Simpson sand beige coat and black silk dress ensemble to wear on Easter Sunday, the item made the news. Mrs. Nixon wore Simpson designs to Russia, China, and Africa, and one of the second Inaugural balls.

While for years the designer favored only pure silk, wool, and cotton in their many variations, she later did admit the merits of synthetic fibers. Simpson always made a point of asking women about their needs and desires in clothing; she credited her belief in Christian Science for setting the standard for beauty and excellence in her work.

After Adele Simpson donated her vast collection of artifacts, costumes, and fashion magazines to the Fashion Institute of Technology in 1978, she continued to oversee the designing, but Donald Hobson became the official designer for the company. His work maintained the Simpson aesthetic, but evolved into even softer, more fluid and youthful lines.

—Therese Duzinkiewicz Baker

SITBON, Martine.

French designer

Born: c.1952. Raised in Casablanca and Paris. **Education:** Graduated in fashion design from the Studio Bercot, Paris, 1974. **Career:** Fashion consultant, then free-lance designer, 1974-84; signature ready-to-wear collection debuted in Paris, 1984; also ready-to-wear designer, Chloé in Paris, from 1987. **Address:** 6 rue de Braque, 75003 Paris, France.

Publications:

On SITBON:

Books

Steele, Valerie, *Women of Fashion: Twentieth Century Designers,* New York 1991.

Articles

Webb, Ian R., "Martine Sitbon," in *Blitz* (London), April 1986.
"Chloé Unveils New Design Team with Martine Sitbon," in *Women's Wear Daily* (New York), 14 May 1987.
Maiberger, Elise, "Sitbon Pretty," in *The Face* (London), June 1988.
Voight, Rebecca, "Martine Sitbon: France's Best Kept Fashion Secret," in *i-D* (London), March 1989.
Gross, Michael, "Paris Originals: Chloé in the Afternoon," in *New York,* 15 May 1989.

*   *   *

Although her early collections bore fairy-tale titles like Cinderella, it is rock music, especially of the 1970s, that is Sitbon's strongest inspiration. Her sculptural suiting, often based on masculine lines, underpins each season's looks but leathers, studs, and swirling sequins are always present, emphasizing both her affinity with the music scene and her skilled use of luxury fabrics.

This manipulation of delicate textiles, mixing soft pastel and metallic shades as artistically as fruitier colours, is seen in both her own name line and the work she produced to breathe life back into the Chloé label from the mid-1980s to the early 1990s. Her use of fine organzas, left to flow and ruffle in petal-like folds at the cuff and collars of blouses, is a recurring element in her work. This reached its apex in the cascading frills that flowed down the back of blouses dotted with overblown silk flowers in her spring/summer 1992 collection. This delicate

femininity was tempered by the cool shine of slim satin trousers, abbreviated skirts, and elongated jackets.

The freedom to use these sensuous fabrics comes from her strong Italian financial backing, enabling her to experiment with expensive 1970s decorative favourites like sequins and embroidery. In 1989 she punctuated cropped leather waistcoats with gold studs, manipulating Hell's Angel motifs to achieve more luxurious results. The idea was developed further in olive suede waistcoats with looped chains that hung down to the bright gold velvet skirts with which they were teamed, demonstrating the subtle use of colour and shade that pervades her work.

More recently, her rock music preoccupations have come into their own, in tune with current retrospective trends that have given an edge to her signature use of flares and bell bottoms. Over the past decade she has shown them in everything from intricate pink and charcoal cut velvet to dazzling gold sequins. In her spring/summer 1993 collection, her look became more attenuated. Slate grey hipster flares were worn with thigh-skimming jackets, severely cut away and held together by black thongs bound across the body, a look which has been very influential. This collection contrasted bondage motifs with fluid chocolate-brown satin and organza skirts, and raised her already impressive profile in Europe, linking as it does with the main elements of current deconstructed styles that put proportions off balance and dress down luxury textiles with rougher detailing and accessories.

Sitbon's work is always carefully accessorized, recently with perspex-heeled platform sandals with black straps criss-crossing up the leg and stringy leather or satin chokers. This attention to detail also inspires the trimmings she uses. For Chloé in 1991 she placed a fluffy hem of marabou on bell-shaped skirted dresses, with neat bustier tops and white lacy crystal-dotted braid attached down the full length of the front. They presented a futuristic image that is a recurring undercurrent. This is often represented in her own line by stretch fit leggings, tops and jackets in soft leather, stitched in circles and stripes, which emphasize the wearer's physique and give a starkly post-modern feel. This sculptural form continues in her suits, tailored to accentuate the shape of the body. This was seen in the soft Prince of Wales trouser suits in 1987 that exploited the cut of men's suits and, more severely, in fitted black jackets and mini skirts defined by white borders and flap pocket edges in 1990. Along with the simple raw silk trousers and supple blouses, they provide a classic foil to her more dandyish designs for Chloé and the more fantastic elements of her main line.

This ability to design strong daywear items as well as more luxurious garments has provided Sitbon with a wide customer base in Europe. The current prominence of her pared-down 1970s-influenced designs should bring her to the attention of the American market where she is less well known. Her skilful manipulation of fabrics and mixing of very contemporary themes makes her an important force in fashion, with a successful record of collections on which to build.

—Rebecca Arnold

SITBON, Sophie.

French designer

Born: Paris, 29 June 1961. **Education:** Attended the Lycée Victor Hugo, Paris; followed a one-year course in screen-writing, Paris,

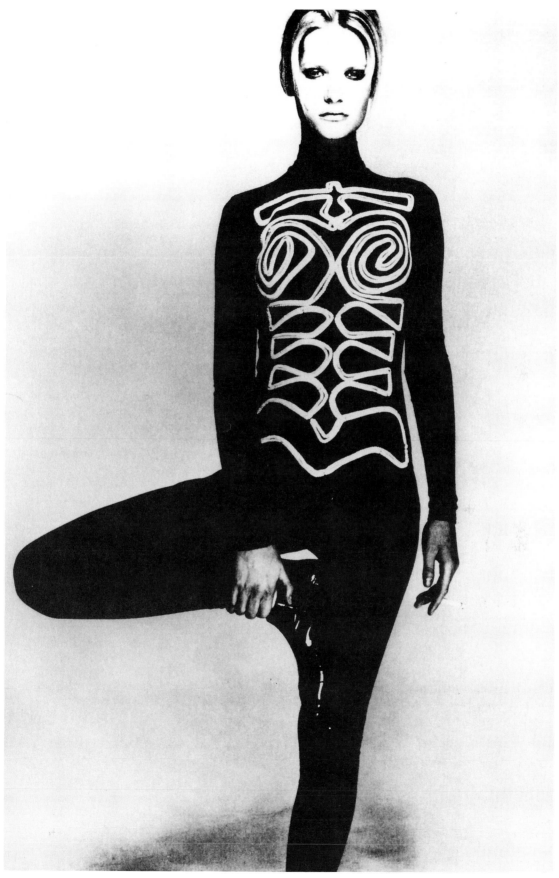

Martine Sitbon: Summer 1990. *Photograph by Nick Knight.*

Sophie Sitbon.

1980; studied fashion design, 1981-83, Paris. **Career:** Launched own fashion line, Sophie Sitbon, 1985. **Exhibitions:** *Modes gitanes,* Carousel des Sources, 1994. **Address:** Sophie Sitbon Sarl, 4, rue de Braque, 75003 Paris, France.

Publications:

On SITBON:

Books

Modes gitanes, Paris 1994.

Articles

Beurdeley, Laurence, "Tête à tête: Sophie Sitbon, une femme d'absolu," in *L'Officiel* (Paris), n.d.
Véran, Sylvie, "...Et les bonheurs de Sophie," in *Gap* (Paris), February 1986.
"Sophie Sitbon," in *Elle* (Paris), May 1987.
"Stylistes: Sophie Sitbon," in *20ans* (France), September 1989.
"Designers' Inspirations: Sophie Sitbon," in *Joyce* (Hong Kong), Summer 1991.

*   *   *

Fashion, to Sophie Sitbon, is functional. Clothes are not a means of artistic expression but a liaison between proportion and harmony and their sole reason for being is to be worn. Clothes are an individual means of expression for the person who wears them. They send out messages that can describe the complex range of subtleties and distinctions that make up the human persona, a signal to other people about the essence of another person.

Sitbon describes her signature look as being seductive. In contrast to sexiness, seduction is subtle and has the power to attract in many directions. She particularly admires the seductive power of Tennessee Williams's writing and the complex, often subversive repression of his heroines. Her designs reflect this, being always provocative yet never blatant.

Movies and television are another strong influence; Sitbon regards her generation as being more audiovisual than literary. The visual impact of glamorous movie stars and movie star wardrobes often tells a more potent story than the written word. She sees clothes as a visual medium for reinterpreting the excitement and vibrancy of movies in real life.

Sitbon loves the drama of black and red, colours she has adopted as her own, "I love black. I loved it before it became fashionable and I will always love it. Black is perennial," she said in an interview with *Joyce* magazine (Paris). Her clothes are simple yet dramatic, classic yet eccentric: a stark, black shift dress, suspended by spaghetti straps, is punctured by tiny holes that follow the dart positions of a dress block and is teamed with matching opera gloves. Another shift dress has a scalloped neckline and is splashed with an asymmetrical, contrast colour shape reminiscent of a Matisse cutout. Always energetic in her approach, Sitbon creates designs that are whimsical yet vital and impudent without being aggressive.

A graduate of the Esmode School of Fashion in Paris, in her final year she was awarded a Gold Medal by a jury of designers including Jean Paul Gaultier and Thierry Mugler at the International Style Competition in Osaka, Japan. She produced her own collection in 1985, financed by a Japanese group and manufactured from a showroom in the Marais district of Paris, aiming to provide a simple, high quality couture look for modern women at affordable prices. Seven years later she declared herself happy with her design success, although her admiration for movie heroines has left her with one unfulfilled ambition—to direct her own movie.

Today Sitbon creates clothes for an independent, self-confident woman who is what she is, rather than what she wears. Her clothes are a proposition rather than an imposed ideal. Her customer interprets Sitbon clothes to create her own independent look. "I prefer people to see someone in my designs and say 'doesn't she look wonderful,' not 'she's wearing Sophie Sitbon,'" the designer declared.

—Kevin Almond

SMITH, Graham.

British milliner

Born: Bexley, Kent, 19 January 1938. **Education:** Studied at Bromley College of Art, 1956-57, and the Royal College of Art, London, 1958-59. **Career:** Worked for Lanvin, Paris, 1958-59; milliner, Michael of Carlos Place, London, 1960-67; own firm established, 1967-81, and from 1991; consultant design director, Kangol Limited, 1981-91. **Address:** 22 Crawford Street, London W1H 1PJ, England.

Publications:

On SMITH:

Books

McDowell, Colin, *Hats: Status, Style, Glamour,* London 1992.

Graham Smith: For Kangol, Spring/Summer 1995; multicolored flowered hat.

Articles

"Haute Hats," in *Cosmopolitan* (London), November 1986.
Rowe, Gillian, "Heads He Wins," in *You* magazine of the *Mail on Sunday* (London), 6 November 1988.

*   *   *

Graham Smith is a milliner's milliner; one examines his hats and finds outstanding craftmanship. These featherweight pieces appear untouched by human hand; no irregularities mar the sheen of the fine straw crowns, and snow-white felts remain pristine after the rigorous hand-blocking which sets them irrevocably into shape. Invisibly-stitched brims and seemingly effortless draping belie hours of painstaking handwork for which there is no substitute if one requires the genuine article.

Nor does Smith's work exhibit technical mastery alone: to walk into his new Crawford Street, London, showroom is to be amazed and amused by the combination of colour, texture, and shape, and by the witty inventiveness of the trims. Smith's shows during the decade of his design directorship of Kangol were stunning parades of the milliner's art and a gift to fashion editors, whether the chosen theme followed a traditional floral path, swooped up into outer space or dived to the bed of a tropical ocean. The staid Kangol beret suddenly emerged as a hot fashion item, whether studded, particoloured or trimmed whimsically with buttons.

Smith left London's Royal College of Art early to work in Paris with Lanvin. After returning to work with Michael, the English couture house, he ran his own business off Bond Street, which soon attracted a distinguished clientèle. Royalty and media stars wear his hats: every leading London store carries them. He has worked with many leading designers, amongst them Zandra Rhodes and Jean Muir, and has often designed for the screen—notably for *Help, The Ruling Class, Goodbye Mr Chips,* and *Casino Royale.* His hats literally travel the world, adorning the heads of British Airways flight attendants. His work is represented in the permanent collection at the Victoria and Albert Museum, and has been photographed for the Pirelli calendar by Norman Parkinson.

To use an inelegant term for an elegant man, Smith might be termed a workaholic; given the time, one could well imagine that he would prefer to do all his own work. Of this he would certainly be more than capable, and he is an exacting master—which does not deter his loyal staff, some of whom have worked with him for more than two decades. His wit and entertaining teaching style endeared him to many fashion students during his time as millinery tutor on the degree course at Kingston Polytechnic.

Graham Smith has thrived on design talent and technical excellence, running a successful business through years when hats were far from obligatory as high fashion accessories. Now that hats are again as important as the clothes they accompany, Smith's faithful clients may continue to wear his hats in the knowledge that they are simply of the highest possible quality; and to reach these heights there are no short cuts.

—Alan J. Flux

SMITH, Paul.

British designer

Born: 1946. **Education:** Attended Beeston Fields Grammar School, Nottingham. **Career:** Opened first menswear shop, Nottingham, 1970; London shop opened, 1979; New York City shop opened, 1987; flagship Tokyo shop opened, 1991; womenswear collection introduced, 1993. **Awards:** British Design for Industry Award, 1991; named Honorary Fellow, Chartered Society of Designers, 1991; named Commander of the British Empire, for services to fashion industry, January 1994. **Address:** Riverside Building, Riverside Way, Nottingham NG2 1DP, England.

Publications:

On SMITH:

Articles

York, Peter, "The Meaning of Clothes," in *Blueprint* (London), October 1983.
"Harris Tweed, Campaign Sign; Paul Smith," in *Fashion Weekly* (London), 13 June 1985.
"Cue: Paul Smith," in *Vogue* (London), 15 September 1985.
"Face to Face," in *Creative Review* (London), June 1986.
Boehlert, Bart, "Mr Smith Comes to New York," in *New York,* 20 April 1987.
Rumbold, Judy, "The Man of Paul Smith's Dreams," in *The Guardian* (London), 9 November 1987.
Mower, Sarah, "The Gospel According to Paul," in *The Observer Magazine* (London), 29 November 1987.
Schneider-Levy, Barbara, "Paul Smith, Anti-fashionist," in *Footwear News* (London), 14 December 1987.
"After Nottingham, the World for Smith," in *Blueprint* (London), December/January 1987-88.
"Wearing Mr Smith," in *The Economist* (London), 9 January 1988.
Jeal, Nicola, "Smith Said 'Cotton,'" in *The Observer* (London), 21 February 1988.
Hamilton, William L., "The Schoolboy's Revenge," in *Metropolitan Home,* August 1988.
Dutt, Robin, "Paul Smith," in *Clothes Show* (London), July/August 1989.
Emmrich, Stuart, "The Hip Little Shop around the Corner," in *Manhattan, Inc.* (New York), February 1990.
Harris, Martyn, "The Designer Guru Who Suits Himself," in *The Sunday Telegraph* (London), 11 March 1990.
Gandee, Charles, "Mr Smith Goes to Italy," in *House and Garden* (London), April 1990.
Fairchild, Gillian, "A Day in the Life of Paul Smith," in the *New York Sunday Times Magazine,* 9 June 1990.
Jordan, Mary Beth, "I Am a Camera: Designer Paul Smith Shoots his New York," in *Metropolitan Home,* August 1990.
Omelianuk, Scott, "Mr Smith Goes Global," in *Gentlemen's Quarterly* (New York), August 1993.
Morais, Richard C., "We're finally ready...," in *Forbes* (New York), 24 April 1995.

*   *   *

The much-used phrase "classics with a twist" was the original design philosophy behind Paul Smith's menswear collections, where the element of classicism did not frighten traditionally conservative British male dressers. With no formal training in fashion design, Smith's fashion career began with his shop in Nottingham in 1970. Unable to find the type of clothes he wanted, he introduced his own designs for shirts and jackets which he had made up in local workrooms.

Smith attributes his personal success to the fact that his early designs were representative of a classical phase in terms of the company's image. His jackets were traditionally styled but he lowered the armholes to make them easier to wear and subtly changed the shape of the trousers. Using wools, tweeds, and fine cottons, Smith's designs retained just the right element of English tailoring traditions with a hint of eccentricity that appealed not only to conservative City types but the newly-emerged yuppie of the 1980s, for whom a Paul Smith suit became an important status symbol. By gradually introducing changes to the male wardrobe, he says he found that his customers slowly became less nervous about adding a patterned tie or a coloured sweater. Richly patterned or embroidered waistcoats, coloured braces, and decorative socks are also examples of Smith's subtle changes to basic menswear items.

The evolution of the Paul Smith label away from classicism, which began in the early 1980s, was prompted by the proliferation of copyists that sprang up on the heels of his initial success. The Paul Smith style was imitated both in England and abroad by companies like Next, Façonnable, and Henry Cotton's. Smith admits that his decision to become a more fashion-oriented label resulted in confusion about the company's image. Although the classic phase of the label has now given way to a higher fashion emphasis, the designer says he is often likened to America's Ralph Lauren because of his earlier image. An indication as to the current standing of the Paul Smith label may be seen in Japan, where his clothes are sold alongside those of Italy's Romeo Gigli, France's Jean Paul Gaultier and Japan's Comme des Garçons. The introduction of two diffusion lines, the Sportswear Collection and Jeans collections, opened up a younger market for the Paul Smith label with lower price ranges than the mainline collection.

Smith's own shops are an integral part of his design strategy and form the backdrop for his fashion designs. His was one of the first fashion shops to sell items other than clothes, including watches and pens, modern sculpture, candlesticks, mirrors, and glassware. The selling of a lifestyle was also greatly imitated during the 1980s, when ordinary everyday objects achieved cult status in the right environment. Smith was responsible for the revival of the Filofax and men's boxer shorts during this period.

—Catherine Woram

SMITH, Willi.

American designer

Born: Willi Donnell Smith in Philadelphia, 29 February 1948. **Education:** Studied fashion illustration, Philadelphia Museum College of Art, 1962-65; studied fashion design, Parsons School of Design, New York, 1965-67. **Career:** Worked as fashion illustrator with designers Arnold Scaasi and Bobbi Brooks, New York, 1965-69; free-lance designer, working in New York, for Digits Inc., sportswear company, Talbott, Bobbie Brooks, 1967-76; with Laurie Mallet established company, WilliWear, Ltd, 1976; added WilliWear men's collection, 1978; first store opened posthumously, Paris, 1987. Also: designed for McCall's, Kroll Associates, Bedford Stuyvesant Workshop, etc. Lecturer, art history, Fashion Institute, London. **Awards:** International Mannequins Designer of the Year Award, New York, 1978; Coty American Fashion Critics Award, 1983; 23 February named Willi Smith Day in New York City, 1988. *Died* (in New York City) *17 April 1987.*

Publications:

On SMITH:

Books

Lambert, Eleanor, *World of Fashion,* New York 1976.
Alexander, Lois K., *Blacks in the History of Fashion,* New York 1982.
Milbank, Caroline Rennolds, *New York Fashion: The Evolution of American Style,* New York 1989.

Articles

Rogers, Susan, "Willi Smith, a Man with Missions," in *Amsterdam News,* 16 June 1979.
"Willi Smith: noir et blanc et en coton," in *Elle* (Paris), September 1984.
"Da New York: Off Off Fashion," in *L'Uomo Vogue* (Milan), March 1985.
"Talents: WilliWear," in *Depêche Mode* (Paris), January 1987.
Filmer, Denny, "Just William," in *Fashion Weekly* (London), 12 February 1987.
Horwell, Veronica, "The Wonder of Willi," in *The Observer* (London), 8 March 1987.
James, George, "Willi Smith, Clothes Designer, Creator of Vivid Sportswear," in the *New York Times,* 19 April 1987.
Rittersporn, Liz, "Designer Willi Smith Dead," in the *New York Daily News,* 19 April 1987.
"Willi Smith," [obituary] in *The Daily Telegraph* (London), 22 April 1987.
O'Dwyer, Thom, "Willi Smith Is Dead," in *Fashion Weekly* (London), 23 April 1987.
Als, Hilton, "Willi Smith, 1948-87," *Village Voice* (New York), 28 April 1987.
Parikh, Anoop, "The Man Who Had Attitude," [obituary] in *The Guardian* (London), 30 April 1987.
Lebow, Joan, "WilliWear without Willi: His Partner, Petite, French and Tough, Looks Ahead," in *Crain's New York Business,* 4 May 1987.
"For Willi, 1948-1987," [obituary] in *Essence* (New York), July 1987.
"Designer Collection: Garments by Willi Smith," in *Elle* (London), October 1987.

Also articles in:

Essence (New York), November 1978.
People (New York), 14 November 1983.
New York Times, 17 November 1984.
Esquire (New York), December 1984.
USA Weekend (New York), 17-19 October 1986.
Washington Post, 30 November 1986.
New York Times, 19 April 1987.
Newsweek (New York), 27 April 1987.
Time (New York), 27 April 1987.

*   *   *

Without respect for race, Willi Smith was one of the most talented designers of his era. With respect to race, he was indisputably, as *New York Daily News* fashion writer Liz Rittersporn wrote at his death in 1987, "the most successful black designer in fashion history." Smith chafed at the attention given to the anomaly of his being a black designer, yet he acknowledged some advantages in sensibility in being an African-American: "Being Black has a lot to do with my being a good designer. My eye will go quicker to what a pimp is wearing than to someone in a gray suit and tie. Most of these designers who have to run to Paris for color and fabric combinations should go to church on Sunday in Harlem. It's all right there." It was all right there for Smith as a quintessentially American designer, of the people and for the people, with a vivid sense of style democracy and eclectic mix.

Perhaps in part due to his Indian cottons and colors, perhaps to his inexhaustible appeal to youth, perhaps just due to his own wit and sense of loose fit, Smith excelled in clothing for summer; his winter collections were especially notable for oversized coats based on classic shapes. Was it wit, racial marginalization, or happy style foolishness that made a WilliWear coat so capacious, its lapels just a little too great, and its time-honored style just hit the edge of loopy?

His WilliWear News for fall 1986 proclaimed with irony his intention to get "serious" with the fall collection. In a sense, Smith never was serious, preferring instead a lively incongruity and surprising mix that he learned from observation and that he refined in affordable clothing made in India. WilliWear, the company he founded with Laurie Mallet in 1976, went from $30,000 in sales in its first year to $25 million in 1986. His soft, baggy looks did not require sophisticated tailoring and benefitted from the Indian textiles that he chose for their supple hand, easy care and comfortable aging, and indescribably indefinite colors. Smith's slouchy softness was a "real people" look, marketed at modest costs with great impact in the 1980s as the informality of designer jeans and other casual wear was replaced by the kind of alternative that Smith's design offered: a drapey silhouette for comfortable clothing with style. While primarily a designer of women's clothing, WilliWear was also influential in men's clothing. In July 1983, he created the clothes for Edwin Schlossberg on his marriage to Caroline Kennedy: Smith designed blue-violet linen blazers to be worn with white slacks and white buck shoes for the groom's party; the groom wore a navy linen double-breasted suit with a silver linen tie, outfits that were both traditional and slightly spoofy and outrageous enough to notice and enjoy.

George James in an obituary in the *New York Times* quotes Smith: "I don't design clothes for the Queen, but for the people who wave at her as she goes by." In Smith's designs there was no equivocation: sportswear was for fun and comfort. He knew this, having first worked for Arnold Scaasi in a rarefied world of fancy dress. Later, he worked for Bobbie Brooks and Digits, among others, but it was on his own, first in a business with his sister Toukie, and later in WilliWear, that Smith found his own voice designing what he affably called "street couture" without apology. Smith created uniforms for the workers on Christo's Pont Neuf, Paris wrapping in 1985. In fact, Smith's work arguably anticipates much that has become casual style in America in the late 1980s and 1990s through The Gap and A/X—loose, slouchy oversizing and mixable possibilities. Hilton Als eulogized Smith in the *Village Voice,* "As both designer and person, Willi embodied all that was the brightest, best, and most youthful in spirit in his field.... That a WilliWear garment was simple to care for italicized the designer's democratic urge: to clothe people as simply, beautifully, and inexpensively as possible" (28 April 1987). In a tragically short life terminated by an AIDS-related death at 39, Smith made little issue or complaint of the social disadvantage and difficulty of being an African-American committed to making a mass-market clothing business—he simply proceeded to make an exemplary life of innovative design that both earned him the Coty Award in 1983 and countless fans of his sportswear style who may never have known—or cared—whether he was Black, White, or any other color.

—Richard Martin

SPOOK, Per.

Norwegian fashion designer

Born: Oslo, Norway, 1939. **Education:** Studied at School of Fine Arts, Oslo, and École de la Chambre Syndicale, Paris. **Career:** Arrived in Paris, 1957, and joined house of Dior soon afterwards. Worked as free-lancer with Yves Saint Laurent and Louis Féraud. Opened own house, 1977. Produces haute couture and ready-to-wear. **Awards:** Golden Needle (Chambre Syndicale, Paris), 1978; Golden Thimble, 1979. **Address:** 6 rue François 1er, 615008 Paris, France.

Publications:

On SPOOK:

Books

McDowell, Colin, *McDowell's Directory of Twentieth Century Fashion,* Englewood Cliffs, New Jersey, 1985.
O'Hara, Georgina, *The Encyclopaedia of Fashion,* New York 1986.

Articles

Greene, Elaine, and Bent Reg, "Coming Home to Norway," in *House Beautiful,* May 1988.
"Paris: C'est tout!," in *Women's Wear Daily* (New York), 22 July 1993.
Ramey, Joanna, "Backer Pulls the Plug on Per Spook Couture," in *Women's Wear Daily* (New York), 27 June 1994.

*   *   *

Per Spook came to Paris in the late 1950s after graduating from the Oslo School of Fine Arts. For him Paris had been a lifelong ambition, the place to go for anyone wanting to work in the fashion industry. After studying at L'École de la Chambre Syndicale de la Couture in Paris, he embarked on a long career as an apprentice and free-lance designer. Experience with revered houses like Yves Saint Laurent, Christian Dior, and Louis Féraud gave him a taste for the haute couture and specialized fashion that created a sensation when he opened his own house at the age of 38 in 1977.

Per Spook clothes were instantly applauded for their new, soft shapes and colour. He established a hallmark for well-cut clothes that were elegantly understated but upheld the characteristics of quality, individuality, and wearability. Distinctive innovations have been his versatile long dresses that include a device that allows them to be taken up for daywear then let down again for an evening look; his Ile de Wight dress, a square-cut white linen dress embroidered with abstract black squares; his Crumple clothes made from a sprousefabric that allows the clothes to fold into a small bundle and pack away without creasing. He also likes to design versatile mix-and-match outfits that can unite to create ensembles ranging from glamorous cocktailwear to daywear.

When it comes to ready-to-wear, the ideal Per Spook customer is a woman who is both realistic and practical. She is active, up to date and, with her international lifestyle and career, needs clothes that are graceful and polished, but also witty and lively. With his couture clothes Per Spook likes to combine his own creativity with the individual personality of a client. He recognizes that each client has a different set of needs and fantasies about how they want to look. Even if designer and client have opposing ideas, it is always possible to create a united design.

Per Spook collections are often fanciful and evoke romantic images of society lifestyles in the 1920s and 1930s. The clothes have a strong resort feel, suggesting leisured times at Deauville or on the Lido at Venice. Figure prints on expensive crêpes and asymmetric details on cross-over crêpe mini dresses have been popular, as have saucy nautical stripes, abstract polka dots and geometrics, like black and white checkerboard jackets or long sequin shift dresses in geometric-patterned fabrics. They evoke references to fashion icons of the past, an updated Duchess of Windsor, Marlene Dietrich or the 1950s model Dovima.

Per Spook's other artistic interests are noteworthy and undoubtedly inspirational when it comes to fashion design, and his design interests are not exclusively fashion oriented. He is an accomplished painter, sculptor, and photographer. Interiors, textiles, and product design capture his imagination and are barometers of inspiration and observation that help form and develop his creative fashion ideas.

In his career Per Spook has been recognized with several fashion awards, including the Chambre Syndicale's Golden Needle and Golden Thimble awards. Ultimately it is in couture that Per Spook excels. To a designer, haute couture is often the inventive lifeblood of the industry, where creativity is unhampered by the limitations of expense or market. Per Spook's approach is down to earth. He enjoys creating couture that combines practicality and realism with creativity and aesthetic vision.

—Kevin Almond

SPROUSE, Stephen.

American designer

Born: Ohio, 1953. **Education:** Attended Rhode Island School of Design for three months. **Career:** Worked briefly for Halston and for Bill Blass; showed first collection, 1983; out of business, 1985-87; showed three lines, S, Post Punk Dress for Success and Stephen Sprouse in own shop, 1987; satellite shop opened, Beverly Hills, 1988; out of business, 1988-92; designer, introducing Cyber Punk line, Bloomingdale's, 1992.

Publications:

On SPROUSE:

Books

Milbank, Caroline Rennolds, *New York Fashion: The Evolution of American Style,* New York 1989.

Articles

"Hot Commodities: Rich Returns," in *Harper's Bazaar* (New York), July 1987.

Goodman, Wendy, "Stephen Sprouse Tries a Comeback with a Bold New Store," in *New York,* 21 September 1987.

"Art & Commerce: Stephen Sprouse," in *Interview* (New York), September 1987.

"All Sproused Up: The Return of Stephen Sprouse," in *i-D* (London), November 1987.

Martin, Richard, "Vicious Icon: Hero and History in the Art of Stephen Sprouse," in *Arts Magazine,* December 1987.

Fressola, Peter, "Glitzy Sprouse," in the *Daily News Record* (New York), 19 April 1988.

Cihlar, Kimberly, "The Many Sides of Stephen Sprouse," in the *Daily News Record* (New York), 12 August 1988.

Young, Lucie, "Corporate Greed: A Fashionable Vice," in *Design* (London), August 1988.

Lender, Heidi, "The Return of Stephen: The Seventies Are Back and So Is Stephen Sprouse," in *Women's Wear Daily* (New York), 30 October 1992.

Norwich, William, "Back to the Future," in *Vogue,* December 1992.

Yarritu, David, and Mariuccia Casadio, "Quick! There's a Sprouse in the House," in *Interview* (New York), December 1992.

Spindler, Amy M., "Rock-and-Roll's Designer-Curator," in the *New York Times,* 9 May 1995.

*   *   *

A much lauded figure on the New York fashion scene in the early 1980s, Stephen Sprouse must be one of the most notorious success-failure stories in the American fashion business. One of a number of designers with their roots in the rural backwaters of Indiana, Sprouse shares his origins with Norman Norell, Bill Blass, and Halston, for whom he worked briefly in the early 1970s. Reputedly already displaying a precocious talent by the age of 12 when he designed leopard-print jumpsuits, Sprouse went on to study for a mere three months at the Rhode Island School of Design before hitting the New York scene as a rock photographer.

In the late 1970s, Sprouse made his name by designing stage clothes for Debbie Harry of the pop group Blondie, having met her in the kitchen of the flats they were sharing in New York's Bowery. His designs included ripped T-shirts, minis, and leotards, paving the way for the first of his collections in 1983.

Sprouse's clothes display a nostalgia for the New York underground of the 1960s, particularly Andy Warhol and the Factory aesthetic, and he almost designs with Edie Sedgewick or Ultra Violet in mind. Revisionist rather than retro, the garments are a witty caricature of the wildest excesses of 1960s fashion, harking back to the days of Betsey Johnson at Paraphernalia, yet tempered by Sprouse's New Wave sensibilities.

Sprouse uses synthetic fabrics, neon hues, and striking graphic prints to give his basic shapes visual appeal, contrasting day-glo colours with black jersey separates such as T-shirts and minis. Press attention has focused primarily on his use of sequins shown on jackets, thigh high boots, and his signature single shoulder strap dresses worn with matching bra tops.

The influence of André Courrèges and Rudi Gernreich is obvious in his use of cutout panels revealing parts of the female torso such as the waist or midriff, or in his redefinition of that staple of the

1960s male wardrobe, the Nehru jacket, coloured hot punk pink by Sprouse in 1985.

Acknowledging the clichés of youthful rebellion, Sprouse toys with items of subcultural style which through overuse in popular imagery have become mainstream. A prime example of this approach is the motorcycle jacket which Sprouse experiments with endlessly, covering it with sequins, 1960s iconography, or pseudo-slang. His use of logos, which seem to be making reference to some magical teenage argot, bemused audiences in 1988 when the meaningless phrase Glab Flack was emblazoned over clothes shown on the catwalk.

Arguably his best work, as worn and publicized extensively by the rock singer Debbie Harry, was the collection in 1983 on which Sprouse collaborated with the celebrated New York graffiti artist Keith Haring to produce day-glo prints of hand-painted scribbles, imagery lifted straight from the subway walls. Matching outfits of miniskirts and tights or shirts and flares for men made the wearer look as if he or she had been caught full force in the fire of a spray can.

Sprouse's designs are strictly club clothes, street fashion at couture prices as a result of the expensive fabrics, applied decoration and handfinishing applied to every garment. He is one of a rare breed of American designers using post-war American history as his source, rather than deferring to European influence and as such should be recognized as an original.

—Caroline Cox

STAVROPOULOS, George Peter.

Greek designer

Born: Tripolis, Greece, 20 January 1920. **Family:** Married Nancy Angelakos, 1960; son: Peter. **Career:** Couturier, Athens, 1949-61; New York couture and ready-to-wear business opened, 1961. *Died* (in New York), *10 December 1990.*

Publications:

On STAVROPOULOS:

Books

Milbank, Caroline Rennolds, *New York Fashion: The Evolution of American Style,* New York 1989.

Articles

"George Peter Stavropoulos," *Current Biography* (New York), March 1985.
Milbank, Caroline Rennolds, and Peter Vitale, "George Stavropoulos: A Master of Classical Line in Manhattan," *Architectural Digest,* September 1989.
"George Stavropoulos Dies; Known for Classic Designs," in *Women's Wear Daily* (New York), 12 December 1990.
"George Peter Stavropoulos," obituary in *Current Biography* (New York), February 1991.

*   *   *

Throughout his career, George Stavropoulos maintained a relatively low, but highly respected profile in the fashion world. He was one of a small number of designers in America who exclusively produced ready-to-wear clothes of the quality and caliber of Parisian haute couture. Stavropoulos presented two ready-to-wear collections, produced in his own *atelier,* each year for 30 years and never ventured into lower priced lines, licensed products, or perfumes, as did many of his contemporaries. Nor did he venture into the further reaches of avant-garde design. While many of his designs were innovative and strikingly beautiful, they were never shocking or arresting and his design innovations were subtle to the degree that they were apparent only to the wearer or noticed either upon close inspection, or when the wearer moved about.

Since he established his business in New York in 1961, having left his native Greece, chiffon evening dresses of every variety were central to his collections. Signature chiffon looks included single shoulder asymmetrically draped toga styles, inspired by models from classical antiquity, many layered body-skimming styles, and dresses with pleats originating at the neckline or shoulders that could be tied at the waist or left flowing freely away from the body. Recurring details included intricate pleats and tucks, wrap and capelet effects, free floating panels that could be thrown across the shoulders as a scarf or wrapped around the waist as a belt, and other multi-purpose convertible details such as cascading drapery that could also function as a shoulder wrap. Evident in his chiffons and central to Stavropoulos's design philosophy were the ideas of comfort, softness, and ease of movement. In 1961 he remarked: "I don't want clothes to be tight, it's not high fashion. A woman must be able to move around in a dress."

In the early to middle 1960s, contrary to the prevailing tendency toward stiffness and a boxy silhouette, Stavropoulos designed unconstraining kimono sleeved jackets and daytime wool suits cut on the bias that subtly draped over the body. Throughout his career, rather than designing evening coats to go over his gowns he preferred the soft and simple cape to finish off his evening looks, often accessorized with a single long strand of black or white pearls. By the mid-1970s, when the trends had caught up with Stavropoulos and fluid simplicity was the rage, the designer presented the ultimate innovation in soft and simple luxury: a gently flaring tank dress in five layers of bias cut white chiffon with a single seam at the center back. Unlike his contemporary Halston however, who presented similar looks around the same time, cerebral, minimal modernism was not the conceptual basis for his design. Instead Stavropoulos was most interested in exploring the ideas of softness and ease of movement (despite the apparent simplicity of Halston's designs and his pretensions to minimalism, many of his garments were a challenge to wear). Although he was most praised for his creations in chiffon, Stavropoulos was adept at working with other fabrics and had a particular liking for taffeta and satin, pleated, tucked, and manipulated on the bias with the same attention to fine detail that he gave chiffon.

Stavropoulos's style remained unchanged in his three decades in business in New York. Demand for his signature body-skimming layered chiffon evening look was so consistent that he found it a challenge to "make the clothes look different" yet still reflect his point of view that "classical design is forever." His clients appreciated the classic and long lasting investment quality of his garments and they are still wearing his clothes today.

—Alan E. Rosenberg

STECKLING-COEN, Adrienne. See **ADRI.**

STEFANEL SpA.

Italian sportswear manufacturer and retailer

Formed in Treviso, 1959, by Carlo Stefanel (1925-87). **Address:** 85 via Postumia, 31047 Ponte di Piave, Treviso, Italy.

Publications:

On STEFANEL:

Articles

"Knitting Patterns," in *The Economist,* 3 October 1987.
Bannon, Lisa, "Stefanel's Fantasy Trip," in *Women's Wear Daily* (New York), 13 March 1992.

*　*　*

Stefanel is today one of Italy's largest fashion companies, manufacturing young, sporty, wearable separates and knitwear for the young menswear and womenswear market. Sold in over 1,500 shops worldwide, the clothing is synonymous with good design in quality fabrics.

The company began in 1959 as a manufacturer of knitwear in Treviso, Italy. The brainchild of Carlo Stefanel, it quickly established a reputation for lively colour and quality. Carlo's son Giuseppe Stefanel entered the business in the mid-1970s, with exciting plans for expansion into the broader fashion market of casual clothing, sportswear, jeans, and ready-to-wear.

Through franchising, Stefanel has developed a competitive distribution system that has resulted in a steady growth in international markets, particularly in the Far East and Europe. Stefanel's development strategy has supported distribution growth by introducing carefully targeted production policies within the textile and clothing sector, constantly widening the breadth of product ranges.

Knitwear still plays a dominant role in Stefanel collections. For both men's and womenswear the look is unisex, homespun, and traditional. Fair Isles, Jacquards, stripes and checks are incorporated into cosy, easy shapes and restyled into modern, young looks. For evening there are slinky gold, ribbed knits and crochet designs teamed with black drainpipes and silky white blouses for a dressed-up look. Pioneer-style denims, chambray, tartans, and tiny paisley prints are the major woven fabrics used in oversize shirts, waistcoats, casual shirtwaist dresses, simple jackets, and wrap over minis with fringed hems. Caban style jackets in heavy wool coating, teamed with fisherman jerseys, give a nautical feel to the range.

Stefanel boutiques mix high tech with traditional in their interiors. Simple wood floors and furniture are mixed with chrome and glass to create a spacious, modernistic shopping environment. The clothing is merchandised in a logical, easy way with garments arranged in colour coordinated sections that make it simple for the customer to put together an outfit.

The company sees the 1990s as a growth area for the number of Stefanel retail outlets in the UK and Ireland. Seven new boutiques opened in the UK in 1991-92 and in January 1993 the company opened its first Irish concession in Arnots, Dublin. The company was also the first manufacturer of consumer goods to open shops in China's largest cities.

Today the group is similar to a publishing house in having several divisions worldwide, each with its own identity, and networks of sales agents to promote the Stefanel trademark. This industrial and commercial growth led to the listing of Stefanel SpA on the international stockmarket, allowing it to sell shares through most of Europe's important exchanges. Although Carlo Stefanel died in 1987 at the age of 62, Giuseppe Stefanel has continued the company's integral philosophy of continued growth.

—Kevin Almond

STEHLE, Gerd. See **STRENESSE GROUP.**

STEWART, Stevie. See **BODYMAP.**

STOCK, Robert.

American designer

Born: The Bronx, New York, 1946. **Education:** Self-taught in design. **Family:** Married Nancy McTague in 1982. **Career:** Apprentice designer, Paul Ressler Pants, New York, c.1966; owner and designer, Country Britches, New York, 1967-73; design assistant, Chaps by Ralph Lauren, 1973-76; designer, Country Roads by Robert Stock, from 1976; co-owner and designer, Robert Stock Designs Ltd., from 1990; women's line introduced, 1992; children's line introduced, 1993; licenses include men's shirts and ties, from 1991, jeans, outerwear, and leather goods, from 1992. **Awards:** American Fashion Critics Coty Award, 1978.

Publications:

On STOCK:

Articles

"Robert Stock: Quiet on the Fashion Front," in *GQ* (New York), April 1981.
"Robert Stock," in the *Daily News Record* (New York), 12 March 1987.
"Robert Stock Forms Firm," in the *Daily News Record* (New York), 19 June 1990.
"Robert Stock Ltd.," in the *Daily News Record* (New York), 4 August 1993.

*　*　*

As a fashion designer, Robert Stock has achieved a remarkably successful about-turn. His first foray into the fashion industry, after an apprenticeship with a trouser company, was to form Country Britches, a company that produced traditional sportswear—including classic slacks and polo shirts—that would fit into almost any traditional department store. Stock later sold the company and went to work with Ralph Lauren, the master of timeless dressing. He aided in the design and development of Chaps, Lauren's lower-priced men's sportswear division which has since become a division of Warnaco.

Country Roads by Robert Stock, a division of Creighton Industries, was the company for which Stock designed after leaving Ralph Lauren. Appropriately, this line followed the same traditional vein—sportswear to appeal to the conventional middle American male.

In 1990 Stock and a partner formed Robert Stock Designs to manufacture men's knitwear. Soon after, sandwashed silk pieces were added and the company grew swiftly from a firm worth ten million dollars into one valued at 100 million.

Although it would be inaccurate to credit Stock as designer of a line consisting chiefly of plain and print sandwashed silk shirts, he should be credited for recognizing that silk, considered a luxury fabric, could be sourced and manufactured in the Far East at a cheaper price than previously thought. By adding this luxury line, Stock offered consumers value at an affordable price, referred to in the market as "perceived value."

Stock has since expanded this offering of silk luxury to both the womenswear and boyswear market and has reintroduced to the menswear market the leisure suit. Robert Stock's version, however, is almost active wear; a sweat- or warm-up suit is offered not in the usual nylon or Gore-tex, but in sandwashed silk. Such a suit, designed for leisure or sport and manufactured in a fabric that implies style and luxury, seems incongruous, yet consumers are snapping them up.

The success brought by sandwashed silk has enabled Robert Stock to enter into licensing agreements in other areas, including tailored clothing, furnishings, neckwear, jeans, knitwear, and leather and cloth outerwear markets.

As an erstwhile traditional designer, Robert Stock is pushing the limits of traditional men's sportswear by changing the face of the fabrics used. He refers to himself as the "Ford or Chevrolet of designers." With the Asian influence in manufacturing and sourcing, a possibly more accurate description would be the Nissan of designers.

—Lisa Marsh

STOREY, Helen.

British designer

Born: Rome, 16 August 1959. **Education:** Graduated with degree in fashion design, Kingston Polytechnic, 1981. **Family:** Married Ron Brinkers; one son. **Career:** Apprenticed to Valentino and Lancetti, Milan, 1981-83. Own label Amalgamated Talent launched, 1984; partner and designer, Boyd & Storey, London, 1987-89; first catwalk show, London, 1990; designer, Jigsaw stores, 1990; menswear collection introduced, 1991; designer, Knickerbox, and Empire stores, 1991; 2nd Life line of recycled clothes introduced, 1992; opened store in King's Road, London, 1992. **Awards:** with

Karen Boyd, British Apparel Export Award, 1989; Most Innovative Designer of the Year Award, 1990; Young Designer of the Year Award, 1990. **Address:** Coates & Storey Ltd., 57 Kings Road, London SW3 4ND, England.

Publications:

On STOREY:

Articles

Wheeler, Karen, "Five Survivors," in *DR: The Fashion Business* (London), 26 August 1989.
Wolford, Lisa, and Mark Borthwick, "West End's Storey," in *Interview* (New York), December 1989.
Hume, Marion, "Shock Tactics," in *The Sunday Times* (London), 17 December 1989.
Armstrong, Lisa, "Success Storey," in *Vogue* (London), May 1990.
Curtis, Anne-Marie, "Love Storey," in *Sky* (London), June 1990.
Bull, Sandra, "Multi Storey," in *Fashion Weekly* (London), 13 September 1990.
Rowe, Gillian, "Storey Lines," in *Shop in Town,* 14 March 1991.
"Great Expectations," in *Women's Wear Daily* (New York), 13 June 1991.
Chunn, Louise, "Bettering by Design," in *The Guardian* (London), 20 May 1992.
Mulvagh, Jane, "From the Rag Trade to Riches," in *The European* (London), 3-6 December 1992.
Dutt, Lalla, "True Storey," in *City Limits* (London), 21-28 January 1993.
Underhill, William, "The Roaring 90s: America's Resurgent Economy," in *Newsweek* (New York), 22 February 1993.
Schiro, Anne-Marie, "Small Houses: Holding in the 80s, or Back to the 70s," in the *New York Times,* 23 February 1993.
Armstrong, Lisa. "One Girl's Storey," in *Vogue* (London), November 1994.

*   *   *

Helen Storey is one of Britain's most innovative and controversial young designers. She has been described as "the next great British hope," and rationalizes her success in characteristic style: "One of the reasons that I am here and a lot of my contemporaries aren't is because I sit on the knife edge between good and bad taste, fashion and theatre, business and imagination."

Trained at Kingston Polytechnic in Surrey, Storey was encouraged by one of her tutors, Richard Nott (of Workers for Freedom) to apply to Valentino as her work seemed out of step with the fashion course at Kingston. Storey says of her work as a student at that time, "I was designing wildly theatrical outfits—I doubt if they could even be made up, let alone washed. I tried to think Marks and Spencer but it always came out wrong." She stayed with Valentino's design studio for two years and was much struck with the contrast between the experience in Rome and her student training: "Valentino designed 65 collections a year and was treated like a lord. I felt sick that this kind of sky's the limit attitude could never happen at home."

When she returned to London, at the high point of international interest in young British designers in 1984, Storey became one of a group to join forces under the umbrella title of Amalgamated Talent where she showed six highly successful collections. In 1987 Storey opened Boyd & Storey in West Soho, London, together with fellow designer Karen Boyd and Caroline Coates. Two years later Helen Storey and Karen Boyd (who were to go their separate ways within the year) won the British Apparel Export Award in recognition of their outstanding export achievements. By May 1990 the Helen Storey for Jigsaw collection was available in Jigsaw stores throughout Great Britain and in October of the same year Storey was to win the Most Innovative Designer of the Year award with her first solo catwalk show during London Fashion Week.

In 1991 Storey designed her first full menswear collection, which was launched at SEHM, Paris. That same year she was commissioned by the underwear chain Knickerbox to design a range and by Empire stores to endorse and design for their mail order catalogues. In the following year, Showroom Seven was appointed as Storey's American agent, and the fall-winter 1992 collection Dreams and Reality was shown in New York, London, Paris, and Düsseldorf.

Storey is preoccupied with recycling: "Fashion is a wasteful image—full stop! So there's a limit to how much you can fly the eco-flag. As a fashion company my problem is how do I keep selling and respond to environmentalism. We must tackle the problem slowly." In June 1992 Storey introduced a range of recycled clothes under the name 2nd Life, and in the same year she began another significant foray into eco-fashion when she became the first British designer to launch and use the most recent Courtauld's fibre Tencel, the so-called "cashmere of denim," for her October 1992 collection. Tencel is the first new manmade textile fibre in 30 years, and Helen Storey describes it as having extraordinary possibilities. "It can be as floppy as silk but has all the robust characteristics of denim." In 1993, Helen Storey continued her innovatory fibre association and marketing with the use of Tencel, Tactel (ICI), and Acetate Novaceta Ltd.

Storey believes "the fashion industry is really a very funny place for me to be," and attempts to explain her work in the following terms: "Basically, people want to see a bit of the impossible in the clothes because it confirms their own sense of reality. I am an instinctual designer; I see that I am attached to the energy of creation, but it also makes me want to give up sometimes because of the amount of unnecessary items we churn out for the sake of another season."

—Doreen Ehrlich

STRAUSS, Levi. See **LEVI-STRAUSS & CO.**

STRENESSE GROUP.

German fashion house

Founded from family clothing company by Gerd Strehle in Nordlingen, 1968; joined by wife Gabriele Strehle as designer, from 1973; launched Strehle Collection, 1976. **Address:** Eichendorffplatz 3, 8860 Nordlingen, Germany.

Publications:

On STRENESSE:

Articles

Drier, Melissa, "Strenesse: Making Marks with Minimalism," in *Women's Wear Daily* (New York), 2 February 1993.

*   *   *

The Strenesse group designs clothes that aim to show the personality of a woman in a way that suits her own style. It is for this reason that the company promotes its label as a style label rather than a designer label, so often only a platform for the creative personality of the designer. A group collection like Strenesse is more concerned with providing the modern woman with a versatile, stylish wardrobe created by a united team of fashion experts.

The company was originally established in 1948 and produced a wearable but unadventurous line of coats and suits. Gerd Strehle took over the company from his parents in 1968 and, with the help of free-lance designers and stylists, established it as a popular fashion label. In 1973 a design graduate from the fashion school in Munich became responsible for the collection. Gabriele Strehle eventually married into the company and became its creative director.

Gabriele established a stylish collection—a mixture of luxury materials, quality workmanship, and a purist, minimalistic look that was intended to emphasize the aura and personality of its wearer. Strenesse collections are timeless and classic. The design principle is that each new piece can be combined and worn with the previous season's look, to create a harmonious continuity of style. It also emphasizes Gabriele Strehle's ecological and cultural sense in for a definitive style that will not date. The clothes themselves are simple and luxurious, sensuous knits, hacking jackets, tailored skirt and trouser suits, and roomy, comfortable coats. Fabrics include tweeds, leathers, chiffons, pinstripe flannels, and cashmeres.

Photographers such as Jacques Olivar and Ellen Von Unwerth are responsible for creating many of the visuals that represent the Strenesse look in both PR and advertising. Classic tailored, mannish looks and elongated, sexy basque dresses are photographed in sharp black and white. Classic movie star references abound: Sophia Loren on a Vespa in Rome, Marlene Dietrich languidly smoking in a darkened railway station, or Ingrid Bergman in a beret from *Arch of Triumph*. These looks suggest to the customer the many different roles she can adopt with her versatile Strenesse wardrobe.

The ideal Strenesse woman is both erotic and confident in her pared-down chic. She does not use fashion as a means to flaunt her success, wealth or status. Like Gabriele Strehle, she believes in the phrase "Less is more." In a world that is taut with recession and environmental constraints, this philosophy has a creative longevity. Fashion gimmicks and short-lived trends are rejected in favour of a forward-looking fashion style that adapts to, but does not radically alter, the personality of its wearer.

Teamwork is very important at Strenesse. Gabriele sees her role as catalyst for her design team's many ideas. The company views group work as being the chief motivation for creativity and, ultimately, productivity. Teamwork is a unity of interpersonal relations and common interests with one aim in mind, that being the extended development of new ideas for the evolution of the Strenesse look.

Strenesse has recently introduced accessory products—belts, shoes, and handbags—to encourage the customer to adopt the

Strenesse lifestyle. In autumn 1993 the company introduced Strenesse Group Blue, a more casual holiday and leisurewear collection. To date the group has approximately 900 worldwide clients, confirming their established popularity and influence on international style.

—Kevin Almond

SUI, Anna.

American designer

Born: Dearborn Heights, Michigan, c.1955. **Education:** Studied at Parsons School of Design, New York, c.1973-75. **Career:** Stylist for photographer Steven Meisel and for junior sportswear firms in New York, 1970s to 1981; sportswear designer, Simultanee, New York, 1981; also designed own line, from 1980; formed own company, New York, 1983; first runway show, 1991; menswear line added, 1992; opened in-store boutique, Macy's, and first free-standing boutique, New York, 1992; second boutique opened, Hollywood, 1993. **Awards:** Perry Ellis Award, 1993. **Address:** 275 West 39th Street, New York, NY 10018, USA.

Publications:

On SUI:

Articles

Casadio, Mariuccia, "Anna Sui: Spectacular Ingredients," in *Interview* (New York), July 1991.
Goodman, Wendy, "Anna Sui Suits Herself," in *House and Garden,* March 1992.
Allis, Tim, "The Sui Smell of Success," in *People* (Chicago), 13 July 1992.
James, Laurie, "Sui Success," in *Harper's Bazaar* (New York), September 1992.
Shiro, Anne-Marie, "On Opposite Sides of the Cutting Edge," in the *New York Times,* 6 November 1992.
"Designer Dish," in *Women's Wear Daily* (New York), 29 March 1993.
"Anna Sui," in *Current Biography* (New York), July 1993.
Shiro, Anne-Marie, "Anna Sui Pounds Out the Beat," in the *New York Times,* 5 November 1993.
Foley, Bridget, "Anna's Time," in *W* (New York), September 1994.
Spindler, Amy M., "Saluting—or Doing In—The Suburban Muse," in the *New York Times,* 4 November 1994.
DeCaro, Frank, "Hairy Situations and Hula Baloos: Anna Sui," in *New York Newsday,* 4 November 1994.
Spindler, Amy M., "Cool Rises to Intimidating Heights," in the *New York Times,* 7 April 1995.
"New York: Anna Sui," in *Women's Wear Daily* (New York), 7 April 1995.

*   *   *

When Anna Sui started her own apparel company in 1980, her mission was to sell clothes to every rock 'n' roll store in the country. "It was right after the punk rock thing and I was so into that," said the designer, who has earned a reputation for bringing a designer's sensibility to wild-child, rock 'n' roll clothes with a vintage spin.

One of three children of Chinese immigrants, Sui knew she wanted to be a clothing designer since she was a little girl growing up in Detroit in the late 1950s and 1960s. She came to New York to attend Parsons School of Design after graduating from high school in the early 1970s—an era whose music-inspired fashion scene, mix-it-up attitude, and free-spirited energy has influenced Sui to a great degree. At Parsons Sui met photographer Steven Meisel—her counterpart in styling ventures then and now.

Upon graduation from Parsons, Sui's first job was with the now-defunct junior sportswear firm Bobbie Brooks, where she worked as a design assistant for about a year. After working for other firms over several years, Sui landed at Glenora, a firm the designer described as "very hip at the time." There she was able to experiment with her interest in clothing with a historical bent, made modern by mixing fresh colors and new shapes with vintage elements.

In 1980, prompted by friends and the praise she received as a stylist for Meisel's shoots for the Italian fashion magazine *Lei,* she started her own company. Greatly influenced by New York's punk scene of the 1970s, Sui's main focus was on selling her funky styles to rock 'n' roll stores, though she continued as a stylist for Meisel. This changed around 1987, when the designer decided to "get serious about being a designer," as she recalled. She moved her line into the Annette B showroom, owned by Annette Breindel, a no-nonsense woman known for nurturing young designers. "Annette helped me enormously," said Sui. "She helped me build my dress business first because that's what she saw as a worthwhile area."

Building that category is what allowed Sui to move her business out of her apartment and into a loft workspace in the garment district of New York. In 1991, Sui staged her first major fashion show during New York show week. Her friends—supermodels Naomi Campbell, Linda Evangelista, and Christy Turlington—walked Sui's runway for free, in exchange for clothes. Influenced by the shows of Thierry Mugler and Jean Paul Gaultier, the designer created a show that was as much about music and theatre as about clothing. She now reigns as the queen of the fashion show extravaganza.

Sui's collection is now sold in many major department and specialty stores, as well as her own two stores—one in New York and one in Los Angeles. Priced moderately, the collection reflects Sui's current concern: "To continue to make these clothes accessible to the people I want wearing them."

—Mary Ellen Gordon

SUNG, Alfred.

Canadian designer

Born: 26 April 1948, in Shanghai, China. Immigrated to Paris, 1966; immigrated to Canada, 1972. **Education:** Studied fashion design at the Chambre Syndicale de la Couture Parisienne, Paris; studied one year at Parsons School of Design, New York, 1967-68. **Career:** Worked in New York City Garment District, c.late 1960s-early 1970s; moved to Toronto, 1972; worked on Spadina Avenue for Lindzon Ltd.; opened own boutique named "Moon"; partnered with Joseph and Saul Mimran forming a company called Monaco, 1979; Licensed with Etac to make and market the Alfred Sung line and Sung sport line, 1991; could not maintain quality and went bankrupt, 1993; Sung and the Mimran's formed Alfred Sung Collections Ltd., 1994; Sung bought back licensing agreements from

Etac and planned to have own line, 1995; company, Alfred Sung Collections Ltd., based in Toronto, Canada. **Awards:** Named one of the top 10 new designers by Saks, 1981.

Publications:

On SUNG:

Articles

MacKay, G., "Alfred Sung: The New King of Fashion," in *Macleans,* 22 August 1983.
Bennett, J., "Designs for an Empire," in *Macleans*, 15 December 1986.
Hastings, N. J., "Sung Style: Like His Fashions," in *Chatelaine,* January 1989.
Wickens, B., "Sung Also Rises," in *Macleans,* 12 September 1994.

*   *   *

Alfred Sung is a Canadian designer with an international following. His firm is called Alfred Sung Collections Ltd. and is based in Toronto. Sung creates designs primarily for women's clothing, though he has produced designs for men, as well as other fashion accessories. He has also developed a very popular perfume called, appropriately, Sung.

The hallmark of this Shanghai-born designer is simple, chic design created to be worn by women who need clothes that are stylish, yet wearable for busy lifestyles. Sung's designs show a classic feeling for line and detail, and his clothes are made from high-quality fabrics that he himself has been known to design. He creates separates, dresses, evening clothes, and jeans. His simple shapes are easy to wear and chosen by people in the public eye because they are neither trendy nor outrageous, and because they are somewhat conservative. In fact, some consider his designs boring. However, these clothes are the clothes of people who want to look and feel good in their apparel and who want clothes that complement rather than overwhelm the wearer. Sung works towards an understated chic in his designs so that they are worn by and not displayed on the wearer. He creates designs for real life, not the life of the runway. His clothing can be found within two major lines created under the Sung label, Alfred Sung and Sung Sports.

Sung is a perfectionist who lives and breathes the world of fashion design and often eschews other concerns of life. He has faced many challenges as his career developed. A native of Shanghai, Sung was originally named Sung Wang Moon, which means "a door in the cloud." When his family moved to the British colony of Hong Kong, his father changed Sung's name to Alfred. From an early age he painted and drew and wanted to continue study in this field. His father sent him to Paris, however, not to study painting but fashion design at the Chambre Syndicale de la Couture Parisienne. There, Sung learned draping, cutting, and sewing garments by hand, obtaining a sound grounding in design and clothing construction basics.

Sung studied at Parsons School of Design for a year, and worked on Seventh Avenue in New York City for several years, eventually moving to Toronto, Canada, where he worked on Spadina Avenue for Lindzon Ltd. Wanting to be self employed, Sung opened a boutique named "Moon." For the three years of operation he was responsible for all aspects of the design process, from designing, cutting and sewing, to marketing. He developed a devoted following of young people who wanted well-designed clothes.

Fortuitously, in 1979 Sung formed a partnership with Joseph and Saul Mimran. These brothers took over the business end of the operation, allowing Sung to concentrate on the design end. Based in Canada, the three men developed an operation that at one point included boutiques under the Alfred Sung name in Boston, Washington D.C., and Short Hills, New Jersey. In 1981 Sung was named one of the top 10 new designers by Saks. Sung licensed luggage designs, sunglasses, and perfume. Unfortunately, the group licensed to manufacture Sung's clothing designs went bankrupt, creating a void in the production and distribution of Sung's work. In spite of this, Sung continued to design. He formed a new operation called Alfred Sung Collections Ltd. with his partners, the Mimran brothers.

Sung's collections are in demand because of their easy to wear, sophisticated elegance. His designs are for people who value good design, who want to look their best, and who want to feel at ease in their clothes.

—Nancy House

SYBILLA.

Spanish designer

Born: Sybilla Sorondo in New York, 1963, to Polish/Argentinian parents; moved to Madrid, age seven; moved to Paris, 1980. **Family:** Married Enrique Sirera in 1992; son: Lucas. **Career:** Apprentice cutter and seamstress, Yves Saint Laurent, 1980; returned to Madrid, 1981, making made-to-measure clothes for friends; first collection, Madrid, 1983; also made first shoe collection; signed production and international distribution agreement with Spanish company, for women's ready-to-wear, 1985; presented first collections in Milan, Paris, New York, 1985. Head designer, Programas Exterioras SA, Madrid, from 1985. Sybilla boutique opened, Madrid,

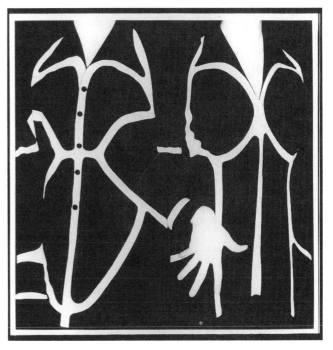

Sybilla.

1987. Signed with Italian company Gibo for women's ready-to-wear, 1987. Begins producing knitwear with Italian company ICAP, 1988; same year starts producing women's shoes and bags with Spanish company Farrutx; also starts designing carpets with German company Vorwerk. Agrees to exclusive license in Japan with Itokin, 1989; opens new shops in Paris and Tokyo, 1991. Opened 20 in-store outlets in Japan. Also designs household items, tableware (for Bidasoa of Spain), childrenswear and accessories. Autumn/winter 1993-94 launched second line for younger people, with 20 shops, called Jocomomola. **Exhibitions:** *50 años de moda,* Cuartel de Conde Duque, Madrid, 1987; *Le monde selon ses créateurs,* Musée de la Mode et du Costume, Paris, 1991. **Collections**: Museo de la Moda, Barcelona; Musée de la Mode et du Costume, Paris; Fashion Institute of Technology, New York. **Awards:** Premio Balenciaga, Best Young Designer of the Year, Spain, 1987; Prix Fil d'Or, France, 1987. **Address:** Jorge Juan 12, 28001 Madrid, Spain.

Publications:

On SYBILLA:

Books

Benaim, Laurence, *L'année de la mode,* Lyons 1988.
Steele, Valerie, *Women of Fashion: Twentieth-Century Designers,* New York 1991.

Articles

"Profile: Sybilla," in *Harper's and Queen* (London), January 1987.
Dreier, Deborah, "Designing Women," in *Art in America* (New York), May 1987.
Chua, Lawrence, "Sybilla: Designing Lady of Spain," in *Women's Wear Daily* (New York), 28 September 1987.
Gordon Lennox, Sarah, "Sybilla Reigns in Spain," in *W* (London), March 1988.
Fuente, Ada de la, "El inevitable éxito de una niña salvaje," in *Vogue* (Spain), August 1988.
Benaim, Laurence, "L'ange couturier," in *Vogue* (Paris), October 1988.
Cocks, Jay, "A Look on the Wild Side: Two Young Designers Liven Up a Groggy Fashion Scene," in *Time* (New York), 16 January 1989.
"Deux grands d'Espagne: Sybilla et Javier Valhonrat," in *Jardin des Modes* (Paris), 1-8 April 1989.
Brantley, Ben, "Spain's New Flame," in *Vanity Fair* (New York), November 1989.
Naeto, Maite, "El triunfo de una chica precoz," in *El Pais* (Madrid), November 1989.

Armstrong, Lisa, "She's a Wizard of Aaah's," in *Harper's Bazaar* (New York), August 1990.
Mower, Sarah, et. al., "The Reign of Spain," in *Metropolitan Home* (New York), February 1991.
Oku, Emiko, "Sybilla's 77 Answers," in *Ryuko Tsushin* (Tokyo), February 1992.
Alvarado, Antonio, "Sybilla, ¡jo, cómo mola!," in *El Mundo* magazine (Madrid), March 1994.

*

I guess that people try to dress up in a way that represents themselves. Somehow we all "paint" our skin with clothes, copying an inner image of ourselves. If you are able to get to this point, you can forget what you are wearing, you can overcome your own image ... at this moment the peace and serenity that you show outside can be condsidered elegance.

—Sybilla

*   *   *

Sybilla has been widely acclaimed as the most exciting designer to have emerged from Spain since Balenciaga. She was born in 1963 in New York City, the daughter of an Argentine diplomat. Her mother was a Polish aristocrat who worked as a fashion designer under the name "Countess Sybilla of Saks Fifth Avenue." When she was seven years old her family moved to Madrid, and she considers herself thoroughly Spanish; her clothes, she says, are also very Spanish—"not *olé olé*" but Spanish in the classical sense.

She served a brief apprenticeship in Paris at the couture *atelier* of Yves Saint Laurent, but recoiled at what she regarded as the "snobbish, cold, and professional" aspects of French fashion. "Paris scares me. 'Fashion' is too serious. In Spain, you can still play." Like filmmaker Pedro Almodovar, Sybilla is a member of the post-Franco generation that launched a creative explosion in the 1980s. "We were the first generation after Franco died, and we tried to be different and creative," recalled Sybilla. With success came greater professionalism. In 1987, Italian fashion manufacturer Gibo began producing Sybilla's clothes en masse in Italy.

At the end of the 1980s, Sybilla became famous for creating what she called "weird and outrageous designs"—such as sculpted dresses with wired hems. But there is also a soft feeling to many of her clothes, which derives both from the colors (tobacco, pumpkin, pale green) and from a tendency towards biomorphic shapes. "The dresses of Sybilla remind you of when you were a child and your mother would tell you fairy stories," says Almodovar actress Rossy de Palma. "But in her dresses you live that, like a dream."

—Valerie Steele

TAKADA, Kenzo. See **KENZO.**

TANG, William.

Chinese designer

Born: Hong Kong. **Education:** Graduated in Economics and Business, University of Guelph, Canada; studied fashion design, London School of Fashion. **Career:** Returned to Hong Kong, 1982, to design for a number of labels, including Sahara Club, Michel Rene and Daniel Hechter. Opened own company, W. Tang Co. Ltd, 1985, designing ladies- and menswear. Labels include William Tang, and W by William Tang; opened Paris boutique, Presence II. **Address:** Flat E, Upper Ground Floor, 14/16 Aberdeen St Central, Hong Kong.

Publications:

On TANG:

Articles

Marshall, Samantha, "Shenzhen: A Look across the China Border," in the *Daily News Record,* 10 January 1994.

*

Fashion itself is an art form that moves and lives with the human body. The fashion business is also art, a form that is based on creative ideas where various commercial aspects are taken into consideration.

—William Tang

*   *   *

Known as the bad boy of Hong Kong Fashion, William Tang has never been one to take the conventional route. After studying economics and business and then hotel management, he decided on a career in fashion. He wanted to develop further his interest in the arts and the choice was between fashion and architecture. To him, fashion seemed closer to the fine arts and fulfilled his childhood love of drawing people. His arrival in London as a fashion student coincided with the style era of the New Romantics. Tang was in tune with their retro brand of flamboyance and glamour.

History and culture are very important to Tang's work. In Western art and design his particular interests include art déco and Georgia O'Keeffe. The Mediterranean is his greatest geographical influence: he holds a special place for Venice, Ancient Greece, and Ancient Egypt. He revived the unique technique of fine pleating originated by the Venetian Mariano Fortuny to create elegant shift dresses inspired by the Ancient Greek *chiton.* For Tang, fashion must be a means of expression, not purely concerned with commercialism. Artistic and personal fulfillment are his major lifetime goals.

Tang goes his own way. Never sticking to one look, he prefers to experiment and innovate. But there is a practical side. His business education provided a sound base for the more pragmatic aspect of fashion. W by William Tang and William Tang are his two retail labels in Asia Pacific, where he sells through major department stores including the Japanese Seibu and Daimaru. He works with the Betu Company in Hong Kong and with Seibu to produce contemporary silk collections aimed at the Japanese and Taiwanese markets. He has recently opened his own workshop in his home base of Hong Kong. His only shop, Presence II, is in Paris. The next project is to open a shop in Hong Kong's fashionable Lan Kwai Fong area. The aim is to encompass the extent of Tang's creativity, including individual couture designs, contemporary daywear, and also his paintings.

His enthusiasms fuel his work. He has reinterpreted clothes photographed by Man Ray to coincide with an exhibition of the artist's work. He has awakened others to the significance of fashion through his designs, lectures, books, and articles. His collections have echoed his knowledge of Chinese history and culture. Shanghai in the 1930s inspired a shocking pink *cheong-sam* dress, trimmed with ostrich feathers and worn with platform shoes, which stunned the catwalks of Hong Kong. Exquisite lace eveningwear, created from fabric hand-crafted in Shandong Province in China, was declared the triumph of the 1989 Hong Kong Fashion Week. As evidence of his diversity, the following year he showed tie-dyed coordinates topped with overvests and leggings made from rubber bands.

It is somewhat surprising that Tang's versatile young look is not better known internationally. Insufficient financial backing and the need for better promotion have proved hurdles to wider recognition. Tang is relaxed about the future. He enjoys his work too much to be concerned about what lies ahead. He has been accused of "stirring things up on the Hong Kong fashion scene" by frequently playing the wild card. But William Tang knows his business. He is aware that "Good fashion should be a combination of artistic ideals and expression, and the commercial process involved in producing a line of clothes that will sell well." In Hong Kong he has become the darling of the press. His personality and presence set him apart from some of his older and more reserved contemporaries. But Tang is no mere showman. His work is lively, fresh, and worthy of greater recognition. Its time is yet to come.

—Hazel Clark

TARABINI, Gianpaolo. See BLUMARINE.

TASSELL, Gustave.

American designer

Born: Philadelphia, Pennsylvania, 4 February 1926. **Education:** Studied at Pennsylvania Academy of Fine Arts. **Military Service:** Served in the U.S. Army. **Career:** Joined Hattie Carnegie, late 1940s, as window-dresser, later designer; designer, Elfreda Fox; designed custom clothes, Philadelphia; sketch artist for Mme. Fath and free-lance sketch artist, Paris, 1952-54; designer, Hattie Carnegie fashion house, New York, 1954-55; managed own design firm, Los Angeles, California, 1956-72; took over design at Norman Norell, New York, after death of Norell, 1972-76; designer, Michael Forrest Furs, 1976. Awards: International Silk Association Award, 1959; Coty American Fashion Critics Award, 1961; Cotton Council Fashion Award, 1963.

Publications:

On TASSELL:

Books

Levin, Phyllis Lee, *The Wheels of Fashion,* Garden City, New York 1956.
Lambert, Eleanor, *World of Fashion: People, Places, Resources,* New York 1976.
Morris, Bernadine, and Barbara Walz, *The Fashion Makers,* New York 1978.
Milbank, Caroline Rennolds, *New York Fashion: The Evolution of American Style,* New York 1989.

Articles

In *Holiday,* June 1962.
In the *New York Times,* 24 January 1974, 6 August 1974, 8 August 1975, 12 July 1976.

*   *   *

White gloves and pearls are the accessories one needs to wear with the refined, graceful designs of American Gustave Tassell. He designs for women who have a built-in serenity and who are not out to shock. His designs go beyond fringe and ruffle and are noted for their sense of proportion, simplicity of line, and refined detail.

Among the notable people who have worn the designs of Tassell were Princess Grace of Monaco and Jacqueline Kennedy Onassis—who was young, beautiful, charismatic, and very influential in the fashion field when she was First Lady of the United States. She wore simple clothes, favoring sleeveless dresses without a defined waistline or a lot of details. Tassell's creations were perfect for the First Lady. They were youthful, elegant, without unnecessary details or defined waistlines. They would glide over the body rather

than hugging it. His designs were elegant and easy to wear.

Tassell had a New York showroom, but the base of his operation was in Los Angeles. There he maintained a small organization and workroom which insured top notch quality at relatively low cost. He did not produce the extremes of fashion. In *Holiday* magazine he says "forget fashion, you can't go around startling people all the time" (Philadelphia, PA, June 1962). Fabrics were important, *peau d'ange* and quilted cotton damask added interest; bugle beads were used, in an understated manner, for eveningwear. Through the use of seams, tucks, and gathers, Tassell was able to create sculptural forms which skimmed over the body, rather than hugging it tightly. The look was graceful and feminine. Skirts could be bell shaped, or gathered gently. The seams of a princess-style dress curved to suggest the bust and waistline. He designed clothes for both evening and daytime wear; separates, dresses, and coats. He designed versions of the black dinner dress, the shirtwaist, culottes, and the reefer coat. His interpretation was always graceful and feminine. In 1961 he received the Coty American Fashion Critics Award.

Tassell did not start out to be a fashion designer, but studied painting at the Pennsylvania Academy of Fine Arts. Moving to New York, he worked in the advertising and display department for Hattie Carnegie, who was well known in the fashion design world for both custom made and ready-to-wear clothes. Seeing the design work of Norman Norell inspired Tassell's decision to create clothes for women.

In the early 1950s Tassell moved to Europe where he did fashion sketches for Geneviève Fath and became acquainted with the American designer James Galanos. It was through the encouragement of Galanos that Tassell eventually began his own business in 1956 in California, though the designs Tassell produced were closer in concept to those of Norell than Galanos.

In 1972, when Norman Norell died, Tassell was asked to come to New York to maintain the line. He did this under the name House of Norell, Gustave Tassell. The Norman Norell line was permanently closed in 1976 and Tassell returned to California where he again turned out his sophisticated designs for a small group of customers.

Currently Tassell is working on a concept of dressing for women of the 21st century. He envisions a design in natural fibers that will serve many purposes. The silhouette will change by the way it is buttoned, seamed, or tucked. Mr Tassell wants to produce an affordable item of clothing which still has a sense of proportion, grace, and design.

—Nancy House

THOMASS, Chantal.

French designer

Born: Chantal Genty in Malakoff, Seine, 4 September 1947. **Family:** Married Bruce Thomass in 1967; children: Louise, Robin. **Career:** Free-lance designer selling to Dorothée Bis, 1966-71; Partner, Ter et Bantine boutique, Paris, 1967, renamed Chantal Thomass, 1975; introduced lingerie and hosiery collections, 1975, maternity wear, 1981, children's clothing line, from c.1982; signed partnership with World Company for distribution, licensing and boutiques in Japan, 1985; second boutique for clothing and household accessories opened, Paris, 1991. **Awards:** named Chevalier des Arts et Lettres. **Address:** 100, rue du Cherche Midi, 75006 Paris, France.

Chantal Thomass. *Photograph by Sylvie Barin.*

Publications:

On THOMASS:

Books

Slesin, Suzanne, and Stafford Cliff, *French Style,* New York and London 1982.
Steele, Valerie, *Women of Fashion: Twentieth-Century Designers,* New York 1991.

Articles

"Les stylistes," in *Elle* (Paris), 23 May 1977.
"Chantal Thomass: la renouveau du froufrou," in *Jardin des Modes* (Paris), October 1982.
Depardieu, Gérard, "Chantal Thomass," in *La Mode en Peinture,* Winter 1982-83.
"Chantal Thomass," in *Profession Textile* (Paris), 18 September 1987.

*   *   *

Chantal Thomass has built a reputation for her tantalizing, flirtatious clothes. Much of her work pays a titillating homage to exotic underwear; there is, however, never a blatant display of overt sexuality. Instead there is always a hint of the naughty schoolgirl or a sensuous allusion to the charms of the teenage seductress, like Carole Baker in *Baby Doll,* or Sue Lyon in *Lolita.* The clothes are often fitted or skimpy, trimmed in frills, ribbons, and flounces, and always produced in the most sophisticated fabrics.

Chantal Thomass has had no formal training in fashion design but as a child dressing up proved enough of a motivation for her to design her own clothes, which were made up by her mother. She began her fashion career at 18, designing clothes for girls of her own age. A year later she married Bruce Thomass, who had studied at the École des Beaux Arts in Paris. Together, they formed a small fashion company called Ter et Bantine that manufactured and sold young and unusual clothes. They created dresses from hand-painted scarves, designed by Bruce, and succeeded in selling them to Dorothée Bis. Thomass also designed dresses with flounced pinafores, schoolgirl collars, and balloon sleeves that were sold from their first boutique on Boulevard Saint Germain in 1967. Actress and French cultural symbol Brigitte Bardot became a regular customer, as did designer Jacqueline Jacobson, who ordered over a hundred dresses in one season alone!

The business was sufficiently successful for the pair to found the Chantal Thomass label in 1975, with Chantal as creative director and Bruce as licensing and sales director. As the profile of the company rose so did the price of the clothes, although they retained their young, enchanting, and highly feminine style.

Thomass declares herself to be motivated by the progression of her own life. Her pregnancy in 1981 led her to develop a line of maternity clothes. As her daughter began growing, Thomass developed a childrenswear division that retained many of the distinctive and theatrical elements of her mainline collections. The company moved into licensing in 1985, joining forces with the Japanese group World as a financial partner. Licensed products that are available throughout Europe and Japan include: fine leather goods, tights, women's shoes, eyewear, watches, children's ready-to-wear, scarves, lingerie, and swimwear. There are now 12 boutiques throughout France, two in Paris.

Chantal Thomass retains her eminence by reflecting fashion changes and adapting her look to suit the prevalent mood. A youthful feel to her clothes keeps her in the forefront of leading Paris-based designers.

—Kevin Almond

TIEL, Vicky.

American designer working in France

Born: Washington, D.C., 21 October 1943. **Education:** Studied fashion design at Pratt Institute, New York, 1961-62, and at Fashion Institute of Technology, New York, 1962-64. **Family:** Married Ron Berkeley in 1971 (divorced, 1986); children: Rex and Richard. **Career:** Settled in Paris, 1964; opened boutique, Mia & Vicky, later renamed Vicky Tiel; fragrance line introduced, 1990; eveningwear bridge line introduced, 1992. Also film costume designer 1960s. **Address:** 21 rue Bonaparte, Paris 6, France.

Publications:

On TIEL:

Books

Leese, Elizabeth, *Costume Design in the Movies,* New York 1991.

On TIEL:

Articles

de Leusse, Claude, "Vicky Tiel: Gentleness on Her Mind," in *Women's Wear Daily* (New York), 3 March 1972.
Grassi, Adriana, "Vicky, Elizabeth and Richard," in *Women's Wear Daily* (New York), 27 June 1972.
Morris, Bernadine, "An American in Paris: The Eclectic Spirit," in the *New York Times,* 18 May 1978.
"Tiel Goes Hollywood," in *Women's Wear Daily* (New York), 31 May 1978.
Johnson, Bonnie, "American in Paris: Vicky Tiel Has Built her Reputation on Gowns a Cut below the Rest," in *People,* 1 September 1986.
Stephens, Suzanne, "Vicky Tiel: American Élan in Paris Apartment," in *Architectural Digest* (Los Angeles), September 1989.
Hunter, Catherine Ellis, "Vicky Tiel: An American in Paris," in *Drug and Cosmetic Industry* (Cleveland, Ohio), August 1990.
Pagoda, Dianne M., "Tiel Lowers Prices as Business Drops," in *Women's Wear Daily* (New York), 30 July 1991.

*   *   *

Vicky Tiel is a unique phenomenon in the international world of fashion. She is, perhaps, the only American to operate her own fashion design business in Paris, and to do so longer than many of her French contemporaries. She holds a unique place in the history of fashion as one of the early boutique/ready-to-wear designers in Paris. Her clothes now occupy a special place between ready-to-wear and couture, both in manufacture and in marketing.

In 1964, having graduated from the Fashion Institute of Technology, New York, Tiel arrived in Paris with the intention of designing costumes for films. During her school years in New York she had already been actively creating youth-oriented clothes, sold in Greenwich Village boutiques. Her designs in this early period included leather skirts with matching fringe vests and a prototypical miniskirt designed in fall 1963, a full season ahead of Mary Quant's mini, introduced in London in the spring of 1964. While looking for film work in Paris, Tiel, together with her friend Mia Fonssagrives, created innovative "youth-quaker"-style ready-to-wear. These clothes caused a stir among the fashion press and in 1965 Tiel and Fonssagrives even appeared on the *Tonight* show with Johnny Carson. At this time fashion in Paris was still dominated by the great couturiers and there were only a few designers, such as Emmanuelle Khanh and Michele Rosier, who were exclusively designing ready-to-wear clothes. Subsequently Mia Fonssagrives married the couturier Louis Féraud who, in a highly unusual move, permitted Tiel and Fonssagrives to use sample-hands and seamstresses from his *atelier* in order to produce their ready-to-wear for sale in their own boutique called Mia and Vicky. Mia Fonssagrives later dropped out and the boutique was renamed Vicky Tiel. As a direct result of this series of events Tiel's clothes have come to hold a unique place in between ready-to-wear and couture: they are clothes, meticulously crafted of the finest fabrics by sewers trained in the tradition of the haute couture. By 1972 Tiel's clothes had moved away from the radically young, kooky 1960s look, toward a traditionally feminine style with a sexy twist as seen in floral printed garden party dresses closely gathered through the bodice, skinny navy jersey tops with white piqué collar and cuffs, and long skirts worn with ruffled shirts. By the mid-1970s dramatically draped dresses in matte jersey had become a major component of her collection. From that period onward Tiel's style has reflected her point of view that a woman can be glamorous, sexual, powerful and feminine all at the same time. Her exemplar for the reification of this concept is the Hollywood screen goddess of the 1940s and 1950s. Her clothes appeal to the consumer's basic fantasy desire, a fantasy of glamor and sexuality mediated by quality and a refined sensibility. In 1978, inspired by a 1940s Frederick's of Hollywood catalog, she designed a collection with the theme Fun Hollywood Trash but remarked that "the look is done in very good taste and in the most expensive fabrics." The collection featured backless tuxedo dresses and evening dresses of contrasting colored chiffon layered over jersey, creating an iridescent look. Her description of the development of her perfume could also serve as a description of her clothes, "I wanted it to reek of femininity and sensuality, but to be soft and romantic, with subtle, not overpowering sex." Her recent designs have continued to reflect this point of view with a large portion of her collection devoted to eveningwear, especially her signature draped jerseys, often enhanced with applied decoration of sequins and embroidery.

Tiel's clothes are sold in her own boutique in Paris and in fine department stores and specialty stores where she often makes personal appearances at trunk shows. Special and custom orders account for a large percentage of Tiel's sales and this personal style of

Vicky Tiel.

marketing is consistent with the caliber of these uniquely luxurious, sensual clothes.

—Alan E. Rosenberg

TIFFEAU, Jacques.

French designer

Born: Chenevelles, Loire Valley, France, 11 October 1927. **Education:** Early training in Paris couture house until World War II. **Military Service:** Served in the French Army Air Force 1939-40. **Career:** Tailor; assistant to Dior, 1945-c.1950; immigrated to the United States; studied figure drawing, Art Students' League, New York; pattern maker, then designer, Monte-Sano & Pruzan coat and suit manufacturers, c.1952-58; partner and designer, Tiffeau and Busch Ltd. for Monte-Sano & Pruzan, New York, 1958-66; launched own firm, 1966-71; taught fashion design, Paris, 1970s; supervisor, Rive Gauche collections, Saint Laurent, 1972-76; designer, Originala, and Blassport lines, New York. Awards: Coty American Fashion Critics Award, 1960, 1966; National Cotton Award, New York, 1961; *Sunday Times* International Fashion Award, London, c.1966; Tobe-Coburn Fashion Award New York. *Died in 1988.*

Publications:

On TIFFEAU:

Books

Bender, Marylin, *The Beautiful People,* New York 1967.
Lambert, Eleanor, *World of Fashion: People, Places, Resources,* New York and London 1976.
Milbank, Caroline Rennolds, *New York Fashion: The Evolution of American Style,* New York 1989.

On TIFFEAU:

Articles

Sheinman, Mort, "Jacques Tiffeau Dies in Paris," in *Women's Wear Daily,* 7 March 1968.

*   *   *

Writing about designer Jacques Tiffeau in the 1960s, fashion doyenne Diana Vreeland once grandly declared, "He's in tune." She was referring to a Tiffeau collection comprised of simple, nonchalant, elegant dresses and daytimes suits, most without bust-darts or extraneous frills, many cut on the bias. The gifted designer, who once turned down an offer to replace Yves St. Laurent at Dior, excelled at creating pared-down, sophisticated, gimmick-free clothes that derived their strong visual impact purely from the designer's manipulation of cut, shape, and color. He was one of the prescient few who understood the importance of trousers for women, including basic trousers in nearly every collection until they were no longer seen as inappropriate for certain occasions. He was also known for his uncluttered coat designs with their clean, graphic silhouettes.

A Frenchman transplanted to America, Tiffeau belonged to the 1960s pantheon of American designers which included Geoffrey Beene, Bill Blass, Donald Brooks, and James Galanos. He embraced the advanced manufacturing technologies of the post-World War II era, eagerly investigating the properties of new materials in his garments: double-knits, rayons, plastics, and polyesters. His clothes were designed with a young, affluent, fashion-conscious consumer in mind, and his styles found ready buyers in America who saw reflected in his streamlined designs the modern spirit they wished to project.

Tiffeau spent many years learning his trade. During the German Occupation of France, the teenaged Tiffeau left his small Loire village and ran off to Paris, where he apprenticed himself to a men's tailor. There he skillfully mastered the art of cutting a toile, the muslin pattern which designers use as a model for the finished pattern. He next moved to New York and became protegé and chief stylist for Max Pruzan at Monte-Sano & Pruzan, an Italian artisan tailor who had built up one of the most expensive women's coat-and-suit houses in the trade. A friendship with Christian Dior led to an offer to design at Dior New York, but Tiffeau felt that his future lay in ready-to-wear. Tiffeau teamed up with Beverly Busch, Pruzan's daughter, and formed Tiffeau & Busch, a successful ready-to-wear line of young, lower-priced coats, dresses, and sportswear separates. The designer spent nearly a decade creating six collections a year between the two concerns before dedicating himself exclusively to Tiffeau & Busch.

Life-drawing art classes combined with his inspired manipulation of toiles as a tailor's apprentice had given the young Tiffeau an excellent comprehension of the body as a mobile, three dimensional object in space. This in-depth knowledge of clothing construction came to set him apart from many other American designers of his generation. Unlike his contemporaries, who would simply give their assistants a sketch to translate into three-dimensions, Tiffeau was able to cut, shape, drape, and sew a garment from start to finish. Buyers loved the fact that Tiffeau's clothing truly fit and rarely needed alterations. But he preferred to think of himself merely as a technician, never as an artist.

He was an inspired designer, however, often using staid gray flannel for elegant separates, making cocktail dresses of zebra-striped velveteen—and he was among the first to use wool for evening dresses. He was an avid collector of ancient Near-eastern and Asian art, from which he claimed to derive ideas about purity of line. He always sought refinement in his designs, an endless paring down, saying, "the secret of good clothes is to keep taking off, simplifying, trimming down—yet capture the shape of the human body." Besides his mentor Christian Dior, he admired Balenciaga, Beene, Courreges, and Norell. His minimalist, almost severe style made him one of the most renowned designers of the 1960s, but as tastes changed in the 1970s he was accused of merely "rehashing" his old styles and was never again able to regain the spotlight.

In 1972 he left New York and returned to France, where he worked for a time for Balmain and Yves St. Laurent. An attempt to revive his career designing coats at Originala in New York was short-lived, though he was praised for his soft, unconstructed styles in tweed, alpaca, and cashmere. Eventually he found himself again in France, this time as a fashion design instructor. He left behind the legacy of a strong-willed and talented man whom his friend artist Robert Motherwell once said was "like having a beautiful leopard in the room."

—Kathleen Paton

TIKTINER.

French fashion designer

Born: Dina Tiktiner Viterbo in Nice, France, "between the wars."
Career: Began family business in Nice, 1949, expanded into sportswear with factories in the South of France. **Address:** 14 avenue de Verdun, 06000 Nice, France.

Publications:

On TIKTINER:

Books

McDowell, Colin, *McDowell's Directory of Twentieth Century Fashion,* Englewood Cliffs, New Jersey, 1985.

Articles

"Tiktiner Fall," in *Women's Wear Daily* (New York), 26 February 1990.

*   *   *

The owners of Tiktiner, a family-run fashion house based in Nice, France, never really considered their position outside the urban fashion center of Paris a liability. The principles, Henri and Dina Viterbo and their daughters Miquette and Vivian, occasionally admitted to the need for stimulation beyond the French Riviera in order to inspire new ideas. But the Viterbos remained committed to their own brand of high-quality, classic-styled, resort-oriented ready-to-wear, and they felt no need to leave Nice or tamper with the relaxed attitude toward clothing that supported them handsomely for over three decades.

The Tiktiner family members each played an important role in the company: Henri was the founder and owner; Dina was the head designer; eldest daughter Miquette, an international attorney married to American Mort Schrader, represented the company in the United States; and younger daughter Vivian co-designed the collections with her mother. Together the Viterbos created and promoted dependable ready-to-wear collections with their own, recognizable "Tiktiner look"—a look based essentially on tailored sportswear separates, with a focus on knits, basic colors, rich weaves, and youthful lines.

The combined inspiration of Vivian and mother Dina resulted in fashion-forward clothes mitigated by classicism, and indeed, Vivian often chided her mother for excessive conservatism. Yet, the pair worked well together. Early collections emphasized the sleek lines in vogue during the 1960s, with clingy jersey tops over slim, hip-hugging trousers and mini-skirts. Tiktiner favored the natural fiber fabrics used in active wear, often experimenting with stretch jerseys and printed piques in their youth-oriented clothes. The polo shirt, that icon of French sportswear popularized by René LaCoste, was even fair game, given a clever twist by Vivian and Dina in their one-piece shirt dress with a polo top and faux skirt designed to look like separates. The "Tiktiner look," though essentially casual, relied on the buyer's familiarity with design classics, and the look was equally at home at a beachside tennis court or a Parisian salon de thé.

However, the company did not design only garments meant for warm weather resorts. The bi-annual collections included autumn/winter lines with thick knits and cold-weather layered looks. In the 1970s Tiktiner made fashion news with their sweater tunics and bulky multicolored sweater coats over plaid shirt jackets in lieu of the traditional cloth coat. Each knitted sweater layer was designed to coordinate, so that a lightweight, slim jersey top might slip over a matching skirt under a fuller mohair coat, all in various shades of amber or other compatible hues. These loose, comfortable, mix-and-match cold weather knits fit perfectly into the youthful fashion mood of the period of the 1970s, when even a simple cloth coat could be seen as bourgeois and confining. But Tiktiner was not averse to more traditional coat designs, and were lauded for their updated, shaped "redingote" of rosy wool chinchilla in 1979.

Tiktiner never wavered from their dedication to style combined with comfort. One clothing group comprised of over 200 pieces highlighted slim waists with drawstring closures, shirred shoulders, and back yokes for easy movement. The collections were frequently hailed for their coordinating palettes; muted earth tones, dusty blues and greens, pale pastels, and paired intensities of the same color figured largely in the Viterbos' vision. The notion of comfort also emerges when considering Tiktiner's attention to travel-minded clothes made from lightweight and packable wool challis, mohairs, and double-knits. Underlying the designs was a philosophy based on ease: ease of fit, of combining colors, of simply getting dressed.

Sophisticated hues; soft knit fabrics; elegant ease—Tiktiner was considered the best at creating their own "South-of France" style of inspired French dressing.

—Kathleen Paton

TIMNEY FOWLER LTD.

British textile design firm

Founded in London in 1979 by husband and wife team Sue Timney (born 9 July 1950) and Grahame Fowler (born 12 January 1956); firm incorporated, 1985. Timney educated at Carlisle College of Art, 1966-67; Newcastle-upon-Tyne Polytechnic 1971-76, B.A.; Heriot Watt University, Edinburgh, postgraduate diploma, textiles, 1976-77; Royal College of Art, M.A., Textiles, 1977-79. Partnership developed Japanese market for print design, clothing and accessories consultancy, 1980-84. Clients included Issey Miyake and Yohji Yamamoto. Opened UK retail outlets and Print Studio Workshop; interior fabric range, 1984. Expanded design services to Yves Saint Laurent, Chloé, Agnes B. Collections produced for Italian designers Bini and Mantero. Also: ceramics, jewellery, scarves, clothes and fabrics, exporting also to Europe and US, and designs for Calvin Klein, Kamali, Saks Fifth Avenue, 1985-88. Designed table- and giftware for Wedgwood, 1990. Fashion accessories launched in USA, 1993. Textile license with Linda McCartney, 1994. Members of Chartered Society of Designers, London; Textile Institute, London; Interior Designers and Decorators Association, London. **Exhibitions:** *Period Homes and Interiors,* Olympia, London, 1992. **Collections:** Victoria and Albert Museum, London; Cooper-Hewitt Museum, New York City; Chicago Art Institute. **Awards:** Roscoe Award, Interior Fabrics, USA, 1988, 1989; Textile Institute Design Gold Medal, 1991. **Address:** 388 King's Road, London SW3 5UZ, UK.

Timney Fowler: 1994, Devoré tunic.

Publications:

On TIMNEY FOWLER:

Books

McDermott, Catherine, *Street Style: British Design in the 80's,* London 1987.
Gordon-Clark, J., *Paper Magic,* London 1991.

Articles

"Timney Fowler Prints," in *Country Life* (London), 16 September 1984.
"England's Fabric," in *Women's Wear Daily* (New York), 3 June 1985.
"Two's Company," in the *Sunday Express Magazine* (London), 15 September 1985.
Hall, Dinah, "Family Classics," in *World of Interiors* (London), April 1988.

Hawkins, Heidi, "Culture Club," in *Graphics World,* September/ October 1988.

Crawford, I., "Artists in Residence: Mission Impossible," in *Elle Decoration* (London), October 1990.

Heinrich-Jost, Ingrid, "Alte Römer und Junge Englander," in *Frankfurter Allemein,* March 1991.

"Duo Tones," in *Metropolitan Home,* December/January 1991-92.

Fitzmaurice, Arabella, "Appearing in Print," in *The Sunday Times* Magazine (London), 1 March 1992.

*

Timney Fowler's distinctive designs draw on the rich symbolism of European art. Neo-classical, architectural and Egyptian images are placed together in unexpected ways to create modern prints. Other designs use hand-drawn symbols to give a softer, more ethnic look. Animals, leaves and other images from the natural world are also used in unexpected ways.

—Timney Fowler

*   *   *

Sue Timney and Graham Fowler are a design team of international repute who began working together after graduating in Textiles from London's Royal College of Art. Timney had earlier studied Fine Art and Fowler, Graphics and Textiles. They launched themselves as free-lance fashion designers in 1979, selling printed fabric on the roll. In 1985 they produced their own range of interior furnishings to sell in their first London showroom in Portobello Road.

Self-confessed "20th-century vultures," their inspiration has been drawn variously from photography, mythology, classicism, and European history, and from the Arts and Crafts and Aesthetic Movements—this eclecticism expressed with bold graphic imagery and in an uncompromising monochrome. "Image rather than colour is our main vehicle for expression," Timney explains. "Black and white keeps colour to its absolute classical minimum,."

If design hype were to be believed, they virtually invented black and white. This striking classical modernism was taken up avidly by the style conscious avant-garde in the early 1980s.

From the early years strong links were established with Japan, from where their work derived many influences. Clients included Yohji Yamamoto and Issey Miyake and the Japanese market remains an important business connection.

The company's design criteria could be said to be embodied in the Neo-Classical Collection, the core of the Timney Fowler fabric range, produced in 1984-85. Drawing extensively on the history and symbolism of European art, the designs were presented in the company's distinctive graphic style, black on white. Greek, Roman, and Florentine objects led by the bestselling Emperor's Heads; twisted columns, sections of architectural buildings plans, elaborate montages of stonework and foliage scrolls, the unexpected and witty juxtapositions of paisley dolphins teamed with acanthus plasterwork.

To complement these classical borrowings was a range of Regency stripes, latticed Victorian ironwork, and small scale heraldic repeats. Linked to all this was a small group of wallpapers, friezes, and borders.

Their aim has always been to produce "20th-century classics, contemporary and exciting in mood but making few concessions to instant fashion." The Neo-Classical Collection features in some of the world's leading museums of modern design.

Over the years Timney Fowler have become truly international, supplying specialist design consultancy services to leading fashion and household names, and their position in the forefront of British design has been recognized in the United Kingdom and internationally with the prestigious Textile Institute Design Medal for "outstanding contributions to textile design and management." Twice they have been the recipients of the Roscoe Award in the United States.

In the late 1980s, Timney Fowler expanded into fashion, with a range of scarves and shawls in wool and silk, silk shirts, ties and T-shirts, waistcoats, and bags. New fabrics included velvet and plastic-coated cotton. Design features included images from Greek and Roman works of art, French tapestries, nautical instruments, along with a strong architectural theme; Russian maps, mosaic floor plans, and in the scarf range the design element which over the years virtually became the company's logo—the clock—all used in a thoroughly modern way. Surprisingly, having traded for so long on their black and white signature, Timney Fowler at this stage introduced colour for the first time into its fashion range. Their shirts and fashion accessories sell worldwide through retail outlets and several collections have been launched in London.

New products continue to emerge, including umbrellas, jewellery, shoes, furniture, lights, and a collection of black and white clothes. Noteworthy are their range of ceramics; mainly neo-classical reference, paralleling the fabrics; insistent architectural imagery. But while the source remains historical, they have here included wit and a sense of the surreal. They are strongly inspired by the etchings of Piranesi, the 18th-century Venetian architect, and capture the romantic characteristics of his work. A new trend for Gothic Revival is to be seen in Lion Man and Dolphin Man. It is all hard-edged and very contemporary.

In the early days Timney and Fowler had applied the transfers and fired the ceramics themselves and the cooperation between designer and manufacturer remains close.

On a much larger scale yet maintaining the same imagery are their gun-tufted rugs—manifestly intended to be centrepieces, perennial designs like Coinhead and Timepiece, all resolutely in black and white, speak for themselves.

The company fast outgrew its original premises in Portobello Road and in 1986 moved to the highly fashionable King's Road, Chelsea where they concentrate on key products suited to this more sophisticated mileu—fashion, scarves, ceramics, tableware and interiors. Timney Fowler describe their design philosophy as "a process of evolution, working through one set of ideas in a kind of natural progression, but without any ups and downs."

Although there has been no let up in the appeal and saleability of their original style theme, much plagiarized by lesser talents, there have been moves to get away from visual typecasting. To this end a major development has been the expansion of the Interiors Collection in the early 1990s, from the original black and white neo-classical themes into new fabrics and colour, including a range of deep dyed cottons and velvets. New themes have emerged based on Rococo and Toiles, 15th-century European fashion portraits and, more recently, 18th-century Byzantine paintings. Colour is creeping into the Timney Fowler scheme of things and, as the designers would have it, not before time. There is also a distinct softening up around the edges. Timney has described her earlier work as "clinical and calculated" and believes that the new ecological awareness, lowering of international barriers, and the recession will make for less ostentation in the 1990s. She sees interiors following fashion's lead towards purer, simpler lines. Elements of their old style are being infiltrated by a new down-played look.

This dynamic married couple have created the unique Timney Fowler look. Their contrasting approaches of the formal intellectual on the one hand and flamboyant practicality on the other—"At the RCA he was always the wackier one," Timney says—have been the recipe for a success story which looks set to go from strength to strength.

—Elian McCready

TINLING, Ted.

British designer

Born: Eastbourne, 23 June 1910. **Military Service:** Served in the British Army, 1939-47, Lieutenant-Colonel. **Career:** Designer of custom dresses and sports clothes, London, 1931-39 and 1947-75; liaison committee member, Wimbledon Tennis Association, London, 1927-49, 1982-90; chef de protocol, International Tennis Federation, 1973; immigrated to the United States, 1975; designer, Virginia Slims Tournament, 1971-78. **Awards:** British Clothing Institute Designer of the Year Award, 1971; International Tennis Hall of Fame Award, 1986. **Collections:** International Tennis Hall of Fame, Newport, Rhode Island. *Died* (in Cambridge, England) *23 May 1990.*

Publications:

By TINLING:

Books

White Ladies, London 1963.
Love and Faults, London 1979.
Sixty Years in Tennis, London 1983.

Articles

columns for *British Lawn Tennis.*
"From Bustles to Bodysuits," with Camille Peri, in *Women's Sports and Fitness* (Boulder, Colorado), US Open special advertising section, September 1986.
"Stay Back to Get Ahead," in *World Tennis* (New York), June 1987.
"The Goddess and the American Girl," [book review] in *Tennis* (New York), April 1988.
"Who's the Best Ever?," in *World Tennis* (New York), March 1989.
Suzanne Lenglen, "Tennis Idol of the Twenties," [book review] in *Tennis* (New York), April 1988.

On TINLING:

Books

Glyn, Prudence, *In Fashion: Dress in the 20th Century,* New York 1978.
Wade, Virginia, *Ladies of the Court,* London 1984.

Articles

"An Interview with Teddy Tinling," in *World Tennis* (New York), December 1954.
Glynn, Prudence, "That Tinling Feeling," in *The Times* (London), 11 June 1971.
Cox, Sue, "Teddy Tinling: The Go-between," in the *Sunday Express Magazine* (London), 26 June 1983.
Flink, Steve, "The Professor of His Profession," in *World Tennis* (New York), June 1985.
Flink, Steve, "You Must Remember This," in *World Tennis* (New York), February 1986.
Bodo, Peter, "Why Tinling Worries about the Women," in *Tennis* (New York), May 1986.
Griggs, Barbara, "Wimbledon's Other Champion," in *The Daily Telegraph* (London), 19 June 1986.
Ciampa, Gail, "Tinling's Shocking Tennis Togs Now Tame Stuff," in the *Providence Journal Bulletin* (Rhode Island), 23 July 1987.
Rothlein, Lewis, "Combining Form with Fashion," in *Women's Sports and Fitness* (Boulder, Colorado), August 1988.
"Ted Tinling," [obituary] in the *New York Times,* 24 May 1990.
Bodo, Peter, "Ted Tinling, the Doyen of Women's Tennis," in *Tennis* (New York), June 1990.
"Died, Ted Tinling," in *Time* (New York), 4 June 1990.
Pignon, Laurie, "Ted Tinling: 1910-1990," in *Women's Tennis* (New York), July 1990.
Flink, Steve, "He Left Them Tinling," in *World Tennis* (New York), August 1990.

*   *   *

Teddy Tinling was a major presence in the world of international tennis from the late 1920s until his death at the age of 79 in 1990. Among the roles he filled were player, umpire, announcer, ombudsman, raconteur, historian, and designer to generations of champions.

His entrance into the professional side of the sport came about wholly by chance. In the absence of a club official, Tinling was asked to referee a match in Nice starring the legendary Suzanne Lenglen. He was 13 years old. The unlikely combination of smitten teenager and temperamental tennis star gelled and Tinling accompanied Lenglen to Wimbledon. In 1927 he became Wimbledon's official liaison between the tournament's players and its committee members. He held the position until 1949.

At the age of 21, Tinling settled on dressmaking as a profession, setting himself up in a bed-sitter in South Kensington, London. His first collection was shown in 1931. By 1939 Tinling had moved to Mayfair where a staff of 100 worked on the wedding gowns and evening dresses which were his specialty.

After World War II, Tinling sought to resume his business. Postwar Utility regulations combined with a shortage of raw materials, however, prevented him from creating luxurious gowns for the carriage trade. Tinling turned instead to the new phenomenon, sportswear. Standard wear at the time for women on the tennis court was a blouse or jersey and a pair of culottes, an outfit which Tinling thought utterly lacking in femininity or style. His heroine Suzanne Lenglen always looked glamorous on or off the court, always dressed as the star she was. Tinling determined to bring these qualities to women's tennis clothes.

His designs were controversial from the outset. Tinling's first commission, for Joy Gannon's Wimbledon debut in 1947, was a dress with a small colored border at the hem. A similar design the following year for champion Betty Hilton's Wightman Cup match so outraged Hazel Wightman that she threatened to ban color—if not Tinling—from future Wimbledon games. Into this brewing storm blew Gertrude "gorgeous Gussy" Moran. Could Ted, she wrote from California, design her a dress for Wimbledon? A very colorful dress? Tinling correctly predicted that an all-white rule would prevail for the 1949 games and so he designed instead a dress in proper white of satin-trimmed rayon, which shimmered, he said, as did Moran herself. Came the fitting, it was apparent that a pair of panties would be required to complete the ensemble. As legend has it, Tinling finished off the pants with a bit of lace edging and with this act inadvertently secured his place in fashion history. Moran was besieged by the press. Photographers crawled behind her on their stomachs to achieve the most advantageous camera angle. Tinling was accused of introducing sin and vulgarity to a gentleman's game and he was banned from Wimbledon for the next 33 years.

His clothes, however, were not banned, and they continued to provoke Wimbledon officialdom as they continued to bring a sense of flair and glamor to center court. Tinling had an easy rapport with the stars of the game. He designed to suit the playing style and personality of the players he came to know so well, matching fabric, trim, and cut to the individual. Between 1952 and 1961 every female champion at Wimbledon and most winners of the US Women's Open wore Tinling's dresses. In 1973 he dressed the winners of every major international tournament.

Tinling continued to subvert the all-white regulations, which he felt led to clothing that lacked spectator appeal and contributed nothing to a player's individuality. In 1950 he conceived a shirt and shorts ensemble of *broderie anglaise* which the United Press dubbed the "peekaboo" suit, thus assuring its later success in the retail market. A few years later Lea Pericoli sported a pink petticoat under her dress for the 1955 Wimbledon games. In 1962 Tinling's designs for Maria Bueno proved too provocative to escape censure. Bueno's Wimbledon costumes were enhanced with colored diamond-shaped petals which appeared in a sunburst pattern on her skirt lining and across her panties. One costume came suspiciously close to the official tournament colors; Bueno's semi-final match was lost amidst outbursts of temper and flashes of hot pink. The committee closed ranks and banned color for a second time.

From 1971 to 1978 Tinling was the official designer for the Virginia Slims circuit. It was here that he was able to introduce color to the game in a significant way. For the Slims circuit Tinling might design 100 dresses per season, each unique to the player, with color as the unifying factor.

When the occasion called for it, Tinling could bring a sense of drama and flamboyance to the game. For Rosie Casals, he created a three-piece ensemble in, of all things, black velvet. Billie Jean King's "battle of the sexes" against Bobby Riggs was fought in a sequined dress which perfectly suited the frivolity of the event, even as it made sure she would be visible to spectators at the top of Houston's vast Astrodome.

Largely because of the Virginia Slims tournament and owing to the efforts of the women themselves, women's tennis in the late 1970s became popular enough for sportswear manufacturers to offer lucrative endorsement contracts to the players. Tinling's career as a custom designer was thus curtailed.

Within the profession Ted Tinling was respected as the supreme arbiter who represented players to management in an official capacity not only at Wimbledon, where he was reinstated in 1982, but at the other three grand slam events as well as on the Slims tour. His encyclopaedic knowledge of tennis and tennis players made him an oral historian of the game, and keeper of its traditions. For 60 years Ted Tinling and tennis were synonymous.

—Whitney Blausen

TISE, Jane. See **ESPRIT.**

TOI, Zang.

American designer

Born: Malaysia, 11 June 1961. **Education:** Studied fashion design at Parsons School of Design, New York, 1981-83. **Career:** Production associate, Mary Jane Marcasiano, New York, 1982-87; freelance designer, Ronaldus Shamask, New York, 1988; opened own business, 1989, introduced diffusion line, Z, 1992. **Exhibitions:** Fashion Institute of Technology Museum. **Awards:** Mouton-Cadet Young Designer Award for outstanding achievement in the arts, 1990. **Address:** 30 West 57th Street, New York, New York 10019, USA.

Publications:

On TOI:

Articles

Starzinger, Page Hill, "New Faces," in *Vogue* (New York), March 1990.
Baker, Martha, "Back to School," in *New York Magazine,* 17 September 1990.
De Caro, Frank, "Fashion New Kids: On the Block," in *Newsday* (New York), 3 October 1990.
Darnton, Nina, "The New York Brat Pack," in *Newsweek* (New York), 29 April 1991.
"Great Expectations," in *Women's Wear Daily* (New York), 12 June 1991.
Goodman, Wendy, "Couture Cuisine," in *House and Garden* (New York), December 1991.
Ezersky, Lauren, "Going for the Glitz," in *Paper* (New York), October 1992.

*

At the house of Toi, it all starts with color. Lavish hues of chartreuse, red, and hot pink ... theoretically should never be seen together. Here they have been combined masterfully with a flair and wit that has won the hearts of both critics and customers alike!!!

Breaking the rules is what I do best. I try not to limit my thinking to the way things have been done before—my customers have come to expect the unexpected. Pioneering in dressing up good old all-American denim in splashy red and hot pink stitched with metalic

Zang Toi: c.1994.

gold stitching into sexy suits and little bustier dress is the chicest way to dress.

The Zang Toi's formula is creating glamourous tailored, classic sportswear with a dramatic twist. With a surprising mixed palette and signature design finishes. Evening at Zang Toi means haute fantasy with a dash of old Hollywood glamour.

It is always a dream of mine to merge my fashion sense with fine food. The magic words here are food is like fashion; clothes are just a piece of cloth until you add the decoration and the look, then it becomes fashion. The same with food, once you start decorating it becomes appetizing. My personal philosophy is that beautiful food and clothes should always be a part of life.

—Zang Toi

*   *   *

Zang Toi has the dubious distinction of being a featured designer in a *Newsday* article of 3 October 1990, "Fashion's New Kids: On the Block," and of being a principal in Nina Darnton's article "The New York Brat Pack" in the 29 April 1991 issue of *Newsweek.* In the *Newsweek* article, Zang Toi has the last word, telling Darnton, "I think women are looking for good prices and styles that are new—not just young people in the same mold as the current stars." Likewise, in the *Newsday* article, Zang Toi's pragmatic and sensible remarks form the article's conclusion when he says, "There are so many young designers who are eager to be stars right away. But ego can be the worst killer to any young designer. You can't let the press and the hype go to your head. If the work doesn't meet the demand and the quality, it doesn't mean anything."

Toi's work resoundingly meets demand and determines desires and styles in the early 1990s. The gifted young designer has demonstrated a color sensibility related not only to Asian textiles (the collection that earned him the Mouton-Cadet Young Designer Award was inspired by Southeast Asian textiles, with rich batiks and embroideries), but perhaps equally to Matisse in his vibrant palette. Toi's color is often and aptly compared to Christian Lacroix's. But Toi has brought his tinted exuberance not, as Lacroix, to almost baroque forms of highly elaborated couture, but to serviceable sportswear separates. For Lacroix, arguably the delectation is in the whole and is a design by ensemble. In Toi's work, the delights are in the elements. Even within, his ingenious and impertinent buttons and extravagant details give punctuation with whimsy. Well-cut jackets, saucy skirts and shorts, spunky sarong skirts with ornament, wonderful vests and trousers provide a sensible dressing from constituents rich in color and texture. It is as if Albers's color cards and Matisse paper cutouts and the richest textile patterns (often with the exquisite horror vacui excess associated with Southeast Asian textiles) have come together in three-dimensional and living form in Toi's beautiful designs. As much as Toi loves glamor, he has also created a diffusion line, Z, launched in 1992, that luxuriates in denim and less expensive fabrication.

Toi did not set out to be a designer. Growing up as the youngest son of seven children of a grocer in a small town in Malaysia, Toi loved sketching and drawing, but dreamed of being an architect or interior designer. His love of fashion came later and always in conjunction with cuisine and other pleasurable arts. He admits to wanting to combine fashion and running a restaurant. Like many designers, however, a lifetime interest in classic movie glamor and stars such as Audrey Hepburn encourage his fashion interests. The Malay tradewinds have always brought rich interactions of British colonialism (apparent in Toi's schoolboy stripes), Chinese, Indonesian, and other converging possibilities. Exoticism and pragmatic synthesis seem to come effortlessly to Toi.

In the West, we have traditionally enjoyed an adulation of the new and Zang Toi is a new designer. But his merit and interest reside in the fact that his design is distinguished not by novelty but by his intense commitment to color. His fashion draws eclectically and with an absorbing anachronism on history and global fashion, always keeping his international eye for color. His practicality and sensitivity to the consumer are hallmarks of smart design for the 1990s. Infinitely personable and charming, Toi also partakes of a Western tradition of the designer as social mixer and gregarious personality. Lauren Ezersky wrote, "I love Zang. Everybody loves Zang. He truly is one of the nicest designers on the scene today. And his designs are as fabulous as his gams, which he displays on a regular basis by wearing shorts" (*Paper,* October 1992).

If he is a new kid on the color block, Toi has the characteristics of precocious aptitude and wise business acumen. Frank de Caro said ungrammatically of Malaysian-born Toi and of his success, "if anyone is the Next Big Thing, it's him" (*Newsday,* New York, 29 April 1991). One could wish that all proclaimed as new and the Next Big Thing were as solid, as self-aware, and as sensible in design exploration and innovation as Zang Toi.

—Richard Martin

TOLEDO, Isabel.

Cuban designer working in the United States

Born: Cuba, 9 April 1961. **Education:** Studied painting and ceramics, then fashion design at the Fashion Institute of Technology and Parsons School of Design, New York. **Family:** Married Ruben Toledo in 1984. **Career:** Showed first collection, 1985. **Awards:** Coty American Fashion Critics "Winnie" Award. **Address:** 31 West 31st St, New York, New York 10018, USA.

Publications:

On TOLEDO:

Books

Steele, Valerie, *Women of Fashion: Twentieth Century Designers,* New York 1991.

Articles

Schiro, Anne-Marie, "Hot New Young Designers," in *Cosmopolitan,* June 1987.
"Storm over Toledo," in *Connoisseur* (New York), February 1992.
Rosenblum, Anne, "Partners in Style," in *Harper's Bazaar* (New York), March 1992.
Gordon, Mary Ellen, "Isabel Toledo's Cottage Industry," in *Women's Wear Daily* (New York), 27 May 1992.
"What Do Women Want?," in *Mirabella* (New York), October 1992.
"The Toledos," in *Mirabella* (New York), January 1993.
Wadyka, Sally, "A Structured Life," in *Vogue* (New York), February 1995.

* * *

The United States is better known for the mass-production of clothing than for nourishing avant-garde talent. Isabel Toledo is one of the few cutting-edge designers working in New York, and financial success has been a long time coming. When she began designing professionally in 1986, Toledo was immediately recognized as a powerful talent; her clothes were featured in magazines like *Vogue* and *Harper's Bazaar* and sold in prestigious stores like Bendel's of New York. Since then, however, she has had legal difficulties with a financial backer, as well as problems with American retail store executives.

Isabel Toledo did not sell a single piece of clothing at retail in the United States for three years in the early 1990s. She and her husband, artist Ruben Toledo, told *Women's Wear Daily* that they just could not afford to take orders from stores that refuse to provide half payment up front. Meanwhile, store buyers worried that her line was too "experimental" for the American market. She survived on the business from sales in Japan and Paris. "It makes sense for us to sell to Japanese and European accounts because when they give you an order, they give you the money," she said. She also had the patronage of about 60 devoted private clients, who are attracted by what she calls her penchant for "practicality disguised as fantasy."

Through it all, Isabel Toledo has been a cult figure among fashion enthusiasts. Her fellow designers admire her tremendously. Todd Oldham calls her "one of America's greatest resources." Both Marc Jacobs and Christian Francis Roth have praised her "incredible" talent and urged retailers to advance her money. Journalists agree: "Best overall collection for our money was Isabel Toledo, who ignored the market and concentrated on a well-edited, very weird, internal vision," raved a reporter for the *Village Voice*. Toledo is a "great designer ... travelling on that new American highway of fashion," argues Kim Hastreiter of *Paper*. Recently, she has begun to achieve the financial recognition that she deserves, and her clothes are now available in Barneys New York (Manhattan, Chicago, and Beverly Hills).

Toledo designs clothes that are structured, even architectural, and sometimes (as she says) "rather severe—a lot of black and strong shapes." She has always started with a shape, usually a circle or a curved line: a circle skirt, a curved bra, a flared apron overskirt, the sweeping arc of a coat. "I'm not a fashion designer," insists Toledo. "I'm a seamstress. I really love the technique of sewing more than anything else." She believes that it is crucial to know fashion from the inside: through cutting, draping, patternmaking and sewing. Among the designers she admires are women like Madeleine Vionnet and Madame Grès, who also worked in three dimensions rather than from a flat sketch. Toledo sees definite advantages in being a woman designer, because they "experience" the way the clothing feels. Men, she believes, tend to be more "decorators of clothing."

Like Claire McCardell, creator in the 1940s of the "American look," the Cuban-born Toledo uses classic materials such as denim and cotton flannel plaid in a modern way. Although inventive tailoring is characteristic of her work, her clothes are not for "an office type of person," she admits, but for someone like herself: artistic and feminine. There is also a futuristic element in her work, which she sees as being related to her experiences as an immigrant to a new country. Unlike many designers, Toledo is not interested in recycling styles from the past, preferring to experiment with the basic materials of her art, and to explore the future of fashion.

Ruben Toledo once did an illustration, "Fashion history goes on strike!" which depicted the styles of the past (from New Look to Mod) marching in a demonstration with signs demanding: "Let us rest in peace! No more retro! Look forward, not backwards!" That sums up Isabel Toledo's approach to fashion.

—Valerie Steele

TOMALIN, Lewis. See **JAEGER.**

TOMPKINS, Susie and Doug. See **ESPRIT.**

TORII, Yuki.

Japanese fashion designer

Born: Tokyo, 3 January 1943. **Education:** Studied at the Bunka College of Art, Tokyo, 1958-61. **Family:** Married Takao Torii in 1974; one child: Maki. **Career:** Free-lance designer, working in Torii Ginza Boutique, Tokyo, founded by grandmother in 1952 (now belonging to Yuki Torii); presented first designs within her mother's collection, 1962. Established Torii Company Ltd, ready-to-wear firm, Tokyo, 1972; first Paris collection, autumn 1975; launched Yuki Torii Deux label, and Yuki Torii International, 1983; opened Yuki Torii Design Studio, Tokyo, 1984; established Yuki Torii France SA, 1985. Designs include ready-to-wear for men and women, printed fabrics, *kimonos,* lacquerware, accessories, interior design items, and childrenswear. Also: designed costumes for theatre and television. Member of NDC (Nippon Designer Club), from 1984. Awards: Fashion Editors Club Award, Paris, 1976; Japan Fashion Editors Club, Best Designer of the Year, 1988. **Address:** Torii Co., Daito Building, 1-5-1 Minami Azabu Minato-ku, Tokyo 106, Japan.

Publications:

On TORII:

Books

The Tokyo Collection: Graphic Sha, Tokyo, 1986.

Articles

Monique, "They Have a Yen for Traditional Japanese Styles," in the *New York Daily News,* 1975.
Monique, "Paris' New Household Word: Yuki," in the *New York Daily News,* 1975.
de Turckheim, Hélène, "Le travail c'est la santé de la mode," in *Le Figaro* (Paris), 9 December 1975.

Yuki Torii: Fall/Winter 1994/95.

Women's Wear Daily (New York), 19 December 1975.
"Mais qu'est-ce qui fait courir les japonais?," in *Gap,* December/
January 1977-78.

*

I create clothes which make women beautiful, happy and gay. My clothes are easy to wear. They are made in beautiful colours, vivid or tender.

Reflecting well the *"air du temps,"* they are trendy and modern, but never provocative. I like femininity and *"le charme"* based on nature and harmony.

There is no age to wear my clothes. They are for women of any age. At first sight, my clothes give the impression of being destined for the very young, because of the bright colours. But they give successfully a young and modern allure to any woman.

My philosophy: the clothes should make the person who wears them beautiful and happy as well as the people who look at her.

—Yuki Torii

* * *

As a child, Yuki Torii had ambitions of becoming a painter. Pattern and colour had always excited her and when she became a professional designer in the early 1960s, her approach always began with the textile or colour, with a defined choice of palette that has ranged from pastels to brights.

Bright, vivid colour has been a recognizable quality in Yuki Torii's work. A distinctive collection was autumn/winter 1986, which mixed vividly coloured tartans and checks for men's, women's and childrenswear. Lively, wearable separates; oversize tartan shirts, tartan trousers, and comfortable cardigans for men; long tartan flounced skirts for women, teamed with long, skinny rib jumpers or oversize Argyle patterned sweaters; tartan pinafore dresses for girls and a weatherbeaten, mountaineering look for boys, layering tartan overshirts over tartan Levi-style jackets.

The vibrant Yuki Torii collection sold as part of Liberty of London's *Japan at Liberty* promotion in 1991 displayed a more sophisticated air, paying homage to the style of Coco Chanel combined with the bold colour combination of Christian Lacroix. Vibrant tweeds in unities of orange, lime green, red, grass green, yellow, pale pink, and fuchsia were made into neat, boxy suits, and separates. Much of the fabric was fringed at the hems of garments and interesting details were flower-shaped tweed emblems appliquéd on to pockets and trims.

Yuki Torii had been the youngest student to enroll at the Bunka Gakuin College of Art in Tokyo when she was 15. This precocious talent led her to sell her first creations in her grandmother's haute couture boutique Ginza in Tokyo. By 1972 she had established her own ready-to-wear business, Torii Co. Ltd., and by 1975 had shown her first collection in the prestigious Paris prêt-à-porter collections.

Yuki Torii is often told that her clothes look best on herself and it is from this perspective that she begins designing. The approach is similar to that adopted by many other female designers, in particular Jean Muir who is renowned for producing clothes women really want to wear and feel comfortable in. Yuki Torii thinks it natural that female designers conceive ideas from themselves and their roles and needs as women. She likes to project an overall image of sweetness in her clothes, a sweetness that is retained in images of

childrenswear but is often lost in adult fashion. She achieves this by never presenting themes that threaten or provoke controversy. Her look instead is a harmonious combination of contrasting colour and fabric that is wearable and flattering but often incorporates the unusual detailing found in children's clothes. For instance, Western cowboy detailing on children's shirts or the naïve flower emblems in her tweed collection.

In 1983 two new brands were created, Yuki Torii Deux and Yuki Torii International. Licensed products like scarves, furs, gloves, belts, eyewear, neckties, and umbrellas were produced from the Yuki Torii Design Studio established in 1984. By 1985 the company was operating from both Japan and France when Yuki Torii France SA was established, together with the opening of the boutique at 38-40 Galerie Vivienne in Paris.

—Kevin Almond

TORRENTE.
French fashion house

Established in Paris by designer Madame Torrente Mett, in the 1960s; licensing contract for men's ready-to-wear signed with French factory, 1971; signed licensing deal with Japan, 1972; childrenswear, leather collection, luxury accessories such as neckties, scarves, glasses, jewellery, and household linens introduced; signed licensing deal with La Callonec and Murier for corporate wear; sells both couture and ready-to-wear lines; Rosette Mett, chief artistic director. **Address:** 9 rue du Faubourg Saint-Honoré, Paris, France.

Publications:

On TORRENTE:

Articles

d'Aulnay, Sophie, "Vestra Weaves Its Global Web," in the *Daily News Record,* 25 January 1993.

* * *

Torrente is a French haute couture and ready-to-wear label. The essence of the company's style is represented by their Haute Boutique situated at 9 rue du Faubourg Saint-Honoré, in Paris. The shop sells the best of both the Torrente couture and ready-to-wear lines, made from the most exquisite, luxurious, and individual fabrics in the world. Many of the clothes are hand finished, which although adding to the cost of the garments, gives the customer a unique and personalized purchase.

Popular and influential styles have included the satin collar; in an abstract floral print on a shapely, turquoise, short skirted suit or a classic cream collar and cuffs on elegant, checked wool coat dresses and two-pieces. Unusual, stiff, gauzy silk fabrics are used on stoles, edged in bead embroidery and thrown over short, strapless bell-skirted raw silk dresses, with matching beading on the hems. Lace is another popular fabric, used mainly in eveningwear and ranging from heavily beaded and encrusted for sculpted looks, to a soft drapable lace used in short empire dresses in cream, with *décolleté* necklines. The drape is positioned centrally at the cleavage and secured with the palest of pink roses. The overall look is very feminine, aimed not at fashion's vanguard, but designed for a woman secure and established in her own style, whose schedule demands a quantity of individualistic, smart occasion wear.

The company was established by its first designer Madame Torrente Mett in the 1960s and the upper echelons of Paris society soon recognized a formidable design talent. Torrente creations began to be seen in places like Maxims and at the Opéra; stylish names like Claudia Cardinale and Marlene Dietrich soon became regular clients at the Haute Boutique. Since the 1960s the company has steadily expanded. In 1971 a licensing contract for men's ready-to-wear was signed with a French factory and in the following year a lucrative deal was clinched with Japan. Childrenswear, a leather collection, and luxury accessories like neckties, scarves, glasses, jewellery, and household linens have since been introduced. The company even branched out into corporate wear, signing a licensing deal with La Callonec and Murier in France.

Madame Torrente Mett was elected a member of the Chambre Syndicale de la Haute Couture in 1971. Today the chief artistic director is Rosette Mett, although Madame Torrente Mett continues to have a valued overview of the design and artistic merit of Torrente products. Her other activities in the fashion world have been as the founder and vice-president of the French Fashion Institute and as a lecturer at the Paris business school, Hautes Études Commerciales.

Items from the haute couture range are available in over 100 shops worldwide. The less expensive ready-to-wear line, Miss Torrente, is sold through over 250 European outlets, and Torrente menswear retails in 400 worldwide outlets. The couture line remains the flagship for the essence of the Torrente style, denoting quality with an international sophistication equally at home at a society wedding in the south of France or at an opera gala in Milan.

—Kevin Almond

TRACY, Ellen. See ALLARD, Linda.

TRANSPORT.

British footwear firm

Founded by Jimmy Sarvea. Opened first shop, Reading, Berkshire, 1970. Firm bought by Allied Shoes Ltd. **Address:** Allied Shoes, 77-79 Great Eastern St, London EC2A 3HU, UK.

*   *   *

Transport Shoes probably epitomized the growth of modern footwear fashion and the looks that we now take for granted as the street level expression of the young. The originator of the label, Jimmy Sarvea, previously a boxer, was first a shoe repairer, became an assistant manager for a major footwear retailer and went on to become one of the leading shoe entrepreneurs of the 1970s and 1980s. From the opening of his first shop in Reading, Berkshire in 1970 to his continued presence on the High Street, Sarvea has helped to ensure that the avant-garde, trend conscious customer is well served.

Whether classic or high fashion, the original Transport shoes, manufactured in Italy, created an impressive turnover. One of the most famous outlets for their men's shoes was Succhi, a mecca for the discriminating. The menswear market in general had become increasingly aware of fashion as the decade progressed, and the individuality of the footwear sold under the Transport label became an essential ingredient of a positive statement. Jimmy Sarvea was joined by Carol Sullivan and the influence they found from streetwear added charisma and a new visual freedom to their shoes. The collection continued to grow, with exciting and innovative designs for both sexes. Many styles were unisex, with wide use of the unexpected, including glitter fabrics, stinging use of colours such as orange and purple, unforgettable last and heel shapes, platform soles, chunky silhouettes, and interesting and unusual use of laces and buckles.

Shoes were featured on *Top of the Pops,* a BBC Television musical programme for the young, and potential customers eagerly sought out the shoes. Transport had created the most anticipatory underground footwear fashion statement of the 1980s. Their ultimate goal, total originality, assisted in attracting the stars of the period, and George Michael, Five Star, Duran Duran, and Ian Dury were the pioneers for those who desired, for personal or professional reasons, that their footwear should be the centre of attention.

—Angela Pattison

TREACY, Philip.

Irish designer working in England

Born: Ireland. **Education:** Attended Royal College of Art. **Career:** Hat designer; has worked for such designers as Karl Lagerfeld, Marc Bohan, and Rifat Ozbek; produces hats for various couture houses and ready-to-wear firms, including the Philip Treacy for Right Impression label. **Address:** c/o Public relations office, Marie-Helene de Taillac, 69 Elizabeth Street, London SW1, England.

Publications:

On TREACY:

Articles

"Treacy: Another Feature at BG," in *Women's Wear Daily* (New York), 15 November 1991.
Fallon, James, "Philip Treacy: The Shape of Things to Come," in *Women's Wear Daily* (New York), 6 July 1990.
Killen, Mary, "Hats Off to Philip Treacy—His Fanciful Designs are Turning Heads," in *Vogue* (New York), October 1991.
McKenna, Joe, "The Big Fat Hat," in *Interview* (New York), November 1991.
Overland, Martha Ann, "Style Makers: Philip Treacy," in the *New York Times* (New York), 5 April 1992.

Bowles, Hamish, "The New Enlightenment," in *Vogue* (New York), March 1993.

Moore, Alison, "London Calling," in the *New York Times Magazine* (New York), 19 December 1993.

"Glad Hatter," in *People Weekly* (Chicago), 4 July 1994.

*   *   *

Ex-Royal College of Art student Philip Treacy was recognized as a talented milliner even before graduating from college where his final show was sponsored by *Harper's and Queen* magazine, London. In the two years since leaving college, Irish-born Treacy has moved to the forefront of the fashion world, producing hats for some of the most prestigious couture and ready-to-wear designers, including Karl Lagerfeld at Chanel, Marc Bohan at Hartnell, and Rifat Ozbek. Described as the Rembrandt of millinery by the established hat designer, Shirley Hex, Treacy's monumental creations for the fashion catwalks often receive as much publicity as the outfits for which they were designed.

Treacy's millinery designs reflect his unquestionably vivid imagination, drawing upon diverse subjects such as surrealism, the dance of Martha Graham, as well as religious and historical imagery. Treacy asserts that to create a modern hat does not require space age influences, preferring to plunder the past for inspiration and then make it appear totally new. A floral hat by Philip Treacy is a crash helmet covered in flowers and butterflies, the traditional guardsman's busby is completely transformed in yellow ostrich feathers, a towering turban is created by an intricately wrapped blanket with fringed edging, a large cluster of black coq feathers are tied together with white feathers to form a brim and crown. Treacy's hats, like those of other British milliners, are often described as eccentric. Treacy attributes this eccentricity to the fact that the British are associated with idiosyncrasy but says that he does not set out to create deliberately unusual hats. Using what he describes as "boring" fabrics, Treacy begins working upon these materials with different treatments—feathers, for example, are singed so that they take on the appearance of very fine gossamer.

An important factor in Treacy's work is his mastery of highly skilled traditional millinery techniques which ensure the correct balance, fit, and proportion for the hat which he concedes are as much mathematical as aesthetic. It is this artisan approach, with the emphasis on craft and technique, that characterizes much of Treacy's work. Treacy currently produces hats for nine different companies—three couture houses and six ready-to-wear firms, one of which is the Philip Treacy for Right Impression label designed for his backer. Treacy's ability to work at all levels of the market, from the costly couture creations to the less expensive ready-to-wear field, illustrates his versatility as a designer for whom price barriers are seen as a challenge rather than an obstacle.

While Treacy's use of imagery and visual effects for his millinery creations is a vital element in his success, fashion critic Brenda Polan claims that Treacy's mastery of technique is what singles him out as a great milliner, stating, "The balance of his hats, their swooping and curving, is perfect. A Treacy hat sits naturally upon the head, its proportions complementing those of the body, its horizontal and vertical lines extending and dramatizing the planes of the face. It is a perfection only an obsessive can achieve."

—Catherine Woram

TRIGÈRE, Pauline.

American designer

Born: Paris, France, 4 November 1912. **Education:** Jules Ferry and Victor Hugo Colleges, Paris, 1923-28. **Family:** Married Lazar Radley in 1929 (separated); children: Jean-Pierre, Philippe. **Career:** Immigrated to the United States, 1937, naturalized, 1942. Trainee clothing cutter, Martial et Armand, Paris, 1928-29; assistant cutter, fitter, in father's tailoring business, Paris, 1929-32; free-lance designer, Paris, 1933-36; design assistant, Ben Gershel, New York, 1937; assistant to Travis Banton, Hattie Carnegie fashion house, New York, 1937-42; co-founder, designer, House of Trigère, from 1942. **Awards:** Coty American Fashion Critics Award, 1949, 1951, 1959; Neiman Marcus Award, Dallas, 1950; National Cotton Council of America Award, 1951; Filene Award, Boston, 1959; Silver Medal, City of Paris, 1972. **Address:** 550 Seventh Avenue, New York, New York 10018, USA.

Publications:

On TRIGÈRE:

Books

Lee, Sarah Tomerlin, *American Fashion: The Life and Lines of Adrian, Mainbocher, McCardell, Norell, Trigère,* New York 1975, London 1976.

Morris, Bernadine, and Barbara Walz, *The Fashion Makers,* New York 1978.

Diamonstein, Barbaralee, *Fashion: The Inside Story,* New York 1985.

Milbank, Caroline Rennolds, *Couture: The Great Designers,* New York 1985.

New York and Hollywood Fashion: Costume Designs from the Brooklyn Museum Collection, New York 1986.

Milbank, Caroline Rennolds, *New York Fashion: The Evolution of American Style,* New York 1989.

Articles

"Designers Who Are Making News," in *American Fabrics and Fashions* (New York), No. 38, 1956.

Alexander, J., "New York's New Queen of Fashion," in the *Saturday Evening Post* (New York), 8 April 1961.

Greene, Gael, and Peter Vitale, "The Style of Pauline Trigère: Enduring Qualities Enliven Her New York Residence," in *Architectural Digest* (Los Angeles), September 1988.

Woods, Vicki, "Vicki Woods Crosses Paths with the Eccentric Pauline Trigère—and Comes Away with an Earful," in *Vogue* (New York), October 1989.

Brady, James, "Most Elegant Pauline," in *Advertising Age* (New York), 21 November 1994.

*

I've always found it difficult to talk or write about FASHION. I think FASHION—clothes, garments—should be enjoyed and worn, and certainly fill a certain purpose in one's life.

I also think that for me, doing it for 50 years or more, proved that I have done it somewhat right.

Pauline Trigère: 1990; white doubleface wool suit with strapless gold embroidered top. *Photograph by Gideon Lenin.*

I love my work, I love designing, I love folding, draping, molding the fabric in my hands and producing new shapes, new designs.

I have never gone up-up, or down-down like a yo-yo. I have tried to keep my women, my customers, happy in their Trigère clothes—hoping that they bought them and wore them with pleasure, and that they were right for their lives—PTA, business meetings, concerts, theater, etc.

In thinking back, I don't think that I would have enjoyed anything else but doing collection after collection, four to five times a year—(oh yes, maybe I could have been an architect, or yes, yes, most certainly a surgeon ...).

—Pauline Trigère

*   *   *

Pauline Trigère is more than a designer of women's clothing, she is a fabric artisan. Trigère left her native France in 1937 and arrived in New York with practical training gathered from her parents' tailoring shop and the Parisian couture house of Martial et Armand, plus a natural talent for working with fabric. She started her own business in 1942 with a collection of just 12 dresses. During World War II, when the American fashion industry was cut off from inspiration normally coming from Paris, Trigère's combination of French elegance and American practicality proved successful. Her constant commitment to excellent design and workmanship has kept her in business for over 50 years.

During the 1940s Trigère become known especially for her impeccable and imaginative tailoring of women's suits and coats. She made use of all weights of wool, from sheer crêpes for eveningwear to thick tweeds for daytime coats. She was recognized early in her career as an innovator for such fashions as evening dresses made of wool or cotton, reversible coats and capes in all shapes and sizes. Another characteristic Trigère feature is the luxurious touch of fur trim at necklines, cuffs, and hems. Before the 1960s, her palette was fairly subdued and she rarely used printed fabrics; during the 1960s and 1970s she began to use more prints and softer fabrics, always retaining a tailored touch. Her use of prints is bold and deliberate, the pattern is often used to complement the structure of the piece. Notwithstanding her extensive use of wool and tailoring techniques, Trigère's clothing is unmistakably feminine. She rarely makes use of menswear details.

While she is an acknowledged innovator of fashions, she is also know for repeating and perfecting her most successful themes. For example, her princess line dress which appears in her collections consistently is considered to have no equal, and her rhinestone bra top, first introduced in 1967, was revived in 1985 and 1992.

Throughout the evolution of fashion in the last half-century, Trigère has worked within the mainstream while retaining her signature style. Simple elegance and timelessness are descriptions often applied to her work, but style is not her only concern. She insists on the highest quality of materials to assure that her clothing will serve her customers for years to come. Her collections are carefully planned so that many pieces will work together, and complement past seasons' collections.

Trigère's work has been compared to that of two legendary French couturiers, Cristobal Balenciaga and Madeleine Vionnet. These designers were known for employing complex and unusual construction techniques to create simple, elegant silhouettes. Trigère herself rarely sketches her ideas; like Balenciaga and Vionnet she designs by draping and cutting the actual fabric on a dress form or live model. The fabric itself is an important part of Trigère's design

process. It is her inspiration and her guide as it reveals what it is capable of doing. Trigère's continued involvement with the creative process and her insistence on quality make her unique on New York's Seventh Avenue.

—Melinda L. Watt

TRUSSARDI, SpA.

Italian leathergoods and accessories manufacturer

Founded in Bergamo, Italy, as glove making firm by Dante Trussardi, 1910. Firm taken over by nephew Nicola Trussardi, 1970. First boutique opened, Milan, 1976; jewelery collection introduced, 1976; men's and women's ready-to-wear collections and Trussardi Junior childrenswear line introduced, 1983; Trussardi Jeans, Trussardi Action and Trussardi Sport collections introduced, 1987; designed Italian Olympic team uniforms, 1988. **Awards:** Nicola Trussardi named Cavalier of the Great Cross, Italy, 1987. **Address:** Piazza Eleanora Duse 4, 20122 Milan, Italy.

On TRUSSARDI:

Books

The Fashion Guide: International Designers Directory, London, Paris, New York, Tokyo 1990.

On TRUSSARDI:

Articles

Frosh, Jennifer, "Camping in with Trussardi," in *Women's Wear Daily* (New York), 8 July 1977.

*   *   *

For over 60 years the Italian family firm of Trussardi manufactured high quality leather gloves. Opened in 1910 by Dante Trussardi in Bergarmo, the company had a limited but well-respected reputation for its goods. In 1970 Nicola Trussardi, a graduate of business and economics from the University of Milan, joined the family firm with ambitions for broadening scope and production. After comprehensive research, Nicola diversified and extended the technical and creative aspects of the company, initiating a wide range of luxury goods made to the highest possible standards of good taste and retailing for extravagant sums of money. Top-quality leather goods like belts, bags, and luggage were introduced followed by umbrellas, foulards, ties, and shoes.

By 1976 the first exclusive Trussardi boutique was opened in Milan and further accessory products, together with gold and silver jewellery, were presented. All merchandise is stamped with a trademark greyhound, the sleek symbol of nobility and antiquity, now well established as a mark for Italian quality. Today there are well over 50 boutiques in Italy alone, plus international boutiques throughout Europe, the United States, and the Far East as well as exports to many luxury department stores.

By 1983 Nicola Trussardi was devoting much energy to the launch of the company's first ready-to-wear collection. Clean-cut and essentially classic, the ranges of men's and womenswear soon diversified to include knitwear, skiwear, eveningwear, and Trussardi Junior, a childrenswear line. The clothes naturally reflect the exclusive luxury of the established leather and accessory goods, yet are modern in feel, casual, and wearable. Favourite fabrics are naturally leathers (often embossed or treated), velvets, wool jerseys, and furs. Recent collections have adopted more avant-garde trends such as Empire line suits in oversize plaids, sleeveless A-line leather slip-overs or a side-split plaid skirt dangerously perched at hipster level. This approach keeps the collection young looking and provides a healthy fashion content, whilst retaining the ever-present sense of lavish expense and exquisite taste.

Trussardi are noted for presenting collections in prestigious sites, organized and participated in by the most noted international names in theatre, cinema, and opera. The first ready-to-wear collection was presented in La Scala in Milan. A 1985 collection was shown in an enormous semi-transparent cube constructed in Piazza Duomo in the heart of Milan. The theatricality of these showings is obviously designed to attract the maximum media coverage for the Trussardi name.

Recent developments in Trussardi have included jeans and the Trussardi sport lines. The company was also responsible for the design of Italy's team uniforms for the 1988 Olympics. Fervently nationalist, Trussardi sponsored the building of the Palatrussardi in 1986, an important centre for sports and entertainment ventures in Milan.

—Kevin Almond

TUFFIN, Sally.

British designer

Born: 1938. **Education:** Studied at the Walthamstow School of Art; graduated from the Royal College of Art, 1961. **Career:** Partner, Foale and Tuffin, 1962-72; opened retail store, 1965; designer, Sally Tuffin, Ltd., mid-1970s.

Publications:

By TUFFIN:

Books

Children's Wardrobe (with Ann Ladbury), London 1978.

On TUFFIN:

Books

Lobenthal, Joel, *Radical Rags: Fashions of the Sixties,* New York 1990.

Articles

"Tuffin Alone," in *Women's Wear Daily* (New York), 10 July 1972.

*   *   *

Sally Tuffin was one of several designers to emerge from Professor Janey Ironside's talented stable of fashion design graduates at London's Royal College of Art in the 1960s. In company with Ossie Clark, Zandra Rhodes, and Bill Gibb she and her business partner Marion Foale (also a RCA graduate) fast came to epitomize the street style and culture of what became the trademark phrase of the decade, "Swinging London."

Based in that hotbed for trendy 1960s happenings, Carnaby Street, Tuffin and Foale produced clothes that celebrated youth culture. "We were dressing ourselves and our friends and it just happened to be the things that people wanted," Tuffin reminisced in the 1980s. The pair recognized that the sudden predominance of street fashion was a reaction to a previous generation's reliance on Paris for ideas. To the young, the couture direction seemed tired and inaccessible. Tuffin and Foale noted that there was a fast-growing younger market which wanted something inexpensive in which to have fun and wear to discotheques.

As designers, they incorporated both modernist and nostalgic ideas into their clothes. Beginning with the Pop Art movement that spawned Pop Art prints and "keyhole" shift dresses, they moved through Op Art, into an art déco phase, and next the romantic dressing made popular by the hippie movement. They created hipster trousersuits, clean-cut crêpe dresses like cycle shirts, or vigorously banded into rugby stripes. They even printed giant Ys across a group of shift dresses that were intended as a pun on the male undergarment, in many ways a forerunner to the witty tactics employed by Moschino today.

Tuffin and Foale's partnership came to symbolize the greater opportunities that became available to young people with ideas and energy in the 1960s. Initially inspired by a lecture on costing garments given by Mary Quant at the Royal College of Art, the pair realized that business could be fun and approached it in a light hearted way. "As students we were trained to see, to explore, to enjoy ourselves. We felt as though we could go off and do anything without restriction," enthused Tuffin.

Tuffin and Foale's clothes sold in many outlets. Their first big break came in 1962 when buyer Vanessa Denza purchased their designs for Woolands 21 shop in London. This was followed by the opening of their one showroom in Carnaby Street and the retailing of their clothes in the famous Countdown boutique on the King's Road, Chelsea and at various department stores throughout England. In 1965 the partners were among the first designers to be stocked in Paraphernalia in New York, where designer Betsey Johnson recalled that they sold out of Tuffin and Foale's clothes almost immediately.

In 1972 the design duo dissolved their partnership. Tuffin went on to produce some collections under her own name label, which closely adhered to the cutting edge young fashion look she and Foale had established in the 1960s. Today she runs a pottery business with her husband.

—Kevin Almond

TYLER, Richard.

Australian designer working in Los Angeles

Born: Sunshine, Australia, c.1948, son of a factory foreman and a seamstress. **Family:** Married Doris Taylor (divorced); married

Lisa Trafficante, 1989; children: (first marriage) Sheriden; (second marriage) Edward. **Career:** Opened store, Zippity-doo-dah, in Melbourne, Australia, late 1960s; designed outfits for rock and roll stars, early 1970s; designed and traveled with Rod Stewart's "Blondes Have More Fun" tour, 1978; started the Richard Tyler collection with wife and partner Lisa Trafficante, late 1980s; opened Los Angeles showroom, Tyler Trafficante, 1988; opened New York City showroom, 1992; named head designer for Anne Klein & Company, 1993; left Anne Klein & Company, 1994. **Awards:** Council of Fashion Designers of America New Talent award, 1993; Council of Fashion Designers of America Womenswear Designer of the Year award, 1994.

Publications:

On TYLER:

Beckette, Kathleen, "Runway Report: My One and Only Hue: Richard Tyler," in the *New York Post,* 4 November 1994.

"New York: Richard Tyler," in *Women's Wear Daily* (New York), 4 November 1994.

Schiro, Anne-Marie, "The V-Shaped Jacket of the 1940s Makes a U-Turn," in the *New York Times,* 5 November 1994.

Spindler, Amy M., "Anne Klein's Designer Departs," in the *New York Times,* 20 December 1994.

LaFerla, Ruth, "Richard Tyler, Perfectionist," in *Elle* (New York), March 1995.

Spindler, Amy M., "Oldham and Tyler Look Super," in the *New York Times,* 6 April 1995.

"New York: Richard Tyler," in *Women's Wear Daily* (New York), 5 April 1995.

Articles also appear in *GQ,* October 1990; *Harper's Bazaar,* October 1992; *New York,* 12 October 1992, 13 September 1993, 11 April 1994; *Newsweek,* 4 April 1994; *People,* 21 February 1994, 5 January 1995; *Vogue,* August 1993, October 1994, February 1995.

*   *   *

"At my age, I'm thrilled," 46-year-old Richard Tyler told *People* magazine when he won the Council of Fashion Designers of America New Talent award in 1993. Just one year later he walked away with the Council's Womenswear Designer of the Year award—one of the fashion world's highest honors. While Tyler's fame may have come later in life than other designers, it has quickly grown, earning him the respect of his peers and the devotion of his customers.

Much of Tyler's initial success was due to his celebrity clients. Julia Roberts, Janet Jackson, Sigourney Weaver, and Oprah Winfrey are just a few of the stars who have publicly praised the exemplary quality and fit of his clothes. "That's the age-old recipe for success in fashion: get the right people to wear your clothes," Patrick McCarthy, the executive editor of *Women's Wear Daily,* told *Newsweek.* While his famous clients might draw new customers in, it is Tyler's attention to detail and fine tailoring that keeps his business growing. Everything on a Richard Tyler piece of clothing is done by hand. Identical and precise buttonholes are a hallmark of his collection, and his fabrics—the finest wools, silks, and linens— boast such details as individual stripes sewn onto the cloth with silk threads.

Tyler was born in Sunshine, Australia, just outside of Melbourne. His mother was a costumer with the Melbourne Ballet, and also sewed wedding dresses, men's suits, and clerical robes. Tyler's father was a plastics factory foreman with one of the best wardrobes in town. It was through his mother that Tyler learned his love for fine quality tailoring. At age 16, Tyler decided to drop out of school and began work as a tailor at a shop that was known for outfitting the Australian prime minister. He also spent some time at a factory, cutting out bras. At the age of 18, with his mother's help, Tyler opened his own store, Zippity-doo-dah, in a run-down section of Melbourne. His father paid the bills and his mother sewed his designs in the back room.

By the 1970s Tyler's shop was beginning to attract a steady clientele. Australian celebrities, and such touring rock and roll stars as Cher, Elton John, and Alice Cooper, began to seek out his lycra and sequined outfits. During this time Tyler married Doris Taylor. The marriage lasted ten years, and they had a son, Sheriden, born in the late 1970s. After Tyler's mother died in 1976, he made many trips to London, continuing to dress rock and roll stars.

In 1978 Rod Stewart asked Tyler to design his "Blondes Have More Fun" tour. When the show stopped in Los Angeles, Tyler fell in love with the city and decided to make it his home. He continued to design for performers, including Supertramp, the Bee Gees, the Go-Gos, and Diana Ross. But as costume demands became increasingly outrageous in the mid-1980s, Tyler began to drop his work for the stars. He stayed in Los Angeles, doing odd jobs and trading his gardening and sewing skills for rent at his friends' guest houses.

Tyler then spent two years in Oslo, Norway, but ended up back in Los Angeles in 1987, with his last $100 and a plane ticket home to Australia. The night before he was to fly home, he met Lisa Trafficante, an actress and businesswoman, who would change his life forever. Together Tyler and Trafficante would soon form a partnership that enabled them to establish the Richard Tyler line of clothing. Trafficante urged Tyler to follow his strengths and design finely tailored menswear. She took it upon herself to come up with a business plan and the necessary capital.

Tyler's clothes were so bold that many buyers thought their customers wouldn't buy them. It was during their last appointment of the day, at the boutique If in SoHo, that Tyler and Trafficante received their first order. If's customers were immediately drawn to Tyler's work, and within two years Chativari in New York City and Wilkes Bashford in San Francisco were also buying from Tyler. In 1988 Trafficante persuaded Tyler that they needed to open their own showroom in Los Angeles. With the backing of Trafficante's sister Michelle and investor Gordon DeVol, they bought a drapery-manufacturing building in an out-of-the-way part of town. They gutted the interior of the art-deco building and created a bare, contemporary setting for Tyler's fashion-forward designs.

The store was named Tyler Trafficante, and it was there that Tyler first became known for his trademark fitted jackets. Diana Rico, writing for *GQ,* described the transformation felt after trying on a Tyler jacket: "Its dashing cut and construction are so comfortable that you feel as though you're barely wearing anything at all. The sensuous silk lining and luxurious hand-tailored details bespeak an old-world emphasis on fine craftsmanship, while the stagy lapels, offbeat colors and elongated silhouette give the piece a daring rock and roll edge."

Although the showroom started without a women's section, so many women came in off the street requesting clothes that the next season Tyler began designing for them. It was the demand for women's clothes that really sparked the growth of Tyler Trafficante. Within five years they had one of the hottest stores in Los Angeles.

In 1992 Tyler decided it was time to introduce his line to New York. The New York fashion world welcomed Tyler and the press lauded his debut show in March of 1993. The reviews were barely in when he was contacted by the upscale women's sportswear line, Anne Klein & Company, asking him to sign on as their new design director. Many in the fashion world questioned the pairing of Tyler, known for his bold, sexy designs, with Klein, a label that manufactures traditional, conservative career clothes for women. The first year Tyler began designing for Anne Klein, store orders rose 30 percent. Despite the immediate jump in sales, the reviews of the Anne Klein line were mixed.

In December of 1994 Anne Klein and Tyler parted company. There were a number of problems that plagued his tenure with Anne Klein. Tyler had difficulty controlling quality and price: his demand for impeccable quality raised the price of an Anne Klein jacket by 15 percent. In addition, he was not used to overseeing a huge staff of patternmakers, tailors, design assistants, and dressmakers. Many speculated that the overriding reason for Tyler's termination, however, was that in his attempt to attract a younger customer, he made too many changes too soon and turned off Klein's traditional customers.

Industry insiders have no doubt, however, that Tyler will rebound. He is known as a survivor. He left Anne Klein with a reported $2.1 million buyout of his contract. In the near future, Tyler plans to launch a secondary line, with a lower price point so that more women can afford his clothes. His tenure with Anne Klein only served to increase his visibility and will undoubtedly help when he launches his new line. As for the quality of the clothes in this new line, Tyler promises that there will be no compromise. As always, his collection will begin with his tailoring skills. "In Richard's work a detail always becomes a major theme in the collection," Trafficante told *Vogue*. "Some designers have theatrical themes, but he has the way he makes his clothes as his theme." The Richard Tyler label continues to grow in popularity, and services accounts all over the globe. The key to Tyler's success was given in *Vogue*: "My mother always said if you have great quality, women will come back."

—Molly Severson

UNDERWOOD, Patricia.

British millinery designer working in New York

___

Born: Patricia Gilbert in Maidenhead, England, 11 October 1947. **Education:** Trained in millinery at Fashion Institute of Technology, New York, 1972. **Family:** Married Reginald Underwood, 1967. Divorced, 1976. Married Jonathan Moynihan, 1980. Married name; Patricia Moynihan. Children: Vivecca Underwood. **Career:** Clerk/typist at Buckingham Palace, 1966-67. Secretary, United Artists, New York, 1968-69. Manufactured hats with Lipp Holmfeld ("Hats by Lipp"), 1973-75. President and designer in own company Patricia Underwood, New York 1976. Launched Patricia Underwood Knit Collection, 1983; Featured collections in Vogue. Designs for Bill Blass, Oscar de la Renta, Carolyne Roehm, Donna Karan, Calvin Klein, Perry Ellis, Bill Blass, and other designers. Patricia Underwood Too line of women's ready-to-wear introduced, 1990. **Exhibitions:** *Hats,* Philadelphia Museum of Art, 1993. **Awards:** Coty American Fashion Critics Award, 1982; Council of Fashion Designers of America Award, 1983, American Accessories Achievement Award, 1992. **Address:** 242 West 36th Street, New York, New York 10018.

Publications:

On UNDERWOOD:

Books

Khornak, Lucille, *Fashion 2001,* New York 1982.
Steele, Valerie, *Women of Fashion,* New York 1991.
McDowell, Colin, *Hats: Status, Style, Glamour,* London 1992.
Muller, F., *Les chapeaux: une histoire de tête,* Paris 1993.
Smith, R., and Smolan, L., *The Hat Book,* New York 1993.

*

I design hats which complement clothing, flatter the wearer, and rely on shape and proportion rather than ornamental trim to achieve this effect. My designs are characterized by clean, elegant lines that enhance a silhouette and complete a sophisticated look. A simplicity of design avoids the pitfalls of a hat becoming a distraction on a wearer. I create hats in a variety of materials since there are also the practical weather related aspects to hat wearing. For instance, one can have chic hats for warmth as well as to shield sun. A hat must be comfortable and easy to wear. This is achieved by using high quality, malleable materials and handcrafted workmanship.

My inspiration for a collection comes from my travels, art, and the international world of fashion. Beautifully tailored clothing, innovative uses of materials and application of finishing details are constant sources of new ideas. Collaborations with talented designers including Bill Blass, Marc Jacobs, the late Perry Ellis, and many others, are a tremendous source of inspiration for me. I am always intrigued by color and certain tones that flatter a complexion to enhance beauty.

We are lucky today that one may choose to wear a hat or not, unlike 50 years ago when a hat was considered a necessity of good grooming. Now hat wearing has become a matter of personal style and a way of stimulating response. For instance, one of my greatest friends, recently divorced, had come to live in New York. She was in an elevator wearing one of my hats, as it happened, when a gentleman entered the elevator and said, "You look wonderful in that hat." A conversation ensued and marriage followed. Hats create amazing possibilities.

—Patricia Underwood

*   *   *

The outstanding characteristic of millinery designer Patricia Underwood's hats is that they are, for the most part, completely unadorned. There are no added trimmings, no flowers, ribbons, or even hatbands on her pieces. The shape and the materials are the statement, they provide all the texture and color that she feels is necessary. Underwood works with a variety of traditional millinery materials; various straw braids, fur felts, real fur, and knitted yarns, in addition to more unusual materials such as fake furs and her signature sewn strips of leather and suede.

Underwood's hats are designed specifically to work with clothing and to complement it. She strives to avoid overwhelming the wearer, and to avoid crossing the fine line between the flattering and the absurd in millinery. She is described by Colin McDowell in *Hats: Status Style, Glamour* as: "Probably the most skilful of the middle-market milliners ... Underwood's approach is entirely practical. Her paramount concern is how the hats will relate to clothing." Underwood herself explains, "Why bother to have a hat ... if it does not go with the clothes?"

Underwood's strength lies in transforming traditional hat shapes and types and creating new interpretations of these classic forms. The change may be made by the use of an unexpected material, or by her subtle manipulation of the form, giving a familiar shape an entirely new look. For example, a cowboy hat for her 1991 collection was made of fine straw braid, the brim slightly wider than normal, the curve of the brim more subtle, the curl of the edge was slightly exaggerated. The overall effect of her cowboy hat was more feminine and sophisticated than a cowboy hat has ever been before. A 1920s-style cloche from the same year was transformed in a similar manner; the crown was squared and the brim became a small visor off the front; the feminine cloche was given a sportier character, suggesting a modern baseball cap. Some other familiar hat types

Patricia Underwood: Fall/Winter 1994; hat in chocolate and heather suede; shawl in autumn mohair/chenille. *Photograph by Evan Sklar.*

that she has used are boaters, nun's coifs, and the wide brimmed picture hat. By changing the expected relationships between the elements of the hat, the crown, and the brim, Underwood creates modern versions of these forms. Her aesthetic is in concert with the minimalist fashions of designers such as Giorgio Armani and Calvin Klein; she takes the forms we are familiar with and eliminates detail until they are reduced to their essential shape.

In response to the frequent pronouncements that "hats are back" as mandatory fashion accessories, Underwood maintains that the hat will not return as a fashion staple, but will continue to exist as an optional accessory. Thus the art of the milliner will survive in modern fashion. Underwood's inspiration is derived from the arts, her travels, and historical fashion. Her palette for the fall-winter 1994 collection was inspired by the work of the painter Modigliani. In general, her preferred colors are muted, natural tones. She has recently added coordinating scarves, shawls, and gloves to her collection. Her work is mostly ready-to-wear, available through department and specialty stores, though she also does custom work. Besides her own collections, Underwood has collaborated with many of the top American fashion designers who appreciate her purity of form.

—Melinda L. Watt

UNGARO, Emanuel.

French designer

Born: Aix-en-Provence, 13 February 1933. **Career:** Worked in his father's tailoring business, Aix-en-Provence, 1951-54; stylist, Maison Camps tailors, Paris, 1955-57; designer, Balenciaga, Paris, 1958-64; head of design, Balenciaga, Madrid, 1959-61; designer, Courrèges, 1964-65; established own firm, 1965; Ungaro Parallèle ready-to-wear collection introduced, 1968; menswear collection added, 1975; sportswear line, Emanuel, introduced, 1991; *Ungaro* perfume introduced, 1977, signature fragrance introduced, 1991; other fragrances include *Diva,* 1983 and *Senso,* 1987. **Awards:** Neiman Marcus Award, Dallas, 1969. **Address:** 2 avenue Montaigne, 75008 Paris, France.

Publications:

On UNGARO:

Books

Perschetz, Lois, ed., *W, The Designing Life,* New York 1987.
Loebenthal, Joel, *Radical Rags: Fashions of the Sixties,* New York 1990.

Articles

Ryan, Ann, "Ungaro," in Ruth Lynam, ed., *Couture: An Illustrated History of the Great Paris Designers and Their Creations,* New York 1972.

Arroyuelo, Javier, "La haute couture: Ungaro," in *Vogue* (Paris), March 1985.

"The Allure of Ungaro," in *Vogue* (New York), April 1985.

Salinger, Pierre, "Emanuel Ungaro, un homme et artiste," in *Vogue* (Paris), September 1985.

Brubach, Holly, "Theme and Variations: Expression of a Unique Style at Ungaro," in *Vogue* (New York), December 1985.

Salinger, Pierre, "Emanuel Ungaro, un homme et un artiste," in *Vogue* (Paris), February 1986.

Salvy, Gérard Julien, "Créer c'est rêver d'une femme," in *Vogue* (Paris), February 1986.

Premoti, Francesca, "Emanuel Ungaro: un'eleganza discreta," in *L'Uomo Vogue* (Milan), October 1986.

Bernasconi, Silvana, "Ungaro la seduzione: *Senso,*" in *Vogue* (Milan), September 1987.

Williamson, Rusty, "Rapping with Ungaro: He Talks of Couture, Fashion and Texas Women," in *Women's Wear Daily* (New York), 16 January 1990.

Howell, Georgina, "Ungaro Fortissimo," in *Vogue* (New York), November 1991.

Prey, Nadine, "Prints Charming," in *Harper's Bazaar* (New York), November 1991.

Gerrie, Anthea, "Sex, Style and a Man Called Ungaro," in *Clothes Show* (London), January 1992.

Yusuf, Nilgin, "Emanuel Ungaro: The British Are So Exotic," in *Marie Claire* (London), January 1992.

Morris, Bernadine, "House of Ungaro at 25: Seductiveness without Vulgarity," in the *New York Times,* 25 March 1992.

Aillaud, Charlotte, "Chez Emanuel Ungaro: Grand Illusions Fill the Fashion Designer's Paris Residence," in *Architectural Digest* (Los Angeles), July 1992.

Menkes, Suzy, "Chanel: Beauty without Gimmicks," in the *International Herald Tribune* (Paris), 25 January 1995.

*   *   *

Upon celebrating 25 years of success in couture, Ungaro could look back and see that he had indeed accomplished his goal of "seducing the woman." His early training in the *atelier* of Balenciaga taught Ungaro about line and color. He still refers to what he learned about draping directly on the model. Later, working with Courrèges, Ungaro participated in the Space Age hard chic of his mentor. It was later suggested that many of Courrèges's successful designs might have been attributed to Ungaro, who created metal bras, skimpy cutout A-line dresses, and white boots in a hard, futuristic manner that even Ungaro himself later dismissed as "false modernism." The influence of two years with Courrèges carried over into the early years of Ungaro's work on his own. He continued to make young, "kicky" fashions, dresses, and coats in bold, interlaced geometrics. His turtleneck and leggings worn underneath a sleeveless pinafore was a 1960s look that was resurrected by other designers to great popularity 20 years later. With the advantage of textile designer Sonia Knapp's artistic fabric designs, Ungaro gradually developed a softness of line that was to fully develop a decade later. Of his early designs, Ungaro prefers to say little, but chenille daisy appliquéd

see-through trouser-suits speak for themselves.

Toward the end of the 1970s, Ungaro began to experiment with the then-taboo mixing of textures and prints, of which he has become the master. Knapp's fabrics had evolved into more painterly, impressionistic florals, abstract smears, luminous colors. In daytime clothing Ungaro would pair a paisley blouse with a plaid suit, or a striped top worn under a tweed jacket with glen plaid trousers. In 1980, this daring approach found full expression in a collection of casual but complex ensembles, featuring fantasy printed, gold-edged jackets over sheer lace blouses, luxuriant paisley shawls wrapped over quilted, fur-lined cardigans, solid chiffon blouses paired with half-patterned, half-striped skirts. For evening, embellished velvet burnooses or wrapped paisley dresses, trimmed in black lace, completed this unusual eclectic look, offered through Ungaro's expensive ready-to-wear line, Parallèle. This risk taking had its early appearance in Ungaro couture, and has continued to the present day. The clothes were designed for women who chose and combined their outfits without regard to what others would think. In the wake of the drab "dress for success" uniform, Ungaro's vision offered the self-confident woman, or one who was not dependent upon conformity for job security, the opportunity for a more personal, individual look. Knapp's special fabrics made the mixtures work. Her colors were rich, with underlying coordinate properties that were not easy to duplicate. Over the years many designers have borrowed from Ungaro's ideas, with varying degrees of success.

Borrowing from the East, in 1981, Ungaro layered fluid chinoiserie patterned tunics over contrasting colorways skirts, draped with tasseled shawls of tiny floral and undulating lines in a riot of colors. The sensual, covered-up looks suggested Gustav Klimt's paintings in their profusion of mosaic colors and patterns. Cummerbund-bound floral skirts topped with lacy blouses under boleros showed a folkloric influence, though less literal than Saint Laurent's Russians a few years before.

Ungaro's designs have been intended to convey sex appeal without being vulgar. He has said that when doing a dress he would always ask himself if the woman in the dress would be seductive. Women and music are his inspiration. One can only guess if a particular collection has been created while Ungaro was listening to Mozart, Beethoven, Wagner, Stravinsky, or Ravel. Certainly his designs possess the contrast and harmony, repose and counterpoint of a musical composition. By the mid-1980s an Ungaro dress could be immediately identified by its diagonally draped and shirred skirt, wide shoulders gathered into gigot sleeves buttoned at the wrist, wrapped V-neckline, jewel-toned silk jacquard fabric. Ungaro wedding dresses were of pale pastel crêpe, sculpted, diagonally draped and caught with self-fabric flowers. At this time he introduced the short black-skirted suit with colorful jackets, both printed and plain. This look continues to be universally chic. To add to the seductiveness of his ensembles, Ungaro's models wore veiled elongated pillbox hats, pushed down over the eyes, an accessory resurrected a decade later for fall.

By 1985 Ungaro seemed to achieve a new serenity, the result of his thoughts and dreams. Since then he has repeated with variations the sleek curvaceous silhouettes, the fluid construction, ingenious cut, original color sense, and print and pattern mixtures without ever becoming boring. The self-confident Ungaro customer is also appealingly vulnerable because the fabric and cut subtly reveal her body. A flirtation with the short bubble floral skirt followed Lacroix's introduction of that silhouette, but Ungaro became even more wildly successful with his short, tightly wrapped dress. Late 1980s spring

Emanuel Ungaro: Spring 1992; black linen daisy applique sundress.

dresses featured short flounced skirts, big puffed sleeves, and bold solids or florals. Ungaro called his style a "new Baroque." Fall 1989 ball gowns were gypsy inspired, with floor-length bouffant floral skirts trimmed with polka dotted ruffles and black lace, puffed sleeved jackets of contrasting florals trimmed with velvet and jewels. In 1990 folkloric flowers trimmed a cape worn over a short black leather skirt and deep red jacket. Voluminous Victorian bustled plaid skirts on strapless evening dresses highlighted Ungaro's 1991 couture, while padded Central Asian coats were offered through his ready-to-wear line. After a cheerful, bouffant skirted spring, Ungaro presented a more somber, but no less luxurious, collection for the fall of 1992. Ungaro Parallèle continued to produce feminine floral brocade dresses and vibrant plaid suits interwoven with gold threads. In 1991 the lower priced Emanuel line was launched, with the famous tight and short Ungaro silhouette typified by a thigh-high shirred houndstooth dress with high neck and long sleeves.

Certainly the body-hugging Ungaro designs require a trim figure, but all the shoulder and hip emphasis can also be flattering to many figures by simulating an hourglass shape. Diagonal lines have a slimming effect. Some of Ungaro's spring dresses have merely skimmed the body, hiding flaws. Slit skirts have flatteringly shown off still-good legs. Ever in search of pleasing the woman, of following his dream, Ungaro has endured because his clothes show profound appreciation and respect for women.

—Therese Duzinkiewicz Baker

UNGER, Kay.

American designer

Born: Chicago, 22 May 1945. **Education:** Studied at Washington University, Missouri, and at Parsons School of Design, New York. **Career:** Worked for Pattullo-Jo Copeland, Gayle Kirkpatrick, and Geoffrey Beene; became designer of Traina Boutique and Traina Sport collections, 1971; created own collection; became partner at Gillian Group, 1972, with Howard Bloom and Jon Levy. Lines include Gillian, Gillian Dinner, Gillian Suits, Gillian Petites, Woman, and two other prominent dress lines, A.J. Bari and GiGi By Gillian. **Awards:** J.C. Penney scholarship and Irish Linen Association scholarship, Parsons School of Design. **Address:** 230 West 38th Street, New York, New York 10014, USA.

Publications:

On UNGER:

Books

Lambert, Eleanor, *World of Fashion: People, Places, Resources,* New York 1976.

Articles

Stiansen, Sarah, "Staying on Top," in *Savvy Woman,* November 1990.

* * *

Kay Unger epitomizes the customer for whom she designs with a clear understanding based on her own busy lifestyle. As the de-

signer and co-owner of Gillian, she balances a schedule that includes the creation and production of five collections per year, extensive community involvement, and family life. Using herself as the customer, she understands the needs of an active lifestyle, whether the woman is involved in a career or not. The specific needs of the Gillian customer are rooted in lifestyle dressing, primarily dresses that can be worn from the office to dinner or appropriate for luncheons or charity functions.

In 1989, recognizing a void in the marketplace for "clean dinner dresses," Kay Unger set out to reinvent the little black dress. She designed a group of understated, tasteful, less-embellished restaurant dresses, brought hemlines down—some to mid calf and ankle length—and successfully replaced the overly opulent, short, and ornamented looks of the 1980s dress market. In addition to the void in p.m. dresses she also filled a void in the daywear market with city short sets or rompers. To unite day and evening she created ensemble dressing: two or three piece outfits sold as one rather than as sportswear separates. This allowed the customer a certain freedom to alter the look of a garment, depending on the occasion.

The Gillian signature fabric is silk, in many guises and in various weaves. Other fabrics she uses are wool crêpe for fall, and linens and linen weaves for spring and summer, always incorporating novelty fabrics and innovative color mixes. Her eye for color and design was honed during early training as a painter and continues to influence the prints that appear in every line, designed in-house by her design team and exclusive to the Gillian Group. They are often influenced by her knowledge of art history as well as home furnishings. New color stories are delivered on a monthly basis to maintain interest in the many different regions in which her clothing is sold. Color is the number one strength of the Gillian line, due to its innovative and saleable quality.

Her clothes are categorized as bridge, falling between top quality ready-to-wear and designer apparel; feminine and classic rather than trendy, street wise, or masculine; dresses that follow trends. Her customer, wherever she lives, is an adult woman, fairly affluent and with good taste. She is classic rather than trendy, but definitely not traditional.

The Gillian collection includes a wide variety of classic designs for daytime, career, and dinner dressing. Comfort and affordability are important considerations for a customer whose day demands polish and professionalism, from early meetings to late night dinners or entertaining. Bold color combinations, quality fabrics, and striking prints have become Gillian trademarks. Certain styles such as the longer shirt dresses, easy chemises, and coat dresses, savvy suits, and understated dinner dresses continue to meet with great success.

The Gillian Group today is one of the largest suppliers of women's apparel in America. Recognizing the various needs of women who span from the northeast to the south and to the west, these regional differences are addressed through a large variety of fabrics and colorations within the different fashion divisions bearing the signature Gillian style and value. They include: Gillian, Gillian Dinner, Gillian Suits, Gillian Petites, Woman, and two other prominent dress lines—A.J. Bari and GiGi By Gillian.

Throughout the Gillian and A.J. Bari collection, Kay Unger focuses on a singular goal: creating a wardrobe for today's woman that stands for femininity, fashion newness, and impeccable quality and value.

—Roberta Hochberger Gruber

VALENTINA.
American designer

Born: Valentina Sanina in Kiev, Russia, 1 May 1904. **Education:** Studied drama in Kiev, 1917-19. **Family:** Married George Schlee in 1921 (died, 1971). **Career:** Dancer, Chauve Souris Theater, Paris, 1922-23; moved to New York, 1923. Opened small couture house, 1925, incorporated as Valentina Gowns, Inc., 1928; introduced perfume *My Own,* 1950; firm closed, 1957. Also: theater designer, leading ladies' gowns, 1934-54, 1964. *Died* (in New York) *14 September 1989.*

Publications:

On VALENTINA:

Books

Milbank, Caroline Rennolds, *Couture: The Great Designers,* New York 1985.
Owen, Bobbie, *Costume Designers on Broadway: Designers and Their Credits 1915-1985,* Westport, Connecticut 1987.
Milbank, Caroline Rennolds, *New York Fashion: The Evolution of American Style,* New York 1989.
Steele, Valerie, *Women of Fashion,* New York 1991.

Articles

"Valentina," in *Current Biography* (New York), December 1946.
Diesel, Leota, "Valentina Puts on a Good Show," in *Theatre Arts,* April 1952.
Pope, Elizabeth, "Women Really Pay Her $600 for a Dress," in *Good Housekeeping* (New York), February 1955.
"Valentina," obituary in *Current Biography* (New York), September 1989.
Morris, Bernadine, "Valentina, A Designer of Clothes for Stars in the Theater, Dies," in the *New York Times,* 15 September 1989.
"Valentina," obituary in *Women's Wear Daily* (New York), 18 September 1989.
"Valentina," obituary in *The Independent* (London), 28 September 1989.

*　　*　　*

Madame Valentina was as exotic as her name. A Russian emigrée, she attracted attention in New York after her arrival in 1923 by looking like a woman at a time when women were trying to look like young boys. For dining in fashionable restaurants or attending the theater and parties with her theater producer husband George Schlee, Valentina wore her own designs—long, high necked, long sleeved gowns with natural waistlines, made of flowing black velvet—in contrast to the short, waistless, beaded flapper fashions that prevailed. Instead of bobbed hair, Valentina emphasized high cheekbones and large soulful eyes by wearing her long blonde hair in a high chignon. Slavic reserve, thick Russian accent, expressive hands, and movement with a dancer's grace completed the personality. She was her own best model and maintained a consistency of appearance throughout her long career.

Interest in Valentina's unusual clothes led to the establishment of Valentina Gowns, Inc. in 1928, on New York's upper East side. Success was immediate. Valentina's clients included luminaries from the theater, opera, ballet, society, and film. Greta Garbo, whom Valentina was said to resemble ("I am the Gothic version"), was one of her customers. Each of Valentina's customers, who numbered no more than 200 at any one time, was granted personal attention. Valentina insisted that she alone knew what was best for the customer and made last-minute changes in color or detail if necessary. Fashion editors were exasperated by Valentina's insistence upon selecting and modeling her clothes herself, but, ultimately, Valentina was right. Her business remained successful for 30 years. Valentina's sophisticated color sense, influenced by Léon Bakst, gravitated toward subtle earth tones, "off-colors," monochromatic schemes, and the ubiquitous black. An evening dress with a bolero might be made of three shades of grey. In the 1950s Valentina began using variations of deep colors of damask and brocade. From a visit to Greece, Valentina learned proportion, which lent an architectural dignity to her gowns. Her couture was original, intricately cut and fitted, and avoided the popular practice of copying French haute couture.

With an innate flair for the dramatic, Valentina successfully designed for the theater. Beginning with a play starring Judith Anderson in 1933, Valentina was known for her ability to suit the character, whether on or off the stage. Critic Brooks Atkinson commented, "Valentina has designed clothes that act before a line is spoken." The clothes she created for Katherine Hepburn in the 1939 stage play, *The Philadelphia Story,* remained in demand by her customers for five years. Timelessness of design was essential. In the 1930s and 1940s Valentina introduced hoods and snoods as headcoverings, wimple-like effects (flattering to mature throats) swathed around tall, medieval-inspired head-dresses. The diamond and emerald Maltese cross brooch she wore almost constantly was widely copied. Drawing inspiration from fine art in European galleries, Valentina created striking evening ensembles along Renaissance lines; a white crêpe floor-length gown fastened down the bodice with small self-fabric bows, topped by a three-quarter length beige wool cape, lined with gold brocade and fastened with an antique gold chain was one example.

Only the wealthy could afford Valentina. A minimum price of 250 dollars was charged per dress in the 1930s, with an average price of 600 dollars in the mid-1950s. Valentina preferred to sell entire wardrobes, presenting a unified look from formal to casual. For ease of travel she introduced the concept of a few coordinating pieces: blouse, bare top, skirt, shorts, and scarf that could be mixed and matched. Valentina disdained fussy, frilly ornamentation, silk flowers, or sequins, relying instead on exquisite line. During the 1930s she borrowed Oriental details such as *obi* sashes and Indian striped embroidery used as sleeve accents. A favorite casual accessory was a coolie hat tied under the chin. In the 1940s she promoted a look that was slightly softer than the popular, mannish, broad-shouldered silhouette, and she introduced the short evening dress, while promoting ballet slippers, which were not rationed, worn with dark rayon stockings.

Valentina's working costume often consisted of a simple black long-sleeved dress with a versatile neckline, cut so it could be pinned high with a contrasting pin, or folded down and worn with a long scarf draped about the head or shoulders for evening. A slice of colored satin lining would be turned *en revers* for contrast with the black. By the 1950s Valentina's evening gowns featured increasingly *décolletage* necklines. Her casual ruffled handkerchief linen blouses, worn with pleated skirts, were widely copied, as were her aproned organdie party dresses. The supple matte fabrics favored by Valentina included crêpe cut on the bias for daytime, wool and satin crêpes, chiffons and damasks. Elegant wraparound silhouettes were created for coats, one of which featured three layers of progressively longer capes falling from the shoulders. Valentina's idiosyncratic, though classic, fashions also included evening gowns with one bare shoulder, the other long-sleeved, dolman sleeves, large fur hats made from sable, the only fur she would accept. Plain necklines lent themselves well to showcasing her client's jewelry.

Often called "America's most glamorous dressmaker," Valentina was recognized to be one of the United States' top couturiers and theater costume designers. She retired in 1957, and died in 1989.

—Therese Duzinkiewicz Baker

VALENTINO.
Italian designer

Born: Valentino Garavani in Voghera, Italy, 11 May 1932. **Education:** Studied French and fashion design, Accademia dell'Arte, Milan, to 1948; studied at the Chambre Syndicale de la Couture, 1949-51. **Career:** Assistant designer, Jean Dessès, 1950-55, and Guy Laroche, 1956-58; assistant to Princess Irene Galitzine, 1959; business established, Rome, 1960; company owned by Kenton Corporation, 1968-73, repurchased by Valentino, 1973; showed first ready-to-wear collection, 1962; Valentino Più, interior décor, textile and gift company established, 1973; ready-to-wear boutiques established, Paris, 1968, Rome, 1972, 1988, Milan, 1979, London, 1987; menswear collection introduced, 1972; signature fragrance introduced, 1978. **Exhibitions:** *Italian Re-Evolution,* La Jolla Art Museum, California, 1982; retrospective, Capitoline Museum, Rome, 1991, and New York, 1992. **Awards:** Neiman Marcus Award, 1967; National Italian American Foundation Award, 1989. **Address:** Piazza Mignanelli 22, 00187 Rome, Italy.

Publications:

On VALENTINO:

Books

Mulassano, Adriana, *I mass-moda: fatti e personaggi dell'Italian Look,* Florence 1979.
Ricci, Franco Maria, editor, *Valentino,* Milan 1982.
Sartogo, Piero, editor, *Italian Re-Evolution: Design in Italian Society in the Eighties* (exhibition catalogue), La Jolla, California 1982.
Alfonsi, Maria-Vittoria, *Leaders in Fashion: i grandi personaggi della moda,* Bologna 1983.
Cosi, Marina, *Valentino che veste di nuovo,* Milan 1984.
Soli, Pia, *Il genio antipatico* (exhibition catalogue), Venice 1984.
Talley, André Leon, *Valentino,* Milan 1984.
Milbank, Caroline Rennolds, *Couture: The Great Designers,* New York 1985.
Perschetz, Lois, editor, *W, The Designing Life,* New York 1987.
Coleridge, Nicholas, *The Fashion Conspiracy,* London 1988.
Aragno, Bonizza Giordani, *Moda Italia: Creativity and Technology in the Italian Fashion System,* Milan 1988.
Howell, Georgina, *Sultans of Style: 30 Years of Fashion and Passion 1960-1990,* London 1990.
Accademia Valentino, *Valentino: Thirty Years of Magic,* Rome 1991.
Martin, Richard and Harold Koda, *Orientalism: Visions of the East in Western Dress* (Exhibition catalogue), New York, 1994.

Articles

"Valentino," in *Current Biography* (New York), November 1973.
Pertile, Marina, "Valentino: 25 anni nella moda compiuti," in *Vogue* (Milan), September 1984.
Etherington-Smith, Meredith, and Caroline Clifton-Magg, "Palace Evolution," in *Harper's and Queen* (London), June 1989.
Ducci, Carlo, and Lele Acquarone, "Valentino 59-89," in *Vogue* (Milan), September 1989.
Rafferty, Diane, "Valentino," in *Connoisseur* (New York), August 1990.
Casadio, Mariuccia, "Valentino, Take a Bow!," in *Interview* (New York), September 1991.
Koenig, Rhoda, "When Valentino Fêtes His Anniversary, There's No Place Like Rome," in *Vogue* (New York), September 1991.
Mulvagh, Jane, "The Sultan of Style," in *The European* (London), 1 November 1991.
Lesser, Guy, "Our Funny Valentino," in *Town and Country* (New York), September 1992.
Shields, Brooke, "Hello, Valentino?," in *Interview* (New York), September 1992.
Schiff, Stephen, "Lunch with Mr. Armani, Tea with Mr. Versace, Dinner with Mr. Valentino," in *The New Yorker* (New York), 7 November 1994.
Menkes, Suzy, "Craft Is in the Details: Artistry is In, Supermodels are Out," in *International Herald Tribune* (Paris), 24 January 1995.
Valentino: The Sophisticated Lady," in *Women's Wear Daily* (New York), 21 March 1995.

Schiro, Anne-Marie, "Yves Saint Laurnet's Shocking New Color: Black," in the *New York Times,* 22 March 1995.

Menkes, Suzy, "YSL Plays Safe While Valentino Shines at Night," in the *International Herald Tribune* (Paris), 22 March 1995.

*   *   *

Both a reverent hush and an excited clamor surround the Italian designer Valentino simultaneously. He enjoys the patronage of a long established clientèle of wealthy and aristocratic women, yet his clothes are never staid and always express a fresh, current style. His collections and his lifestyle embody the grandeur and serenity of eternal Rome, where he works from his salon near the Spanish Steps, and at the same time represent the up-to-the-minute point of view of a jet-setting citizen of the world. In 1991 Valentino celebrated 30 years in business. The anniversary was celebrated in characteristically Valentino style in Rome with a magnificent retrospective exhibition, a lavish formal dinner, and an all-night dance party. The press reported this event with detailed descriptions of the proceedings and participants, who had flown in from around the globe to pay homage to the designer they devoutly refer to as "The Chic." Valentino's various homes, in London, Capri, Gstaad, and New York, are regularly featured in magazines and newspapers, an indication that "Valentino" is not just a style of dressing, but rather a style of living.

In 1960, when Valentino opened his first salon in the Via Condotti, Rome was the center of fashion in Italy. The ready-to-wear designers of Milan, the industrial center, did not come to prominence until a decade later. Thus the fashion world in Italy was the world of the couture in Rome. After having served as an apprentice in Paris for five years with Jean Dessès and two years with Guy Laroche, Valentino's design foundation was firmly set in the haute couture tradition of quality, luxury, and a dose of extravagance. He immediately began to attract clients who came to him for his finely crafted, colorful, and elegant designs. By the mid-1960s he introduced his signature trousersuits for day and evening.

In 1968 he created a sensation with his White Collection which featured short dresses shown with lace stockings and simple flat shoes. That same year Jacqueline Kennedy chose a lace-trimmed silk two-piece dress with a short pleated skirt, for her marriage to Aristotle Onassis. Red has become Valentino's signature color, a rich shade of crimson with vibrant overtones of orange. He uses it throughout his collections, especially in his lavish evening designs, which are characterized by magnificent embroideries and meticulous detailing. A section of his retrospective exhibition was devoted to evening jackets covered entirely in elaborately beaded decorations. Typical Valentino details include scalloped trims and hems, raglan sleeves, circular ruffles, complex plays of proportion, and extravagant pattern and texture mixes; for example, the combination of lace, velvet, and houndstooth in a single outfit.

Valentino's devotees flock to him for couture and ready-to-wear and a vast array of products and accessories including menswear, innerwear, leather goods, eyewear, furs, and perfumes. He reaches the youth market through his Oliver line of clothes that are casual but still marked with distinctively refined Valentino sensibility. He produces a special collection of eveningwear called Valentino Night, in which the luxury of his couture designs is adapted for a wider audience. All of his designs, throughout all of his collections, express a singularly opulent view of the world. Valentino's sensibil-ity embraces both timelessness and originality, filtered through a dedication to a luxurious way of life and the commitment to express that lifestyle in his collections.

—Alan E. Rosenberg

VAN DEN AKKER, Koos.

American designer

Born: The Hague, Netherlands, 16 March 1939. **Education:** Studied at the Netherlands Royal Academy of Art, 1956-58; worked in department stores in The Hague and in Paris; studied fashion at L'École Guerre Lavigne, Paris, 1961. **Military Service:** Served in the Royal Dutch Army, 1958-60. **Career:** Apprenticed at Dior, Paris, 1963-65; returned to The Hague and maintained own boutique, 1965-68; immigrated to the United States, 1968, naturalized, 1982; lingerie designer, Eve Stillman, New York, 1969-70; freelance designer, from 1971; first New York boutique established, Columbus Avenue, 1971-75; relocated to Madison Avenue, 1975; opened second shop, Beverly Hills, California, 1978; opened second New York boutique, 1979; added line of handbags, 1986; introduced diffusion line, Hot House, 1983. Also: designer of bedlinen, lingerie and home furnishings. **Awards:** Gold Coast Award, 1978; American Printed Fabrics Council "Tommy," Award, 1983. **Address:** 550 7th Avenue, 18th Floor, New York, New York 10018, USA.

Publications:

On VAN DEN AKKER:

Books

Khornak, Lucille, *Fashion 2001,* London 1982.

Articles

de Llosa, Martha, "Designer Koos van den Akker: Berserk on the Surface," in *American Fabrics and Fashions* (New York), Spring 1980.

Revson, James A., "The Uncrowned King of Collage," in *Newsday* (New York), 9 August 1984.

Coffin, David Page, "Koos, the Master of Collage," in *Threads* (Newtown, Connecticut), December/January 1989-90.

"New York Now," in *Women's Wear Daily* (New York), 9 April 1990.

Struensee, Chuck, "Koos Comes Back," in *Women's Wear Daily* (New York), 23 March 1993.

*   *   *

Koos Van Den Akker is known for his painterly delight in mixing colors, patterns, and textures in unusual, often one of a kind, garments. Since his arrival in the United States in 1968 with just a sewing machine, he has been delighting clients who want something a bit different to wear. His styles have not changed much, simple shapes being more amenable to rich surface manipulations. Having learned the basics of good fit and cut as an apprentice with the house of Christian Dior, Van Den Akker was able to proceed confidently with the fabric collages which have become his signature. Although his Koos garments recall the art-to-wear movement, they remain free of the sometimes heavy-handed messages inherent in the artifacts that seem more suitable for gallery walls: they are meant to be worn and appreciated for their beauty.

Conservatively styled suits consisting of cardigan jackets and gored skirts might be covered with textured mixtures of fur, quilted fabric, leather strips, or pieces of wool. A dress of lace might be dramatized by bold appliqué. As many as six materials might be combined in collages of cotton, wool, furs, tweeds, sequins, and leather. Some of the results are reminiscent of grandmother's "crazy quilt," but they are carried out with a true designer's skill and artistic sensitivity. Indeed, Van Den Akker has admitted that the designs just flow, working themselves out through the process of creation, perhaps reflecting a hereditary affinity with Dutch national costume.

Six years at The Hague selling his own custom-made dresses in a boutique gained Van Den Akker the experience to open a Madison Avenue shop, one in Beverly Hills, and a men's boutique during the 1970s. In 1983 he presented a moderately priced collection, Hot House. By 1986 he was designing lingerie, daytime and evening clothes, furs, sheets, and home furnishings. Women's clothes were made of beautiful fabrics with colorful print and lace inserts, sometimes following the lines of the garments in harmony and balance, other times contrasting shapes versus line. During the 1980s Van Den Akker collected a following among show business personalities including Gloria Vanderbilt, who at one point surrounded herself with patchwork, Elizabeth Taylor, Cher, Madeleine Kahn, Barbara Walters, Marilyn Horne, and Glenn Close. Bill Cosby wore Van Den Akker's sweaters on *The Cosby Show*.

Van Den Akker has been eager to share the joy he attains from his craft. Designer Christian Francis Roth was his apprentice for several years before venturing on his own. In late 1989 Van Den Akker showed the home-sewing public how to make their own creative clothing in a detailed article in *Threads Magazine*. The next year signaled a broadening of his range to include simpler ready-to-wear sportswear: tweed dresses and coats, coats of blanket materials, matching suede jackets and skirts, and short floral dresses with just a hint of the Koos play with fabrics in a mixed-print collar.

Van Den Akker continues to refine his artistry, developing a ready-to-wear sportswear collection for DeWilde that is more subtle and interchangeable. Toned-down collage effects and texture appliqués lend interest to classic pieces in wool and cashmere, even sheer georgette.

—Therese Duzinkiewicz Baker

———

VARTY, Keith. See **BYBLOS.**

———

VASS, Joan.

American designer

———

Born: New York City, 19 May 1925. **Education:** Attended Vassar College and graduated in philosophy from the University of Wis-

consin, 1942; did graduate work in aesthetics at the University of Buffalo. **Family:** Children from first marriage: Richard, Sara, Jason. **Career:** Assistant curator, drawing and prints, the Museum of Modern Art, New York; free-lance editor, Harry N. Abrams publishing house, New York; columnist, *Art in America,* New York. Began designing hand knits in the early 1970s with sales to Henri Bendel, New York; company incorporated as Joan Vass, Inc., 1977; labels include Joan Vass Sporting, Joan Vass New York, men's and women's clothing; Joan Vass USA, lower priced women's line, introduced, 1984; Joan Vass USA For Men introduced, 1988; New York flagship store opened, 1989. **Awards:** Smithsonian Institution, Extraordinary Women in Fashion Award, 1978; Coty American Fashion Critics Award, 1979, 1981; Prince Machiavelli Prix de Cachet Award, 1980. **Address:** 485 Seventh Avenue, New York, New York 10018, USA.

Publications:

On VASS:

Books

Milbank, Caroline Rennolds, *New York Fashion: The Evolution of American Style,* New York 1989.
Steele, Valerie, *Women of Fashion,* New York 1991.

Articles

Oliver, Richard K., "Style," in *People* (Chicago), 29 October 1979.
Etra, Johnathan, "Vass Horizons," in *House and Garden* (New York), January 1989.
Infantino, Vivian, "A Vass Landscape: Designer Joan Vass Paints Her Fashion Philosophy," in *Footwear News* (New York), 28 August 1989.
Hastreiter, Kim, "Vass Appeal," in *Mirabella,* January 1995.

*   *   *

Joan Vass is an American designer who believes the only purpose for a label in a piece of clothing is to show which way to put it on. Her easy-to-wear designs for both men and women are beautifully crafted, in simple, elegant lines.

In college, Vass studied philosophy and aesthetics. She worked as an assistant curator of drawings and prints at the Museum of Modern Art in New York. At the same time she edited art books for Harry N. Abrams and wrote columns about art auctions for *Art in America*.

Joan Vass began a cottage industry in the early 1970s when she brought her personal interest in hand knits and crochet to women who needed an outlet for their marketable skills. Vass created designs for hats and mufflers which these women crocheted. Marketed at Henri Bendel, New York, they quickly sold out. She went on to create designs for sweaters for both men and women, having them produced under the label Joan Vass New York. Vass provided the designs, the yarns and buttons if necessary. Her cadre of workers, ranging in age from 20-70, came from a variety of backgrounds including housewives and artists. They would knit, crochet, or hand-loom the design, incorporating their personal style. The production for this line was limited, selective, and not accessible to everyone. The Joan Vass New York line continues today with some of the original craftspeople still creating the designs provided by

Joan Vass. It remains a small-volume, selective design business which now includes woven materials. All of the designs from the past are still available to be produced.

The return to natural fibers, the individuality in American fashion expression, the use of knits for more than just the travel wardrobe, plus a new-found appreciation for hand-made items during the 1970s all helped create a welcoming environment for Vass's designs. Her work was unique, practical, and beautifully crafted.

Vass created her own company in 1977. In the 1980s, a mid-priced licensed line was first produced on a large scale by the Signal Knitting Mills in South Carolina. Working with Joan Vass designs these clothes carry the label Joan Vass USA. They are made of beautiful fine-gauged, natural fiber, knitted and woven fabrics. Today there is a third design line called Joan Vass Sporting. This is a more casual line which includes more details. Though natural fibers are still used, the designs also use some of the new synthetic fibers such as chinchilla, a 100 percent polyester fabric.

Whether Joan Vass New York, Joan Vass USA, or Joan Vass Sporting, the designs she creates are simple and easy to wear. They are predominantly made of natural fibers, usually in subtle colors, in unstructured shapes. There are no extras such as shoulder pads. Besides sweaters, she designs trousers, skirts, and shorts and dresses. Her stated aim is to produce interchangeable, ageless designs which evolve from season to season. Reviews in the *Daily News Record* describe Vass's designs as classic. When the clothes are old, she wants them to be worn for gardening.

In an interview for *House and Garden,* Vass says, "If you notice me I am not well-dressed" (Johnathan Etra, "Vass Horizons," January 1989). She feels that style is something that lasts. This does not preclude a sense of humor in her design work, as she has been inspired by iguanas and has created bizarre and funny hats. Joan Vass is an American woman who has strong ideas and concerns which are reflected in her designs.

—Nancy House

VENET, Philippe.

French fashion designer

Born: Lyons, France, 22 May 1929. **Education:** Apprentice tailor, age 14, at Pierre Court, Lyons, until 1948. **Military Service:** Served in French Army, 1948-50. **Career:** Assistant designer Schiaparelli, Paris, 1951-53; master tailor for Givenchy, 1953-62. Established Philippe Venet couture house, Paris, 1962; launched menswear collection, 1990s. Awards: Dé d'Or, Paris, 1985. **Address:** 62 rue Francois 1er, 75008 Paris, France.

Publications:

On VENET:

Books

McDowell, Colin, *McDowell's Directory of Twentieth Century Fashion,* Englewood Cliffs, New Jersey 1985.
O'Hara, Georgina, *The Encyclopaedia of Fashion,* New York 1986.
Stegemeyer, Anne, *Who's Who in Fashion,* New York 1992.

Articles

L'Officiel (Paris), March 1992.

*   *   *

Philippe Venet had a long apprenticeship in fashion before opening his own couture house in 1962, at the age of 33. Born in Lyons, France, he was apprenticed at 14 to an established and respected dressmaker in the town, Pierre Court, where he was taught about fabric, manufacture, and cut, as well as learning the rudiments of tailoring, a major feature of his later work. Pierre Court held the rights to the Balenciaga label and it was Venet's association with this Parisian couture house that led him to the fashion capital to pursue his design career.

His first job was at the house of Schiaparelli. Elsa Schiaparelli had been one of the most important and influential designers of the 1930s, when her witty surrealist and avant-garde designs broke new ground in fashion. By the 1950s, however, Schiaparelli's influence was waning and the house was soon to close. For Venet the job was a stepping stone in his career. It was at Schiaparelli that he met the young Hubert de Givenchy, who was also an employee. When Givenchy opened his own couture house in 1953, he employed Venet as his master tailor.

The 1950s were Givenchy's heyday, a success to which Philippe Venet undoubtedly contributed. Givenchy is perhaps most notable for his association with Audrey Hepburn whom he first dressed in the 1954 film *Sabrina Fair.* Together, the design house and actress created a gamine look that typified the style of the late 1950s and 1960s. It was young elegance, long-legged and sophisticated, ranging from Audrey's beatnik look in the 1957 film *Funny Face,* to her little black dress look in the 1961 film *Breakfast at Tiffany's.*

Philippe Venet finally opened his own couture house at 62 rue François 1er in 1962. His experience and respect for the traditions of haute couture were a mainstay of his work from the beginning, as were his superb tailoring skills. His cut is always innovative and imaginative and a range of beautifully cut and tailored coats have always featured in a collection. Distinctive pieces from the 1960s were his kite coats, plastic diamonds attached edge to edge to thick white, short, and full length coats. A strong coat theme from the 1970s was geometry, oversize capes and jackets in flannel and reversible wools, with square and dolman sleeves and triangular pocket details. His suits and coats in the 1980s and 1990s are romantic and flirtatious, in refreshing colours.

Venet's eveningwear is often inspired by flora and fauna. In a black organza dress, the skirt is folded into layered petals and secured with a belt. A baby doll dress is made from a country garden flower-print taffeta, strapless and suspended by a huge bow at the bust. The overall look is romantic but sophisticated, smart but with a hint of naughtiness, and designed for a wealthy clientèle.

Venet was awarded the Dé d'Or Award in January 1985. This award not only recognized his aesthetic contribution to the fashion industry but applauded the detailed attention he brings to every aspect of the business; closely monitoring the creation of each outfit and personally attending all the fittings.

Today Venet divides his time between France and the United States. A third of his clients are American, and he presents a collection once a year in both Los Angeles and New York. Expansion of the business in the 1990s has included a menswear line to complement the womenswear ranges.

—Kevin Almond

Gian Marco Venturi: Spring/Summer 1995.

VENTURI, Gian Marco.

Italian fashion designer

Born: Florence, c.1955. **Education:** Studied at the Istituto Tessile Butti in Prato; degree in economics and commerce from Florence University. **Career:** Worked for Italian firms Domitilla, Lebole, Erreuno. Own label ready-to-wear established, 1979, Milan. Launched leather goods and accessory line, 1981; men's jeans and sportswear, 1982; ladies' jeans and sportswear, 1985; activewear and lingerie lines, 1988. Awards: The Oner Best Designer Award, Milan, 1983; Catherine de Medici Perfume Award, Milan, 1986. **Address:** Via della Spiga 31, 20121 Milan, Italy.

Publications:

On VENTURI:

Articles

"Gian Marco Venturi: gessati et jabot," *Donna* (Milan), 7 August 1987.
Muritti, Elisabetta, "Venturing on His Own," in *Donna* (Milan), March 1989.

* * *

Gian Marco Venturi worked for many companies as a designer/stylist before his own ready-to-wear label was launched in 1979. Born in Florence, Italy, he attended the Istituto Tessile Butti in Prato, then took a degree in business and economics at the University of Florence. He did not enter the fashion business until 1974 when he was 28. Instead, he spent time travelling the world, gaining a rich variety of cultural and aesthetic experience that has provided useful inspiration for his subsequent design career.

Venturi first began designing for a firm called Domitilla. The company produced jersey clothes very much in the style of Emilio Pucci. It was Venturi's task to update the range and give it the right look for the mid-1970s. The first collection was shown in the Palazzo Pitti in Florence. He then went on to work on leather garments (leather has always been a strong feature in his work) for Sander's; at the same time he also designed knitwear for Beba. Graziella Ronchi hired Venturi in 1979 to design for her Erreuno collections. Working with the company for six seasons it was Venturi who helped develop and establish the soft, neutral look combined with architectural correctness for which the company is known today.

Venturi's women's ready-to-wear is stylish and expensive: sexy, sometimes sensuous and suggestive, sometimes blatant or tarty. His sensuous side is perhaps best exemplified in his autumn-winter 1989-90 collection. A masculine, black snakeskin jacket with astrakhan collar and cuffs is belted over black trousers and sweater, highlighted with a white shirt collar. Black snakeskin gloves, dark glasses, and a model with a short black bob give the impression of Louise Brooks on a black and white aviation excursion. Dark glasses are the distinctive accessory that runs through a collection which also includes fit and flare double breasted coats with astrakhan cuffs then, in a softer vein, reversible cashmere with huge shawl collars and patch pockets in sand and warm grey.

Another distinctive Gian Marco Venturi ready-to-wear collection was spring-summer 1993. It featured hipster chain mail belts slung over skirts and tabards, in a red, white, and blue colour palette. Also featured were blue leather safari jackets, boldly printed Capri trousers, skinny ribbed knits with chain mail embroidery, topped off with gold leather jerkins, belts, and lots of gold jewelery. It was a fun, dynamic, swingy look, that suggested a star or Opera diva lost in Miami and featured favourite fabrics such as white lace and organza.

Venturi's menswear is usually classic and traditional but is sometimes highlighted by a touch of ornamentation, such as crests and stars lifted from the naval styles or a gold ribbon embroidered waistcoat. The clothes are disciplined and produced in seasonal colours. Favourite fabrics include linens, flannels, and gabardines. Sober jackets, waistcoats, close fitting trousers, and blouses are the main separates, coordinated to create these looks.

Gian Marco Venturi also produces lines of leather garments, jeans, casual clothing, sportswear, and perfume all marked by the label Gian Marco Venturi Made in Italy in black on a white ground. He has been awarded several prizes during his career including The Oner for best designer of 1983 and the Catherine de Medici prize for the greatest sales of men's aftershave in 1986. The company moved from Florence in 1983 and now occupies studios on the prestigious Via della Spiga in Milan.

—Kevin Almond

VERDÙ, Joaquim.

Spanish designer

Born: Barcelona, Spain. **Education:** Attended Feli's fashion school; studied anatomical drawing and painting; apprenticed under Pedro Rodríguez. **Career:** Became known for knitwear; own label manufactured by Pulligan, beginning 1991. **Address:** Riera del Pinar, 12, 08360 Carnet de Mar, Spain.

Publications:

On VERDÙ:

Articles

Klensch, Elsa, "España!," in *Vogue,* October 1988.

* * *

Joaquim Verdù is rare among fashion designers in showing a preference for knitted rather than woven fabrics—to the extent that, since his label started to be manufactured by Pulligan in 1991, Verdù has devoted himself exclusively to knitting. Underlying the eminently wearable collections is a philosophy of less is more. The keynotes are well-defined volumes, fluid lines, and immaculate detailing; colours are mostly plain. What interests the designer is the knitted fabric in its own right, rather than knitting as a vehicle for multicoloured jacquards and intarsias. Apart from occasional stripes or prints, if Verdù combines colours it is on a large scale. He might, for example, use a different shade for each part of an outfit, or for each garment of a range. That he had intended to be a painter is always apparent in the subtle choice and juxtaposition of brights, pastels, or neutrals.

Previous collections have been more exuberant, with a clever mix of knitted and woven materials. When mixing fabrics Verdù tends to play a teasing game of "spot the knitting." He chooses knitted fabrics that look so much like weaves that only a very close inspection reveals what they are; then he reverses traditional roles and takes us light years away from the woven suit teamed with a sweater. In a Verdù runway, knitting, identifiable or not, is always the star of the show. Weaves become complementary or, at best, equal partners.

Handling knitting in this way is a difficult exercise, especially when tailoring is involved, and Verdù has been known to dress male models in suits entirely made out of jersey. The very same qualities that make knitting feel like a second skin turn it awkward in the workroom. Knitted fabrics can be unpredictable. Pressing can stretch them. Some curl, others have a sideways slant, difficult to control and impossible to correct. Half the time the fabric needs to be designed from scratch, and here lies the greatest challenge: to start a garment not from a bale of jersey but from a cone of yarn.

Verdù designs for the straight knitting machine show him in complete control of the fabric and of the manufacturing process. This is one of the aspects that make his work so successful, but there are others. One is his skill at producing infinite variations on a theme, however simple. Verdù devotees know for a fact that, in any given range, they will find something to fit their age, lifestyle, and bone structure. Then there is the way in which the designer combines chic with exquisite comfort, something which international models appearing in his shows have been quick to point out. Finally there is the clearly distinctive signature, the very personal imprint Verdù leaves on everything he does because, except for making the clothes, he actually does everything. From the moment he chooses a yarn or fabric and reaches for the sketch pad, up to the final fitting, nobody else works on the design. In the era of the franchise, a Joaquim Verdù label means exactly what it says.

As a young man, Verdù started his studies at Feli's fashion school. He had not been there more than a few weeks before his potential was spotted by one of the lecturers. Pedro Rodríguez obtained permission from the school to take Verdù to his own couture house, where he personally introduced him to the intricacies of cut and drape. On his death, many years later, Rodríguez left him his scissors. The man who shares with Balenciaga the honour of being the father of Spanish couture could not have paid Joaquim Verdù a greater compliment.

—Montse Stanley

VERINO, Roberto.

Spanish fashion designer

Born: Manuel Roberto Marino, Verin, Spain, May 1945. **Family:** Children: Cristina, Jose Manuel. **Career:** Began business management studies and fine arts in Paris, but returned home in 1967 to take charge of parents' leather garments business. In 1970s, worked for MARPY Jeans. Launched ready-to-wear collection for women, Roberto Verino; a year later, opened his first shop in Paris. Collections represented in over 20 countries. Specializes in women's ready-to-wear. **Awards:** T for Triumph (*Telva* magazine, Spain), 1991 and 1994; Aguja de Oro (Golden Needle), Spanish Press, 1992. **Address:** Amaro Refojo 12, 36200 Verin (Orense), Spain.

Publications:

On VERINO:

Articles

Mattioni, Marina, "Roberto Verino," in *Donna* (Milan), June 1990.

*   *   *

Roberto Verino is a Spanish designer who first trained in Paris before returning to take over the family leather clothing business in northern Spain. Through the 1970s he built up a small concern into a prosperous local industry; then, in 1982, Verino launched his first collection of prêt-à-porter. His success was almost immediate, and year by year his fame has grown so that in 1994 he is the premier Spanish fashion designer.

From the beginning Roberto Verino has set himself the highest standards of artistry. He has collaborated with well known Spanish painter Xaime Quesada and as early as 1984 designed his prototype around the work of Joan Pere Viladecans for display at the Barcelona International Cotton Institute. In recent years, designs for his new collections have been drawn by Arturo Elenor whose style is similar to the British political cartoonist Gerald Scarfe, so that the fashion plates are not just design drafts but art in their own right.

As well as this strong accent on artistry, Roberto Verino makes clothes that are both practical and comfortable. To these ends, he looks to masculine fashion to create feminine clothes. All his designs are a clash of male and female. Masculine lines, female detail, male fabrics, feminine cuts, masculine shape, feminine colours.

Roberto Verino prides himself on his use of cotton and linen; no longer, if ever, uniquely masculine fabrics, except Roberto Verino prefers black, grey and brown, pin-striped, flecked, or even tartan colours and patterns. Roberto Verino's favourite clothing is jacket and trousers, double-breasted, broad lapels, wide collars, neither cuffs nor turn-ups. Eschewing the traditional suit, the cut is pure feminine, the trousers fit snugly at the waist then flare at the ankle, or hug the waist in layers of wrap-around fabric that sculpt the leg down to a tight ankle fit. The jackets have tailored waists and soft shoulders to enhance feminine profiles.

Comfort and practicality should never preclude stylishness and it is the feminine detail of Roberto Verino's creations that make his work so original. Sparkling gems and brooches replace buttons, waistcoats shimmer and shine, shirts have full-flowing sleeves and lace collars, coats have satin linings, trousers and skirts are split high to reveal first ankle, *tibia,* and thigh. It would be wrong to give the impression that Roberto Verino uses uniquely dark colours. He has, in fact, built entire collections around white, contrasting male versus female by mixing male form with female colours. His collection includes royal blue trousers and coats, poppy red double-breasted jackets, angel-white suits, and yellow-gold waistcoats. For all his use of masculine materials, his adoption of male styles, Verino's clothes are pure female.

If Verino's masculine fabrics pay homage to Giorgio Armani, he is by no means a satellite of this Italian designer. Armani's reinvention of male fashion has inspired designers across Europe but Verino's genius is to twist Armani's ideas into a uniquely feminine creation. Many other influences are also apparent. Verino takes a pinch of humour from Moschino, mixes and matches colours in the style of Christian Lacroix, draws on the same sources of subtlety and so-

Roberto Verino: Fall/Winter 1994/95.

phistication as Sybilla and Claude Montana. Further geographic influences are readily apparent to northern Europeans: the delicate jewelled sandals straight out of a *souke;* the flowing gowns, high necklines, and modesty-preserving tops so reminiscent of heroines from Arabian Nights. The latest 1994 collection shows new influences from Asia and the Far East, square jackets, long lines, intricate toggle buttons, marvellous gold, red and orange silks.

Verino's collections have been shown in Paris and Madrid, Barcelona and London, but his work is not uniquely haute couture. In effect, he designs for three main markets. First is Sport and Urban, where Verino makes maximum use of male shapes to create practical styles for women. The Look Comfortable is a younger line, with emphasis on comfort. Miniskirts turn out to be shorts, blouses are long, light and full. Espadrilles, rope and canvas sandals are *de rigueur.* Finally comes his Night-time collection, where elegance meets comfort and seduction is inevitable. So reads the advertising copy, but it is clear that Roberto Verino designs with a woman's wants as well as needs in mind. 1993 saw the launch of a line of Roberto Verino cosmetics. Together with his clothes, this is to be found in shops and boutiques in the United Kingdom, Germany, Benelux, France, and Japan, making Roberto Verino a truly European designer.

—Sally Anne Melia

VERSACE, Gianni.

Italian designer

Born: Reggio Calabria, Italy, 2 December 1946. **Education:** Studied architecture, Calabria, 1964-67. **Career:** Designer and buyer in Paris and London, for his mother's dressmaking studio, 1968-72; free-lance designer, Callaghan, Complice, Genny, Milan, 1972-77; formed own company, Milan, 1978; showed first womenswear collection, 1978, first menswear collection, 1979; signature fragrance introduced, 1981; home furnishings collection launched, 1993. Also theatrical costume designer, La Scala and Bejart Ballet, from 1982. **Exhibitions:** Galleria Rizzardi, Milan, 1982; Studio La Città, Verona, 1983; Galerie Focus, Munich, 1983; *Gianni Versace: dialogues de mode,* Palais Galliera, Paris, 1986; retrospective, Fashion Institute of Technology, New York, 1992-93. **Awards:** Occhio d'Oro Award, Milan, 1982, 1984, 1990, 1991; Cutty Sark Award, 1983, 1988; Council of Fashion Designers of America International Award, 1993. **Address:** Via Gesu, 20121 Milan, Italy.

Publications:

By VERSACE:

Books

Vanitas: lo stile dei semsi, with Omar Calabrese, Rome 1991.
Versace Signatures, with Omar Calabrese, Rome 1992.
Designs: Gianni Verace, Milan 1994.
The Man without Tie, Milan 1994.
Men without Ties, New York, 1995.

On VERSACE:

Books

Mulassano, Adriana, *I mass-moda: fatti e personaggi dell'Italian Look,* Florence 1979.

Alfonso, Maria-Vittoria, *Leaders in Fashion: i grandi personaggi della moda,* Bologna 1983.
Giacomondi, Silvia, *The Italian Look Reflected,* Milan 1984.
Soli, Pia, *Il genio antipatico* (exhibition catalogue), Venice 1984.
Palais Galliera Musée de la Mode, *Gianni Versace: dialogues de mode* (exhibition catalogue), Milan 1986.
Pasi, Mario, *Versace Teatro* (two volumes), Milan 1987.
Coleridge, Nicholas, *The Fashion Conspiracy,* London 1988.
Bocca, Nicoletta, and Chiara Buss, *Gianni Versace: l'abito per pensare,* Milan 1989.
Martin, Richard, and Harold Koda, *Infra-Apparel,* New York, 1993.
Martin, Richard and Harold Koda, *Orientalism: Visions of the East in Western Dress* (exhibition catalogue), New York, 1994.

Articles

Carlsen, Peter, "Gianni Versace: Disciplined Negligence," in *Gentleman's Quarterly* (New York), August 1979.
Withers, Jane, "The Palace of Versace," in *The Face* (London), December 1984.
Simpson, Helen, "Gianni Versace: ordito e trama," in *Vogue* (Milan), October 1985.
Petkanas, Christopher, "A Dialog with Gianni Versace," in *Women's Wear Daily* (New York), 22 October 1986.
Del Pozo, Silvia, "Gianni Versace: l'immigrato eccellente," in *L'Uomo Vogue* (Milan), October 1987.
Phillips, Kathy, "The Satanic Versace," in *You,* magazine of the *Mail on Sunday* (London), 19 March 1989.
Martin, Richard, "Sailing to Byzantium: A Fashion Odyseey, 1990-1991," *Textile and Text,* 14 February 1991.
Servin, James, "Chic or Cruel? Gianni Versace's Styles Take a Cue from the World of S&M. Some Women Say It Makes Them Feel Powerful; Others Find It Demeaning," in the *New York Times,* 1 November 1992.
Morris, Bernadine, "The Once and Future Versace," in the *New York Times,* 8 November 1992.
"Gianni Versace," in *Current Biography* (New York), April 1993.
Schiff, Stephen, "Lunch with Mr. Armani, Tea with Mr. Versace, Dinner with Mr. Valentino," in *The New Yorker* (New York), 7 November 1994.
Forden, Sara Gay, "Very Versace: Making America No. 1," in *Women's Wear Daily* (New York), 1 November 1994.
Gandee, Charles, "Versace's Castle in the Sand," in *Vogue* (New York), December 1994.
"Book Preview [*L'Uomo Senza Cravatta*]," in *L'Uomo Vogue,* November 1994.
"Milan: Versace, Versus/Istante," in *Daily News Record* (New York), 18 January 1995.
Menkes, Suzy, "Versace's Pastiche Amid Couture Upheaval," in the *International Herald Tribune* (Paris), 23 January 1995.
Spindler, Amy M., "Versace: Clean and Mean for Fall," in the *New York Times,* 8 March 1995.
"Gianni Versace: The Right Stuff," in *Women's Wear Daily* (New York), 8 March 1995.
Van Lenten, Barry, "Gianni's American Dream," in *Women's Wear Daily* (New York), 10 April 1995.

*   *   *

Gianni Versace's work is both metaphorical opera and real clothing, the first in its larger-than-life exuberance and design *bravura* and the latter in its unpretentious, practical application to the comfort of the wearer and the expressiveness of the body. Versace has made all the world a stage for flamboyant and fascinating costume with the knowledgeable pageantry of the Renaissance, a Fellini-like sensuality of burlesque, and the brilliant notes of operatic color and silhouette. Richly cultivated in historical materials and vividly committed to the hedonism of late 20th-century culture, Versace creates a distinctive, at-the-edge design that achieves the aesthetic limit of the avant-garde and the commercial success of viable apparel. As Peter Carlsen argued in 1979, a Versace garment is of its time, is part of a "pure" design continuum pursued by Versace, and incorporates elements of history. ((*Gentleman's Quarterly,* August 1979.)

Versace has expressed his admiration for Poiret, the fashion revolutionary who in a brief *éclat* of design genius combined a theatrical fantasy with *legerdemain* eclecticism. Similarly, Versace functions as a kind of impresario to his own style, commanding authority over his image and advertising, menswear, womenswear, and other products. His apparel design is characterized by a particular interest in bias, itself a means of revealing the body in dramatic, sexy clothing for women. His embroideries (and metal mesh) harken back to the art déco, but also come forward to the conversationals of recent magazine covers. Likewise, his fascination with black-and-white grids and alternations recalls the 1920s and 1930s. His abundant swathings suggest Vionnet, Madame Grès, and North Africa. Line is important, with many Versace suits, dresses, and coats marked by lines as if the bound edges of fabric would in outline define waistlines, shoulders, or center front. Like any great prestidigitator on stage, Versace is also concerned with metamorphic clothing; that which can be worn or perceived in several different ways. In these respects, it is clear that the Milanese designer looks to Tokyo as well as to Milan and Paris. His metallics, trousers for women (ranging from voluminous pantaloons to cigarette-trouser leg wrappings), leather for women, and chunky, glittery accessories have created an image of women as a cross between Amazon and siren.

The boldness of silhouette in his womenswear is only reinforced in his work with photographers to represent the clothing, generally against a pure white field to grant further starkness and aggressiveness. But, in person and in the individual item, Versace's clothing is far less *diva* and dominatrix than it might seem. Versace's jewel-like colors, his line in geometry in pattern, his recurrent fascination with the asymmetrical collars engendered by bias, and his flamboyant juxtapositions of pattern are elegant traits. Likewise, Versace employs luxurious textiles, a proclivity to classical references, bias in its mediation between the hard edge of geometry and the soft rendering of the body (even as practised in trousers on the bias), and such combinations as leather reversible to wool, embroidery-encrusted bodies and soft flowing skirts, and anomalous fashion history in skirt-trouser combinations with blazer and wrapped waist, a piquant pastiche of fashion elements. When Diana Vreeland reportedly commended Versace, saying that no one could wrap cloth like him and that wearing a Versace blouse made her feel 20 years old again, Vreeland identified the bias as his most trenchant attribute and as a trait precious in fashion history since Vionnet.

Versace's menswear is also accented by leather, body wrapping for sensuality, audacious silhouette, and oversizing for comfort. Even in menswear, Versace plays with asymmetry and the bias-influenced continuous rotation around the body, rather than a disjunctive front and back. Versace's menswear in particular is sometimes criticized as being futuristic with its big shoulders and technological detailing seeming to suggest science fiction. However,

Versace employs the most elegant menswear materials in a loose, capacious drape that defies any outer-space uniforms. Rather, his design recalls Thayaht and the Futurist ideal of clothing fully realized for the first time with sensuality and practicality.

Versace is an encyclopaedist of classical tradition. His insistence upon directing all aspects of the fashion communication, his books and exhibitions interpreting his one work, and his theatrical work in its virtuoso diversity testify to a philosophy of fashion as expressed in his exhibition and book *Gianni Versace: L'abito per pensare.* Versace is neither a secluded scholastic, though, nor merely the glittery dresser of stars and celebrities that some have perceived. The truth is somewhere in between, in a design imagination of brilliant theatrical insight, probing and analytical interest in bias, and a desire to reconcile the use of fashion history with the making of a clothing aesthetic for today. Versace has brought theatrical delirium and delight to the classical tradition in a way that reminds us of the ceaseless energy and entertainment of human adornment. In Versace, a dynamic classicism survives and a jubilant theater triumphs.

—Richard Martin

VICTOR, Sally.

American milliner

Born: Sally Josephs in Scranton, Pennsylvania, 23 February 1905. **Education:** Studied painting in Paris. **Family:** Married Sergiu Victor in 1927; son: Richard. **Career:** Saleswoman, then millinery buyer, Macy's, New York, 1923-25; assistant millinery buyer, 1925, and head buyer, 1926, Bamberger's, Newark, New Jersey; designer, Serge millinery, New York, 1927-34; opened own made-to-order millinery establishment, 1934; Sally V ready-to-wear line introduced, from 1951; firm closed, 1968. **Exhibitions:** the Brooklyn Museum, 1942. **Awards:** Fashion Critics Millinery Award, 1943; Coty American Fashion Critics Award, 1944, 1956. *Died (in New York) 14 May 1977.*

Publications:

On VICTOR:

Books

Lambert, Eleanor, *World of Fashion: People, Places, Resources,* New York and London 1976.
McDowell, Colin, *Hats: Status, Style, Glamour,* London 1992.

Articles

"Sally Victor," in *Colliers* (New York), 11 March 1939.
"Sally Victor," in *Current Biography* (New York), April 1954.
Sheppard, Eugenia, in the *New York Herald Tribune,* 25 March 1964. "Sally Victor," [obituary] in the *New York Times,* 16 May 1977.

*   *   *

Just as the American sportswear designers were establishing the American look in mix-and-match separates during the 1930s and

1940s, American milliners, especially Sally Victor, established the look in their own craft. Learning millinery first from the point of view of the buyer and customer, while working at Macy's in New York, Victor focused on what she knew women wanted, "designing pretty hats that make women look prettier," as she once described her principal objective, a quote considered appropriate enough for her career to be found in her *New York Times* obituary on 16 May 1977. Although Eugenia Sheppard reminded her *New York Herald Tribune* readers in her 25 March 1964 column that Victor was "sometimes accused of designing too pretty, too feminine, too becoming, too matronly hats," she went on to give her credit for reviving the Ecuadorean economy by making the Panama straw hat popular again, even with the young women of the mid-1960s. Her customers included Mamie Eisenhower, Mrs Eleanor Roosevelt, Queen Elizabeth II, Judy Garland, and Helen Hayes. As well as being pretty, there was a sophistication and cleanness to the line of many of her designs that was usually described as being especially "American." She was called "a magnificent sculptress of straws and felts" by *The New Yorker* in 1954.

Influences on her work were many and varied, and among those she readily acknowledged were art exhibitions and architecture. The 1948 exhibition of art from the museums of Berlin at the Metropolitan Museum of Art, New York inspired her to create hats in a Franco-Flemish mode, with coifs and beret-like shapes taken from the paintings. In 1952 she did a series, in commemoration of Marco Polo's birth, on oriental themes using shapes inspired by fans, lanterns, and pinwheels. In the late 1950s and early 1960s she looked for inspiration to such buildings as Frank Lloyd Wright's Guggenheim Museum, which she interpreted in straw.

From early in her career she was counted with Lilly Daché and John Fredericks among the most important American milliners. Sally Victor hats were used to accessorize the catwalk models of American designers from Hattie Carnegie to Anne Klein. She was not only prolific in the variety of her made-to-order hats for each season, but was also among the first to establish a ready-to-wear line, Sally V. Her retirement in 1968 coincided with the demise of the hat as an essential fashion accessory and the increasing casualness of the American lifestyle.

—Jean Druesedow

VICTORIO Y LUCCHINO.

Italian fashion design company

Founded by José Luis Medina del Corral (born in 1954 in Seville) and José Victor Rodríguez Caro (born in 1952 in Cordoba). Met in 1972, working for a Seville design group. *Carmen* perfume, launched, 1992. **Exhibitions:** *Sevilla Barroca,* Museo de Ferrocariles, Madrid, 1986; British Designers Fair, Olympia, London, 1987, 1988, 1989; Cibeles Fashion Show, Madrid, 1987-91; *Festa de la moda,* Barcelona, 1988; *IGEDO,* Dusseldorf, 1989, 1990; *Mode Woche,* Munich, 1990; *Fashion Coterie,* New York, 1990; *Milanovende,* Milan, 1991; *Festival de Disenadores Hispanos,* Washington, D.C. 1991; Expo 92; Hotel Ritz, Barcelona, 1992. **Address:** Padre Luis Mallop, 4 Casa Natal de Velazquez, 41004 Seville.

Publications:

On VICTORIO Y LUCCHINO:

Articles

"Victorio & Lucchino," in *Vanidad,* No. 1, 1992.
"Pasarela Cibeles: la moda esta de moda," in *¡Hola!,* 4 March 1993.
"Victorio y Lucchino suspiran por Espana," in *El Pais* (Madrid), 19 February 1994.

*   *   *

Victorio y Lucchino are a Spanish design duo, combining the talents of the founding partners, José Victor Rodríguez Caro and José Luis Medina del Corral. Caro comes from Palma Del Rio in Córdoba. Born during the early 1950s, he was originally inspired by the Parisian designers of the decade who dominated the pages of Spanish fashion magazines. As a teenager, he worked as an assistant for several fashion companies, collaborating in the preparation of their collections.

Del Corral, also born in the 1950s, hails from Seville. From an early age he, too, felt that his vocation was to be in fashion design. After his studies, he began work with a Seville design company where Caro was also working and, after several months at the company, the pair decided to join forces and create their own line, "Victorio y Lucchino."

The Victorio y Lucchino style is purely Spanish in origin. They are particularly inspired by the spirit of Andalucia in the southern region of Spain where they live and work. The bright light creates very rich shadows, colours and textures, awakening the senses to the tastes, touches, and smells that stimulate exciting design. The visual imagery also inspires, like the religious rituals, such as the slaves of the Phoenician Goddess of Estarte as they bedeck her in heavy jewels amidst a haze of incense, myrrh and amber. The duo themselves declare: "We create our fashions amid scents of geraniums, basil, and myrtle. Our influences are mixed and melted together to form ideas reminiscent of the streets, squares, and the river bejewelled with stars."

Luscious opulence is reflected in the type of fabrics Victorio y Lucchino choose to work with. Smooth velvets in burgundies, dark olive greens, and sunlit yellows and oranges. Iridescent velvets that reflect the light and ribbed and stripped velvets that shimmer. Crinkled and bubbled organza, and organza with tone on tone marble effects. Satin, and the luxurious effect of chenille, are other popular fabrics.

Sensuous eveningwear is a favourite look. Bustiers with long, attached sleeves leaving shoulders revealed and lots or room for full straps. Clingy, sculpted dresses and lily-shaped jackets are other popular innovations. The Victorio y Lucchino woman is calm, deep, and sensual; she is dressed to make an impact on a Spanish balcony or on the street. It is an outdoor, Mediterranean glamour, born of a bright and orange scented afternoon.

The nationalistic flavour of Victorio y Lucchino collections is enhanced by recurring themes plucked from Spanish culture. Ranges have been christened with titles such as Spanish Barroca, The Comb and Manstilla, Carmen, and Vestales Hispalenses. In 1992 the design duo even launched a perfume called Carmen, paying homage to Bizet's famous opera and his fiery heroine.

The design label has points of sale in Europe, Hong Kong, Japan, Kuwait, and the United States. They show seasonally at the Cibeles

Victorio y Lucchino.

fashion show in Madrid as well as other popular international trade shows, such as the Fashion Coterie in New York and Milanovendemoda in Milan. The design duo also have their own shop selling the label in Seville.

—Kevin Almond

VIONNET, Madeleine.

French designer

Born: Chilleurs-aux-Bois, 22 June 1876. **Family:** Married in 1893 (divorced, 1894); one child (died); married Dmitri Netchvolodov in 1925 (divorced, 1955). **Career:** Dressmaker's apprentice, Aubervilliers, 1888-93; dressmaker, House of Vincent, Paris, 1893-95; cutter, then head of workroom, Kate Reilly, London, 1895-1900; saleswoman, Bechoff David, Paris, 1900-01; head of studios under Marie Gerber, Callot Soeurs, Paris, 1901-05; designer, Doucet, 1905-11; designer, Maison Vionnet, 1912-14, 1919-39; retired, 1940. **Exhibitions:** *Three Women: Madeleine Vionnet, Claire McCardell and Rei Kawakubo,* Fashion Institute of Technology, New York, 1987; retrospective, Musée de Marseille, 1991. *Died* (in Paris) *2 March 1975.*

Publications:

On VIONNET:

Books

Latour, Anny, *Kings of Fashion,* London 1958.
Milbank, Caroline Rennolds, *Couture: The Great Designers,* New York 1985.
Koda, Harold, Richard Martin, and Laura Sinderbrand, *Three Women: Madeleine Vionnet, Claire McCardell, and Rei Kawakubo* (exhibition catalogue), New York 1987.
Demornex, Jacqueline, *Madeleine Vionnet,* Paris 1989.
Kirke, Betty, *Vionnet,* Tokyo 1991.
Steele, Valerie, *Women of Fashion: Twentieth Century Designers,* New York 1991.
Alaia, A., *Madeleine Vionnet* (exhibition catalogue), Marseille 1991.

Articles

Chatwin, Bruce, "Surviving in Style," in *The Sunday Times Magazine* (London), 4 March 1973 (version "Madeleine Vionnet" republished in Bruce Chatwin, *What Am I Doing Here?,* London 1989).
"Madeleine Vionnet, A Revolution in Dressmaking," in *The Times* (London), 6 March 1975.
Imatake, S., "Inventive Clothes 1909-1939," in *Idea* (Concord, New Hampshire), September 1975.
Weinstein, Jeff, "Vionnet, McCardell, Kawakubo: Why There Are Three Great Women Artists," in *Village Voice* (New York), 31 March 1987.
Drier, Deborah, "Designing Women," in *Art in America* (New York), May 1987.
Kirke, Betty, "A Dressmaker Extrordinaire," in *Threads* (Newtown, Connecticut), February/March 1989.

*   *   *

Bruce Chatwin once commented: "A Vionnet dress looks [like] nothing in the hand. It contains no artificial stiffening and flops limply on the hanger" (*The Sunday Times Magazine,* London 4 March 1973). Vionnet's inexorable synergy is the body in the dress. Her draping on the bias gave stretch to the fabric, a fully three-dimensional and even gyroscopic geometry to the garment, and a fluid dynamic of the body in motion as radical as Cubism and Futurism in their panoramas on the body. Her work inevitably prompts the analogy to sculpture in its palpable revelation of the form within. Some accused Vionnet of a shocking *déshabillé,* but Vionnet was seeking only the awareness of volume. Chatwin wrote: "No-one knew better how to drape a torso in the round. She handled fabric as a master sculptor realises the possibilities latent in a marble block; and like a sculptor too she understood the subtle beauty of the female body in motion and that graceful movements were enhanced by asymmetry of cut."

The only rigidity that ever obtained for Vionnet was her definite sense of self: she closed her couture house in 1939, although she lived until 1975. She lamented the work of other designers and disdained much that occurred in fashion as unprincipled and unworthy; and she was a true believer in the modern, scorning unnecessary adornment, seeking structural principles, demanding plain perfection. Fernand Léger said that one of the finest things to see in Paris was Vionnet cutting. He used to go there when he felt depleted in his own work.

Vionnet draped on a reduced-scale mannequin. There she played her cloth in the enhanced elasticity of its diagonal bias to create the garment. In creating the idea in miniature, Vionnet may have surpassed any sense of weight of the fabric and achieved her ideal and effortless rotation around the body in a most logical way. When the same garments achieved human proportion, their sheerness, the avoidance of decorative complication, the absence of planes front and back, and the supple elegance of fabric that caresses the body in a continuous peregrination were distinctive of Vionnet.

While bias cut was quickly emulated in the Paris couture, Vionnet's concepts of draping were not pursued only by Claire McCardell (who bought Vionnets to study their technique) before World War II, Geoffrey Beene, Halston, and other Americans in the 1960s and 1970s, Azzedine Alaïa in France, and Japanese designers Issey Miyake and Rei Kawakubo in the 1970s and 1980s (alerted to Vionnet by her strong presence in *The 10s, 20s, 30s* exhibition organized by Diana Vreeland at The Costume Institute of the Metropolitan Museum of Art in 1973-74).

One of Vionnet's most-quoted aphorisms is "when a woman smiles, her dress must smile with her." By making the dress dependent on the form of the wearer rather than an armature of its own, Vionnet assured the indivisibility of the woman and the garment. It is as if she created a skin or a shell rather than the independent form of a dress. Like many designers of her time, Vionnet's external references were chiefly to classical art and her dresses could resemble the wet drapery of classical statues and their cling and crêpey volutes of drapery.

At Doucet, she had discarded the layer of the underdress. In her own work, Vionnet eliminated interfacing in order to keep silhouette and fabric pliant; she brought the vocabulary of lingerie to the surface in her *détente* of all structure; she avoided any intrusion into fabric that could be avoided. Darts are generally eliminated. In a characteristic example, her "honeycomb dress," all structure resided in the manipulation of fabric to create the honeycomb, a pattern that emanates the silhouette. Elsewhere, faggoting and drawnwork displace the need for darts or other impositions and employ a decorative field to generate the desired form of the garment. The fluidity of cowl neckline, the chiffon handkerchief dress, and hemstiched blouse were trademarks and soft symbols of a virtuoso designer.

In insisting on the presence of a body and on celebrating the body within clothing, Vionnet is an early-century revolutionary in the manner of Diaghilev, Isadora Duncan, and Picasso. But there is also a deeply hermetic aspect to Vionnet who remains, despite the prodigious research revelations of Betty Kirke, a designer's designer, so subtle are the secrets of composition, despite the outright drama of being one of the most revolutionary and important fashion designers of the century.

—Richard Martin

VITTADINI, Adrienne.

American designer

Born: Adrienne Toth, in Budapest, Hungary, 1944. Immigrated to the United States, 1956. **Education:** Studied at the Moore College of Art, Philadelphia, 1962-66; received academic scholarship to apprentice with Louis Feraud, Paris, 1965. **Family:** Married Gianluigi Vittadini in 1972. **Career:** Designer, Sport Tempo, New York, 1967; designer, SW1 line for Rosanna division, Warnaco, New York, 1968-71; designer, Adrienne Vittadini collection for Avanzara division, Kimberly Knits, New York, 1976-79; with partner Victor Coopersmith, established own firm, AVVC, 1979, bought out partner, renamed company Adrienne Vittadini, 1982; formed Vopco Inc., franchising company, New York, 1987. First boutique opened, Beverly Hills, California, 1987. Also designer, Adrienne Vittadini swimwear collection for Cole of California. **Awards:** Coty American Fashion Critics Award, 1984. **Address:** 1441 Broadway, New York, New York 10018, USA.

Publications:

On VITTADINI:

Books

Milbank, Caroline Rennolds, *New York Fashion: The Evolution of American Style,* New York 1989.

Articles

Conant, Jennet, "Sweaters for the Self Assured," in *Newsweek* (New York), 3 February 1986.
Boyes, Kathleen, "Adrienne Vittadini: From Aesthetics to Reality," in *Women's Wear Daily* (New York), 25 January 1988.
Schiro, Anne-Marie, "Adrienne Vittadini: From Sweaters to an Empire," in the *New York Times,* 19 July 1988.
Pattrinieri, Anita, "A Magic Moment for Adrienne," in *Donna* (Milan), November 1989.
White, Constance C. R., "Adrienne Vittadini: The Power of Knits," in *Women's Wear Daily* (New York), 7 August 1991.
Schiro, Anne-Marie, "On Opposite Sides of the Cutting Edge," in the *New York Times,* 6 November 1992.

*   *   *

To the industry and the fashion press, Hungarian-born Adrienne Vittadini is known as the Queen of Knits. In 1979, after working with several knitwear firms, Vittadini started her own knitwear company, always asserting that knitwear is more than just sweaters. As a knitwear designer she is also a textile as well as a fashion designer. Vittadini maintains, "creating fabrics, then silhouettes, is the essence of fashion." She begins with a concept or theme for a collection, based on a mood or a feeling, which she then connects with a particular inspiration. The inspiration can evolve from an individual artist, an artistic movement, or her travels. Once she decides on a theme, intense research in libraries, museums, books, and magazines begins. Her collections have been inspired by the works of Alexander Calder, Pablo Picasso, Joan Miró, and Max Bill as well as Norwegian design and early Russian embroidery. She also taps into contemporary pop culture for ideas, such as the line she designed based on the cartoon character Dick Tracy.

After establishing a theme, Vittadini creates the knit fabric by selecting and creating unusually textured yarns with Italian yarn spinners. She then oversees the dyeing to obtain her own distinctive colorings and often supervises the initial samples off the knitting machines. Once the color and pattern are finalized, the fit, finishing, and quality are considered. This allows her to maintain a sense of control over the design process from start to finish. Vittadini likens this entire process to painting, relating to her background in fine arts study at Moore College of Art in Philadelphia.

The Vittadini look is characterized by knitwear that is of all-natural fiber, a certain practical, casual ease, and contemporary design with a feminine appeal. Her trademark knit silhouettes are loose-fit sweaters worn over short skirts, sophisticated ensembles, and sweater dresses which can all be interchanged. Vittadini asserts that knits are the most modern way of dressing. In her collections, she balances her love of European elegance in design with American practicality and ease by creating clothes which are "feminine without fussiness, a certain cleanness and pureness without hardness." Vittadini's simple knit silhouettes create a seductive look as they mold to the shape of the body.

First and foremost, Vittadini design is defined by the textile. She has expanded the knitwear industry by inventing and developing new computer knitting techniques in textures, prints, and patterns as well as shapes and colors. Vittadini cites Lycra as the most important development in knitwear. She uses it as a technological and functional tool to keep shape in her knits—especially trousers. Vittadini has expanded the fabrics used in her collections to include wovens, prints, suedes, and leathers. Her lines now include licensing arrangements for cotton swimwear, accessories, girlswear, sleepwear, sunglasses, home furnishings, wallcoverings, and decorative fabrics. Roughly 60 per cent of her line is knits.

Adrienne Vittadini has always stressed the advantage she has as a woman designer. She states that, because she is a woman, she knows innately what other women want: clothes which reflect their modern lifestyles.

For many years, knits were looked upon by the industry as dowdy. Since Vittadini revolutionized the power of knits, many Seventh Avenue companies now include knits in their collections. By promoting the ease and practicality of knits as well as the fact they travel well, the Vittadini customer is both suburban and city, housewife and businesswomen, with a diverse set of needs from clothes. Adrienne Vittadini has recognized the importance of sportswear to her American customer by offering a quality, well-designed product.

—Margo Seaman

VIVIER, Roger.

French footwear designer

Born: Paris, 13 November 1913. **Education:** Studied sculpture at l'École des Beaux Arts, Paris. **Military Service:** Performed military service, 1938-39. **Career:** Designed shoe collection for friend's shoe factory. Opened own atelier, 1937, designing for Pinet and Bally in France, Miller and Delman in USA, Rayne and Turner in United Kingdom; designed exclusively for Delman, New York, 1940-41 and 1945-47. Studied millinery, 1942; opened New York store, Suzanne and Roger, with milliner Suzanne Remy, 1945; returned to Paris, 1947, designing free-lance; designed for Dior's new shoe department, 1953-63; showed signature collections, from 1963; reopened own business in Paris, 1963. Designs collections for couture houses, including Grès, St Laurent, Ungaro, and Balmain. **Exhibitions:** Musée des Arts de la Mode, Paris, 1987 (retrospective). **Awards:** Neiman Marcus Award, 1961; Daniel & Fischer Award; Riberio d'Oro.

Publications:

By VIVIER:

Books

Vivier, Roger, and Cynthia Hampton, *Les souliers de Roger Vivier* (exhibition catalogue), Paris 1987.

On VIVIER:

Books

Swann, June, *Shoes,* London 1982.
McDowell, Colin, *Shoes: Fashion and Fantasy,* New York 1989.
Trasko, Mary, *Heavenly Soles: Extraordinary Twentieth-Century Shoes,* New York 1989.
Provoyer, Pierre, *Vivier,* Paris 1991.

Articles

In *Vogue,* July 1953, March 1954, September 1958, September 1962.
In *Harper's Bazaar* (New York), November 1960.
Cassullo, Joanne L., "Four Hundred Shoes," in *Next,* December 1984.
Bricker, Charles, "Fashion Afoot: Roger Vivier, the Supreme Shoemaker Comes to New York," in *Connoisseur* (New York), December 1986.
Buck, Joan J., "A Maker of Magic," in *Vogue* (New York), December 1987.
"Styles," in the *New York Times,* 9 August 1992.
Menkes, Suzy, "Master Cobbler Sets Up Shop Again," in the *International Herald Tribune* (Paris), 24 January 1995.

*   *   *

Roger Vivier: c.1992. *Photograph by Eric Delorme.*

Roger Vivier has been perhaps the most innovative shoe designer of the 20th century. Vivier's shoes have had the remarkable ability to seem avant-garde yet destined at the same time to become classics. He has maintained an eye for the cutting edge of fashion for nearly six decades. Vivier looks back into the history of fashion and forward to the disciplines of engineering and science for inspiration. The shoes may seem shocking at first; however, it is the way that they complete the silhouette that has made Vivier so coveted by top fashion designers of the 20th century. With a sophisticated eye for line, form, and the use of innovative materials, Vivier has created footwear which has been worn by some of the most stylish and prestigious people of the 20th century, among them red *faux* snakeskin boots for Diana Vreeland, gold kidskin shoes studded with rubies for the coronation of the Queen of England, "Ball of Diamonds" shoes for Marlene Dietrich.

Vivier has worked with some of the most innovative fashion designers of the 20th century: these have included Elsa Schiaparelli, Christian Dior, and Yves Saint Laurent, at the height of their careers. Schiaparelli was the first designer to include Vivier's shoes in her collection. Vivier was working for the American firm Delman at the time. Delman rejected Vivier's sketch of the shocking platform shoe which Schiaparelli included in her 1938 collection. In 1947 Vivier began to work for Christian Dior. The New Look by Dior brought new emphasis to the ankle and foot. Vivier created a number of new heel shapes for Dior, including the stiletto and the comma heel. During their ten-year association, Dior and Vivier created a golden era of design. In the 1960s Vivier created the low heeled "pilgrim pump" with a square silver buckle. This shoe is often cited as fashion's most copied shoe.

Vivier was one of the first designers to use clear plastic in the design of shoes. His first plastic designs were created in the late 1940s after World War II; however, in the early 1960s he created entire collections in plastic. Vivier popularized the acceptance of the thigh-high *cuissarde* boot in the mid-1960s, a fashion which had been considered unacceptable for women since the time of Joan of Arc (Trasko, Mary, New York 1989). Vivier teamed with Delman again in 1992. The mood of his collections continues to be imaginative and forward thinking. Drawing his inspiration from nature, contemporary fashion, the history of fashion, painting, and literature, Vivier has updated some of his earlier designs and he is constantly creating new designs which challenge the ideas of shoe design.

Vivier studied sculpture at the École des Beaux-Arts in Paris and later apprenticed at a shoe factory. It was this solid base of training in both aesthetics and technical skills that led Vivier to become known for precision fit as well as innovative design. A *Vogue* ad for his shoes in 1953 educates the viewer to look beyond the design. Showing the shoes embraced in callipers and other precision tools the ad reads, "Now study the heel. It announces an entirely new principle—the heel moved forward, where it carries the body's weight better." In another ad from *Vogue* (1954) the experience of owning a pair of Vivier shoes is likened to owning a couturier suit or dress, "a perfection of fit and workmanship." Vivier's shoes not only have the ability to complete a silhouette with an eloquence that makes a whole, but the beauty of their line, form, and craftsmanship make them creations that stand alone as objects of art. Vivier's strong combination of design and craftsmanship allows his shoes to stand prominently in the permanent collections of some of the world's most prestigious museums: the Costume Institute of the Metropolitan Museum of Art, New York; the Victoria and Albert Museum, London; and the Musée du Costume et de la Mode of the Louvre, Paris.

—Dennita Sewell

VOLLBRACHT, Michaele.

American designer

Born: Michael Vollbracht in Quincy, Illinois, 17 November 1947. **Education:** Studied at Parsons School of Design, New York, 1965-67. **Career:** Design assistant in New York to Geoffrey Beene, 1967-69, to Donald Brooks, then back to Beene and Beene Bazaar line, then returned to Brooks, 1969-71. Designed for Norman Norell until Norell's death in 1972; illustrator, Henri Bendel, 1972-74, and Bloomingdale's, 1975; Vollbracht Design Studios, producing garments from hand printed silks (by Belotti) of his design launched, 1977, New York; swimwear designer, Sofere company, 1979; launched Vollbracht Too division of Manhattan Industries, 1981; Michaele Vollbracht Sport line introduced, 1983; has also designed sheets for Burlington Industries, table linens for Audrey Company, Dallas. **Awards:** Golden Thimble Award, Parsons School of Design, 1967; Coty American Fashion Critics Award, 1980; American Printed Fashion Council's "Tommy" Award, 1984. **Address:** M.V. Swimwear, c/o A. H. Schrieber, 460 West 34th Street, New York, New York 10001, USA.

Publications:

By VOLLBRACHT:

Books

Michaele Vollbracht's Nothing Sacred, New York 1985.

On VOLLBRACHT:

Books

Khornak, Lucille, *Fashion 2001,* New York 1982.

Articles

Schiro, Anne-Marie, "And Then They Turned to Clothes," in the *New York Times,* 8 July 1978.
Langway, Lynn, "A Fashion Comet Returns," in *Newsweek* (New York), 25 May 1981.
Heiderstadt, Donna, "The Tranquil Force Behind Michaele Vollbracht's Bold Art," in *California Apparel News* (Los Angeles), 19 August 1983.
Radakovich, Anka, "Vollbracht Perfects a 'Starring Role' for Every Fashion Fantasy," in *Apparel News South* (Atlanta, Georgia), March 1985.
Larkin, Kathy, "Michaele Vollbracht," in the *New York Daily News,* 29 December 1985.

Lavina, Bettijean, "Portrait of a New Life," in the *Los Angeles Times,* 16 October 1992.

*   *   *

Dubbed "a fashion comet" by *Newsweek* magazine in 1981, Michaele Vollbracht blazed across the New York fashion scene for a ten year period beginning in 1977. When he left Parsons School of Design, New York, towards the end of the 1960s, Vollbracht logged time as a design assistant on Seventh Avenue, found it not to his liking, and turned instead to fashion illustration and graphic design. A shopping bag he created for Bloomingdale's department store in 1975 became an instant conversation piece and collector's item. It pictured an idealized woman's face, the artist's signature, and no other identifier, least of all the store name. The bag became the all purpose tote, a symbol of reverse chic, acceptable *because* it carried no advertising, although everyone knew what it represented.

By 1977, Vollbracht was one of the top illustrators in the field. At the same time, sensing that women were ready to turn away from the conservative, monochromatic look which had characterized much of the 1970s, Vollbracht established his fashion company in that year. "We have been beiged to death," he told Priscilla Tucker for the 8 May 1978 issue of the *New York Daily News.*

Bringing his skills as a graphic artist to the new company, Vollbracht created huge patterns in bright colors, hand screened onto lengths of silk, then cut into simple kaftan or *kimono*-like shapes, sometimes further embellished with sequins or bugle beads. These were entrance-making clothes with humor and panache for a confident clientèle. Vollbracht's celebrity customers included movie star Elizabeth Taylor, actress and singer Diahann Carroll, and comedienne Joan Rivers. For his first collection in 1978, many of Vollbracht's prints consisted of a single stylized element, such as a palm frond or a panther's head, enlarged to full body proportion and placed asymmetrically at the shoulder or side seam so that the motif was not quickly perceived—and the negative space of the ground formed a pattern of competing interest.

By the early 1980s Vollbracht's work included more sophisticated shaping and traditional fabrics in addition to his enormous signature prints. "I had to prove that I'm not just some outrageous designer, waving fabric over women's heads," he told *Newsweek* in 1981, "I want to demonstrate that I can cut an armhole and shape a dress—maybe not as beautifully as Givenchy, but I *can* do it." Indeed he could: a black velvet dress from his 1980 collection was softly draped diagonally across the back from the left shoulder almost to the waist at right, presenting the bare back as a piece of sculpture.

At the height of his career in the mid-1980s, Vollbracht was responsible for three ready-to-wear lines, Vollbracht Too, Michaele Vollbracht Sport, and Overs by Michaele Vollbracht, as well as a line of swimwear for the American manufacturer Sofere. His licensing agreements included sheets, towels, table linens, and a line of women's blouses. Vollbracht's whimsical, eye catching prints characterized his swimwear just as they did his custom line.

In 1985 Vollbracht parted company with his backer. Apparently unable or unwilling to obtain financing elsewhere, he discontinued his custom business. In 1987 Vollbracht retired from Seventh Avenue for the second time to concentrate on illustration and portrai-

ture. His work can be seen in *The New Yorker* and in *Vogue* as well as in his 1985 illustrated memoir *Nothing Sacred.*

—Whitney Blausen

VON FURSTENBERG, Diane.

Belgian designer working in the United States

Born: Diane Michelle Halfin in Brussels, 31 December 1946. **Education:** Studied at the University of Madrid, graduated in economics, University of Geneva. **Family:** Married Prince Egon Von Furstenberg in 1969 (divorced, 1983); children: Alexandre, Tatiana. **Career:** Immigrated to the United States, 1969; owner, designer, Diane Von Furstenberg Studio, 1970-77, and from 1985; established couture house, 1984-88; signature cosmetics line produced, 1977-83; *Tatiana* fragrance introduced, 1977. **Awards:** Fragrance Foundation Award, 1977; City of Hope Spirit of Life Award, Los Angeles, 1983; *Savvy* Magazine Award, New York, 1984, 1985, 1986, 1987, 1988; Einstein College of Medicine Spirit of Achievement Award, New York, 1984; Mayor of the City of New York's Statue of Liberty Medal, 1986. **Address:** 745 Fifth Avenue, suite 2400, New York, New York, 10151, USA.

Publications:

By VON FURSTENBERG:

Books

Diane Von Furstenberg's Book of Beauty, New York 1976.
Beds, New York 1991.

On VON FURSTENBERG:

Books

Reeves, Richard, *Convention,* New York 1977.
Morris, Bernadine, and Barbara Walz, *The Fashion Makers,* New York 1978.
Milbank, Caroline Rennolds, *New York Fashion: The Evolution of American Style,* New York 1989.

Articles

Rothmyer, Karen, "Once Upon a Time a Princess Made It with the Hoi Polloi," in the *Wall Street Journal* (New York), 17 January 1976.
Francke, Linda Bird, with Lisa Whitman and Sari Gilbert, "Princess of Fashion," in *Newsweek* (New York), 28 March 1976.
Rowes, Barbara, "Women Buy, but Men Dominate ... Then Came DVF," in *People,* 14 May 1979.
Wallach, Leah, "What Makes Diane Run?," in *Metropolitan Home* (New York), September 1982.
Blandford, Linda, "I Was Very Very Clever and Very Very Devious," in *The Guardian* (London), 9 March 1983.
Scholl, Jaye, and Paula Span, "The Savvy 60: The Top US Businesses Run by Women," in *Savvy* (New York), February 1984.

Diane Von Furstenberg.

Alai, Susan, "Fashion's Shy Di: DVF through the Ages," in *W,* October 1985.

Szabo, Julia, "Diane Von Furstenberg," in *Vogue* (New York), January 1991.

Dyett, Linda, "Women of Style: Princess Di and Her Daughter," in *Lears,* June 1991.

Podolsky, J. D., "Not Lying on Her Laurels," in *People,* 7 December 1991.

*

I got into fashion almost by accident, inspired to create the pieces I wanted, but couldn't find, in my own wardrobe. From my original 1970s knit wrap dress, to my new 1990s stretch "sock dress," I believe in marrying fashion and function—chic style and easy comfort, maximum impact and minimum fuss. Today I look to the modern woman. Pulled in many different directions in the course of a day, she juggles multiple roles depending on the situation, but always knows who she is and what's really important in her life.

I like to say that "I design a line the way I pack a suitcase," visualizing all of the different places I'm going to be, and then creating the appropriate outfits. My clothing must be timeless and versatile, so that a few simple pieces add up to many different looks. I think building a wardrobe should be like compiling a scrapbook of your life—over the years you accumulate favorite pieces, like old friends, that you always come back to for their unfailing ability to make you feel safe or confident, sexy or secure, depending on what you need.

Fabrics are key, since they're like a second skin, and should always be soft to the touch and breatheable. Colors should be beautiful and harmonious, and silhouettes simple, allowing the body to move freely. All in all, clothes should complement a woman, the perfect accessories to her beauty and lifestyle.

—Diane Von Furstenburg

*   *   *

When Diane Von Furstenburg married Prince Egon Von Furstenburg in 1969, she became Princess Diane Von Furstenburg. This aristocratic title proved no mean asset when she embarked on a fashion career in 1969, after moving from Europe with her husband to the United States. The cachet of "Princess" on a label proved especially potent to American buyers, aware of the American public's fascination with titles.

Putting the preeminence of rank aside, Von Furstenburg began her career with no fashion training. Her qualifications were a degree in economics from the University of Geneva and a fluency in five languages. She did, however, have a knowledge of international high society and culture. For a short period after her marriage both she and her husband were celebrities amongst the party-going jet set of the late 1960s, and for a time there was not a party that they did not attend. Von Furstenburg started her business during this period with a range of simple dresses that she had made up in Italy. They were a reaction to the jeans dressing so prevalent then, providing an easy, elegant alternative for women who wanted to wear a dress. Selling the clothes herself by tugging a sample rail around various American stores, she became an immediate success and a known designer name almost overnight.

Her philosophy was simple: she wanted to create elegant ease for all women. "There was a need for my things, for very simple dresses everyone could wear," she said in an interview for the book *The Fashion Makers* (New York 1978). Both slim and large women could wear the clothes, senator's wives or secretaries. They were sexy and chic regardless of the customer because they were designed to be sexy, accessible, and easy-to-wear.

Von Furstenburg's business quickly flourished and expanded. Highly successful lines of cosmetics, scent, handbags, shoes, jewellery, table linen, furs, stationery, wallpaper, and designs for *Vogue Patterns* were produced. She even produced a *Book of Beauty* in 1976 which detailed many of her philosophies towards life and design. She established herself as a liberated role model for many women. When she declared, "You don't sit around in little white gloves and big hats and try to look fashionable. You have a job, a husband or lover and children," she was stressing the practicality with style needed to adapt to modern life, which in many ways sums up her design philosophy.

Von Furstenburg resumed her business in the 1990s selling via television. Her contribution to fashion rests on a universal practicality. She believes in the importance of finding a style that is right for the individual, which is why many of her collections have featured very simple, flattering clothes. They can be dressed up or dressed down and are versatile enough for all sorts of women to feel attractive in. "Stick with them," she advises her customers when they have found Diane Von Furstenburg clothes to suit them.

—Kevin Almond

VUITTON, Louis.

French luggage and accessory firm

Founded by Louis Vuitton in Paris, 1854. Vuitton born in 1811. Vuitton arrived in Paris at age 16, apprenticed to several luggage makers; began designing flat luggage for use on new railways, diverging from traditional iron hooped trunks used on horse-drawn coaches. Company has kept abreast of changes in travelling habits, with innovative designs for new methods of transport, from the railway to steamers, the motor car, and the airplane. Designs range from watertight trunks to semi-rigid, expanding suitcases. **Address:** Grande Arche de la Défense, Cedex 41, 92044 Paris, France. *Died in 1892.*

Publications:

On VUITTON:

Books

A Journey through Time, Paris 1983.
Vuitton, Henry L., *La malle aux souvenirs,* Paris 1984.
Sebag-Montefiore, Hugh, *Kings on the Catwalk: The Louis Vuitton and Moët-Hennessy Affair,* Chapmans 1992.

Articles

"French Capital Markets: Bags of Bubbly," in *Euromoney,* January 1987.
"Fashionalbe Takeover," in the *Economist,* 16 July 1988.
Toy, Stewart, "Avant le Deluge at Moët Hennessy Louis Vuitton," in *Business Week,* 24 April 1989.
Carson-Parker, John, "Dese, Doms and Diors," in *Chief Executive,* November/December 1989.
Toy, Stewart, "Meet Monsieur Luxury," in *Business Week,* 30 July 1990.
Berman, Phyllis, and Zina Sawaya, "Life Begins at 77," in *Forbes,* 27 May 1991.
Caulkin, Simon, "A Case of Incompatibility," in *Management Today,* February 1993.

*   *   *

The French firm of Louis Vuitton has been making prestigious luggage since the middle of the 19th century. The firm's eponymous founder, Louis Vuitton, first came to Paris in 1837, in the year in which stage and mail coach travel was to be transformed by the opening of the first railway line in France, from Paris to St Germain, to passenger traffic. Louis Vuitton became an apprentice *layetier,* or luggage packer, to the prominent households of Paris at a time when journeys could take many months and require endless changes of wardrobe. He established such a reputation in this work that he was appointed by the Emperor of France, Napoleon III, as *Layetier* to his wife, the Empress Eugenie. Vuitton thus acquired expert knowledge of what made a good travelling case and started to design

luggage, opening his workshops to the general public in 1854 to provide luggage suitable for a new age of travel. Vuitton designed the first flat trunks that could be easily stacked in railway carriages and in the holds of ocean liners. Made of wood and covered in a new distinctive canvas called "Trianon Grey," this trunk superseded the dome-shaped, cumbersome trunks originally designed for the stage coach.

So successful and prestigious did this luggage become that other trunk makers began to copy Louis Vuitton's style and designs, a problem that still has to be dealt with over a century later. In 1876 Louis Vuitton responded to the imitators by changing the "Trianon Grey" canvas to a striped design in beige and brown. However, the problem persisted and in 1888, Louis Vuitton adopted another canvas: a checkerboard pattern with the words "Marque deposée Louis Vuitton" interwoven through the material. When George Vuitton took over the family firm on his father's death in 1892, imitation of the company's products was still a major problem, and four years later he designed and took out worldwide patents on the now legendary Louis Vuitton canvas, which featured his father's initials against background motifs of stars and flowers. This innovative design had the effect of stopping all imitations until the 1960s, when counterfeiting became a serious problem. Louis Vuitton takes a serious view of all counterfeiting and employs a team of lawyers and special investigation agencies to actively pursue offenders through law courts all over the world. The company allocates half of its communications budget to counteracting piracy. Louis Vuitton luggage and travel accessories can only be bought in a Louis Vuitton shop, unless sold as antiques.

Methods of manufacture have not changed since the 19th century. Suitcases are still made by hand; the craftsmen line up the leather and canvas, tapping in the tiny nails one by one and securing the five-lever solid pick-proof brass locks with an individual handmade key, designed to allow the traveller to have only one key for all his or her luggage. The wooden frames of each trunk are made of 30-year-old poplar that has been allowed to dry for at least four years. Each trunk has a serial number and can take up to 60 hours to make, and a suitcase as many as 15.

Although the luggage collection has always offered extensive choice, Louis Vuitton has been creating special made-to-order hard-sided luggage since 1854. The Congo explorer Pierre Savorgnan de Brazza (1852-1905) commissioned a combined trunk and bed from the company, and in 1936 for the American conductor Leopold Stokowski's travels, Gaston Vuitton designed a travelling *secrétaire,* measuring a mere 94x45x41 cm when closed. When opened, this extraordinary design reveals two shelves for books, three drawers for documents and musical scores, and a vertical compartment to store a typewriter. The gate-legged table which completes the instant workstation folds into the door.

Today over 50 Louis Vuitton shops in the major cities of Europe, America, and the Far East continue to supply prestigious luggage, incorporating high-performance materials developed for the advanced technologies of aeronautics and space, with the traditional expertise which has distinguished its products since the 19th century.

—Doreen Ehrlich

WALKER, Catherine.

French designer working in London

Born: Catherine Marguerite Marie-Therese Baheux-Lefebvre, in Pas de Calais, France. **Education:** Graduated in philosophy from Lille University, and received Maître-ès-Lettres in aesthetics, Aix-en-Provence. **Family:** Married John David Walker in 1969 (died, 1975); children: Naomi and Marianne. **Career:** Worked in Film Department, French Institute, London, 1970; Lecture Department, French Embassy, London, 1971. Designed childrenswear, 1977-86; opened shop, The Chelsea Design Co., 1977; first womenswear collection, 1980, under label The Chelsea Design Co. Ltd; opened bridal shop, Fulham Road, London, 1986. **Awards:** Designer of the Year Award for British Couture, 1990-91, and for Glamour, 1991-92. **Address:** The Chelsea Design Co., 65 Sydney Street, London SW3 6PX, England.

Publications:

On WALKER:

Books

McDowell, Colin, *A Hundred Years of Royal Style,* London 1985.
Coleridge, Nicholas, *The Fashion Conspiracy,* London 1988.
Debrett's Illustrated Fashion Guide—The Princess of Wales, London 1989.

Articles

Jobey, L., "Designing Women," in *Vogue* (London), July 1987.
Alexander, H., "When Discretion Is the Better Part of Glamour," in *The Daily Telegraph* (London), 26 November 1987.
Modlinger, J., "Di's Designer Walker," in the *Daily Express* (London), 7 March 1988.
Menkes, Suzy, "Who Dresses Princess Diana?," in the *International Herald Tribune* (Neuilly, France), 8 November 1988.
Darnton, Nina, "Fashion Fit for a Princess—Di's Secret Designer," in *Newsweek* (New York), 27 March 1989.
Jeal, N., in *The Observer Magazine* (London), 16 September 1990.
Hauptfuhrer, Fred, and Louise Lague, "She Designs Dresses to Di For," in *People Weekly* (New York), 6 May 1991.
"Designer Aims for Elegance of Simplicity," in *The Independent* (London), 16 July 1991.
Hume, Marion, "Joely Richardson Puts Sex into Catherine Walker," in *Tatler* (London), July/August 1991.
Mower, Sarah, "The Discreet Charm of Catherine Walker," in *Vogue* (London), November 1991.

Armstrong, Lisa, "A Couture Fairy Tale (Princess Included)," in *The Independent* (London), 16 July 1992.

*

My initial interest in fashion revolved around two things: to elongate the body, and the general underlying technical composition of clothes. This took its own course towards designing glamorous, lean, fluid (1930s inspired) suits, cocktail and evening dresses, and a penchant towards couture.

I try to focus on making the above relevant to the lifestyle of today, that is to design clothes which give poise to women without being rigid, and which are poetic without being overworked.

Fashion is fast moving but also very uniform for the short time when a trend is "in." I like women who wear make-up and clothes for their own pleasure regardless of fashion—women who are themselves—and while one notices the individuality of their clothes you also feel they belong. I believe that this is where modern couture fits into fashion today and where I want my work to be.

—Catherine Walker

*   *   *

French-born couturier Catherine Walker established the Chelsea Design Co. Ltd in London in 1977 with no formal training in fashion design. Her educational background was in philosophy, for which she took a Maître-ès-Lettres, roughly the equivalent to a UK doctorate. Walker claims that the title of her company, which did not bear her own name until 1993, was in deference to her lack of experience as a fashion designer.

The decision to start her own company was made when Walker was widowed in 1975 and left with two young children. She began making childrenswear, and the transition to making maternity wear was in fact a natural one, according to Walker, since the pregnant female form resembles the generally shapeless figure of a child. Walker affirms that it was many years before she thought of herself as a fashion designer, and that it was a purely technical interest in the construction of garments that initially inspired her.

During the first 12 years of business Walker consolidated her knowledge of pattern cutting, fitting, and sewing, and later couture dressmaking, and tailoring. As her reputation grew by word of mouth she attracted press attention, and British *Vogue* first photographed one of her dresses for its January 1982 issue. Although the designer's clothes have been regularly featured in editorial fashion pages, Walker is renowned for her dislike of publicity and has never held a catwalk show. She views her personal development as a designer in a series of stages—first dressing, then tailoring, followed by embroidered decoration and, finally, draping.

It is her tailoring and decorative use of beading that have become the hallmarks of Walker's designs. There is always an emphasis on

Catherine Walker. *Photograph by Terence Donovan, courtesy of British Vogue (c) The Condé Nast Publications Ltd.*

the midriff, which Walker attributes to her French background. This structured effect around the waist, which though not fitted, gives the illusion of elongating it, is apparent not only in her tailored jackets but on both day dresses and evening gowns. British journalist Lisa Armstrong maintains that her skill as a couturier lies in her ability to create cloths that possess the subtle, unlaboured tailoring that on the surface seems not to be doing anything much but somehow manages to eliminate unwanted contours and add curves. (*The Independent* [London], 16 July 1992).

Another characteristic of Walker's designs is her use of plain colours such as black, navy, cream, and red, which are enhanced not through the use of printed textiles but with applied decoration such as hand-embroidery, heavy beading, and frogging. Her attention to detail is legendary. Articles about the designer mention the fact that she has been known to fly to Paris to find three buttons for a particular jacket.

While the bulk of her business is the made-to-measure couture collection, Walker also produces a ready-to-wear range called De Luxe and designs hats that are made for her by Mailson Michel in Paris. She designs both fine jewellery and a collection of costume jewellery, which include earrings and bracelets to accessorize the clothes. Walker also designs a collection of couture wedding gowns which she launched in 1986 with the opening of a second shop on London's Fulham Road. She was responsible for designing, amongst others, the wedding dress worn by Lady Helen Windsor at her marriage in July 1992.

Walker is perhaps best known for her creations for the Princess of Wales, which have attracted widespread publicity for her as a couturier, although she has always tried to avoid this aspect of the fashion world. It is important to note, however, that a close study of the Princess of Wales's wardrobe designed by Walker would not produce an accurate image of the designer. The requirements of the public royal wardrobe that the wearer stand out from the crowd—particularly important for television cameras and photographers—has meant that strong, often harsh colours have been used, which are not typical of Walker's style. However, the draped gowns, column evening dresses, and decorated tailored jacket worn by the Princess of Wales on numerous occasions illustrate the designer's signature use of beading and embroidery as well as her cutting technique of emphasizing the midriff and waistline.

Catherine Walker's impressive clientele, which lists not only British but foreign royalty, bears testament to her skill as a designer, despite the fact that she did not consider herself one for the first 12 years of business.

—Catherine Woram

WEITZ, John.

American fashion and industrial designer

Born: Berlin, Germany, 25 May 1923; immigrated to Britain, 1934, and to the United States, 1940; naturalized American, 1943. **Education:** Studied at The Hall School, 1936, at St. Paul's School, London, 1936-39; apprenticed to Edward Molyneux, Paris, 1939-40. **Family:** Married Susan Kohner, 1964; children: Paul and Christopher; also, children Robert and Karen, from a previous marriage. **Military Service:** Served in the United States Army, 1943-46; became Captain. **Career:** Designer of women's sportswear, working with several companies in London and New York, until 1954;

founder-designer and chairman, John Weitz Designs, Inc., men's fashion designs, New York, from 1954. Also a yachtsman and ex-race car driver. **Awards:** *Sports Illustrated* Award, 1959; NBC *Today* Award, 1960; Caswell-Massey Awards, 1963-66; *Harper's Bazaar* Medallion, New York, 1966; Moscow Diploma, 1967; Coty American Fashion Critics Award, 1974; Cartier Design Award, 1981; Mayor's Liberty Medal, New York, 1986; First Class Order of Merit, Germany, 1988; Dallas Menswear Mart Award, 1990; Fashion Institute of Technology President's Award, New York, 1990. **Address:** 600 Madison Avenue, New York, NY 10022, USA.

Publications:

By WEITZ:

Books

Sports Clothes for Your Sports Car, New York 1959.
The Value of Nothing, New York and London 1970.
Man in Charge, New York 1974.
Friends in High Places, New York 1982.
Hitler's Diplomat, London 1992.

Articles

"Auto Motives," in the *New York Times Magazine,* 27 March 1988.
"Jocks and Nerds: Men's Style in the Twentieth Century" (book review), in the *New York Times Book Review,* 3 December 1989.
"Home Away from Home," in *New York Magazine,* 19 February 1990.
"Fashion Statements," in *Town and Country* (New York), July 1994.

On WEITZ:

Books

Bender, Marilyn, *The Beautiful People,* New York 1968.

Articles

Talley, André Leon, "John Weitz," in *Interview* (New York), March 1983.
Gross, Michael, "Design for Living," in *Gentleman's Quarterly* (New York), September 1985.
Ferrari, Lynn, "John Weitz: Image of Distinction," in *Millionaire,* December 1987.
Brady, James, "In Step with John Weitz," in *Parade Magazine,* 31 July 1988.
Christy, Marian, "A Stylist with the Power of Politeness," in *The Boston Globe,* 9 April 1989.
Harris, Joyce Saenz, "The Novel Life of John Weitz," in *The Dallas Morning News* (Texas), 8 April 1990.
Simon, Cecelia Capuzzi, "Can You Explain John Weitz? Yes. You're Kidding," in *The New York Observer,* 10 September 1990.
Parola, Robert, "The Way It Was: John Weitz," in the *Daily News Record* (New York), 22 May 1992.
Van Lenten, Barry, "Men's Wear's Designer Pioneers: John Weitz," in the *Daily News Record* (New York), 18 January 1995.

*   *   *

John Weitz explained to *The Boston Globe* (9 April 1989) that he never wears a formal dress shirt with his tuxedo. "I wear white business shirts. I can't take the time to fiddle with front studs. The last thing I want is to be controlled by fashion." No one would say—and certainly no one would dare say in his presence—that Weitz is controlled by fashion. Rather, he has treated fashion as a chosen field, one among many. He abandoned the competitive field of womenswear for a mannerly, self-invented calling in menswear. Even there, he has stayed slightly aloof, choosing to be the debonair gentleman rather than fashion victim/victimizer. He has become two rare personalities: a late New York intellectual and a natural aristocrat who has seen aristocracies disintegrate, but who persists in imagining new ones.

Since the 1940s, Weitz has spoken a gentlemanly common sense about fashion for men and women. First encouraged by Dorothy Shaver of Lord & Taylor (New York) in the 1940s to pursue women's sportswear with his demanding sense of a contemporary post-war lifestyle, Weitz carried his marrow of American practicality within the genteel spirit of his own European and English cultivation. A polymath, as much a man of letters and ideas as of fashion, once an adventurer who drove race cars and was solicited to portray James Bond, a paragon of elegance often compared in appearance to Gregory Peck and Cary Grant, Weitz is a consummate gentleman in the sometimes less than genteel world of fashion.

While his great achievements in apparel in the 1950s were women's sportswear, he became one of the first men's fashion designers in the early 1960s, shifting his emphasis to this field for its capability to fulfil his interest in classic looks, utmost practicality, and no-nonsense durability. Until Giorgio Armani and Ralph Lauren in the late 1970s and 1980s, no designer was as faithful as Weitz to menswear as the germinal center of design and of a practical approach to wardrobe. In personal style as well as his design, Weitz exemplifies the refined, but unpretentious, good taste that comes of humane attention to what is important in life, with clothing following as a consequence of those values. Even in the extreme years of menswear in the late 1960s and early 1970s, Weitz's vision was always tempered.

If Weitz was first a visionary of the disciplines of sportswear for women in America, creating car coats, playsuits, jeans, button-down shirts for women in pink satin, and other practical items in the 1950s, he transferred his allegiance to menswear at the early moment in 1962-63 when a number of designers recognized for women's apparel were testing the waters of menswear, among them Geoffrey Beene and Bill Blass in America, Hardy Amies in England, and Pierre Cardin in France. Weitz alone gave his primary attention to menswear, a field where his own principal ideas had first come from observing the Duke of Windsor. Long before absorbing and ultimately creating the ethos of sportswear, Weitz had been an assistant to Molyneux in London. There, he was a part of fashion that was fastidious, client-driven, and rich in protocol and money. When asked in *Interview* (March 1983) if he considered himself a couturier, Weitz replied, "Good God, no. I'm a modern-day creature that emerged from an old couture assistant into a sort of inventive concept, which I don't mind at all." Weitz is his own creation: his acumen for business and licensing has enabled him to build an empire in menswear and cognate products with, in fact, a minimum of participation from the designer. His own engaging and cosmopolitan charm establishes only the guidelines for product development. In many ways, Weitz was the first to be such a designer: god-like prime cause, thereafter far removed from the world of his own creation. Weitz makes a point, however, of wear-

John Weitz.

ing his own clothes: this is a matter of honor for a man of boyscout, even knightly, integrity. With selfeffacing grace, he explained this phenomenon to Cecelia Capuzzi Simon in *The New York Observer* (10 September 1990): "You can survive beautifully being dead. I had no intention of taking that as a specific or as a quantum leap into the future. Now, eventually I have to perform that."

Alive and well, Weitz offers a graceful conceptual model of a fashion designer. To some, Weitz exemplifies effete or feigned aristocratism. But he is rather more of the special individuals Paul Fussell described in *Class* (1983) as "X," an open class that many could join though they have not understood that they have been invited. This class resembles E. M. Forster's "aristocracy of the sensitive, the considerate, and the plucky" who are "sensitive for others as well as themselves, ... considerate without being fussy." That's John Weitz.

—Richard Martin

WESTWOOD, Vivienne.

British designer

Born: Vivienne Isabel Swire in Glossop, Derbyshire, 8 April 1941. **Education:** Studied one term at Harrow Art School, then trained as a teacher. **Family:** Children: Ben, Joseph. **Career:** Taught school before working as designer, from c.1971. With partner Malcolm McLaren, proprietor of boutique variously named Let It Rock, 1971, Too Fast to Live, Too Young to Die, 1972, Sex, 1974,

Seditionaries, 1977, and World's End, from 1980; second shop, Nostalgia of Mud, opened, 1982; Mayfair shop opened, 1990. First showed under own name, 1982; first full menswear collection launched, 1990. Professor of fashion, Academy of Applied Arts, Vienna, 1989-91. **Exhibitions:** Retrospective, Galerie Buchholz & Schipper, Cologne, 1991; retrospective, Bordeaux, 1992. **Awards:** British Designer of the Year Award, 1990, 1991; Order of the British Empire (OBE), 1992. **Address:** Unit 3, Old School House, The Lanterns, Bridge Lane, Battersea, London SW11 3AD, England.

Publications:

By WESTWOOD:

Articles

"Youth: Style and Fashion, Opinion," in *The Observer* (London), 10 February 1985.
"Paris, Punk and Beyond," in *Blitz* (London), May 1986.
"Pursuing an Image Without Any Taste," in *The Independent* (London), 9 September 1989.
"My Decade: Vivienne Westwood," in the *Sunday Correspondent Magazine* (London), 19 November 1989.
"Vivienne Westwood Writes...," in *The Independent* (London), 2 December 1994.

On WESTWOOD:

Books

Polhemus, Ted, *Fashion and Anti-Fashion,* London 1978.
McDermott, Catherine, *Street Style: British Design in the 1980s,* London 1987.
Howell, Georgina, *Sultans of Style: 30 Years of Fashion and Passion 1960-1990,* London 1990.
Steele, Valerie, *Women of Fashion: Twentieth Century Designers,* New York 1991.

Articles

Sutton, Ann, "World's End: Mud, Music and Fashion: Vivienne Westwood," in *American Fabrics and Fashions* (Columbia, South Carolina), No. 126, 1982.
Gleave, M., "Queen of the King's Road," in *The Observer* (London), 8 December 1982.
Warner, M., "Counter Culture: Where London's Avant-garde Designers Get Their Ideas," in *Connoisseur,* May 1984.
McDermott, Catherine, "Vivienne Westwood: Ten Years On," in *i-D* (London), February 1986.
Mower, Sarah, "First Lady of Punk," in *The Guardian* (London), 11 December 1986.
Buckley, Richard, and Anne Bogart, "Westwood: The 'Queen' of London," in *Women's Wear Daily* (New York), 17 March 1987.
Franklin, Caryn, "Rule Britannia Viv Rules OK," in *i-D* (London), March 1987.
"Vivienne Westwood," in *The Face* (London), May 1987.
Barber, Lynn, "Queen of the King's Road," in the *Sunday Express Magazine* (London), 12 July 1987.
"Royal Flush," in *i-D* (London), August 1987.
Mower, Sarah, "The Triumphal Reign of Queen Vivienne," in *The Observer* (London), 25 October 1987.

Brampton, Sally, "The Prime of Miss Vivienne Westwood," in *Elle* (London), September 1988.
Roberts, Michael, "From Punk to PM," in the *Tatler* (London), April 1989.
Barber, Lynn, "How Vivienne Westwood Took the Fun Out of Frocks," in *The Independent* (London), 18 February 1990.
Ash, Juliet, "Philosophy on the Catwalk: The Making and Wearing of Vivienne Westwood's Clothes," in Juliet Ash and Elizabeth Wilson, editors, *Chic Thrills, A Fashion Reader,* Berkeley, California 1993.
Fleury, Sylvia, "Vivienne Westwood," in *Flash Art* (Milan), November-December 1994.
Spindler, Amy M., "Four Who Have No Use for Trends," in the *New York Times,* 20 March 1995.
Menkes, Suzy, "Show, Not Clothes, Becomes the Message," in the *International Herald Tribune* (Paris), 20 March 1995.

*   *   *

Vivienne Westwood's clothes have been described as perverse, irrelevant, and unwearable. Westwood's creations have also been described as brilliant, subversive, and incredibly influential. Westwood is unquestionably among the most important fashion designers of the late 20th century.

Westwood will go down in history as the fashion designer most closely associated with the punks, a youth subculture that developed in England in the 1970s. Although her influence extends far beyond that era, Westwood's relationship with the punk subculture is critically important to an understanding of her style. Just as the mods and hippies had developed their own styles of dress and music, so did the punks. But whereas the hippies extolled love and peace, the punks emphasized sex and violence. Punk was about nihilism, blankness and chaos, and sexual deviancy, especially sadomasochism and fetishism. The classic punk style featured safety pins piercing cheeks or lips, spiky hairstyles, and deliberately revolting clothes, which often appropriated the illicit paraphernalia of pornography.

Westwood captured the essence of confrontational anti-fashion long before other designers recognized the subversive power of punk style. In the 1970s Westwood and her partner Malcolm McLaren had a shop in London successively named Let It Rock (1971), Too Fast to Live, Too Young To Die (1972), Sex (1974), and Seditionaries (1977). In the beginning the emphasis was on a 1950s-revival look derived from the delinquent styles of 1950s youth culture. "I was making Malcolm Teddy Boy clothes," recalled Westwood. "Remember, I was a first time round Teddy Girl." In 1972 the shop was renamed after the slogan on a biker's leather jacket, heralding the new brutalism that would soon spread throughout both street fashion and high fashion. Black leather evoked not only anti-social bikers like the Hell's Angels, but also sadomasochistic sex, which was then widely regarded as "the last taboo."

Westwood's Bondage collection of 1976 was particularly important. Working primarily in black, especially black leather and rubber, she designed clothes that were studded, buckled, strapped, chained, and zippered. Westwood talked to people who were into sadomasochistic sex and researched the "equipment" that they used: "I had to ask myself, why this extreme form of dress? Not that I strapped myself up and had sex like that. But on the other hand I also didn't want to liberally *understand* why people did it. I wanted to get hold of those extreme articles of clothing and feel what it was

Vivienne Westwood: An exhibition at one of Westwood's stores. *Photograph by Lothar Schnepf.*

like to wear them." Taken from the hidden sexual subculture that spawned it and flaunted it on the street, bondage fashion began to take on a new range of meanings: "The bondage clothes were ostensibly restricting but when you put them on they gave you a feeling of freedom."

Sex was "one of the all-time greatest shops in history," recalled pop star Adam Ant. The shop sign was in padded pink letters and the window was covered, except for a small opening, through which one could peep and see items like pornographic T-shirts. Westwood, in fact, was prosecuted and convicted for selling a T-shirt depicting

two cowboys with exposed penises. Other T-shirts referred to child molesting and rape, or bore aggressive slogans like "Destroy" superimposed over a swastika and an image of the Queen.

Sex was implicitly political for Westwood; when she renamed the shop Seditionaries, it was to show "the necessity to *seduce* people into revolt." Westwood insisted: "Sex is fashion." Deliberately torn clothing was inspired by old movie stills of "film stars looking really sexy in ripped clothes." She also launched the fashion for underwear as outerwear, showing bras worn *over* dresses. From the beginning she exploited the erotic potential of extreme shoe fashions, from leopard-print stiletto-heeled pumps to towering platform shoes and boots with multiple straps and buckles.

"When we finished punk rock we started looking at other cultures," recalled Westwood. "Up till then we'd only been concerned with emotionally charged rebellious English youth movements.... We looked at all the cults that we felt had this power." The result was the Pirates Collection of 1981, which heralded the beginning of the New Romantics Movement. The Pirates Collection utilized historical revivalism, 18th-century shirts and hats, rather than fetishism, but like the sexual deviant, the pirate also evoked the mystique of the romantic rebel as outcast and criminal. Meanwhile, in 1980 the shop was renamed World's End, and in 1981 Westwood began to show her collections in Paris, finally recognized internationally as a major designer.

Like pirates and highwaymen, Westwood and McLaren wanted "to plunder the world of its ideas." The Savages Collection (1982) showed Westwood gravitating toward a "tribal" look; the name was deliberately offensive and shocking; the clothes were oversized, in rough fabrics, and with exposed seams. Subsequent collections, like Buffalo, Hoboes, Witches, and Punkature, continued Westwood's postmodern collage of disparate objects and images. Models dressed in layers of mud-colored, torn clothing, with rags in their hair—and bras worn over their dresses.

In 1985 Westwood launched her "mini-crini," a short hooped skirt inspired by the Victorian crinoline, and styled with a tailored jacket and platform shoes. "I take something from the past which has a sort of vitality that has never been exploited—like the crinoline," she said. Westwood insisted that "there was never a fashion *invented* that was more sexy, especially in the big Victorian form."

She also revived the corset, another much maligned item of Victoriana—and an icon of fetish fashion. "I never thought it powerful to be like a second-rate man," said Westwood. "Feminine is stronger." Certainly her corsets and crinolines forced people to reexplore the meaning of controversial fashions. As she moved into the late 1980s and early 1990s, Westwood continued to transgress boundaries, not least by rejecting her earlier faith in anti-establishment style in favour of a subversive take on power dressing. Like "Miss Marple on acid," Westwood appropriated twinsets and tweeds, and even the traditional symbols of royal authority.

—Valerie Steele

WHISTLES.

British retailing firm

Established by Lucille Lewin, in George Street, London, 1976. Lewin studied fine art in South Africa, moved to the United States, sold furniture in Cambridge, Massachusetts; joined Conran Group, London; worked for Harvey Nichols as a buyer, until 1976. In-house range of clothes introduced, 1985. Chain includes 12 stores in the UK and in-store boutiques at Harrods, Selfridges, and Fenwicks, all in London. **Awards:** Design Led Retail Award, 1994. **Address:** 12 Saint Christopher's Place, London W1M 5HB, England.

Publications:

On WHISTLES:

Articles

McDowell, Colin, "Whistling," in *Country Life* (London), 5 February 1987.

Polan, Brenda, "Lucille Has a Ball," in *The Independent* (London), 16 December 1988.

Pascal, Béatrice, "La Chaine Anglaise Whistles reve de Vendre sa Mode a Paris," in *Dossier,* 14 October 1991.

"Cost Effective: The Designer," in *Marie Claire,* November 1993.

"The Latest Wrinkle," in *Women's Wear Daily,* 24 November 1993.

*   *   *

Uncomplicated, classic, and comfortable are words often used to describe the clothes designed by Lucille Lewin and sold under the Whistles retail label. Lewin combines her own moderately priced designs with other top name designer garments to create individual style for what is described as the confident and independent woman. Inspired by the fine arts, history, and culture, Lewin's collection is designed along a narrow colour range, setting the foundation and tone for each season in Whistles' nine shops. In many respects, Whistles may be compared with other British retailers such as Terence Conran and Joseph Ettedgui—all of whom are concerned with creating identities and consistency of style.

Lewin was originally a fine arts student from South Africa. After a brief period in the United States, Lewin and her husband moved to London and opened the first of the Whistles shops in 1974. Lewin gained considerable retail experience at Harvey Nichols' 21 Shop in London, and developed an aptitude for finding new talent. Owning her own shop has provided an opportunity to stock clothes by young, often virtually unknown, designers. In the early 1970s the careers of British designers Wendy Dagworthy, Betty Jackson, and Ally Capellino were launched by Lewin, and more recently designs by the French designer Myrène de Prémonville have proven to be major sales successes.

To reinforce the Whistles identity, Lewin began producing her own range of clothes in 1985. The collection consists of tailored garments, knitwear, swimwear, accessories, and shoes, with cuts ranging from classic to baggy. Natural fabrics, such as cotton and linen, are the mainstay of the collection, but Lewin is not averse to experimenting with new synthetic fabrics she deems appropriate to achieve the looks and the feel of a collection.

Lewin draws inspiration from a variety of sources reinforced by her training as a fine artist. Morocco, India, and Tunisia have inspired desert-coloured jersey sarong skirts and wrapover tops. In contrast, her designs of crisp, sporty navy and white garments in gabardine, linen, and cotton are influenced by baggy sailor trousers and tailored jackets from the 1920s. Another influence may be traced in her tweed suits, which are reminiscent of Chanel's simple and classic tailoring.

Lewin promotes her designs as mix-and-match pieces—not only with her own designs but with those of other designers. In effect, Lewin is acting as fashion "editor," both buying and designing garments. Her approach provides greater flexibility and choice in responding to individual preferences and budgets. In addition, through carefully considered colour groups and fabric selections, overall moods may be more easily and effectively established than if garments were designed as self-contained sets. Her approach is similar in attitude to the collections of American designer Donna Karan, and has provided British women with affordable, casual apparel preserving classical appeal.

Lucille Lewin's contribution to British fashion is recognized on two levels at least. Firstly, she has provided a moderately priced retail shop for women who want to create an individual look without succumbing to trendy fashions. Secondly, her unique approach to fashion retailing enables her to design under the Whistles label, thereby establishing and maintaining a strong and consistent foundation for the designers' garments bought for each season. This combination of retail and design distinguishes her work from that of other contemporary British fashion designers.

—Teal Triggs

WORKERS FOR FREEDOM.

British design firm

Founded October 1985 by Richard Nott (born in Hastings, England, 3 October 1947) and Graham Fraser (born in Bournemouth, 20 July 1948). Nott studied at Kingston University; design assistant to Valentino, Rome, 1972-75; principal lecturer, Kingston University Fashion School, 1975-85. Fraser studied accountancy and fashion retailing; worked as buyer/accountant, Feathers Boutique, London, 1970-71; assistant buyer, Harrods, London, 1975-78; buyer for Wallis Shops, London, 1978-81; advertising manager, Fortnum and Mason, London, 1981-82; fashion director, Liberty, London, 1982-85. Nott and Fraser operated first Workers for Freedom shop, Soho, London, 1985-92; introduced mens- and womenswear wholesale collections for Littlewoods Home Shopping catalogue, beginning in summer 1993; womenswear collection for A-Wear, Dublin, summer 1994. **Exhibitions:** Dayton Hudson, Minneapolis, USA, 1991; Fenit, São Paolo, Brazil, 1992. **Awards:** British Fashion Council Designers of the Year Award, 1990; Viyella Designer of the Year Award, 1990. **Address:** 6 Spice Court, Ivory Square, Plantation Wharf, London SW11 3UE, England.

Publications:

On WORKERS FOR FREEDOM:

Books

Coleridge, Nicholas, *The Fashion Conspiracy,* London 1988.
Wilson, Elizabeth, and Lou Taylor, *Through the Looking Glass,* to accompany BBC TV series, London 1989.

Articles

Lorna, James, in *The Independent* (London), 20 February 1987.
Cenac, Laetitia, in *Madame Figaro* (Paris), October 1988.
Fallon, Jim, in *Women's Wear Daily* (New York), 19 October 1989.
Roberts, Nancy, "Workers White," in *Marie Claire* (London), April 1990.
Smith, Liz, in *The Times* (London), 15 May 1990.
Flett, Kathryn, in *The Sunday Times Magazine* (London), 2 September 1990.

*   *   *

Graham Fraser and Richard Nott launched their company, Workers for Freedom, in 1985, leaving behind their respective former careers as merchandising manager for fashion and accessories at Liberty in London and principal fashion lecturer at Kingston University in Surrey. Nott came from an art school background, and also worked for three years as design assistant to Valentino in Rome.

The company name was chosen to emphasize what they saw as their freedom from the large companies for whom they had previously worked. Their former experience in the fashion field left them well qualified to set up their own fashion company which, amongst other things, earned them the title Designer of the Year at the British Fashion Awards in 1990. The reason behind the formation of their own label, according to Nott and Fraser, was their mutual disillusion with what was happening in the field of menswear design at that time and their aversion to very "preppy" styles with little or no decorative adornment. Their first collection, which was sold through their retail shop in Lower John Street in London's Soho district, was comprised solely of menswear. The garment that was to become their hallmark was the embroidered shirt, in black on white or white on black combinations. The success of this first collection, which attracted both male and female customers, prompted Workers for Freedom to extend the next collection to womenswear, at the request of the American and Japanese buyers who bought their collections.

Nott and Fraser have always stressed that their designs are outside mainstream fashion trends, and that their customers are not concerned with being in fashion. The evolutionary nature of their designs has meant that each season the customer may add an outfit or single garment to those from previous collections. Nott describes Workers for Freedom's clothes as being "very gentle" and admits that at one point during the 1980s, with the advent of designers like Christian Lacroix, their designs seemed somewhat out of place with what was happening in fashion as a whole.

According to Richard Nott, who is responsible for designing the collections (Fraser handles the administrative and promotions side), the inspiration for his designs has always come from the fabric itself, which ultimately determines the shape or form of the garment. Nott views each garment within a collection as an individual piece, since he does not start out to create a certain look. Each garment is designed as a separate item and the collection is styled afterwards. At this point a certain garment, such as a shorter skirt for example, may be added if it is deemed necessary. The fabric for which Workers for Freedom is best recognized is silk, which they have used continually both in its plain state and in Nott's textile prints. Their signature colours have always been subtle, with a predominant use of black, brown, ivory, and indigo blue.

In October 1991 Workers for Freedom began working for Littlewoods mail order catalogue, for whom they have continued to design a separate collection each season. The Littlewoods connection is viewed by Nott and Fraser as being rather like a diffusion collection, which is produced at a lower price range and also helps maintain their name at High Street level. This has left them free to make the mainline collection to be what they describe as more rarefied, since the sportswear element is now incorporated into other ranges such as Littlewoods and a collection for A-Wear shops in Ireland, which is distributed by the company Brown Thomas.

The decision by Workers for Freedom to move to France in 1992 attracted a considerable amount of publicity from the British press. Nott and Fraser had sold their shop in Soho and considered moving the business to Toulouse where they found a château that they decided to buy and establish the company base there. This fell through when the exchange rate dropped and they found themselves unable to sell their London house. During this period Nott and Fraser kept a low profile, did not produce a collection for fall/winter 1993 and moved the company headquarters to Battersea, South London. The six-month break from producing a collection enabled a reevaluation period for Workers for Freedom, and their succeeding collections indicate a definite change in direction. Their signature use of embroidery has been dropped ("because everyone has it now," says Nott), and there is an emphasis on shape using bias-cutting that Nott sees as the new softer alternative to stretch Lycra fabrics. The fall/winter collection for 1994-95 by Workers for Freedom was produced entirely in black and brown, without embroidery or other form of decoration.

Having always considered themselves to be on the outside of high fashion, it is somewhat ironic that the gentle, almost handcrafted image perpetrated by Workers for Freedom has become totally relevant to fashion in the 1990s, with the final demise of power dressing that dominated fashion in the late 1980s.

—Catherine Woram

WRIGHT, Trevor. See FENN WRIGHT AND MANSON.

XYZ

XÜLY BET. See KOUYATÉ, Lamine.

YAMAMOTO, Kansai.

Japanese designer

Born: Yokohama, 1944. **Education:** Studied civil engineering and English, Nippon University; graduated from Bunka College of Fashion, 1967. **Career:** Apprenticed with Junko Koshino and Hosano; designer, Hisashi Hosono, c.1968-71; opened firm, Yamamoto Kansai Company, Ltd., Tokyo, and showed first collection, London, 1971; first Paris showing, 1975; opened Kansai Boutique, Paris, 1977. **Awards:** Soen Prize, Bunka College of Fashion, 1967; Fashion Editors Award, Tokyo, 1977. **Address:** 4-3-15 Jungumae, Shibuya-ku, Tokyo 150, Japan.

Publications:

On YAMAMOTO:

Books

Koren, Leonard, *New Fashion Japan,* Tokyo 1984.

Articles

Queen, Bobbie, "Kansai Confidence," in *Women's Wear Daily* (New York), 28 January 1985.
Steber, Maggie, "Future Shock, with the Brilliant Innovators of Japanese Fashion," in *Connoisseur,* September 1986.
DuCann, Charlotte, "Zen and the Art of the Real Shirt," in *The Independent* (London), 29 June 1989.
Strauss, Frédéric, "Au vrai chic wendersein," in *Cahiers du Cinema* (Paris), December 1989.
Martin, Richard, "Sailing to Byzantium: A Fashion Odyssey, 1990-1991," *Textile and Test,* 14 February 1991.

*   *   *

Kansai Yamamoto's presentation of his fall-winter 1981-82 collection was divided into 14 parts, among them "Peruvian Geometry," "Sarraku" (Japanese 17th-century painter), "Korean Tiger," "Ainu," and "Sea Foam, 5 Men Kabuki Play." Kansai declared in the accompanying program notes: "True originality is almost impossible to imitate as it is the expression of the creator's personal experience and cultural environment. As a Japanese, I always seek the 'oriental quality' that is within me." Yet, Kansai's personal sensibility is a single aspect of Orientalism and reflects a style relatively little known in the West in Asian forms, but comparable to many traditions of the West. Kansai is Kabuki in his overt theatricality, flamboyant sense of gesture and design, and brilliant colorful design as much to be read from afar as admired at close range. Leonard Koren said, "For Kansai, fashion means creating a festival-like feeling using brightly colored clothes with bold design motifs inspired by the *kimono,* traditional Japanese festival wear, and military clothes" (*New Fashion Japan,* Tokyo 1984). Gaudy by desire, larger-than-life by theatre's intensity, and virtually to Japanese culture what Pop style was to Anglo-American culture, Kansai has consistently cultivated a fashion of fantastic images, extravagant imagination, and sensuous approach to both tradition and a view of the future.

Unabashed entertainer and impresario (long a familiar product spokesman on television in Japan), Kansai achieved cult status in Japan in the 1970s for his worldly transmission of Japanese culture. Kansai's selections of favor in his indigenous culture have not been the refined natural dispositions of materials so much favored in the West as the alternative to Western materialism, but the aspects of Japan that are expressive, grandly symbolic, and vernacular. In fact, Kansai's work has often been controversial in Japan inasmuch as it is thought to promote and exploit images of Japanese vulgarity internationally. Is Kansai creating an "airport art," expensive exoticism for the West that still thinks of an East Asia of bright colors, lanterned festivals, Kabuki masks, and fabulist stories with dragons and tigers? Kansai seems poised between traditional Japanese culture, the Pop sensibility of the late 20th century, and a longing for a millennial future. Central to Kansai's work is his delight in mass entertainment and popular culture, a sense of both following and leading the ordinary population whether in graphic T-shirts or the convenience of knitwear. His stadium coats are the hyperbole of an American sportswear vocabulary; his fall-winter 1979 stegosaurus coat, with shoulder and sleeves built into a crenellation of triangles, harkens back to animal tales and prehistory; his fish and bird forms seem exotic, but merge with spiky punk. His silhouettes for both menswear and womenswear are extreme, suggesting either the most wondrous last *samurai* or the most magnificent first warriors for intergalactic futures; and his appliqués have been in the ambiguous realm between primitive art and 20th-century abstraction.

In a West frightened by Japanese militarism (no Yukio Mishima, but no Buddhist monk either, Kansai has drawn inspiration from firemen's uniforms and other easily identified work vestments traditional in Japanese subcultures of conformity) and prone to disregard any popular culture if not its own, Kansai became a designer of special, but limited, interest in the 1980s. His less-than-solemn work is anathema to some, celebratory to others. Cerebral, spiritual, aestheticized Japan (as represented by Issey Miyake or Rei

Kawakubo) seemed more ideal, especially to the West. Kansai's plebeian flash was for many in the West the worst of two worlds.

Kansai's sensibility, however, is universal. If he was the first fashion designer to bring Kabuki circus-like joy and impertinence and Japanese common culture to international fashion, he has remained a significant figure in espousing such conspicuous love of theatre, love of life, love of exaggeration. His aggrandizements begin in delight and exuberance and end in celebration of the most universal kind. They benefit from a relationship to costume, though Kansai is always grounded in the wearability of his clothing. They often function as happy graphic signs, emblems of the most bold in fashion. On the opening of his Madison Avenue boutique in 1985, Kansai remarked to *Women's Wear Daily*, "My clothes are no good for someone who loves chicness." If we understand chic to be slightly haughty and narrowly sophisticated, Kansai misses the mark by express intention. Rather, he is seeking an earthy, populist ideal of clothing created in the grand gesture for the great audience. "I am making happiness for people with my clothes," he told *Women's Wear Daily* in 1985. "If you walk through Central Park in them you create a 'wow.'" Kansai achieves exclamatory, spectacular visual statement. Wow!

—Richard Martin

YAMAMOTO, Yohji.

Japanese designer

Born: Yokohama, Japan, 1943. **Education:** Graduated in Law, Keio University, 1966; studied at Bunka College of Fashion, Tokyo, 1966-68, won Soen and Endu prizes; earned scholarship to Paris, 1968, studied fashion, 1968-70. **Career:** Designer, custom clothing, Tokyo, from 1970; formed ready-to-wear company, 1972; showed first collection, Tokyo, 1976; launched men's line, 1984; Yohji Yamamoto design studio, Tokyo, established, 1988; also opened Paris boutique. **Exhibitions:** *A New Wave in Fashion: 3 Japanese Designers,* Phoenix Art Museum, Arizona, 1983. **Awards:** Fashion Editors Club Award, Tokyo, 1982; Mainichi Grand Prize, 1984. **Address:** San Shin Building 1, 1-22-11 Higashi Shibuya-ku, Tokyo, Japan.

Publications:

On YAMAMOTO:

Books

Phoenix Art Museum, *A New Wave in Fashion: 3 Japanese Designers* (exhibition catalogue), Phoenix, Arizona 1983.
Koren, Leonard, *New Fashion Japan,* Tokyo 1984.
Fraser, Kennedy, *Scenes from the Fashionable World,* New York 1987.
Sparke, Penny, *Japanese Design,* London 1987.
Coleridge, Nicholas, *The Fashion Conspiracy,* London 1988.

Articles

"In Pursuit of Excellence," in *i-D* (London), May 1987.

"Yohji Yamamoto: Fashion Designer," in *Blueprint* (London), February 1987.
"Mr. Yamamoto Comes Back to Town," in *Blueprint* (London), December 1987.
"Yohji Yamamoto: La vie d'artiste," in *Elle* (Paris), 19 September 1988.
Montagu, Georgina, "A Life in the Day of Yohji Yamamoto," in *The Sunday Times Magazine* (London), 26 February 1989.
Flett, Kathryn, "Yohji by Knight: Photography at Work," in *The Face* (London), April 1989.
Deslaudieres, Ainree, "Le long voyage à la rencontre de Yohji Yamamoto," in *L'Officiel* (Paris), May 1989.
"Yohji Yamamoto: Les femmes et moi," in *Vogue* (Paris), November 1989.
Sudjic, Deyan, "Go Yohji, Go!," in *The Sunday Times Magazine* (London), 2 December 1990.
"The Paris Collections: The Ideas of March: Yohji Yamamoto," in *Women's Wear Daily* (New York), 17 March 1995.

*   *   *

Part of a pioneering fashion sensibility that erupted onto the Parisian catwalks of the early 1980s, Yohji Yamamoto has a philosophical approach to fashion that makes him interested in more than just covering the body: there has to be some interaction between the body, the wearer, and the essential spirit of the designer. With Issey Miyake and Rei Kawakubo, Yamamoto is exploring new ways of dressing by synthesizing Western clothing archetypes and indigenous Japanese clothing. Refusing to accept traditional ideas of female sexual display and reacting against the Western notion of female glamour as expressed in titillating figure-hugging garments, Yamamoto employs a method of layering, draping, and wrapping the body, disguising it with somber, unstructured, swathed garments based on the *kimono* that ignore the usual accentuation points.

Uncompromising to Western eyes, Yamamoto is in fact investigating the traditional Japanese conviction in beauty being not naturally given but expressed through the manipulation of the possibilities of the colours and materials of garments. Consequently, Yamamoto's clothing construction is viewed in the round rather than vertically, not from the neck down as in Western fashion, but a rectilinear, two dimensional approach that explores the visual appeal of asymmetry, the notion of the picturesque that plays an important part in Japanese design philosophy where irregular forms are appreciated for their lack of artifice and thus closeness to nature. Therefore, Yamamoto's garments have strange flaps, pockets, and layers, lopsided collars and hems, set off by the body in motion, and the labels inside are inscribed with the epithet, "There is nothing so boring as a neat and tidy look."

By not referring to Western fashion but to a fixed form of Japanese dress that has been developed and refined over the centuries, Yamamoto produces anti-fashion—non-directional garments that ignore contemporary Western developments of the silhouette but influence Western designers in turn. Beauty is more indefinable, to be found in the texture of materials rather than applied decoration, with the use of fabrics like linen and rayon that have been deliberately chosen and developed for their likelihood of wrinkling and heavy knitted surfaces. Like a number of Japanese designers, Yamamoto is interested in developing new materials.

Yamamoto's source material is idiosyncratic and derives from a vast library that he draws on for inspiration. One book to which he consistently refers is a collection of photographs by August Sander, a photographer based in Cologne in the early 20th century, who took photographs of representative types in the everyday clothes that sharply reflect their lives. Yamamoto is also inspired by utilitarian outfits such as the protective clothing worn by women munitions workers in the 1940s, and has been known to reproduce the coat lapel worn by Jean-Paul Sartre discovered in an old photograph.

Notable for his relentless use of black, a colour traditionally associated in Japanese culture with the farmer and the spirit of the *samurai,* Yamamoto's move into navy and purple in the 1980s was shortlived—he found it roused too many complicated emotions for him!

His company, launched in 1976, now produces the experimental, idiosyncratic Yohji Yamamoto line, the Y and Y line for men that is moderately priced and extremely successful, made up of an easy to wear mixture of integrated separates and the Workshop line of casual leisurewear.

—Caroline Cox

ZAHM, Herwig. See MONDI TEXTILE GmbH.

ZEGNA, Ermenegildo.

Italian designer/company

Company founded in 1910 by Ermenegildo Zegna (1892-66) in Trivero, Biellese Alps, Italy. Ermenegildo turned business over to sons, Aldo and Angelo, who expanded into ready-to-wear clothing, menswear line, 1960s; opened branches in Spain, France, Germany, Austria, United States, Japan, and United Kingdom; group-controlled production units opened in Spain and Switzerland, 1968. Company specialises in menswear fabrics in natural raw materials, ready-to-wear for men: suits, jackets, trousers, shirts, ties, accessories. First U.S. boutique launched, 1989; fragrance, *Zegna;* E.Z. line, designed by Kim Herring, launched 1993. From 1980s, Angelo's son Gildo became responsible for Formalwear Division; Aldo's son Paolo became President of the Textile Division; Gildo's sister Anna responsible for image and communication of the Group and Zegna shops worldwide; Benedetta, Angelo's youngest daughter, responsible for coordinating the fully owned and franchised Zegna stores in Italy. Oasi Zegna, land recovery program, Trivero, launched, 1993, to provide sports and leisure facilities to visitors and local population. **Exhibitions:** *Made in Italy,* Pier 84, New York, 1988; *Wool Bicentennial,* Barcelona, 1990; *The Meandering Pattern in Brocades and Silk,* Milan, 1990-91; and at the Fashion Institute of Technology, New York, 1992. **Collections:** The Power House Museum, Sydney; Museo della Scienza e della Tecnica, Milan. **Awards:** Cavaliere del Lavoro (to Ermenegildo Zegna), 1930. **Address:** Via Pietro Verri 3, 20121 Milan, Italy.

Publications:

On ZEGNA:

Books

Storie e favole di moda, Italy 1982.
Giacomoni, Silvia, *The Italian Look Reflected,* Italy 1984.
Canali, Renato, *La Panoramica Zegna,* Italy 1985.
Enciclopedia della moda, Milan 1989.
Villarosa, R., and Angeli, G., *Homo elegans,* Milan 1990
Chaille, F., *La grande histoire de la cravatte,* France 1994.

Articles

"Fuori la stoffa, ragazzi," in *Panorama* (Milan), 24 May 1992.
"Der Kaschmir-Clan," in *Stern* (Germany), September 1992.
"Zegna alla Conquista della Cina," in *La Stampa* (Turin), 7 July 1993.
"La seconda conquista dell'America," in *L'indipendente,* 26 November 1993.
Siow, Doreen, "High Price Can be a Strong Suit," in *The Sunday Times* (London), 13 December 1993.
"Ecology: The Best Strategy," in *Newsweek* (New York), 31 January 1994.
"La ricerca Zegna sui materiali," in *Il Sole 24 Ore* (Italy), 15 March 1994.
Dubini, Laura, "La géneration verte," in *Jardin des Modes* (Paris), April 1994.
Gellers, Stan, "There's Hard Business Sense Behind the Soft Suit," in *DNR* (New York), 25 April 1994.
"Zegna quota 500 miliardi nel '94," in *Il Sole 24 Ore* (Italy), 17 May 1994.
Levine, Joshua, "Armani's Counterpart," in *Forbes* (New York), 4 July 1994.

*

Ermenegildo Zegna was founded in 1910 as a company which created and produced woolen fabrics.

With the passing of time, the subsequent generations of the family encouraged the diversification of the company's activities, leading to the introduction of a complete line of menswear. Our philosophy has always been based on quality and the search for excellence.

What makes Zegna unique is the fact that it is the only company of its type in the world specialized in the direct purchase of natural raw materials on their markets of origin, with a totally verticalized creative and production cycle going from raw materials to cloths, clothing and accessories, which are internationally distributed through Zegna's salespoints and other selected menswear shops.

Our style is classical but modern; international but deeply rooted in the Italian tradition. It is a style which fully respects the individual personality of each of our clients, based on care over details, comfort, and personalization of our products. It is for this reason that we offer a "made-to-measure" service which is capable of satisfying even the most demanding and sophisticated consumers. And while we are talking of service, we also guarantee the post-sale of our customers' wardrobes, because Zegna products are faithful companions designed to last, deserving all of the care and attention that can be given them.

Ermenegildo Zegna: "Collezione Sartoriale," Spring/Summer 1995. *Photograph by Aldo Fallai.*

Finally, Zegna is also characterized by its sensitivity and respect for the environment. As early as 1930, Ermenegildo Zegna established and financed a vast project for the reclamation of the mountain overlooking Trivero, the village in the Alpine foothills of Biella where Zegna's headquarters are located. And now, following in the footsteps of the company's founder, the younger generations of the family have created *Oasi Zegna,* a project designed to protect nature over an area of about 100 square kilometres.

—Ermenegildo Zegna

* * *

"Our typical client believes in understated classic styles," says Gilda Zegna. "That's why they like Ermenegildo Zegna." Ermenegildo Zegna is not a brand of radical fashion statements; on the contrary, very classic tailoring, rich and supple fabrics, and obsessive attention to detail make Ermenegildo Zegna the Rolls Royce of menswear, and image Zegna is quick to reinforce. All their marketing and advertising copy speaks of wool spun into strands so fine that one kilo stretches 150,000 metres, hand-sewn buttons, and the hand pressing of each jacket before leaving the factory. The latter, we are told, takes 45 minutes, but then suit prices are high. Ermenegildo Zegna has built a reputation on catering only to the richest of businessmen, well-established celebrities, and the world's royalty.

So how does Zegna differentiate from the hundreds of companies vying for this same market sector? Zegna clothes are quintessentially English, from the suits of a world-class banker to the casualwear of a world-beating yachtsman or horsemaster. The fabrics are Italian, made for lightweight softness and presoaked in the waters of the Italian Alps, whose mineral-free quality has been sought after by Italian cloth merchants since the middle ages. The craftsmanship is Swiss—accurate, precise, always correct. Colours change year on year. Winter 1993 was brick, brown, tobacco, evergreen, billiard green, emerald. Winter 1994 was eye-blue, cobalt, stone grey, tobacco, some red, more browns. Raw materials are taken from the world over—wool from Australia, cashmere from China, mohair from South Africa. Although most upmarket men's fashionwear use similar resources and methods, when one discovers that Zegna's preferred cashmere is that of a Chinese goat, aged between three and five years, one understands that these are not just professionals but inspired visionaries of men's clothing.

The fact remains that Ermenegildo Zegna is successful in a highly competitive sector. The market for men's suits costing over one thousand dollars is, in 1994, considered one million units per year. Ermenegildo Zegna currently sells 300,000 such suits or 30 percent of the market. To maintain and grow in this sector, their marketing is more than just subtle. Ermenegildo Zegna sponsors a yacht race at Portofino, Italy. The sponsorship is discrete, no banners and posters, just models walking through the crowd wearing Zegna blazers with the small white EZ motif. The seat covers for the Saab 9000 car are made by Zegna. Saab salesmen are drilled in the virtues and qualities of Zegna fabrics, information passed on to Saab buyers. Above all, Zegna mails sample swatches, possible combinations jackets, ties, and shirts to their best customers, several times a year. Perhaps Zegna's strength is its size; they remain resolutely small and claim to have no desire to be a popular brand.

In recent years, however, Zegna has started to expand into new markets with soft suits, the casual cut, and mix 'n' match coordinates now so popular in the United States, France, and Italy. Specifically for the United States market, Zegna designs sportswear to compete with Hugo Boss, Giorgio Armani, and Calvin Klein: shirts, slacks, and sports and outerwear jackets are all aimed at the 35 plus market. To complete a man's wardrobe, Zegna makes natural cotton undergarments, high quality corporate gifts (for example, Paco Rabanne ties), and more recently a fragrance.

Ermenegildo Zegna's originality lies in its manufacturing process. Unusually, the company is completely vertically integrated. It buys its own raw materials, makes its own fabrics, designs its own clothes, and runs its own boutiques. The company is forward-looking, yet steeped in tradition. It uses the most advanced databases to maintain and update customer measurements, purchases, and personal details. Satellite communication allows such data to be transferred at the touch of a button from Singapore to Switzerland. A Computer-Aided Design (CAD) program is used to adjust a pattern to the customer. Yet wool fabrics are washed and suits finished by hand. Salesmen visit businessmen in their offices and homes. And still Zegna looks for improved speed in delivering clothes or bringing a new collection to market.

Perhaps Zegna's unique strength is the family that holds this tight-knit, perfectionist company together. The Zegna company employs both sons of Ermenegildo Zegna and five of his eight grandchildren. As yet there is no indication that such reliance on home-grown talent has led to stagnation. If anything, the enthusiasm of the young Zegnas, educated in universities and colleges across Europe, is tempered and modeled by the experience of the older family members. Gilda Zegna, quoting an Italian proverb, essentially states the company's philosophy: "Qui va piano, va sano, e va lontano" ("He who goes slowly, goes safely, and will last longest").

—Sally Anne Melia

———

ZEHNTBAUER, John A. and C. Ray. See **JANTZEN, INC.**

———

ZEIGLER, Mel and Patricia. See **BANANA REPBULIC.**

———

ZORAN.
American designer

Born: Zoran Ladicorbic in Banat, Yugoslavia, 1947. Immigrated to the United States, 1971. **Education:** Studied architecture at the University of Belgrade. **Career:** Worked variously in New York as coat checker at Candy Store club, salesman at Balmain boutique, accessory designer for Scott Barrie, salesman and designer for Julio, 1971-76. Free-lance designer in New York, from 1976; first collection shown, 1977; Washington, D.C. showroom established, 1982; also maintains studio in Milan.

Publications:

On ZORAN:

Books

Milbank, Caroline Rennolds, *New York Fashion: The Evolution of American Style,* New York 1989.

Articles

Morris, Bernadine, "Zoran and Kamali: Success with the Offbeat," in the *New York Times,* 4 January 1983.
"Cue: Zoran Design for Living," in *Vogue* (London), March 1983.
"Zoran: The Wizard of Ease," in *Vogue* (New York), March 1983.
Barron, Pattie, "Style: Less Is Good for You," in *Cosmopolitan,* June 1983.
Watters, Susan, "Zoran Entertains at the Capital," in *Women's Wear Daily* (New York), 19 October 1988.
Brantley, Ben, "Zoran Zeitgeist," in *Vanity Fair* (New York), March 1992.
Giovannini, Joseph, "Brilliant Emptiness," in *House Beautiful* (London), March 1994.

*		*		*

Zoran Ladicorbic was born in Banat, Yugoslavia in 1947. The designer, who goes by his first name, was trained in his native country as an architect, and a love of geometric shapes and straight lines is evident in his clothing design.

Zoran came to the United States in 1972. Although he had no formal education in fashion, he worked for the first few years in retail. He was also an accessories designer for the 1970s women's fashion designer, Scott Barrie.

In 1976 Zoran started his own collection, using only the best and most luxurious fabrics. Cashmere, satin, velvet, and high-quality wool are staples of his collection. He creates two collections a year, spring and fall, and shows them in his New York loft-workplace located in the downtown SoHo neighborhood.

He is obsessive about cutting and finishing a garment. His clothes create a feeling of luxury through perfect craftsmanship and materials, not through ostentatious embellishment, bright color, or showy fabrics. He uses the same muted color palette over and over: black and white, ivory, gray, and navy, with an occasional washed-out pastel such as pale pink or celery thrown in to liven the mix.

Zoran has kept to this minimalist aesthetic even during the more flamboyant 1980s. In the somewhat more abashed 1990s, his designs have gathered more momentum and his customer base has increased. His designs are not cheap, but he has a loyal following that snaps up his designs year after year. Among the Zoran devotees are model-actresses such as Lauren Hutton, Candice Bergen, and Isabella Rossellini, the painter Jennifer Hartley, socialite Amanda Burden, and Tipper Gore, the U.S. vice-president's wife. His clothes are sold by high-level, slightly avant-garde stores such as Barney's and Henri Bendel in New York, as well as out of his workplace.

Zoran believes that his typical customer visits him once a year and buys several thousand dollars' worth of pieces at one time. Like the color palette, the silhouettes vary only slightly from season to season. Core pieces include a cardigan jacket, a T-shirt, crewneck cashmere sweaters, loose trousers, loose shorts, and a sarong skirt, which the designer claims he wore himself for a year to make sure the fit was correct.

The designer eschews the typical New York fashion life. He prefers solitude and is said to keep a constant supply of Stolichnaya vodka close at hand at all times of the day. He has an apartment in New York and a house in the resort community of Naples, Florida.

—Janet Ozzard

NAME INDEX

NATIONALITY INDEX

AMERICAN

Abboud, Joseph
Adolfo
Adri
Adrian, Gilbert
Alfaro, Victor
Allard, Linda
Anthony, John
Badgley Mischka
Banana Republic
Banks, Jeffrey
Barnes, Jhane
Barrie, Scott
Bartlett, John
L.L. Bean
Beene, Geoffrey
Blass, Bill
Brigance, Tom
Brooks Brothers
Brooks, Donald
Bruce, Liza
Burrows, Stephen
Carnegie, Hattie
Cashin, Bonnie
Cassini, Oleg
Catalina Sportswear
Cesarani, Sal
Champion
Claiborne, Liz
Cole of California
Costa, Victor
Daché, Lilly
Danskin
di Sant'Angelo, Giorgio
Ellis, Perry
Esprit
Estevez, Luis
Fabrice
Fassett, Kaffe
Fezza, Andrew
Flusser, Alan
Fogarty, Anne
Freis, Diane
Galanos, James
The Gap
Garratt, Sandra
Gernreich, Rudi
Guess, Inc.
Halston
Hardwick, Cathy
Harp, Holly
Hawes, Elizabeth
Head, Edith
Heisel, Sylvia
Henderson, Gordon
Hilfiger, Tommy
Jacobs, Marc
James, Charles
Jantzen, Inc.
Javits, Eric
Joan & David

John, John P.
Johnson, Betsey
Julian, Alexander
Kahng, Gemma
Kaiserman, Bill
Kamali, Norma
Karan, Donna
Kasper, Herbert
Kelly, Patrick
Kieselstein-Cord, Barry
Klein, Anne
Klein, Calvin
Kloss, John
Knecht, Gabriele
Kors, Michael
Lane, Kenneth Jay
Lars, Byron
Lauren, Ralph
Leiber, Judith
Leser, Tina
Levi-Strauss & Co.
Mackie, Bob
Mad Carpentier
I. Magnin
Mainbocher
Marcasiano, Mary Jane
Maxwell, Vera
McCardell, Claire
McClintock, Jessica
McFadden, Mary
Miller, Nicole
Mizrahi, Isaac
Morris, Robert Lee
Natori, Josie Cruz
New Republic
Norell, Norman
Oldham, Todd
Parnis, Mollie
Pedlar, Sylvia
Pomodoro, Carmelo
Pulitzer, Lilly
Rentner, Maurice
Restivo, Mary Ann
Robinson, Bill
Roehm, Carolyne
Roth, Christian Francis
Rowley, Cynthia
Sachs, Gloria
Scaasi, Arnold
Schnurer, Carolyn
Simpson, Adele
Smith, Willi
Sprouse, Stephen
Stock, Robert
Sui, Anna
Tassell, Gustave
Tiel, Vicky
Toi, Zang
Trigère, Pauline
Unger, Kay
Valentina

NOTES ON CONTRIBUTORS

ALMOND, Kevin. Fashion director, Leeds College of Art and Design. Designer, Enrico Coveri, 1988-89, assistant designer, Woman Hautwell Ltd., 1989-90. Senior lecturer in fashion/fashion promotions, University of Central Lancashire, 1990-94. Contributor of "Camp Dressing" article to *Components of Dress,* 1988. **Essays:** Ally Capellino; John Anthony; Jacques Azagury; Sheridan Barnett; Rocco Barocco; Scott Barrie; Bellville Sassoon-Lorcan Mullany; Alistair Blair; Blumarine; Bodymap; Jean Cacharel; Oleg Cassini; Corneliani SpA; Giorgio Correggiari; Paul Costelloe; Enrico Coveri; Jules François Crahay; Wendy Dagworthy; Myrène de Prémonville; Oscar de la Renta; Christian Dior; Erreuno Scm SpA; Escada; Luis Estevez; Louis Féraud; Gianfranco Ferré; David Fielden; John Flett; Georgina Godley; Norman Hartnell; Daniel Hechter; Peter Hoggard; Betty Jackson; Bill Kaiserman; Jacques Kaplan; Donna Karan; Herbert Kasper; Christian Lacroix; Guy Laroche; Jürgen Lehl; Lolita Lempicka; Marcel Marongiu; Mondi Textile Gmbh; Popy Moreni; Jean Muir; Bruce Oldfield; Benny Ong; Arabella Pollen; Nina Ricci; Marina Rinaldi Srl; Gloria Sachs; Mila Schön; David Shilling; Sophie Sitbon; Per Spook; Stefanel Spa; Strenesse Group; Chantal Thomass; Yuki Torii; Torrente; SpA Trussardi; Sally Tuffin; Philippe Venet; Gian Marco Venturi; Victorio y Lucchino; Diane Von Furstenberg.

ARNOLD, Rebecca. Lecturer in fashion history and cultural theory, Kent Institute of Art and Design. **Essays:** Dirk Bikkembergs; Marc Bohan; Liza Bruce; Joe Casely-Hayford; Chloé; Nick Coleman; Ann Demeulemeester; Dolce & Gabbana; John Galliano; Romeo Gigli; Pam Hogg; Joseph; Michiko Koshino; Karl Lagerfeld; Helmut Lang; Hervé Léger; Hanae Mori; Pepe; Emilio Pucci; John Richmond; Martine Sitbon.

ARSENAULT, Andrea. Professor of Fashion Design, School of the Art Institute of Chicago. Designer. Former chair of the Fashion Department, and the Faculty Senate, School of the Art Institute of Chicago. Contributor, *Jean Charles de Castelbajac Album;* contributor and advisor, *Contemporary Designers* and *Contemporary Masterworks.* **Essay:** Jean-Charles de Castelbajac.

BAKER, Therese Duzinkiewicz. Associate professor/extended campus librarian, Western Kentucky University, Bowling Green, Kentucky. Author of journal articles on library service for off-campus students. Book reviewer in decorative arts for *Library Journal.* Contributor to *Dictionary of American Biography.* **Essays:** Adri; Gilbert Adrian; Jacqueline de Ribes; Norma Kamali; Emmanuelle Khanh; Mainbocher; Jessica McClintock; Mary McFadden; Norman Norell; Thea Porter; Jean-Louis Scherrer; Adele Simpson; Emanuel Ungaro; Valentina; Koos Van Den Akker.

BLAUSEN, Whitney. Independent writer and researcher. Former administrator, The Costume Collection, Theatre Development Fund. Contributor of numerous articles to various periodicals, journals, and books, including *Theatre Crafts International, Fiber Arts, Surface Design Journal, Dictionaire de la mode au xxc siècle,* 1995, *50 American Designers,* 1995, and *Dictionary of Women Artists,* 1996. **Essays:** Bianchini-Férier; Donald Brooks; Bonnie Cashin; Danskin; Fabrice; Elizabeth Hawes; Edith Head; Betsey Johnson; Bob Mackie; Sylvia Pedlar; Zandra Rhodes; Rodier; Cynthia Rowley; Ted Tinling; Michaele Vollbracht.

BODINE, Sarah (with Michael Dunas). Independent lecturer and writer in design and craft studies and criticism. Teacher, senior thesis studio, University of the Arts. Visiting lecturer and critic at various institutions, including Cleveland Institute of Art, Akron University, Tyler School of Art, RISD, Cranbrook Academy of Art, University of Michigan, Alfred University, Massachusetts College of Art, Parsons School of Design, Miami University, and Moore College of Art. Whitney Library of Design, 1973-79. Editor, *Metalsmith,* 1979-92; editorial director, Documents of American Design, 1988-91. Contributor to numerous periodicals and volumes, including *Industrial Design* and *Design Book Review.* **Essays:** Agnès B; Rei Kawakubo.

BROWN, Mary Carol. Free-lance essayist based in England. **Essays:** Laura Ashley; "Coco" Gabriel Bonheur Chanel; Salvatore Ferragamo.

BURNS, Jane. B.A. in ecology and environmental studies, University of Georgia; studied fashion design at Fashion Institute of Technology. Designed Christmas windows for Hermès, New York; worked as a dresser for the Macy's Thanksgiving Day parade. **Essays:** Badgley Mischka; Patrick Kelly.

CARLANO, Marianne T. Formerly Curator of Costume and Textiles at both the Wadsworth Atheneum in Hartford and the Museum of Fine Arts, Boston. Textile scholar. Author of catalogue essays and articles in *Art Journal* and *Arts Magazine.* **Essays:** Joseph Abboud; Gruppo GFT; Carmelo Pomodoro.

CAVALIERE, Barbara. Free-lance writer on art and design, New York City. Associate editor, *Womanart* magazine, 1976-78; contributing editor, *Arts Magazine,* 1976-83. Fellowship in art criticism, National Endowment for the Arts, 1979-80. Author of exhibition catalogues. **Essay:** Mariuccia Mandelli.

CLARK, Hazel. Head of School of Design, Hong Kong Polytechnic University, Hong Kong. Contributor to various journals, including *Journal of Design History, Design, Design Week, Design Review, Monument,* and *Women's Art Journal.* Author of "Selling Design and Craft" and "Footprints Textile Printing Workshop" in *Women Designing: Redefining Design in Britain between the Wars,* 1994. **Essays:** Sylvia Ayton; Jeff Banks; Sandy Black; Sarah Dallas; Diane Freis; Ragence Lam; Ralph Lauren; Mickey Lee; Walter Ma; Judy Mann; Muji; Mary Quant; William Tang.

CLEVELAND, Debra Regan. Contributing editor and book reviewer, *The Lady's Gallery Magazine* and *The Vintage Gazette* newsletter; feature writer/correspondent, *The Antiques Journal* and *Antique Week;* free-lance writer specializing in period fashion and antiques. Co-founder of the first New England vintage clothing show and sale and of *The Vintage Gazetter* newsletter. Contributor of free-lance and in-house work for antiques and marketing trade publications, including *Antiques and Collecting Hobbies* and *Costume Society of America, Region 1 Newsletter.* **Essays:** Catalina Sportswear; Jantzen, Inc.; Lacoste Sportswear.

COLEING, Linda. Free-lance essayist. **Essays:** Ossie Clark; Emma Hope.

COLEMAN, Elizabeth Ann. Curator, Textiles and Costumes, Museum of Fine Arts, Houston, Texas; former curator of Costumes and Textiles, The Brooklyn Museum. Adjunct professor, Fashion Institute of Technology, New York. Rice University Fellow. Author of *The Genius of Charles James,* 1982, and *The Opu-*

lent Era: Fashions of Worth, Doucet, and Pingat, 1989. **Essay:** Charles James.

COOPER, Arlene C. Consulting curator, European Textiles and Shawls, Museum for Textiles, Toronto, Ontario, Canada. President, Arlene C. Cooper Consulting (consultant to museums and private collectors of shawls, European textiles, and 20th-century fashion). Senior research assistant for textiles, Department of European Sculpture and Decorative Arts, Metropolitan Museum of Art. Author of "The Kashmir Shawl and Its Derivatives in North American Collections," 1987, and "How Madame Grès Sculpts with Fabric," in *Great Sewn Clothes from Threads Magazine,* 1991. **Essays:** Junichi Arai; Hubert de Givenchy; Sonia Rykiel.

COX, Caroline. Free-lance essayist based in England. **Essays:** Azzedine Alaia; Giorgio Armani; Hugo Boss AG; Pierre Cardin; André Courrèges; Jean-Paul Gaultier; Rudi Gernreich; Hobbs Ltd.; Margaret Howell; Hiroko Koshino; Maxfield Parrish; Franco Moschino; Rifat Ozbek; Paco Rabanne; Yves Saint Laurent; Fernando Sanchez; Stephen Sprouse; Yohji Yamamoto.

DENNIS, Fred. Coordinator of Costume Collections, Museum at Fashion Institute of Technology, New York. **Essay:** Gabriele Knecht.

DRUESEDOW, Jean L. Director, Kent State University Museum. Associate curator in charge, The Costume Institute, Metropolitan Museum of Art, New York, 1984-92. Adjunct full professor, New York University. Author of *Jno. J. Mitchell Co. Men's Fashion Illustrations from the Turn of the Century,* 1990, and "Who Wears the Pants," chapter in *Androgyny,* 1992. **Essays:** Roberto Capucci; Vera Maxwell; Sally Victor.

EHRLICH, Doreen. Tutor in Art and Design History, Hillcroft College. Author of *Twentieth Century Painting,* 1989, and *The Bauhaus,* 1991. **Essays:** Burberrys; Liz Claiborne; Nicole Farhi; Fenn Wright And Manson; Brigid Foley; French Connection; Jaeger; Alexander Julian; Liberty of London; Mulberry; Pringle of Scotland; Helen Storey; Louis Vuitton.

ELLIOTT, Mary C. Curator of Historic Costume and Textiles, Mount Mary College, Milwaukee, Wisconsin. **Essay:** Lucien Lelong.

FLUX, Alan J. Free-lance essayist. **Essays:** Lilly Daché; Stephen Jones; Stephen Linard; Anthony Price; Graham Smith.

GORDON, Mary Ellen. Free-lance writer. Associate editor, *Women's Wear Daily,* 1989-94. Contributor to periodicals, including *Elle, Self, InStyle,* and *Paper Magazine.* **Essay:** Anna Sui.

GRUBER, Roberta Hochberger. Assistant professor, Fashion Design, Drexel University. Co-director, Design Arts Gallery, Drexel University. Free-lance designer and fashion illustrator. Curator of several exhibitions, including *Fashion Imagery,* 1991, *Hat Formation,* 1993, and *Designer Sketchbook,* 1995. **Essays:** Mariano (y Madrazo) Fortuny; Nicole Miller; Robert Lee Morris; Elsa Schiaparelli.

HAMADA, Yoko. Fashion journalist involved in the connections between Japanese fashion and New York (deceased). Author of *HiFashion* and *Men's Club.* **Essays:** Giuliano Fujiwara; Yoshiyuki Konishi.

HILL, Chris. Senior lecturer, Cordwainers College, London. Company Director, Fancy Footwork Ltd. **Essays:** Patrick Cox; Charles Jourdan; Sara Navarro; Andrea Pfister; Sir Edward Rayne; Red or Dead.

HOUSE, Nancy. Adjunct faculty, Art History, Wilmington College; also taught at Ohio State University and Salem State College, Massachusetts. **Essays:** Banana Republic; Brooks Brothers; Anne Fogarty; Joan & David; John Kloss; Levi-Strauss & Co; I. Magnin; Carolyne Roehm; Alfred Sung; Gustave Tassell; Joan Vass.

KIRKE, Betty. Retired Head Conservator, Edwarde C. Blum Design Laboratory, Fashion Institute of Technology. Created and taught graduate curriculum in costume conservation at Fashion Institute of Technology, in the 1980s. Author of *Vionnet,* 1991. **Essays:** Jacques Griffe; Lanvin.

MARKARIAN, Janet. Textile specialist. Taught textile studies at many colleges and universities. Taught master's program at The Costume Institute, Metropolitan Museum of Art, and New York University. Worked in the Metropolitan Museum's Ratti Textile Center, 1995. **Essays:** Linda Allard; Kenneth Jay Lane.

MARSH, Lisa. Sportswear reporter with *Women's Wear Daily* (New York). **Essays:** Champion; Perry Ellis; David and Elizabeth Emanuel; Alan Flusser; Guess, Inc.; Robert Stock.

MARTIN, Richard. Curator, The Costume Institute, Metropolitan Museum of Art. Among numerous other posts: Editor of *Arts Magazine,* 1974-88; editor of *Textile & Text,* 1988-92. Executive director of the Shirley Goodman Resource Center, 1980-93, and professor of art history, 1973-93, at the Fashion Institute of Technology. Taught at Columbia University, New York University, School of Visual Arts, The Juilliard School, Parsons School of Design, and the School of the Art Institute of Chicago. Books include *Fashion and Surrealism* and *The New Urban Landscape.* More than 300 essays have appeared in various journals, including *Vogue* (Munich), *Journal of American Culture, Los Angeles Times, International Herald Tribune,* and *Artforum.* **Essays:** Akira; Walter Albini; Victor Alfaro; Cristobal Balenciaga; Jeffrey Banks; Jhane Barnes; John Bartlett; Geoffrey Beene; Laura Biagiotti; Bill Blass; Tom Brigance; Brioni; Stephen Burrows; Byblos; Calugi e Giannelli; Nino Cerruti; Sal Cesarani; Cole of California; Han Feng; Andrew Fezza; Fontana; Irene Galitzine; The Gap; Marithé & François Girbaud; Madame Grès; Halston; Jacques Heim; Gordon Henderson; Tommy Hilfiger; Isani; Marc Jacobs; Eric Javits; John P John; Wolfgang Joop; Gemma Kahng; Kenzo; Barry Kieselstein-Cord; Calvin Klein; Yukio Kobayashi; Michael Kors; Junko Koshino; Lamine Kouyaté; Byron Lars; André Laug; Judith Leiber; Mad Carpentier; Mitsuhiro Matsuda; Missoni; Issey Miyake; Isaac Mizrahi; Edward H Molyneux; Claude Montana; Josie Cruz Natori; Nikos; Todd Oldham; Elsa Peretti; Lilly Pulitzer; Mary Ann Restivo; Marcel Rochas; Christian Francis Roth; Ronaldus Shamask; Simonetta; Willi Smith; Zang Toi; Gianni Versace; Madeleine Vionnet; John Weitz; Kansai Yamamoto.

McCREADY, Elian. Painter and textile designer. Churchill fellow, 1985. Design writing includes *Glorious Needlepoint,* 1987, *Kaffe Fassett at the V & A,* 1988, *Glorious Inspiration,* 1991, *Fruits of the Earth,* 1991, and *Ehrman Tapestry Book,* 1995. **Essays:** Caroline Charles; Kaffe Fassett; Bill Gibb; Patricia Roberts; Timney Fowler Ltd.

MELIA, Sally Anne. Science and culture free-lance journalist and author. Contributor to *St. James Guide to Fantasy Writers,* 1994, *Larousse Encyclopedia,* 1995, *Lexus Dictionary of French Life and Culture,* 1995; author of celebrity interviews and articles for magazines in the United Kingdom and the United States, including *SF Chronicle* and *Interzone.* **Essays:** Sueo Irié; René Lezard; Roberto Verino; Ermenegildo Zegna.

OZZARD, Janet. Graduate of Bryn Mawr College; M.A. in fashion history, Fashion Institute of Technology. Reporter for *Women's Wear Daily* (New York). **Essay:** Zoran.

PATON, Kathleen. Writer, researcher, and editor specializing in cultural history. Free-lance graphic designer, since 1988. M.A. in Museum Studies, State University of New York, Fashion Institute of Technology, 1993. Research and essays for *In A Rising Public Voice: Women in Politics Worldwide.* **Essay:** Christian Aujard; Franck Joseph Bastille; Jean Baptiste Caumont; Jacques Esterel; Olivier Guillemin; Hermès; Guy Paulin; Bernard Perris; Gerard Pipart; Georges Rech; Jacques Tiffeau; Tiktiner.

PATTISON, Angela. Lecturer in design. Program leader, Cordwainers College. International design consultant. Trained as a fashion designer in the early 1960s. Specializes in trend predictions, fashion forecasting, and designing footwear and accessories with major manufacturers and retailers throughout the world. **Essays:** Manolo Blahnik; Elio Fiorucci; Jan Jansen; Transport.

ROSENBERG, Alan E. Studied fashion design at The Fashion Institute of Technology and art history at Hunter College of the City University of New York. Director of the Metropolitan Historic Structures Association for several years. Studying for master's degree in museum studies, Fashion Institute of Technology. **Essays:** Adolfo; Dorothée Bis; Carven; Elisabeth de Senneville; George Peter Stavropoulos; Vicky Tiel; Valentino.

SALTER, Susan. Writer/contributor to several reference series, including *Contemporary Authors, Newsmakers,* and *Major Authors and Illustrators for Children and Young Adults.* **Essay:** Esprit.

SEAMAN, Margo. Graduate of the College of Wooster; master's degrees from the Fashion Institute of Technology and Bank Street College of Education. Teacher and free-lance writer. **Essays:** Pierre Balmain; Carolina Herrera; Anne Klein; Claire McCardell; Jean Patou; Paloma Picasso; Adrienne Vittadini.

SEVERSON, Molly. Free-lance writer. **Essay:** Richard Tyler.

SEWELL, Dennita. Graduate of the University of Missouri and Yale School of Drama. Collections Manager in The Costume Institute, The Metropolitan Museum of Art, since 1992. **Essays:** Cathy Hardwick; Roger Vivier.

SHAW, Madelyn. Collections Manager, The Textile Museum, Washington, D.C. Former member of the curatorial staff, The Museum at the Fashion Institute of Technology, New York, and The Gallery of Cora Ginsburg, Inc., New York. Instructor, Boston University School of Theatre Arts, Boston, Massachusetts. Also involved in free-lance exhibition consultation and preparation. Contributor to *A World of Costume and Textiles: A Handbook of the*

Collection, 1988, and of "Women's Flying Clothing: 1910-1940," in *Cutter's Research Journal,* 1992-93. **Essays:** Hattie Carnegie; Jean Dessès; Tina Leser; Robert Piguet; Maurice Rentner; Maggy Rouf; Carolyn Schnurer.

SKELLENGER, Gillion. Free-lance wallpaper and fabric designer, Chicago. Instructor, Fashion Department, School of the Art Institute of Chicago, beginning in 1977. **Essays:** Prada; Cinzia Ruggeri.

STANLEY, Montse. Director, Knitting Reference Library, Cambridge, United Kingdom. Author of *Knitting Your Own Designs for a Perfect Fit,* 1982, and *The Knitter's Handbook,* 1986. **Essay:** Joaquim Verdù.

STEELE, Valerie. Author and professor at New York's Fashion Institute of Technology. Author of *Fashion and Eroticism,* 1985, *Paris Fashion,* 1988, *Women of Fashion,* 1991, and *Fetish: Fashion, Sex and Power,* 1995. Co-editor of *Men and Women: Dressing the Part,* 1989. **Essays:** Jacques Fath; Martin Margiela; Jil Sander; Sybilla; Isabel Toledo; Vivienne Westwood.

TRIGGS, Teal. Course Leader, School of Graphic Design, Ravensbourne College of Design and Communication, London. Design historian. Editor, *Communicating Design,* 1995, and (post-conference publication) *Rear Window: American and European Graphic Design,* 1995. Author of "Framing Masculinity: Herb Ritts, Bruce Weber and the Body Perfect" in *Chic Thrills: A Fashion Reader,* 1992. Contributor of articles to numerous periodicals and books, including *Eye* magazine, *Visible Language, Contemporary Designers,* and *Contemporary Masterworks.* **Essays:** Benetton; Jasper Conran; Sylvia Heisel; Marimekko; Whistles.

VASILOPOULOS, Vicki. Senior fashion editor, *Daily News Record,* Fairchild Fashion Group. **Essays:** C.P Company; New Republic; Bill Robinson.

VOTOLATO, Gregory. Essayist. Head of Art History, Buckinghamshire College, High Wycombe. **Essays:** L.L Bean; Adolfo Dominguez; Barbara Hulanicki; Thierry Mugler.

WALKER, Myra J. Associate Professor of Fashion History, School of Visual Arts at the University of North Texas in Denton. Director, Texas Fashion Collection. Curator, "The Art of Fashion: The Radical Sixties," Kimbell Art Museum, 1990. Exhibition organizer, JC Penney National Headquarters, 1993-95. Specialist in 20th-century fashion history. **Essays:** Victor Costa; Giorgio di Sant'Angelo; Sandra Garratt; Holly Harp; Arnold Scaasi.

WATT, Melinda L. Study storage assistant, The Costume Institute, Metropolitan Museum of Art. M.A. in Costume Studies from New York University. **Essays:** Willy Bogner; Pauline Trigère; Patricia Underwood.

WORAM, Catherine. Free-lance fashion writer/stylist. Author of *Wedding Dress Style,* 1993. **Essays:** Hardy Amies; Aquascutum, Ltd.; English Eccentrics; Fendi; Bella Freud; Genny Spa; Ghost; Gucci; Katharine Hamnett; Lachasse; Max Mara Spa; Digby Morton; Next PLC; Jenny Packham; Paul Smith; Philip Treacy; Workers for Freedom; Catherine Walker.